Microsoft® Exchange Server 2007
Tony Redmond's Guide to Successful Implementation

Microsoft® Exchange Server 2007
Tony Redmond's Guide to Successful Implementation

Tony Redmond

ELSEVIER

Amsterdam • Boston • Heidelberg • London • New York • Oxford
Paris • San Diego • San Francisco • Singapore • Sydney • Tokyo

Digital Press is an imprint of Elsevier

Digital Press

Digital Press is an imprint of Elsevier
30 Corporate Drive, Suite 400, Burlington, MA 01803, USA
Linacre House, Jordan Hill, Oxford OX2 8DP, UK

∞ Recognizing the importance of preserving what has been written, Elsevier prints its
books on acid-free paper whenever possible.

Library of Congress Cataloging-in-Publication Data
Application Submitted.

British Library Cataloguing-in-Publication Data
A catalogue record for this book is available from the British Library.

ISBN: 978-1-55558-347-7

For information on all Elsevier Digital Press publications visit our Web site at
www.books.elsevier.com

Printed in the United States of America
07 08 09 10 11 12 10 9 8 7 6 5 4 3 2 1

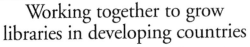

Contents

Preface   **xvii**

Foreword   **xxi**

1 Introduction   **1**

   1.1   A decade and counting of Exchange deployments   1
       1.1.1   The way we were   2
       1.1.2   The protocol wars   2
       1.1.3   Ever increasing mobility   4
       1.1.4   Third-party products and management   6
       1.1.5   Some interesting projects   6
       1.1.6   The not so good points   7
       1.1.7   Exchange's connection with the Active Directory   10
       1.1.8   Reviewing predictions made in 1996   11
   1.2   Microsoft's themes for Exchange 2007   12
       1.2.1   The happy prospect of a migration   18
   1.3   Preparing for Exchange 2007   20
   1.4   Installing Exchange 2007   22
       1.4.1   Modifying and removing servers   27
       1.4.2   Validating the installation   27
       1.4.3   Third-party software   28
   1.5   Server roles   28
       1.5.1   Services   32
   1.6   Licensing   36
       1.6.1   Version numbers   40
       1.6.2   32-bit Exchange 2007?   41
   1.7   Support   42
   1.8   Challenges for Exchange 2007   42
   1.9   Into the future   45

2   Exchange, Windows, and the Active Directory   **47**

2.1   Active Directory and Exchange   47
    2.1.1   Domain Designs   48
2.2   Active Directory replication   50
    2.2.1   Replication basics   51
    2.2.2   When Active Directory replication happens   53
    2.2.3   Active Directory naming contexts   55
    2.2.4   Transforming Domain controllers into
Global Catalogs 58
    2.2.5   USNs and replication   60
    2.2.6   Urgent replication   64
    2.2.7   Intrasite and Intersite replication   65
    2.2.8   High-watermark vector and up-to-date vector tables   68
    2.2.9   Changes in Active Directory replication in Windows 2003   70
2.3   Exchange's Active Directory Topology service   71
    2.3.1   DSAccess (or ADAccess)   72
    2.3.2   How many Global Catalog servers do I need?   75
    2.3.3   Where are my Global Catalogs?   76
2.4   Recovering deleted Active Directory accounts   78
2.5   Exchange and the Active Directory schema   80
    2.5.1   Updating the schema with an installation   80
    2.5.2   Changing the schema   82
    2.5.3   Active Directory custom attributes for Exchange   85
    2.5.4   Updating the schema to allow Ambiguous
             Name Resolution   86
    2.5.5   Exchange-specific permissions   87
    2.5.6   Exchange property sets   88
2.6   Longhorn and Exchange 2007   90
2.7   The very important LegacyExchangeDN attribute   91
2.8   Brain surgery for the Active Directory: ADSIEDIT   93
    2.8.1   LDP and LDIFDE   96
    2.8.2   Active Directory for Exchange   98

3   The Basics of Managing Exchange 2007   **99**

3.1   Exchange Management Console   100
    3.1.1   The importance of filters   104
    3.1.2   Managing mixed organizations   109
    3.1.3   Running EMC remotely or on a workstation   112
    3.1.4   No more AD Users and Computers   113
    3.1.5   Changing columns   115

	3.1.6	Visual effects	116
3.2		Why some options have disappeared from EMC	118
	3.2.1	Coping with change	122
3.3		Changes in the Exchange delegation model	124
3.4		Customized Recipient Management	128
	3.4.1	Adieu RUS	130
	3.4.2	Recipient types	132
3.5		Moving users	133
	3.5.1	Moving mailboxes	134
	3.5.2	Logging mailbox moves	138
3.6		Using distribution groups	140
	3.6.1	Forming groups	142
	3.6.2	Group changes in Exchange 2007	145
	3.6.3	Expanding distribution lists	147
	3.6.4	How many objects can I have in a group?	148
	3.6.5	Managing group membership	149
	3.6.6	Protected groups (and users)	152
3.7		Using groups for permissions	154
	3.7.1	Managing distribution groups from Outlook	154
3.8		Dynamic distribution groups	156
	3.8.1	Changing filters and conditions for dynamic distribution groups	157
	3.8.2	A note on OPATH	159
	3.8.3	A new UI for dynamic groups	160
	3.8.4	Creating New dynamic groups	162
	3.8.5	Using dynamic Distribution groups	167
3.9		Mailbox quotas	168
	3.9.1	Setting mailbox quotas	170
3.10		Email address policies	173
	3.10.1	Mailbox moves and email address policies	178
	3.10.2	Queries that drive email address policies	178
3.11		Address lists	183
	3.11.1	Upgrading Address Lists to Exchange 2007 format	187
3.12		User naming conventions	188
3.13		Server naming conventions	192
3.14		Moving from the basics	194
4		**The Exchange Management Shell**	**195**
4.1		EMS: Exchange's management shell	197
	4.1.1	Working with PowerShell commands	199
	4.1.2	Exchange shell commands	204

4.1.3   Command editing   208
4.1.4   Getting at more information about something   210
4.1.5   Using common and user-defined variables   214
4.1.6   Identities   217
4.1.7   Working in a multi-domain forest   219
4.1.8   Profiles   221
4.1.9   PowerShell in batch   223
4.1.10   Execution policies   224
4.1.11   Sending email from the shell   226
4.2   Learning from EMC   229
4.3   Using EMS to work with mailboxes   232
4.3.1   Creating a new mailbox with a template   232
4.3.2   Setting and retrieving mailbox properties   234
4.3.3   Other ways of interacting with mailboxes   244
4.3.4   Get-Recipient   245
4.3.5   Moving mailboxes   245
4.3.6   Accessing another user's mailbox   249
4.3.7   Different commands and different properties   251
4.3.8   Contacts   252
4.4   Working with distribution groups   253
4.4.1   Working with dynamic distribution groups   257
4.4.2   Advanced group properties   262
4.5   Delegation through the shell   265
4.6   Creating efficient filters   267
4.7   Bulk updates   270
4.7.1   Creating sets of mailboxes   273
4.8   Reporting mailbox data   275
4.8.1   Special properties   282
4.9   Using the shell for other management tasks   284
4.10   Command validation   287
4.11   Working with remote servers   290
4.12   Working with non-Exchange 2007 servers   291
4.13   Testing Exchange 2007   292
4.13.1   Client connections   294
4.13.2   Mail Flow   295
4.13.3   Miscellaneous test commands   297
4.14   PowerShell for Exchange administrators   297

5   The Store   301

5.1   Introducing the Store   301
5.2   Differences in the Exchange 2007 Store   306

	5.2.1	Are 64 bits that important?	307
	5.2.2	Trading memory for I/O	312
	5.2.3	The decrease in storage costs	317
5.3	No more streaming database		318
5.4	Tables and items		320
5.5	Storage groups		323
	5.5.1	Creating a new storage group and database	327
	5.5.2	Working with storage groups and databases	329
5.6	Transaction logs		331
	5.6.1	Circular logging	335
	5.6.2	Creating new transaction logs	337
	5.6.3	Reserved logs	338
	5.6.4	Transactions, buffers, and commitment	339
	5.6.5	Transaction log I/O	341
	5.6.6	Protecting transaction logs	341
	5.6.7	Transaction log checksum	342
	5.6.8	Maximum database size	343
5.7	Database portability		345
	5.7.1	Zero database pages	349
5.8	MAPI connections and logons		349
5.9	The Deleted Items cache		350
	5.9.1	Cleaning the Deleted Items cache	356
	5.9.2	Recovering items and mailboxes	357
5.10	Background maintenance		360
	5.10.1	Background tasks	364
	5.10.2	Tracking background maintenance	367
5.11	Fixing failed databases		368
5.12	Exchange 2007 content indexing		375
	5.12.1	Using content indexing	380
5.13	Public folders		383
	5.13.1	Public folders and Exchange 2007	384
	5.13.2	Changes in public folders administration since Exchange 2003	386
	5.13.3	Calming replication storms	388
	5.13.4	Managing public folders with Exchange 2007	392
	5.13.5	Permissions on top-level folders	405
	5.13.6	Referrals	405
	5.13.7	Migrating public folder content	406
5.14	Removing database size limits		408
5.15	Backups		408
	5.15.1	NTBackup	410

5.15.2	Other commercial backup products	410
5.15.3	Creating a backup strategy	413
5.15.4	Backups and storage groups	415
5.15.5	Checkpoint file	421
5.15.6	The future of streaming backups	426
5.16	Moving from the Store	427
6	**Exchange Transport and Routing**	**429**
6.1	The evolution of routing	429
6.2	Change through experience	430
6.2.1	Hidden administrative and routing groups	433
6.3	Exchange 2007 transport architecture	435
6.3.1	The critical role of hub transport servers	438
6.3.2	Receive connectors	440
6.3.3	Send connectors	447
6.3.4	Linking Exchange 2003 and Exchange 2007	453
6.3.5	Multiple routes into Exchange 2003	458
6.3.6	Decommissioning Exchange 2003 routing groups	458
6.3.7	Handling Exchange 2003 link state updates during migration	458
6.3.8	Foreign connectors	459
6.3.9	Authorization	460
6.3.10	Accepted domains	460
6.3.11	Transport storage	461
6.4	Routing ABC	464
6.4.1	Resolving multiple paths	467
6.4.2	Most specific connector	467
6.4.3	Connector cost	469
6.4.4	Closest proximity	469
6.4.5	The role of hub routing sites	470
6.4.6	Site link costs versus routing costs	471
6.4.7	Instructing mailbox servers	472
6.4.8	Bypassing some connections	472
6.4.9	Protocol logging	473
6.4.10	X.400 support	474
6.4.11	Bifurcation	475
6.4.12	Header firewalls	476
6.5	Transport configuration	476
6.5.1	Transport configuration file	481
6.5.2	Routing logs	483
6.6	Queues	485

6.6.1	The Queue Viewer	488
6.6.2	The Unreachable queue	491
6.6.3	Poison messages	493
6.7	Back Pressure	494
6.8	Delivery Status Notifications	496
6.8.1	Customizing DSNs	501
6.8.2	Postmaster addresses	504
6.9	Transport agents	505
6.10	Transport summary	506
6.11	Edge servers	506
6.11.1	Edge or hub?	508
6.11.2	Basic Edge	510
6.11.3	Edge Synchronization	511
6.11.4	Basic Edge security	518
6.11.5	Fighting spam and email viruses	518
6.11.6	Defense in depth	522
6.11.7	Microsoft's approach to mail hygiene	523
6.11.8	Forefront for Exchange	528
6.11.9	Mail Hygiene Agents	533
6.11.10	Agent logs	535
6.11.11	Connection filtering	536
6.11.12	Sender filtering	538
6.11.13	Address Rewrite agent	539
6.11.14	Sender ID agent	541
6.11.15	Content filtering	547
6.11.16	Content Filter updates	550
6.11.17	Per-user SCL processing	553
6.11.18	Safelist Aggregation	554
6.11.19	Sender reputation	557
6.11.20	Recipient filtering	559
6.11.21	Blocking file attachments	560
6.11.22	Attachment filtering	562
6.11.23	Edge transport rules	563
6.11.24	Available Edge	565
6.12	Client-side spam suppression	567
6.12.1	Outlook's Junk Mail Filter	568
6.12.2	Postmarks	573
6.12.3	Restricting OOF and other notifications	574
6.13	Routing onwards	580

7   Clients   581

7.1	Outlook	583
	7.1.1	Outlook web services	585
	7.1.2	Understanding Outlook's relationship with Exchange	591
	7.1.3	Deploying cached Exchange mode	596
	7.1.4	Address caching	599
	7.1.5	MAPI compression and buffers	600
	7.1.6	Conflict resolution	602
	7.1.7	Preventing MAPI clients from connecting	603
	7.1.8	Outlook 2007 and Exchange 5.5	607
7.2	Offline and personal Stores	608
	7.2.1	Personal folders	609
	7.2.2	Mail delivery to personal folders	611
	7.2.3	Configuring PSTs	615
	7.2.4	PST archiving	617
7.3	Offline folder files	619
	7.3.1	OST synchronization	621
	7.3.2	When things go wrong with your OST	623
7.4	Out of Office changes	624
	7.4.1	The big question: Is Outlook 2007 worth the upgrade?	625
7.5	The Offline Address Book (OAB)	626
	7.5.1	Downloading the OAB	627
	7.5.2	OAB files on the PC	628
	7.5.3	The evolving OAB format	630
	7.5.4	OAB and cached Exchange mode	632
	7.5.5	OAB generation and distribution	634
	7.5.6	Creating a customized OAB	640
	7.5.7	Allocating OABs to users	642
7.6	Outlook Anywhere	645
7.7	Outlook Web Access	650
	7.7.1	New features in Outlook Web Access 2007	652
	7.7.2	Outlook Web Access Light	658
	7.7.3	International versions	662
	7.7.4	Accessing legacy data	664
	7.7.5	Managing Outlook Web Access	666
	7.7.6	Authentication	667
	7.7.7	Segmentation	671
	7.7.8	Notifications	675
	7.7.9	Controlling attachments	677
	7.7.10	Themes	680
	7.7.11	Client settings	684

7.8	Internet client access protocols	684
7.8.1	IMAP4	685
7.8.2	The Exchange 2007 IMAP server	689
7.9	Mobile clients	694
7.9.1	Selecting mobile devices	696
7.9.2	Server-based ActiveSync	698
7.10	Windows Mobile 6.0 and Exchange 2007	702
7.10.1	ActiveSync policies	706
7.10.2	Managing mobile devices through EMC	711
7.10.3	Moving mailboxes to Exchange 2007 and ActiveSync	713
7.10.4	Estimating network traffic for mobile devices	715
7.10.5	Analyzing ActiveSync logs	717
7.10.6	Wiping mobile devices	719
7.10.7	Debugging synchronization	721
7.11	Comparing Windows Mobile and BlackBerry	723
7.11.1	Processing the mail	725
7.11.2	Other messaging options for Windows Mobile	730
7.11.3	Power management	731
7.11.4	Input flexibility	732
7.12	Unified Communications	735
7.13	Unified Messaging	737
7.13.1	Client Access to voicemail	741
7.13.2	Dealing with voicemail	745
7.13.3	Voice synthesis	747
7.13.4	Pure voicemail	748
7.13.5	The magic of SIP	749
7.13.6	Speech Grammars	752
7.13.7	Phonetic names	754
7.13.8	Cross-forest UM	756
7.14	Special mailboxes	756
7.15	Clients and users	759
8	**Managing Users**	**761**
8.1	Room and equipment mailboxes	762
8.1.1	Managing properties of room and equipment mailboxes	765
8.1.2	Converting old mailboxes to rooms	770
8.2	Helping users to use email better	771
8.2.1	Eliminating bad habits	771
8.2.2	Disclaimers	779
8.2.3	Out-of-Office Notifications	781
8.2.4	The last few bad email habits	781

8.3		Customizing display templates	782
8.4		Exchange 2007 and compliance	787
	8.4.1	The growing need for compliance	789
	8.4.2	Transport rules	792
	8.4.3	Using a rule to add disclaimer text to outgoing messages	794
	8.4.4	Capturing selected messages	795
	8.4.5	Becoming more complicated	797
	8.4.6	Creating an ethical firewall	800
	8.4.7	Transport rule storage	803
	8.4.8	Rules and the shell	804
	8.4.9	Journal rules	808
8.5		Messaging Record Management	815
	8.5.1	Managing default folders	818
	8.5.2	Managing custom folders	824
	8.5.3	Allocating managed folders with policies	826
	8.5.4	Applying policies to users	827
	8.5.5	The Managed Folder Assistant	829
	8.5.6	Logging Managed Folder activity	831
	8.5.7	Using Managed Folders	833
	8.5.8	Harvesting information from managed folders	835
8.6		Message classifications	837
	8.6.1	Adding intelligence to classification through rules	844
8.7		Copying user mailboxes	848
	8.7.1	Auditing	853
8.8		Free and busy	853
	8.8.1	Looking at free and busy data	855
	8.8.2	Free and busy in Exchange 2007	861
	8.8.3	Changes in Outlook 2007	863
	8.8.4	Cross-forest free and busy	866
9		**Hardware and Performance**	**867**
9.1		Moving toward 64-bit Exchange	867
9.2		Buying servers for Exchange 2007	870
9.3		The storage question	876
9.4		RPC pop-ups	881
9.5		Clusters and Exchange	882
9.6		Continuous replication and Exchange 2007	888
	9.6.1	Concepts	889
9.7		Deploying Local Continuous Replication (LCR)	892
	9.7.1	How LCR works	897
	9.7.2	LCR operations	900

	9.7.3	LCR restrictions	903
	9.7.4	LCR database transition	904
9.8	Deploying Cluster Continuous Replication (CCR)		906
	9.8.1	Comparing CCR and traditional clusters	910
	9.8.2	CCR in practice	912
	9.8.3	CCR failovers	915
	9.8.4	Lost Log Resilience	919
	9.8.5	The transport dumpster	921
	9.8.6	Standby Continuous Replication	924
9.9	Continuous Log Replication: Good or bad?		924
9.10	Virtual Exchange		925

10 More useful things to Know about Exchange   929

10.1	Automated analysis		929
	10.1.1	SSCP	932
	10.1.2	Microsoft's Release to Web (RTW) strategy	933
10.2	The Exchange Toolbox		935
	10.2.1	Updates	936
	10.2.2	Database Recovery Management	937
	10.2.3	Database Troubleshooter	942
	10.2.4	Mail Flow Troubleshooter	943
10.3	Messaging tracking logs		945
	10.3.1	Generating message tracking logs	947
	10.3.2	Log sizes and ages	950
	10.3.3	Keeping track of message subjects	951
	10.3.4	Accessing message tracking logs	951
	10.3.5	Using the Troubleshooting Assistant to track messages	952
	10.3.6	Tracking messages with EMS	956
	10.3.7	Message delivery latency	959
10.4	Management frameworks		959
10.5	Utilities		963
	10.5.1	Performance testing	963
	10.5.2	The MFCMAPI utility	965
	10.5.3	MDBVU32	968
	10.5.4	ExMon—Exchange User Monitor	968
	10.5.5	PFDavAdmin	971
	10.5.6	LogParser	973
	10.5.7	Outlook Spy	978
10.6	Bits and pieces		978
	10.6.1	Where the Exchange team hangs out	978
	10.6.2	Online Forums	979

10.7   Conferences   979
       10.7.1   Magazines   980
       10.7.2   How Exchange uses registry keys   980
10.8   Good reference books   981

A   Appendix   **983**

A.1   Message Tracking Log Format   983
A.2   Events noted in Message Tracking Logs   985

B   Important Exchange PowerShell commands   **987**

B.1   Recipient management commands   987
B.2   Exchange server administrative Commands   990
B.3   Databases and Storage Groups   993
B.4   Address Lists and Email Policies   995
B.5   Queues and Messages   995
B.6   Edge Synchronization   996
B.7   Routing   997
B.8   ActiveSync   998
B.9   Public folders   999
B.10   Transport and journal rules   1000
B.11   IMAP and POP   1001
B.12   Active Directory commands   1002
B.13   Testing Exchange 2007   1003
B.14   Basic PowerShell   1004
B.15   PowerShell control commands   1005

Index   **1007**

Preface

By their very nature, every book that seeks to describe how technology works face challenges during its creation. Dealing with beta software and attempting to resolve the difference between how the software works and how the developers say it will work in the final version is a problem faced by any author, which is one reason why it is often best to wait to finalize text after you have a chance to work with released software. Looking back at this project, in some ways, this has been the hardest book of the seven that I have written about Exchange. I think that there are four reasons why this might be so.

First, Exchange 2007 marks the boundary for substantial architectural change within the product, so it is similar to the degree of change that we experienced when we moved from Exchange 5.5 to Exchange 2000. Second, the nature of software is that it becomes more complex over time as the developers add new features and this is certainly true of Exchange 2007. The new features have to be considered, probed, and documented, all of which takes time. Third, the Exchange development team has done an excellent job since 2004 to document all aspects of Exchange in a more comprehensive manner than ever before. The Exchange 2007 help file, TechNet, MSDN, and the excellent Exchange team blog at http://msexchangeteam.com/default.aspx are interesting and productive hoards of information for authors to mine. Unfortunately, there is often too much material (a good complaint to have) and the material needs to be interpreted and analyzed in the light of your own experience with Exchange. Engineers write great blogs, but the scourge of cognitive dissonance often means that they omit some detail that makes all the difference to a newcomer in understanding why a component works the way that it does.

Last but not least, you should not underestimate the degree of cultural change that Microsoft has incorporated into Exchange 2007 in the transition from a predominantly GUI-centric approach to server management to the use of the PowerShell scripting language as the basis of many management operations. The need to understand and appreciate the change has to occur before you can adequately document and describe the benefits and this increases the effort required to write the book. I must admit that it took me time to realize the full benefit of interacting with Exchange through the shell, but now I am at the point where I wonder why Microsoft never provided such a powerful interface in the past!

The degree of change that exists in Exchange 2007 means that it is difficult to cover everything in one book. I have therefore elected to cover the parts of Exchange that I think are of most interest to the majority of administrators and have left other components for you to discover through the material that Microsoft publishes or perhaps another book, written by me or someone else. Please accept my apology if I have not covered something that you think is important and treat this as a challenge and opportunity for you to write about the topic yourself. There are many magazines, blogs, and other ways of spreading information about Exchange.

From time to time, I wander back down the path to consider some aspect of Exchange 2003. While this book is firmly focused on Exchange 2007, the vast majority of companies that will deploy Exchange 2007 will do so by migrating from Exchange 2003 and will therefore run both products alongside each other for some period. For large organizations, the period might extend to a year or more as it is unlikely that few will complete their migration to a pure Exchange 2007 environment quickly. With this in mind, it is fair and reasonable to document how things work with Exchange 2003, especially when these servers operate with Exchange 2007.

So what is in the book? To set the context, Chapter 1 starts with an overview of the development of Exchange from 4.0 to 2007 and then describes the themes that Microsoft employed to focus the development priorities for Exchange 2007 and some of the changes that occur in this release. All successful deployments of Exchange since Exchange 2000 operate on a solid Active Directory foundation, so Chapter 2 reviews some of the critical intersection points between Exchange and the Active Directory including replication, the schema, and Global Catalogs. Chapter 3 goes into the basics of managing Exchange 2007 through the Exchange Management Console. Chapter 4 takes the management topic further by exploring the ins and outs of the new Exchange Management Shell, perhaps the most fundamental change to the product that Microsoft has made in Exchange 2007. Chapter 5 goes to the heart of Exchange and reviews how the Store works including topics such as databases, storage groups, and transaction logs to content indexing and backups. Chapter 6 looks at how the new transport system routes messages and includes topics such as the Edge server and anti-spam protection. Chapter 7 explains how clients from Outlook to Outlook Web Access to mobile devices allow users to work with their mailboxes. Chapter 8 then moves on to consider some elements of user management, including the important topic of compliance and records management. Chapter 9 addresses one of the more difficult topics in hardware and performance. It is difficult because hardware capabilities change so rapidly that it is hard to give any advice about performance in anything other than outline detail. Finally, Chapter 10 wraps things up with some miscellaneous items that are important to Exchange, or at least that I think are important for Exchange administrators to know. I hope that the book hangs together as a coherent whole.

It is inevitable that I have omitted some topics that you might like me to have covered. There is so much technology in and around Exchange 2007 that it would take a 2,000 page book to cover it in any detail.

My experience is mostly in the enterprise space, so it should not be a surprise that many of the opinions expressed in the book reflect that bias. One of my reviewers noticed this point, and complained that I did not think that POP3 was an important protocol. Using Exchange 2007 as a hosting platform is a pretty specialized business and I apologize in advance if I offend anyone by my concentration on how to deploy Exchange 2007 most effectively for medium to large enterprises.

All errors and omissions are mine, especially in the code samples selected to illustrate the power of the Exchange Management Shell. PowerShell samples are indicated in the courier typeface like so:

```
Get-Mailbox –id Redmond | Select DisplayName
```

Any output from the commands is shown as follows:

```
DisplayName:        Tony Redmond
```

While all the code worked on one or more test systems, experience tells me that errors can creep in the process required to take code from a system through editing and publishing to the final content in a book. This is especially so when the underlying code changes from build to build as the engineers push to finish the product and generate a knock-on effect of changes to commands and individual parameters. This book does not pretend to be a comprehensive guide to PowerShell programming or to the Exchange Management Shell and the examples are there to give you a taste of what you can now do to automate management operations, so any errors that do creep in should be pretty obvious and easily solved—I hope!

Books do not happen overnight and they represent a lot of work. I have gained enormously from being able to work alongside some tremendous experts in enterprise messaging, both inside and outside HP. I acknowledge the contribution of groups such as my own team, who humored me when I was writing. The Exchange 2007 academy tutors allowed me to ask many questions as I probed the content that they generated to train HP consultants and customers. I must also acknowledge the huge contribution made by the enterprise messaging team at HP including Kathy Pollert, Mike Ireland, and Stan Foster (an honorary member), who let me into the details of how Exchange 2007 into the huge Windows infrastructure that HP operates. There are many people at Microsoft who patiently answered questions even if they didn't realize that this was happening; the amount of information that Microsoft now generates in help files, blogs, MSDN, TechNet, and Knowledge Base articles is truly staggering and has become a big challenge for people to understand and assimilate. It is great that the information is there, but just sometimes…. I should also acknowledge and thank the mass of enthusiasts who attend conferences such as Windows and Exchange Connections who asked about an Exchange 2007 book and eventually prompted me to start writing.

Foreword

On my first day with the Exchange team in 2001, I was handed a copy of Tony Redmond's Exchange 2000 book, "Here, read this!" It did take me a while to make my way through that tome, but I still recall thinking that it was well worth the time, as it laid the foundation for everything that was to come for me in Exchange.

They were obviously there before me, but I can personally attest that since that day, Tony's team at HP have been outstanding partners with us in designing Exchange 2003 and 2007, helping us test the software throughout the development, and ultimately working with many customers on their deployments, migrations, and operations.

We designed Exchange 2007 with three audiences in mind:

- The IT executive looking for cost reduction, security, and compliance.
- The IT professional looking for operational efficiency.
- The end user looking for anywhere access to their email.

I hope you will find with your deployment of Exchange 2007 that we've delighted all three. Since 2005, we've been testing Exchange 2007 with more organizations and more end users than any previous release of Exchange. The end result is a product that we are very proud of here in Redmond, Washington. We look forward to receiving your feedback about Exchange 2007 over the coming years.

On behalf of the entire Exchange team, thank you for choosing Microsoft Exchange!

Terry Myerson (terry.myerson@microsoft.com)

General Manager, Exchange Server

Microsoft Corporation

Introduction

1.1   A decade and counting of Exchange deployments

Microsoft shipped Exchange 4.0 in March 1996 after a gestation period of some four years. The new messaging server went through many different design phases. Microsoft grappled with the challenge of enterprises and small companies, figured out what they had to do to be competitive, understood how best to migrate users from other platforms (including their own), and achieved the necessary performance and scalability levels—albeit limited by the capabilities of Windows NT 3.51 and the available hardware.

Exchange replaced Microsoft Mail and went into immediate competition with other messaging systems such as those favored by large corporations (IBM PROFS, Digital Equipment Corporation's ALL-IN-1 and MailWorks, and HP OpenMail) and the PC LAN-based systems such as Lotus cc:Mail, Banyan Vines, Novell GroupWise, and Lotus Notes. Exchange 4.0 was the first version that implemented the initial Exchange architecture and this generation subsequently spanned Exchange 5.0 and 5.5, released in March and November 1997 respectively. The second generation arrived with Exchange 2000 in 2000 and Microsoft developed this version of the architecture further with Exchange 2003. Exchange 2007 advances the state of the art by implementing the third distinct architecture for Exchange.

It is hard to realize just how much progress messaging technology has made since 1996. Exchange has improved its capabilities dramatically in terms of functionality, robustness, security, and connectivity since 1996. We have also seen other important advances in the standards that dictate how systems connect together, the networks that we use, Windows and associated technology such as IIS, the power and usefulness of the devices that we connect to our mailboxes, and the other technology that has established the type of world we work in. The web is the best and most pervasive example of a technology that has influenced Exchange. The volume and depth of change over the decade has posed a challenge for administrators to keep up to date with new developments, and hopefully the articles published about Exchange and associated technologies in that time have helped to bridge the gap.

I.I.I   The way we were

The messaging market was more fragmented in 1996 than it is in 2007. The administrator who set out to deploy Exchange 4.0 had to cope with a plethora of competing standards, connections, and clients. Companies such as SoftSwitch (later bought by Lotus), WorldTalk, and LinkAge (later bought by Microsoft as part of their push to migrate companies from Notes) built healthy businesses by producing software to connect different email systems so that companies could communicate together. The war between the proponents of the international messaging standards (X.400 and X.500) and the Internet standards hadn't reached a satisfactory conclusion in 1996, so we struggled to communicate in a world where you needed a great deal of magic incantations to send even a plain text message addressed to a single recipient to a foreign email system.

Government and telecommunications bodies led the charge toward a common standard for directories that eventually resulted in the X.500 standard. While X.500 offered the potential that it could eventually result in a global directory standard that everyone used to connect directories to, directory synchronization was another black art in 1996. It was common to have weekly or monthly synchronization runs to merge directory data to provide a common view of users across multiple systems. Email addresses were more convoluted (mine was then Tony.Redmond@dbo.mts.dec.com) than today as most organizations now use the standard SMTP convention of first-name.last-name@domain. Of course, X.500 has long since faded into the background and LDAP is now the most widely used standard for directory access and interoperability. We can still see the influence of X.500 in some enterprise directories and in the design principles that Microsoft followed to build the original Exchange Directory Store and then the Active Directory, but few Exchange administrators bother about X.500 now.

The ease of connectivity established by SMTP, its extensions (ESMTP), and the easy access that we now enjoy to the Internet has revolutionized email. This is true for corporate users and personal users. Ten years ago it would have been difficult to predict the success and ease of access that people around the world enjoy to email systems such as Hotmail, Gmail, and Yahoo mail.

I.I.2   The protocol wars

MAPI is the great survivor of the protocol wars. MAPI is actually an API, but many people refer to MAPI as a protocol, in the same way as they refer to

IMAP4 or POP3; MAPI is also a message format as used in Exchange, so the email community uses the term in different ways. Microsoft introduced the first version of MAPI in Microsoft Mail, but this was a very simple version of the API that Outlook clients use today as it only supported twelve functions. Capone, the original Exchange client shipped with Exchange 4.0, was the first client to exploit the full range of MAPI capabilities as made available in the MAPI 1.0 release. Microsoft developed the Exchange RPC protocol to wrap around MAPI and Exchange 2007 continues to use Exchange RPCs (often called MAPI RPCs or often just MAPI) to connect Outlook clients to servers. There's also server-side MAPI, which is what Exchange servers use for server applications that need to access the Store, such as the System Attendant and the Exchange management console. The server variation of MAPI in Exchange 2003 is tuned to support the kind of multi-threaded applications that you find on servers better, but the difference between the MAPI library distributed with Exchange and the version that came along with Outlook confused administrators in the past. For example, you could not install Outlook on an Exchange server because the two versions of the MAPI library would cause a conflict when they were loaded into the same process space.

Exchange 2007 introduces MAPI.Net—a thoroughly modern version of server-side MAPI that Exchange uses for communication between servers. For instance, all of the traffic between mailbox and hub transport servers is via MAPI.Net RPCs. A side effect of the new version of MAPI is that you can now install Outlook quite happily on an Exchange 2007 server because the two versions do not clash anymore. While it's still possible (but difficult and time consuming) to write highly efficient and effective MAPI code to run on the server, Microsoft's strategy is to move programmers away from MAPI to use Exchange Web services. The promise is that code will be easier to write and debug, will deliver better performance, and should be more supportable over the long term. Microsoft tuned the server variation of MAPI in Exchange 2003 to better support the kind of multi-threaded applications that servers run, but the difference between the MAPI library distributed with Exchange 2003 and the version that came along with any version of Outlook confused administrators in the past.

Exchange 2007 introduces MAPI.Net—a thoroughly modern version of server-side MAPI. Back on the client side, Microsoft referred to the Capone client as a "viewer." This seemed to be an odd name to give to a client, but it reflected a software engineering perspective that the client was an application that allowed users to view Exchange data. Capone was elegant, simple, and precise, but the first release of Outlook in 1997 rapidly passed out the original Exchange client in terms of functionality. Today Outlook boasts a range of features that most users (except Sue Mosher, the guru of Outlook) find all the features difficult to comprehend, let alone use. Despite rumblings over the years (many from within Microsoft), that Exchange should drop MAPI and use Internet protocols for its clients instead, no Internet client protocol has emerged that could deliver the same functionality as MAPI, so it continues to be the foundation for Exchange 2007 and Outlook 2007. MAPI remains a mystery to many, so if you're interested in finding out more, head over to www.insidemapi.com, the Web site dedicated to *Inside MAPI*, the definitive book on the API (out of print for many years).

Of course, Outlook is not the only client that you can connect to Exchange. Ever since Microsoft realized that they had to support the Internet after the famous memo written by Bill Gates galvanized Microsoft's engineering groups in 1996, Exchange has been able to support other client protocols. Exchange 5.0 (released in early 1997) was the first version to support Internet protocols. Today, Exchange 2007 supports a broad range of Internet protocols from POP3 and IMAP4 on the client side to SMTP as the basis for messaging connectivity and transport, to HTTP for Web access, plus extensions that provide better security and functionality, like ESMTP and HTTPS.

The Outlook Web Access (OWA) client is a real success story for Microsoft. Like many other projects that come out of Redmond, the initial version (shipped with Exchange 5.0 and then improved significantly in 5.5) was slow. This was due to some aspects of its architecture, its interaction with the Store, and various implementation details, all of which combined to limit its scalability to be less than the number of MAPI clients that a server could support. The version of Outlook Web Access that shipped with Exchange 2000 marked a dramatic step forward in the UI and performance and Outlook Web Access became a client that you could actually use as a replacement for Outlook. Microsoft made further improvements to Outlook Web Access in Exchange 2003, not least to respond to the needs of the service providers who wanted to deliver segmented functionality to their users, and further improvements, not least in an upgraded and highly functional user interface, are delivered by Exchange 2007. Some suggest that it is difficult to tell the difference between Outlook Web Access 2007 and Outlook 2007. The test works at a distance (of at least five feet), if not when you actually start to use the two clients where Outlook is still the superior client. Nevertheless, the bottom line with Outlook Web Access is that many users who work in offices with reliable network connections find that they do not need to use Outlook as all the functionality that they need is in Outlook Web Access.

1.1.3   Ever increasing mobility

We were just getting used to having cell phones in 1996 (but cell phone bills were dramatically more expensive than today), so Exchange 4.0 and the versions that followed really did not have to do much to accommodate mobility. Alphanumeric pagers were the most common mobile device that people carried if they needed to keep in touch with the office. RIM (www.rim.net) was founded in 1984 and developed its BlackBerry device as a solution that was initially targeted at executives. Today, BlackBerry has become a term that people understand to mean constant connection to the office and many of those connections are to Exchange. Of course, Black-Berry is not the only mobile device that Exchange supports. The GoodLink server (www.good.com—now owned by Motorola) connects BlackBerry devices to Exchange along with its own devices and those running Palm OS and Microsoft-powered PDAs. You can choose from a wide range of Smart-Phones as well.

Microsoft continues to focus on mobile access to information as one of its key development strategies for Exchange. They have poured in a huge amount of effort to improve connectivity for mobile devices from Exchange 2003 onwards, especially for devices that run Windows Mobile 5.0 or later releases. The good news is that the combination of new devices and Exchange 2007 deliver even better functionality and performance, if not quite yet to the standard that BlackBerry delivers.

In Chapter 7, we explore how Exchange 2007 delivers even more functionality for mobile users, as long as you are prepared to buy devices that run the latest version of Windows Mobile. Exchange 2007 also includes Microsoft's first venture into the unified messaging market to deliver an integrated inbox that accommodates voicemail as well as email, plus the ability for users to access their mailbox and calendar data through Outlook Voice Access. Microsoft's favorite demo for unified messaging is to show how you can ring Exchange while you are en route to the office and cancel all your appointments for the day, perhaps because you are feeling ill. Having such a wide range of connectivity options is very convenient for users, but the sheer number of connections that an Exchange server now supports has put a huge load on kernel mode resources that Windows finds hard to satisfy. Increasing the server's ability to support client connections is one of the primary reasons why Microsoft made the decision to make Exchange 2007 available only on the x86-64[1] Windows platform. It is also fair to say that the increase in the number of options available to users to connect to Exchange made server and network administration more complex because of the increased number of places where things can go wrong and disrupt the messaging flow. Security of data, especially data carried around on mobile devices, is also a concern, largely because of the number of mobile devices that are lost annually. It is a personal disaster to lose your contacts because you mislaid a phone; it is a professional and business disaster if your SmartPhone contains the company's business plan and you have not protected the device.

---

1.   Exchange 2007 runs only on the 64-bit Intel and AMD platforms. It does not run on the IA64 "Itanium" platform.

1.1.4　Third-party products and management

Exchange began with a sparse ecosystem surrounding the product. In 1996, the threat horizon was not what it is today, so there was not the same need for anti-virus and spam-suppression products. Management software was limited to the basic Exchange administration program. Developers had not even begun to think about the range of reporting and analysis software that we enjoy today. In short, the only add-on software that was available for Exchange was some messaging connectors and migration products to help Microsoft migrate customers from other email systems.

The situation today is very different and we now enjoy a huge range of add-on software that help administrators to deploy, operate, manage, report, and debug their installations. Many software companies have come and gone and a wave of recent mergers and acquisitions has reduced the number of companies who create add-on products, amongst them HP (with its Open-View suite) and Quest Software (www.quest.com), which sells many useful products for an Exchange environment. Microsoft has been active in this area too and despite some false starts when it comes to APIs, Microsoft has created a lot of helpful software that it makes available to customers through Web downloads from www.microsoft.com/exchange (see Chapter 10). Taken with the improvements in the base software, the upshot of all the third-party activity is that it is easier to manage an Exchange server than ever before.

1.1.5　Some interesting projects

Like any technology, Exchange is useless until you deploy it in projects to solve customer business problems. The early projects were all about migration and usually contained some interesting technical problems. For instance, one European post office wanted to replace PROFS with Exchange, but they only had 2Kbps connections to each post office. The link was OK for "green screen email," but could not handle the RPCs that Exchange and MAPI clients depend on. Later on, we faced the challenge of bringing Exchange and Windows together as Exchange 2000 absolutely depended on a solid implementation of Active Directory before it could function. Active Directory posed a huge learning curve for administrators, system designers, and consultants alike, but we have past it now and the combination of Windows 2003 and Exchange 2003 is a much more stable platform. The new combination of 64-bit Windows and 64-bit Exchange 2007 will take some time for administrators to become accustomed to, but it should be at least as stable as Windows 2003/Exchange 2003 in terms of its performance in production environments.

Introducing Exchange to the world of Internet service providers (ISPs) broke a lot of new ground around the turn of the century. Microsoft had not designed the first versions of Exchange to deal with the demands of ISPs, yet they expected Exchange to replace MCIS, their previous email solution for ISPs. The world of ISPs is significantly different to enterprise deployments as the focus is all about short connections for huge numbers of POP3 and IMAP4 clients instead of the leisurely-extended connections enjoyed by corporate users. Maybe the most interesting project was the system deployed to provide email to political parties. Even within the same party, users did not trust each other and the politicians were not happy to have their email stored on the same computer as data owned by other politicians. This was not a technology challenge, except in convincing users that Exchange and Windows could provide the necessary security to isolate everyone's data and keep it secure, but there were many interesting debates along the way.

1.1.6 The not so good points

Not everything has gone well for Exchange since 1996. Public folders are probably the biggest piece of functionality that has underperformed and disappointed across a large number of deployments. When Microsoft was stoking the market before they shipped Exchange 4.0, they made enormous play about the capabilities of public folders, especially when you linked them to the power of the 16-bit Visual Basic–like Electronic Forms Designer (EFD). With EFD, you could quickly put together a form such as a travel request or expense claim, link it to a public folder, and allow users to create and use the form much more efficiently than paper equivalents. With replication, you could move that information around your organization and collate it centrally. It all looked promising, but in practice EFD was a disaster as it generated forms that performed well with a couple of users or with a small number of items in a folder, but rapidly ran out of steam after that. EFD sank quickly while public folders have lingered on. Microsoft has made a couple of runs at improving public folders, most notably when they introduced multiple folder hierarchies in Exchange 2000, but no one seemed to be interested because public folders are difficult to manage and maintain and it did not seem like a good idea to introduce more complexity with the extra folder hierarchies. The net result is that many companies have large numbers of public folders, but no good way to audit, clean up, report on, or effectively manage their contents. We will not mourn the passing of public folders when Microsoft eventually puts a bullet through them, as long as migration utilities exist to allow companies to move their data to a new platform. Exchange 2007 marks the start of the phase-out process for public folders, albeit one that may take several more versions before Microsoft can finally pull the plug on this functionality. Microsoft has promised to support public folders until at least 2016, so you can take that as an indication of the work that Microsoft and customers have to do to transition the contents of public folders and whatever applications still depend on public folders to new platforms. Other technologies, such as SharePoint Portal Server, did not exist in 1996 and do a much better job of categorizing, searching, and managing data, so it will be a relief to move.

Clustering is a disappointment on the hardware side. I had great hopes for Microsoft clustering when the original "Wolfpack" release appeared alongside Exchange 5.5 in late 1997. Part of my optimism arose from my history at Digital where OpenVMS clustering set a bar in the mid-1980s that Microsoft clustering has still approached today. My optimism went alongside a realization that Exchange was vulnerable to hardware failure, especially in the disk subsystem where the disks that were available in 1997 were not as reliable or intelligent as they are today and few companies had started to use Storage Area Networks (SANs) as the backbone of their Exchange deployment. Vulnerability increased as we increased the user load on servers, which had reached a point where even the basic 32-bit Pentium II–based servers could cheerfully accept the load of several thousand concurrent users. Microsoft's original implementation of clustering was expensive because you could only run two servers in a cluster and one of those was passive, waiting for its twin to fail. The passive server had to be licensed and have a similar configuration to its partner, so only deployments that absolutely needed the highest protection against failure stumped up the necessary investment to implement clustering.

Microsoft revamped clustering in Windows 2000 and 2003 and upgraded Exchange 2000 and 2003 to take advantage of active-active clusters. Active-active means that every node in a cluster can support work and despite being limited to four Exchange servers in a cluster, it seemed like an advance. However, problems with virtual memory fragmentation led to the inability to transfer storage groups from a failed node and Microsoft revisited its support of Exchange on clusters to impose an active-passive model where you had to keep at least one passive server in the cluster to accept the workload should a failure occur. Obviously, this was a retrograde step because it increased the cost of clustering again as you could not use all of the hardware in a cluster as productively as before. Another problem was that not all third-party software was cluster aware, which caused problems for companies who wanted to deploy clusters but also wanted to use a common set of software for purposes such as monitoring, anti-virus, or backup. Finally, some of the Exchange components did not run on clusters (like messaging gateways), so introducing a cluster became an expensive business when you counted the extra servers that were required to support the complete environment.

To their credit, Microsoft made a commitment to use clusters for their internal deployment of Exchange and demonstrated that they could support 16,000 mailboxes on a seven-node cluster (four active nodes running Exchange, one passive node, two servers performing backup and other administrative work). Of course, the cynics pointed out that it would be easy to deploy and manage such a cluster if you had the Windows and Exchange development groups on site all the time. The net is that clustering began with great hopes and has receded to a point where it is useful to those who can afford to deploy the necessary hardware and understand the somewhat special administrative environment that clusters represent. It would have been great if clustering had become the de facto standard for Exchange deployments, but the obvious deficiencies in the implementation and the cost premium meant that this could never happen.

Exchange 2007 now offers a choice between "traditional" clusters where the databases are located on shared storage, and cluster continuous replication (CCR), a feature that allows you to deploy a cluster built from two physical nodes and keep the database used by a virtual Exchange server up to date on both nodes through asynchronous log shipping. CCR lays the foundation for stretched clusters and allows for a new level of protection against physical datacenter outages. Exchange 2007 also includes local continuous replication (LCR) to provide an additional level of protection against a disk failure that affects the Exchange Store to address the most obvious single point of failure in all previous versions of Exchange. Chapter 9 covers these technologies in some detail.

Because of the very nature of the beast, disaster recovery is always difficult, but it is the role of software to automate recovery operations to guide administrators and assist them in getting servers back online as quickly as possible while also avoiding mistakes like overwriting transaction logs. Until the introduction of the Recovery Storage Group in Exchange 2003, you had to maintain extra servers to use if a disaster occurred, and in the early days of virtualization this required physical hardware. Better hardware and fewer software bugs steadily reduced the number and impact of database corruptions, but it is surprising that we have had to wait until Exchange 2007 for features such as log shipping (as employed in both CCR and LCR) and the database troubleshooting assistant. Even though we've had to wait, now that we have the ability to deploy CCR and LCR, it will be interesting to see how these technologies are used to build a new level of resistance to database outages.

APIs are the other disaster area for Exchange. Microsoft needed Exchange to have great programming capabilities to help wean companies off Lotus Notes. Notes is not a great messaging engine, but it has extremely strong collaborative and programming capabilities that companies exploit to put together mail-enabled applications that take advantage of the Notes replication engine (also better than the replication implemented in Exchange public folders). We have endured multiple attempts by Microsoft to deliver an equivalent development platform for Exchange. To give Microsoft credit, they are persistent, and they have been very persistent, but also have a very awful track record with the APIs that have shipped with Exchange. We have seen CDO^2, CDOEXM, Exchange Routing Objects, the infamous EFD, WMI, client-side MAPI and server-side MAPI, WebDAV, and so on. The highest figure I ever heard was that there have been 32 different ways a programmer can write code to access Exchange data over the years. I cannot verify the count, but it does not surprise me.

Microsoft knows that they have a mess on their hands and the advent of PowerShell (see Chapter 10) support in Exchange 2007 means that we have a solid and robust interface that we can use to build a new set of management scripts and other tools. Exchange 2007 also delivers a new set of Web services that may mark the start of the process of breaking Exchange up into a series of Web services that other applications can consume. Decomposing a mammoth application will take time, but Microsoft has made a good start in Exchange 2007. Outside of the limited set of Web services that can only access a tiny portion of the overall functionality of Exchange, there is still no good way to develop mission-critical client side applications that exploit the storage and messaging power of Exchange and we await developments in this area.

1.1.7   Exchange's connection with the Active Directory

When Microsoft moved Exchange away from its own directory store to support the Active Directory in Exchange 2000, some predicted that the transition would make Exchange harder to manage and deploy. To some extent, this assertion is true as the need to deploy Active Directory first slowed down the migration from Exchange 5.5 to Exchange 2000. Indeed, some companies have not yet migrated away from Exchange 5.5!

Over time, I think that Active Directory has been good for Exchange. After the initial set of hiccups that slowed adoption, the body of knowledge around the Active Directory grew and some solid deployments ensued. This is not to say that the deployments were perfect and certainly some have corroded over time in terms of their effectiveness. The transition to Exchange 2007 is a perfect opportunity to revisit Active Directory deployments to ask the question whether they are as effective as they could be if they reflect current best practice, and to consider whether you can consolidate sites, domains, and servers to reduce complexity and cost from the infrastructure. You realize the worth of Active Directory to Exchange 2007 in the new dependency that exists on the site topology and site links as the basis for message routing, replacing the routing group structure used by Exchange 2000/2003.

The only big problem that I now have with the Active Directory is the inflexible way that Exchange uses it. Exchange uses a container in the Active

---

2.   CDO 1.2.1 remains supported for use with Exchange 2007, but only on 32-bit platforms.

Directory configuration naming context to store its configuration data. Exchange gains great value from this implementation, not least because the Active Directory replicates all of Exchange's configuration data automatically to domain controllers around the forest. However, no one has ever been able to explain to me why the Active Directory can host only a single Exchange organization, as it does not seem to be complex to store several containers, one for each organization, in the directory. It would be nice to see this restriction lifted in the future, if only to remove the requirement to deploy multiple forests (and the hardware to support multiple forests) if you need to support multiple Exchange organizations. Sometimes it is good to have the separation between organizations that different Active Directory forests afford, but it would be better to have the option to store everything in one place.

1.1.8   Reviewing predictions made in 1996

Scary as it seems, I have been writing about Exchange since 1996. The vast bulk of my scribbling has appeared in *Windows IT Pro* magazine (and its predecessors—see www.windowsitpro.com) and the *Exchange Administrator* newsletter, and I hope that the articles have helped you understand and exploit Exchange to the maximum over the years. However, my first article appeared in a publication called *Exchange Manager* that did not last very long. I wrote an article called "Scaling Exchange" where I looked at the practical issues involved in scaling Exchange 4.0 to deal with hundreds of users (my advice was not to support more than 300 users on a server). I wrote: "Lots of people get hung up about the 16GB limit for the Information Store…. I don't, because it's a limit that most of us will never encounter." I was right in one respect because Microsoft only upped the 16GB limit to 75GB for the standard edition of Exchange in Exchange 2003 SP2 (and then removed the limit completely in Exchange 2007), but the sheer number of messages that we send and the average size of those messages has exploded since 1996. Then, most messages in corporate email systems were between 5KB and 10KB. Now, they are bloated through a mixture of user indiscipline (horrible autosignature files, too many replies to replies, etc.) and huge attachments.

I went on to ask: "What was the last time you saw a Windows NT system that had more than 100GB of disk attached? Or more than 4 CPUs? Or even more than 256MB of memory or 512MB on a RISC system?" How times have changed. In my defense, our first Exchange servers boasted 66MHz 486 CPUs, had 64MB of memory, and 4GB of disk. Today, the best advice is to buy powerful 64-bit servers to run Exchange 2007, preferably with multi-core processors, gigabytes of memory, and lots of disk. In their justification (see the commentary in http://blogs.technet.com/exchange/archive/2005/12/29/416613.aspx) for the move to an exclusive 64-bit platform for Exchange 2007, Microsoft cites the fact that they believe that 500GB disks will be standard when Exchange 2007 ships and that 1TB disks will be available. Note that 64-bit means the x64 platform as Exchange 2007 does not support the Itanium (IA64) platform. Support for a version of Exchange running on IA64 may come in the future as SQL has already demonstrated the huge scalability potential of the IA64 platform.

I looked into the future by predicting that: "In the long term, the evolution of Windows NT to support 64-bit computing will raise the performance bar even further and allow people to consider even larger systems ... systems that can support thousands of users on a daily basis." I went on to ask Microsoft to consider raising the limit on the Information Store from 16GB to 16TB (Microsoft did this for the Enterprise version in Exchange 2000); support clustering (Microsoft shipped Wolfpack clustering in 1997 with Exchange 5.5, but the Exchange clustering story has been an uneven success since); support a single mailbox restore (possible with third-party products), since 1997; PSS generated the ExMerge utility in 1998 (a utility that Microsoft no longer supports in Exchange 2007); the Mailbox Recovery Center arrived in Exchange 2003; provide better support for multiple processors (done in Exchange 5.5 and much improved since); and optimize the code for non-Intel processors. Alas, the multi-platform play for NT and Exchange terminated after Windows NT 4.0/Exchange 5.5 when Microsoft halted their support for Windows NT on the Alpha CPU, but the 64-bit AMD and Intel platforms are now a great success for Exchange 2007. Looking back, it was not a bad list to ask for.

1.2   Microsoft's themes for Exchange 2007

Over the last ten years, the environment surrounding Exchange has evolved in many dimensions. Here are just a few of the most important technology influences that have affected the evolution of Exchange.

- The base operating system has moved from Windows NT 3.51 on a 32-bit platform to Windows 2003 R2 on a 64-bit platform.

- Storage has moved from small and expensive direct attached storage to a huge range of solutions spanning anything from JBOD (just a bunch of inexpensive disks) to very large SANs.

- Systems that might have been lucky to operate with 128MB of memory have moved to a point where many email servers are equipped with 8GB or more, and Microsoft's recommendations for memory for some Exchange 2007 servers will make 32GB or 64GB a common configuration in the near future.

- Microsoft has poured enormous engineering effort to bring Exchange through three distinct generations of software from the original focus on PC LAN-centric deployments and the need to migrate from competing products such as Lotus cc:Mail to the ability to deal with massive corporate deployments.

- Exchange's administrative model has moved from a purely graphical interface that dealt well with the needs of a few hundred users but struggled with large organizations to a point where Exchange 2007 complements an administrative GUI with a sophisticated shell that administrators can program to automate many management operations.

- The protocols that are important to Exchange have moved from a mishmash of messaging and directory protocols, both proprietary and international, to a point where we deal with a consistent set of Internet protocols such as SMTP, LDAP, HTTP, and IMAP.

- The computing model for Windows has evolved from an approach that usually focused on a one-server, one-application model to something that more closely resembles the kind of deployments seen on other corporate computing platforms.

- The range of clients that Exchange supports has expanded dramatically from a single Microsoft client that could only run on Windows to a variety of clients that accommodate the spectrum of user needs from traditional PC workstations to many variations of handheld devices.

When Microsoft began to design the third generation of Exchange, they decided to use three broad themes as the general thrust for the development effort. These are:

Built-in Protection: While Exchange has long had good protection against viruses and spam through third-party products and Exchange 2003 offers good filtering capabilities to block incoming messages from undesirable parties, Microsoft knew that they had to offer out-of-the-box protection for Exchange to remain competitive and to protect customers. Some of this work started with the release of the Internet Message Filter (IMF) for Exchange 2003 and the SmartScreen junk mail filtering technology that Outlook 2003 and 2007 incorporate into their code.

After they had released Exchange 2003, Microsoft's original plan was to deliver a server designed for deployment within the DMZ (the original Edge project). Microsoft based the original Edge project on Exchange 2003 technology, but they cancelled the project in late 2005. Microsoft bought market-leading anti-virus and anti-spam technology in-house through the acquisition of Sybari Software Inc. in 2006. They have since refined its capabilities since to produce the ForeFront Security for Exchange product, which is bundled with the Enterprise edition of Exchange 2007. In addition, Microsoft has dedicated considerable engineering effort to research how best to defend against email threats and contributed to projects such as the Sender ID initiative. While the result of this work is spread throughout Exchange 2007, much of it is focused in the Edge and hub transport server roles. The Edge server essentially completes the project that Microsoft started out to build some years ago with the added advantage that it is built on the Exchange 2007 code base. The bottom line is that Microsoft intends Exchange 2007 to be the most secure email server available anywhere. This is a laudable goal, but given the evolving nature of network threat, we will not really know whether Microsoft has succeeded until companies have moved to Exchange 2007 and moved away from the previous generation of servers.

Anywhere Access: This theme reflects the mobile nature of the world that we live in today rather than the tethered nature of traditional email access. Exchange has offered Web-based access since 1996 and support for handheld devices since 1999, first with RIM BlackBerry devices and then later Windows Mobile handhelds, but only through add-on products. Exchange 2003 introduced server-based ActiveSync and Outlook Mobile Access (support for WAP browsers). Neither offering was on par with the leaders in the market. Outlook Web Access was a reasonable Web-based interface, but it needed to move away from protocols such as WebDAV that had seemed the way forward when Microsoft introduced WebDAV support in Exchange 2000 but had now been bypassed, and create a new user interface based on the latest Web technologies such as ASP.NET. However, while increasing the functionality and power of Outlook Web Access and ActiveSync reflected some immediate technical imperatives of this theme, the more interesting aspect was the desire to incorporate voice technology into the Exchange platform for the first time. This was not a new technical challenge because third parties such as Nortel and Avaya had created good voicemail integrations with Exchange and Outlook as far back as 1998. The interesting challenge was to create a different type of integration than merely playing back received voicemail through Outlook messages and PC speakers. As they set out to create the Exchange 2007 Unified Messaging server, Microsoft wanted to deliver an integrated server that used the Exchange Store as the repository for voice and data and the Exchange messaging infrastructure to move voice messages around. On the client side, Outlook Voice Access lets users access their messaging, calendar, and directory data through a range of telephones from the latest SmartPhone to a plain old touch-tone phone.

Operational Efficiency: Even its best friends would not hold Exchange 2003 up as the best example of an operationally efficient messaging system. Exchange 2003 offers great functionality to end users at the expense of a lot of hard work by administrators at the back end. Issues included:

- Common administrative tasks such as moving mailboxes were hard to automate.

- The user interface presented by the administrative tools were sometimes confusing; there were too many black boxes in Exchange (think of how the Recipient Update Service stamps email addresses on newly created mailboxes).

- There are far too many places where Exchange suddenly enabled features if an administrator would only update the system registry with a magic key.

- Performance of some of the tools was acceptable for small to medium businesses but not for large organizations.

Sometimes you felt that the developers had simply lost interest when the time came to write the system management components of Exchange because they all wanted to create cool new features that were appreciated by users. This is quite a litany of complaints. I have had practice in composing this list because I have been quite vocal on the point both when speaking at conferences and when talking with the Exchange developers. Exchange 2003 is not bad software to have to manage, as long as you know its quirks and took the time to learn all about how it works. The trouble was that many people did not make the necessary effort to learn Exchange and the inevitable result was dissatisfaction, product issues, and system outages.

Perhaps the biggest change in attitude and focus that Microsoft has made since the release of Exchange 2003 is the effort that the development group has poured into making Exchange more automated, more manageable, and easier to deploy. Microsoft has pumped out a huge increase in wizards, automated management and analysis tools, and documentation since 2005. A new attitude seems to have infused the development group with the desire to improve the administrative characteristics of Exchange and you can see the result in Exchange 2007. While the most obvious change is in the Exchange Management Console, the real magic is in the introduction of the Exchange Management Shell because this is the basis for a new era of automation for common and not so common administrative tasks.

Figure 1.1 illustrates an example of how Microsoft has made Exchange 2007 more manageable than any previous version. Users receive nondelivery messages all the time, but the content of messages generated by older versions is often not too helpful to the average user. Exchange 2007 generates messages that are easy for users to understand what problem has occurred and include some additional information for administrators to figure out why the problem has occurred. For example, the bottom portion of the message shown in the left-hand screen of Figure 1.1 includes the error text, and then a trace of all of the servers (not illustrated) that the message passed through

Figure 1.1
Some improved system messages from Exchange 2007

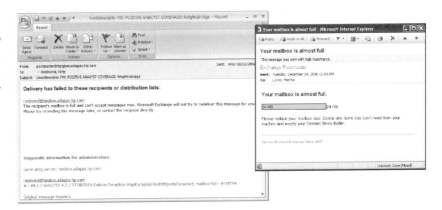

before Exchange detected the error. You see the same attention to detail in other places too, like the diagnostics information available from Outlook Web Access (Figure 1.2) to help administrators figure out why things may not be working as normal, the mailbox quota exceeded messages sent to users (the right-hand screen in Figure 1.1), and so on.

Figure 1.2
Outlook Web Access reveals all to help administrators fix problems

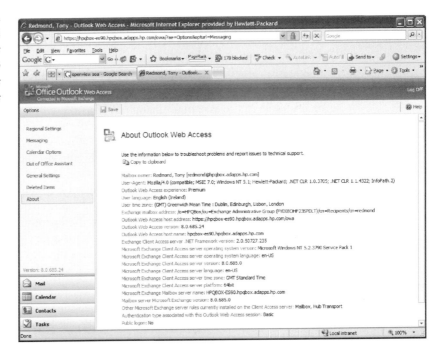

Microsoft has removed two major distinguishing features of the Exchange 2000/2003 architecture in Exchange 2007. When Microsoft introduced Exchange 2000, they had to provide backwards compatibility with

Exchange 5.5 in terms of management and routing, so they introduced the concept of administrative groups (comparable to Exchange 5.5 sites) and routing groups (comparable to Exchange 5.5 sites in terms of the routing topology). Unfortunately, the original plans to make administrative groups more flexible in terms of server management never quite worked out. As implemented in Exchange 2000 and 2003, administrative groups are an unintelligent container for servers and not much else. Experience with administrative groups has demonstrated that they were far too rigid in operation (you could not move a server between administrative groups) and not granular enough when it came to server management (delegation applied to all of the servers in the group rather than down to the individual server). The result is that many Exchange administrators ignored administrative groups and kept all the servers in the default administrative group.

According to surveys conducted by Microsoft at events like TechEd, the only administrators who paid much attention to administrative groups worked in large enterprises where the sheer number of servers and their distribution across multiple physical sites meant that administrative groups offered some benefits. Administrators of small to medium Exchange organizations often did not know about administrative groups because they never needed to do anything else but install all their servers into the default administrative group. The experience with routing groups was more positive because they offered flexibility and a way to control the routing topology but they required quite a lot of manual intervention to set up and manage. In addition, the move to a new SMTP routing engine that leveraged the Active Directory and used point-to-point TCP connections to create a full-mesh routing network based on deterministic routing meant that routing groups were no longer required. As we will see later on, a default administrative and a default routing group still linger on within Exchange 2007, but only as a method to allow management and routing to continue seamlessly in a mixed-mode organization.

Better security was another important focus for Exchange 2007. Microsoft has steadily increased the default level of security in its products to cope with the increased level of threat that exists within the network today. You will find that Exchange 2007 components are secure by default. For example, Outlook Web Access connects via HTTPS instead of HTTP as previously used; POP3 and IMAP4 clients connect over secure ports rather than the insecure default ports for these protocols; Exchange servers authenticate and connect securely before they transfer messages; and connectors are secure out of the box. Overall, Exchange 2007 is a much more secure product than its predecessors are. This is not to say that administrators are unable to punch holes in Exchange's security by removing restrictions, but even if you leave the default security settings, you will find that your installation is more secure than before. Tools provided by Microsoft to review and tighten security (such as the Windows 2003 Security Configuration Wizard) are helpful to ensure that you do not leave holes open on Exchange 2007 servers.

It is important to point out that Microsoft management gave these three major focus areas to Microsoft engineers to create cohesion in very large software engineering projects. However, you should not attribute the same degree of importance to these areas because they may not be critical to your organization. In fact, there may be specific areas inside Exchange 2007 that Microsoft thinks are hypercritical and you think are unimportant—such is the nature of very large and complex software products. You can often measure the real success of software in its longevity. Microsoft shipped Exchange 5.5 in 1997 and perhaps Microsoft's relative lack of success in persuading companies to move off Exchange 5.5 is due to its usability and relative ease of management. It will be interesting to see how Exchange 2007 has fared ten years after customers first deploy it and compare whether administrators feel the same positive way about it as many clearly do about Exchange 5.5.

1.2.1   The happy prospect of a migration

I doubt that there is a single administrator of a messaging system in the world who can honestly say that they enjoy the process of moving an email system from one software version to another. Over the three generations of Exchange, we have experienced relatively easy migrations, such as upgrading servers from Exchange 5.0 to 5.5 or from Exchange 2000 to 2003. These migrations required careful planning to ensure no disruption for users, but the actual mechanics of the upgrade were simple and easy to perform because there was no change to the fundamentals of Exchange—the operating system, hardware, or internal architecture. On the other hand, some migrations have caused massive upheaval because of the degree of change in those same fundamentals. Upgrading an Exchange organization from 5.5 to 2000 was not easy because of the requirement to install the Active Directory, which required a change in the base platform from Windows NT to Windows 2000. Administrators had enough of a steep learning curve to understand how Active Directory worked, especially around security boundaries and replication, and when you heaped the massive change in the Exchange architecture that Microsoft introduced in Exchange 2000, you had a recipe for many long hours of work to plan, deploy, and support the migration. From Microsoft's perspective, their decision to base Exchange 2000 around Active Directory was a great move because it forced many companies to introduce a corporate directory service long before they might have wanted to do so. Any company that wanted to use Exchange was forced to deploy the Active Directory first. The long-term effect is that the Active Directory is an embedded part of the core IT for any company who uses Exchange.

In the most part, we have mastered Active Directory now. While Exchange 2007 does not require disruption of the kind seen when you introduce a new corporate directory that simply has to work before applications can function, it does include two huge changes. First, Exchange 2007 only runs on 64-bit Windows on x64 servers. Second, Microsoft has torn up the administrative model used in Exchange 2000 and 2003 in favor of a simplified GUI for the management console and a whole new focus on a highly programmable scripting language implemented through a UNIX-like command shell. Administrators therefore face the need to refresh their server hardware inventory completely for both Exchange and Windows while at the same time they need to learn a whole bag of new tricks to work with and manage Exchange 2007.

The server refresh is not straightforward because you should not simply replace 32-bit servers for 64-bit models on a one-for-one basis. Such an approach could be an incredible waste of money and negate many of the advantages of the new platform. Exchange 2007 is an opportunity to completely revamp the original Active Directory and other base Windows infrastructure components laid down to support Exchange 2000 and 2003 with the intention of simplifying the infrastructure through consolidation of servers into a much smaller set of domain controllers, global catalog servers, DHCP servers, and the like. Consolidation is possible because a 64-bit Windows server is able to handle much more work than its 32-bit counterparts are and additional cheap network capacity usually makes it possible to bring the work to a smaller set of servers than to distribute it around the network. For the same reason, the same kind of consolidation may be possible with Exchange 2007. In one way, the introduction of server roles prompts you to think about the number and function of servers to deploy for Exchange 2007. How many mailbox servers will you deploy? How many servers of the other roles will you need and should you run multi-role servers or single-role servers? For example, if you want to deploy CCR on MNS clusters, these servers will be single-role mailbox servers whereas you can use LCR on multi-role servers. How will you take advantage of the larger memory model to support more mailboxes? How can you exploit SANs better to support the data requirements for consolidated servers in a datacenter? Exchange 2007 requires more memory than ever before to compensate for a large reduction in I/O operations. This leads on to a dramatically different I/O profile in terms of the demands that Exchange 2007 makes on storage subsystems. Large SANs will be able to support more servers and you can build servers around newer storage technologies that offer better performance and lower cost. There is quite a bit of work to do to figure out the most appropriate configuration for Exchange 2007 servers in any organization.

With so much upheaval caused by the transition to 64-bit servers, you should take the opportunity to have a long hard look at the server and storage infrastructure you use for Exchange 2003 and think about how you can consolidate to remove cost, complexity, and administrative overhead. You cannot upgrade an Exchange 2003 server to Exchange 2007 server, so you have to use the move mailbox function to get user data across to the new servers. With this in mind, there is an obvious opportunity to plan for a smaller number of mailbox servers that support larger user communities.

Another point that you should consider is whether the time is right for you to virtualize some of your Windows infrastructure, including domain controllers and Global Catalog servers. There is no doubt that virtual servers will gradually replace physical servers over time in order to maximize the use that we can get from increasingly powerful hardware. The capabilities of the virtual server software that is available today are incredible, even if it is not all from Microsoft. Virtual servers should definitely be on your agenda to support test servers at the very least, but it is now time to take a hard look at your Windows servers to figure out what you can deploy on virtual servers and what has to stay on physical servers.

Of course, server consolidation is not easy and you need to do a lot of planning to make sure that you deploy and populate new servers with data without causing disruption to users. The end goal is worthwhile because fewer servers are easier and cheaper to manage, so the lower operational costs may pay for some or all of the overall migration effort.

The impact of the change in the administrative model is harder to predict. Some administrators will take to the Exchange Management Shell with gusto and will become very comfortable with the 360+ new commands that Microsoft has made available to manage Exchange 2007 through PowerShell. Other administrators will be like lost lambs in a storm, wondering where their familiar graphical management console has gone and struggling with the syntax of the shell. To a large degree, the change is in terms of culture and philosophy as well as technology, and it will take people time to adjust.

To return to the original point—migrations are not easy and we face some big changes in Exchange 2007 that make the migration to this version more difficult to plan for. However, the good thing is that careful planning, attention to detail, and dedication to mastering the new technology will bring success, albeit at the expense of a lot of time and effort.

1.3   Preparing for Exchange 2007

Because of its dependence on the Active Directory, just like Exchange 2000 and 2003, you have to prepare the forest and every domain that will host mail-enabled objects before you can install Exchange 2007. Consult the Exchange 2007 documentation and the release notes to get the most up-to-date information on what you need to do to install Exchange 2007. In general, the major considerations that you need to incorporate into a deployment plan are:

- Ensure that the schema master, domain controllers, and Global Catalogs in any domain that will support an Exchange 2007 server runs Windows 2003 SP1, R2, or later.

- Ensure that the Active Directory functional level for the forest is Windows 2003. This is not a strict prerequisite. However, I recommend that you move the forest to Windows 2003 functional level before you deploy Exchange 2007.

- Ensure that any legacy Exchange servers are running Exchange 2003 SP2 or Exchange 2000 SP3 with the post-SP3 update rollup (available from Microsoft's Web site).[3] No Exchange 5.5 servers can be in the forest. Unless Microsoft supports you through a beta program, you will have to remove and reinstall any servers that run beta versions of Exchange 2007.

- Ensure that you have a Global Catalog server in every Active Directory site that you intend deploying an Exchange 2007 server. Note that Exchange 2007 setup will fail if the Active Directory site contains a Windows 2000 domain controller. You should upgrade these servers to Windows 2003 SP1 before you deploy Exchange 2007.

- Run Setup /PrepareAD in the forest root to prepare the forest creating forest-wide objects used by Exchange 2007.

- Run Setup /PrepareSchema to extend the Active Directory schema to support Exchange 2007. You need to take this step even if you have extended the schema to support Exchange 2000 or 2003.

- Run Setup /PrepareDomain for every domain in the forest that will host mail-enabled objects.

- If you are installing Exchange 2007 into an existing Exchange 2000/2003 organization, you have to run Setup with the /PrepareLegacyExchangePermissions switch.

- Install the first Exchange 2007 server into an Active Directory site that is close (in network terms) to the site that supports the schema master.

- Exchange 2007 has its own SMTP stack, so you should remove the standard Windows SMTP server or the SMTP server installed by IIS before you install Exchange hub transport or Edge servers.

You can run ExBPA, the Exchange Best Practice Analyzer tool, to verify that your organization is ready to deploy Exchange 2007. ExBPA performs

---

3.   It is important that legacy Exchange servers run the latest service packs because this software includes the updates to allow the Exchange System Manager console to deal with Exchange 2007 objects correctly.

checks against the Active Directory, validates that you have the correct version of software deployed on legacy servers, and generally checks that you will not meet any surprises when you come to install your first Exchange 2007 server. See Chapter 10 for more information on ExBPA.

It is important that servers run at least Windows 2003 SP1 because Exchange 2007 depends on its notification mechanism to advise components that an update has occurred in the Active Directory. In addition, Outlook Web Access 2007 depends on improvements made in Windows 2003 SP1 to exploit a feature called VLV (Virtual List View) to perform more efficient lookups against the GAL.

While you must install Exchange 2007 on new 64-bit servers, you do not necessarily have to deploy 64-bit domain controllers and Global Catalog servers, as Exchange is happy to use the Active Directory on 32-bit servers. There is no doubt that 64-bit Windows servers are much more scalable than their 32-bit equivalent, largely because they can cache even very large Active Directory databases completely in memory and so improve performance for applications that depend on the directory, like Exchange. It is a good idea to plan for the introduction of 64-bit Windows servers to provide the essential infrastructure to support Exchange 2007 and to deploy this infrastructure well before you plan to install Exchange 2007, just to make sure that the supporting infrastructure is fully bedded down.

1.4   Installing Exchange 2007

In some respects, the task of the engineers who created the Exchange 2007 setup program was simple. After all, because it is not possible to upgrade an old 32-bit Exchange 2000 or 2003 server to Exchange 2007, they only had to build a program to install Exchange on brand-new 64-bit servers, and conceptually, there is nothing easier than taking software off an installation kit and arranging it across the available space on a disk. Of course, it is easy enough to say, but difficult to do, especially when you want to create an installation procedure that is intelligent, robust, and difficult for administrators to make mistakes when they install Exchange. The latter point is important for Microsoft because a good installation program reduces the number of support calls that they receive, especially after the launch of a new version of a product. Support costs are very expensive because they often require human intervention to solve the reported problem.

The Exchange developers have done a good job with the Exchange 2007 installation program. A lot of intelligence is incorporated into the program so that even before you begin to get near to installing Exchange, the program does a comprehensive job of scanning the target server to ensure that you have already installed all the necessary pre-requisite software (such as PowerShell version 1.0, version 2.0 of the .NET framework or later, and MMC

3.0). The program also checks the Active Directory to ensure that the schema is at the necessary version. Even better, unlike other installations that tell you that something is wrong and then promptly exit to leave the poor administrator to figure out how to fix the problem, a strong point of Exchange 2007's installation program is its integration with Microsoft's support network. When it detects a problem, the installation program points you to the right Web page to download the components that are necessary to fix the problem. Of course, this will not do you much good if you have to install Exchange 2007 in a secure location that's isolated from the Internet, but it's great for the vast majority of installations.

Figure 1.3

*Installing
Exchange 2007*

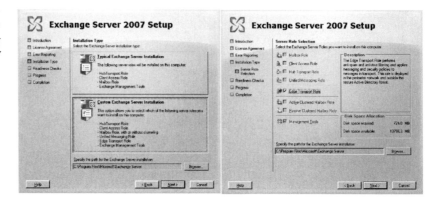

The user interface that allows you to select the options for the installation are well thought out and easy to follow. Figure 1.3 shows how you can select a typical installation (install the hub transport, client access, and mailbox roles, and the Exchange Management Console, Help files, and the Exchange Management Shell extensions for PowerShell) or a customized installation. If you select a customized installation, you can decide what roles to install on a server and, if you want to create a mailbox server, whether you want to use a cluster configuration. Custom installation is also the place to go when you want to deploy an Edge server or Unified Messaging server.

Before beginning the actual installation, the program checks to see whether any new best practice advice is available from Microsoft and downloads the advice if Microsoft has updated it since they built the installation kit. This is a good example of how Microsoft is leveraging the investment that they have made since 2003 in building intelligent analysis and reporting tools for Exchange because the installation program can access the same knowledge base as the Exchange Best Practice Analyzer to find out about nonsoftware items that have to be resolved before a successful installation can proceed. For example, Figure 1.4 shows that an installation of an Edge server detected two problems before proceeding. In both cases, the installation program can connect you to a Web page that contains the steps necessary to fix the problem. In this case, because Microsoft designed the Edge server to operate within the DMZ and because Exchange 2007 uses its own SMTP stack, it is necessary to turn off the standard SMTP service that is part of IIS. If you install a server that supports multiple roles, the installation program will determine the order that it installs the roles. However, if you install a single-role server and then decide to install other roles on that server, the suggested order to do this is Client Access Server, Hub Transport, and Mailbox followed by Unified Messaging if required.

Figure 1.4

An error detected by the Exchange 2007 setup program

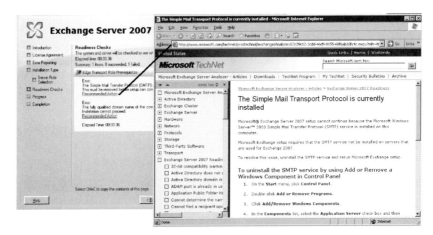

Note that you must have at least one hub transport server in an Active Directory site if the site supports a mailbox server. A mailbox server cannot communicate on its own and needs the hub transport server to act as its point of contact with the rest of the organization. A hub transport server is also required if you deploy a Unified Messaging server. Exchange 2007 uses server-side RPCs to connect servers together within the same site. Microsoft has never optimized RPCs to work over extended WAN connections that you might expect between Active Directory sites. For this reason, if you have an Active Directory site that supports a small number of users, you will deploy either a single multi-role server (mailbox, hub, and client access) or route client connections to servers in another site.

Exchange 2007 supports command line installations if you do not like the GUI. Command line installations are very useful if you want to use unattended installations. You have to log onto the target server and then execute Setup, passing the options that you want to use for the installation. For example:

```
Setup.com /Mode:install /Roles:C, H, M /On:XYZ /dc:GC-
Dublin.xyz.com /EnableLegacyOutlook /
LegacyRoutingServer:Exch2003BHS /DisableErrorReporting
```

This command line tells the installation procedure to:

- Install the Client Access, Hub Transport, and Mailbox roles in the XYZ organization.
- Use GC-Dublin.xyz.com as the domain controller.
- Enable support for legacy Outlook clients (Outlook 2003 and previous). Essentially, this means that Exchange 2007 will be installed with public folders as legacy clients are heavily dependent on public folders.
- Create a routing group connector to link back to legacy Exchange servers; the Exch2003BHS server is the bridgehead on the legacy side of the connector.
- Disable the option to report errors back to Microsoft for inclusion in their quality improvement program (some companies have internal rules that stop them from reporting error data in this way).

Exchange 2007 also has the ability for an administrator to assign the responsibility for completing the installation of a server to another user with the /NewProvisionedServer command switch. In this scenario, an enterprise administrator executes the heavily permissioned parts of the installation procedure to create the server object and add the delegated account to the local administrators group on the target server. The delegated user account is also added to the Exchange View Only administrators group. Effectively, the enterprise administrator delegates enough authority to allow the designated user to run Setup to complete the actual creation of the physical server (such as moving files to the right location on the disk, etc.). The other user only has the necessary permission to be able to complete the installation of the designated server and can take no other action. See the section on "Changes in the Exchange Delegation Model" in Chapter 3 for more information.

Behind the scenes, the Exchange 2007 installation program writes a vast amount of information into a set of log files that it creates in the \Exchange-SetupLogs directory on the drive that you use to install Exchange. Amongst the files that you'll find there are some PowerShell scripts (the exact number depends on the kind of installation that you perform on the server) that Exchange generates to install itself. Figure 1.5 shows an extract of a script generated during the installation of the mailbox role on a server. You can see commands to stop services that must not be running when Exchange is being installed followed by commands to precompile the software components used by Exchange.

Overall, Microsoft has done an excellent job to create a nice tool for administrators in the Exchange 2007 installation program. Running the installation program should not cause many concerns for your deployment and may be the easiest part of the process. Following the installation, you normally have some work to do that is more complicated. For example, if you do not want to configure a routing group connector to link your first Exchange 2007 server with a legacy organization during the installation, you could do it after you have checked out the newly installed server and made sure that everything is working as expected. Another task to support legacy clients is to configure the Offline Address Book for legacy Outlook clients. Other tasks include making sure that the Availability service is running smoothly, installing some anti-virus software, setting up an Edge server, or even plunging into the new world of Unified Messaging to allow Exchange users to access their mailbox through the phone. We will get to all of these tasks later on in the book.

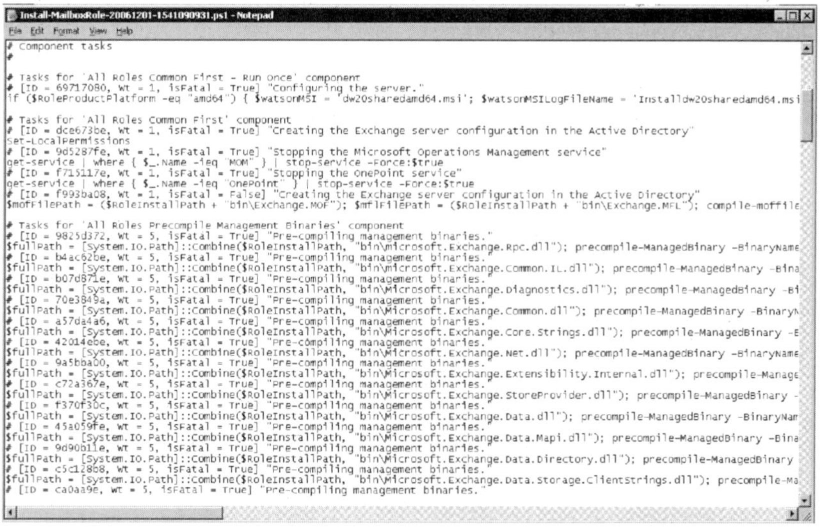

Figure 1.5

Extract of a PowerShell script used to install Exchange 2007

After you complete a server installation, you should consider running the Microsoft Security Configuration Wizard (SCW) to harden the server. Exchange 2007 includes support for SCW, so you can follow the directions in the installation guide to run SCW and configure security for the different server roles. Before you begin using SCW, you need to register the SCW extensions for the server roles. You can do this with these commands. The first command registers the extensions for any role except the Edge server; the second registers the extension for the Edge server.

```
Scwcmd register /kbname:"Ex2007KB" /kbfile:"%programfiles%\
Microsoft\Exchange Server\scripts\Exchange2007.xml"

Scwcmd register /kbname:"Ex2007EdgeKB" /
kbfile:"%programfiles%\Microsoft\Exchange Server\scripts\
Exchange2007Edge.xml"
```

1.4.1   Modifying and removing servers

To modify or remove an existing Exchange 2007 server, you can use either the Windows Control Panel (to add/remove software) or the ExSetup program, which you'll find in the \Program Files\Microsoft\Exchange Server\Bin directory. This program has several modes:

- /Install: Add a new role to an existing Exchange 2007 server.

- /Uninstall: Remove a role or a complete Exchange 2007 server. For example, to remove the client access role from a server, use ExSetup / Mode:Uninstall /Roles:CA.

- /Upgrade: Upgrade to a new release.

- /Recover Server: Recover a server using the information about it stored in the Active Directory.

- /Clustered: Designate an active role in a cluster.

1.4.2   Validating the installation

After the installation process checks, you may want to validate the installation by testing that the installation procedure has generated a functioning Exchange server. The installation procedure logs all of the operations that it performs in the Exchange setup log file at C:\ExchangeSetupLogs\ExchangeSetup.log. It is certainly possible to review the setup log, but it is verbose in the level of detail that it captures. You can filter the application event log for events written by MSExchangeSetup and check for events 1000 (starting to install a server role) and 1001 (successfully installed a server role). Alternately, you can use a PowerShell script called Get-SetupLog.ps1[4] to parse the contents of the setup log and report the entries found there. Figure 1.6 shows what you can expect to see from both the Get-SetupLog script and the application event log.

Of course, another way of looking at things is to say that you have not installed a server until it works and that the only good test validates that

---

4.   Located in \Program Files\Microsoft\Exchange Server\Scripts. You can find details of how to use the script in TechNet or in the header of the script.

Figure 1.6
*Checking the
installation log*

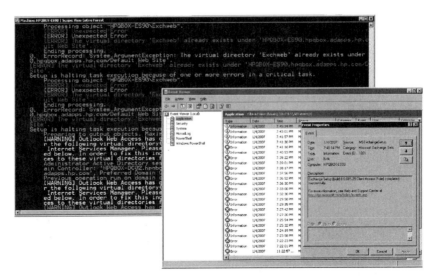

the server works in all its various roles. You can use some simple tests for this purpose. First, use the `Get-ExchangeServer` PowerShell command to see whether the output of the command includes the new server in the list of Exchange servers in the organization. Second, log onto the server and use the special test commands supported by the Exchange Management Shell work as expected. You can find details of how to use these commands in Chapter 4.

1.4.3 Third-party software

Migrations can only proceed at the pace of the slowest component and often that slowest component is some essential piece of third-party software that's used with Exchange in your production environment. Table 1.1 lists a representative sample of third parties that engineer software that supports Exchange 2007 in some way. This list is likely to grow over time, so you should consult the online list that Microsoft maintains at http:// www.microsoft.com/exchange/partners/default.mspx for the latest information. In addition, you need to check with the vendor to ensure that they do not have any special prerequisites for deployment alongside Exchange 2007, such as an inability to support clusters, a requirement to deploy on a single role server, or anything else.

1.5 Server roles

The notion of giving a server a particular role to fulfil within a messaging infrastructure is not new and messaging architects have assigned roles such as

Table 1.1 *Representative sample of third-party product support for Exchange 2007*

Software Category	Products
Anti-virus	Microsoft ForeFront Security for Exchange, TrendMicro, McAfee, Symantec, GFI, Kasperski, Sophos, F-Secure
Archiving (compliance)	HP, Commvault, Symantec, Hummingbird, Mobius, Overtone, Atempo, AXS-One, Zantaz
Content Filtering	IXOS, Meridio
FAX Gateway	Fenestrae, GFI, Captaris, BNS Group
IP/PBX Gateway	Audiocodes, Dialogics
Line of Business Applications	Newsgator (RSS), nCipher, K2 (workflow)
Management	Quest Software, NetIQ, Computer Associates, HP, Zenprise
Migration from Legacy Exchange to Exchange 2007	Quest Software
Mobile Clients and Management	RIM (BlackBerry), Good (GoodLink)
Public Folder Migration	Quest Software, Tzunami
Secure Messaging	nCipher, RSA, CheckPoint
Storage (Backup, Disaster Recovery, High Availability)	HP, NetApp, Hitachi, CommVault, Symantec, Doubletake, Computer Associates, UltraBack, F5, Teneros, Azaleos, Cemaphore, Xiotech, Mimosa

front-end servers, mailbox servers, and mail hygiene servers within their designs for years. The difference in Exchange 2007 is that Microsoft has defined server roles within the product so that, for example, you now manage and view servers through ESM according to roles. To make the definition of roles effective, Microsoft has divided the Exchange code base so that you only install and operate the code on a server that is absolutely necessary. There is no doubt that the more code you run on a server, the higher potential exists for you to uncover bugs, some of which are urgent problems such as security holes that need to be plugged with hot fixes. In addition, if you have a service pack or hot fix to apply, it is a lot easier when you only have to apply it to a server that hosts the role that requires the updated code.

The previous generation of Exchange became more and more like a monolithic messaging behemoth as Exchange 2000 went through four service packs, evolved into Exchange 2003 and added a new set of service packs, not to mention the inevitable collection of bug fixes. Microsoft's decision to divide Exchange's functionality into different roles allowed them to reduce the code that runs on a server to just the set that is required to implement the desired functionality and no more. Over the long term, deploying Exchange in this way should increase server stability and remove complexity (because you will not have unexpected or unwanted options appearing on servers), so the introduction of server roles is rather more strategic than a simple exercise in packaging.

In practice, because an Exchange 2007 server can take on multiple roles, there is nothing to stop you deploying from Exchange 2007 servers in exactly the way that you have deployed Exchange 2000 or 2003 servers in the past. Many small to medium companies will deploy multi-role servers because they don't want to operate multiple physical computers just for Exchange. The advantage of dividing Exchange functionality into different roles is really for the enterprise market where companies commonly operate tens or hundreds of servers within a distributed network. Apart from the Edge role, you can install and remove roles from a server to meet changing circumstances, assuming that the servers have enough hardware capacity to take on the new workload.

The set of server roles in Exchange 2007 are:

- Client Access servers: These servers are responsible for proxying client connections to the servers that host user mailboxes, much like Exchange 2003 front-end servers handle incoming connections from POP3, IMAP4, Web, and mobile clients before relaying them to back-end servers that host user mailboxes. Client Access servers do the work to render the Outlook Web Access user interface for Web clients and they also provide the Exchange 2007 Web services such as the Availability service to clients. Users whose mailboxes are on Exchange 2003 servers can access their mailboxes through Exchange 2007 Client Access Servers. Microsoft does not support access to Exchange 2007 mailboxes through Exchange 2003 front-end servers.

- Mailbox servers: These servers are responsible for managing user mailboxes and handling MAPI connections to mailboxes and public folders. Mailbox servers are the only role that you can run on a cluster.

- Hub transport servers: These servers form the basis of the messaging topology and are responsible for routing messages between mailbox servers inside the organization and the transmission of messages via connectors to external messaging systems.

- Edge transport servers: These servers are designed to operate in standalone mode and are not part of the Exchange organization or the Active Directory forest, so they can be placed outside the firewall inside the DMZ to act as the first point of contact in the messaging infrastructure. Edge servers run anti-spam and anti-virus agents to cleanse the incoming message stream before handing it over to hub transport servers for routing within the internal Exchange organization. No other server role can exist on an Edge server.

- Unified messaging servers: This is a new server role for Microsoft, but UM is not a new technology and other vendors such as Nortel, Adomo, and Cisco have offered integration between PABX and Exchange for years. The unified messaging servers are responsible for the routing of messages between a PABX and Exchange so that you can use the phone to communicate with Exchange through a new product offering called Outlook Voice Access. You need to deploy a gateway (IP-PBX or VoIP) to connect the UM server with your PBX before you can use Outlook Voice Access.

The suggested deployment order for the most common roles is Client Access server, mailbox server, and hub transport server. If you deploy server roles on different physical servers, you need to ensure fast network links between them. For example, you need at least 100Mbit links between Client Access and mailbox servers—1Gbit is better.

You can only deploy mailbox servers on clusters (both traditional clusters—SCC—and the new continuous log replication—CCR—clusters), largely because Microsoft has not done the testing to support the other roles on when clustered. In addition, you can argue that server roles that typically deal only with transient data (such as hub transport servers) do not need the resilience to storage failure that clusters can deliver for mailbox servers. You can achieve the necessary degree of resilience for other server roles without clustering. For example, you can deploy several hub transport servers in a site to load balance the messaging workload—if one of the hub transport servers fails, the remaining hub transport servers take up the workload. The same is true for Client Access and Edge servers.

Apart from the Edge server, you can combine server roles on a single physical computer (similar in concept to the way that you deploy Exchange 2003 servers that host mailboxes and connectors) except clustered servers. The design and code base of the Edge server is very different to the other roles. There is some debate as to what is the best practice for installing an Edge server. Some administrators advocate installing Edge servers into a Windows workgroup to keep them well isolated from the production environment. Others prefer to install a separate version of the Active Directory for the DMZ and install the Edge server into that domain. In either case, every Edge server has its own and separate instance of ADAM (Active Directory Application Mode) to hold a read-only copy of the Exchange organization configuration (so that it can participate in routing) that is synchronized from a hub transport server through a push process. The ADAM instance also holds configuration data specific to the Edge server. To complete the picture, Table 1.2 summarizes how each of the server roles interacts with Active Directory.

1.5.1   Services

Following a successful installation, you will find that a number of separate services related to Exchange 2007 are active on your server. A Windows service is an executable file designed to run independently as a background process that Windows can launch during system start-up or when an application starts. The exact set of Exchange services that you find on a server depends on the roles that the server supports. All previous versions of Exchange have

Table 1.2   *How different Exchange 2007 server roles interact with Active Directory*

Role	Active Directory Use
Mailbox	Authentication of MAPI client connections. Retrieval of information about mail-enabled objects from the directory plus the necessary data required to enforce email address policies.
Client Access	Authentication of non-MAPI client connections (IMAP, POP, ActiveSync, Outlook Web Access, Outlook Voice Access). Lookup of server that hosts target mailbox.
Hub Transport	Lookup against the directory during message categorization. Expansion of distribution groups. Execution of queries against the directory to populate dynamic distribution groups. Expansion of groups used in transport rules plus storage of transport and journal rules in Exchange configuration data. Use of Active Directory site topology as the fundamental underpinning for routing.
Unified Messaging	Storage for global configuration such as dial plans, IP gateways, and hunt groups. Active Directory is also used to build speech grammars that are used to find users and to match telephone numbers to accounts.
Edge	Uses an ADAM instance rather than Active Directory to hold its configuration and other data, but synchronizes recipient and configuration information from the production Active Directory so that the Edge server understands how to route messages effectively. Edge synchronization also includes safe list information generated by users to improve the effectiveness of anti-spam processing.

used a similar set of services; the difference is that Exchange 2007 uses rather more services as a by-product of server role segmentation. Figure 1.7 illustrates a set of services active on a server that supports the mailbox, Client Access, and hub transport server roles. Some services such as IMAP4 and POP3 access are not used extensively with Exchange in most enterprises outside companies that provide hosting services. It is quite safe to leave these to be started manually until you find that they are needed. Others, such as the Store and System Attendant, represent the fundamental core of Exchange 2007 and run on any server. The Transport service is the other critical component, but this only runs on hub and Edge servers.

Figure 1.7
*The set of
Exchange services*

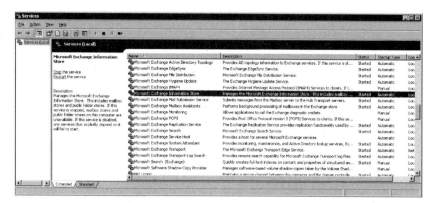

Table 1.3 lists the full set of Exchange services with a brief description of what the service does, the server roles that it is valid for, and a note whether the service is required or optional.

Table 1.3   *Exchange 2007 services*

Service name	Description	Server Roles	Notes
Active Directory Topology (MS-ExchangeADTopology)	Runs under LocalSystem. Interrogates the Active Directory and returns configuration and other data to Exchange.	MBX, CAS, HT, UM	Required
ADAM (ADAM_MSExchange)	Network service. Manages data about Exchange configuration and recipient data that is synchronized from the Active Directory to an Edge Transport server.	ET	Required (only by ET servers)

Table 1.3　*Exchange 2007 services (continued)*

Anti-spam Update service (MS-ExchangeAntiSpamUpdate)	Runs under LocalSystem to automatically download anti-spam updates from Microsoft.	HT, ET	Optional (you have to license the anti-spam service)
Credential service (EdgeCredentialSync)	Runs under LocalSystem to monitor any credential changes that occur in ADAM and then implements the changes on the Edge Transport Server	ET	Required (only by ET servers)
EdgeSync (MSExchangeEdgeSync)	Runs under LocalSystem on a HT server to connect via LDAP to an ADAM instance on an ET server to synchronize data from the Active Directory to ADAM. Depends on AD Topology service.	HT	Required (only if ET servers are used)
File Distribution Service (MS-ExchangeFDS)	Runs under LocalSystem to copy the files that make up Offline Address Books to Web distribution points. Also distributes any custom prompts used by Unified Messaging. Depends on AD Topology and workstation services.	CAS, UM	Required
IMAP4 (MSExchangeIMAP4)	Runs under LocalSystem to allow IMAP4 clients to connect to mailboxes. Dependent on AD Topology service.	CAS	Optional
Information Store (MSExchangeIS)	Runs under LocalSystem to manage mailboxes and public folders. Dependent on several Windows services including NT LM Security, RPC, Server, and workstation.	Mailbox	Required
Mail submission service (MsExchangeMailSubmission)	Runs under LocalSystem to transfer messages from a mailbox server to a HT server. Dependent on AD Topology service.	Mailbox	Required
Mailbox Assistants (MsExchangeMailboxAssistants)	Runs under LocalSystem to manage the calendar, resource booking, OOF, and managed folder assistants. Dependent on AD Topology service.	Mailbox	Required

Table 1.3 *Exchange 2007 services (continued)*

Monitoring (MSExchangeMonitor-ing)	Runs under LocalSystem to provide an RPC server that can be used to execute diagnostic commands on a server.	All	Optional
POP3 (MSExchangePOP3)	Runs under LocalSystem to allow POP3 clients to connect to mail-boxes. Dependent on AD Topology service.	CAS	Optional
Replication (MSExchangeRepl)	Runs under LocalSystem to manage the process of transaction log ship-ping at the heart of LCR (Local Con-tinuous Replication) and CCR (Cluster Continuous Replication). Dependent on AD Topology service.	Mailbox	Required
Search (MSFTESQL-Exchange)	Runs as LocalSystem to insert new items provided by the Search Indexer into the full-text index maintained for mailbox databases. This is a cus-tomized version of the general-pur-pose Microsoft Search engine and is dependent on the RPC service.	Mailbox	Optional (if you want to use content indexing).
Search Indexer (MSExchangeSearch)	Runs under LocalSystem to provide new items to the Search service. Dependent on AD Topology and Search services.	Mailbox	Optional (if you want to use content indexing)
Service Host (MSExchangeService-Host)	Runs under LocalSystem to manage the RPC virtual directory in IIS and the registry data required for Outlook Anywhere. Dependent on the AD Topology Service.	Mailbox, CAS	
Speech Engine (MSS)	Runs as network service to provide UM speech processing services. Dependent on Windows WMI ser-vice.	UM	Required (for UM)
System Attendant (MSExchangeSA)	Runs under LocalSystem to provide monitoring, maintenance, and direc-tory lookup services for Exchange. Dependent on the same set of Win-dows services as the Store.	Mailbox	Required

Table 1.3   *Exchange 2007 services (continued)*

Transport (MSExchangeTransport)	Runs as network service to manage the Exchange SMTP service and the transport stack. Dependent on the AD Topology service.	HT, ET	Required
Transport Log Search (MSExchange-TransportLogSearch)	Runs under LocalSystem to allow administrators to trace the path of messages through the message tracking log.	Mailbox, HT, ET	Optional (must be running before message tracking can work)
Unified Messaging (MS-ExchangeUM)	Runs as LocalSystem to manage the Exchange UM engine and provide the services that make up Outlook Voice Access. Dependent on the AD Topology and Speech Engine services.	UM	Required (for UM)

Just for the sake of comparison, Exchange 4.0 had just four core services (System Attendant, MTA, Information Store, and Directory Store). The Internet Mail Connector (for SMTP) was an optional extra that you had to pay for and we did not have to worry so much about spam and viruses. Things have certainly changed since 1996.

1.6   Licensing

There are two different versions of Exchange 2007: the standard edition and the enterprise edition. Microsoft targets the standard edition at small to medium companies and is the version that is included in Microsoft Small Business Server. The enterprise edition is more appropriate to the messaging needs of large corporations. As you can see from Table 1.4, the major differences between the two editions occur within the Store. Because the enterprise edition focuses on large corporations, it is logical that it should support a much larger amount of storage groups and databases.

Apart from deciding on what server edition to run, you also have to make sure that every user (or device) has a client access license (CAL). There are two types of CAL: standard and enterprise. The standard CAL provides access to the basic functionality that makes Exchange an email server. The enterprise CAL is additive, meaning that you have to purchase a standard CAL first and then add the enterprise CAL to gain access to the enterprise-level features. Table 1.5 lists the functionality enabled by each CAL type.

Table 1.4 *Exchange database features in standard and enterprise editions*

Feature	Standard	Enterprise
Maximum number of Storage Groups	Up to five	Up to fifty
Maximum number of databases	Up to five	Up to fifty
Maximum size of an individual database	No software limit	No software limit
Clusters	Not supported	Support for both MNS (CCR) and traditional (SCC) clusters
Continuous replication	LCR (local) only	LCR (local) and CCR (cluster)

Table 1.5 *Functionality gained through standard and enterprise CALs*

Feature	Standard CAL	Enterprise CAL
Email	Included	Included
Calendar	Included	Included
Tasks	Included	Included
Contacts	Included	Included
Outlook Web Access	Included	Included
ActiveSync	Included	Included
Unified Messaging		Included
Per-User/Per-Group Journaling		Included
Managed Folders		Included
Exchange Hosted Filtering		Included
Forefront Security for Exchange Server		Included

Exchange hosted filtering and Forefront Security for Exchange Server are not covered by licenses sold in the retail channel. You have to purchase licenses from Microsoft through their Volume Licensing Program if you want to use these features. Hosting filtering means that Microsoft takes responsibility for filtering email traffic en route to an organization by passing it through a set of servers that Microsoft operates before redirecting the mes-

Figure 1.8
EMC detects an
unlicensed server

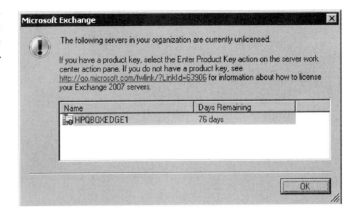

sage stream to its original destination. This is a similar offering to that of other companies such as Postini, Symantec, and MessageLabs.

Exchange 2007 is more demanding in terms of license enforcement. It prompts administrators that they need to take corrective action if their servers remain unlicensed. Every time the Exchange Management Console starts, it checks all of the current servers in the organization and reports any that are unlicensed, as shown in Figure 1.8. All servers are unlicensed immediately after you install them. You move them to licensed status when you input a valid product key (a standard 25 character alphanumeric string in five groups separated by hyphens) that you purchase from Microsoft. You can select a server and enter the product key or use the Set-ExchangeServer PowerShell command to enter the product key. For example, this command enters a product key for the ExchMbxSvr1 server:

```
Set-ExchangeServer —id ExchMbxSvr1 —ProductKey '10554-212-
7070916-06623'
```

Unlicensed editions expire 120 days after you install them, but you can continue running these versions in environments such as test laboratories as long as you can tolerate the constant nagging to enter a product key. Alternatively, you can remove and reinstall the test servers to start an extra 120 days of nag-free work.

You can perform the same check as EMC with a single line of Power-Shell code:

```
Get-ExchangeServer | Where {$_.AdminDisplayVersion —iLike '*8.0*' —and
$_.ProductId —eq $Null} | Select Name, Edition, RemainingTrialPeriod
```

Name	Edition	RemainingTrialPeriod
HPQBOXEDGE1	Unknown	76.03:49:54.4808287

We'll get to do a lot more to work with Exchange data through Power-Shell in Chapter 4, but for now it's enough to know that this command queries the Exchange configuration data in the Active Directory for a list of Exchange servers in the organization. A filter then reduces the set to just the servers that run Exchange 2007 and have a blank ProductId property, which indicates an unlicensed state. Edge servers always return a blank ProductId property until they have taken out a subscription to a hub transport server and joined the organization. The synchronization process between the Edge and hub transport servers inserts the licensing information from the Edge server into the Exchange configuration so that Exchange acknowledges the license and EMC ceases to worry about the status of the server. The valid edition types[5] are "Unknown," "Standard," "Standard Evaluation," "Enterprise," and "Enterprise Evaluation."

Another interesting difference in the Exchange 2007 license that may affect more companies is that it no longer includes a client license for Outlook. All previous versions of Exchange have included a PC client from the original Capone client distributed with Exchange 4.0 to Outlook 2003 with Exchange 2003. Microsoft believes that Outlook Web Access has progressed to a state where it delivers so much functionality that it serves as an adequate replacement, but as covered in Chapter 7, the inability to use the client offline and lack of support for public folders until SP1 will make Outlook Web Access a bad swap for many companies. The choice that you have is to continue to use Outlook 2003 with Exchange 2007 or to negotiate a separate upgrade with Microsoft to use Office 2007. As always with licensing, the conditions and licenses that companies have vary greatly, so your company should have a discussion with your local Microsoft representative to understand exactly what your Software Assurance or Enterprise Agreement covers in terms of upgrades to new software versions.

---

5.   Use the [Enum] ::GetValues([Microsoft.Exchange.Data.ServerEditionType]) shell command
      to retrieve the valid edition types.

1.6.1 Version numbers

Exchange 2007 is Exchange 2007, or is it? Well, it all depends what version number you look at. The code name for the product was Exchange 12, which is the version that Microsoft used until their marketing team made a decision about the real product name. Internally, if you ask PowerShell to report the two properties that contain version information for an Exchange 2007 server, you get different answers in different formats:

```
Get-ExchangeServer —id ExchMbxSvr1 | Select ExchangeVersion,
AdminDisplayVersion


ExchangeVersion                          AdminDisplayVersion
---------------                          -------------------------
0.1 (8.0.535.0)                          Version 8.0 (Build 685.24)
```

Figure 1.9
What version is Exchange 2007?

The data reported in the ExchangeVersion property is not a product version at all. Instead, it is the minimum version of Exchange that can read the object. In this case, any version of Exchange from 8.0.535 can read the object, which is an Exchange 2007 server. Microsoft refers to Exchange 2007 as Exchange version 8; Exchange 2003 is version 6.5, Exchange 2000 is version 6.0, and so on through 5.5, 5.0, and 4.0. The AdminDisplayVersion property reports the build number as well, so we know that this server is running the RTM[6] release because that is build 685.24—or maybe 685.25 (as always reported by an Edge server). Then you look at the Help About screen and Exchange reports itself to be running build 685.018 (Figure 1.9). All in

---

6. RTM means Release to Manufacturing. This is the version that the engineering team builds to deliver to customers at the end of their development cycle. The fact that Exchange 2007 reports 685.24 in the Admin-DisplayVersion property is due to a bug.

all, the different version numbers are slightly confusing and a good source for a Trivial Pursuit question.

1.6.2   32-bit Exchange 2007?

All through its development, Microsoft insisted that the only version of Exchange 2007 that they would support would be on the 64-bit x64 platform. They would provide a 32-bit version during the development period to allow partners to understand the new release without deploying a 64-bit environment, to support training facilities where it would be too expensive to deploy 64-bit servers, to allow for installation on laptops (often used for test environments), or to run on a virtual server. At the end of development, Microsoft generated two versions of the RTM code: a 32-bit version and the expected 64-bit version. What happened?

When the time came to release Exchange 2007, Microsoft discovered that they could not keep to a hard line on 64-bit everywhere because it just was not practical in real life. Administrators had 32-bit Windows XP workstations that they wanted to run the EMC console on and they wanted to run the Exchange setup program on 32-bit Windows 2003 servers that supported the Active Directory to prepare the Active Directory for Exchange 2007 (extend the schema, etc.). These are obvious examples of why Microsoft needed to provide 32-bit versions of Exchange 2007. A far less obvious example is the limited support that Microsoft permits for using the 32-bit version of Exchange 2007 to run test servers to try out Exchange 2007 clusters (SCC and CCR), even though the 32-bit version is only provided for the Standard Edition of Exchange 2007 that doesn't support clustering. You can also use the 32-bit version to try out Unified Messaging. In effect, this decision was a pragmatic step by Microsoft to help customers get to grips with new technology in the hope that customers would then accelerate their adoption rate for Exchange 2007. However, you still cannot install a 32-bit Exchange 2007 server into production and there is absolutely no guarantee or commitment that Microsoft will ever update the 32-bit code base to incorporate service packs or new functionality. Other missing functionality includes no support for automatic anti-spam updates (you do not need automatic updates because you are not going to run this software in production) and the same restriction on the number of storage groups and databases as you have with the standard edition of Exchange 2007.

See http://www.microsoft.com/technet/technetmag/issues/2007/01/ExchangeQA/ for more information about the conditions under which Microsoft supports the use of 32-bit Exchange 2007.

1.7   Support

Exchange 2007 incorporates a new support mechanism. Instead of issuing separate hot fixes for individual issues as they are reported, Microsoft plans to create cumulative fixes that they will issue regularly, perhaps every six to eight weeks at the start (when new software always has most bugs that need to be fixed) and potentially less often thereafter. Cumulative means that the kits contain every fix that Microsoft has made to Exchange 2007 since they released the original version. Kits are cumulative from one to another, so Kit 5 contains all the fixes in Kits 1 through 4. You will be able to download the fixes from Microsoft Update.

This approach simplifies life for administrators because you will know that a patch kit will be available at regular intervals that you can incorporate into regular server maintenance windows rather than having to constantly check for new Microsoft Knowledge Base articles that document a new bug and often mean that you have to install a patch.

1.8   Challenges for Exchange 2007

No one ever deploys a software product without encountering some upheaval. The situation is more interesting because Exchange has a large installed base of customers as well as the companies that service those customers with products of their own. In short, because Microsoft has elected to change the architecture of Exchange, including the APIs that allow other products to connect to and use the services offered by Exchange, the complete ecosystem undergoes a transformation around Exchange 2007. Challenges exist for Microsoft, their customers, service partners, and independent software vendors (ISVs) to prepare for and then deploy Exchange 2007.

In some respects, the challenge before Microsoft is the simplest and most straightforward. They have to deliver a high-quality, reliable, scalable, and robust product that interfaces well with previous versions. They have to perform the necessary testing and quality control to ensure that all of the features work as designed, that they achieve the necessary interoperability with previous versions and other messaging systems so that clients can connect as expected, that the bug count is within acceptable boundaries, and that the software appears on time. This is an enormous effort, which is why Microsoft has hundreds of engineers working on the Exchange 2007 project, but it is a development effort that Microsoft has gone through many times before with products such as Exchange, SQL, SharePoint, and Windows, so the task is within expected boundaries. The biggest challenge facing Microsoft is the smooth transfer from older versions of Exchange as customers migrate to Exchange 2007. Migrations have always caused problems, but this migration is more difficult because of the move to the 64-bit platform. Exchange has moved from one architecture to another before, as when we migrated from Exchange 5.5 to Exchange 2000, but that operation could proceed on the same Windows platform (if you upgraded to Windows 2000 first). With Exchange 2007, we have to install new 64-bit servers, deploy the necessary surrounding infrastructure (anything from Global Catalog servers to anti-virus software), and then move mailboxes. Microsoft cannot build utilities to transform a 32-bit Windows 2003/Exchange 2003 server to Exchange 2007, so they have to test and document to be sure that everyone understands what needs to be done and when it has to be done to achieve a graceful migration.

Customers will take the information provided by Microsoft and put it into context with their own infrastructures to build a tailored migration plan. Complexity increases because there are so many different ways to deploy and use Exchange, including international and multi-lingual scenarios. Customers have to train their system administrators and support staff so that they understand the new architecture. They have to make a decision whether they need outside help from external consultants to plan and deploy Exchange 2007. They need to build and agree on hardware budgets so that 64-bit hardware is available when the deployment commences.

Possibly the most fundamental decision for any deployment of Exchange 2007 is how long the migration project will take and when to start. These decisions drive many other activities, such as training and hardware procurement. You also have to consider user training if you plan to deploy new clients alongside Exchange, especially if you want to perform a desktop refresh and change operating systems at the same time perhaps to deploy a combination of Office 2007 and Vista. Other issues come into play if you plan a desktop refresh, such as cost, the sheer work involved in deploying new desktop hardware, how to distribute and install the client software, and so on.

Service partners (such as HP) track the development of new software products carefully because they have to be ready to assist customers before the formal ship date in projects such as Microsoft's Technology Adoption Program (TAP), which is the formal way that Microsoft engages customers to test and comment on new versions of products like Exchange. As the product approaches its official ship date, service partners have to be ready to scale up to support customer deployments. Some service partners depend on Microsoft to train their consultants while others build their own training programs, as they want to include their own consulting methodologies and best practice for Exchange. In either case, the trick is to have people ready at the right time. If training happens too early, the risk exists that Microsoft has not fully completed the software, so training cannot be complete. It is also true that best practice evolves over time and with experience, so early training often cannot cover best practice because it does not exist (or is pure guess-work). On the other hand, if you train people too late, you miss the chance to take "first mover" advantage and the market may perceive you to be a follower rather than an influence.

The change in Exchange architecture automatically throws any existing infrastructure into some doubt because you have to validate that the plan that you used to deploy Exchange 2000 or 2003 will be equally successful with Exchange 2007. Given the fundamental nature of the change in the underlying operating system, hardware platform, Exchange software, and influences such as increased automation and virtualization, it's a stretch to imagine that a design laid down a few years ago that focused on Exchange 2000 or 2003 will be right for Exchange 2007. Best practice changes over time as our knowledge evolves about how we use software in production, so this is another thing to take into account. For example, early designs for Active Directory deployments assumed that domains represented security boundaries, but we soon discovered that the forest is the only real security boundary that you can depend on once Active Directory was subjected to the stress and strain of real-life deployments. This discovery had a huge impact on designs. Another truth about IT architectures is that time has a corrosive effect on their effectiveness. The architectures work well best on the first day that you deploy them, but they tend to degrade afterwards as users load servers with data, administrators make mistakes, software upgrades and patches are applied, and new products are introduced to the mix. The best architectures survive the longest by being most resistant to influence of change, but all architectures inevitably come around to the point when it is time to rebuild and refresh. The combination of the move to the Windows 64-bit platform, the new design for Exchange 2007, and the demands for more mobility, more security, and more functionality is a good indicator that now is a good time to take a fresh look at the architecture that underpins any existing Exchange deployment and ask whether the migration to Exchange 2007 can be used as a catalyst for improvement.

In seeking the right type of change to make, it is always attractive to see if you can drive cost out of the infrastructure by eliminating components that you no longer need or that you can consolidate into a smaller set of servers. For example, Exchange 2007 offers the potential to consolidate many 32-bit servers to a smaller set of more scalable 64-bit servers. The same is true of the basic Windows infrastructure, where you can look at consolidating 32-bit domain controllers and Global Catalog servers onto a smaller set of 64-bit equivalents. Seeking opportunities for server consolidation is enough reason to conduct a review of any current infrastructure.

The move from routing groups to Windows sites as the basis for message routing requires attention because it is unlikely that your Windows sites map the routing infrastructure as implemented in routing groups. You probably need to review your management procedures and validate that they work as well with Exchange 2007 as they did with Exchange 2003.

ISVs face another balancing act. They want to be ready to support a new version when Microsoft ships the product, but they do not want to invest too early because they will have to work against incomplete code. Some ISVs are ready with an upgraded version of their product when Microsoft ships the final code, others have a policy where they delay until the first service pack on the basis that many customers opt to wait for this version before they want to upgrade.

1.9 Into the future

Overall, working with Exchange since Microsoft introduced Exchange 4.0 in 1996 has been a real blast. Even though Microsoft has gone down some blind alleyways (with application programming interfaces in particular) and we still don't fully understand how and when public folders will shuffle out of the product, there is no doubt that the software has improved consistently and usually has been easy to work with. In addition, I have met great people across the Exchange community and enjoyed the projects that I have worked on with customers around the world. Microsoft has taken a big step forward with Exchange 2007, but before we go into the details of what they have done, we need to set the foundation for success—and that is in a solid deployment of Windows and the Active Directory.

Exchange, Windows, and the Active Directory

No server software operates in a vacuum. Exchange depends on a solid deployment of Windows to underpin the success of its own ecosystem. In this chapter, we review the essential interoperation between Exchange and Windows and the critical points where Exchange depends on Windows. In particular, we will look at how Exchange uses the Active Directory, how Active Directory replicates data, the role of domain controllers and Global Catalog servers, and how Exchange updates and extends the Active Directory for its own purposes.

2.1 Active Directory and Exchange

A good design and efficient operation of the Active Directory has been core to any deployment of Exchange ever since Exchange 2000. Exchange makes extensive use of the Active Directory to:

- Store the configuration data for the Exchange organization. The Active Directory stores this information in the "Microsoft Exchange" container (Figure 2.1) in the configuration naming context and replicates it to every domain controller in the forest. Among the configuration data, Exchange holds information about valid routing paths and connectors that the transport system uses to determine how best to route messages.

- Store permissions used to access Exchange data such as server objects.

- Store information about mail-enabled objects—user accounts (mailboxes), public folders, contacts, distribution groups, and dynamic distribution groups.

The most fundamental difference that exists between Exchange 2007 and previous versions when it comes to the Active Directory is the depen-

Figure 2.1
*Exchange
configuration
data in the
Active Directory*

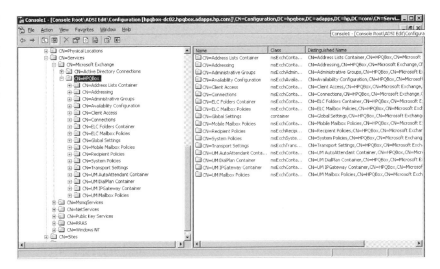

dency that Exchange 2007 now has on the site definitions that you apply within a forest. Previously, sites are interesting because they tell Exchange servers where the closest Global Catalog and domain controller servers are, but now Active Directory sites provide the information Exchange needs to route messages when direct connections between hub transport servers are unavailable using the IP subnet information that you define as the foundation of each site (Figure 2.2). In effect, the Active Directory site structure that you deploy lays down the routing topology for your Exchange organization and every Active Directory site that contains a hub Exchange 2007 server can participate in message routing.

It's fair to say that any Active Directory design made before the advent of Exchange 2007 will not have taken message routing into consideration, so it is a good idea to review the existing site layout and decide what sites will host hub transport servers and what sites will remain outside the routing topology.

2.1.1   Domain Designs

The classic Active Directory design deploys a root domain to hold the FMSO servers and business or geographic-centric domains to hold the user accounts. This design is based on the logic that you isolate enterprise components into the root domain, where you can protect the components against inadvertent administrative mistakes by restricting access to the domain to a small set of enterprise administrators. All of the application servers and the user accounts are then deployed in one or more domains under the root domain. Another reason that proved erroneous was the idea that domains represented a security boundary, something that Microsoft eventually

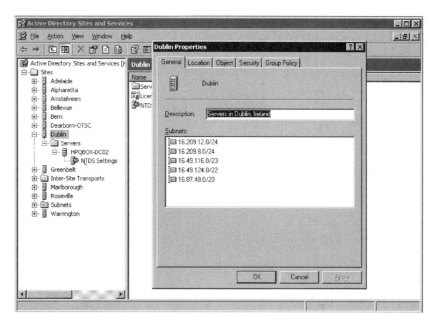

Figure 2.2
IP subnets define an Active Directory site

acknowledged to be untrue in 2001—but it is amazing that in some people's minds, the myth that the domain is a security boundary still persists. The forest represents the only true security boundary for the Active Directory, so if you need to operate multiple security domains, you will be forced to deploy multiple forests, with all the attendant overhead of cross-directory synchronization, authentication, and so on.

The multi-domain model is certainly valid and it has proven its worth in deployments in some very large enterprises since Active Directory first appeared in 1999 and the design continues to work in companies such as HP where three regional-based domains (for the Americas, Europe, and Asia-Pacific) organize user accounts on a geographic basis. Indeed, the multi-domain design is the only way to implement specific features, such as applying different password policies to each domain. If you do decide to deploy multiple user domains, make sure that you restrict the number of Enterprise Admin accounts to as few a number as possible and use delegation to allocate the rights to allow administrators to take control of the elements that they need to manage, such as an organizational unit or server. You should also establish clear rules for situations where decisions are needed that influence multiple domains, such as the appointment of a new enterprise administrator or the allocation of rights over the root domain, as you do not want situations to arise where an inadvertent action on the part of an administrator impacts multiple domains.

In the light of experience and in the spirit of removing complexity whenever possible, the advice now is to have as few domains as possible and place the FSMO servers in the same domain structure as user accounts. Instead of depending on domain access to protect sensitive components, you place the components into Organizational Units that you protect with appropriate access controls. The ideal situation in most situations is to deploy a single domain for everything.

Microsoft designed Exchange 2000 to support a single organization per Active Directory forest and the one-directory, one-organization restriction remains in place with Exchange 2007. Many companies find it limiting to be only able to deploy a single Exchange organization, as they want to segment users across multiple messaging systems and connect the systems with SMTP. While it might appear that dividing users across multiple systems generates increased cost and complexity in operations, email address synchronization, and message transport, in some cases it is the right solution because a real need exists to maintain separate messaging communities within the one company. For example, a financial services company might have divisions that handle trading and investment banking and need to control the communications between the two divisions to satisfy legislative or regulatory requirements. Setting up two messaging systems is one approach, as is the deployment of specialized software to monitor communications between the two sides. However, if you elect to go with two messaging systems and want to use Exchange, you have to deploy two Active Directory forests.

2.2   Active Directory replication

The Active Directory replicates configuration data about itself and applications such as Exchange together with information about objects such as users, contacts, and distribution lists (groups) between domain controllers in a domain and to Global Catalog servers within the forest. Replication is the term that describes the propagation of data from an originating server to other connected servers, in this case within a Windows domain or forest of domains. We could spend a lot of time diving into the details of how Active Directory replication works, but this topic deserves its own book. Instead, we will look at the basics of Active Directory replication between domain controllers and Global Catalog servers.

Understanding how the Active Directory replicates information is important for Windows and Exchange administrators alike. If replication does not flow smoothly then Exchange or any other application that depends on the Active Directory will experience problems. Successful Exchange projects invariably have a solid and well-managed Active Directory deployment in place before the installation of the first Exchange server. The move to use Active Directory sites as the basis for the routing topology in Exchange

2007 further underlines the need to make successful replication a high-priority item for any Exchange 2007 deployment.

2.2.1 Replication basics

The goal of any replication mechanism is to propagate data as quickly as possible so that all participants in replication receive updates and can build their own synchronized copy of the data. After replication has finished, all copies should be consistent. In a fast-moving networked environment where users and computers update data all the time, it is difficult to achieve a state of perfect replication, so you can consider the Active Directory partition hosted on any individual domain controller to be in a state of loose consistency. In other words, while the vast majority of the data in the Active Directory is consistent and synchronized with the server's replication partners, it is likely that outstanding replication operations are en route somewhere in the network. In a perfect world, we would have only one copy of the directory (unlikely a worldwide deployment) or be able to freeze changes for a time to allow all servers to perform any outstanding replication operations to achieve perfect synchronization throughout the network. Unfortunately, we do not live in a perfect world, so we have to be satisfied that the Active Directory is loosely consistent at any point in time.

Windows domain controllers are responsible for initiating and participating in replication operations. Each domain controller holds a complete read-write copy of the objects for its domain and acts as a replication partner for the other domain controllers within the domain. Replication only occurs between domain controllers as member servers do not hold a copy of the Active Directory.

Global Catalog servers hold a partial read-only copy of the objects for the other domains in the forest as well as the fully writable set of objects for its own domain. We say partial copy because Windows replicates a subset of the full attribute set of objects from domains to every Global Catalog along with a complete copy of all objects from its own domain. You can change the Active Directory schema to force replication of additional attributes. See page 80 for details.

The Active Directory performs attribute-level replication to reduce the amount of data that a replication partner sends or receives after a change has occurred. This means that the Active Directory only replicates the content of changed attributes, plus the GUID to identify the object and data to track replication rather than replicating the complete object including all the attributes that haven't changed. For example, if you change the display name for a user account, then the Active Directory only sends that attribute to replication partners. The net effect is that the Active Directory throttles back network traffic to only the size of the changed data and a buffer (perhaps 600 bytes in total, depending on the attribute that you update). In addition, the Active Directory uses a multi-threaded replication agent to be able to handle a high volume of replication requests. Given the speed of the network that connects many Windows servers today, you might not think that it's important to save a couple of thousand bytes on the wire here and there, but you have to remember that the Active Directory continues to hold more data about objects as applications exploit its ability to act as a repository for information. Exchange 2007 allows users to publish their safe lists as attributes in the Active Directory so that Exchange can then synchronize this information with Edge servers, which then use the data to check the sender information on incoming messages to detect spam. Exchange 2007 also introduces the Unified Messaging server and this adds a slew of new attributes to the Active Directory. The average size of an Active Directory object is getting larger as time goes by and there are many more attributes that applications can update, so attribute-level replication is a very important feature.

To help monitor and control the flow of replication, the Active Directory maintains a high watermark vector table on each domain controller. The table contains a row for every replication partner of the domain controller, including the partner's highest known USN (unique serial number). A USN is a 64-bit number maintained by each controller to indicate how many changes have occurred on the domain controller. The Active Directory also maintains USNs for every object in the directory and for every attribute in an object, so multiple USNs are involved in the replication process. Maintaining USNs at an attribute level allows the Active Directory to control replication at that level rather than replicating complete objects.

As you can see in Figure 2.3, the Active Directory tracks the changes made to an object and you can see both the USN value when the Active Directory first created the object (73,476) and the current USN (1,019,026,971). These USN values are specific to a domain controller and you will see other values for the same object if you connect to a different domain controller in the same domain. However, if we take the figures at face value, then this domain controller (part of HP's cpqcorp.net forest) has processed nearly a billion separate changes that have been replicated to this domain controller in 76 months. Some of these changes originated on the domain controller, but given the size of HP's Active Directory and the number of domain controllers in the four domains that make up the domain, the majority of changes are likely to have originated on other domain controller. Another way of looking at this is that the domain controller processed over 465,000 changes in each of the 2,316 days since the object was originally created. This kind of churn in the directory is indicative of major change within an organization that is typical when mergers and acquisitions occur.

It is common to see such a heavy volume of changes in a large organization and this illustrates the replication traffic that the Active Directory can

Figure 2.3
*Active
Directory
USNs*

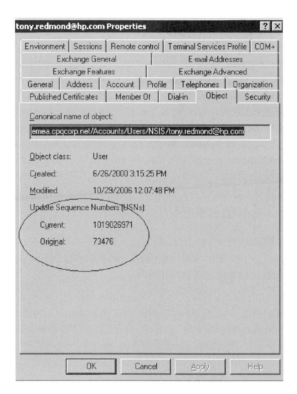

handle, plus the wisdom of using a 64-bit number (a GUID) to hold USNs. Technically, when the number overflows because of the number of changes applied to a controller, the USN reverts to one and starts over again. This will provoke a huge amount of replication to occur within a network as the controller will ask its replication partners for "any change since USN 1," but you shouldn't worry too much about this situation as it is extremely unlikely to occur in our lifetime (just like Y2K!).

2.2.2 When Active Directory replication happens

The Active Directory does not dispatch replication updates immediately after changes occur. If this was to happen, replication updates might swamp the network if a program applied many changes over a short period. Consider what happens when you synchronize data from an external directory with the Active Directory. The typical synchronization routine process uses a load file or another mechanism (such as a direct LDAP connection) as input to a program that synchronizes the content of another directory with matching entries in the Active Directory. For example, HP's LDSU (LDAP Synchronization Utility) is able to synchronize the Active Directory with any LDAP-compliant directory or any directory that can generate an LDIF-format load file. During the synchronization process, the Active Directory process instructions are to add, change, or delete objects very quickly (programs have been written to add objects at well over 500 objects per second), and if replication were triggered after each individual update, the network would grind to a halt due to all of the replication updates. Instead, the replication mechanism on a domain controller gathers changes together and sends out packages of replication data that its replication partners can apply. The exact method depends on whether the Active Directory needs to replicate data within a single Windows site or between Windows sites, but in all cases, the Active Directory packages groups of updates together instead of sending individual changes.

Any change to the Active Directory provokes some replication activity. The basic operations are:

- Object creation: For example, when you create a new user object, contact, or group.

- Object modification: For example, when you add a new SMTP address to a user, or add a user or contact to a mail-enabled group, or if you move a user from one organizational unit to another.

- Object deletion: The Active Directory does not remove an object immediately. Instead, it creates a tombstone for the object and replicates the tombstone to other domain controllers to inform them that the object has been marked as deleted. Tombstones have a default expiry time of 60 days, and after this time, the Active Directory permanently removes all trace of the object and completes the deletion by replicating the final state change.

The Active Directory makes a distinction between two types of write operations. When you initiate an operation on a domain controller, the update that the Active Directory applies to its local copy is called an originating write. A replicated write is an operation that occurs as the result of incoming data that arrives from a replication partner for application to the local Active Directory database. For example, if we increase the mailbox quota for a user on the HPDC1 domain controller and then replicate the information to the HPDC2 domain controller, we refer to the update applied on HPDC2 as a replicated write.

The Active Directory maintains two internal GUIDs for each controller, one for the server itself and one for the database. The server GUID remains constant, even if the server name changes. The Active Directory allocates a unique Server GUID to each domain controller and uses it to reference and identify specific controllers during replication operations. The Active Directory also creates a GUID to identify the copy of a database on a domain controller and sets it to be the same value as the Server GUID. If you ever need to restore a database from a backup, the Active Directory alters the database GUID to inform other domain controllers that you have restored the database, which may therefore be in an inconsistent state and need to generate some backfill requests to recover some updates that occurred after the backup was taken.

2.2.3   Active Directory naming contexts

In Windows 2000, the Active Directory organizes data into three separate naming contexts (NC). Windows 2003 introduces the application NC. A naming context is a tree of objects. In some definitions of directory terminology, a naming context represented the level of replication or referral within the directory.

- The configuration NC contains the objects that represent the structure of the directory (controllers, site topology, etc.). Because it uses the Active Directory as its repository and stores information about its organization (servers, roles, rules, and so on) in the configuration NC, this part of the Active Directory is very important to Exchange 2007.

- The schema NC contains all the classes and attributes that define individual objects and their attributes.

- The domain NC defines all the other objects such as users, groups, contacts, and computers. A separate domain NC exists for each domain in the forest.

Domains act as partitions within the Active Directory. To some degree, domains also act as a replication boundary, but not for the schema, which the Active Directory shares throughout the forest, or for the partial set of domain data that the Active Directory replicates to Global Catalogs throughout the forest. Of course, if your deployment manages to use just one domain across a high-speed network then the replication issue becomes very simple indeed and you will probably not have to worry about where you replicate data to and how long it takes to get there. On the other hand, even a single domain can run into replication issues if low-bandwidth links connect the sites and the topology is overly complex.

When Microsoft first shipped Windows 2000, best practice for corporate deployments recommended the use of multiple domains arranged into a single forest. This approach was liked by administrators because in some respects, it mimicked the way that Windows NT domains divided up the

administrative workload and responsibilities. As time has gone by, best practice focused more on removing complexity within the Active Directory as
much as possible by reducing the number of domains, so a design exercise
started today is less likely to create multiple domains within a forest than previously. Even if you have just two domains within a forest, the scope of replication becomes a very important issue, especially when you deploy an
application that makes extensive use of the Active Directory (like Exchange)
on top of the basic Windows infrastructure. For example, if Active Directory
replication does not work predictably across the forest, then the contents of
the GAL are likely to be inaccurate.

Naming contexts set boundaries for data replication. The configuration
and schema are unique within a forest, which means that the Active Directory must replicate these contexts to every domain controller in the forest,
so they have a forest-wide scope. In Exchange terms, this means that an
Exchange server can query any domain controller to discover a complete
picture of the Exchange organization data. The Active Directory only replicates domain objects to the controllers within a domain, so this naming
context has a domain-wide scope. Besides storing the domain NC of its own
domain, the Active Directory includes a partial replica of all other domain
NCs in the database held by a Global Catalog to build a complete picture
across the forest. The partial replica of a domain NC contains roughly 30%
of the data stored in the full replica of the NC, so each Global Catalog that
you create incurs a replication penalty that grows with the number of
domains in the forest.

Exchange exploits the fact that the Global Catalog provides a full view
of the user objects in a forest to build address lists like the GAL through
LDAP filters that it applies to the copy of the Active Directory hosted on a
Global Catalog. The LDAP filter essentially "finds" every mail-enabled object
known to the Global Catalog whose showInAddressBook flag is set to true.
Because its content forms the basis of the GAL, the Global Catalog is
extremely important to Exchange. For example, when Outlook clients want
to look up an address in the GAL, behind the scenes Exchange fetches the
information from the Global Catalog and responds to the client. The
Exchange transport engine makes heavy use of Global Catalog data because it
needs to check email addresses in message headers to decide how best to
route messages.

A typical forest that supports Exchange has one GAL, but you can create
more address lists by specifying filters that focus in on a specific collection of
mail-enabled objects. This feature is often used by service providers that supply an email service to companies so that each company is able to see their
own users but no one else. In a Windows 2003 forest, the technical limit for
the number of GALs or address lists in the forest is 1,300. However, this is a
theoretical limit and you would quickly lose yourself in a flurry of address

Figure 2.4
*Exchange routing
information in the
configuration NC*

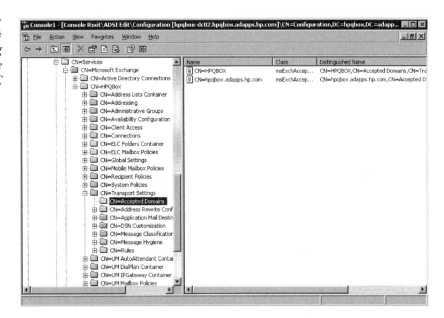

lists if you attempt to create that many. The vast bulk of Exchange implementations are happy with just one GAL.

While Exchange makes heavy use of the Global Catalog for address validation and message routing, it also needs to access configuration data for management and other operational purposes. For example, you cannot navigate through a complete view of the organization if the EMS console cannot read it from the data held in the Microsoft Exchange container in the configuration NC. Figure 2.4 illustrates how Exchange stores information about the domains that Exchange 2007 will process email for in the configuration NC in the Transport Settings section under "Microsoft Exchange." When you use the EMC to manage Exchange, EMC reads the configuration data from the nearest domain controller. Generally, the larger the Exchange organization, the slower EMC performs because of the amount of data it fetches from the Active Directory.

Generally, you should only work with Exchange configuration data through EMC or through shell commands as the console and commands will stop you doing something silly, like deleting essential information from Exchange's configuration data. Sometimes, the need might arise to eradicate completely all traces of Exchange from a forest, perhaps because you have made a mistake (like using the wrong organization name) when you first installed Exchange and you want to start over. You can use the ADSIEDIT utility (see page 88) to remove Exchange from an organization very quickly. Simply select the "Microsoft Exchange" container, right-click, and select "Delete" from the menu. Afterwards, you need to wait for replication to occur to complete the removal of Exchange from the forest. This action will not roll back the schema changes that Exchange makes to the Active Directory, but it does mean that you can restart the deployment of a brand new organization. Note that removing Exchange in this way is a very drastic option, so be sure that you have good reason to remove the organization in this way before you proceed. Knowledge Base article 312878 documents the approved Microsoft method to remove an Exchange organization from the Active Directory, while article 260378 also provides some useful background information.

2.2.4　Transforming Domain controllers into Global Catalogs

You turn domain controllers into Global Catalogs by changing the server's NTDS Settings property through the Active Directory Sites and Services console. Navigate to the site that holds the server, select the server, and view its NTDS Settings properties, as shown in Figure 2.5. Check the "Global Catalog" box to make the controller start to pull information from other domains. If you clear the checkbox, the server will revert to become a domain controller and the Active Directory will flush data belonging to other domains from the local database. This process may not happen quickly because it depends on the number of objects from other domains that exist in the local database. The Knowledge Consistency Checker (KCC) component removes these objects every time it runs and spreads the load by deleting about 8,000 objects an hour. It is therefore obvious that it can take some days before a DC finally purges data for other domains from its database and during this time, you cannot reverse the process and make the domain controller into a Global Catalog again. In large forests and especially where a relatively low-bandwidth connection exists between the server that you're working with and the nearest domain controller, it may be faster to remove the domain controller completely, reinstall the server from scratch, and then reload the Active Directory from media!

Transforming a domain controller into a Global Catalog generates replication activity. If you add a second Global Catalog to a site, the new Global Catalog copies the partial replicas of other domain NCs from the existing Global Catalog rather than requesting data from outside the site. This step avoids the need to broadcast replication requests outside the site boundary and thus potentially generate a flood of replication data within the forest. Otherwise, the exact impact on a network and Windows infrastructure depends on the complexity of the site topology, the number of domains in the forest, and the number of controllers involved in the replication process.

There is no good answer to how quickly the Active Directory can replicate data from one part of a forest to another. Microsoft recommends using tools like the Performance Monitor to review the performance of the NTDS Objects (such as DRA Outward Bytes Total and DRA Inward Bytes Total, or the total bytes consumed in outward and inward replication activity). However, this is a rudimentary approach to the problem and it is better to use the more sophisticated tools from companies like Quest Software or NetPro. In addition, to help gain an insight into potential problem areas for replication between sites and controllers, you can use tools like HP's OpenView Active Directory replication monitor to measure end-to-end replication latency and the overall effectiveness of replication inside a forest.

Figure 2.5
Setting the Global Catalog property for a domain controller

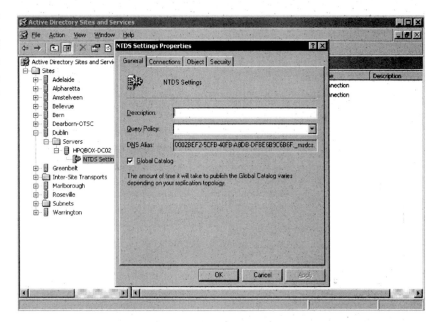

Exchange's dependency on consistent availability of Global Catalogs and the underlying reliable replication of Active Directory data illustrates the point that you cannot approach a design exercise for the Active Directory in isolation from the applications that depend on the infrastructure. This is a major and far-reaching change for any company that traditionally keeps infrastructure design teams separated from application design teams—and we see the same issue arising with Unified Messaging where successful deployments depend on a close working relationship between the telephony and messaging teams. The intimate dependency of Exchange 2007 on the Active Directory means that successful design teams treat the infrastructure as a whole rather than as separate parts. It is worth noting that while Exchange has a tremendous dependency on proper Active Directory deployment and operation, you also have to manage other Windows and network components to bring everything together. For example, if you do not deploy DNS properly, Exchange may not be able to locate domain controllers and Global Catalogs to read information about the organization's configuration and mail-enabled objects.

2.2.5 USNs and replication

As mentioned earlier, the Active Directory uses USNs to track changes made to its objects. Two different USNs are maintained for each object. The domain controller sets the value of the *USNCreated* attribute for a new object to the value of the server USN when it creates the object and then updates the *USNChanged* attribute each time it processes an update for the object. When an object is replicated to another domain controller, the Active Directory on the receiving controller sets the value of *USNChanged* to the value of the server USN of the server where the originating write occurs. You can see the value of a server USN by examining server properties, as shown in Figure 2.6. Now that we know the basics, we can track what happens during a simple set of replication operations.

Figure 2.6
Server USN

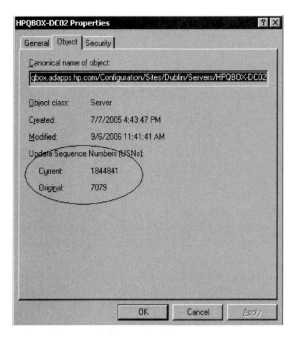

This scenario uses two controllers in a domain called HPDC1 and HPDC2. The servers have been in operation for some time, so the values of the server USNs reflect the number of AD updates. For this example, we assume that HPDC1 begins with USN 10925 and HPDC2 starts with 11933.

We begin replication by creating a new user object on HPDC1. The Active Directory automatically allocates the next USN in sequence based on the server USN, or 10926. Note that the allocation of a USN is a one-time operation and the USN can never be reused even if the create operation is interrupted and fails to complete. The next update on HPDC1 increases the USN by one. Table 2.1 lists a subset of the values maintained in the user object table in the database on HPDC1.

Table 2.1   *User Table in Active Directory*

Attribute	Value	USN	Version	Timestamp	Originating DC GUID	Originating USN
First name	John	10926	1	200208311245	HPDC1 GUID	10926
Surname	Doe	10926	1	200208311245	HPDC1 GUID	10926
Mailbox server	HPDC1	10926	1	200208311245	HPDC1 GUID	10926
SMTP address	John.Doe@acme.com	10926	1	200208311245	HPDC1 GUID	10926

The extract illustrates a number of important points:

- The originating domain controller automatically adds a number of values to each attribute to control replication.

- Each attribute populated as the Active Directory creates the new user object receives the USN allocated to the object. The "Originating" USN is set to the same value because the operation is initiated on the local server. This value will change as the Active Directory updates attributes over the lifetime of the object.

- The Active Directory populates the "Originating DC GUID" with the GUID from the server where it creates the object. Again, this value can change if another domain controller updates an attribute.

- The version number is set to "1" because the originating domain controller has just created the object. This number is incremented as updates are applied. The Active Directory uses the version number to resolve replication conflicts that might occur if two or more controllers attempt to update the same attribute at roughly the same time.

Conflicts are resolved by accepting the update with the highest version number. This is especially important when resolving conflicts for multivalued attributes (such as groups). For example, if you make two changes to a group on one domain controller that overwrites a single change made to the same group on another domain controller later on.

- A timestamp extracted from the current date and time on the server is saved. The Active Directory uses timestamps as a last resort to resolve replication conflicts that might occur if two or more controllers attempt to update the same attribute at roughly the same time and end up with a version number that is the same. Conflicts are resolved by accepting the last update according to the timestamps, using the timestamp from the originating write to arbitrate the conflict.

Note also that the Active Directory assigns the new object the current value of the server USN (10926) in its *USNCreated* and *USNChanged* attributes. We now replicate the information to HPDC2, which inserts the new information into its copy of the directory. Table 2.2 shows the values from HPDC2.

Table 2.2　　*User Table in Active Directory (2)*

Attribute	Value	USN	Version	Timestamp	Originating DC GUID	Originating USN
First name	John	11934	1	200208311247	HPDC1 GUID	10926
Surname	Doe	11934	1	200208311247	HPDC1 GUID	10926
Mailbox server	HPDC1	11934	1	200208311247	HPDC1 GUID	10926
SMTP address	John.Doe@acme.com	11934	1	200208311247	HPDC1 GUID	10926

The Active Directory changes the USN to reflect the server USN on HPDC2 and also assigns this value (11934) to the *USNChanged* attribute because this is the initial creation of the object on this controller. The timestamp now contains the date and time when HPDC2 applied the update. The originating DC GUID and the originating USN are still the values from HPDC1 because this is the controller where the update originated. We now see the difference between an originating write and a replicated write.

Table 2.3   *User Table in Active Directory*

Attribute	Value	USN	Version	Timestamp	Originating DC GUID	Originating USN
First name	John	11934	1	200208311245	HPDC1 GUID	10926
Surname	Doe	11934	1	200208311245	HPDC1 GUID	10926
Mailbox server	HPDC1	11934	1	200208311245	HPDC1 GUID	10926
Title	Consultant	11935	1	200208311255	HPDC2 GUID	11935
SMTP address	John.Doe@acme.com	11934	1	200208311245	HPDC1 GUID	10926

Table 2.3 demonstrates what happens after you update the user's title on HPDC2. We populate a previously blank attribute, which forces the USN on HPDC2 to move to 11935. The Active Directory also updates the *USN-Changed* value to 11935 and then sets the originating DC GUID for this attribute to HPDC2 because the update originates from this controller, so the Active Directory also updates the originating USN to the USN from HPDC2. Eventually, replication will occur back to HPDC1, which results in the values shown in Table 2.4. The timestamp is set to the value of the originating write.

Table 2.4   *User Table in Active Directory*

Attribute	Value	USN	Version	Timestamp	Originating DC GUID	Originating USN
First name	John	10926	1	200208311245	HPDC1 GUID	10926
Surname	Doe	10926	1	200208311245	HPDC1 GUID	10926
Mailbox server	HPDC1	10926	1	200208311245	HPDC1 GUID	10926
Title	Consultant	10927	1	200208311255	HPDC2 GUID	11935
SMTP address	John.Doe@acme.com	10926	1	200208311245	HPDC1 GUID	10926

The important things here are that the USN has been incremented according to the server USN for HPDC1, but because the write originated on HPDC2, the Active Directory takes its server GUID and USN and uses them to update the database on HPDC1. The Active Directory also updates the timestamp. However, the Active Directory leaves the *USNCreated* value for the object unaltered at 10926, but updates the *USNChanged* value to 10927. Note that the Active Directory leaves all the other attributes alone, as it only needs to update the value of the Title attribute. While it may seem obvious to keep track of the controller that last updated an attribute by holding the server GUID, the role of the originating USN might be more obscure. The way that the Active Directory uses the originating USN becomes more important as you increase the number of domain controllers that participate in replication. In fact, the Active Directory uses the originating USN for propagation dampening, or the ability to stop replication operations progressing if the Active Directory has already updated the local database after an interchange of replication data with another controller. Propagation dampening is very important in large networks as it eliminates unnecessary traffic and reduces the amount of system resources that are required to keep the directory in a consistent state.

2.2.6 **Urgent replication**

The normal replication process is sufficient to ensure that the Active Directory replicates updates to attributes such as telephone numbers, titles, or even email addresses between DCs reasonably quickly. Two situations exist when fast replication is required. These are when a user account is locked out and when a new set of identifiers is issued by the RID master.

The Active Directory supports the concept of "forced" replication to get updates to domain controllers as quickly as possible after you lockout or disable accounts. This feature exists to prevent users being able to move between domain controllers and log in after an administrator has disabled or locked their account. If the Active Directory depended on normal replication in these instances, the danger exists that the newly locked out user could still authenticate against a controller that has not yet received the update and so continue to access resources. You should realize that this mechanism does not prevent users who previously logged onto the network from accessing the resources until their Kerberos ticket lifetime expires. In case of NTLM authentication, the users can continue to access resources until they logoff.

Note that the Active Directory does not consider password updates as urgent. When you update your password, the controller that you make the change to replicates the new password to the PDC emulator master, which then replicates the updated password to other domain controllers in the next replication cycle. Note that the site topology might prevent a controller communicating with the PDC emulator, but normal inter-site replication will eventually get the change through.

Finally, if the RID master issues a new set of identifiers to a domain controller to allow it to generate unique identifiers for new accounts, the Active Directory must send that information quickly to its destination. In all these cases, fast replication or rather a faster form of replication is performed by immediately sending out change notifications to replication partners, which then respond by pulling the update from the originating controller.

2.2.7   Intrasite and Intersite replication

Exchange 4.0 introduced the notion of a site to reflect locality in terms of network connectivity. The Active Directory also uses the concept of a site, but with some subtle differences. An Exchange 4.0 site was defined as a collection of servers that share good network connectivity, often because all the servers in the site are in a common location (office, city, country, or even continent). The definition of a Windows site is somewhat stricter. An Active Directory site is composed of a collection of one or more IP subnets, but like an Exchange site, an Active Directory site shares LAN-quality bandwidth between the servers.

In logical terms, a Windows infrastructure builds sites on top of the physical network and sites map the physical network to create the Active Directory site topology. Another way of thinking about this is to remember that sites are collections of servers in a location whereas domains are collections of objects that may exist across multiple sites. In actuality, when you deploy your first Windows domain, it goes into the default site (called "default-first-site"). New domain controllers are also installed into the same site unless you decide to create other sites to accommodate the requirements of the network. You introduce a domain into a site by creating a replica (domain controller) for the domain in the site. A domain may span many sites, and a site can host multiple domains as long as a domain controller for each domain is present in the site. Exchange 2007 imposes another requirement by mandating that one of the domain controllers in the site must also be a Global Catalog before the site can participate in message routing.

Windows limits domain NC replication to synchronous RPCs. This means that you can only include servers in a domain if they can establish RPC connectivity with the other servers in the domain. The connection is not limited to a LAN, but within a WAN, you find that RPCs are sensitive to latency and network availability and may time out or otherwise fail to complete. The requirement to support RPC connectivity means that some designs use domains to restrict replication and end up with more domains than strictly necessary. The Active Directory can replicate the configuration and schema NCs through asynchronous SMTP messages, so replication can truly span the world. In this case, the Active Directory uses the Windows SMTP service to send the messages containing replication data.

When you first create the forest, Windows creates a default site link. You cannot create a site without associating it with at least one site link, so you can either use the default link or create new ones. Site links connect together to allow replication to proceed. The existence of a site link indicates that network connectivity is available between the two sites. Unlike the automatic connection objects created by Windows to replicate data between two partners in a specific NC, you must create site links before intersite replication can proceed.

The Knowledge Consistency Checker (KCC) manages the creation of the intrasite topology and works with the ISTG (Inter-Site Topology Generator, a subprocess of the KCC) to ensure that Windows optimizes Active Directory replication. The KCC is a service that runs on every domain controller to generate and optimize the Active Directory replication topology by creating connection agreements between domain controllers. Costs range from 1 to 32767, with 100 being the default. In general, the lower the cost, the better the network connectivity that exists between sites. Because they link sites, which are IP subnets, you can think of site links as WAN connections. Each site link has a cost, and the ISTG uses the cost and site link schedule to determine which connection objects it must create to enable replication. The connection objects created by ISTG to link the different sites form a spanning tree, designed to avoid message looping as updates flow between bridgehead servers in the sites. This is important with asynchronous replication (see below), where messages that contain replication data may take some time to reach their final destination. Administrators can also create connection objects, but the usual approach is to let the ISTG create a default set and only interfere if necessary afterwards.

Because good network connectivity is assumed, directory replication occurs automatically and frequently inside and between sites. Replication partners notify each other when they have updates, and the partners then pull the data from the originating server to update their directory. Even if no updates exist for replication, the domain controllers in a site exchange details of their latest USNs to update their vector tables and ensure that they miss no data. The Active Directory uses the same pull mechanism for intesite replication. In this case, bridgehead servers hold data until their replication partners (bridgehead servers in other sites) request updates and then pull the data.

Because the Active Directory assumes good connectivity exists between servers in a site, it never compresses replication data and uses RPCs to communicate between servers. By default, if there are two domain controllers in a site, they replicate every 5 minutes. If more than three domain controllers are present in the same site, the KCC will set up the replication connections to ensure that changes from any domain controller within the site reach all other domain controllers within three hops. That is, any changes replicate to all domain controllers within 15 minutes. On the other hand, the Active Directory always performs intersite replication according to a schedule, which allows administrators to distribute changes when they feel appropriate. If replication data is over 50KB, the Active Directory compresses it to between 10–15% of its original size before transmission, trading network consumption against the processing to compress and decompress the data.

The Active Directory can replicate synchronously or asynchronously between sites. Synchronous replication occurs between two bridgehead servers within the same NC. The bridgehead server acknowledges receiving the data and then distributes it to other domain controllers in the site. Synchronous replication can only happen over a reliable and relatively high-speed connection. Asynchronous replication allows replication to occur over slow or unreliable links by sending SMTP messages using a component called Inter-Site Messaging (ISM-SMTP). ISM generates messages containing replication data and sends them through the basic SMTP service included in every Windows. However, you cannot replicate the domain NC over SMTP and the experience gained in enterprise deployments demonstrates that few if any large companies use SMTP replication for the Active Directory. Because Active Directory replication is so important, most large companies deploy domain controllers within the parts of their networks that have best connectivity to ensure that replication works predictably. The reduced cost of network experienced in most countries since Microsoft introduced Windows 2000 has also reduced the attractiveness of asynchronous replication, so to some degree you can consider this a feature that may help in very specific circumstances (such as Active Directory deployments over extended low-speed networks), but one that has hardly been proved in practice. Table 2.5 summarizes the differences between intra- and intersite replication for the AD.

Table 2.5   *Characteristics of Active Directory replication*

	Intrasite	Intersite
Transport	RPC	RPC or SMTP
Topology	Ring	Spanning tree
Replication timing	Automatic when necessary (every 5 minutes by default)	According to schedule as defined by administrator
Replication model	Notify and Pull	Store and Forward
Compression	None	Full (if over 50KB)

Within a site, Windows sets the default schedule for domain controllers to send notifications of updates to their replication partners to 300 seconds (5 minutes). You can change this interval for all members of a site, but there is little reason to do this normally unless you want to tune back the amount of replication traffic that the Active Directory generates. One exception to the rule is when you want to send changes to the bridgehead server in the site so that it begins to replicate with its partner sites as soon as possible. This technique can propagate changes faster within a distributed Active Directory, but you need to test and measure results before committing it to deployment.

Each site link and connection object has a schedule (Figure 2.7), which defines when the domain controllers associated with the connection object will replicate. Each time a replication slot occurs in the schedule, the domain controllers inside the site exchange information with each other to establish whether they need to replicate. The site link schedule takes precedence over the connection object schedule for intrasite replication.

Figure 2.7
Connection Object
Schedule

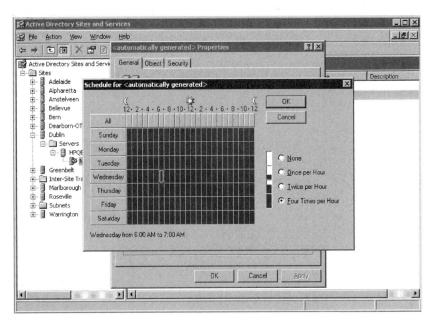

2.2.8 **High-watermark vector and up-to-date vector tables**

The Active Directory incorporates a number of propagation dampening mechanisms to control the amount of replication within the network. Propagation dampening means that a domain controller can suppress or ignore unnecessary replication under specific circumstances. In other words, if a domain controller receives information that it already knows about, such a request to create a new user object in their copy of the Active Directory, the domain controller can discard the update. Elimination of unnecessary replication activities becomes more important as the number of controllers increase. Duplicating some work between two controllers is probably not important, but involving a hundred or two hundred controllers in a replication mechanism that generates "n" unnecessary activities per replication partner is a recipe for disaster.

Windows uses two tables to control propagation—the high-watermark vector table and the up-to-date vector table (also sometimes called the state vector table), and maintains the two tables on every domain controller. The contents of the tables represent the current state of replication as known to an individual domain controller. The Active Directory increments the controller USN as it actions each change, no matter whether it is to add, update, or delete an object. It then stores the USN with the object and any updated attributes. Increments also happen for unsuccessful operations, such as the failure to create a user account.

The high-watermark vector table tracks the highest known USN from each replication partner. This information allows a domain controller to know whether it needs to request additional information from a replication partner to backfill data that may be missing, perhaps because of a failure to replicate properly in the past. The Active Directory uses the high-watermark vector table to detect recent changes on a replication partner. If a domain controller has not received a recent update from a replication partner, it broadcasts its highest known USN to the partner. The receiving DC can then verify this data against its own high-watermark vector table to discover whether any outstanding replication exists. If this is true, the domain controller can then request the information from a replication partner.

Knowing the USN from a replication partner also allows a controller to request precisely the data required to update its own directory without having to request "all changes." For example, if the highest known USN on controller DC20 is 17754, and a replication notification arrives from DC20 saying that its current USN is 17794, then the receiving domain controller knows that it still has to apply 40 updates to its copy of the directory and is able to issue a request to DC20 to provide the missing information.

The up-to-date vector table maintains a list of all replication partners and the highest originating write on each. When Windows has fully synchronized all of the controllers in a domain, the up-to-date table is the same everywhere. Each domain controller sends its up-to-date vector table to its replication partners as part of the replication cycle. The replication partner matches the USN in the up-to-date vector table with its high-watermark vector table to identify any missing data. If the replication partner finds that some replication operations are outstanding, it will request updates. Otherwise, if the replication partner has already received the data—through replication with another domain controller—then it makes no further attempt to replicate because of propagation dampening.

Within a small domain, these tables are not very important. However, their importance grows in line with the number of domain controllers. Each domain controller is likely to have a set of different replication partners, so replication data can flow along many different paths. If no mechanisms were in place to stop unnecessary replication, then a domain controller might process updates multiple times after it contacts different replication partners, all of whom want to provide the domain controller with the same information.

2.2.9 Changes in Active Directory replication in Windows 2003

Most Exchange servers run on Windows 2003 today and you have to upgrade to Windows 2003 to deploy Exchange 2007. While it is possible to run a very effective Active Directory infrastructure on Windows 2000, Windows 2003 introduces many important Active Directory upgrades, enhancements, and fixes. The following are the most critical changes in terms of operation and deployment:

- You can now promote a Windows 2003 server to become a domain controller using a copy of the Active Directory on removable media. This makes it much easier to deploy controllers in a large network because it removes the replication load necessary for the Active Directory to populate a database on a new DC. For example, within HP's forest, network based replication using Windows 2000 used to take between three and five days to complete to promote a new controller. Using the load from media feature, a new controller is online within an hour.

- The Windows 2003 Active Directory is better at cleaning up "lingering" objects (ones that do not disappear completely in all controllers after the replication process completes) that remain in the database after deletion.

- Intersite replication is more efficient and consumes less bandwidth.

- The overall size of the Active Directory database is usually smaller because the database engine is more efficient and uses mechanisms like single-instance storage of security descriptors. For example, when HP moved its Windows forest into native Windows 2003 mode, the DIT file shrank from 12GB to 7.5GB.

- Global Catalog servers do not commence a full synchronization when you add new attributes to the partial attribute set defined in the Active Directory schema, such as those added by the schema upgrade required to support Exchange 2007. Large forests feel the effect of this change most because of the number of controllers that participate in replication. Where changes to the partial attribute set in Windows 2000 might create a replication storm over five days before all of the Global Catalogs have a fully populated database, now you can assume that replication completes in under a day, assuming no network outages.

- Last logon timestamps are replicated.

- ITSG makes better decisions about the site connections that it creates.

- The Active Directory supports per-value replication for multi-value attributes. This is very important for groups (and Exchange makes extensive use of distribution groups), which hold group membership in a single multi-value attribute. Therefore, any change to group membership used to force the Active Directory to replicate the complete membership now just replicates the changed value.

While the Active Directory is a critical component of successful Windows infrastructures, it is not the only component to manage. File Replication Services (FRS), which replicates SYSVOL and policies, is also a dependency for many applications. For example, if FRS replication is not working properly, then the changes to server security policies applied by the Exchange installation program will not replicate from the server that you perform the installation on to other servers in the domain. One side effect of this failure is that you may be able to start the set of Exchange services on other servers, but you will not be able to mount the Store databases because the services will not possess the necessary privileges!

2.3   Exchange's Active Directory Topology service

Exchange 2007 uses an Active Directory API to access information that is stored in Active Directory. The Active Directory Topology service runs on all Exchange 2007 servers. This service reads information from all Active Directory partitions. The data that is retrieved is cached and is used by Exchange 2007 servers to discover the Active Directory site location of all Exchange services in the organization. The Active Directory Topology service checks the site membership attribute on the Exchange server object when the server starts. If the site attribute has to be updated, the Active Directory Topology service stamps the attribute with the new value. The Active Directory Topology service verifies the site attribute value every 15 minutes and updates the value if site membership has changed. The Active Directory Topology service uses the Net Logon service to obtain current site membership. The Net Logon service updates site membership every 5 minutes. This means that up to a 20-minute latency period may pass between the time that site membership changes and the new value is stamped on the site attribute.

2.3.1   DSAccess (or ADAccess)

DSAccess was a pretty important component for Exchange 2000 and 2003 because it manages the interaction between Exchange and the Active Directory. It also managed a cache of recipients that were read from the Active Directory as the transport engine resolved message headers to decide how best to route messages. Over time, Exchange built up a cache of recipient information that the transport engine could access from memory without having to make an expensive call to a Global Catalog server. Renamed as ADAccess, DSAccess is still used in Exchange 2007, but its recipient cache is no more. Instead, four services load ADAccess to gain a consistent view of the current topology data from the Active Directory and to make sure that a single consistent view of the topology is shared by all services running on a server:

- Active Directory Topology
- Information Store
- System Attendant
- Client Access server (through the WWW Publishing service)

The role of ADAccess is to:

- Perform suitability testing to determine that a selected domain controller and Global Catalog server can function correctly before ADAccess uses them (see below).
- Manage load balancing of LDAP requests within the local Active Directory site if more than ten domain controllers and Global Catalog servers are present.
- Perform graceful failovers to a new domain controller or Global Catalog server to minimize the impact on clients and other Exchange components such as the transport service. ADAccess uses information about Windows site links and connection costs to determine the most appropriate controller to fail over to.

- In failover situations, ADAccess monitors for the local domain controller and Global Catalog to detect when they are available again. If this happens within 5 minutes, ADAccess automatically reconnects to that controller.

- Diagnostic logging to help troubleshoot problems.

Figure 2.8

ADAccess discovers
Active Directory
servers

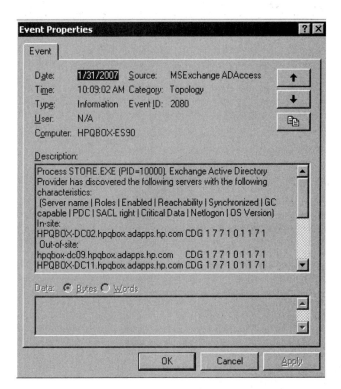

Every 15 minutes, ADAccess scans the Active Directory to build a view of the current topology. ADAccess divides the servers that it discovers into those that are in the same Active Directory site as the Exchange server and those that are outside the site. Figure 2.8 illustrates the data returned by ADAccess:

- The name of the server: A list of the FQDNs of the controllers that are available inside and outside the Exchange server's Active Directory site. For example, dc1.xyz.com.

- The roles that this server can fulfill: D indicates that the server is a domain controller, G means Global Catalog, C means that the server is acting as the Configuration DC. In this case, CDG means that the selected server is able to act as the Configuration domain controller, a regular domain controller, and as a Global Catalog server.

- Whether or not the server is reachable: This value is a bit mask where "1" means that the server is reachable via LDAP as a Global Catalog through port 3268, "2" means that it is reachable as a domain controller through port 389, and "4" means that it can act as a configuration domain controller (through port 389 also). A value of "7" indicates that the server is reachable through all ports and can act in any role. A value of "0" indicates that the server is completely unreachable and therefore ADAccess cannot use it.

- Whether or not the server is synchronized: The same bit mask values are used, so "1" means that the Global Catalog is synchronized, "2" that the domain controller is synchronized, and "4" that the configuration domain controller is synchronized. A value of "7" means that the server is completely synchronized.

- Whether the server is capable of acting as a Global Catalog: "1" indicates that it is.

- Whether or not the server is the PDC emulator for a domain: "0" indicates that it is not.

- Whether the server passes the SACL (System Access Control List) test: This test determines whether the server resides inside a domain that you have prepared to host Exchange servers. A value of "1" indicates that the SACL test passed.

- Whether the server hosts critical data: A value of "1" indicates that the Microsoft Exchange container exists in the configuration naming context on this domain controller. The Exchange container stores critical data such as server names and roles, routing information, and so on that must be available for the transport service to work. ADAccess only selects a domain controller if it hosts this container.

The set of services that rely on ADAccess are used throughout Exchange 2007, so ADAccess is a very important component, but a curious feature of its introduction is the elimination of Exchange's ability to use cached recipient data. Instead of using a centralized cache for data fetched from the Active Directory, Microsoft allows each service running inside Exchange 2007 to decide how long they want to keep data for as long as they need it and no longer. Microsoft believes that this approach results in more predictable and better performance, keeps code simpler, and that it ensures that the data used is always up to date (in other words, there is no danger that it has aged in the cache). In the case of the Exchange 2007 transport engine, it only retains recipient information for as long as it takes to route a message, which is very different to the behavior of Exchange 2003. If services need to keep Active Directory data for extended periods, they can subscribe for notifications from the Active Directory so that they know when to refresh. In addition, they can perform periodic checks to ensure that the data that they use is consistent with the data in the Active Directory.

Perhaps Microsoft believes that the migration of Active Directory to 64-bit Windows servers will remove the general need for Exchange to cache information because, assuming that enough memory is available to the server, it is far more possible to cache the complete Active Directory database in memory on a 64-bit Global Catalog than it is on a 32-bit Global Catalog. Thus, even if Exchange needs to make a massive amount of directory requests to resolve recipient addresses, the requests will flow across a short network hop to a Global Catalog that can respond immediately because the necessary data is in its cache. It's entirely possible that this is true, but it does underline the need to deploy sufficient high-performance Global Catalog servers in any Active Directory site that hosts several hub transport servers. How many is sufficient? Only time, experience, planning, and some realistic data gained through testing will answer that question for your company, so be prepared to do some work to find out.

2.3.2   How many Global Catalog servers do I need?

The best advice that I ever heard was to avoid skimping on Global Catalog servers for any medium- to large-scale Exchange deployment. This is an attitude that perhaps runs contrary to the approach taken by Windows administrators, who may not understand the vital role that Global Catalogs play in Exchange, especially in GAL interaction (for example, to update a distribution group or lookup the properties of a recipient) performed by clients and address validation performed by Exchange to route messages efficiently. There are many instances when deployments start with a relatively small number of Global Catalogs and everything proceeds smoothly until Exchange servers begin to operate. Up to this point, the demand on the Global Catalogs is relatively small and is generated largely by client logins and replication. Immediately you introduce an Exchange server and start to use it to send and receive mail, the load on the Global Catalogs increases dramatically.

The general rule of thumb to determine the number of Global Catalogs was originally one Global Catalog per four Exchange servers. As experience with Exchange deployments grew, the rule changed to one Global Catalog CPU per four Exchange CPUs. In other words, if you have two dual-CPU Exchange servers, you need a Global Catalog. If you have six dual-CPU Exchange servers, you need three Global Catalog servers, and so on. The Global Catalog servers do not have to be heavy-duty systems and it is easy to build relatively inexpensive servers to carry the load—nd even deploy some as virtualized servers running on much bigger systems. The important thing is to be resilient to failure as nothing stops Exchange working as quickly as a Global Catalog outage, and to make sure that there is enough capacity to handle the peak load generated by Windows, Exchange, and any other application that uses a Global Catalog.

Another issue to consider is the placement of Global Catalogs alongside Exchange servers. The rule of thumb here is simple too. If you have an Exchange server, you need a Global Catalog on the same WAN segment. In other words, you must ensure that any network outage has a minimal effect on Exchange. Satisfying the rule may not always be possible, especially if you feel that you have to place an Exchange server in a branch office (to speed up email for local users) and cannot afford to add a Global Catalog. In this case, you may want to channel Active Directory lookups to the Global Catalog across a WAN link. However, while it seems an attractive option to use the network in this way, it will inevitably lead to outages and user dissatisfaction and the better options are to either deploy a local Global Catalog or centralize Exchange and Global Catalogs together in one location and use clients such as Outlook in cached Exchange mode to connect over the WAN.

2.3.3   Where are my Global Catalogs?

Because you need to have at least one Global Catalog server in each site that supports an Exchange 2007 server, Global Catalog servers are a critical component of your Exchange 2007 deployment. As you roll out servers to support Exchange 2007, you may want to investigate what Global Catalogs are deployed within your infrastructure. Some of these computers may not be required as you can normally consolidate the workload done by several 32-bit Global Catalog servers into a smaller number of 64-bit servers. This is especially valuable when your Active Directory includes more objects than can be cached in the memory available to 32-bit Windows servers. It's difficult to be precise as to exactly how many objects this represents because the average size of an Active Directory object depends on the object type (user objects are bigger than contacts or groups, for instance) and how many of their properties are populated. A good rule of thumb is deploy 64-bit Global Catalogs when the forest contains more than 100,000 objects. Of course, over time, the natural server replacement cycle will replace the 32-bit version of Windows with 64-bit servers and the process will complete naturally, but it's certainly a good idea to move faster when you have large directories to manage.

As an example, tests inside HP's production Windows environment showed that a single 64-bit Global Catalog server (dual CPU, either Opteron or IA64, equipped with 14GB of memory) can handle the load previously processed by eleven 32-bit servers for 20,000 users in a single large campus site. In HP's case, the size of the DIT (AD database file) varies between 10 and 11GB to hold approximately 350,000 objects, depending on the amount of white space in the database, so it is possible to cache the entire database if the server is equipped with enough physical memory. Normal Exchange messaging activity in a reasonably busy site will populate the cache on a Global Catalog server quickly and once the cache is populated, further access is very fast indeed. Depending on the size of your Exchange and Active Directory infrastructure, your mileage will vary, so do not take these figures as anything more than a guideline to what might be possible. It's also obviously not a good idea to depend on a single large Global Catalog to handle the workload generated by a set of Exchange servers as a failure on the Global Catalog will affect thousands of users, so in a production environment, you'd have at least two or three Global Catalogs for a site that supports 20,000 users, even if one can handle the workload.

Before you can decide what Global Catalogs to refresh or consolidate, you need to know where they are. There are at least three ways of discovering what Global Catalog servers exist inside the forest. First, you can use the NSLOOKUP utility to check what servers have registered themselves as offering a Global Catalog service:

```
NSLOOKUP gc._msdcs.<ROOT DOMAIN>
```

The difficulty here is that servers might have registered themselves as Global Catalogs at some point in the past and subsequently ceased this role but never removed their information from Active Directory. You can go to every Domain Controller and query it to see if its isGlobalCatalogReady attribute is true, but this can be quite a lot of work.

Microsoft also provides the REPLMON utility as part of the Windows support tools. You can add a server to its list and then right click on the server and select the "Show Global Catalog Servers in the Enterprise" option to view the data. Other products such as the HP OpenView Smart plug-in for Active Directory are able to graphically chart the replication topology and show you what's going on inside your network. These approaches work equally well with both before and after you deploy Exchange 2007. Once you start to deploy Exchange 2007, you'll be able to use PowerShell, the new Windows scripting language. There is much more coverage of PowerShell and how you can use it to manage Exchange 2007 from Chapter 4 onwards. For now, we should recognize that PowerShell has a huge influence over how you will manage Windows, Exchange, and other components going forward, so it's not surprising to discover that you can use PowerShell to interrogate the Active Directory and find out what Global Catalog servers exist.

After you start up PowerShell, we start off by populating a variable with details of the forest:

```
$Forest =
[System.DirectoryServices.ActiveDirectory.Forest]::GetCurrent
Forest()
```

You can view details of the forest by typing the name of the variable and this reveals some interesting information that you can capture by piping the output to a text file:

```
$Forest > c:\temp\Forest.txt
```

You'll see something like this:

```
Name                  : xyz.com
Sites                 : {San Francisco, Dublin, Atlanta,
Amsterdam, Bellevue, Warrington, Adelaide, Paris, London,
Chicago, Zurich}
Domains               : {xyz.com}
GlobalCatalogs        : {DC01.xyz.com, DC02.xyz.com,
DC03.xyzcom, DC04.xyz.com, DC05.com}
ApplicationPartitions : {DC=DomainDnsZones,DC=xyz,DC=com,
DC=ForestDnsZones,DC=xyz,DC=com}
ForestMode            : Windows2003Forest
RootDomain            : xyz.com
Schema                : CN=Schema,CN=Configuration,DC=xyz,
DC=com
SchemaRoleOwner       : DC02.xyz.com
NamingRoleOwner       : DC01.xyz.com
```

This list is easy to understand in a small organization, but it can be difficult to interpret in more complicated environments, so we can break out the Global Catalogs and list them as follows:

```
$GClist = $Forest.FindAllGlobalCatalogs()
ForEach-Object ($GC in $GClist) { $GC.Name }
```

2.4   **Recovering deleted Active Directory accounts**

Even the best administrator can make a mistake and if you delete an AD account in error, you will find that it is difficult to restore the account quickly and simply. Sometimes, the quickest recovery method is to recreate the account from scratch, but this means that the account loses the access it has to different resources because the SID for the recreated account is different from the original. Another problem is that the new account does not have membership of the different groups that the original group belonged to, something that is easier to cope with albeit only if you know all the groups to add the account to.

The normal method used to recover a deleted account from a backup tape is to perform an authoritative restore on a domain controller and then use the NTDSUTIL program to recover the account. You can only do this if you know the full DN of the account, as you need this information to retrieve the data from the backup. However, there are other difficulties to overcome even after you recover the deleted account as its group membership may not be intact and therefore the account may lose access to some resources.

In large organizations, where the potential for accidental deletions is higher, you may want to consider setting up a special Windows site that contains a domain controller. The delayed site replicates with the rest of the domain once or twice a week so that its copy of the AD database is complete after replication finishes. If you catch the error before replication to the delayed site occurs, you know that a copy of the deleted account still exists in the copy of the AD in the delayed site, so you do not have to restore any backup tapes. Instead, you can log onto the domain controller in the delayed site to find the deleted object (and establish its DN) and note its group membership, then boot the domain controller into Directory Services Restore Mode and use the NTDSUTIL program to run an authoritative restore for the object. The effect of this operation is to increase the USN for the restored object by 100,000, which means that the update to the object in the delayed site will win any replication conflict caused by updates from other sites. After the restore, you reboot the domain controller as normal and then force replication to replicate the data back into the rest of the domain. After replication is complete, you can reestablish the account's membership of the groups that it lost because of the accidental deletion.

A variation of the delayed site technique is to deploy domain controllers in two different sites, each with different replication schedules. For example, the first site might replicate every Tuesday, while the second replicates every Friday. With this setup, even if you do not catch the accidental deletion quickly and replication occurs to one site, you have a backstop to rescue you. However, there is obvious additional cost to maintain the second site that rules this variation out for all but the largest Windows deployments.

Even in its simplest form, the delayed site technique is not for every organization. If you have a small company, it is unlikely that you will want to maintain the overhead to create a delayed site as you probably will not realize much of a benefit. Virtualized servers can help because it is possible to host multiple domain controllers for different sites on one large physical server.

The bottom line is that in return for some extra cost, the technique may save you hours of work especially in large multi-site organizations.

2.5   Exchange and the Active Directory schema

Schemas define the structure of a database, including the object classes and the attributes held for each object. The AD schema is extensible by applications or enterprises to allow it to hold additional information. For example, you could extend the directory to add a new "Birthday" attribute for user objects, and then write an AD-enabled application that ran when a user logged on to check whether it was their birthday, generating an appropriate message on the day in question. First, generation Exchange includes 15 "custom" attributes for mailboxes that you can use for similar purposes, but you cannot extend the schema of the Exchange Directory.

Exchange was the first application to extend the AD schema by adding new attributes that can then be associated with recipients (users, contacts, and groups) as well as configuration information about Exchange such as administrative and routing groups. For example, Exchange extends the user object with storage attributes to allow users to be associated with the Store where their mailbox is located as well as any quotas placed on the mailbox. Exchange also extends the schema to accommodate the requirements of its own subsystems, such as the changes to hold information about Exchange ActiveSync and the mobility policies that Exchange can impose on certain mobile devices. Schema extensions for Exchange must be in place (and replicated throughout the forest) before you can install Exchange servers into an AD forest, so this is a step that you have to include in your deployment plan. If you have Exchange 2003 servers already in the forest, there are just a few extensions to install and replicate before you can install Exchange 2007, but there are well over 2,000 changes necessary to prepare a brand new AD forest for Exchange 2007.

2.5.1   Updating the schema with an installation

The easiest way to update the schema is to just go ahead with the first Exchange server installation in a forest, but you can update the schema beforehand by utilizing two options that are included in the Exchange installation procedure. You execute SETUP with these options from an administrator account that has full permission to modify the Active Directory. Once the Active Directory is prepared, you can perform subsequent installations of Exchange using accounts that have local administrative access, but are not privileged to change forest-wide settings such as updating the schema or adding the Exchange container to the configuration-naming context.

The options are:

- Setup /PrepareAD: This option runs in the root domain of the forest (or the domain that hosts the schema master, which is normally the root domain). /PrepareAD performs the set of changes to the schema, instantiates the Exchange organization, adds the Exchange container to the configuration naming context, and creates the security groups used by Exchange. You cannot execute this command unless you are able to log on with Enterprise Admin and Schema Admin privileges.

- Setup /DomainPrep: You run this option in every domain where an Exchange 2007 server is located. The option performs tasks such as creating the global groups used for Exchange administration. You must be a domain administrator to be able to run this option.

- If you are installing Exchange 2007 into an existing Exchange 2000/2003 organization, you have to run Setup /PrepareLegacyExchange-Permissions to ensure that the correct security context is created to support a mixture of server versions. In particular, this process allows the Exchange Enterprise Server and Exchange Domain Servers security groups access to the new property sets that Exchange creates in the Active Directory and ensures that the Recipient Update Service can continue to stamp attributes on new objects after Exchange 2007 joins the organization. Note that if you add a new domain to the forest and install Exchange 2003 servers into the domain, you must run Setup /PrepareLegacyExchangePermissions in this domain to allow the Recipient Update Service to work.

- If you install Exchange 2007 in a domain in another forest to the forest that holds your user accounts, you have to run Setup /Foreign-ForestFQDN in the forest that holds the user accounts to allow the accounts to access their mailboxes in the other forest.

The /PrepareAD option is a useful thing to execute if you want to replicate schema updates throughout the forest before you begin server installations. The sheer number of changes applied to the schema (Exchange adds 57 attributes to the Windows Partial Attribute Set that is replicated to all Global Catalogs and creates over 500 new object identifiers, including 13 indexed attributes) is a good reason to perform the installation (or schema update) of the first Exchange server close (at least in network terms) to the schema master as this will speed up processing of the schema changes. Windows makes schema changes to the configuration container of the Active Directory on the target controller and then replicates them to the other controllers throughout the forest.

Figure 2.9 shows the ADSIEDIT utility examining the properties of the container used to hold configuration details for Exchange. Every object in the Active Directory has a distinguished name, so the container used to hold Exchange data is named *<domain-name>/Configuration/Services/Microsoft Exchange* and it holds a number of other containers to store details of entities such as policies, address lists, connectors, and so on.

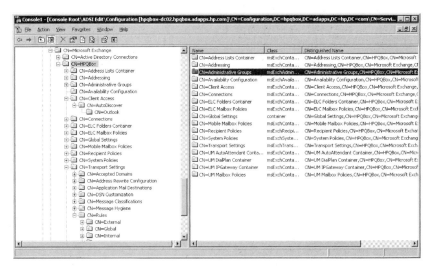

Figure 2.9
The Exchange configuration container

2.5.2 Changing the schema

The provision of an extendible schema is a major feature of the Active Directory, but whereas it is great to be able to customize the Active Directory, the feature introduces some new issues for consideration. Updating the schema does not impose a performance penalty. The new attributes occupy no space in the database unless you populate the attributes with data. Changing the schema is something that you must treat very seriously and only perform when a change is justified and you fully understand the ramifications. For this reason, you should agree any change up front with all of the domain administrators. Ideally, someone within the organization should take responsibility for arbitration of schema changes and anyone who wishes to make a change should first consult that person. Schema anarchy is not a pretty sight! For this reason, some companies keep the membership of the Schema Admins group empty until they know they need to make a change, whereupon they add the necessary user to the group until after the change when they revoke the membership.

It is also a good idea to apply as many schema changes as possible at the start of an implementation as this means that every new domain controller will inherit the fully updated schema as part of the DCPROMO procedure. The alternative is to make schema changes as the need arises, but this means that you have to let the Active Directory replicate each set of changes throughout the forest before you can proceed to deploy applications that depend on the schema update.

Attributes can be single-valued (like your home telephone number) or multi-valued (like the membership of a group). Before you change the schema to add a new attribute, you need the following information:

- The name of the new attribute and its purpose: In directory terminology, this is the common name. You can provide a separate description, although in many cases for the standard set of attributes used by Windows or Exchange, the description is very similar to the name.

- Because the roots of Active Directory are in X.500, each attribute and object has a unique X.500 object identifier, or OID. A national registration authority, such as the American National Standards Institute (ANSI)[1], issues OIDs. You can make up the value for an OID, and as long as the value does not clash with the OID of another attribute, then you will not have a problem. However, if an application comes along in the future and attempts to add an attribute with an existing OID, then you will have a problem and the application will not be able to add the new attribute to the schema. One method that is sometimes used is to take the base OID for the DSA provider and append your company's international telephone number plus some sequence number to it to create the new OID. This method usually guarantees uniqueness.

- The type or syntax of the attribute and its maximum and minimum range: For example, an attribute held as string values will be stored as Unicode strings and can range in size from 1 to whatever number of bytes is required to hold the maximum string length.

- Whether or not the Active Directory should replicate the attribute to Global Catalog servers: Clearly, the more attributes that are replicated, the more data is transmitted across the network. Some attributes are not required enterprise-wide and can be restricted to an object's home domain. The Active Directory has to replicate others, like the attribute that holds details of an Exchange user's home mailbox server, throughout the forest to enable specific functionality, like message routing.

- Whether the Active Directory indexes the attribute and includes it in the Ambiguous Name Resolution (ANR) process. Exchange has supported ANR since Exchange 4.0.

---

1. See http://www.ansi.org/public/services/reg_org.html.

Before we look at the detail of how to change the schema, we need to update the system registry on the server where we want to apply the change. Ideally, you should apply all updates to the schema at the schema master. If not, the server that you use to make the change needs a fast connection to the schema master to make the change. Applications like Exchange often include commands to update the schema in their installation procedures. Exchange 2007 updates the Active Directory and extends the schema when you run the Setup program with the /PrepareAD switch. After the schema is updated, you can browse through it, as shown in Figure 2.10, to view details of the additional attributes used for Exchange. Figure 2.10 shows the schema snap-in loaded in an MMC console, which is how we are able to view details of the schema. You may find that MMC doesn't list the schema snap-in when you go to load it. This is probably because the schema snap-in is not registered for use with MMC. To solve the problem, issue this command at the command prompt:

```
C:> \WINNT\SYSTEM32\REGSVR32 SCHMMGMT.DLL
```

Figure 2.10
Viewing Exchange attributes in the AD schema

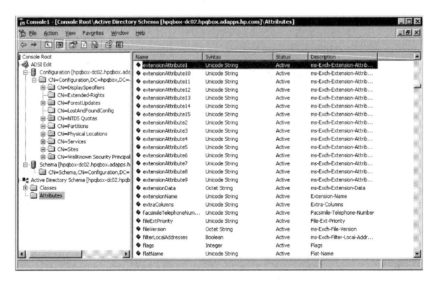

The schema is loaded into memory on every domain controller in an area called the schema cache. To ensure that clients access changes promptly, the Active Directory reloads the schema cache from disk every five minutes. If you change the schema, you can force the Active Directory to reload the cache immediately from an option in the Schema snap-in. This ensures that all the changes are active before you attempt to use them.

2.5.3 Active Directory custom attributes for Exchange

Exchange has always provided a set of custom attributes that you can use to store information about users in the directory. It is highly unlikely that the designer of any directory will ever incorporate a set of attributes that satisfies every possible customer, so the Active Directory includes 15 custom attributes that you can populate according to your needs. Prior to Exchange 2007, you fill in the attributes by first selecting the advanced view for AD Users and Computers and then viewing the Exchange Advanced property page. In Exchange 2007, you select the object using EMC, edit the properties, and click on the "Custom Properties" button (Figure 2.11).

Before anyone begins to add values to the custom property set, you should clearly define what these values will hold and how to populate them. Otherwise, one administrator may think that custom attribute 1 holds an employee badge number whereas everyone else uses custom attribute 2 for this purpose. Other common uses for these attributes include cost center identifiers, whether a user is a permanent or temporary employee, social security numbers (some countries bar you by law from holding personal information like this in a general-purpose directory), job codes, and so on.

Figure 2.11

Setting values for custom properties

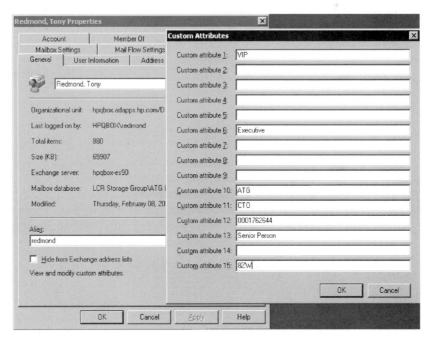

2.5.4   Updating the schema to allow Ambiguous Name Resolution

Ambiguous Name Resolution (sometimes called Automatic Name Resolution) is the process used by Exchange to search the Active Directory to find addresses that match information provided by users. In other words, Exchange searches the Active Directory against a number of different fields to find any or all matching addresses. If Exchange finds a number of matching addresses we have an ambiguous name, and Exchange prompts the client to present the addresses to the user in a dialog for them to make the final selection.

Exchange checks attributes such as the first name, surname, display name, and mailbox alias during the ANR process. ANR is invoked whenever a user presses the CTRL/K sequence, or when an unresolved address is detected in the TO:, CC:, or BCC: fields of a message header. Outlook and Outlook Web Access clients support ANR. In Figure 2.12, you can see how Outlook Web Access supports ANR in Exchange 2007 (left) and Exchange 2003 (right). Outlook Express also performs ANR if you configure the client to check names against the Active Directory before it sends messages.

Figure 2.12
Ambiguous names detected by Outlook Web Access

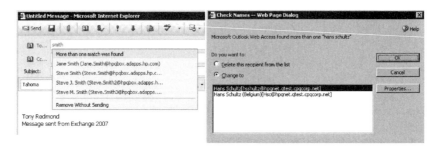

It may be advantageous to alter the schema to include a customized field in the ANR process. You could populate one of the extension properties with details such as a department code and add this attribute to the ANR process, if this makes sense within the company. Remember that changes to the schema are forest-wide and you cannot reverse a change once made, so be sure to consider all aspects of making the change before implementation.

Three different properties govern whether Exchange can use an attribute for ANR.

Figure 2.13 illustrates these properties as set for one of the custom extension properties. You might wonder why I say that three properties govern ANR when only one is marked as such. The reason is simple. The Ambiguous Name Resolution property determines whether the ANR process uses the attribute, but it is not very intelligent to mark an attribute for ANR

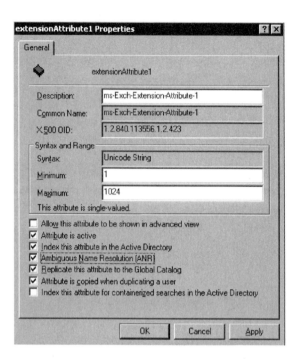

Figure 2.13
Where to enable ANR resolution for a selected attribute

if it is not indexed, and only slightly more intelligent to keep an attribute used by ANR out of the Global Catalog. After all, if the Active Directory does not index the attribute, any attempt to check a name against the attribute will be very slow and frustrate users, and if the attribute is restricted to one domain, its value is useless anywhere else in the forest. For best effect, check all the properties.

2.5.5 Exchange-specific permissions

Along with an upgraded schema, Exchange also adds a set of permissions to the Active Directory to allow administrators to perform operations such as managing databases. The permissions, which Microsoft refers to as "extended rights," exist in the configuration container under "Extended-Rights," as shown in Figure 2.14. All of the rights that Exchange uses have an "ms-Exch" prefix, so they are easy to find.

Property sets are a special type of extended rights. A property set is a group of object properties that you can use to define access control on an object by manipulating multiple permissions in a single operation. For example, if you enable the Exchange Information (a property set) permission on a user object, you actually enable users to see the values in the object's email addresses, manager, and common name attributes. Exchange uses property sets extensively to simplify administrative operations. If it did not, we would

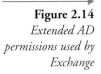

Figure 2.14
*Extended AD
permissions used by
Exchange*

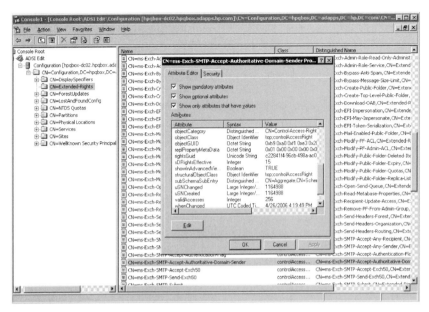

be constantly updating permissions on Active Directory objects to try to
assign the necessary rights to get work done.

2.5.6   Exchange property sets

Chapter 3 reviews how Exchange and the Windows administrators perform
different tasks in an Exchange 2000/2003 environment. The split administrative model is not natural in that Microsoft didn't build a comprehensive
design for administrative delegation that spans both Exchange and Windows.
Instead of being able to assign some out-of-the-box roles such as "Administrator of a Branch Office" that incorporates the necessary permissions to perform all the tasks that you'd expect someone in this role to have to be able to
do, it's a case of creating a roll-your-own solution by assigning different permissions over different objects to different people on a very individual basis.
You can argue that this is the right approach because every company is different and all have their own way of managing servers. While this assertion is
correct, it would still be nice to have a flexible administrative framework to
work within.

The problem in solving the problem through selective allocation of
permissions to individuals is that you run the danger of bloat in access control lists. In other words, to assign administrators a fine level of control
over the attributes of mailboxes and other recipient types, you have to
assign permissions over a large number of individual attributes. The result
is that the access control lists increase in size and become difficult to man-

age. The Active Directory database file, NTDS.DIT, also grows in size to accommodate the expanded Access Control Lists. Exchange 2007 solves this problem by defining property sets that cover the vast majority of attributes associated with mail recipients. A property set is a grouping of attributes that can be controlled by setting a single Access Control Entry (ACE) on the set rather than setting individual ACEs on each attribute. An attribute can only be a member of a single property set. For example, the Personal Information property set includes information such as the given name, company name, telephone number, and department name, all of which are attributes of user objects. Exchange recipient administrators need to be able to work with these attributes, so by grouping all of the attributes that a recipient administrator needs to work with into a property set, we can set the necessary ACE to allow recipient administrators to work with those attributes in a single operation.

Exchange 2003 did not use specific property sets. Instead, the Exchange 2003 installation added some Exchange-specific attributes to the standard Active Directory Personal Information and Public Information property sets. On the surface, this seems like a good idea, but the problem is that Exchange has no control over these property sets, which may be amended by a future version of Active Directory that generates a subsequent knock-on impact for Exchange. Exchange 2007 resolves the problem by creating two new property sets, Exchange Information and Exchange Personal Information, that are installed into the forest when you run Setup /PrepareAD. These property sets contain attributes that are defined by the Exchange schema extensions to Active Directory and are under the control of Exchange. These property sets are created when you extend the Active Directory schema prior to installing the first Exchange 2007 server in an organization. Attributes that were added by Exchange 2003 to the standard Active Directory property sets are removed from these property sets and incorporated into the new Exchange property sets. Examples of the attributes that are in the Exchange Information property set are:

- MailNickName
- HomeMDB
- ExtensionAttribute1
- ForwardingAddress

While examples of the attributes in the Exchange Personal Information property set include:

- MsExchangeMessageHygieneFlags

- MsExchangeSafeRecipientsHash
- MsExchangeSafeSendersHash

The last two of these attributes are interesting because they allow Exchange to capture and store details of users' safe recipients and safe sender data in their accounts in the Active Directory. Subsequently, Exchange can synchronize this data to the ADAM instance used by Edge servers so that they can integrate user data into the tests that the Edge servers use to detect and suppress spam.

Creating a new Recipient Administrator role provides a logical solution to the problem, and that is what you get in Exchange 2007, where you can grant a user the Exchange Recipient Administrator role through EMC or by using the `Add-ExchangeAdministrator` command. Having Microsoft determine what permissions are required to perform the recipient management task is a much more secure solution than each organization figuring out what ACLs have to be set on Active Directory objects or permissions held by user accounts. It is inevitable that mistakes will occur along the way when multiple attempts are made to solve the problem and mistakes lead to loopholes in security, which can lead to further issues with data integrity and so on.

2.6   Longhorn and Exchange 2007

Longhorn is the code name for the major release of the Windows server operating system that Microsoft anticipates shipping in late 2007 or early 2008. Dates are always difficult to predict when it comes to the availability of a new version of an operating system as much depends on the quality of the software and the kind of bugs that the developers encounter as they drive to meet the ship date.

Because Longhorn was still in the beta development phase when Microsoft shipped Exchange 2007, it is logical that you cannot deploy Exchange 2007 on servers that run Longhorn, nor can you deploy Exchange 2007 servers inside an Active Directory site that supports Longhorn domain controllers or Global Catalogs. After all, the Exchange developers can test Exchange 2007 on the latest version of Longhorn that is available to them when they put the final changes on Exchange 2007, but that is no guarantee that code will run on the final version. There is no doubt that a future version of Exchange 2007 (probably a full-service pack) will support Longhorn, so you can therefore factor Longhorn into your long-term plans for your Windows infrastructure.

Even though you cannot use Longhorn as a platform to run the first release of Exchange 2007 and have to wait until Exchange 2007 SP1 for

Microsoft to support the two software releases working together, you can use Longhorn to solve specific issues. For example, Longhorn supports a read-only version of a domain controller that is well suited for deployment within a DMZ when you want to allow applications access to the Active Directory to retrieve account information, but you don't want to allow applications to write into or update the Active Directory in case the DMZ is compromised by an attacker. Exchange 2007 could use this functionality to support its Edge server role but as Longhorn is not available, Exchange 2007 uses ADAM instead.

2.7 The very important LegacyExchangeDN attribute

The original Exchange architecture allocated a fixed distinguished name to every object in the directory and used this value as the primary key for the object in the directory. Exchange composed distinguished names from the names of the containers along the path to an object in the directory. Primary keys are difficult to change and this implementation led to some problems in terms of flexibility. You could not change the name of an Exchange 5.5 site or move users between containers because these operations required the object to be deleted and then recreated with a new distinguished name that reflected the new location of the object within the directory.

During Exchange's transition to use the Active Directory, the developers were careful to avoid the same issue. While the Active Directory still uses distinguished names to reference objects, the distinguished name is no longer the primary key. Instead, when it creates a new object, the Active Directory allocates a GUID (Global Unique Identifier) to it. You can move objects around the directory between containers as much as you want, which results in multiple changes to their distinguished names, but their GUIDs remain constant. Unlike previous versions of Exchange, no correlation exists between a user's distinguished name and a site or other administrative, security, or routing boundary.

You can view the distinguished name for an object using the ADS-IEDIT utility. Select the object and then look at the value of the "distinguished name" attribute. You will see values like this:

```
CN=Tony Redmond,OU=Exchange Users,DC=xyz,DC=com
```

There is no correlation between distinguished names and email addresses. The change in distinguished name format occurs automatically as accounts are migrated and Exchange hides the change in distinguished name format from users. However, many different pieces of the messaging puzzle store the old Exchange-format distinguished name (such as the headers of old messages and MAPI profiles) to ensure backwards compatibility.

Because two different formats are in use, some method is needed to ensure that the older addresses stored within the infrastructure are still valid. The Active Directory accomplishes this goal by maintaining a separate attribute for every Exchange object called the *LegacyExchangeDN*. You can think of LegacyExchangeDN as the "old" name for an Exchange object; something to ensure backwards compatibility by always having something that an older version of Exchange, older clients, or a utility built for an older version of Exchange can recognize and use. Another way of considering the attribute is to think of it as the equivalent of a SID for MAPI because all versions of MAPI clients and servers built to date can use the LegacyExchangeDN to locate objects. As an example, here are two LegacyExchangeDN values for a mailbox created in an Exchange 2007 organization and the special administrative group that Exchange 2007 uses for backwards compatibility with Exchange 2000/2003. The values that you see in legacy organizations will be slightly different.

```
/o=xyz/ou=Exchange Administrative Group (FYDIBOHF23SPDLT)/
cn=Recipients/cn=EPR

/o=xyz/ou=Exchange Administrative Group (FYDIBOHF23SPDLT)
```

The Active Directory indexes the LegacyExchangeDN attribute to enable fast lookup and automatically searches the index if a client attempts to search the Active Directory using a distinguished name in the old format. Thus, MAPI profiles continue to work and clients can continue to reply to messages using old addresses because the Active Directory responds to the search executed by the transport engine when it attempts to resolve the address.

It is possible that Exchange will move away from using the LegacyExchangeDN attribute in future versions, but the need to retain backwards compatibility means that we'll probably run a new convention (like an SMTP address) in tandem with the old LegacyExchangeDN addresses for at least two versions. To do this, Microsoft will have to create parallel code to be able to handle both formats and they will have to move to a position where a new version of Exchange cannot support previous versions of Outlook. Even though LegacyExchangeDN is used throughout Exchange, creating parallel code is a well-understood engineering technique that Microsoft already uses in the availability service so that the previous method of free and busy lookups work for older Outlook clients and the new method used by Outlook 2007. However, the big issue is that there are many older Outlook clients used with Exchange and customer response to a forced upgrades a new version of Outlook is unlikely to be positive. The net result is that this a difficult problem to solve and that the LegacyExchangeDN attribute is likely to be with us for a while yet.

2.8   Brain surgery for the Active Directory: ADSIEDIT

Normally, you access the Active Directory through consoles such as the AD Users and Computers snap-in. The user interface of MMC and the snap-ins enforce rules and restrictions that stop administrators from making mistakes when they work with important data. In most conditions, it is perfectly acceptable to work with the regular consoles, but sometimes you want or need to be able to go behind the scenes to interrogate the Active Directory in order to find out how things really work and that is where ADSIEDIT proves its value.

ADSIEDIT allows administrators to browse and manipulate raw Active Directory data, such as the configuration data for an Exchange organization or a single attribute setting for a storage group. ADSIEDIT is a double-edged sword: While it allows you to interrogate and view details of any Active Directory data, it is also very possible to change something best left untouched. You could do much the same thing with the original Exchange ADMIN program by running it in raw mode as this exposed the contents of the Exchange directory that the user interface normally blocked. However, when you can work with raw data, you can make some raw mistakes, such as deleting something important that affected the way that Exchange works. Occasionally, mistakes required a complete restore of the directory to fix the problem. The same power and potential for problems exists with ADS-IEDIT, and an inadvertent slip of the finger can stop Exchange working if you make a mistake in the wrong place. The best idea when working with ADSIEDIT is to practice safe directory access by never changing an object unless you know the exact consequences of the action.

Before you can use ADSIEDIT, you have to install the Windows Support Tools. You can get the Windows Support Tools from the Windows 2003 server CD or by downloading the kit from Microsoft's Web site. Once installed, you load the ADSIEDIT snap-in by starting MMC, clicking on the Add/Remove Snap-in option on the File menu, then clicking on the "Add" button to view the snap-ins that are available on the server, and then select the ADSIEDIT snap-in from the list (Figure 2.15). Click Add, Close, and then OK to make the snap-in active in the console.

After you have loaded ADSIEDIT into MMC, you need to connect to a naming context before you can work with the Active Directory. Right-click on the ADSIEDIT root and select the "Connect to" option to force ADS-IEDIT to display the Connection Settings dialog shown in Figure 2.16.

Figure 2.15
Adding the ADSIEDIT snap-in to a console

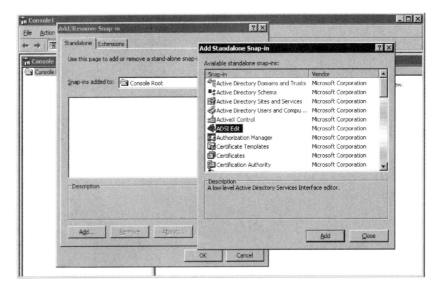

Figure 2.16
Connecting ADSIEDIT to a naming context

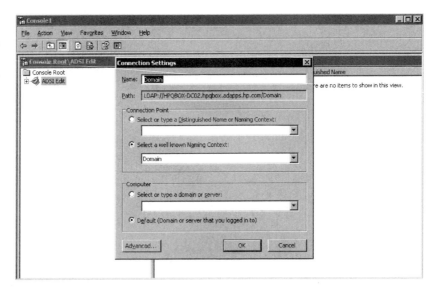

If you want to work with account and contact information, you connect to the Domain naming context; if you want to work with configuration information, such as Exchange organizational data, then you connect to the configuration naming context. By default, ADSIEDIT attempts to connect to a Global Catalog in the local Windows site. You can click on the "ADSI Edit" root and connect to another controller elsewhere in the forest by typing the full name of the server. Note that the default connection is to the domain naming context for the selected server and that ADSIEDIT maintains any existing connections, including to the schema and configuration naming contexts unless you use the "Remove" option to release the connection. Once connected, you can browse the contents of each of the naming contexts in the same way as any other MMC console. Figure 2.17 shows ADSIEDIT loaded into an MMC console being used to browse user account information through the domain naming context. Once you have connected to the Active Directory, you can use ADSIEDIT to browse the contents of each of the naming contexts in the same way as any other MMC console. Figure 2.17 shows the contents of the domain naming context, so objects like user accounts are listed. Note the dynamic distribution group object shown here.

Figure 2.17
*Accessing Active
Directory data
with ADSIEDIT*

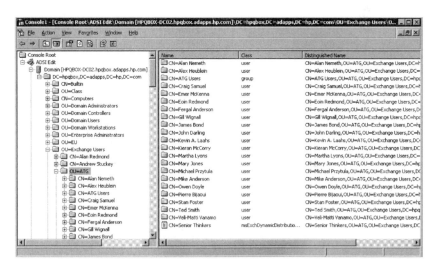

Administrators most commonly use ADSIEDIT to examine the properties of objects and verify that the right values exist in the various attributes. There are many and varied reasons why you use ADSIEDIT for this purpose. Even the Advanced View of AD Users and Computers only reveals a limited selection of the attributes of an object so you have to use a different tool if you want to examine the hidden attributes, and ADSIEDIT is very convenient for this purpose. Many of these attributes are very important in directory synchronization projects. For example, if you are using your own procedures to synchronize the Active Directory with another metadirectory, you may want to check that the synchronization process is writing values from the metadirectory into the correct attributes in the Active Directory.

As an example, let us assume that the metadirectory holds information about business units and we have implemented code to transfer this data to the extensionAttribute15 attribute in the Active Directory. To check that the synchronization code works correctly, we use ADSIEDIT to select any user object and then view its properties, selecting the appropriate attribute as shown in Figure 2.18. As you can see, the string "Thinker" exists in extensionAttribute15. If this is the value in the metadirectory, we know that the synchronization code works. Of course, if the wrong value is present we have entirely another problem to solve!

Figure 2.18
*Using ADSIEDIT
to view properties
of a user object*

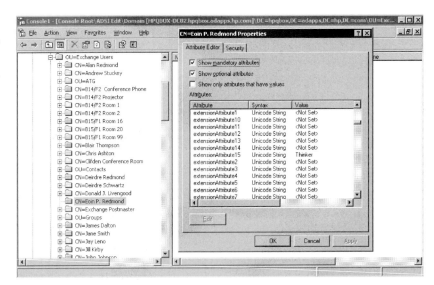

Windows administrators also use ADSIEDIT for many purposes. For example, assume that a domain controller suffers a catastrophic hardware failure and you do not want to reinstall the server. Because an administrator has not run the DCPROMO process to demote the server, it still exists in the Active Directory as a domain controller with all of the associated roles and responsibilities such as acting as a replication partner. In this case, you could use ADSIEDIT to remove all references of the server from the AD. Later on, if you wanted to reintroduce the controller, you can rebuild the server and then run DCPROMO to make it a domain controller.

Note that you shouldn't run DCPROMO on a server that has Exchange 2007 installed because Microsoft doesn't support this operation. In fact, Microsoft is pretty emphatic that you shouldn't run Exchange on a server that supports the Active Directory. See TechNet for more details.

2.8.1   LDP and LDIFDE

If you want to get even closer to raw data, the LDP utility is available. While ADSIEDIT is quite capable of performing brain surgery on the AD, LDP is able to examine individual nerves. LDP is a good example of a utility that works brilliantly in the hands of a software engineer or someone who knows their way around LDAP and needs to retrieve diagnostic information. If you just want to poke around the innards of the AD for a casual browse, use ADSIEDIT. LDP is just too dangerous because the GUI does not protect you, so a simple slip or mistype of one character can have enormous consequences. The big difference between the two utilities is that you can examine many attributes together for an object with ADSIEDIT whereas you can look at many together with LDP. In addition, even though the Windows 2003 version of LDP is improved, its user interface is very basic and it is easy to make a mistake. For example, you have to type in the name of an attribute when you modify it, whereas ADSIEDIT allows you to select the attribute through from lists. Knowledge Base article 224543 is a good introduction to LDP and explains many of its functions.

Figure 2.19
LDP utility

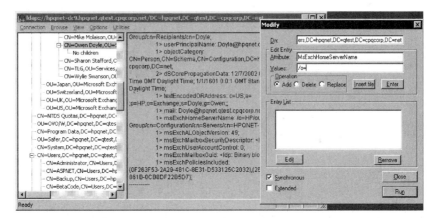

Figure 2.19 shows the LDP utility connected to a DC. In this case, I began searching in the OU that holds some user accounts, selected one, and then began to modify an attribute. The Browse menu allows you to add, delete, or modify attributes for selected objects, but in most cases, you simply want to interrogate the AD to discover information about objects. You can see the contents of the OU in the tree view in the left-hand pane and some of the attributes and their values in the right-hand pane.

When you examine a user object, you can see a large amount of data, including the links to the distribution groups that the user belongs to and any organizational data that exists (their manager and direct reports). You can also look at security descriptors, while the replication option allows you to see replication metadata. This information is very valuable if you need to provide it to Microsoft PSS to help solve a complex problem, but it is not usually very valuable in day-to-day administration. After you have investigated the AD with LDP, you may want to change the values of some attributes. You can certainly do this with ADSIEDIT, but again you have to operate on one object at a time.

LDIFDE is a utility that exports or imports LDAP-compliant data into the AD. Knowledge Base article 237677 gives you a good overview of the process, but you will also need to become conversant with LDAP syntax and the set of attributes supported by the AD to process anything other than simple exports and imports. RFC2254 is the authoritative source for information about LDAP search strings, while you can discover the names of the attributes that you want to work with by examining the properties of a selected object with ADSIEDIT or LDP.

LDIFDE works on very basic principles. You create a file that contains the operations you want to perform against the AD and then feed it to LDIFDE for execution. In most cases, the easiest way to accomplish the goal is to export data about the objects you want to process first, use a text editor to make whatever changes you want, and then run LDIFDE again to import the file and make the changes.

2.8.2   Active Directory for Exchange

The Active Directory continues to provide the fundamental underpinning for Exchange 2007, just as it has done since Exchange 2000. Seven years or so later, we don't have to experience the same trauma that occurred when everyone had to upgrade to Windows 2000 and the Active Directory before they could deploy Exchange 2000, and most Active Directory deployments are in good shape now. Exchange also depends on the Active Directory for its permissions model and to provide the link to Edge servers so that anti-spam protection works smoothly, if you decide to deploy Edge servers for this purpose. For all these reasons and more, the Active Directory still deserves and requires attention from an Exchange administrator.

The big change for Exchange 2007 is the dependency on Active Directory sites as the basis for the message routing topology. If Active Directory replication works efficiently today, you should be in good shape to move forward with Exchange 2007. Moving to the 64-bit version of Windows may be a more interesting challenge because of the potential that exists to consolidate domain controllers and Global Catalogs into a smaller set of physical servers and it will be interesting to see how administrators approach this work. Leaving Active Directory behind (but always lurking in the background), we move on to discuss the basics of managing Exchange 2007.

3

The Basics of Managing Exchange 2007

Managing Exchange has often been a challenge for system administrators, especially in large corporate environments. Because of the huge variety of companies that use Exchange, Microsoft had to perform a balancing act when they built the management tools that they provide with Exchange. They had to create tools that administrators could use in any situation from the small deployments based on the version of Exchange integrated with Microsoft Small Business Server to deployments that spanned the world and hundreds of thousands of users. This is a very difficult problem to crack because it is not easy to create software that can adapt to a huge variety of different operating circumstances, yet this is what Microsoft attempted to do in Exchange 2000 and 2003 with the Exchange System Manager (ESM) console. As a system management tool, ESM was okay, but no more. ESM reflected the view of the world in 1998–99 and was not flexible enough to deal with the demands of the largest Exchange deployments.

To Microsoft's credit, they recognized that the development approach that resulted in ESM had run out of steam and needed to be changed. ESM represents an inflexible object-centric view of management that limits administrators to working with objects such as servers, connectors, databases, and mailboxes within the boundaries set by the GUI built by the Exchange developers. If you want to go outside the GUI, you face the hurdle of incomplete and undocumented programming interfaces that have changed across different versions of Exchange and that require a good deal of knowledge before you can attempt even the most fundamental of tasks, such as retrieving a list of mailboxes from a server. Microsoft's response in Exchange 2007 can be broken down into two major pieces—a radically redesigned management console that looks a lot better and behaves more intuitively than previous versions and an automation shell. For Exchange 2007, Microsoft created EMS, the Exchange Management Shell, on top of the standard Windows PowerShell scripting language. The idea is that you can use EMS to program common management tasks quickly and easily. The interesting thing is that Microsoft has built the Exchange Management Console (EMC) from the task-based commands that they expose through

PowerShell. For the first time, because Microsoft built EMC on the same code as they use for the PowerShell commands, Exchange administrators are able to create scripts that automate tasks to meet the demands of their own operating environment without having to depend on an Exchange developer doing the job for them.

The complete overhaul of the management console takes some time for even experienced Exchange administrators to become used to. It is not just the change in the appearance of EMC or the introduction of newly formalized concepts such as server roles or the appearance of multiple wizards to perform tasks. In addition, you have to become accustomed to the new terminology that Exchange uses throughout the product allied to the new focus on programmability. Finally, it is the fact that you can only perform some tasks through PowerShell. Apart from the challenge of understanding the new interface and terms, administrators have the option of becoming a GUI "whimp" or an EMS wizard. With this in mind, this chapter explores how to use the Exchange Management Console to perform common management tasks and how to use Exchange PowerShell to automate the same tasks.

3.1   Exchange Management Console

The Exchange Management Console is the latest version of the administrative tool for Exchange servers. It replaces the Exchange System Manager (ESM) console that features in Exchange 2000 and 2003 that replaced the original ADMIN.EXE administration program used by Exchange 4.0 to 5.5. EMC and ESM are both MMC snap-ins. EMC is based on Version 3.0 of the Microsoft Management Console (MMC) framework and shares some of the design philosophies seen in other consoles, such as those used for ISA 2004 or 2006, MOM 2005 or 2007, and Windows Storage Server. MMC 3.0 is included in Windows 2003 R2 and also supports Windows 2003 SP1, where it requires you to install the .NET framework (version 2.0.50727 or higher).

Experience with the original version of ESM demonstrated that it worked well for small to medium organizations but had some performance problems in larger organizations (more than a hundred servers). ESM was also handicapped in that you cannot create new mail-enabled Active Directory objects from the console, so you ended up in a split management model where some tasks (such as creating a new user account) were performed with the AD Users and Computers console and others (like creating a new messaging connector) were performed with ESM. While you could argue that the split in responsibilities was logical because you wanted those who administered the Active Directory to have full control over the objects that were created, in practice the split was not terribly logical and ended up confusing more people than it helped. Finally, it was not always easy to find information within ESM as getting to a specific option might require seven or eight different navigation operations to expose the desired data. Microsoft's goal was to make EMC better performing and to simplify navigation within the console.

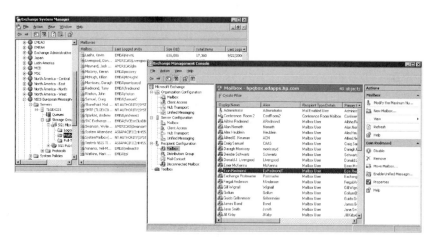

Figure 3.1
Exchange 2003 ESM and Exchange 2007 EMC

Figure 3.1 demonstrates the difference in design philosophies in console layout between Exchange 2003 and Exchange 2007. The Exchange 2003 ESM (left) has a traditional tree that you navigate down through to reach the administrative group, then the server, then the storage group, and then the database before you can do any real work. As it happens, ESM reveals more information about mailboxes in a database when you eventually get there, because it displays the mailboxes and data such as mailbox size and total items alongside. However, you have had to do quite a lot of clicking to get there. The Exchange 2007 EMC (right) has a cleaner design that organizes information into four distinct nodes or sections:

1. Organization Configuration: This area holds all the global or system-wide configuration data such as email address policies[1], address lists, and accepted domains. The sub-tree in this area shows servers categorized by role so that you can see all the configuration data for a server role in one place. The top level of the tree holds all the general global settings that do not map to a server role, much as it does when you work with organizational settings in the Exchange 2003 version of ESM.

---

1.   Recipient Policies are the rough equivalent in Exchange 2000 and 2003.

2. Server Configuration: As the name implies, this area holds configuration settings for individual servers such as the databases that are present on the servers. It also allows you to work with servers to enable options such as local continuous replication for a storage group (see Chapter 9 for more details on how local continuous replication works). Like the organization area, the server area presents servers grouped in roles, but you can also click on the Server Configuration node to see an aggregate view of all servers in the organization. Think of how you work with individual servers in ESM; the difference is that you can get to an individual server more quickly because you don't have to navigate through administrative groups.

3. Recipient Configuration: This is where you manage all types of mail-enabled recipients such as mailboxes, distribution groups, and contacts. EMC groups the various recipient types under the Recipient Configuration node and if you click on the node, you see a list of all recipients, or at least, up to the first 1,000 recipients in the organization. This operation could take a long time in a large organization, but Microsoft is confident that they have tweaked the performance of the predefined filters included in Exchange 2007 (for example, show only mailboxes) to deliver the necessary responsiveness. As we will discuss later on in this chapter, you can create tailored filters to match the exact requirements of your environment and speed things up even further. One small concern is the naming convention that Microsoft has chosen for the "Disable" and "Remove" options (Figure 3.2) because the "Disable" option really means, "Leave the Active Directory account there, but remove the Exchange-specific attributes" whereas "Remove" means "Delete the Active Directory account and the mailbox completely." Apart from the obvious removal of access to a mailbox, removing a mailbox can have other consequences. For instance, if you use the mailbox as a journal recipient, its removal has an obvious effect on the ability of Exchange to journal messages to that destination.

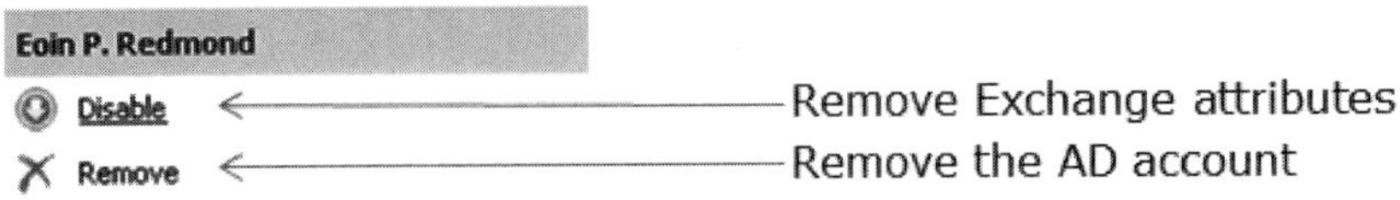

Figure 3.2
*Disable and
Remove a mailbox*

Eoin P. Redmond

Disable ⟵——————————— Remove Exchange attributes
Remove ⟵——————————— Remove the AD account

EMC lists any disconnected mailboxes in this node. Disconnected mailboxes are mailboxes that exist in a mailbox database but do not have a connection to an Active Directory account. You can use this node to connect these mailboxes with an account after the mailbox was previously disabled or following a disaster-recovery exercise. Because entries for disconnected mailboxes do not exist within the Active Directory, Exchange queries a specific mailbox store to discover any disconnected mailboxes that may exist in that database's mailbox table. If you suspect a database includes some disconnected mailboxes that do not show up in EMC, you can use the `Clean-MailboxDatabase` shell command to scan the database to check for disconnected mailboxes. This is the equivalent to the Run Cleanup Agent option in the Exchange 2003 ESM. You can then delete the disconnected mailboxes with the `Remove-Mailbox` command.

4.   Exchange Toolbox: Some refer to this node as a "launching pad" for additional tools from Microsoft (and potentially third parties) that you can use to manage Exchange. For example, Microsoft includes troubleshooting, diagnostics, and analysis tools such as the Message Tracking Center, the Exchange Best Practice Analyzer tool, and the Queue Viewer. See Chapter 10 for an explanation of these tools. ESM supports the Message Tracking Center, but Microsoft has only created many of the tools that you now find in the Toolbox since they shipped Exchange 2003. Previously, you would have to download each tool separately from Microsoft's web site and install it onto selected servers.

The four task areas do not include anything to do with the Edge server role. This is because Edge servers operate in a standalone mode quite separate from the rest of the Exchange organization. Edge servers share in the configuration of the organization through the EdgeSync process that pushes the data from the Active Directory to individual Edge servers, but they play no part in the organization as a whole and are therefore omitted from EMC.

Microsoft implemented the new layout for EMC because they believe that this is a logical division of labor across common tasks for Exchange administrators. They refer to each area as a "work center," which Microsoft defines as a top-level tree node with sub (or child) nodes. A major difference in EMC is that any dynamic data that results as you navigate through different object types is shown in the result pane rather than appearing as part of the tree. For example, if you enable a mailbox for ActiveSync, an option to allow you to work with properties of the mobile devices associated with the mailbox appears in the action pane. EMC divides its screen estate into the navigation tree, the result pane, and the action pane (which you can turn off by customizing the console view if you prefer to use the right-click context-sensitive menu to reveal the options that are available to work with objects). The server node also reveals a separate work pane to allow you to view details

Figure 3.3
*EMC Error
provider in action*

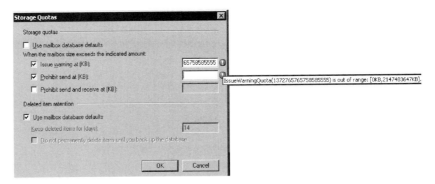

of objects related to individual servers, such as the databases on a mailbox server. EMC now offers a tabbed view to group similar features and data together in some cases, such as when you view the configuration details of a server role. The result of all the changes is that EMC navigation now goes just three levels deep rather than eight or more as was the case in ESM. The change takes a little to get used to, but it is reasonably intuitive.

One nice touch in EMC that did not exist in ESM is the addition of an error indicator when a value that you enter into a field is incorrect. As you can see in Figure 3.3, I attempted to enter a huge value for the "Issue warning at" storage limit. EMC flags the error with an exclamation mark in a red icon and if you move the mouse pointer over the icon, you see some explanatory text. In this case, the limit for a quota ranges from 0KB to 2,147,483,647KB, or just under 2,048GB, which should be enough for anyone.

3.1.1   **The importance of filters**

For performance reasons, EMC only attempts to fetch the first 1,000 items that match the filter in use. The same limit of 1,000 items exists everywhere that Exchange fetches information from the Active Directory, including PowerShell commands. The default filter for EMC is to "get everything," so EMC limits itself to working with the first 1,000 mailboxes, contacts, or groups when you access these nodes under Recipient Configuration, or a combination of all mail-enabled objects when you work at the Recipient Configuration level.

For performance reasons, EMC uses a feature called "list view virtual page" to avoid the need to render the items until it needs to display them, so even if you ask for more items, you will not take on much more of a performance penalty until EMC has to display the new items. The default approach of showing the first 1,000 items is perfectly reasonable in a small Exchange organization, such as those operating in small businesses or in test environments. In any medium to large organization, it is likely that you will want to apply a filter to restrict the items that EMC displays in order to not slow down the responsiveness of EMC. Alternatively, if you really need to view thousands of items, you will have to specify that EMC should process a larger number of items from the Active Directory. Once you find a filter that works well in your environment, you can save it as the default view (use the Save Current Filter as Default option on the View menu to do this). For example, opting to view all the mailboxes on the server that you manage is a common option to take.

Figure 3.4 shows two ways to define what data you want to work within EMC. First, you can set the scope for the organizational unit to fetch users from the default (access everything from the top-level organizational unit down, so all mail-enabled objects in the directory are fetched) to another point in the OU structure. This approach works well if you have administrative responsibility over a domain or organizational unit and do not need EMC to scan the entire directory. It is also an important point for administrators who work with Exchange inside a multi-domain forest. The default starting point for the recipient scope is the domain that the Exchange server is located in, so if you want to work with objects from another domain, you have to click on the "Modify Recipient Scope" option at the Recipient Configuration level and select the domain that you need.

The other option to control the set of objects that you work with allows you to increase the number of items that EMC fetches from the Active

Figure 3.4

Increasing the numbers of items and applying a new scope to EMC

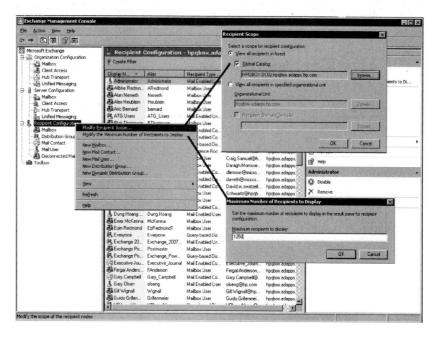

Directory. The default number of items returned is 1,000 and if there are more objects available (as defined by the current recipient scope), you will see the error displayed in Figure 3.5. However, you can increase the size of the set that EMC fetches by setting the "Modify the Maximum Number of Recipients to Display" option, so that even if you select a very large organizational unit to work with, you can fetch all the items. As we will see in Chapter 4, you can do the same thing when you work with shell commands by specifying a number for the set of objects that you want to work with through the –ResultSize parameter.

Figure 3.5
Too many objects in the current scope

Do not rush to fetch a larger number of items from the Active Directory. Depending on network conditions and the load on the Global Catalog server that Exchange connects to, it could take EMC a long time to fetch more than the default set of 1,000 items. For example, I changed the maximum number of recipients setting to force EMC to fetch and display 60,000 recipients in a very large organization (Figure 3.6). EMC took approximately two minutes to fetch all the recipients, but it displayed them without a problem. If you do set too high a figure to load, you can always use the "Stop Loading" button to stop and then click on F5 or the "Refresh" option to get going again.

Figure 3.6
Allowing EMC to display sixty thousand recipients

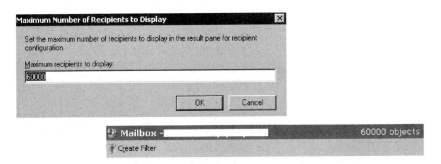

Once you have the complete set cached, EMC does not go back to the Active Directory unless you explicitly ask for the set to be refreshed. In another test, I increased the number of recipients to 30,000 and EMC took about a minute to load these objects. I then increased the number to 50,000 and EMC took approximately 30 seconds to load the first 30,000 and then slowed down to load the last 20,000 in just over another minute. Even though EMC still verified the objects, the first 30,000 objects loaded faster because they were already in memory whereas the last 20,000 had to come off disk.

You do not want to wait around for EMC to load, so when your organization spans more than a few thousand users, it is more efficient to create and apply a filter to work with the objects that you need. Figure 3.7 shows how to focus in on a set of objects to work with. In this case, we have defined a filter to show only the users who work in a department starting with "L." Examples of other common filters are "all mailboxes on server ExchMbxSvr1" or "All users in London" to focus in on a specific set of users. Because it is difficult to know exactly what filters you need, EMC allows you to use a wide range of properties to build filters.

Figure 3.7
Applying a filter to EMC

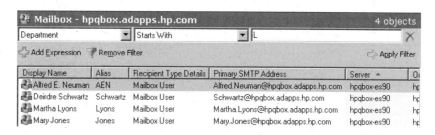

For example, if you work at the Recipient Configuration level, you can filter based on the following properties:

1. ActiveSync Mailbox Policy

2. Alias

3. City

4. Company

5. CustomAttribute1 to CustomAttribute15

6. Database

7. Department

8. Display Name

9. Email Addresses

10. External Email Address

11. First Name

12. Last Name

13. Manager

14. Managed Folder Mailbox Policy

15.   Name

16.   Office

17.   Recipient Type Details

18.   Server

19.   State or Province

20.   UM Enabled

21.   Unified Messaging Mailbox Policy

22.   User logon name (pre-Windows 2000)

23.   User logon name (User Principal Name)

Some of these properties are available for certain recipient types. For example, the 15 custom attributes are only available for mailboxes, so if you create a filter based on one of these attributes, the filter will only return mailboxes and contacts and groups will be ignored. The same is true for a server, because only mailboxes are associated with a server. When you build filters, you can use the following operators to compare values:

- Contains
- Does Not Contain
- Does Not Equal
- Ends With
- Equals
- Starts With

Not all of the operators are available for every property. For example, you can create a filter of "City Equals Dublin" or "Office Starts with L," but you can only use the "Equals" and "Does not Equal" operators with the Server property. However, to make things easier, EMC does at least provide a browse button for you to select the server that you want to include in the filter. After you add a filter, you apply it by clicking on the "Apply Filter" button. You can add additional expressions for the filter by clicking on the "Add Expression" button. The left-hand screen in Figure 3.8 shows a two-step filter that searches for mailboxes that have an office starting with "Bel" and a city containing "Dub." In fact, this is not a very efficient filter because EMC has to do a lot of work to scan records any time you use the "Contains" operator. This filter works, but it would be more efficient (and precise) if we change the second expression to "City starts with Dub." You will not notice the per-

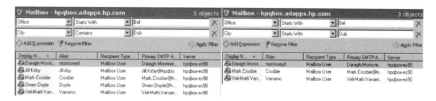

Figure 3.8
*Adding expressions
to the filter*

formance hit on a test system, but you will on a production system if you support more than a few thousand users.

Note that you can add multiple expressions that operate against the same property, in which case Exchange treats the filter as an implicit OR operation. If you create multiple expressions against different properties, Exchange treats the filter as an AND expression. Look at the right-hand screen of Figure 3.8 and see that because we have changed the expression that compares the value of the City property from "Contains" to "Starts with," the number of found items falls from five to three because the filter now drops the two items that contain "Dub" somewhere in the City property.

You can add up to ten additional expressions for your filter. Each expression adds to the complexity of the filter and may slow its performance, so you should ensure that you only add expressions that are absolutely required to zero in on the objects that you want to see. EMC is optimized to use server-side filtering whenever possible, meaning that Exchange executes the filter on the server rather than bringing all possible items to the client and then applying the filter. This approach minimizes network traffic and maximizes performance, but even so, an inefficient filter is never going to execute quickly. Removing the filter to revert back to the default filter is simply a matter of clicking the "Remove Filter" button.

3.1.2 Managing mixed organizations

As Figure 3.9 illustrates, if you operate a mixed mode organization to migrate legacy Exchange servers, Exchange 2007 servers are visible through the Exchange 2000/2003 management console. You will also notice that the Exchange 2007 servers occupy their own special administrative and routing group that allows them to participate in routing within a mixed mode organization. However, while you can view organizational information, the version of ESM provided in Exchange 2003 automatically blocks any attempt to edit an object that is under the control of Exchange 2007. You should always manage Exchange 2007 objects through EMC or EMS. Here are some recommendations on how to approach management when you have a mixture of servers in your Exchange organization:

Figure 3.9
*Exchange 2007
servers listed
in ESM*

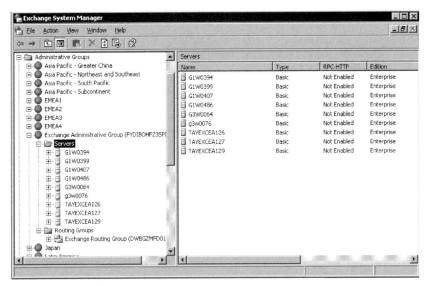

- Do not attempt to use ESM to manage Exchange 2007 storage groups and databases. These objects have been modified to function correctly on an Exchange 2007 server. If you attempt to use ESM to view the properties of these objects, Exchange returns an error similar to the one shown in Figure 3.10.

Figure 3.10
*ESM cannot deal
with an Exchange
2007 server*

- Always manage Exchange 2007 mailboxes with EMC or EMS. Why? Because if you attempt to manage them with AD Users and Computers on a Windows 2003 server that has the Exchange 2003 add-ins loaded, you may corrupt some important attributes. Microsoft does not impose a block on editing Exchange 2007 mailboxes from AD Users and Computers, but you do this at your own peril.

- You can edit, remove, or move Exchange 2003 mailboxes with EMC or EMS, but do not attempt to create a mailbox on an Exchange 2003 server with EMC or EMS. Why? Because the RUS has to process new mailboxes on an Exchange 2003 server and if you create it through EMC or EMS, the mailbox may not be fully functional.

- You can manage mail-enabled contacts from either Exchange 2003 or Exchange 2007.

- You can manage mail-enabled groups from either Exchange 2003 or Exchange 2007. However, be careful managing dynamic distribution groups because the recipient filters differ between the two versions. Exchange 2003 uses LDAP filters and Exchange 2007 use OPATH filters. See page 156 for more information on this topic.

- Do not use the Exchange 2003 move mailbox feature to move mailboxes to an Exchange 2007 server. Always use the Exchange 2007 move mailbox feature (or the `Move-Mailbox` shell command), because it is the only method that can move data between both server versions.

- Apart from the `Move-Mailbox` command, a number of other shell commands work against legacy Exchange servers. We will get to more detail on this topic in Chapter 4, but in general, you should not expect shell commands to work, if only because the majority of the commands focus on Exchange 2007 objects and data structures.

- Do not edit objects such as the Default Offline Address List or Email Address policies with ESM after you update them with Exchange 2007.

- Do not attempt to use the ESM functions to monitor servers or view queues on an Exchange 2007 server, as these functions will not work.

- You can look at the details of the routing group connector that links your Exchange 2003 servers with the Exchange 2007 servers, but you cannot modify it. ESM flags the problem with the dialog shown in Figure 3.11, which indicates that you need to use a server running Exchange version 8 (2007) to work with the object.

Figure 3.11
Unable to edit an object with ESM

The Exchange 2003 version of ESM understands the difference in object version numbers, so it is able to stop you editing Exchange 2007 objects. However, the Exchange 2000 version of ESM has no knowledge about object version numbers or Exchange 2007 unless you have updated your servers to run Exchange 2000 SP3 and the August 2004 hot-fix roll-up (described in Microsoft Knowledge Base article 870540). In addition to the servers, you obviously need to update any workstations that run the Exchange 2000 version of ESM.

While you can use EMC to manage objects on an Exchange 2003 server, if you want predictable results, it is best to follow the old advice of using management tools designed for a particular environment to manage that environment. In other words, use the mixture of AD Users and Computers and ESM to manage Exchange 2003 objects and use EMC and EMS to manage Exchange 2007 objects. The bottom line is that you should keep ESM to manage the Exchange 2003 and 2000 servers until they are decommissioned and to administer components that have been deprecated in Exchange 2007, such as public folders (see Chapter 4 for a discussion on how to manage public folders through the Exchange Management Shell).

3.1.3   Running EMC remotely or on a workstation

You can install the Exchange 2007 management tools on a server that does not support Exchange 2007 or onto a workstation to allow you to perform Exchange management remotely. To do this, you run the Exchange 2007 installation program and select the option to install only the Administration components. You can download the x32 version of the Administration components (EMC, EMS, Exchange Best Practice Analyzer, Exchange Troubleshooter, and the Exchange help files) and install them on the following platforms:

- Windows Server 2003 with SP1 or SP2 (x86 or x64 versions)
- Windows XP SP2 (x86 and x64)
- Vista[2]

In all cases, you must already have installed MMC 3.0, PowerShell 1.0, and at least version 2.0 of the .NET framework, and whatever hot fixes are required when you are installing the Exchange management tools. If you install on an XP workstation, you also have to install IIS common services (use the Add/Remove Windows components from the Add/Remove software option in Control Panel and make sure that you do not install other IIS components such as the SMTP server). If you want to manage some third-party components that link to Exchange, you may have to install some of their management code to integrate with EMC and that code may not be supported on a workstation.

Figure 3.12 shows a mixture of Outlook 2007, EMC, and EMS running on a Windows XP workstation. Everything progresses smoothly and the only issue that I ever see is a slight delay caused by the extended WAN connection between my PC (in Dublin) and the server (in Houston). After careful net-

---

2.   Microsoft will not support Vista as a platform for Exchange administration until they have had time to test Vista workstations. Expect formal support as part of an early service pack, or expect to pick up tips on how to install and configure the necessary 32-bit components to get EMC and EMS working on Vista as the result of testing and persistence within the Exchange community.

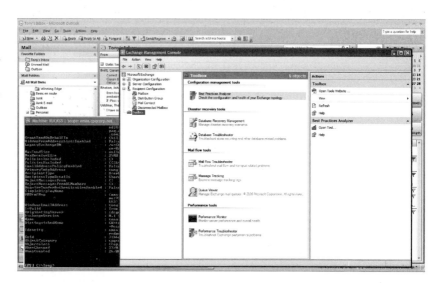

Figure 3.12
*Running EMC,
EMS, and
Outlook 2007 on
Windows XP*

work planning, HP consolidated all its Exchange 2007 servers into three datacenters in the US, so all client traffic to an Exchange server flows over extended connections..

You can only install the Exchange management tools on a workstation that is part of an Active Directory forest. The management tools depend on the schema extensions for Exchange 2007, so you must deploy them first. When you start up EMC or EMS on the workstation, it automatically connects to the Exchange organization if one is present in the forest. There is no way (that I have found) to tell EMC and EMS to connect to another Exchange organization, such as one that you might run in a test forest.

Another equally effective method is to use the inbuilt terminal services capability of Windows 2003 servers to allow Windows XP Professional and Vista workstations to log onto an Exchange server and be able to perform administrative activities remotely. This approach works very well and is a great way of being able to manage Exchange without the need to install anything on a workstation.

3.1.4   No more AD Users and Computers

We touched on the split in responsibilities between Active Directory management and Exchange management that occurs in ESM. Another important aspect of the introduction of EMC is that you do not need to use the AD Users and Computers console to work with the Active Directory objects that are important to Exchange. In the past, you had to create user and other objects through AD Users and Computers and ESM was only able to list objects and report on their properties. If you needed to update an object, you had to go back to AD Users and Computers, so administrators needed to move continually between the two consoles to get work done. Obviously, if you wanted to delegate access to another administrator and allow them to manage mailboxes, you had to grant access to both consoles. The split in operations between AD Users and Computers and ESM was confusing for administrators and difficult to manage in some production environments if you wanted to allocate different responsibilities to different administrators.

Exchange 2007 allows you to work with mailboxes, contacts, and groups through EMC without ever having to go near AD Users and Computers. In fact, the Exchange 2007 installation program does not install the add-ins that Exchange 2000 and 2003 use to allow AD Users and Computers to work with Exchange properties, so you can only use AD Users and Computers to work with properties that are not used by Exchange. For anything specific to Exchange 2007, such as enabling features like ActiveSync (Figure 3.13), you have to access mailbox properties through EMC, or indeed use the PowerShell commands that Exchange provides to work with the objects. You still need to use AD Users and Computers, but only for tasks that are fundamental to the Active Directory, such as creating a new organizational unit.

Figure 3.13
Working with
Exchange mailbox
properties

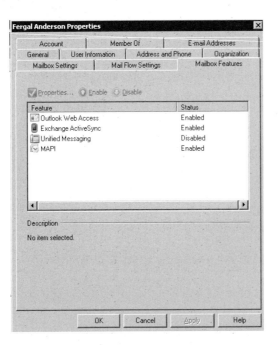

If you create users through AD Users and Computers, you can use the New Mailbox option in EMC to mail-enable them. As shown in Figure 3.14,

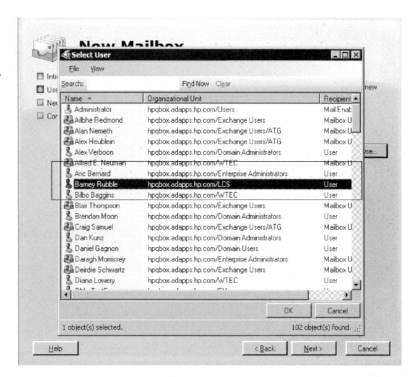

Figure 3.14
*Selecting a
Windows user to
be mail-enabled*

you can select "Existing User" rather than "New Mailbox" to be able to choose a user who is not mail-enabled and assign them a mailbox.

One small note about creating new mailboxes through EMC – the wizard that creates the mailbox only supports the default UPN suffix even though a forest can support multiple UPNs. In addition, the UI (Figure 3.15) uses a drop down list for the UPN suffix that obviously indicates that Microsoft planned to include this functionality. However, it is just a small UI bug that has crept into Exchange 2007. If you want to create new mailboxes that use a non-default UPN suffix, you will have to do this by using the shell New-Mailbox command that we will explore in Chapter 4. Alternatively, you could create a non-mail enabled user object through the AD Users and Computers console and set the UPN there before using EMC (or the shell) to mail-enable the new user. Microsoft addresses the issue in Exchange 2007 SP1 and you will be able to select a UPN from a drop-down list that an administrator can create.

3.1.5 Changing columns

Like any MMC console, you can use the Add/Remove option on the View menu to change the columns that you see when you access different types of

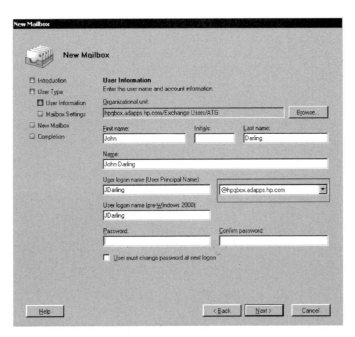

Figure 3.15
*Problem—only
one UPN
suffix allowed!*

objects. In Figure 3.16, we are positioned at the mailbox node under Recipient Configuration. The default columns are Display Name, Alias, Recipient Type Details, Primary SMTP Address, Server, and Organizational Unit. You can actually only see the first three of these columns in the picture because of limited screen real estate, but EMC would display them if enough space was available.

As you can see, you can remove some of the default columns and replace them with others that might be of more use to you. For example, some administrators replace the alias column with department because they manage mailboxes on the basis of department and so want to be able to sort what EMC displays by department order (you can sort on any available column by clicking on its heading).

Because EMC deals with different types of objects depending on where you are positioned, it is logical that it offers different columns. Figure 3.17 shows the columns available when EMC is positioned on the hub transport node under Organizational Configuration. You can see that the columns that are available here are very different to those available when EMC displays mailboxes.

3.1.6   Visual effects

EMC offers a visual effects option on the View menu that allows you to chose whether these effects are always on (default), never used, or automatic

Figure 3.16
Changing the columns used by EMC

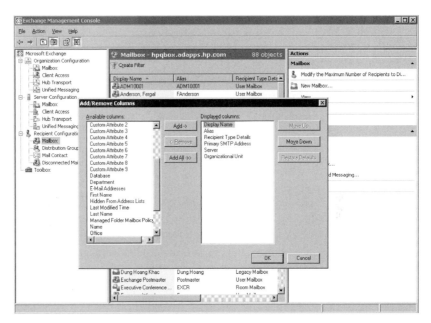

Figure 3.17
Columns available for send connectors

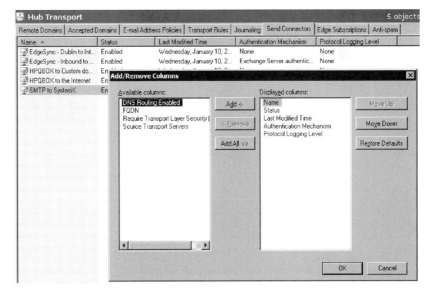

(meaning that EMC selects). Visual effects control whether the Exchange wizards use the "Exchange 2007 skin" or classic Windows look. Figure 3.18 illustrates the difference. On the left, you see the classic Windows look as a wizard creates a new mail-enabled contact. On the right, you see the Exchange 2007 skin.

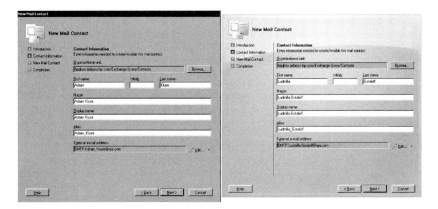

Figure 3.18
*Classic Windows
and Exchange
2007 visual effects*

You see the big difference in the two effects when you work over a low-speed connection such as when you manage an Exchange server using Windows Remote Desktop Connection across the public Internet via a VPN. While the Exchange developers believe that their skin is cool, it is also slow and gets in the way because it takes too long for the wizard to paint screens.

3.2   Why some options have disappeared from EMC

You can manage Exchange 2007 objects through EMC or EMS, but you have to understand that EMC is a subset of the capabilities offered by EMS. The result is that administrators have to be comfortable with EMS if they want to exert maximum control over Exchange 2007, because the more you look at Exchange 2007, the more you discover that there are many tasks that can be only performed through EMS. The introduction of EMS is therefore a huge influence on Exchange administration.

Even accepting that EMS is the most powerful tool at the disposal of Exchange administrators, it is still a tremendously interesting aspect of the transition from ESM to EMC that Microsoft has removed a number of options that used to feature in ESM. You cannot assume that everything that you used to be able to do through the GUI is still possible in Exchange 2007. For example, you cannot alter server properties to enable message tracking for a server. In Exchange 2007, you enable this feature through EMS (see the discussion on message tracking in Chapter 10). As you can see from Figure 3.19, there is no diagnostics tab available when you view server properties, so you cannot turn up diagnostics on a server to force Exchange to log more information into the application event log. Like every other time when you discover a missing feature that used to be in the GUI, you now have to resort to EMS. In this case, you would use the `Get-EventLogLevel –Server` command to return the current diagnostic level on a server and the `Set-EventLo-`

Figure 3.19

Server properties— no diagnostics!

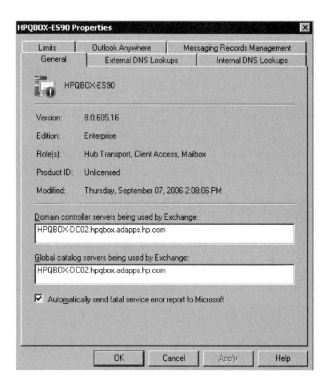

gLevel command to set a new diagnostic level (lowest, low, medium, high, or expert) for a selected component. For example:

```
Set-EventLogLevel –id 'MSExchangeTransport\Categorizer'
–Level High
```

Of course, you may not know what components you can tweak to increase the diagnostic level, but you can check this with the Get-EventLogLevel command, passing the desired server name as a parameter:

```
Get-EventLogLevel –Server ExchMbxSvr1
```

Other examples of options that are available in the ESM GUI in Exchange 2003 that are not supported by EMC in Exchange 2007 include managing the properties of Exchange's POP3 or IMAP4 servers as well as almost anything to do with routing management such as organizing servers into routing groups (which have disappeared from Exchange 2007 anyway). Another example is the inability to view or set permissions on Exchange objects through the GUI. In Exchange 2000 and 2003, you can set a registry value to force ESM to expose a "Permissions" property page when you view objects, but the Exchange developers didn't have time to complete this work for Exchange 2007. Instead, you have to use the `Add-AdPermission`, `Get-AdPermission`, and `Remove-AdPermission` commands to work with permissions.

In addition to permissions, there are a number of other management tasks that you can only perform through PowerShell, such as managing Cluster Continuous Replication or managing public folders. In fact, if you want to manage public folders through a GUI, you have to use the Exchange 2003 ESM or tools such as PFDavAdmin running on an Exchange 2003 server. That is, until Microsoft updates Exchange 2007 to incorporate some GUI to manage public folders through EMC, an update that is expected in a future service pack.

The developers did not make the changes lightly. They wanted to create a streamlined, powerful, and uncluttered console that included all of the operations that Exchange administrators perform most often. This was not always the case. For example, administrators can perform Outlook Web Access management in Exchange 2003 with the OWAAdmin tool, a separate utility that you have to download and install before you can use it. There are many other examples where administrators had to change Exchange's behavior by making changes to the registry or to Exchange's configuration data in the Active Directory. Often, Microsoft had documented these settings poorly or had not documented them at all, which made Exchange 2003 more difficult to support, especially if administrators made mistakes when they edited configuration data. Finally, there are parts of ESM that are difficult to extend to add new functionality because business logic is buried alongside the user interface.

As they designed EMC and decided what options to present through the GUI, the developers put features into four buckets:

1.   Options that would remain and EMC might be able to enhance. For example, you can now control what features Outlook Web Access presents to users. In addition, EMC displays some information that is not covered. For example, if you view mailbox details, EMC displays the last login time for the user, the total items in the mailbox, and the consumed quota (Figure 3.20). This is a nice feature, but it can slow you down if the mailbox data is not cached as EMC is then forced to retrieve the data from the Store.

2.   An option that most administrators never needed to use. For example, Microsoft discovered that the Recovery Storage Group was not used by many administrators, so it is now available as

part of the Toolbox. However, you never see the Recovery Storage Group as all of the interaction with it is via a wizard. Another example is configuration of the IMAP and POP protocols. Few enterprise installations use IMAP to access Exchange and fewer use POP, so it makes sense to move these options into EMS. These options helped ESM to become over complicated in parts, so moving them out helps to create the streamlined UI that we see today.

3. An option that was no longer required by Exchange 2007. The best example is the elimination of the Recipient Update Service. Although they will be around for some time to come, you might also consider the removal of public folder management to be in this category.

4. An option that has been replaced by a better solution in Exchange 2007. The inclusion of recipient management in EMC is a good example because it removes the split of Exchange 2003 management operations that exists between AD Users and Computers and ESM and it allows Exchange to use a common code base to work with recipients in EMC and EMS. System policies are no longer required because you can use shell commands to perform bulk management of servers, mailboxes, contacts, and groups.

If they just removed features from the console, the developers would have created an easier console to use but a less powerful management environment. The advent of EMS is a mitigating factor because it offers the developers a way to include all the seldom used features in Exchange and a way to replace making changes to Exchange's configuration with tools like ADSIEdit. Do not read these comments as being critical of the developers who built ESM in Exchange 2000 and 2003 as they did their best with the technology available at that time. Exchange leverages the MMC framework as much as it can through components like the snap-ins for AD Users and Computers to add the Exchange property pages, but there is a limit to what you can do with a graphical user interface. The review done for Exchange 2007 identified opportunities to improve matters using new technology, new approaches, and feedback gleaned from the experience of many thousands of customers who have managed Exchange since 2000.

The Exchange developers believe that EMC is a much better working environment for administrators and that the combination of EMC and EMS delivers the power and flexibility to manage even the largest and most complex Exchange organization. Microsoft also believes that they will be far better able to extend Exchange in the future in a way that they never have to resort to the kind of add-on utilities and registry hacks that we've experienced in the past. If they are right, then we'll all be happy.

Figure 3.20
*Viewing
mailbox
details*

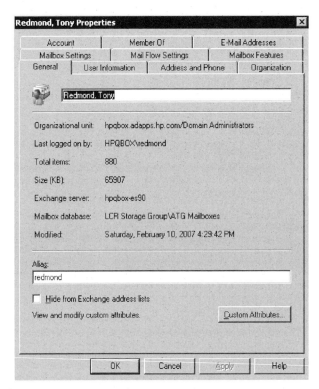

3.2.1 Coping with change

Like every other human, administrators accumulate habits over time and we all have our own methods to manage Exchange that we have honed over time. The changes that the developers have made to the console and the fact that some options are missing force you to go and learn where the equivalent functionality exists in Exchange 2007.

Microsoft provides a huge array of commands to handle all the work to deploy and manage Exchange. There is huge power and flexibility now available for those who want to roll their sleeves up and write scripts to build management the way that they see best fit, but others, especially part-time administrators, will feel that it would have been nice had Microsoft provided a more comprehensive and feature-rich GUI for EMC. Such an attitude rather misses the essential point of what has occurred for Exchange management. The transition from GUI options to EMS commands is a fundamental cultural transformation. Griping about the new GUI and the missing options that used to be available in Exchange 2003 ESM is only a waste of time. The real value of EMS is not in one-off tasks: The value of EMS comes about through the ability to automate common tasks, especially when you need to process more than one object at a time. Once you discover how to perform a task through EMS, you can capture the necessary commands in a script and reuse that script time after time, something that becomes a lot more interesting than the alternative of clicking your way through the GUI multiple times.

For example, while ESM can list information about mailboxes in a selected mailbox store, it cannot give you a complete list of all mailboxes across the organization, so you need to select every mailbox store to retrieve this data and then combine the data that you extract from each mailbox store to form the complete picture. If you have 20 mailbox servers that host 3 mailbox stores each within your organization, you have to repeat the select, open, export operations 60 times before you can even begin to combine the data. By comparison, you can combine the `Get-ExchangeServer` and `Get-MailboxStatistics` commands to extract and report data from all servers in one operation. It might take the script some time to complete the processing necessary to fetch data from all your servers, but it is a lot easier when the computer does the work.

Another example of how the `Get-MailboxStatistics` command helps to locate specific data quickly is how to discover how many disconnected mailboxes exist within a mailbox database. You would not expect to have a GUI option for this operation because it is not something that administrators need to perform often, but you can do it with a single command line:

```
Get-MailboxStatistics —Database 'VIP Mailboxes' | Where-
Object {$_.DisconnectDate —ne $Null}
```

Do not worry too much about the syntax of EMS commands for now, as we will get to explore the finer points of working with the shell in Chapter 4. The point is that you can execute commands like this to do things that were not possible in previous versions of Exchange without writing a lot of code. Here is another example to illustrate the point. With Exchange 2003, unless you have just one server with just one mailbox database, it is very hard to get a quick snapshot of the distribution of mailboxes across the different mailbox stores in an organization. To complete the task, you have to go to every server, open up each mailbox store, record the data, and then collate it. With Exchange 2007, you can use the `Get-Mailbox` command to do the job like this:

```
Get-Mailbox | Group-Object database | Sort Count -descending
| Format-List Count, Name
```

Again, this is a command that will take some time to execute in a large organization, but it is not something that you will do every day.

All of this goes to prove that a fundamental change in system management philosophy occurs in Exchange 2007. The changeover from expecting to perform management through a GUI that is limited by the imagination of the developers to working through a powerful shell poses a cultural and learning challenge for administrators. There is no doubt that you can do many things with just a few lines of PowerShell, but Microsoft's strong and frequent assertions that administrators will find that the change from GUI to PowerShell makes Exchange easier to manage understates the dimension of the problem that faces administrators as they move to Exchange 2007. I suspect that a little bit of cognitive dissonance may have crept in here because the Microsoft developers have worked with PowerShell for so long. The changeover in thinking from GUI to shell is a challenge for us all; some will struggle to get to grips with PowerShell and it will take everyone some time to discover how to get things done effectively and efficiently through the shell.

3.3   Changes in the Exchange delegation model

Exchange 2007 includes many changes to the delegation model that enables administrators to work with servers and other Exchange data. The major changes are:

- Creation of a wider and more useful set of out-of-the-box roles (Table 3.1) for common administrative tasks such as taking backups and working with recipients. The logic here is that many large organizations delegate tasks like these to help desk personnel, who do not need complete administrative control over a server to do these jobs. The permissions therefore reflect role-specific tasks that you can assign to individuals through the Permission Delegation Wizard (Figure 3.21).

- Implementation of a clearer separation between Exchange and Windows properties in recipient management: While Exchange depends on a large set of properties for mail-enabled Active Directory objects, the separation between the set of attributes that Exchange administrators need to work with and those required by Windows was not clear in previous versions. Exchange 2007 is more definitive in this respect and you cannot access a Windows property unless you are a Windows administrator. Apart from anything else, the separation of Exchange and Windows properties for mail-enabled objects means that there is less chance of inadvertent errors.

Figure 3.21
Adding a new delegate administrator

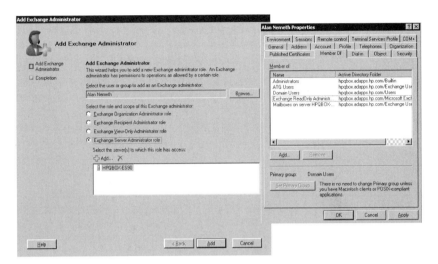

- Exchange 2007 creates an Exchange Servers universal group to hold all Exchange servers and to replace the previous Exchange Domain servers and Exchange Enterprise servers groups. This change reflects experience of Exchange in production. There must have been a good reason to have several groups previously, but that reason is lost in the mists of time.

- Implementation of simpler recipient provisioning: Creating new mail-enabled objects in Exchange 2003 is a complex multi-step process that requires an administrator to create the object followed by processing by the Recipient Update Service (RUS), which takes care of creating email addresses according to policy. Exchange 2007 uses simplified email address policies to define the format of email addresses to apply immediately after an administrator creates a new mail-enabled object. If you modify a template, Exchange applies the change to all recipients covered by the policy. In effect, the RUS is neutered—and not before time! See page 130 for more information about how Exchange 2007 now performs the functions previously taken care of by the RUS.

The changes in the delegation model will be most useful in enterprise deployments where there are multiple administrators and multiple roles. In smaller deployments, where one or two people administer Windows and Exchange and do everything, you can continue as before in the "all-powerful" Exchange Full Administrator role.

Exchange automatically assigns the Exchange Organization Administrator role to the account that installs the first Exchange server in an organiza-

Table 3.1   *Exchange administrative roles*

Role	Scope	Description
Exchange Organization Administrator	Organization	This is the highest level of permissions within an Exchange organization and is designed to manage data with a global scope, so it has full control over the Exchange configuration container in Active Directory. This role is able to modify any setting for Exchange at global or local level, for example, create new managed folders, set policies, establish a new connector, or set a new global restriction for message size.
Exchange Server Administrator	Server	Designed to perform administrative tasks tied to a specific server. Is able to modify any setting on that server.
Exchange Recipient Administrator	Organization	Is able to perform administrative operations on mail-enabled objects (for example, set a new mailbox quota) or execute recipient management operations for the complete organization. This role is facilitated through access to the Exchange Personal Information and Exchange Information property sets (see later in this chapter).
Exchange View-Only Administrator	Organization	Is able to view information about the complete organization. One "viewlike" option that these administrators cannot take is Message Tracking, as this requires authorized access to the Exchange Transport Log Search service on the server where the search is being performed.

tion. Subsequently, you can use this account to delegate administrative roles to other accounts. Behind the scenes, the /PrepareAD phase of the Exchange installation program creates Windows universal security groups to support the roles in the Microsoft Exchange Security Groups OU in the domain where /PrepareAD runs. The groups shown in Figure 3.22 are:

- Exchange Organization Administrators: Accounts that hold the Exchange Organization Administrator role are members of this group.

- Exchange Recipient Administrators: The delegation wizard adds accounts that hold the Exchange Recipient Administrator role to this group.

- Exchange View-Only Administrators: The delegation wizard adds accounts that you grant the Exchange View-Only Administrator role to this group. In addition, the wizard adds accounts that hold the Exchange Server Administrator role for a specific server to the group to allow a server administrator to be able to view the complete organization.

- ExchangeLegacyInterop: Used to secure operations between Exchange 2007 and legacy (Exchange 2003 and 2000) servers.

- Exchange Servers: This group contains all Exchange 2007 servers in the organization.

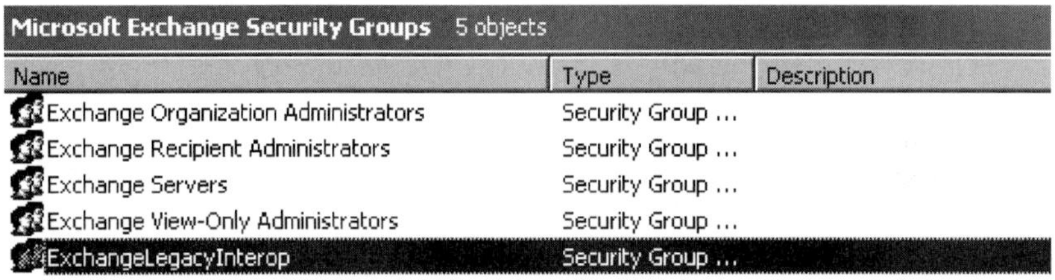

Figure 3.22
Exchange Security
Groups

Microsoft Exchange Security Groups	5 objects	
Name	Type	Description
Exchange Organization Administrators	Security Group ...	
Exchange Recipient Administrators	Security Group ...	
Exchange Servers	Security Group ...	
Exchange View-Only Administrators	Security Group ...	
ExchangeLegacyInterop	Security Group ...	

The addition of the ability to delegate administrative permission for a specific server to an individual solves a major issue that often occurred in Exchange 2000/2003 deployments where a single Exchange server was deployed in branch offices to support a small community. In these cases, it was common practice to create a separate administrative group to host the server and then allocate administrative control over the administrative group to a user in the branch office. This approach was logical because the administrative group represents the boundary for server administration in Exchange 2000/2003. However, even though it was logical to create small administrative groups, the result was a proliferation of administrative groups and complicated organizations. Exchange 2007 does not use administrative groups, so something had to change, which is why servers are now the basic administrative entity for Exchange 2007.

Following on the ability in Exchange 2007 to restrict administration rights to a single server, the Exchange developers added an interesting option to define who can install an Exchange 2007 server. This functionality is extremely useful when you need to delegate the ability to install a server to someone else in the organization or you simply want to prepopulate the entire organization with servers that you will eventually get around to installing.[3] To perform the delegation, you run the ExSetup program and specify the FQDN of the server that you want to install and the account name (which has to be a member of the Local Administrators group for the target server) that you want to be able to install the server. For example:

---

3.   There is an excellent entry in the Exchange team's blog that describes scripts to prepopulate an Exchange organization using the provisioned server feature.

```
ExSetup /NewProvisionedServer:ExchMbxSrv2.xyz.com /
ServerAdmin xyz\Redmond
```

The ExSetup program then creates the necessary entries in the Exchange configuration in the Active Directory and assigns the appropriate permissions to allow the nominated account to run the installation on the server. The delegated account is also granted the Exchange Server Administrator role for the target server and the Exchange View-Only Administrators role for the organization. To reverse the process, you can run the ExSetup program with the /RemoveProvisionedServer switch:

```
ExSetup /RemoveProvisionedServer:ExchMbxSvr2.xyz.com
```

You can also delegate administrative access to the organization, recipients, and specific servers through the Exchange Management Shell. See Chapter 4 for details.

In addition to the groups created in the Microsoft Exchange Security Groups container, you will find another group in the Microsoft Exchange System Objects container called Exchange Install Domain Servers. When you install an Exchange 2007 server, the installation procedure adds the server's computer account to the Exchange Servers universal security group. The Exchange Servers group is hosted in the root domain of the forest, but if you install a server into another domain, the Exchange services may fail to start because the LocalSystem account is not authorized to run these services. The normal root cause is that the Active Directory has not been able to replicate the updated membership of the Exchange Servers group to the local domain. As you can see from Figure 3.23, the Exchange Install Domain Servers group is not designed for general viewing. Its purpose is to ensure that Exchange can start its services immediately and avoid the dependency on Active Directory replication. Logically, in a multi-domain forest, you can expect to find an Exchange Install Domain Servers group in each domain.

3.4   **Customized Recipient Management**

As discussed earlier, a split permissions model exists in Exchange 2000/2003 where administrators perform some operations with ESM and some through the AD Users and Computers console. Recipient management is therefore sometimes a challenge in Exchange 2000/2003 if you were not a Windows administrator who had the necessary access to the Active Directory to be able to update the Exchange-specific properties on mail-enabled objects. This wasn't a problem for small to medium deployments because it is usual to have the same administrators taking care of Windows and Exchange, but

Figure 3.23

*The Exchange
Install Domain
Servers group*

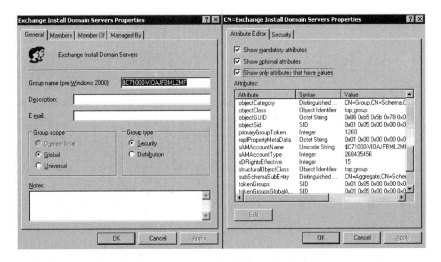

larger deployments tend to separate out responsibilities to different teams and want to do things such as allocate the power to update user properties to help desk personnel. Microsoft supports different administrative roles for Exchange 2000/2003, so you can assign users to hold the roles of Exchange Server Administrator, Exchange View-Only Administrator, and Exchange Organization Administrator. These roles are implemented as canned sets of Windows permissions that Exchange gathers together so that you can assign the roles to users to enable them to perform different types of management activities. However, the roles defined in Exchange 2000/2003 are focused on server rather than recipient management, so while you could be allocated a role to perform Exchange server management, you had to receive another set of Windows permissions to be able to create users, contacts, and groups. Recipient Management is better organized in Exchange 2007. First, you can assign the Exchange Recipient Admin role to users who need to perform this role. Second, you can create a customized console that brings together all of the functionality required to work with Exchange mailboxes, groups, and contacts. Follow these steps to create the console:

1. Open MMC.

2. Add the Exchange Server 2007 snap-in to the console.

3. Select the Recipient Configuration node and right click. Select "New Window from here" to force MMC to open a new window and display just the Recipient Configuration node.

4. Select File. Options to give the new console a suitable name and to lock it down to User Mode, single window, with limited access.

5.   Save the console as an .MSC file. You can distribute the .MSC file to any user who needs to act as a Recipient Administrator.

You can see the effect of the customized console in Figure 3.24.

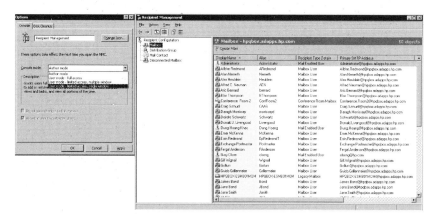

Figure 3.24
Creating a customized Recipient Management console

3.4.1 Adieu RUS

Exchange 2000 was the first version to use the Recipient Update Service (RUS) to discover and provision mail-enabled objects with email addresses according to recipient policies and to ensure that the new objects joined whatever address lists they should belong to. Mail-enabled objects created through AD Users and Computers are in a state of "email limbo" until the RUS stamps them with an email address and other key properties such as HomeMDB (pointer to the database that holds a user's mailbox) and LegacyExchangeDN (legacy Exchange distinguished name) that are required to make them fully functional for Exchange.[4] In Exchange 2000/2003, the RUS is implemented as an API that calculates the value for the properties used by Exchange and a process that runs as part of the System Attendant that scans for new and updated objects and then updates their properties to comply with recipient policies. The two-step process was necessary in Exchange 2000/2003 because of the split between Active Directory and Exchange management of objects. Exchange 2007 uses a different approach that removes the need for the RUS process because it takes full responsibility for the management of any mail-enabled object through EMC or EMS.

When you create a new mail-enabled object on an Exchange 2007 server through EMC or EMS, the new object is immediately fully provisioned and

---

4.   See Microsoft Knowledge Base article 253770 for more details about the processing that the RUS performs for new mail-enabled objects created on Exchange 2000 or 2003 servers.

able to function. There is no need for the RUS process to run asynchronously to validate that the email addresses on the new objects comply with email address policies, that the new objects possess a full array of Exchange properties, or that they have joined address lists such as the GAL. Behind the scenes, the commands that create new mail-enabled objects call the RUS API to calculate values for the properties before the Exchange stamps them onto the objects. The advantage of incorporating a synchronous process to update new mail-enabled objects is obvious: Once an administrator creates a new mail-enabled object, the user can access their mailbox immediately. This is much simpler for all concerned. With the benefit of hindsight, even the most ardent defender of the RUS would probably admit that it is the way that things should have been done from the start.

Recipient policies provided a major input to the RUS in Exchange 2000/2003. In their place, Exchange 2007 uses Email Address Policies to define what form of email proxy addresses you want to create within an organization. The wizard provided in Exchange 2007 to work with Email Address Policies create a much more structured way of defining and setting email proxy addresses and you do not run the risk of wreaking havoc within an organization after changing a recipient policy. Changing a recipient policy to alter an email proxy address forces the RUS into action to apply the new policy, but unfortunately the RUS often seemed to ignore some email addresses. If an administrator wanted to be sure that all email addresses compiled with policy, they would have to apply it explicitly through ESM. In Exchange 2007, if you update an Email Address Policy, you have a choice of updating objects immediately or at a future time that you schedule, so you know when updates will occur. In addition, you can have confidence that the underlying commands will enforce the new Email Address Policy every time an administrator adds or updates a mail-enabled object through EMC or EMS. See page 173 for more information on Email Address Policies.

The change to remove the RUS from the mailbox creation and update process is not before time. When it worked everything flowed smoothly and new mail-enabled objects could be used reasonably soon after they were created, but when the RUS stopped functioning or merely hiccupped, it was enormously difficult to determine what was going on. The root of the problem was that Microsoft never documented the RUS in any depth, so it became one of the black boxes that ran on an Exchange server. The lack of documentation or feedback from the RUS meant that you could never be quite sure when the RUS would wake up to process new or amended mail-enabled objects, which lead to administrator confusion and frustration. Depending on your environment, the RUS might take anything from a few minutes to a few hours before it had stamped a new object with the email addresses that the object needed to become email-enabled.

It is possible that you run another process to create new mail-enabled objects, perhaps as part of a system that provisions new users across multiple systems. For example, a new employee joins and is entered into a HR system that automatically spawns jobs to create a new user in the Active Directory. In the past, the RUS would find the new mailbox and stamp the object with the necessary properties to mail-enable the object. Because the RUS no longer runs in Exchange 2007, you will have to periodically run the `Update-EmailAddressPolicy` and `Update-AddressList` commands through EMS to detect new recipient objects that have to be updated. These commands apply the appropriate email proxy address and address list policies to any object that they determine should be processed. For example, the command:

```
Update-EmailAddressPolicy 'Default Policy' —Domain XYZ-DC1
```

Looks for objects and applies the default email address policy to create new email proxy addresses when required. Note that the domain controller to provide information about recipients and where to apply the updates is specified with the –Domain parameter. This command can take some time to execute for any moderately large organization. Perhaps the best advice is to test how best to integrate these commands into whatever procedures you operate today in order to ensure that provisioning continues to work after you introduce Exchange 2007.

One final point—you can see Exchange 2007 servers through ESM so you may be tempted to select an Exchange 2007 server to host the RUS. Do not do this as the Exchange 2007 server has no knowledge of how the Exchange 2003 RUS functions and you will only create a brain-dead non-functioning RUS.

3.4.2 Recipient types

Exchange 2003 really offers just one mailbox type: a mailbox used by a human being to store messages. However, in the real world, it is common to find different types of mailboxes in use, and Exchange 2007 recognizes this by supporting several implicit mailbox types that you can use as a filter when viewing mailboxes through ESM:

- User mailbox: A standard mailbox hosted on an Exchange 2007 server.

- Room mailbox: A mailbox associated with a disabled Active Directory account used to schedule a conference room.

- Equipment mailbox: A mailbox associated with a disabled Active Directory account used to schedule an item of equipment.

- Linked mailbox: A mailbox accessed through an account in a different Active Directory forest that is accessible through a two-way trust.

- Shared mailbox: These are mailboxes that multiple user accounts have permission to log on to. The actual account that is associated with the shared mailbox is usually disabled because no one uses this account to log on to the mailbox.

- Legacy mailbox: These are mailboxes that are homed on Exchange 2000 or 2003 servers. Even though they are fully functional user mailboxes, they are called "legacy" because the Exchange 2007 ESM cannot apply all features to these mailboxes. Once migrated to an Exchange 2007 server, these mailboxes become standard mailboxes. If you ever find that you have a mailbox shown as "Legacy" that you have definitely migrated to Exchange 2007, you can upgrade it with the shell command:

```
Set-Mailbox —id Old-Mailbox —ApplyMandatoryProperties
```

This command only works with mailboxes that are hosted on an Exchange 2007 server.

A similar model of implicit typing applies when it comes to distribution groups, breaking them out into:

- Mail-enabled universal security group.
- Mail-enabled universal distribution group.
- Mail-enabled nonuniversal group (global or domain local groups): These groups are not recommended for use by Exchange because the expansion of group membership is unpredictable unless you can guarantee that you always connect to a DC that holds a complete copy of the group membership.
- Dynamic (or query-based) distribution group.

Contacts are much simpler because they are objects with an associated email address.

3.5   Moving users

You're going to have to move mailboxes if you migrate from a legacy version of Exchange to Exchange 2007. Once you get to Exchange 2007, normal messaging operations will dictate the need to move mailboxes for business reasons, to balance the load on servers, or to redistribute mailboxes across databases.

3.5.1 Moving mailboxes

Because you can't upgrade an Exchange 2003 mailbox server to be an Exchange 2007 mailbox server, the only way that you can transfer existing mailboxes to Exchange 2007 is to use the Move Mailbox feature. You can move mailboxes from Exchange 2000 (SP3 or later), Exchange 2003 (SP1 or later), or Exchange 2007 servers to Exchange 2003 (SP3 or later), Exchange 2003 (SP1 or later), or Exchange 2007 servers. You can also move mailboxes between different Exchange organizations, providing that the necessary trusts exist between the two forests.

In most cases, you'll be moving to Exchange 2007, but it's nice to know that you can use the feature to move mailboxes between older servers if necessary. To move a mailbox to an Exchange 2007 server, your account needs to hold administrative permissions for the target server and you'll obviously need administrative permission to access the source mailbox. Apart from migrations, common reasons to move mailboxes include rebalancing across databases on a server or across servers within the organization, or to move mailboxes off a server that is being decommissioned for some reason such as a datacenter consolidation.

You can use two approaches to move mailboxes in Exchange 2007: the traditional wizard-based method available through EMC or by using the `Move-Mailbox` shell command (see Chapter 4 for details). Because they are based on the same code base, both methods get the job done, but you can specify additional parameters to exert more control using the `Move-Mailbox` command. In most cases, you won't need the additional degree of control to move a few mailboxes around on an ad-hoc basis, but the extra parameters become more important as you dive into the possibilities that scripting offers to automate moves for hundreds of mailboxes during the migration to Exchange 2007.

Microsoft made many improvements such as support for multiple threads to the Move Mailbox wizard in Exchange 2003. Exchange 2007 adds prevalidation checking to ensure that any obvious errors that could stop a successful mailbox move are detected before the move commences. The checks include:

- Verify that the user account exists and that they have a valid mailbox.

- Check that the user performing the move has sufficient permissions to perform the move. This check is done by connecting to both source and target server.

- Check the mailbox quota limit on the target database to ensure that the mailbox does not exceed the quota.

- Stop attempts to move system mailboxes.

- Check that the target database is mounted and available to accept the incoming mailbox.

The Move Mailbox wizard always performs these checks before it attempts to move a mailbox. If you use the `Move-Mailbox` shell command, you can specify the –ValidateOnly parameter to force Exchange to make the checks.

Figure 3.25
*The Exchange
2007 Move
Mailbox Wizard*

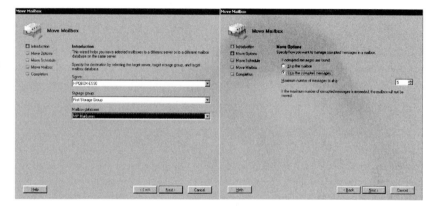

Figure 3.25 illustrates the first two screens of the Exchange 2007 Move Mailbox wizard.

- The first choice to make is what are the target server and database. As long as a network link is available, you can move a mailbox. My own mailbox was transferred from a server in Dublin, Ireland, to a server in Houston, Texas, during HP's migration to Exchange 2007 but clearly, the closer the two servers are in terms of network connectivity and bandwidth, the faster that the move can progress.

- The wizard can continue processing and move the mailbox even if it encounters some corrupt messages in the mailbox. You can decide how many corrupt messages the wizard should skip. In Exchange 2003, the wizard had a hard-coded limit of 100, but Exchange 2007 allows you to specify much higher figures (the highest that I have gone is 1,000). Clearly, if you meet a mailbox that has many corrupt messages, it is a sign that the underlying mailbox store is probably suffering from some sort of corruption that deserves your attention.

Note that if the wizard skips any corrupt messages, it generates a report to show you what those messages are.

■ You can schedule moves to occur at a particular time. The System Attendant tracks and performs scheduled jobs at the requesting time, allowing you to ensure that mailboxes move when users are asleep!

■ You can move multiple mailboxes concurrently by selecting multiple mailboxes and then taking the "Move Mailbox" option. Of course, you can achieve further acceleration by using multiple workstations to move mailboxes. The Move Mailbox wizard uses up to four threads per session to move mailbox content (you can increase the number of threads if you move mailboxes with the `Move-Mailbox` command). Figure 3.26 shows how to set a schedule through the wizard and how EMC reports details of a multi-mailbox move as it progresses.

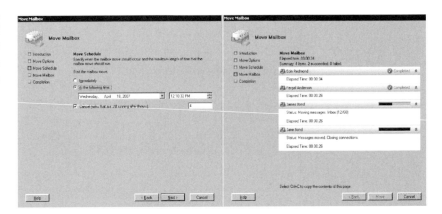

Figure 3.26
Setting a schedule and multiple mailbox move

Depending on system load, moving large mailboxes (> 100 MB) will take between five and ten minutes to perform if the two servers share the same LAN, up to approximately 500 MB an hour. Moving a mailbox is a binary operation—it either works or not. If a failure occurs somewhere along the process, you have to start again. Note that you need Exchange administrator permission for the administrative group for both the source and target server to be able to perform the move. Always make sure that you ask the mailbox owner to log off before commencing the move, and ensure that enough disk space is available to accommodate all the transaction logs that the move operation generates. Each transferred message is a transaction for both the source and target databases, so the disk that holds the transaction logs will handle a substantial I/O load during the transfer. One small thing that occasionally trips people up is the fact that when you move mailboxes, the contents of the deleted items cache remain behind in the source database. Therefore, a user is not able to retrieve a deleted item after their mailbox is moved.

If users run Outlook 2003/2007 and have a cached Exchange mode mailbox, it is possible for them to continue working in a disconnected state while Exchange moves their mailbox. Exchange will not deliver new messages to the mailbox and queues them on the source server while the move proceeds. When it has moved the mailbox, Exchange releases the messages and delivers them from the queue. Exchange notifies Outlook when the moved mailbox is ready to use, and Outlook then switches across (transparently) to access the new server and then transmits any messages that the user sent during the mailbox move. While it is possible to move Outlook 2003/2007 users who do not work in cached Exchange mode while they are online, it is definitely something that tempts fate and invites problems. Therefore, it is always a good idea to have users disconnect before the move starts and have them set their connection status to "Work Offline." In addition, if a user attempts to log on during a mailbox move (as opposed to continue working during the move), the Store detects the connection attempt and logs event 9660, identifying the user name and distinguished name. The Store also flags an error to tell the user that a mailbox move is under way. Finally, you should ask users to wait for 20 minutes after their mailbox is moved to a new server before attempting to connect. This step allows any cached credentials to expire and forces Outlook to refresh its information about the user's mailbox and so discover that the mailbox is now on a new server.[5]

After Exchange has moved the mailboxes, it is best to leave a period of at least 15 minutes before you attempt to access them on the new server. This is because the Store process caches information about mailboxes so that it does not have to go back to Active Directory each time a user requests to access their mailbox. If a mailbox is not accessed in 15 minutes, the Store removes the data from its cache. When you move mailboxes, Active Directory replication may create a slight time-lag before it reflects the true location of the mailbox across all domain controllers, which may then lead to a situation where a user attempts to log on to their mailbox but cannot because Active Directory is still pointing to the old location. The Store caches the incorrect login data and will refer to this data if the user makes another attempt to access their mailbox. The net result is confusion and frustration, so it is best to wait for replication to occur before you attempt to access a moved mailbox.

After a mailbox move, Exchange redirects Outlook Web Access connections to the new server the next time that a user attempts to logon to their mailbox, but you have to update settings manually for IMAP4 and POP3 cli-

---

5. Some installations have reported that Outlook 2003/2007 clients that work with RPC over HTTP have difficulty connecting to Exchange 2007 after a mailbox move. It may be that Microsoft fixes this problem in a service pack, but if you encounter the issue, the easiest solution is to delete the user's profile and recreate it to point at the new server.

ents. In some cases, administrators report that newly moved mailboxes use larger quotas (in other words, the same number of messages occupy more space) when hosted by Exchange 2007 than on a legacy server. This is anecdotal evidence that is not reported consistently from implementation to implementation and is probably highly dependent on the type and format of items stored in a mailbox. In any case, it is a good idea to check mailbox quotas before and after the move to ensure that users can keep working.

3.5.2 Logging mailbox moves

In addition to the prevalidation checks, Microsoft has improved the logging of mailbox moves. All movements are logged in the application event log (Figure 3.27), including the deletion of any Active Directory objects such as source mailboxes involved in cross-organization moves. Exchange 2003 generates XML reports (Figure 3.28) for mailbox moves and the detail is improved in Exchange 2007 because the report now includes items such as the domain controllers and Global Catalog servers referenced in the move, the mailbox size, the number of mailboxes moved, time taken, and so on. By default, Exchange puts the move mailbox logs in the \Logging directory under the installation directory, but if you use the `Move-Mailbox` command, you can specify the –ReportFile parameter to select a different location.

Figure 3.27
A mailbox move
is logged

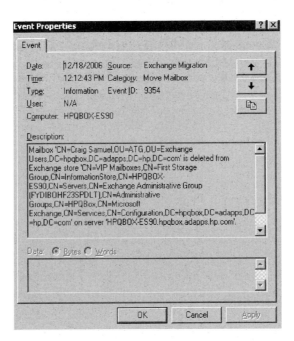

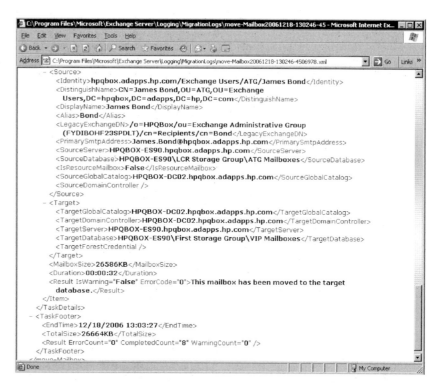

Figure 3.28
*Move Mailbox
XML report*

In addition to the XML report, Exchange 2007 generates a detailed text format log of all operations performed in the move that is helpful when troubleshooting failures. This log is stored in the same directory with a file name of Move-MailboxHHMMSS.log. An example extract of what you can expect to find in the troubleshooting log is shown below:

```
[12/18/2006 1:03:26 PM] [0] [Bond] Updating attributes.
[12/18/2006 1:03:26 PM] [0] [Bond] Messages moved. Closing connections.
[12/18/2006 1:03:26 PM] [0] [Bond] Trying to unlock mailbox:
    szServer: HPQBOX-ES90.hpqbox.adapps.hp.com
    pguidMdb: {903F6615-A656-4F08-84FD-26069DEFFBC3}
    pguidMailbox: {E33F05B7-59DC-4961-B9B1-A6E1EA4867C9}
[12/18/2006 1:03:26 PM] [0] [Bond] Mailbox was unlocked successfully.
[12/18/2006 1:03:26 PM] [0] [Bond] Deleting mailbox from mailbox database:
    szServer: HPQBOX-ES90.hpqbox.adapps.hp.com
    pguidMdb: {DC280469-1A69-426E-BB84-DF3406FE47FC}
    pguidMailbox: {E33F05B7-59DC-4961-B9B1-A6E1EA4867C9}
[12/18/2006 1:03:26 PM] [0] [Bond] Mailbox '{E33F05B7-59DC-4961-B9B1-
A6E1EA4867C9}' was deleted successfully.
```

[12/18/2006 1:03:26 PM] [0] [Bond] The operation has finished.

[12/18/2006 1:03:26 PM] [0] Searching objects "hpqbox.adapps.hp.com/Exchange Users/ATG/James Bond" of type "ADUser" under the root "$null" using "HPQBOX-DC02.hpqbox.adapps.hp.com".

[12/18/2006 1:03:27 PM] [0] Searching objects "HPQBOX-ES90.hpqbox.adapps.hp.com" of type "Server" under the root "$null" using "HPQBOX-DC02.hpqbox.adapps.hp.com".

[12/18/2006 1:03:27 PM] [0] [Bond] Before applying RUS, the proxy addresses are:

    smtp:JB@xyz.com

    SMTP:James.Bond@hpqbox.adapps.hp.com

[12/18/2006 1:03:27 PM] [0] Applying RUS policy to the given recipient "hpqbox.adapps.hp.com/Exchange Users/ATG/James Bond" with the home Domain Controller "HPQBOX-DC02.hpqbox.adapps.hp.com".

[12/18/2006 1:03:27 PM] [0] The RUS server to apply policies on the given recipient is "HPQBOX-ES90.hpqbox.adapps.hp.com".

[12/18/2006 1:03:27 PM] [0] [Bond] After applying RUS, the proxy addresses are:

    smtp:JB@xyz.com

    SMTP:James.Bond@hpqbox.adapps.hp.com

3.6   Using distribution groups

As shown in Table 3.2, Windows supports four types of groups. For email purposes, you need to mail-enable groups before users can send messages to the members of the group. Groups also hold security principals, so you can use them to control access to resources. However, we will focus on the use of groups for email purposes in this discussion.

Universal groups are available anywhere within a forest. In other words, you can use a universal group to control access to any resource in the forest. Windows publishes details of universal groups in the Global Catalog, and clients resolve membership of universal groups when they log-on by reference to a Global Catalog. This step ensures that a client receives a full set of credentials and is able to access resources through membership of any universal group they may hold.

Somewhat confusingly given the name, Windows does not publish details of global groups in the Global Catalog. Similar to the definition of global groups as used in Windows NT, global groups can be present in the ACL of any object in the forest, but they can only contain members from the domain that "owns" the group. Domain local groups are the most restricted as they only apply within the domain in which they are created. Again, Windows does not publish details of domain local groups in the Global Catalog. Domain local groups can contain universal or global groups along with individual users. There is no real value in attempting to use domain local or global groups with Exchange. Unless you operate inside a single-domain forest, universal groups are the only logical type of

Table 3.2   *Groups*

Group type	Exchange Group Type	Use
Universal group	MailEnabledUniversalSecurityGroup or MailEnabledUniversalDistributionGroup	The preferred group type for Exchange 2007
Global group	MailEnabledNonUniversalGroup	Not useful for Exchange unless in a single domain forest
Domain local group	MailEnabledNonUniversalGroup	Not useful for Exchange unless in a single domain forest
Query based group	MailEnabledDynamicDistributionGroup	Group whose membership depends on the execution of an OPATH query against the Active Directory

group to use for email-enabled recipients because you can guarantee that Exchange will always be able to expand the membership of the group accurately by reference to a Global Catalog. Exchange 2007 is the first version of Exchange to enforce this requirement.

Here is why the problem exists for Exchange 2000 and 2003. In these releases, you can use AD Users and Computers to create mail-enabled global groups or mail-enabled domain local groups. Everything works if you operate in a single domain, but if Exchange operates in multi-domain forests and mail-enabled objects exist in multiple domains, you can experience problems when Exchange attempts to expand the contents of groups to build the recipient list for message delivery. Everything will go well and Exchange will be able to expand the group to determine its full membership if the Global Catalog server that Exchange queries holds a complete copy of all the group members. However, if Exchange connects to a Global Catalog that has an incomplete copy (for example, a universal group that contains a link to a nested domain local group from a different domain), then it is impossible to resolve the group to its complete membership. Even worse, users will see different results from one Exchange server to another. Enforcing a common approach to groups is the reason why Microsoft changed Exchange 2007 to require you to use universal groups. It is also the reason why Microsoft requires you to operate the Active Directory in native mode. If you have non-universal groups in use, you can use the Set-Group command to convert these groups. For example:

```
Set-Group —id 'Exchange Gurus' —Universal:$True
```

This command converts the "Exchange Gurus" group to be a universal group if it is not already. If it is, you will get an error.

If you want, you can scan for mail-enabled groups that are not universal with this command:

```
Get-DistributionGroup —Filter {RecipientTypeDetails —eq
'MailNonUniversalGroup'}
```

If you add the command to set the group to universal, you can scan and convert all at one time:

```
Get-DistributionGroup —Filter {RecipientTypeDetails —eq
'MailNonUniversalGroup'} | Set-Group —Universal:$True
```

As you can see from Figure 3.29, Windows also defines groups by type. If a group is a "security" type, it means that the group holds a security principal and you can use it to control access to resources. A group that is a "distribution" type does not have a security principal, but you can use it with Exchange as a way to distribute messages, which is very close in style to the original definition of an Exchange distribution list. Figure 3.29 also shows that a security group can be mail-enabled (the group has a published email address that is obscured in the picture). A mail-enabled universal group that holds a security principal is the most powerful group. It is available anywhere in the forest, can be used to secure resources, and you can use the group as a traditional e-mail distribution list. Of course, you do not create groups using AD Users and Computers when you work with Exchange 2007. Instead, you can use either EMC or EMS to create and manage both security and distribution groups. All the groups that Exchange 2007 creates are universal.

Because they provide a convenient way to address large numbers of users in a single operation, groups or distribution lists have always been tremendously important to email systems. Exchange is no different in this respect. For example, Microsoft IT report that they have some 175,000 groups in use in their Exchange environment and HP has over 150,000 (90,000 of which have been created since I last wrote on this topic some four years ago). While these are two very large deployments of Exchange, they prove the point of the importance of groups and provide us with a good reason to look into groups in some detail.

3.6.1 Forming groups

Windows groups are composed of a set of backwards pointers to individual directory objects (other groups, users, and contacts) that form the group. The

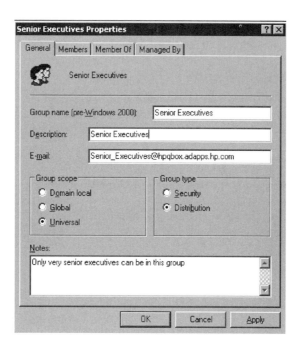

Figure 3.29

General properties of a Windows Group

left-hand screen in Figure 3.30 shows group membership as viewed through EMC. The right-hand screen shows the membership of the same group, this time viewed through the ADSIEDIT utility. Here we see that the Active Directory holds the membership of a group in a single multi-valued attribute called "Member" and that the attribute is formed by the distinguished name of each of the members. The AD uses the distinguished name as the pointer to the records for the individual members when it has to resolve or expand group membership. Because Windows builds a group through a set of pointers to Active Directory objects you have to be careful if you need to perform an authoritative restore of the Active Directory to recover from a database failure, as you may affect group membership if the restore removes some of the pointers. For this reason, you should take great care to check important group membership after completing any restore of the Active Directory.

The Active Directory uses attribute-level replication, but any change made to the membership of a group results in essentially the complete object being replicated because the membership is held in a single attribute. This is a true statement for Windows 2000, but the situation is a little different in Windows 2003, which includes a new mechanism called linked value replication (LVR). LVR addresses some of the problems associated with large distribution groups that span more than a few hundred members. People tend to leave and join groups on a regular basis, so the "churn" in membership generates an obvious issue in excessive network traffic to handle replication of the membership attribute. In addition, because the Active Directory is a

Figure 3.30
*Viewing group
membership*

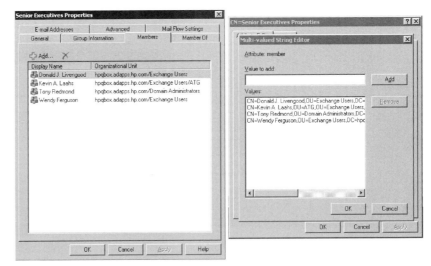

multi-master directory where any replica (on a domain controller) can originate an update, the danger exists that the Active Directory ignores updates when users make changes to group membership in multiple places at approximately the same time.

In this situation, the Active Directory must reconcile changes coming in from multiple places without the benefit of human intelligence, and it does not always make the right decision. In Windows 2000, the Active Directory is handicapped because it only updates one attribute—the membership—for each of the changes it must reconcile. Thus, the change originating from the New York domain controller looks the same as the change from London. Which change should win? The Active Directory uses its normal conflict-resolution techniques to decide the "winner" (the update that is finally made). Timestamps eventually help to resolve the conflict, and the Active Directory uses the last timed update to the group membership and applies that update to the group. Administrators may only know about a reconciliation snafu when a user complains that they are not able to access a public folder or that they do not receive email sent to a list. LVR helps to solve the conflict issue because the Active Directory is now able to resolve changes at the level of individual members rather than handling the complete group as one entity.

At this point, it is also worth noting that restoring the Active Directory in a multi-domain environment may lose some updates applied to any data that the Active Directory holds in a multi-value attribute. An authoritative restore will recover any links associated with the domain that you perform the restore for, so the problem only arises for links that tie objects together across multiple domains. Group membership is the obvious example, but Exchange uses multi-value attributes for data such as organizational structures (reporting relationships between manager and employee, for instance). When you restore data, you essentially roll back to the point in time when the backup occurred. Many changes may take place between that time and the current time and there is no guarantee that the Active Directory replication mechanism will be able to reconcile everything accurately because (unlike public folders) there is no concept of a backfill request to allow one replica of the directory to request a complete refresh from another replica. There is also no way that you can know whether the Active Directory is in an inconsistent state. For these reasons, it is a good idea to practice restores of the Active Directory and to have a plan to take frequent backups of the system state of a domain controller from every domain in the forest, as you will rely on this data during restores. You may also want to check with companies that build Active Directory utilities to see if they have a program to help with this problem. With all of this in mind, it makes sense from a pure Active Directory perspective to limit the amount of updates applied to groups whenever possible, especially for universal groups as the Active Directory replicates them to every Global Catalog in the forest. However, universal groups are very important to Exchange, as they are the only way to implement secure access to public folders and as email distribution lists within multi-domain implementations.

You can reduce the replication load by building the membership of universal groups from a set of global groups. This means that the effect of changes to group membership are restricted to the host domain of the users or contacts in the group, and the only replication to the Global Catalog occurs if a global group is added or removed from the universal group. Seeking to reduce replication in this way is a great example of where the needs of the base operating system do not match the need of applications. If you include nested global groups in a universal distribution group, only Exchange servers in the same domain will be fully able to resolve group membership. This leads to a situation where you can send email to the same group from accounts in different domains and have messages delivered to different sets of people! Even worse, neither users nor administrators will be aware of the problem because no problem exists in purely technical terms and Exchange signals no error messages. For this reason, it is best practice only to use universal groups with Exchange.

3.6.2 Group changes in Exchange 2007

Up to Exchange 2007, you worked with mail-enabled groups through the AD Users and Computers console, just like any other Active Directory object. With Exchange 2007, you should work with groups through EMC to ensure that the correct set of attributes is stamped on groups when you create or work with them. Part of the reason for the change is that the Exchange Management Console (EMC) now performs the work that the Recipient

Update Service (RUS) does in Exchange 2000 and 2003. Part is because Exchange exercises much closer control over Active Directory objects when they are managed completely through the EMC interface than when administrators go behind the scenes and update objects with AD Users and Computers, ADSIEDIT, or any other utility.

Figure 3.31
*Comparing the
properties of
two groups*

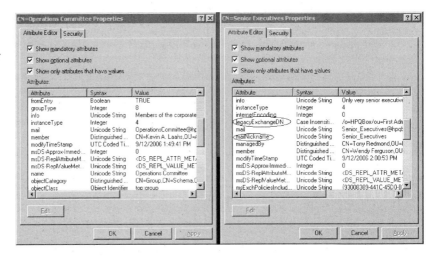

Even in an Exchange 2007 environment, AD Users and Computers allows you to continue creating distribution groups and you can even assign them a valid email address. However, any group that you create through AD Users and Computers is not functionally equivalent to a group created through EMC. On the surface, everything looks similar, but below—in the set of properties stamped on an object when you create or update a group using EMC—things are very different.

For example, compare the properties of the two groups as viewed through ADSIEDIT shown in Figure 3.31. The "Operations Committee" group (left) was created with AD Users and Computers. The "Senior Executives" group (right) was created with EMC. Two immediate and important differences are apparent. The Senior Executives group has values for the MailNickName and LegacyExchangeDN attributes. If we scroll down through the list of properties, you would find other differences, such as the presence of a value for MsExchPoliciesIncluded, MsExchRecipientDisplayType, MsExchRequireAuthToSendTo, and so on. These properties complete the process of making a standard Windows group into a fully-fledged Exchange object, and while it is entirely possible for you to set the necessary properties manually, there is a huge risk of error that then leads to further difficulties. If you send a message to an object that is not fully mail-enabled, you will receive an NDR that says something like this:

```
Diagnostic information for administrators:
Generating server: ExchMbxSvr1.xyz.com
operationscommittee@xyz.com
#550 5.1.1 RESOLVER.ADR.RecipNotFound; not found ##
```

The rule is therefore to use AD Users and Computers to work with objects that are unique to Windows and to use EMC to maintain those required by Exchange. See page 100 for more information about how to work with EMC.

3.6.3 Expanding distribution lists

Exchange expands the membership of any distribution group that a user includes in a message header by checking a Global Catalog to find the preferred email address of each object in the lists. As Figure 3.32 shows, you can assign the task of group expansion to a particular server. When a server is defined for group expansion, Exchange routes any message addressed to that group to the specified expansion server, which then expands the group into the individual addressees. If the expansion server is not available, Exchange queues the message until the server becomes available again.

Most groups do not have an expansion server specified, so Exchange can expand the group on the first hub transport server (or Exchange 2003 server) that the message is routed through en route to its destination. To expand a group, the transport engine decomposes it into the set of individual email addresses for each member in the group and then uses the email addresses to help determine the optimum routing path for the message to reach each recipient. All of this work occurs in memory.

Exchange does not update message headers sent to groups with the details of the individual group members for two good reasons:

1. Adding email addresses for the group members would increase the size of the message header. It is much more efficient to transport a single address than a complete set.

2. Group membership changes over time, so keeping the group address in the header ensures that Exchange always uses up-to-date membership if a user replies to a message.

If you use a personal distribution list to address a message, Outlook (or the client you use) must expand the contents of the distribution list and add addresses for all of the recipients to the message header before it can submit the message to Exchange. You can see the impact of list expansion on the size

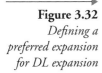
Figure 3.32
*Defining a
preferred expansion
for DL expansion*

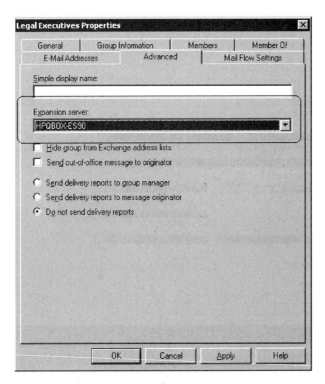

of a message by comparing similar messages sent to a group and a list, each containing 20 members. The message sent to the group is always far smaller.

In the past, the expansion of large distribution groups (that contain more than a few hundred members), or those that contain nested groups, could impose a considerable demand on system resources. Given the speed of current computers you shouldn't see any problem unless you use groups that expand to literally thousands of users. Even so, users can notice a delay when they send a message to a large list (if they are a member of the list), as Exchange can take up to a minute or so to deliver a copy of the message back to the originator.

3.6.4 How many objects can I have in a group?

The AD Users and Computers UI imposes a limit of approximately 5,000 objects for membership of a group, although you can manipulate the member attribute of a group programmatically to add more entries. However, because of some technical issues involved in replicating group membership, Microsoft recommends that you avoid building groups with 5,000 entries. My own opinion is a little stronger on this topic—the limit is technical, not realistic, and you create the potential for problems if you insist on using very large groups. Best practice is to keep group membership under 1,000 to make everything (membership, replication, update collisions, traffic) a lot easier to control. This is particularly true in large multi-domain implementations.

Note the use of the word "objects" when referring to group membership. An object can be a user account or contact, but it can also be another group, so you can build groups from a collection of nested groups and build very large logical groups in this manner. Nested groups greatly expand the total possible user population that you can address through a single directory entry. However, while it is nice to know that it is technically possible to create a mega-distribution list to address thousands of users at a single keystroke, once a list contains more than 200 users or so, it is also a weapon waiting for people to use as a form of internal spam.

Windows does not impose a hard-coded limit to the number of groups that can exist in a forest, but you can run into a situation called "token bloat" that can prevent users logging on. Token bloat occurs when the number of groups that a user belongs to is so large that Windows cannot fit all the groups into the security token. Because they are so useful for email, an Exchange environment is likely to use far more groups than a simple Windows deployment, and you may run into token bloat when you migrate from an earlier version of Exchange and Windows upgrades the distribution lists to groups. This is good reason to review group membership and remove users from groups that they do not need to belong to. Note that you are less likely to run into a problem with tokens on the Windows 64 platform because Windows has more memory available to deal with AD structures.

3.6.5 Managing group membership

It is easy to set up new distribution groups but some forget the hard work to maintain membership. In theory, updates should be automatic and the Active Directory adjusts group membership as it deletes accounts and contacts. The normal problems include:

- Adding new members: Whom should someone contact if they want to join the list? An easy way to inform people is to include instructions in the "Notes" section of the list's properties as this text is visible to Outlook when you look at its properties through the GAL (Figure 3.33).

- Note that a user is only able to manage groups that are part of the user's own domain and that you can control the ability for a manager to update the membership list by an attribute of the list. You cannot manage groups from other domains because you are using an incomplete copy of the group replicated to a local Global Catalog rather

Figure 3.33
*Details of a list
maintainer*

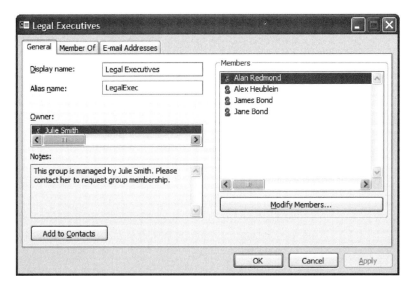

than the full copy maintained by domain controllers in the owning domain. In addition, the group maintainer must have the correct Windows permissions (Allow Read Members and Allow Write Members) to be able to change the membership. You can grant these permissions at either the organizational unit (if the same maintainer takes care of multiple groups) or individual group level.

- The informational text can state whether the potential member should email a request to the maintainer or take another action to join the list. Some companies have sophisticated web-based applications to allow users to maintain their own group membership, using LDAP-based utilities or PowerShell scripts to communicate with the Active Directory behind the scenes.

- You know you have a problem when the list begins to receive "please let me in" messages from people who want to join as this is a good indication that your procedures are not well known or do not work.

- You need to know who the members of the list are. This is easy for small lists, but it becomes increasingly difficult as the numbers grow because the standard tools for list maintenance (through Outlook or EMC) have no way to generate membership reports. You can use the `Get-DistributionGroupMembership` command to list the members of a distribution group and then export by piping the output to the `Export-CSV` command to create a CSV file that you can manipulate with another program for formatting purposes, such as Excel or Access. Figure 3.34 shows how `Get-DistributionGroupMembership` lists the members of a group. If you want to see all the properties for each member, pipe the output to the `Format-List` command. For example:

```
Get-DistributionGroupMembership 'Senior Executives' | Format-
List
```

- Removing obsolete members: If your practice is to disable accounts and keep mailboxes for a period after their owners leave the company, you should remove them from all groups to prevent the mailboxes receiving unwanted copies of email. It is best practice for group owners to review the list regularly to remove recipients who no longer work for the company. Apart from filling Store databases with messages that no one will ever read, this step prevents the other group members from becoming annoyed when they send messages to the group only to receive multiple nondelivery notifications back. The most common reason for NDRs is that Exchange cannot deliver messages to the mailboxes of the disabled accounts (perhaps because the mailboxes have exceeded their quotas with all the messages that have arrived since the owner left the company).

Figure 3.34
Listing group membership

You can block most nondelivery notifications by setting the "Advanced" properties (Figure 3.35) of the distribution group to:

- Suppress notifications completely;
- Send notifications back to the message originator; or
- Send notifications to the owner of the group as defined in the "Group Information" property page.

The easiest option is to suppress nondelivery notifications for distribution lists, but this means that you never see any indication that someone has a problem—their mailbox quota is exceeded or Exchange makes an attempt

Figure 3.35
Properties of a
distribution group

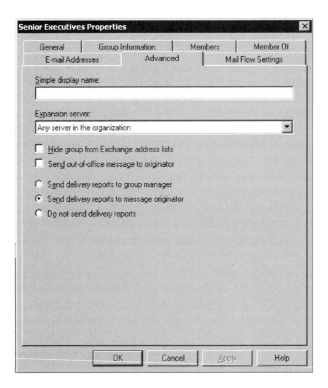

to deliver to a mailbox that no longer exists, which could mean that directory replication is not working. Sending notifications back to the owner is acceptable if that person can take appropriate action. For example, if you allocate ownership to an administrative assistant and they do not have the correct Windows permissions to modify group membership, then you will end up doing the work to maintain the group. Note that these properties are only valid for a single forest and single Exchange organization. If you operate in an environment where you use multiple Exchange organizations, the settings you make in one organization do not replicate to the others and you will still see notifications unless you turn them off everywhere.

3.6.6   **Protected groups (and users)**

Sometimes, the SMTP address of a distribution group gets outside a company. Apart from the obvious irritation if spam (otherwise called unsolicited commercial email) starts arriving for everyone on the list, there is a danger that unauthorized users could exploit the list to identify personnel within the company, for example, by a recruiter looking for specific talent. The first attempt to block messages from unauthorized users was implemented in Exchange 2000, which allows administrators to configure delivery restrictions for groups by checking that it could resolve the sender's address against the directory, but spammers can work around this check by spoofing their identity by inserting a perfectly valid email address in a message's "From:" field. For example, you might restrict a group so that only senior executives can send messages to it, only to be embarrassed when a spammer uses your chief executive's email address (which is often published or known externally) to address the troops. In Exchange 2007, you can put a deny permission called ms-Exch-SMTP-Accept-Authoritative-Domain-Sender on send connectors that process incoming traffic from the Internet if you want to block this kind of message. Send connectors are discussed in Chapter 6.

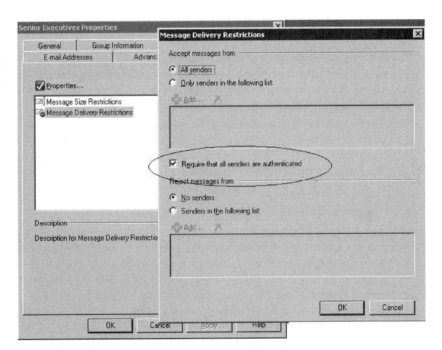

Figure 3.36
Limiting a group to authenticated users only

With Exchange 2003 and Exchange 2007, you can block such access by only allowing authenticated users (those who possess recognized NT credentials) to send messages to the list. For Exchange 2003, use AD Users and Computers to select the group you want to protect and set the "From authenticated users only" checkbox on the Exchange General property page. For Exchange 2007, use EMC to select the group and access the Message Delivery Restrictions options from the Mail Flow property page (Figure 3.36). This feature depends on a new attribute that Exchange 2003 introduced for user and distribution group objects (ms-Exch-Authenticated-Only), so you can only set authenticated restrictions on a group when working on a server that has the Exchange 2003 or Exchange 2007 management components installed.

You can implement the same restrictions on an individual user's mailbox. For example, it is reasonably common to create two mailboxes for senior executives. One is their "working" mailbox, which they and their support staff use for day-to-day email. Access to this mailbox is restricted to specific users and groups. The second mailbox is intended for public access so that anyone can send a message to it. Messages that arrive in the public mailbox are screened by a member of the executive's support staff before they are forwarded to the working mailbox for a response.

3.7 Using groups for permissions

Because Exchange treats them like any other recipient, mail-enabled security groups are a useful way of maintaining permissions on public folders, much along the same lines as delivery restrictions. When you give permission to a group, all members of the list inherit the permission. The advantage lies in the fact that it is very much easier to grant permission to a single entity, the group, than it is to manage separate permissions for each individual in the group. Better still, when people join a group, they automatically inherit the permissions held by the group and so have access to all of the public folders that are available to the group. Later on, when you remove some members from the group, Windows revokes the permissions they inherit from the group and there is no danger that someone will gain access to confidential information after they no longer need this privilege.

3.7.1 Managing distribution groups from Outlook

I use Outlook to manage distribution groups all the time because it is a quick and effective way to manage group membership. Outlook does not differentiate between distribution and security groups; all it cares about is whether the group is mail-enabled, and if it is, then Exchange includes the group into the GAL and so Outlook accesses and manages it.

You need to have the appropriate permissions before you can manage a group with Outlook. This means that you either are an administrator of the OU that the group belongs to or an administrator explicitly allocates you the permission to manage and update the group by updating the group's properties through EMC as shown in Figure 3.37.

Note that it is also possible to update the group's maintainer through PowerShell. For example, we could assign the group to Julie Smith and tell people who to go to if they want to be included in the group with this command:

```
Set-Group -Id 'Legal Executives' -ManagedBy 'Julie Smith' -Notes
'This group is managed by Julie Smith. Please contact her to request
group membership'
```

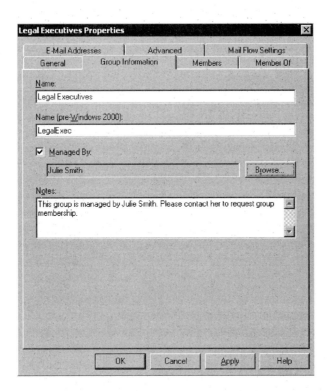

Figure 3.37
*Permissions to
manage a group*

Once the permissions are set, you should be able to update group membership from Outlook unless your account belongs to a different domain to the domain that owns the group. The inability to manage groups across domains, even in the same forest, is a major flaw that has existed in all versions since Exchange 2000. The problem exists because of the way Exchange proxies connections from some versions of Outlook to a Global Catalog server through the DSProxy mechanism. DSProxy exists to support older Outlook clients that assume a direct connection to the directory, as existed with Exchange 5.5. The Global Catalog that Exchange connects an Outlook client to contains details of all of the mail-enabled objects in the forest, but only a partial read-only attribute set of objects from domains outside the Global Catalog server's own domain. When a user updates group membership from Outlook, DSProxy relays an NSPI request to perform the update to the Active Directory, but the NSPI request fails if it goes to a Global Catalog that cannot update the target group (because the Global Catalog only has a read-only copy of the group). The failure is silent, meaning that the user will not be aware that the update failed unless they check the group membership afterwards.

Updates to user objects, such as adding delegates (to allow other users to process email on your behalf) to your mailbox, can exhibit the same problem if Outlook connects to a Global Catalog that does not belong to the same domain as the target user object. Once again, you attempt to make the change with Outlook and everything seems to go okay only for the interaction between Exchange and the Global Catalog to fail. The delegate information remains unaltered and the user is unaware of the problem unless they check afterwards that Exchange updated the Active Directory.

It is best to manage groups with accounts that are in the same domain and never to create an Active Directory design that places users from one domain into a situation where they are likely to connect to Global Catalogs that belong to another domain. This is one reason why some experts recommend that you place all user accounts in one domain.

3.8 Dynamic distribution groups

Large companies like HP use distribution groups (or lists) extensively to create email-addressable objects that reach many people who share a common need or interest. However, it is typical to find a proliferation of distribution groups in any large email deployment, leading to a situation where people spend a lot of time updating the groups to make sure that the right people receive the right data all the time. For example, the HP GAL includes over 150,000 distribution groups, all of which have different maintainers. Some maintainers are very conscientious about how they maintain membership and the group is always accurate; others are less so and you can never be sure that the group contains everyone that it should.

Conscientious maintainers remove members who no longer want to receive messages sent to the group or those who have left the company. Others simply leave the groups to degrade gently until they are no longer wanted. At that point, system administrators have to clean up the directory by removing redundant groups. However, cleaning up the directory or maintaining group membership are low-priority tasks for hard-pressed administrators, so they are easy tasks to overlook. The result is a directory cluttered with obsolete groups and groups that do not reach the right membership. Exchange 2003 introduced support for query-based distribution groups to help automate list maintenance. Only Exchange 2003/2007 and Exchange 2000 (SP3 onwards) can use dynamic distribution groups as the Active Directory must have the necessary schema extension to support these lists (object type ms-Exch-Dynamic-Distribution-List).

The only difference a user sees between a dynamic group and a normal group is that you cannot view the membership of a dynamic group from its GAL properties. This is quite logical because the GAL has no way of resolving the query to determine group membership. From an administrative perspective, you cannot use dynamic groups to control access to objects like connectors and you cannot nest these groups inside other distribution groups.

3.8.1 Changing filters and conditions for dynamic distribution groups

When users submit a message addressed to a dynamic distribution group, the message travels from the originating mailbox to a hub transport server where the transport system identifies that the group requires a query to determine the addresses to receive the message. The categorizer component then expands the group membership into individual addresses by using the query to interrogate the Global Catalog server. The categorizer can then use the group membership to create the list of recipients and decide how to best route the message. The need to execute the query to build a list before message submission increases load on both the hub transport server and the Global Catalog server and delays the message slightly, but this is usually a justifiable trade between usefulness and overhead.

In Exchange 2007, Microsoft renames the query-based distribution groups that they introduced in Exchange 2003 to be "dynamic" distribution groups. The name may have changed, but the resolution of the group into individual routable addresses still depends on queries that Exchange executes against the Active Directory. The big difference is that Exchange 2003 query-based distribution groups use queries that are expressed in LDAP format while Exchange 2007 dynamic distribution groups use queries in OPATH format.

You may ask the question why Microsoft has changed query types from LDAP to OPATH in Exchange 2007. After all, this is a move away from a standard for queries that is well understood and supported by many products, including utilities that you can use to build queries against LDAP-compliant directories. It seems strange that Microsoft would want to move away from LDAP to use OPATH and require administrators to master new skills. OPATH isn't difficult, but it is something more to learn.

The complete answer is probably pretty complicated, but I think that the history of how Exchange queries the Active Directory reflects the components that the developers had to work with when they introduced query-based distribution groups in Exchange 2003. They didn't have the time to create a wizard or other UI to help administrators create new groups, so they used the Active Directory LDAP picker to create the criteria for the queries. The groups were managed through AD Users and Computers, just like all of the other mail-enabled objects used by Exchange, and they were forced to use LDAP because it was the only directory query language available. Everything worked, but the implementation was flawed. Four years later, the Exchange developers have a completely new environment to work in. First, PowerShell has arrived to provide the scripting and automation language for Windows and application such as Exchange. As discussed in Chapter 4, Exchange 2007 does an impressive job of extending the basic PowerShell framework to include support for mail-enabled objects, servers, and other messaging components. OPATH is the filtering syntax used by PowerShell, so it is a natural progression for Exchange 2007 to embrace OPATH as its preferred syntax, especially as it also removes the need for administrators to learn and master the somewhat obscure and opaque queries that LDAP often generates. The change to OPATH allows administrators to learn one query syntax and use it everywhere, whether they want to write one-line PowerShell commands that filter objects or complex filtering expressions used in scripts or to drive objects such as dynamic distribution groups, email address policies, address lists, and global address lists.

Query-based distribution groups never made much of an impact in many organizations that deployed Exchange 2003, so now is as good a time as any to change the filter syntax. You can use the LDIFDE utility to gain an insight into the information that the Active Directory holds about dynamic distribution groups. Figure 3.38 shows an edited version of LDIFDE output generated for a group by running the command:

```
C:> LDIFDE -v -d "CN=Exchange Power Users,
OU=Groups,OU=Exchange Users,DC=hpqbox,DC=com" -f x.tmp
```

Figure 3.38
LDIFDE output
for a dynamic
distribution group

```
dn: CN=Exchange Power Users,OU=Groups,OU=Exchange
Users,DC=hpqbox, DC=com
objectClass: msExchDynamicDistributionList
cn: Exchange Power Users
instanceType: 4
displayName: Exchange Power Users
mailNickname: Exchange_Power_Users
name: Exchange Power Users
objectCategory:
 CN=ms-Exch-Dynamic-Distribution-
List,CN=Schema,CN=Configuration,DC=xyz,DC=com
mail: Exchange_Power_Users@xyz.com
msExchQueryFilter:
 ((RecipientType -eq 'UserMailbox' -and Department -eq
'Exchange') -and -not(Name -like 'SystemMailbox{*'))
msExchDynamicDLFilter:
(&(objectCategory=person)(objectClass=user)(mailNickname=*)(msE
xchHomeServerName=*)(department=Exchange)(!(name=SystemMailbox{
*)))
msExchRecipientDisplayType: 3
```

As you can see, many of the attributes that you expect for any other distribution group including email addresses also exist for dynamic groups. The big difference is the value of the msExchQueryFilter attribute, which holds the OPATH filter that the Active Directory resolves to determine the membership of the list. The msExchDynamicDLFilter holds the equivalent LDAP query to allow an Exchange 2003 server to expand the group membership. While the effects of the two filters are the same, the difference in syntax can be a learning hurdle for administrators who want to convert older query-based distribution groups to new dynamic distribution groups. The LDAP filter is a read-only property that also allows administrators who are experienced with LDAP to compare and understand the syntax of the OPATH filter. Exchange generates the value of the LDAP filter when it creates the OPATH filter and you should not attempt to set the LDAP filter with other tools as you may generate incompatible or unusable results.

3.8.2 A note on OPATH

Dynamic distribution groups are the most obvious opportunity for Exchange administrators to use OPATH. Exchange uses the same filtering behavior for email address policies, address lists, and global address lists, so clearly OPATH is a big thing for Exchange administrators to get to know (and maybe love). All of these objects support precanned filters and all allow you to build custom filters using the same syntax and filtering properties. If you learn how to build OPATH filters for dynamic distribution groups, you can use the same techniques with the other objects.

Some basic points about OPATH syntax for building custom recipient filters are:

- OPATH requires a hyphen before –and, –or, and –not operators.

- Comparison operators include –eq (equal), –ne (not equal), –lt (less than), –gt (greater than), –like (like), –ilike, and –notlike. –Like and –notlike are wildcard string compares. –iLike and –inotLike are case insensitive.

- The RecipientFilter property specifies the OPATH query specified in the syntax given above and including the properties and values that we want to filter on. Specify the filter within braces. For example, {Office –eq "Dublin"} means that we want to filter on objects whose "Office" property is set to "Dublin." When you create a dynamic distribution group through EMC, Exchange automatically generates the necessary filter and stores it in the RecipientFilter property.

- The RecipientContainer property specifies the scope of the query within the Active Directory. For example, if you pass "Exchange Mailboxes" in this property, the query covers the "Exchange Users" organizational unit and all its child organization units below.

■ The IncludedRecipients property allows you to specify the type of recipients to include in the query. For example, if you pass "Mailbox-Users" in this property, the query includes only mailboxes.

Do not worry too much about how to construct OPATH queries for now, as we will review many examples of filters in action when we enter the world of PowerShell in Chapter 4. For now, all we have to realize is that you have to update older LDAP filters created for dynamic distribution lists in Exchange 2003 to use OPATH filters if you want to support them in Exchange 2007. You cannot edit a query-based distribution group created with Exchange 2003 with EMC or EMS unless you use the `Set-DynamicDistributionGroup` command to force an upgrade of the group using the –ForceUpgrade parameter. At this point, you might find that you need to provide a new query because Exchange can't automatically convert the LDAP query to OPATH format. Note that whenever you upgrade a filter to use OPATH format, Exchange automatically translates the OPATH filter into LDAP syntax so that legacy Exchange servers can continue to use the query.

As you migrate to Exchange 2007, the best plan is to remove the old query-based distribution groups and replace them whenever possible with new Exchange 2007 dynamic distribution groups. Because the Active Directory properties for both types of groups contain queries that Exchange 2003 and 2007 can execute, you can use both types of group during the migration period. Over time you will want to phase out the Exchange 2003 servers and will therefore lose the ability to manage the older query-based distribution groups, so you will need to change them over. In some cases, the process to create new equivalent dynamic distribution groups is a matter of point and click through the Exchange 2007 Management Console; in other cases where complex queries are required to build the membership for dynamic groups, you will need to create and manage the new groups through PowerShell.

3.8.3 A new UI for dynamic groups

At the same time as they moved to OPATH, the Exchange team was designing a new administration GUI. This allowed them to get rid-of -components that they can't control, like AD Users and Computers. It also allowed them to focus on the question of how to help administrators create well-structured and high-performing queries and to avoid some of the overly complex queries that were generated in Exchange 2003.

When you create a dynamic group for Exchange 2003, you have a huge amount of flexibility in creating the query used to expand group membership. The Active Directory query builder allows you to construct very sophisticated and precise searches against the Active Directory, but on the other hand, an unsuspecting or careless administrator is able to build queries that take hours to execute. For example, using the Active Directory Finder, you can create Exchange 2003 dynamic groups based on queries that examine:

- Objects in a particular department or set of departments.

- Users who have mailboxes on a specific Exchange server.

- Users and contacts who have a specific title (for example, all marketing managers).

- Identify users who are temporary employees or full-time employees, using a customized attribute to locate the members of either set. You might like to restrict the ability to send to a group to certain users or groups (see Figure 3.36). For example, you could limit the ability to send messages to full-time employees to authenticated users so that someone outside the company cannot send a message to all employees.

- Objects in a particular country.

- Queries that use values in the set of customized attributes reserved for your own deployment purposes. For example, you could store employee job codes in one of the customized attributes and search against these values.

You can also combine searches for values in different attributes. For example, find everyone named Tom who has a mailbox on a specific server and lives in Ireland. The Active Directory is able to resolve such a query but it will take some time. Real-life experience showed that it was all too easy for Exchange administrators to fall into the trap of creating queries that stressed servers as the Active Directory attempted to build lists of thousands of matching objects followed by Exchange sending each object a copy of a message. You could create a query that ended up addressing a message to every user in your organization—something that is probably okay for anyone to do inside a small company, but definitely a problem if you have tens of thousands of recipients. The problem was compounded by the fact that the processing that ensued after a user sent a message to a dynamic group was a black hole and administrators could not get any insight into what was happening or their servers, nor could they halt the processing of a dynamic group after a user submitted a message.

Flexibility often results in complexity, and in turn, can lead to some of the problems discussed above. The new wizard-driven UI in the Exchange 2007 EMC leads administrators through the steps to create dynamic distribution groups based on three questions. The answers to these questions determine the OPATH query that the wizard generates.

1. What is the organizational scope for the recipients that should be included in the query? The scope is established by an organizational unit in a domain and all of its child organizational units. Scope cannot extend across domain boundaries, so if you need groups that cover multiple domains, you need to create separate groups for each domain and then combine the groups together into a "super group."

2. What sort of recipients are included in the query? Are they just mailboxes or can mail-enabled contacts be included as well?

3. What additional properties of the recipients should be used to select the right people?

The aim of the GUI is to enable administrators to create the vast majority of all of the dynamic distribution groups that they will need by providing enough flexibility to handle most scenarios. The filters that the wizard creates are "precanned" rather than "custom" and are tuned for performance. You can only edit precanned filters through the wizard, so if you need to make a change to a filter that can't be done with the options presented by the wizard, you will have to delete the original group and create a new one through PowerShell and specify the necessary recipient filter then.

3.8.4 Creating New dynamic groups

Before creating a new dynamic group, you should know what purpose you want the group to serve as well as the attributes that you will use to query the Active Directory to build the group. In an Exchange 2003 organization, you create dynamic distribution groups through the AD Users and Computers console. After you install Exchange 2007 on a server, the option to create a dynamic (query) distribution group still exists in AD Users and Computers, but the necessary add-in code that allows AD Users and Computers to create new mail-enabled objects that was previously installed by Exchange 2003 is missing on an Exchange 2007 server. You can choose the option, but you will not be able to create the group. Some administrators like to create one or more organizational units (OU) to hold the query-based groups instead of holding them with other objects in "regular" OUs. For example, you might call this OU "Dynamic Groups" to make its purpose obvious. This decision is a matter of taste and policy and is not a requirement to use these groups.

To create a new Exchange 2007 dynamic group, open EMC and click on Distribution Groups under the Recipient Configuration node (Figure 3.39) to launch the new object wizard. The first step is to select the OU where you want to create the new object along with its name and alias. It is a good idea to create groups in a logical structure within the Active Directory

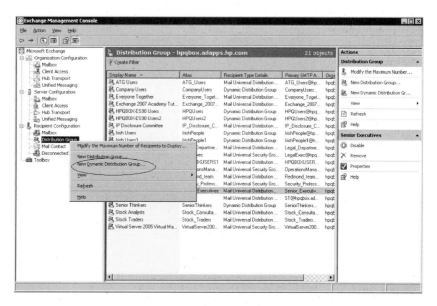

Figure 3.39
Creating a new dynamic distribution group

and you may well want to keep all the dynamic groups together in a specific OU. You then decide what type of objects will be included in the query. In most cases, you will probably want to address recipients with Exchange mailboxes although you can also select other object types such as mail-enabled contacts or equipment mailboxes. The next stage is to create the LDAP query that determines group membership. Exchange will execute against the Active Directory to group membership. It is at this point that the biggest change occurs between Exchange 2003 and Exchange 2007.

The use of a wizard-driven GUI may make you assume that Exchange 2007 dynamic groups are less flexible than their Exchange 2003 counterparts. This is true to some degree (but any gap can be addressed by creating a dynamic group through PowerShell). In any case, it is possible to create dynamic distribution groups in Exchange 2007 that are flexible and powerful. The major difference is that the UI restricts you to creating relatively simple and well-bounded queries for dynamic distribution groups, but at least you'll know that the queries will work and you won't have to grapple with OPATH syntax as Exchange will generate the necessary code for you.

Microsoft's decision to restrict the ability to build dynamic groups based on simple queries through EMC is easier to understand when you reflect on the type of dynamic groups that administrators actually create. In most cases, the queries are reasonably straightforward. Microsoft analyzed the queries and realized that the majority can be satisfied by the following conditions:

Figure 3.40
Setting query
parameters

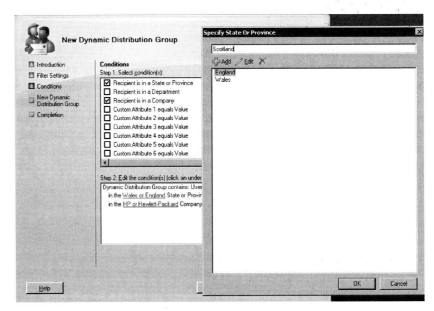

1. A specific organizational scope (for example, a domain, or an organizational unit and its children).

2. A specific collection of recipient types (for example, mailboxes, groups, contacts, or any mail-enabled object).

3. Checks against a number of popular Active Directory fields that are most commonly used to create dynamic groups:

   a. Recipient is in a specific State or Province (check against the StateOrProvince property in Active Directory). This value is stored in the ConditionalStateOrProvince property in the filter.

   b. Recipient is in a specific Department (check against the Department property in Active Directory). This value is stored in the ConditionalDepartment property in the filter.

   c. Recipient is in a specific Company (check against the Company property in Active Directory). This value is stored in the ConditionalCompany property in the filter.

   d. Checks against any of the 15 customized attributes (CustomAttribute1 through CustomAttribute15) created for use with Exchange. These values are stored in the ConditionalCustomAttribute1 through Conditional-CustomAttribute15 properties in the filter.

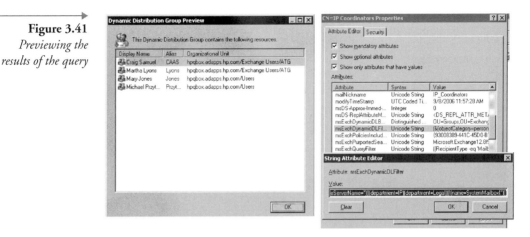

Figure 3.41
Previewing the results of the query

The wizard helps administrators to create dynamic groups based on the conditions described above. Figure 3.40 illustrates the dynamic group wizard in action. In this case, we have already decided the scope for the query and the collection of objects that we want to select. In this step of the wizard we have the opportunity to refine the collection further by comparing values against the three Active Directory properties that we just discussed. In all cases, you can specify multiple values, such as looking for recipients who are in both the "Legal" and "Law" departments. You can also combine the different criteria. For example, the query specified in Figure 3.40 searches for any recipient in the four countries that constitute the United Kingdom provided that they also have HP or Hewlett Packard specified in the company field. When you have defined the query parameters, you can test a query with the "Preview" button. Exchange executes the OPATH query and outputs the result as shown in the left-hand screen of Figure 3.41. It's a good idea to test the query to ensure that it generates the expected list of names, if only to avoid the possibility that users send messages to unintended recipients. Of course, the membership of dynamic groups change as administrators update the underlying Active Directory objects and can only function as you expect if data is correctly populated and maintained in the directory.

After it creates the new dynamic group, EMC displays the PowerShell command that it uses. You can use CTRL/C to copy this command to review it or to use the code as the basis for scripting the creation of future dynamic distribution groups. For example, here's the code that EMC generated to create the group that we just reviewed:

```
New-DynamicDistributionGroup -Name:'UK employees'
-OrganizationalUnit:'hpqbox.adapps.hp.com/Users'
-DisplayName:'UK employees' -Alias:'UK_employees'
```

```
-IncludedRecipients:'MailboxUsers' -Company:'HP','Hewlett Packard'
-StateOrProvince:'England','Scotland','Northern Ireland','Wales'
-RecipientContainer:'hpqbox.adapps.hp.com/Groups'
```

The OPATH filter for the group is specified in the –IncludedRecipients parameter. If you do not believe the query conditions that you see through EMC, you can check behind the scenes to examine the queries that Exchange generates by looking at the Active Directory group object with ADSIEDIT. The LDAP query is held in the MsExchDynamicDLFilter attribute, as shown in the right-hand screen of Figure 3.41 and we can see the OPATH filter by looking at the msExchQueryFilter attribute. It is very easy to make a mistake if you update attributes through ADSIEdit, so it is not a good idea to attempt to change either the OPATH or LDAP filters through ADSIEDIT (and with Exchange 2007, the OPATH filter is the one that is important), even if you are the world's best and most fluent expert in these syntaxes.

The thought might now cross your minds as to what Exchange 2007 does with the LDAP query that you established when you created dynamic groups in Exchange 2003 if you subsequently edit the groups using the Exchange 2007 EMC. The answer is that the Exchange 2007 EMC can only generate simple queries and cannot display the kind of complex queries that administrators often built using the Active Directory finder. You therefore cannot update older query-based distribution groups using EMC and have to update them with EMS. If you want to create a dynamic distribution group that is functionally equivalent to a query-based distribution group, you will have to translate the LDAP recipient filter contained in the msExchDynamicDLFilter attribute of the group and write the equivalent OPATH recipient filter into the msExchQueryFilter attribute with the Set-DynamicDistributionList command. For this reason, you should review the use of query-based distribution groups in Exchange 2003 and determine how you can create equivalent Exchange 2007 dynamic distribution groups with new OPATH queries as replacements during your migration to Exchange 2007. Remember that it is possible to make a mistake and create queries that generate different results for Exchange 2003 and the new Exchange 2007 groups, so some careful testing is required.

Note that Exchange 2007 limits the recipients that can be included in a dynamic distribution group to a single domain. In other words, if you operate in a multi-domain forest and want to create and use dynamic distribution groups, you will have to create separate groups for each domain that contains recipients that you want to include and then create a separate "all-in" normal distribution group that contains all the dynamic distribution groups for the different domains.

3.8.5 **Using dynamic Distribution groups**

Outlook 2007 and Outlook Web Access 2007 clients support dynamic groups completely. The support in the 2003 versions of these clients is less complete. For example, while you can view the dynamic groups in the Outlook 2003 GAL, if you view their membership, the list appears to be blank. By comparison, if you view the membership of a dynamic group through Outlook Web Access 2007, you see all the members. It is possible that the masking of group members will cause users some concern, but this is an easy point to cover in training, as long as your users accept that some magic happens behind the scenes to get their messages to the right recipients. Figure 3.42 illustrates what you can expect to see for a dynamic group using Outlook Web Access 2007 (left) and Outlook 2003 (right).

Because a dynamic group only "exists" when an application like Exchange resolves its membership against the AD, it follows that you cannot maintain group membership in the same way as users can update membership of regular groups by selecting the list from the GAL and then modifying its properties using Outlook. You have to make any change to a dynamic group through EMC.

Outlook Express and other non-Microsoft POP3/IMAP4 clients do not support dynamic groups, so these clients have some problems when you attempt to address or send email to these groups. For example, you cannot use the CTRL/K feature with Outlook Express to check the name of a dynamic group against AD. In addition, the Outlook Express interface to AD (a straightforward LDAP search) cannot find these entries, so it is best to create personal contacts that include the dynamic group's SMTP address if you want to use dynamic groups often. You can then use the contact or type

Figure 3.42
Viewing a dynamic group from Outlook Web Access 2007 and Outlook 2003

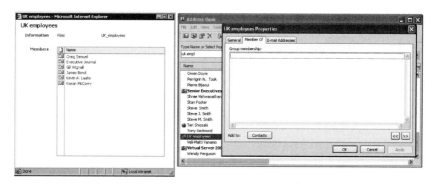

in the SMTP address into a message header and Exchange will safely deliver the message by expanding the group membership after it resolves the address on the incoming message against the AD.

Dynamic distribution groups cannot hold Windows security principals so you cannot use them to control access to public folders or other resources such as file shares. In a similar manner, you cannot use dynamic groups to place restrictions on objects like connectors. In addition, you cannot nest dynamic groups and cannot add them to global or universal distribution groups: they stand on their own. Finally, the data captured by Exchange to chart the progress of a message sent to a dynamic group in a server's message tracking logs is the same as for regular groups.

Dynamic distribution groups are a useful feature that enables administrators to create self-maintaining groups. Like anything that depends on a directory, the accuracy of directory information will dictate the effectiveness of dynamic groups in practice. For example, if you want to create a dynamic group to address all users in a particular country, the group can only be successful if you identify every user in that country by updating their user objects with the necessary information in the directory.

3.9   Mailbox quotas

Mailbox quotas have grown from the 25–30MB typically assigned to corporate users on an Exchange 4.0 server to a point where many companies consider a 1GB mailbox to be a nice round figure to use for a mailbox quota and 5GB is not a very unusually large mailbox. One of Microsoft's big reasons for going to the 64-bit platform is to allow users to have bigger mailboxes. In short, Microsoft recognizes that we are human packrats who cannot survive within the confines of a 100MB mailbox and need far more space to hold all the important information that we accumulate through work and personal activities. The truth, of course, is different. Users need larger mailboxes because they are not disciplined enough to clean out their mailboxes and keep them somewhat under control, and anyway, storage is cheap, so what is the problem with having a large inbox? It's hard to get agreement on what people consider to be a large mailbox or rather a large quota. A user thinks that their mailbox is large enough when they don't get messages to say that their quota is exceeded; an administrator thinks that mailboxes are too large at this point because they are responsible for backing up mailbox content to protect the data; and managers often look at cost and don't think about mailbox sizes at all!

The real reason why users and administrators struggle to agree on mailbox quotas may lie between lack of discipline on the user side and the time that administrators spend figuring out how to manage mailbox data. In some cases, the lack of user discipline may actually be due to lack of time for users to be able to review and clean out old mailbox content. If this is the case, then perhaps administrators should concentrate on growing mailbox quotas gracefully to meet user demand so that the Exchange servers are not stressed, that backups can proceed quickly, and that data can be restored efficiently in case of disasters. This is perhaps the core reasoning behind Microsoft's argument that they need to support very large mailboxes in Exchange 2007.

If we take the opportunity presented by cheaper storage and the ability of Exchange 2007 to manage more data to allocate larger storage quotas for user mailboxes then perhaps we can eliminate the security problem that PSTs pose. The limitations of PSTs are well known, yet users continue to create these files and populate them with information because they cannot keep the data on the server as their mailbox quotas are too small. From a philosophical perspective, I would cheerfully trade server storage to eliminate PSTs because I could then:

- Assure users that they can access their mailbox information from a variety of clients instead of being restricted to Outlook.

- Assure the legal department that the Exchange deployment can satisfy any legislative requirements for the company to achieve compliance because all messages stay on the server and can be captured in a journal on the server instead of some being delivered to PST inboxes.

- Provide better resilience to failure than you can get from any file that is hosted on a local hard drive of a workstation or a laptop.

- Provide better protection against viruses because the anti-virus scanners can access all messages and attachments in server mailboxes. This is much preferable to attempting to scan every PST in the organization (which can be done, if the anti-virus scanners can gain access to all the PSTs).

- Provide better all-round security to data because information in mailboxes is far harder for someone to break into than a PST, which can be opened (even if it is password protected) very easily.

The list goes on (and we discuss this topic in detail in Chapter 7), but the point is that Exchange 2007 presents administrators with an opportunity to change user behavior for the better. However, to be effective, you will have to use a group policy setting to disable PST use from Outlook. The answer lies in the DisablePST registry value that Outlook 98 (and all versions from then) supports. This value is under the HKEY_LOCAL_MACHINE\Software\ Microsoft\Office\11.0\Outlook subkey (this is for Outlook 2003, use 10.0 for Outlook XP, 9.0 for Outlook 2000, and 12.0 for Outlook 2007). You create the value if it is not present and set it to 1 to disable PST access. As you might imagine, the default is "0" to allow access. The net effect is that DisablePST turns off the ability to archive to a PST, to export or import data to and from a PST, and to create a new PST. Smart users can get around the disabling block by opening an existing PST through the File.Open.Outlook Data File command, so a complete solution to the issue requires you to use group policy to disable the Outlook Data File command by blocking the ID for the command (5576). This is a little complex, but it works and it stops users messing with PSTs, which is what you want to achieve.

3.9.1 Setting mailbox quotas

Exchange has a structured flow to set and respect mailbox quotas. When you create a new mailbox, it automatically inherits the default storage limits set for the database that hosts the mailbox, and as you can see in Figure 3.43, the default limits are quite high. Exchange 2007 is the first version that sets default limits as these values are left blank for databases created by previous versions of Exchange. Table 3.3 lists the default storage limits together with their meaning. The table also lists the EMS shell parameter that you use to retrieve information about a user's current quota consumption with the Get-Mailbox command and the Active Directory property that stores the storage limits for the user object.

Microsoft set the default storage limits by beginning with an assumption that users will have large 2GB mailboxes, which is aligned with their general idea that Exchange 2007 is better able to support such large mailboxes and that the move toward unified messaging means that more items will end up in mailboxes. This assertion is true, if you decide to deploy Exchange 2007 Unified Messaging. However, voicemail messages do not generally take up much extra space in a mailbox, so it's hard to accept that mailbox quotas need to increase quite so much to accommodate voicemail.

Table 3.3 *Default mailbox storage limits*

Active Directory Property	EMS Shell Parameter	Meaning and Default Value
mDBStorageQuota	IssueWarningQuota	Issue a warning that you are close to the limit when the mailbox reaches 1.9GB
mDBOverQuotaLimit	ProhibitSendQuota	Stop the user sending new messages when the mailbox reaches 2GB
mDBOverHardQuotaLimit	ProhibitSendReceiveQuota	Stop the user sending and receiving messages when the mailbox reaches 2.3GB
mDBUseDefaults	UseDatabaseQuotaDefaults	Flag to control whether mailbox uses default storage quotas set for the database; default is "true"

After settling on a default mailbox size of 2GB, Microsoft then calculated the point to start issuing warnings by assuming that an average user receives a hundred 50KB messages a day, or about 5MB daily and 100MB over 20 days. The gap between a warning starting at 1.9GB and a user being unable to send new messages at 2GB is sufficient for even the tardiest user to take note of the warnings and clean up their mailbox. They then decided to leave a gap of 0.3GB before the next restriction kicks in and the user is unable to receive new mail to accommodate the situation when users take extended vacations and are unable to clean out their mailbox.

You may decide that Microsoft's calculations are off and come up with your own default values for what limitations should be applied to mailboxes within the organization. In any event, once you have decided on quotas, you should apply the values by policy before you start to move users to Exchange 2007 so that the new mailboxes inherit the desired quotas. For specific users, you can set different quotas by editing mailbox properties and clearing the "Use mailbox database defaults" checkbox and setting new values for warning, prohibit send, and prohibit send and receive. If you want to create a mailbox that has a truly unlimited quota, then clear the "Use mailbox database defaults" checkbox and set no values for warning, prohibit send, and prohibit send and receive.

Figure 3.43
How mailbox quotas are applied

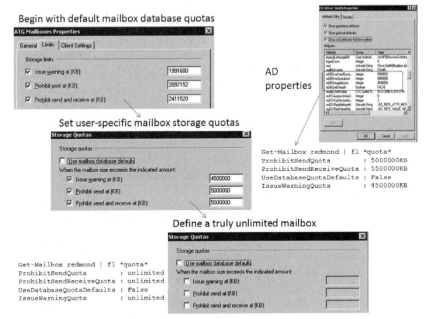

When a user exceeds their mailbox quota, Exchange logs event 8528 in the application event log (Figure 3.44). Users also see a notification about their quota problem the next time they connect to Exchange with Outlook or the premium edition of Outlook Web Access 2007 (Figure 3.45). The light edition of Outlook Web Access, IMAP and POP clients will not detect a problem with mailbox quota until a user attempts to create and send a new message.

Apart from scanning the event log regularly to detect users that exceed their quotas, you can take a more proactive approach by checking with a PowerShell command. We will get to the details of how to use PowerShell with Exchange 2007 in some detail in Chapter 4, but for now, you can use a command like this to check for problem mailboxes on a server:

```
Get-MailboxStatistics —Server ExchMbxSvr1 | Where-Object
{$_.StorageLimitStatus —eq 'MailboxDisabled'} | Select
DisplayName
```

This one-line PowerShell command scans the ExchMbxSvr1 server to look for disabled mailboxes because they have exceeded quota. We can do a lot more with PowerShell to help us identify mailboxes that need some administrative intervention, but we will leave the details of how to create more powerful scripts until Chapter 4.

Figure 3.44
Event logging
mailbox quota
exceeded

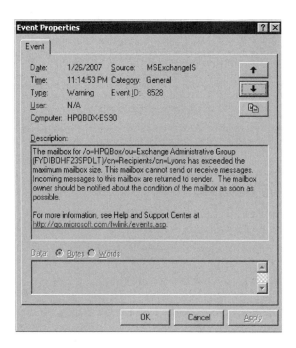

Most users who struggle to keep under quota will probably admit that their Inbox and Sent Items folders are stuffed full of messages that they really do not need to retain. On Exchange 2007 servers, you can use managed

Figure 3.45
*Outlook Web Access
flags a quota
problem*

folder policies to help users keep some control of these folders by expiring and deleting messages after a defined period (for instance, 60 days). Managed folder policies are discussed in Chapter 8.

3.10 Email address policies

Email address policies dictate the primary email address of mail-enabled objects in an Exchange organization. Objects can have many different SMTP addresses that can be used to receive email, but one address is always primary and is the address that is stamped on outgoing messages. When you install a new organization, Exchange automatically creates a default email address policy that creates addresses of the form:

```
Object alias + organization name
```

For example, if you are in an organization called xyz.com and you create a new mailbox with an alias of "Redmond," then the default email address policy stamps the new account with an SMTP primary address of Red-mond@xyz.com.

An organization can have multiple address policies and each policy has a priority so that Exchange knows the order in which to apply the policies. Figure 3.46 shows how EMC lists email address policies. As you can see, the default policy has lowest priority, meaning that it is applied last if no other policy covers an object being processed. Exchange creates the default email address policy automatically for you when you install the organization to ensure that all new mail-enabled objects receive valid email addresses. The default policy serves as a backstop, meaning that Exchange applies this policy to create an email address for new objects if no other policy applies.

Part of creating a policy is to establish a filter that determines what objects Exchange will apply the policy to. You can create a policy that applies to every mail-enabled object in the organization, a specific type such as mailboxes or contacts, or a filter based on an attribute such as department or

Figure 3.46
*Email address
policies*

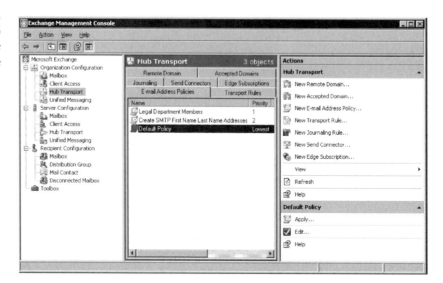

Figure 3.47
*Email address
policies in the
Active Directory*

country. For example, you can create a policy that creates email addresses specifically for mailboxes belonging to users in the Legal Department in China.

You define Email Address policies at organizational level, so they apply to all Exchange servers within the organization. Exchange stores details of the email address policies in its configuration data in the Active Directory (Figure 3.47), so the policies are replicated to all domain controllers in the forest. The Active Directory Topology service is responsible for refreshing policy information to local mailbox servers so that they can implement the policies as mail-enabled objects are added or updated. The Recipient Update Service is responsible for stamping objects with email addresses according to policy on Exchange 2000 and 2003 servers and the reliance on an additional service meant that an unpredictable interval (anything from a few minutes to an hour or more) often occurred before a new object received its email address and could be used. Exchange 2007 avoids this problem by incorporating policies directly into the process that updates the attributes of mail-enabled objects, so that if you call Set-Mailbox, Set-Contact, or the other commands that work with these objects and update an attribute, Exchange checks for policy and updates email addresses to comply with policy.

Figure 3.48

Creating a new email address policy

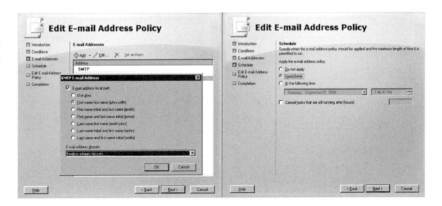

Apart from deciding what objects the policy applies to, the most important part of an email address policy is the format of the email address that the policy will generate for the objects. As you can see in Figure 3.48, Exchange supports a number of different formats for SMTP addresses. The most common format used by large organizations is "first name.last name," so that's the format selected here. Note that the email domain that you specify here must be in the list of accepted domains defined under the Hub Transport node under the Organization Configuration in EMC.

You can apply the new policy immediately as the last step in the wizard or schedule the update to occur at some point in the future (Figure 3.49). If you opt to update immediately, the wizard will cycle through every object covered by the scope of the policy and update the primary SMTP address for each object. The advantage is that the policy is enacted immediately; the disadvantage is that you could have to wait a long time for the wizard to finish. Some simple tests revealed that Exchange processes between 25 and 35 objects per minute, so applying a policy to 5,000 mailboxes might take between 142 and 200 minutes to complete! Your mileage will vary.

It is also possible to create, amend, and apply email address policies through the shell. You can invoke the Update-AddressList shell command if you want to update a set of users (identified by a known address list). To find out what email address policies exist within the organization, the format of email addresses they generate, and their priority, use the command:

```
Get-AddressList | Select Name, EnabledEmailAddressTemplates,
Priority
```

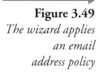

Figure 3.49
*The wizard applies
an email
address policy*

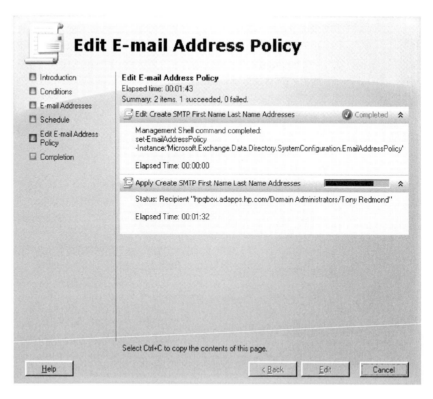

If conflicts arise when the email address policy is applied to existing objects or as new objects are created because the policy results in duplicate email addresses, Exchange resolves the conflicts by adding a number starting at 2 to the address and continues to do this until it generates a unique email address. For example, if you have three users named John Smith, the email addresses generated by Exchange under a first name.last name@xyz.com policy will be:

```
John.Smith@xyz.com
John.Smith2@xyz.com
John.Smith3@xyz.com
```

Mail-enabled objects can have several email addresses and several email addresses of the same type. Figure 3.50 shows a mailbox with three SMTP addresses and one X.400 address. The bolded SMTP address is the default reply address that Exchange uses to identify the user in outgoing messages. The checkbox "Automatically updated email addresses based on recipient policy" allows you to control whether or not Exchange applies its email address policies to an object. If you clear this checkbox, you take full responsibility for the format and content of the email addresses given to the object. If the checkbox is set, Exchange automatically validates any email addresses that you add or update to ensure that policies are respected. Exchange also validates that email addresses are unique in the organization to ensure that a condition never occurs when objects share email addresses. The ability to state that the email addresses for an object are not under the control of a policy is a change in behavior as performing a rebuild of email addresses with the RUS in previous versions of Exchange processed all objects, whether or not you wanted the RUS to do anything with those objects.

Figure 3.50
Email addresses for a mailbox

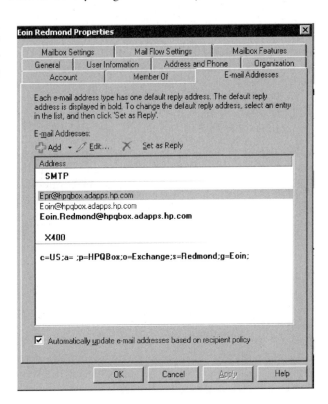

There are situations where companies will provision and update mailboxes as part of automated HR processes that control all of the steps necessary to bring a new employee on board and may not want to use email address policies. In other cases, companies may want to use an email address format that isn't included in the wizard and will write their own code to stamp the mailboxes for new users with email addresses in the desired format. These procedures should also make sure that the EmailAddressPolicyEnabled property of the mailbox is set to False. As we will see in Chapter 4, setting a property for a mailbox requires a one-line PowerShell command:

```
Set-Mailbox —id 'James Bond'
—EmailAddressPolicyEnabled:$False
```

It's hard to satisfy everyone, but the basic email address policies provided by Exchange do enough to satisfy the needs of 90% or more of deployments.

3.10.1 Mailbox moves and email address policies

One interesting side-effect of moving mailboxes from an Exchange 2003 server to Exchange 2007 is that the mailboxes will be processed by an email address policy. Given the somewhat erratic way that Exchange 2003 applies recipient policies, it is entirely possible that you move some mailboxes that have not had policies applied to them. Exchange 2007 offers far less latitude (or loopholes) about how email address policies are applied so when the mailboxes are moved they may be stamped with a new email address to comply with policy and perhaps even a new primary SMTP address, which could cause confusion for users.

To avoid the problem, you can use the AD Users and Computers console on the Exchange 2003 server to amend the mailbox properties so that policies are not applied or you can run a shell command to do the same thing as explained in the last section. Even better, if you know that you are moving a group of mailboxes and you can identify them (all in a CSV file, all mailboxes from a server or database, everyone in a distribution group), then a piped command such as the one shown below will work:

```
Get-Mailbox —Database 'VIP Mailboxes'  |  Set-Mailbox
EmailAddressPolicyEnabled:$False
```

After the mailboxes move to Exchange 2007, you can decide whether or not to reenable email address policies for them or leave them alone.

3.10.2 Queries that drive email address policies

Behind the scenes, each email address policy has a recipient filter that allows Exchange to determine what objects are under the control of the policy. For example, the default email address policy has a very broad recipient filter because it has to apply to any object that Exchange can apply no other email address policy to. The recipient filter for the default email address policy is very simple as the filter catches everything. You can see details of the policy with the Get-EmailAddressPolicy command:

```
Get-EmailAddressPolicy —id 'Default Policy' | Select Name,
*Filter*, *Exch*


Name                            : Default Policy
RecipientFilter                 :
LdapRecipientFilter             : (mailnickname=*)
LastUpdatedRecipientFilter      :
RecipientFilterApplied          : False
RecipientFilterType             : Legacy
ExchangeVersion                 : 0.0 (6.5.6500.0)
```

The interesting thing about this output, which you will see if you look at the default policy in an Exchange organization that contains legacy servers, is that:

- The default email address policy does not include a recipient filter. As we learned earlier on in this chapter, Exchange 2007 uses OPATH syntax recipient filters instead of the LDAP filters used by Exchange 2003. Because this organization contains legacy servers, the LDAP filter remains in place and will be translated into OPATH on the fly by Exchange 2007 mailbox servers when they need to apply it to new objects. We can also see that the RecipientFilterType is "Legacy" and that the ExchangeVersion property specifies 6.5, which indicates that the object can be worked with by legacy servers.

- The LDAP recipient filter (mailnickname=*) is exactly what you'd expect to find for every object in the organization, so it applies to every object if Exchange has not been able to apply a previous policy.

If you attempt to edit this email address policy, EMC signals an error as shown in Figure 3.51. This does not mean that you have to take immediate action to upgrade or otherwise change the policy because it is quite valid to retain the policy in its current form until you decide that you want to use the Set-EmailAddressPolicy command to upgrade the policy, perhaps after you have removed the last legacy Exchange server from the organization. Use this command to perform the upgrade:

```
Set-EmailAddressPolicy —id 'Default Policy' —
IncludedRecipients AllRecipients
```

Exchange will prompt you to confirm that you want the upgrade to occur. If you agree, Exchange will rewrite the email address policy and

Figure 3.51

EMC detects a
legacy email
address policy

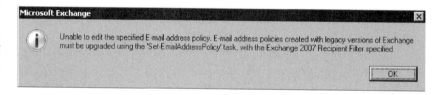

Figure 3.51

EMC detects a
legacy email
address policy

upgrade its version and the RecipientFilter. You can suppress the question by
including the –ForceUpgrade parameter, which is provided to allow you to
upgrade email address policies in a script, however, it does nothing to automatically write new recipient filters and you have to provide that information
yourself. Do not worry about upgrading the default email address policy even
if you still have some legacy Exchange servers. The fact that Exchange maintains an LDAP filter within the email address policy allows the Recipient
Update Service to continue to stamp email addresses for new objects created
on the legacy servers. However, because of the upgrade, you will not be able
to edit the default email address policy using ESM.

On the other hand, rewriting the default email address policy in this
way will not allow you to edit the recipient filter through EMC either
because you have programmatically set the filter conditions. If you need to
adjust the recipient filter in future, you will have to do it with the Set-
EmailAddressPolicy command. This should not be a problem because
most organizations never change their default email address policy after it
is first set.

You can check for email address policies that are still in legacy status
with the following command:

```
Get-EmailAddressPolicy | Where {$_.ExchangeVersion –Like
'*6.5*'} | Select Name, *Filter*
```

If you look at an email address policy that EMC created, you see some
differences in the filters:

```
Get-EmailAddressPolicy –id 'Legal Department Members' |
Select Name, *Filter*, *Exch*
```

```
Name                        : Legal Department Members
RecipientFilter             : (RecipientType -eq 'MailboxUser'
-and (Department -eq 'Legal' -or Department -eq 'Law'))
LdapRecipientFilter         :
(&(objectCategory=person)(objectClass=user)(mailNickname=*)(m
sExchHomeServerName=*)(|(department=Legal)(department=Law)))
RecipientFilterApplied      : False
```

```
RecipientFilterType      : Precanned
ExchangeVersion          : 0.1 (8.0.535.0)
```

Remember that the OPATH syntax used by email address policies is the same as that used by dynamic distribution groups and the other Exchange objects that use recipient filters, so the form taken by the recipient filter should be familiar. Looking at the details of the email address policy that we created through EMC, we see that:

- The email address policy contains a recipient filter in both OPATH and LDAP format. The two filters generate the same result when applied to find users. However, we are still functioning in an organization that contains legacy servers, so the Recipient Update Service will continue to use the LDAP filter.

- Exchange has upgraded the ExchangeVersion property to 8.0 to indicate that we can manage the policy with EMC.

- The recipient filter is "Precanned," meaning that it has been generated by setting conditions through the wizard that EMC calls to allow you to define what objects are covered by a policy. Figure 3.52 shows the wizard editing the email address policy to set the conditions that eventually result in the recipient filter shown above.

If you need to apply a very complex filter for an email address policy that the wizard does not support, you can create the policy with the New-EmailAddressPolicy shell command and specify the recipient filter that you need. In this situation, the syntax rules that apply are the same as those used to specify recipient filters for dynamic distribution groups. See the section on using the shell to manipulate dynamic distribution groups in Chapter 4 for more information. As an example, let's assume that you want to create an email address policy that only applies to mailbox users in the Dublin office. You could use this command:

```
New-EmailAddressPolicy —Name 'Users in Dublin'
—RecipientFilter {Office —eq 'Dublin' —and
RecipientTypeDetails —eq 'UserMailbox'}
—EnabledPrimarySMTPAddressTemplate 'SMTP:@dublin.xyz.com'
```

This command creates an email address policy with a custom recipient filter, so you will not be able to edit the policy through EMC afterwards. Therefore, if you need to update the recipient filter subsequently, you will have to do it by writing a new recipient filter with the Set-EmailAddress-Policy command. If we examine the details of the email address policy cre-

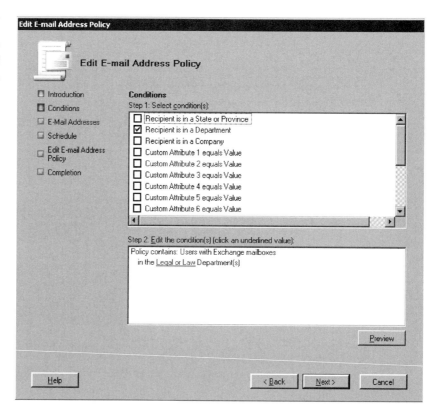

Figure 3.52
Setting a query for an email address policy

ated with the above command, we see the output shown below. Note that Exchange has generated the appropriate LDAP filter and that the Recipient-FilterType is now "Custom."

```
Name                     : Users in Dublin
RecipientFilter          : (Office -eq 'Dublin' -and RecipientTypeDetails -eq
'UserMailbox')
LdapRecipientFilter      :
(&(physicalDeliveryOfficeName=Dublin)(objectClass=user)(objectCategory=person)(ma
ilNickname=*)(msExchHomeServerName=*)(msExchRecipientTypeDetails=1))
RecipientFilterApplied   : False
RecipientFilterType      : Custom
ExchangeVersion          : 0.1 (8.0.535.0)
```

3.11 Address lists

Exchange uses address lists to segment the set of available addressees within an organization into different types of useful lists such as All Users, All Contacts, Public Folders, and the Global Address List itself. All of these lists are available in Exchange 2003. Exchange 2007 adds the All Rooms Address List to allow users to access a list of available room mailboxes. You work with Address Lists through the Mailbox section of the Organization Configuration node in EMC (Figure 3.53). Each Address List has a recipient filter that establishes the objects included in the list. You can create new Address Lists by providing Exchange with the necessary recipient filter to build the list.

Figure 3.53
Address Lists

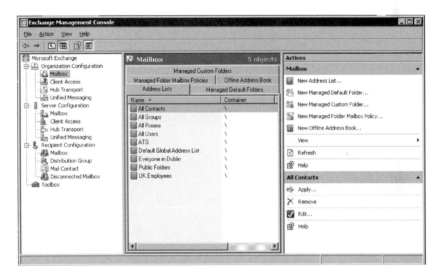

Conceptually, an Address List is similar to a dynamic distribution group in that Exchange uses a recipient filter to locate all of the objects to form the Address List. Whereas a dynamic distribution group is transient and its membership only exists when Exchange expands the group to add the recipients to a message addressed to the group, Address Lists are more persistent as users can access them through a client. Figure 3.54 shows how Outlook presents the set of available Address Lists.

You can see the same information through the Exchange Management Shell with the Get-AddressList command:

Figure 3.54
*Address lists as
shown through
Outlook*

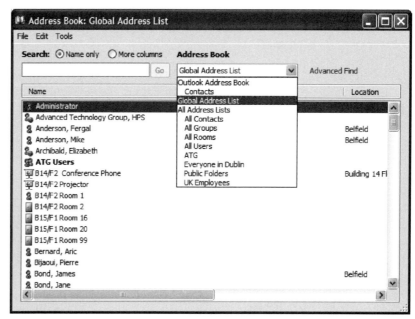

```
Get-AddressList | Select Name, RecipientFilter
```

Name	RecipientFilter
All Rooms	
All Users	
Everyone in Dublin	(RecipientType -eq 'MailboxUser' -and StateOrProvince -eq 'Dublin')
All Groups	
All Contacts	
Public Folders	
UK Employees	(((Alias -ne $null -and (Company -eq 'Hewlett Packard' -or Company...
ATG	(RecipientType -eq 'MailboxUser' -and Department -eq 'ATG')

As you can see, some of these Address Lists have custom recipient filters. The standard Address Lists provided by Exchange use precanned recipient filters. We can see this by examining the properties of one of the lists:

```
Get-AddressList —id 'All Users' | Select Name, *Filt*, *Exch*
```

Name   : **All Users**

RecipientFilter   :

LdapRecipientFilter   : **(& (mailnickname=*) (|**
(&(objectCategory=person)(objectClass=user)(!(homeMDB=*))(!(msExchHomeServerN
ame=*)))(&

(objectCategory=person)(objectClass=user)(|(homeMDB=*)(msExchHomeServerName=*
)))))

LastUpdatedRecipientFilter :

RecipientFilterType   : **Legacy**

ExchangeVersion   : **0.0 (6.5.6500.0)**

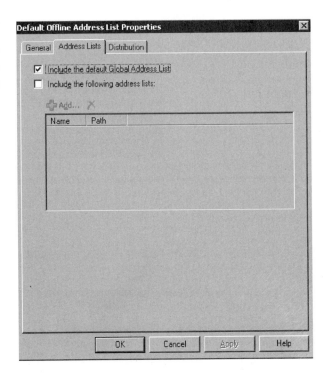

Figure 3.55
Properties of the
Default Offline
Address List

Just like Email Address Policies, we can see that this Address List is managed by a legacy Exchange server and that the filter is provided in LDAP format. We will examine how to upgrade these Address Lists later on in this section.

To create a new Address List, go to the Mailbox section under the Configuration node in EMC and click on the New Address List option. Creating a new Address List is very similar to creating a dynamic distribution group in that you specify the types of recipients that you want to include in the list and then the filter that Exchange will use to build the list. You also specify the schedule that Exchange uses to build the list. Figure 3.56 shows the first two steps in the wizard used to create a new Address List. Note the Preview option on the right-hand screen that allows you to verify that the filter you create selects the right objects to include in the list.

Companies that provide a hosted Exchange service to other companies often use customized Address Lists to create customized Offline Address Books. In this case, if we examine the Address List that we have just created, we will see some differences between it and the standard Address Lists.

```
Get-AddressList –id 'Everyone in Dublin' | Select Name, *Fil*, *Exch*
```

```
Name                          : Everyone in Dublin
RecipientFilter               : (RecipientType -eq 'MailboxUser' -and
StateOrProvince -eq 'Dublin')
LdapRecipientFilter           :
(&(objectCategory=person)(objectClass=user)(mailNickname=*)(msExchHomeServerN
ame=*)(st=Dublin))
RecipientFilterType           : Precanned
ExchangeVersion               : 0.1 (8.0.535.0)
```

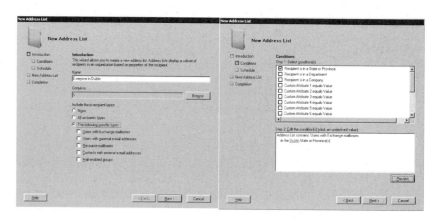

Figure 3.56
Creating a new
Address List

Note that the version number has increased to 8.0, meaning that you cannot manage this Address List in Exchange 2003. The recipient filter is in both OPATH and LDAP syntax and because it is a precanned filter, we know that we can manage it through EMC.

3.11.1 Upgrading Address Lists to Exchange 2007 format

As with Email Address Policies, the Address Lists created by a legacy Exchange organization will function quite happily under Exchange 2007. If you want to upgrade them to Exchange 2007 format, you take roughly the same approach as to upgrade Email Address Policies by using the `Set-AddressList` command to update the Address List with a new recipient filter. For example:

```
Set-AddressList —id 'All Users' —IncludedRecipients
MailboxUsers -ForceUpgrade
```

If you don't supply the —ForceUpgrade parameter, you'll be prompted to go ahead with the upgrade. After the upgrade, you can examine the properties of the Address List to see what happened. We'll see that a recipient filter in OPATH format exists, the older LDAP format is also available to support Exchange 2003 servers, and the Exchange version has been upgraded. Once again, because we have upgraded the Address List through the shell, we can only change the recipient filter in the future with `Set-AddressList`.

```
Get-AddressList —id 'All Users' | Select Name, *Filt*, *Exch*

Name                        : All Users
RecipientFilter             : RecipientType -eq 'UserMailbox'
LdapRecipientFilter         :
(&(objectClass=user)(objectCategory=person)(mailNickname=*)(m
sExchHomeServerName=*))
RecipientFilterType         : Precanned
ExchangeVersion             : 0.1 (8.0.535.0)
```

There are two Address Lists that you have to take special care with when you upgrade them from their legacy versions: Public Folders and the Default Global Address List. No precanned filter exists for mail-enabled public folders, so you have to specify the filter:

```
Set-AddressList —id 'Public Folders' —RecipientFilter
{RecipientType —eq 'PublicFolder'}
```

The Default Global Address List is a little more complex, as we see when we examine its properties with the `Get-GlobalAddressList` command, and we see the following:

```
Get-GlobalAddressList | Select Name, *Filter*, *Exch*
```

Name   : **Default Global Address List**

RecipientFilter   :

LdapRecipientFilter   : **(& (mailnickname=*) (|**
(&(objectCategory=person)(objectClass=user)(!(homeMDB=*))(!(msExchHomeServerN
ame=*)))(&
(objectCategory=person)(objectClass=user)(|(homeMDB=*)(msExchHomeServerName=*
)))(&(objectCategory=person)(objectClass=contact))(objectCategory=group)(obje
ctCategory=publicFolder)(objectCategory=msExchDynamicDistributionList)))

RecipientFilterType   : **Legacy**

ExchangeVersion   : **0.0 (6.5.6500.0)**

The syntax for the LDAP recipient filter looks complicated because it includes all the different recipient types that are included in the GAL. To upgrade the Default Global Address List, we have to use the following command to specify the new recipient filter in OPATH format:

```
Set-GlobalAddressList -id 'Default Global Address List'
-RecipientFilter { (Alias -ne $null -and (ObjectClass -eq
'User' -or ObjectClass -eq 'contact' -or ObjectClass -eq
'msExchDynamicDistributionList' -or ObjectClass -eq
'Group' -or ObjectClass -eq 'PublicFolder' ))}
```

You may have custom Address Lists that you created with Exchange 2003. The process that you take to upgrade custom Address Lists to Exchange 2007 format is exactly that described above. You have to determine what the recipient filter is in OPATH format and then use the `Set-Address-List` command to add the new recipient filter to the object. To help you figure out the correct syntax for OPATH recipient filters, Microsoft has published a PowerShell script on the Exchange team's blog. You can use this script to convert an LDAP filter to OPATH format.

3.12 **User naming conventions**

Email Address policies allow you to define and apply different patterns for SMTP addresses, however, Exchange 2007 does not allow you to define policies to control the generation of display names. The default pattern for display names is %g %s—in other words, first name <space> last name, or "Tony Redmond." This is an acceptable naming convention for small implementations where everyone knows each other and it is easy to find the correct recipient by browsing the GAL, but problems arise as the number of directory entries increases. Even though they have a very large GAL, Microsoft actually uses this naming convention, but I suspect that this is more to do with tradition than design.

On balance, more variation within any messaging community occurs in surnames rather than given names. Users are accustomed to browse through telephone directories by surname, so it makes sense to organize the GAL by surname. Think of a common given name, like "John" or "Mary," and imagine how many times they occur in a large GAL. If the GAL is sorted by given name, you might have to look through several hundred entries before you locate the right recipient. It is easier to search using a surname, even with common surnames, like "Smith," "Chan," or "Ng."

Exchange builds the GAL from Active Directory data. Because Exchange 2000 and 2003 use the AD Users and Computers console to create user objects, the DisplayName attribute dictates the way that display names are generated when new objects are created and therefore dictates the sort order for the GAL. In these versions, it was common practice to change the pattern that Active Directory uses to create display names by altering the properties of the User-Display attribute of the "Display Specifier" object in the configuration naming context with the ADSIEDIT utility and change the pattern to %<sn>, %<givenname> as this then forces Active Directory to create new display names in Surname, First Name format, which then generates the GAL in the desired format. The same trick is possible for contacts and if you make a change for user objects, you should make the same change for contacts in order to maintain consistency in the GAL. Groups are normally left alone because you don't normally assign surnames to groups.

The problem that we encounter with the naming of user objects when we upgrade to Exchange 2007 is that EMC now has full control over the creation of mailbox objects. Therefore, the changes that you make to Active Directory to effect how the Active Directory creates display names for new objects don't apply and are ignored by EMC.

A further complication for organizations that run Exchange in multiple languages arises because the Exchange 2007 EMC includes logic to respect locales so that name-related edit boxes are reordered to reflect language-specific naming conventions. EMC supports the following languages:

- Chinese (Simplified)
- Chinese (Traditional)
- English
- French
- German
- Italian

- Japanese

- Korean

- Portuguese

- Russian

- Spanish

The language that you run EMC in determines the fields that are exposed when you create new objects and the order that the fields are used. For example, EMC doesn't display the initials field in the French version. If you create Chinese users, the boxes are presented by EMC in surname, initials, and first name order, which is exactly what some organizations who run everything in English would like to use. However, you can't force this order to occur for other locales as the ordering is hard-coded in EMC. Thus, if you want to apply a different naming convention, you can either:

- Allow EMC to create the mailboxes and contacts as normal and then edit the Display Name.

- Create mailboxes and contacts using shell scripts so that you have complete control over the format used for display names.

Changing the display name pattern only effects the display name for objects created after you make the change, so in either case, you may have existing mailboxes and contacts that do not have display names that comply with your desired naming convention. Here is a simple script that can do the job of changing the display names for mailboxes and mail-enabled contacts objects to the last name, first name standard:

```
$Users = Get-User -Filter {RecipientTypeDetails -eq 'UserMailbox' or
RecipientTypeDetails -eq 'LegacyMailbox'}
ForEach-Object ($U in $Users)
{
   $Mailbox = $U.Name
      $DN = $U.LastName + ", " + $U.FirstName
   Write-Host "Setting display name for mailbox " $DN
   Set-User $Mailbox -DisplayName $DN
   $DN = $Null


}
$Contacts = Get-Contact -Filter {RecipientTypeDetails -eq 'MailContact'}
```

```
ForEach-Object ($C in $Contacts)
{
   $Contact = $C.Name
         $DN = $C.LastName + ", " + $C.FirstName
   Write-Host "Setting display name for contact " $DN
   Set-Contact $Contact -DisplayName $DN
   $DN = $Null

}
```

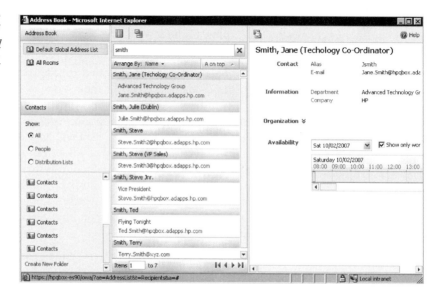

Figure 3.57
A well-ordered GAL

Apart from groups, you may also want to leave resource and equipment mailboxes unchanged, again because they don't have surnames. There may be other circumstances where you have mailboxes that you don't want to use the last name, first name convention, such as those used for journaling, but these can be dealt with on an exception basis. Figure 3.57 shows an example of a GAL with a mixture of users and groups where the mailboxes and contacts use the last name, first name convention and the groups use the default.

Of course, at any time, you can change the display name for objects to make them consistent or indeed to input any value you like to help users identify the correct user. For example, you could include a department name, location, job title, or other identifier to help resolve users that share the same name. Thus:

```
Smith, John (Glasgow)
Smith, John (Security Department)
Smith, John (VP, Technology)
```

3.13 Server naming conventions

Is it important to have a naming convention for all the servers in your infrastructure or for both servers and workstations? The answer depends on the number of servers in the infrastructure. If you only have a small number of servers, you probably know each server intimately and you will be able to recognize the location of the server and its relative importance to the infrastructure if a problem arises. In these cases, you can afford to deploy whimsical names such as calling all the servers after characters in Star Trek, Lord of the Rings, or whatever your favorite film happens to be.

However, things are more complicated in large, distributed infrastructures that span hundreds of servers. In these cases, you need some help to locate a server if your beeper goes off to notify you that your monitoring service has identified a problem with a specific system. For example, if the beeper says "problem with SERVER27," you will have to rack your brains to figure out where SERVER27 is physically located and what it does. If SERVER27 is a backup server for a production system, maybe you do not have to rush to fix the problem, but if it hosts Exchange for senior management, you probably have a different response. Being able to find servers quickly when things go wrong is the best and most practical reason to use a naming convention.

The next step is to decide what kind of naming convention to use. Here are some:

- Office or location codes: If you work in a company that has many offices, you may be able to use office or location codes to identify where servers are located. For example, one company that I worked in used location codes such as "ZKO," "MRO," "REO," "DBO," and so on. If several buildings exist in a location, you can add a number to identify the exact building, giving values such as "REO1," "DBO2," etc. The problem with office or location codes is if your company closes down an office and you relocate servers elsewhere.

- Geographic names: The best thing about geographic names like "London", "Paris", and "New York" is that they are highly unlikely to change before you need to replace a server. For this reason, many companies use three or four-character abbreviations of geographic names as the base of their naming convention, resulting in values such as "LON", "PAR", and "NYC." Again, you can combine these values with an indicator of what building the server is located in to make the name more effective.

- Function indicator: Knowing where a problem server is valuable, but knowing its function is even more valuable. Many companies use values such as those listed below to indicate how important the server is to the infrastructure.

  - EXMBX—Exchange mailbox server
  - EXCAS—Exchange Client Access Server
  - EXBHS—Exchange bridgehead server (Exchange 2003)
  - EXHUB—Exchange Hub transport server
  - EXPFS—Exchange public folder server (Exchange 2003)
  - EXCH—Exchange multiple role server
  - EXEDGE—Exchange Edge server
  - GC—Global Catalog Server
  - DC—Domain Controller
  - DHCP—DHCP server
  - WS—individual workstation

- Identifier: You may have more than one server of a specific type in a location, so you need to allocate a value to create a unique identifier. Some companies number their servers, while others assign values that provide more information about the server. For example, they might use "CL1" to indicate the first node in a cluster, or "PL380-4" to indicate that the server is a 4-way ProLiant 380. Going to this degree of specificity is somewhat excessive and the simple numbering scheme is usually sufficient.

Putting everything together, you have a naming convention that names servers like this:

```
NYC1-EXMBX1
```

Meaning that this server is located in building 1 in New York City and is the first Exchange server in the office. Note that hyphens in server names are not a problem for Windows infrastructures but they can pose an issue for legacy environments. Other administrators think that it is a good idea to include an indication of the user community that Exchange servers support, so they add suffixes such as "-VIP" (VIP mailboxes), "-FIN" (Financial Department mailboxes), and so on, meaning that you might decide to have a naming convention that named servers like:

```
NYC-EXMBX-FIN1
```

On a cautionary note, before you include the server's role in your naming convention, make sure that your security team is happy for this to happen as some security teams believe that adding information like this makes certain servers more of a target for attack. Security teams also dislike location indicators in server names, as they hate to expose any data to potential attack. However, it is fair to say that security teams are paranoid due to the very nature of their business and that they would prefer you to give servers names like:

```
AAAZZZ-ZXYY-003-AAZ
```

In fact, if Windows would allow you to include some special characters in server names, the security team would want you to take advantage of that feature too. As always, the important thing is to achieve a balance in your naming convention between utility, ease of management, and security. It is wise not to be too hung up on if servers do not follow the naming convention precisely as few organizations manage to achieve 100% compliance.

Some administrators approach the question of server naming with the attitude that it is not important what name you start with because it is possible to rename servers. This is true, but in practice, most administrators do not want to do the work that is involved to rename a server and leave servers with their original names until the servers gently degrade over time and eventually leave the infrastructure when they become obsolete. For this reason, it is best to select a naming convention that is most resilient to change while meeting whatever restrictions others in the organization (such as your auditors or IT security) place upon you.

3.14 Moving from the basics

The Exchange 2007 management console is an easy tool to work with. The changes that the Exchange developers have made may confuse at first sight, but rapidly become familiar. With a solid grasp of the basics of how to approach the management of Exchange 2007 servers, it is time to move onto something more complex. We met some aspects of PowerShell when we discussed recipient filters and the wonders of OPATH when used with dynamic distribution groups, Email Address Policies, and Address Lists. It is now time to move into PowerShell in some detail because you cannot spend all your time working through the management console if you expect to manage an Exchange 2007 organization effectively.

4

The Exchange Management Shell

The original Exchange administration program, ADMIN.EXE, did a good job of managing small groups of servers (a site), but Microsoft did not design the ADMIN program for the enterprise, so it faltered in large deployments because it struggled to deal with large numbers of servers or a very distributed environment. ADMIN did not support a generally available API, so what you got with ADMIN was what you used. Things improved somewhat in Exchange 2000 with the introduction of the Exchange System Manager (ESM), based on the MMC (Microsoft Management Console) framework. ESM uses many different APIs such as CDOEXM and WMI (Windows Management Instrumentation), but while ISVs could build their own snap-ins for MMC, the average Exchange administrator still could not customize ESM. You still had to acquire a lot of knowledge about programming interfaces and languages before you could attempt to automate even the simplest task. For example, managing public folders has always been a nightmare for Exchange because there was no way to roll your own administrative utilities when the product failed to deliver.

The split between Active Directory management, which is where you create user accounts, groups, and so on, and Exchange management, where you deal with the details of mailboxes, stores, and the configuration of the organization, further complicates matters. Because of the reliance that Exchange had on IIS, another set of inconsistencies existed in the split of management of web protocols between ESM and IIS. As Microsoft approached the issue in the Exchange 2007 design cycle, what seemed to be missing was a single way of managing the entire set of objects that live inside an Exchange ecosystem, preferably something that functioned in an open and extensible manner.

Microsoft's response that we see Exchange 2007 is to provide broad and deep support for PowerShell (previously called Monad[1]) that works alongside

---

1. The name Monad comes from The Monadologya book by Gottfried Wilhelm Leibniz, one of the inventors of Calculus. The idea describes components that could be combined to solve complex problems, which is what the PowerShell developers set out to do—provide commands that can be combined in scripts and programs to get work done.

the new Exchange Management Console to deliver a new administrative framework. PowerShell is a new Windows shell that supports a powerful scripting language that allows administrators to build their own tools to manage Exchange and other Windows components.

PowerShell supports many different system objects on the Windows platform, including COM objects, WMI objects, and .NET objects. Access to these objects, plus the ability to extend over time to other objects such as those now supported for Exchange, give administrators the ability to automate administrative tasks in the same way as has long been common for other enterprise-class operating systems. Administrators of operating systems such as OpenVMS and UNIX have been able to write scripts to automate operational procedures for years, and some pretty complicated applications have been written completely in scripts. You can argue that the provision of a comprehensive scripting language is a sign of growing maturity in the ability of Windows to satisfy the demands of enterprise computing, or you might regard PowerShell as Microsoft's acknowledgment that it is impossible to cover all administrative options for an operating system through a GUI. There is no way that a developer sitting in Redmond, even though Microsoft has some very gifted people, can determine every single option that customers will want to perform to manage servers, so providing a way to allow customers to build their own management tools allows Microsoft to provide a much more complete management framework. This aspect is especially visible in Exchange, where the product has been handicapped by the inability of administrators to do anything but the options provided by the GUI since the product first shipped. A few registry hacks and some command line tools do not provide a way to automate common management operations, but a powerful scripting language certainly does.

To achieve the goal of being able to automate administrative tasks, PowerShell provides a single consistent scripting interface to Windows and applications. This step eliminates the need for a mass of competing and confusing interfaces from ADSI and WMI for Windows to CDOEXM and WebDAV for Exchange. Another goal behind the introduction of PowerShell was to create a programmable scripting language for Windows that delivers similar capabilities to languages such as Perl and Python on other platforms. We are only at the beginning of the PowerShell era and it will take time for applications to expose their objects (through COM, .NET, or WMI) that administrators can work with every application that they need through PowerShell, but a good start has been made.

The promise is that you should only have to learn PowerShell syntax and structure once to be able to use it across the complete range of applications that support PowerShell. In fact, you only have to use PowerShell to the level that makes sense to you. It is possible that some administrators will never use PowerShell, perhaps because they can do everything that they need or want to do through EMC. If your server only supports 20 or 30 mailboxes, you may never need to go into PowerShell mode. Perhaps you will not be able to because the server that you manage has been locked down to meet security requirements. Another set of administrators will be happy to write one-line commands all the time or maybe build some quick and dirty scripts by recording the commands that they have used to save them from having to figure out the necessary syntax and commands again. Others will have the time to investigate the language to a deeper level and end up by developing complex scripts to automate administrative operations. These scripts may be complete with error handling and support parameters so that the scripts can deal with a range of situations. These scripts may end up becoming part of the formal operations framework used to manage production servers and be treated in the same way that any mission-critical piece of code should be. A few will go into the depths of .NET programming and extend PowerShell with new commands. You can compare the different styles of PowerShell usage to other shells—one-liners like bash, scripting like Perl, and programming like any of the .NET languages. The great advantage of being able to employ PowerShell in many different ways is that you can begin with a small knowledge base and gradually evolve over time as your experience of using the language increases to a point where you can take on new challenges. No knowledge is wasted and everything contributes to improvement. Another point is that it's easy to share PowerShell one-line commands and scripts on web sites and blogs, so people can gain from the overall knowledge of the network community rather than having to do everything themselves.

At the end of the day, PowerShell is just a tool and even the most experienced PowerShell users will use one-line commands because it is often the best way to get things done. Microsoft refers to the range of usage from one-line scripts to compiled code as the Admin Development Model; not because it's limited to system administrators in any way, but because the activities that PowerShell helps with are critical to administrators. Of course, you only have to go near PowerShell if the standard tools do not do what you want them to, and many Exchange 2007 administrators will continue to use the new EMC for all their administrative duties. However, as discussed earlier in this chapter, some options that appear in previous versions of the Exchange management console are not supported in the Exchange 2007 GUI (like configuring transport settings or exporting the contents of mailboxes), so you will end up in PowerShell, even if you don't want to at first.

4.1   EMS: Exchange's management shell

On an Exchange 2007 server, the following components contribute to form the basic management infrastructure that you can exploit through scripts and programs or execute interactive commands through a command line interface:

- PowerShell and PS, the PowerShell runtime engine.

- Other components that call PowerShell cmdlets, such as the Exchange 2007 Exchange Management Console.

- The script and command parser, which processes language constructs such as scripts and predicates.

- The Extended Type System (ETS), which provides a standardized view of objects through an interface that allows users to work with properties and methods of cmdlets, no matter what differences exist in their underlying data structures or without knowledge of the underlying data structure. For example, a script can use information extracted from the file system or the system registry and combine it with information retrieved from Exchange. Good examples of ETS in action are provided by the `Sort-Object` and `Group-Object` cmdlets, which are able to sort objects returned by any PowerShell command despite the vast difference in the type of object that these cmdlets might be asked to process.

- The session state manager, which manages the data sets used by cmdlets when they execute.

- Namespace providers, which provide file system like interfaces to sets of stored data such as the system registry. You can get a list of the available namespace providers with the `Get-PSProvider` command.

- Cmdlets[2], which provide the way to gain access to and operate on objects associated with applications that expose their objects to PowerShell using a supported interface such as COM. Applications like Exchange 2007 support PowerShell directly with a set of cmdlets, while other applications such as the Active Directory support PowerShell indirectly because you have to work with their objects through an intermediate interface like .NET.

The structure described above seems complex, but its value is that PowerShell commands are easy to work with once you get used to the philosophy behind the language and its syntax, even when you use PowerShell to work with data gathered from multiple sources. Writing scripts that call PowerShell commands is similar to writing command line scripts on a UNIX[3] or Linux server, or even like DCL command procedures from OpenVMS. Understanding the structure of scripts and getting to know how to use the

---

2.   Cmdlets are also called "commands," which seems like a more intuitive name for them. The two names are used interchangeably.

3.   According to Bruce Payette in Windows PowerShell in Action, the developers started with the shell grammar defined for POSIX, which is a subset of the UNIX Korn shell, and then optimized PowerShell for the Windows environment in the same way that UNIX shells are optimized for UNIX.

full power of PowerShell takes a little time, but there is no doubt that access to Exchange information is more programmable and easier than ever before, especially if you want to automate common management procedures or create batch processes.

You can expect that you will write your own scripts, borrow others that you find in blogs or elsewhere in the net, or learn about them from books. You will be able to take scripts that come along with products (like those provided with Exchange 2007) and amend them to suit your own purposes. Over time, you will build up a library of scripts that help you manage Windows and Exchange much more effectively than you have ever been able to do before, especially for Exchange.

4.1.1 Working with PowerShell commands

Cmdlets are .NET classes and not standalone executables. They are the smallest unit of execution in PowerShell. While each cmdlet has a specific purpose (such as to move a mailbox or change a property of a mailbox), you can "assemble" shell commands together to automate common management processes through scripts. The default version of PowerShell that you might run on a Windows server does not include any of the commands required to work with Exchange data as any application that wants to use PowerShell has to load its command set into the basic shell. Behind the scenes, when you start the Exchange Management Shell (EMS), PowerShell starts the core shell and then loads the set of Exchange commands through a snap-in (an assembly of commands) using the command:

```
Add-PSSnapin Microsoft.Exchange.Management.PowerShell.Admin
```

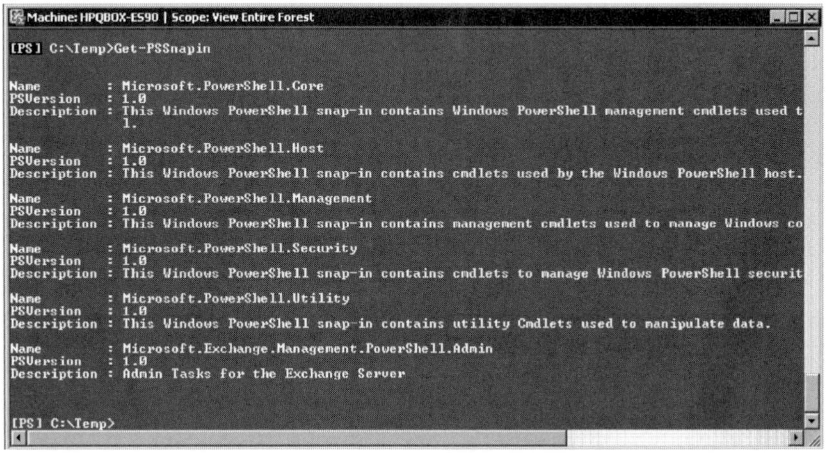

Figure 4.1

Listing the set of snap-ins loaded into PowerShell

The Get-PSSnapin command returns the list of snap-ins that PowerShell has loaded on top of the core shell. You can use the Remove-PSSnapin command to remove a snap-in from the core.

The latest version of PowerShell and some additional information is available at http://www.microsoft.com/windowsserver2003/technologies/management/powershell/default.mspx. You have to install PowerShell on a server before you can install Exchange 2007, if only because Microsoft built EMC on top of PowerShell. You can run PowerShell and EMC on Windows XP or Vista[4] workstations, so you can use these workstations to manage Exchange through the shell or the GUI, as long as you also install PowerShell and the Exchange management components on your workstation.

Figure 4.1 shows the list of PowerShell snap-ins generated by the Get-PSSnapin command on an Exchange 2007 server. You might have other snap-ins listed if you install other applications that support PowerShell, such as the Virtual Machine snap-in or those from third-party software vendors that extend the capabilities of PowerShell, such as PowerGadgets.

The Get-Process command is a good example of one of the standard set of commands available to work with Windows. This command lists all of the active processes running on a server. You can then group the output so that you know the company who generated the software that is running in the processes. For instance, here's the result of scanning the processes active on an Exchange 2007 server. You can see components from the hardware provider (HP and Compaq), anti-virus (Symantec), and base Windows (Microsoft), among others.

```
Get-Process | Group-Object Company

Count Name                   Group

----- ----                   -----

   5  Symantec Corporation       {ccApp, ccEvtMgr, ccSetMgr, DefWatch,
  11  Hewlett-Packard Company    {cissesrv, cpqnimgt, CpqRcmc, cpqteam,
   7                             {csrss, csrss, esmagent, Idle, System,
  47  Microsoft Corporation      {ctfmon, ctfmon, EdgeTransport, explorer,
   4  Apache Software Founda...  {rotatelogs, rotatelogs, rotatelogs,
   1  Compaq Computer Corpor...  {sysdown}
   1  WinZip Computing, Inc.     {WZQKPICK}
```

You can also find information about the top processes that are consuming most CPUs on a server. For example:

---

4. As pointed out in Chapter 3, Microsoft will not formally support using Vista workstations to manage Exchange until at least service pack 1 for Exchange 2007.

```
ps | Sort CPU —Descending | Select —First 15
```

The output from running this command on an Exchange 2007 server is shown in Figure 4.2 where we can see three interesting processes appear in the list. The first is the Exchange log replay service, so we know that this server runs either LCR or CCR to protect its databases. The second is the Microsoft Search service, which generates the content indexes for databases on the server. The last is the process that synchronizes Active Directory content from a hub transport server to an Edge server. Because of the presence of the second process, we know that this server is a multi-role server that supports both the mailbox and hub roles. The server must therefore be running LCR. We know this because CCR only runs on a clustered mailbox server that can't support the hub transport role, so this particular server can't synchronize with an Edge server. LCR and CCR are explored further in Chapter 9. Of course, as we'll learn when we get into the details of PowerShell syntax, you could isolate the Exchange processes that run on a server by including a filter through the Where command:

```
PS | Where {$_.ProcessName —Like '*Exchange*'} | Sort CPU -
Descending
```

Figure 4.2
Output from PS command

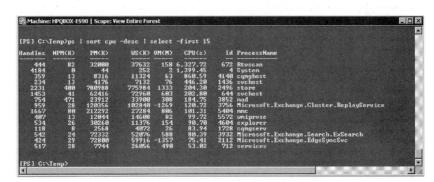

Getting into the details of how you can build filters and the properties that you can use is a stretch for now, given what we have covered for Power-Shell so far. Moving on, ps is an alias or shorthand for the Get-Process command. You can define aliases for your favorite PowerShell commands to cut down on the amount of typing you have to do or rely on the default set.[5] The Get-Alias command returns a list of all of the currently defined aliases, including the ones that PowerShell creates for you, such as ps and commands

---

5.   The O'Reilly Monad book by Andy Oakley (ISBN 0-596-10009-4) contains a nice appendix that describes basic Windows PowerShell commands and their aliases.

that you will use very often when you view Exchange data, such as `ft` for `Format-Table`. You can create a handy text file that contains all the aliases with this command:

```
Get-Alias > c:\temp\Alias.txt
```

Another example of using a PowerShell command to work with Windows is how to return the current status of the set of services that composes an Exchange server:

```
Get-Service *Exch* | Select DisplayName, Status
```

```
DisplayName                                      Status
-----------                                      ------
Microsoft Exchange Active Directory Topology     Running
Microsoft Exchange EdgeSync                       Running
Microsoft Exchange File Distribution              Running
Microsoft Exchange IMAP4                          Running
Microsoft Exchange Information Store              Running
Microsoft Exchange Mailbox Assistants            Running
Microsoft Exchange Mail Submission Service        Running
Microsoft Exchange Monitoring                     Running
Microsoft Exchange POP3                           Stopped
Microsoft Exchange Replication Service            Running
Microsoft Exchange System Attendant               Running
Microsoft Exchange Search                         Running
Microsoft Exchange Service Host                    Running
Microsoft Exchange Transport                      Running
Microsoft Exchange Transport Log Search           Running
Microsoft Search  (Exchange)                      Running
```

As we will see later on in this chapter when we discuss how to use PowerShell to test different aspects of Exchange 2007, the `Test-ServerHealth` command provides another way to discover whether all the Exchange services are running. In Chapter 2, we met an example of how PowerShell is able to query the Active Directory and how to extract a list of Global Catalog servers. Here's an example of how to retrieve information about the current Active Directory forest by loading information into a variable that you can subsequently interrogate to retrieve precise data. It is a good thing to record this information regularly so that you know exactly the exact state of the forest.

```
# Active Directory Forest
$Forest =
```

```
[System.DirectoryServices.ActiveDirectory.Forest]::GetCurrentForest()
#
# Get information on the Forest
#
$Forest.Sites                          # List of AD sites
$Forest.ForestMode                     # Forest mode
$Forest.Domains                        # List of all domains
$Forest.GlobalCatalogs                 # List all GCs
$Forest.get_Applicationpartitions()    # List all partitions
```

It's somewhat frustrating to have to work with Active Directory objects in such a clunky manner (through their .NET classes), but Microsoft is aware of the problem and may include PowerShell extensions for Active Directory in the "Longhorn" release of Windows server.

You can use PowerShell to launch applications that are associated with a particular file extension. For example, assuming that Word is installed on a system, here's how you can launch Word to edit a specified document:

```
Invoke-Item c:\Temp\Exchange.doc
```

You can even ask PowerShell to count the number of words in a Word document:

```
Type c:\temp\Exchange.doc | Measure-Object —Line -Word
```

Another interesting way to use PowerShell is when you want to interrogate the Event Log to check for a particular event. For example, here's how to look through the Application Event Log for event 701, which is generated by the Store after it finishes a background defragmentation run against a database. You can use the same technique for any event. The command shown here may seem complex initially, but you will soon get used to combining the Where command (to apply a filter on a data set), the Select command (to pick out records to work with), and the Format-List command (to format output data in a list) as you work with Exchange data.

```
Get-Eventlog Application | Where {$_.EventId  -eq 701} |
Select -First 5 | Format-List
```

We can also output the details of the event that Exchange provides so that you can see the name of the database that is processed. In this instance, we are more specific that the source of the events that we want to see is ESE (the Store database engine) rather than other parts of Exchange (like the transport engine) that generate the same event. In addition, we trim the output of the message property to remove a blank line that you'd see otherwise.

```
Get-Eventlog Application | Where { ( $_.EventId -eq 701) -and
($_.Source -eq 'ESE') } | Select -First 5 | Format-List
TimeGenerated, Username, @{ Expression= {$_.Message -replace
"`n", "" } ;  Label = "Message"}
```

4.1.2 Exchange shell commands

When we discussed the topics of Email Address Policies and Address Lists in Chapter 3, we ran into Exchange PowerShell commands because they are the only way to get some of the management tasks done for these objects in Exchange 2007. Now we'll plunge into the details of how to use the commands made available through the Exchange Management Shell to work with many of the more common objects that an administrator deals with on a daily basis.

When you install Exchange 2007 onto a server, you add over 370 commands[6] to the standard set of PowerShell commands, including commands to work with the system registry, the file system, variables (including environmental variables), and so on.

Some examples (in no particular order) of Exchange 2007 commands include:

- `Get-ExchangeServer`: Return a list of Exchange Servers in the organization.

- `Disable-Mailbox`: Disable a user's mailbox.

- `Remove-AdPermission`: remove an Active Directory permission from an account.

- `Move-Mailbox`: Move a user's mailbox from one database to another.

- `Add-DistributionGroupMember`: Add a new member to a distribution group.

- `Set-Mailbox`: Set a property of a user's mailbox.

- `Get-MailboxDatabase`: Retrieve properties of a mailbox database.

---

6.   Use the command `Get-ExCommand | measure-object -line` to find out exactly how many commands are added by Exchange. Use the command `Get-Excommand > c:\temp\ ExCommands.txt` to create a listing of all the commands.

- **Get-MailboxStatistics**: Return statistics about user mailboxes such as the total item count, quota used, etc.

- **Get-TransportConfig**: Return properties that control how the transport service processes messages.

- **Get-ExBlog**: Launches a browser to bring you to the Exchange development team's blog.

Note the consistent syntax of verb (Get, Set, Move, Remove, Disable) and noun (Mailbox, User, etc.). Along with commands that operate on objects, you find commands that help you to work with data, such as Where-Object, Sort-Object, and Group-Object and Import-CSV and Export-CSV. Where-Object, Sort-Object, and Group-Object, are commonly shortened by using their aliases of Where, Sort, and Group. You can type Help followed by a command name at any time to get help on the syntax of the command, and you can use the Get-Help command to list all the commands available to work with a specific type of Exchange object:

```
Get-Help —Role *Mailbox*
Get-Help —Component *Recipient*
```

In fact, you'll find that the Exchange developers have done a nice job to make help for the EMS commands very accessible. Apart from the default way of getting help shown above (which displays what the command does and the syntax you should use), there are other ways of looking at help:

- Use Help *mailbox* to get help about commands that work with mailboxes. The same technique works to find commands that deal with different types of objects that you'll need to work with and you'll see the actions that you can take with these objects. For example, if a Get- command exists, you can retrieve properties for the object, but if there isn't a Set- equivalent, you won't be able to set a property, so you know that this is a read-only object:
  - Help *database* - database commands
  - Help *server* - server commands
  - Help *user* - user account commands
  - Help *contact* - contact commands
  - Help *group* - distribution group commands
  - Help *public* - public folder commands
  - Help *exchange* - Exchange system commands
  - Help *transport* - transport commands

- ■ Help *connector* - connector commands
- ■ Help *rule* - transport and journal rule commands

- ■ Use the –Detailed switch to get more detailed help about a command. For example: `Get-Help Get-CasMailbox –Detailed`

- ■ Use the –Full switch to have EMS return every bit of information it knows about a command: `Get-Help Get-DistributionGroup –Full`

- ■ Use the –Examples switch to see whatever examples of a command in use EMS help includes: `Get-Help Get-MailboxServer –Examples`

- ■ Use the –Parameter switch to get information about a selected parameter for a command: `Get-Help Get-Mailbox –Parameter Server`. This switch supports wildcards, so you can do something like `Get-Help Set-Mailbox –Parameter *Quota*`

You will probably begin by using the full view of commands to get to know what each command does. After you learn more about the commands, you can move on to the default view once you become more accustomed to working with EMS. Remember that the Exchange 2007 help file contains information about all the EMS commands. The advantage of using the help file (which is always present on a server) is that you can use the help file's index and search for specific entries.

Most of the time, you'll probably work with commands by invoking EMS interactively and then typing in whatever individual commands or scripts are necessary to get something done. After you become used to working with EMS, things flow smoothly and it is easy to get work done and it is usually faster to start EMS and issue the necessary commands to change a property on a mailbox or a server than to start EMC and navigate to the right place to make the change through the GUI. Executing commands through EMS is especially valuable if you have to perform management operations across an extended network link when waiting for the GUI to display can be painful. If you have a programmatic mind, you can also call shell commands through C# code, which is how Microsoft invokes them in the EMC console and other places throughout Exchange, such as setting up servers and databases in the setup program. In the past, the different groups that contributed to Exchange had to build their own programming interfaces whereas now everyone uses PowerShell.

You'll note that shell commands focus on performing tasks rather than taking the more object-focused approach implemented in the GUI, something that reflects a desire to accommodate the needs of administrators who think about how to do things rather than how to work with objects. After all, it is only human nature to think in terms of the task of moving a mailbox to a different server rather than thinking about how to manipulate the properties of a mailbox object to reflect its new location.

Shell commands accept structured pipelined input from each other in a common manner to allow them to process data in a consistent manner, no matter what command provides the data, and there is even a command to read data in from a CSV format file (and another one to export data to a CSV file). Programmers therefore do not have to worry about reformatting data for input to specific commands, so the task of assembling different commands together into a script to do a job is much easier. Microsoft built PowerShell around the concept of objects, so its commands accept objects as input and its commands output in the form of objects that you can then pipe to other commands as input objects. Even if the output from a PowerShell command looks like plain text, what you see is one or more objects that you can manipulate in a much more powerful manner than you can ever work with text output. The implementation is really very elegant.

The pervasive nature of EMS means that administrators can access all management operations through the command shell for the first time. Previous versions of Exchange support interfaces such as CDOEXM or WMI, but no previous interface delivers the same range of functions as is now available through PowerShell. In addition, because Microsoft has implemented the GUI options presented in EMC or the Exchange setup program through one or more shell commands, you can do more with a single line of script that calls a command than you could do with twenty lines of WMI code. Another advantage gained by providing a set of task-oriented commands is that other programs can call these commands to perform work rather than writing their own code.

The availability of a powerful interface to administrative functions is also attractive to third-party software providers who traditionally have written a lot of code to integrate their products with Exchange or provided a separate management utility. If you want to integrate a product in the Exchange 2003 administrative environment, you have a range of APIs to deal with, including CDOEXM, which includes functions used for provisioning recipient and databases, and WMI, which offers functions to retrieve and report information about the infrastructure. However, the combination of CDOEXM and WMI does not deliver the functionality that exists in the Exchange 2003 version of ESM and you will have to use other interfaces, such as ADSI, if you want to access configuration information about the Exchange organization. Another issue for developers is that there was no good or approved method to integrate a new management feature into ESM. The result is that the Exchange 2003 administrative vista is not consistent because it has multiple interfaces, tool sets, and programs. PowerShell is the unifying theme for automation of administrative procedures and the base upon which third parties extend the Exchange administrative framework by combining out-of-the-box commands provided by Microsoft with their own code. This, at least, is the theory, and it will be interesting to see how quickly third-party developers move to adopt PowerShell as their interface of choice.

4.1.3 Command editing

It should already be obvious that you could do a lot of typing to enter commands into PowerShell, make the inevitable mistakes, correct, and try again. To make life a little easier, PowerShell supports the same kind of command line editing as CMD does. The different keys that you can use are described in Table 4.1.

Table 4.1 *Command editing keystrokes for PowerShell*

Keyboard Command	Effect
F7	Pops up a list of the last ten commands that you have used to allow you to select a command to reuse
Tab	Requests PowerShell to attempt to complete a command based on what you've typed
Left/Right arrows	Move the cursor left and right through the current command line
Up/Down arrows	Move up and down through the history of previous commands
Delete key	Deletes the character under the cursor
Insert key	Toggles between character insert and character overwrite mode
Backspace key	Deletes the character behind the cursor

Most of these keys are pretty basic and straightforward. The two most interesting keys are F7 and Tab. F7 pops up a list of the last ten commands that you executed (Figure 4.3) so that you can both see what you've done in the immediate past and select one of the commands to reexecute. The Up and Down arrow keys serve a similar purpose in that they navigate through the command history. At times it's more convenient to use the Up and Down arrow because you can retrieve more commands and have the chance to edit a command before executing it (F7 selects the command and executes it immediately).

Tab completion is a wonderful feature that PowerShell inherited from the Windows command shell (CMD). Tab completion means that you can partially enter a command and then hit the tab key to have PowerShell try to fill in the rest of the command. For example, type:

Figure 4.3
PowerShell F7

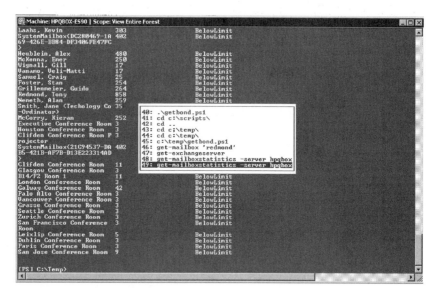

```
Get-Dist
```

This isn't a valid command, but it is the root of several commands, so when you hit tab, PowerShell completes the first valid command that matches and inserts:

```
Get-DistributionGroup
```

If you hit tab again, PowerShell moves to the next command that matches and inserts:

```
Get-DistributionGroupMember
```

If you hit tab again, PowerShell returns to Get-DistributionGroup because there are only two valid matches. However, things get even better because PowerShell supports completion for parameters as well. If we insert – to indicate a parameter value after Get-DistributionGroup and hit tab, PowerShell starts off with the first parameter and will continue through all valid parameters. If you tab too many times and pass by the parameter that you want to use, you can use SHIFT-TAB to go back through the parameter list. If we add some characters to help PowerShell identify the parameter, it attempts to complete using that value. For example:

PowerShell completes `Get-DistributionGroup —Ma` into
`Get-DistributionGroup —ManagedBy`

Even better, tab completion is context-sensitive, so it understands the structure of the object that you are navigating. For example, if you want to move through the system registry, tab completion understands the hive structure, so you can type a location in the registry and then use the tab key to move through the available choices from that point. For example, type:

```
CD HKLM:\Software\Microsoft\Exchange
```

Now press tab and PowerShell will lead you through all of the registry locations used by Exchange.

Finally, PowerShell will complete variables and even the properties of variables (such as their length) in a similar way to the way that the Microsoft Visual Studio Intelligence feature works. If you type the incomplete name of a variable and hit tab, PowerShell will attempt to complete it from the list of known variables. For example, if we fill a variable with details of a mailbox like so:

```
$Mailbox = Get-Mailbox —Id Redmond
```

And then type $Ma and hit tab, PowerShell will complete and return $Mailbox. This is a very useful feature if you forget the names of variables that you've defined. To see how properties are completed, type:

```
$Mailbox.Di
```

Hitting tab now will request PowerShell to go through the list of properties beginning with "Di." For a mailbox, the list is "DistinguishedName" and "DisplayName."

4.1.4   Getting at more information about something

Any command like `Get-EventLog` that retrieves some information about an object will output a default set of properties about the object (or references to an object). Sometimes those properties are not the exact ones that you want to examine, so you will inevitably end up using the `Format-List` and `Format-Table` commands to expand the set of properties returned by a command. For example, if you use the `Get-Mailbox` command to view the properties of a mailbox, the information returned isn't all that interesting:

```
Get-Mailbox —identity Bond
```

Name	Alias	ServerName	ProhibitSendQuota
James Bond	Bond	hpqbox-es90	unlimited

However, if you specify the `Format-List` command after the `Get-Mailbox` command, you see a lot more information (an edited version of the output follows):

```
Get-Mailbox —identity Bond | Format-List
```

```
Database                          : ExchMbxSvr1\First Storage Group\VIPMBX
DeletedItemFlags                  : DatabaseDefault
UseDatabaseRetentionDefaults      : True
RetainDeletedItemsUntilBackup     : False
DeliverToMailboxAndForward        : False
ExchangeUserAccountControl        : None
ExternalOofOptions                : External
RetainDeletedItemsFor             : 14.00:00:00
IsMailboxEnabled                  : True
OfflineAddressBook                : \VIP Users
ProhibitSendQuota                 : unlimited
ProhibitSendReceiveQuota          : unlimited
RecipientLimits                   : unlimited
UserAccountControl                : NormalAccount
IsResource                        : False
SamAccountName                    : Bond
AntispamBypassEnabled             : False
ServerLegacyDN                    : /o=XYZ/ou=Exchange Administrative Group
(FYDIBOHF23SPDLT)/cn=Configuration/cn=Servers/cn=ExchMbxSvr1
ServerName                        : ExchMbxSvr1
UseDatabaseQuotaDefaults          : True
IssueWarningQuota                 : unlimited
RulesQuota                        : 64KB
Office                            : Belfield
UserPrincipalName                 : Bond@xyz.com
UMEnabled                         : False
AddressListMembership             : {UK Employees, Default Global Address
List, All Users}
Alias                             : Bond
```

```
OrganizationalUnit                          : xyz.com/Exchange Users/Spies
DisplayName                                 : James Bond
EmailAddresses                              : {smtp:JB@xyz.com}
HiddenFromAddressListsEnabled               : False
LegacyExchangeDN                            : /o=XYZ/ou=Exchange Administrative Group
(FYDIBOHF23SPDLT)/cn=Recipients/cn=Bond
PrimarySmtpAddress                          : JB@xyz.com
RecipientType                               : UserMailbox
Name                                        : James Bond
DistinguishedName                           : CN=James Bond, OU=Exchange
Users,DC=xyz,DC=com
Identity                                    : xyz.com/Exchange Users/Spies/James Bond
```

It's easy to list every property downwards, but when you have limited screen estate across, you need to be more selective about the properties that you want to output, and that's why it's often a good idea to use the Select-Object command to select the data that you really need before you use the Format-Table command. In this case, we use the Select alias for Select-Object, just because this command is used so often and it is nice to have the chance to use shorthand.

```
Get-Mailbox —Identity Bond | Select Name, PrimarySmtpAddress, Database | Format-Table

Name                    PrimarySmtpAddress        Database
----                    ------------------        --------
James Bond              James.Bond@xyz.com        ExchMbxSvr1\First Storage Group\VIPMBX
```

Another way of extracting and then working with data is to direct the output of a command into a variable, in which case you have a complete picture of the object's properties in the variable. For example, this command loads all of the available information about the server called ExchMbxSvr1 into the $Server variable:

```
$Server = Get-ExchangeServer —id 'ExchMbxSvr1' -Status
```

We can now extract additional information about the server to use as we please by stating the name of the property that we're interested in (by the way, specifying the —Status parameter requests Get-ExchangeServer to provide some additional information about the current domain controller and Global Catalog that the server is using). For example, to get the domain that the server belongs to:

```
$Domain = $Server.Domain
$GC = $Server.CurrentGlobalCatalogs
```

You can also use a variable as an array and populate the array with a call to a command. In this example, we populate an array called $Mailboxes with a call to Get-Mailbox, using a filter to ensure that we only include actual mailboxes (and not room or equipment mailboxes). We do include legacy mailboxes (those that have not yet moved to Exchange 2007 servers such as those that use Exchange 2000 or Exchange 2003). Remove the check for legacy mailboxes to exclude these users:

```
$Mailboxes = Get-Mailbox —Filter {RecipientTypeDetails —eq
'UserMailbox' —or RecipientTypeDetails —eq 'LegacyMailbox'}
```

Once populated, you can then navigate through the array as follows:

```
$Mailboxes[0]
$Mailboxes[1]
$Mailboxes[2] etc etc etc.
```

Or reference specific properties of the objects using the "." operator.

```
$Mailbox[2].Name
$Mailbox[53].PrimarySmtpAddress
```

Some values need a little more processing before you can use them directly. For example, if you look at the PrimarySmtpAddress property of a mailbox, you see a value like this:

Length	Local	Domain	IsValidAddress
19	James.Bond	xyz.com	True

To make the property more useful, you have to convert it to a string. For example, creating a string from the value as follows:

```
$Address = $Mailbox[53].PrimarySmtpAddress.ToString()
```

Gives us something more familiar:

```
James.Bond@xyz.com
```

4.1.5   **Using common and user-defined variables**

PowerShell includes a number of variables that you will use a lot. $True and $False are variables that you can pass to shell commands and scripts to check for true and false conditions. Usually, $True is equivalent to setting a check box for an option in EMC and $False is equivalent to clearing a check box. If you prefer numeric values, you can replace $True and $False with 1 (one) and 0 (zero). Other global variables that you commonly meet as you work with PowerShell include $Null (no value), $home, which returns the user's home folder, and $pwd, which returns the current working folder. Important Exchange 2007 variables include:

- $ExBin: Points to the Exchange 2007 bin directory (usually \Program Files\Microsoft\Exchange Server\bin)

- $ExScripts: Points to the Exchange 2007 scripts directory (usually \Program Files\Microsoft\Exchange Server\Scripts)

- $ExInstall: Points to the Exchange 2007 installation directory (usually \Program Files\Microsoft\Exchange Server)

You can use these variables to access files in these directories. For example, to see a list of scripts provided by Exchange, type:

```
Dir $ExScripts
```

Checking that a value is $True or $False is a common occurrence. For positive conditions, you can shorten the check by just passing the property to check against and PowerShell will assume that you want to check whether it is true. For example, let's assume that we want to find out what mailboxes are enabled to use Outlook Web Access. We can use this command and as you can see, there is no mention of $True, but it works:

```
Get-CasMailbox | Where-Object {$_.OWAEnabled} | Select Name
```

Note the use of $_ in the last command. $_ is a very important variable because it points to the current object in the pipeline. For example, if you create a filter to look for people in a certain department because you want to update the name of the department, you might do something like this:

```
Get-User | Where-Object {$_.Department —eq 'Legal'} | Set-User
    —Department 'Law'
```

Notice that the Department property is prefixed with $_ to indicate that we want to check this property for every object that the call to the Get-User command passes through the pipeline. We actually use $_. as the prefix because it includes the "." operator to specify that we want to access a property. If we just passed $_, then the comparison would not work because PowerShell would compare "Legal" against the complete object.

User-defined variables can be integer, decimal, or string—you decide by passing a value to the variable you want to use. For example:

```
$Tony = 'Tony Redmond'
$Figure = 15.16
```

This obviously creates a string variable while the second variable holds a decimal value. Variables are case insensitive and case preserving. Using the example shown above, I can refer to $Tony as $TONY or $tony or even $ToNY and PowerShell will refer to the same variable. Variables are local unless you declare them to be global by prefixing them with Global, as in:

```
$Global:Tony = 'Tony Redmond'
```

Once a variable is global, you can reference it interactively and in scripts that you can. Be careful how you use quote marks in PowerShell because while it may appear that double and single quotes are interchangeable, there is a subtle difference that may catch you out. Single quotes represent a literal string, one that PowerShell will use exactly as you provide it. Double quotes mean that PowerShell should examine the string and resolve any variable that it finds inside through a process called variable expansion. Consider this example:

```
$n = Now
$n1 = 'Right now, it is $n'
$n1
Right now it is $n
$n2 = "Right now it is $n"
$n2
Right now, it is Tue Jan 16 17:59:54 2007
```

You see the difference a little quote mark makes? Best practice is to use single quotes whenever you are sure that you want a string variable to stay exactly as you have typed it and to use double quotes elsewhere. You cannot mix and match the different types of quotation marks to enclose a variable as

PowerShell will refuse to accept the command if you try. You will not do any great harm if you use double quotes instead of single quotes, but it is best to use single quotes as the default. Moving away from strings:

```
$Tony = 1
```

Creates an integer, and to create a decimal variable, we can do something like this:

```
$Tony = 17.55
```

You can even perform a calculation, as in $C = 17*5 or $Sum = (2*7.15)/4. By the way, do not include hyphens when you name variables, as PowerShell will interpret the hyphens as parameters. In other words, $ServerName is a good name for a variable while $Server-Name is not.

Like any good scripting language, PowerShell supports conditional checking with IF and ELSEIF that you will mostly use in scripts. It's easy to generate code that goes through a certain number of iterations with constructs such as `1..100 | ForEach-Object <command..>`. We will go through examples of these constructs as we use more sophisticated PowerShell commands in later chapters.

Another thing that catches the PowerShell novice is how to call a script. The basic rule is that if the script is in the working directory (the directory that you are currently in), then you prefix the name with ".\"

```
.\Get-All-Users.ps1
```

If you're not in the right directory, you can move to where you want to be with the **cd** command:

```
cd c:\Scripts\
```

Alternatively, you can supply the full path to where the script is located:

```
c:\Scripts\Get-All-Users.ps1
```

One of the few things that PowerShell misses is comprehensive debugging capabilities. About the only thing that you can do is to use the **Set-PSDebug** command before you run a script to step through commands. Don't get too excited because if you've been used to set debug points in programs or step backward and forward through instructions to examine the results of commands, change the value of variables, and so on, you'll be disappointed with what you can do to debug PowerShell scripts during development. In some respects, writing a PowerShell script is a matter of trial and error. See the help file for more details about the Set-PSDebug command. For now, the way that I use it as is follows:

```
Set-PSDebug –Trace 2 –Step
```

4.1.6   Identities

You may have noticed the –Identity parameter in use in some of the commands that we have reviewed. Objects like mailboxes, groups, contacts, connectors, and even Exchange servers have identities that allow you to focus in and work with on a specific object within a set of objects (think of a pointer to an item in an array). For example, if you issue the Get-ExchangeServer command, you retrieve a list of all of the Exchange servers in the organization. If you want to work with one server, you have to tell the shell what server that is by passing its identity. For example, to work with just the server named ExchMbxSvr1:

```
Get-ExchangeServer –Identity ExchMbxSvr1
```

If you want to, you can retrieve a list of objects and store them in a variable and retrieve the values as you wish. The variable holds the objects as an array. For example, to populate a variable with a set of mailboxes hosted by a server:

```
$Mbx = Get-Mailbox –Server ExchMbxSvr1
```

To retrieve the different objects in the array, pass the number of the object that you want to work with, starting from zero. For example, to fetch the first mailbox in the array:

```
$Mbx[0]
```

Being more specific, you can ask for one of the object's properties. For example, to get the identity of the first mailbox in the array:

```
$Mbx[0].Identity
```

```
Rdn                 : CN=Tony Redmond
Parent              : xyz.com/Exchange Users
Depth               : 5
DistinguishedName   : CN=Tony Redmond,OU=Exchange
Users,DC=xyz,DC=com
DomainId            : xyz.com
ObjectGuid          : a4e64295-2cbe-4962-8306-26f18ce8ae92
Name                : Tony Redmond
```

You may be surprised by the amount of information returned here for the mailbox's identity (it's all defined in the schema), but it contains all of the ways that you can navigate to this object via its relative distinguished name (rdn), distinguished name, GUID, and name. Normally, you'll just use the name of a mailbox to find it, but you can use the other methods and Exchange will find the mailbox. There is no requirement to parse out the part of the identity that you want to use or trim values before you use them to find information—PowerShell does it all for you. For example, you can use an identity to discover the groups that a user belongs to. Here's the code:

```
$U = (Get-User —id Redmond).Identity; Get-Group —Filter
{Members —eq $U}
```

The first command loads the user's identity into a variable, the second scans through all groups to discover any that include the user in their membership. As you can see from Figure 4.4, EMC displays similar results when it displays the "Member Of" property page for the same mailbox. Scanning the membership list of groups to discover string matches using the Get-Group command is never going to be as quick (and will get slower and slower as the number of groups in the forest grows) because a string compare will never get close to the backward pointers that the GUI uses to display group membership when it comes to speed of access, so don't be surprised if scanning for group membership in this way takes some time to complete.

The great thing about identities is that you sometimes don't need to bother about using them! This situation occurs when you pipe information fetched from one command for processing by another command because the shell understands that it needs to operate on the current object that has been fetched through the pipe. Fetching objects with one command and processing them with another is a very frequent thing that you'll do as you work with Exchange data. For example, let's assume that you want to change the value of the Office property for a set of users who have moved to a new building. It would be tedious if you had to fetch the identity of each user individually, retrieve their identity, and then use that to make the change. A simple pipe does the trick because PowerShell knows that it can use the

Figure 4.4
*Using an identity
to discover group
membership*

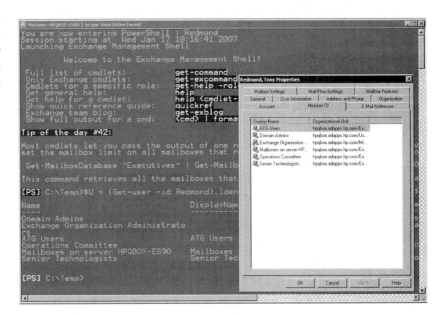

stream of data from one command to identify the objects that it has to process with another. Here's how we might update the Office property for a complete set of users without any mention of an identity!

```
Get-User —Filter {Office —eq 'Building A'} | Set-User —Office
"Building B"
```

4.1.7 Working in a multi-domain forest

By default, when you start EMS, Exchange sets the scope for queries performed against Active Directory to be the domain that the server belongs to. This is fine if you operate a single domain forest, but it is definitely not okay if you have to manage objects in a multi-domain forest because it means that any query that you perform will only return objects from the local domain. For example, let us assume that you have a classic forest implementation where a root domain has three child domains to support accounts for the regions Europe, America, and Australia. Your Exchange servers are installed in the regional domains. If you log into a server installed into the Australian domain and execute:

```
Get-User | Where {$_.StateOrProvince —eq 'TX'} | Select Name
```

You would expect this command to return a list of users who reside in Texas. Naturally, these accounts are in the domain that hosts American users. Because your scope is set to the Australia domain, the command returns nothing, or maybe some Australian users who have decided to relocate to Texas.

Another interesting example is when you have mailboxes from multiple domains hosted on an Exchange server that is in one of the domains (or a completely different domain). In this example, we search for anyone whose mailbox is on a server in the Americas domain and is located in Sydney.

```
Get-Mailbox —Server AmericasMbx1 | Where {$_.Office —like
'Sydney'} | Select Name
```

The only mailboxes returned by this search will be accounts that belong to the Americas domain. Any accounts in the Australia domain that happen to be hosted by the Exchange server in the Americas domain will be ignored until you set the scope of the query to cover the entire Active Directory forest.

The scope used by Exchange is set in the ADminSessionADSettings.ViewEntireForest global variable that Exchange defines in the Exchange.PS1 file in the \Bin directory of the location where you installed Exchange. EMS runs the commands in the Exchange.PS1 file as a bootstrap to load commands and define a number of variables that EMS uses to control different aspects of its environment. You can edit the ViewEntireForest property of the AdminSettingADSettings variable to set the scope to view the entire forest as follows:

```
## Reset the Default Domain
$global:AdminSessionADSettings.ViewEntireForest = $True
```

Setting the proper scope is important if you want to retrieve the right information from your queries. To reset the scope so that Exchange only uses objects from the local domain, type:

```
$AdminSessionADSettings.ViewEntireForest = $False
```

Creating the proper scope for Active Directory lookups is critical for some commands. For example, the `Update-SafeList` command gathers safe list information from user accounts and aggregates them to pass to an Edge server so that the anti-spam agents running on the Edge server can use this information to filter out spam. If you execute `Update-SafeList` with the wrong scope, you will synchronize only the safe list data from the in-scope domain to the Edge server and the anti-spam agents may end up blocking some valid messages as spam.

If you do not want to set your scope to the entire forest, a workaround is to specify a Global Catalog server in the remote domain to perform the query there. Taking our previous example, if we changed it to include a domain controller in the Americas domain, then we would be able to retrieve the right data at the expense of missing out on the Australians who want to live in Texas:

```
Get-User —DomainController GC01.America.xyz.com | Where
{$_.StateOrProvince —eq 'TX'} | Select Name
```

The natural question at this point is whether changing scope will affect how you work with EMS. The answer is yes because when you set a forest-wide scope, you work with data from across the forest rather than the local domain. Unless you use parameters to focus in on particular groups of objects, such as specifying that you want to work with the mailboxes from one server, you will probably have to wait longer for a response from any command. This is because you will ask EMS to process commands that deal with servers, mailboxes, databases, or storage groups across a complete forest rather than just one domain, but in most cases the wait is worthwhile because you see the big picture and don't run the risk of missing something.

4.1.8   **Profiles**

As we have just seen, when you start EMS, Exchange runs a PowerShell script called Exchange.PS1 to load the Exchange snap-in and define a set of variables used by EMS. You can see how EMS calls Exchange.PS1 by examining the properties of the EMS option that the Exchange installation adds to the Start menu, as shown in Figure 4.5. Note the property pages to control font, layout, and colors. These are settings that you can use to change the appearance of the EMS command window to use a more readable font, use a larger font size, or use different colors.

We have already seen how the $AdminSessionADSettings global variable is set in the Exchange.PS1 file to set the scope for Active Directory lookups during an EMS session. You can define other variables for your own purpose in your personal PowerShell profile, which is located in \My Documents\WindowsPowerShell\Microsoft.PowerShell_Profile.PS1[7]. Windows does not create your personal PowerShell profile automatically, so you will have to create the file manually by using an editor such as Notepad. Afterwards, you can edit the file to create whatever variables you need or

---

7.   Earlier versions of PowerShell used a file called Profile.PS1. Either filename works.

insert other commands to create your personal working environment. Power-Shell uses a global variable called $Profile to point to your profile, so once the file is created, you can edit it from within EMS by typing the command:

```
Invoke-Item $Profile
```

Figure 4.5
Properties of EMS

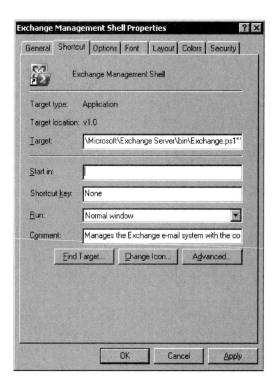

The contents of a sample profile are shown below. You can see the effect of these commands in Figure 4.6. The commands contained in your profile are effective the next time you launch EMS. Note that PowerShell executes your profile first and will then execute the commands in Exchange.PS1.

```
# welcome message
'You are now entering PowerShell:' + $env:Username
$Global:Start = Now

Write-Host "Session starting at $Start"
Set-Location c:\temp\
```

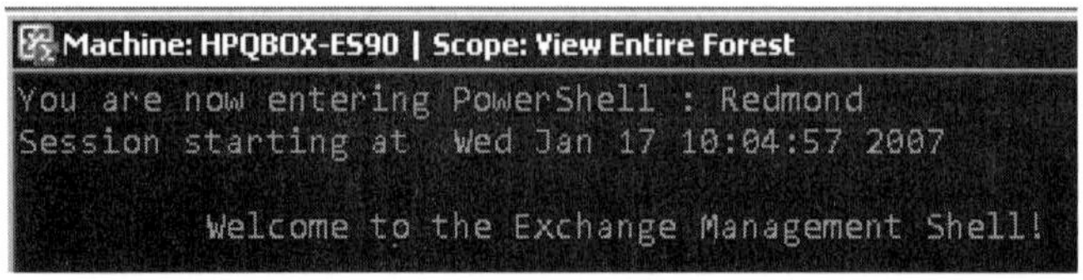

Figure 4.6
The effect of a
personal profile

You can scan the Internet to discover the many different customizations that people have applied through their personal profile such as defining new aliases that they like to use as command shortcuts, creating a different prompt, and so on.

4.1.9   PowerShell in batch

If you write a script that uses Exchange PowerShell commands that you want to execute in batch mode, you have to call the `Add-PSSnapin` command to load the Exchange PowerShell snap-in before you attempt to work with Exchange as otherwise PowerShell won't know anything about the Exchange commands like `Get-Mailbox`, `Get-MailboxDatabase`, and so on. For example, if you wrote a script to report on mailbox quotas for everyone on the organization, it might be something like this:

```
Get-MailboxServer | Get-MailboxStatistics > c:\temp\
AllMailboxes.txt
```

It all looks very simple and this one-line command will work interactively, but won't generate a thing if you run it in batch. In fact, PowerShell does not provide a command to run a script in batch mode, so you have to rely on the Windows scheduler to submit a BAT (batch file) for processing. The batch file calls PowerShell and passes the name of the script as a parameter, so the kind of batch file that we need is:

```
PowerShell.Exe c:\Script\Get-All-Mailboxes.Ps1
```

Inside the script file, we still have some work to do because we have to tell PowerShell about the `Get-MailboxStatistics` command by loading the Exchange snap-in:

```
Add-PSSnapin Microsoft.Exchange.Management.PowerShell.Admin
Get-MailboxServer | Get-MailboxStatistics > c:\temp\
AllMailboxes.txt
```

Adding the Exchange snap-in is not an intuitive thing to do when you come to design scripts that run in batch, but when you think a little, it's logical that you should have to create the same environment for the batch script that you'd have when you work with EMS interactively. As explained above, when you start EMS, it loads PowerShell and then the Exchange snap-in, so you have to do the same in your scripts. Note that it's also a good idea to establish the exact scope of the forest that you want commands to work for within scripts.

4.1.10 Execution policies

By this point, you're probably convinced that EMS is pretty powerful and that just a few lines of code can affect many objects, so the thought might have crossed your mind about how to control the ability of users to execute EMS command. PowerShell supports a concept called Execution Policies to control how users can execute commands. Execution policies define the conditions under which PowerShell loads files for execution. There are four policies: *Restricted, AllSigned, RemoteSigned*, and *Unrestricted.*

By default, Microsoft configures PowerShell to run under the Restricted execution policy, which is the most secure mode. In this mode, PowerShell operates as an interactive shell only and you cannot call scripts. In fact, all you can do is issue PowerShell commands interactively at the shell prompt. Table 4.2 lists the alternate modes together with the potential trade-off in security that you may have to make.

Table 4.2   *PowerShell execution policies*

Execution Policy	Execution Context
Restricted	Users can issue commands at the PowerShell prompt. Users cannot call scripts.
AllSigned	Users can run scripts, but the scripts and any configuration files must be signed by a trusted publisher.
RemoteSigned (default for Exchange)	Users can run scripts. Scripts and configuration files that are downloaded from communications applications such as Outlook, Outlook Express, IE, and Messenger must be signed by a trusted publisher.
Unrestricted	Users can run scripts. Scripts that are downloaded from communications applications can be run after the user acknowledges that this content may be dangerous. No signature is required.

You can use the `Get-ExecutionPolicy` command to discover what the default execution policy is on an Exchange 2007 server. If you attempt to run an unsigned script that doesn't comply with policy, PowerShell signals that it cannot load the script. Scripts are signed with the `Set-AuthenticodeSigna-ture` command, but you need to get a valid certificate first. The certificate can be one that you generate yourself or one that you buy in from a commercial vendor, such as Verisign. See the Microsoft documentation for details of how to generate and apply certificates to sign scripts.

Execution policies are not a way around Exchange permissions and you will not be able to execute anything through EMS that you can't do through EMC. For example, if you don't have at least view-only permission for a server, EMS will return an error if you attempt to retrieve any information that isn't part of the organization configuration (which you gain access to by having view-only permission). To see what I mean, assume that you have view-only permission for a server but not for the server called ExchHub1. This command works:

```
Get-ExchangeServer —ExchHub1
```

But this command does not work:

```
Get-ExchangeServer —ExchHub1 —Status
```

The reason is that the first command reads from the Exchange organization configuration in the Active Directory. The second combines the first set of information with some additional information from the system registry from the target server. You don't have permission over that server, so the command fails with an error.

Obviously, running an Exchange server with an unrestricted execution policy is a horribly bad idea. In fact, you should avoid any deviation from the default policy unless you have an excellent reason why you need to change. To change the policy, use the `Set-ExecutionPolicy` command to update the default execution policy on an Exchange 2007 server. This command updates the registry. For example:

```
Set-ExecutionPolicy —ExecutionPolicy AllSigned
```

The change to the execution policy will come into effect immediately. Be sure to test any change that you want to make before putting the change into production because it may break scripts that you or applications depend on. Note that any update to the registry can be overridden by group policy, which is the way to implement a consistent execution policy across a large organization.

4.1.11   Sending email from the shell

It may seem awfully obvious for an email system to provide some method to create and send messages when it enhances a scripting language, but EMS provides no special commands to create and send messages. Everything has to be done with the basic SMTP commands for Windows that PowerShell includes. We already reviewed an example of what the SmtpClient .NET class can do in a couple of lines of script. For example:

```
$SmtpClient = New-Object System.Net.Mail.SmtpClient
$SmtpClient.host = 'ExchSvr1.xyz.com'
$From = 'MoneyPenny@xyz.com'
$To   = 'James.Bond@xyz.com'
$Title = 'Answer to your questions'
$Body = 'Status Message follows — Here is some important
information'
$SmtpClient.Send($From, $To, $Title, $Body)
```

These commands work if you point them to an SMTP server that is willing to relay messages for clients. Most Exchange servers and especially Exchange 2007 hub transport servers will restrict the ability of clients to relay messages, especially unauthenticated clients. However, you can pass credentials by either setting the UseDefaultCredentials property to $True (the default is $False), which tells Windows to fetch whatever default network credentials are cached for the current logged-on user or you can pass explicit credentials by setting the property with the necessary values for username and password. For example:

```
$SmtpClient.UseDefaultCredentials = $True
```

or

```
$credentials = New-Object
System.Net.NetworkCredential('Redmond@xyz.com', 'Password')
SmtpClient.Credentials = $Credentials
```

Including credentials in plain text in a script isn't very secure. You can do a much better job by prompting the user for credentials to use:

```
$Credentials = Get-Credential
```

This command puts up a standard Windows login dialog for the user to input their username and password. We can then fetch the data and store it as follows:

```
$Username = $Credentials.Username
$Password =$Credentials.GetNetworkCredential().Password
$Credentials2 = New-Object
System.Net.NetworkCredential($UserName,
   $Password)
SmtpClient.Credentials = $Credentials2
```

So far we've sent a pretty simple message. What about if we want to read addresses for all the mailboxes in a container and send a message to them. We can use a container such as a distribution group (use Get-Distribution-GroupMember to fetch the names) or from an organizational unit as shown below. This script is one that I use to generate a set of messages to load test systems. The script differs from the simple examples that we have used to date by also adding an attachment to the message and by reading in some content from a text file to become the body of the message. Note that if you want a copy of the message, you have to include your mailbox in the recipient list as the code shown here generates and sends a basic SMTP message.

```
# Spam lots of users
# Get a list of the members of a distribution group

$MbxSet = Get-Mailbox –OrganizationalUnit 'Exchange Users'
–Filter {RecipientTypeDetails –eq 'UserMailbox'}

Write-Host "About to spam $($MbxSet.Count) users..."

$Title = 'Very Important and Critical Message to Important
People:'

# Determine who's sending the message
$SourceMailbox = Get-Mailbox -id 'Redmond'
$SourceAddress = $SourceMailbox.PrimarySmtpAddress.ToString()

# What's the address of our SMTP server (that will relay mail)
$SmtpServer = "Smtp-Relay.xyz.com"
```

```
# Load some text into the message body
$Item = Get-Item c:\temp\objects.tmp
$MsgBody = Get-Content $Item.Fullname

# Create an attachment
$File = 'C:\temp\Information.txt'
$MsgAttachment = New-Object System.Net.Mail.Attachment
($File)

$MbxCount = $MbxSet.Count - 1
$X = 1

# Create a set of addresses in the format expected by email
$Recipients = 0..$MbxCount | ForEach-Object
{$MbxSet[$_].PrimarySmtpAddress.ToString()}
$ToRecipients = [String]::Join(",",$Recipients)

Write-Host "Spamming $($ToRecipients)..."

1..100 | ForEach-Object {
  $Subject = $Title + " " + $_
  Write-Host "Generating Message $_ )"
  $Msg = New-Object System.Net.Mail.MailMessage
    ($SourceAddress,
    $ToRecipients, $Subject, $MsgBody)
  $Msg.Attachments.Add($MsgAttachment)
  $SmtpClient = New-Object System.Net.Mail.SmtpClient
    $SmtpServer, 25
  $SmtpClient.Send($Msg)
}
```

Of course, if you do not want to get involved in scripting, you can simply create a message in the proper format (containing all the necessary fields) and put it into the SMTP pickup directory on a hub transport server. Exchange will find the file there and assuming that it does not contain any invalid or illegal lines, Exchange should send the message for you.

The lesson from all of this is that you do not need standalone programs such as MAPISend or BLAT that administrators have used with previous versions of Exchange to generate and send email to report the status of jobs, that various events have occurred, or any other message that they needed to generate as part of operations. The scripting capabilities of PowerShell and the ability to access and process Exchange data through the shell are much more powerful than anything we've had in the past, short of breaking out the MAPI programming manuals and writing some heavy-duty code, which seems excessive if you only want to generate a message.

Now that we have an insight into how PowerShell can work with standard Exchange objects and other important concepts such as variables and identities, we can plunge into the detail of how PowerShell dramatically enhances the management framework for Exchange 2007.

4.2   Learning from EMC

As we know, EMS commands provide the foundation for the options offered through EMC. It is therefore logical to assume that we can gain an insight into how shell commands function by working with EMC – at least for the tasks that you can perform through EMC. Let's assume that you want to create a mail-enabled account. This option is available through EMC and a browse through the Exchange 2007 help file reveals that the New-Mailbox command creates mail-enabled accounts. You also know that you need to populate a number of fields in the Active Directory object for the new account. These fields include:

- Name: The common name (CN) of the account.
- Database: The distinguished name of the mailbox store to host the new account.
- UserPrincipalName: The name of the user in SMTP address format.
- OrganizationalUnit: The organizational unit within the Active Directory into which to place the new account.
- Password: The password to assign to the new account.

Note that equipment mailboxes and room mailboxes have simpler requirements in terms of creation because they are disabled Active Directory objects. However, these mailboxes have their own distinct set of properties that you can manipulate that don't exist for regular mailboxes.

The Exchange 2007 help file describes how you can provide the necessary values to populate these fields when you call New-Mailbox. However, the syntax of New-Mailbox can be hard to understand, so it's nice to be able to get a hint about how to start and that's where EMC comes in. If you create a mailbox with EMC, you provide the necessary values through the GUI. Afterwards EMC creates the mailbox by calling New-Mailbox.

A really neat feature of EMC is that it displays the code that it uses when it completes a task and prompts you to use the CTRL/C keystroke to copy

Figure 4.7
*Extracting
PowerShell code
from EMC*

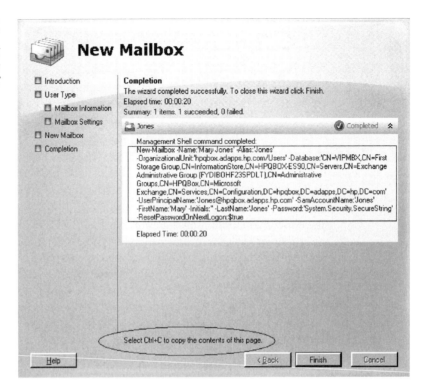

the commands. The Exchange help file is another great source of examples of PowerShell code and you also can cut and paste the code from the help file. The sample code in the help file is more generic than the code that EMS generates inside your own organization, but it provides a useful starting point for the more esoteric commands.

Figure 4.7 shows the actual code generated to create a mailbox for a user called "Mary Jones." You can start up any editor and paste the commands to begin the process of automating the creation of new mailboxes. We now have some code to work with. You might assume that you can simply edit the code to add the appropriate values for a new user but there is one minor challenge that stops us doing this. Passwords have to be secure and they would not be secure if you could enter them in plain text within a script. PowerShell allows you to declare a variable as a secure string but you can't just assign a value to it in a script by specifying a simple text string that remains readable in the script.[8] For now, the easiest way to provide a password is to use the Read-Host command to prompt for a password when the script runs to create the

---

8.   It is possible to use the `ConvertTo-SecureString` command to convert a plain text string to a secure string, but we still have the security problem of the plain text value in the file, so overall it's best to prompt the user to provide the password.

new account. Later on in this chapter we'll discuss how to use more complex code to compose a secure string based on some data read in from a load file and then to use the secure string for a password when you perform a bulk creation of new accounts.

Providing a single password to a prompt or encoding strings fetched from a load file during a bulk load operation are not ways around password policies that the Active Directory may enforce. If you input a password that doesn't comply with policy (too short, not containing the right character mix, etc.), New-Mailbox will fail when it attempts to create the new account in the Active Directory. The complete code that EMS generates to create a new account is therefore:

```
$password = Read-Host "Enter password" -AsSecureString

New-Mailbox -Name:'James Bond' -Alias:'Bond'
-OrganizationalUnit:'xyz.com/Exchange Users/Users'
-Database:'CN=Mailbox Store 1,CN=First Storage
Group,CN=InformationStore,CN=XYZ-MBX-1,CN=Servers,CN=Exchange
Administrative Group (FYDIBOHF23SPDLT),CN=Administrative
Groups,CN=XYZ,CN=Microsoft Exchange, CN=Services,
CN=Configuration,DC=London,DC=adapps,DC=XYZ,DC=com'
-UserPrincipalName:'Bond@xyz.com' -SamAccountName:'Bond'
-FirstName:'James' -Initials:'' -LastName:'Bond'
-ResetPasswordOnNextLogon:$True -Password $password
```

As you will see as we investigate different examples, the code that EMC generates to create a new mailbox is a tad verbose in the way each parameter is fully spelt out and objects like the target database are identified precisely. You normally don't have to be quite so exact because EMS is pretty good at interpreting input to know what you mean. For instance, if there is only one database on the local server that's called "VIP Mailboxes," then that's all you have to specify unless you really want to spell out the full distinguished name or GUID of the database.

Creating a customized script is not the way to do the job if you only have one or two accounts to create. Using PowerShell becomes much more compelling when you need to process lots of objects at one time or you need to automate the provisioning of user accounts, perhaps by linking the creation to a feed from an HR system.

Similar commands are used to create equipment, room, shared, and linked mailboxes with slightly different parameters being required to identify these mailbox types. For example, when you create a room mailbox, you specify the –Room parameter; an equipment mailbox takes the –Equipment parameter; and you must pass the –LinkedMasterAccount parameter to create a linked mailbox. You can discover the exact format of these commands by creating a mailbox of the required type with EMC and examining the commands that the GUI generates.

4.3   Using EMS to work with mailboxes

The shell provides many commands to maintain mailboxes and distribution groups. While we have already explored how to use PowerShell to report mailbox data and to create a new mail-enabled account, many other examples of PowerShell commands in use are dotted throughout the book. An exhaustive description of PowerShell and the Exchange 2007 Management Shell would require a separate thousand-page book to describe adequately. Instead of attempting that task, I want to look at some specific examples that illustrate the power of EMS and investigate how you can use shell commands to automate common Exchange administrative tasks. The aim here is to help you make the cultural transition from a point where we look for an option in the GUI to do everything to an appreciation of how you can use EMS to get your work done. The structure of the EMS commands look similar to other scripting languages and those who have ever had the chance to administer a UNIX or Linux server will be at home with PowerShell commands.

Before starting, we should note that you have to connect to a server that supports the mailbox role before you can work with mailboxes, recipients, or distribution groups and the account that you log into must possess at least Exchange Recipient Administrator permission for the server that you want to use.

4.3.1   Creating a new mailbox with a template

When you create a new mailbox with Exchange 2003, you can use the Copy option in the AD Users and Computers console to copy an existing user account and create a new account that inherits all of the Exchange properties. You cannot do this any longer because Microsoft has removed the Exchange add-ons from the AD Users and Computers console. Furthermore, the EMC console does not offer administrators the opportunity to create a new mailbox from a copy.

Instead, you have to use the –TemplateInstance parameter to point to an existing mailbox when you create a new mailbox with the New-Mailbox command.

```
$Password = Read-Host 'Enter Password:' -AsSecureString
```

```
New-Mailbox —Alias 'DPR' —OrganizationalUnit 'Exchange Users'
—DisplayName 'Redmond, Deirdre' —FirstName 'Deirdre'
—LastName 'Redmond' —Database 'VIP Mailboxes'
—UserPrincipalName 'dpr@xyz.com' —Name 'Deirdre Redmond'
—TemplateInstance (Get-Mailbox —id Redmond) —Password
$Password
```

As you can see, you still have to specify many other parameter values, so it is not just a case of pointing to a mailbox and copying everything from that mailbox. Later on, when you examine the new mailbox, you will find that specifying another mailbox as a template tells Exchange to copy selected properties, but not others. The properties that Exchange copies include:

- Mailbox quota limits
- Protocol settings (for example, what version of Outlook can connect to the mailbox)
- Language setting for Outlook Web Access
- Outlook Web Access feature segmentation
- Spam Confidence Level settings
- Address list membership
- The set of 15 Exchange custom attributes
- Maximum send and receive size

For some companies, the change in behavior caused by the move from a simple copy operation to the requirement to use a template with the New-Mailbox command will be an annoyance. For others, especially companies that depend on the ability to copy mailboxes in every detail as part of their user creation process, it will provoke some unexpected change. The good news is that it is possible to script the complete creation process to generate an exact replica from a template mailbox; the bad news is that you have to build the script to meet your company's needs.

One small bug in using a template mailbox with the New-Mailbox command is that Exchange does not create a primary SMTP address for the new mailbox. Microsoft will fix this Exchange 2007 bug in SP1. For now, you have to update the mailbox after you create it to add the address.

4.3.2 Setting and retrieving mailbox properties

First, here is an example of a single line of script that accomplishes a task that you would need many lines of ADSI code to do in Exchange 2003. We want to update a user's mailbox to give "Send on Behalf" permission to another user. The command is:

```
Set-Mailbox —identity XYZ\Redmond —GrantSendOnBehalfTo
smith@xyz.com
```

This command uses the `Set-Mailbox` command to look for the user account that belongs to XYZ\Redmond (we could also pass a UPN or an SMTP address as the identity to find the account) and set the Send on Behalf permission to the user account identified with the SMTP address smith@xyz.com. UPNs are probably the easiest way to identify mailboxes, especially if they match users' SMTP addresses. Note that you can shorten parameters as long as they remain unique. For example, when you create a new mailbox, you can use –id for –identity or –org for –organizational unit. The shell will prompt you for a value if you fail to provide one for a mandatory parameter. Some parameters like –identity are positional so you do not need to specify them. In other words, the following command is as good as our earlier example because `Set-Mailbox` assumes that the first parameter passed is the identity of the mailbox to work with.

```
Set-Mailbox 'Jane Bond' —GrantSendOnBehalfTo 'James Bond'
```

My own preference is to be specific about the identity parameter, so I tend to use it all the time. If you give someone the ability to send mail for another user, you will also need to give them the appropriate Active Directory permission if you want to allow them to access your mailbox and work with its contents.

```
Add-AdPermission —id 'Jane Bond' -ExtendedRights Send-As
-User 'James Bond'
```

Knowing the name of the available parameters that an individual command supports can be difficult. As we learned earlier in this chapter, PowerShell makes it easy to discover what parameters are available for a command by allowing you to use the tab key to cycle through the available parameters. This feature is especially useful for commands that have many parameters, such as those that deal with mailboxes. For example, if you type:

```
Set-Mailbox —
```

Now press the tab key, EMS starts to go through the available parameters. Moving on to a much simpler command, if you need to disable a mailbox, you can do it with a one-line command:

```
Disable-Mailbox 'James.Bond@xyz.com'
```

And if you have to disable a whole set of mailboxes quickly, you can do it with `Disable-Mailbox` too. Here we disable all of the mailboxes on the "MbxServer1" server:

```
Get-Mailbox MbxServer1 | Disable-Mailbox
```

Now that we have a few disabled mailboxes, we can enable selected ones again with the `Enable-Mailbox` command:

```
Enable-Mailbox James.Bond@xyz.com -database 'Mailbox
Database'
```

We can also process mailboxes for a complete server:

```
Get-Mailbox —Server MbxServer1 | Enable-Mailbox
```

`Get-Mailbox` is a very useful command that gets used a lot. For example, to list all the users on a specific server:

```
Get-Mailbox —Server MbxServer1 | Format-Table
```

Or just one database:

```
Get-Mailbox —Database 'VIP Mailboxes' | Format-Table
```

You can be more specific about a database and identify that it comes from a different server:

```
Get-Mailbox —Database 'ExchMbxSvr1\Storage Group 1\VIP
Mailboxes'
```

Or even just the mailboxes that belong to a certain organizational unit on a specific server:

```
Get-Mailbox —Server ExchMbxSvr1 —OrganizationalUnit
Executives
```

Another useful trick is to search for mailboxes using Ambiguous Name Resolution (ANR). In other words, you provide EMS with a value and it finds any mailbox that might possibly match the value in its name or alias. For example:

```
Get-Mailbox —Anr 'Red'
```

Another special case is where you simply want to search based on name. Microsoft did some work in EMS to allow you to pass a command like this:

```
Get-Mailbox *James*
```

This command performs a wildcard search for any user that has "James" in their name or SMTP address! You can even pass wildcard characters to specify what fields you want output, as in:

```
Get-Mailbox *Ja* | Format-Table Name, *depart*, *quota*
```

This command lists the name, department, and all the quota properties of any user who has "Ja" in their name or SMTP address. You probably won't use this kind of command often, but it's interesting to see just how much can be done in a few characters of code (older programmers who worked on Digital operating systems may remember the late lamented Teco language, which could do some of the same tricks).

Unfortunately, you can't use `Get-Mailbox` to discover what mailboxes exist in the databases within a specific storage group. However, we can solve the problem with a combination of the `Get-MailboxDatabase` command to interrogate the databases on a specific server and a loop through the databases to return the mailboxes for the storage group that we are interested in:

```
Get-MailboxDatabase -Server MailboxServer1 | Where
{$_.StorageGroup.Name -eq 'VIP Storage Group'} | ForEach-Object
{Get-Mailbox -Database $_.Name} | Select Name, Alias, Database
```

By eliminating the –Server parameter, you could execute a command to look for mailboxes that belong to a storage group with a specific name that occur on any server in the organization. For example, you could look for mailboxes from the "First Storage Group," the default name given to storage groups on all Exchange servers. Such a command is likely to take a long time to execute and you will see an error if a server is unreachable for any reason. Even if the $Error variable is always available to check if things go wrong, the degree of error checking and handling in one-line PowerShell commands is normally not great! As a great example of how elegant PowerShell can be, one of the book's reviewers pointed out that a faster solution to the problem is provided by:

```
Get-Mailbox –Server (Get-StorageGroup 'VIP Storage
Group').Server | Select Name, Alias, Database
```

In this case, we rely on the fact that the `Get-StorageGroup` command can return the name of the server where the storage group resides and can use that as input to `Get-Mailbox`. Another example is where you want to find out how many mailboxes are allocated to a server or database. Here we use the `Group-Object` command to collect the mailboxes according to the unique values in the property that we specify:

```
Get-Mailbox | Group-Object ServerName
Get-Mailbox | Group-Object Database
```

The ability to group objects is very useful because you can apply it to any property that an object returns. For example, we might want to discover how many mailboxes have been assigned a managed folder policy:

```
Get-Mailbox | Group-Object ManagedFolderMailboxPolicy

Count Name                       Group
----- ----                       -----
   39                            {Gary Olsen, Dung Hoang Khac, Administrator, Liffey
   45 Business Planning          {Aric Bernard, Conference Room 2, Tony Redmond, Jane
    1 Clean out calendar fol...  {Leixlip Conference Room}
```

We can see here that 39 mailboxes don't have a managed folder policy assigned (you can find more details about how to create and apply these policies in Chapter 8). EMS reports the names of some of the mailboxes but truncates the list, so we need to generate a complete list if we want to discover the names of the mailboxes that don't have a managed folder policy assigned. We can execute another command using `Get-Mailbox` for this purpose. In this case, we eliminate room and equipment mailboxes, but you can use a similar filter to identify these mailbox types if you want to apply specific managed folder policies to them:

```
Get-Mailbox | Where {$_.ManagedFolderMailboxPolicy –eq $Null
–and $_.RecipientTypeDetails –eq 'UserMailbox'} | Select Name
```

A problem with any command that sets out to process a large number of mailboxes is that you might blow the limit for the total number of items that `Get-Mailbox` returns. As with all EMS commands that return items, the default set is 1,000 items (this is the same as the default filter size applied to EMC) and it's easy to find servers or mailbox databases that support more than 1,000 mailboxes. If you know that you need to process more than 1,000 mailboxes, you can increase the limit to a set value:

```
Get-Mailbox –ResultSize 5000
```

Or, if you are very brave or just don't know how many items are likely to be retrieved:

```
Get-Mailbox –ResultSize Unlimited
```

Better practice is to restrict the number of mailboxes that are returned by applying a suitable filter. For example, the example given above to return counts of mailboxes per database will scan all of the servers in the organization. You'll get a much quicker result if you scan just one server by changing the command to include the –Server parameter:

```
Get-Mailbox –Server ExchMbxSvr1 | Group-Object Database
```

Count	Name	Group
35	ExchMbxSvr1\SG4\DF	{kathy.pollert@xyz.com, pierre.bijaoui@xyz.com...
158	ExchMbxSvr1\SG2\Pilot	{shaun.duncan@xyz.com, tony.redmond@xyz.com, k...
125	ExchMbxSvr1\SG6\DB6	{richard.beijer@xyz.com, maria.jordan@xyz.com,...
22	ExchMbxSvr1\SG3\UM	{jonathan.bradshaw@xyz.com, soren@xyz.com, wen...
2	ExchMbxSvr1\SG1\DB1	{Test Mailbox 1, Test Mailbox 2}

You can export data that you retrieve with shell commands in CSV or XML format, which makes it easy to then load the output into a program like Excel (CSV) or an XML reader. For example:

```
Get-Mailbox —id Bond | Export-CSV c:\temp\Bond.csv
Get-Mailbox —id Bond | Export-CliXML c:\temp\Bond.xml
```

You can use the ability to export data in CSV or XML format to report information about a mailbox using the Get-MailboxFolderStatistics command. This command goes through the folders in a mailbox and reports information such as the number of items in the folder, the size of the folder, and the timestamp for the newest item in the folder. For example:

```
Get-MailboxFolderStatistics —id Bond | Select Identity,
FolderSize, ItemsInFolder, NewestItemReceiveDate | Export-CSV
c:\temp\Bond.csv
```

The default operation for Get-MailboxFolderStatistics is to report on every folder in a mailbox. You can restrict processing to a single folder, but only if it is one of the default folders or a custom-managed folder (see Chapter 8). For example:

```
Get-MailboxFolderStatistics —id Redmond —FolderScope Inbox

Date                       : 1/15/2007 6:25:28 PM
Name                       : Inbox
Identity                   : redmond\Inbox
FolderPath                 : /Inbox
FolderType                 : Inbox
ItemsInFolder              : 71
FolderSize                 : 9396867B
ItemsInFolderAndSubfolders : 71
FolderAndSubfolderSize     : 9396867B
OldestItemReceivedDate     : 10/18/2006 1:17:20
NewestItemReceivedDate     : 1/15/2007 5:14:29 PM
ManagedFolder              : Inbox
```

Once you have the data in CSV format, you can edit it using Excel or another similar tool as shown in Figure 4.8. Another example where CSV output comes in handy is where we want to generate a quick list of all the users on a server:

```
Get-Mailbox -Server ExchMbxSvr1 | Select LastName, FirstName,
Phone | Export-csv c:\temp\UserList.csv
```

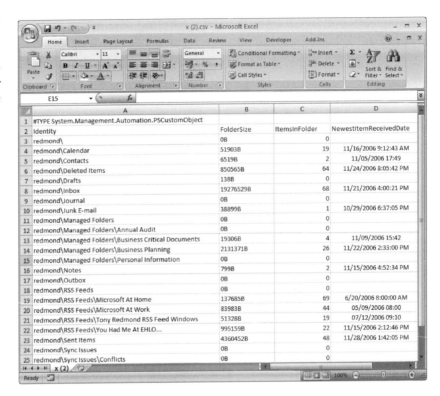

Figure 4.8
*CSV output from
Get-
MailboxFolder
Statistics*

You can also use `Get-Mailbox` to return a quick count of all of the mailboxes assigned to different databases within the organization. As scanning all the servers in the organization might take some time, you may want to restrict the scope of the command to a single server by specifying the –server parameter:

```
Get-Mailbox –Server ExchMbxSvr1 | Group-Object Database |
Format-Table Name, Count
```

The same approach that we took to retrieve mailbox information with the `Get-Mailbox` command applies if we need to remove mailboxes. When we want to remove just one mailbox, we use the `Remove-Mailbox` command and specify their UPN. For all delete and disable operations that affect mailboxes and other mail-enabled objects, EMS will prompt you to confirm the operation before it proceeds.

```
Remove-Mailbox 'Tony.Redmond@xyz.com'
```

And to do the same thing to all mailbox-enabled users on a specific server:

```
Get-Mailbox —Server MbxServer1 | Remove-Mailbox
```

It should now be obvious that you will use the `Get-Mailbox` command frequently to fetch information about mailboxes and as we know, `Set-Mailbox` is its counterpart when it comes to updating a property of a mailbox. Let's review some other examples of `Set-Mailbox` in action. For example, we can assume that I want to set a very large quota on my mailbox:

```
Set-Mailbox —id 'Tony.Redmond@xyz.com'
—UseDatabaseQuotaDefaults:$False —IssueWarningQuota 5000MB
—ProhibitSendQuota 5050MB
—ProhibitSendReceiveQuota 5075MB
```

After we set quotas for mailboxes, we can check to see if any user has exceeded a quota using the `Get-MailboxStatistics` command:

```
Get-MailboxStatistics | Where
{"IssueWarning","ProhibitSend","MailboxDisabled" —Contains
$_.StorageLimitStatus} |
Format-List Displayname, Itemcount, TotalitemSize
```

When we discussed the topic of how Exchange 2007 controls mailbox quotas in Chapter 3, we encountered a one-line PowerShell command that identified mailboxes that Exchange had disabled because they have exceeded quota. Now that we know a little more about PowerShell, we can develop the command a little more to give us more information about disabled mailboxes on a server and to tell us what we need to do to correct the problem.

```
$Mbx = Get-MailboxStatistics —Server ExchMbxSvr1 | Where-Object
{$_.StorageLimitStatus -eq 'MailboxDisabled'}
 Foreach-Object ($U in $Mbx)
{
   $M = $U.DisplayName
   $PSquota = (Get-Mailbox -id $M).ProhibitSendQuota.Value.ToKB()
   $MbxSize = $U.TotalItemSize.Value.ToKB()
   $Increase = $MbxSize - $PSQuota + 100
```

```
Write-Host $M " has quota of $PSQuota KB and has used $MbxSize KB -
allocate at least an extra $Increase KB"


}
```

This script loops through all of the mailboxes on a server to detect the ones that are disabled. The mailbox quota and the value for the Prohibit-SendQuota property are retrieved and converted to kilobytes (Exchange allows you to pass quota values in KB, MB, and GB, but it returns the total size of the mailbox in bytes). We then output a message to tell the administrator what they have to do. You can see the effect of running the script in Figure 4.9.

Figure 4.9
Checking for disabled mailboxes

Speaking of quotas, we might want to restrict the ability of a user to send and receive very large messages. This might be dangerous for someone who works for a marketing department, who seems to love circulating large PowerPoint attachments for everyone to admire. In any case, here is how we restrict the maximum sizes for sending and receiving messages to 5MB.

```
Set-Mailbox James.Bond@xyz.com -MaxSendSize 5MB
-MaxReceiveSize 5MB
```

Many users like to create rules to process incoming messages as they arrive into their mailbox. In previous versions of Exchange, the rules had to fit into a 32KB space. In Exchange 2007, Microsoft increases the available space for rules to a maximum of 256KB with the default limit increased to 64KB. You can check on the quota for any mailbox with the Get-Mailbox command.

```
Get-Mailbox -id Redmond | Select Name, RulesQuota
```

If the user needs more headroom to store rules, you can increase their quota with the Set-Mailbox command. Exchange will signal an error if you attempt to increase the quota past 256KB:

```
Set-Mailbox -id Redmond -RulesQuota 128KB
```

A common administrative task is where you want to add a new forwarding address to a mailbox.

```
Set-Mailbox Jane.Smith@xyz.com
—DeliverToMailboxAndForward:$True
—ForwardingAddress Jack.Abel@xyz.com
```

In this case, we have told EMS to add a new forwarding address to a mailbox and to ensure that mail is copied to both the original mailbox and to the forwarding address. Sometimes when you change mailbox properties, you want to add something to the property rather than simply overwriting existing data. Adding a new SMTP address to a mailbox is a good example of this kind of processing. All mailboxes that are under the control of an email address policy will have their primary SMTP address automatically configured by Exchange to ensure compliance with the policy, so you cannot change the primary email address unless it complies with policy. It doesn't make sense to change the primary address anyway because Exchange will only update it when it enforces the policy. However, you can add a new address to the secondary SMTP addresses:

```
$MbxData = Get-Mailbox 'James.Bond@xyz.com'
$MbxData.EmailAddresses += 'JB@xyz.com'
Set-Mailbox — id 'James.Bond@xyz.com' —EmailAddresses
$MbxData.EmailAddreses
```

This code is definitely not an example of a one-line command, but you probably will not be doing complicated manipulation of mailbox properties interactively except when you test individual commands. It is much more likely that you will manipulate mailbox properties in scripts if you want to do anything complicated. With this in mind, we can look at these commands and see that we:

- Retrieved the properties of the James.Bond@xyz mailbox and stored them in the $MbxData variable. We can now access all of the properties by referencing them in the variable, as in $MbxData.Email-Addresses.

- Appended a string containing the new SMTP address (JB@xyz.com) to the existing addresses.

- Updated the mailbox with the new set of email addresses with the Set-Mailbox command using the collection of addresses held in the $MbxData.Emailaddresses property.

A somewhat more elegant way of doing the same job is to pipe data returned from `Get-Mailbox` to return the existing email addresses appended with the new address back into `Set-Mailbox`:

```
Set-Mailbox 'James.Bond@xyz.com' -EmailAddresses ((Get-
Mailbox 'James.Bond@xyz.com').EmailAddresses + 'JB@xyz.com')
```

This simply proves that there is more than one way to skin a cat or even to set email addresses. Across all these examples you can see how pipelining allows us an elegant way to combine fundamentally simple commands to perform more complex operations.

If you are in doubt about the type of data contained in a variable or property, you can use the `Get-Member` command to return details of the type. This is valuable information when you want to know what kind of methods you can use to process the data. For example, if we want to know about the type of information contained in the email addresses for a mailbox so that we understand how to update it, we can do:

```
$MbxData = Get-Mailbox -id 'James.Bond@xyz.com'
$MbxData.EmailAddresses | Get-Member
```

PowerShell will then list all the information that we need to know about the different types of proxy addresses supported by Exchange.

4.3.3 Other ways of interacting with mailboxes

There are other commands that interact with mailboxes that we will mention in passing here. The `Get-MailboxPermission` command returns the permissions (such as delegate access) that Active Directory accounts holds over a mailbox. In this example, we're scanning for any mailboxes that Bond's account has access to.

```
Get-MailboxPermission -User Bond | Format-List User,
Identity, AccessRights, Deny
```

We use the `Set-CasMailbox` command to work with mailbox properties that interact with Client Access servers. For example, if you want to determine the options of Outlook Web Access that a mailbox can use such as the option to use the premium client, or to enable a specific feature of Exchange like ActiveSync. For example, here's how to enable a mailbox to use ActiveSync:

```
Set-CasMailbox James.Bond@xyz.com —ActiveSyncEnabled $True
```

4.3.4 Get-Recipient

EMC has a catch-call category of "recipients" that it uses if you click on the Recipient Configuration node. The `Get-Recipient` command is also available to you to retrieve information about every type of recipient and it exposes a fuller set of properties about a recipient. The normal use is to call `Get-Recipient` and specify the type of recipients that you want to view:

```
Get-Recipient —RecipientType UserMailbox
Get-Recipient —RecipientType DynamicDistributionGroup
```

Among the set of properties that are returned are some that you can't retrieve with other commands. For example, you can view the hashed values for the safe sender list stored for a user mailbox that Exchange synchronizes to Edge servers for use in anti-spam filtering by doing:

```
$Hash = Get-Recipient —id Redmond
$Hash.SafeSendersHash
```

You may not find many uses for the `Get-Recipient` command, but it's nice to know that it's there!

4.3.5 Moving mailboxes

We already discussed how to use the Move Mailbox wizard that is available through EMC to move mailboxes in Chapter 3. Moving mailboxes is a very common administrative task and the `Move-Mailbox` command offers administrators some additional flexibility to script mailbox moves. In addition to the options presented through the wizard, the `Move-Mailbox` command allows you to specify these additional parameters:

- GlobalCatalog: Specifies the name of the Global Catalog to be used during migration.

- DomainController: Specifies the name of the domain controller to be used during migration.

- MaxThreads: Define the number of threads to be used to move mailboxes simultaneously (default is 4).

- ValidateOnly: Run the validation code to check that a mailbox can be moved.

- ReportFile: Change the directory and/or file name for the XML report generated for mailbox moves.

- AllowMerge: The default is for Exchange to create a new mailbox in the target database and import the content from the source mailbox into the new mailbox. However, we can specify this parameter to force Exchange to merge the content from the source mailbox into an existing mailbox.

- BadItemItem: Specify the number of "bad items" that Exchange can ignore during the mailbox move. If Exchange encounters more than the specified value, Exchange aborts the mailbox move. Exceeding a reasonable limit (such as between 5 and 8 items) is a good indication that there is a problem with the source mailbox that we should investigate before attempting to move it again.

- ExcludeFolders: The default is for Exchange to move everything from the source mailbox, but we can decide that a mailbox move should ignore specific folders.

- IncludeFolders: You can also specify that only certain folders should be extracted and moved to the target mailbox.

- StartDate and EndDate: We can also apply a filter so that Exchange only moves items from the source mailbox that match a specified date range.

- IgnoreRuleLimitErrors: Exchange 2003 mailboxes have a 32KB limit for rules, which is increased to 64KB for Exchange 2007 mailboxes. If you attempt to move a mailbox from an Exchange 2007 server to an Exchange 2003 server, the rules limit may be exceeded, so this parameter allows you to move a mailbox without its rules and so avoid an error condition.

The basic syntax for the `Move-Mailbox` command is straightforward. To move a mailbox immediately, we simply identify the mailbox to move and the target database and server. In this example, we want to move the user with the SMTP address "Jane.Moneypenny@xyz.com" to a database on server ExMbxSvr1:

```
Move-Mailbox –id 'Jane.Moneypenny@xyz.com' –TargetDatabase
'ExMbxSvr1\VIP Mailboxes Database'
```

In a migration scenario, it could be pretty boring to sit waiting for each mailbox to move before typing the command to move the next—and it's hard to be sure that you process all the mailboxes that you need to. Pipelining comes in handy here as we can take all the mailboxes from a specific database and move them to our new Exchange 2007 server in a single command. As always, make sure that you have enough disk space on the target server to receive all the mailboxes that you are just about to transfer. Here we use the `Get-Mailbox` command to read a list of mailboxes from a server and then pipeline that data to the `Move-Mailbox` command so that it can perform the move.

```
Get-Mailbox —server Exchange2003MbxSvr | Move-Mailbox
—TargetDatabase 'ExMbxSvr1\Exchange 2007 Mailboxes'
```

Another variation on the move mailbox theme that comes into play in disaster recovery situations is when you want to move information about mailbox properties in the Active Directory to point a database on another server (or another location on the same server). This is a nice change in Exchange 2007 because it allows you to quickly transfer mailbox information to another server in disaster recovery scenarios when, for instance, you have experienced a database outage and you want to allow users to continue to send and receive email. The advantage gained by having a single command to replace the many varied scripts that administrators had to write to deal with moving mailboxes after a database outage in previous versions of Exchange is obvious. In an Exchange 2007 environment, you can use the `Move-Mailbox` command to update the configuration data for the mailboxes to point to another server so that Exchange can allow users access on that server. Later on, when the failed database is available again, you can use the Recovery Storage Group option to load the database and merge information back into the user mailboxes (see Chapter 10 for more information about the Recovery Storage Group). Alternatively, you can use the new database portability feature to move the production location for a failed database to a new server (see Chapter 5 for more information on database portability). For example, to move pointers to user mailboxes from the ExchMbxSvr1 server (which we assume has experienced a failure) to the ExchMbxSvr2 server, you could use this command:

```
Get-Mailbox -Server 'ExchMbxSvr1' | Move-Mailbox
-TargetDatabase 'ExchMbxSvr2\Mailbox Database'
-ConfigurationOnly:$True
```

You might also have to move users based on their department or other organizational information such as their location. In these cases, it's a good idea to understand how many mailboxes you might actually move and their mailbox sizes before you actually perform the move. You can do this by specifying the –ValidateOnly parameter. For example:

```
Get-User | Where {$_Department -eq 'Technical Sales'} | Move-Mailbox
-TargetDatabase 'ExchMbxSvr2\Mailbox Database 2' -ValidateOnly
Get-Mailbox -Filter {Office -eq 'Dublin'} | Move-Mailbox
-TargetDatabase 'ExchMbxSvr1\Dublin Mailboxes' -ValidateOnly
```

The –ValidateOnly parameter generates quite a lot of information, but you can capture it by piping the output to a text file where you can review the details including mailbox size, etc. An (edited) example of the information that you can expect to see is shown below:

```
Identity                           : xyz.com/Exchange Users/ATG/Martha Lyons
DistinguishedName                  : CN=Martha Lyons,DC=xyz,DC=com
DisplayName                        : Martha Lyons
Alias                              : Lyons
LegacyExchangeDN                   : /o=xyz/ou=Exchange Administrative Group
(FYDIBOHF23SPDLT)/cn=Recipients/cn=Lyons
PrimarySmtpAddress                 : Martha.Lyons@xyz.com
SourceServer                       : ExchMbxSvr1.xyz.com
SourceDatabase                     : ExchMbxSvr1\First Storage Group\VIP Mailboxes
SourceGlobalCatalog                : XYZ-DC02.xyz.com
SourceDomainController             : XYZ-DC02.xyz.com
TargetGlobalCatalog                : XYZ-DC01.xyz.com
TargetDomainController             : XYZ-DC01.xyz.com
TargetMailbox                      :
TargetServer                       : ExchMbxSvr2.xyzcom
TargetDatabase                     : ExchMbxSvr2\Technical Mailboxes
MailboxSize                        : 25411KB
IsResourceMailbox                  : False
MoveType                           : IntraOrg
MoveStage                          : Validation
StartTime                          : 12/18/2006 1:38:46 PM
EndTime                            : 12/18/2006 1:38:47 PM
StatusCode                         : 0
StatusMessage                      : This mailbox can be moved to the target database.
```

When you're happy that everything is ready to go, you can remove the –ValidateOnly parameter and execute the remaining command to perform the move.

When you move mailboxes between forests, you have to provide more information to allow Exchange to authenticate itself correctly. In this example, we want to move a mailbox from the "ABC.Com" forest to our

Exchange organization. The first thing we have to do is to collect the credentials that Exchange will use to identify itself to the source forest. We can do this with the `Get-Credential` command, which prompts with a standard Windows dialog to collect a username and password that we can store in the $AbcCredentials variable. We then call the `Move-Mailbox` command and pass the name of a Global Catalog server in the other forest to help find the mailbox that we want to retrieve and the credentials to identify ourselves to the remote forest. The complete command looks like this:

```
$AbcCredentials = Get-Credential
Move-Mailbox —id 'ABC\Smith' —TargetDatabase 'ExchMbxSvr2\VIP
Mailboxes' —SourceForestGlobalCatalog'ABC-GC1.abc.com'
—SourceForestCredentials $AbcCredentials —BadItemLimit 9
—NTAccountOu 'Exchange Users'
```

4.3.6 Accessing another user's mailbox

The `Add-MailboxPermission` command allows you to grant permissions to users to access the mailboxes of other users. For example, to grant full access to user Bond to user Smith's mailbox:

```
Add-MailboxPermission —id Smith —AccessRights FullAccess —
User Bond
```

You obviously need permission to be able to log onto another user's mailbox, either by creating a new MAPI profile to allow Outlook to open the mailbox or by selecting the Outlook Web Access option[9] (Figure 4.10) to serve the same purpose. You need to grant full access to a mailbox if you want the user to be able to open the mailbox through Outlook Web Access.

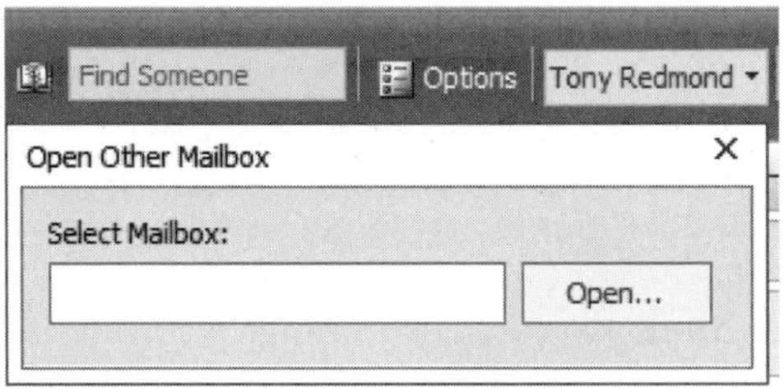

Figure 4.10
Opening another mailbox with Outlook Web Access

---

9.   You can also open another user's mailbox with Outlook Web Access by passing the URL https://server-name/owa/user-name@domain. For example: https://ExchMbxSvr1/owa/Jane.Smith@xyz.com

The FullAccess permission grants a user to work with the contents of any folder in the target mailbox, including the ability to delete items, but it does not include the right to send messages on behalf of a user. Any attempt to send a message on behalf of the user will result in the error illustrated in Figure 4.11. If you want to grant that permission, you either have to use EMC to grant the Send on Behalf permission through the Delivery Options settings for the mailbox or use the `Set-Mailbox` command:

```
Set-Mailbox —id Smith —GrantSendOnBehalfTo Bond
```

The reason why the two-step process is needed to allow someone to send email on another user's behalf is that the first operation (`Add-Mailbox-Permission`) establishes a right for the specified user within the Store. The second step (`Set-Mailbox`) establishes an Active Directory right. Another way of accomplishing the second step is to use the `Add-AdPermission` command to add the extended Send As right to the user who you want to grant control over the mailbox. Note that you may need to wait for the Store to clear its cache of user information before these rights become fully effective.

```
Add-AdPermission —identity Smith —AccessRights ExtendedRight
—ExtendedRights Send-As —User Bond
```

You can use the `Get-MailboxPermission` command to check the permissions on a mailbox:

```
Get-MailboxPermission —id Smith
```

Or to find out what permissions exist on a mailbox for a specific user:

```
Get-MailboxPermission —id Smith —User Bond | Format-List
```

As you look at permissions, you will note that some are explicit and some are inherited, or granted to an account for some reason, such as membership of the Exchange Organization Administrators group. The mailbox's owner receives their permissions through "SELF." You may also see an explicit deny, meaning that a user has been blocked from a permission. You can use the `Remove-MailboxPermission` command to remove an explicit permission from a mailbox:

```
Remove-MailboxPermission —id Smith —User Bond —AccessRights
FullAccess
```

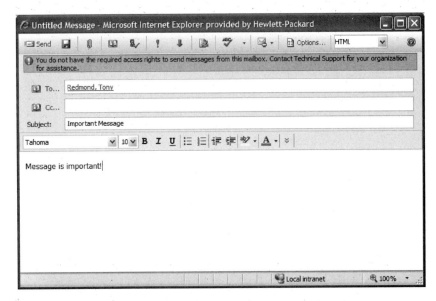

Figure 4.11
*Unable to send
email because you
don't have the right*

4.3.7 Different commands and different properties

From our discussion, you might assume that Get-Mailbox is top of the list of the Exchange administrator's all-purpose commands. However, mailboxes only exist as attributes of Active Directory user objects, so it should come as no surprise that separate commands exist to retrieve and set the basic properties of user objects (including those that are not mail-enabled) and the properties that transform user objects into mailboxes.

- Get-User and Set-User operate on the broad set of user object properties.

- Get-Mailbox and Set-Mailbox operate on a set of properties that relate to mailboxes.

- Get-CasMailbox and Set-CasMailbox operate on a limited set of properties that control access to the protocols managed by the Client Access server.

- Get-UmMailbox and Set-UmMailbox operate on the properties used by the Unified Messaging server.

It can be hard to know when to use one of these commands instead of another. For example, you might assume that the Department property is under the control of Get-Mailbox because the EMC GUI displays this information when you look at the properties of a mailbox. This isn't the case because Department is a property that non-mailbox-enabled Active Directory objects can possess, so you will not see it displayed if you type:

```
Get-Mailbox | Select Name, Department | Format-Table
```

EMS will execute the command, but you will see many blank values listed in the "department" column even if you are quite certain that you have populated this property. This is because Get-Mailbox does not include the Department property in its property list and so treats it as a custom variable. If you type:

```
Get-User | Select Name, Department | Format-Table
```

You now see a lot more information because Get-User is able to work with any user objects (not just those that are mailbox-enabled) and it knows about the department property. The rule is that you can use a Set- command to manipulate any property that you see listed by its Get- counterpart. In other words, if the Get-Mailbox command can retrieve a value for a property, then you can use the Set-Mailbox command to set a new value for that property.

You will use the Get-Mailbox and Set-Mailbox commands to work with mailboxes most of the time. However, you need to use the Get-CasMailbox and Set-CasMailbox commands to access the properties that control the protocols managed by the Client Access server, such as a user's ability to use POP3 or IMAP4 to get to their mailbox, the features available to mailboxes through Outlook Web Access, and the settings that control how mobile devices access mailboxes through ActiveSync. You cannot use the Get-Mailbox and Set-Mailbox commands to work with the properties that control protocol access. In addition, you cannot use the Get-CasMailbox and Set-CasMailbox commands to work with the general set of Exchange properties for mailboxes. It can be sometimes confusing to know exactly what you can do with what command, but you quickly get used to picking the right command.

4.3.8 **Contacts**

Mail-enabled contacts are Active Directory objects that point to someone outside our organization that we want to communicate with, such as users of a different email system within the same company or users in an external company that we do business with. Contacts have SMTP email addresses and appear in the GAL. Providing that you know the email address of the contact, creating it through EMS is trivial.

```
New-MailContact —Alias SeanD —Name 'Sean Doherty' —Org Contacts
—ExternalMailAddress 'Sean.Doherty@other-company.com'
```

If you have an existing contact in Active Directory, you can enable it for mail with the `Enable-MailContact` command:

```
Enable-MailContact —id 'JFS' —ExternalEmailAddress
'Jfs@millionaires.com'
```

To disable a mail contact, use the `Disable-MailContact` command:

```
Disable-MailContact —id 'JFS'
```

Disabling a mail contact leaves them in the Active Directory but removes the properties that allow users to email the contact and allow Exchange to list the contact in the GAL. If you want to remove a contact completely, use the `Remove-MailContact` command:

```
Remove-MailContact —id 'JFS'
```

Use the `Set-MailContact` command to perform subsequent operations to update existing contacts. For example, to set a contact so that they always receive MAPI rich text format messages:

```
Set-MailContact —id 'Sean Doherty' —UseMAPIRichTextFormat
Always
```

Note that the `New-Contact` and `Get-Contact` commands are also available. These commands operate on the basic contact objects in the Active Directory and do not manipulate the properties used by Exchange.

4.4 **Working with distribution groups**

Creating a new distribution group is a two-step process. First, we need to create the new group and ensure that it has a type of "distribution" rather than "security" so that Exchange allocates an email address to the new group.

```
New-DistributionGroup —alias SeniorExec —name 'Senior
Executives'
—Type Distribution —org 'xyz.com/Users/Groups'
—SamAccountName SeniorExec
```

If you already have a Windows group and want to mail-enable it for use with Exchange, you use a command like this to populate the group with the properties that make it available for use with Exchange:

```
Enable-DistributionGroup —id SeniorExec
```

Once we create the new group it is immediately functional in that you can send email to it, but the message will go nowhere because the group does not contain any members. We therefore have to add members to make the group useful. The basic operation is to add members one at a time.

```
Add-DistributionGroupMember —id SeniorExec —Member Bond
```

The last parameter is the identification of the user that you want to add to the list. The default is to use the account alias, which is unique to Windows, so whatever user whose alias is "Bond" will be added to the list. However, it is easy to make mistakes with aliases when you work with large user communities, so it is usually a better idea to pass the UPN as this parameter.

```
Add-DistributionGroupMember —id SeniorExec —Member
'Tony.Redmond@xyz.com'
```

You can obviously cut and paste the required Add-DistributionGroup-Member commands to add the members of the group or you can import the membership in from a prepared CSV file and loop through the data to add each member using the technique outlined for bulk mailbox loads on page 285. Another trick that you can use when you have multiple members to add to the group is to create a table and pipe the table as input to the Add-DistributionGroupMember command. For example:

```
"John Smith", "Amy Cater", "Ollie Harding" |
Add-DistributionGroupMember —id 'Senior Exec'
```

As you would expect, you use the Get-DistributionGroup command to retrieve properties of a group and the Set-DistributionGroup command to set the properties of a group. For example, to set one of the custom attributes on a group:

```
Set-DistributionGroup —id SeniorExec —CustomAttribute1 'VIP'
```

In the same way that we encountered differences between using the Set-Mailbox command to set Exchange-specific properties on an Active Directory user account and the Set-User command to set basic Active Directory properties, the Set-Group command is sometimes required instead of Set-DistributionGroup. For example, to change the user who is responsible for managing a group, we need to use Set-Group because this action creates a link to another Active Directory account who will manage the group. You can assign a manager to any group even if it is not mail-enabled.

```
Set-Group —id SeniorExec —ManagedBy Bond
```

Taking this example a little further, let's assume that you want to assign the responsibility for managing all of the groups that belong to a department (such as the Legal department) to a user. We can do this with a combination of three commands:

```
Get-DistributionGroup | Where {$_.Name —Like '*Legal*'} | Set-Group
—ManagedBy Bond
```

Another situation is where we want to discover what groups a user belongs to. This is easy to do in the Active Directory when you view the properties of an account because the Active Directory maintains pointers to the groups in the MemberOf property (and the MemberOf property is not available through the Get-User command). It is not quite so straightforward in PowerShell, but you can scan as follows:

```
$User = (Get-User —id Bond).Identity ; Get-Group —Filter {Members —eq $User}
```

Once you have groups populated, you can use them as the basis for some management operations. For example, let's assume that you want to assign a managed folder policy (see Chapter 8 for information about how managed folders and managed folder policies work) to users. You can do this individually, but if all the target users are in a group, you can use the group as the basis for the operation. In this example, we use the Get-Distribution-Group command to select the group that we want to use, the Get-DistributionGroupMember command to expand the group into individual members, and then the Set-Mailbox command to assign the managed folder policy.

```
Get-DistributionGroup —id 'Senior Executives' | Get-
DistributionGroupMember | Set-Mailbox —ManagedFolderMailboxPolicy
'Senior Leader Records Management'
```

Deleting a member from a group is easy too.

```
Remove-DistributionGroupMember —id SeniorExec —Member Bond
```

One common request is to create a group that contains all the mailboxes on a particular server. Administrators use groups like this to let users know when a server is going to be unavailable for some reason, such as when a service pack or hot fix needs to be applied. We can create and populate such a group with a couple of commands. First, we create the new group:

```
New-DistributionGroup -Type Distribution
-SamAccountName 'ExchMbxSvr1Users'
-Name 'Mailboxes on server ExchMbxSvr1' -OrganizationalUnit 'Groups'
```

To add all the mailboxes to the group, we call the Get-Mailbox command to fetch the names of all of the mailboxes on the server and pipe these names to the Add-DistributionGroupMember command. This is exactly what we did before to add a single user to a group only now we do it for a whole set of mailboxes.

```
Get-Mailbox —Server ExchMbxSvr1 | Add-DistributionGroupMember
-Identity ExchMbxSvr1Users
```

You might not include mailboxes in the group that you don't want to ever receive messages, such as those used for room and equipment resources. With this point in mind, we should amend our original command to add a filter to exclude these mailboxes:

```
Get-Mailbox —Server ExchMbxSvr1 —Filter {RecipientTypeDetails —eq
'UserMailbox' —or RecipientTypeDetails —eq 'LegacyMailbox'}| Add-
DistributionGroupMember -Identity ExchMbxSvr1Users
```

It is great to have the new group created and ready to go, but you know that the accuracy of the group's membership immediately starts to degrade as you add new mailboxes to the server or move mailboxes to another server. Adding or moving mailboxes do not automatically update group membership in the same way as mailbox deletes do. Recall that group membership is formed by a set of backward pointers to the underlying Active Directory objects that form the group, so if you delete a mailbox and its user account, the Active Directory automatically removes the pointer and so maintains group membership. Therefore, if you want to keep the group up to date you either have to:

1.   Integrate group membership updates into the process that you use to move mailboxes between servers (you need to remove the mailbox from one group and add it to another) and the process that you use to create new mailboxes.

2.   Regenerate the groups on a regular basis. You can do this by creating a script to delete the group and recreate it using the commands that we have just described. Note that this approach may cause some problems with Active Directory replication if you delete a group that someone else is updating elsewhere in the forest.

3.   Use a dynamic group.

The last option is the most interesting because it requires least work on the part of an administrator.

4.4.1   **Working with dynamic distribution groups**

When we discussed dynamic distribution groups in Chapter 3, we reviewed the wizard that Microsoft provides in EMC to create and maintain dynamic groups and the limitations that Microsoft has imposed on the queries that you can create to generate dynamic groups through EMC to ensure that the filters generated to create these groups work and deliver great performance. All of the dynamic groups generated by EMC have precanned filters because the filter created by EMC is constrained to using a limited number of properties. The net result is that you can only edit these groups through EMC and if you want to create a dynamic distribution group that uses any other property than those supported by EMC in the filter, then you have to create and maintain the group through PowerShell.

As we think about creating groups through the shell, it is good to remind ourselves of the three principles that guide the creation of any dynamic distribution group:

1.   What organizational scope will the recipients come from? We will state this in the RecipientContainer property of the query.

2.   What types of recipients will be included in the query? We will state this in the IncludedRecipients property.

3.   What other properties are involved in the filter? We pass these values in the RecipientFilter property. Because we are creating a custom filter through the shell, essentially we have made the decision that we need to use more than the set of properties supported by the EMC wizard.

First, we start by reviewing how to create a new dynamic distribution group using the New-DynamicDistributionGroup command. Here is the one-line command to create a group that contains a recipient filter that includes anyone who works for HP.

```
New-DynamicDistributionGroup -Alias 'CUserDL' -Name 'Company Users'
-RecipientFilter {Company -eq 'HP' —and RecipientTypeDetails —eq
'MailboxUsers'} -RecipientContainer 'HP.COM'
-OrganizationalUnit Groups
```

This isn't a very exciting query because it could easily have been generated by the EMC wizard. We haven't done anything very intelligent in terms of creating a complex query. Note that the RecipientContainer parameter specifies the objects that will form part of the dynamic group based on their position in Active Directory. In this case, we have specified the root of the domain, meaning that any object under this point will be included. After creating the new dynamic distribution group, you can determine whether the query used is precanned or custom by using the Get-DynamicDistribution-Group command:

```
Get-DynamicDistributionGroup —id 'Company Users' | Format-List
DisplayName, RecipientFilterType, RecipientFilter,
LDAPRecipientFilter
```

```
DisplayName        : Company Users
RecipientFilter    : ((Company -eq 'HP' -and RecipientTypeDetails -eq
'UserMailbox') -and -not(Name -like 'SystemMailbox{*') -and -not(Name
-like 'CAS_{*'))
LdapRecipientFilter :
&(company=HP)(objectClass=user)(objectCategory=person)
(mailNickname=*)(msExchHomeServerName=*)(msExchRecipientTypeDetails=1
)(!(name=SystemMailbox{*))(!(name=CAS_{*)))
```

Even though we created this dynamic distribution group through the shell, it shows up as a precanned filter, just like all of the filters generated by the EMC wizard. The reason is that Exchange optimizes the filters as much as possible and has recognized this filter as precanned because it does not use any properties outside the set of conditional properties that precanned filters support. As you will recall from the discussion about creating dynamic distribution groups through EMC in Chapter 3, the conditional properties that are available for filtering when you use EMC are:

- ConditionalDepartment
- ConditionalCompany
- ConditionalStateOrProvince
- The fifteen custom attributes (ConditionalCustomAttribute1 to ConditionalCustomAttribute15)

The reason why this set of special conditional properties exists is very simple. A dynamic distribution group is a recipient object itself and you can set properties for recipient objects, including the properties that you might want to use when you create a filter. The potential for confusion is obvious, so the Exchange developers added the special filtering properties to make it obvious when you want to set a property of the group and when you want to set a property used in a filter.

To tweak the filters programmatically to take them past the point that you can achieve with EMC, you can create a dynamic distribution group and create a filter using whatever properties you need and then pass the filter in the RecipientFilter property. Note that if you create a custom filter and want to pass it in RecipientFilter, you cannot combine it with a precanned filter like –IncludedRecipients. The reason is that Exchange will compute the filter for you and then write it into the RecipientFilter property, so you can't pass one set of values for Exchange to compute and then pass another value (that might be completely different) in RecipientFilter. For example, you can't do this:

```
New-DynamicDistributionGroup -Alias 'CUserDL' -Name 'Company
Users'
-RecipientFilter {Company -eq 'HP'}
-RecipientContainer 'HP.COM'
-IncludedRecipients 'MailboxUsers'
-OrganizationalUnit Groups
-ConditionalCompany 'HP'
```

The rules of thumb for building filters for dynamic distribution group are therefore:

- The easiest way to build a filter is to use the special conditional properties, if only because you break out the filter for each property into a separate parameter. For example:

```
Set-DynamicDistributionGroup —id 'UK Employees'
—ConditionalStateOrProvince 'England', 'Wales', 'Scotland'
—ConditionalCompany 'HP', 'HP UK', 'Hewlett-Packard',
'Hewlett Packard'
—ConditionalCustomAttribute1 'Employee'
—IncludedRecipients 'MailboxUsers'
```

  In this example, the query that Exchange uses to build the group is: Any account from England, Wales, or Scotland who belongs to the company called HP, HP UK, Hewlett-Packard, or Hewlett Packard, and who has the value "Employee" in custom attribute 1. This type of query that has to check multiple values for a property is evidence of a certain lack of standards in the population of mailbox data. Remember the caveat that while dynamic distribution groups are great ways to address changing populations, they can be slow for the transport service to resolve against the Active Directory if more than a couple of hundred addresses result or you add many conditions. This is one case where simpler is better.

- As shown in the last example, you can restrict a dynamic distribution group to send messages to a certain set of recipient types by specifying the —IncludedRecipients parameter. You can then select from one or more of the following values: AllRecipients, MailboxUsers, Resources, MailContacts, MailGroups, MailUsers, or even None (which would be a kind of non-op).

- If you use —RecipientFilter to state a filter to use with a dynamic distribution group, then you can include a broader range of properties within the filter. You can combine properties to create a filter that is as complex as you like. For example:

```
—RecipientFilter {Company —eq 'HP' —and Office —eq 'Dublin' —and
Department ne 'Sales' —and ServerName —eq 'ExchMbxSvr1' —and
CustomAttribute15 —eq 'Employee'}
```

■ You cannot combine –RecipientFilter and the special filter properties in a dynamic distribution group.

Moving on to work with something that is of immediate interest to most administrators, the command to create a new dynamic distribution group with a recipient filter that includes all the mailboxes on an Exchange 2007 server is:

```
New-DynamicDistributionGroup -Name 'Mailboxes on ExchMbxSvr1'
-Alias MbxSvr1 -RecipientContainer 'xyz' -OrganizationalUnit Groups
-RecipientFilter {ServerName -eq 'ExchMbxSvr1'}
```

Figure 4.12
Filter for a dynamic distribution group

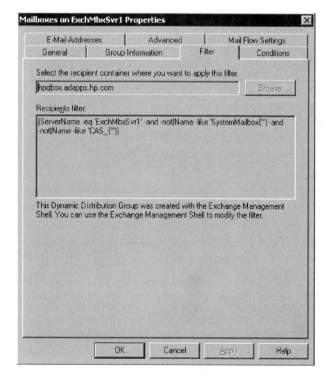

You cannot use EMC to edit a custom recipient filter created for a dynamic distribution group. As you can see in the group properties shown in Figure 4.12, you can see the custom filter, but you cannot do anything else. The only way that you can edit the group's custom recipient filter is to create a new recipient filter and update the group with the Set-DynamicDistribution-Group command.

There is no equivalent to the `Get-DistributionGroupMember` command for dynamic distribution groups, so if you want to discover the membership of a dynamic group, you have to invoke a command such as `Get-Mailbox` and pass it to the appropriate filter.

4.4.2   Advanced group properties

Apart from membership, Exchange allows you to set many other properties for groups that you can do when you create the group or afterwards. For example, the "Advanced" property tab of the GUI offers options to set these properties:

- Hide group from Exchange distribution list: Users can always send to the group if access to the group is not restricted to a certain list of correspondents and they know its SMTP address. This option removes the group from the GAL and any other Exchange address lists.

- Send Out of Office notifications to originator: You can suppress OOF[10] messages for messages sent to the group by setting this property to be false. The default is to allow notifications to flow back to anyone who sends to the group.

- Send delivery reports to group manager: Before you can set this property, you have to specify what account manages the group. The default is that the group will not have a manager.

- Send delivery reports to message originator: This is the default behavior, meaning that Exchange will return non-delivery and other reports back to the message originator.

- Do not send delivery reports: Set this property to suppress any reports for messages sent to the group.

Before we start to work with properties of the group, it is a good idea to check out the current values of the properties and the names of the properties that we want to work. The easiest way to do this is with a command like this:

```
Get-DistributionGroup SeniorExec | Format-List
```

Along with the set of regular properties, you will notice that distribution groups support the set of 15 customized attributes that are available to

---

10.   OOF means "Out of Facility." Logically, we should be using OOO for out of office, but OOF has been around since before Exchange appeared (the term was used on Microsoft's previous Xenix email system) and will not change now.

you to store data of your choice. You should also see that the value of both the RecipientType and RecipientTypeDetails properties is "MailUniversal-DistributionGroup" and that the value of GroupType is "Universal." If you use the group to assign permissions over objects, it will be a mail-enabled security universal group, so the value of the RecipientType and Recipient-TypeDetails property is "MailSecurityUniversalGroup." Here is how to set the properties to hide the group from the GAL and to suppress reports going back to anyone.

```
Set-DistributionGroup SeniorExec
-ReportToOriginatorEnabled:$False
-ReportToManagerEnabled:$False
-SendOOFMessageToOriginatorEnabled:$False
-HiddenFromAddressListsEnabled:$True
```

We have already seen that some properties need to have data appended to them rather than simply overwriting the data. You can restrict access to distribution groups so that only specific users or distribution groups are able to send messages to them. It is quite common for companies to restrict the ability of users to send messages to senior executives. You can set restrictions on who has the ability to send messages to a group by selecting the group and then accessing the Message Delivery Restrictions option of the Mail Flow tab. Here's what we would do to add a new user to the list of accepted senders for our distribution group through EMS:

```
Set-DistributionGroup SeniorExec -AcceptMessagesOnlyFrom ((Get-
DistributionGroup SeniorExec).AcceptMessagesOnlyFrom + 'James Bond')
```

If you want to restrict access to a distribution group, it is easier to use another distribution group as the control point for the restriction and import the members of that group into the restriction list. To do this, we use much the same code but specify the AcceptMessagesOnlyFromDLMembers parameter and pass the name of the distribution group that we want to use instead of a specific user.

```
Set-DistributionGroup SeniorExec -AcceptMessagesOnlyFromDLMembers ((Get-
DistributionGroup SeniorExec).AcceptMessagesOnlyFromDLMembers + 'Legal
Executives')
```

There are two important points to note here. First, importing members from another group to add them to the restriction list for a group is a one-time operation. Exchange expands the membership of the group that you specify and adds each of the members of the group to the set of users who can send messages to the target group. If you make a subsequent change to the membership of the group that you import, Exchange does not automatically add the new member to the restriction list. For example, if I add the user "Jack Smith" to the "Legal Executives" group after I use the "Legal Executives" group as the basis for restricting email address to the "Senior Executives" group, Jack Smith is unable to send email to "Senior Executives" until I add their name separately.

The second point is that `Set-DistributionGroupMember` will fail if a user that you import from another group already exists in the restriction list. You could avoid this problem by setting the AcceptMessagesOnlyFromDLMembers property to $Null first before you specify what the value should be.

Because PowerShell's error handling is a tad basic, it's a good idea to check that everything went smoothly and that the right users are allowed to send messages to the group after you make any changes. I like to do something like this:

```
Get-DistributionGroup SeniorExec | Select Name, AcceptMessagesOnlyFrom |
Format-List
```

```
Name                     : Legal Executives
AcceptMessagesOnlyFrom : {Ailbhe Redmond, James Bond, Tony Redmond, Daragh
Morrissey}
```

Note that you can also explicitly prohibit specific individuals from sending messages to a group by setting the RejectMessagesFrom property. For example:

```
Set-DistributionGroup SeniorExec -RejectMessagesFrom ((Get-
DistributionGroup SeniorExec).RejectMessagesFrom + 'Mary
Jacobs')
```

Working with group membership provides a nice opportunity to explore pipelining further. For example, let's assume that we have made the decision to give all of our senior executives a very large mailbox quota. We have a group called "Senior Executives" that all the necessary mailboxes are members of, so the logic we need is:

- Open the "Senior Executives" group.
- Read all the members of the "Senior Executives" group.

- Update each mailbox with the new quota.

This is a good example of an administrative activity that can be a real pain to execute through the GUI if we have to process a large group. With EMS we can say:

```
Get-DistributionGroup 'Senior Executives' |
Get-DistributionGroupMember | Set-Mailbox —IssueWarningQuota
5000MB —ProhibitSendQuota 5050MB
—ProhibitSendReceiveQuota 5075MB
—UseDatabaseQuotaDefaults:$False
```

Note the –UseDatabaseQuotaDefaults parameter—setting this parameter to "False" tells Exchange to use the specific quotas we have now set on the mailbox. If you did not set this value, Exchange would continue to apply whatever default quotas the mailboxes inherited from the database where they reside.

4.5 Delegation through the shell

Chapter 3 discusses the Exchange delegation model that allows different users to have administrative control over the organization, servers, and recipients and how to use EMC to delegate access to users. You can also delegate access through EMS. For example, to get a complete list of all users who possess any sort of administrative permission for an Exchange server within the organization, you issue the `Get-ExchangeAdministrator` command. I find it most convenient to pipe the output to a text file as follows:

```
Get-ExchangeAdministrator | Format-Table > c:\Temp\
ExchangeAdmins.txt
```

As you scan the entries, you find users who have control over the complete organization:

```
Identity : xyz.com/Domain Administrators/Tony Redmond
Scope    :
Role     : OrgAdmin
```

Users who have control over recipients:

```
Identity : hpqbox.adapps.hp.com/Exchange Users/Ailbhe Redmond
```

```
Scope     :
Role      : RecipientAdmin
```

And others who have administrative control over servers. In this case, the users have view-only access to the organization (so that they can navigate through the organization with EMC) and specific control over particular servers.

```
Identity : xyz.com/Exchange Users/Management/Mark Crosbie
Scope     :
Role      : ViewOnlyAdmin
Identity : xyz.com/Exchange Users/Management/Mark Crosbie
Scope     : ExchMbxSvr1
Role      : ServerAdmin
```

Naturally, you can also use `Get-ExchangeAdministrator` to return information about a specific user:

```
Get-ExchangeAdministrator —id 'Tony Redmond'
```

The `Add-ExchangeAdministrator` command delegates access to a new user. For example, to add Jane Smith to the list of administrators for the ExchMbxSvr1 server, you type the command shown below. After you add the account to the list of administrators, make sure that you add the account to the built-in local Administrators group for the server.

```
Add-ExchangeAdministrator —id 'Jane Smith' —Role ServerAdmin
—Scope ExchMbxSvr1
```

The `Remove-ExchangeAdministrator` command removes a user's administrative access.

```
Remove-ExchangeAdministrator —id 'Jane Smith' —Role
ServerAdmin —Scope ExchMbxSvr1
```

See Chapter 3 for more information about how to delegate administrative access to an Exchange 2007 server.

4.6 Creating efficient filters

PowerShell supports server- and client-side filters. Any time that you see the Where command used like all the examples we have discussed so far, you know that you are executing a client-side filter. Client-side filters are the standard for PowerShell and all PowerShell commands that can filter data support client-side filters. Exchange has different characteristics to standard Windows management because of the potential number of objects that you can ask a query to process. It is one thing to ask for all of the processes that are active on a server and quite another to ask for all of the mailboxes on a server. This is the reason why Exchange supports server-side filters.

The big difference between the two types of filters is that client-side filters bring all of the requested data set from the server to the client before applying the filter to generate the final data set, which the command that you call then processes. The client and server do a lot of work to isolate the necessary data. Server-side filters ask the Exchange server to filter the data set before passing the resulting filtered data to the client for execution and therefore reduce the amount of data that traverses the network for the client to process. Only a limited number of commands that deal with users, other mail-enabled objects, and queues support the –Filter parameter that invokes a server-side filter and not all of the properties returned by these commands support filtering. Without filters, these commands can generate a huge amount of data in any medium to large organization and be quite slow to execute, so server-side filtering helps by focusing on a specific set of objects and doing the work on the client. It is worth mentioning that Exchange generates the most efficient queries that it can for OPATH filters. All of the precanned filters generated for dynamic distribution groups, Address Lists, and Email Address Policies use server-side filters.

For example of server and client-side filtering in action, two methods are available to find all the mailboxes with "James" in their name. We can use either of these commands:

```
Get-Mailbox –Filter {Name –like '*James*'} –ResultSize 5000

Get-Mailbox –ResultSize 5000 | Where {$_.Name –like
'*James*'}
```

On the surface, these two pieces of code seem similar, but they are very different in reality. First, they use different filters. Second, the effect of the filters can generate very different results. If we omitted the –ResultSize parameter, you generate the same query: find all the mailboxes with a name that contains "James." The server-side filter will execute faster than the client-side filter, which proves the point that server-side filtering is faster. When we add the –ResultSize to limit the size of the collection that we process (which you would probably want to do if you work with a large organization), then the queries that Exchange generates to locate data are very different.

- The first (server-side) filter returns the first 5,000 mailboxes that it finds that include James in the mailbox name.

- The second (client-side) filter fetches data for the first 5,000 mailboxes to the client and then applies the filter to find the mailboxes that include James in the name. However, the filter only applies to the set that the client fetched and may not find all of the mailboxes that we actually want to discover.

Even though we ask the server-side filter to do more work (because it will have to process significantly more data to find the mailboxes that we have asked for), it still executes faster! For example, when I executed the two commands shown above against a very large Exchange organization (170,000 mailboxes), the server-side filter completed in 43 seconds and the client-side filter in 81 seconds.

Sometimes people make the mistake of assuming that the client-side filter is faster because server-side filters provide the data in one motion after the server processes all the data. You therefore wait for a while without seeing anything and then see all the filtered records at one time. By comparison, the client-side filter fetches and filters data continuously and so you see some output on the screen as the command finds each matching record. However, the important indicator of performance is how long each type of filter takes to complete and server-side filters are always faster.

The commands that you are most likely to use with server-side filters are:

- `Get-User` –Retrieve basic Active Directory properties for any user account, including mail-enabled accounts.

- `Get-Mailbox` –Retrieve Exchange-specific properties for mailboxes.

- `Get-MailContact` –Retrieve Exchange-specific properties for mail-enabled contacts.

- `Get-DistributionGroup` –Retrieve Exchange-specific properties for mail-enabled groups.

Each of the commands that you can use to work with user accounts, groups, and mailboxes supports a different set of filterable properties. To discover what properties are available for filtering, you can use PowerShell to query the properties of a returned object. For example:

```
Get-Mailbox -id Redmond | Get-Member | Where-Object
{$_.MemberType —eq 'Property'} | Sort-Object Name | Format-
Table Name
```

This set of commands calls a command to return some information about an object. It then pipes the information returned by the first command to the Get-Member command, which extracts information about the properties. We sort the properties by name and output them in table format. The output looks like this:

```
Name

----

AcceptMessagesOnlyFrom

AcceptMessagesOnlyFromDLMembers

AddressListMembership

Alias

AntispamBypassEnabled
CustomAttribute1

CustomAttribute10

CustomAttribute11

CustomAttribute12

CustomAttribute13
CustomAttribute14
...
WindowsEmailAddress
```

This method works for the Get-Mailbox, Get-CasMailbox, Get-User, Get-Recipient, Get-DistributionGroup, and Get-DynamicDistribution-

Group commands. You can use any of the values reported in a –Filter statement. For instance, the all that we just made to Get-Mailbox reports that the custom attributes are available, so to find all mailboxes that have a value in the CustomAttribute10 property, we can generate a command like this:

```
Get-Mailbox –Filter {CustomAttribute10 –ne $Null}
```

If you look at the filterable properties reported by the Get-Dynamic-DistributionGroup command, you can see that the ManagedBy property is available for this dynamic distribution group whereas it is not for mailboxes. Hence, we can execute a filter like this:

```
Get-DynamicDistributionGroup –Filter {ManagedBy –ne $Null}
```

When you create a filter, it is best to be specific as possible. You can state several conditions within a filter. Another example of a server-side filter that returns all the mailboxes in the Dublin office where the user name contains "Tony" is shown below. The Get-User command also works with this filter, but Get-Mailbox executes a tad faster because the server does not have to process accounts that are not mail-enabled.

```
Get-Mailbox –Filter {Office –eq 'Dublin' –and Name –like
'*Tony*'}
```

After you have mastered server-side filtering, you will find that you use it all the time to work with sets of users. For example, let's assume that you want to give a new mailbox quota to members of a certain department but no one else.

```
Get-User –Filter {Department –Eq 'Advanced Technology'} |
Set-Mailbox -UseDatabaseQuotaDefaults:$False –
IssueWarningQuota 5000MB –ProhibitSendQuota 5050MB –
ProhibitSendReceiveQuota 5075MB
```

4.7   Bulk updates

Anyone faced with the task of bulk updates (either to create a lot of new mailboxes or other objects, or to modify many existing objects) in Exchange 2000/2003 had quite a lot of work ahead of them because Exchange offered no good way to perform the work. You could create CSV or other load files and use utilities such as CSVDE or LDIFDE to process data in the files against the Active Directory, or you could write your own code to use CDOEXM or ADSI to update the Active Directory. Either approach involved a lot of detailed work where it was quite easy to make a mistake. The alternative (to use the ESM or AD Users and Computers consoles to make the necessary changes through a GUI) was just boring and also an invitation to make a mistake. The root cause of Exchange's problems with bulk changes was the lack of a programmable way to automate common management operations, something that changes with the arrival of EMS.

You can combine the `Get-User` and `Set-Mailbox` commands effectively to solve many problems. Here is an example where you need to update the send quota property on every mailbox for a set of users whose business group has decided to fund additional storage. You can identify these users by their department, which always starts with "Advanced Tech" but sometimes varies into spellings such as "Advanced Technology" and "Advanced Technology Group." Conceptually, the problem is easy to solve.

1. Look for all users who have a department name beginning with "Advanced Tech."

2. Update the send quota property for each user.

With Exchange 2000/2003, we can use the "Find" option in AD Users and Computers to build a suitable filter to establish the set of users. The problem here is that you then have to open each user located by AD Users and Computers to update their quota through the GUI, something that could become very boring after ten or so accounts. You could also export a CSV-formatted list of users to a text file, then manipulate the file to find the desired users, and then process that list through CSVDE to make the changes, but you have to search for all matching users across the complete directory first. There is a lot of work to do.

The process is easier in EMS. First, you use the `Get-User` command with a suitable filter to establish the collection of mailboxes that you want to change. The following command returns all users who have a department name that begins with "Advanced Tech" and then updates the ProhibitSend-Quota property to the desired amount (let's say 1,000MB). Because we have a collection of user objects established, we can chain on the necessary `Set-Mailbox` command to perform the update. Note that some of these users may not be mailbox-enabled, but error handling is another day's work.

```
Get-User | where {$_.Department -like '*Advanced Tech*'} |
Set-Mailbox -ProhibitSendQuota 1000MB -
UseDatabaseQuotaDefaults $False
```

Mergers, acquisitions, and internal reorganizations pose all sorts of problems for email administrators. EMS won't solve the big problems, but it can automate a lot of the mundane tasks that occur. For example, department names tend to change during these events. EMS makes it easy to find all users who belong to a specific department and update their properties to reflect the new organizational naming conventions. If only executing organizational change was as easy as this one-line command, which transforms everyone who works for the "Old Designs" department to now belong to the "Cutting Edge Design" department:

```
Get-User | Where {$_.Department —eq 'Old Designs'} | Set-User
—Department 'Cutting Edge Design'
```

Note the use of $_.Department. This indicates a value fetched from the current pipeline object. In this case, it is the department property of the current user object fetched by Get-User.

To verify that we have updated all the users that we wanted to (and maybe provide a report to HR or management), we can use a command like this:

```
Get-User | Where {$_.Department —eq 'Cutting Edge Design'} |
Select Name, Department | Sort Name | Format-Table > c:\temp\
Cutting-Edge.tmp
```

A variation on this theme is to output the data to a CSV file to make the data easier to work with Excel or Access or another tool that can read in CSV data.

```
Get-User | Where {$_.Department —eq 'Cutting Edge Design'} |
Select Name, Department | Sort Name | Export-CSV c:\temp\
Cutting-Edge.CSV
```

Things are even easier if you just need to change everyone's company name after your company is acquired.

```
Get-User | Set-User —Company 'New Company'
```

You can even do things like only alter the users whose mailbox belongs to a particular database:

```
Get-Mailbox —database 'VIP Mailboxes' | Set-User —company
'Big Bucks'
```

    —Department 'Executives'

All of the examples discussed so far depend on you being able to identify some property that you can use as the basis for a filter. But what about the situation where you do not have a common property value to check for? In this case, you can build a simple list of mailbox names (or any other format that the –identity parameter will accept such as a UPN) and use the Get-Content command to read the names one by one and pipe these values to whatever other command you need to use. For example, here is how we can use that trick to enable ActiveSync access for a set of users:

```
Get-Content c:\temp\Users.txt | Set-CasMailbox —
ActiveSyncEnabled $True
```

Another place where EMS excels is where you want to apply a common setting across all servers in your organization. For example, let's assume that you want to apply a new retention limit for items of sixty days (perhaps mandated by the legal department) to all servers:

```
Get-MailboxDatabase | Set-MailboxDatabase —ItemRetention
60.00:00:00
```

These simple examples demonstrate the value of having a scripting language that supports automation of common management tasks.

4.7.1 Creating sets of mailboxes

We already discussed how to use PowerShell to create a new mailbox, but what happens when you have a whole set of mailboxes to create at one time, perhaps to populate a new mailbox server? In this case, you can use a combination of the Import-CSV and New-Mailbox commands to do the job. The Import-CSV command reads data in from a CSV-formatted file and New-Mailbox creates the new mailbox. The ConvertTo-SecureString command reads the password provided in the file and converts it to a secure string so that it you can pass it as an acceptable value for a password. A sample input file in CSV format looks like this:

```
Id, FullName, LastName, FirstName, Password
MAnderson, Mike Anderson, Anderson, Mike, Testing123
FAnderson, Fergal Anderson, Anderson, Fergal, Testing234
```

Sometimes it is good to check that the list is populated with the correct data and can be read as we'd expect. One way to do this is to call the Import-CSV command to process the data to populate a variable and then see what that variable contains:

```
$MyData = Import-CSV c:\temp\users.csv
$MyData | Format-Table
```

Here's the code to read the CSV file and create the mailboxes (and of course, the underlying Active Directory accounts):

```
# Set up variables

$data = Import-CSV c:\temp\Users.csv
# Database where we are going to put the user mailboxes
$mdb = 'ExchMbxSvr1\Database1'
$ou = 'XYZ.com/Exchange Users/XYZ'

# Import the data and create the new mailboxes

ForEach-Object ($i in $data)
{
 $ss = ConvertTo-SecureString $i.password -AsPlaintext -Force
 $upn = $i.id + "@xyz.com"
 New-Mailbox -Password $ss -Database $mdb
 -UserPrincipalName $upn -name $i.fullname -
OrganizationalUnit $ou
 -SamAccountName $i.id -FirstName $i.firstName
 -LastName $i.lastname -Displayname $i.fullname
}
```

Note that New-Mailbox populates a limited number of attributes in the new Active Directory object and you may want to call Set-Mailbox afterwards to populate attributes such as mailbox quotas. This script is a little complex but you only need to write it once (or reuse it from somewhere else). While the necessary code is much simpler, you can take the same approach to create a bulk load of mail-enabled contacts. Assume that you have a CSV load file in the following format:

```
Name, First, Last, Alias, SMTPAddress
Bob Hope, Bob, Hope, BH, Bob.Hope@xyz.com
```

Terry Smith, Terry, Smith, TSM, Terry.Smith@xyz.com

This code is enough to read the load file and create mail-enabled contacts.

```
Import-CSV c:\temp\Newcontacts.csv | ForEach-Object {New-
Mailcontact
-Alias $_.alias -Name $_.Name -ExternalEmailAddress
$_.SMTPAddress
-First $_.first -Last $_.last -Org Contacts}
```

As you can imagine, you can repurpose much the same code for other situations.

4.8   Reporting mailbox data

Perhaps one of the more dramatic examples of how the focus for management has changed in Exchange 2007 from the GUI to the shell is the loss of the ability to view mailbox statistics and logons through the console, which has been a feature of Exchange management since 1996. The Recipient Configuration node of EMC lists mailboxes, contacts, and groups, but it does not tell you anything about them in terms of who's currently connected to a server, the number of items in their mailbox, and how much quota they use. To get this information, you now have to use the `Get-MailboxStatistics` and `Get-LogonStatistics` commands to extract and report data rather than browsing information through the GUI.

The logic behind why Microsoft eliminated the display of user statistics from EMC has to do with how EMC retrieves information from the server and the overall change in design philosophy for the management console. To fetch information about a mailbox, the Exchange 2003 console makes RPC calls to the database that hosts the mailbox to retrieve information like the mailboxes in the database plus properties such as the item count, quota used, deleted item count, and the size of deleted items for each mailbox. This approach is acceptable if you restrict your view to a single database on a server, but EMC treats recipients on an organization-wide basis and its default mode is to display the first 1,000 mailboxes in the organization when you click on the Mailbox node under Recipient Configuration. EMC makes an LDAP request to fetch data about mailboxes from the Active Directory and does not have to access the Store at all until you decide that you want to view the properties of a mailbox, in which case EMC displays the properties that it retrieves from Active Directory alongside the mailbox information. You will notice that a small pause often occurs between requesting the properties and their display, caused by the need to access the mailbox and fetch the total item count, quota used, and time of last logon. You see the same pause when you execute a `Get-MailboxStatistics` command against the mailbox because this is effectively what EMC has to do to retrieve information about the mailbox from the Store.

Because the design philosophy behind EMC is to treat mailboxes on an organizational basis, there is no guarantee that the mailboxes that you view when you open EMC will come from any particular server or database on a server. EMC normally orders mailboxes alphabetically by their Display Name, so you fetch mailboxes starting with "A" and continue until you hit the limit for the number of items that EMC is willing to process. If you want EMC to fetch mailboxes from your local server, you have to apply a filter. Although you can argue a good case that EMC should always apply a filter, it is not currently the default behavior for EMC, so the performance implications of having to make up to 1,000 RPC calls to different databases scattered around the organization to fetch storage details for the mailboxes before EMC can display anything are unconscionable. Avoiding horrible performance is the reason why Microsoft dropped the ability to browse mailbox and logon statistics through the console. The official line is that they mitigated the issue somewhat by displaying information about the quota used and items in a mailbox when you look at its properties and that you can always use PowerShell to retrieve the information. However, Microsoft has received a huge amount of negative feedback on this issue, especially from administrators who do not look after Exchange full-time and those do not care to learn shell programming. It would not come as a surprise if Microsoft upgrades EMC so that it can report statistics in a future release.

If you want to retrieve the kind of mailbox statistics that you are able to view with Exchange 2003 ESM, you use the `Get-MailboxStatistics` command. Like many other shell commands, the first impression of `Get-MailboxStatistics` is that it is somewhat verbose in terms of the volume of data that it generates on anything but a very small server, so if you want to look at data interactively, you need to provide a filter by database or server to reduce the amount of information that you have to deal with. In most cases, it is more convenient to pipe the output to a file and use an editor to go through the contents. For example, here is what the output from `Get-MailboxStatistics` looks like when you pipe it through the `Format-list` command to show you all the properties that `Get-MailboxStatistics` can report. In this example, we extract information for just one mailbox:

```
Get-MailboxStatistics –id Redmond | Format-list > c:\temp\
MailboxStatistics.tmp


AssociatedItemCount    : 524
```

```
DeletedItemCount         : 3429
DisplayName              : Redmond, Tony
ItemCount                : 15723
LastLoggedOnUserAccount  : xyz\Tredmond
LastLogoffTime           : 1/12/2007 11:59:28 AM
LastLogonTime            : 1/12/2007 11:59:22 AM
LegacyDN                 : /O=xyz/OU=Europe/CN=RECIPIENTS/CN=Redmond
MailboxGuid              : 4ea5e87d-5aa0-4d50-9966-0d0b93166129
ObjectClass              : Mailbox
StorageLimitStatus       : BelowLimit
TotalDeletedItemSize     : 585519749B
TotalItemSize            : 1269649497B
Database                 : ExchMbxSvr1\LCR Storage Group\Users
ServerName               : ExchMbxSvr1
StorageGroupName         : LCR Storage Group
DatabaseName             : Users
Identity                 : 4ea5e87d-5aa0-4d50-9966-0d0b93166129
IsValid                  : True
OriginatingServer        : ExchMbxSvr1
```

Not all of these properties are necessarily interesting, so we can select specific properties and use the Format-table command to generate the output as a table. For example, when we extract information for all of the mailboxes in a specific database, we can format the information to make it appear more attractive:

```
Get-MailboxStatistics –Database "Mailbox Store 1" | Select
DisplayName, ItemCount, TotalItemSize | Sort ItemCount |
Format-Table @{Expression="DisplayName"; width=30; label
="Name"}, @{Expression="ItemCount"; width=10; label =
"Items"},
@{Expression={ [math]::round(
[double](([string]$_.TotalItemSize).split("B")[0]) /1KB , 2)}
; width=15; label="Size(KB)"} > c:\temp\Mailbox-Report.tmp
```

In this case, we want to output just three pieces of information per mailbox and to sort by item count. We format the output fields with headers that describe the content better than the default names. We also take the default output for the TotalItemSize field (normally returned in bytes) and format it to display in kilobytes. Using the code shown above, we get a report like this:

Name	Items	Size(KB)	Database
Heublein, Alex	254	144322.91	ExchMbxSvr1\LCR Storage Gro...
Smith, Jane (Techology Co-O...	28	34495.39	ExchMbxSvr1\LCR Storage Gro...
Bond, James	405	26612.84	ExchMbxSvr1\First Storage G...
Walker, Karen	9	12586.35	ExchMbxSvr1\First Storage G...
Morrissey, Daragh	35	10102.26	ExchMbxSvr1\First Storage G...
Smith, Steve Jnr.	8	8394.89	ExchMbxSvr1\First Storage G...
Nemeth, Alan	33	7762.14	ExchMbxSvr1\LCR Storage Gro...
Crosbie, Mark	7	4201.99	ExchMbxSvr1\First Storage G...
Lyons, Martha	32	900.59	ExchMbxSvr1\LCR Storage Gro...
Grillenmeier, Guido	37	657.9	ExchMbxSvr1\LCR Storage Gro...

While you review these code examples, the thought may occur to you that the reports that we can generate using PowerShell commands are not as pretty as the GUI output from the Exchange 2003 ESM console. This is true. It is also true that you can extract data from ESM and export it to Excel to manipulate it further to create colorful reports and graphs. You can do this work with a couple of mouse clicks much more easily than grappling with the convoluted formatting requirements of the Format-Table command, including its ability to generate HTML output. Such a conclusion is natural, but it ignores the fact that you can write a PowerShell script once to create a report and then reuse it many times afterwards. You do not see the true value of the shell when you execute once-off commands; it only appears when you automate operations through scripts.

Once you have written a script to perform the desired operation, it is easy to reuse the script time after time. In this case, automation is best when you can process data for many different databases with one command or process all of the Exchange servers in the organization. Before explaining what is going on, the complete code for our script is:

```
Get-ExchangeServer | Where-Object {$_.ServerRole -like
'*Mailbox*'} | Get-MailboxStatistics | Select DisplayName,
ItemCount, TotalItemSize, Database | Sort TotalItemSize
-Descending | Format-Table @{Expression= 'DisplayName';
width=30; label = 'Name'}, @{Expression= 'ItemCount';
width=10; label = 'Items'}, {Expression={
[math]::round([double](([string]$_.TotalItemSize).split("B")[
0]) /1KB , 2)} ; width=15; label = 'Size(KB)'}, @{expression =
'database'; width=30; label = 'Database'} > C:\TEMP\
MBXStats.TMP
```

To explain what the script does:

1. We call the `Get-ExchangeServer` command to retrieve a list of all the Exchange servers in the organization.

2. We impose a filter with the `Where-Object` command to filter out any servers that do not support the mailbox role. This command also removes any legacy Exchange servers because these servers return "None" in the ServerRole property. The filter is required because we do not want to access servers that do not support the `Get-MailboxStatistics` command (such as legacy servers and Edge servers).

3. `Get-MailboxStatistics` fetches mailbox data from all of the Exchange servers that pass the filter. We select the display name for each mailbox, the count of items in the mailbox, the total size of the items, and the name of the database that hosts the mailbox.

4. We sort the data by mailbox size.

5. We format the data into a table. The fields are given headers and the total size field is formatted to turn bytes into kilobytes.

6. We pipe the report to a text file.

Proving that the shell is very flexible as well as powerful, EMS allows you to pipe the mailbox statistics that you extract to a file in CSV format with the `Export-CSV` command. In this case, you would amend the script to do something like this:

```
Get-MailboxStatistics —Database 'Mailbox Store 1' | Select
DisplayName, ItemCount, TotalItemSize | Export-CSV c:\temp\
MailBoxStats.csv
```

Everything we have done so far generates simple text output, but proving that the shell can output data in multiple ways, you can use another function called `ConvertTo-HTML` to generate HTML format data that is generated by another command. Here's an example:

```
Get-MailboxStatistics | Sort TotalItemSize —Descending |
Select —First 10 | ConvertTo-HTML —Property DisplayName,
ItemCount, TotalItemSize > C:\TEMP\Stats.htm
```

This command calls `ConvertTo-HTML` to process some sorted and selected output from `Get-MailboxStatistics`. We specify the properties that we want to format and then output the HTML to a temporary file that you can then view through a browser, as shown in Figure 4.13.

Figure 4.13
*HTML output
from Get-
MailboxStatistics*

There are many examples available on the Internet to show how to pipe the HTML direct to an IE window that you can define as a custom script and call instead. For example, here's the code for a script called Out-IE.PS1, which leverages the fact that you can use the `New-Object` command to invoke a new instance of an application through COM. In this case, we're calling Internet Explorer:

```
$ie = New-Object -com InternetExplorer.Application
$ie.navigate("about:blank")
while ($ie.busy) { sleep 1 }
$ie.visible = $true
$ie.document.write("$input")
$ie
```

Of course, you could also use the `Invoke-Item` command to call Internet Explorer. This way saves typing:

```
Invoke-Item c:\temp\Stats.htm
```

HTML output is a step forward from plain text but it's not very exciting. Third-party software providers such as PowerGadgets (www.powergadgets.com) have written PowerShell snap-ins that add the ability to generate customizable charts and other graphic output. These add-ons are a useful way to report data extracted from Exchange 2007 servers. Figure 4.14 shows a simple example of how the PowerGadgets Out-Chart command charts the output from the Get-MailboxStatistics command. The command used to produce this graph was:

```
Get-MailboxStatistics —Database 'VIP Mailboxes' | Select
DisplayName, ItemCount | Sort ItemCount | Out-Chart —Title
'Total Items in Mailbox' —Values ItemCount —Label DisplayName
```

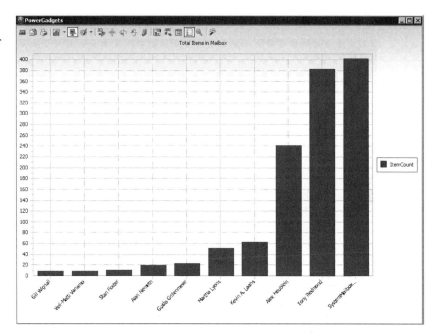

Figure 4.14
*Example of
PowerGadgets Out-
Chart command*

You can play around with different variations using the Get-Mailbox-Statistics command to generate different reports. For example, here is how to select the top ten consumers of mailbox quota on a server.

```
Get-MailboxStatistics -Server ExchMbxSvr1 | Sort
TotalItemSize -Descending | Select -First 10
```

In this example, we count all the mailboxes in a database and return the maximum, minimum, and average size of the mailboxes in the database. The figures reported are in bytes:

```
Get-MailboxStatistics —Database 'VIP Mailboxes' | Measure-
Object TotalItemSize —Average —Maximum -Minimum
```

```
Count     : 16
Average   : 18805567.75
Sum       :
Maximum   : 148691039
Minimum   : 0
Property  : TotalItemSize
```

If you need to scan a database to discover all the mailboxes that are larger than a certain size, you can do it by using a combination of the Get-MailboxStatistics and Where-Object commands. In this example, we report all of the mailboxes on a server that are over 100MB.

```
Get-MailboxStatistics —Server ExchMbxSvr1 | Where-Object
{$_.TotalItemSize —gt 100MB} | Select DisplayName, ItemCount,
TotalItemSize
```

The Get-LogonStatistics command produces equally ugly output as Get-MailboxStatistics, at least when compared to the ability to browse information about users that are currently logged on to Exchange through ESM, but once more, you have it in your hands to decide how to extract and use the data that EMS provides when you ask for it. As an example of how you might use the Get-LogonStatistics command, assume that you want to find out what users have logged in to their mailbox on a server since a specific date. A command like this will do the trick:

```
Get-LogonStatistics —Server 'ExchMbxSvr1' | Where
{$_.Logontime -gt '1/1/2007'}
```

4.8.1   Special properties

When we built our report using the Get-MailboxStatistics command, we found that the TotalItemSize property outputs data in bytes. TotalItemSize is actually one of the special properties that crop up in Exchange from time to time, and while a byte size is interesting when you want to be exact, few administrators actually think about mailbox sizes, message sizes, or quotas in terms of bytes. For this reason, we usually convert the value TotalItemSize to make it more understandable. One common method is shown above, another that involves the use of the ToKB method to transform bytes into kilobytes is:

```
Get-MailboxStatistics —Database 'Mailbox Store' | Format-
Table DisplayName, @{Expression={$Size =
$_.TotalItemSize.Value; $Size.ToKB()} ; Label = "Size (KB)"}
```

Other properties that report sizes in bytes include anything to do with mailbox quotas. While reporting these properties can take some extra work, it is much easier to set values because you can specify what you need in bytes, kilobytes, megabytes, or gigabytes. For example, to set the new default prohibit send quota size for a database:

```
Set-MailboxDatabase —id 'VIP Mailboxes' —ProhibitSendQuota 500MB
```

Another example of where you might need to execute some special processing is the ServerName property, which you might want to use to list all the mailboxes on a server:

```
Get-Mailbox —Filter {ServerName —eq 'ExchMbxSvr1'}
```

This is a convenient and quick way to focus in on a group of mailboxes. Remember that EMS, like EMC, returns a default set of the first 1,000 matching objects for a command, so if you have more than 1,000 mailboxes on the server, you would have to pass the ResultSize parameter to set the size of the set you want to process. For example:

```
Get-Mailbox —Filter {ServerName —eq 'ExchMbxSvr1'}
—ResultSize 5000
```

Let's say that you now want to interrogate a set of servers to get a complete listing of mailboxes. You do not want to use client-side filters because this would take too long, so you execute a server-side filter to find all mailboxes on servers with a name like "ExchMbx":

```
Get-Mailbox —Filter {ServerName —like '*ExchMbx*'}
—ResultSize Unlimited
```

Problem! EMS responds to say that the ServerName property does not support a text filter. This seems strange—you have just executed another server-side filter with the —eq operator. What is the issue with the —like operator? Well, the reason is that the ServerName property is a calculated property that Exchange takes from the ServerLegacyDN property that is stored with the mailbox. The ServerLegacyDN property means a lot to Exchange, but because it identifies the server in X.500 format, it is very long and unwieldy to process. Microsoft recognized that most administrators would prefer not to go to the bother of working with the full ServerLegacyDN. They therefore provide the ServerName property as a convenient shortcut that you can use in places such as EMC filters. However, shortcuts do not come with the full set of features, so you cannot use it with the –like operator. Because ServerLegacyDN is a "proper" property, the command that we actually need is:

```
Get-Mailbox —Filter {ServerLegacyDN —like '*ExchMbx*'}
—ResultSize Unlimited
```

The good news is that these are the most obvious examples of where you will run into strange gotchas with Exchange shell commands. Over time, Microsoft will probably clean things up and these issues will go away.

4.9   Using the shell for other management tasks

The influence of the shell permeates throughout Exchange 2007, so it is impossible to discuss how to manage Exchange through the shell in one point. Instead, it is more sensible and logical to discuss how to use appropriate shell commands for different management tasks as we meet those tasks in the remaining chapters of this book. For example, we review details of how to use shell commands with objects such as databases and storage groups in Chapter 5, transport and connector settings in Chapter 6, protocol settings in Chapter 7, managed folder policies and other user management tasks in Chapter 8, hardware-related tasks in Chapter 9, and other server management tasks in Chapter 10.

To complete an overall picture of the range of commands supported by EMS, we can say that:

- EMS supports all of the traditional management tasks for the Store such as creating new databases or setting the properties of a database. Because Microsoft has based EMC on the same code as the EMS, you can execute equivalent shell commands for any option available through EMC. For example, to set circular logging for a storage group:

```
Set-StorageGroup 'Unimportant Mailboxes'
—CircularLoggingEnabled $True
```

- You have to perform many of the new management features that Microsoft has introduced in Exchange 2007, such as the synchronization of Active Directory configuration and recipient information between hub transport servers and edge servers, through EMS. There are exceptions to this rule where the options also appear in EMC, such as setting up Local Continuous Replication for a mailbox database.

- EMS is a flexible management tool whenever you want to interrogate data across a range of servers or other objects. For example, to find all of the servers in the organization that support the Client Access server role:

```
Get-ExchangeServer | Where {$_.IsClientAccessServer -eq
$true}
```

The same technique can be used to check for other server roles in the organization using the IsMailboxServer, IsHubTransportServer, IsEdgeServer, and IsUnifiedMessagingServer properties. You can also check server properties to determine whether the server runs Exchange 2007 or later (IsExchange2007OrLater) or is clustered (IsMemberOfCluster).

To return a count of all the servers in the organization grouped by the edition of Exchange that the servers run:

```
Get-ExchangeServer | Group-Object Edition
```

Another way to view servers in the organization is by the server roles that they support:

```
Get-ExchangeServer | Group-Object ServerRole
```

It is also useful to be able to execute a quick command to discover when the databases on a server were last backed up:

```
Get-MailboxDatabase —Server ExchMBXSvr1 —Status | Format-List
*Back*
```

We can also report on what version of software and edition the Exchange servers in the organization are running:

```
Get-ExchangeServer | Format-Table Name, ExchangeVersion,
Edition
```

- EMS is a powerful ally when you need to execute the same command for a number of objects. For example, let's assume that you want to mount all of the mailbox databases that belong to a server called ExchMbxSvr1:

```
Get-MailboxDatabase —Server ExchMbxSvr1 | Mount-Database
```

Another example is where you want to set the same deleted item retention period on every mailbox database across the entire organization:

```
Get-MailboxDatabase | Set-MailboxDatabase —ItemRetention
45.00:00:00
```

- A nice example of how you can use Get-MailboxDatabase to return information that you might not expect is when you scan a server to discover the size of mailbox databases and return the information sorted from largest to smaller:

```
Get-MailboxDatabase -Server ExchMbxSvr1 | ForEach {Get-
ChildItem $_.EdbFilePath | Select-Object Name, Length} |
Sort-Object
-Property Length -Descending
```

- EMS provides separate commands to manipulate the different server roles that exist within the product:

    `Set-/Get-MailboxServer` works with the properties of mailbox servers

    `Set-/Get-ClientAccessServer` works with Client Access servers

    `Set-/Get-TransportServer` works with hub transport and Edge servers

    `Set-/Get-UMServer` works with UM servers

- The most exciting prospect offered for administrators by EMS comes through the ability to automate common procedures that you could not have even thought about in previous releases of Exchange. You can now create a set of commands to perform an operation once, capture the commands in a PowerShell script, and use the script whenever you need to perform that work.

Apart from speeding things up, if you create the necessary commands in a script to automate common procedures, you eliminate some of the potential for administrator error and ensure consistency of application of policy by different administrators across the organization. Of course, you have to get the commands right to perform any particular operation in the first place, but it is easier to spend the effort to write and test a script once and reuse it everywhere than to have multiple administrators all attempt to do the same thing in slightly different ways.

4.10 Command validation

It is not always easy to test a complex command to a degree of certainty that you know exactly what the command will do. Some EMS commands that work with mailboxes support the –validate parameter, which allows you to request EMS to inform you what will happen if the command executes. You can see a list of the commands that support –validate by typing:

```
Get-ExCommand | Where {$_.Definition -Like '*Validate*'}
```

The most important command that you will want to validate is Move-Mailbox because you do not want to go ahead with the move of one or maybe multiple mailboxes, all of which could be quite large, to another server if things are not exactly right. The value of a GUI is that it can incorporate checks to stop you doing silly things but you are on your own when you work with the command shell, so it is nice to have a check. For example:

```
Move-Mailbox —id 'Jane Smith' —Targetdatabase 'New mailboxes'
-Validate
```

EMS will pause to tell you that it is about to move the mailbox from its current location to the target database and ask you to confirm that this operation should proceed. If you confirm, nothing will happen apart from Exchange performing checks to ensure that it could move the mailbox. As you can see from Figure 4.15, Exchange completes the command by issuing a status message, which in this case indicates that everything is okay if you want to move the mailbox. Apart from stopping you from making a mistake, using the –validate parameter is a way to check your syntax before starting an operation such as moving mailboxes that can take some time to complete.

A much larger group of commands support the –Confirm parameter, which prompts you with "Do you want to perform this action" before proceeding. To see the list of commands that support –Confirm, type:

```
Get-ExCommand | Where {$_.Definition -Like '*Confirm*'}
```

For example:

```
Get-User *Bon* | Set-User –department –eq 'Flying Tonight' –
Confirm
```

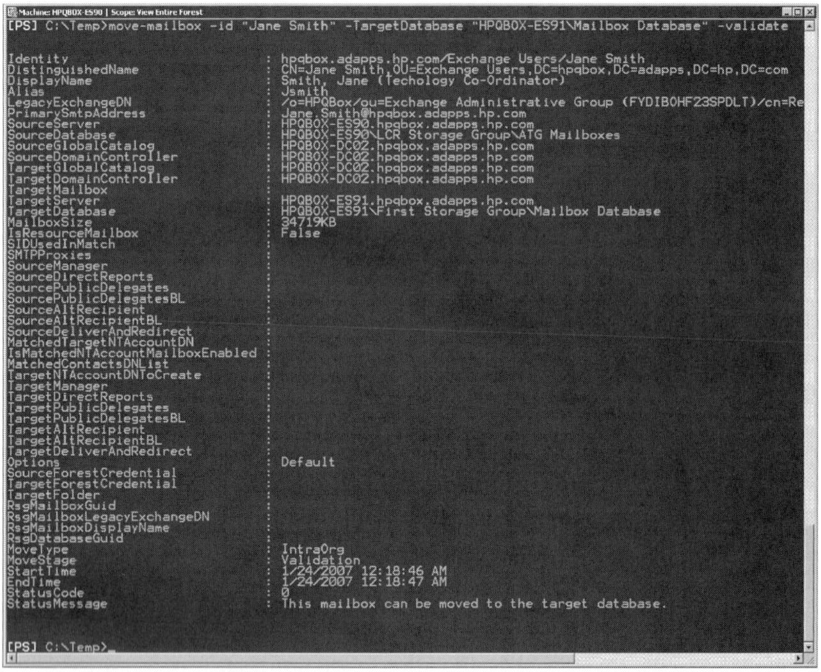

Figure 4.15
Command validation

Remember that you can use command validation with non-Exchange commands as well. For example, adding the –confirm parameter to the Stop-Process command might stop you killing a process like the Information Store when you really do not want to.

```
Stop-Process 5468 -Confirm
```

The –Whatif parameter is available to allow you to "ask" PowerShell what will happen if you execute a command. For example, if you type the command to move a mailbox and append –Whatif

```
Move-Mailbox —id 'Bond' —TargetDatabase 'ExchMbxSvr1\
Database1' —Whatif
```

EMS will tell you that the operation could take a long time to complete and that the mailbox will be inaccessible until the move is complete. The current release of PowerShell does not support the –WhatIf and –Confirm switches for commands that you include in scripts, so you have to be sure about what your code does before you incorporate it into a script, especially if the code deletes objects or otherwise affects the system. Jeffrey Snover, Microsoft's PowerShell architect, acknowledges that the lack of support for confirmation switches may be a problem and supplies a solution in the PowerShell blog at http://blogs.msdn.com/powershell/archive/2007/02/25/supporting-whatif-confirm-verbose-in-scripts.aspx.

Another form of validation is to record everything that you do when you work inside EMS, just in case you have to account for something that you did later on. To start capturing information:

```
Start-Transcript c:\Temp\LogofAdminActions.tmp —Append
```

EMS signals that all actions are now being captured in the file that you pointed to. To stop EMS capturing actions:

```
Stop-Transcript
```

The captured information looks like this:

```
**********************
Windows PowerShell Transcript Start
Start time: 20070112223353
Username  :XYZ\Redmond
Machine   : ExchMBXSvr1 (Microsoft Windows NT 5.2.3790 Service Pack 1)
**********************
Transcript started, output file is c:\temp\LogOfAdminActions.tmp
[PS] C:\Documents and Settings\redmond.xyz>get-mailboxdatabase

Name                 Server          StorageGroup       Recovery
----                 ------          ------------       --------
VIP Mailboxes        ExchMBXSvr1     First Storage Group  False
```

```
ATG Mailboxes          ExchMBXSvr1    LCR Storage Group    False
Rooms and Resources    ExchMBXSvr1    First Storage Group  False
Mailbox Database       ExchMBXSvr1    First Storage Group  False


[PS] C:\Documents and Settings\redmond.xyz>get-mailboxstatistics

DisplayName                ItemCount    StorageLimitStatus    LastLogonTime
-----------                ---------    ------------------    -------------
Thompson, Blair            54                   BelowLimit
Redmond, Alan              24                   BelowLimit


[PS] C:\Documents and Settings\redmond.xyz>Stop-Transcript
**********************
Windows PowerShell Transcript End
End time: 20070112223444
********************** **********************
```

4.11 Working with remote servers

The default set of PowerShell commands that support Windows operate on the local server and cannot execute remotely. For instance, you cannot use the Get-Process command to return the list of active processes on another computer. In the eyes of some, this is a weakness that the PowerShell developers should address in a future release, but in the meantime, many Exchange commands can work with remote servers. The reason why is probably because Exchange has always embodied the concept of remote administration, whether it was the ability of an administrator to manage all the servers in a first-generation Exchange site, or the ability of an enterprise administrator to work with all of the servers in an organization in Exchange 2000 and 2003.

Clues that show you when you can work with remote servers include the presence of the –Server parameter, where you can pass the name of the remote server that you want to retrieve information from or set a property on, or the presence of a target for data to move to or to be used as a source. Examples include Get-MailboxServer, Get-TransportServer, Get-MailboxStatistics, Export-Mailbox, Set-Mailbox, Move-Mailbox, and so on.

The ability of EMS to work with remote servers out of the box is a strength of the product that should not be overlooked.

4.12 Working with non-Exchange 2007 servers

Another interesting aspect of PowerShell is that you are not restricted to working with Exchange 2007 servers. Recall that previous versions of Exchange support WMI and that you can use WMI to access information about an Exchange server, such as the list of mailboxes on a server. Power-Shell supports access to WMI objects, so you can put the two together to access some information about Exchange 2000 and 2003 servers from a Pow-erShell script. Access to legacy Exchange data is limited because WMI can't access some of the information on these servers, nor can it perform some of the operations that are commonplace on Exchange 2007 servers, such as creating a new mailbox or a storage group. Nevertheless, you can still do some useful work. For example:

```
get-WMIObject -class "Exchange_mailbox" -namespace
"root/MicrosoftExchangeV2" -computerName "ExchServer01"
—Credential "XYZ\Smith" | Format-Table  MailboxDisplayName,
@{e={[math]::round ($_.Size / 1KB , 2)} ; Label ="Size"}
```

This example uses PowerShell to access the WMI object and read information about Exchange mailboxes from the ExchServer01 computer. The command passes a set of credentials for the domain that owns ExchServer01. PowerShell then pipes the output from the WMI query through the format-table command to generate a formatted table, dividing the size of the mail-box (in bytes) by 1KB to return the size in kilobytes. The point about using PowerShell in this way is that you should not restrict yourself to looking at PowerShell exclusively for Exchange 2007.

Apart from working through WMI, a small selection of the standard EMS commands work with legacy Exchange servers. For example, here is an edited version of the details that the Get-ExchangeServer returns about an Exchange 2003 server:

```
Get-ExchangeServer ExchSvr2003 | Format-List

Name                          : ExchSvr2003
DataPath                      : C:\Program Files\Exchsrvr
Domain                        : xyz.com
Edition                       : Enterprise
ExchangeLegacyDN              : /O=xyz/OU=Exchange/nn=Configuration /
cn=Servers/cn=ExchSvr2003
Fqdn                          : ExchSvr2003.xyz.com
IsHubTransportServer          : False
```

```
IsClientAccessServer                 : False
IsExchange2007OrLater                : False
IsEdgeServer                         : False
IsMailboxServer                      : False
IsMemberOfCluster                    : No
IsProvisionedServer                  : False
IsUnifiedMessagingServer             : False
OrganizationalUnit                   : xyz.com/ExchSvr2003
AdminDisplayVersion                  : Version 6.5 (Build 7638.2: Service Pack 2)
Site                                 :
ServerRole                           : None
IsExchange2007TrialEdition           : False
IsExpiredExchange2007TrialEdition    : False
RemainingTrialPeriod                 : 00:00:00
IsValid                              : True
OriginatingServer                    : DC23.xyz.com
ExchangeVersion                      : 0.0 (6.5.6500.0)
ObjectClass                          : {top, server, msExchExchangeServer}
WhenChanged                          : 9/18/2006 5:23:44 PM
WhenCreated                          : 2/21/2003 3:46:28 PM
```

The Get-Mailbox and Get-CasMailbox commands work for mailboxes on legacy Exchange servers but other commands such as Get-MailboxStatistics and Get-MailboxDatabase do not. Because you cannot be sure that all of the EMS commands will work against legacy servers, the best idea is to follow the guideline of managing legacy Exchange servers with legacy tools and managing Exchange 2007 servers with Exchange 2007 tools.

Because PowerShell supports many different providers through a consistent interface, you can write code that mixes and matches data from multiple sources to automate reports, provisioning of servers, and other administrative operations. While it is true that you will encounter some limitations (such as the fact that using WMI to work with Exchange 2003 servers has not the same potential as using PowerShell to work directly with Exchange 2007 servers), there is still a lot of useful work that PowerShell can do in a multi-version Exchange environment.

4.13   Testing Exchange 2007

Exchange 2007 provides a set of shell commands that you can use to verify that everything is working correctly on a server. This is the first time that Microsoft has provided commands to help administrators check that Exchange is working properly and as you look at the comprehensive suite of test commands available in Exchange 2007, you can't help reflecting that it has taken Microsoft a long time to fill in this particular gap. You need to have Exchange administrative permissions over a server before you can execute these commands.

The first step in testing a system is to check that all the necessary components are present and are at the right revision level. The `Test-System-Health` command helps by scanning a server to verify that it is running the correct versions of software (related to Exchange 2007) and to detect some other conditions that may cause Exchange 2007 a problem. Before it runs, the `Test-SystemHealth` command checks the Microsoft web site for any updates that it should know about to be able to test a server accurately.

Figure 4.16 shows the result of running `Test-SystemHealth` on a server that runs a beta version of Exchange 2007 and you can see how the command reports this issue. More importantly, `Test-SystemHealth` reported that a driver is present (for HP Remote Insight Manager) that does not meet the Microsoft standards for some reason. There may be a good reason why the driver is not compliant, but it is always best to check out errors that Exchange flags like this.

Figure 4.16
The results of the Test-SystemHealth command

From the perspective of Exchange, the most basic test that you can perform is to determine whether all the services that collectively make up the different server roles in Exchange 2007 are running on a server. Use the `Test-ServerHealth` command for this purpose. As you can see, Exchange responds with the server roles that are installed on the target server and a list of services that are running plus any that are not currently operational.

```
Test-ServerHealth —Server ExchMbxSvr1
```

Role	RequiredServicesRunning	ServicesRunning	ServicesNotRunning
Mailbox	True	IISAdmin	
		MSExchangeADTopology	
		MSExchangeIS	
		MSExchangeMailboxAssis	
		tants	
		MSExchangeMailSubmissi	
		on	
		MSExchangeRepl	
		MSExchangeSA	
		MSExchangeSearch	
		MSExchangeServiceHost	
		MSExchangeTransportLog	
		Search	
		MSFTESQL-Exchange	
		W3Svc	
Client Access	True	IISAdmin	
		MSExchangeADTopology	
		MSExchangeFDS	
		MSExchangeIMAP4	
		MSExchangePOP3	
		MSExchangeServiceHost	
		W3Svc	
Hub Transport	True	MSExchangeADTopology	
		MSExchangeEdgeSync	
		MSExchangeTransport	
		MSExchangeTransportLog	
		Search	

4.13.1   Client connections

The Test-MapiConnectivity command verifies that clients can make MAPI connections to a database. If you run this command on a mailbox server, Exchange attempts to make a connection to every mailbox database on the server and reports how quickly it can make the connection. You can specify the name of a server or a mailbox database to focus in on a specific issue. If you do not specify the name of a mailbox to connect to, then Exchange connects to the special system mailbox in the database. This command runs a quick check against a selected mailbox server:

```
Test-MapiConnectivity –Server ExchMbxSvr1
```

MailboxServer	Database	Result	Latency(MS)	Error
ExchMbxSvr1	VIP Mailboxes	Success	5	
ExchMbxSvr1	new Mailboxes	Success	4	

The `Test-PopConnectivity` and `Test-IMAPConnectivity` commands allow you to check that a Client Access server is able to service incoming requests from POP3 and IMAP4 clients, including their ability to make LDAP requests to search the Active Directory. In this example, note the use of a pipelined call to the `Get-Credential` command to force Exchange to prompt for credentials to log onto the XYZ\Redmond account.

```
Test-PopConnectivity —ClientAccessServer ExchCAS1
—MailboxCredential(Get-Credential XYZ\Redmond)

And

Test-IMAPConnectivity ClientAccessServer ExchCAS1
—MailboxCredential(Get-Credential XYZ\Redmond)
```

CasServer	MailboxServer	Scenario	Result	Latency(MS)	Error
ExchCAS1	ExchMbxSvr1	Test IMAP4 Connectivity	Success	390.62	

The `Test-OWAConnectivity` command tests that Outlook Web Access connections are functioning as expected, including the ability to log onto a mailbox with Outlook Web Access or that a Client Access server provides the correct URLs to allow clients to connect. You can test a specific server or all servers (mailbox and Client Access) in an Active Directory site. For example, this command tests the ability to log onto a mailbox on a specific server for the stated user. You will be prompted by EMS to provide the credentials before the command executes:

```
Test-OWAConnectivity —MailboxCredential(Get-Credential Xyz\Redmond)
—MailboxServer ExchMbxSrv1
```

ClientAccessServer	MailboxServer	URL	Scenario	Result	Latency (ms)	Error
ExchMbxSvr1		https://ExchMbxSvr1. xyz.com/owa/	Logon	Success	5031.12	

4.13.2 Mail Flow

The `Test-MailFlow` command allows you to test whether the transport service is functioning correctly by logging on to the system mailbox in the first mailbox database on a server to create and send a test message from one server to another or to an external email address. The test also reports the time taken to send the message and whether the test used an external address. Figure 4.17 shows the resulting message, including the disclaimer applied by the transport system through a transport rule. You can find out more about how to create and manipulate transport rules in Chapter 8.

```
Test-MailFlow —TargetEmailAddress Tony.Redmond@xyz1.com


TestMailflowResult          MessageLatencyTime                   IsRemoteTest
------------------          ------------------                   ------------

Success                     00:00:03.6331338                     True
```

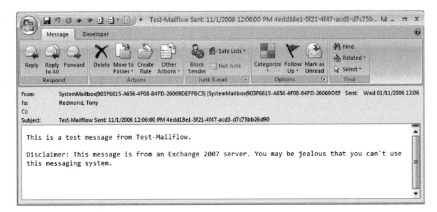

Figure 4.17
Message generated by the Test-Mailflow command

The `Test-OutlookWebServices` command tests whether the set of web services (AutoDiscover and Availability) that Outlook 2007 and Outlook Web Access clients depend on to locate services such as an OAB distribution point and free and busy data are working. In this example, we test that the services are running on a target Client Access server and state that we want to use the email address "Tony.Redmond@xyz.com" to test the Outlook provider (the service that handles requests from Outlook clients). In addition, we want to use the Availability service to check the free and busy data for the user "James.Bond@xyz.com."

```
Test-OutlookWebServices —ClientAccessServer ExchCAS1 —Identity Tony.Redmond@xyz.com —
TargetAddress James.Bond@xyz.com
```

Id	Type	Message
--	----	-------
1003	Information	About to test AutoDiscover with the ...
1007	Information	Testing server ExchCAS1.xyz.com...
1019	Information	Found a valid AutoDiscover service c...
1018	Information	The SSL certificate on ExchCAS1.xy...

```
1006                              Information Contacted AutoDiscover at https://Ex...
1016                              Success Successfully contacted the AS servic...
1013                              Error When contacting http://ExchCAS1...
1015                              Error Error when contacting the OAB servic...
1014                              Success Successfully contacted the UM servic...
1006                              Success Successfully tested AutoDiscover.
```

Among the commands that you can use to verify different aspects of the transport system are `Test-IPAllowListProvider` and `Test-IPBlockListProvider`, which tests the connection to an external third-party provider of an IP allow or block list that you may want to use on a hub or Edge server. In both cases, you pass the name of the provider and an IP address of a suspected problem server to test. The result of the test will be a true or false to indicate that a connection to the provider is possible and another true or false if the lookup for the IP address was successful.

`Test-SenderID` is a useful command if you use checks against Sender ID records in DNS to verify that servers are not sending spam. For example:

```
Test-SenderID —PurportedResponsibleDomain Microsoft.com
—IPAddress 65.55.238.126
```

If you deploy Exchange edge servers, you can run the `Test-EdgeSynchronization` command on a hub transport server to verify that any edge servers that synchronize their copy of Exchange configuration and recipient data with Active Directory (in their local copy of ADAM) are up to date. We will review details of how Edge synchronization works in Chapter 6.

4.13.3 Miscellaneous test commands

If you have deployed Exchange Unified Messaging, you can use the `Test-UMConnectivity` to check that everything is working. Likewise, if you have deployed Outlook Anywhere, you can use the `Test-OutlookAnyWhereConnectivity` command to test that it is functioning correctly.

The `Test-ExchangeSearch` command verifies that Exchange content indexing and retrieval is working properly. See Chapter 5 for details.

4.14 PowerShell for Exchange administrators

After all of these examples of EMS in action, what can we conclude about PowerShell from the perspective of an Exchange administrator?

First, PowerShell is simply something that you have to learn. At the start, you may want only to execute a couple of one-line commands, but gradually (unless you work with a very simple server), you'll find that EMS becomes part of your daily working life and that your command-line skills increase so that you do something more complex, such as writing your first script. You'll check out web sites to find tips from other administrators and sample scripts that you can adapt for your own environment. Eventually, because PowerShell is just so useful, it will be a natural way for you to solve many of your day-to-day administrative problems.

Second, PowerShell is powerful—maybe too powerful at times. If you have permission over the Exchange organization or even just a server, you can wreak havoc with a PowerShell command that does something that you didn't expect, perhaps because you made a mistake with syntax and moved hundreds of mailboxes to a server that couldn't accommodate the load when you really wanted to move just ten. The –Confirm and –Validate parameters are there to provide administrators with protection, but only to confirm that you have typed commands correctly and have not missed out any important parameters. They will not stop you doing something stupid, but they may cause you to pause before you commit to a command. Human nature being what it is, some won't use these parameters to check commands before execution, just like some drivers persist in thinking that seat belts are for wimps. Take your time and master PowerShell before you rush into anything that could cause damage to your organization. Learn the commands, learn the parameters, and test, test, and test again.

To help you to get used to PowerShell and to understand the power that it can have over your environment, it's a great idea to deploy a test lab that accurately reflects the characteristics of your organization. If you run clustered servers or a unified messaging server, then they should be in your test environment. It is not difficult today to create a set of virtualized test servers that run on a single large computer or even on a powerful laptop, and this will make all the difference to you when you test how PowerShell commands work with Exchange data. It is always better to screw up in a test environment than to inflict damage to a production system.

Third, you are going to accumulate scripts over time. You will develop some and find others on blogs and web sites that you then adapt for your own purposes. PowerShell scripts are like programs and should be treated as such. Make sure that only administrators use them and that you exercise some degree of version control (and testing, as described above) over the scripts that you plan to use for operational control. It is not great to discover that you cannot find the script that you wanted to use because someone has deleted or moved the file, so take the time to store copies of important scripts in a safe place.

Fourth, PowerShell is great, but let's realize that it is in its early days. Like the first version of any product, PowerShell will evolve over time and remove some of the problems that you can see today, such as syntax inconsistency in places. Another annoyance is that some commands cannot output to a file. For example, you can execute `Get-Mailbox > c:\Mailbox.txt` to create a list of mailboxes, but you cannot do `Get-SendConnector > c:\Send.txt` or `Get-ReceiveConnector > c:\Receive.txt` to create a list of send or receive connectors. However, if you pipe the output of these commands through the `Format-Table` command (`Get-SendConnector | Format-Table > c:\Send.txt`), the output appears. It's all very frustrating at times.

Last, the Exchange developers have done a great job of embracing and extending PowerShell for Exchange 2007. You can also use PowerShell to manage Windows and there is evidence that a solid ecosystem of third-party products will grow up around PowerShell to help fill in any gaps that exist. However, not every Microsoft product supports PowerShell today and you can expect that legacy versions of Microsoft products will not support Power-Shell in the future, so you can predict that Microsoft's fragmented administrative model will continue to exist until all of the product development groups figure out how they will incorporate support for PowerShell. Even then, to get to a more integrated administrative model, you will have to upgrade to the product versions that support PowerShell, and we all know how long that can take.

The net is that PowerShell marks the start of a new scripting experience for Exchange administrators. It will do great things when used correctly, but don't expect PowerShell to address all the sins of Microsoft's curiously deficient administrative past.

5

The Store

At its core, Exchange is a database application, albeit one that is highly tuned for the kind of transactions that a messaging system generates. The Information Store, or simply "the Store," lies at the heart of Exchange. Without a well-configured and managed Store, an Exchange server cannot provide a reliable and robust service to users.

Exchange 2007 introduces a number of changes for the Store, including an increase in the number of supported storage groups, internal changes that result from the move to the 64-bit platform, and database portability between servers. In this chapter, we review the core components of the Store and discuss how you can manage these components most effectively. Some of the other important changes, specifically continuous log replication, are in Chapter 9.

5.1 Introducing the Store

While Exchange is a database application, it is important to stress that the kind of transactions that Exchange users generate are very different to those of other, more structured databases. For example, the kind of transactions in a banking database where each transaction is broadly similar in terms of data and contains fields such as date, account number, transaction type, narrative, and amount. In the case of Exchange, a transaction can be radically different to the preceding transaction because one message might contain a simple "Hi" and goes from one user to another, and the next is a message sent to a large distribution list and has three paragraphs of text in the message body and a large PowerPoint attachment. Microsoft designed the Store to be able to deal with widely different transactions in a scalable and robust manner and this aspect of Exchange has contributed a great deal to the product's success.

Since Exchange 4.0, the Store has used a database engine called ESE (Extensible Storage Engine), which is a variant of Microsoft's JET (Joint Engine Technology) generalized database engine that provides the specialized features required by Exchange. The different layers in the Store take the following responsibilities:

- ESE organizes low-level database structures. ESE is a multi-user ISAM (Indexed Sequential Access Method) database with full Data Manipulation Language (DML) and Data Definition Language (DDL) capabilities.

- The Jet implementation of the database engine organizes the ESE database structures into pages and trees. The specific implementation of Jet for Exchange was referred to as "Jet Blue" up to the version shipped with Exchange 5.5 (ESE97) to distinguish it from other variants such as "Jet Red." From Exchange 2000 on, Exchange's database engine is simply "ESE." All versions are designed to optimize the storage of loosely-formatted, semi-structured data, which is a tad different from the very structured approach to data preferred by other databases, such as SQL.

- The Store organizes its database pages into tables that hold messages and attachments. The Store uses a hierarchical arrangement with mailboxes holding folders and folders holding the messages and attachments belonging to messages. The hierarchical model is not unique to Exchange and many other messaging implementations have used it, so this model is very much the traditional approach.

Other Microsoft products use JET technology. The Active Directory is the best and closest example to Exchange as its internal structure and arrangement is very close to the Store. Access is another example of JET technology in action, but you should not assume that the database engine used by Access is anywhere close in functionality to the version used by Exchange. There is, after all, a world of difference in the technology required to drive personal databases and that are needed by very large messaging servers. During the evolution of Exchange, Microsoft has used different versions of ESE. For example, the version used in Exchange 2000 and 2003 is "ESE98." While the versions changed, the basics of the underlying structure of the Store remains the same, with some important differences in Exchange 2007 that we will come to shortly.

ESE arranges database pages into a relatively shallow B-tree (balanced tree), a relatively common database construct (Figure 5.1). Exchange uses a variant called B+ tree, which provides a higher degree of efficiency by limiting the extent of the internal hierarchy within the database. The pages are of fixed size (4KB in all versions of Exchange prior to Exchange 2007, 8KB from Exchange 2007 onwards—the same size as Microsoft uses in the Active Directory database). In the B-tree, the first two pages are the database header, followed by a single page (logical database page 1) at the root level that contains pointers to the pages that make up the internal structure of the database. Each page has a 40-byte header that contains the page number, a count of free bytes available in the page, and a checksum. The page checksum plays an important role in maintaining the overall integrity of the database. The page header also contains information about adjacent pages to allow ESE to navigate to these pages quickly.

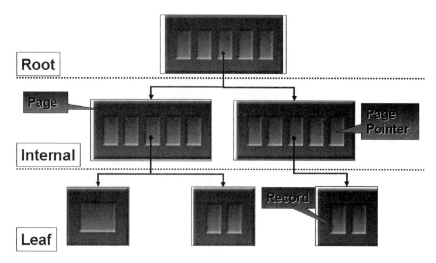

Figure 5.1
The B-tree structure within an ESE database

Within the internal structure of an ESE database, there are pages that contain pointers to the leaf pages, which hold data as database records. An individual page can contain up to 400 pages to leaf pages. The design of the database structure allows ESE to access any page quickly with a minimum number of referrals within the database (from root to internal to leaf). If ESE needs to fetch data from contiguous pages, it can do so by using the forward and backward links stored in the pages. Interestingly, ESE does not support the notion of data locality within its databases, as the ESE does not divide into pages indexes and data pages. In addition, ESE arranges database pages in a random manner so that the Store does not write new data in any particular order and it can assign data to any available page in the database. These facts make it difficult for storage arrays to cache critical data, such as an index, and so can make it more challenging to scale up an Exchange server to cope with large numbers of users that generate many I/O transactions. The move to the 64-bit platform offers ESE more headroom to cache data and so may make it easier to scale up larger servers.

Microsoft designed the Store to meet the ACID (Atomicity, Consistency, Isolation, and Durability) test for database transaction integrity. Atomic means that the Store only applies transactions to the database if they are complete and intact. A transaction is a series of modifications to the database that leaves the database in a consistent state. These modifications are called operations. When you send a message, the Store effects your command by executing the operations to assemble all of the MAPI properties for the message, such as the subject, recipients, author's email address, and so on, and whatever body parts are required, and posting the message in what you perceive to be a single logical step. Behind the scenes, the Store hands off the message for transport to its eventual recipients and then it updates the Sent Items folder in your mailbox with a copy of the message. An operation is the smallest change that an application can make to an ESE database. Operations include insert, delete, replace, and commit. A database is in an inconsistent state if ESE does not execute all of the operations required to make up a transaction, as in the case when a sudden power outage causes a server to fail. In such a circumstance, the Store replays as many operations as possible from the contents of a database's transaction logs, but it will ignore any transaction that is incomplete. The Store maintains consistency by insisting that transactions must be complete and it achieves isolation by not making a database change visible to users until it is complete. The presence of the transaction logs and the dual-phase commit for transactions into the Store databases achieves durability, the final part of the ACID[1] test.

ESE uses dual-phase commit for transactions. The first phase writes the data for the updated or deleted pages that contain the data that forms the transaction from the volatile cache[2] in memory into a transaction log file. These pages are referred to as "dirty" or being in a dirty state, and the vast majority of transactions in Exchange affect more than one page. The second phase then updates pages in the database using the data held in the database cache (memory) and writes the updates to disk. Both phases can occur simultaneously and enable ESE to commit transactions to disk rapidly, even under load. Note that ESE never commits a transaction to the database unless it is able to commit the entire transaction; if ESE committed a partial transaction then it would both fail to meet the atomic part of the ACID test and run the risk of introducing corruption into the database. The presence of the data in the transaction logs allows Exchange to recover data to a failed database after an administrator recovers it from a backup copy by replaying the transactions stored in the log files into the recovered database until the database is up to date.

At the logical level, the Information Store uses ESE to organize database pages into a series of tables that organize data in a form that Exchange can

---

1.   ACID means that the ESE is a transactional-based database that implements atomic, consistent, isolated, and durable transactions. See Transaction Processing: Concepts and Techniques, Gray and Reuter, 1983.

2.   The msExchESEParamLogBuffers parameter (an attribute that Exchange maintains for each storage group) determines the size of the volatile cache. See Microsoft Knowledge Base article 328466 for more information on how to tune the parameter. The size of the cache influences the I/O profile of the Store; a larger cache encourages fewer large I/O operations while a smaller cache generates a larger number of small I/O operations.

consume. For example, all of the mailboxes in a mailbox store have entries in a mailbox table. The entry for an individual mailbox acts as a pointer to a separate table that holds entries for all of the folders in the mailbox. When an Outlook client connects to Exchange, it accesses the mailbox table to locate the pointer to its folder table and then reads all of the folder information to build the folder hierarchy for display to the user. The Outlook client can then access the pointer in the folder table to the inbox folder and use that to read information about all the messages in the inbox folder. If the user then decides to read a message, Outlook takes the pointer for the message and uses it to extract the MAPI properties for the message and to populate the message form that it displays to the user. If the message has attachments, Outlook uses the pointers to the entries in the attachment table to fetch the attachments and display them in the message form. ESE maintains different tables for any custom views that users create. Unlike the standard tables (mailboxes, folders, etc.), users can create views[3] at any time and can order a view by any field that they include in the view. Exchange supports nested folders, or subfolders within folders, with pointers providing the necessary link from a child folder back to its parent. From the description above it is easy to imagine how many different tables that ESE has to manage in a typical Exchange mailbox database. There will be at least one table per mailbox, and it is likely that there will be tens or even hundreds of tables per mailbox. As you might expect, the tables that store messages and attachments occupy over 90% of the typical Exchange database. The dynamic nature of views and the sheer number of tables in the database pose a major performance challenge for any database, and one that Exchange has been able to address over the years, but not without some pain.

For example, views are an excellent user feature and they work very well. However, once a user has a large mailbox that has more than a few thousand items in some of the critical mail folders (inbox, sent items, calendar, deleted items), then it becomes very performance intense for ESE to generate a new view for the folder. Multiply this requirement by several thousand users accessing a server concurrently and you understand the challenge. The fact that mailboxes are increasing steadily in size as users store more information compounds the performance challenge. The advent of cached Exchange mode in Outlook 2003 addressed some of the problem by offloading activity to the client, but the need still exists for ESE to perform a huge amount of processing on the server. For example, no matter how many client-side operations Outlook takes care of, the server still has to handle the insertion of new messages as they arrive into user mailboxes to generate appropriate notifications, update the views, and so on.

Experience demonstrates that the best Exchange administrators have a good knowledge of the Store and of how ESE works. It is logical to assume

---

3. Only MAPI clients support views.

that anyone who attempts to administer a database application will understand the fundamental underpinnings of the application, but not always the case in practice.

5.2   Differences in the Exchange 2007 Store

When Microsoft began the design process for Exchange 2007, their original plan was to use this version to change the Store over to use the "Yukon" version of SQL (as implemented in SQL 2005) as the database engine. The plan (the "Kodiak" project) was very logical because it had the potential to deliver great savings to Microsoft as they standardized on a single database platform. With a single database platform for multiple applications, Microsoft would simplify development and eliminate a lot of cost that they incur in testing, packaging, and support. They would also be able to take advantage of some of the higher transactional capability that SQL delivers, especially on high-end systems. However, the engineering complexity of moving Exchange from ESE to SQL proved too much to bite off and Microsoft decided to continue with ESE in Exchange 2007. One major issue is that ESE accommodates all the quirks and foibles of the way that MAPI organizes data into properties and allows users to create their own views of data, such as sorting by received date, author, or item size. If the Store had only to deal with simple clients like those that use the IMAP protocol, it would be much easier to swap database engines. However, MAPI clients like Outlook can create different views for each folder and on a server that supports thousands of mailboxes, each of which can hold thousands of folders, the database might end up by having to deal with millions of folder views. As we can see from the experience with ESE, handing thousands of dynamic views is not an insurmountable problem, but it is challenging for a database like SQL that is designed to deal with the kind of predictable transactions that exist in traditional database applications. Note that changing folder views is a feature executed on the client when Outlook operates in cached Exchange mode, so there is less of an immediate impact on the server as the new view can be synchronized in the background. New views created by Outlook Web Access clients impact the server more heavily because the change occurs immediately, resulting in more work for ESE to create the view and return the result to the client—and a lot of processing results if the folder contains a lot of items. Microsoft's recommendation is to keep less than 5,000 items in a folder, but users aren't often aware of this point and probably couldn't care less.

All these reasons underline that there is no point in going ahead with a changeover in underlying database technology if you cannot guarantee that you can achieve at least comparable performance and functionality, and this was not possible in the Exchange 2007 timeframe. Microsoft could have persisted with the project to make Exchange 2007 use SQL, but only with the prospect of slipping eventual product availability to an unknown date and with no real guarantee of achieving the necessary performance, even on a 64-bit platform. The decision to stay with ESE is therefore very understandable, but we may yet see a move to SQL in a future version of Exchange, once Microsoft has had the chance to figure out how to solve the technical issues. Because of the complexity involved in making the transition from ESE, it is unlikely that the changeover will occur in the next version of Exchange, but you never know after that.

Instead of the radical transformation required to move the Store to use SQL, Microsoft took on the technical challenge of how to improve the ESE-based code to take advantage of 64-bit servers. Clearly, the extended address space on a 64-bit platform compared to a 32-bit platform provides an enormous increase in the memory available to any application, so the question is how Exchange could take maximum advantage of the available memory. Microsoft's answer in Exchange 2007 is to trade I/O operations for memory and so address a performance bottleneck that has always afflicted Exchange, the need for huge amounts of I/O capacity before a powerful server can handle the load generated by large numbers of concurrent mailbox connections. In addition, Exchange 2007 offers some hope that we can reduce the expense of deployments by increasing the ability of low-end storage configurations to provide the necessary power to service Exchange. In effect, you do not always have to deploy a SAN to provide storage to Exchange 2007, as a lower-priced and less complex storage configuration may be able to provide the necessary I/O capacity and throughput. However, you should not read this to be a general recommendation to move away from SAN deployments for Exchange because there are many good reasons to continue to use SANs, such as increased resilience to hardware failure, more configuration options, and the ability to consolidate storage requirements for multiple applications into a single infrastructure.

5.2.1 Are 64 bits that important?

Exchange has been down the 64-bit path before as Exchange 4.0 through 5.5 all supported the Digital Alpha 64-bit platform from 1996 to 2000. Indeed, Digital engineers did a lot of work to help Microsoft solve some major scalability problems in the Exchange 5.5 Information Store. However, Microsoft made the decision that Windows 2000 would not support Alpha and the consequence was that Exchange 2000 and subsequent releases reverted to 32-bit only.

The Alpha platform was the fastest system of its time, but it was handicapped by the fact that Microsoft merely recompiled programs like Exchange to run on Alpha as Microsoft did not want to incur the additional cost of maintaining two different code bases for 32-bit and 64-bit versions. For this reason, the Alpha version of Exchange could never take full advantage of the Alpha processor, and while the CPU delivered raw speed, the overall package was handicapped by the fact that the Exchange code never attempted to maximize its use of Alpha by, for example, caching more of the Store or directory databases in memory. Alpha enthusiasts regretted the situation and Alpha's speed advantage was gradually eroded by Intel's 32-bit CPUs, but it is fair to ask whether Exchange could have actually taken full advantage of a 64-bit platform at this point in its evolution. After all, many companies were still migrating from products such as Microsoft Mail and Lotus cc:Mail, storage was more expensive and delivered less capacity than is available now, mailboxes were smaller, and the number of mailboxes supported by a server was generally fewer than today. All in all (and with the benefit of hindsight), the 32-bit versions of Exchange 5.5, 2000, and 2003 provided the necessary combination of speed, performance, and supportability for the state of messaging technology as it existed.

Across the board, many of the parameters that dictate the performance that a messaging server like Exchange can deliver have changed in the last decade. For example:

- Message size is greater: Many organizations that migrated to Exchange 4.0 in 1996 came from "green screen" email systems where the average message size was in the 2KB–4KB range. Today, in the intensely graphic world we live in, the average message size (including attachments) is closer to 100KB and can go higher as users cheerfully shuttle large PowerPoint presentations, MP3 music files, digital photos, and other attachments around.

- Mailbox size is greater: While administrators attempt to limit mailbox size so that backup and restore times stay reasonable, the demand from users for more space grows. The fact that storage is much cheaper today than it was even three years ago means that it is often cheaper to deploy more disks than to ask users to spend the time necessary to clean up their mailboxes. The net result is that the average mailbox size has grown from 25MB in 1996 to well over 100MB in most organizations today. Indeed, multi-gigabyte mailboxes are not unknown and the largest mailbox is now well into the tens of gigabyte range.

- Client features encourage users to consume disk space in a wasteful manner. For example, Outlook's default behavior is to incorporate the complete text of a mail thread in a message. This is sometimes useful because you can scan all of the previous messages to see the flow of a discussion, but it also generates larger messages. If Outlook had some intelligent filter that allowed it to extract the essential points in a debate and present them then we could move away from ever-expanding messages, but software engineering has not cracked that problem yet.

- Consolidation is a continuing theme: The advent of Exchange 2000 began a phase of consolidation as administrators attempted to remove complexity from their organization by reducing the number of servers. Consolidation has been helped by cheaper network costs, so Exchange servers deployed in branches have gradually been pulled back into centralized datacenters. The result is that today's Exchange servers support a larger number of mailboxes than they have in the past. Storage is tied to consolidation as there has been a move to use larger and more complex storage systems to provide the consolidated servers with the I/O performance and raw storage capacity that these servers require. In addition, storage networks have become more complex as administrators seek to deploy more resilient configurations such as clustered servers, both the simple variety as well as stretched or geographic clusters.

- We access mail more often and through more varied ways: In 1996, the average user probably accessed Exchange from a desktop PC and may have spent four hours working with their email. Today, we increasingly access email using laptop PCs more than desktop PCs, so we can be online and access our mailboxes for longer. We also use mobile devices like PDAs, Blackberries, and SmartPhones, so there are more ways to get to our inboxes and we stay connected more. A further consequence is that servers have to support more concurrent authenticated connections than ever before. For example, as I type this document, I am connected to Exchange via Outlook and via my Windows Mobile 6.0 SmartPhone. Many of these devices constantly poll the server, which creates a different type of workload than normal user activity and another consequence is that because we are more connected, we generate more messages. The introduction of cached Exchange mode in Outlook 2003 has also increased connections as Outlook now maintains multiple connectivity threads to the server for background synchronization operations. Each connection increases demand for kernel memory, which becomes a limited commodity on a 32-bit server. The problem caused by multiple client connects is well illustrated in Microsoft Knowledge Base article 912376, which describes why Exchange 2003 SP2 runs out of kernel mode memory when the paged pool is exhausted due to too much memory being allocated to client access tokens. Another issue arises because Windows 32-bit servers have limited capacity to support HTTPS connections and top out at between 17,000 and 20,000 connections due to kernel memory exhaustion. This limits the number of clients that can connect to a server using RPC over HTTP clients (each client will consume at least 10 TCP connections and may consume more to handle the RPC threads that allow Outlook to accept and send messages at the same time).

Table5.1 summarizes how different configuration guidelines have altered since Microsoft shipped 4.0 in 1996. This data comes from various articles that I have written about Exchange over the period and the data are not specific to any one organization, so your mileage will vary. However, they are an illustration of the growing pressure on Exchange in terms of dealing with more mailboxes, bigger messages, and more data than ever before. Together with the need to support more client connections—and more intelligent clients—should we be surprised that the 32-bit Exchange architecture, especially in the Store, is creaking and groaning?

Table 5.1   *Bigger mailboxes from bigger messages*

	Exchange 4.0 (1996)	Exchange 5.5 (1997)	Exchange 2000	Exchange 2003
User mailboxes per server	50–500	200–1000	50–3000	Up to 4,000
Average mailbox size	25MB	50MB	75MB	100MB
Average message size	4KB	10KB	25KB	100KB
RAM	Up to 256MB	Up to 512MB	1GB	1–4GB

Larger mailboxes and message sizes also mandate a need for additional storage on servers. If you consider following some of the commentary from Microsoft and look at increasing mailbox quotas to something like 1GB, you might also look at removing PSTs. I am on record that I do not like PSTs because these files are insecure and prone to failure. It is much better to move the data from PSTs to server mailboxes and take advantage of the greater resilience and security that servers deliver compared to client-based storage.

Through product briefings from late 2005 onwards, Microsoft communicated that Exchange 2007 would be the first true 64-bit version of Exchange. Their dilemma was whether to continue with a 32-bit version of Exchange. Keeping two different code bases increases Microsoft's engineering expenses as they develop, test, debug, package, and translate Exchange. From an engineering perspective, if Microsoft had retained a 32-bit version[4], they would not have been able to address some of the problems that prevent the Store scaling up, such as the virtual memory fragmentation issue that limits cluster state transitions in Exchange 2000 and 2003 or increasing the number of databases that a single Exchange server can support. Windows allocates virtual memory in contiguous address blocks. Every time the Store mounts a storage group and its databases, it requests 10MB of free virtual memory to

---

4.   As discussed in Chapter 1, Microsoft provides a 32-bit version of Exchange 2007 for testing purposes. Microsoft does not support this version for production use.

perform the operation. If the largest block of free virtual memory on the server is less than 10MB, the Store cannot mount the storage group, even if Windows is able to provide 10MB composed of smaller noncontiguous address blocks. As a server comes under load, it allocates virtual memory to all the processes that request memory, and eventually you get to a point where large chunks of contiguous virtual memory are unavailable. The only solution is to reboot the server and start the process of allocating memory to processes again.

In addition, 32-bit Exchange servers experience some problems with kernel mode memory, including providing the memory required to handle delegate access to calendars and mailboxes or the number of client connections that arise when users access Exchange through a variety of different devices. One indication of when a 32-bit Exchange server is under strain is if you see errors such as paged pool allocation failures in the event log during times of peak load (such as 9AM to 11AM every morning when users first connect to their mailboxes). Virus scanners, which are an absolute necessity for Exchange servers, also use kernel mode memory and decrease the amount available to other processes. Full-text indexing and archiving can also occupy resources that Exchange could otherwise dedicate to clients.

Over time, we have seen that Windows increasingly takes up more kernel memory as it loads more drivers. For example, Windows 2003 SP1 has 10% less kernel memory available for applications because Windows enables IPSec by default and loads additional storage drivers. Another problem that is sometimes seen with Exchange 2000 and 2003 is the kernel mode exhaustion that can happen if you attempt to serve more than 10,000 mailboxes with a single public folder server (by making the public folder server the default public store for these mailboxes).

Microsoft struggled with virtual memory issues in Exchange since they released Exchange 2000 and they issued a number of patches to address problems with components such as client access tokens that consumed virtual memory (for an example of the kind of virtual memory management problems experienced by Exchange 2003, see Microsoft Knowledge Base articles 912376 and 912480). The 64-bit version of Windows supports eight terabytes of user-mode memory and eight terabytes of kernel-mode memory, which means that an Exchange 2007 server can handle many more concurrent client connections and practically eliminates any of the current issues that Exchange 2003 experiences with virtual memory fragmentation and kernel mode exhaustion. Greater ability to accommodate load and the growing inability of the 32-bit Windows platform to deal with the demands of applications like Exchange is probably the most compelling reason to move to the 64-bit platform.

You could argue that the easy answer would have been for Microsoft to retain the 32-bit version because this would allow customers to continue to use their existing hardware to move to Exchange 2007. Microsoft could have made Exchange 2007 the last version to support 32-bit hardware and use it to prepare the user community to move in the release that follows Exchange 2007. On the other hand, the next major release of Exchange might not appear until 2010 and today's server hardware is ready to run 64-bit Windows and Exchange, and indeed, it is difficult to buy servers that only run 32-bit Windows now. While the initial reaction of administrators to Microsoft's decision to support only 64-bit platforms with Exchange 2007 was to take a sharp breath, after everyone had the chance to think through the issues a little more, the community concluded that Microsoft's decision was logical and broadly welcomed it.

5.2.2   Trading memory for I/O

For years, the Exchange development team has worried about the number of I/O operations per second (IOPS) that users generate, especially on large servers. One problem is that ESE for Exchange 2003 uses a 1GB cache that cannot be extended on 32-bit systems.[5] The Store maps its cache into virtual memory and its objective is to prevent expensive disk activity by allowing the Store to access commonly used and recently accessed data from in the cache instead of having to go to disk. The limitations of 32-bit Windows restrict Exchange 2003 to a maximum of 3GB of addressable user-mode virtual address space, given that Windows takes about 1GB itself. In this respect, it is interesting to look at an end-user application like Outlook, which will cheerfully use as much memory as you care to throw at it (and many desktop and laptop computers can provide 1GB for Outlook), while we support thousands of Exchange users in an equivalent amount of memory on server computers. Exchange 2003 does a reasonable job of managing the memory that is available to it through code such as Dynamic Buffer Allocation, but on heavily loaded systems there never seems to be enough memory to accommodate all demands.

The buffer manager, a component of the Store, manages the database pages in the cache using an algorithm called Least Recently Used Reference Count (LRU-K). ESE flushes pages from the cache if it calculates that the pages have not been used recently, while it retains pages that processes (users or internal Store processes) have accessed. Due to the relatively flat nature of the page hierarchy within an ESE database, ESE needs no more than four I/Os to navigate from the root page to the page that contains data that you need. These I/Os are eliminated if the pages are in the cache, so a large cache is a good thing.

---

5.   The theoretical size of the cache on an Exchange 2003 server is 2.1GB. However, Microsoft recommends that you tune the cache back to closer to 1GB (896MB)—see Microsoft Knowledge Base article 266768.

Another issue in the Exchange 2003 Store is that JET organizes data in a series of 4KB pages and has done so since Exchange 4.0 shipped in 1996. At that time, the average message size in corporate messaging systems was usually around 4KB, so the Store could pack entire messages into a single page. Now, the average size is much larger (in some organizations, it has grown to over 100KB), and it is impossible for the Store to hold any but a small percentage of messages in single pages. Even taking the message body alone (the text of the message without attachments), because users often reply and include previous text, the average Exchange 2003 message will not fit into a single page. For example, if you send a message whose body text is more than 4KB, ESE cannot fit it into a single page in an Exchange 2003 database and must therefore split the content across two pages—and those pages are not necessarily contiguous within the database. Splits also occur for large attachments, so ESE must divide a 1MB PowerPoint attachment across 250 pages on an Exchange 2003 server or 125 pages on an Exchange 2007 server. Retrieving a large attachment therefore generates a lot of work for the Store and if the data is not in the cache, it can generate many I/O operations. To help address the problem of how to manage ever-increasing message sizes, Exchange 2007 increases the Store page size from 4KB to 8KB. Microsoft believes that the change will allow the Store to hold more than 50% of all messages in a single page, with a subsequent decrease in the number of read and write operations that the Store generates for each message. Changing the page size is not an earth-shattering update for Exchange because other database applications (such as Oracle 9*i* and SQL Server) use this page size and Microsoft already had plenty of experience with it in the Active Directory database. In addition, because you cannot upgrade Exchange 2000 or 2003 servers to Exchange 2007, Microsoft does not have to convert existing databases to the new format.

While ESE attempts to locate data in the most efficient manner, it does not help performance to have ever-increasingly large messages split across multiple pages, and on Exchange 2003 servers, many pages in the database are extensions for other pages. Because of the page splits, we end up with a pattern of random access across the entire database, which means that cache optimization techniques such as those implemented in RAM or storage controller caches, do not help as much as they could to speed access to Exchange data. The overall result of the original 4KB page size is that the Exchange 2003 Store processes more I/O requests to read and write messages across multiple pages. To compound matters, we know that messages are unlikely to get smaller as attachments grow larger, users compose message bodies with graphical editors like Word, and Microsoft starts to push unified messaging technology so that we have voice messages in our mailbox as well. Because of all these factors, we end up with larger mailboxes, larger databases, and a huge demand for I/O, with the typical design figure for Exchange 2003 being 0.5 to 1.0 IOPS per concurrent active client. The problem with a growing demand for I/O is that while storage density has increased dramatically in the last decade so that 1TB disks are on the horizon, we have not seen a similar increase in the ability to process I/Os.

All of this is fine if you only need to run a small server because current server and disk technology can easily support several hundred Exchange mailboxes at a very cost-effective price. However, once you start to scale up to servers that support more than a thousand mailboxes, sheer storage capacity is not the limiting factor or most costly item. Instead, the critical area becomes the capability of the storage subsystem to process the I/O demand generated by users. If the storage subsystem cannot handle the I/O demand, then users see degraded performance because of bottlenecks in the Store. You can certainly design and deploy storage subsystems that are capable of dealing with 4,000 concurrent users on an Exchange server, as long as you are willing to spend a lot of money. The expense of providing and managing sufficient storage that can handle the I/O load generated by very large Exchange servers is one of the reasons why Exchange 2003 "tops out" at around the 4,000 mailboxes per server mark. There are other important reasons that limit the number of mailboxes that you want to host on a single server, including the time required to perform backup and restore procedures, but storage expense is a real constraint to building larger Exchange servers. Microsoft is more than aware of the I/O problem, if only because they have gone through a massive consolidation process for their own internal Exchange deployment.

The interesting thing about moving to a 64-bit platform is that Microsoft believes that the 64-bit platform holds the key to solving many of the longstanding problems in the Exchange Store. With more addressable memory, there should be far less of a problem with fragmentation of virtual memory, so Exchange 2007 supports more storage groups and databases (see Table 5.2). Email databases are big and getting bigger all the time and on the 32-bit platform the Store has to do a lot of processing to move data pages in and out of its cache as users make requests, which then results in I/O operations as the Store fetches data from the database and commits page updates from the cache. A larger cache means that more pages can stay longer in the cache (database professionals say that there is less risk of "data eviction," which is a nice way of thinking about what's going on). Reading a page from disk to find the next item in a user's inbox takes at least 1,000 times longer than retrieving the data from memory, so Exchange becomes more responsive to requests. The net is that the extended memory model achieved by running Exchange on the 64-bit Windows platform allows the Store to cache far more user data than it can today, with the result that Exchange 2007 generates (on average) a quarter of the same I/O operations as an Exchange 2003 server does for the same number of users.

Table 5.2 *Storage group and databases in Exchange 2003 and 2007*

Version	Maximum Number of Storage Groups	Maximum Number of Databases	Maximum size of Database
Exchange 2003 Standard	1	2 (1 mailbox, 1 public folder)	16GB, then 75GB after SP2
Exchange 2003 Enterprise	4	20 (maximum of 5 per storage group)	Limited only by hardware
Exchange 2007 Standard	5	5 (maximum of 5 databases in a storage group)	Limited only by hardware*
Exchange 2007 Enterprise	50	50 (maximum of 5 databases per storage group)	Limited only by hardware

* While the database size is unlimited, Microsoft recommends that no database should exceed 100GB unless you use LCR/CCR, in which case their recommended maximum is 200GB. In real life, there are many examples of production databases that exceed 250GB comfortably. It all depends on the degree of risk you are prepared to take.

As an example of what caching data means to a server, Microsoft calculated that if a Exchange could cache the contents of every user's inbox, the rules that typically process messages arriving into the inbox, and the most current 50 messages, they could reduce the number of I/O operations significantly because the Store could then provide this data from memory instead of constantly going to disk. One calculation from the Exchange engineering group shows that the 32-bit JET cache can store 250KB per user on a server that supports 4,000 mailboxes. By comparison, on a 64-bit Windows server equipped with 16GB of RAM,[6] the expanded ESE cache can hold 3.5MB per user for the same number of mailboxes, a 14-times increase in the amount of data that the Store can access from memory rather than having to go to disk. Typical user access to Exchange concentrates on a reasonably small number of folders such as the Inbox, Sent Items, and Calendar—something that is even truer for mobile clients. The ability to cache these folders in memory will lead to much improved performance all round, no matter what client you use. Note that the extended cache does not automatically mean that the Store will generate 14 times fewer I/Os, but it is obviously a good thing to trade expensive storage I/O for relatively cheap memory access. Consider this fact: Accessing data through an I/O operation (disk read) usually takes something like 14 milliseconds and incurs some CPU cycles; reading a data page from memory takes 50 nanoseconds and no CPU. It's an easy trade-off to swap memory for disk I/Os.

---

6. User mode virtual address space on a 64-bit Windows server can theoretically grow as large as 8TB. However, the actual space available to Exchange depends on the available RAM. Large Exchange 2007 servers will have lots of RAM, so they will have large caches and so be better able to handle I/O loads by trading memory for I/O.

I/O coalescing is the ability to group read or write operations to contiguous pages together so that you deal with everything in a single I/O operation rather than generating multiple I/Os. As we have discussed, optimizing I/O operations is a major concern for Microsoft when they engineered Exchange 2007. The Exchange 2003 version of the ESE engine coalesces up to 64KB of data in a single I/O, while the additional size of the ESE cache enables Exchange 2007 to handle up to 1MB (128 pages), which contributes to a reduction in the IOPS requirement per user. Another change is an increase in checkpoint depth, which governs the amount of dirty pages that the Store maintains in its cache. Checkpointing is just a way to manage changed pages efficiently until a database can commit the pages to disk. Exchange 2007 uses a checkpoint depth of 20MB (of transaction logs) per storage group. Making the checkpoint depth deeper increases the chance that users will update these pages multiple times before the Store eventually flushes them into the database and so allows ESE to combine multiple transactions into one write operation. Batching write operations allows Exchange to eliminate some unnecessary writes and drives a further reduction in I/O operations. For example, you would probably agree that you update your inbox and calendar folders frequently. If the Store can cache the pages that represent the contents of these folders (especially the pages that hold the top of your inbox and this week's appointments, which are highly likely to change) and update the pages in memory rather than constantly going to disk all the time, it's easy to see how extra checkpoint depth can help performance. Multiply the effect by the number of concurrent users accessing a server and you can realize that this can have a big impact. In passing, it is worth noting that an application-specific cache, such as the one that Exchange 2007 uses to optimize database writes, is very different to the application-independent data cache that you find on intelligent storage controllers. Hardware caches take care of data from multiple applications and do not attempt to optimize write activity at an application level.

All of the changes made to optimize the Exchange 2007 Store mean that you will probably install more memory on an Exchange 2007 server than you will for previous versions. While it is too early to say just how much physical memory you need to install on an Exchange 2007 server to achieve optimum performance, Microsoft provides guidance of 5MB per active concurrent user plus 2GB for Exchange, so a server supporting 2,000 concurrent users needs 10GB for the users plus 2GB = 12GB. As this is merely guidance, you should discuss memory requirements with an Exchange performance expert to arrive at accurate memory sizing for any particular server. Along the same lines, it will take time to test systems to get real production data to verify exactly what impact 64-bit Exchange makes on IOPS. Educated feedback from those involved with Microsoft engineering put the figure at between 0.3 and 0.25 IOPS/user, according to data gathered from some of Microsoft's own systems[7]. These systems had been operating at 1 IOPS/user on a 32-bit platform, so these results are very positive. After all, if you can reduce the I/O demand to a third or quarter of that current for Exchange 2003, the theory is that you can reduce your storage costs. It is interesting to note that larger mailboxes increase the number of I/Os generated per mailbox for clients that do not operate in cached Exchange mode, which is a good reason to insist that all Outlook clients are configured to use cached Exchange mode if you want to use large mailbox quotas. The increase in I/O demand is likely to be due to Exchange having to cope with more data in the mailbox (more folders and more items in each folder), more user activities (if a user can store more in their mailbox, they will do things like subscribe to online mailing lists), and the side-effect of having more items in mailboxes such as content indexing. Benchmarks that seek to test I/O performance may be based on small mailboxes that contain relatively few items; a different I/O pattern is likely when your users behave like human packrats and each has a mailbox containing 200 folders with up to 5,000 items per folder.

Experience with early deployments demonstrates that it is difficult to achieve the full amount of theoretical cost savings in storage that better I/O performance in Exchange 2007 might enable. You are hardly likely to jettison all your existing storage and replace it with lower cost alternatives. Instead, you will keep the same storage infrastructure and if the I/O demand drops, then you may be able use the storage to host more servers or to handle the increased workload of new applications, such as unified messaging. Consolidation and extended storage lifetime rather than the installation of cheaper storage solutions are where the real cost savings will be produced through the changes that Microsoft are making in Exchange 2007.

5.2.3   The decrease in storage costs

IDC predicts that the storage industry will ship 15 exabytes of storage in 2006–2008. To put this amount into perspective, it is more than the industry has shipped in aggregate since it started. Servers have more storage than ever before because users want to store more data than ever before and the decrease in storage costs has allowed administrators to configure servers with more and more storage.

Exchange 2007 trades memory for I/O operations to drive down the overall IOPS figure for a server. While you may have to provide more storage to satisfy user demands, you may be able to take advantage of cheaper storage subsystems to support larger servers. With Exchange 2003, if you want to deploy large Exchange servers that support thousands of mailboxes, you incur much of the capital cost for the project to buy the necessary stor-

---

7.   Your mileage will vary from Microsoft's experience depending on user performance characteristics and the other software that is active on the server alongside Exchange. For example, anti-virus software can exert a significant performance load on a server.

age technology that can supply the I/O requirements to handle the desired number of concurrently active mailboxes. The fact is that while storage technology has seen huge advances in capacity (measured in both cost per GB and the average size of disks—500GB or larger disks are available now) since 1996, storage technology has failed to drive performance at anything like the same rate. The disks that we have today are bigger and less prone to failure, but their I/O performance is not much better than those that we used ten years ago. The upshot is that if you want to provide lots of I/O capacity, you have to invest in upscale storage technology, and that comes with a big price tag.

In some cases, the costs of the storage for large deployments is much higher than the servers, so much so that Microsoft says that 80% of the hardware costs of many Exchange deployments is due to storage. Of course, costs vary greatly from deployment to deployment, but there is no doubt that SANs are expensive to deploy and operate. They are more complex, they require more expertise, but they offer more features and functionality than simple direct attached storage does. The question for administrators is whether you want to trade functionality, performance, and complexity for cost and simplicity. Other factors such as resilience to failure also come into the equation.

Any step that eliminates cost for an implementation is welcome and companies will be interested in investigating how they can take advantage of Exchange 2007's reduced I/O demands to reduce costs. However, I do not imagine that companies that operate SANs for Exchange 2003 will dump their SANs and rush to deploy low-cost storage for Exchange 2007 as the need still exists to deliver a balance of cost versus robustness and resilience for production environments.

5.3   **No more streaming database**

Up to Exchange 2000, the product only used the EDB or MAPI property database. Exchange 2000 introduced the concept of the STM file, or streaming database. Exchange 2000 also introduced ExIFS, the Exchange Installable File System, which it used to access data in the STM. The idea behind a streaming database was very logical. Up to that point, the vast majority of content generated by Exchange users was through MAPI clients and was very suited to storage as MAPI properties in the EDB. For example, the title of a message is a MAPI property, as is its author, the recipients, the message body, and even pointers to any attachments that the message might have.

Exchange 5.5 was the first version of Exchange to support a wide array of clients that preferred Internet protocols such as POP3, IMAP4, SMTP, and MIME, so Exchange had to do an increasing amount of work to convert these protocols into MAPI properties before the Store was able to accept the data. Microsoft therefore decided that they would give the Store the ability to handle Internet protocols in their native format and that the Store would do no conversion unless it was necessary, such as in the case when an Outlook client requested a message that an IMAP4 client had originally created and sent. MAPI clients continued to use the Store and the EDB database in much the same way that they always had, but messages generated in Internet formats by IMAP4 and POP3 clients went into the STM file, with just a few basic MAPI properties (such as message subject and author) being "promoted" into the EDB. On Exchange 2000 and 2003 servers, every EDB database has a partner STM file and the Store provides the software layer to mask the complexity of format translation and the different storage paths. The implementation of the dual database was fine and did not cause any problems, but the advantages of increased processing power and memory availability generated by the move to the 64-bit platform for Exchange allowed Microsoft to review the situation to decide whether Exchange still required the STM file.

The engineering answer was that Exchange no longer requires the STM file as the upgraded Store is capable of handling Internet formats as easily as it handles MAPI. In addition, the power of current hardware platforms means that extra CPU cycles are available to handle the processing load of format conversion. The major advantage gained by the elimination of the STM file is simplification of the file structure within the Store. This advantage is not apparent if you have a small server with just one database, but it is clearer on larger servers that support 20 databases or more. As you cannot upgrade an Exchange 2003 server to Exchange 2007, you never see an STM file on an Exchange 2007 server. The move mailbox operations that transfer content from older Exchange servers to Exchange 2007 mailboxes takes care of the data transformation from STM to EDB format en route. A consequence of the elimination of the STM is that Microsoft has also retired ExIFS. This decision is a good one because ExIFS never delivered on the promise that it (or Microsoft developers) held out to provide fast access to data in the Store for applications, including the ability to map mailbox data through the DOS prompt, something that became a favorite party trick at Microsoft demonstrations. Some administrators took Microsoft at their word and attempted to backup Exchange databases through ExIFS only to find that while backups occurred, they did not contain information that Exchange could use to restore a database.

One potential drawback of the elimination of the STM file is the requirement for a high-performance TEMP location that the Store can use to convert MAPI content to native Internet content for consumption by IMAP4 or POP3 clients. This is only a problem if you have a server that supports large populations of these clients and servers that support a predominantly Outlook client base do not have to concern themselves about the issue.

5.4   **Tables and items**

When a client makes an authenticated connection to a mailbox in the Store, it builds a hierarchical representation of all of the folders in the mailbox from the tables that hold the data. The major tables that clients interact with to read and send messages are:

- The mailbox table: Each row in the table represents a mailbox.

- The folders table: Each row represents a folder in a mailbox and each folder has a unique identifier. One table holds details of every folder in the database. A parent/child scheme supports nested folders so that a subfolder maintains a pointer to its parent folder. For example, in Table 5.3, the Articles folder in TonyR's mailbox is a child folder of the Publicity folder and the Exchange folder is a child folder of the Microsoft folder. The count of new items in the table allows a client to bold the folder name to give the user a visual indication that there is new content to be read in the folder.

- The message table: Each row represents a message in a folder. Again, one table holds every message in a database.

- The attachments table: Each row represents an attachment to another item.

- A set of message/folder tables: The Store holds a separate message/folder table for every folder in a database.

Table 5.3   *Sample contents of the Folders table in a mailbox database*

Folder ID	Folder Name	Folder Owner	Count of items	Count of New Items	Parent Folder ID
10445872	Inbox	TonyR	1,954	11	0
10446633	Publicity	TonyR	10	0	0
10457766	Articles	TonyR	15	1	10446633
10577446	Microsoft	TonyR	651	0	
10578764	Exchange	TonyR	28	1	10577446
10579438	Inbox	KevinL	2,330	176	0
10584466	Deleted Items	KevinL	15	0	0

Public folder databases also organize into folders and rows. However, the major client interaction is with mailboxes, so this is what we investigate here.

Pointers link data in different folders together. The use of pointers is the basis of the single instance storage model, which means that the Store holds only a single copy of any unique content (such as a message body or an attachment) and uses pointers to link all of the mailboxes that have an interest in the content. The benefit is that you do not have to duplicate content across multiple mailboxes. The Store manages the pointers so that as users delete items from their mailboxes, the Store reduces the "usage count" for pointers to a piece of content until the content is no longer required. At this point, the Store erases the content from the database. Single instance storage was a big feature for the first generation of Exchange but its importance has decreased since Exchange 2000 introduced support for multiple databases on a server. Obviously, if Exchange delivers a message to multiple mailboxes that exist in different databases, it must create the content in each database, and so eliminating some of the benefit of the single-instance storage model.

Table 5.4   *Contents of a message/folder table*

From	Subject	Received	Size	Priority	Attachment Flag	Message Identifier
Kevin Laahs	Exchange 2007 academy	1-Dec-2006	4KB	High	No	24646484
Kieran McCorry	Training for administrators	1-Dec-2006	2KB	Normal	No	24647744
Personnel	New cafeteria	1-Dec-2006	6KB	Low	No	24647764
Ken Ewert	LCS is great!	1-Dec-2006	5KB	Normal	Yes	24648174
Marketing	New brand	1-Dec-2006	10MB	High	Yes	24649444

The Store holds header information for each folder in a separate table, called a message/folder table (Table 5.4). The header information is composed of a set of MAPI properties, such as Size, From, Received, and so on. Maintaining this information in a separate table allows the Store to support a separate sort order or view for each folder. When a client requests information about a folder from the Store, they read information from the message/folder table.

The message identifier in a row in a message/folder table links the message properties with the content, which the Store holds in the Message table (Table 5.5). Note that the message body content is always in RTF (Rich Text Format), even if you use Word as your message editor.

Table 5.5   *Contents of the Message table*

Message identifier	To	Message Body Content	Usage Count	Attachment Pointer
24646484	Tony Redmond	We have just started to train people…	1	0
24647744	Tony Redmond; Kevin Laahs	Training for administrators is…	2	0
24648174	Tony Redmond	LCS is a new way of contacting…	1	64472464
24649444	All employees	Our new brand is ready for launch!	22	68364646

Figure 5.2 illustrates the interaction between the different tables in the Store to populate the Outlook user interface. The folder tree, including nested folders, comes from data in the folder table. The messages in the folder displayed in the right hand pane come from the data in the message/folder table for the folder (in this case, the folder is "Tony's Inbox"). When the user clicks on a message to read it, Outlook combines the message header data with the content, including an XLS attachment, to build the message form that the user sees.

Figure 5.2
How Outlook combines data from different Store tables into its UI

message body part and attachment taken from the messages and attachments tables

5.5 Storage groups

Up to Exchange 2000, administrators dealt with a single mailbox database and a single public folder database per server. Exchange 2000 introduced the concept of storage groups, or an instance of the database engine running within the Information Store process that can manage up to five databases within the group, all of whom share a single transaction log set. With the Enterprise Edition of Exchange 2000 and 2003, you can deploy up to 4 storage groups on a server, or a maximum of 20 databases.

Microsoft's original design for Exchange 2000 envisaged that a server could support many more databases, but memory restrictions forced the developers to limit Exchange to 4 storage groups. As we have seen, the additional memory that is available for the Windows 64-bit platform has eased this restriction quite considerably to a point where Exchange 2007 now supports up to 50 storage groups per server, each with its accompanying set of transaction logs. Each storage group occupies some virtual memory. Apart from the obvious issue of how to manage large numbers of storage groups especially in terms of the number of storage LUNs required to accommodate the groups, there is no technical reason why Exchange 2007 could not have supported 100 storage groups or more. After all, the headroom made available by the move to the 64-bit platform makes a lot more memory available to the Store, and it could have used the memory to accommodate more storage groups. In short, Microsoft settled on 50 as a reasonable compromise between manageability and functionality, but the architecture allows them to increase the number of supported storage groups in a future version of Exchange, if demand justifies such a change.

It is still possible to allocate multiple databases to a storage group, but experience with Exchange 2003, especially in terms of easier disaster recovery, demonstrates that it is better to deploy fewer databases per storage group and Microsoft's best practice is to deploy one database per storage group. Some mailbox servers in organizations that support legacy servers will continue to support a public folder database in one of the storage groups on the server.

The situation was not always so simple. Immediately Exchange 2000 introduced the ability to support multiple databases divided across multiple storage groups. The debate erupted as to which was the better approach: to deploy multiple databases in a single storage group, or to spread the databases across multiple storage groups. Memory management overhead and some bugs in Exchange 2000 meant that Microsoft's recommendation at that time was to avoid creating more storage groups than you absolutely needed. Exchange 2003 fixed the software problems and Exchange 2007 provides even more headroom so now you can select whatever option for storage group deployment that seems right to you.

The debate still rages and it is hard to set any hard-and-fast rules because every deployment differs in its needs and constraints. Here are some points to take into account as you consider how to deploy storage groups within your organization.

- Adding complexity to a deployment is always a bad thing unless it is necessary. For example, CCR and LCR require storage groups that host just one mailbox database, so if you decide to deploy continuous log replication, you are more likely to deploy additional storage groups. Extra storage groups mean extra sets of transaction logs to manage and deploy. In particular, you have to ensure that you deploy the logs and databases across available storage in such a way that user activity does not generate excessive I/O to any spindle and that a failure will not compromise more than one storage group.

- Splitting user load across multiple databases usually results in smaller databases, which are easier to manage, especially if you have to restore from tape after a failure. Plan on a restore speed of 20GB/hour to establish the SLA that you can meet; you will probably do better in practice as tape technology improves, but it is good to know the worst case. However, the availability of Volume ShadowCopy Services and support for hot snapshots means that it is easier to restore very large databases, so the database size may not be a concern to you if you deploy the necessary technology to support hot snapshots.

- The more databases you deploy, the fewer the users affected by any database failure unless hardware causes the failure and affects multiple databases. You can compare supporting all users in one or two very large databases to putting all of one's eggs into a single basket. Everything is okay until a database failure.

- User mailbox quotas are growing, so the size of your databases today will be larger in the future. Plan on 300% growth over three years and you will not go far wrong, and then use that figure as the basis for planning.

- Sometimes, depending on the storage technology that you use, you simply have to spread the I/O load across multiple streams, including multiple transaction logs. In this case, you have to deploy multiple storage groups as each storage group has its own transaction log set. Having additional transaction log sets should not increase the time required to replay transactions after a failure as Exchange generates roughly the same number of transaction logs whether you have one or four storage groups. There is some additional complexity in restoring transaction logs, but only if you have to restore logs for several storage groups.

- Some people believe that Exchange can take a long time to replay transaction logs in case of failure because the logs contain interleaved transactions from all of the databases in the storage group; restore performance is therefore faster if the transaction logs only contain data for one database. This was certainly the case for Exchange 2000, but from Exchange 2003 SP1 onwards log replay is rapid—the improvement went from a minute per log to 10–15 logs per minute on many systems.

- The backup and restore solution that you deploy may influence how you use storage groups. For example, if you deploy a VSS-based solution, you have to dismount all of the databases in a storage group to perform a restore, even if you want only to restore a single database. This is a significant difference when compared to how traditional streaming backup and restore programs work.

Different people have different views on the best approach to take to storage groups, mostly based on their own experience. In the case of Exchange 2007, we can now configure many more storage groups on a server, so the debate is different. For example, consider the situation where you have an Exchange 2003 server that supports ten mailbox databases of up to 80GB each. You have 500 users assigned to each database, so the server supports 5,000 users. In this scenario, you have to manage the databases in four storage groups, so two of the storage groups have three databases and the other two support two databases. You also have four sets of transaction logs to manage. On an Exchange 2007 server, you could assign each database to its own storage group, or you can opt to create 20 storage groups and have one 40GB database in each group, or 50 storage groups that each has a 20GB database, or indeed 20 storage groups where each storage group supports two 20GB databases. The design decision is whether to shrink the database size by creating more storage groups and if so, at what point the number of storage groups (and their associated transaction log sets) becomes unmanageable. Some argue that it makes perfect sense to limit each storage group to one database because you then have isolation of all data belonging to the database in the storage group, while others believe that Exchange manages interleaved transactions in the logs well enough to support multiple databases in each storage group.

Another way to look at storage groups is to determine how many mailboxes of what size you want to deploy and then to calculate how many storage groups you need to create to support the mailboxes. We can include the maximum reasonable size for a database in the equation (as determined by how large you are willing to let a database grow in terms of backup times). Microsoft now recommends that you configure storage groups with just one database, so that is another factor to take into account. Table 5.6 shows a rough calculation of the number of single-database storage groups required to support different sizes of mailboxes for different user communities using databases of different sizes. It is no surprise to see that the larger the mailbox, the fewer mailboxes we can support in a database, and the more storage groups we need. What may be a surprise is how quickly we get into a situation where the server has to support twenty or more storage groups. Microsoft's white paper covering their internal deployment of Exchange 2007 mentions that they configure their "mailbox I" server type with 28 storage groups and their "mailbox II" server type with 42 storage groups, which backs up the assertion that we will see a big increase in the number of storage groups as companies deploy Exchange 2007.

Table 5.6   *Storage Groups and mailbox sizes*

	Maximum Database Size in Storage Group				
Mailboxes	50GB	75GB	100GB	125GB	150GB
1,000 × 250MB	5	3	3	2	2
2,000 × 250MB	10	7	5	4	3
3,000 × 250MB	15	10	8	8	5
4,000 × 250MB	20	13	10	8	7
1,000 × 500MB	10	7	5	4	3
2,000 × 500MB	20	13	10	8	7
4,000 × 500MB	40	27	20	16	13
1,000 × 1GB	20	13	10	8	7
2,000 × 1GB	40	27	20	16	13
4,000 × 1GB	80	53	40	32	27
1,000 × 2GB	40	27	20	16	13
2,000 × 2GB	80	53	40	32	27
4,000 × 2GB	160	107	80	64	53

Remember that an Exchange 2007 server can support up to 50 storage groups. Looking at our table, we therefore conclude that we have to be prepared to let databases grow to 100GB or more if we want to offer even 1GB mailboxes to users. We can also see that the total number of storage groups requires exceeds the maximum supported by Exchange as we go past 2,000 mailboxes on the server. The other point of concern is the number of disks that are required to support so many storage groups. We can use mount points to get past the disk letter limitation, but the prospect of managing so many disk locations for databases and transaction logs is not attractive. Of course, we can configure storage groups to host multiple databases, but then we cannot use continuous log replication. What you gain on the swings, you lose on the roundabouts.

Optimizing disk I/O is another factor to take into the equation. Exchange 2007 trades memory for I/O and has a radically different I/O profile than Exchange 2003. If you use a single database per storage group then the full transaction log checkpoint depth (the size of the in-memory database cache) is available to that database. The Store therefore has a higher likelihood that it will find a page to update in the cache where it holds dirty database pages because the pages stay in the cache until the checkpoint forces the Store to write the pages into the database. If multiple updates can be applied to a page in memory, the Store needs only to write the last page update to the database and so generates a single I/O instead of the multiple I/Os that it would otherwise need if it were forced to commit more updates to disk to accommodate the transactions for multiple databases.

We have a lot of experience of multi-database storage groups from operating Exchange 2000 and 2003, but there is no doubt that Microsoft is heading to a position where one database per storage group becomes the rule. The challenge is to balance your database storage requirements with management and to deploy enough storage groups to support users without going completely overboard.

5.5.1 Creating a new storage group and database

Creating a new storage group is easy, but a little bit of planning goes a long way. The first thing to consider is the disk location where you will put the storage group. Best practice is to:

- Keep the transaction logs and database files for a storage group on separate disks so that a failure on one disk will not compromise all of the files.

- If a server supports multiple storage groups, put the storage groups on different disks.

- Keep storage groups away from drive C: whenever possible. In most cases, the default location suggested by Exchange is under the \Program Files\Microsoft\Exchange Server\Mailbox directory, so you need to move away from here.

Other considerations also come into play when you plan the position of a storage group, such as the need to balance I/O operations across available disks, the overall configuration for SAN deployments, the requirements of other applications, and so on. The key point is for you to understand where you want to put the storage group before you start rather than making a key decision halfway through its creation. You can move a storage group after it is created, but it is human nature to leave things alone, which is a good enough reason to get things right from the start.

Figure 5.3
Storage group and database files immediately after creation

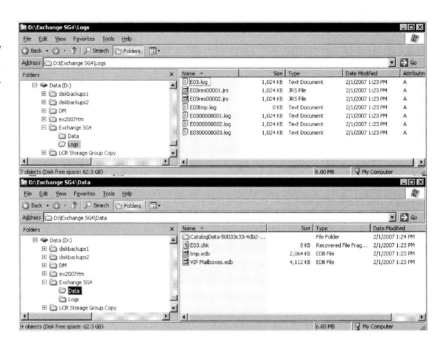

After you decide on the physical location for the storage group, you should create whatever directories are required to hold the transaction logs, system files, and databases. It is a good idea to use a consistent naming standard for this purpose. For example, you could use a simple convention of naming the directory "SG" plus a number, as in "SG1," "SG2," "SG3," and so on. If you think it a good idea to make an explicit reference to Exchange to make it obvious what application uses the directory, you might use Exchange as a prefix, as in "Exchange SG1" and "Exchange SG2." Some administrators prefer to include the Exchange server name in the names for storage groups and databases, as they believe this to be useful if they ever have to mount databases in the Recovery Storage Group and because it makes the server that owns the databases obvious when you work with many databases through shell commands. This naming convention results in names such as "ExchMbxSvr1-SG1" and "ExchMbxSvr1-SG1-

DB1." Selecting the right naming convention is largely a matter of what works for you and is often influenced by legacy servers and databases, but it is a good thing to consider as you create new Exchange 2007 servers, storage groups, and databases.

Under the root directory for the storage group, it is a good idea to create a set of subdirectories to hold the transaction logs and databases. Figure 5.3 illustrates a typical on-disk structure for a storage group containing a single mailbox database. This situation is immediately after Exchange has created the database, so you can see the initial set of transaction logs in the \Logs directory and the newly created database in the \Data directory.

Once you know where all the files are to go, creating a new storage group and adding a database is easy with the EMC wizard. It is more interesting to look at the shell commands that you can use to script the creation of a storage group and a mailbox database. First, you use the `New-StorageGroup` command to create the storage group:

```
New-StorageGroup -Server 'ExchMbxSvr2' -Name 'Critical
Mailboxes'
-LogFolderPath 'D:\Exchange SG4\Logs'
-SystemFolderPath 'D:\Exchange SG4\Data'
```

With the storage group in place, we can create a new mailbox database with the `New-MailboxDatabase` command.

```
New-MailboxDatabase -StorageGroup 'ExchMbxSvr2\Critical
Mailboxes'
-Name 'VIP Mailboxes'
-EdbFilePath 'D:\Exchange SG4\Data\VIP Mailboxes.edb'
```

If we want to use local continuous replication for the database (and it is the only database in the storage group), then we would also specify the –HasLocalCopy and –CopyEdbFilePath parameters. See Chapter 9 for more information on local continuous replication. If you want to create a public folder database instead of a mailbox database, you need to specify the –PublicFolderDatabase parameter.

5.5.2 Working with storage groups and databases

After you create a new mailbox database, you can mount it with the `Mount-Database` command:

```
Mount-Database -Identity 'Critical Mailboxes\VIP Mailboxes'
```

The storage group and mailbox database are now ready for you to populate with mailboxes. You can check its status with the `Get-MailboxDatabase` command:

```
Get-MailboxDatabase —id 'Critical Mailboxes\VIP Mailboxes'
```

If you are unhappy with a property of a database, you can change it with the `Set-MailboxDatabase` command. For example:

```
Set-MailboxDatabase —id 'Critical Mailboxes\VIP Mailboxes'
—ProhibitSendQuota 1995MB
```

If you are completely unhappy with the database, you can dismount it and then delete it.

```
Dismount-Database —id 'Critical Mailboxes\VIP Mailboxes'
Remove-MailboxDatabase —id 'Critical Mailboxes\VIP Mailboxes'
```

The apparent inconsistency in the naming of commands that work with databases is because the `Mount-Database` and `Dismount-Database` commands work with mailbox and public folder databases. There is a separate `Remove-PublicFolderDatabase` command to delete public folder databases, just like there are commands to create (`New-PublicFolderDatabase`), and fetch and set properties (`Get-PublicFolderDatabase` and `Set-PublicFolderDatabase`). In any case, after you delete a database, you have to complete the clean-up operation by deleting the physical files on disk.

Of course, after we delete the database, we may want to clean up completely by deleting the storage group. We can do this with the Remove-StorageGroup command:

```
Remove-StorageGroup —id 'ExchMbxSvr2\Critical Mailboxes'
```

Other notable commands that you may want to use in scripts include `Move-DatabasePath`, which moves database files from one disk location to another, and the `Clean-MailboxDatabase` command, which checks a mailbox database for any disconnected mailboxes that exist in the database that are not properly marked. The command then corrects their status. A disconnected mailbox is a mailbox that exists in a database but does not have an associated Active Directory account. You can connect a disconnected mailbox to an Active Directory account with the `Connect-Mailbox` command. The `Move-StorageGroupPath` command is available if you need to move the location of transaction logs or system files.

5.6   **Transaction logs**

Exchange has always featured transaction logs as the method that the Store uses to capture transaction data before the Store commits transactions to its database. Transaction logs capture all transactions—new items, modifications to existing items, and deletions—for both mailboxes and public folders. Because of the asynchronous way that the Store saves transactions to the log while batching transactions for efficient committal to the database, it is entirely possible for users to read and write messages in memory without the Store ever going to disk to fetch data. Fast, efficient, and secure access to data is the major advantage delivered by the write-ahead logging model used by Exchange, and it is important that every administrator understands how the model works.

The Store never commits an item to a database unless it first saves the data to a transaction log. This means that until the Store commits data to a database, the only durable place that the data exists is in the transaction log. Of course, the data is in the Store's cache, but the cache can quickly disappear through hardware failure. The major function of the transaction logs is therefore to allow the Store to use the data in the logs to replay transactions and so preserve data by rebuilding a database from the combination of a backup copy and the transaction logs. Obviously, this is only possible if you take care to preserve the transaction logs in the same way that you take regular backups of the databases.

Every time the Information Store service starts up, the Store automatically checks the databases as it mounts them to verify that the databases are consistent. A flag in the database header indicates whether the database is consistent or inconsistent, depending on whether the Store was able to shutdown the database cleanly the last time it shutdown. A clean shutdown flushes all data from the Store's cache and commits any outstanding transactions into the database to make the database consistent. An inconsistent database is one that has some outstanding transactions that the Store has not yet committed. If the Store detects that a database is inconsistent, it attempts to read the outstanding transactions from the transaction logs to replay the transactions into the database and so make the database consistent. This operation is referred to as a soft recovery and while it happens less frequently today than with earlier versions of Exchange, soft recoveries occur from time to time, usually after a software or hardware failure has caused Exchange to terminate abruptly. In most instances, you are unaware that the Store has performed a soft recovery and you will not find out unless you check the event log to see whether the Store replayed any transactions after it mounted a database. If you are unsure whether a database is consistent, you can run the ESEUTIL utility with the /MH parameter to check the database header.

The only way that you can be sure that a database is consistent is to perform a controlled shutdown of the Information Store service (which makes all databases consistent) or to use ESM to dismount a specific database. At this point, the Store makes sure that it commits any outstanding transactions that exist within its cache before it shuts down the database. Taking a full backup creates a somewhat similar situation in that the database after the backup is consistent. However, because the database is still online, the Store will continue to commit transactions immediately after the backup finishes, so the database is only consistent for a very short time.

ESE deals with transaction logs as if they formed one very large logical log, which the Store divides into a set of generations to be more convenient to manage. On Exchange 2000/2003 servers, transaction logs are 5MB whereas they are 1MB on Exchange 2007 servers. Each log represents a single generation that ESE assigns a sequential generation number to for identification purposes. Obviously, a single message that has a number of large attachments can easily span many log files. ESE manages the split of data across the logs automatically and is also able to retrieve data from several logs to form the single message and its attachment if the need arises to replay the transaction into a database. On a busy server, millions of transactions might flow through the logs daily, and it is common to see hundreds if not thousands of logs created each day. Apart from the activity generated by users, transaction logs capture background and maintenance activity such as the generation of NDRs, mailbox moves, the import of mailbox data from other messaging systems, and so on. Any operation that causes data to flow in and out of a database is captured in a transaction log. If you want to estimate the number of transaction logs that a server will generate daily, you can use the rule of thumb of five 5MB of data (or five logs) per active user per eight-hour working day. This rule assumes that you remove transaction logs through daily full backups and has stood the test of time. You will not go far wrong if you use it.

Each storage group has its own set of transaction logs and the Store interleaves the transactions for all of the databases in the storage group within the transaction logs. Thus, the first transaction in a log may belong to mailbox database 1, the next belongs to mailbox database 2, the next to mailbox database 1, and the next to mailbox database 3. You cannot separate out the transactions for one database from a transaction log—the Store does this automatically when it needs to replay transactions into a database. Transaction logs are tied to their storage groups in two ways. First, ESE writes a unique identifier (the signature) into each log as it creates the file. The log identifier must match the signature of the storage group before ESE can use the contents of a log to recover transactions. Second, ESE records the path to the directory where the database is located in the transaction logs. You can find information about identifiers and locations by running the ESEUTIL utility with the /ML parameter to dump the header information from a transaction log as shown in Figure 5.4.

Figure 5.4
Output from ESEUTIL /ML dump of transaction log header

```
Initiating FILE DUMP mode...

      Base name: e01
      Log file: c:\temp\e010000aa15.log
      lGeneration: 43541 (0xAA15)
      Checkpoint: NOT AVAILABLE
      creation time: 01/03/2007 08:50:58
      prev gen time: 01/03/2007 08:50:57
      Format LGVersion: (7.3704.10)
      Engine LGVersion: (7.3704.10)
     Signature: Create time:12/01/2006 21:00:37 Rand:85169237 Computer:
      Env SystemPath: H:\SG2-Logs\
      Env LogFilePath: H:\SG2-Logs\
      Env Log Sec size: 512
      Env
(CircLog,Session,Opentbl,VerPage,Cursors,LogBufs,LogFile,Buffers)
         (    off,     852,   42600,   24960,   42600,    2048,
             2048,2000000000)
      Using Reserved Log File: false
      Circular Logging Flag (current file): off
      Circular Logging Flag (past files): off
      1 H:\Data\DB2\DB2.edb
             dbtime: 105576739 (0-105576739)
             objidLast: 161066
             Signature: Create time:12/01/2006 21:00:37
                Rand:85161050 Computer:
             MaxDbSize: 0 pages
             Last Attach: (0x1B53,9,86)
             Last Consistent: (0x1B51,6B8,149)

      Last Lgpos: (0xaa15,7FF,0)

Integrity check passed for log file: c:\temp\e010000aa15.log
```

The Store creates file names for transaction logs using a naming scheme that combines the prefix for the storage group with a sequential log number in hex, so you can have over a million log files before the Store has to reuse file names within a storage group. For example, E00 is the prefix of the default storage group. The current transaction log for the default storage group is E00.LOG. Exchange 2007 changes the naming convention for log files. Exchange 2000 and 2003 use an eight-character name composed of the storage group prefix and the log generation number, resulting in names such as E0007E71.log. On an Exchange 2007 server, the names are ten characters long (such as E00000002A.log). The difference is accounted by the requirement to avoid the potential that log file names are recycled and overwritten. In reality, a low potential for this situation existed beforehand, but it did increase when the number of log files expanded by five due to the reduction in size from 5MB to 1MB. The extra characters allow Exchange to create over four billion logs before any possibility exists for name reuse. Figure 5.5 illustrates the different file size and naming convention used by Exchange 2007 (left) and Exchange 2003 (right).

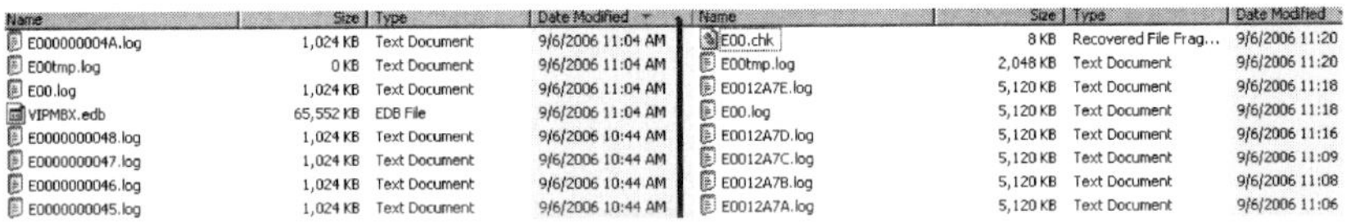

Figure 5.5
Transaction logs from Exchange 2007 and Exchange 2003

Name	Size	Type	Date Modified	Name	Size	Type	Date Modified
E000000004A.log	1,024 KB	Text Document	9/6/2006 11:04 AM	E00.chk	8 KB	Recovered File Frag...	9/6/2006 11:20
E00tmp.log	0 KB	Text Document	9/6/2006 11:04 AM	E00tmp.log	2,048 KB	Text Document	9/6/2006 11:20
E00.log	1,024 KB	Text Document	9/6/2006 11:04 AM	E0012A7E.log	5,120 KB	Text Document	9/6/2006 11:18
VIPMBX.edb	65,552 KB	EDB File	9/6/2006 11:04 AM	E00.log	5,120 KB	Text Document	9/6/2006 11:18
E0000000048.log	1,024 KB	Text Document	9/6/2006 10:44 AM	E0012A7D.log	5,120 KB	Text Document	9/6/2006 11:16
E0000000047.log	1,024 KB	Text Document	9/6/2006 10:44 AM	E0012A7C.log	5,120 KB	Text Document	9/6/2006 11:09
E0000000046.log	1,024 KB	Text Document	9/6/2006 10:44 AM	E0012A7B.log	5,120 KB	Text Document	9/6/2006 11:08
E0000000045.log	1,024 KB	Text Document	9/6/2006 10:44 AM	E0012A7A.log	5,120 KB	Text Document	9/6/2006 11:06

When you create a new storage group, ESE allocates it a separate prefix to use for transaction log naming (you cannot assign your own prefix), so the second storage group uses E01, the third E02, and so on. Figure 5.6 shows that the log file prefix for the "LCR Storage Group" is E02, so we know that this is the third storage group created on the server. Note that if you create a storage group and then remove it, Exchange may not reuse its log file prefix. Assigning a different prefix to the logs for each storage group allows you to keep all the transaction logs from every storage group in the same directory and avoid any problems that might occur if the storage groups used the same naming convention. However, cluttering up a single directory with thousands of log files is not a good idea. It is best practice to place the transaction logs for each storage group into a separate directory.

Despite the growing size of messages and message volume, Exchange log files have been 5MB since Exchange 4.0. Microsoft changed the log file size downwards to 1MB for Exchange 2007 to accommodate the requirements of log file shipping and the continuous replication features that are now available. In particular, to ensure that any data divergence that might occur as a result of an interruption in log replication can be quickly resolved and that it is less likely that data will be lost if a log file cannot be copied or is corrupted through hardware or software failure. Any variation from the expected file size is an indication that the file might be corrupt for some reason. If you see unexpected log sizes, you should stop the Information Store service and check the event log, database, and disks for errors.

In all cases, you should take care to place the transaction logs on separate physical disk devices to their databases (or two disk logical units on a SAN). Apart from the performance issue caused if too much I/O goes to one device, you need to ensure that you lay out important Exchange files in a way that you create maximum resilience to failure. You can have an accident and lose a database through disk corruption or an administrative failure, and if so, you can proceed to recover the database from a backup and replay all the transactions from the log files. However, if you lose a database and then find that you cannot recover the transactions, users end up by losing data and you may end up by losing your job. With this in mind, be sure to maintain clear separation in storage terms between databases and their transaction logs.

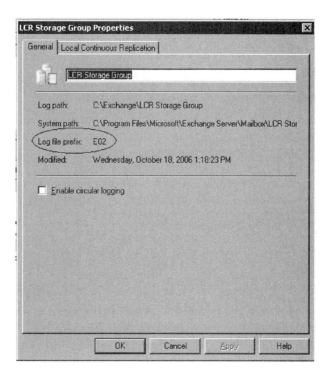

Figure 5.6
Storage group log file prefix

5.6.1 Circular logging

The Store supports the concept of circular logging, which means that instead of creating a new transaction log for every 1MB of transaction data, the Store reuses a set of transaction logs to save disk space. In other words, as the Store commits all of the transactions in a log file to the database, that transaction log file becomes a candidate for reuse. Under anything other than heavy load, the Store uses a set of transaction logs. However, if the server or the Store comes under heavy load, the Store may not be able to commit transactions as quickly as it normally does into the database, and in these circumstances, the Store may create and use additional log files. In all cases, the Store only uses a limited number of logs, so you can be sure that the server will never run out of disk space because of log usage.

Because all of the databases in a storage group share a common set of transaction logs, you cannot set circular logging for a specific database. Instead, you enable circular logging by selecting a storage group and updating its properties as shown in Figure 5.7. You can also effect the change with the `Set-StorageGroup` command:

```
Set-StorageGroup —id  'ExchMbxSvrl\First Storage Group'
—CircularLoggingEnabled $True
```

The reason why circular logging exists is to restrict the amount of disk space that the Store consumes to hold transactions. This reason was very important in the time when storage was expensive and disks were small. On a server running Exchange 4.0 or 5.0 in 1996, the prospect of running out of disk space was very real and administrators paid a lot of attention to services that consumed storage because if less than 10MB is available on the disk that hosts transaction logs, the Store service shuts down. However, given that most server computers have much larger amounts of disk space available today, the need to keep such a close eye on available disk space is not as necessary. Exchange does a good job of removing obsolete transaction logs if you take regular backups and most companies assign the necessary disk space (with a good buffer) to handle the storage of at least three days worth of transaction logs just in case backups do not happen. Experience of Exchange in production proves that the prospect of losing valuable data through the unavailability of a transaction log and being unable to restore a storage group completely after a disk outage is a more frequent occurrence than exhausting space on the disk that hosts transaction logs.

This does not mean that you do not have to monitor the space consumed by transaction logs because there are occasions when the Store can generate many more logs than normal. For example, if you decide to move a large amount of mailbox data from one server to another, the act of moving the mailboxes generates transactions on both the source and target servers (usually a transaction log for every megabyte of mailbox data that moves), resulting in the generation of a large number of logs on both computers. For this reason, it is a good idea to take a full backup of both computers after the move is complete to remove the transaction logs and to ensure that you can restore the servers to a postmove state, just in case a problem occurs.

The golden rule is never to enable circular logging for a storage group on anything other than a test server or a storage group that holds transient data that you can afford to lose. For example, you can safely enable circular logging on a storage group on a front-end server that does not host mailboxes. Never use circular logging for a mailbox store unless it hosts only test mailboxes.

Figure 5.7
Enabling circular logging

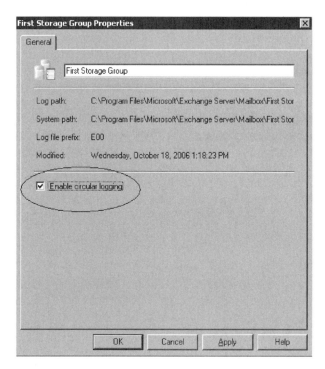

5.6.2 Creating new transaction logs

If you enable circular logging for a server, the Store uses a small set of transaction logs to capture database transactions. The set varies in number depending on the transactional load on the server, but it is usually between four and six logs that the Store switches in and out to become the current log as it commits transactions into the database. Circular logging is not a good idea on a production mailbox server but is common on test servers and those that handle purely transient traffic, such as Edge servers.

When circular logging is disabled, the Store continuously creates new transaction logs as it fills the current log with data. The Store performs the following steps to create a new log and switch it to become the current log. First, the Store advances the checkpoint in the checkpoint file to indicate that it has committed the transactions in the oldest log into the database. Next, the Store creates a temporary file called <storage group prefix>tmp.log or E00tmp.log for the default storage group. The Store switches this file into use to become the current log when the Store closes off the current log and ensures that the Store can continue to write transactions into a log without pausing. If the Store fails to create the temporary file, it usually means that no more disk space is available on the disk that holds the transaction logs. In this case, the Store will proceed to an orderly shutdown of the Information

Store service and uses the two reserved log files to hold transaction data that it flushes from its cache during the shutdown.

When the temporary log file is created, the Store initializes its log header with the generation number, database signature, and timestamp information. When the current log file is full, the Store stops writing transactional data and renames the current log file (always E00.log for the default storage group) to incorporate the generation number in its file name (for example, E000007E71.log). The Store then renames the temporary log file to be E00.log to make it the current transaction log and then resumes writing transaction data into the current log file, flushing any transactions that have accumulated in the short time required to switch logs.

The Store continues with the process of creating the temporary log file and switching it to take the place of the current log file until the Information Store service shuts down. The number of logs created on a server varies according to message traffic and other activity, such as mailbox moves and public folder replication. Busy and large servers may generate tens of gigabytes of transaction logs daily, so this is obviously an important factor to take into account when you size storage for servers. However, the space occupied by transaction logs is released when the files are deleted after successful full backups. The logic here is that you do not need the transaction logs any more if you have a full backup because the database is consistent and you have a backup copy if a problem arises. The backup copy also contains the transaction logs that are necessary to allow the Store to make the database consistent if you need to restore it.

5.6.3   Reserved logs

In Exchange 2000/2003, every storage group has two special log files called RES1.log and RES2.log that the Store uses to reserve some storage in case it is unable to create new transaction logs for any reason, usually space exhaustion on the storage device that holds the transaction logs. Running out of disk space was a reasonably common occurrence in the early days of Exchange because disks were small and expensive, but such an event is a much less common experience for today's Exchange administrator. Most administrators now monitor free disk space on all disks used by Exchange and take action to release space if less than 250MB is available. Exchange 2007 renames the reserved logs (which now only occupy 1 MB each) to SGprefixres00001.jrs   and   SGprefixres00002.jrs   (for   example, E00res00001.jrs is the first reserved log file for the default storage group).

5.6.4 **Transactions, buffers, and commitment**

After a client submits a message to Exchange, an ESE session that is responsible for the transaction follows a well-defined order to apply the transaction to commit the new message to the Store. The same order is followed for other transactions such as deletes and moves. First, ESE obtains a timestamp using the internal time (called a "db-time" held in an 8-byte value) maintained in the database header. In order to modify a page, ESE must calculate a new db-time based on the current value in the header. Once it has calculated the new db-time, ESE writes the records that make up the transaction into the current transaction log. After this operation completes, the session can go ahead and modify the appropriate pages in the database. Page modifications occur in an in-memory cache of "dirty pages," so ESE may first have to fetch the necessary pages off the on-disk database.

Eventually, ESE flushes the modified pages from the in-memory cache and writes them into the database. The database write cannot occur before the transactions are first committed into a transaction log to ensure that data is always protected. If you look at the steps that make up a complete transaction, you see that the last step is to commit the transaction for an individual ESE session to disk. For example, the last step shown in Figure 5.8 is a commit command for ESE session 8. Other prior steps begin a transaction for session 8 and insert some data to replace an existing page. The commit is a synchronous operation, so no other transaction can occur for that session until the write to disk is complete. Enabling write-back caching on the disk that holds the transaction logs improves performance by allowing the write to complete in the controller's memory and so release the synchronous wait. The controller is then responsible for writing the data to disk.

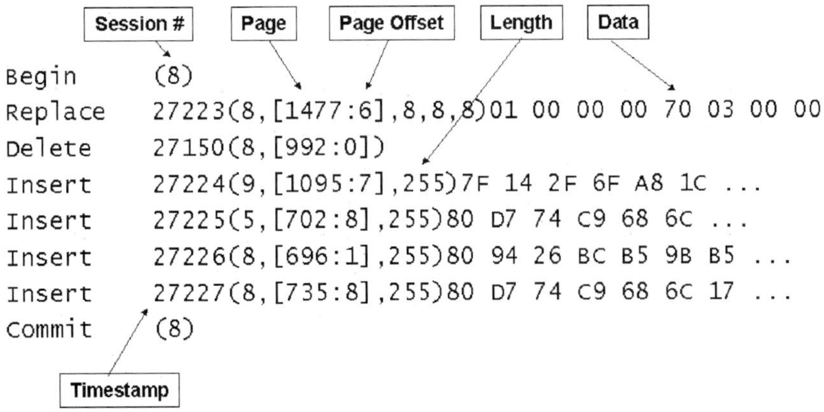

Figure 5.8

Data in a transaction log

```
                    Session #    Page    Page Offset    Length    Data

Begin       (8)
Replace     27223(8,[1477:6],8,8,8)01 00 00 00 70 03 00 00
Delete      27150(8,[992:0])
Insert      27224(9,[1095:7],255)7F 14 2F 6F A8 1C ...
Insert      27225(5,[702:8],255)80 D7 74 C9 68 6C ...
Insert      27226(8,[696:1],255)80 94 26 BC B5 9B B5 ...
Insert      27227(8,[735:8],255)80 D7 74 C9 68 6C 17 ...
Commit      (8)

                    Timestamp
```

The delivery of a single new message causes ESE to modify many different pages since many tables (Inbox, message folder table, and so on) are updated. ESE also updates the index for each table and if the message contains a large attachment, its content will be broken up into several long value chunks, all of which generate log records and the Store generates a set of log files to hold all the pages that it updates with the new content. On the other hand, if you delete an item that has a very large attachment, Exchange only needs to capture the page numbers of the pages that now contain deleted data and the actual content does not appear in the logs. As you can see from Figure 5.8, records for different transactions are interspersed throughout a log file, so replaying a transaction is quite a complex matter. These records are low-level physical modifications to the databases in a storage group. Each transaction log contains a sequential list of operations that the Store performs on pages in memory. The log captures details of when a transaction begins, when it is committed, and if the Store needs to roll it back for some reason. Each record in the log is of a certain type. Record types include begin (a transaction is starting), replace (some data in a page is being updated), delete (data is removed), insert (data is added), and commit. In addition to interleaved transactions from multiple databases in a storage group, transactions from multiple sessions are interleaved throughout a transaction log. This means that the "begin" record type also identifies the session that performed a transaction. You can think of a session as a thread running within the Store process. The session forms the context within which ESE manages the transaction and all of the associated database modifications. Each session could be tied back to a particular client, but the database has no knowledge of individual clients (MAPI or otherwise), as all it sees are the threads that operate on its contents.

Regretfully, there is no tool provided to interpret a log file. Figure 5.8 illustrates how a set of transactions might appear in a log. In this example, the first transaction in session 8 (or thread 8) is replacing a record in the database. Every physical modification to a database is time stamped. ESE uses timestamps later if it has to replay transactions from a particular point in time. The page number and an offset within the page are also recorded. The length of the data to be replaced is then noted and is then followed with the actual binary data that is inserted into the page. The next transaction is a record delete. The set of insert transactions demonstrates that transactions from multiple sessions are intermingled within a log. Sessions write data into the log file as they process transactions. Any dump of a log file from even a moderately busy server will record transactions from scores of sessions.

When the Store replays transactions from logs to make a database consistent, it has to interpret the contents of all the different transaction logs that have accumulated since the last good backup to find the transactions that it requires and then assemble the different records for those transactions from the logs and replay them into the database.

5.6.5　**Transaction log I/O**

ESE always writes transactions in sequential order and appends the data to the end of the current transaction log. All of the I/O activity is generated by writes, so it is logical to assume that the disk where the logs are located must be capable of supporting a reasonably heavy I/O write load. In comparison, the disks where the Store databases are located experience read and write activity as users access items held in their mailboxes. You should never place transaction logs on a compressed drive, as Exchange will have to decompress them each time it needs to access the content, which only slows down processing.

On large servers, the I/O activity generated by transaction logs is usually managed by placing the logs on a dedicated drive. This solves two problems. First, the size of the disk (today, usually 100GB or greater) means that free space should always be available. If you accumulate 100GB of logs (100,000 individual log files) it means that either your server is under a tremendous load or you haven't taken a full online backup in the recent past. Full online backups remove the transaction logs when they successfully complete. Second, in all but extreme circumstances, a dedicated drive is capable of handling the I/O load generated by transaction logs. I cannot think of a reason why a dedicated drive could become swamped with I/O requests from log activity. In any case, if such a load was ever generated on a server, the I/O activity to the Store is probably going to be of more concern than the log disk.

Of course, having a dedicated drive for log files is a luxury that you might not be able to afford. But the logic applied to justify the drive—reserve enough space for log file growth and keep an eye on I/O activity—should be remembered when you decide where the logs should be stored on your system. For example, it's a bad idea to locate the logs on the same drive as other "hot" files, such as a Windows page file. Also, never place the logs on the same drive as a database. Keeping the logs with their database may seem like a good idea, but it risks everything. If a problem afflicts the disk where the stores are located, the same problem will strike down the transaction logs and you will lose data.

5.6.6　**Protecting transaction logs**

Apart from the fundamental first step of separating the transaction logs away from their databases through placement on different physical volumes, best practice is to deploy the necessary hardware to provide the Store databases with maximum protection against disk failure.

You also need to protect transaction logs, but they usually do not need RAID-5, as the overhead generated by RAID-5 will slow the write activity to the logs. However, it is possible that a specific storage controller will dictate that you should use RAID-5 on the drive that you use for transaction logs for a reason particular to that controller, which illustrates the need to consider the performance characteristics of your hardware and the way that the hardware handles read and write operations before making a firm decision. In the same vein, using RAID 0+1 to protect transaction logs is also overkill. In most cases, all you need to do is to allocate two disks for the transaction logs to create a mirror set. You can place transaction logs on an unprotected drive, but if you do this, you must understand that any problem on that drive may render the logs unreadable. In this situation, if you then have to restore a database for any reason, you will not be able to replay transactions from the logs into the restored database and data will be lost.

As discussed earlier, the default behavior for ESM is to create transaction logs and databases on the same volume. Exchange places the default storage group and its transaction logs on the same volume when you first install a server. You should therefore review log placement on a regular basis with an aim of assuring both maximum protection and performance.

I may seem a touch paranoid when I discuss protection for the databases and transaction logs, but I look at it a different way. Consider how much money it costs to recover data if a drive fails. Now factor in the cost in terms of loss of productivity, the strain on everyone involved, and the sheer lack of professionalism that exists in any situation where you might compromise data integrity. With these points in mind, I think I am right to be paranoid about protecting data!

5.6.7 **Transaction log checksum**

Every transaction log contains a checksum that ESE validates to ensure that the log data is consistent and valid. Microsoft introduced the checksum to prevent logical corruption occurring as the Store replays transactions into a database during a recovery process. The checksum also prevents administrators replaying a selective set of logs back into the Store after a restore, something that used to be possible up to Exchange 5.5. Selective replays are a bad idea because the Store interleaves transactions from all databases in a storage group into a single set of logs, so it is possible to miss parts of a transaction if the Store does not replay the complete set.

ESE uses a type of "sliding window" algorithm called LRCK (Log Record Checksum) to validate checksums for a selected group of records in a log to ensure log integrity. ESE reads and verifies these checksums during backup and recovery operations to ensure that invalid data is not used. If ESE detects invalid data through a checksum failure, it logs a 463 error in the system event log. If ESE fails to read the header of a transaction log and is unable to validate the checksum, it signals error 412 in the application event log. Transaction log failure inevitably leads to data loss, as the only way to recover from this error is to restore the last good backup. All of the transactions since that backup will be lost.

5.6.8 Maximum database size

Microsoft makes the point that the 64-bit larger memory model of Windows and the changes made in the database engine enables Exchange 2007 to support larger mailbox quotas. One interesting aspect of the introduction of continuous replication is Microsoft's assertion that you can double the size of the mailbox databases that you operate from Microsoft's usual recommended 100GB[8] maximum size for databases that are not on an LCR server to 200GB. If you allocate 1GB mailbox quotas, these limits mean that you can only support 100 or 200 mailboxes per mailbox database, which does not seem a lot. Of course, you may run into other problems if you deploy very large mailboxes, such as the number of storage groups that you need to use.

Once you run the Enterprise Edition of Exchange 2007, the software does not enforce any limit for a mailbox database size. In fact, the theoretical limit for a database on an Exchange Enterprise server is 16TB, so there is plenty of room to grow from 100GB. The operational requirements that surround the deployment of very large mailbox databases means that it is unusual to see a mailbox database that exceeds 300GB, but there are instances of Exchange 2003 servers that support mailbox databases that are larger than 1TB. Microsoft's suggested limit of 100GB for a standard mailbox database is a somewhat arbitrary value because the limits are influenced by:

- The desire of the Exchange engineering group for customers to operate manageable databases on production servers. It is reasonable for an engineering group to tell customers to remain within well-defined limits for supportable database sizes because it reduces the possibility that customers will deploy very large databases. In addition, if a bug or hardware failure affects a database, users lose less data when databases are smaller.

- Experience gained from the internal deployment of Exchange within Microsoft and the way that Microsoft IT manages their Exchange servers and storage. It is natural to take lessons such as the time required for backup and restore operations from a well-functioning deployment and represent them as best practice.

- The focus that the Exchange engineering group had a focus on enabling low-cost storage as a suitable platform for Exchange 2007 to

---

8. Some consultants use a lower 75GB maximum for a database.

drive down cost. If you deploy low-cost storage, you are using storage that is less resilient than a Storage Area Network, so it makes sense to limit database sizes. It is reasonable to create a 50GB database on direct attached storage and less of a good idea to create a 200GB on the same platform.

- The larger the database, the longer it will take you to perform offline operations such as defragmentation (with ESEUTIL). While you should not need to perform these operations very often, you also do not want to have to spend days to process a 300GB database.

- Experience gained with problems within the database with Exchange 2000 and 2003. For example, in a very large mailbox database, ESE has to manage a huge fee page lookaside list (the list of free pages that are available for new items), and this caused some performance and stability issues if the database is stressed.

It is true that the basic problem with large databases is that the larger the database, the longer it takes to perform online and offline backups and restore operations. Restore operations usually take much longer than backups. In addition, Exchange may struggle to perform the nightly background maintenance operations such as the removal of deleted items past their retention date within the maintenance window for these tasks. Even with these caveats, you can support very large mailbox databases through rigorous management practices.

Microsoft doubles their recommendation for maximum database size to 200GB when you use LCR to protect a server because LCR allows you to recover much more quickly from a database failure by swapping the local replica in to take the place of the failed database. However, even using continuous replication, Microsoft is careful to set expectations as to what practical maximum size of a production database should be because of the time required to reseed the database replica if this is required. For example, if a failure occurs on the drive that supports the replica, you need to reseed the replica before LCR can restart, and this requires you to take a block copy of the production database (using a file level copy or with the `Update-Storage-GroupCopy` command, which uses the ESE streaming backup functionality to copy the database). Copying a very large database can take a long time even on fast storage[9], hence a big reason for Microsoft's preference that you limit the size of production databases.

Continuous replication provides a solution for hardware failure that affects mailbox stores, but only if you place the replicated files on a different

---

9.   A good estimate is to expect to be able to copy 25MB/second for a single database, with speeds up to 100MB/sec for multiple parallel database seeds on a gigabit network.

device that is not affected by the failure. One assertion that I have heard is that the use of continuous replication removes the need to perform daily full backups because another copy of the database is always available and up to date. Conceptually, this position may be accurate in terms of the technology, but it absolutely fails to consider the requirement that companies have to preserve and protect business critical data, which often mandates the need to take full daily backups followed by the removal of the backup media to an offsite location.

The big problem with Microsoft's recommendation for maximum database sizes is that there are many examples of deployments that routinely use larger databases with both Exchange 2000 and Exchange 2003. Given good management practices in design, deployment, and operation, especially hosted on SAN-based storage, there usually are not problems with very large mailbox databases, so there is no need to reduce mailbox database sizes as you migrate from Exchange 2003 to Exchange 2007.

In summary, Microsoft's suggested limits for maximum database size are reasonable to use for planning purposes and you should have good reasons before you decide to use higher limits.

5.7   Database portability

Database portability is a new feature in Exchange 2007. It means that you can move a database from one Exchange 2007 server and remount it on another Exchange 2007 server in the same organization or in a different storage group on the same server. You can then reconnect users to mailboxes in the moved database. Database portability is only available for mailbox databases—you cannot move a public folder database between servers as this would cause havoc for the replication mechanism. Databases in all previous versions of Exchange are static and tied to the storage group and server where they are created. You cannot move databases from one Exchange 2003 server to another, except in the very limited circumstances permitted when a database is mounted in the Recovery Storage Group to allow an administrator to recover mailbox contents. Users cannot access a database mounted in the Recovery Storage Group, so you cannot consider this database as portable. You also cannot move a database from an Exchange 2003 server to an Exchange 2007 server because of the different database formats (such as the change in page size made by Exchange 2007).

Database portability is important because it allows you to recover from a server failure by moving database files (and their mailboxes) to another server and so restore service to users. Database portability also allows you to split up the databases in a storage group by moving the mailboxes from one database to a database in another storage group. You may want to do this to split up a storage group that contains several databases into a set of storage groups that each contains one database so that you can use LCR with one or all of the storage groups to improve database resilience. See Chapter 9 for more information about LCR. Of course, you can move mailboxes from one database to another with the `Move-Mailbox` command, but this approach generates a lot of processing for the server and a pile of transaction logs. It is easier and faster to move the physical files from one disk to another than to move mailboxes, especially if the two locations are on the same server. Database portability is a situation where operating Exchange 2007 on a SAN is better than on direct-attached storage as it is much easier to remap the LUN that holds a database and redirect it to another server.

Database portability depends on some additional capabilities introduced in the Store in Exchange 2007 and the ability of the `Move-Mailbox` command to move configuration data for mailboxes, which is also a new feature in Exchange 2007. To move only the configuration data for mailboxes, you use the –ConfigurationOnly parameter with the `Move-Mailbox` command. For example:

```
Move-Mailbox —id Redmond —TargetDatabase 'ExchMbxSvr2\New
Database' -ConfigurationOnly
```

Exchange maintains pointers in the Active Directory to associate a user account with the database where its mailbox is located. When you move configuration data, it means that you move the pointer that ties a mailbox to a database to a different database. The next time an Outlook 2007 client attempts to connect to the mailbox, the AutoDiscover service will redirect it to the database that you have moved the mailbox to. Older Outlook clients should be able to switch databases automatically, but you will have to reconfigure the profiles of IMAP4 and POP3 clients to update them with the new database location.

Of course, you have not physically moved the mailbox (yet), just a pointer. Of course, after you use the `Move-Mailbox` command to move configuration data, the Active Directory has to replicate the changes around the organization. If something such as a network outage stops the Active Directory from being able to replicate the data, users will not be able to connect to their mailboxes on the new server until replication completes.

You can use these steps to move mailboxes in a database to a different server or to move the database from one disk to another on the same server:

1.   If it is possible, take a full backup, just in case. Apart from anything else, this step will reduce the number of transaction logs that you have to copy from the old to the new location.

2. Create a list of all of the mailboxes and their contents (number of items and mailbox sizes) from the database that you plan to move. The easiest way to do this is with the `Get-MailboxStatistics` command.

3. Create a new database on the target server (or in the desired location on the same server). You must give the new database the same name as the database that you want to move. You are going to overwrite this database with the database that you move, so this step is to ensure that the configuration data in the Active Directory matches the name of the moved database. For the same reason, make sure that the properties of the new database include the "this database can be overwritten by a restore" setting.

4. Dismount the database in the target location and delete the .EDB file.

5. Move the user mailboxes, remembering to specify –Configuration-Only.

6. Dismount the database that you want to move plus any other database that is in the storage group, including a public folder database if present. All of the databases in a storage group share a common set of transaction logs, so if you do not dismount all of the databases, you will not be able to copy the logs.

7. If you are unsure that the database has shut down cleanly (for example, the server crashed unexpectedly), you can run the ESEUTIL utility with the /R switch to commit transactions from any log files that are needed and put the database into a clean state.

8. Copy the database files including transaction logs and content indexing catalog files to the new location.

9. Mount the database in the new location.

10. Check that all the mailboxes that you wanted to transfer have moved across. Use the `Get-MailboxStatistics` command to generate a report on the mailbox contents (see below).

11. The more paranoid (or wise) administrators would now take another full backup on the basis that you can't be too sure about things and a good full backup is always a reassuring thing to have.

12. You can now clean up the old database files by first removing them through EMC or with the `Remove-MailboxDatabase` command, and then deleting the files.

You probably will not move just one mailbox to access the moved database. Instead, it is more likely that you will want to move all of the mailboxes from the database on the old server to the new server. For example, this command moves the configuration data for all of the mailboxes belonging to "Database1" on server ExchMbxSvr1 to use the same database name on server ExchMbxSvr2:

```
Get-Mailbox —Database 'ExchMbxSvr1\Database1' | Move-Mailbox
—TargetDatabase 'ExchMbxSvr2\Database1' —ConfigurationOnly
```

After moving the mailbox database and logs and remounting it in the new location, you can check that the contents are in place. `Get-Mailbox-Statistics` should show you that all of the mailboxes are now in place in the moved database. If you took a list of the mailboxes before the move, you can now compare that list to the report generated after the move.

```
Get-MailboxStatistics —Database 'ExchMbxSvr2\Database1'
```

Figure 5.9

Mixed transaction logs after a move

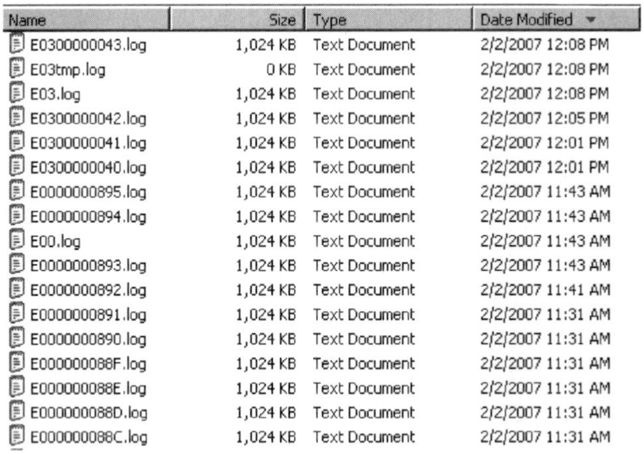

Name	Size	Type	Date Modified ▾
E0300000043.log	1,024 KB	Text Document	2/2/2007 12:08 PM
E03tmp.log	0 KB	Text Document	2/2/2007 12:08 PM
E03.log	1,024 KB	Text Document	2/2/2007 12:08 PM
E0300000042.log	1,024 KB	Text Document	2/2/2007 12:05 PM
E0300000041.log	1,024 KB	Text Document	2/2/2007 12:01 PM
E0300000040.log	1,024 KB	Text Document	2/2/2007 12:01 PM
E0000000895.log	1,024 KB	Text Document	2/2/2007 11:43 AM
E0000000894.log	1,024 KB	Text Document	2/2/2007 11:43 AM
E00.log	1,024 KB	Text Document	2/2/2007 11:43 AM
E0000000893.log	1,024 KB	Text Document	2/2/2007 11:43 AM
E0000000892.log	1,024 KB	Text Document	2/2/2007 11:41 AM
E0000000891.log	1,024 KB	Text Document	2/2/2007 11:31 AM
E0000000890.log	1,024 KB	Text Document	2/2/2007 11:31 AM
E000000088F.log	1,024 KB	Text Document	2/2/2007 11:31 AM
E000000088E.log	1,024 KB	Text Document	2/2/2007 11:31 AM
E000000088D.log	1,024 KB	Text Document	2/2/2007 11:31 AM
E000000088C.log	1,024 KB	Text Document	2/2/2007 11:31 AM

It is entirely possible that the prefix used by the storage group that you move the database to may differ from that used by the source server. In this case, you will see that new transaction logs created after you mount the database take the prefix used by the new storage group rather than persisting with the prefix used on the old. This is quite logical because transaction logs always use the prefix of the storage group that creates them. Figure 5.9 shows what the prefix switch means in action. You can see that the directory contains a set of transaction logs created with the E0 prefix, which means that they belong to the default storage group. This set of logs terminates at E00 and E00000895 at 11:43AM. The next transaction log starts at E030000040, created at 12:01PM. You can see that the prefix changes from E0 to E3 and that the log name has gone backwards in terms of the sequence number. All of this is logical because the new logs have taken the prefix of the storage group that the database now belongs to, but it can be a little confusing the first time you see this happen.

5.7.1 Zero database pages

If you view the properties of a database through the Exchange 2003 GUI, you can set a checkbox to have Exchange zero out deleted database pages. This means that the Store writes zeros into deleted pages to overwrite any data that exists in the pages and remove the possibility that someone could dump the database to work out what those pages contain. Zeroing out pages in this manner adds a small amount of overhead to Store processing, so Exchange does not enable this feature for databases by default. Generally, only administrators of highly secure Exchange servers opt to use page zeroing and this is the reason why Microsoft removed the option from the Exchange 2007 GUI.

If you want to zero out deleted database pages in Exchange 2007, use the Set-StorageGroup command as follows:

```
Set-StorageGroup —id 'VIP Storage Group' —ZeroDatabasePages
$True
```

As the name of the command implies, all of the databases in the storage group now zero out deleted pages.

5.8   MAPI connections and logons

It would be simple if one MAPI connection from a client like Outlook was reflected in a single link to the server. However, MAPI is a reasonably complex protocol and the work done by a single client is usually represented through multiple connections, a fact that can be somewhat confusing to the unwary administrator.

When a MAPI client connects to Exchange, it establishes a MAPI session (otherwise known as a connection). The session is an object that contains information about the user including the mailbox that they access and their security credentials. After it establishes a session, the client is able to log on to the session. A client is able to establish multiple logons to a server within a single session and there can be multiple active sessions per user. For example, a user is connected through Outlook and also has a session established through the BlackBerry Enterprise server so that new messages can be delivered to their handheld device. Each logon provides the connection to a mailbox, public folders, or another user's mailbox (to access their calendar, for instance). Remember that remote clients may logon to a server to access a folder on the server, which increases the total sessions that a server has to support. All of the logons are terminated to end the session when the client exits. The ability to maintain several distinct connections to a server within a single session is the reason why you see Exchange report multiple connections from a single Outlook client. In general, if you want to understand the connections that exist on a server, you can look at them through the following relationship:

```
Number of logons >= Number of sessions >= Number of users
accessing the server.
```

With this statement in mind, Table 5.7 describes the major Performance Monitor counters that you can use to assess the current workload of an Exchange server.

5.9   The Deleted Items cache

The Deleted Items cache is a temporary resting point where items remain between the time that a user deletes them from their mailbox and the time that the Store removes the items from a database. The deleted items retention period is the time that the items remain in the cache. The ability to recover deleted items from the cache has saved me on innumerable times to retrieve a message that I deleted that suddenly became important again.

When a user deletes an item, their client moves the item into the Deleted Items folder. The item remains in the Deleted Items folder until the user makes an explicit choice to empty the folder or the client automatically empties the folder the next time it exists. Outlook controls this behavior through the option shown in Figure 5.10. Best practice is to encourage users to set the option to empty their Deleted Items folder automatically, if only to help keep under their mailbox quota, but some users like to keep items in the Deleted Items folder for quite a period, perhaps because they want to review these items before they make the decision to delete them finally. Note that you will not be able to recover an item if you move it into a PST and then delete it from that location (either by using the Shift-Delete key combination when working with items in a folder or by emptying the PST's Deleted Items folder). This is because PSTs delete items immediately and finally and do not have the ability to keep items until a retention period expires as the Store can.

Table 5.7   *MAPI Connections and logons*

Performance Counter	Meaning
MSExchangeIS Mailbox\Active Client Logons	The number of logons that have issued a MAPI request within the last 10 minutes. As a client can maintain multiple logons, this number may be more than the number of mailboxes on a server. The number is incremented for each logon and decremented after a logon has been inactive for 10 minutes.
MSExchangeIS Mailbox\Client Logons	The number of client processes, including system processes, that have initiated MAPI logons to sessions. A single Outlook client normally maintains several logons.
MSExchangeIS\Active User Count	The number of unique users that have logged onto the server and been active in the last 10 minutes. If the server maintains public folder replicas, remote users may connect to these replicas and increase the active user count. The count also includes remote users who connect to calendars on the local server.
MSExchangeIS\Active Anonymous User Count	The number of anonymous users (those who do not authenticate) who have connected to the server and been active in the last 10 minutes.
MSExchangeIS\User Count	The number of users currently connected to the Store, including users connected to public folder replicas and those who are logged on to other users' mailboxes.
MSExchangeIS\Anonymous User Count	The number of anonymous users currently connected to the Store.
MSExchangeIS\Connection Count	The number of current connections to the Store. A user may maintain multiple connections if they use different protocols such as MAPI and IMAP.
MSExchangeIS\Active Connection Count	The number of connections that have been active in the last 10 minutes. Generally, the active count is less than the total connection count.

Figure 5.10
*Outlook 2007
option to empty
Deleted Items
folder*

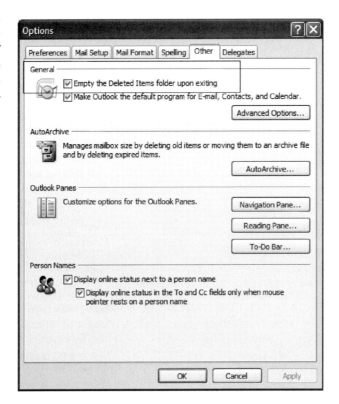

Up to Exchange 5.5, the story stopped here. Once deleted, items stayed deleted. However, users make mistakes and sometimes they delete items when they should not. When this happened, administrators had a simple choice: Either tell the user that they could do nothing to recover the deleted item or go ahead and restore the mailbox database on another server, find the item, export it to a PST, and provide it to the user. Given these options, most administrators chose not to restore databases and the user suffered—unless they held a sufficiently high position in the organization to be able to convince the administrator to change their mind. Since Exchange 5.5, Exchange servers have supported the option to maintain a cache of deleted items that remain in the Store until a set deleted retention period expires, at which point the Store removes the items from the database. This is a great feature for both users and administrators alike because it saves work for everyone.

To allow deleted items recovery, the Store uses a flag (a MAPI property) to enable "soft" or two-phase deletes. When a client empties their Deleted Items folder, the Store initially hides the items from view by setting the delete flag. This step has the effect of placing the items into the Deleted Items cache. The cache is logical rather than physical and does not exist in a separate area in the Store. Instead, the items remain in the Deleted Items folder but you cannot see them because the Store does not reveal their existence unless you use the "Recover Deleted Items" option. The Deleted Items folder does not exist for public folders, but an administrator can still recover a deleted item for a public folder from the cache by opening the public folder that it was deleted from and then using the Recover Deleted Items option.

By default, Exchange 2007 applies a 14-day retention period to all new databases, which means that the Store keeps items in the cache and then expires them, which then allows the regular nightly background maintenance tasks to remove the items from the database. Because you cannot upgrade older servers to run Exchange 2007, every database begins with the default retention period. Microsoft sometimes mentions that they selected the 14-day period because they wanted to reduce the number of times that administrators had to recover items for users by restoring backups, but in most cases, large companies have operated 7- to 10-day retention periods since Exchange 2000, so the change to 14 days will not have much impact.

Increasing the deleted items retention period has an impact on database size. The Store has to retain deleted items for longer and these items occupy pages. To calculate the expected impact, you can estimate based on the average daily message traffic received by users. If this is 20MB and you have 2,000 mailboxes on a server, then the database grows by 20MB × 2,000 = 40GB daily. Users will delete some of these messages. If we assume that they keep half, then the actual database growth is closer to 20GB and 20GB moves into the deleted items cache, so we end up with 280GB of cache storing items deleted in the last 14 days. This amount stays constant because deleted items move in and out of the cache, but you have to account for this overhead in terms of overall database size and backup times. If you assign 1GB mailbox quotas, this amounts to 14% additional overhead. All of these calculations are highly specific to the quotas and behavior that apply within an organization, but they may help you to understand the potential impact.

If you want to change the deleted items retention period for a database, you do so through EMC by selecting the database and modifying the limit through the Limits property tab, as shown in Figure 5.11. You can also set the retention period for deleted mailboxes here. By default, Exchange 2007 retains deleted mailboxes in a database for 30 days after an administrator deletes them, just in case someone makes a mistake and removes a mailbox early. Thirty days is an appropriate period for most companies. You can use the following command to find out what deleted item settings exist for user mailboxes within your organization.

```
Get-Mailbox —ResultSize UnLimited —Filter
{RecipientTypeDetails —eq 'UserMailbox' —or
```

```
RecipientTypeDetails —eq 'LegacyMailbox'} | Select
DisplayName, DeletedItemFlags, RetainDeletedItemsFor,
RetainDeletedItemsUntilBackup
```

Note the use of the ResultSize parameter to ensure that we can handle more than 1,000 mailboxes and the filter applied so that we do not check room or equipment mailboxes. A scan like this on a large organization can take some time to complete and we probably want to pipe the output to a text file for review. The kind of information you will see is like this:

DisplayName	DeletedItemFlags	RetainDeletedItemsFor	RetainDeletedItemsUntilBackup
Bernard, Aric	DatabaseDefault	14.00:00:00	False
Morrissey, Daragh	DatabaseDefault	14.00:00:00	False
Redmond, Tony	DatabaseDefault	14.00:00:00	False
Laahs, Kevin	DatabaseDefault	14.00:00:00	False
Doyle, Owen	DatabaseDefault	14.00:00:00	False
Kirby, Jill	RetainUntilBackup	60.00:00:00	True

The last mailbox in this report has flags set to keep deleted items for 60 days and an explicit flag set to keep deleted items in the database until you backup the database. Naturally, you can manipulate these properties through the Set-Mailbox command if you find that you want to set certain values for a mailbox:

```
Set-Mailbox —id 'Doyle, Owen' —RetainDeletedItemsFor
120.00:00:00
—RetainDeletedItemsUntilBackup $True
—UseDatabaseRetentionDefaults $False
```

You can also set the deleted items retention period for a database through the shell with the Set-MailboxDatabase command. For example, the next command sets a deleted items retention period of 120 days on a database. It also sets the retention period for deleted mailboxes to 60 days. Finally, the command sets the flag to instruct the database to retain deleted items until an administrator takes a successful backup, even if this causes the items to exceed their retention period. This is a good option to take because it ensures that a deleted item will be kept as long as is necessary until it is safely stored in another location that you can recover it from if required.

```
Set-MailboxDatabase —id 'VIP Mailboxes' —ItemRetention
120.00:00:00
—DeletedItemRetention 60.00:00:00
```

```
—RetainDeletedItemsUntilBackup:$True
```

To set the deleted item retention for all databases on a server, add a call to Get-MailboxDatabase:

```
Get-MailboxDatabase —Server ExchMBXSvr1 | Set-MailboxDatabase
—DeletedItemRetention 120.00:00:00
```

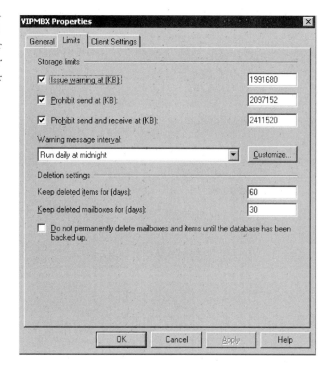

Figure 5.11
*Setting a specific
retention period for
a mailbox*

It is often useful to be able to assign a special deleted items retention period to one or more mailboxes. Because it takes time to set limits on individual mailboxes, this is not a recommended option and you should only take it on an exception basis. For example, during a legal discovery action, your legal department may compel you to be able to recover all messages sent and received by particular users such as the officers of the company or those involved in particular deals. You can either group all the affected users into a single mailbox store or apply the desired retention period to the database, or you can edit the properties of each mailbox. The latter option is preferable if the target accounts use mailboxes on a set of distributed servers, perhaps spread across a wide geographic area. You can set a deleted items retention period for a mailbox in three ways:

1. Accept the default retention period inherited from the database that hosts the mailbox.

2. Use EMC to modify the deleted items retention period for the mailbox as shown in Figure 5.12. In this instance, the retention period is set to be 60 days.

3. Use the `Set-Mailbox` command to set the deleted items retention period. For example, to set the retention period to be 60 days for the "Bond" mailbox:

```
Set-Mailbox —id Bond —RetainDeletedItemsFor 60.00:00:00
-UseDatabaseRetentionDefaults $False
```

Figure 5.12
*Setting Deleted
Items retention for
a mailbox*

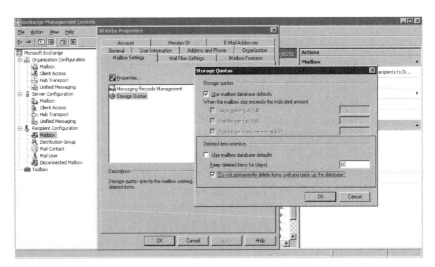

The Store does not calculate the size of items in the deleted items cache when it applies quotas to user mailboxes. Some users exploit this fact when they come close to exceeding their quota by selecting large items from their mailbox, deleting the items, emptying the Deleted Items folder, and then performing whatever actions they wish. Later on, when their quota frees up, they can recover the items from the cache.

5.9.1 Cleaning the Deleted Items cache

The background Store maintenance tasks performed by the System Attendant remove items in the cache after their retention period expires. The exact schedule that controls background processing is set through a database property and it is usually started nightly just after midnight. In database terms, removing items from the deleted items cache are "hard deletes" because the Store removes the items from its database tables and you cannot recover them later without performing a database restore. You can get an idea of the cleanup processing done by the Store by looking for event 1207, which reports the number of items and their size in the cache before and after scanning for items with an expired retention period. Figure 5.13 shows how the Store reports the cleanup for a database. In this case, the Store did not remove anything because no item exceeded the deleted item retention period!

Figure 5.13

Items removed from the Deleted Items cache

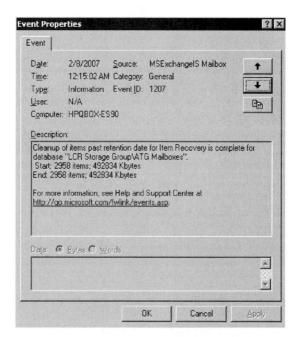

5.9.2 Recovering items and mailboxes

Pushing work down to users is always popular with administrators and all MAPI clients from Outlook 98 onwards support the option to recover deleted items from the cache. Outlook Web Access also supports this functionality. Anyone who uses a client like Outlook Express that does not support deleted item recovery will have to log on with a client that does and Outlook Web Access is usually the preferred option.

When you use the Recovered Deleted Items option (Figure 5.14), Exchange provides a list of all the deleted items in your mailbox that have not yet exceeded their retention period. The items listed were deleted from the folder that you run the option from, so if you take the option from the Deleted Items folder, you see the majority of the items that you have deleted. On the other hand, if you attempt to recover deleted items from the

Inbox, Outlook only lists the items that were deleted directly from this folder and never went through the Deleted Items folder. You can only recover items when you connect to a server. If you run Outlook in cached Exchange mode, Outlook connects to Exchange to recover items. Items recovered in cached mode take a little time to reappear in the Deleted Items folder because Outlook has to synchronize the items from the server into the client-side folder replica.

Figure 5.14
*Recovering
deleted items*

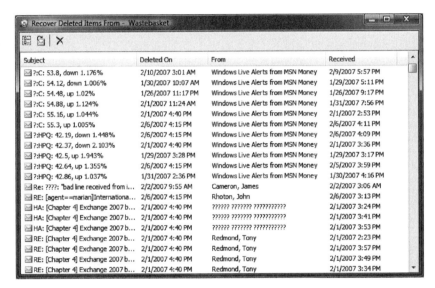

By default, the Deleted Items folder is the only folder enabled for item recovery. However, clients can delete an item in place in any folder (use the Shift/Delete combination instead of the Delete option), meaning that the item does not progress through the Deleted Items folder before it enters the cache. If users are accustomed to delete items in place, you may want to enable deleted items recovery for every folder to allow users to recover items in their original folders. Enabling this feature is a good idea for users who operate in cached Exchange mode because deleting in place avoids the network overhead of synchronizing the items that move into the Deleted Items folder. It also makes Outlook faster to exit because there is less to delete in the Deleted Items folder. Note that if you delete an item in place and want to recover it later on, you have to access that folder and then use the Recover Deleted Items option rather than attempt to recover the item from the Deleted Items folder.

To enable deleted items recovery for every folder, create a new DWORD value at the following registry location on the client PC and set its value to "1"—this works for all versions from Outlook 98 through Outlook 2003. You don't need to make this change for Outlook 2007 because it enables the dumpster for all folders, even when it is not connected to Exchange 2007.

```
HKEY_LOCAL_MACHINE\Software\Microsoft\Exchange\Client\
Options\DumpsterAlwaysOn
```

Outlook versions prior to Outlook 2003 do not filter the cache when you attempt to recover items into any other folder than the Deleted Items folder. In other words, you see everything in the cache rather than just the items deleted from the folder that you want to recover items for. Outlook 2003 and 2007 filter items, so you only see the items deleted from the folder rather than the complete cache.

You can use the `Get-MailboxStatistics` command to list any mailboxes that have been deleted. For example:

```
Get-MailboxStatistics —Database 'Executives' | Where
{$_.DisconnectDate —ne $Null}
```

Use the `Connect-Mailbox` command to reconnect a deleted mailbox to an Active Directory user account.

```
Connect-Mailbox —Database 'VIPMBX' —identity 'George Smith'
```

In this case, the name of the disconnected mailbox is "George Smith." We haven't told Exchange what Active Directory account to connect the mailbox to, so Exchange searches the Active Directory to discover a suitable account using the LegacyExchangeDN and Display Name values that it retrieves from the disconnected mailbox. If Exchange can find a match, it prompts you to confirm that you want to proceed to reconnect. If Exchange can't find a match, you will have to provide the name of the Active Directory account to use by passing the value in the —User parameter.

EMC also supports an option to reconnect a deleted mailbox. In this case, you open the Disconnected Mailbox node under Recipient Configuration to see the list of deleted mailboxes that are available to connect (Figure 5.15). You can then select a mailbox and take the connect option to launch a wizard to select the user account to reconnect the mailbox with. As with the shell, you can search the Active Directory using the LegacyExchangeDN and Display Name values to find a match or select a new account.

Figure 5.15
*Reconnect a
deleted mailbox*

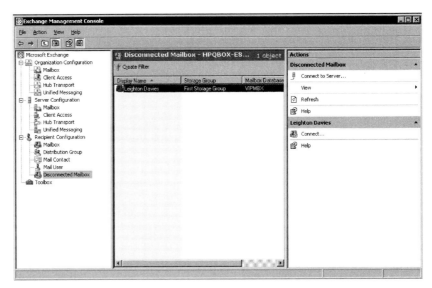

5.10   **Background maintenance**

All databases have internal structures that require some degree of maintenance and Exchange is no different. You can take a database offline to rebuild
it with the ESEUTIL utility or verify its internal structures with the ISIN-
TEG utility, but these operations require you to deprive users of access to
their mailboxes. As Microsoft designed Exchange to be highly available with
as little downtime as possible, it is obvious that some online maintenance
operations are required to keep the databases efficient while allowing users to
continue working. The Store performs online maintenance as a background
task nightly to ensure logical consistency within the mailbox and public store
databases and to remove unwanted data. As shown in Table 5.8, the Store
performs 12 background maintenance tasks nightly.

Table 5.8   *Background maintenance tasks*

Task	Mailbox Store	Public Store
Purge indexes	Y	Y
Perform tombstone maintenance	Y	Y
Purge the deleted items cache	Y	Y
Expire outdated public folder content	N	Y
Expire tombstones in public folders	N	Y

Table 5.8 *Background maintenance tasks (continued)*

Public folder conflict aging	N	Y
Event history cleanup	Y	N
Update server versions	N	Y
Secure folders	N	Y
Purge deleted mailboxes	Y	N
Check for obsolete messages	Y	Y
Database defragmentation	Y	Y

While the Information Store process controls background maintenance, it actually only executes the first 11 tasks and executes the last by calling ESE to perform defragmentation, an action the Store takes after at least one of the 11 tasks is complete. The purpose of background defragmentation is to reorganize pages within the database so that they are in the most efficient structure. At the end of the pass, Exchange reports how much free space is available in the database. Figure 5.16 shows that the database has 262 megabytes of free space. In other words, Exchange can store an additional 262 megabytes of information in this database before it will be forced to extend the file size of the database. You cannot recover the free space and return it to the file system without taking the database offline and processing it with the ESEUTIL utility to perform a complete rebuild. In the bad old days when Exchange background defragmentation was not as efficient as it is now and file space was more costly, administrators often rebuilt databases to recover disk space, but this is not required today.

In concept, the difference between the tasks performed by the Store and those executed by ESE is similar to how ISINTEG understands the structure of tables and indices that the Store assembles pages into while ESEUTIL deals with pages in the database at a lower level. Obviously, background maintenance can generate a huge amount of updates to Store contents. Like any other database update, the Store captures the details in transaction logs, which accounts for why you will see more transaction logs generated during the maintenance window than you can account for through user activity (which is usually low at this time) or even through public folder replication. Note that the "secure folders" task is now obsolete as it only applies to public folders that are homed in Exchange 5.5 sites. Once you eliminate Exchange 5.5 servers from your organization, the need for this task goes away.

You can take backups at the same time as background maintenance tasks are active with the exception of background defragmentation, which clashes with backups because of the way that ESE rearranges data in pages as it

Figure 5.16
*Online
defragmentation*

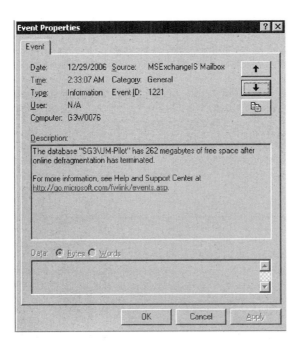

defragments the database. If defragmentation is active when you start an online backup, the Store suspends it until the backup finishes. If the Store cannot complete all the tasks during the allocated time, it finishes the last running task and records where processing stopped so that it can pick up from that point at the next maintenance period.

The event history cleanup task is the only addition to the background maintenance performed by Exchange 2007. The Store maintains a list of event notifications such as a new outbound message or new calendar request that the transport service and the Exchange assistant processes use to understand when they have to take action. Over time, the table that holds these events accumulates entries for events that have expired, so the event history cleanup task goes through the table to find and delete expired events.

By default, Exchange schedules background maintenance for between 1AM and 5AM local time. You can set up a separate custom schedule for each server by selecting the database properties through EMC, and then set the maintenance window as shown in Figure 5.17. Unlike Exchange 2000 or 2003, Exchange 2007 does not support server policies, so if you want to apply the same maintenance schedule to a set of mailbox or public folder databases, you have to use the Set-MailboxDatabase and Set-PublicFolderDatabase commands. Use the Get-MailboxDatabase or Get-PublicFolderDatabase commands to retrieve the current schedule. For example:

```
Get-MailboxDatabase —id 'VIP Mailboxes' | Select Name,
MaintenanceSchedule
```

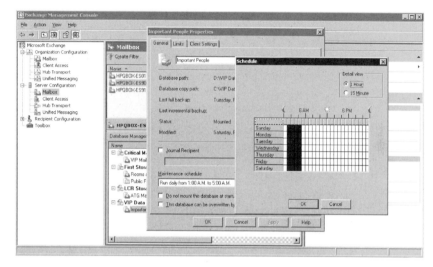

Figure 5.17
*Setting the
maintenance
window for a
database*

For example, to set the maintenance window to between 1AM and 7AM
daily for a group of databases on a server, you can use a command like this:

```
Get-MailboxDatabase —Server 'ExchMbxSvr1' | Set-MailboxDatabase
—MaintenanceSchedule 'Sun.1:00 AM—Sun.7:00 AM, Mon.1:00 AM—Mon.7:00
AM, Tue.1:00 AM—Tue.7:00 AM, Wed.1:00 AM—Wed.7:00 AM, Thu.1:00 AM—
Thu.7:00 AM, Fri.1:00 AM—Fri.7.00 AM, Sat.1:00 AM—Sat.7.00 AM,
Sun.1:00 AM—Sun.7:00AM'
```

This syntax is useful because it allows you to be extremely precise about
the exact time when maintenance can occur. However, the syntax used to
specify the date/time settings is a little fussy. Always leave a space between the
minutes and "AM" (as in 7:00 AM) and have a hyphen between the first time
and the day for the second time (as in AM-Wed).

Fortunately, Microsoft has provided a shortcut to express maintenance
windows by allowing you to use a number of predefined windows. For
example:

```
Get-MailboxDatabase —Server 'ExchMbxSvr1' | Set-MailboxDatabase
—MaintenanceSchedule@([Microsoft.Exchange.Data.Schedule]DailyFrom1AMto5AM)
```

In this case, the special "DailyFrom1AMto5AM" expression sets a maintenance window from 1AM to 5AM daily. The complete set of special expressions available to set maintenance windows are:

```
Never
Always
Daily10PM
Daily11PM
Daily12PM
DailyAtMidnight
Daily1AM
Daily2AM
Daily3AM
Daily4AM
Daily5AM
DailyFrom11PMTo3AM
DailyFrom1AMTo5AM
DailyFrom2AMTo6AM
DailyFromMidnightTo4AM
EveryFourHours
EveryHour
EveryTwoHours
FridayAtMidnight
SaturdayAtMidnight
SundayAtMidnight
DailyFrom8AMTo5PMAtWeekDays
DailyFrom9AMTo5PMAtWeekDays
DailyFrom9AMTo6PMAtWeekDays
DailyFrom8AMTo12PMAnd1PMTo5PMAtWeekDays
DailyFrom9AMTo12PMAnd1PMTo6PMAtWeekDays
```

5.10.1   Background tasks

Now that we understand what happens during background maintenance and when it happens, we can consider some of the details. Clients like Outlook make extensive use of the Store's ability to generate indexes or views on a dynamic basis. For example, if you decide that you want to view your inbox by author rather than by date, Outlook requests the Store for this view. If the Store has previously generated the view and has it cached, the response is very quick, but the Store is able to process quickly a request for a brand new view. Over time, the Store accumulates large numbers of views—each folder in every mailbox can have several views. It is not desirable to retain all of the views because each view occupies space within the database. In addition, users may not require a view after its first use. The Store assigns an expiry time to each view and monitors this data in an internal table called the index-aging table. When background maintenance runs, the Store scans the index-aging table to discover views that are older than 40 days and removes any view that has expired. Of course, if a client accesses a view, the Store resets its expiry time.

The next task is to perform tombstone maintenance. The Store maintains a list of deleted messages for each folder and a list of "tombstones" to indicate that a message was deleted. The tombstone list is most important for replicated folders, such as public folders, because it provides the Store with a list of message delete operations that it must replicate to every server that holds a replica of the folder. After successful replication, the Store can clear the entries from the tombstone list. Background maintenance ensures that the lists are accurate.

When a client deletes a message, the Store sets a flag to hide the message from the mailbox (a soft delete). Clients can retrieve messages from the deleted items cache by clearing the flag, thus causing the message to reappear in the mailbox. During background maintenance, the Store examines every message that has the deleted flag set (if enough time is available in the maintenance window, the Store processes the entire contents of the deleted items cache) to determine whether its retention period has expired. If this is true, the Store removes the message from the Store (a hard delete) and makes the pages used to hold the message available for reuse. You can set retention periods on a per-mailbox, per-database, or per–public folder basis, and can control these setting through EMC or with shell commands.

Figure 5.18 shows the limits set on a public folder database. You can see the deleted retention time is set at 14 days. Exchange also allows you to set a retention period for content in a public folder either per database or per folder. The idea here is that you may use some public folders to hold content that ages out in a systematic way, such as a feed from an NNTP service. By aging out content from a public folder, you impose a check on how large the folder grows to. To set a new age limit for a public folder database to 365 days:

```
Set-PublicFolderDatabase —id 'Public Folders'
—ItemRetentionPeriod 365.00:00:00
```

To set a specific age limit for a public folder:

```
Set-PublicFolder —id '\Exchange 2007\Admin Discussions'
—AgeLimit '365.00:00:00' —UseDatabaseAgeDefaults $False
```

Figure 5.18
Public Store limits

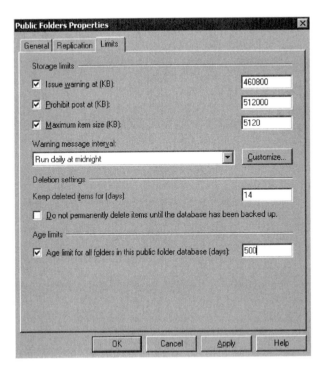

If you want to set an age limit for a set of public folders from a known root, you can use a combination of the Get-PublicFolder and the Set-PublicFolder commands. Note the use of the –Recurse parameter to walk down through the child folders.

```
Get-PublicFolder —id '\Exchange 2007' —Recurse | Set-PublicFolder
—AgeLimit '365.00:00:00' —UseDatabaseAgeDefaults $False
```

Background maintenance also checks for deleted folders that have exceeded their retention period and then removes them. Much the same processing occurs for deleted messages in public folders. The Store also checks for deleted mailboxes, which have a default retention period of 30 days, and removes any that have expired. Removing obsolete folders and mailboxes cleans up the internal table structure of the database and increases efficiency.

The next check is for deleted public folders that have expired. By default, if you delete a public folder, the Store creates a tombstone for the folder. This allows the replication mechanism to propagate the deletion properly to servers that hold replicas. Because replication may not occur quickly in some circumstances, the Store retains the tombstone for 180 days (default value). If replication has not propagated the tombstone in 180 days, your organization is experiencing fundamental replication difficulties and a few erroneous tombstones are of little concern. During background maintenance, the Store checks for folder tombstones that have expired and removes them. However, the Store only removes a maximum of 500 tombstones per 24-hour period.

Public folder replication is somewhat of a black art and it is easy for conflicts to occur; for example, if multiple users modify the same item in different replicas of a public folder or if multiple users attempt to simultaneously save an item in the same replica. When a conflict happens, the Store sends a conflict-resolution message to the users that provoked the problem to ask them to resolve the issue. It is easier for human beings to decide which change is more important and so resolve the conflict. While the human beings decide what to do, the Store maintains the different versions of the items in conflict. However, if the humans fail to respond, the Store examines each item in conflict and resolves them automatically, usually by accepting the most recent version.

The next task is to update server versions for the public stores. This process updates any version information that is necessary to maintain the system configuration folder. The Store incurs no great overhead and you cannot control the process.

The Store uses a single-instance storage model, meaning that it keeps a single copy of message content and uses pointers in user mailboxes to the content. The Store tracks the number of mailboxes that have pointers to content through a reference count and physically removes the content from the database when the reference count reaches zero. In any database, there is the potential for pointers to become unsynchronized, so background maintenance checks for lingering messages that have a zero reference count and then removes up to 50,000 of these items per day. The final and most compute-intensive task is for the Store to invoke ESE to perform online defragmentation.

5.10.2 Tracking background maintenance

Like any other operation in Exchange, the selected level of diagnostics logging determines how much information the Store writes about maintenance operations into the Application Event Log. You set the level for diagnostic logging using the `Set-EventLogLevel` for the "MSExchangeIS\9000 Private\Background Cleanup" and "MSExchangeIS\9001 Public\Background Cleanup" settings. Change the value from "Lowest" to "Expert." For example:

```
Set-EventLogLevel —id 'MSExchangeIS\9000 Private\Background
Cleanup' —Level 'Expert'
```

After applying the new setting, the Store begins to generate events the next time it runs background maintenance. Except on very large or heavily loaded servers, many of these tasks complete quickly. The obvious exception is background defragmentation. This is the most intense activity and can last a number of hours, depending on whatever other load the server is under, hardware configuration, and the size of the databases that the Store processes.

5.11 Fixing failed databases

A database failure has always been the source of bad dreams for Exchange administrators. It's not just the failure and the work required to restore service to users there's the inevitable inquiry as to why the failure occurred—was it a software bug, fault in a disk drive or controller, a lapse in administrative procedures, or something else that needs to be understood and protected against in the future. Database failures were reasonably common in the early days of Exchange (4.0 through 5.5 and even into 2000), but things have improved significantly as the software matured and, even more importantly, hardware (especially disks and controllers) has become much more reliable. At this point, it's fair to assert that a database failure comes as a surprise rather than a common occurrence for most Exchange administrators, assuming that normal best practice in hardware maintenance and monitoring is carried out. Even so, it's good to be aware of the tools that you can use to recover from a database failure should the need arise.

Transaction logging is one of the great strengths of the Exchange Store. With a full set of transaction logs and some good backups, you should be able to handle the vast majority of failures. Simply swap in some new hardware to replace the dud components, restore the database from backup, replay the transaction logs to bring the database up to date, and restart services. Of course, there are different variations on the restore theme, including dial-tone restores (to restart services with blank mailboxes and eventually recover the missing contents behind the scenes as users continue to work), but everything revolves around the ability to restore a copy of the failed database from a backup successfully. Troubles truly begin if you discover that you can't restore the database from a backup or Exchange refuses to start up with the backup copy. Not having a good backup to restore from, finding that the backup media is damaged, or perhaps that the backup failed for some reason and no one noticed are all reasons to update your resume.

Even with the reliability and robustness of today's hardware, nothing quite beats the feeling of confidence that a good backup brings—or the calmness that happens when you know that solid backups are available in an off-site location. But let's assume that you have managed to restore a copy but that Exchange won't mount the database for some reason. What can you do then? The answer lies in two utilities that have been part of the product since

Exchange 4.0. ESEUTIL is the ESE database utility and ISINTEG is the Store integrity checker. Both executables are located in the Exchange program files directory. These are command line utilities that can only run when a database is not mounted by the Store, so when these utilities run, users don't have access to their mailboxes. Microsoft has tweaked ESEUTIL and ISINTEG over the years and the latest versions provided with Exchange 2007 are the best and fastest yet. Never use a program from one version of Exchange to work with databases from a different version of Exchange as it is highly unlikely that the programs will work and you run the risk of doing some damage to a database.

ESEUTIL operates deep down within the bowels of the ESE database to fix problems at the page and records level; ISINTEG operates at a much higher level to fix problems with the logical arrangement in data within the database that turns tables and pointers into mailboxes, items, and attachments. Another way of comparing the two utilities is to say that ESEUTIL takes care of physical corruption while ISINTEG fixes logical corruption. While neither utility is able to fix problems caused by fundamental hardware failure (fixing a few corrupt pages won't get around the widespread corruption that a failed disk controller can cause), the utilities are very good at fixing the kind of problems that stop Exchange databases working the way that they should. It's common to find administrators who think of these utilities as panaceas for any problem that may afflict a database, a situation that couldn't be further from the truth. For example, five or six years ago, it was common practice to run ESEUTIL regularly to compact databases and recover disk space to the system. In fact, there are even third-party products that wrap ESEUTIL with a GUI and run it on a schedule to compact databases. This is certainly an action that was beneficial with early versions of Exchange when the Store's internal processing wasn't particularly efficient or effective at reusing "white space" within the databases, but any version from Exchange 2000 SP2 onwards is very good at maintaining its databases and you should never need to run ESEUTIL as a matter of course.

The situation you're in is that you've restored a backup copy of the database but the Store won't mount it for some reason. Before we panic, make sure that the database really is not going to work. Sometimes the database is fine but something else isn't and that's what stops the database working. The first thing to do is to check to see if Exchange has reported any problems in the application event log. Perhaps the restore operation didn't complete properly and you have an incomplete copy of the database on disk; perhaps the database is missing some files, such as transaction logs, that the Store needs to verify that it can replay any missing transactions into the database. Exchange is pretty good at noting problems in the event log and you can check the error number and descriptions reported in the log against the Microsoft Knowledge Base to see if there are any recommended actions to take.

Another action that you can take is to restart the server. This may be a case of clutching at straws, but a server restart has been known to clear out random problems. In any case, it doesn't hurt to put the server back into a good known state before you take any further action to cure the problem. After the reboot, we will proceed with the following actions:

- Copy database files.
- Run ESEUTIL to fix any database corruptions that it can.
- Run ESEUTIL to defragment and rebuild the database (optional).
- Run ISINTEG to correct any pointers.
- Take a full backup.

To start the repair process, make a copy of the database files—the EDB, the STM (if on an Exchange 2000 or 2003 server), and the transaction logs. The database utilities don't offer a sophisticated GUI that protects administrators from mistakes so it's important that you have something that you can revert to if required. Put these files in a safe place and then check that you have enough disk space available on the drive where the database is located to make a repair. As a general rule of thumb, try to have 120% of the size of the EDB file available for use when you run ESEUTIL. If you need to rebuild the database, ESEUTIL will recreate a new version that is likely to be around the same size as the original. Reserving an extra 20% is just to be sure that ESEUTIL has enough space to expand into if it needs to. ESEUTIL allows you to redirect temporary files to another disk through command line switches, so you can always take this option if you don't have enough free space on the disk that holds the database. While it's easiest if the EDB and STM files are in the same directory, they don't have to be and ESEUTIL has command line switches to allow you to specify different locations for the files.

You're now ready to run ESEUTIL in /P or repair mode. Here's an example of a command to repair a database[10]:

```
ESEUTIL /P F:\DATA\Mailbox1.EDB /T:E\TEMP\Fixed.EDB
```

This command:

- Tells ESEUTIL that it is running in repair mode.

---

10.   See http://support.microsoft.com/kb/317014 for the full set of command line switches for ESEUTIL.

- Points ESEUTIL to F:\DATA\Mailbox1.EDB as the input database. On an Exchange 2000 or 2003 server, ESEUTIL assumes that the STM file is in the same location as the EDB. If not, you can point ESEUTIL to the right location with the /S command switch.

- Instructs ESEUTIL to create E:\TEMP\Fixed.EDB as the output database. All of the processing performed by ESEUTIL is captured in a file called <database name>.integ.raw in the same location as the input database. While this file is unlikely to be of great interest to you, it may be useful to Microsoft PSS if you encounter problems in repairing a database and need help to resolve an issue.

On an Exchange 2000 or 2003 server, it is possible to proceed and repair an EDB database even if its matching STM is unavailable by specifying the /CreateSTM command switch. This forces ESEUTIL to create a brand new STM and while you will end up with a fully functional EDB, any content that clients created in the STM will be missing. The exact impact that this will have on clients depend on the client type. If you use Outlook and Outlook Web Access, then the demise of the STM is unlikely to have a major effect because these clients don't create data in the STM. On the other hand, if you use IMAP4 and POP3 clients, the reconstruction of the STM will remove all of their data because the STM is the default storage location for these clients. Exchange 2007 doesn't use the same rendering mechanism for MIME protocols as Exchange 2000/2003 do, and the data for all clients is now stored in the EDB, so this situation doesn't arise in Exchange 2007.

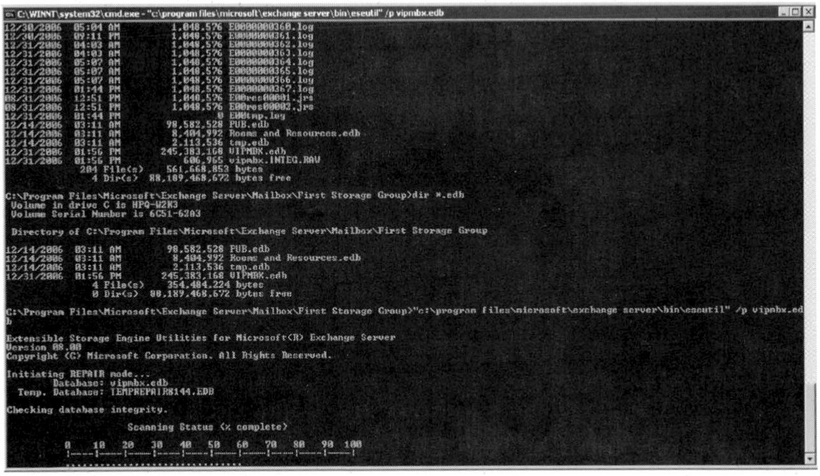

Figure 5.19
Running ESEUTIL

ESEUTIL has never been a fast utility in terms of how quickly it processes data (Figure 5.19), but it gets things done pretty rapidly when it performs a repair and you can expect ESEUTIL /P to execute at approximately 1–2GB/minute. Things get slower when you rebuild a database with ESEUTIL /D and you can expect the utility to do this work at around 20GB/hour—your mileage will vary depending on CPU and disk speed. Even with the fastest CPU, multiple cores, and fast disks, ESEUTIL won't set any speed records, so be prepared to wait. In fact, the slowness of ESEUTIL is one of the factors that many administrators take into account when they calculate the maximum size of a database that they are happy to manage in production. It's all very well to generate a massive database that's 200GB or more, but if it takes more than eight hours to run a procedure against the database, then you start to wonder how you'll ever meet your SLAs.

The repair operation won't fix every problem that may be lurking in the database. In particular, the resulting database won't be as space efficient as it could be, so you can run ESEUTIL with the /D switch to defragment and rebuild the database to create its most effective structure. Once again, you'll need enough disk space available to hold the output database. This is usually between 10% and 20% smaller than the original database, but you may not see this shrinkage as it all depends on how efficient the original database was.

If you want to get an idea about how much the database is likely to shrink, you can run ESEUTIL /MS to create a "space dump" of the database. A space dump can generate a lot of information, so it is best to pipe the output to a text file where you can examine it later on. The interesting data that you're looking for is at the start of the dump, where you'll find the available pages in the database. Figure 5.20 shows that roughly 26% of the database pages (7,684) are free and will be recovered if the database is rebuilt. Multiply this value by 8,192 (the size of a page in an Exchange 2007 database is 8KB; for Exchange 2000 or 2003 use 4,096 as these versions use 4KB pages). In this case, roughly 60MB of free space is available and will be recovered if the database is rebuilt. These figures are never exact, but they give you a good idea of what is likely to happen.

Figure 5.20
Output from ESEUTIL /MS

```
Extensible Storage Engine Utilities for Microsoft(R) Exchange Server

Version 08.00

Copyright (C) Microsoft Corporation. All Rights Reserved.


Initiating FILE DUMP mode...
        Database: vipmbx.edb

******************************* SPACE DUMP *******************************
Name               Type   ObjidFDP   PgnoFDP  PriExt     Owned  Available
========================================================================
vipmbx.edb         Db            1         1  256-m      29696       7684
```

Rebuilding a database is an optional step, but it's a good idea to do so just to be sure that the database is in its most efficient state before users are allowed to access it. To rebuild a database, ESEUTIL /D must read the input database page by page, verify the checksum and the physical integrity of the page, and then write it into a temporary output database. Any page that fails the checks is dropped, which then leads to the potential for data loss. A page that doesn't contain any data won't matter, but a page that holds information about a message or even details about messages in a folder is clearly a different matter. The upside of running ESEUTIL to rebuild a database is that it fixes database problems and that it returns disk space to the file system; the downside is that you may end up with a number of black holes in user mailboxes. To make sure that an administrator understands that some risk exists in running a repair, ESEUTIL flags a warning as shown in Figure 5.21.

Figure 5.21
A warning from ESEUTIL

After all the pages are processed from the input database, ESEUTIL copies the temporary output database to take the place of the original. If you have been able to keep all the files on the same disk, the copy happens quickly but clearly it will be a lot slower if you've had to put the temporary database on another drive, especially if the database is larger than a few gigabytes.

The last step is to run the ISINTEG utility to fix any logical issues that exist within the tables in the database, such as correct counts for items in a folder or pointers to items that don't exist. Run the command as follows:

```
ISINTEG —S "Server Name" — Fix —Test -Alltests
```

As you can see from Figure 5.22, ISINTEG lists the databases on the server and allows you to select the one that you want to process, which must still be dismounted at this point. However, behind the scenes, ISINTEG mounts the database to access its content through the Store process and then dismounts it afterwards. Users aren't aware that the database has been mounted and the Store blocks access anyway. ISINTEG processes data rapidly. It's a verbose utility because it was originally created by Microsoft as an internal test utility to verify the integrity of a database in the days when there were more software bugs that caused logical errors in the Store than there are today. At the end of a successful ISINTEG run, you should see very few or zero errors reported. If there are errors, you can run ISINTEG again to see

Figure 5.22
Running
ISINTEG

whether ISINTEG can fix the errors, but if persistent errors continue it may be an indication that a fundamental corruption is still present in the database. In this case, you can either run ESEUTIL again followed by ISINTEG to see whether the problem disappears or, if time is pressing and users want to get to their mailboxes, proceed to mount the database. If users report further problems, you should move mailboxes to another database until you are able to delete the database. If the problem database hosts public folders, you can move the replicas to a public folder database on another server, let replication finish, delete the replicas from the problem database, and then finally delete the database.

The final thing to take care of is to perform a full online backup after you have remounted the database. All of the transaction logs created before you started working with ESEUTIL and ISINTEG are nullified if you rebuild the database and you don't want to have to repeat all the work that you've just done, so take a full backup immediately before the database is back online. Apart from anything else, the checks that the backup API does as information is streamed out of the database will give you an extra feeling of confidence that you've restored the database to good health.

If you run Exchange 2003 on your servers, you have to perform a database repair step by step using the raw utilities. Exchange 2007 is a different matter because the Toolbox node of EMC includes a Database Recovery Management that will lead you through the entire process of running ESEUTIL and ISINTEG. All you'll have to do is make sure the target database is dismounted before starting the utility, mount it again after successfully running the utility, and complete the job by taking a full backup. Figure 5.23 shows the results page of the Troubleshooting Assistant after it performed exactly the same operations as we covered in this section. See Chapter 10 for more information about the Exchange Toolbox.

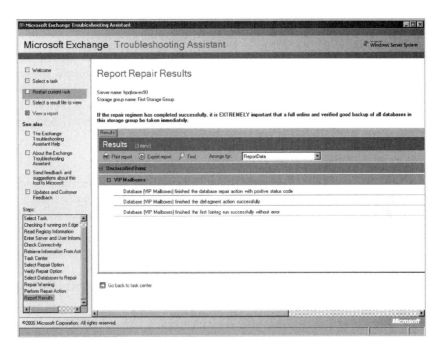

Figure 5.23
Results of a database repair

5.12 Exchange 2007 content indexing

Microsoft introduced content indexing (also called Exchange Search) for mailbox and public databases in Exchange 2000. This implementation used an early version of the Microsoft Search engine, but it proved to be unsuccessful in production because of the load that indexing generated on the server. Over time, we have seen increases in server performance, better knowledge and implementation of search algorithms, and the appearance of efficient desktop search engines that are capable of indexing mailbox data, such as Microsoft's own Windows Desktop Search and the LookOut add-in for Outlook that Microsoft purchased in 2005, plus competitors such as Google Desktop. Microsoft includes the ability for Outlook 2007 to use Windows Desktop Search, but the big issue with desktop indexers is the potential performance impact desktop indexing can provoke on the server. To the server, a desktop indexer can seem to be like a voracious user who keeps on demanding information in a seemingly endless stream of requests from the desktop to the server. It makes sense that it is more efficient to perform indexing once, on the server, and have clients use that index rather than generating local indexes, but users will not move away from local indexes unless they are sure that the server-based equivalent works. Therefore, to avoid the proliferation of local client-based indexes, we need tremendously efficient and responsive server-based indexing. This never happened in

Exchange 2003, where indexing was so slow that even Microsoft realized that it was best to disable the feature by default.

Apart from desktop searches, Microsoft supports Exchange search folders and programming interfaces to allow external programs to search within the Store. Huge differences exist between Exchange 2007 content indexing and in-Store searches. Here are some of the major differences. The first three are the most important in practice—content indexing is faster, more accurate, and can look through attachments:

- Content indexing is invariably faster because it uses indexes to locate requested information while Store searches have to perform serial scans through everything in the mailbox or folder that you search.

- Content indexing allows searches based on words, phrases, and sentences while a Store search uses a stream of bytes. Content indexing therefore ignores punctuation marks and spaces and is case insensitive while Store searches look for exact matches of all supplied characters.

- Content indexing supports filters for a number of common attachment types so it can index and search the content of those attachments. Store searches look through MAPI properties, which include message bodies but not attachments. On the other hand, because Store searches can access MAPI properties, you are not limited to content searches and can check date ranges and other properties such as importance, flags, etc.

- Content indexing is usually more accurate because it uses word prefix matches as well, so a search for "star" will also discover items that contain "starlet" or "stargazer," but not "filmstar." Store searches will find all three instances unless a prefix match is explicitly specified.

- Content indexing understands non-English languages, which gives it the ability to support correct searches against content that contains double-byte characters such as Japanese and Chinese. The byte stream searches performed by the Store have great difficulties with double-byte languages.

While content indexing offers major advantages in search accuracy, customers will enable it only if it responds quickly to user requests and does not overload the server. These were the major issues with content indexing in previous versions of Exchange, so Microsoft rewrote the entire subsystem for Exchange 2007 based on Version 3.0 of the Microsoft Search engine, which SQL Server 2005 also uses. SharePoint Portal Server 2007 also uses Microsoft Search 3.0 together with some of its own technology.

Microsoft also rewrote the software layer that connects the indexing engine to the Store so that it is much more efficient in how it accesses data. The net effect is that indexing is smooth and consistent and up to 35 times faster (Microsoft's own estimate) in indexing activities. The only real downside is the requirement to allocate between 25% and 30% of the size of the databases for the index. Because indexing now only takes between 3% and 5% of server CPU when it is running in a steady state to keep the indexes up to date, Microsoft now enables indexing by default. From a user perspective, searches return within seconds rather than minutes, so there is a reduced desire to use a desktop search albeit recognizing that desktop search engines remain useful when PCs operate disconnected from the network.

Exchange 2007 uses two services to perform indexing.

- The Exchange Search Indexer is responsible for creating and maintaining the search index. It monitors the Store for new items and invokes the necessary processing to update the index. For example:
  - The Indexer adds any new items that arrive into mailboxes through email delivery or item creation.
  - The Indexer scans the complete mailbox if a new mailbox is added to a database. This step ensures that any mailbox moved to a server has its contents incorporated into the index as soon as possible.
  - The Indexer scans new databases that are added to the Store.

- The Indexer is responsible for locating new items for indexing. When it discovers items that have not been indexed, it sends sets of pointers to these items to the MS-Search engine, which is responsible for indexing the content. Exchange creates a separate catalog folder that contains multiple index files for each mailbox database and the index files occupy between 5% and 10% of the size of the mailbox database.

  To retrieve the content, the MS-Search engine uses a special protocol handler to fetch the items from the Store and then pours the content through a set of filters that can understand specific formats such as Word, PDF, HTML, PowerPoint, Excel[11], and so on (at the time of writing, the new Office 2007 formats are not supported—Microsoft may address this omission in Exchange 2007 SP1). It is possible to customize indexing by adding new filters for new formats, but if you add a new filter (which requires you to buy in the filter

---

11.   See the registry value HKLM\Software\Microsoft\Exchange\MSSearch\Filters for the set of file types supported by Exchange.

code or install a new service pack or hot fix), Exchange will only index new content in that format unless you recreate the entire index.

The output of the filters is plain text content, which MS-Search then processes using a set of word breakers that identify the individual words in the content. The word breakers are able to handle content in different languages, including Japanese and Chinese. One possible complication for content indexing arises when documents are in one language but marked as being in another. For example, if you create an English-language document on a PC that runs the Dutch version of Word, Word marks the document as Dutch. Then content indexing applies its Dutch word breakers and you cannot guarantee that the words that are discovered will make sense for the purpose of searching.

If you look at processes running on an Exchange server, you will see two processes taking up CPU and memory to perform indexing. MSFT-ESQL.EXE is the core indexer, while MSFTEFD.EXE is a filter daemon that pours content from the Store through the filters and word breakers. Apart from a radical improvement in performance, the biggest difference in the implementation is the move from a "crawl" model (periodic updating of the index) to an "always up-to-date" model, which means that the Store indexes new items automatically as users create them in the database. A new message is usually indexed within 10 seconds of its arrival into an inbox. Of course, because of the increase in data cache enabled by the 64-bit platform, new items can be kept in the cache long enough for them to be indexed, so indexing generates no additional I/O, and new items appear in indexes very soon after they are created.

An Exchange server can encounter various situations that cause a mailbox database to undergo automated or manual maintenance and some of these situations can provoke the need for Exchange to rebuild the content indexes. Table 5.9 summarizes these situations. Note that Exchange does not automatically include the catalog folder in online backups taken using the Exchange backup API, so this is the reason why a full rebuild of the index is required if you have to restore a database from backup. If you take a file-level backup with acquiescent databases, you have the choice to include other files along with the databases and can include the catalog folder. In this scenario, if you have to restore the databases after a failure, you can restore the catalog folder too and so avoid the need for an index rebuild.

Performing a full crawl of a server to populate an index from scratch consumes a lot of CPU and memory and can generate a lot of I/O activity. Depending on the other work that the server is doing, crawling has the

Table 5.9 *Effect of database operations on indexing*

Scenario	Action	Result
Online backups	Backup taken with VSS or streamed to tape.	Re-index required if a database is restored from a backup.
File level offline backups	Offline backup to disk or tape.	Index data can be backed up and restored (without requiring an update) along with mailbox databases.
Fast recovery	Dial-tone recovery using blank mailbox database followed by recovery of the failed database.	Exchange creates a new index for the blank database and re-indexes once the failed database is recovered.
LCR	Log shipping and application of transactions to local copy of a mailbox database.	Exchange creates a new index if you have to switch over to the passive copy.
CCR	Switch to copy of the database on a passive node in a MNS cluster.	Search continues to work after transition. For lossy failovers, the index is okay and will be updated provided that the loss duration is less than seven days.
SCC	Switch to passive node (shared copy cluster).	Because only the active node is indexing, the transition causes Exchange to rebuild the index.

potential to disrupt email throughput. To avoid this problem, indexing throttles back its processing demands in periods when server load is high. During normal indexing, the indexer regulates the load that it places on the server by controlling the number of items that it attempts to process per unit of time. A monitoring thread keeps track of the load on each mailbox database by measuring the average latency required to retrieve a document from the database. If the latency crosses a specific threshold (20 milliseconds is the default value), then the indexing engine reduces the load on the server by delaying requests to retrieve information from the Store. Before attempting to fetch a document from the Store, the indexer checks the current processing delay and if it is larger than zero, the indexer goes to sleep for a short time before attempting the fetch. This kind of throttling only occurs during full crawls as the immediate updates to maintain the index do not impose significant load on a server.

Interestingly, content indexing does not index items that Outlook's junk mail filter detects as spam and moves into the Junk E-Mail folder. However, if you find that a message has been wrongly detected as spam and you move it from the Junk E-Mail folder to any other folder, content indexing will detect the move and include the message in its index.

5.12.1 Using content indexing

Content indexing is configured by default for all databases, so no work is required to set it up. You can check on the current indexing status for all mailbox databases on a server with the `Get-MailboxDatabase` command:

```
Get-MailboxDatabase —Server ExchMbxSvr1 | Select Name,
IndexEnabled
```

The databases that are shown with IndexEnabled = True are obviously those that Exchange is currently indexing. To disable content indexing temporarily, you use the `Set-MailboxDatabase` command:

```
Set-MailboxDatabase 'VIP Mailboxes' —IndexEnabled $False
```

Remember to reenable content indexing later on by setting the Index-Enabled property to "True." If for some reason you want to disable content indexing for all databases on a server, you can either set the IndexEnabled flag to False with the one-line shell command:

```
Get-MailboxDatabase —Server ExchMbxSvr1 | Set-MailboxDatabase
—IndexEnabled $False
```

Alternatively, you can stop the "Microsoft Exchange Search Indexer" service. Users will experience a radical reduction in performance if they conduct online searches when the indexing service is unavailable, especially when searching through large folders, and they will only be able to search message subjects rather than content. Outlook Web Access signals the potential performance degradation with a pop-up, as shown in Figure 5.24.

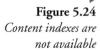

Figure 5.24
Content indexes are not available

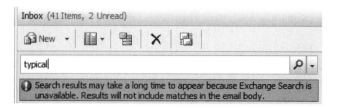

Another interesting shell command allows you to test the performance of a search operation for a specific mailbox (and the underlying mailbox database). You need to have the permissions to write into the mailbox that you want to test:

```
Test-ExchangeSearch 'Tony Redmond'
```

Exchange responds to the test by reporting whether it was able to perform a search and the search time. A result of 10 or less for the search time is acceptable. A reported search time of −1 indicates failure!

Figure 5.25
Building a complex search with Outlook 2007

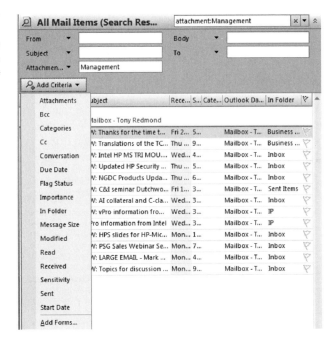

Now that we understand how to enable and test content indexing, we need to understand when it is used. If the mailbox database that hosts the mailbox is enabled for content indexing, all searches executed by Outlook Web Access clients connected to mailboxes in the database use content indexing. This is easy enough to understand because Outlook Web Access works in online mode. Things get a little more complicated with Outlook because it supports online and cached Exchange modes.

When Outlook clients (any version from Outlook 2000) operate in online mode, the vast majority of searches use content indexing providing that the mailbox database is indexed and the Exchange Search service is enabled for the database. In addition, the search query must contain fields that are actually indexed. Most fields are indexed, so this is not usually a problem. However, some queries exist that content indexing cannot satisfy, especially those that invoke complex combinations of NOT, AND, and OR checks against fields or any query against a field that is not indexed, such as a date field. In these cases, Outlook reverts to a Store search. Figure 5.25 shows the Outlook search builder in operation—you can build very complex queries to narrow in on the right information, but it's also probably as easy to confuse users.

Outlook 2003 and 2007 clients that operate in cached Exchange mode use client-side linear scans similar to those performed by the Store. Performance is often better than Store searches, but these clients never use Exchange content indexing. You can, of course, install an add-in product that indexes Outlook data and use that to achieve better performance.

Windows Desktop Search uses the same basic indexing and search technology as SharePoint and Exchange, but obviously on a less massive basis. Windows Desktop Search is included in Windows Vista and can be downloaded and installed on Windows XP clients and controlled through Group Policy. On a purely unscientific basis, it seems that Windows Desktop Search functions more smoothly under Vista than Windows XP because it seems to place less strain on the operating system when it indexes items.

Figure 5.26
Outlook 2007
Search Options

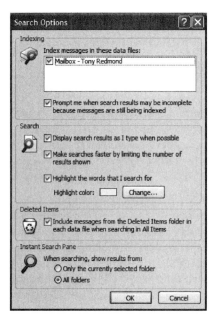

Figure 5.26 shows the options that you can configure with Outlook 2007 to control how search operates. Outlook 2007 clients that operate in

cached Exchange mode do not use server-based content indexing and use Windows Desktop Search instead. Windows Desktop Search relies on the cached copy of the mailbox plus any PSTs to include messaging data into its index. Note that it is possible for a client to generate searches using Exchange-based indexes and local indexes. For example, if you run Outlook 2007 in online mode and execute a search across your mailbox and a PST, Outlook uses Exchange content indexing to search mailbox content and Windows Desktop Search to search the PST.

5.13 Public folders

Public folders have been part of Exchange since the product's earliest days. The best definition that I can offer is that a public folder is a special form of shared mailbox that Exchange manages within a public folder hierarchy. Unlike mailboxes, which users can only access by connecting to a specific server that hosts the desired mailbox, Exchange can replicate the hierarchy and content of public folders to multiple servers within the organization so that users can access the data from their local server rather than connecting to a remote server. Exchange synchronizes modifications made to local folder replicas to ensure that data remains constant throughout the organization.

During the 1995–96 period, Microsoft often referred to public folders as "public fora" to indicate their intended use as a fulcrum for discussion and debate. Microsoft also emphasized the potential of public folders to be an application development platform through electronic forms that operated on the data stored in public folders. The theory was that you could generate the electronic forms necessary to automate common tasks such as expense processing by creating a suitable form to provide users with the ability to work with data in a public folder, taking advantage of the replication facility to keep information up to date across an organization. Microsoft's vision of what public folders could do was sophisticated and many demo applications probed the possibilities of public folders. In fact, there was even a chess application that users could play across the network by entering moves through an electronic form. Exchange stored the moves in a public folder and replicated them between servers so that players could see the latest state of the game and update their positions. Sadly, the limited nature of the 16-bit Electronic Forms Designer (EFD), the lack of development from the initial launch, and the black box that public folder replication became all conspired to block public folders from fulfilling the grand plan. Public folders slipped back to take up more mundane tasks such as providing a rudimentary shared document repository, archiving messages that users sent to distribution lists, and so on.

However, while it was easy to create new public folders and to populate the folders with data, companies found it more difficult to manage the proliferation of public folders if they allowed users to create folders without control. The result is that some companies that deployed Exchange early have ended up with hundreds of thousands of public folders. Exchange management consoles have never provided great insight into what public folders are used for or what they contain. In some cases, public folders may hold very important corporate information, but it's difficult to be sure unless you go and check every folder (which is a very difficult task if you have thousands of folders to review). Understanding what data exists in public folders is an important task for administrators as they contemplate the long-term future for this repository and that leads on to the next task, which is to decide where to store the data in the future.

Their relative lack of success has caused Microsoft to consider the future of public folders many times over Exchange's history. Microsoft attempted to reignite the potential of public folders by introducing support for multiple top-level folder hierarchies (TLHs) in Exchange 2000, with the intention that the standard hierarchy (called the MAPI TLH) would continue to host "standard" public folders while programmers would create and use new TLHs to host applications. Unfortunately, a lack of programming capabilities to exploit public folders did not accompany the new folder hierarchies, so they never succeeded. Given the lack of success, a lack of tools to manage public folders effectively, and the advent of other Microsoft solutions for collaboration such as mail-enabled document libraries in SharePoint 2007, you can see why Microsoft might want to move their products and customers away from public folders as soon as they can.

5.13.1   Public folders and Exchange 2007

In an Exchange 2007 environment, you only need public folders for two reasons:

1.   To support legacy Exchange 2003 or 2000 servers.

2.   To support legacy Outlook clients (anything pre-Outlook 2007).

To give customers some comfort about the future of public folders, Microsoft states that they will fully support Exchange 2007 for 10 years after first product release, so you can continue to use public folders with Exchange 2007 until 2016. However, you have to put this statement into context with Microsoft's overall support strategy (see http://support.microsoft.com/default.aspx?pr=lifecycle), which limits mainstream support to 5 years after which a product moves into extended support. Exchange is no different to other Microsoft business and developer products and 10 years is a reasonable time horizon to plan for an application. However, when all is said and done, the fact remains that Microsoft is still "de-emphasizing" public folders in Exchange 2007, which means that Microsoft will continue to look for an opportunity to move public folders out of one of the next major releases of Exchange. Originally, Microsoft intended to remove public folders from the next major release of Exchange (codenamed Exchange 14), probably due in the 2009–10 timeframe. Customer pushback and the lack of mature and easily attainable migration targets forced a rethink and so it is now likely that we will not see public folders fully removed from Exchange until a release in the 2011–13 timeframe, so there is plenty of time to prepare for a migration. Plans may easily change in this area, so it's something to keep an eye on.

While it might be desirable, Microsoft cannot eliminate public folders if they want to maintain a high degree of backwards compatibility for Exchange. For example, all MAPI clients up to and including Outlook 2003 require a connection to a public folder server to access components that these clients depend on, including the offline address book, free/busy data, Outlook security settings, and the organization form library. When you install the first Exchange 2007 server, the setup program prompts you to indicate whether you want to support legacy Outlook clients (anything before Outlook 2007). If you respond that you have legacy clients, the setup program creates a public folder database and populates the hierarchy with the public folders that these clients expect. If you say that you have no legacy clients, the setup program does not create a public folder database and it sets up a block to prevent legacy clients connecting to the Store. Basically, Exchange checks for the presence of a public folder hierarchy when the Information Store service starts and if it can't find the hierarchy, the Store blocks any attempt by a legacy client to log on to a mailbox. Legacy clients can't really function effectively without public folders (you can create and send mail, but many features are crippled by the lack of public folders), so it makes sense to block access.

Microsoft designed Outlook 2007 to work in a new manner with Exchange 2007, so these clients do not require access to public folders because they incorporate different mechanisms to get to shared data such as free/busy information. When connected to Exchange 2007 servers, Outlook 2007 clients can use a BITS (Background Intelligent Transfer Service)[12] connection to a web distribution point on an Exchange 2007 Client Access server to fetch a copy of the Offline Address Book; they access free/busy information through the Exchange 2007 availability web service, and retrieve Outlook security settings from the registry. As the first step in phasing out public folders, organizational forms are not available in Exchange 2007, so it is time to move from these forms to something more modern, such as InfoPath. All of this means that you have to wait until you can upgrade your MAPI clients to Outlook 2007 before you can even think

---

12. See http://www.microsoft.com/windowsserver2003/techinfo/overview/bits.mspx for more information on BITS.

about a retirement strategy for public folders. See Chapter 7 for more information about how Outlook 2007 interacts with Exchange 2007 when public folders are not present.

Microsoft offers customers some guidance about what to do with public folders and you can expect the story to mature and develop as we gain experience with Exchange 2007 and people experiment with long-term alternatives for public folders. At the time of writing, Microsoft recommends that you migrate to Exchange 2007 and Outlook 2007 as quickly as possible to remove the dependency that older Outlook clients have on public folder servers. Microsoft also recommends that customers develop new forms-based workflow applications with the .NET framework. Existing applications that use a combination of Outlook forms and public folders will continue to work as long as you keep the organizational forms library in a system public folder. Finally, you should keep a close eye on developments as Microsoft figures out how best to move data from public folders to new repositories.

If you decide that Exchange 2007 is a good time to move from public folders, you can consider Office SharePoint Server 2007 or its predecessor (for example, a SharePoint site makes a pretty good archive location for messages sent to an Exchange distribution list). This seems to be the logical path forward from public folders because SharePoint offers much better document management and search features, and SharePoint has a solid development plan that has delivered real progress since SharePoint Portal Server 2001. In addition, SharePoint leverages the .NET development platform, so you can be confident that any application that you build around SharePoint will use the latest programming techniques and libraries. Even when you select a new target platform, you still have to figure out how to move the data that has accumulated in public folders. One approach is to leave the data where it is and plan to obsolete the data gradually. In other words, do not create any new public folders and redirect data away from public folders to a new repository whenever possible. You can also create a review and retirement program for public folders with the aim of eliminating as many folders as you can in the short term.

5.13.2   Changes in public folders administration since Exchange 2003

In some ways, maintaining public folders is a case of Microsoft applying enough oxygen to the patient to keep it alive until new software rescues the situation. Some manageability improvements appeared for public folders in Exchange 2003 SP2, including:

- The ability to stop and resume content replication.

- The ability to apply delta changes on a recursive basis throughout the public folder hierarchy.

- The ability for an administrator to decide to synchronize the public folder hierarchy.

- Better control over the removal of servers that hosted public folders from an organization.

- Logging of public folder deletions.

It can be argued that most if not all of these features should have been included in Exchange from the first release and that their omission led to some of the problems that have resulted in the bad reputation that public folders enjoy today. In the same timeframe as SP2, Microsoft released the PFDavAdmin[13] tool to help administrators understand the data that their servers store in public folders. This tool closed a gap in the product that had existed since Exchange 4.0. PFDavAdmin is a useful tool in planning a migration because it gives you the hard data to analyze just what content you have to deal with. Running the tool is not difficult and it completes quickly. For example, a run against HP's Exchange infrastructure took an hour to discover and report on 160,000 public folders. This may seem like a large number of folders, but HP is similar to many companies that have run Exchange since 1996 and deployed public folders as the basis for applications or data sharing, often because it was a better answer than file shares. The interesting item that PFDavAdmin allows you to identify is the date when content last changed in a public folder. This is useful data because it indicates whether the folder is still in use. If someone has not accessed a folder and updated it in two years, the folder is probably not in use and you can delete it safely. See Chapter 10 for more details on the PFDavAdmin tool.

If you decide to move away from public folders and use a tool like PFDavAdmin to analyze and then clean up the public folder hierarchy, you can figure out what to do with the remaining public folders. Some advocate leaving the data in the public folders to decay gently over time by not encouraging users to use public folders and by preventing creation of new public folders. The theory here is that you will eventually be able to remove all of the public folders, providing you are willing to wait long enough. A more proactive approach is to look for a new repository, and Windows Share-Point Services and SharePoint Portal Server are good solutions that can take on many of the functions public folders serve today. Forms-based applications that use public folders remain an issue, but Microsoft proposes Info-Path forms as the way forward here. The problem with forms-based

---

13. DAV stands for "Distributed Authoring and Versioning" and is an extension to HTTP that Microsoft uses extensively with Outlook Web Access in Exchange 2000 and 2003.

applications is the need to recode the forms and application logic and not the data, which may need a one-time conversion from its current home in a public folder to a new repository. Finally, you need to consider network connectivity for users to the data and applications. Public folders use replication to get data and applications close to the user, but solutions like SharePoint Portal Server do not have the same replication capability, so you are likely to end up bringing users over extended network links to a central server. Given that today's network connections are probably more capable than those that existed when you originally deployed the application, this may not be an issue, but it may still be a problem for users in branch offices at the end of a hub and spoke network.

5.13.3   Calming replication storms

Public folder replication is a black art at the best of times and lack of knowledge about what happens to replicate content around an organization has led to many horror stories, such as the administrator who replicated the entire set of public folders from New York City to Australia for a very large financial institution. Replication took forever and it took even longer to rehome the public folders back to the servers where they should have been. Few Exchange system administrators understand how and when replication occurs and the Exchange administrative tools, especially the Exchange 2003 ESM console, are weak in this area, perhaps because Microsoft realized that public folders were not as successful as they had originally anticipated in the early days of Exchange and that there were other more usable repositories, such as SharePoint Portal Server. From Exchange 2000 onwards, Microsoft knew that they would eventually move away from public folders and so never gave this component the attention that other parts of Exchange have received. Overall, it is difficult to get a good picture of public folder replication to know when processing is proceeding as expected and when problems occur. Some companies have put together their own early warning systems based on data extracted from the application event log and WMI counters, but it is not a satisfactory situation, especially as the Exchange 2007 management console does not include any ability to manage public folders, so you have to manage public folders either through EMS or by keeping an Exchange 2003 server in the organization so as to be able to use its console. Neither approach is completely satisfactory.

There is a small but significant feature in Exchange 2003 SP2 that can help administrators to manage the phenomenon known as a "public folder replication storm." Replication storms occur when an uncontrolled or unexpected amount of replication activity is generated within the organization so that network links are swamped with the amount of data that public folder servers replicate to update the folder replicas on these servers. The typical cause of a storm is a change that an administrator makes that triggers the replication of many folders and items in those folders. Sometimes a replication storm is the result of a planned activity, such as when you add a new public folder server to the organization and need to replicate a large amount of data to that server in order to populate its set of folder replicas. Other times the storms occur by accident, such as when an administrator creates a new replica of a very large folder at 9AM on Monday morning, right in the middle of peak-time user demand when the servers are busy handling requests by Outlook clients to refresh their caches and process mail created offline. Sometimes replication storms occur without your knowledge and without any impact to the messaging infrastructure. This is especially true when the public folder servers that participate in replication are connected through high-speed, low-latency network links that can handle the peak demand generated by a limited replication storm.

You can control public folder replication storms to some degree by taking actions such as starting replication at a time when you know that the network is quiet and no other major activity is planned. Storms only cause problems when they are unplanned, especially if a large amount of data is channeled across an unreliable or slow network link or a link that is high latency. Bugs in Exchange have been known to cause replication storms in the past, but Exchange 2000 SP2 and later versions are pretty reliable in this respect and most storms are now caused by administrative error, such as the scenario around the creation of a large public folder described above. Of course, you can argue that if Exchange offered better management facilities for public folders (including the ability to monitor and throttle replication as required) then administrators would not make mistakes, and while this assertion is probably true, even the best administrator makes mistakes sometimes. For example, in a moment of weakness, you might create a new replica of a very large folder on a server that's at the end of a high-latency link. The intention is good—you probably want to allow users of that server to enjoy local access to the folder data—but the effect might be a replication storm. Exchange 2003 SP2 includes a public folder replication stop/start feature to allow you to address the problem. You can stop replication across your entire organization, fix the problem by reversing the changes that you made (in this case, remove the folder replica from the remote server), and then resume replication.

Microsoft implemented the ability to stop public folder replication as an organization-wide setting. This is logical because you want to stop replication on all servers. The options to stop and restart public folder replication are therefore revealed through the organization object in ESM. As shown in Figure 5.27, select the organization object and right click to see the option to stop public folder replication. This is the normal state of affairs as ESM only displays the option to resume replication when a stop operation is in effect. As we will see in a little while, EMS provides com-

Figure 5.27
*Exchange 2003
ESM option to stop
a replication storm*

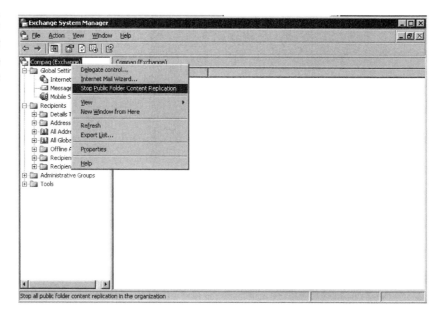

mands to allow you to stop and restart replication through the shell, which
has the same effect as the ESM commands.

If you click on the "Stop Public Folder Content Replication" option,
ESM displays a warning to ensure that you understand the effect of the
action that you are about to launch, which is to stop content replication
between all of the public folder servers in the organization. It is critical to
underline the organization-wide impact of your action before you proceed.
Clearly you don't want every administrator in the organization clicking on
this option just to see what it does, so you need Exchange Organization
Admin permission to be able to execute the option to stop a replication
storm. If an unprivileged administrator attempts to execute the option, ESM
issues an "LDAP Provider issue" message, which is ESM-speak to say that the
user doesn't have the right permissions.

Assuming that you have the right permission, ESM proceeds by setting
an organization property to indicate that public folder content replication is
disabled and then sends a "cease and desist" message to every server that hosts
a public folder database in the organization. The cease and desist message
stops servers responding to backfill requests from other servers. Each backfill
request asks a server to provide some data to update a public folder replica on
a remote server, so if the server stops responding to backfill requests, it has
the effect of nullifying any replication requests that the server would normally handle. Servers still send out backfill requests to request other servers
to provide backfill updates for their replicas, but the receiving server never
answers the requests. Of course, it is only as the servers receive and action

this message that replication gradually decreases and eventually stops. Note that changes to the public folder hierarchy are still replicated around the organization. This is because hierarchy updates go to every server that hosts a public folder database, are relatively tiny in terms of the data that these updates contain, do not contain folder content, and are necessary to allow administrators to adjust the replica lists to stop the replication storm recommencing when replication restarts.

Servers that run versions prior to Exchange 2003 SP2 do not understand the "cease and desist" message or the organization setting that prevents content replication, so these servers continue to respond to backfill requests. The non-SP2 servers also continue to broadcast details of changes that occur to the public folder replicas that they host. Your ability to suppress a public folder replication storm effectively is therefore linked to the percentage of Exchange 2003 SP2 servers in your organization—the higher the percentage, the more effective you will be.

You can verify that Exchange 2003 SP2 servers that host public folders are not responding to replication requests by checking for event 3118 in the application event log on these servers. The Store logs event 3118 whenever a backfill request arrives that the Store cannot respond to because of the organization setting to suppress public folder replication.

A replication storm is bad but you do want public folder replication to proceed when network conditions are stable. Without replication, functions such as free/busy information won't work properly because servers will be unable to replicate data between each other. After replication has been halted, you can start replication again by clicking on the organization object in ESM and selecting the "Resume Public Folders Content Replication" option. You can only see this option after you have successfully issued a stop replication command. ESM will then display a dialog to ask you to confirm that you want to proceed to restart replication and if you confirm that replication should resume, ESM sends a message to public folder servers to tell them to start replication again. Servers resume replication according to their usual replication schedule, so if you have configured servers to replicate data once a day at midnight, they will not resume replication until that time arrives. Before you restart replication, you should ensure that you have addressed any problems that caused the original replication storm.

When replication begins again, the Store logs event 3119 in the application event log to indicate that replication has been reenabled. Replication should quickly settle down into its normal pattern in small organizations, but large distributed organizations that have more than a few public folder servers may take several hours to resume normal service. It is conceivable that very large organizations or those that depend on high-latency or low-bandwidth links to reach some servers may take some days before replication settles down.

The fact that we have an option to control replication storms is nice, but you can't ignore the fact that public folders have a short expected lifetime left within Exchange. With this fact in mind, perhaps you should use the introduction of Exchange 2007 to implement a policy that prohibits the creation of any new replica folders (which will effectively halt the potential for future replication storms) and direct the data that might be held in public folders to another repository.

5.13.4 **Managing public folders with Exchange 2007**

Compared to the ability to manage public folders in the Exchange 2003 ESM, the options presented by the first version of the Exchange 2007 EMC are sparse and limited. You can create a new public folder database if a server does not already have one (you can only have one public folder database per server). You can mount and dismount a public folder database or move database files, and you can amend some of the properties of the public folder database as shown in Figure 5.28 to determine a replication schedule and set limits on the database. But there's no ability to create new replicas or to navigate through the folders in the database or to examine how much storage each folder occupies or to see the items in the folder.

Figure 5.28
Public folder database properties in Exchange 2007 EMC

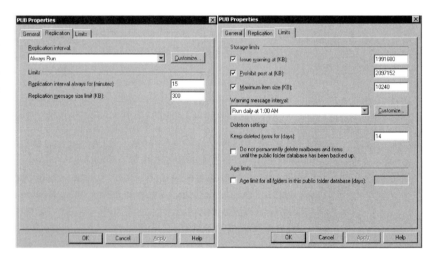

If you want to gain an insight into the content of the public folders rather than just knowing what folders exist in the public folder hierarchy, you have to resort to Exchange 2003 ESM or use an Outlook client to see the information. Figure 5.29 shows what you can expect to see from Outlook when you view folder sizes. Note that Microsoft provides no interface to access public folders in Outlook Web Access 2007, nor can you access public folders using IMAP or POP clients.

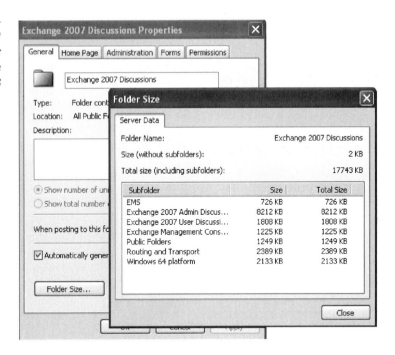

Figure 5.29
Viewing public folder sizes from Outlook 2003

It is common knowledge that Microsoft has deprecated the use of public folders within Exchange, so the lack of support for managing public folders through EMC shouldn't come as a complete surprise, nor should the inability to work with public folders through Outlook Web Access 2007. Microsoft plans to introduce support for public folder management in Exchange 2007 SP1 and this will be a welcome relief to administrators. Until then, if you operate a mixed organization where you have some Exchange 2003 servers, you can continue to use ESM to manage public folders. You can even argue that you should keep one Exchange 2003 server for this purpose until you migrate off public folders to another repository and there is some sense in this approach. However, if you move to a pure Exchange 2007 organization and retain public folders, you have to be prepared to manage public folders through the shell. With this point in mind, we need to examine how to perform some of the most common public folder management operations with EMS. Microsoft provides some sample scripts with the Exchange 2007 installation kit[14]. You can use these scripts to work with public folders or as the basis to develop scripts that meet your unique needs. Table 5.10 lists the sample scripts and their intended use.

While it is useful to have some sample scripts to work with, you still need to understand the basic EMS commands that work with public fold-

---

14. The default location for the example scripts is C:\Program Files\Microsoft\Exchange Server\Scripts.

Table 5.10   *Sample public folder management scripts*

Script	Description
AddReplicaToPFRecursive	Adds a server to the replication list for a public folder, including all the child folders under the folder.
RemoveReplicaFromPFRecursive	Removes a server from the replication list for a folder, including all the child folders underneath. If the server is the only one in the replication list, the script leaves the list unchanged.
MoveAllReplicas	Replaces a server in the replication list for all public folders with a new server (includes system folders).
ReplaceReplicaOnPFRecursive	Replaces a server in the replication list for a folder with a new server, including all the child folders underneath. If the server that you want to replace is not listed, nothing is changed.
AddUsersToPFRecursive	Adds a user to a folder's permission list including all child folders. If the user is already listed, their permission is updated to the set specified in the script.
ReplaceUserWithUserOnPFRecursive	Replaces a user with a new user on a folder's permission list, including all child folders. Folders that do not contain an entry for the specified user are not altered.
ReplaceUserPermissionOnPFRecursive	Replaces the permissions of a user with a new set of permissions, including all child folders.
RemoveReplicaFromPFRecursive	Removes a user from a folder's permission list, including child folders. The "Default" and "Anonymous" permissions cannot be removed, although an attempt to remove them reduces their permissions to "None."

ers. The most basic command is to create a public folder database on a server that hosts the mailbox role. You also have to have the necessary permissions to manage the target server. If a server does not have a public folder database, you can create the database with the New-PublicFolderDatabase command. This command creates a new public folder database in the default Storage Group.

```
New-PublicFolderDatabase 'Public Folders' —StorageGroup
'First Storage Group'
```

To validate that the new database exists, you can use the `Get-Public-FolderDatabase` command. Type the command without a parameter to see all the public folder databases that exist within the organization. By default, Exchange does not return the names of public folder databases that reside on Exchange 2003 servers, so if you want to see this information, you have to specify the –IncludePreExchange2007 parameter as follows:

```
Get-PublicFolderDatabase —IncludePreExchange2007
```

You can pass the name of a specific public folder database to retrieve more information about the database. The best way to do this is to include the format-list command. In this instance, we pass the display name of the public folder database as you see in EMC (see Figure 5.30), so the command is:

```
Get-PublicFolderDatabase —id 'Public Folders' | Format-List
```

If you want to specify a public folder database on a server, include the server name in the –identity parameter.

```
Get-PublicFolderDatabase —id 'ExchSvrPF1\Public Folders' |
Format-List
```

Now that we have a public folder database, we can populate it with folders using the `New-PublicFolder` command. For example:

```
New-PublicFolder '\Exchange 2007 Discussions' —Path
'\Discussions' -Server 'ExchSvrPF1'
```

This example creates a new public folder called "Exchange 2007 Discussions" under the "Discussions" top-level public folder and hosts the initial replica on the server called ExchSvrPF1. The root folder must exist on the target server. After you create the public folder, you can check its presence with the `Get-PublicFolder` command.

```
Get-PublicFolder —id 'Exchange 2007 Discussions'
```

Alternatively, you can check all of the child folders that exist under a root folder. For example:

```
Get-PublicFolder —id '\Exchange 2007 Discussions' —Recurse
```

In this example, we are working with a top-level public folder immediately under the root. It is unlikely that you will be in this situation as top-level public folders probably exist already and you will not be in a hurry to create more. It is more likely that you will work with folders some way down the public folder hierarchy and will therefore have to specify the full path to the folder in order to work with its properties. For example:

```
Get-PublicFolder —id '\Top\Second\Third\Fourth\Fifth'
```

Get-PublicFolder and other commands that manipulate folder properties execute reasonably quickly because they interrogate the public folder hierarchy. Exchange replicates a copy of the public folder hierarchy automatically to every server in the organization that hosts a public folder database, so you are always working with local data when you retrieve information about a folder. The ability to scan through a complete copy of the hierarchy comes in handy if you need to locate a public folder but you do not know where exactly it is. For instance, assume that you need to find a public folder called "Critical Documents." You can use a command like this to scan from the root folder downwards to locate every folder that matches the folder name.

```
Get-PublicFolder \ -Recurse | Where {$_.Name -eq 'Critical
Documents'}
```

Like many of the EMS commands, you could consider the output of Get-PublicFolder to be pretty verbose. Here is an edited extract that shows the presence of two child folders under the \Discussions top-level folder:

```
HasSubFolders                    : False
HiddenFromAddressListsEnabled    : False
MailEnabled                      : False
Name                             : Exchange 2007 Discussions
ParentPath                       : \Discussions
PerUserReadStateEnabled          : True
```

```
Replicas                        : {PUB}
UseDatabaseAgeDefaults          : True
UseDatabaseQuotaDefaults        : True
UseDatabaseReplicationSchedule  : True
UseDatabaseRetentionDefaults    : True
Identity                        : \Discussions\Exchange 2007 Discussions
ObjectState                     : Unchanged
IsValid                         : True
HasSubFolders                   : False
HiddenFromAddressListsEnabled   : False
MailEnabled                     : False
Name                            : Exchange 2007 User Discussions
ParentPath                      : \Discussions
PerUserReadStateEnabled         : True
Replicas                        : {PUB}
UseDatabaseAgeDefaults          : True
UseDatabaseQuotaDefaults        : True
UseDatabaseReplicationSchedule  : True
UseDatabaseRetentionDefaults    : True
Identity                        : \Discussions\Exchange 2007 User Discussions
ObjectState                     : Unchanged
IsValid                         : True
```

If a folder has many child folders, it is better to be selective in the data you output:

```
Get-PublicFolder —id '\Exchange 2007 Discussions' —Recurse | Select Name,
Identity
```

```
Name                               Identity
----                               --------
Exchange 2007 Discussions          \Exchange 2007 Discussions
EMS                                \Exchange 2007 Discussions\EMS
Exchange 2007 Admin Discussions    \Exchange 2007 Discussions\Exchange 2007 Admin...
Exchange 2007 User Discussions     \Exchange 2007 Discussions\Exchange 2007 User ...
Exchange Management Console        \Exchange 2007 Discussions\Exchange Management...
Public Folders                     \Exchange 2007 Discussions\Public Folders
Routing and Transport              \Exchange 2007 Discussions\Routing and Transport
Windows 64 platform                \Exchange 2007 Discussions\Windows 64 platform
```

In very large organizations, it is possible that a call to `Get-PublicFolder` that uses the —Recurse or —GetChildren parameters to force EMS to list all of the folders that exist under the specified root will result in the output of a huge number of folders. By default, EMS limits the maximum number of folders returned to 10,000, but you can override this by passing the desired number of folders to output through the –ResultSize parameter. From the output reviewed so far, you may have noticed that the Get-PublicFolder command does not return information about the servers that host the databases where the public folders are stored. You can get at the data, but only if you dig through the full set of folder properties. Given that the name of most public folder databases is "Public Folders" and they are usually located in the default "First Storage Group," you can see that it sometimes can be difficult to find the public folder that you really want. It would have been nice if Microsoft had given the Get-PublicFolder command the ability to be more obvious about where the folders are located, but maybe this option will come in the future.

Exchange uses two types of public folders: system and nonsystem. Exchange uses system folders to store information such as the Offline Address Book and free/busy information. You can view system folders by specifying the Non_IPM_Subtree root. For example:

```
Get-PublicFolder -Identity \NON_IPM_SUBTREE -Recurse |
Format-List Name
```

As we examine the properties of public folders, we may find that we need to change some of those properties. For example, we may want to mail-enable the folders (so that users can create new items in the folder by email, something that often happens when you use a public folder as a repository for discussions). We may also want to impose quotas on the folders. To mail-enable a public folder, use the Enable-MailPublicFolder command:

```
Enable-MailPublicFolder '\Exchange 2007 Discussions'
```

You can check that the command executed correctly with this command:

```
Get-PublicFolder –Identity '\Exchange 2007 Discussions' |
Select Name, MailEnabled
```

To reverse the process, use the Disable-MailPublicFolder command. You can use the Get-MailPublicFolder command to view all of the public folders that are mail-enabled. This command is likely to return many items and the data includes the set of system folders that are mail-enabled.

```
Get-MailPublicFolder | Select Name
```

You can also execute this command for an individual folder if you know its name:

```
Get-MailPublicFolder '\Exchange 2007\User Debates' | Format-
List
```

While you should see that the value of the MailEnabled property for the folder is "True," one problem with mail-enabling a public folder with Exchange 2007 is that the details returned by the `Get-PublicFolder` command do not include the email address. You are therefore in the dark as to the right address to use to send items to the public folder unless you examine the folder properties with ESM or through the GAL. If you know the Email Address Policies in effect, you can guess as to what email address Exchange stamps on the public folder. In this case, it was Exchange_2007_Discussions@xyz.com! You may not want mail-enabled public folders to appear in the GAL, so you would set another property to effect this option:

```
Set-PublicFolder —id '\Exchange 2007 Discussions'
—HiddenFromAddressListsEnabled $True
```

Remember that you can always use email to post an item to a public folder even if it does not appear in the GAL by using its SMTP address to send messages. Some administrators have a practice of adding a mail-enabled public folder to a distribution group through Outlook while the folder is still listed in the GAL and then to hide it to prevent users inadvertently sending new messages to the folder. The hidden public folder remains in the group thus serving the purpose of acting as a repository for any message sent to the group.

5.13.4.1 Public folder permissions

By default, Exchange assigns owner permission to the user who creates a public folder. You probably need to assign permissions to other users to allow them to add information to the folder and you can do this with the `Add-PublicFolderClientPermission` command. Here is how to set two different types of permission on a public folder. The second command assigns the contributor permission to a distribution group, which is the permission that you need to set if you wanted to use the public folder as a repository for messages sent to the group.

```
Add-PublicFolderClientPermission —id '\Exchange 2007
Discussions'
—AccessRights 'Owner' —User 'James Bond'
Add-PublicFolderClientPermission —id '\Exchange 2007
Discussions'
—AccessRights 'Contributor' —User 'Legal Executives'
```

You can check permissions with the `Get-PublicFolderClientPermission` command:

```
Get-PublicFolderClientPermission —id '\Exchange 2007
Discussions'
```

If you make a mistake, you can use the `Remove-PublicClientFolderPermission` command:

```
Remove-PublicFolderClientPermission —id 'Exchange 2007
Discussions'
—AccessRights 'Contributor' —User 'James Bond'
```

Note that EMS prompts you to confirm this action before it will remove the permission. Apart from assigning permissions for clients to work with public folders, you may also want to assign permissions for users to manage public folders and perform operations such as creating new replicas, changing the deleted item retention period, or modify the storage quota. Exchange provides the `Add-PublicFolderAdministrativePermission` command for this purpose. For example, assume that you want to give a user full permission to alter any property related to the Store for a folder:

```
Add-PublicFolderAdministrativePermission —User Bond —id '\
Exchange 2007' —AccessRights AllStoreRights
```

The AllStoreRights access option does not allow the user to assign administrative permissions to another user. If you want to give them full administrative permission, you use the –AccessRights AllExtendedRights option. To check what management permissions exist on a public folder:

```
Get-PublicFolderAdministrativePermission —id '\Exchange 2007'
```

To remove an administrative permission from a public folder, use the

`Remove-PublicFolderAdministrativePermission` command:

```
Remove-PublicFolderAdministrativePermission –id '\Exchange
2007' –User Bond –AccessRights AllStoreRights
```

5.13.4.2   Deleting public folders

You can delete a public folder with the `Remove-PublicFolder` command. EMS will refuse to execute the command if you attempt to remove a public folder that has child folders, so in this instance you need to specify the Recurse parameter:

```
Remove–PublicFolder –Id '\Exchange 2000 Discussions'
–Recurse:$True
```

As this command can wipe away valuable content held in the public folders, EMS prompts for confirmation before it proceeds to delete the folders. Removing a folder also removes any replicas that exist, although the exact point when Exchange has removed all replicas from all servers depends on replication across the organization. You can delete folders on a remote server by specifying its name.

```
Remove–PublicFolder –Id '\Exchange 2000 Discussions' –Server
ExchPubPF1 –Recurse
```

Before you can remove a public folder server from the organization, you usually have to make sure that replicas of the folders that the server holds exist on other servers. If you proceed to delete without checking, you may remove the only copy of a folder that exists within the organization, and that may be a bad thing. Assuming that you have checked and that it is okay to delete every public folder on a server, two commands will clean up the server. The first command is to remove all of the nonsystem folders in the public folder tree (starting from the "\" root); the second removes copies of any system folders such as the OAB or free/busy from the server. Note that we allow Exchange to process more than 1,000 folders. We also instruct Exchange to keep on processing if an error occurs when it deletes a folder.

```
Get-PublicFolder –id '\' -Server ExchPubPF1 -Recurse
-ResultSize Unlimited | Remove-PublicFolder -Recurse
-ErrorAction SilentlyContinue

Get-PublicFolder –id '\Non_Ipm_Subtree' –Server ExchPubPF1 -
Recurse
```

```
-ResultSize Unlimited | Remove-PublicFolder -Recurse
—ErrorAction SilentlyContinue
```

Before you delete the folders, you may want to execute just the `Get-PublicFolder` command to check exactly what folders it finds. If there are too many folders to check on the screen, you can create a report that lists the folders together with the number of items in each folder, their size, and the last access time with the following command:

```
Get-PublicFolder —id '\' -Server ExchPubPF1 -Recurse
-ResultSize Unlimited | Get-PublicFolderStatistics | Select
Name, ItemCount, TotalItemSize, LastModificationTime > C:\
Temp\PFReport.txt
```

5.13.4.3   Setting limits on public folders

As we can see from Figure 5.22, public folders can accumulate a lot of data and we do not want the folders to become a dumping ground where users can store large files that would otherwise blow their personal mailbox quota. The default that Exchange 2007 assigns for the maximum size of an individual item that a user can post to a public folder is very large (10MB). In addition, the size that an individual folder can grow to before Exchange starts to issue warnings and then to prohibit further posts are very large at 1.9GB and 2.0GB, respectively. It is therefore a good idea to restrict these properties for public folders to more reasonable levels. For example:

```
Set-PublicFolderDatabase —id 'PUB' -IssueWarningQuota 450MB
-ProhibitPostQuota 500MB -MaxItemSize 5MB
```

But what if we want to allow users to post large items to a specific public folder? We can set limits that override the database default and double the limits that apply to a specific folder as follows:

```
Set-PublicFolder —id '\Exchange 2007 Discussions'
—StorageQuota 990MB
—PostStorageQuota 1GB —MaxItemSize 10MB
```

If you examine the properties of the folder afterwards, you'll see the new quotas and that the UseDatabaseQuotaDefaults property is set to False.

5.13.4.4   Managing public folders on a remote server

You are not limited to executing the `Set-PublicFolder` or `Set-PublicFol-derDatabase` commands on a local server as EMS is quite happy to execute commands on any server for which you have administrative permission. Remember that if you want to execute commands for a database on a remote server, you have to specify the full name of the database, including the name of the server where the database resides. For example, if I want to set new default quotas for the "PUB-2" database on server ExchPFSvr2, I would refer to the database as "ExchPFSvr2.xyz.com\PUB-2." Here is another example to prove the point. EMC presents no ability to create a new replica of the public folder that we have just created and this is an operation that you could never perform with Outlook, so we have to do it with EMS. A moderately complex one-line command does the job:

```
Set-PublicFolder -id '\Exchange 2007 Discussions' -Replicas
((Get-PublicFolder -id '\Exchange 2007 Discussions').Replicas
+ 'ExchPFSvr2.xyz.com\PUB-2')
```

In this case, we retrieve the current set of replicas with `Get-Public-Folder` and then call `Set-PublicFolder` to add the new replica to the list and you can see how we specify the target public folder database to host the new replica.

Of course, creating a set of public folders, altering their properties so that they match our needs, and setting up appropriate replicas is only the start of the management challenge. Over time, users will populate the public folders with content using Outlook clients. The next issue that we have to deal is to understand what content is being stored and how this affects storage. If you have a limited set of folders in a well-arranged hierarchy, it is easy enough to browse public folders and investigate what they contain (Figure 5.31).

5.13.4.5   Public folder statistics

To get a more comprehensive overview of public folders, you can use the `Get-PublicFolderStatistics` command. For example, here's how to use the command along with some formatting instructions to create relatively pretty output, but possibly not as comprehensive or as pretty as that generated by the Exchange 2003 PFDavAdmin utility.

```
Get-PublicFolderStatistics | Select Name, ItemCount,
TotalItemSize | Sort TotalItemSize | Format-Table
@{expression="Name"; width=30; label ="Public Folder"},
@{expression="ItemCount"; width=10; label = "Items"},
```

Figure 5.30
*Viewing public
folder content*

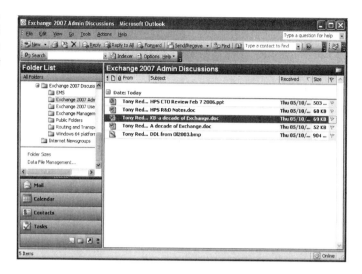

```
@{expression={
[math]::round([double](([string]$_.TotalItemSize).split("B")[
0]) /1K , 2)} ; width=15; label="Size(KB)"}
```

Public Folder	Items	Size(KB)
internal	0	0
globalevents	0	0
StoreEvents{B25A72F7-5DBC-4...	0	0
OWAScratchPad{B25A72F7-5DBC...	0	0
Exchange 2007	0	0
Exchange 2007 Discussions	5	490.03
EMS	3	816.82
Store	4	5636.31
Admin	16	12318.5
Transport	17	13008.95

On page 388, we discuss changes in Exchange 2003 SP2 to allow administrators to control replication storms. EMS offers the same facilities. To suspend public folder replication:

```
Suspend-PublicFolderReplication
```

EMS prompts to confirm that you want to suspend replication before executing the command. After you have completed the changes that are necessary to reduce replication activity and calm the storm, you can resume replication with:

```
Resume-PublicFolderReplication
```

Finally, if you ever need to force replication of the public folder hierarchy, you can do this with the `Update-PublicFolderHierarchy` command.

In reading about all of these commands, you might conclude that public folder management is a lot harder in Exchange 2007. In some respects this is true because if you don't take the time to understand how EMS works and the commands that EMS has to work with public folders, there is no doubt that public folder management will be a nightmare. On the other hand, if you are shell-literate and willing to experiment, you can automate public folder operations to a far higher level than was possible with any other version of Exchange. And as most companies will migrate relatively slowly from Exchange 2003 to Exchange 2007, you will be able to fall back onto the Exchange 2003 ESM to perform public folder management if you really want to.

5.13.5 Permissions on top-level folders

For whatever reason, the lack of a GUI seems to have made it very difficult to allocate the permission to a user (outside Exchange administrators) to create new top-level public folders. You may argue that you don't want people to create any more top-level public folders, but if you do, you can allocate the necessary permission with a command similar to the one shown below, which assigns the right to create a top-level public folder on the folder hierarchies object. There may be a more effective or efficient way to do this, but this way works!

```
Add-ADPermission -id "CN=Public Folders,CN=Folder
Hierarchies,CN=Exchange Administrative Group
(FYDIBOHF23SPDLT),CN=Administrative
Groups,CN=xyz,CN=Microsoft
Exchange,CN=Services,CN=Configuration,DC=xyz,DC=com" -User
Redmond
-ExtendedRights ms-exch-create-top-level-public-folder
-AccessRights readproperty,genericexecute
```

5.13.6 Referrals

Exchange 2003 supports the concept of referrals to allow a client to connect to a remote public folder server to retrieve content. Exchange chooses the public folder server to provide the content by reference to the connector costs that exist between the routing group of the server that hosts the user's mail-box and the routing group that hosts the public folder replica. Exchange 2003 also uses these costs when it needs to backfill content into a public folder. Administrators have some control over referrals by disallowing public folder referrals across a connector or by giving a server a preferred list of pub-lic folder servers to use.

Exchange 2007 does not use routing groups, so the Store has changed to use Active Directory site costs. However, there is no concept of a setting to disallow public folder referrals across a link. If you want to stop the Store referring clients to a very remote public folder server, then you need to set the cost of the site link connector (the Exchange site cost) to a high enough value that the Store will disregard the link when it comes to com-pute the available referral paths because the connection is "too expensive." In this respect, high enough means 50 or higher, assuming that site costs are normally 10 or under.

5.13.7 Migrating public folder content

There is no silver bullet available to answer the question of how to migrate the data that has accumulated in public folders since 1996. Every company uses public folders differently and every company will need to develop their own plan.

The first challenge is to understand the public folders that are in the hierarchy and which ones are actually in use. You can run a program like PFDavAdmin on an Exchange 2003 server to generate reports about public folders that are a good first step in understanding the scope of the problem. However, PFDavAdmin will not tell you why the public folder was created, who created it, who manages it now, and the business value of the data held in the folder. These are all questions that you will have to answer through patient and detailed investigation.

Part of the challenge is to categorize public folders in terms of their use in order to help determine how and where you might eventually migrate the data. Common usages include:

- Repositories for forms-based applications, sometimes workflow in nature. These applications are much more common in companies who deployed Exchange before 2000 because Microsoft placed a heavy emphasis on how to use public folders with Outlook forms early on.

- Project document repositories. These folders probably store an eclec-tic set of items in varying formats from mail messages to Word docu-ments to Excel worksheets. Users post items to the folders on an on-demand ad hoc basis by dragging and dropping from an Exchange mailbox folder or Windows Explorer.

- Archives for discussion groups. Exchange has never offered list server functionality, but people created their own basic implementation by using distribution groups as the list and a public folder (automatically copied on every post by including the SMTP address of the folder in the list) as the list archive.

If you discount the options to ignore all the data held in some or all public folders or to leave the data in place until it gradually ages to a point where it is no longer required, you have to figure out how to move it out of Exchange. Unfortunately, there is no equivalent to the Export-Mailbox command to process public folder data and export it to another repository. Microsoft and third parties have written extractors to move data to Share-Point. Now, exploring a move to SharePoint is the route that most companies will look into, if only because it is a Microsoft solution. SharePoint Portal Server is quite a good option because it offers some extra functionality to help manage data, such as better programmability and customization and radically better search facilities. Aside from moving data to SharePoint, the drawing board is bare, although there's certainly a possibility that further offering will appear to fill the gap as companies realize that the public folder issue is something that they have to deal with.

The final issue is how to replace the functionality made available through public folders. Some answers are available in Exchange 2007 and you can anticipate that Microsoft will respond to customer demand by providing more features to handle public folder migration in future versions of Exchange. However, we cannot count on any such features today, so what can you do now? If you have any forms-based applications, you will probably have to redevelop the application to use a different forms package and a different repository. Replication originally solved the issue of getting data close to the user at the expense of other problems, such as conflicts caused by users making changes in multiple places concurrently. Thankfully, better and cheaper networks have made replication less necessary, so it is now conceivable to run an application from a central server that stores all the data.

Windows Team Services provide a solution for project repositories. Team Services are simple to deploy and use but suffer from some of the same management challenges as public folders, because it is not easy to know what team sites are in use, what they store, and what the data is used for. Nevertheless, Team Services is a more than adequate replacement for project repositories. You might also experiment with Managed Folders to see whether they can help address some needs in this area.

There is no silver bullet available today to assist you to migrate data from public folders but it is not yet time to become desperate as there is no doubt that some keen minds will focus on the problem before Microsoft ceases support for Exchange 2007. In the interim, the best idea is to stop using public folders wherever possible, investigate possible routes forward, and to do a lot of experimentation.

5.14   Removing database size limits

Prior to Exchange 2003 SP2, the limit of a mailbox store in the Standard Edition of Exchange was always 16GB. This limit had been in place since Exchange 4.0, so it was obviously outdated and inappropriate in a world where the average size of a message has grown, average disk size has increased, and the cost per GB has decreased enormously since 1996. Microsoft's response was to increase the limit to 75GB in Exchange 2003 SP2. The new limit also applies to the version of Exchange included in Microsoft Small Business Server. It is nice to have a bigger limit for the store, but even a 59GB increase does not match the growth in average message size. In 1996, the average message in most corporations was around 10KB and now it is 100KB or larger, so just to keep pace Microsoft should have increased the store limit to 160GB or more.

Once Exchange hits its store size limit, the Information Store service gracefully halts and you have to reduce the size of the store to allow Exchange to restart. The easiest way to shrink a store database is to run ESEUTIL to remove all the white space from the database, but this is only a short-term fix as it is unlikely that you will recover more than 1GB unless you recently removed many mailboxes. The long-term fix is to ask users to remove old messages from their mailboxes, and if they don't cooperate, to help them by implementing the Exchange 2003 Mailbox Manager so that their mailboxes are automatically cleaned even if they don't want them to be.

Given Microsoft's focus on developing the Store as an all-purpose repository for anything from email to voicemail, and their view that users will demand much larger mailboxes than they have today, it was a very rational decision for Microsoft to remove all software limits for database sizes from the standard and enterprise versions of Exchange 2007. The only database limits that you will ever meet now are the amount of storage that you can make available to Exchange and the operational window for backups and restores that you want to apply.

5.15   Backups

A very wise person once said that an important difference between email and word processing applications was that the effect of a word processor failure is limited to a single user and a small quantity of documents. When an email system collapses, everyone connected to that system is affected. Usually, people at the top of a company notice the problem fastest (and complain quickest). Having a large server go offline because of a hardware problem creates lots of extra work for administrators and users alike. Not being able to recover data because no backups exist or discovering that you cannot restore the data for some reason are fundamental lapses in system management discipline that can lead to instant dismissal for an administrator. There is simply no excuse for not taking backups, and no excuse for not ensuring that backup media is valid and restorable.

Email systems depend on many different hardware and software components to keep everything going. If any element fails to operate in the required manner, data corruption can occur. If the hardware suffers a catastrophic failure, or some disaster such as an electricity outage afflicts the location where the computers are, you will need to know the steps necessary to get your users back online as quickly as possible. In all these instances, system backups are a prerequisite.

In their purest sense, backups are snapshots of a system's state at a certain point in time. All of the data available to the system should exist in the backup and should be restorable to exactly the same state if required. You can write backups out to many different forms of magnetic or other media, although the most common media for small to medium organizations is some form of high-density magnetic tape while large servers may first backup to disk and then move the backup media to tape.

Exchange has always supported online backups, which generally proceed without causing any discomfort or impact to clients connected to the server. There is no reason to take Exchange offline just to perform a backup. In fact, taking Exchange offline is not a good thing to do. First, it reduces overall system availability because users cannot connect to their mailboxes. Second, each time you bring the Store service online, the Store generates public folder replication messages to request updates from replication partners. Finally, the Store calculates checksums for each page before streaming them out to media during online backups, and if a checksum does not match, the Store will halt the backup operation. Best practice is always to perform online backups, and to perform daily full online backups if possible, mainly because it is much easier to restore from a single tape than have to mess around with incremental backups. Microsoft believe that the introduction of continuous log replication technology in Exchange 2007 (see the section on LCR and CCR in Chapter 9) reduces the requirement to take full daily backups to a point where you only need full weekly backups, but this is only true if a) you deploy continuous replication and b) your auditors and data retention experts agree that you don't need the daily backups. The problem is that many organizations routinely move daily backups of critical data offsite to a secure vault and do so to ensure that they can recover from a catastrophic failure and that they can meet legislative or regulatory requirements for data security.

Apart from the introduction of continuous replication technology, the biggest difference in Exchange 2007 that may influence your backup strategy is the ability to move any database to any live server in the same organization. This was an impossible task in the past because of the close link between the server name and databases.

5.15.1   NTBackup

When you install Exchange, the installation procedure enhances NTBACKUP.EXE, the standard Windows backup utility so that it can process online backups of Exchange databases. These enhancements are:

- Support for the transactional nature of the Store: In particular, the capacity to deal with storage groups, mailbox stores, transaction logs, and transactions that might still be queued in memory.

- The ability to perform online backups: In other words, to copy online databases to tape without having to shut down Exchange services. Users continue to work during backups.

- Extension of the NTBACKUP.EXE user interface to allow system administrators to select which servers and databases they wish to backup or restore.

NTBackup also includes support for hot backups taken through Windows Volume Shadow Copy Services.

5.15.2   Other commercial backup products

NTBackup is a basic backup engine that is very suitable for small to medium organizations. Larger organizations, especially those that want to use a single backup product to deal with many different types of data, tend to consider other commercial backup products.

Exchange provides two DLLs that are for use by backup utilities to access Exchange data. These are ESEBACK2.DLL, which interfaces with the Store to perform a backup or to restore files, and ESEBCLI2.DLL, which provides the interface to the backup client. Exchange-aware backup utilities load these DLLs when they start. The DLLs include the API necessary for backup utilities to process Exchange data. The following functions illustrate the flow of a backup operation:

- *HrESEBackupPrepare:* Establishes an RPC connection to Exchange and returns a list of the available databases available for backup.

- *HrESEBackupSetup:* Used by the backup utility to tell Exchange which storage group it wishes to backup. Each storage group uses its own backup set. You can perform a restore operation of a single database by selecting it from the list held in a backup set.

- *HrESEBackupOpenFile:* Opens the selected database for read access. Both EDB and streaming file are included.

- *HrESEBackupReadFile:* Reads the database in 64K chunks. This function also performs checksum calculation and verification.

- *HrESEBackupCloseFile:* Closes the database.

- *HrESEBackupGetLogAndPatchFiles:* Get a list of all the log file names to include in the backup set. ESE backs up these files using the *HrESEBackupOpenFile*, *HrESEBackupReadFile*, and *HrESEBackupCloseFile* functions.

- *HrESEBackupTruncateLog:* Delete any obsolete transaction logs after a full backup. Truncation only happens after ESE successfully backs up all selected databases. If you do not backup all of the databases in a storage group for any reason, ESE cannot delete the logs.

- *HrESEBackupInstanceEnd:* End the backup for the instance (storage group or selected database).

- *HrESEBackupEnd:* Disconnect from the RPC connection to Exchange.

Exchange provides a similar set of functions to restore databases from backup sets, including *HrESERestoreOpen*, *HrESERestoreAddDatabase*, and *HrESERestoreOpenFile* to support the restore of a single database or a complete storage group. While it is technically possible to run multiple concurrent restore operations, best practice suggests that it is safer to concentrate on a single restore at a time, just to reduce the potential for error. The Exchange backup API is comprehensive and is utilized by all of the major vendors of backup software, as shown in Table 5.11. Use the web address to get information about the latest product features (including the precise version that supports Exchange 2007) to help you to decide which product best meets your needs.

It can be difficult to justify the additional expense of buying in a package to replace a standard utility, especially when the standard utility does the job in an adequate manner. The cost of deploying, managing, and supporting the new utility across multiple servers also has to be taken into account. It is a mistake to use different products to backup Exchange within an orga-

Table 5.11   *Selected third-party backup products for Exchange 2007*

Company	Product	VSS Aware	Web Address
CommVault	QiNetix	Yes	http://www.commvault.com
Symantec	Backup Exec	Yes	http://www.symantec.com
EMC	Networker Module for Microsoft Exchange	Yes	http://www.emc.com
HP	Data Protector AppRM	Yes Yes	http://www.hp.com
Computer Associates	ArcServe Backup Agent for Exchange	Yes	http://www.ca.com
BEI Corporation	Ultrabac	Yes	http://www.ultrabac.com

nization as this makes it much more difficult to move data between servers. Due to the different ways that software manipulates data, it is highly unlikely that one backup package will be able to read a tape created by another. Once you allow diversity, you create a potential situation where you cannot restore a backup for one reason or another. Moreover, Murphy's Law dictates that this situation occurs just after a server hosting thousands of users has crashed and you cannot bring it back online quickly. For this reason, you should standardize on a single backup product and use the same backup media (tapes and drives) to gain maximum flexibility. You never know when you will need to move data onto a different server and it is embarrassing to discover that you cannot because the target server is not equipped with a drive that can read the backup media.

A specialized package often provides very useful features that are missing in the standard utility. In practice, third-party backup products usually provide four major enhancements over NTBackup:

- Scheduling
- Speed
- Control
- Ability to take VSS hot backups

In addition, third-party backup products may provide features to help you manage clusters and continuous log replication. Specialized backup products tend to support high-end features such as unattended backups, automated loading and unloading via tape libraries, and network backup to very large storage silos (juke boxes or similar). Such features are not critical to small or medium servers, but you need to consider them for any server that hosts large databases.

It is important to understand that while third party backup software can provide some valuable advantages, it is another piece to fit into your system configuration matrix. New releases of the backup software must be qualified against existing versions of Exchange, and then against new versions of Exchange. You should also check the backup software against service packs of both Exchange and Windows. The Exchange development team cannot check their product against every third-party product or extension, so it is entirely possible that the installation of a service pack will introduce a problem that only becomes apparent when a backup operation is attempted. On the other hand, even worse, a problem that suddenly appears during a restore. The complex interaction between Exchange, Windows, and any third-party product adds weight to the argument that you should test all combinations of software products (including patches) before they are introduced to production servers.

5.15.3 Creating a backup strategy

All hardware systems can expect hardware failures to occur over time. When it is your turn to experience a failed server, you will be glad that backups exist. System failures come in three broad categories.

- Disk or drive controller failure.

- Other noncritical system component failure, for example, the video monitor for the server develops a fault.

- Critical system component failure, for example, the motherboard or other associated component experiences a fault that you cannot quickly rectify.

Any failure situation requires some fast but calm thinking in order to make the correct decisions to get everything up online again. If you cannot bring the system back online, can you substitute another similar system and restore application data? If it is a particular system component, is a replacement available or can you change the system configuration to work around the problem? Having backups around will not replace making the right decision, but they are a great safety net.

The MTBF (Mean Time between Failures) rate for disks improves all the time and new storage technologies guarantee an ever-increasing resilience to unexpected failure. The advent of hot snapshots through Windows Volume ShadowCopy Services and the introduction of continuous log replication in Exchange 2007 creates new tactics to consider for backup strategies. These developments do not mean that you will never experience a disk failure, but it does mean that you are less likely to have one over any particular period or that you can recover from failures more rapidly than before. A high MTBF is no guarantee that the disk will not fail tomorrow, so the challenge for system administrators is to have a plan to handle the problem when it arises. Without a basic RAID array or more sophisticated storage technology, if something does go wrong with a disk you will have to stop and fix the problem or swap in a new drive. Once the hardware problem is fixed you will have to restore the data, and of course, this simple statement assumes that you have copies of all the application files that were stored on the faulty drive, and possess the capability to move the data onto the new drive. The value of good backups is instantly obvious at this point! Of course, none of the protection afforded by storage technology is viable if you do not deploy the right hardware, such as hot-swappable drives and the best controller you can buy.

The database-centric nature of Exchange poses a particular challenge for restore operations. There is no getting away from the fact that if a restore is necessary it is going to take much longer than you may realize. The length of time that it takes an administrator to backup or restore databases from a large production Exchange server may come as a surprise to some. It is easy to forget just how long it takes to move data to backup media. Databases have the capacity to expand quickly, so your backup times will grow in proportion. After a server has been in production for a number of months, you might find that it is time to consider looking for faster or higher-capacity media to help reduce backup times.

Remember too that it is not just the Exchange databases that you have to backup to ensure that you can recover a system. The Active Directory database, other Windows data, the IIS metabase, Exchange binaries, user data, and other application data all contribute to the amount of data and length of backup operations. In line with best practice, most Exchange servers are not domain controllers or Global Catalogs, so you may not have to restore the Active Directory after a failure on an Exchange server.

It is also important to apply the correct levels of service packs to Windows and Exchange on the recovery server before commencing any restore operation. The internal database schema has changed a number of times in Exchange's history. In general, you cannot restore a database from a backup taken with a higher software revision level. In other words, do not expect to be able to restore a backup taken with Exchange 2007 to a server running

Exchange 2003. This rule does not hold true for all combinations of service packs and versions, but there is enough truth in it to make a strong recommendation that you should maintain servers at the same software levels in order to ensure that you can always restore backups.

You must account for all of the factors discussed here in the operational procedures you employ at your installation. Restores are equally as important as backups, but all the attention goes on backup procedures and backup products. Administrators usually only look into the detail of restores when a disaster happens, which is exactly the wrong time to begin thinking about the issue. Consider this question: How long will it take to restore one gigabyte of data from your backup media using the backup software you employ? Now, how long will it take to restore 3GB, or maybe 10GB, or how about a full-blown 100GB mailbox store? And what about a public store? Do you have procedures in place to handle the restore of the different permutations of the Active Directory? And the data for all the other applications you may want to run on a server such as the IIS metabase?

In most circumstances, even when suitable hardware is waiting to be hot-swapped into your production environment, the answer for how long it takes to restore a server is counted in hours. Even when the restore is complete, you may have other work to do before Exchange is available for use again. For instance, the Store must replay transaction logs to roll forward messages and other items that are not fully committed to the database. The Store does this automatically, but applying masses of transactions at one time delays the start-up operation (depending on processor speed and other load, a set of 100 logs might take between 20 and 30 minutes to process on a slow server). Users will be yelling at you to get the system back online as quickly as possible, so it's going to be a time when stress levels are rising, which just adds to the piquant nature of the task. These are the facts of system management life. You must be prepared and able to conduct a well-planned restore of essential data in order to be successful. No one wants to explain to a CIO why the messaging system was unavailable for one or two days while staff fumbled their way through a restore. Knowing how to properly use and safeguard backup media is an important part of a backup strategy. Think of the following questions: After you perform backups, who will move the media to a secure location? Is the secure location somewhere local or remote? When will you use the tapes or other media for backup purposes again? How can you recover the backup media quickly if a disaster occurs?

5.15.4   Backups and storage groups

Exchange permits you to take a granular approach to backup and restore operations as it is possible to backup or restore a single database instead of the entire Store. Figure 5.32 shows how you can select individual databases within a storage group for backup using the Windows Backup Wizard. When one or more databases from a storage group are processed, all of the transaction logs belonging to the storage group are also included in the backup media to ensure that the backup includes all transactions, including those that are not yet fully committed to the database. Therefore, it does not make sense to backup individual databases unless you have good reason to do so. Always process backups on a storage group level whenever possible. Note that NTBackup lists all of the servers in the organization and you can perform a remote backup across the network, if you choose to do so. However, this is not a good option unless you have a very capable high-speed link between the source database and the target backup device.

Figure 5.31
*Using the Windows
Backup Wizard to
select databases*

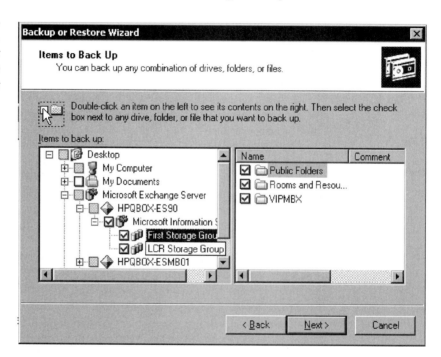

Exchange reserves an additional special storage group for restore operations. When you restore a database, the Store overwrites the failed database with the database from the backup set and moves the transaction logs from the backup set into the temporary directory. The Store can then replay transactions from the logs, commit changes to the database, and make the database consistent and up to date. When the database is ready, the restore storage group turns over control to the normal storage group and operations recommence. This technique ensures that the other databases on a server continue to be operational when you have to restore a failed database.

5.15.4.1 Backup operations

The exact process to take a backup depends on the software that you use. To illustrate the process, this section describes how to take a full backup of an

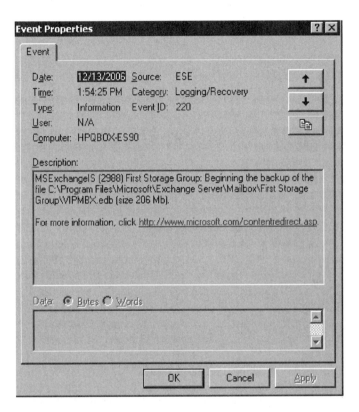

Figure 5.32
*A full backup is
about to start*

Exchange storage group. You can compare the steps outlined here with the way that the software that you use behaves when you use it to perform a backup:

- The backup agent (NTBackup or a third-party utility) performs its own processing to prepare for the backup. This includes establishing the type of backup (incremental, full, or differential) and the target media (tape or disk).

- The backup agent makes a function call to ESE to inform the storage engine that it wishes to begin a backup. ESE logs event 210 to indicate that a full backup is starting.

- The current transaction log is closed and the Store opens a new transaction log. The Store then directs all transactions that occur during the backup to a new set of logs that will remain on the server after the backup completes.

- The backup process begins (Figure 5.33). The backup agent requests data and the Store streams the data out in 64K chunks. ESE writes event 220 to the application event log (Figure 5.32) as it begins the backup of each database, noting the size of the file. A backup to disk uses shared memory and is registered by Exchange 2007 as event 907.

- As the Store processes each page, it reads the page to verify that the page number and CRC checksum are correct to ensure that the page contains valid data. The page number and checksum are stored in the first four bytes of each page, and if either is incorrect, the Store flags a -1018 error to the Application Event Log. The backup API will then stop processing data to prevent you from taking a corrupt backup. This may seem excessive, but it stops administrators blithely taking backups of databases that potentially contain internal errors. There is no point in taking a backup if you cannot restore the data, and restoring a corrupt database is little use to anyone.

- ESE logs event 221 as the backup of each database completes.

- After all the pages from the target databases (a complete storage group or individually selected databases) are written to the backup media, the backup agent requests ESE to provide the transaction logs, which are then written to the backup media. ESE then logs event 223.

- ESE only writes the set of transaction logs present when the backup starts to the backup media. If this is a full backup, ESE then deletes these logs (and notes the fact in event 224, which also notes the file names of the logs that are deleted) to release disk space back to the system. It is quite safe to do this as the transactions are committed to the database and are available in the logs in the backup set. Of course, if a situation occurs where a backup copy of a database is corrupted in any way (perhaps due to a tape defect), then you will need copies of every log created since the last good full backup to be able to perform a successful restore. For this reason, some administrators take copies of transaction logs to another disk location before a backup starts. Some may regard this behavior as a touch paranoid; others point to the failure rate for tapes and consider it a prudent step to ensure full recoverability.

- The backup set is closed and normal operations resume. Successful completion is marked in event 213.

When it completes processing, the backup utility usually reports the details of its work. For example, an NTBackup report of the successful backup of an Exchange storage group is shown below:

```
Backup Status
Operation: Backup
Active backup destination: File
Media name: "Storage Group 1 created 3/21/2007 at 11:37 AM"

Backup of "ExchSvrMbx1\Microsoft Information Store\Storage
Group 1"
Backup set #1 on media #1
Backup description: "Set created 3/21/2007 at 11:37 AM"
Media name: "Storage Group 1 created 3/21/2007 at 11:37 AM"

Backup Type: Normal

Backup started on 3/21/2007 at 11:38 AM.
Backup completed on 3/21/2007 at 11:53 AM.
Directories: 3
Files: 6
Bytes: 9,221,460,426
Time:   15 minutes and 22 seconds
```

Figure 5.33
A backup in progress

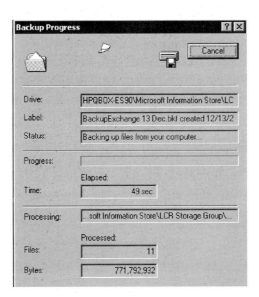

Incremental and differential backups only copy transaction logs to backup sets. Incremental backups copy the set of logs created since the last backup, while a differential backup copies the complete set of logs created since the last full backup. Thus, to restore Exchange databases you need:

- The last full backup, or
- The last full backup plus all incremental backups taken since then, or
- The last full backup set plus the last differential backup.

Obviously, a full backup is the easiest way to restore because there are fewer tapes to handle and less opportunity to make mistakes. However, if you rely exclusively on full backups, it is possible that you will miss some log files you need to recover back to a time before the last full backup. For this reason, it is best practice to take differential backups between full backups, leading to a backup schedule where you might take a daily full backup at 6PM, with a differential backup at lunchtime when system load is often lower.

Exchange 2003 and 2007 both stamp databases with the date and time after each successful backup. You can view the timestamp by selecting a database and viewing its properties through EMC. Exchange records times for the last full and last incremental backups, as shown in Figure 5.35 (in this case, the database is obviously backed up by a regime that favors full backups instead of incremental backups). Apart from anything else, the existence of the timestamp gives you confidence that a successful backup exists as well as telling you how old it is.

Another way of checking on whether backups are being taken properly is to scan the organization with the `Get-MailboxDatabase` command, specifying the –Status parameter so that Exchange includes details of each database's current status. For example:

```
Get-MailboxDatabase —Status | Select Name, StorageGroup, Mounted, LastFull
Backup
```

```
Name               StorageGroup              Mounted LastFullBackup
----               ------------              ------- --------------
DB1                ExchMbx1\SG1                 True 4/9/2007 7:00:18 PM
DB3                ExchMbx1\SG3                 True 4/9/2007 7:19:15 PM
DB4                ExchMbx2\SG4                 True 4/9/2007 7:23:12 PM
DB1                ExchMbx2\SG1                 True 4/10/2007 12:00:...
DB3                ExchMbx2\SG3                 True 4/8/2007 1:00:14 AM
DB2                ExchMbx2\SG2                 True 4/8/2007 12:30:1...
DF                 ExchMbx3\SG4                 True 4/10/2007 1:40:1...
```

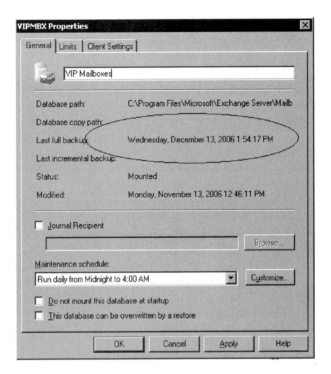

Figure 5.34
*Last good
backup timestamp*

DB6	ExchMbx4\SG6	True 4/10/2007 2:30:1...
DB7	ExchMbx4\SG7	True 4/9/2007 3:59:49 PM
DB1	ExchMbx5\SG1	True
DB1	ExchMbx6\SG1	True
DB2	ExchMbx6\SG2	True
DB6	ExchMbx6\SG6	True
DB3	ExchMbx6\SG3	True

Assuming that we executed this command around March 10, the status looks acceptable for the first four servers (we might ask why two of the three databases on server ExchMbxSvr2 lag two days behind in backups), but we can see that no one has taken a backup of servers ExchMbxSvr5 and ExchMbxSvr6.

5.15.5 Checkpoint file

The checkpoint file (E00.CHK is the file used by the default storage group) maintains a note of the current log file position so that ESE knows the last committed transaction written to the databases in a storage group. ESE maintains a separate checkpoint file for each storage group. If you enable continuous replication for a storage group, ESE maintains a checkpoint file for the database replica.

The primary role played by the checkpoint file is during "soft" recoveries, when databases have closed down in an inconsistent manner through some system failure that has not resulted in a corrupt database. When the Information Store service restarts, ESE opens the checkpoint file and retrieves the location of the last committed transaction, and then begins to replay transactions from the logs from that point. While this is convenient, the checkpoint file is not mandatory for replays to occur, as ESE is able to scan the complete set of transaction logs to determine the point from which replays should commence. ESE does not write the checkpoint file to a backup set because it serves no purpose during a "hard" recovery. In this scenario, you restore databases and transaction logs to different locations, so the ESE instance that controls the restore depends on the log information contained in the database header to work out what logs it should replay. In addition, ESE checks that all necessary log generations are present and available before beginning to replay transactions and will not proceed if gaps exist. Other Windows components such as DHCP, WINS, and the Active Directory that use ESE also maintain checkpoint files.

Figure 5.35
Selecting a database for restore

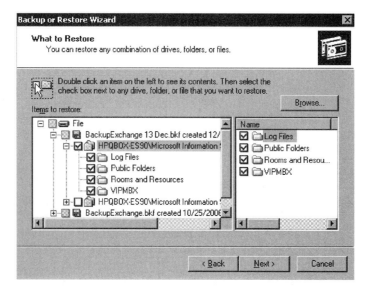

5.15.5.1   Restoring a database

The Store is responsible for restore operations and ESE uses a reserved storage group to enable online restores. The following steps occur to perform a database restore using NTBackup, which streams the data out of a backup set to recreate the database and any required transaction logs in a recovery location on disk:

- The database or storage group affected by the failure is dismounted by the administrator or is rendered unavailable by a hardware problem, such as a disk failure. In this case, you must fix the hardware problem before a restore can proceed. The Information Store service must be running.

- If you have a corrupt database in place, you probably want to overwrite the file on disk. Alternatively, you may prefer to take a copy of the corrupt database (EDB, STM, and associated transaction logs) before the restore overwrites the file and move it somewhere safe for later investigation. A database property controls whether the Store will allow the backup agent to overwrite a database. Either access the store's properties and set the necessary checkbox, or simply delete the corrupt file before beginning the restore.

- The backup agent initializes and displays details of the backup sets that you can restore from the available media. Figure 5.36 shows NTBackup in operation. The backup set is from a full backup operation because both databases and transaction logs are available. Incremental and differential backup sets only hold transaction logs. We can now select whatever data we need to restore.

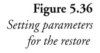

Figure 5.36
Setting parameters
for the restore

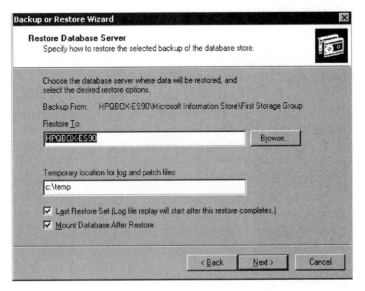

- The backup agent notifies ESE that it wishes to begin a restore operation. The Store then launches an ESE recovery instance to manage the special recovery storage group. The recovery storage group only exists during restore operations.

- The backup agent begins to stream data out of the backup set into the necessary databases, using direct Win32 file system calls to copy the files into the appropriate locations. This operation proceeds under the control of the Store, which uses the special reserved storage group for this purpose. You restore differential and incremental sets first, followed by the most recent full backup. If you follow best practice, and always take full backups whenever possible, restore operations are much simpler. Figure 5.37 shows how you direct the backup set to the target restore server. Note that because this is the last backup set that must be restored, we can set the "Last Backup Set" checkbox to tell the backup agent that it does not have to look for any other backup sets and can complete the recovery operation once the databases have been restored. For NTBackup, this checkbox is a critical part of the restore operation because ESE will perform none of the fix-up processing to make the database consistent until you tell ESE that it is okay to proceed by checking this box. However, if a database proves to be inconsistent after a restore, you can use the ESEUTIL utility to try to correct any errors[15]. Note that the user interface of some third-party backup utilities do not include the "Last Backup Set" checkbox because the utility controls the entire restore operation, including the decision when to begin post-restore fix-up processing. You can also check the "Mount Database After Restore" checkbox to get the restored mailbox store into operation as quickly as possible after the restore is complete.

- ESE restores the EDB and streaming files to the production directory, but the transaction logs are not, as they might overwrite logs that contain transactions that ESE later needs to replay. You must therefore provide a temporary location to hold the transaction logs from the backup set for the duration of the restore. Make sure that the temporary location (for example, C:\TEMP\BACKUP) has enough disk space to accommodate all of the log files in the backup set.

---

15.   The usual indication that you have to take some action to fix a database is when you cannot mount it following a restore. You will probably see error 544 signaled by Exchange when you attempt to mount the database with the Mount-Database command. This error should also appear in the application event log and it indicates that you need to perform a hard recovery before Exchange can mount the database. You should have a restored database and a set of transaction logs accumulated since the time of the last backup on disk, so you can perform the necessary recovery by replaying the transactions from the logs into the restored database and so make the database consistent and fully up to date. You can perform the hard recovery with the ESEUTIL /CC /T<storage group instance> command or by running the database recovery utilities in the Exchange 2007 toolbox.

- ESE creates a file called *restore.env* in the temporary location to control the processing of transaction logs during the restore. The *restore.env* file contains information about the databases, paths, signatures, and other information used by the restore and replaces the older registry key used by previous versions of Exchange to signal that a restore operation was in progress. ESE creates a separate file for each restore operation. You can dump the contents of *restore.env* with the ESEUTIL utility.

- The next step is to process any transaction logs required to bring the database up to date. During this process, ESE validates the log signature and generation sequence to ensure that the correct transaction logs are present and are available to recover transactions. If a log signature does not match the database signature, ESE returns error – 610, and if it discovers a gap in the log generations, ESE signals error –611. If either of these errors is encountered the recovery process is stopped. ESE has not yet replayed any transactions into the database, so you have a chance to fix the problem and start the restore again. Fixing the problem may need you to check the signatures on the databases and logs to ensure that they match, or discover why a gap exists in the log generations.

ESE actually reads two sets of logs during the restore. First, it processes the logs held in the temporary location, and then the logs in the normal location that have accumulated since the backup. Transaction logs contain data for all of the databases in a storage group, so if you are restoring a single database, ESE must scan all the data in the logs to isolate the transactions for the specific database and then proceed to apply them. ESE ignores all of the other data in the logs. This phase of the operation may be the longest of all, depending on the number of transaction logs that have to be processed.

Once the data in the transaction logs has been applied, the recovery storage group performs some cleanup operations, exits, and returns control to the primary storage group (the storage group that is being restored), which is then able to bring the newly restored databases back online. ESE also deletes the files in the temporary location. ESE notes details of all of the recovery operations in the Application Event Log.

In the case of differential or incremental restores, only the transaction logs are loaded into the temporary location and processed there. At the end of a successful restore, ESE writes event 902 into the application event log. ESE also records the details of the restore operation in a text file (the file is named after the backup set). To be certain that everything is okay before you allow any users to connect to the store, check that ESE logs event 902 and that ESE has recorded no errors in the text file.

Given the growing size of databases, the focus for Exchange backup and restore operations is moving from the traditional streaming approach as used by programs such as NTBackup to the snapshot or cloning approach offered by backup programs that support Windows Volume ShadowCopy Services (VSS). Streaming backups are all that small to medium servers require, but if you work with databases that are larger than 50GB, you should consider moving to VSS-based backups, if only because they deal with large volumes of data much more efficiently and faster than streamed backups.

5.15.6   The future of streaming backups

Companies have used NTBackup and other streaming backup utilities to take online backups of Exchange servers since 1996. Even large companies like the flexibility of being able to use NTBackup to take a backup to disk and then complete the process by moving the backup file from disk to tape or to a tape SAN. Microsoft's future direction for streaming backups is not certain because there the new Windows Backup utility that is part of Longhorn cannot generate streamed backups. In addition, the Longhorn version of NTBackup may be restricted to only being able to read and restore from existing backup sets and will not be able to generate new backups.

The logic is that Microsoft wants to move towards block-level backups that are taken with VSS. This means that you will only be able to backup complete volumes in the future. VSS-based utilities will create backups as images of the source volumes in the form of VHD (Virtual Hard Disk) files. The meaning of these changes is that you will not be able to store backup sets on the same volume as the original data or on any other disk except a volume that you dedicate for backup purposes. While medium to large enterprises will be able to find the required disk resources easily enough, this evolution adds extra cost to small deployments.

While it is true that Microsoft never intended that NTBackup to become an enterprise-capable backup utility (which is one of the reasons why so many other backup products exist), the fact still remains that NTBackup is a popular choice for Exchange deployments. The move to VSS-based backups will require companies to change their procedures for backup and restore operations and to spend time to select and test software to use. They will experience additional cost if they decide to use a third-party backup product and they will have to invest in some extra disk. None of this seems like a good idea, but you could argue that streaming backups are yesterday's technology and that it is time to move on to something more modern. In any case, this is an area to keep an eye on as Longhorn matures and its effect is felt by Exchange 2007.

5.16 Moving from the Store

The Store provides a great repository for the messages and other items generated on an Exchange server, but an email system does not exist purely on its ability to act as a repository as it has to be able to transfer messages to other servers and different email systems. The Store has a great connection to the Exchange transport system, which is our next stop.

6

Exchange Transport and Routing

While the Store is the heart of Exchange, the Transport engine is its lungs. In this chapter, we review how Exchange 2007 transports and routes messages from origination to destination.

6.1 The evolution of routing

In terms of flexibility, the way that messaging systems route email has evolved greatly over the last ten years. Mapping developments against the history of Exchange, a rough timeline is as follows:

- **Pre Exchange:** Message routing is quite inflexible and administrators need to sit down and map out the path of messages from one server to another within an organization to understand how messages flow. Routing messages to another company or to a different email system within the same company usually requires a connector to link incompatible systems and rewrite email addresses. Satisfactory message interchange is often only possible in 7-bit plain text format and attachments are usually unsupported.

- **Exchange 4.0–5.5**: The X.400 protocol provides the basis for message routing. Messages flow between servers in the same site automatically, but administrators have to create paths between sites with connectors. The routing topology, even within the same organization, is still inflexible and a server outage can have a huge impact on reliable message routing. Connectors are required to link to other email systems. It is easier to pass rich text format messages between different email systems, but interoperability remains a challenge.

- **Exchange 2000–2003**: SMTP provides the basis for message routing. Messages flow within the same routing group automatically and a great deal of flexibility exists within the organization because Exchange servers send link state information to each other to update servers about problems along routing paths. Servers can then change the routing topology to accommodate changing conditions. Connectors are still required, but less traffic flows across connectors, as SMTP has become the lingua franca of the email world. Greater support for SMTP makes message interoperability much easier.

- **Exchange 2007**: SMTP remains the foundation for message routing. Exchange 2007 drops its own routing topology, adopts the topology that Windows uses to replicate Active Directory information, and favors direct connections between email servers whenever possible. Exchange 2007 introduces the concept of hub transport servers that are responsible for the routing of all messages within an Exchange organization. Exchange 2007 also introduces the Edge server, a specialized version of a hub transport server that Microsoft has designed to operate in the DMZ and be the first port of contact for incoming messages. While they offer the best degree of integration with an Exchange organization and deliver strong SMTP performance and good protection against spam and viruses, Edge servers are optional and you do not need to deploy them unless you do not have another way to protect your organization against the polluted mail streams that arrive in from the Internet.

The bottom line is that message flow is more integrated with the operating system today than ever before, leading to less administrative overhead (because you have only one infrastructure to manage) and faster transmission (less overhead to get in the way). At the same time, the adoption of SMTP everywhere makes it easier to connect different email systems together.

6.2   Change through experience

The first generation of Exchange servers supported SMTP, but only through a separate connector (the Internet Mail Connector, or IMC). The second generation made SMTP the default protocol for email transmission and supported SMTP on every server. Instead of using sites[1] as the basis for the routing topology, Exchange 2000 introduced routing groups, each of which included a server that acts as the routing group master. To build the routing topology, you link the routing groups together with connectors. A server inside each routing group is nominated as the routing group master and is responsible for tracking the current state of the topology by exchanging link state information with other routing group masters. These specially encoded messages contain link state updates that provide the routing group masters

---

1.   An Exchange site (4.0–5.5) is a collection of servers connected together by Windows RPCs.

with new data about the network, such as connector outages or new connectors. The concepts of link state routing, OSPF (Open Shortest Path First), and link state propagation used by Exchange 2000/2003 provide a routing topology that is much more flexible than the fixed nature of the GWART (Gateway and Routing Table) that Exchange 5.5 generates nightly.

There is no doubt that Exchange 2000 and 2003 servers are capable of routing very high volumes of messages and that link state routing works, but administrators encountered three problems in production. First, the propagation of link state information is advantageous in networks that experience changing conditions because it keeps the mail flowing around potential bottlenecks. Knowing that a connector is unavailable can prevent messages accumulating on a queue when an alternate route is available. If your network is stable, you don't gain any advantage from link state updates and incur the overhead to propagate the information between servers.

In complex networks with many routing groups, especially those built on hub and spoke networks where connections to the spokes might not be consistently available, the overhead created by link state updates can create network bloat. When an outage occurs in a leaf and spoke network no alternative network routes exist, because once a connection to a spoke is unavailable, Exchange cannot transfer email to that leaf node, no matter how many link state updates flow between servers. From Exchange 2003 onwards, you could turn link state routing off for these networks by making a change to the registry.

The second issue is the need for administrators to build and maintain routing groups to create the routing topology. This is not a major problem because the majority of work often occurs at the start of a messaging project and then the work reverts to simple maintenance, but it is another administrative task that only delivers value to large enterprises. Companies that run one or two Exchange servers may not even understand that routing groups exist!

The last problem is the ability of administrators to troubleshoot routing problems. Because link state routing implies that routes between servers can change at any time, you are never quite sure about how messages flow. This is not an issue when everything is working well, but it can be if you have a problem and you do not quite know where to start debugging the issue. The lack of good administrative tools in Exchange 2000 and 2003 to debug message flow and reveal the current routing topology compounded this problem.

The issues that administrators discovered with the Exchange 2000/2003 transport engine are irritating rather than disastrous and Microsoft could have fixed or ameliorated the problems by taking steps such as tuning the propagation of link state information or providing better administrative tools. However, developments elsewhere meant that Microsoft had to change part of the core of the transport engine. Microsoft took the decision to rewrite the complete transport engine and base it on the .NET framework rather than to upgrade the older code base used in Exchange 2000/2003. The immediate impact of this change is that if you have any customized code created for Exchange 2000/2003 (such as event sinks for the transport service), you will have to rewrite it for Exchange 2007. The same issue arises if you have code that modifies SMTP attributes in the IIS metabase because Exchange no longer depends on IIS for the SMTP protocol. Exchange 2007 now includes all of the code necessary to support a comprehensive SMTP service in its own code base.

Microsoft cites the following advantages about the Exchange 2007 transport engine:

- The code base is now managed code, so it is more secure and robust. For example, managed code generates no buffer overflow conditions for hackers to exploit. The APIs used in the .NET framework are more consistent and easier for programmers to work with, so the code base is easier to maintain and extend.

- The routing topology created with routing groups and connectors is not needed by many Exchange organizations. Everyone has to deploy the Active Directory before they can install Exchange and the Active Directory has its own topology created from sites and site links. Eliminating the separate Exchange routing topology simplifies matters and removes a task from the administrative workload.

- SMTP is the default transport protocol for Exchange 2007. The type of networks deployed today permit point-to-point connections between servers, especially when you use an efficient protocol like SMTP.

- Point-to-point connections create a much simpler routing infrastructure because you have a full-mesh network where any hub transport server can contact any other hub transport server in another Active Directory site to transfer messages. It also leads to better scalability. The Exchange 2003 transport engine has problems when there are more than 100,000 messages in a queue. You might not hit this problem in a small to medium enterprise, but it can be an issue for large enterprises and hosted deployments.

- Administrative tools such as queue viewers are easier to write for simpler routing environments.

- The new transport engine has the ability to detect and handle "poison" messages. These are badly formed or illegally-formatted SMTP messages that can cause the previous routing engine to stop.

- It made sense for Exchange 2000 to rely on IIS for the SMTP service because it allowed Microsoft to ship Exchange 2000 faster. Over time, the complications of managing the interaction between IIS, Exchange, and Windows to control a relatively simple service surpassed the original advantage, so creating an Exchange-specific SMTP service that only runs on hub transport and Edge servers simplifies matters all around. Exchange 2007 servers disable the standard IIS SMTP service and replace it with an upgraded SMTP service that runs inside MSExchangeTransport.EXE. If they need to, Microsoft can upgrade the Exchange SMTP engine without affecting IIS and potentially other applications.

Compliance and message tracking was another big issue that Microsoft could not address in an adequate manner with their old code base. In an Exchange 2000/2003 environment, both the Store (local delivery) and the transport engine (remote delivery) can handle messages, so it is extremely difficult to introduce software to monitor and trace the path of messages and be able to satisfy the requirements of auditors and legislators. Many companies in the financial industry developed transport events to impose Chinese Walls (otherwise known as ethical walls) between different parts of the companies (brokers and traders, for instance) or to process messages to ensure that they complied with legislation. Code like this works very well for any message going to an external address, but because the Exchange 2003 Store handles local delivery and Exchange does not invoke transport events for these messages, it is difficult for Exchange to comply with some regulatory requirements. To be fair to Microsoft, no one could have predicted the growth in the need for compliance in email systems when they designed Exchange 2000 and every other email system has faced a struggle to achieve compliance. The net result is that it made a lot of sense for the developers to rewrite the transport engine in Exchange 2007 and to deliver a much simpler and straightforward SMTP-based routing environment that incorporates new functionality to add support for compliance through transport and journal rules.

6.2.1 Hidden administrative and routing groups

Of course, it is difficult to move from one transport architecture to another without leaving some traces behind. In the case of Exchange 2007, the designers had to support backwards compatibility with routing and administrative groups to allow Exchange 2007 servers to coexist inside an organization with Exchange 2003 servers. The solution was to create a hidden administrative group and a hidden routing group to hold Exchange 2007 servers as they were installed into the organization. You can see the hidden groups if you examine the details of the Exchange organization through the

Active Directory or look at them through ESM. A minor but important detail was to come up with a suitable name for the hidden administrative and routing groups, and the Exchange designers decided to call them:

```
Exchange Administrative Group (FYDIBOHF23SPDLT)
Exchange Routing Group (DWBGZMFD01QNBJR)
```

On the surface, it looks as if the designers used the same algorithm as is used to generate the alphanumeric keys for Windows licenses, but the Trivial Pursuit answer is that they used a simple Caesar cipher[2]. Thus, the actual meaning of the names are:

F	E		D	E
Y	X		W	X
D	C		B	C
I	H		G	H
B	A		Z	A
O	N		M	N
H	G		F	G
F	E		D	E
2	1		0	1
3	2		1	2
S	R		Q	R
P	O		N	O
D	C		B	C
L	K		J	K
T	S		R	S

All of this goes to prove that at least some humor was applied during the design of Exchange 2007.

After you install Exchange 2007 into an Exchange 2003 organization, the installation procedure updates the ESM console to prevent you renaming the special administrative and routing groups. Some administrators have asked if it is possible to change the name of the special administrative and routing groups because the names, while cute, are somewhat clumsy, especially if you want to use LDAP to interrogate the directory. It is obviously much easier (and less likely to make a mistake) to type in a name like "Ex2007Admin" instead of "Exchange Administrative Group (FYDIBOHF23SPDLT)." The special

---

2.   When Caesar sent sensitive messages around, he used a simple code created by shifting letters one position forward or backwards in the alphabet to encode the message. You reverse the process to decrypt the message.

names aren't just in a few places as they are scattered across the Active Directory in use in LegacyExchangeDN properties for many objects. Microsoft's answer is that it is impossible to change the names because they are hard-coded in some places like the setup program, which expects to install servers into the special administrative group.

Note that the creation of the hidden administrative and routing groups to support Exchange 2007 servers will result in a full OAB download for any client like Outlook 2000 or XP that uses OAB format 2 or 3.

6.3 Exchange 2007 transport architecture

You have to consider the change in the transport architecture alongside the introduction of server roles in Exchange 2007 and Microsoft's desire to split functionality up so that a server only runs the code that it absolutely must in order to perform its role. As discussed in Chapter 1, previous generations of Exchange servers are complete messaging servers in that Microsoft designed an architecture that ran the complete system on a single computer. You can still keep things simple by deploying multiple roles on an Exchange 2007 server, but the overall design philosophy is to move toward specialized server roles, and the hub transport[3] server is critical to the ebb and flow of messages within the Exchange organization. In large deployments, hub transport servers are operated as separate servers, but in smaller deployments, it is more common for a server to support both mailbox and hub transport server roles. These servers may also take on the Client Access server role to provide a complete messaging service within an Active Directory site. Note that you cannot deploy the hub transport role on a clustered server.

Figure 6.1
Message flow through the Exchange 2007 transport system

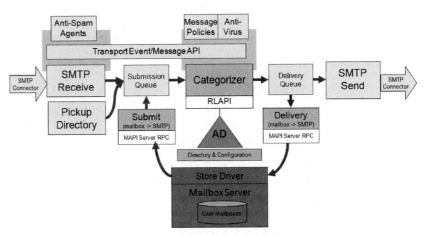

---

3. Hub transport servers perform the same work as bridgehead servers in previous versions of Exchange.

Figure 6.1 illustrates a simplified view of message flow between Exchange 2007 mailbox and hub transport servers. The major points that you need to understand from this diagram are:

- Exchange 2007 mailbox servers do not transport mail. Instead, when a mailbox server has a message that it needs to send to either a mailbox on another Exchange server or a recipient in another email system, the Microsoft Exchange Submission service that runs on the mailbox server informs a hub transport server that it has a message to be fetched. The Submission service indicates the database, mailbox, and message identifier to point to where the new message is waiting. The transfer of the message between mailbox and hub transport server is the responsibility of the Store driver. Note that the mailbox server performs the same processing for remote and local deliveries because if it did not then Exchange 2007 would have the same problems with compliance systems. In effect, outgoing mail goes into an "outbox" folder in the Store where it is fetched by the Store driver and moves the message to the hub transport server, where the message ends up on the submission queue. The transport service retrieves the messages from the submission queue, categorizes them, and then routes the mail by placing the messages onto the appropriate delivery queues for onward transmission.

- Mailbox and hub transport servers within an Active Directory site communicate together using server-side RPCs. The need to accommodate Exchange RPCs requires the servers to be connected by LAN-quality bandwidth as otherwise you run the risk of RPC timeouts and failure.

- If multiple hub transport servers are available in the site, the Mail Submission Service selects one on a load-balancing basis. This provides a level of fault tolerance for the transport service. If a server hosts both the mailbox and hub transport role, Exchange uses the local hub transport server to process messages.

- The Active Directory Topology Service is responsible for providing the transport service with information about the current site topology by reference to an Active Directory domain controller/Global Catalog server. The interface used is RLAPI.

- Outgoing messages leave via SMTP to other hub transport servers, through a routing group connector to legacy Exchange servers, an SMTP connector to other SMTP email systems, or to a purpose-built gateway for transmission via other means, such as FAX.

- The transport service applies message policies when the categorizer has expanded the set of addresses for messages. The policies are applied through transport rules that can perform processing from the mundane (apply disclaimer text to outgoing messages) to complex (block messages from travelling between different groups of users). The transport service also invokes any journal rules that you define to capture message traffic at this stage.

- Message policies are applied when the categorizer has expanded the set of addresses for messages. The policies are applied through transport rules that can perform processing from the mundane (apply disclaimer text to going messages) to complex (block messages from travelling between different groups of users). Journal rules to capture message traffic are also invoked at this stage.

- A new version of the Exchange Virus Scanning API (VSAPI) is available to scan incoming and outgoing messages on hub transport and Edge servers.

- All of the hub transport servers in the organization share a common configuration that dictate settings such as the maximum message size that Exchange can transport, the maximum number of recipients on an incoming message, and the connectors that are available to Exchange including connectors hosted by Edge servers. The configuration settings, including details of transport and journal rules, are held in the Active Directory. Edge servers operate as isolated entities that are loosely connected to the organization but don't share configuration settings. If you deploy Edge servers, you have to configure each Edge server separately.

Exchange 2007 determines available routing paths for messages by reference to the Active Directory topology and does not use the link state routing algorithm employed by Exchange 2000 and 2003. Link state update data is not exchanged between hub transport servers to keep them abreast of potential connector outages. The routing topology created from routing groups and routing group connectors (and less commonly, SMTP and X.400 connectors) is replaced by simple point-to-point connections between Exchange 2007 hub transport servers. If a point-to-point connection between hub transport servers is unavailable for some reason, Exchange determines how close to the eventual destination it can transport a message by reference to the Active Directory site topology, but only includes sites that include an Exchange hub transport server. To determine the best routing path, Exchange 2007 uses the costs assigned to the links that connect Active Directory sites. From this discussion it's obvious that a well-designed and properly functioning Active Directory site topology is now a critical success factor for Exchange 2007.

6.3.1   The critical role of hub transport servers

In order to go deeper into the Exchange 2007 transport architecture, it's important to fully understand the work that the hub transport server and the components that collectively form the Exchange transport services do in an Exchange 2007 organization. We will get to the details of many of these operations, such as setting up SMTP connectors, as we move through the remainder of this chapter.

Hub transport servers are responsible for:

- **Mail Flow:** Hub transport servers process every message sent inside an Exchange 2007 organization before the messages are delivered to mailboxes or routed outside the organization. There are no exceptions to this behavior; Exchange always directs messages through a hub transport server to determine and execute routing. Obviously, this means that you must install a hub transport server inside every Active Directory site that contains a mailbox server.

- **Message Submission:** Messages flow into hub transport servers in four ways. The first is through SMTP submission via port 25 through a receive connector (or port 587 in the case of POP3 and IMAP4 clients). Connectors handle messages flowing in from other hub transport servers or an Internet connection or through a routing group connector that allows messages to flow in from legacy Exchange servers in a mixed organization. The second is when applications place properly formatted SMTP messages in the Pickup or Replay directories. The third method is via the Store driver, which handles outgoing messages that the driver fetches when MAPI clients connected to mailbox servers send messages. The Store driver fetches the messages from the outbox folders in user mailboxes in MAPI format and converts them to TNEF format before submitting them. The last is when an agent creates a message. In all instances, the message ends up on the Submission queue for processing by Transport services. Edge servers accept messages only through a receive connector.

- **Message Categorization:** The Categorizer performs all address resolution for recipients by checking the addresses for internal recipients in message headers against a Global Catalog server. It expands distribution groups, including resolving the queries necessary to provide the membership of dynamic distribution groups, and checks these addresses against the Global Catalog. Once it knows the set of addresses it has to deal with, the categorizer resolves the best routing path for messages and performs any content conversion that is necessary (for example, to ensure that a user receives messages in a preferred format). The categorizer is also responsible for message bifurcation, if this is required for efficient message delivery. All messages that move through a hub transport server pass through the categorizer. Before the categorizer places a message onto a delivery queue, it checks to see whether the message has to be processed by a transport or journal rule and then performs whatever processing is required.

- **Message Delivery:** When a hub transport server determines that a message is to be delivered to an Exchange 2007 mailbox, it either notifies the Store driver if running on the same server to effect delivery to a local mailbox (a local mailbox is a mailbox on any server in the same Active Directory site as the hub transport server) or it transfers the message via a send connector to another hub transport server in a different Active Directory site, which then takes responsibility for onward delivery to the destination mailbox. Messages going to non-Exchange recipients are delivered through an SMTP connector, routed to an Edge server, or routed to an external gateway that has responsibility for transmission to a foreign email system. You don't have to do anything to configure the connectors between hub transport servers in different Active Directory sites, because all hub transport servers know about each other through the configuration information held in Active Directory and the connectors are automatically configured by Exchange. You do have to create SMTP connectors for outgoing communications. All communication between hub transport servers is via SMTP and is automatically secured with TLS and Kerberos. Again, you don't have to do anything to configure the secure connections.

- **Protection:** Hub transport (and Edge) servers are the only Exchange 2007 servers that can be configured with anti-spam agents to filter and cleanse the messaging stream before messages are routed to recipients. Hub transport servers can host anti-virus software to provide a further level of protection. Mailbox servers can also host anti-virus software. We will discuss how to deploy anti-spam and anti-virus software on hub transport and Edge servers later on in this chapter.

- **Message Recovery:** The hub transport server has a facility called the transport dumpster that is used in conjunction with mailbox servers running Cluster Continuous Replication (see Chapter 9). The dumpster is used to recover messages that were in transit when a cluster outage occurs so that they can be redelivered to the mailbox server.

- **Messaging Records Management:** Hub transport servers provide a single point of contact for Exchange to be able to apply transport and journal rules to messages as they flow through the organization. Transport rules can apply disclaimers, take selective copies of messages, prevent groups of users communicating with each other, and so on. Journal rules allow Exchange to take full copies of message traffic and move the data to another repository, such as an HSM system. There's a lot more detail about Messaging Records Management explored in Chapter 8.

While you can describe the Store as the heart of Exchange, the message flow capability provided by hub transport servers are the lungs because they provide the means for Exchange to function and get work done as a messaging system.

6.3.2   Receive connectors

All versions of Exchange support SMTP connectors to allow bidirectional email communications with other messaging systems that support SMTP. Exchange 2000 made the fundamental switch in focus from X.400 to SMTP and since then, SMTP has been the major method of communication for Exchange. Exchange 2003 servers support SMTP virtual servers and SMTP connectors that you configure to use the virtual servers to send and receive messages. Exchange 2007 servers take a different approach.

Figure 6.2
*Receive connectors
and properties*

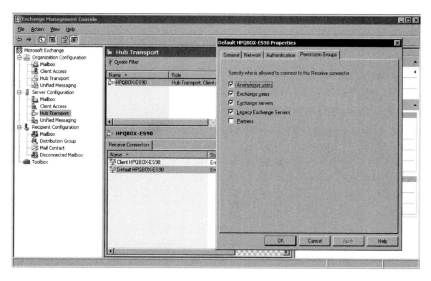

You can configure a receive connector to accept accepting incoming messages from other Exchange 2007 servers, other SMTP servers, or POP3/IMAP4 clients. Each receive connector is a "listener" that monitors a specific port for incoming connections, so you'd configure a connector for SMTP traffic to listen on port 25 and a connector to handle POP3/IMAP4 clients on port 587. Unless you want to support unauthenticated connections, the normal approach (and a change from the default configuration used by Exchange 2000 and 2003) is to force POP3 and IMAP4 clients to authenticate before they can connect to port 587 and use an Exchange 2007 receive connector. As we will see later on, you can also restrict the range of IP addresses that a connector will accept connections from.

Receive connectors are scoped to a particular server and establish what incoming messages that hub transport or Edge server is willing to accept. When you install the hub transport role on a server, the installation creates two receive connectors to allow the hub transport server to communicate with other Exchange 2007 servers and to support clients. The two connectors are the "default" receive connector for interserver communications and a receive connector for clients. The properties of a connector establish the connections that it can handle. As you can see in Figure 6.2, the default connector on this hub transport server can handle connections from:

- Anonymous users
- Exchange users
- Exchange servers
- Legacy Exchange servers

You can use the Get-Connector command to view details of the connector properties. For example:

```
Get-Connector —Server HPQBOX-ES90

Identity                        Bindings          Enabled
--------                        --------          -------
HPQBOX-ES90\Default HPQBOX-ES90  {0.0.0.0:25}      True
HPQBOX-ES90\Client HPQBOX-ES90   {0.0.0.0:587}     True
```

By default, receive connectors on hub transport servers are configured to accept authenticated connections from other Exchange servers, including legacy Exchange servers in the same organization. In this respect, the default configuration differs from the configuration shown in Figure 6.2 because the "Anonymous users" permission group is excluded. Because of its outward facing role, the receive connector on an Edge server is configured automatically to accept anonymous connections.

A permission group is a predefined set of permissions (in this case, for the connector) that is granted to well-known security principals such as a user or group. Exchange 2007 uses permission groups to make it easier to configure access to a connector. You can find details of all of the permission groups and the permissions that each includes in TechNet online. For now, Table 6.1 describes the AnonymousUsers and ExchangeUsers permission groups.

Table 6.1   *Example permission groups*

Permission Group	Security Principal	Included Permissions
AnonymousUsers	Anonymous User Account	Ms-Exch-SMTP-Submit Ms-Exch-SMTP-Accept-Any-Sender MS-Exch-SMTP-Accept-Authoritative-Domain-Sender Ms-Exch-Accept-Headers-Routing
ExchangeUsers	Authenticated User Accounts	Ms-Exch-SMTP-Submit Ms-Exch-SMTP-Accept-Any-Recipient Ms-Exch-Bypass-Anti-Spam Ms-Exch-Accept-Headers-Routing

The default configuration for hub transport servers works well if all the hub transport servers need is to receive incoming SMTP traffic on port 25 from other Exchange servers. However, if you want to receive incoming messages from other SMTP servers inside the company, including servers in another Exchange organization, then you have to either update the receive connector to include the "Anonymous users" permission group by selecting its checkbox on the Permission Group property page, as shown in Figure 6.2 or create another receive connector to handle the connections. If you don't configure a receive connector to allow anonymous connections, users who send messages from the other email systems will receive nondelivery notifications with an error code of 5.7.1, which means that the sending server was unable to authenticate itself to Exchange and so the connection was terminated. Figure 6.3 shows the error message generated by an Exchange 2007 organization for a message that it couldn't send to a user in another Exchange 2007 organization, both within the same company.

It might seem logical to you that the receive connector on hub transport servers should be able to accept anonymous connections. Microsoft took a deliberate decision to force administrators to upgrade the connectors if they wanted to support anonymous connections to emphasize their philosophy of "secure by default" and the role of the Edge server, which is explicitly designed to accept and process incoming messages from external servers. With security in mind, Microsoft's recommendation is that you create a specific receive connector to handle connections from external SMTP servers. In

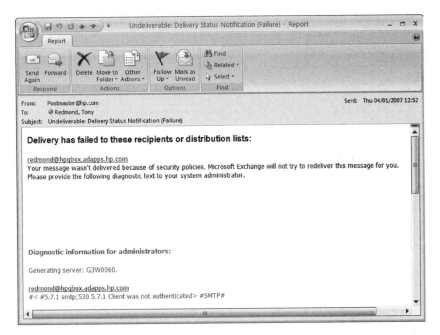

Figure 6.3

A receive connector won't handle unauthenticated connects

reality, it's quite acceptable to update the default receive connection to permit anonymous connections. Allowing anonymous connections effectively means that "it's okay to accept messages from other SMTP servers that aren't part of this Exchange organization." If you prefer, you can use the Set-ReceiveConnector command to do the same thing:

```
Set-ReceiveConnector  -id "Default HPQBOX-ES90"
-PermissionGroups AnonymousUsers, ExchangeUsers,
ExchangeServers, ExchangeLegacyServer —Comment "Updated
Connector to allow Anonymous Connections"
```

Updating the default receive connector to allow anonymous connections is the easy solution to the problem of accepting incoming messages from external SMTP servers. However, this approach means that you use the same configuration for internal and external messages. You may want to treat external messages differently, for instance, you may allow users to send 10MB messages internally but want to restrict incoming messages to 5MB. In this circumstance, you can create a separate receive connector and customize it to meet your requirements.

To create a new receive connector, select the hub transport server that you want to host the connector in EMC and then select the "New Receive Connector" option. The wizard that creates the connector first prompts for a

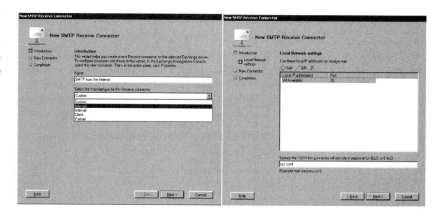

Figure 6.4
*Creating a new
receive connector
for external SMTP
traffic*

name and usage type. The usage type determines the permission groups that
Exchange assigns to the connector. Table 6.2 lists the usage types defined by
Exchange 2007 and their meaning for a connector.

Table 6.2   *Receive connector usage types*

Usage type	Meaning	Default Permission Groups	Authentication
Client	A connector to support IMAP4 and POP3 clients. This type cannot be used on Edge servers because Edge servers don't support client connections.	ExchangeUsers	TLS Basic plus TLS Integrated Windows
Custom	A connector tailored by the administrator to meet specific needs. For example, to connect two Exchange 2007 organizations together.	None (needs to be determined by the use of the connector)	None (needs to be determined by the use of the connector)
Internal	A connector to link Exchange 2007 and Exchange 2003/2000 servers.	ExchangeUsers ExchangeLegacyServers	Exchange Server authentication
Internet	A connector to handle SMTP traffic from external (non-Exchange) servers.	AnonymousUsers Partner	None or externally secured
Partner	A connector to secure SMTP communications with a partner organization.	Partner	Requires TLS with a remote domain

The connector illustrated in Figure 6.4 is of the Internet usage type and
will listen on port 25. The shell command used to create the connector is
shown below. Note the value passed in the –Usage parameter:

```
New-ReceiveConnector -Name 'SMTP from the Internet' -Usage
'Internet' -Bindings '0.0.0.0:25' -Fqdn 'xyz.com' -Server
'ExchHub1'
```

We're not quite done when the connector is created because its settings might not be fit for our purpose. We can check the complete configuration with the Get-ReceiveConnector command, which outputs a lot of information that is not revealed by EMC:

```
Get-ReceiveConnector —id 'SMTP from the Internet' | Format-List
```

```
AuthMechanism                            : Tls
BinaryMimeEnabled                        : True
Bindings                                 : {0.0.0.0:25}
ChunkingEnabled                          : True
DeliveryStatusNotificationEnabled        : True
EightBitMimeEnabled                      : True
DomainSecureEnabled                      : False
EnhancedStatusCodesEnabled               : True
Fqdn                                     : xyz.com
Comment                                  :
Enabled                                  : True
ConnectionTimeout                        : 00:10:00
ConnectionInactivityTimeout              : 00:05:00
MessageRateLimit                         : unlimited
MaxInboundConnection                     : 5000
MaxInboundConnectionPerSource            : 100
MaxInboundConnectionPercentagePerSource  : 2
MaxHeaderSize                            : 64KB
MaxHopCount                              : 30
MaxLocalHopCount                         : 3
MaxLogonFailures                         : 3
MaxMessageSize                           : 10MB
MaxProtocolErrors                        : 5
MaxRecipientsPerMessage                  : 200
PermissionGroups                         : AnonymousUsers
PipeliningEnabled                        : True
ProtocolLoggingLevel                     : None
RemoteIPRanges                           : {0.0.0.0-255.255.255.255}
RequireEHLODomain                        : False
RequireTLS                               : False
Server                                   : ExchHub1
SizeEnabled                              : Enabled
TarpitInterval                           : 00:00:05
AdminDisplayName                         :
ExchangeVersion                          : 0.1 (8.0.535.0)
Name                                     : SMTP from the Internet
```

We can now see that TLS is the authentication mechanism selected for the connector and that it will accept messages from anonymous senders. This is an appropriate setting if the external servers that we want to communicate with support TLS, but we may want to start off by removing TLS as this will allow any SMTP server to connect. Other parameters that we can tweak include the maximum message size, the number of recipients allowed per message, and the number of connections that we are willing to accept. If the external SMTP servers generate older format messages that don't support extended SMTP, we may want to disable 8-bit MIME support, binary MIME support, and chunking. All of these changes can be done with the `Set-ReceiveConnector` command. Here's an example that tunes the maximum message size down to 5MB, allows 250 recipients per message (if more recipients are on a message, Exchange will accept for the first 250 and it's up to the sending server to resend for the remainder), and turns off TLS and any other authentication. We also add a comment so that other administrators understand the use of the connector and update the FQDN that is sent back to a server after it makes a successful connection.

```
Set-ReceiveConnector -id 'SMTP from the Internet'
-MaxMessageSize 5MB -MaxRecipientsPerMessage 250
-AuthMechanism None -Comment 'Connector to support external
SMTP servers' -fqdn 'mail.xyz.com'
```

Figure 6.5
Updating a receive connector

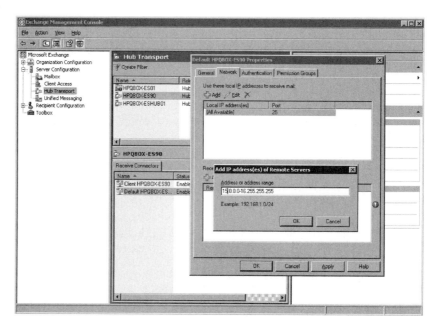

If you're concerned about opening up a receive connector to accept connections from any SMTP server, you can restrict the connections that it will accept by defining a set of IP addresses that you're willing to accept messages from. Do this by removing the standard mask (0.0.0.0–255.255.255.2555) and then adding the IP addresses that identify the servers that you want to accept messages from. You can do this with individual IP addresses, IP address ranges, an IP address together with a subnet, or an IP address in Classless Interdomain Routing notation (for example, 17.1.16.0/24). Enter the IP address data through the Network property page for the receive connector, as shown in Figure 6.5.

The command to restrict access to a range of IP addresses for the default connector on the hub transport server called ExchHub1 is:

```
Set-ReceiveConnector —id "ExchHub1\Default ExchHub1"
—RemoteIPRanges "19.0.0.0–19.255.255.255"
```

6.3.3   Send connectors

Every hub transport server operates a default send connector. You will not see any trace of this connector if you look for it through EMC, but you realize that it must exist because Exchange 2007 is able to send messages off the server. In fact, the default send connector is an integral part of the transport system and is present in memory. You can get details of the default send connector with the `Get-TransportServer` command:

```
Get-TransportServer —Server ExchHub1 | Format-List
```

Like many other EMS commands, the output generated is verbose, but provides an excellent insight into the properties that you can control for the default send connector. An edited version of the output from `Get-TransportServer` is shown below.

```
Get-TransportServer —Server ExchHub1 | Format-List

Name                              : ExchHub1
AntispamAgentsEnabled             : True
DelayNotificationTimeout          : 04:00:00
InternalDsnSendHtml               : True
MaxConcurrentMailboxDeliveries    : 30
MaxConcurrentMailboxSubmissions   : 20
MaxConnectionRatePerMinute        : 1200
MaxOutboundConnections            : 1000
MaxPerDomainOutboundConnections   : 20
```

```
MessageExpirationTimeout                    : 2.00:00:00
MessageRetryInterval                        : 00:01:00
MessageTrackingLogEnabled                   : True
MessageTrackingLogMaxAge                     : 30.00:00:00
MessageTrackingLogMaxDirectorySize          : 250MB
MessageTrackingLogMaxFileSize               : 10MB
MessageTrackingLogPath                      : C:\Program Files\Microsoft\Exchange
Server\TransportRoles\Logs\MessageTracking
MessageTrackingLogSubjectLoggingEnabled : True
OutboundConnectionFailureRetryInterval      : 00:10:00
IntraOrgConnectorProtocolLoggingLevel       : None
PickupDirectoryMaxHeaderSize                : 64KB
PickupDirectoryMaxMessagesPerMinute         : 100
PickupDirectoryPath                         : C:\Program Files\Microsoft\Exchange
Server\TransportRoles\Pickup
PoisonMessageDetectionEnabled               : True
PoisonThreshold                             : 2
QueueMaxIdleTime                            : 00:03:00
ReceiveProtocolLogMaxAge                    : 30.00:00:00
ReceiveProtocolLogMaxDirectorySize          : 250MB
ReceiveProtocolLogMaxFileSize               : 10MB
ReceiveProtocolLogPath                      : C:\Program Files\Microsoft\Exchange
Server\TransportRoles\Logs\ProtocolLog\SmtpReceive
ReplayDirectoryPath                         : C:\Program Files\Microsoft\Exchange
Server\TransportRoles\Replay
RoutingTableLogMaxAge                       : 7.00:00:00
RoutingTableLogMaxDirectorySize             : 50MB
RoutingTableLogPath                         : C:\Program Files\Microsoft\Exchange
Server\TransportRoles\Logs\Routing
SendProtocolLogMaxAge                       : 30.00:00:00
SendProtocolLogMaxDirectorySize             : 250MB
SendProtocolLogMaxFileSize                  : 10MB
SendProtocolLogPath                         : C:\Program Files\Microsoft\Exchange
Server\TransportRoles\Logs\ProtocolLog\SmtpSend
TransientFailureRetryCount                  : 6
TransientFailureRetryInterval               : 00:05:00
```

Use the `Set-TransportServer` command to update properties. As we will see in Chapter 10, one common use of this command is to change the properties that control the generation of message tracking logs:

```
Set-TransportServer —id ExchHub1 —MessageTrackingLogPath 'L:\
Logs\MessageTracking'
```

Apart from the default send connector, custom send connectors are all SMTP-based. You can create new send connectors to connect Exchange 2007 to the Internet (or to transfer messages to foreign SMTP-based email systems) on a hub transport server in much the same way you'd create an SMTP connector hosted on an Exchange 2000/2003 bridgehead server, but there are some differences:

- Send connectors can be configured on hub transport or Edge servers and you configure and manage the two sets of connectors separately. It's likely that the Edge servers will be synchronized with a hub transport server to be able to route incoming messages for an organization. In this case, you configure connector settings on the hub transport server and synchronize details out to the Edge server through the EdgeSync process. In fact, you can't configure connectors on an Edge server if it has established synchronization with a hub transport server.

- Unlike receive connectors, which are created automatically when you install a hub transport server and remain bound to that server, send connectors are created at the organization level and are available for any server to route messages across. However, before a server can use a send connector to route messages, you have to add it as a valid source to the send connector's properties. Figure 6.6 shows that two servers are able to send messages via the "HPQBOX to the Internet" send connector. Both EMC and EMS flag warnings if you add a hub transport server that is not in the same Active Directory site as the hub transport servers that are already registered. The warning is to notify you that you may have created a nonoptimum routing because the transport service always uses deterministic routing and always picks one Active Directory site to route messages. Therefore, the transport service cannot load balance messages across two sites. Instead, the transport service selects the first Active Directory site in the connector's source hub transport list and always routes messages via that site.

If you know that the new source server has adequate network connectivity to support routing of messages from other Active Directory sites across the connector, it is acceptable but not best practice to add it. Note that even if a hub transport server is not registered as a valid source, it can still route messages across the connector, but it must route the messages via one of the valid source hub transport servers.

In most cases, a single custom send connector to handle external messages will suffice, but you can configure connectors to handle messages for specific domains. When you configure a custom send connector, you need to think about the settings to apply to the connector:

Figure 6.6
Source servers for a
send connector
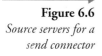

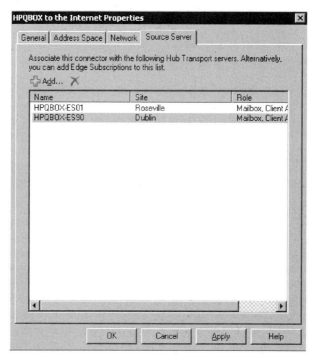

- Like a receive connector, the usage of the send connector determines the permission group for the connector: Internal means that the connector will connect to other Exchange servers; Internet means that anonymous connections will be accepted; Custom means that you will define permissions manually.

- The address space that a connector supports allows you some control over what messages flow across the connector. If you use an address space of "*", then the connector can handle any message to any domain[4]. You may want to establish a connector that routes messages to a specific domain, in which case, you would create a new connector and define the appropriate address space on that connector. Figure 6.7 shows a connector being configured to send messages to a domain called SystemX.xyz.com. However, let's assume that you had the need to connect to a specific domain in system.xyz.com and want to be sure that the messages go through a certain connector. You can accomplish your goal by creating a connector that hosts the exact address of the domain that you want to reach (for example, finance.systemx.xyz.com). After you create the connector and estab-

---

4.   Exchange 2007 doesn't support SMTP address spaces of "*.*" or "@*.*". Always use "*" if you want a connector to be able to route messages to any SMTP domain.

lish the address space, Exchange has two available routes that it can use for messages to finance.systemx.xyz.com: the default SMTP connector and the one specifically created for this domain. Exchange always routes messages across a connector with the most precise address space, even if choosing this connector incurs a higher routing cost, so any message sent to xyz.com will go across the default SMTP connector and any addressed to finance.systemx.xyz.com will always travel across the connector that you've just created. This is not new behavior in Exchange 2007 as this is the way that routing has worked since Exchange 5.0.

- Whether to use DNS MX ("mail exchange") records to route email or to send email through one or more smart host servers. A smart host is a server that is able to route SMTP traffic on behalf of other servers. Typically, this is a service offered by your ISP or a server that acts as a central point for routing within a company.

- The hub transport servers that are associated with the connector. You can decide to create an association with an Edge subscription at this point so that the connector is published through a hub transport server to become known to an Edge server.

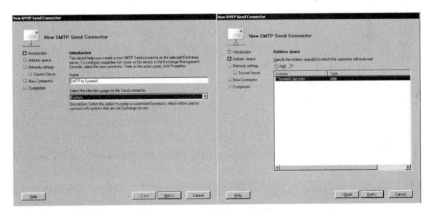

Figure 6.7
*Creating a new
SMTP send
connector*

If you opt to use a smart host to route SMTP messages to external destinations, Exchange asks you to specify what kind of authentication mechanism to use when it connects to the smart host. It may be that you have an SMTP server that's set up as an open relay for general use within the company, in which case you won't have to use authentication (the case shown in Figure 6.8) or you may have to provide a username and password for basic authentication. The smart host can be another Exchange server, in which case you'd use Exchange Server Authentication, or it might support IPSec for encrypted communication between the two servers.

Figure 6.8
Authentication settings to route via a smart host

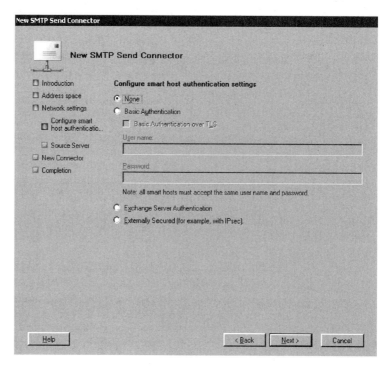

The shell command to create the send connector that we have just explored is:

```
New-SendConnector -Name 'SMTP to SystemX' -Usage 'Custom'
-AddressSpaces 'smtp:systemx.xyz.com;1' -DNSRoutingEnabled
$False -SmartHosts 'smarthost.xyz.com'
-SmartHostAuthMechanism 'None' -UseExternalDNSServersEnabled
$False -SourceTransportServers 'ExchHub1'
```

We can see the properties of the connector with the Get-SendConnector command. As we experienced when working with receive connectors, you have the opportunity to tweak many more settings through EMS than you do through the GUI.

```
Get-SendConnector -id 'SMTP to SystemX'

AddressSpaces              : {smtp:systemx.xyz.com;1}
AuthenticationCredential   :
Comment                    :
```

```
ConnectedDomains              : {}
ConnectionInactivityTimeOut   : 00:10:00
DNSRoutingEnabled             : False
DomainSecureEnabled           : False
Enabled                       : True
ForceHELO                     : False
Fqdn                          :
HomeMTA                       : Microsoft MTA
HomeMtaServerId               : ExchHub1
Identity                      : SMTP to SystemX
IgnoreSTARTTLS                : False
IsScopedConnector             : False
IsSmtpConnector               : True
LinkedReceiveConnector        :
MaxMessageSize                : 10MB
Name                          : SMTP to SystemX
Port                          : 25
ProtocolLoggingLevel          : None
RequireTLS                    : False
SmartHostAuthMechanism        : None
SmartHosts                    : {smarthost.xyz.com}
SmartHostsString              : smarthost.xyz.com
SourceIPAddress               : 0.0.0.0
SourceRoutingGroup            : Exchange Routing Group (DWBGZMFD01QNBJR)
SourceTransportServers        : {ExchHub1}
UseExternalDNSServersEnabled  : False
```

If we need to change any settings, we can do it with the Set-SendConnector command. Let's assume that we want to reduce the maximum message size that flows across the connector to 5MB. The command is:

```
Set-SendConnector –id 'SMTP to SystemX' –MaxMessageSize 5MB
–Comment 'SystemX mailboxes are limited to 5MB'
```

6.3.4 Linking Exchange 2003 and Exchange 2007

During a migration project, you will have to decide how to connect Exchange 2007 servers into the existing routing infrastructure. Exchange 2007 servers install into a special hidden routing group that is exposed to Exchange 2003 servers to allow them to communicate with Exchange 2007. When you install the first Exchange 2007 server with the hub transport role, you are asked which routing group you want to connect to so that the installation program can create a routing group connector between the Exchange 2007 routing group and the routing group that you nominate.

The simplest and best approach is to select a hub routing group to act as the point of connection between Exchange 2003 and Exchange 2007. Remember that this connector will act as the message interchange between Exchange 2003 and Exchange 2007 and a lot of traffic will flow across the connector during the migration, so you need to select a routing group that is both appropriate for this role and one that can handle the load. The servers in the routing group need to have solid, reliable, and fast network connections with the rest of the Exchange 2003 organization. Picking a non-optimum routing group isn't a disaster—at least not immediately—but it could have ramifications as you ramp up the message load across the connector as more and more users migrate to Exchange 2007. For example, you may decide to connect the first Exchange hub transport server with a routing group that is not part of the core network, perhaps even a small routing group that occupies a network spoke. Things will work just fine with a small group of users sending mail from Exchange 2007, but as traffic ramps, it doesn't make sense to funnel all messages from Exchange 2007 down into a network spoke and back up again for delivery to other routing groups.

On the Exchange 2007 side, it is equally important that the hub transport server at the other side of the routing group connector is able to handle the traffic, so you should also install this server into a core network site.

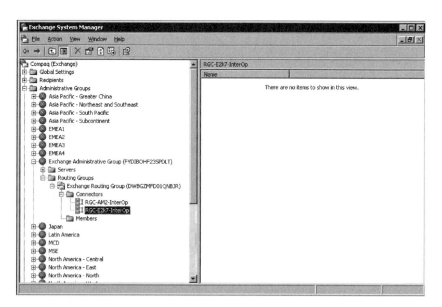

Figure 6.9
Exchange 2003 ESM displays the special routing group

Exchange 2007 installs its servers into a special administrative group that includes a routing group. You can't see these objects through EMC, but they do appear through ESM (Figure 6.9). However, as noted earlier, you can't work with these objects through ESM as Exchange applies a block to stop you doing anything except viewing their properties. For example, if you click on a routing group connector that is created in the special routing group to link Exchange 2007 and legacy servers, you can view all the properties, but you can't change anything (Figure 6.10).

The question therefore is how do you create such a specialized connector? The answer is in the `New-RoutingGroupConnector` command, which is designed to handle all the work to establish bidirectional connectivity between Exchange 2007 and legacy servers. Because all of the details of the Exchange 2007 servers are available to ESM, you can go through the process of setting up a routing group connector using ESM to connect a bridgehead in another routing group with a hub transport server in the special Exchange 2007 routing group, but you will also need to add the name of the legacy bridgehead server to the ExchangeLegacyInterop security group (Figure 6.11) afterwards as otherwise messages won't flow across the connection. The `New-Routing-GroupConnector` command takes care of all the details, so it's the recommended way to accomplish the task. For example:

```
New-RoutingGroupConnector —Name "RGC Exchange 2007 <->
Legacy" —SourceTransportServers "ExchHub1"
—TargetTransportServers "E2003Svr1" —Cost 50 —Bidirectional
$True
```

Figure 6.10
Properties of the special RGC

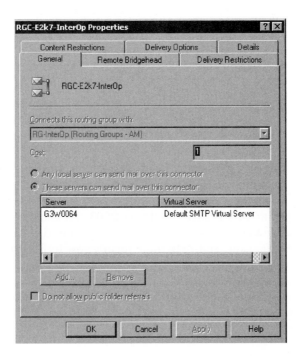

This command creates a new routing group connector that links the Exchange 2007 hub transport server called ExchHub1 with the Exchange 2003 bridgehead server called E2003Svr1. The cost of the link is set to 1 because we want this to be the default connection between the two parts of the organization (we might create another routing group connector between two other servers with a higher cost to act as a backup) and we've told Exchange to create the necessary connectors on both sides. Afterwards, you can check the properties of the connector with the Get-RoutingGroupConnector command (an edited version of the output is shown below):

```
Get-RoutingGroupConnector —id "RGC Exchange 2007 <-> Legacy"  |  Format-List
```

```
TargetRoutingGroup              : RG-InterOp
Cost                            : 50
TargetTransportServers          : {E2003Svr1}
ExchangeLegacyDN                : /o=xyz/ou=Exchange Administrative Group (FYDI
                                  BOHF23SPDLT)/cn=Configuration/cn=Connections/cn=
                                  RGC Exchange 2007 <-> Legacy
PublicFolderReferralsEnabled    : True
SourceRoutingGroup              : Exchange Routing Group (DWBGZMFD01QNBJR)
SourceTransportServers          : {ExchHub1}
ExchangeVersion                 : 0.1 (8.0.535.0)
Name                            : RGC Exchange 2007 <-> Legacy
Identity                        : RGC Exchange 2007 <-> Legacy
ObjectCategory                  : xyz.com/Configuration/Schema/ms-Exch-Routing
                                  -Group-Connector
ObjectClass                     : {top, msExchConnector,
msExchRoutingGroupConnector}
OriginatingServer               : ExchHub1.xyz.com
IsValid                         : True
```

Note that the cost of the connector is set reasonably high at 50 rather than the default cost of 1 that is usually assigned to a new routing group connector. The logic here is that you do not usually want to use the routing group connector between Exchange 2003 and Exchange 2007 as a backbone connection as it's best to keep messages within their native environment as much as possible and only route them across to Exchange 2007 when their final destination is on an Exchange 2007 server. Of course, a time will come during the migration when Exchange 2007 is performing the majority of routing or you take the decision to make Exchange 2007 the backbone mail router for the organization, and in this case you can reduce the connector

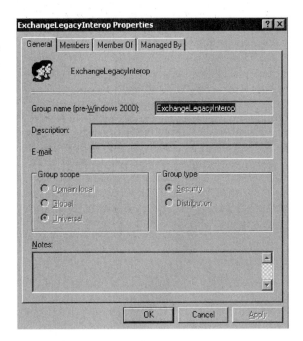

Figure 6.11
The Exchange LegacyInterop security group

cost to allow Exchange 2003 servers to transfer messages across the connector more often.

Remember that all of the Exchange 2007 servers appear to be in a single routing group, so we've just created two connectors between that routing group and the rest of the Exchange 2003 routing topology. Because we have two routes that Exchange 2003 can take into Exchange 2007, we have created a situation where any outage might convince the Exchange 2003 servers to route messages in a non-optimal manner and potentially even create a loop. You can assume that no connectors will ever experience an outage, in which case you don't have to do anything, or you can take the pragmatic view that software and networks tend to meet problems from time to time. In this case, you want to stop link state updates propagating so that the Exchange 2003 servers never attempt to recalculate routes and will always use the topology that you've just created.

There really isn't anything more than that to setting up bidirectional message flow between Exchange 2007 and legacy servers, unless you still have some Exchange 5.5 servers deployed. In this case, you'll have to continue to route messages from Exchange 5.5 through an Exchange 2003/2000 bridgehead server on to Exchange 2007 as there is no way to establish a direct routing group connection between Exchange 2007 and Exchange 5.5.

6.3.5   Multiple routes into Exchange 2003

As long as you only have a single routing group connector between Exchange 2003 and Exchange 2007, you do not have to worry about link state information. Exchange 2003 will continue to send link state updates between its routing groups but Exchange 2007 will simply drop the updates and ignore them. The two sides will operate independently of each other and maintain separate routing topologies. Operating a single connector will be sufficient for small to medium organizations but things often become more complex with larger organizations because of the need to handle bigger volumes of traffic and to route messages efficiently within geographical network segments. In this situation, you probably need to configure additional routing group connectors between appropriate Exchange 2003 servers and Exchange 2007 hub transport servers.

6.3.6   Decommissioning Exchange 2003 routing groups

Eventually, you will come to a point where you can start eliminating routing group connectors because you have decommissioned Exchange 2003 servers and emptied some routing groups. Another challenge now awaits you: how to decommission servers without creating islands of link state replication. If you remove connectors between Exchange 2003 routing groups and force the Exchange 2003 servers that are left behind to route messages via Exchange 2007, mail will flow but link state updates cannot because Exchange 2007 ignores these updates. The upshot is that, in terms of routing topology, the Exchange 2003 servers will exist in a moment frozen in time and will never be aware of any topology changes that occur elsewhere in the organization. This may not be a bad thing if you are decommissioning servers fast and don't expect the servers to have to function in the mode for long, but in most cases (especially in large organizations), you can't switch over to Exchange 2007 quickly enough to avoid the potential that messages will be routed ineffectively (or conceivably end up in a black hole because Exchange can't figure out where to send them). For this reason, any time you remove a routing group connector, make sure that the Exchange 2003 servers that are left behind have an alternative connector that they can use to receive link state updates.

6.3.7   Handling Exchange 2003 link state updates during migration

You don't have to care about link state updates if you are in a pure Exchange 2007 organization, but you do have to pay attention to them during migrations from Exchange 2003. Link state updates are a concept that Microsoft introduced in Exchange 2000 where servers that act as routing group masters in an organization communicated information about the routing topology with each other so that servers would know when problems existed in the topology, such as a connector being down or otherwise unavailable, and would then be able to adjust the way that they routed messages to avoid the problems. Dynamic routing was a great idea and it made a lot of sense as a natural evolution from the static GWART (gateway and routing table) used by Exchange 5.5. The problem with using a fixed view of the routing topology is that servers can send messages to a destination where they become stuck until a connector is fixed and brought back into service.

Exchange 2007 doesn't use link state information to decide how to route messages. As we know, Exchange 2007 uses the underlying network as defined in Active Directory sites to perform least cost routing between sites. Microsoft's view is that this approach puts routing decisions closer to the network layer so any problems become easier to diagnose. Instead of trying to understand how changing network conditions and connector outages may have caused Exchange to reroute messages, all you have to do is understand how the network connects sites together (and sites are IP subnets, so you can go down to that level) and you can figure out how messages flow. It's also easier to estimate where messages are because you know that Exchange 2007 will queue them at the closest point of failure instead of attempting to reroute them dynamically across nonoptimum routing groups. Collectively, these steps make it much easier to understand message routing in complex networks that span hundreds of Exchange servers. In smaller networks, where you only operate a few servers, everything should run automatically and you probably won't care too much after you connect your sites together.

If you want to stop link state propagation, you have to make a registry change on every Exchange 2003 bridgehead server. To do this, go to `HKEY_LOCAL_MACHINE\SYSTEM\CurrentControlSet\Services\RESvc\Parameters` and add a new DWORD value called SuppressStateChanges. Set the value to 1 (one) and then restart the Exchange Routing Engine, the SMTP service, and the Exchange MTA service. Servers will continue to send link state updates to each other but they will ignore any connector outages that might force a topology change. If a connector experiences an outage, Exchange will either reroute via another available connector or queue messages at that point until the connector is available again.

6.3.8 Foreign connectors

Foreign connectors link Exchange to other messaging systems. In the past, installing foreign connectors was a necessary evil because different email systems used different protocols. Microsoft provided the Exchange Development Kit (EDK) to allow third parties and their own engineers to build connectors for email systems such as Lotus Notes, Novell GroupWise, Lotus cc:Mail, Fax, Short Message Service, and so on.

The growing acceptance of SMTP as the de facto standard for email exchange plus the addition of other Internet-driven standards such as iCal permit much better out-of-the-box connectivity between email systems today and have eliminated the need to operate many bespoke gateways. Microsoft has removed support for gateways developed with the Exchange 2003 EDK, so if you use one of these gateways, you will have to get an updated version that can connect to the Exchange 2007 transport system. Microsoft has new versions of their interoperability and connectivity tools for major systems such as Lotus Notes and Novell GroupWise, and you can expect that the other software vendors who have provided tools in the past will upgrade their products to support Exchange 2007. Note that connectivity is just one part of the interoperability picture when you have to support multiple email systems. It's relatively easy to pass messages between the different systems, but achieving the finer details such as directory synchronization and support for message that contain meeting requests takes more effort.

6.3.9 Authorization

The Exchange transport service uses Windows permissions to allow different operations to proceed depending on where they originate. The permissions model extends to the different SMTP verbs or events that occur during message processing. For example, the transport service checks permission to establish whether a sender is allowed to submit messages from a particular email domain or submit a message of a certain size. The transport service can perform authentication on a session basis to establish the permissions that are available, which allows it to assign one set of permissions to messages submitted by anonymous Internet senders and another set of permissions to internal users.

6.3.10 Accepted domains

Accepted domains are email domains that you define to be those that you are willing to accept email for and establish what recipients Exchange 2007 deems to be internal and what it deems to be external. In previous versions of Exchange, we configured SMTP address spaces on connectors, but in Exchange 2007, if you specify an accepted domain, you create an entry in the Exchange organization's configuration that says that the domain is one of three types:

1. An authoritative domain is one that is hosted by the Exchange organization. When you install the first Exchange 2007 hub transport server in the organization, the installation procedure automatically adds the FQDN of the forest root as an authorita-

tive receive domain, meaning that this Exchange organization is able to receive and process incoming email sent to that domain. You need to specify other authoritative domains if you want Exchange to process incoming messages sent to these domains. Any recipient that belongs to an authoritative domain is deemed to be an internal recipient.

2. An internal relay domain is one that you are willing to accept messages for recipients who do not have mailboxes, but are registered as mail-enabled contacts.

3. An external relay domain is one that you are willing to accept messages and then relay them to a separate server for onward routing and delivery.

You create additional domains on a hub transport server (at the organizational configuration level) and synchronize them to Edge servers through EdgeSync. Figure 6.12 illustrates how to create a new accepted domain. Behind the scenes, EMS creates the domain with:

```
New-AcceptedDomain -Name:'HPQBOX' -DomainName:'hpqbox.com'
-DomainType:'Authoritative'
```

In this case, we declare that our Exchange organization is willing to accept messages sent to the hpqbox.com domain, so presumably there are some users in the organization who have hpqbox.com email addresses. It is reasonably common for an organization to support multiple email domains. For example, an organization might include users who have joined the company through acquisition and you have allowed those users to retain the email addresses from their old company (as secondary email addresses), so that they can continue to receive messages from correspondents who only have those addresses.

Edge servers reject incoming messages (with a DSN of 550 5.7.1 Unable to Relay) that are addressed to domains that they do not recognize, so it is clearly important to understand what domains you support and then to populate those domains out to the Edge servers.

6.3.11 Transport storage

Exchange 2003 stores messages in file system directories. Exchange 2007 uses a Jet database called mail.que (similar to those used by the Active Directory and the Store) as its repository, writing messages from memory into the database in 20MB batches or as required. For example, a message that causes a

Figure 6.12
Creating a new
accepted domain

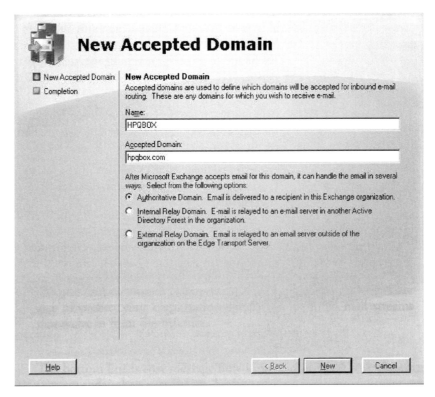

problem during delivery such as those regarded as "poison" (see section later in this chapter), are written into the database immediately.

As shown in Figure 6.13, the default location for the mail.que database is stored in \Program Files\Microsoft\Exchange Server\TransportRoles\Data\ Queue. If you look at the number of transaction logs that the transport service generates on a server, you can get some sense of how busy the server is. In the case illustrated here, we know that the server is lightly trafficked because it has only generated 104 (hex value of 67 plus the current log) 5MB logs since the server was installed.

The vast majority of the transactions that flow through the mail queue database are transient, so the database uses circular logging and 5MB transaction logs instead of the 1MB used by the Store. The current transaction log is trn.log and, just like the Store databases, Exchange uses two reserved logs to ensure that processing can continue even if disk space runs out. Given the amount of available storage on most Exchange servers today, administrators do not normally have to worry too much about the disk space occupied by mail.que or its transaction logs unless you operate a very busy hub transport server that handles a huge volume of messages. An Edge server that handles thousands of messages per hour will have a large message queue database,

Figure 6.13

Transport queue files

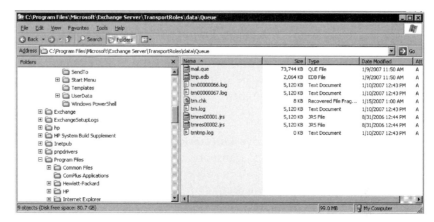

especially if you want to build in some capacity to handle an outage situation when the Edge server cannot communicate with the hub transport servers behind the firewall. For example, if your average message size is 100KB and you want to hold a queue of up to 100,000 messages, then the message queue database will be approximately 100GB. Your mileage will vary depending on the average message size and the volume of traffic.

When the server has sufficient memory, the transport service stores incoming messages in memory and commits them to the transaction logs, using a similar mechanism to that employed by the Store to work with its transactions. If memory becomes scarce and a back-pressure situation exists, the transport service throttles back on its memory demands by caching only the first 128KB of a message in memory and storing the remainder in the database. In all cases, the transport service writes the message data into the transaction log. When the transport service needs the complete message, it streams the data out of the database and performs any content conversion that is required using the TEMP directory (the directory pointed to by the %TEMP% variable). For this reason, it is best for performance to colocate the message queue database on the same disk LUN as the TEMP directory. On the other hand, you should separate the message queue database and its transaction logs.

The really interesting thing about the mail queue database is that you can take it from one hub transport server and load it on any other Exchange 2007 hub transport server to have that server attempt to process any queued mail in the database. Providing that the addresses on the messages are valid, the hub transport server will route them to their final destination. This is a valuable weapon to have in disaster-recovery scenarios, where you may have problems on a hub transport server that require you to take it out of service because you can move the mail queue database to the replacement server to ensure that any waiting messages are processed.

6.4   **Routing ABC**

Before we look at different routing scenarios, we have enough detail to present a picture of how the major components link together to establish message flow in an example Exchange organization. Before we begin, let's recap some points:

- The Active Directory Topology Service provides information to the Exchange transport service about sites and site links. Exchange uses this data to calculate the least-cost path for a message and to understand whether any hub routing sites occur along the path and if it needs to bifurcate a message at any point.

- Hub transport servers make point-to-point connections with other hub transport servers to transfer messages as close as possible to the final destination.

- If a hub transport server is unavailable in the destination site, then the message goes to a hub transport server in the closest site (as dictated by routing costs). If Exchange can't reach a hub transport server in the closest site, then it "backs off" and attempts to transfer the message to a hub transport server in the next closest site, and so on until the message is eventually on its way. If it is impossible to transfer a message to another site, Exchange queues it until a connection is possible.

- Messages that arrive into an intermediate hub transport server stay there until Exchange can transfer them to their final destination or to a hub transport server in a closer site.

Figure 6.14 shows Exchange 2007 servers installed into four Active Directory sites (Dublin, Paris, London, and Prague). Recall that you don't need to configure the send and receive connectors that allow messages to flow between the hub transport servers between sites as this is done automatically when you install the hub transport role on a server. Each of the sites support some mailbox servers and the Dublin site hosts two other connectors: one is a custom SMTP connector to route messages onwards to a smart host for delivery to Internet addresses; the other links Exchange 2007 to the legacy servers in the rest of the organization through a routing group connector. In this example, Dublin and Paris are hub routing sites. Now that we have a mental picture of how to link everything together, let's see how routing works in practice.

The simplest routing situation for the transport service is where a message sent on a mailbox server in Paris is addressed to a mailbox in Dublin.

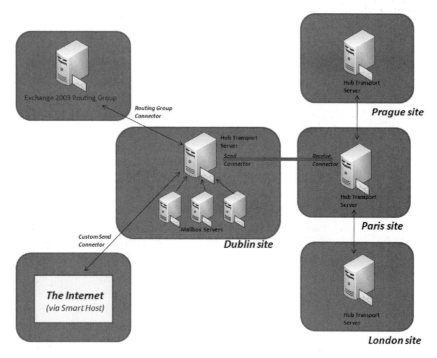

Figure 6.14
How the routing pieces fit together

The message travels from the mailbox server to the Paris hub transport server and is then transferred using a point-to-point SMTP connection over to the Dublin hub transport, which then delivers it to the mailbox server that hosts the destination mailbox.

Slightly more complex, a message from a mailbox in London to a mailbox in Dublin or Prague must travel through the hub transport server in Paris because it is a hub routing site en route to Dublin. The same is true for messages generated in Prague, which flow through Paris en route to Dublin or London. If the Paris hub transport server is unavailable, then messages queue up because they cannot be transferred. If Paris was not defined as a hub routing site, then the hub transport server in London could make direct connections to the hub transport server in Prague or Dublin.

All messages to Exchange 2003 must flow through the Dublin hub transport server because it is the only hub transport server that is associated with the routing group connector. All messages flowing in from Exchange 2003 travel through the Dublin hub transport server, which then makes the necessary connections to Paris to transfer messages that are not addressed to recipients in Dublin. Remember that Paris is a hub routing site, so messages from Exchange 2003 that are destined for mailboxes in Prague and London flow through Paris. The same situation exists for Internet traffic, which all travels through the send connector that the Dublin hub transport server supports.

If Dublin supported two hub transport servers, each of which supports the Internet and the routing group connector, then the transport service load balances any messages flowing into Dublin across the two hub transport servers. If one of the hub transport servers goes offline for some reason, the transport service diverts all traffic through the online hub transport service. The component called the Edge Connection Manager running within the transport service is responsible for establishing connections to remote servers, such as hub transport servers in remote Active Directory sites and smart SMTP routing hosts. It is the Edge Connection Manager that figures out how to load balance connections so that messages flow as quickly as possible. For example, if Paris has 60 messages queued to go to Dublin, it divides the number of waiting messages by 20 to calculate the number of connections that it should use. Dublin has two hub transport servers available, so Paris will establish two connections to one hub transport server and one connection to the other. Each connection delivers the messages one at a time off the queue and will disconnect when the queue empties. The number of messages that is actually handled by a connection depends on the size of the message and its attachments, the speed of the connection, and how quickly the other connections process messages off the queue.

The number of connections that a hub transport server can establish at any time can be controlled by a number of transport server parameters:

```
Get-TransportServer —id ExchHub1 | Select Max*

MaxConcurrentMailboxDeliveries   : 30
MaxConcurrentMailboxSubmissions : 20
MaxConnectionRatePerMinute       : 1000
MaxOutboundConnections           : 1000
MaxPerDomainOutboundConnections : 20
```

The important parameters here are:

- MaxPerDomainOutboundConnections limits the number of connections that can be established for a single queue.

- MaxOutboundConnections limits the total number of outbound connections that can be established by the server.

If you have good reason, use the `Set-TransportServer` command to set a different value:

```
Set-TransportServer —id ExchHub1 —MaxOutBoundConnections 1200
```

6.4.1 Resolving multiple paths

Exchange 2007 routing is deterministic in that it always picks a path to route a message. The examples that we have explored to date have involved relatively simple routing decisions because only one real path has been available from one site to another. The question now is how does Exchange make a decision on the routing path when multiple connectors are available?

- Most specific connector: Use the connector that supports the most specific address space when compared to the address for the message.

- Connector cost: The sum of the cost is the cost of the link to the connector plus the cost of the address space. The link cost is zero when the connector is hosted in the same Active Directory site.

- Closest proximity: Use a local connector whenever possible in the following order—connector hosted on local server, connector within the same Active Directory site, connector in a remote Active Directory site. Note that it is possible to give a connector a local scope, meaning that it is only available to hub transport servers in the same site. This is similar to the scoping functionality that is supported by Exchange 5.5 and Exchange 2000/2003.

- Alphanumerically lowest: To break ties, if all else is equal, pick the connector with the alphanumerically lowest name. For example, Dublin wins over Paris.

- An Exchange 2007 connector is always selected before routing across an Exchange 2003 connector. If Exchange 2007 is forced to route via Exchange 2003, it selects the lowest-cost Exchange 2003 connector that is available. If two connectors have the same cost, the one with the lowest alphanumeric connector name is chosen.

To help illustrate how messages are routing, Figure 6.15 provides a more complex routing environment than the previous example.

6.4.2 Most specific connector

Most specific means that Exchange looks at the address provided by a message and attempts to find the connector that most closely matches the address. Our example routing topology has two routes that messages can take

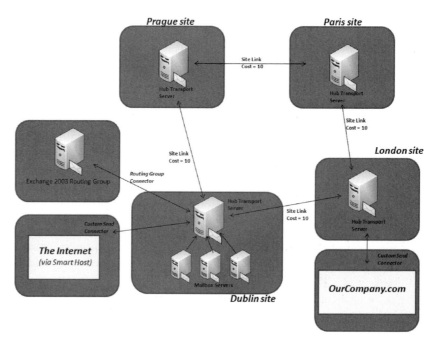

Figure 6.15
*A more complex
routing example*

to external addresses. The Dublin site hosts an SMTP connector that routes via a smart host, and its address space is configured as "*", meaning that it can handle messages sent to any domain. The London site has another SMTP connector that routes messages to just one external domain, ourcompany.com, so its address space is configured to be "ourcompany.com." You might have this kind of situation where you're acquiring a company and want a connector in place to handle traffic during a period of due diligence before you can progress to full integration.

If a user in Prague sends a message to a recipient in xyz.com, Exchange routes the message from Prague to Dublin and then out through the SMTP connector to the smart host. If a user in Prague wants to send to a recipient in ourcompany.com, the SMTP connector in London is selected because its address space is an exact match for the destination domain. The same is true for any message generated in the organization that goes to a recipient in ourcompany.com, even though the message may have to transit other sites en route and so incur a higher routing cost and even for messages sent by users in Dublin, despite the presence of a local SMTP connector that can handle external traffic. Of course, if all links are available, the hub transport server in Prague will make a direct connection to the hub transport server in London to transfer the message.

6.4.3 **Connector cost**

Exchange calculates the cost of routing a message as the cost of the site link that the message has to transit plus the cost of using a connector. If two connectors are available that can handle a message, Exchange chooses the one with the lowest total cost. For example, if the Paris site also hosted a connector to ourcompany.com and assuming that both connectors have the same cost, Exchange would route messages from Prague via that connector rather than London because the total site link cost of getting from Prague to London is (10 + 10) = 20 + connector cost, whereas the site link cost to Paris is 10.

6.4.4 **Closest proximity**

Microsoft has supported the concept of connector scoping since Exchange 5.5, which can limit the availability of a connector to a site. Exchange 2000 and 2003 support connector scoping on a routing group basis. In Exchange 2007, you can limit the availability of a connector to the hub transport servers in a specific Active Directory site. The only problem is that EMC does not expose this feature and you have to apply scoping by either setting a scope when the connector is created with the `New-SendConnector` command or later on by updating the scope of the connector with the `Set-SendConnector` command.

In this example, we update the address space for a connector so that it handles traffic to the xyz.com domain. Prefixing the address space with "local:" means that Exchange will not publish the availability of the connector outside the local Active Directory site. The effect of scoping this connector as local is that the hub transport servers outside the local Active Directory site will ignore this connector even for messages addressed to the xyz.com domain that would otherwise be routed via this connector following the principle of "most specific connector."

```
Set-SendConnector –id 'SMTP to Custom Domains' –AddressSpaces
'local:xyz.com'
```

After the command completes, we can view the address spaces supported by the available SMTP send connectors in the organization with the `Get-SendConnector` command:

```
Get-SendConnector | Select Name, AddressSpaces, Enabled, IsScopedConnector

Identity                    AddressSpaces        Enabled   IsScopedConnector
--------                    -------------        -------   -----------------
SMTP to the Internet        {smtp:*;1}           True      False
```

```
EdgeSync - Dublin to Internet {smtp:*;100}         True       False
EdgeSync - Inbound to Dublin  {smtp:--;100}        True       False
SMTP to Custom domains        {Local:smtp:xyz.com;1} True     True
```

As you can see, the "SMTP to custom domains" connector is scoped to be local and the IsScopedConnector flag is set to inform hub transport servers that they need to be aware of scoping when they generate routing paths.

6.4.5 The role of hub routing sites

Administrators exercise control over routing in Exchange 2000/2003 organizations by creating routing groups and connectors. The move to base message routing on Active Directory sites in Exchange 2007 removes routing groups from the equation, but the need still exists for administrators to be able to exercise control over message routing in situations such as leaf and spoke networks. Microsoft's answer is the hub site, a new property that you can set on an Active Directory site to give the site a special role within the Exchange routing topology.

When you configure an Active Directory site as an Exchange hub site, any Exchange 2007 servers located in other Active Directory sites that connect directly to the hub site via site links will send their messages through hub transport servers in the hub site instead of making direct connections to hub transport servers in other sites. Servers in sites that are not adjacent to a hub site will continue to make direct connections with each other. For example, if we enable London as a hub site, messages from Dublin to Paris will always flow through London, but messages from Prague to Paris will go through a direct connection. Hub routing sites, scoped connectors, and connector costs are the only levers that you can use to influence the path messages take. For instance, you cannot, force selected hub transport servers to serve selected mailbox servers unless you group these servers together into sites and then configure costs and sites to channel messages along that path.

You enable an Active Directory site to be a routing hub site with the Set-AdSite command. For example, to set the London Active Directory site to be a routing hub:

```
Set-AdSite —id London —HubSiteEnabled $True
```

To check that the Set-AdSite command has had the desired effect, use the Get-AdSite command:

```
Get-AdSite —id London | Format-List
```

Look for the HubSiteEnabled property to check that it is True.

Hub routing sites are the closest things that we have in Exchange 2007 to Exchange 2000/2003 routing groups, but it would be a mistake to replace routing groups on a one-for-one basis with Active Directory hub sites. Instead, the better idea is to sit down and figure out the optimum routing topology for your Exchange 2007 organization after you have completed your migration to Exchange 2007 and have implemented whatever server consolidation is possible during the migration. You can then select obvious hub sites and implement them slowly, keeping an eye on overall message delivery performance and throughput as you implement the hubs.

6.4.6   Site link costs versus routing costs

Administrators do not necessarily configure Active Directory site link costs for optimal mail routing, so it is possible to configure Exchange to use a different value to base its routing decisions. You do this by setting a value for the ExchangeCost property for the site link by running the Set-ADSiteLink command on a hub transport server. For example:

```
Set-ADSiteLink —id 'London to Paris' —ExchangeCost 1
```

This command tells Exchange to use a cost of "1" (one) when calculating routing costs rather than the normal site link cost as used by Active Directory replication. You cannot see the ExchangeCost value if you look at the properties of the site link through the Active Directory Sites and Services console, so you have to use the Get-ADSiteLink command to view this information. For example:

```
Get-ADSiteLink | Format-List

Cost                : 10
ADCost              : 10
ExchangeCost        : 1
Sites               : {Bern, Adelaide, Warrington, Bellevue, Amstelveen, Dublin}
AdminDisplayName    :
ExchangeVersion     : 0.0 (6.5.6500.0)
Name                : Core Site Link
Transports,CN=Sites,CN=Configuration,DC=xyz,DC=com
Identity            : xyz.com/Configuration/Sites/Inter-Site Transports/IP/Core
Site Link
ObjectCategory      : xyz.com/Configuration/Schema/Site-Link
ObjectClass         : {top, siteLink}
OriginatingServer   : dc02.xyz.com
IsValid             : True
```

In this instance, there is an Active Directory site link cost of 10 and an Exchange cost of 1.

6.4.7   Instructing mailbox servers

The default is for mailbox servers to be able to connect to any hub transport server in a site. Sometimes, you may want to reserve hub transport servers for a special purpose, such as to handle the message traffic in and out of an Exchange organization. In large organizations, you may be able to justify setting aside one or more hub transport servers for this purpose because of the sheer volume of messages. Another advantage that you can gain with dedicated hub transport servers for external traffic is that during a virus attack, you can close off the connections to these hub transport servers without affecting the flow of messages within the Exchange organization.

You can use the `Set-MailboxServer` command to configure mailbox servers so that they can connect only to a restricted set of hub transport servers. For example, this command instructs the ExchMbxSvr1 mailbox server to submit messages only to the ExchHub1 and ExchHub2 hub transport servers:

```
Set-MailboxServer —id ExchMbxSvr1
—SubmissionServerOverrideList ExchHub1, ExchHub2
```

To check that the setting is what you expect, use the `Get-Mailbox-Server` command:

```
Get-MailboxServer —id ExchMbxSvr1 | Select Name, Submission*

Name                       SubmissionServerOverrideList
----                       ----------------------------
ExchMbxSvr1                {ExchHub1, ExchHub2}
```

6.4.8   Bypassing some connections

Exchange 2007 ignores Active Directory sites that do not include a hub transport server. In the scenario described, we could have Active Directory sites in Lisbon, Brussels, and Amsterdam (perhaps hosting Exchange 2003 servers), but because these sites don't include an Exchange 2007 hub transport server, the Active Directory Topology service excludes them from the data that it provides to the transport service to determine available routing costs and paths. This fact identifies an issue to take into account when you review an existing Exchange 2003 routing topology. You should look at the Active Directory site layout and map it against the Exchange 2003 routing group structure to determine whether the two are comparable (or compatible). The review will allow you to figure out if any changes are necessary, such as if an Active Directory site needs to host a hub transport server to enable messages to flow through the site. During the same review, it is a good idea to attempt to simplify the routing topology as much as possible, as it is possible that the legacy of previous designs generated a nonoptimal topology that has not been touched since you implemented it for Exchange 2000 or 2003.

If you operate in a mixed-mode organization, Exchange 2007 takes this fact into account when it calculates the best path for messages and will select the route that keeps messages under the control of Exchange 2007 as far as possible as they progress toward their destination. In other words, Exchange 2007 favors routing a message across an interim Active Directory site instead of across a connector into Exchange 2003. In addition, Exchange 2007 knows if a destination mailbox is on an Exchange 2007 server and will never route messages to these mailboxes across a legacy connector, even if the legacy connector has the lowest connection costs.

Exchange 2007 routing is straightforward to the extreme and that everything proceeds on a predictable basis—once you understand how your Active Directory sites are arranged and connected together, you will understand how Exchange routes messages.

6.4.9 Protocol logging

Normal behavior is for the transport engine not to log protocol events as messages come in to receive connectors or dispatched through send connectors. You can turn the protocol logging level from "None" to "Verbose" by changing the properties of a connector, as shown in Figure 6.16. Turning on verbose logging can be a useful way to gain information about why a connector is failing to send or receive messages. For example, you may be able to see that Exchange is declining to accept an incoming SMTP connection because of a problem with authentication.

Alternatively, you can use the `Set-SendConnector` and `Set-Receive-Connector` commands to set the protocol logging level on selected send and receive connectors. For example:

```
Set-ReceiveConnector —id 'SMTP from External Servers'
—ProtocolLoggingLevel Verbose
Set-SendConnector —id 'Outgoing SMTP' —ProtocolLoggingLevel
Verbose
```

Figure 6.16
Setting protocol logging

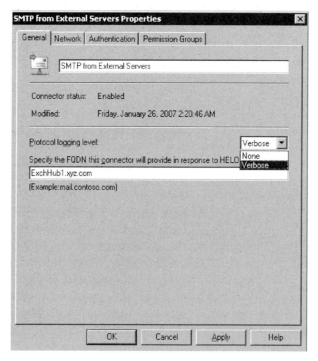

After you set the protocol logging level to verbose, the transport service logs the protocol event in log files in the C:\Program Files\Microsoft\ Exchange Server\TransportRoles\Logs\ProtocolLog\SmtpReceive directory for receive connectors and C:\Program Files\Microsoft\Exchange Server\ TransportRoles\Logs\ProtocolLog\SmtpSend for send connectors. Figure 6.17 shows the output from a receive connector log. In this case, you can see that a message has come in through the "SMTP from External Servers" connector from a server called Oldhub1.xyz.com. You can see the protocol events occur as the two servers negotiate a connection, including passing the ESMTP verbs that are supported during the connection.

Protocol logging can consume a significant amount of disk space on busy hub transport or Edge servers. Some organizations report that they see between 5 and 15GB of information generated daily, so you have to keep an eye on this activity if you decide to enable protocol logging.

6.4.10 X.400 support

Exchange 2007 does not support an X.400 connector, so if you need to route messages to X.400 recipients, you have to keep an Exchange 2003 server in the organization to host an X.400 connector. Unlike previous versions of Exchange, the X.400 addresses that are assigned to users are not

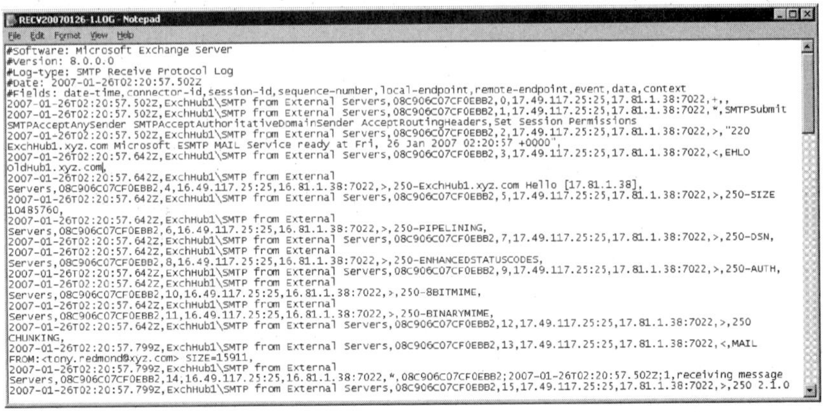

Figure 6.17
Output from protocol log

required for routing, so if you don't have a need for these addresses, you can safely remove them.

6.4.11 Bifurcation

Exchange performs message bifurcation to better utilize network connections and bandwidth. Bifurcation occurs automatically within the transport system and users are not aware that it has occurred unless they examine message headers to determine the path that a message takes to get to different mailboxes. The basic concept is that Exchange transports a message to a single optimum point within the network and then splits the message to deliver individual copies to mailboxes. Active Directory site costs determine where the optimum point is within the network for bifurcation to occur, but it is usually the site furthest along the message's path to final delivery.

The simplest example of bifurcation is when a message goes to two recipients whose mailboxes are in different sites. Using our sample routing topology, if a user in Dublin sends a message to users in Paris and Prague, Exchange can send a single copy of the message to the hub transport server in Paris. When the message arrives on the Paris hub transport server, Exchange then sends another copy to go to Prague. Clearly, this is a very simple example and things get more complex in large routing networks with many sites and route permutations. For instance, once you introduce hub sites, you will see that messages flow through the hub transport servers and may be bifurcated there or at the next link in the routing chain. Bifurcation can occur for other reasons than routing. If recipients chose different formats to receive messages in (some clients can select to receive messages in plain text, some like HTML), then Exchange has to create separate copies of the message to deliver in the recipients' chosen format.

6.4.12 Header firewalls

The transport service deploys header firewalls to protect Exchange against the possibility that a hacker will spoof an x-header and cause Exchange to perform some processing that it should not. X-headers are user-defined (usually application-defined) unofficial header fields that SMTP messages transport in the message header. As we will see when we discuss the Exchange 2007 anti-spam agents, Exchange places x-headers such as a value for the spam confidence level in message headers to indicate that its anti-spam agents have processed messages. If you examine a message header after it has passed through a hub transport server or Edge server where the anti-spam agents are active, you will see x-headers such as x-MS-Exchange-Organization-Antispam report.

Header firewalls remove x-headers from inbound messages that enter Exchange from untrusted sources. They also process outgoing messages to remove x-headers generated by Exchange if the messages go to untrusted destinations. The decision whether to remove headers is dictated by the permissions that apply to the send or receive connector that the messages flow through.

6.5   Transport configuration

In Exchange 2000/2003, the Global Message settings define properties such as the maximum message size. Exchange 2007 does not provide the ability to set global messaging defaults through EMC. Instead, you use the Set-TransportConfig command to define transport configuration settings for the organization and Get-TransportConfig to report on the current values. In a mixed-mode organization, the existing settings for the maximum size of an incoming message, the maximum size of an outgoing message, and the maximum number of recipients allowed per message are retained, but in a new Exchange organization the value for these parameters is set to be "unlimited." For example, the settings reported by Get-TransportConfig might look like this:

```
Get-TransportConfig

ClearCategories               : True
GenerateCopyOfDSNFor          : {}
InternalSMTPServers           : {15.0.0.0-16.255.255.255}
JournalingReportNdrTo         : <>
MaxDumpsterSizePerStorageGroup : 0B
MaxDumpsterTime               : 00:00:00
MaxReceiveSize                : unlimited
MaxRecipientEnvelopeLimit     : unlimited
```

```
MaxSendSize                      : unlimited
TLSReceiveDomainSecureList       : {}
TLSSendDomainSecureList          : {}
VerifySecureSubmitEnabled        : False
VoicemailJournalingEnabled       : True
Xexch50Enabled                   : True
```

Setting a new value is easy:

```
Set-TransportConfig —MaxSendSize 50MB
```

Table 6.3 lists the properties that you can set with the `Set-Transport-Config` command and their meaning.

Table 6.3   *Parameters for Set-TransportConfig*

Parameters	Meaning
ClearCategories	Setting controls whether the transport engine clears Outlook categories during content conversion. The default is $True.
GenerateCopyOfDSNFor	Defines whether any DSN messages are copied to the Postmaster mailbox (as defined by `Set-TransportServer`). The desired DSNs are defined by their code (for example 5.1.1). By default, no messages are copied.
InternalSMTPServers	The list of IP addresses of SMTP servers that the anti-spam agents consider to be internal.
JournalingReportNdrTo	The mailbox that the journaling agent will send journal reports to if the journal mailbox is unavailable.
MaxDumpsterSizePerStorageGroup	The maximum size of the dumpster used by CCR to recover in-transit messages in case of lossy failures. Only used when CCR is configured.
MaxDumpsterTime	The maximum time that messages remain in the transport dumpster. Only used when CCR is configured. To enable the transport dumpster, the size of the dumpster must be greater than 0B (it should be something reasonable such as 100MB) and the dumpster time has to be nonzero. A good default value is 0.00:10:00, or 10 minutes.

Table 6.3   *Parameters for Set-TransportConfig (continued)*

Parameters	Meaning
MaxReceiveSize	The maximum size of message that can be received by the organization.
MaxRecipientEnvelopeLimit	The maximum number of recipients that can be in the header of an incoming message (including the results of group expansion—groups are counted as 1 even if there are many recipients in the group).
MaxSendSize	The maximum size of message that can be sent within the organization.
TLSReceiveDomainSecureList	List of domains that are configured for mutual TLS authentication through receive connectors.
TLSSendDomainSecureList	List of domains that are configured for mutual TLS authentication through send connectors.
VerifySecureSubmitEnabled	Set to $True to force MAPI clients to submit messages over a secure channel (encrypted RPCs). The default is $False. By default, Outlook 2007 uses a secure channel, but previous versions do not.
VoicemailJournalingEnabled	Defines whether voicemail messages should be journalled by the journal agent.
Xexch50Enabled	Defines whether backwards compatability should be enabled for Exchange 2000/2003 servers. The default is $True.

Like the Global Message settings in Exchange 2003, these transport configuration properties apply to all Exchange 2007 hub transport servers within the organization. Other commands influence the way that messages are processed by the transport engine. For example, you can configure receive connectors with parameters such as the maximum number of recipients for a message and the maximum number of connections it will accept in total or from one source. For example:

```
Set-ReceiveConnector –id 'Internet Connector for
Organization'
–MaxRecipientsPerMessage 250
```

After making this change, if the connector is presented with a message that has more than 250 recipients, it accepts the message for the maximum permitted (250) and rejects the rest of the message. Most modern SMTP senders will then resend the message up to the permitted maximum and continue in this loop until all of the message recipients have been processed. After the receive connector has accepted the message (end of data transfer), it checks to see whether the message is too large (size is greater than MaxMessageSize). Even here, there are other checks that have to happen because you can configure an individual mailbox to reject messages that are smaller than the organization's acceptable maximum size. For example, if I did this:

```
Set-Mailbox –id Redmond –MaxReceiveSize 2MB
```

Then Exchange will reject any message sent to that mailbox that is over 2MB in size even if the receive connector and the global transport settings allow the message. Note that authenticated users can also have a maximum permitted message send size that Exchange will respect even if it blows the limits that apply to connectors. I guess that the logic here is that an administrator must know what they are doing when they allow certain mailboxes to send very large messages, so Exchange should treat these situations as exceptions and permit them to pass.

Being able to send a very large message is no guarantee that the message will be able to reach its final destination unless it is within the Exchange organization because it is very likely that the message will encounter a limit on an external connector or server along its path that will result in a rejection[5]. Even within an Exchange organization, if a user who has the ability to send a 10MB message sends such a message to a mailbox that has a lower receive limit configured, then Exchange will reject the message because it is the recipient's limit that governs their ability to receive and you'll receive a message similar to the left-hand screen shown in Figure 6.18. By comparison, the message generated by Exchange 2003 to report the same problem is shown in the right-hand screen. You can see that the quality and comprehensiveness of the delivery service messages generated by Exchange 2007 is in a different world to those generated by previous versions. These messages are clear and contain enough information for even a nontechnical user to figure out what's gone wrong, which is not always the case before.

The normal default value for maximum message size used for Exchange 2007 send and receive connectors is 10MB. To change this value on a send connector:

---

5.   You may also encounter problems sending large messages to legacy Exchange 2003 servers within the same organization. See the Exchange 2007 release notes for details.

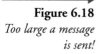

Figure 6.18
*Too large a message
is sent!*

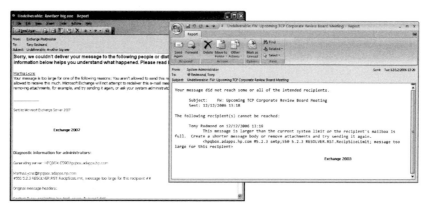

```
Set-SendConnector —id 'Outbound to Legacy' —MaxMessageSize
20MB
```

And for a receive connector:

```
Set-ReceiveConnector —id 'Inbound from XYZ' —MaxMessageSize
15MB
```

If you don't know the identifiers for the various connectors in the organization, use the `Get-SendConnector` or `Get-ReceiveConnector` commands to list all of the current connectors, including those hosted by Edge servers.

It is possible for a message size to fluctuate as it makes its way from initial entry via an Edge or hub transport server to final delivery. Format conversion, encoding, and agent processing are reasons why message size can increase and you wouldn't want Exchange to reject a message just because of some internal processing. Exchange therefore stamps a message with an X-header called X-MS-Exchange-Organization-OriginalSize and stores the size of the message when it is first encountered there. Downstream checks performed by hub transport servers in other sites use this data instead of the current message size when they decide whether or not to block a message. Note that some messages bypass checking—system messages, agent-generated messages, and anything to do with journaling and message quarantining.

The MaxRecipientEnvelopeLimit determines the maximum number of individual recipients that can be in the P1 envelope for a message. The exact number of recipients is unknown until any distribution groups are fully expanded. Some problems occurred in Exchange 2000/2003 where partial delivery could happen if a user sent a message to a group and the subsequent expansion generated enough recipients to exceed the limit.

Some members of the group (up to the maximum recipient limit) received the message while the remainder did not. This is clearly not desired behavior as you would always want to allow delivery to a group if a user has the necessary permission to send to that group, no matter how large the group. Exchange 2007 changed its processing so that each group in a message header is treated as one recipient for the purpose of checking against the maximum recipient limit.

6.5.1 Transport configuration file

Exchange 2007 hub transport and Edge servers maintain a routing configuration file called EdgeTransport.Exe.Config located in the \bin directory. As shown below, the file holds details such as the default retry interval for queued messages.

```
<configuration>
    <runtime>
        <gcServer enabled="true" />
    </runtime>
    <appSettings>
        <add key="AgentLogEnabled" value="true" />
        <add key="ResolverRetryInterval" value="30" />
        <add key="DeliverMoveMailboxRetryInterval" value="30" />
        <add key="ResolverLogLevel" value="Disabled" />
        <add key="ExpansionSizeLimit" value="20000" />
        <add key="MaxIdleTimeBeforeResubmit" value="12:00:00" />
        <add key="MailboxDeliveryQueueRetryInterval" value="00:05:00" />
        <add key="PFReplicaAgeThresholdHours" value="48" />
        <add key="DeferredReloadTimeoutSeconds" value="5" />
        <add key="MaxDeferredNotifications" value="20" />
        <add key="MaxQueueViewerQueryResultCount" value="250000" />
        <add key="RoutingConfigReloadInterval" value="12:00:00" />
        <add key="DumpsterAllMail" value="false" />
        <add key="DumpsterAllowDuplicateDelivery" value="false" />
        <add key="DatabaseCheckPointDepthMax" value="20971520" />
        <add key="DatabaseMaxCacheSize" value="134217728" />
        <add key="DatabaseCacheFlushStart" value="3" />
        <add key="DatabaseCacheFlushStop" value="5" />
        <add key="QueueDatabaseBatchSize" value="40" />
        <add key="QueueDatabaseBatchTimeout" value="100" />
        <add key="QueueDatabaseMaxConnections" value="4" />
        <add key="QueueDatabaseLoggingFileSize" value="5242880" />
```

```
    <add key="QueueDatabaseLoggingBufferSize" value="524288" />
    <add key="QueueDatabaseMaxBackgroundCleanupTasks" value="32" />
    <add key="QueueDatabaseOnlineDefragEnabled" value="true" />
    <add key="QueueDatabaseOnlineDefragSchedule" value="1:00:00" />
    <add key="QueueDatabaseOnlineDefragTimeToRun" value="3:00:00" />
    <add key="ContentConversionCacheEnabled" value="false" />
  </appSettings>
</configuration>
```

Normally, you should not have to touch the transport configuration file unless you need to change a parameter that cannot be updated through a shell command. For example, if you want to move the location of the transport queue database, you will find that there is no parameter to change through the Set-TransportConfig command. Instead, you will have to open the transport configuration file with a text editor and add the necessary commands to tell the transport service where the files are located. The lines shown below move the transport queue database and its transaction logs to new locations on drive D:

```
<add key="QueueDatabasePath" value="D:\Data\TransportQueue" />
<add key="QueueDatabaseLoggingPath" value="D:\Data\TransportLogs" />
```

After making the change to the transport configuration file, you have to stop the transport service and move the queue database and its associated files to the new locations before you restart the transport service.

Another common customization is to include lines in the transport configuration file that affect how the transport service works when hub transport and Edge servers come under load. Exchange 2007 incorporates the concept of back pressure, which means that when a server is under load, it will stop accepting new connections in order to reduce load on the server. Eventually, the conditions that cause the back pressure to mount will ease and the transport service will resume normal working. Conditions such as free disk space and available memory are used to determine when a back-pressure condition exists. For example, if less than 4GB free (disk and database) space exists on the drive that holds the message queue database, Exchange applies back pressure. You can alter this behavior by customizing the transport configuration file.

As an example of how you can customize the values that control back pressure, here are the lines necessary to determine thresholds for normal working (less than 75% memory used), medium pressure (less than or equal to 78% memory used), and high pressure (83% or greater memory used).

```
<add key="PercentagePrivateBytesUsedNormalThreshold" value=75>
<add key="PercentagePrivateBytesUsedMediumThreshold" value=78>
<add key="PercentagePrivateBytesUsedHighThreshold" value=83>
```

It is very easy to make a mistake when you edit configuration files and you will not see any indication that you have caused a problem until the transport service attempts to read the configuration file and potentially fails. Be very careful when you make changes and always test the change on a test system before you apply it in production.

6.5.2 Routing logs

Exchange 2007 calculates its routing table every 12 hours and maintains the routing table in memory. Updates can also be provoked if something changes in the routing configuration, such as the addition of a new connector somewhere in the organization, installation of a new hub transport or Edge server, or if the transport service is restarted.

After it regenerates the routing table, Exchange writes a copy of the table into an XML format log file that you can find in the C:\Program Files\ Microsoft\Exchange Server\TransportRoles\Logs\Routing directory. The log is composed of 22 sectors that collectively form Exchange's knowledge of the current routing topology. Microsoft has not provided a GUI or other tool to interpret and analyze the routing log, so the only way of accessing its contents to gain an insight into how Exchange routes messages is to open the routing log with a browser (Figure 6.19) or other XML editor.

The sections in the routing log are:

1. Routing tables: links server names[6], mailbox databases, legacy servers with server routes.

2. Exchange topology: links server names with topology servers (servers that can participate in routing).

3. Topology servers: lists the Exchange servers that can participate in routing.

4. Topology sites: lists all the Active Directory sites, including those where an Exchange hub transport server is not present.

5. Topology Site Link: lists all the Active Directory site links.

6. Active Directory Site Relay Map: lists the Active Directory paths to every site containing an Exchange server.

6.   Distinguished names are used to identify servers.

7.   Active Directory Topology Path: Lists routes to every remote Active Directory site.

8.   Target Site: Lists Active Directory sites that contain hub transport servers.

9.   Routing Group Relay Map: Lists the routing groups for legacy Exchange servers.

10. Routing Group Topology Site: Lists every routing group and their connectors.

11. Routing Group Topology Link: Lists the links between routing groups.

12. Routing Group Topology Path: Links routing groups with connectors.

13. Routing Group Connector Route: Lists routes to next hop for connectors.

14. Server Route: Lists every Exchange server and a route to it.

15. Connector Routing: Lists every connector route in the organization.

16. Connector Route: Lists every connector in the organization.

17. SMTP Send Connector Configuration: Lists every SMTP Send Connector in the organization.

18. Address space: List all the address spaces and type available within the organization.

19. Legacy Gateway Connector: List every Notes and GroupWise connector used by Exchange 2000 or 2003 in the organization.

20. Non-SMTP Gateway Connection: List all connectors that use the drop directory.

21. Address Type Routing: Maps address types to SMTP connector index.

22. SMTP Connector Index: Maps each part of SMTP address space to a node and associates it with a connector. For example, xyz.com will generate nodes for "xyz" and "com."

It is possible that Microsoft will provide a utility program in the future to help administrators understand the contents of the routing log, but until then it is best to leave the routing log alone, unless you want to give yourself a headache by figuring out the connections that lead from one part of the file to another.

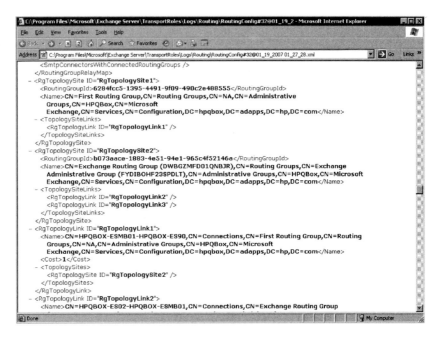

Figure 6.19
Routing log content

6.6   Queues

Once the transport service has categorized and processed messages, they are placed on queues for onward delivery. Queues are of two types: local queues hold messages that are going to mailbox servers (any mailbox server) and remote queues hold messages going to an external SMTP server. Because of the speed that Exchange processes messages, you should only find messages hanging around on queues if problems exist to stop Exchange moving them to the next hop to their destination. Perhaps the problem is a temporary network glitch; maybe the destination hub transport server is unreachable because it is down to have a service pack applied the link to the Internet might be unavailable or some other problem might be present. If Exchange encounters a problem sending a message off a queue, it retries connections four times at 15-second intervals and then pauses for an hour to see if whatever condition is causing the queue to build up goes away. Local delivery queues are an exception to this rule as they continue to retry every 5 minutes.

The easiest way to find out what is happening with queues is with the `Get-Queue` command. This command asks Exchange to return the current status of all the queues on the current server. If you are not running on a hub transport server, you will have to include the name of the server that you want to view the queues for or you will see an error indicating that the

Microsoft Exchange Transport Service is not started. In this example, we ask about the queues on a server and specify that Exchange should provide the queue information sorted by message count so that any problem queues are at the top.

```
Get-Queue —Server HPQBOX-ES90 —SortOrder:-MessageCount


Identity                  DeliveryType Status MessageCount NextHopDoma
--------                  ----------- ------ ------------ -------------
HPQBOX-ES90\821           SmartHost... Retry  6           smtp1-americas.xyz.com
HPQBOX-ES90\823           MapiDelivery Ready  0           hpqbox-s90.hpqbox.adapps.hp.com
HPQBOX-ES90\Submission    Defined      Ready  0           Submission
```

We can see three queues. One of these (the MAPI Delivery queue) only exists when clients have submitted messages that have been transported to the hub transport server via MAPI. Exchange tears this queue down when it is not needed. The submission queue is there to accept messages from other servers. In this instance, the queue that we have a problem with is obviously queue 821 (Exchange allocates the queue number sequentially), which we can see is queuing messages for onward delivery to a smart host (the delivery type tells us this). We can also see the name of the smart host. The "Retry" status is one immediate indicator that a problem exists. If the queue status is "Active," then we know that Exchange is processing messages off the queue, even if the queue was increasing. A queue that increases while active may simply be an indication that the system is under load, that users are sending many messages, or that something is slowing mail flow elsewhere in the network. A growing Submission queue deserves investigation because it may indicate that the categorizer is experiencing difficulty resolving recipient addresses against the Active Directory (this error can only occur on hub transport servers, as Edge servers do not attempt to resolve recipients against the Active Directory). In this case, you will see errors such as "AD transient failure during resolve" noted in the LastError property of the Submission queue.

You may also want to look at the set of messages that are on a queue with the Get-Message command. By default, Get-Message retrieves all messages from all queues, but in this case we only want messages from the queue where we're having the problem, so we pass the queue name and also specify that we want to have the results returned sorted by size (the + sign indicates an ascending sort, – means do a descending sort):

```
Get-Message —Queue HPQBOX-ES90\821 —SortOrder:+Size
```

Each message has a separate identifier composed of the queue name plus a number. We need the message identifier if we want to perform operations such as suspend, resume, or remove a message.

The normal root cause with smart host queues is that a network problem is stopping Exchange connecting to the smart host, so we can check this out with a quick PING to the server. If PING responds, then we can check with TELNET to see whether we can establish a connection to port 25. If that test succeeds, we have to look elsewhere to determine where the problem lies. Perhaps the name of the smart host is wrong (a not uncommon problem when configuring smart hosts for the first time) or something more esoteric has happened. Of course, the first thing we should do before we plunge into a series of tests is to review whatever details the Get-Queue command can reveal to us about our problem queue. For example:

```
Get-Queue –identity 'HPQBOX-ES90\821' –Server HPQBOX-ES90 | Format-List

Identity          : HPQBOX-ES90\821
DeliveryType      : SmartHostConnectorDelivery
NextHopDomain     : smtp-americas.xyz.com
NextHopConnector  : 9ce1cbe0-3a24-4791-9a92-95525114476c
Status            : Retry
MessageCount      : 6
LastError         : 451 4.4.0 DNS query failed. The error was:
SMTPSEND.DNS.NonExistentDomain; nonexistent domain
LastRetryTime     : 1/8/2007 2:56:37 PM
NextRetryTime     : 1/8/2007 3:01:37 PM
IsValid           : True
ObjectState       : Unchanged
```

We can immediately see the root cause of our problem because DNS has reported that it cannot resolve the same of the smart host that we have configured on the send connector. Another common cause that you may see reported is when the remote server simply won't respond to a request to connect and send messages is:

"421 4.2.1 Unable to connect. Attempted failover to alternate host, but that did not succeed. Either there are no alternate hosts, or delivery failed to all alternate hosts."

The NextHopDomain property reported is either the name of a mailbox server, an SMTP server, or the name of the Active Directory site that Exchange is trying to transfer the message to. In the latter case, if there is only one hub transport server in the site, you'll know that it is the server that's causing the problem, otherwise it could be any of the hub transport servers in the site. Hub transport servers reject connections if they begin to exhaust resources using a feature called "Back Pressure" (see page 494), so this is another item for your checklist. If the problem server is a mailbox server, you should verify that the Store is running on the server, as it may be possible that the database that hosts the recipient's mailbox is dismounted or inoperative for some reason.

It may also be possible that some other administrator has suspended the queue for some reason. If this is the case, the queue status will be "Suspended" and you will have to determine why the queue was suspended and if you can resume it. You can resume a queue through the Queue Viewer or with the Resume-Queue command:

```
Resume-Queue —Identity 'HPQBOX-ES90\821'
```

Note that Exchange will clear queues automatically and immediately the underlying problem goes away and will tear down the queue after a couple of minutes if it is no longer required. Queues are transient objects that Exchange creates on demand, so the next time that someone sends a message to the smart host, Exchange creates a new queue and may allocate it number 825, 826, or whatever the next number is in sequential order. Exchange also clears queues when messages expire, which occurs by default after a message is more than two days old. The logic here is that a two-day-old message is not very useful to the recipient, so it is better to return it to the sender so that they can contact the intended recipient using another mechanism.

6.6.1   The Queue Viewer

EMS is a great way to perform a fast scan of queues or the messages on a queue to see if everything is okay, but if a server has more than a few messages queued, you may find that the Exchange Queue Viewer is a more convenient way to look at the queues (Figure 6.20). The Queue Viewer is one of the options that you access through the Toolbox section of EMC. You can connect to any hub transport server that you have at least view-only administrative permission for to view its queues. On busy hub transport servers there may quite a few messages in the queues and it can be difficult to locate the exact message that you are interested in. The Queue Viewer supports filters similar to those used by EMC. Figure 6.21 shows a filter that uses two properties, the sender's address, and the message subject, to locate a message.

Once you find the message you want, you can double-click on its entry in the list to see more details. The general properties of a message (Figure 6.22) allow you to see information such as the sender, recipients, and the date that the message was placed on the queue and when it will expire. The

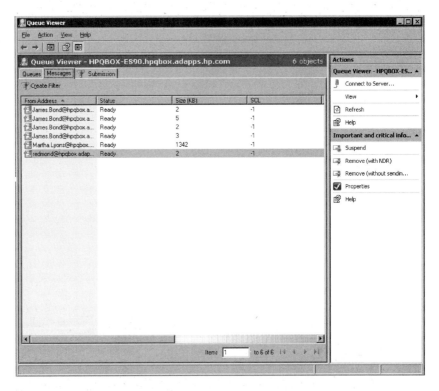

Figure 6.20
Exchange 2007 Queue Viewer

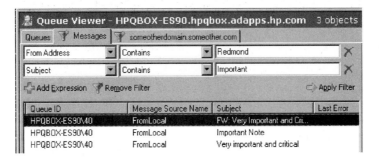

Figure 6.21
Applying a filter to find a message in a queue

information displayed here is identical to that returned by the `Get-Message` command if you pass it the message identifier. For example:

```
Get-Message —id 'HPQBOX-ES90\21\65' —IncludeRecipientInfo |
Format-List
```

After viewing the properties of a message, you may decide to remove it from the queue (with or without an NDR going back to the sender), or suspend it so that the message remains on the queue until you decide to either

Figure 6.22

*Properties of a
queued message*

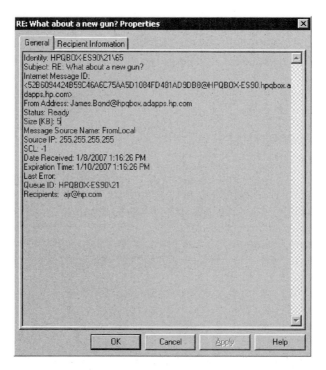

release (with the Resume option) or remove it. As shown in Figure 6.23, the Queue Viewer tells you exactly what it will do when you choose to remove a message from a queue.

You can also suspend a message with the `Suspend-Message` command by passing the message identifier. Exchange lists the message identifier when you execute the `Get-Message` command.

```
Suspend-Message —id 'ExchHub1\60\55'
```

After you fix the problem, you can release the message again with the `Resume-Message` command:

```
Resume-Message —id 'ExchHub1\60\55'
```

The `Remove-Message` command is used to delete a message from a queue. In this example, we send an NDR back to the sender to tell them what's happened. If you set the —WithNDR parameter to $False, Exchange deletes the message without sending an NDR:

```
Remove-Message —id 'ExchHub1\60\65' —WithNDR $True
```

You do not have to suspend a message before you can delete it.

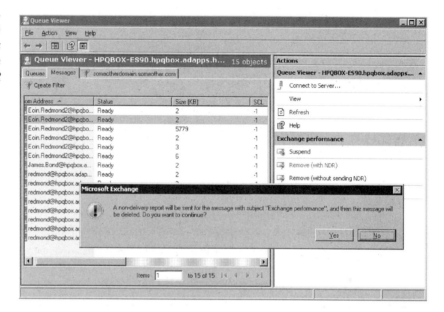

Figure 6.23
Removing a message without an NDR

You might expect that you can use the Queue Viewer if you have Exchange View-Only Administrator permissions on a server but this is not the case. Instead, you need to hold at least the Exchange Server Administrator role for the server that you run the Queue Viewer on and your account must be a member of the local Administrators group for the server.

6.6.2 The Unreachable queue

If Exchange can't work out how to route a message for any reason, it places the message onto the Unreachable queue. Messages remain on the Unreachable queue until a viable route exists and the Transport engine has updated its routing tables to include the new information. For example, it is possible that some messages are addressed to an Internet domain that isn't supported by any of your connectors, so you may add a new connector (or the domain to the address space served by an existing connector) that makes it possible for Exchange to route the message. If the problem is with a message to an Exchange recipient, it indicates that there's an issue with the site topology for hub and mailbox servers that you need to investigate and debug.

You can use the `Get-Queue` command followed by `Get-Message` to find out the reason why messages have been put into the Unreachable queue.

```
Get-Queue —id ExchHub1\Unreachable | Get-Message | Format-List
```

```
Identity                      DeliveryType Status MessageCount NextHop     Domain
--------                      ------------ ------ ------------ ----------  ---
ExchHub1\Unreachable          Unreachable  Ready  36           Unreachable Domain
```

If you look for the last error, it should tell you the reason why Exchange has placed that particular message into the Unreachable queue. If there are multiple reasons (possibly because multiple recipients for the message have caused the message to go into the queue), you can check what recipients are associated with the problem domains by specifying –IncludeRecipientInfo to force Exchange to include the recipient information for the queued messages. We write the output to a text file so that we can browse the content with an editor:

```
Get-Queue —id ExchHub1\Unreachable | Get-Message —
IncludeRecipientInfo > c:\Temp\UnreachableInfo.txt
```

Exchange records a lot of data about the queued messages. We are interested in the recipients and the last error as these pieces of information will help us to understand why Exchange believes that it cannot deliver a message. Here's what you might see:

```
Recipients        : {ajr@xyz.com}
Status            : Ready
Size              : 17741B
LastError         : A matching connector cannot be found to route
the external recipient
```

In this instance, we can see that Exchange has determined that no connector is available to route to the address "ajr@xyz.com." It may be that this organization has no SMTP connector available to route to the xyz.com domain or that there's no SMTP connector available to route to any external recipients.

Another (less common) example may occur for mailboxes within our own organization:

```
Recipients        : {EoinP@xyz.com}
Status            : Ready
Size              : 167975B
LastError        : The mailbox recipient does not have a mailbox
database
```

This kind of error indicates a problem with the Active Directory because the user account that Exchange is trying to deliver to is marked as a user mailbox without a value to tell Exchange what database their mailbox is located in. You shouldn't see an error like this very often, but it does demonstrate the kind of worthwhile information that you can gain by interrogating the queues if problems occur with message flow.

6.6.3 Poison messages

Exchange 2007 maintains a special queue that it uses to hold messages that it cannot deal with. These messages are called "poison messages" because they cause the worker process that is handling the message to crash after the message has been committed into the mail queue database. Exchange recovers from the crash by spawning another worker process. At the same time, Exchange writes the message identifier for the problem message into the system registry and increments its poison count by 1. When the new worker process starts to process messages from the queue, it checks the registry using the message identifier so it can recognize that a particular message caused a crash. The worker process attempts to process the message again, and the same steps happen if a crash occurs again. The next time a worker process attempts to deal with the message, it will see that its poison count is set at 2, which is a hardcoded threshold that says "there's something flaky with this message," so the worker process moves the message to the poison queue rather than attempting to process it again. You'll also see entries like this in the application event log:

```
Event Type: Warning
Event Source: Transport
Event Category: PoisonMessage
Event ID: 10001
Date:   10/01/2007
Time:   10:27:43
User:   N/A
Computer: EXCHEDGE1
Description:
PoisonCount - 2 for the message (RecordID: 772) has reached or
exceeded the configured poison threshold - 2. Moving the message
to the poison queue.
```

Clearly, you want to know what caused the crash to avoid it in the future. There are many potential causes: bugs in the Exchange code, servers that generate and send badly configured SMTP messages, and so on. During the development of Exchange 2007, meeting requests from other email systems caused some problems because of their formatting. This indicated that messages that use special formatting to invoke specific processing for their native system have the potential to cause problems, so clearly this is a point to test as you investigate interoperability between Exchange 2007 and other email systems during migration projects.

The poison queue exists so that Exchange can capture these messages for later examination by an administrator. You can decide to pass the messages to Microsoft so that they can fix any bugs and ensure that the transport engine can handle the type of message that caused the problem. Poison messages are not dangerous in themselves unless they are evidence that an attacker is attempting to compromise a server by exploring some security hole in SMTP that can crash Exchange or reveal secure data. It is a good idea to check occasionally to see whether the transport service has captured any poison messages, if only to ensure that you do not accumulate a large queue of these messages pointing to a problem somewhere in your messaging system. If you find any poison messages, you can figure out what to do with each message. To check for poison messages, issue this command:

```
Get-Queue –id Poison
```

You can then export all of the messages to temporary files for examination. This is required if you want to pass the messages to Microsoft to help them find bugs in Exchange or understand why Exchange considered the message to be poisonous.

```
Get-Message –Queue:Poison | Export-Message –Path 'C:\Temp'
```

Messages stay on the Poison queue until they are removed or resumed by an administrator. You should not resume a poison message until you are sure that it does not contain dangerous content. It is possible that a resumed message will be handled correctly and delivered to its destination. If not, Exchange will put it back on the Poison queue and you should delete it from there.

6.7   Back Pressure

Whereas the transport engine in Exchange 2007 is designed to accommodate large volumes of messages, there are circumstances where it may not have the physical capability to handle incoming or outgoing messages. The hub transport server may come under load from another source that consumes much of the available memory or the disk space on some drives may come close to be exhausted. In these circumstances, Exchange 2007 applies a new feature called "Back Pressure" to allow the transport service to continue running normally and process queued messages while it temporarily rejects incoming connections to stop new messages being queued. In this scenario, the sending

SMTP servers have to queue the messages until the situation that caused pressure on Exchange is relieved. For example, if load on the server reduces to free memory or disk space becomes available because some files are deleted, then Exchange begins to accept incoming connections to receive new mail.

Table 6.4 shows how hub transport servers react to medium and high back pressure conditions. As you can see, under medium load, basic message flow is preserved because hub transport servers can connect to send mail to each other and are also willing to accept messages from mailbox servers. However, they will not accept incoming traffic from other SMTP servers. As pressure builds, the hub transport server will eventually stop accepting connections and wait until pressure decreases.

Table 6.4 *The effect of back-pressure settings on hub transport servers*

Resource Utilization	Connections from Other HT Servers	Connections from Other SMTP Servers	Store Driver Connections from Mailbox Servers	Pickup and Replay Submissions	Internal Mail Flow
Medium	Allowed	Rejected	Allowed	Rejected	Working
High	Rejected	Rejected	Rejected	Rejected	No flow

How do you know when a back-pressure condition exists? The answer is in the application event log where you'll see events such as 15002 from the resource manager component in the Exchange Transport system. This event will tell you what resource is causing Transport to have to apply back pressure. For example, you might see something like this:

```
Queue database and disk space ("F:\Exchange\TransportRoles\
data\queue\Mail.Que") = 81% [High] [Normal = 70% Medium High =
72% High = 74%]
```

In this instance, the problem is that the disk that holds the mail queue database is 81% full and has exceeded the threshold for "high" usage of 74%. While there's still 19% free space left on the disk, the possibility exists that some other application could take the space or that if Exchange continues to accept messages, the mail queue database could grow to fill the space. In some respects and given the size of disks today, you might regard these events as unlikely, but it's best to be cautious when you want to keep a messaging system running. The solution is to move some files off the disk to reduce usage to under 74%.

Another indication is if you see the Mail Submission component report event 1009 on mailbox servers. This event is flagged when Exchange is unable to submit messages to a hub transport server in the local Active Directory site. Either the hub transport server is down, the transport service is stopped, or it is experiencing a back-pressure situation that prevents it accepting any more messages from mailbox servers. Of course, the mailbox and hub roles may be on the same physical server, in which case the messages will be queued in the Store until the back-pressure situation is relieved unless another hub transport server is available in the same site.

Note that an Exchange mailbox server always prefers to submit messages to the local hub if this role is installed on the same physical server and will only use other hub transport servers if the local server cannot accept messages. In this case, the other hub transport servers are used on a round-robin basis until the local server can accept messages again.

6.8   Delivery Status Notifications

Over time, it is inevitable that Exchange will not be able to deliver some of the messages that arrive. The destination mailbox may be full, the mailbox has been disabled or removed or the recipient address is invalid, and so on. These messages normally result in the generation of Delivery Status Notification messages (DSNs) to inform the sender that something unexpected has occurred with their message. DSN messages fall into five categories:

- Group expansion: Administrators can define that Exchange sends notification to either the group manager or users who send to the group when the group is successfully expanded.

- Relayed: These DSNs are generated when a user requests a delivery receipt for a message that passes out of the Exchange organization to a remote SMTP server. Delivery notification is no longer possible, so Exchange notifies the user that their message has been relayed that far.

- Delayed: These DSNs are generated when the configuration of a transport server (use the Set-TransportServer command) is set to create delay notifications to users if messages are delayed past the period specified in the delay notification interval (default is four hours).

- Success: These DSNs are generated when a user requests a delivery receipt for an outgoing message. The DSN is an indication that Exchange has definitely delivered the message to the destination mailbox.

- Failed: These are nondelivery reports (NDRs) that state that delivery failed for some reason such as quota exhausted for the destination mailbox or lack of authorization to send to a recipient. The transport engine automatically generates these messages and includes the original message for the user to deal with, including the ability to use client-specific features to resend the message after correcting the fault that caused the NDR.

Exchange 2007 has improved the quality and readability of the DSNs that it generates when compared to previous versions and allows administrators to set some of options that control how Exchange formats and sends DSNs. Most of these options are per-server settings, so you need to apply them with the Set-TransportServer command to all hub transport servers in the organization (and to Edge users, if they are in use). The internal settings apply to messages deemed by Exchange to originate from internal email servers and the external settings for external servers. To see what domains are regarded as internal, use the Get-AcceptedDomain command.

Table 6.5   *Parameters for DSN control*

Parameter	Meaning
InternalDSNDefaultLanguage ExternalDSNDefaultLanguage	Exchange generates DSNs in the language specified for the recipient's mailbox. You can change the default language for DSNs to tell Exchange what to use when a user-specified language cannot be determined.
InternalDSNLanguageDetection ExternalDSNLanguageDetection	You can instruct Exchange to override the user setting and use the default language set by the server.
InternalDSNMaxMessageAttachSize	Specifies the maximum size that a DSN message can be including the original message if it needs to be returned to the originator.
InternalDSNReportingAuthority ExternalDSNReportingAuthority	The internal version of this parameter is normally populated with the FQDN of the server , while the external version includes the domain. These values are sent back along with a DSN to indicate the name of the server that generates the DSN. Some companies prefer not to expose this information outside the company, so you can suppress or change it.
ExternalPostmasterAddress	Specifies the address that the DSNs show in their FROM field for external recipients.
InternalDSNSendHTML ExternalDSNSendHTML	Specifies whether Exchange creates DSNs in HTML or plain text. The default is to create HTML messages.
GenerateCopyOfDSNFor	Specifies whether you want to collect copies of NDRs in the Postmaster mailbox. By default, copies are not collected.

To collect copies of DSNs for analysis, you use the `Set-TransportConfig` command and pass the set of DSN codes that you want to collect messages for to the –GenerateCopyOfDSNFor parameter. For example:

```
Set-TransportConfig —GenerateCopyOfDSNFor  "5.1.4", "5.2.0",
"5.2.4", "5.4.4", "5.4.6", "5.4.8"
```

However, one small problem exists here. Exchange does not know what recipient to copy the DSNs. Before you can capture DSNs, you have to configure a suitable recipient using the `Set-OrganizationConfig` command. For example, this command determines that copies of DSNs go to the "Postmaster@xyz.com" address.

```
Set-OrganizationConfig
—MsExchangeRecipientReplyRecipient 'PostMaster@xyz.com'
```

As shown in Figure 6.24, Exchange 2007 DSNs are split into three section: some human-friendly information to explain the problem to the recipient in terms that they can understand, some branding to show that the DSN came from Exchange 2007, and diagnostics information that can help administrators understand what conditions caused the DSN to be generated. The user information is deliberately placed first so that users who receive these messages see the important information first (that their message didn't get through) without having to wade through a pile of diagnostic information that they probably don't care about. This is good for all clients and very important for handheld devices where you want to minimize the amount of data transmitted to the device and maximize the use of screen real estate to present critical information first.

All in all, an Exchange 2007 DSN is much more understandable than the DSNs generated by previous versions of Exchange or other messaging systems. It is possible to see "pretty" DSNs that look like those generated by Exchange 2007, but if they don't contain the branding between the user and diagnostic information, it means that the DSNs were generated by a legacy Exchange server or another messaging system and re-rendered by Exchange 2007 to provide the diagnostic information. For example, if a user on an Exchange 2007 sends a message to an address on an Exchange 2003 server that is rejected for some reason (quota exceeded, address doesn't exist, and so on), then Exchange 2007 takes the inbound NDR and maps the reason to its own settings and appends the SMTP diagnostic information to create the DSN. The reason why Exchange 2007 re-renders DSNs is to ensure that users receive consistent DSNs, including any customized text that you have created for system messages, no matter what the source of the DSN is.

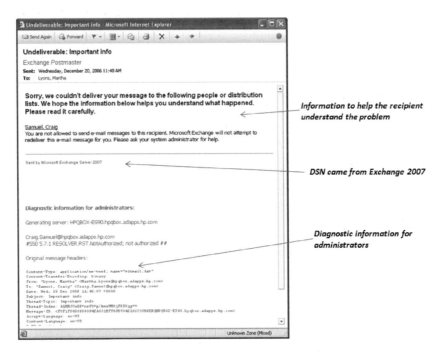

Figure 6.24
Exchange 2007
DSN layout

The diagnostic section in a DSN provides administrators with information to help them understand why the DSN occurred. In this section you'll find:

- Generating server: The name of the server that actually detected the problem and generated the DSN. This may be the Exchange 2007 hub transport server that accepted the message from the Exchange 2007 mailbox server and has failed to transfer it onwards, or it may be another server along the message's path, such as a bridgehead server for another organization that has detected that the intended recipient doesn't exist.

- The DSN status and the enhanced error code. In the example shown in Figure 6.24, the status is 550 and the error code is 5.7.1.

- The SMTP response: In our example, the server was unable to deliver to the recipient because the sender is not authorized. The "Resolver.RST" information is generated by Exchange 2007.

- The SMTP headers: The header information for the original message that caused the DSN is included so that you can see exactly where the message was going to.

- Remote server information: If the message passes from one hub to another, or to an Exchange 2003 bridgehead server, or to a remote SMTP server, all of the communications between the servers are captured including the IP address. If you see that the message was "Received… with MAPI" it indicates a transfer from an Exchange 2007 mailbox server to a hub transport server (this communication occurs with Exchange RPCs; all other communication with servers is via SMTP).

There are about 50 different reasons why Exchange 2007 can't deliver a message. Table 6.6 lists the most common error conditions that you'll meet.

Table 6.6   *Common causes for message delivery to fail*

DSN Code	Reason
4.4.7—Message Expired	Exchange was not able to deliver the message within two days (the default) so the message expired off the queue. Alternatively, an administrator deleted the message from a queue for some reason. The user should resend.
5.1.1—Wrong email address	The intended recipient cannot be found in the directory of the receiving system so the message cannot be delivered. The user may have mistyped the address or even used an outdated message from Outlook's nickname cache. In either case, they will have to fix the address and resend the message.
5.1.3—Wrong format for address	Exchange believes that the format for the address is incorrect so it can't be delivered. The user has to fix the address and resend.
5.1.4—Duplicate address	The receiving email system has detected a duplicate address. The user can't do much about this problem as the remote administrator has to resolve the duplicates before anyone can send to this address.
5.1.8—Bad sender address	For some reason, a remote server isn't able to accept mail from the sender. The only thing that anyone can do is to read the diagnostic information and attempt to figure out what happened.
5.2.0—Generic failure to deliver	All sorts of problems with mailboxes can cause this to occur, including a missing SMTP address, an invalid SMTP address, or an invalid forwarding address. The administrator will have to check the recipient's mailbox to verify that everything is correct.

Table 6.6   *Common causes for message delivery to fail (continued)*

DSN Code	Reason
5.2.2—Mailbox quota exceeded	The recipient's mailbox is full and can't accept incoming messages. They have to reduce the mailbox under quota or have the quota increased to accept new messages.
5.2.3—Message too large for recipient or sender	Either the recipient or the sender is not allowed to send such a large message.
5.2.4—Dynamic distri-bution group query is wrong	Exchange is unable to resolve the query to populate the recipients in a dynamic distribution group. The administra-tor will have to fix this problem.
5.3.4—Message too large to route	Some component along the message path was unable to route the message because of a size restriction. It could be a connector, it could be the organization configuration, or it could be a remote server.
5.4.4—Unable to route	Normally this is because a user attempts to send a message to a domain that doesn't exist anymore so Exchange is unable to route the message.
5.5.3—Too many recipients	There are too many recipients in the message header. Reduce the number and retry. Remember that distribution groups count as one recipient no matter how many recipients they include, so use distribution groups whenever possible.
5.7.1—Lack of authorization	The sender doesn't have the necessary authorization to send to a recipient.

6.8.1 Customizing DSNs

You can customize the text that Exchange 2007 inserts for error conditions. For example, the standard text for a 5.1.1 DSN error is:

"It looks like you might have typed the wrong email address. Please check the address and try again, or ask your system administrator for help."

This is a very nice informational message for users to receive, but let's assume that we want to spice it up a bit. We can do this with the Set-Sys-temMessage command. In this case, the command changes the English lan-guage (en) message used in DSNs that report failures to send to internal recipients. The result is seen in Figure 6.25 and notice that you can't modify the hardcoded bolded text above the erroneous address.

```
Set-SystemMessage —id 'en\Internal\5.1.1' —Text 'Eeek! Can't
find that person — try again!'
```

Figure 6.25

*Customized system
message in a DSN*

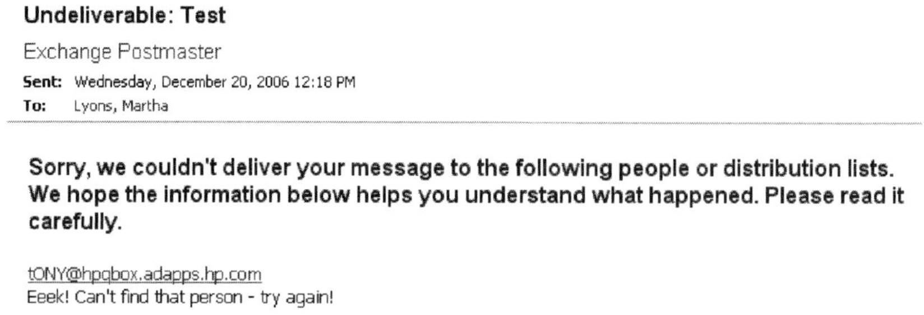

Undeliverable: Test

Exchange Postmaster

Sent: Wednesday, December 20, 2006 12:18 PM
To: Lyons, Martha

**Sorry, we couldn't deliver your message to the following people or distribution lists.
We hope the information below helps you understand what happened. Please read it
carefully.**

tONY@hpqbox.adapps.hp.com
Eeek! Can't find that person - try again!

If you want to use the same customized message for external messages,
execute the same command but pass "en\External\5.1.1." as the identity of
the message that you want to change. After the command executes, Exchange
uses the customized text when it generates a DSN for error code 5.1.1 (see
Figure 6.25). If you want to remove the custom code, you can use the `Set-SystemMessage` command:

```
Set-SystemMessage —id 'en\Internal\5.1.1' —original $True
```

To see the full set of system messages defined on a server, type the `Get-SystemMessage` command:

```
Identity            Text
--------            ----
en\External\5.5.1      A communication failure occurred during the delivery of this
message. Microsoft Exchange will not attempt to redeiver this e-mail message for you.
Please try resending this email message later, or ask your system administrator for
help.

en\Internal\5.5.1      A communication failure occurred during the delivery of this
message. Microsoft Exchange will not attempt to redeliver this e-mail message for
you. Please try resending this email message later, or ask your system administrator
for help.

en\Internal\5.1.1    Eeek! Can't find that person - try again!


en\External\5.1.1       It looks like you might have typed the wrong e-mail address.
Please check the address and try again, or ask your system administrator for help.
```

In reviewing the list of system messages, you will notice that it includes the customization for DSN 5.1.1. that we created a little while ago but that it doesn't include entries for many of the other common DSN codes reviewed in Table 6.6 such as the 5.7.1 failure shown in Figure 6.24. If we want to create a customized message for these codes, we have to use the `New-System-Message` command. For example:

```
New-SystemMessage —DSNcode 5.7.1 —Language en —Internal $True

—Text 'No way that you can send to that person...'
```

If you use `Get-SystemMessage` after executing this command, you will notice an internal entry for 5.7.1 listed. If we attempt to send a message to a mailbox that we are not authorized to send to, we will see something like Figure 6.26. You can compare the difference in the text shown in Figure 6.24 to see that the customization is effective.

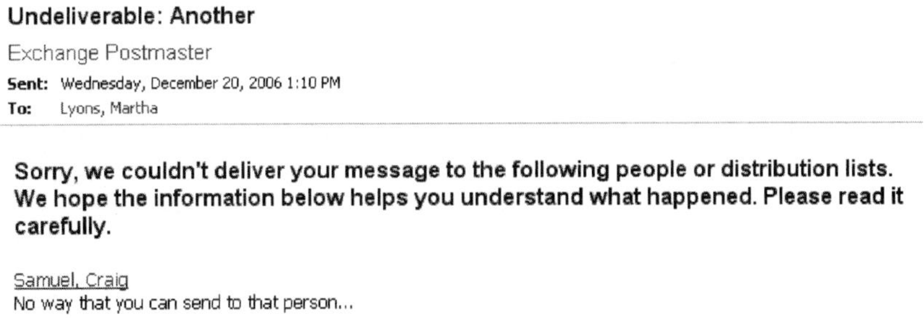

Figure 6.26
Example of a customized new system message

Undeliverable: Another

Exchange Postmaster

Sent: Wednesday, December 20, 2006 1:10 PM
To: Lyons, Martha

Sorry, we couldn't deliver your message to the following people or distribution lists. We hope the information below helps you understand what happened. Please read it carefully.

Samuel, Craig
No way that you can send to that person...

You can also use the `New-SystemMessage` command to alter the text of several messages that Exchange generates when mailbox or public folder quotas are exceeded. In previous versions of Exchange, you had to ask Microsoft for a replacement DLL that contained the customized text that you wanted to use for messages and run the risk that the use of the customized DLL might compromise support. In addition, you had to go through the exercise of deploying the customized DLL to every server in the organization and you had to do this after every software upgrade, including service packs and potentially hot fixes. This was clearly not a good situation and it is surprising that Microsoft took so long to fix the problem. However, with Exchange 2007, you can execute the `New-SystemMessage` command to customize any of the messages specified in Table 6.7.

Let's assume that you want to change the warning message that people who send a message to a mailbox receive if the mailbox exceeds its quota. We can accomplish our goal with this command:

```
New-SystemMessage —QuotaMessageType WarningMailbox —language
En —text 'Too much data to consume!'
```

Table 6.7　　*Quota messages*

Message Code	Generated When
ProhibitSendMailbox	Issued when a mailbox that has a prohibit send quota exceeds the mailbox size.
ProhibitPostPublicFolderIssued	Issued when a public folder that has a prohibit send quota exceeds the specified folder limit.
ProhibitSendReceiveMailbox	Issued when a mailbox that has a prohibit send quota and prohibit receive quota exceeds the specified mailbox send and receive size limit.
WarningMailboxUnlimitedSize	Issued when a mailbox that has no prohibit send quota or prohibit receive quota exceeds the specified mailbox warning limit.
WarningPublicFolderUnlimitedSize	Issued when a public folder that has no prohibit send quota or prohibit receive quota exceeds the specified public folder warning limit.
WarningMailbox	Issued when a mailbox that has a prohibit send quota or prohibit receive quota exceeds the specified mailbox warning limit.
WarningPublicFolder	Issued when a public folder that has a prohibit send quota or prohibit receive quota exceeds the specified public folder warning limit.

6.8.2　Postmaster addresses

Hub transport and Edge servers generate DSNs. The default is to assign an address of "Postmaster@domain" as the sender for DSNs. For instance, the DSNs generated by servers installed into the xyz.com domain have sender addresses of "Postmaster@xyz.com." It may be more convenient for you to have Exchange use a different address. For example, you may want to use an address for a real mailbox so that external recipients can send replies back to the address if they want help. You use the `Set-TransportServer` command to change the address for postmaster messages. For example:

```
Set-TransportServer —Id ExchHub1 —ExternalPostMasterAddress
'PostMaster-ExchHub1@xyz.com'
```

The postmaster address used for messages generated externally is specific to a server. Exchange has another address (the default name is "Microsoft Exchange") that it uses as the sender for NDRs and other service messages such as notifications generated by UM servers that go to internal users. The internal postmaster address is a special value held as part of the organization configuration. You can see the configuration details with the `Get-OrganizationConfig` command:

```
Get-OrganizationConfig | Select Name, Microsoft*

Name                                          : XYZ
MicrosoftExchangeRecipientEmailAddresses      : {X400:C=US;A=
;P=XYZ;O=Exchange;S=MicrosoftExchange329e71ec88ae4615bbc36ab;, SMTP:
 MicrosoftExchange329e71ec88ae4615bbc36ab6ce41109e@xyz.com}
MicrosoftExchangeRecipientReplyRecipient      :
MicrosoftExchangeRecipientPrimarySmtpAddress  :
MicrosoftExchange329e71ec88ae4615bbc36ab6ce41109e@xyz.com
MicrosoftExchangeRecipientEmailAddressPolicyEnabled : True
```

It is possible to use the `Set-OrganizationConfig` command to update the MicrosoftExchangeRecipientPrimarySmtpAddress property with a different SMTP address. However, you create a problem if this address points to a mailbox because you now have a situation where Exchange believes that two objects share the same email address, which Exchange does not permit.

6.9   Transport agents

Transport agents operate under the control of the transport system to perform specific processing on messages at different points of their passage through the transport system. The most important agents are those that execute transport rules and perform journaling. We will get to discuss how to create and use transport rules and journaling when we review how to use Exchange 2007 to achieve better compliance with regulatory or legislative requirements in Chapter 8. For now, it is sufficient to recognize that these components exist. You can use the `Get-TransportAgent` command to discover the list of transport agents that are operating on a hub or Edge server. You'll see a list of agents returned together with whether they are currently enabled and the priority order that Exchange processes messages through the agents.

```
Identity                                 Enabled         Priority
--------                                 -------         --------
Transport Rule Agent                     True            1
Journaling Agent                         True            2
```

Some additional insight can be gained by requesting information about a specific agent:

```
Get-TransportAgent -id 'Transport Rule Agent'

Identity              : Transport Rule Agent
Enabled               : True
Priority              : 1
TransportAgentFactory :
Microsoft.Exchange.MessagingPolicies.TransportRuleAgent.TransportRuleAgentFactory
AssemblyPath          : C:\Program Files\Microsoft\Exchange Server\TransportRoles\
agents\Rule\Microsoft.Exchange.MessagingPolicies.TransportRuleAgent.dll
```

6.10 Transport summary

At the start of this chapter, we looked at a simplified version of the Exchange 2007 transport service illustrated in Figure 6.1. Now that we have considered the components of the transport service in detail, we can fill in some more detail. Figure 6.27 presents a more comprehensive view of how the transport service functions on a hub transport server. There are some components illustrated here that we have not yet discussed. For example, the transport dumpster is associated with continuous log replication on CCR servers, so you can find details about it in Chapter 9. Message log tracking is discussed in Chapter 10.

Now that we understand the full breadth of the Exchange 2007 transport service as implemented on hub transport servers, we can move on to review the new Edge server.

6.11 Edge servers

As is obvious from the discussion in this chapter, the combination of Exchange 2003 SP2 and the Intelligent Message Filter (IMF) are able to suppress spam. However, no rational human being (unless you worked for Microsoft and had a point to prove) would deploy an Exchange 2003 server

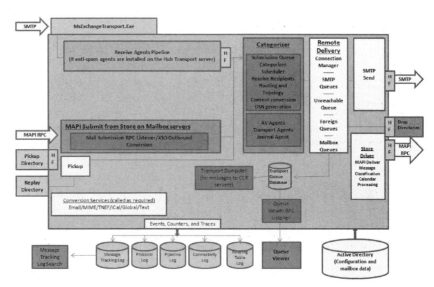

Figure 6.27
The full Exchange 2007 transport service

in a DMZ and use it as the first server to receive and process an unfiltered message stream from the Internet. The reliance of Exchange 2003 on the Active Directory produces a huge attack surface for a hacker to exploit if they penetrate the DMZ, so it is a lot easier to keep Exchange 2003 servers secure on the right side of the DMZ behind an array of firewalls and intrusion detection systems.

Microsoft began a project to develop a specialized version of Exchange 2003 that was hardened to allow deployment inside a DMZ but they never completed the project. Exchange 2007 was on the horizon and too much engineering effort was required. However, the idea of producing a specialized server that could safely handle and clean unfiltered message streams did not go away, and now we have the Exchange 2007 Edge server. This is a highly customized version of Exchange designed for deployment as a bastion email host within the DMZ to process incoming email. You cannot install the Edge server alongside other Exchange server roles and you cannot install the Edge server in a forest that supports other Exchange servers. In fact, the Edge server is best deployed in a totally standalone domain that has no user accounts to reduce the potential attack surface. If an attacker compromises an Edge server, they cannot exploit the penetration to get any further into your Exchange organization or compromise data such as the Active Directory. To help you deploy an Edge server, Microsoft includes an extension to the Windows Security Configuration Wizard (SCW) to automate the process of hardening the server and make it suitable for deployment within the DMZ. Finally, you can deploy Edge servers alongside ISA Server 2006[7] to create a nice combination of firewall and bastion mail server.

Microsoft wants customers to deploy a complete Exchange solution for email and not to have to deploy different servers from other vendors such as Tumbleweed or CipherTrust Ironmail as the first port of call in the DMZ for incoming traffic. The Edge server contains a lot of decent functionality and it is well suited for the task of cleansing an incoming email stream in the DMZ, but the problem that Microsoft faces is to displace existing systems that are installed and operational today. Most companies will not rush to rip out part of their DMZ infrastructure to install new servers just because they come from Microsoft, and it will take time for Microsoft to establish their reputation as a solid player in the mail hygiene space and for companies to deploy Edge servers. Some help to establish the necessary track record will come from Microsoft's own deployment of a set of Edge servers to filter all incoming traffic addressed to microsoft.com, where they report good results.

Over time, as systems age and everyone gains more experience with Edge servers, possibly by installing them to protect a part of the infrastructure, it is likely that the cost advantage that you can gain by going with a pure Microsoft solution will tip the balance and allow Edge servers to displace other systems. However, if you operate a heterogeneous messaging environment, you may not be attracted by the notion of using Edge servers in the DMZ and prefer to continue with your current solution to solve the needs of both Exchange and non-Microsoft email systems.

6.11.1 Edge or hub?

Microsoft has designed the Edge and hub transport server roles to occupy very different positions within an Exchange organization. On the surface, the two server roles seem to overlap because each can perform a lot of the same processing, such as hosting SMTP connectors, running anti-spam agents, and so on. Table 6.8 provides an overview of each server role.

Table 6.8   *Edge versus hub transport*

	Edge Server	Hub Transport
Routing	Outwards facing, designed to accept incoming messages from the Internet.	Inwards facing, designed to manage routing of messages within an Exchange 2007 organization.
Mail processing	Always active—implemented through agents.	Some of the same agents can run on the hub.
Security	Isolated in the DMZ, protected by a firewall; uses credentials to communicate with hub.	Behind the corporate inner firewall; uses Active Directory security (Kerberos/TLS) to communicate with mailbox servers.

7.   ISA Server 2006 is a 32-bit release so you cannot deploy it on the same physical computer as an Edge server. Microsoft expects to release a 64-bit version of ISA Server in the future.

Table 6.8 *Edge versus hub transport*

Policies	None.	Journal and Transport rules.
Focus	External protection.	Internal routing and compliance.
Active Directory	Server installed into separate forest or workgroup; operates with ADAM; synchronization through special EdgeSync process.	Server integrated with the rest of the Exchange organization through the enterprise Active Directory, synchronized using standard Active Directory processes.

The big difference is that the Edge server is deployed inside the DMZ whereas hub transport servers never are, so the code that runs on each server type is very different, and even where similar functionality exists, Microsoft normally uses different default settings for the two server roles. For instance, subject to the connections permitted by its IP block lists, because they are Internet-facing, an Edge server is essentially open to a connection from any mail server that wants to send messages to it. A hub transport server is much more secure because it serves the internal routing needs of an organization, so it doesn't accept messages from unauthenticated (anonymous) or untrusted sources.

Connectors can exist on either a hub or Edge server. You always configure hub-based connectors on a hub transport server, but Edge-based connectors are configured slightly differently. If you operate an Edge server as a standalone system that is not synchronized with the Exchange organization, then you configure any connectors that you need on that server. On the other hand, if you introduce an Edge server as a logical part of your Exchange organization by synchronizing configuration information to the Edge server, then all connectors are configured on the hub transport server that maintains the subscription to the Edge server and are propagated to the Edge server through the synchronization process.

The Edge server is really a much simpler beast than the hub transport server. This follows the principle of only running the code that is absolutely necessary on a server to restrict the possibility of bugs and reduce the surface that you expose to potential attackers. For example, while the Edge server has some knowledge of how to route messages, its ability is very restricted when compared to a hub transport server because the Edge server lacks the categorizer, routing engine, and Store driver component, so it can only match incoming messages with connectors rather than find the best route to a server, public folder, or mailbox. The Edge server's lack of a direct connection to the Active Directory is a strength rather than a weakness and it can run the full suite of anti-spam tools whereas the hub transport server is restricted because some of the agents (like the address rewriting agent) are not supported on a hub transport server. Microsoft's view is that while the hub transport server can run many anti-spam rules, its major focus is on rules that enforce compliance with regulations rather than the cleansing task undertaken by the Edge. You could point an unclean mail stream direct from the Internet to a hub transport server and it would cope, but it doesn't seem to make sense to take on the processing load of cleansing spam when the hub transport servers have a lot more work to do.

6.11.2 Basic Edge

Fundamentally, you can look at the Edge server as being composed of three major components:

- A high performance SMTP engine – the same basic engine as operates on the hub transport server, tailored to handle an incoming Internet mail stream.

- A sophisticated, multi-layered message hygiene cleansing ability to remove spam, viruses, and other suspicious or unacceptable content from incoming messages.

- Read-only access to information about the Exchange organization to enable Edge to route messages to Exchange, plus information about recipients, so Edge can recognize the mailboxes that it can accept messages for. The Edge server only synchronizes enough data from an organization's Active Directory to allow it to perform anti-spam processing. A unique feature introduced by Exchange 2007 is the ability for users to publish their own safelists to the Edge so that these lists can be incorporated into the mail hygiene process.

The Edge server does not hold a complete copy of the Active Directory. Maintaining a writeable copy of the Active Directory, such as the Global Catalog, within the DMZ is a bad idea. Penetrating a Global Catalog could offer a way for an attacker to give themselves elevated privileges through compromised accounts or accounts that attackers create for their own purpose. The solution is found in ADAM, or Active Directory Applications Mode, a form of the Active Directory designed to support applications but doesn't require the full range of functionality offered by the Active Directory. ADAM provides the Edge server with a repository for a read-only partial replica of the Active Directory that can store configuration data about the Exchange organization, user email addresses, and other information used in email filtering such as accepted domains and user safelists. When you install an Edge server, the ADAM database is empty, and you have to populate it through an EdgeSync process that runs on a hub transport server behind the firewall. EdgeSync is a one-way synchronization process that populates the ADAM database on the Edge server with information about the Exchange organization and recipients. You need to configure synchronization between the Active Directory and every Edge server that you deploy by configuring an edge subscription to permit synchronization between a hub transport server and the Edge server. A single hub transport server can support edge subscriptions to multiple different Edge servers. Creating an Edge subscription and performing synchronization are manual tasks that you can easily automate with PowerShell scripts if you need to deploy multiple Edge servers. Note that even if it is not part of the Exchange organization, an Edge server can only support a single Exchange organization. Therefore, if you want to deploy multiple Exchange organizations, you need to deploy different sets of Edge servers to support these organizations.

You can configure Edge servers to support multiple Exchange organizations. However, Edge can only cleanse and deliver messages onwards to multiple organizations. You can only synchronize information such as safelist data from one Exchange organization with the ADAM instance that runs on an Edge server.

Edge servers need to have three TCP ports open to communicate with the Internet and the Exchange organization:

- Port 25 for SMTP connections from the Internet.
- Port 50389 for LDAP and port 50636 for secure LDAP; these ports are used for synchronization between Active Directory and ADAM.

6.11.3 **Edge Synchronization**

The EdgeSync service is designed to synchronize data between hub transport servers and Edge servers through periodic one-way (hub to edge) replication of recipient and configuration data from Active Directory to the ADAM instance running on the Edge server. Only information that is absolutely required is synchronized to allow the Edge server to accept messages for valid recipients, to perform mail hygiene tasks on incoming messages, and to perform simple routing of messages that pass through the hygiene scans to a hub transport server. Synchronization occurs according to a schedule agreed between the hub and Edge servers that is defined in the form of a "subscription." An Edge subscription is a set of configuration settings that defines the relationship between an Edge server and a hub transport server. Because of the one-way nature of the communication, you initiate the subscription on the Edge server with the New-EdgeSubscription command, giving the name of an XML-format file to export the information that is required for the target hub transport server to support the subscription (Figure 6.28).

Before running any synchronization operation, make sure that all of the dates and times on the servers that will connect together are synchronized. Ideally, because date and time is a fundamental influence on any synchroni-

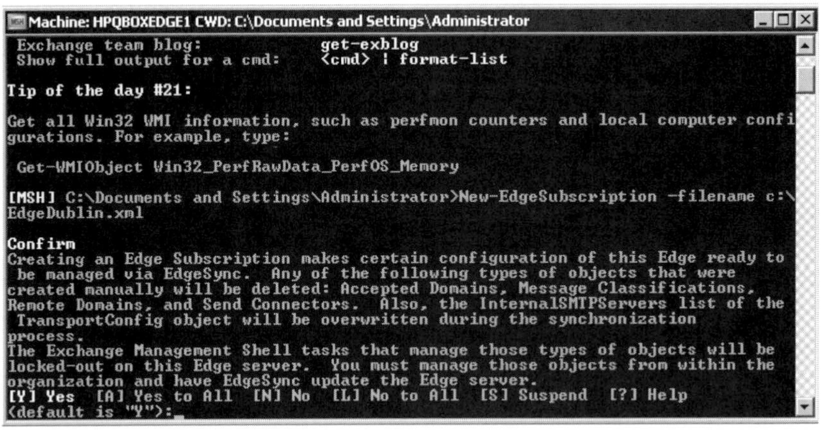

Figure 6.28
*Running New-
EdgeSubscription*

```
Machine: HPQBOXEDGE1 CWD: C:\Documents and Settings\Administrator        _ □ X
Exchange team blog:             get-exblog
Show full output for a cmd:     <cmd> | format-list

Tip of the day #21:

Get all Win32 WMI information, such as perfmon counters and local computer confi
gurations. For example, type:

Get-WMIObject Win32_PerfRawData_PerfOS_Memory

[MSH] C:\Documents and Settings\Administrator>New-EdgeSubscription -filename c:\
EdgeDublin.xml

Confirm
Creating an Edge Subscription makes certain configuration of this Edge ready to
 be managed via EdgeSync.  Any of the following types of objects that were
created manually will be deleted: Accepted Domains, Message Classifications,
Remote Domains, and Send Connectors.  Also, the InternalSMTPServers list of the
 TransportConfig object will be overwritten during the synchronization
process.
The Exchange Management Shell tasks that manage those types of objects will be
locked-out on this Edge server.  You must manage those objects from within the
organization and have EdgeSync update the Edge server.
[Y] Yes  [A] Yes to All  [N] No  [L] No to All  [S] Suspend  [?] Help
<default is "Y">:
```

zation process, you need the servers to be within a minute of each other. You also need to ensure that all of the servers are registered in DNS and that you can ping the IP addresses successfully from the different servers. Once you are ready to proceed, export the subscription information to start the synchronization process:

```
New-EdgeSubscription —FileName 'C:\EdgeSub.XML'
```

The contents of the XML file generated by the New-EdgeSubscription command (Figure 6.29) include the server name and FQDN of the Edge server, the number of the SSL port that the hub transport server which supports the subscription can use to communicate with ADAM, the certificates that allow the servers to establish secure connections, the account to use for synchronization, and the credentials required to allow the hub transport server to bind to ADAM and push information to the Edge server.

After you create a subscription file, you have to transport it in some manner to the hub transport server. Some people use a USB drive or other transportable media for this purpose, while others start up Outlook Web Access on the Edge server and email the XML file as an attachment to themselves. Whatever method you employ to transfer the file from Edge to hub transport server, you have to use the file to create a subscription by importing the file on the hub transport server before the credentials that are included in the file expire. Normally, you have 24 hours (1,440 minutes) to perform the import. Take the file that the Edge server generates and import it with the "New Edge Subscription" wizard that you can find in the Organizational Configuration section of EMC. The wizard (Figure 6.30) requires you to select an Active Directory site so that the Edge server is associated with the hub transport servers in that site. After the subscription is established, other servers in the organization will be able to route messages to the hub transport servers in the selected site for onward transmission to the Edge server and through the Edge to the Internet.

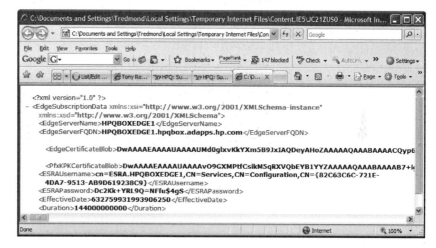

Figure 6.29
Contents of an Edge subscription XML file

If you do not want to use EMC, you can import the XML file containing the subscription data from the Edge server by executing the `New-Edge-Subscription` command on the hub transport server that will serve as the synchronization partner for the Edge server. When you import an XML file from an Edge server to instantiate a subscription on a hub transport server, you have to specify the name of the Active Directory site that the Edge server will join logically for routing purposes (usually the Active Directory site of the hub transport server):

```
New-EdgeSubscription —FileName 'C:\Temp\DublinEdge.XML' —Site
'Dublin'
```

The process of creating a subscription between an Edge and an hub transport server sets up the necessary authentication mechanism to allow synchronization to occur. Another effect is that the Edge server becomes a virtual member of the Active Directory site, albeit only for the purposes of routing topology and Exchange management. You can see how the subscription brings the Edge server into the organization in a logical sense by executing the `Get-ExchangeServer` command, in which case you might see something like the output shown below. You can see that three servers are listed: a legacy Exchange 2003 server, a multi-role server, and an Edge server. The Edge server and the multi-role server (which must support the hub transport role to be able to take out the subscription to connect to the Edge) are in the same Active Directory site. Thus, from a management perspective,

Figure 6.30
*Importing a
subscription XML
file*

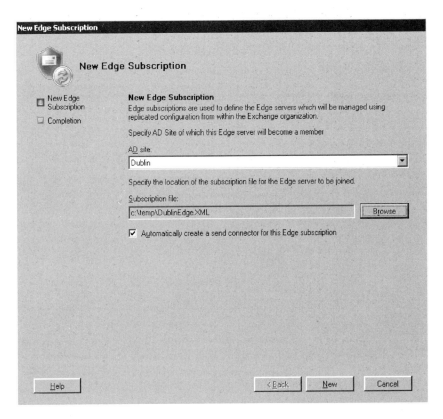

despite the fact that the two servers exist in radically different Active Directory environments, they seem to be part of the same Exchange organization.

Name	Site	ServerRole	Edition	AdminDisplayVersion
----	----	----------	-------	-------------------
ExchMbx23		None	Enterprise	Version 6.5 (Bui...
ExchMbxSvr1	Dublin	Mailbox,...	Enterprise	Version 8.0 (Bui...
ExchEdge1	Dublin	Edge	Unknown	Version 8.0 (Bui...

The Edge server is never a member of a domain within the same forest that supports the Exchange organization. A single Edge server can have subscriptions with multiple hub transport servers in an Active Directory site and may do so in order to have some tolerance to failure for one of the hub transport servers, but it cannot have subscriptions that span multiple Active Directory sites. While it may seem surprising that an Edge server can be subscribed to multiple hub transport servers, everything works because the synchronization process takes out a lock on the Edge server. Thus, if one hub transport server is synchronizing with the Edge server, another hub transport server is blocked by the lock and will have to wait its turn. Exchange uses USNs (see Chapter 2 for details on Active Directory replication) to track the changes that it needs to apply to bring an Edge server up to date, and when the turn of the second hub transport server comes, it is conceivable that all of the updates to Active Directory objects that are waiting on the hub transport server have already been processed by the Edge. The two servers connect, compare USNs, and finish.

Once the subscription is established, you can start to synchronize data from the Active Directory to ADAM with the Start-EdgeSynchronization command on the hub transport server. There is no GUI option to start this process. One result of synchronization is the creation of two send connectors and one receive connector on the Edge server. Figure 6.31 illustrates what you might see through EMC and when you execute the Get-SendConnector and Get-ReceiveConnector commands on the Edge server. These connectors serve the following purpose:

- Send connector inbound to site: This connector handles traffic from the Internet that is accepted by the Edge server, cleansed, and passed fit for transmission to the Exchange organization.

- Send connector site to Internet: This connector handles outgoing traffic from the site to the Internet. Exchange hub transport servers within the organization (and any Exchange 2003 routing group masters) will be able to route messages to the Internet over this connector because they know of its presence through configuration replication and that it can handle any domain as its declared address space is SMTP:*.

- Default internal receive connector: This connector provides the final hop to move messages that have been routed to the hub transport server for onward delivery to the Edge server.

Edge synchronization usually does not take a long time. The initial synchronization requires most effort because it has to populate the ADAM instance with content about all recipients plus the Exchange configuration. Microsoft's tests establish that you can expect to synchronize between 80,000 and 100,000 objects per hour between reasonably configured (in terms of hardware) hub and Edge servers. Your mileage may vary, but this kind of synchronization speed has been observed in a number of Exchange 2007 implementations, so it is safe to plan on this basis.

After the initial load is performed, all subsequent synchronizations only involve delta changes since the last update, so much less data is transferred. The hub transport server synchronizes updated configuration data to Edge servers every hour and recipient data every four hours. You can validate that

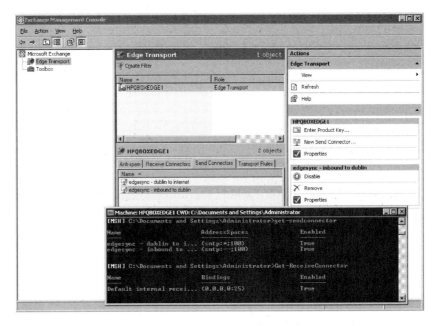

Figure 6.31
*Connectors on an
Edge server
following initial
synchronization*

synchronization is occurring as planned by checking the Event Log for event 1,000 (Figure 6.32) that is generated by the EdgeSync process following a successful update. Remember that Edge servers maintain their own separate copy of ADAM and do not synchronize between each other, so even if you deploy multiple Edge servers in the DMZ to provide load balancing for incoming email traffic, you have to synchronize each Edge server separately.

Information held in the ADAM instance on an Edge server is secured to prevent any possibility that attackers could gain access to Active Directory information such as user names and email addresses. The Edge server hashes the recipient information for incoming messages and uses these values to lookup the information in ADAM to be able to apply per-recipient settings during the mail hygiene scans. You can view this information by connecting to ADAM using the ADSIEDIT version that supports ADAM. Specify that you want to connect to \OU=MSExchangeGateway using Port 50389 and you'll be able to navigate through the information synchronized from the Active Directory. As you can see from Figure 6.33, the hashed data represents user, contact, and group objects plus accepted domains, remote domains, safe sender lists, and connectors. This is all the data necessary to understand the domains that the organization processes email for and to perform sender lookup to ensure that any message coming from a sender that a user has indicated is safe is allowed through and pass these messages through to a hub transport server.

Figure 6.32
Successful EdgeSync

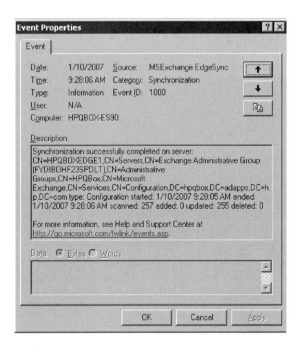

Figure 6.33
Hashed Active Directory information in ADAM

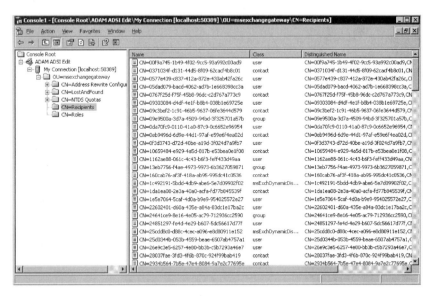

Hashing is a high-performing method to achieve per-recipient checking and does not impact the ability of Edge servers to handle a heavy load of incoming traffic. Microsoft's data indicates that an Edge server can handle up to 360 messages per second, but this figure has to be put in context with the widely differing types of traffic seen in different companies. Nevertheless, it's high enough for you to assume that an Edge server will be able to handle a heavy traffic load and if a single Edge server isn't capable of handling the load for your organization, you can deploy several Edge servers and load-balance the traffic across the available set.

6.11.4   Basic Edge security

The Edge server is deployed within the DMZ and can handle incoming connections from many different email systems. When Edge creates a connection with another server for outbound email, it uses what Microsoft calls "opportunistic and automatic TLS" to establish a secure connection whenever possible. In other words, Edge attempts to set up a TLS session by sending a "STARTTLS" command to the other server. Hopefully the other server supports TLS and if this is the case, the session is secured. If not, a regular SMTP session is used. For inbound connections, all Exchange 2007 servers have an installed SSL certificate, so this can be used to encrypt incoming messages, providing the remote server supports TLS.

When Edge wants to communicate with a hub transport server, it uses a mechanism called Direct Trust. This means that Exchange uses self-signed certificates to establish secure encrypted communications between the Edge and hub transport servers. The certificates are stored in the Active Directory (for hub) and ADAM (for Edge) and synchronized between the servers using the EdgeSync process. An Edge server has copies of all the certificates for the hub transport servers that it communicates with.

As mentioned in Chapter 1, Microsoft includes support for the Windows Security Configuration Wizard (SCW) in Exchange 2007. This is an especially valuable feature for Edge servers because it allows you to secure the server tightly against possible compromise.

6.11.5   Fighting spam and email viruses

Mail hygiene is the term that describes the steps that administrators can take to disinfect the message stream before content gets to user mailboxes. When the message stream enters an organization from the Internet, it is normally pretty polluted—as dirty as the most unclean harbor in the world. You wouldn't drink from an unclean harbor and in the same light, you probably wouldn't want to deal with all the junk that a dirty message stream contains if it was delivered to your mailbox.

Whether we like it or not, spam (or unsolicited commercial email or UCE, to give its legal name) and computer viruses that are transmitted along with valid email are not going to go away soon. The reason for spam is simple: The people who generate and send spam to millions of recipients can make considerable amounts of money with relatively little work. If you consider that a spammer can buy a distribution list of two million email addresses for about $100, they only have to convince a small percentage of the recipients to accept whatever offer the message contains to make a profit. For example, if the message is an invitation to sign up for a restricted site that holds adult content and the spammer receives $14.95 for each person who signs up, then 200 successful signups will generate $2,890 for the spammer. Now consider that the spammer has freeware or low-cost tools that can send messages to the two million recipients in a couple of hours and that they probably use someone else's hardware and network to take the load of the distribution (by using a hijacked relay server), then the profit margin and the attractiveness of the business model becomes apparent. Of course, not all spamming campaigns will earn a spammer several thousand dollars, but if a spammer hits pay dirt twice a week, then they can generate $200,000 profit a year. Given the nature of their activities, you can bet that these people do not report this income to the tax authorities, so they can have a nice lifestyle.

Figure 6.34 *A rather clumsy attempt at phishing*

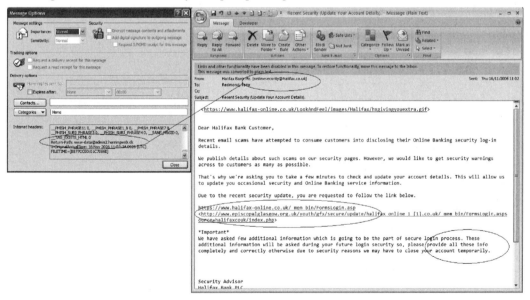

Some of the email that spammers generate to fool recipients are laughable, but only to professionals. Figure 6.34 shows a message that Outlook 2007 moved into my Junk E-Mail folder. The author of this spam didn't do a good job in their attempt to represent the message as a communication from the security department in a large U.K. bank. The message phrasing is not of the professional standard that you'd expect from a company like a bank, the link that the message directs readers to obviously does not belong to the bank, and the spammer didn't bother to disguise the return path for the message so we can see that the apparent sender address is not connected in any way to the return domain, which seems to be somewhere in Denmark. There are many variations on this theme floating around the Internet alleging to come from banks, eBay, PayPal, utility companies, and other organizations.

Figure 6.35
A classic email scam

All want to grab some personal details from the recipient to be used for some nefarious purpose.

Figure 6.35 illustrates an example of what has become a classic scam. Originally the scammers reached their targets via telex or postal mail but ever since email became generally available in the mid 1990s, we have seen a continuous stream of messages turning up in mailboxes from people who claim to offer an incredible deal. All you have to do is send some money to someone you have never met before who lives in a country that you probably have never visited and they will be delighted to use your money to liberate a substantial sum that a relative, friend, or guardian hid away. You will be richly rewarded for your investment and can look forward to an early retirement. These messages are generated in their millions by people in Internet cafes. They are invariably poorly written and don't look like a professional message, but they contain a very tempting offer and it probably should come as no surprise that thousands of victims are duped yearly. This kind of spam is often referred to as "419 email" because of the section in the criminal code that Nigeria was forced to introduce after so many spammers started to operate in Nigeria. Unfortunately, the existence of a crime is no guarantee that it will be prosecuted and the Nigerian spammers continue unabated together with colleagues from elsewhere around the world. Variations on the theme include messages that inform you that you've won a huge amount of money in a lottery, but you need to send some cash to pay for administrative fees, or messages that tell of a great inheritance that just needs some legal fees to be paid before it can be released. No one has ever gained anything from one of these messages and no one is likely to gain anything anytime soon.

The fact that so much spam is in circulation, even spam that is easy to detect, indicates that a viable business model continues to exist for spammers and that they will continue their activities until the business model becomes unprofitable. Government legislation makes spamming more dangerous from a legal perspective, but legislation has to be enforced to be effective and spammers can offset that risk by moving their activities offshore. Lawsuits from companies like Microsoft threaten major spammers by going after their assets, but as long as the activity remains profitable, small- to medium-scale spammers will continue. The existence of easy-accessible spamming toolkits and an active market in distribution lists of email addresses that are either harvested from Internet sources (for example, newsgroups) or generated automatically means that spamming remains an easy business to get into.

The attraction of email as a propagation mechanism for virus authors is that it is a quick and successful way to spread their creation to a large number of people without much effort on their part. There is some "me to" in email viruses as well as many of the viruses that exist are variants on a previous virus. It is all too easy for someone to create an email virus by downloading source code from a web site and adapting it for their own purpose.

Another aspect worth considering is the changing attitude of people in general to data. Where once all essential data lived securely in the data-center, it is increasingly so that users view data as something that lives in the Internet cloud and they are not concerned where precisely the data actually resides. If this was not the case, then social networking sites such as MySpace or Bebo would not be as successful as they are. It's a sweeping generalization to say that the younger you are, the less concerned you are with data storage and protection, but a fair amount of truth lies in this remark. Younger users are faster to trust their data to locations that they have no control over, have no real knowledge about the companies who run the site, and no guarantee that their data will exist tomorrow. Compare this attitude to anyone who grew up in the "green screen email" era! Maybe the easy trust of Internet applications is one of the reasons why email addresses are easy for spammers to harvest and so contribute to the growth of spam traffic.

All of this means that email administrators face an increasing volume of message traffic that contain spam and viruses. The techniques used to transmit this unwanted content are ever changing, so administrators face another challenge simply to understand what's going on and figure out how to best deal effectively with the threat. The ratio of unwanted messages addressed to major corporations that fail-first pass tests (from well-known sources of spam, contain easily detectable content that is objectionable, or have dangerous attachments such as known viruses) is now 70% or above. In some educational institutions, the percentage of rejected email has surpassed 80%, perhaps because of the trusting nature of younger users. If so, this may be a pointer to a future security challenge for corporations as new employees come in with less exacting attitudes to security than their predecessors.

6.11.6   Defense in depth

The classic approach taken by companies to defend against email viruses and spam is to establish defense in depth, with multiple layers of increasingly more sophisticated protection scanning the message stream before final delivery. Most large organizations deploy bastion servers at the edge of the network to suppress these messages before they get into internal networks. Another technique is to outsource the problem by buying a service that allows you to pass the message stream through servers operated by companies that specialize in spam and anti-virus suppression. The cleaned stream of email is then delivered to your network for internal email servers to process. In either case, some spam will get through because the spammers invent new techniques to beat spam traps on an ongoing basis. The only effective way to beat spam is therefore to deploy defense in depth. This means that you:

- Deploy bastion servers (servers that intercept all email traffic en route to your network to filter it and drop any obvious messages that contain spam, viruses, or other objectionable content) or use a managed security service to clean as much of the incoming email traffic before it enters your company's network.

- Run anti-spam and anti-virus software on your email servers to suppress spam that gets into your network. Ideally, use different anti-spam and anti-virus engines on multiple points along the message path. For example, if you operate bastion servers (using Exchange 2007 Edge servers or another technology), then you should run a different anti-virus scan on those servers to those that you run on the hub or mailbox servers that lie behind the firewall. Some anti-virus engines, like Microsoft's own Forefront Security for Exchange Server, allow you to run different anti-virus engines. If you use this approach, make sure that you run one set of anti-virus engines on

Edge or hub transport servers and another on the mailbox servers. If the anti-virus engines operate on the "Don't scan if it's done already" principle, you won't incur much additional overhead if you operate a scan on multiple-level defense.

- Encourage users to use client-side spam filters such as Outlook's junk mail feature to suppress the last few unwanted messages that sneak through. Make sure that the data files that drive virus detection are kept up to date.

The goal is to suppress as much of the unwanted traffic at the network edge to avoid having to transport and store spam within the network. Ideally, end users should see no more than one or two obvious pieces of spam weekly and you should encourage users to report what spam gets through to their inbox so that you can take whatever action is necessary. The messages that get through to inboxes indicate either a weakness in your mail hygiene protection or a new attack technique. For example, the first outbreak of phishing got through most anti-spam filters because the messages seemed to be very legitimate and no one expected to receive invitations to send their personal banking details to rogue servers.

6.11.7 Microsoft's approach to mail hygiene

Since 2000, Microsoft has poured an increasing amount of development resource into upgrading the ability of Exchange to suppress unwanted traffic, a project that they sometimes refer to as the Coordinated Spam Reduction initiative. The enhanced filtering capabilities delivered in Exchange 2003 marked a huge step forward and we have seen even more progress since with the provision of tools such as the Intelligent Message Filter, support for Sender ID, more improvements to the connection and recipient filters, and so on. Microsoft's goal is simple. They would like mail administrators to consider Exchange to be a viable mail server to deploy anywhere inside an infrastructure. This means that Exchange has to be able to handle mail traffic safely at the network edge as well as it can behind firewalls. Some years ago, most mail administrators considered Exchange to be too easy a target for hackers to place servers inside the DMZ, but the changes in Exchange and Windows means that you can safely deploy Exchange anywhere in an infrastructure, providing you pay attention to all of the other pieces that have to be in place for a secure network (properly configured firewalls, intrusion detection systems, and so on).

Table 6.9 *Protection layers*

Layer	Protection

Table 6.9   *Protection layers*

0	External filtering
1	Connection filters
2	SMTP filters
3	Anti-spam/Content
4	Anti-virus/Content
5	Client protection

Table 6.9 lists the different layers of protection that you can deploy inside an Exchange environment. You can deploy multi-layer protection with both Exchange 2003 or 2007. As you'd expect, Exchange 2007 offers more features, is more integrated, and is a little more sophisticated all round. Let's explore the details of the six layers.

- Layer 0 (external filtering) means that the mail traffic stream is cleansed before it is delivered to Exchange. For Exchange 2003, this function is usually accomplished by deploying bastion servers that are responsible for intercepting the mail stream en route into a company with the intention of performing a first pass to drop messages that contain obviously unwanted content. Dropped messages are not acknowledged. Alternatively, you can employ a managed service such as that provided by companies that specialize in virus and spam suppression in an email stream such as Postini, Symantec (Brightmail), or MessageLabs or indeed use Microsoft's own Exchange Hosted Filtering service, which is available to Enterprise customers. You can continue to protect yourself in the same way after you move to Exchange 2007, or you can deploy Exchange 2007 Edge servers to replace the bastion hosts. See page 506 for a discussion about the functionality that the Edge server provides.

- Layer 1 is enabled through connection filters. These filters use DSN Block lists (otherwise known as Real Time Block lists) from specific providers to identify traffic coming in from known spammers. Exchange allows you to customize the filters to add your own blocks and also to specific global accept and deny lists, with exceptions. Exchange 2003 and 2007 both support connection filters. The Exchange 2007 implementation is completely different due to the upgrade of the transport architecture. Exchange 2007 uses a Connection Filter agent that runs on an Edge server to examine the IP address of incoming connection requests to decide whether to accept or drop the connection. You can define lists of IP addresses to block. Connection filtering is on by default for any unauthenticated messages.

- Layer 2 is enabled through recipient and sender filters, which you can deploy on both Exchange 2003 and 2007 servers. The attention turns from where the message comes from to who the messages are addressed to. Exchange checks that incoming messages are well formed according to the RFC specifications that govern SMTP to block attempts to slip by checks through malformed headers. You can create sender filters to block specific SMTP addresses from being able to send messages to users in your organization and to reject messages from specific domains. Exchange can block messages with blank addresses or those that are spoofed (appear to come from a different address than they actually originate from). You can decide to drop messages completely or archive them for further examination. The new Exchange 2007 transport architecture implements recipient and sender filters as agents, but perhaps the most interesting change is the ability to incorporate the safe sender and safe recipient lists generated by users into the checking process. One of the changes made to the Active Directory schema for Exchange 2007 allows users to publish their safelists in hashed format as attributes of their user object. The hashed lists can then be sent to Edge servers through the EdgeSync process to allow Exchange to use this data when it checks incoming messages. The advantage of using this data to filter messages on the Edge server is that it avoids the need for potential spam to enter the organization and be delivered to mail servers. Sender filtering can generate NDR messages from blocked senders or accept the message and increase its spam confidence level (SCL), a value that the Store and Outlook can later examine to decide whether the message really is spam. Recipient filtering is only applied for messages sent to domains that are specified as authenticated, so to avoid the rejection of legitimate messages, you should run the Sender Filter agent in conjunction with the Sender ID agent.

- Layer 3 is enabled by examining incoming messages to detect spam. The Exchange 2003 Intelligent Message Filter (IMF) was Microsoft's first anti-spam suppression technology designed for deployment inside an Exchange organization. IMF is not part of the standard Exchange kit and you have to download it from Microsoft's web site and install it separately. IMF uses the same SmartScreen[8] technology that protects Hotmail. At this point, message headers have passed the previous tests, so Exchange accepts the message content to review it for signs that it contains spam or objectionable content such as por-

---

8.   SmartScreen is technology based on the careful analysis by Microsoft of billions of messages that flow through email systems to detect patterns that identify suspect messages that may contain viruses or spam.

nography. IMF determines an SCL value that is stored with the message attributes. If the SCL exceeds a threshold set by an administrator, IMF drops the message and otherwise passes it on for delivery to the end user. IMF is also able to check for messages that seem valid but are actually the source of phishing attacks. Phishing is an attempt to get users to transmit confidential personal information to a destination that might reuse the data to defraud the user. For example, some phishing attacks ask users for credit card information that is later used to charge their accounts. IMF calculates a PCL (phishing confidence level) that influences the eventual SCL that decides whether IMF passes or drops a message.

Exchange 2007 does not use the IMF. Instead, its functionality is incorporated into the Content Filter agent. Apart from checking for spam, the Content Filter understands the email postmarks applied by Outlook 2007 clients to mark email as legitimate. Postmarks are computed values transported in the message header, and if a postmark exists, the Content Filter considers the message as unlikely to be spam. The Content Filter is able to use the safe sender data gathered from users as part of its check and does so on the basis that if a user has specified a correspondent as a safe sender, then the Content Filter can safely regard any incoming message from that person to be safe. The Content Filter includes a quarantine mechanism that captures suspicious messages that an administrator can later review to decide to delete or release to the end user. Reviewing suspicious traffic for any large organization could occupy a considerable amount of administrator time, so it is a feature that needs to be tested before you deploy it. Both the IMF and Content Filter agent depend on regular updates of the data file that contains data about spam types and techniques to remain at maximum effectiveness. You have to download and apply updates for the IMF manually, but the Content Filter is able to update itself automatically.

■ Layer 4 occurs through anti-virus software that runs on Exchange servers to monitor message and attachment content for viruses. In addition, servers and user PCs are likely to run file-level anti-virus software to protect against infected files that are created when a user reads an attachment. The big change in Exchange 2007 is that anti-virus products that are "Exchange 2007 aware" (such as Microsoft's own Forefront Security product) can examine messages as they transit the transport system and can suppress virus-bearing messages before they are delivered to mailboxes, which reduces the risk that users will inadvertently infect their PCs by opening a message and triggering a virus. Exchange 2007 also includes a new agent that runs on the Edge server to filter attachments. See page 560 for details.

■ Level 5 is enabled by client-side junk mail filters. Outlook 2003 and 2007 both include a good junk mail filter that uses SmartScreen technology and there are many other third-party offerings for Outlook and other clients that use a range of techniques, including Bayesian logic, to detect and suppress spam. Microsoft offers an add-in that you can install in Outlook 2003 and 2007 called the "Junk Mail Reporting Tool" that you can download from their Download Center. This add-on allows you to report a spam message that you receive to Microsoft so that its characteristics can be checked against the SmartScreen database and added if it represents a new type of attack. A new button is added to your Outlook menu bar so that when new spam arrives that isn't detected by Outlook's Junk Mail filter, you can click on the button to remove the message from your inbox and have it sent automatically to FrontBridge, a Microsoft subsidiary (Figure 6.36). You'll receive an automated message afterwards to acknowledge the submission.

Figure 6.36

Reporting spam to Microsoft

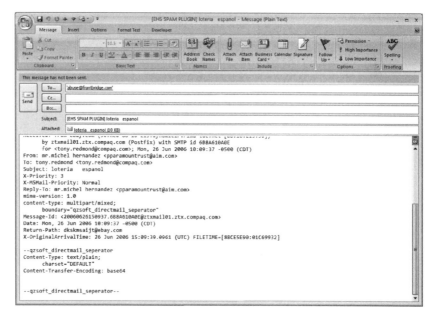

Table 6.10 summarizes how Microsoft has steadily built up the range of mail hygiene features since spam and viruses exploded on the world. In some respects, you can argue that Microsoft has simply evolved Exchange to keep pace with the volume and tactics of spammers and virus authors but that would be a misrepresentation of the degree of engineering effort that has

been expended to create defense in depth for Exchange. A better description is to say that the mail hygiene features offered by Exchange 2007 represent a continuum of improvement since the first defenses erected by Exchange 2000. The agent technology used to implement mail hygiene are easier to control and understand than the transport sinks used previously and you have the option to deploy protection on Edge or hub transport servers standalone or in conjunction with other technology that you already might use. The exact details of the implementation at each layer will differ from company to company and is dependent on their existing email infrastructure, current practice, and the tools that are available. The point is that multi-layer defense is the only proven technique that can prevent users having to process

Table 6.10   *Evolution of inbuilt Exchange mail hygiene features*

Exchange 5.5 (1997)	Exchange 2000 (2000)	Exchange 2003 (2003) and SP1 (2004)	Exchange 2007
Third-party anti-virus products required to protect Exchange; no ability to suppress spam or unwanted connections.	Sender Filters	Sender Filters from Exchange 2000 plus: ■ Connection Filters (real-time block lists) ■ Protect groups with authenticated connections ■ Sender ID (SP1) ■ Content Filter (IMF – SP1) ■ Client-side junk mail filters in Outlook 2003 and Outlook Web Access	Functionally equivalent agents for Exchange 2003 features plus: ■ Attachment Filter ■ Sender Reputation ■ User safelist aggregation ■ Suspicious email quarantine capability ■ Edge server role

large quantities of unwanted or dangerous messages. While Microsoft will continue to improve the mail hygiene features in Exchange, it's up to you to decide how to deploy and use the technology within the context of your IT infrastructure.

6.11.8   Forefront for Exchange

To give the product its full title, Microsoft Forefront Security for Exchange Server is an evolution of the Sybari Antigen product that Microsoft acquired when they bought Sybari Software in 2005. Sybari was a company that had become the leader in Exchange anti-virus protection because of their innovation in anti-virus protection. The first Sybari breakthrough was the introduction of a hook into the Store that allowed Antigen to achieve much higher levels of performance and protection than was possible with the approaches that other anti-virus products took at that time. Over time, Microsoft recognized the value of Sybari's work and introduced their own version in the VSAPI (Virus Scanning API) that all Exchange anti-virus products use today.

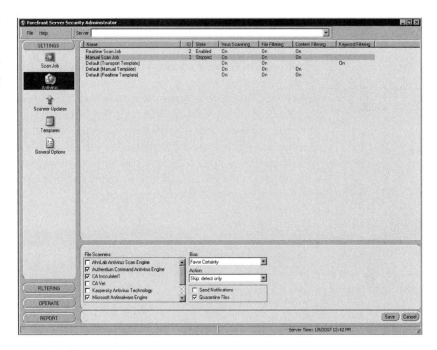

Figure 6.37
Configuring anti-virus engines for Forefront

Another key Sybari feature was their use of multiple anti-virus engines to scan the email stream. Most other products were confined to their own anti-virus engine, but as Sybari did not own or engineer an anti-virus engine, they were able to make licensing deals with vendors who did the necessary research and development to build anti-virus engines and then combine the different engines together to achieve more comprehensive coverage against new viruses. The version of Forefront that is now available combines the best of the existing Sybari technology with an even closer integration with Exchange, so it's a pretty good option if you're looking to deploy an anti-virus product that can scan incoming messages and the Exchange Store. Forefront is included in the Exchange Enterprise CAL and downgrade rights exist to use Antigen on Exchange 2003 servers if you purchase the Exchange 2007 Enterprise CAL. Other versions of Forefront are available to protect SharePoint Portal Server and Live Communications Server against viruses that may be transmitted through those routes.

Figure 6.37 shows the Scanner Updates options that are available to Forefront. As you can see, a large number of engines are available for use with Forefront. You can deploy up to five engines on a server. You can configure Exchange to download and apply updates for these engines automatically to maximize protection against new viruses. Real-time scanning occurs in memory using multiple threads. The theory is that real-time scanning does not delay message delivery. While it is true that users are not aware that real-time scanning has intercepted and processed their messages, it is also true that some administrators do not deploy real-time scanning on mailbox servers in order to maximize the performance of these servers. In these scenarios, the administrators depend on anti-virus scans performed on hub transport servers (or on bastion servers at the edge of the network) to provide the necessary degree of protection against viruses. If you think that some infection has occurred or when you know that a virulent virus attack is underway, you can perform a manual scan of a database, selected mailboxes, or public folders to detect any infected messages that have managed to get through. As Figure 6.38 shows, you can also create a customized message to inform users when a scan detects an infected message in their mailbox. At the time of writing, Forefront supports 11 different languages.

Figure 6.38
Setting up a manual scan and a customized message

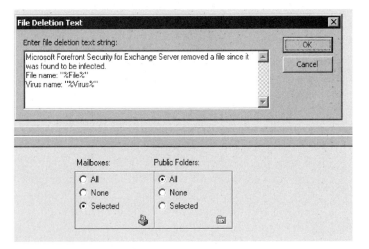

Figure 6.39 illustrates some of the general options that are available to configure how Forefront operates on a server. You can deploy Forefront on Edge, hub, and mailbox servers. Some administrators believe that it does not make sense any more to deploy anti-virus software on mailbox servers because agents process the mail stream multiple times en route to mailboxes. This is certainly even more of a valid point to consider with Exchange 2007 because you now have a guarantee that all messages pass through hub transport servers, which was not the case before. Exchange 2007 includes the con-

cept of anti-virus stamps, meaning that as a server processes a message with an anti-virus engine, it stamps the message to show that it has processed the message. The stamp is stored as a MAPI property that Exchange transports with the message, so that if another server subsequently opens a message for scanning, the server can examine the stamp and pass the message without further scanning. For example, if an Edge server runs Forefront scans and passes a message, the stamp applied by the Edge server stops scanning by hub or mailbox servers further along the message delivery path. The same type of processing occurs for outbound messages, so that a scan applied by a mailbox server will stop processing by the hub and Edge servers. If scanning fails at any point, the lack of a stamp will cause the next server to scan the message. Exchange removes stamps on outgoing messages so that they do not cause a receiving Exchange organization to bypass processing. All anti-virus processing occurs after anti-spam agents have cleansed the message stream so that Exchange does not consume CPU cycles to scan messages that an anti-spam agent will suppress.

Figure 6.39
General options for
Forefront

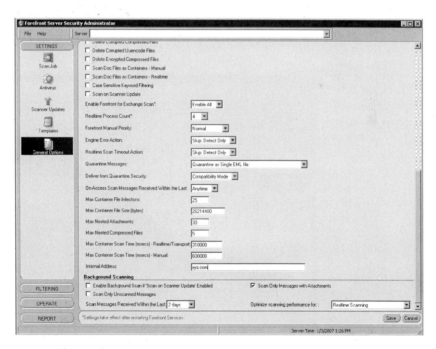

If an anti-virus outbreak occurs, it may be that attachments contain the virus. You can configure Forefront to filter out specific attachment names or file types, and this is a useful thing to do to prevent infected messages circulating within the organization or being sent out to other companies, or coming into the organization if you do not run Edge servers or another type of bastion server that can filter attachment types. You can configure the Attachment Filter agent on Edge servers (see page 562) to process incoming messages and remove attachments, so the ability of Forefront to remove attachments is another weapon in the administrator's armory. Forefront is easier to work with because you can input the names of attachments or attachment types through a GUI; you configure the Attachment Filter agent through shell commands. You can argue that it is better for an administrator to configure the Attachment Filter agent once through a script and then reuse the script on all Edge servers than to have to go to every server that runs Forefront to configure an attachment block through the GUI. The proponents of scripting say that scripts deliver predictable results (after you debug them); those who prefer the GUI say that a user interface lets you see exactly what you have done. It all comes down to personal choice.

You would like to know that something good has come from all your hard work to set up comprehensive anti-virus protection. Forefront provides reasonable facilities to report the viruses that it detects. Figure 6.40 shows the Forefront Incidents screen, where we can see that two viruses have been detected recently (you can move across the screen to discover the sender to be able to contact them to tell them that they may have a problem on their PC). You can also see the statistics for scanning activity on this server.

Figure 6.40
Reporting detected viruses and other statistics

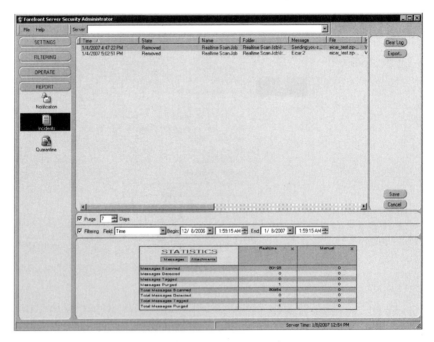

Forefront is not the only anti-virus product that can protect Exchange and it's important that you review the other products that are available to establish which is the best for your organization. If you operate a heterogeneous environment, you may find that you prefer to use a single anti-virus product that can protect all platforms; you may decide to source anti-virus software for both clients and servers from the one vendor; or you may find that other products integrate better into your preferred management framework.

6.11.9 Mail Hygiene Agents

A mail hygiene agent is a piece of code that scans a message for one or more characteristics in order to help make a decision whether Exchange should eventually accept the message. Agents scan messages in order, starting from the time that a remote server initiates an SMTP connection to transfer a message and finishing after the full content of the message has been transferred to the Edge or hub transport server where the agents run. In Exchange terms, the agents "fire" as specific transport events occur and in the following order:

1. Connection Filtering
2. Sender Filtering
3. Address Rewriting Inbound (Edge server only)
4. Recipient Filtering
5. Protocol Analysis and Sender Reputation
6. Sender ID
7. Edge Rules
8. Content Filtering
9. Attachment Filtering (Edge server only)

As shown in Figure 6.41, the set of anti-spam agents are managed from the Organization Configuration node in EMC so that the settings you make for an agent are replicated along with the rest of Exchange's configuration throughout the organization. By default, the anti-spam agents are automatically installed on every Edge server, but if you want to run the agents on a hub transport server, you have to install them. To do this, run the Install-AntiSpamAgents.ps1 script from the \Program Files\Microsoft\Exchange Server\Scripts directory. This script installs the necessary code to allow the agents to run on a server and runs the `Set-TransportServer` command to set the AntiSpamEnabled flag on the server. If you decide to later remove the agents from a hub transport server, use the Uninstall-AntiSpamAgents.ps1 script from the same directory.

Use the `Get-TransportAgent` command to view the set of agents installed on a server. This command shows whether each agent is enabled and the priority order for the agents to execute:

```
Identity                            Enabled        Priority
--------                            -------        --------
Connection Filtering Agent          True           1
Address Rewriting Inbound Agent     True           2
Edge Rule Agent                     True           3
Content Filter Agent                True           4
Sender Id Agent                     True           5
Sender Filter Agent                 True           6
Recipient Filter Agent              True           7
Protocol Analysis Agent             True           8
Attachment Filtering Agent          True           9
Address Rewriting Outbound Agent    True           10
```

Figure 6.41

Anti-spam agents installed on a hub transport server

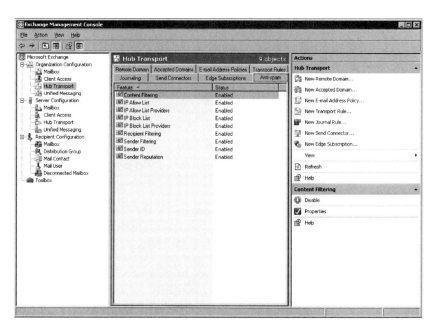

You can use the same command to view additional configuration information for each agent. For example:

```
Get-TransportAgent —id 'Connection Filtering Agent'
```

```
Identity              : Connection Filtering Agent
Enabled               : True
Priority              : 4
TransportAgentFactory :
Microsoft.Exchange.Transport.Agent.ConnectionFiltering.ConnectionFilteringAge
ntFactory
AssemblyPath          : C:\Program Files\Microsoft\Exchange Server\
TransportRoles\agents\Hygiene\Microsoft.Exchange.Transport.Agent.Hygiene.dll
```

You can see the transport events that agents are associated with by using the `Get-TransportPipeline` command. Figure 6.42 shows the output from executing `Get-TransportPipeline` on a hub transport server. The first 15 events fire as messages and are accepted by the receive connector. The last two fire as the categorizer begins to process and finishes processing messages.

Figure 6.42
Output from Get-TransportPipeline command.

```
Event                             TransportAgents
-----                             ---------------
OnConnectEvent                    {Connection Filtering Agent}
OnHeloCommand                     {}
OnEhloCommand                     {}
OnAuthCommand                     {}
OnEndOfAuthentication             {}
OnMailCommand                     {Connection Filtering Agent, Sender Filter Agent}
OnRcptCommand                     {Connection Filtering Agent, Recipient Filter Agent}
OnDataCommand                     {}
OnEndOfHeaders                    {Connection Filtering Agent, Sender Id Agent, Sender Fil...
OnEndOfData                       {Content Filter Agent, Protocol Analysis Agent}
OnHelpCommand                      {}
OnNoopCommand                      {}
OnReject                          {Protocol Analysis Agent}
OnRsetCommand                     {Protocol Analysis Agent}
OnDisconnectEvent                 {Protocol Analysis Agent}
OnSubmittedMessage                {Journaling Agent}
OnRoutedMessage                   {Transport Rule Agent, Journaling Agent}
```

It is possible to change the priority order that the agents fire with the `Set-TransportAgent` command, but this is not a good idea unless you have a logical reason to alter the interaction between the different agents. Each agent operates on different parts of incoming messages and if you change priority, you may cause an agent to fire before full data is available for it.

Configuration changes that you apply on a hub transport server will be replicated throughout the organization. Configuration changes to Edge servers are particular to that server, and if you want to make the same change on all Edge servers, you either have to make the changes manually or create scripts to do the work.

6.11.10   Agent logs

Exchange captures the results of agent processing in a set of log files in the \Program Files\Microsoft\Exchange Server\TransportRoles\Logs\AgentLog directory. The log files are called AgentLogYYYYMMDD-1.LOG. You can interrogate these logs to get an idea of what the agents do when they process mail. For example, to discover what messages are being dropped because they have exceeded the SCL threshold to be deleted, you'd scan the agent log as follows:

```
Get-AgentLog | Where {$_.Reason —eq
'SCLAtOrAboveDeleteThreshold'} | Select MessageId,
P1FromAddress
```

On an active server that processes a stream of incoming messages from the Internet, this command is likely to generate a lot of entries, so if you want to get more detail, you can select an individual log entry using its message identifier and have a look at what it reveals. For example:

```
Get-Agentlog | Where {$_.MessageId -eq
"<BA0F808C82DE9A48A4DAA1542B243182029795B5@Exch2003.xyz.net>"}
```

```
Timestamp        : 12/20/2006 3:07:05 PM
SessionId        : 08C8DAC8E38B7F66
IPAddress        : 11.25.5.6
MessageId        :
<BA0F808C82DE9A48A4DAA1542B243182029795B5@Exch2003.xyz.net>
P1FromAddress    : tony.redmond@xyz.com
P2FromAddresses  : {True}
Recipients       : {True}
Agent            : Content Filter Agent
Event            : OnEndOfData
Action           : RejectMessage
SmtpResponse     : 250 2.6.0
<BA0F808C82DE9A48A4DAA1542B243182029795B5@Exch2003.xyz.net>
Queued mail for delivery
Reason           : SclAtOrAboveDeleteThreshold
ReasonData       : 9
```

6.11.11 Connection filtering

Connection filters examine the IP addresses presented by remote SMTP servers who initiate SMTP sessions with Exchange to decide whether to accept the message that the remote server wishes to send. Connection filtering is applied to all connections that come in from unauthenticated SMTP servers. The Connection Filter agent fires when the OnConnect transport event occurs and extracts the underlying IP address used to initiate the SMTP session and then compares the IP address against IP block lists (to decide whether to drop the session) and IP allow lists (to accept the session). If the IP address is on a block list, Exchange continues to accept data until all recipient information (the RCPT TO data) is received so that it can check if any of the intended recipients has set the bypass spam filter parameter on their mailbox. Any messages for these recipients is accepted for further processing.

```
Set-Mailbox —id Bond —AntiSpamBypassEnabled:$True
```

If the IP address is on an IP allow list, Exchange will not apply any other anti-spam filters because an administrator is assumed to know what they are doing when they add the address to the allow list. The agent can also check with third-party providers who specialize in assembling lists of IP addresses used by well-known spammers. These lists are known as real-time block lists (RBLs) and have been in use for years. The accuracy and up-to-date nature of the lists vary from provider to provider so some care has to be taken before you select a provider to use. Apart from satisfying yourself of the accuracy of the information (there is a lot of information about RBLs available on the Internet), you need fast response to queries and some guarantee of availability if you are to rely on the chosen provider. If the IP address is found on these lists, Exchange will drop the session as before. Exchange always checks its own lists first before checking with a third party.

Figure 6.43
Setting IP blocks

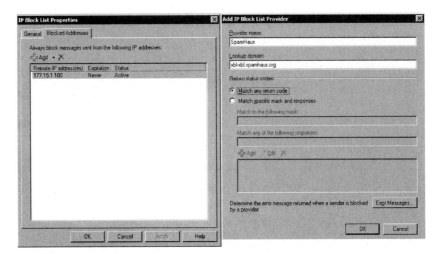

Figure 6.43 shows how to establish IP blocks through EMC. In the left-hand screen, we define that we never want to accept messages that originate from IP address 177.51.1.100. In the right-hand screen we define an IP Block List provider. Note that we can decide to match on any status code returned by the provider or look for a specific code, such as one that indicates that the IP address is on an IP block list or points to an SMTP server that is configured to act as an open relay.

EMC also allows you to set up an IP Allow List, which is the reverse of the IP Block List, and IP Allow List Provider, which serves a similar purpose to the IP Block List provider except that it defines a set of IP addresses that the provider can testify to be safe.

Using the shell, you can view the current IP Block List entries with the `Get-IPBlockListEntry` command, add new IP addresses to the block list with the `Add-IPBlockListEntry` command, and remove them with the `Remove-IPBlockListEntry` command. Similar commands exist for the IP Allow List and to configure the IP Block List and IP Allow List providers. However, it's easier to do this work through the GUI.

6.11.12 Sender filtering

Connection filters protect by blocking the IP addresses used by well-known spammers. Sender filters add protect by blocking the email addresses and domains that spammers use. The Sender filter agent fires on the OnMail-Command event when the MAIL FROM data is available for a message and works by comparing the sender email address (both MAIL FROM and the From: field in the message—these are not necessarily the same and are often not for spam) against a list of addresses that the administrator defines as "bad." You can block individual addresses, like SexyChicks@hotbabes.com, or a complete domain, such as any message from hotbabes.com, or even any sub-domains, such as *.hotbabes.com. Figure 6.44 shows two blocked senders defined: a complete domain (badpeople.com) and an individual called Sales@horribleproduct.com.

Figure 6.44
Defining blocked senders

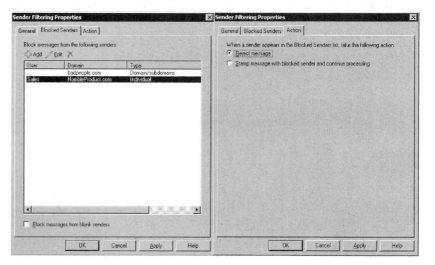

After you identify offending messages, you then have to decide how to handle them. You can decide to reject the message immediately with a "Sender Denied" response or you can accept the message with the proviso that it comes from a blocked sender. The Content filter agent will then take this fact into account when it calculates an SCL value for the message. In all likelihood, the message's SCL value will be increased and may lead to it being blocked at a later point in the anti-spam cycle because its SCL value exceeds the threshold for acceptance.

From the shell, you can use the `Get-SenderFilterConfig` command to see values that are set for the agent. Some of the important parameters are shown below, including the blocked senders that we configured through EMC. You can also see that the configuration for this agent states that filtering occurs for external messages (ExternalMailEnabled=True) and not for internal messages that come from domains defined as being authoritative for the Exchange organization.

```
Name                              : SenderFilterConfig
BlockedSenders                    :
{Sales@HorribleProduct.com}
BlockedDomains                    : {}
BlockedDomainsAndSubdomains       : {badpeople.com}
Action                            : Reject
BlankSenderBlockingEnabled        : False
Enabled                           : True
ExternalMailEnabled               : True
InternalMailEnabled               : False
```

You can use the `Set-SenderFilterConfig` command to set parameters for the Sender Filter agent. For example, let's assume that you have another address to add to the list of blocked senders. We can do this:

```
$Original-List = (Get-SenderFilterConfig).BlockedSenders
$New-List = $Original-List += 'Marketing@ReallyBad.com'
Set-SenderFilterConfig -BlockSenders $New-List
```

6.11.13 Address Rewrite agent

The Address Rewrite agent only runs on an Edge server where it can rewrite the RCPT TO addresses on incoming messages or the MAIL FROM addresses on outgoing messages. This functionality is broadly similar to the token replacement capability offered by U*X-based email systems such as SendMail. Organizations may decide not to reveal internal email addresses to the outside world and provide users with addresses that are sufficient to route messages to the edge of the organization but no further. A process, running either on another email server or the Edge server, then takes responsibility for rewriting the addresses in message headers so that when the messages are passed from the network edge into the organization, email servers are able to route them to their final destination. Another example is where senior executives or other users don't want messages going directly to their mailbox without being screened by someone. In these situations, it's common to have separate internal and external addresses. Internally, the users can be addressed by reference to the GAL and messages go direct to their mailbox but external messages are diverted with a rewrite rule to a special mailbox to be checked.

For example, let's assume that you provide users with outward-facing addresses like:

```
John.Smith@xyz.com
```

But internally, the mailbox is identified as Smith-JohnA @Exchange.Email.xyz.com. Clearly, the first form is much easier for the user to remember and for correspondents to address messages with. If John Smith wanted their messages to be screened first, we might direct any message arriving for them to a mailbox like John.Smith-External@xyz.com.

The Address Rewrite agent can rewrite addresses for individual users or for complete domains. There is no GUI available to control this agent, so you have to do everything through the `New-AddressRewriteEntry` command. Here's what we might do to create a rule for a specific user. Note that in this instance the rule applies bidirectionally for incoming and outgoing messages:

```
New-AddressRewriteEntry —Name "John Smith External" —
InternalAddress "John.Smith-External@xyz.com"    —
ExternalAddress "John.Smith@xyz.com"
```

Another example is where you use `New-AddressRewriteEntry` to rewrite information for complete domains. In this example we create a rule to handle rewrites for an internal routing domain to take on a domain name that's known externally. This might be done in the case of a company merger when you want to replace the domain name used by the company being acquired by the domain name for the acquiring company. Unlike our previous rule, this rule only processes outbound messages (the –OutBoundOnly parameter is set to $True) because we aren't interested in preserving the obsolete domain names for the acquired company:

```
New-AddressRewriteEntry -Name "Rewrite External Address Only"
-InternalAddress *.OurInternalDomain.com -ExternalAddress
OurExternalDomain.com —OutboundOnly $True
```

You can use the `Get-AddressRewriteEntry` command to list all of the rewrite rules that exist on an Edge server and the `Remove-AddressRewrite-Entry` command to remove a rule and remember that any change made to a configuration on an Edge server has to be copied to other Edge servers that function for the organization. Note that the Address Rewrite agent is not enabled by default, so you have to enable it before any of the rewrite rules apply.

6.11.14 Sender ID agent

The Sender Filter agent checks the MAIL FROM information in messages to detect spam, but spammers routinely misrepresent themselves by manipulating addresses. Therefore, you need another way to detect whether the person sending you email really is who they say that they are, and that's when the Sender ID agent comes into play. Sender ID is the amalgamation of two similar proposals aimed at helping organizations to detect SPAM more easily by making it harder to spoof addresses: Sender Policy Framework (SPF[9]), authored by Meng Weng Wong (Singapore) and CallerID for email from Microsoft. Microsoft submitted Sender ID to the IETF as an Internet draft titled "MTA Authentication Records in DNS," but the IETF working group rejected the submission for many reasons, including some worries about intellectual property rights claimed by Microsoft. An effort continues within the IETF to bring the original SPF framework forward into a fully-fledged RFC, but this has not yet been granted. In the meantime, Microsoft supports Sender ID in all versions of Exchange from Exchange 2003 SP2 onwards.

The problem that Sender ID attempts to address is to make it harder for a spammer to spoof email addresses whereby messages come in from addresses that seem to be legitimate but really originate from people with whom we would prefer not to communicate. The core of the problem is that largely because of the simplicity and openness of SMTP, it is very easy for a spammer to spoof email addresses so that their messages appear to come from someone else. Some senders use spoofing to disguise the real originator of spam to make sure that the recipients will read the content, while others exploit spoofing to lure recipients into disclosing financial or other information that the spammers can then abuse.

No solution, including Sender ID, is likely to stop spammers sending messages. The intention behind Sender ID is to make it easier for organizations to detect spam at the point where it enters a network so that the mes-

---

9.   SPF is sometimes referred to as "Sender Permitted From."

sages can be rejected there. Blocking messages at the network perimeter avoids the overhead of accepting and storing the messages, an important factor given that most analysts accept that between 60% and 70% of all messages transmitted in the Internet are spam. Today, mail servers for organizations have to accept the messages to allow anti-spam software like Exchange's Intelligent Message Filter to examine their content before deciding to reject the messages. Even still, some spam gets through to user desktops and has to be dealt with by software such as Outlook's junk mail filter. Because Sender ID emphasizes the acceptance of email from validated domains it is best to regard this technology as part of an overall approach to the elimination of email forgeries, such as the messages used in phishing scams and not as a deterrent to all the other types of spam that afflict corporate and personal email recipients.

Sender ID is implemented in three steps:

1. Companies publish the details (IP addresses) of their email servers that send outbound messages in a format laid down by Sender ID in DNS.

2. Receiving systems can examine messages to determine the purported responsible address (PRA), or the address of the mailbox that sent the message.

3. The PRA includes the domain name of the sender (known as the purported responsible domain, or PRD), so receiving systems can query DNS to determine whether the message came from a valid email server for that domain. If not, then the message is likely to be spoofed and can be rejected or subject to additional checks, such as validation through traditional anti-spam software.

To make this structure work, companies have to publish details of their email servers in DNS in a format known as an email policy document (a structured XML record), a text DNS record. The specification describes the exact structure of the XML record, but in its simplest form, a record looks like this:

```
<ep>
<out>
<m>
<mx>
</m>
</out>
</ep>
```

The <ep> element marks the container for the policy document while the <out> element specifies the details of the policy. The <m> element is the most important part as it specifies the email servers that are permitted to send outbound messages for the domain. <mx> means that the only authorized hosts are those specified in the domain's MX records, but you can also specify IP addresses or ranges of IP addresses with <a> and <r> elements. A very simple policy document registering a single outbound email server of test.example.com might look like:

```
<?xml version="1.0" charset="us-ascii"?>
<root xmlns="urn:ietf:params:xml:schema:marid-1">
  <ep>
    <out default="fail">
      <m result="pass">
        <a>test.example.com</a>
      </m>
  </ep>
</root>
```

You can find many other variations and examples by searching the Web[10].

Sender ID uses a special subdomain called "_ep" to hold the email policy documents, so HP would publish our records under _ep.hp.com. This is the easiest way to publish an email policy document as the Sender ID checks look for the _ep subdomain and it avoids the risk of confusing email policy documents with the other DNS records.

When a message arrives at a server that supports Sender ID, it goes through a five-step validation process to determine the PRA.

1. Examine the Resent-Sender header.

2. Examine the Resent-From header.

3. Examine the Delivered-To, X-Envelope-To, and Envelope-To headers.

4. Examine the Sender header.

5. Examine the From header.

The order in which these headers are examined is determined by the difficulty of spoofing each, so the From header is the easiest for a spammer to spoof (as obvious in the example SMTP commands on page 1). In all cases,

---

10.   http://www.jhsoft.com/tutor/calleriddocs/callerid_senders.pdf is a good place to start, as are the specifications themselves.

the idea is to parse the header and examine its contents to determine whether the information can be resolved to a single PRA that the Sender ID agent can verify. The header information has to be "well formed" and unambiguous. Multiple values in the header will cause the Sender ID agent to move to the next header.

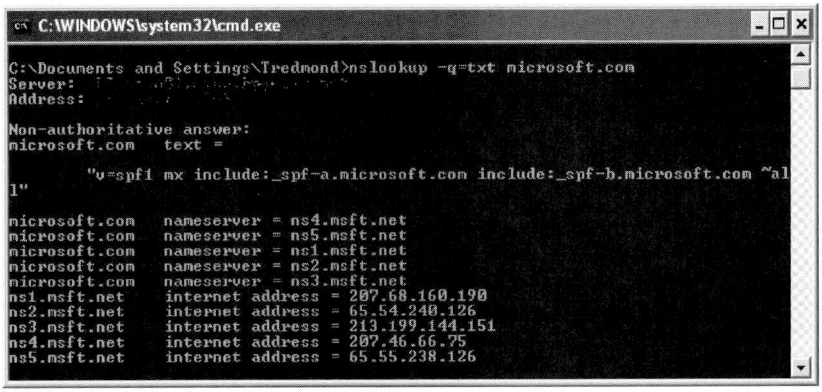

Figure 6.45

Checking whether a domain supports Sender ID

```
C:\WINDOWS\system32\cmd.exe                                          _ □ ×

C:\Documents and Settings\Tredmond>nslookup -q=txt microsoft.com
Server:
Address:

Non-authoritative answer:
microsoft.com    text =

          "v=spf1 mx include:_spf-a.microsoft.com include:_spf-b.microsoft.com ~al
1"

microsoft.com    nameserver = ns4.msft.net
microsoft.com    nameserver = ns5.msft.net
microsoft.com    nameserver = ns1.msft.net
microsoft.com    nameserver = ns2.msft.net
microsoft.com    nameserver = ns3.msft.net
ns1.msft.net     internet address = 207.68.160.190
ns2.msft.net     internet address = 65.54.240.126
ns3.msft.net     internet address = 213.199.144.151
ns4.msft.net     internet address = 207.46.66.75
ns5.msft.net     internet address = 65.55.238.126
```

After the Sender ID agent determines a valid PRA, it can then extract the PRD (domain) and use it to perform a DNS query to look for the email policy document. If the query returns an email policy document, the mail server then has a list of authorized IP addresses that it can use to decide whether to accept the message. Different error codes generated by the Sender ID agent help to make the decision. For example, a network error could happen during the check, in which case Sender ID returns a "transientError" status. A "Fail" status means that an email policy document exists, but it does not match the PRD, a strong indication that the message is spoofed and should be rejected with an SMTP 500 error. Of course, if no email policy document exists (a "neutral" status means that not enough information exists to make a decision, probably because no email policy document exists), the server can accept the message and pass it through whatever anti-spam procedures are in place to filter incoming messages. Users know nothing about Sender ID as all the work is done by system administrators to define and publish email policy documents and then upgrade SMTP servers to begin checking headers according to the Sender ID standard.

Speed of adoption for Sender ID is clearly a limiting factor for its effectiveness because the overall resilience of the Internet to spam is gated by the number of unprotected domains that spammers can attack. Microsoft checks inbound messages sent to hotmail.com, msn.com, and microsoft.com addresses and other large email providers are expected to do likewise. To check whether a domain supports Sender ID, use the NSLOOKUP command as shown in Figure 6.45.

Adding a Sender ID record for a domain is very straightforward and does not require software upgrades, so there is really no good reason not to do so, even if you employ the services of a third-party company to cleanse the incoming email stream for your company. Checking for Sender ID is another matter because many SMTP servers in use today still do not support it, although this issue will wane over time. As of October 2006, Microsoft-collected data indicates that some five million domains used Sender ID to verify their email, responsible for generating some 36% of the legitimate email traffic annually. Achieving this level of acceptance is actually an impressive feat and it indicates that Sender ID will pass the 50% mark sometime in early 2007 and become the most commonly used method of verifying email soon afterwards. Upgrading infrastructures to use SMTP servers that support Sender ID is an important step for the Internet as a whole. As Sender ID checking becomes more pervasive, older servers may not be able to generate the appropriate headers to get through the checks. Another concern is that many of the mailing lists and forwarding services will break after Sender ID checks begin. The solution is to include a "Resent-From" header in the messages that come from these services, but again, it will take time before everything is updated.

Companies such as HP that maintain large and diverse messaging infrastructures face other difficulties. It is easy enough to implement a technique such as Sender ID if you control the number of gateways that can transmit external email on behalf of your company. But if your company operates many different email systems and has many different points where messages can be sent into the Internet stamped with your company's domain, then the task is much harder. In HP's case, we have a large corporate deployment of Microsoft Exchange, but we also have email systems that run on UNIX, Linux, and OpenVMS systems, all of which are Internet-enabled. No one IT department is responsible for all of these systems. In addition, there are SMTP-enabled web servers that interact with customers and marketing systems that dispatch messages on behalf of HP from servers outside the HP domain. To implement Sender ID everywhere within our infrastructure, HP will have to track down every single point of transmission to ensure that all the servers support Sender ID and then make sure that any company that did email-based work (such as sending marketing information) on behalf of HP also supports the standard. The conclusion is that implementing Sender ID inside complex email infrastructures takes substantial planning and careful maintenance.

To configure Sender ID on an Exchange 2007 server, use EMC to select the Sender ID agent and go to the Action property page to select the action that you want to take if a message fails Sender ID validation (Figure 6.46). The equivalent action in the shell is:

```
Set-SenderIDConfig –SpoofedDomainAction Reject
```

Figure 6.46
Configuring
settings for
Sender ID

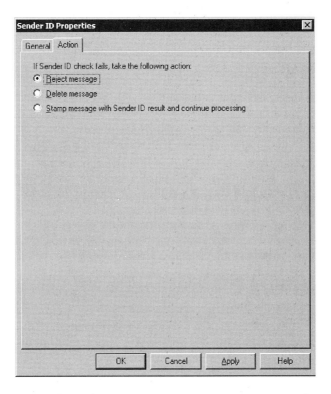

EMS exposes more configuration options for Sender ID than EMC does. For example, you can define a set of up to 100 recipient addresses that the Sender ID agent will not process. For example:

```
Set-SenderIDConfig —BypassedRecipients "Bond@xyz.com,
Smith@xyz.com"
```

You can also define a set of up to 100 sender domains that the Sender ID agent will ignore. For example:

```
Set-SenderIDConfig —BypassedSenderDomains "xyz.com, xyz1.com"
```

By default, all messages generated by authoritative domains within your organization are ignored by the Sender ID agent (because you assume that you know where these messages come from), but you can enable checking for these messages:

```
Set-SenderIDConfig -InternalMailEnabled:$True
```

Naturally, the reverse is true for nonauthoritative domains, which the Sender ID agent checks by default. Again, you can reverse this setting, even if it renders the Sender ID rather useless. To check on the current complete Sender ID configuration:

```
Get-SenderIDConfig | Format-List
```

When the Sender ID agent runs, it checks the SPF records for the purported sending domain to establish whether the IP address of the sender is authorized. The following results can be attained:

- Pass: the IP address of the sender is in the authorized set.
- Neutral: inconclusive.
- Soft Fail: the IP address may be in the NOT permitted set.
- Fail: the IP address is in the NOT permitted set.
- TempError: transient error occurred during the check, for example, DNS is not available.
- PermError: a permanent error occurred, for example, the SPF records are in an illegal format and cannot be properly read.

Following the check, Exchange may decide to Reject the message, delete the message (without any indication to the sender), or stamp the Sender ID status onto the message as a MAPI property. If Sender ID is not configured for the sending domain, that fact is noted in the Sender ID status too. Outlook later uses the Sender ID status as part of its calculation of the message's SCL value. For example, a Fail or SoftFail result contributes to a higher SCL value. However, there is no way for an administrator to define that Exchange should set a specific SCL value for any Sender ID status.

6.11.15   Content filtering

The Content Filter agent is the last in the anti-spam cycle. This agent is a development of the Intelligent Message Agent (IMF) that Microsoft launched for Exchange 2003 SP1. The IMF, the Content Filter agent, and the Outlook Junk Mail Filter (and Hotmail's Junk Mail agents) are all based on Microsoft's SmartScreen technology. As mentioned earlier, SmartScreen uses a database extracted from billions of messages to understand the characteristics of both legitimate messages and spam and uses these characteristics to assess the probability that any message is or is not spam.

The Content Filter agent uses SmartScreen to examine all parts of the message and is therefore the most processing intense of any of the agents. However, because it is the last in the anti-spam cycle, the Content Filter agent will not have to process messages that have already been rejected by other agents such as the Connection Filter and Recipient Filter. Unlike the IMF, the Content Filter is able to use the aggregated safelist data that can be gathered from user mailboxes and synchronized into ADAM on an Edge server to avoiding marking messages as spam if their senders are on a safelist. We'll discuss how you can aggregate and synchronize safelist to ADAM on an Edge server later in this chapter. If you run the Content Filter agent on a hub transport server, it can validate the message sender against the recipient's safelist data in the Active Directory. In effect, any message from someone on a user safelist will pass through the Content Filter unscathed.

Figure 6.47
*Blocking and
allowing words for
the Content Filter*

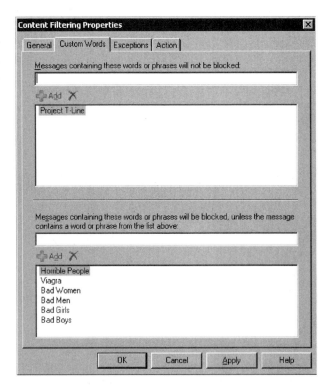

You know when the content agent has found a safelist match because the Content Filter agent adds a value of "AllRecipientsBypassed" in the X-MS-Exchange-Organization-Antispam-Report x-header in the message header. The same header is stamped if the recipient mailboxes have the ByPassAnti-

SpamEnabled flag set on their mailbox (you can set this flag with the Set-Mailbox command). Being able to use user safelists makes the Content Filter far more precise than the IMF. Another difference from IMF processing is the ability of the Content Filter to validate messages by checking the computational postmarks in the message header inserted by clients such as Outlook 2007. Computational postmarks are explained in the section on client-side anti-spam suppression later on in this chapter.

In addition to using the SmartScreen[11] data to detect spam, you can add words or phrases that you want to block or allow through if they occur in messages through the Custom Words page of the Content Filter properties (Figure 6.47). Note that the allowed words take priority over the blocked words, so the Content Filter will allow messages through that contain blocked words if they also contain an allowed word or phrase.

The output from the Content Filter agent is an SCL value for the message, which is added to the MAPI properties of the message. The value of the SCL ranges from 0 to 9 where 0 means that the message is absolutely not spam and 9 means that it absolutely is spam. You control the action that Exchange takes with a message by adjusting three different thresholds (Figure 6.48):

- Delete: Exchange deletes the message when its SCL value equals or exceeds this threshold. No notification is sent to the originating system. If the SCL value is lower than the Delete threshold, compare it to the Reject threshold.

- Reject: Exchange deletes the message and sends a rejection response to the originating mail server when the SCL value equals or exceeds the Reject threshold. If the SCL value is lower than the Reject threshold, it is then compared to the Quarantine threshold.

- Quarantine: Exchange quarantines the message by sending it to a special quarantine mailbox if its SCL value equals the quarantine threshold. Administrators can review the messages that are deposited in this mailbox from time to time (daily is suggested) to establish whether the SCL thresholds are appropriate.

If a message's SCL is lower than the quarantine threshold, the Content Filter agent passes it for onward delivery to the user's mailbox. At this point, Outlook will review the SCL value and decide whether it wishes to classify the message as spam.

---

11. Microsoft refreshes the SmartScreen data regularly and is downloaded by the Anti-Spam Update service from the Microsoft Update web site.

Figure 6.48
*Setting SCL
thresholds*

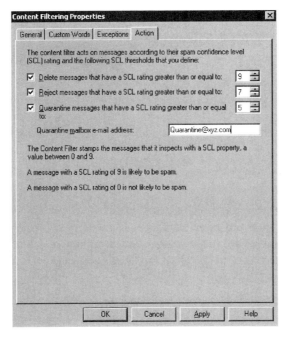

Setting SCL thresholds is a balance between achieving a high level of protection against spam (users complain very quickly when they begin to receive a high level of spam) and avoiding false positives. In addition, it doesn't make sense to set the quarantine threshold so high that vast quantities of messages end up in the quarantine mailbox waiting for an administrator to review and decide whether to pass the message on to the addressee.

To define the mailbox that you want to use for quarantine operations, use the `Set-ContentFilterConfig` command:

```
Set-ContentFilterConfig –QuarantineMailbox Quarantine@xyz.com
```

The email address for the quarantine mailbox does not have to be an Exchange 2007 mailbox. The only requirement is that the address is a valid routable address that Exchange can send messages to.

6.11.16 Content Filter updates

The tactics used by spammers change constantly, so frequent and timely updates of the patterns used to detect spam are a critical part of maintaining an effective anti-spam defense. Microsoft offers updates for the Content Filter running on Edge servers. The exact update that you can receive depends on the CAL that you have brought. Table 6.11 details the updates that are available for Standard and Enterprise CALs; the basic difference is that when you buy an Enterprise CAL, you purchase Forefront Security for Exchange, which includes a suite of anti-virus and anti-spam protection, so you get more frequent updates for the filter definitions plus the updates for spam signatures and IP reputations.

Table 6.11 *Anti-spam updates available from Microsoft*

Update Type	Standard CAL	Enterprise CAL
Content filter definitions	Biweekly	Daily
Spam signatures	Not available	As needed according to spam activity, could be multiple times per day
IP reputation	Not available	Multiple times per day

The content filter agent can run on both hub and Edge servers, but you can only enable automatic anti-spam updates on Edge servers. The logic here is that hub transport servers are designed for deployment behind the firewall, so they need only to provide a second layer of protection. Edge servers are designed to cleanse the incoming mail stream and removing spam is a critical part of this activity, hence the need for updates.

Figure 6.49
Enabling anti-spam updates on an Edge server

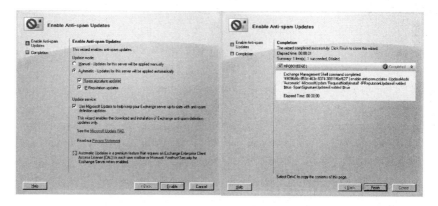

To enable anti-spam updates, select the Content Filter agent on the Edge server and take the "Enable Anti-Spam Updates" option in the action pane to launch the wizard shown in Figure 6.49. The wizard allows you to select whether to download spam signatures and IP reputations and whether you want to apply the updates manually or automatically. In most cases, you should take the default option to apply updates of both types automatically as it doesn't make sense to have updates available to you and not to use them. The wizard then calls the Enable-AntiSpamUpdates shell command to con-

Figure 6.50
*Properties of the
Edge server*

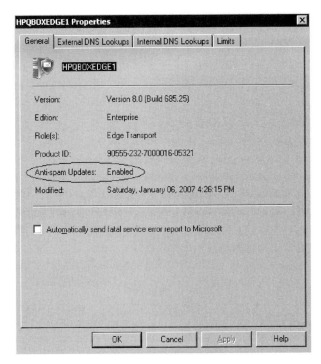

figure the chosen options. You can't enable anti-spam updates until you enter a valid product key for the server.

After automatic anti-spam updates are configured, the Exchange Anti-Spam Update service scans the Microsoft Update site every hour for available updates that should be applied to the server. If an update is available, the service downloads it and applies it automatically if you have configured this option. If you want to force an update, you can stop and restart the Anti-Spam service as the service always checks Microsoft Update for available updates when it starts. The Anti-Spam service logs details of its activities in the Application Event log. Figure 6.51 shows that the service has fetched and applied an update for anti-spam signatures. You can use the version number reported in the event log to determine whether all your Edge servers are consistent. Another way of checking version numbers is with the Get-AntiSpam-Updates command, which reports details about the configuration plus the versions that are active on a server.

```
Get-AntiSpamUpdates

UpdateMode                  : Automatic
LatestContentFilterVersion  : 3.3.4903.660
```

```
SpamSignatureUpdatesEnabled  : True
LatestSpamSignatureVersion   : 3.3.4904.868
IPReputationUpdatesEnabled   : True
LatestIPReputationVersion    : 3.3.4904.020
MicrosoftUpdate              : Configured
```

While you shouldn't normally have to disable anti-spam updates, it's easy to do so with either the `Disable-AntiSpamUpdates` command or by taking the EMC update to do the same thing.

Figure 6.51
Event reporting application of anti-spam updates

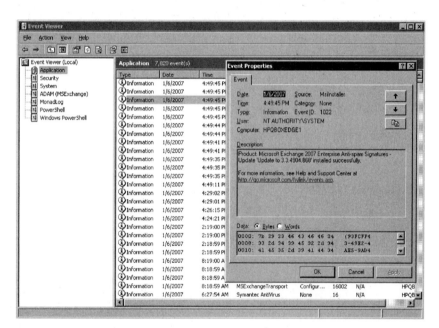

6.11.17 Per-user SCL processing

Exchange 2007 allows you to override the organizational SCL thresholds on a per-user basis through the `Set-Mailbox` command. For example, let's assume that you want to set more rigorous thresholds for a mailbox than the organizational thresholds of 9 (Delete), 7 (Reject), and 6 (Quarantine). The command looks something like this:

```
Set-Mailbox —id Redmond —SCLDeleteEnabled:$True
—SCLDeleteThreshold 8  —SCLRejectEnabled:$True
—SCLRejectThreshold 6
—SCLQuarantineEnabled:$True —SCLQuarantineThreshold 5
```

The SCLJunkThreshold property governs the threshold that Outlook uses to decide whether to put incoming messages into its Junk E-Mail folder. In this case, Outlook will move any message with an SCL value equal to or greater than 4:

```
Set-Mailbox —id Redmond —SCLJunkEnabled:$True
—SCLJunkThreshold 4
```

6.11.18 Safelist Aggregation

The process of gathering and synchronizing safelists from user mailboxes is called safelist aggregation. This feature is designed to reduce the number of false positives (a legitimate message that is determined to be spam) that occur during anti-spam processing and is based on the principle that if a user has added a sender to their safe sender list, it is safe for the organization to accept a message from that sender. Comparison with the Exchange 2003 Intelligent Message Filter (which does not use safelist aggregation) shows that Exchange 2007 anti-spam processing generates far fewer false positives, which in turn creates extra user confidence in the system because legitimate messages from their correspondents will get through.

Figure 6.52
How to populate the safe senders list

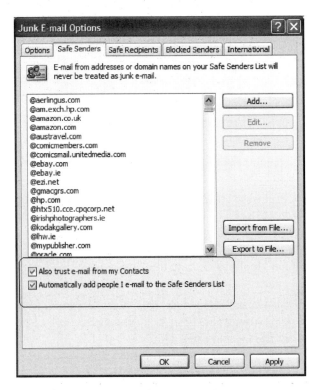

Users populate their safelist data through the Junk Mail options in Outlook or Outlook Web Access (Figure 6.52). The data stored in a user's safelist collection includes their safe senders, any domains that they regard as being safe, external contacts that are stored in their contacts folders, and (optionally) contacts that are captured by Outlook as they are addressed in messages. You can deploy an option through an Outlook Group Policy to force Outlook to add the user's contacts to their safelist.

To make sure that user safelists are available to the Content Filter agent, you have to gather the safelist data from user mailboxes, populate it into the Active Directory, and then wait for Edge synchronization to occur. You can use a batch job to gather data and update the Active Directory (the best approach) or do this on an on-demand basis. The commands to gather and update are very simple:

```
Get-Mailbox | Update-SafeList –Type SafeSenders
```

Before executing the call to Get-Mailbox interactively or in a script, make sure that your domain scope for PowerShell is set correctly as described in Chapter 4, as otherwise you may fail to provide a full update from all mailboxes for synchronization. Note that if you attempt to use the Update-SafeList command on a mailbox that is not hosted by an Exchange 2007 server, Exchange will be unable to complete the command because Exchange 2003 mailboxes do not support the Active Directory attributes that Exchange uses to hold the hashed safe list data. In this event, you will see the following error:

```
Property SafeSendersHash cannot be set on this object because
it requires the object to have version 0.1 (8.0.535.0) or
later. Current version of the object is 0.0 (6.5.6500.0).
```

Each user can have up to 1,024 entries in their safelist. Of course, gathering and storing safelist data from thousands of mailboxes spread across a large enterprise can take some time, so this is an operation best performed in the background. The Update-SafeList command reads the safelist data from the set of user mailboxes that you select. In this case, the lack of parameters supplied to Get-Mailbox means that every mailbox in the organization is processed, but you can obviously apply a filter to process a different set of mailboxes. Note also that we specify that we only want the Update-SafeList command to process user safe sender data. This is because the Content Filter agent only uses safe sender data and does not act on safe recipient data, so there is no point in generating this data and replicating it around the organization.

After the safelist data is read, each entry is hashed using the SHA-256 algorithm, sorted in an array set to provide efficient access to the data, and then converted to a binary attribute, which are then checked against the MsExchangeSafeRecipientHash and MsExchangeSafeSenderHash attributes in the user's Active Directory account to determine whether an update is required. If the safelist data has changed, Exchange updates the Active Directory. The use of hashing means that the sizes of the attributes are not large. For example, the data held in Active Directory for a user who has 200 entries in their safelist is approximately 800 bytes.

Figure 6.53
The link between aggregrated safelists and anti-spam checking

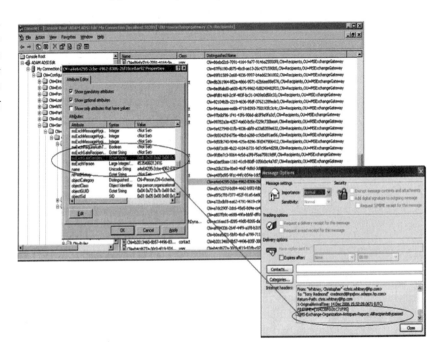

Once in the Active Directory, the safelist data is replicated around the organization and is available to the Content Filter agent running on any hub transport server that has the anti-spam agents installed. The safelist data will be synchronized to any Edge server that has a subscription to a hub transport server. After synchronization, you can see the hashed values appear in the MsExchangeSafeRecipientHash and MsExchangeSafeSenderHash attributes for user entries in ADAM. Figure 6.53 shows the hashed values as they appear in ADAM. The right-hand screen shows the x-header informati[12]on written into incoming messages as they pass through the Content Filter agent to indicate that the agent found a safelist match, and so stamps the header so

---

12.   -MS-Exchange-Organization-Antispam-Report: AllRecipientsBypassed.

that later anti-spam agents that run on other servers know that messages can pass through without further checking.

Hashing the safelist data generates unique fixed-length output fields that are very difficult for malicious attackers to access and abuse. The limited size of the data does not impose a heavy load on the synchronization processing yet allows Exchange to make very fast comparisons between a sender address on a message and the safelist data for the user the message is addressed to. If an inbound hash matches, the Content Filter agent passes the message.

6.11.19 Sender reputation

Exchange 2003 and Outlook 2003 support the concept of Spam Confidence Level (SCL), a value calculated by the Intelligent Message Filter and acted upon by the Store or Outlook to suppress messages that exceed thresholds set by administrators. The Sender Reputation Level (SRL) is a new value that the Sender Reputation agent calculates based on the accuracy of reverse DNS data for a given sender, whether the server that the sender uses appears to be an open proxy[13], the correctness of the EHLO or HELO connection (senders who use many different and unique EHLO commands are likely to be spammers; regular traffic from nonspammers tend to use the same EHLO command consistently), and the SCL ratings that Exchange has calculated using the Content Filter agent for previous messages from the same sender. A message that comes in with a high SCL rating may cause the sender's SRL to be adjusted downwards; a message with a low SCL rating may cause the opposite effect.

The Sender Reputation agent can only run on an Edge server. The agent stores the data that it gathers about senders in a database called SenderReputation.edb that is located in C:\Program Files\Microsoft\Exchange Server\TransportRoles\data. Over time, a sender's reputation can improve or degrade based on the type of messages that they send and go from 0 (zero), indicating that Exchange believes this sender to be 100% legitimate and a highly unlikely source of spam, to 9, which probably means that any message from this sender is not going to improve your life. A value of 4 indicates that Exchange is neutral about this sender. All senders start at 0 and the agent starts to calculate a the SRL for a sender after Exchange captures 20 messages from them. The agent actually fires at two points: after the MAIL FROM: command (so that the agent knows who the message is supposedly coming from) and after the end of data command is received, so that the agent knows the SCL that the Content Filter agent has calculated for the message.

---

13.   An open proxy is a proxy server that accepts connection requests from any other server and forwards the SMTP traffic as if it originated from the local host.

Through the properties of the Sender Reputation agent (Figure 6.54), you can configure the agent with an SRL threshold to indicate your level of tolerance to spam. The default setting is 9, which means that Exchange takes a cautious approach to deciding that a sender's reputation is bad enough to block them. Setting a lower level may cause senders to be blocked when they shouldn't. If a sender reaches the threshold, the Sender Reputation agent flags the sender to the Sender Filtering agent so that it can add the sender's IP address to the blocked senders list for a temporary period, which is 24 hours by default. You can adjust the blocking period to be higher or lower as you require up to a maximum value of 48 hours. Senders whose IP addresses are in Microsoft's own SRL list are automatically added to your blocked list.

Figure 6.54
Sender Reputation
configuration
options

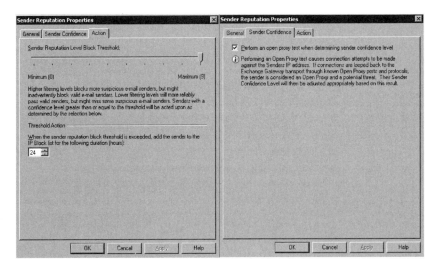

The `Get-SenderReputationConfig` command reveals more about the configuration that Exchange uses for the Sender Reputation agent. You'll notice that the agent is enabled by default for external mail and disabled for internal mail.

```
Get-SenderReputationConfig

Enabled                   : True
SrlBlockThreshold         : 9
OpenProxyDetectionEnabled : True
SenderBlockingEnabled     : True
SenderBlockingPeriod      : 48
Socks4Ports               : {1081, 1080}
Socks5Ports               : {1081, 1080}
WingatePorts              : {23}
HttpConnectPorts          : {6588, 3128, 80}
```

```
HttpPostPorts            : {6588, 3128, 80}
CiscoPorts               : {23}
ProxyServerName          :
ProxyServerPort          : 0
ProxyServerType          : 0
ExternalMailEnabled      : True
InternalMailEnabled      : False
```

You can set properties for the agent with the `Set-SenderReputation-Config` command. For example, this command sets the SRL Block Threshold to be 8 and the blocking period to be 36 hours:

```
Set-SenderReputationConfig —SrlBlockThreshold 8
—SenderBlockingPeriod 36
```

Because the result of a sender exceeding the SRL threshold is to be placed on the blocked senders list, the configuration for the Sender Filter determines how Exchange will handle messages from these senders. The default action is to reject new messages, but you can also elect to stamp the messages with a status as coming from a blocked sender and allow them to continue onwards.

6.11.20   Recipient filtering

Recipient filters work on the RCPT TO: field in messages that contain the addresses that messages are destined for. The recipient filter compares the addresses against administrator-defined Recipient Block lists (Figure 6.55) and the Active Directory to determine if any action is necessary on an inbound message. In most cases, Exchange will decline to accept messages addressed to users that it cannot find in the directory.

The Recipient Filter agent also includes tarpitting functionality. This is the ability to throttle back server response after potential spam communication patterns are detected. For example, if a remote server attempts to conduct an address harvest attack whereby it "tests" thousands of addresses against Exchange to see whether Exchange will accept any of the addresses. Normally, the remote server will use a pattern to compose addresses so that it can test multiple possible combinations for potential users. The idea is for spammers to discover what addresses are valid so that they can add these addresses to their lists and either use them for future spam or to sell to other spammers. Tarpitting is designed to slow down the communication process so that the remote server gives up because the directory attack takes too long and there are other easier targets to attack.

To discover the current tarpit interval on a server:

Figure 6.55
*Setting up the
recipient filter*

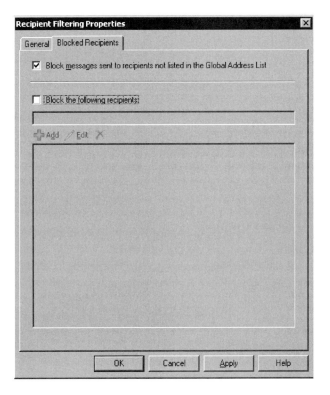

```
Get-ReceiveConnector | Select Server, TarpitInterval

Server                  TarpitInterval
--------                --------------------
ExchEdge1               00:00:05
```

In this case, the tarpit interval is 5 seconds.

6.11.21 Blocking file attachments

Anti-virus systems give administrators the option of blocking certain file
attachments that often contain dangerous or contaminated content. Given
the amount of threat that exists in the Internet today, it is preferable to block
content by either deleting the complete message or passing it through without any attachments than to let an infected message penetrate the messaging
system. With this thought in mind, the next thing to do is to decide what
content to block. Table 6.12 lists a set of file extensions that many large corporations block, including the obvious candidates such as executable, batch,
command, and screen saver files as well as executable code in Visual Basic

and Windows script files. Other important files are those that might install software on a computer or update the system registry, as these may introduce spyware or other undesirable threat vectors onto a server. Less obvious file extensions include Windows Help files and compiled (or compressed) HTML Help files, as these can contain links to web sites that can lead users to inflection.

Table 6.12 is not intended to be a definitive list. You probably have your own ideas about what file extensions should feature on the list and the list will evolve over time as hackers find new ways to attack computer systems. Exchange 2007 introduces a transport agent designed to filter attachments. The attachment filter agent runs on an Edge server and can filter based on file name, file extension, or MIME type. You can decide to block messages that the filter traps (and generate an NDR back to the sender), strip the attachment but allow the message to pass through to the user, or delete the message silently so that neither the sender nor recipient is aware of its fate.

Table 6.12 *Suggested attachment types to block*

.bat	Microsoft Batch File	.chm	Compressed HTML Help File
.cmd	Command file for Windows NT	.com	Command file (program)
.cpl	Control Panel extension	.exe	Executable File
.hlp	Help file	.hta	HTML Application
.js	JavaScript File	.jse	JavaScript Encoded Script File
.lnk	Shortcut File	.msi	Microsoft Installer File
.pif	Program Information File	.reg	Registry File
.scr	Screen Saver (Portable Executable File)	.sct	Windows Script Component
.shb	Document Shortcut File	.shs	Shell Scrap Object
.vb	Visual Basic File	.vbe	Visual Basic Encoded Script File
.vbs	Visual Basic File	.wsc	Windows Script Component
.wsf	Windows Script File	.wsh	Windows Script Host Settings File

Note that dropped messages or stripped attachments are processed in memory and are not written to disk, so you cannot recover these files for examination after they are dropped. There is no UI available to configure the Attachment Filter agent, so you have to set it up with EMS on every Edge server that you want to run the agent on. Filter settings are per-server and not shared elsewhere within the organization.

6.11.22 **Attachment filtering**

The Attachment Filter agent only runs on an Edge server. In some respects, the Attachment Filter is an odd beast because it is the only agent that can only be managed through the shell. In addition, this agent cannot distinguish between internal and external messages and it does not log its activity in the agent log like the other agents. The Attachment Filter is no less effective because of these small oddities, but it is strange that Microsoft has not included it in the set of agents that are visible through EMC. Because of this, you will want to build a set of scripts to help populate the filter list that drives the Attachment Filter agent and control its configuration if you want to apply the same settings across multiple Edge servers.

The job of the Attachment Filter agent is to stop unwanted attachments getting through to users. You can block attachments based on the file name or extension (such as Nicegirls.jpg or *.jpg) or based on the MIME content type (such as image/jpeg). Exchange 2007 provides a set of out-of-the-box attachment types that are blocked. You can view this list with the Get-AttachmentFilterEntry command.

The default action is to reject attachments on the filter list. Unfortunately, you can only select one action to take for all attachment types, so you cannot say that you will take one action for a certain type and another for a different type. The actions that you can take are:

- Reject: Block the entire message and attachments and send a DSN to the sender to explain that the message didn't get through because of the attachment.

- Strip: Pass the message through, but remove the attachment. In this case, the agent adds a text file to the message to explain that the attachment was removed.

- SilentDelete: Delete the message and its attachments and don't send a DSN to the sender.

To set a new action, use the Set-AttachmentFilterListConfig command:

```
Set-AttachmentFilterListConfig —Action Strip
```

You can view the text sent in the DSN for the reject option and to the recipient for the strip option with the Get-AttachmentFilterListConfig command and set new values with the `Set-AttachmentFilterListConfig` command. For example:

```
Set-AttachmentFilterListConfig —AdminMessage "Attachment
removed due to potentially objectionable content."
```

The `Set-AttachmentFilterListConfig` command also allows you to define that the Attachment Filter does not operate on messages that pass through certain connectors by setting the ExceptionConnectors parameter. This might be done if you wanted to allow certain attachment types within the organization but not to come in from outside.

Use the `Add-AttachmentFilterEntry` command to add new file names, attachment types, or MIME types to the filter list.

```
Add-AttachmentFilterEntry —Name BadContent.exe —Type FileName
Add-AttachmentFilterEntry —Name image/jpeg —Type ContentType
Add-AttachmentFilterEntry —Name LovePotions.doc —Type FileName
```

There is no way that an administrator can retrieve a blocked message or a stripped attachment.

6.11.23 Edge transport rules

A spam or virus outbreak that incorporates a new technique to outfox anti-spam detection agents can occur at any time and there is no way today that any anti-spam or anti-virus technology can automatically adapt itself to handle the new threat. Instead, the normal approach is to wait for vendors to update the pattern or other files that contain the characteristics that the software uses to detect unwanted messages. Edge transport rules do not replace anti-spam or anti-virus software. Instead, they allow you to implement a fast block to span the time before vendors can update their software and avoid the possibility that your servers will be swamped by spam or viruses that get past the normal defenses.

In the same way that you can run transport rules on a hub transport server to check message properties to identify whether or not the rule applies, Edge rules examine message properties to look for a characteristic that identifies a problem message. For example, messages containing the infamous Melissa virus had "I Love You" in the subject (Figure 6.56), so it is possible to implement a rule to block any messages that have this text in their subject. You might also be able to identify messages from the domain that they come from or by a type of attachment that they contain. Once identified, the messages are dropped.

Figure 6.56
*Creating a rule on
an Edge server to
suppress the
Melissa virus*

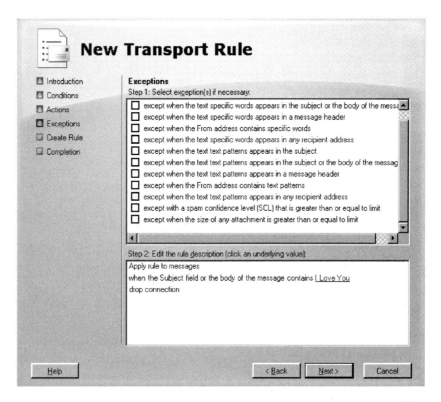

You manage transport rules on an Edge server in exactly the same manner as transport rules on a hub transport server through either EMC or the
shell. Because they are part of the Exchange configuration, transport rules
created on a hub transport server are automatically shared throughout the
organization. Edge servers do not have access to the full configuration data of
the organization, so if you operate multiple Edge servers, you have to build a
rules set on one server and then export the collection to an XML file that you
can take and import on the other servers. For example, to export the current
rules collection from an Edge server:

```
Export-TransportRuleCollection —FileName c:\Temp\
EdgeRulesSet.XML
```

To import an XML file containing a rules collection on another Edge
server:

```
Import-TransportRuleCollection —FileName c:\temp\
EdgeRulesSet.XML
```

6.11.24 **Available Edge**

If you operate a small Exchange organization, a single Edge server can protect you and adequately handle the volume of inbound messages. In larger or more distributed organizations, you may need additional Edge servers to handle the inbound traffic or to avoid creating a single point of failure. Additional servers also allow you to handle the installation of software upgrades and patches or to deal with any hardware outages that may occur.

Edge servers are anti-spam software appliances that operate in isolation. However, you can use round-robin DNS to spread inbound traffic over a set of Edge servers. You can also connect multiple hub transport servers in an Active Directory site to the Edge servers to handle the sanitized email stream. You can also have hub transport servers from multiple Active Directory sites establish synchronizations to Edge servers so that if one site is unavailable, synchronization continues from another site. This sounds complicated, but it's based on the fact that only one hub transport server can synchronize with an Edge server at one time. To do this, the hub transport server takes out a lock on the ADAM instance on the Edge server and only proceeds with synchronization if it can establish the lock. If the lock is declined, it may indicate that another hub transport server is currently synchronizing with ADAM, so the hub transport server will then proceed to the next subscription that it holds for an Edge server and attempts to take out a lock on that server. This process continues until all subscriptions are satisfied. Because the same data is being synchronized into ADAM no matter what hub transport server is used, it doesn't matter if a hub transport server misses its opportunity to synchronize. This mechanism allows you to spread the synchronization load across hub and Edge servers and ensures a certain robustness in the synchronization process. However, while it's pretty straightforward, it is something that you should test before putting into production to ensure that everything works as you expect. To test resilience, you can remove servers, disconnect network links, and otherwise provoke some disruption in the synchronization process and then observe what happens.

An Internet outage is another scenario that you need to cater for. If you lose connectivity to the Internet, outbound messages will begin to queue up on the Edge servers. You have to ensure that the Edge servers have enough disk space to accommodate an outage that lasts at least three days (or maybe more, depending on your tolerance to failure and your prediction of the likelihood that such a failure will occur).

The next issue to consider is how to recover an Edge server quickly. An Edge server doesn't maintain any configuration information in the Active Directory so you can't use the normal Exchange server recovery technique[14] to rebuild a server after failure. Almost all of the data on an Edge server is

Figure 6.57
*XML configuration
data exported from
an Edge server*

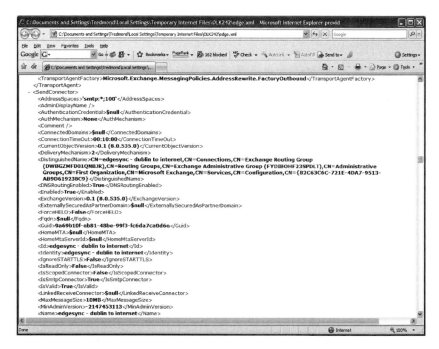

transient. Messages pass through quickly and don't linger unless there is a network outage. The log files are not critical because you can track messages within the organization using the logs contained on hub transport servers. The only data that we need to worry about are the changes that you make to the configuration of the various agents. Microsoft provides a script for this purpose, so the procedure is:

1. Run the ExportEdgeConfig.ps1 script on a regular interval to save details of the Edge configuration to an XML file. Figure 6.57 illustrates a sample of the information that you'll see exported to the XML file.

   ```
   .\ExportEdgeConfig.ps1 —CloneConfigData "c:\temp\
   EdgeServer1.xml"
   ```

2. Move the XML file off the server to a safe location.

---

14.   Run the setup program with the /m:RecoverServer switch.

3. If the Edge server needs to be rebuilt, perform a fresh install of the Edge role to new (or fixed) hardware, using the original server name.

4. Import the saved configuration data from the XML file:

```
.\ImportEdgeConfig.ps1 –CloneConfigData "c:\temp\
EdgeServer1.xml"
```

5. Run the EdgeSync subscription process to create a new subscription to the newly rebuilt Edge server.

6. Run the Start-EdgeSynchronization command from the hub transport server to populate the fresh ADAM instance on the rebuilt Edge server with data from the Active Directory.

After successfully completing these steps, you should have a fully operational Edge server that has the same configuration settings as the failed server.

6.12 Client-side spam suppression

Even with the best possible array of bastion and anti-spam edge servers arranged to suppress incoming spam before it penetrates your network, it is inevitable that some percentage of spam will get through to user mailboxes. For this reason, client-side spam suppression is an important part of the overall defense mechanism against spam. Every version of Outlook includes some rule processing capability that allow users to create some degree of automation in handling incoming messages. In the early days, rules took care of tasks such as filing messages into appropriate folders and we never really had to deal with the electronic version of junk mail, unless the messages from some of our regular correspondents fell into that category. The typical approach taken with rules is to look for a keyword in the message subject and use its presence to decide whether the message should be deleted. However, as spam became more pervasive, Outlook rules just couldn't handle the complexity of detecting the many variations of spam that got past corporate anti-spam filters to arrive in user mailboxes. The need therefore arose for an intelligent client-side anti-spam filter and that's what Microsoft delivered in Outlook 2003 and has continued to update since. Junk mail processing is also available in Outlook Web Access 2003 and 2007 and both Outlook and Outlook Web Access respect the same user preferences, albeit working in a slightly different manner. For example, you can only use Outlook's junk mail filter when you work in cached Exchange mode because Outlook must download messages before it can process them through the filter.

6.12.1   Outlook's Junk Mail Filter

Some junk mail is very easy to detect and that's why rules were able to do the job when junk mail was reasonably uncommon. The earliest spam was crude and unsophisticated. Examples include in-your-face invitations to buy drugs or notifications that you have the opportunity to work with someone you have never met in your life before to extract vast sums from an African country, and so on. It always interests me that so many people fall prey to invitations to part with their money when the invitations are badly written, only use uppercase letters, and contain lots of misspellings. As discussed earlier in this chapter, anti-spam software relies on a variety of techniques to detect unsolicited commercial email. Microsoft uses a version of their SmartScreen technology and shrunk it to fit the needs of Outlook. Unlike rules, which are reasonably slow when they execute, the Junk Mail Filter is compiled code and executes quickly enough not to create any perceivable delay in the delivery of new mail.

The raw data that allows Outlook to filter messages is contained in a file called Outfldr.dat, which holds a large dictionary of keywords and phrases that the Junk Mail Filter uses. You cannot add to the filter file so you cannot train Outlook to respect your preferences. Instead, Microsoft issues regular updates for the filter file as part of its update service for Office (www.microsoft.com/officeupdate), so as long as you download and install the updates, you will benefit from the latest ways to detect spam.

Assuming that you opt to use the Junk Mail Filter, Outlook checks new messages as they arrive. The default protect level is "Low," but I prefer to run at "High" as experience with the filter has shown me that it does a pretty good job. As shown in Figure 6.58, the difference between Low and High is that the first setting filters only the really obvious spam while the second does a much more thorough filtering job. You have the option to delete any mail that the filter catches immediately or have Outlook put these messages in your Junk E-Mail folder. While I usually opt to delete messages immediately, from time to time I take the option to capture messages just to see what kind of spam is arriving.

While you can't update the filters that Outlook uses to detect spam, you can help Outlook to improve its accuracy when it comes to filter the incoming message stream to your inbox by indicating who you think are safe senders (people that you always want to receive email from) and users and domains that you regard as nuisances (those that have sent you spam). Outlook uses this data when it runs its checks to filter messages. The order of the checks are as follows:

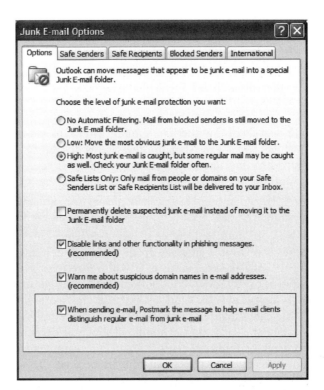

Figure 6.58
Junk mail options

- Check the sender against your contacts—any message from a contact is assumed to be okay because you have taken an explicit action to mark someone as a contact and you would not do this if you didn't want to receive email from them.

- Check the sender against the GAL—Outlook assumes that you are willing to read a message sent by another user in the same organization (note that you cannot use the filter to block messages from another user in the organization—to do this, you have to create a rule).

- Check the sender against your "Safe Senders" list—if you add someone to this list, you tell Outlook that you always want to receive email from them, and Exchange will publish this data to the Active Directory so that it can be used in anti-spam processing.

- Check the sender against your "Safe Recipients" list—if you add an address to this list, you tell Outlook that it's okay to accept any message that contains the address.

- Check the sender against your "Blocked Senders" list—Outlook blocks any message from anyone on this list. The Junk Mail Filter also checks for incoming messages that are from any blocked domains or contain specific character sets. For example, because anyone I know in Russia sends me email in English, I block any other message that arrives in the Russian Cyrillic character set.

- Run the junk mail filter to detect messages that have got this far but might still be spam.

The result of the filter is a ranking (think of a number between 1 and 100, where 100 means that the message is absolutely spam) that Outlook uses to determine whether a message is spam. If you opt for "Low" protection, Outlook is cautious about and the ranking has to be very high before Outlook regards a message as spam. If you opt for "High" protection, then Outlook is more aggressive and moves the ranking bar downwards.

Outlook's junk mail filter is pretty effective. It even works when you attempt to recover a message from the deleted items cache—if Outlook thinks that the message is spam, it will not recover the message. If you use BlackBerry or Windows Mobile handheld, you get an idea of how much spam is suppressed by Outlook because the spam that gets through the server-side anti-spam agents is delivered to the handheld. It is annoying that you receive the spam on the handheld, but this demonstrates that Outlook has to download messages before it can detect junk email and you then realize how effective the junk mail filter is because the spam you see on the handheld does not appear in Outlook's inbox.

While Outlook's Junk Mail Filter is effective most of the time, occasionally you'll find that Outlook moves messages into the Junk E-Mail folder when you think that the message is perfectly legitimate. The opposite situation also occurs and spam ends up in the inbox, despite being totally obvious spam to the human eye. Either situation might cause you to question the effectiveness of the Junk Mail Filter. Here are some reasons why these situations occur:

- Messages generated by applications are regarded as spam: For example, expense reports, notifications from SharePoint Portal Server, subscription updates, distributions from newsgroups, and so on. Messages like this are often generated when an application makes an unauthenticated SMTP connection to a server to submit email and because the connection is unauthenticated, they are suspicious because a spammer might have attempted to hijack what seems to be a perfectly valid internal email address and use it for their purposes. In addition, the content of automatically-generated messages may contain little text context, have URLs for pointers to application data, and do not have a "From:" field specified in their header, all of which are indications that a message might be spam. The solution is to add the sending address to the Safe Senders list or have the administrator of the application change it to use an authenticated SMTP connection.

- Obvious spam that is not caught by the filter: This may simply be due to a new tactic created by a spammer to outwit filters and unfortunately spammers succeed in this respect all the time. In a company that operates a comprehensive anti-spam defense, you can expect to see one or two messages a week sneak through and anything more is an indication that the defenses need to be updated. For example, you may need to download and install the latest version of the Outlook Junk Mail Filter data file.

- Illogical message moves between folders: If you still use mailbox rules to process incoming messages, you can encounter a condition where Outlook downloads message headers (to provide sufficient data for rules to process messages) and then proceeds to download the full content (required for the Junk Mail Filter to process messages), only to find that rules move some messages to specific folders followed by a subsequent move to the Junk E-Mail folder after Outlook has run the junk mail filter. The behavior is logical in computer terms, but the result can baffle users.

Given that spammers invent new techniques to get past filters all the time, even the best anti-spam defenses let some messages through. You can capture addresses from messages that you know to be spam and add these addresses or complete domains to the Blocked Senders list, as shown in Figure 6.59, to gradually build up your own list of spammers. You can export any of the Safe Sender, Blocked Sender, and Safe Recipients lists to a text file that can then be imported by another user.

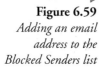

Figure 6.59
Adding an email address to the Blocked Senders list

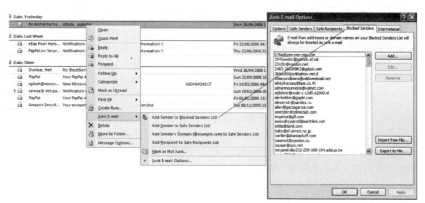

The use of the Blocked Senders and Safe Senders list is apparent, but the purpose of the Safe Recipients list is less so. Essentially, a safe recipient is a way to identify messages sent to a particular destination, often a distribution list or newsgroup that you are part of and want to receive the messages. You do not control the membership of the list or group, but you assume that whoever administers the list will make sure that it is not used for spam and that therefore any message that is addressed to the list is okay. If you couldn't mark the list as being safe, then Outlook might assume that its messages are spam and so suppress them. By marking the address of the list or any other similar address as a "Safe Recipient" you tell Outlook that it can ignore messages from this address when it applies its filters.

Exchange uses the contents of a user's Blocked Senders and Safe Senders lists in tandem with the SCL and PCL values set by the IMF (for Exchange 2003) or an Exchange 2007 Edge server as they process messages. The SCL, or spam confidence level, indicates how strongly Exchange believes that the message is spam, while the PCL, or phishing confidence level, indicates whether it might be a phishing message. If a message gets to Outlook, it means that Exchange considers it to be reasonably okay as otherwise Exchange will have suppressed the message either at the edge or when it arrived into the mailbox store. The Store checks the Blocked Senders list for each mailbox as it delivers messages and suppresses messages if it matches the address of the sender against the list, so Outlook never gets to process these messages (suppression at this point saves Outlook the overhead of having to download the messages to process them locally). The Store uses the Safe Senders list to check messages with a high SCL to see whether the user wants to receive messages from the originator, and if the Store finds that an address is on the Safe Senders list, it passes the message and Outlook can pick it up the next time it synchronizes the inbox.

While the Exchange 2003 IMF uses its own data to check messages, users can contribute to spam suppression by publishing their own safelists data to Edge servers, which can then use this data to check incoming messages. This step allows Exchange to avoid blocking messages that originate from a trusted sender and to avoid letting a message through from an address that a user has positively identified as being bogus. See page 554 for more information about safelist aggregation.

Outlook 2003/2007 and Outlook Web Access look for web beacons in HTML format messages. Web beacons are very small (usually transparent and sized at one pixel by one pixel) and include a URL to a remote site to force you to download image files before Outlook can format and display the full message content. The original purpose of web beacons was to provide some indication to a web site administrator of the traffic that the site received. The fact that you connect and download a file indicates to the message sender that your email address is valid, which is a very valuable piece of information to a spammer as their stock in trade are lists of valid email addresses.

Outlook's Automatic Picture Download setting controls whether Outlook downloads pictures and other graphics automatically in email. The default is not to download, and there is no good reason to change this setting. You can control whether to download from sites in specific Internet zones or for messages from trusted senders, so if you expect to get lots of email from eBay, you can add eBay to your Safe Senders list.

6.12.2 Postmarks

Outlook 2007 includes the ability to stamp an outgoing message with a postmark, a hashed value generated by a computationally intense algorithm that's included in the x-headers (in the x-cr-hashedpuzzle and x-cr-puzzleid attributes) of a message that allows a receiving server to have more confidence that the message is not spam because spammers wouldn't go to the effort and computational load required to generate postmarks on the millions of messages that they send. The theory is that spammers just want to send as many messages to as many addresses as they can and that they can't afford the resources that are necessary to add the postmarks. This may be correct today, but the growing availability of low-cost computing resources may mean that it is less so over time. The option to control whether to generate postmarks is included along with the other Junk E-Mail options (see the highlighted part of Figure 6.58). Depending on the speed of the PC, users may experience a slight delay in message sending, but in most cases they will notice no difference through postmark generation.

Figure 6.60 shows the kind of information that Outlook inserts into a message header for a postmark. Outlook combines multiple attributes of a message when it computes these values. This is a good thing because the more attributes that are used, the more computational resources are required to generate a postmark. The additional load is acceptable for a PC that only generates a hundred postmarks daily, but it becomes more of a problem for a spammer who wants to generate postmarks for millions of messages.

Outlook does not generate a postmark for every outgoing message. It only applies postmarks to messages that you send to a safe recipient (one of your contacts). The logic here is that postmarks aren't required internally, nor are they required for messages to one-off recipients, nor if the content is not spamlike. Remember that the goal is to be able to use postmarks as an indication that the message is valid and it therefore makes most sense to add them to messages that might look like spam or those going to people that you correspond with commonly. Processing the postmarks to ensure their validity is a lot less computationally intense than their original generation so email servers do not take on much additional load to support this feature. Some

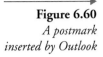

Figure 6.60
A postmark
inserted by Outlook

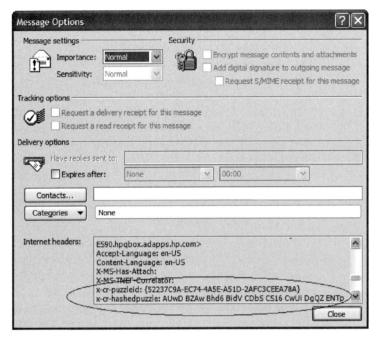

receiving email servers, beginning with Exchange 2007 and Hotmail obviously, recognize postmarks now and treat these messages with a higher degree of confidence by reducing their SCL. Microsoft's hope is that more email servers will support postmarks over time.

6.12.3   Restricting OOF and other notifications

Everyone agrees that OOF (out of office) notifications are very useful within a company because they provide a way to learn when colleagues are absent and unable to respond to messages. When you configure OOF notifications correctly, they also provide correspondents with information about how long you will be absent and what action they can take if they need something to happen while you are away. Unfortunately, the information that you insert in your OOF is also tremendously valuable to external parties who want to learn more about you or the company. For example, valid email addresses are the stock in trade for spammers and phishers and using OOFs may lead to an increase in spam directed to a company. There is some evidence that phishers use personal information extracted from OOF notifications in the messages that they send in an attempt to convince recipients of their bona fides on the basis that if you receive a message from someone who clearly knows something about you, it is more likely to be valid.

Organizational data such as your job title, location, and telephone numbers are of interest to people who want to sell to your company. More alarmingly, criminals can use corporate data to pretend to represent your company or indeed as the entry point to a social engineering attack, where the attacker uses the data that they have learned about your company to reassure people that they target that they actually belong to the company. Once they have reassured their contact, the criminals may then progress to look for sensitive information or convince the contact to help them gain access to systems. For example, they may say that they have forgotten their NT password or the steps that they need to take to access a particular system. They then try to convince their contact to help them reset the password or gain access to the system.

IT administrators therefore have to walk a fine balancing line between providing a useful feature and securing data. With Exchange 2003, many companies suppressed OOFs by updating the default SMTP message format through ESM to disable notifications for general SMTP traffic (Figure 6.61). This step prevents Exchange sending OOFs to all SMTP domains unless you define a specific message format for trusted domains that you know will not abuse the data. For example, you can define a message format for hp.com and allow OOF responses for that domain. In general, best practice is to disable OOF and automated replies for the default message format and to create specific message formats for the domains that your company needs to provide this information to. However, be aware that a large company invariably exchanges email with a very large number of domains, so creating a specific message format for each domain can become a huge task, so think about the workload to create and maintain message formats before you make a final decision on this point. Message format settings apply for all servers in an Exchange 2003 organization, so it is a good way to apply a global policy for OOFs.

Message formats also control whether Exchange responds to incoming messages with delivery and nondelivery reports. Spammers can use these notifications to test the effectiveness of their distribution lists by monitoring whether their messages get through. Of course, users depend on delivery reports to know whether their messages get through too and it is a big call for an administrator to suppress delivery and nondelivery reports as suppression basically makes your company a black hole for incoming messages, both valid business traffic and spam.

Microsoft has made a number of changes in Exchange 2007 and its associated clients to the way that Exchange generates OOFs and how you can control OOFs on a per-user and system-wide basis. From a client perspective, the new Out of Office Assistant allows users to:

- Schedule OOF messages for a specific period. You can now set a start and end date for Exchange to generate OOF messages. Figure 6.62

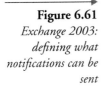

Figure 6.61
*Exchange 2003:
defining what
notifications can be
sent*

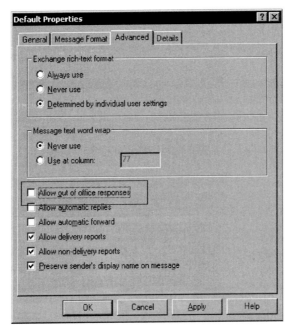

shows that I have set OOFs to be generated while I am away on vacation for the Christmas holidays. The great thing about this feature is that I do not have to create the OOF notification just before I leave for vacation—it can be set anytime in advance. Also, I don't have to remember to turn off OOF after I return to the office as Exchange will automatically stop sending OOF messages after the specified period elapses.

- Support for different OOF messages to be sent to external and internal correspondents. Figure 6.62 shows that I have two different OOF messages. The one that goes to internal correspondents includes some information that might be company confidential, such as the address of an internal web site. The OOF message for external correspondents merely tells them that I will respond when I return after vacation.

- Send only to external contacts. To preserve your privacy, you can specify that Exchange should generate external OOFs but restrict them to correspondents who appear in your contacts list.

Another small but important change is that OOF messages are in HTML format.

Users of older clients such as Outlook 2003 can only access the OOF functionality that is incorporated in that client's GUI. Outlook 2007 users

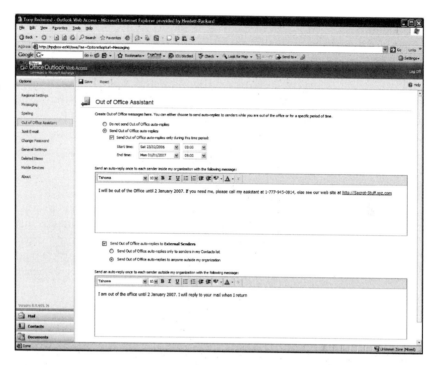

Figure 6.62
OOF settings viewed through Outlook Web Access 2007

who connect to Exchange 2003 or 2000 will see a customized UI that restricts the user to setting a single OOF that applies to external and internal correspondents.

The system-wide OOF settings are functionally equivalent to the OOF control in message format settings in Exchange 2003. On an individual per-user basis, you can use the `Set-Mailbox` command to suppress OOF for a mailbox, so you can decide that some users, such as those who work with external customers, are able to send OOFs. Outside of the selected users, you can restrict OOF generation for everyone else so that potentially confidential data does not go outside the company. The default setting for mailboxes is to allow Exchange to generate OOFs for all messages that arrive when the user has created an OOF and the OOF is active, but you can stop this as follows:

```
Set-Mailbox —id Tony.Redmond@xyz.com —ExternalOOFOptions
InternalOnly
```

This command prevents Exchange sending an OOF notification for any external message addressed to Tony.Redmond@xyz.com, no matter what client is used. To reenable OOF generation for the user, you use the External parameter with the same command:

```
Set-Mailbox —id Tony.Redmond@xyz.com —ExternalOOFOptions
External
```

On a system-wide basis, you can control the exact type of OOF data that can be sent in response to messages coming from a specific domain with the `Set-RemoteDomain` command. These settings apply to all users in the organization. For example:

```
Set-RemoteDomain —Identity 'ABC1' —AllowedOOFType
InternalLegacy
```

Note that the domain identifier that you specify to the `Set-Remote-Domain` command is not the FQDN of the domain. Instead, it is the identifier that you allocated when you created an entry for the domain when you defined it as a new Remote Domain in the hub transport node at the organization level of EMC or created it with the `New-RemoteDomain` command. You can choose the wildcard '*' for the target domain if you want your per-domain OOF settings to apply to all external domains. The OOF suppression types are as follows:

- External (the default): This setting allows only external OOF messages that Outlook 2007 and Outlook Web Access 2007 clients create to be sent to the specified domain. It blocks any internal OOF messages and any OOF messages set by earlier clients such as Outlook 2003. Use this setting for any domain that you had previously blocked with Exchange 2003.

- InternalLegacy: This setting allows only internal OOF messages set by Outlook 2007 and Outlook Web Access 2007 and all OOF messages set by earlier clients to go to the specified domain. This setting is best used when you have a close partner company (perhaps one that is part of a common conglomerate where several different Exchange organizations are in use) where it is not a problem if users in that company receive OOF messages that contain company-confidential information such as phone numbers, office addresses, and so on.

- ExternalLegacy: This setting allows external OOF messages set by Outlook 2007 or Outlook Web Access 2007 clients and the OOF messages set by earlier clients to be sent to the specified domain. You should use this setting if you allowed OOF messages to go externally with Exchange 2003 so as to avoid any disruption to users of Outlook 2003 or earlier clients.

- None: This blocks all OOF messages to the target domain.

The per-domain settings override user-specific settings. Unlike many other management operations in Exchange 2007, defining an OOF setting for a domain is something that you can do through EMC. Figure 6.63 illustrates how the GUI shows the new OOF setting that we created using the `Set-RemoteDomain` command above.

Figure 6.63
OOF settings for a domain

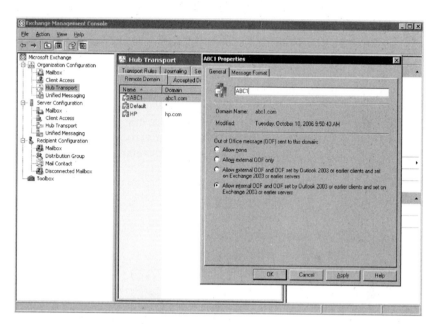

In addition, OOF responses are now more secure because Exchange 2007 performs the following two checks:

1. OOF messages will not be sent in response to server-detected junk e-mail. If Exchange Server 2007 detects a message as Junk or if the message sender is in the user's Block list, no OOF response is sent.

2. OOF messages are not sent as responses to Internet mailing lists. Exchange Server 2007 does not send OOF responses for incoming messages with the Precedence:bulk header set. However, if this header is missing, it is possible that OOF responses may be sent out because there is no reliable way of determining that the message was sent to a mailing list.

The `Set-RemoteDomain` command also allows you to control other aspects of messages that Exchange can send to a domain. For example:

```
Set-RemoteDomain 'ABC1' —AutoReplyEnabled:$True
—AutoForwardEnabled:$True
```

6.13 **Routing onwards**

The story is coming together—we know how to store and how to route messages and we've touched on how messages are generated by clients. Some Exchange administrators take the view that they don't have to worry about clients because clients are deployed and managed by departments with names like "End User Computing." While this is true, it's also true that if you don't know how messages are generated for an email server, you cannot know how to effectively manage that server to realize its full potential. As we move into an era where users expect always-available, always-connected access to their data from a myriad of clients, it's also clear that Exchange administrators need to understand how clients from web browsers to SmartPhones to Outlook interact with Exchange servers, so let's move on to Chapter 7.

Clients

7

My first email client was VAXmail (later VMSmail), a character-based client that was a part of the VAX/VMS operating system when I first begin working with it in the early 1980s. VAXmail was simple and straightforward and got messages through. In fact, you always knew that VAXmail had delivered your messages because it made a direct network connection to the recipient's mailbox in real time, so if VAXmail returned without an error after you sent the message, you knew it was in the recipient's mailbox waiting to be read. Life wasn't perfect in the golden days of "green screen email" and today's clients are definitely a horse of a different color, but sometimes we don't seem to have come a lot further than worrying whether our messages have been delivered.

Life moves on and green-screen email has faded into the past. Over the last 12 years I've connected many different clients to Exchange to read my email. Exchange 2007 supports a very wide range of clients because it supports a wide range of client access protocols. Despite frequent predictions over the years that Internet client protocols would eventually take its place, MAPI (Microsoft's Messaging Application Programming Interface[1]) remains the API that delivers most features and functionality. Microsoft designed the Exchange RPC protocol to exploit MAPI in a highly efficient manner, including access mechanisms that closely mimic the MAPI semantics. The investment made in the Exchange RPC protocol and its dependency on MAPI is a major reason why Microsoft has never moved to replace them with less proprietary protocols. Another reason is that the available nonproprietary messaging protocols are simply not as functional as the Exchange RPC/MAPI combination. Many of the features in Outlook depend on properties exposed through MAPI and depend on the Exchange RPC protocol, so it is hard to see Microsoft moving away from MAPI in the medium term.

---

1. See the Wiki entry on MAPI to learn some of MAPI's history and background. http://en.wikipedia.org/wiki/
Messaging_Application_Programming_Interface.

Apart from MAPI, the other major client families are:

- IMAP4: An Internet client access protocol that is used by most independent clients such as Eudora. Also used by Microsoft's Outlook Express client.
- POP3: An earlier Internet client access protocol that provides a lower level of functionality.
- HTTP: The best-known web protocol and used by clients such as Outlook Web Access.
- ActiveSync: Microsoft's access protocol for mobile clients such as SmartPhones and PDAs.

When you approach a design project for Exchange, you have to understand what clients are going to be used and why. Each client poses its own deployment and management challenges and they have their own implementation and support costs. Clients will change over time and updates will arrive, but you shouldn't worry too much about having to update client versions after the project starts, because in many cases, email client software is tied to desktop upgrades. Except for small groups, it's just too expensive to go and deploy a new version of an email client unless it's part of a planned regular desktop refresh. Thus, many companies upgraded to Office 2003 (and therefore Outlook 2003) as part of their move to Windows XP on the desktop and the same thing is likely to happen with Office 2007 and Vista. Another reason why you shouldn't worry too much about client versions is that Microsoft has an excellent record of supporting older clients in new versions of Exchange. Indeed, you can connect the oldest MAPI client (the "Capone" client or the "Exchange Viewer") distributed with Exchange 4.0 to Exchange 2007. While you won't be able to take advantage of features that newer clients can use, such as cached Exchange mode, you will be able to send and receive email. Almost every browser can connect to Exchange 2007 and run Outlook Web Access, and even the oldest POP3 client can connect to Exchange 2007.

After your deployment is complete, the next challenge is to deflect all the user demands to connect the latest and greatest gadgets to Exchange. In fact, the technical challenge is not difficult because most of the PDAs, phones, and other email-capable devices that appear use IMAP4, POP3, or even ActiveSync, if the manufacturer has licensed it from Microsoft. The challenge is support from the initial connection to the inevitable problems that occur as users attempt to download email, upload email, synchronize their contacts and calendars, and use applications such as Windows Live Messenger. The help desk has probably never seen the devices that users want to connect, so apart from giving some basic support ("are you connected to the network," "is the device turned on," and so on) they can't really help. To compound matters, it's often executives who demand support for these devices, so it's hard to tell them that their favorite toys are unsupported. With this thought in mind, let's consider the details of some of the more common clients that you'll want to connect to Exchange 2007.

7.1 **Outlook**

Outlook continues to be the predominant client for Exchange. Its popularity is due to the high level of functionality that Outlook offers coupled to its presence as one of the core Microsoft Office applications. It's impossible to know how many people use one of the many versions of Outlook that Microsoft has shipped since 1997, but it's safe to say that it's well over a hundred million. The sheer size of the Outlook installed base makes it an attractive target for companies who sell email servers to create the necessary code to connect Outlook to their server.

Exchange 4.0 and 5.0 included a MAPI client along with the server. The original client was known as a "viewer" and it was a functional and straightforward email client that is still in use today. However, Microsoft didn't believe that it made much sense for a server group to develop a client that really belonged as part of the Office application suite and transferred responsibility for client development (apart from Outlook Web Access) to the Office team in 1996. The first Outlook client appeared in 1997 and has been refreshed alongside the other Office applications since. The newest version is Outlook 2007, which is part of the Office 2007 suite. My favorite new feature in Outlook 2007 is automatic server detection or automatic configuration of email accounts through the AutoDiscover service. This means that Outlook is able to interrogate network resources to discover what server hosts the user's mailbox. We'll see more about the AutoDiscover service in just a few pages.

The other new features delivered in Outlook 2007 are incremental improvements to existing features or tweaking of the user interface to make Outlook easier to use. For example, using Word as a common editor makes sense (even though the actual content of message bodies remains RTF or HTML) because users have only to learn one editor. I do like the preview feature for attachments and the anti-spam filters are better. The improvements to the calendar make schedules easier to follow and the ability to add pictures to contacts makes it slightly faster to locate a contact, but none of the user interface features make Outlook 2007 a fundamentally better email client. Of course, this is a personal opinion and Outlook 2007 may well include a feature that makes a real difference for you.

Figure 7.1
MAPI profiles

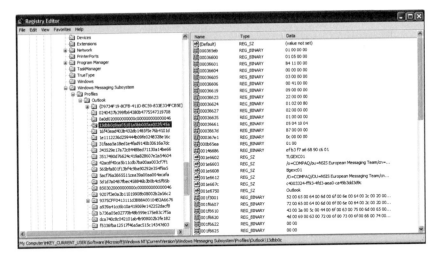

Outlook continues to depend on MAPI profiles to hold many user settings. MAPI profiles are stored in a PC's system registry. In some respects, the use of a PC-specific profile that depends on the system registry is a throwback to a time when it was common to build applications to use the system registry or Windows initialization (.INI) files to hold user preferences and little thought was given to moving users around from PC to PC or from client type to client type. For example, Outlook and Outlook Web Access need to share settings such as junk mail filter preferences and out-of-office notification data so it is inappropriate to store these settings in the system registry because you never know what device a user might want to use with Outlook Web Access. For this reason, Microsoft has moved many of the newer settings into hidden items in the user's mailbox that clients can fetch and interpret after they connect to the mailbox. Given the wide spectrum of clients and device types now in use, this is obviously a much better approach, but we still have to deal with MAPI profiles, if only for backwards compatibility. Figure 7.1 illustrates some sample information from a MAPI profile on my own PC. The information is reasonably complex and doesn't make much sense when you view it through REGEDIT, so you juggle with danger if you edit a setting without knowing exactly what you are doing.

Microsoft doesn't document all of the settings in a MAPI profile in a single place, but you can find a lot of information about different settings in individual Knowledge Base articles, albeit with a lot of research work. The Outlook Resource Kits that Microsoft release for each version contain tools that are the best way to tweak settings through the wizards in the kits. Administrators can also apply settings (for example, to enable or disable options that are available to users) through group policy objects and these settings go into a special section of the registry under the HKEY_CURRENT_USER\Software\Policies key. Separate policy settings are held for each version of Outlook. Outlook 2003 settings are under the \Office\11.0\ key while Outlook 2007 settings go under the \Office\12.0\ key. Administrators who are interested in learning more about using group policy objects to configure and manage Outlook should read the excellent books by Sue Mosher on the subject.

7.1.1 Outlook web services

Exchange 2007 and Outlook 2007 are the first server-client combination to use non-MAPI mechanisms to communicate as Microsoft has started the process of moving some functionality to web services. Outlook 2007 can consume five web services through a Client Access server:

- The AutoDiscover service: AutoDiscover is designed to assist in setting up client applications such as Outlook to work with Exchange by returning configuration data that is necessary for applications to function properly without requiring users to know where to fetch that data, such as the discovery of the server that hosts a user's mailbox.

- Unified Messaging: If your mailbox is enabled to use Exchange 2007 Unified Messaging, you can use Outlook 2007 to play a voice message back to a phone. You can also change your voicemail PIN from Outlook.

- OOF: The ability to set out-of-office messages is controlled by a new web service.

- The Availability service: Outlook 2007 clients can use HTTPS to connect and download free and busy data for other users through the Availability service. See Chapter 8 for more information.

- OAB distribution: Outlook can use HTTPS to locate and download the Offline Address Book (OAB) from a web distribution point. See page 626 for more information.

The last two web services allow Exchange 2007 to avoid the need to deploy public folders. Of course, if you already have public folders because you run older Exchange servers and need to support older Outlook clients, Outlook 2007 has the ability to connect to the public folders to access the Offline Address Book and free and busy data.

The AutoDiscover web service delivers brand-new functionality to Exchange and solves a very real problem that any medium to large enterprise faces. If you have a small deployment, it is easy to communicate server information to users so that they can set up their profile to point to the right place. Outlook's AutoConfiguration option combines AutoDiscover with another process called "GuessSmart" to retrieve information about mailboxes by scanning for predictable combinations of server and protocol information. AutoConfiguration can discover settings for POP3 and IMAP4 accounts (with AutoDiscover and GuessSmart) or the Active Directory (with AutoDiscover) for settings for Exchange accounts. The principles behind GuessSmart are very straightforward. Let's assume that you want to create a new IMAP account. Your ISP will allocate you an email address such as James.Smart@xyz.com. There is a reasonable chance that the IMAP server is called imap.xyz.com or mail.xyz.com and the SMTP server will be smtp.xyz.com or mail.xyz.com. Therefore, Outlook can scan for these servers using the ports that the protocols use (like port 25 for SMTP and 110 for IMAP) to see whether these combinations generate a configuration that works. For most ISPs, guessing what the configuration might be works quickly. As you can see from Figure 7.2, the AutoDiscover service is able to provide the URLs to allow Outlook to contact resources such as the Availability service and the web distribution point for the Offline Address Book. If you configure a Client Access server to support Outlook Anywhere, the AutoDiscover service will populate the profile with the information necessary for Outlook to connect to Exchange using RPCs over HTTP.

Figure 7.2

Results from the Outlook 2007 AutoConfiguration option

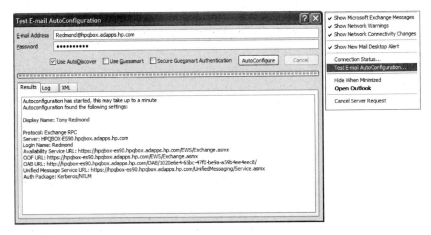

Finding out about your ISP email account is interesting, but the major value of AutoDiscover occurs in an Exchange 2007 environment. As we have seen, MAPI profiles contain many items about a client's configuration including the server name, the distinguished name of the user's mailbox, the location of the OAB, whether Outlook needs to open any PST files and their location, and so on. Outlook can populate some parts of a MAPI profile automatically by contacting a Client Access server (using the Exchange configuration information that is available in the Active Directory) and using the AutoDiscover service on that server to retrieve information about the user from their Active Directory object. The Active Directory object holds all the information that Outlook needs to reconstruct the MAPI profile. Outlook calls AutoDiscover any time that the details in the MAPI profile do not work for any reason. For example, if an administrator moves your mailbox to another server, the server name in the profile is obviously incorrect. In this case, Outlook will fetch the new server name from the Active Directory and update the profile. Outlook will also validate other settings in the profile and update as necessary.

Exchange 2007 Client Access servers are critical to the AutoDiscover service. The first step is for Outlook to discover the list of Client Access servers that are available to the client[2]. After it makes a network connection, Outlook queries the Active Directory (Figure 7.3) to locate Service Connection Points that Client Access servers have registered. A Service Connection Point (SCP) is an Active Directory object that allows applications to discover a service that they may be interested in using. When you install a Client Access server, the installation creates an SCP object in the Active Directory. Note that the AutoConfiguration option can use DNS to find an SCP if the check against Active Directory fails for some reason. In addition, the installation procedure created an AutoDiscover virtual directory in IIS. Figure 7.4 shows the SCP information for a server as viewed through ADSIEDIT. To find this information, open the configuration naming context, navigate to Services, then Microsoft Exchange, then the Administrative Group, then the server name, then Protocols, and finally AutoDiscover.

If Outlook cannot find a Client Access server to connect to, it can make an intelligent guess by taking the user's email address (either from the profile or by prompting the user) and then using that information to form an FQDN to attempt to find a Client Access Server. If this step does not work then Outlook cannot use AutoDiscover. Outlook then attempts to read details of the Exchange server using the Active Directory that you authenticated against, but if this step fails, then the user will have to configure their profile manually.

You can use the `Get-ClientAccessServer` shell command to gain an insight into the configuration data that Exchange maintains about these servers. Here is an edited version of the output that you might see:

```
Name                        : EXCHCAS1
OutlookAnywhereEnabled      : False
AutoDiscoverServiceCN       : EXCHCAS1
AutoDiscoverServiceClassName : ms-Exchange-AutoDiscover-Service
```

---

2.   If the workstation that you run Outlook on is not a member of the forest that supports Exchange, you may have to create an entry in the local hosts file to allow Outlook to find the AutoDiscover service. The format of this entry is the IP address followed by Autodiscover.domain. For example, 10.1.1.7 Autodiscover.xyz.com.

Figure 7.3
*Outlook in the
AutoDiscover
process*

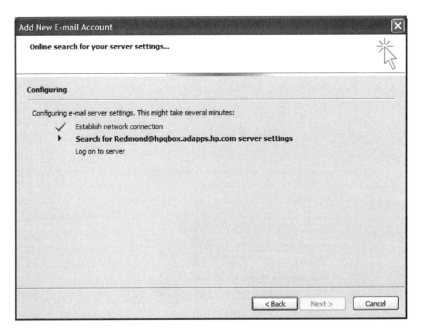

Figure 7.4
AutoDiscover SCP

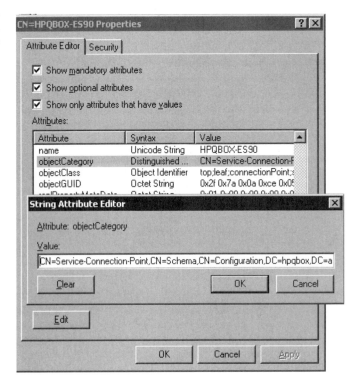

```
AutoDiscoverServiceInternalUri : https://exchcas1.xyz.com/Autodiscover/Autodiscover
                                   .xml
AutoDiscoverServiceGuid         : 77378f46-2c66-4aa9-a6a6-3e7a48b19596
AutoDiscoverSiteScope           : { Dublin}
IsValid                         : True
OriginatingServer               : EXCHCAS1.xyz.com
ObjectCategoryName              : msExchExchangeServer
DistinguishedName               : CN=HPQBOX-ES90,CN=Servers,CN=Exchange Administrative
Group (FYDIBOHF23SPDLT),CN=Administrative Groups,CN=XYZ,CN=Microsoft
Exchange,CN=Services,CN=Configuration,DC=XYZ, DC=com
Guid                            : 7f2d3b6c-d52c-4f8e-a3cf-a7e1df0930d1
ObjectCategory                  : xyz.com/Configuration/Schema/ms-Exch-Exchange-Server
ObjectClass                     : { top, server, msExchExchangeServer}
IsReadOnly                      : False
```

We can see two interesting pieces of information here. The first is the site scope (Dublin), which indicates that this Client Access Server is best to serve requests from clients that belong to the Dublin Active Directory site. You can set a different site scope with the Set-ClientAccessServer command. The second piece of information is the URI (Uniform Resource Identifier) to the virtual directory for the AutoDiscover service.

Outlook uses the Active Directory site scope to discover the best Client Access server to connect to. If the Active Directory returns a number of servers that are available for the site, Outlook selects one at random and attempts to connect to it via HTTPS. Once connected, Outlook can call the AutoDiscover service running on the Client Access Server with a using the value returned in the AutoDiscoverServiceInternalUri property (URI that points to the AutoDiscover service—see the value returned by the Get-ClientAccessServer command above for an example).

AutoDiscover uses the email address to locate the user's Active Directory object and returns the necessary data to populate the settings necessary for Outlook to connect to Exchange, including the LegacyExchangeDN property, which is a critical piece of data for backwards compatibility purposes if you have ever moved the mailbox. AutoDiscover returns the data in XML format. The data contains information about server-side objects such as Exchange itself and the OAB. Executing the Get-OutlookProvider command reveals some information and you will see entries for common services such as EXCH (client connect to Exchange server using TCP/IP) and EXPR (client connect to Exchange using RPC over HTTP). Note that the data returned by AutoDiscover is only sufficient to connect successfully to an Exchange mailbox. There are many other settings that you can make in a MAPI profile (such as the ability to use PSTs). These can be set either by the user or through a group policy.

The AutoDiscover service removes a major hassle for users, who often do not know the name of their mailbox server and definitely will not know the server name if an administrator ever moves their mailbox to a new server. The AutoDiscover service returns the name of the Exchange server where the user's mailbox is located and Outlook proceeds to connect. Outlook 2007 accommodates connections to Exchange 2000 or 2003 servers (which do not offer an AutoDiscover service) by presenting users with the older profile creation screen to allow them to specify the name of the server that hosts their mailbox if Outlook's attempt to contact AutoDiscover returns an error. Some assistance is provided if Outlook 2007 is run on a machine that's part of the forest that supports Exchange and the user is currently logged on as Outlook can consult the Active Directory to retrieve the name of the mailbox server, if not the complete suite of information available for Exchange 2007 servers.

7.1.1.1   Authentication

MAPI clients traditionally authenticate themselves to servers with the NTLM (NT LAN Manager Challenge-Response) mechanism, using cached credentials if available on the PC. The user sees a password prompt only if the credentials are unavailable or have expired. As shown in Figure 7.5, Outlook clients can use native-mode Kerberos authentication when they connect to Exchange (2003 or 2007) servers. The left-hand screen shows the options when connected to an Exchange 2003 server; the right-hand screen shows the options when connected to an Exchange 2007 server. The ability to use Kerberos is important in deployments that use multiple Active Directory forests where accounts belong to one forest and wish to connect to Exchange servers that belong to another forest. Naturally, you need cross-forest trust relationships for such connections to work. NTLM authentication also works between forests, but is less efficient than Kerberos, which is also a more future-proof authentication mechanism.

It is not a good idea to switch Outlook over from NTLM to Kerberos authentication unless every Exchange server in the organization runs on Windows 2003 (which must be the case for an Exchange 2007 deployment that supports no legacy servers), including all public folder servers. In the meantime, you are best to leave clients to use NTLM.

To improve security slightly, Microsoft encrypts RPCs between Outlook and Exchange 2007. This is a change from previous versions, which disabled RPC encryption by default. However, as you can see from Figure 7.5, you can control this per-user setting from Outlook. Administrators can also require RPC encryption for any client connection to a mailbox server with the `Set-MailboxServer` command. For example, to require encrypted RPCs for all connections to the server called ExchMBXSvr3:

Figure 7.5
*Outlook
authentication
modes*

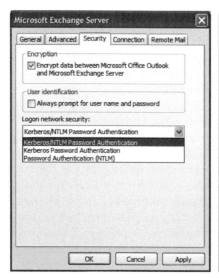
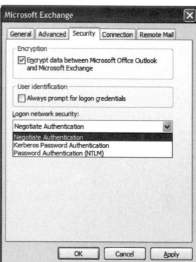

```
Set-MailboxServer —id ExchMBXSvr3 —MapiEncryptionRequired
$True
```

You can use the Get-MailboxServer command to identify the mailbox servers in the organization that have MAPI encryption enabled:

```
Get-MailboxServer | Select Name, MAPI*
```

Name	MAPIEncryptionRequired
----	----------------------
ExchMBXSvr1	False
ExchMBXSvr2	False
ExchMBXSvr3	True

7.1.2 Understanding Outlook's relationship with Exchange

Looking at clients from a server perspective, you always want to understand how the different clients connect to the server and the load that they are likely to place on the server. Traditionally, communication between MAPI clients and Exchange occurs using Exchange RPCs over a TCP/IP or Net-BIOS connection. The model used assumed that networks are reasonably stable and have low latency. In less robust network conditions, there is a danger that RPCs will be dropped due to network interruptions or time-outs. Early versions of Outlook produced a "chatty" client in terms of client-server communications and this facet of Outlook caused much user frustration when they used Outlook to connect to Exchange over slow dial-up connections or over extended, high-latency links. For example, if you use Outlook 2000 to connect to Exchange over a slow link, it is quite common to experience a "hanging RPC" where Outlook freezes because it is waiting for some operation to complete. Sometimes, you might have to kill the Outlook process in order to continue, which leads to other problems with potential corruption of your OST. Outlook 2002 introduced the ability for a user to cancel an RPC request and resume working, but this was hardly the perfect solution. Issues caused by RPC failures became worse as wireless-equipped laptops and tablet PCs replaced traditional desktop PCs as the most popular user device. Outlook 2003 was the first client to address the problem with its introduction of cached Exchange mode and intelligent over-the-wire compression together with changes made to Exchange 2003 to support clients better, even if it could not work the magic necessary to deliver good responsiveness to clients that share a low-bandwidth connection. When I wrote my Exchange 2003 book, I still referred to the need to connect over 28.8kbps dial-up connections. Looking back, it seems like a very long time since I used such a connection as broadband access and wireless connectivity have become so widespread across the world. However, there are still places where dial-up connections are needed, and Outlook has to be able to function efficiently across these links. This is one of the reasons why Microsoft has continued to improve client-server network connectivity in the Outlook 2007 and Exchange 2007 releases.

Cached Exchange mode, which has been the default connection mode for Outlook clients since Exchange 2003, means that Outlook's focus moves from the server mailbox to a local replica or cache of the user mailbox maintained in an OST. In other words, when the user sends or reads email or schedules an appointment, they work with local data rather than fetching data over the network. Because the user works with local data, performance is more consistent and predictable and is isolated to a large degree from network failures. Behind the scenes, Outlook keeps the local replica up to date by fetching data using four synchronization threads and uses an additional "fast thread" to fetch data immediately if required. For example, if you download only headers to your mailbox and decide that you want to read the complete copy of a specific message, Outlook uses the fast thread to connect and fetch that content in the foreground while the four other threads continue to synchronize other data in the background. Figure 7.6 illustrates the options that users have to control how Outlook synchronizes items.

The size of the OST on disk is roughly 20 to 30 percent larger than your mailbox. The OST file structure is not particularly efficient as Microsoft designed it when mailboxes were much smaller. With the size of mailboxes today, OSTs can struggle to deal with large mailboxes, and once an OST file exceeds 1GB, the inherent inefficiency of the internal file structure is compounded by the relatively slow speed and I/O capability of the disks that are installed in laptop PCs. Sometimes, the sheer CPU speed of the PC can mask some of the performance problems caused by OST inefficiency, but it is likely that you will notice heavy disk activity on any laptop used by someone who is a heavy mail user with a large mailbox. Initially, Outlook 2007 experienced slow performance due in some part to OST inefficiency when dealing with large files. Microsoft released a fix for this problem in April 2007 (KB933493). By default, Outlook creates your OST on the C: drive under your Documents and Settings directory, but if your PC supports multiple disks, you may get a performance boost by moving the OST to a less-heavily loaded disk. To move an OST, you have to turn off cached Exchange mode (to stop Outlook using it), then exit Outlook, move the OST to the desired location, restart Outlook, update your mailbox settings so that Outlook points to the new location, and then turn on cached Exchange mode again to have Outlook start to use the OST again.

Figure 7.6
Outlook synchronization settings

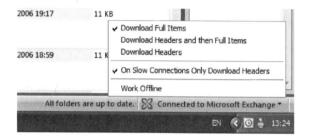

Unlike previous versions of Outlook, Outlook 2003 and 2007 are able to detect problems with items during the synchronization process and work around the bad item where older clients stop working. Outlook 2003 and 2007 are less chatty than previous clients and support what Microsoft refers to as improved replication semantics, which means that the clients are tuned to reduce the amount of data sent over the wire. In addition, users can opt to download message headers only, headers and then full content, or full items depending on the kind of network connection they have at the time. In the office or when using a broadband connection, you can safely use the option to download full items all the time without noticing any delay or performance degradation. If you opt for headers first followed by full items, Outlook uses an algorithm called "drizzle synchronization" to keep the cache up to date.

Drizzle synchronization essentially means that Outlook fetches small pieces of data over a period of time to slowly but steadily populate the cache. It's a mode of working that is very suited to high-latency or low-throughput connections.

If you use a local cache with a TCP/IP connection, Exchange will notify Outlook to initiate synchronization any time that new items arrive in the server mailbox. Outlook does not synchronize immediately if it receives a number of notifications in quick succession as it is more efficient to make one connection to synchronize a number of new items. To pick up new content, Outlook first downloads the message header, including the first 254 bytes of the message content, to load this information into the inbox (so you can see who sent the message) and reading pane, and to allow junk mail filtering and rules to work. The header information does not contain the number of attachments, the size of attachments, or their type, but it does contain the overall message size, which is enough for a user to decide whether they want to download the full content.

Outlook uses an algorithm called Incremental Change Synchronization (ICS) to control synchronization operations with Exchange. ICS sets checkpoints to allow Outlook to know what data is synchronized and what remains to be fetched. In older versions of Outlook, the synchronization process was very crude insofar as any interruption between client and server forced the complete synchronization operation to terminate. Now, synchronization proceeds between small checkpoints (set after every successful network buffer download) so that even if the network connection breaks at a point before synchronization is complete, Outlook can pause at the last checkpoint and resume from this point when it reestablishes the network connection. The user benefits by being able to work with whatever data has been synchronized up to the last good checkpoint. To complete synchronization, Outlook checks every folder in the cache against the server each time it connects to Exchange to ensure that the contents are up to date and then makes whatever adjustments are necessary.

While Outlook 2003 made enormous strides in synchronization and the reduction of traffic across the wire, it did not completely address the problem of partial item upload, which relates to the amount of network activity that is generated between the client and server when a property on an item is changed. For example, if you set a flag on an item, it does not make much sense for the client to copy the complete item up to the server. It is much more logical and efficient if the client copies only the changed data. Outlook 2003 solves the problem for items that are uploaded to Exchange and Outlook 2007 solves the problem for downloads. This means that if you use another client to work with items, you will not generate a lot of network activity to copy any item that you worked with the next time that Outlook resynchronizes with the server. Another positive change in Outlook 2007 is that the client no longer copies a complete item twice when a message is sent (once to send the item and then again to refile it into the Sent Items folder). As items and attachments get larger, this becomes a very important change. Finally, Outlook 2007 now includes the intelligence to know when a message will cause a user to exceed their mailbox quota and will not incur the cost of sending the message up to Exchange only for Exchange to detect the quota problem and return the message back to Outlook. Now, if you are about to send a message that will exceed your quota, Outlook tells you that you have a problem and saves the network costs of sending and receiving the message.

Figure 7.7
Outlook
Connection Status

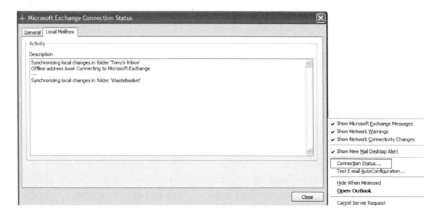

When Outlook 2003 or 2007 synchronizes with Exchange, the Outlook icon in the system tray changes to reflect messages passing up and down to the server. If you hold down the CTRL key and right-click on the icon, you can see what folders that Outlook is currently processing. The right-hand of Figure 7.7 shows the options that you see after pressing CTRL+right-click on the icon. Click on "Connection Status" and Outlook displays the screen shown in the left-hand part of Figure 7.7. In this case, you can see that Outlook is synchronizing changes for two folders[3] and the Offline Address Book.

If a network interruption breaks the connection between Outlook and Exchange, the client continues to work with data in the local cache and then pauses its attempt to synchronize new data into the cache. Users are often unaware that Outlook has gone offline, as the performance that they see when they work with Outlook remains the same. The lack of a connection to Exchange only becomes obvious when users notice that messages that they thought are sent have not been synchronized with the server and are stuck in the Outbox. Users receive another clue when they want to see server data such as the organizational details of another user contained in the GAL. Outlook uses the OAB instead of the server GAL whenever possible to validate email addresses and display user details, so it is important that the OAB is regularly downloaded. As we will discuss later on in this chapter, Outlook 2003 and 2007 download updates for the OAB daily.

---

3.   I renamed my Inbox and Deleted Items folder with the very first version of an Exchange client in 1996 and have used these folder names since. Regrettably, Outlook doesn't allow you to play around with default folder names now.

An important change in Outlook 2003 reflected the need to support people who work from home. Outlook 2003 and 2007 support RPC over HTTP connections, a mechanism that wraps Exchange RPCs with HTTP to allow them to pass across VPN connections to a front-end Exchange 2003 server or an Exchange 2007 Client Access server (Exchange 2007 calls this feature "Outlook Anywhere"; Exchange 2003 refers to it as RPC over HTTP). Because HTTP is used as a wrapper, system administrators do not have to open up firewalls to expose other ports, which is a major advantage from this implementation. You need PCs running Windows XP SP1 or later to be able to use RPC over HTTP connections. Outlook Anywhere is reviewed later on in this chapter.

An interesting and worthwhile feature is the ability of Outlook 2003 and 2007 to compress graphic attachments so that Outlook transmits a much-reduced version. Given that most digital cameras are capable of generating a 3MB or larger JPEG image and that email is a very effective way of sharing photos with your family and friends, the ability to compress graphics is a feature that makes a lot of sense. Compression occurs on the client, so this feature works no matter what server version of Exchange you connect Outlook 2003 or 2007 to.

From a user perspective, it is interesting to note some behavioral changes in how people use folders after the introduction of cached Exchange mode. With previous versions of Outlook, users tended to focus on the Inbox and Sent Items folders and keep many items in these folders because Outlook automatically synchronized them along with the calendar to their OST. Now, Outlook synchronizes every folder in a user's mailbox, so there is less of a tendency to maintain massive Inbox and Sent Items folders to hold every piece of information that you might need when travelling and a more thoughtful use of folders to organize information in a logical manner.

Overall, the synchronization process between the latest versions of Exchange and the latest versions of Outlook are much more intelligent than previous versions. Users do not realize any great difference between message delivery times to a PC running Outlook in cached Exchange mode and a PC running Outlook connected to a server mailbox. Indeed, the only time that you might be aware of a speed difference is if you have a handheld device and compare the time when a message appears in Outlook's cached copy of the inbox and when it appears on the handheld. My experience is that message delivery to handhelds is sometimes faster, but not by a lot.

7.1.3 Deploying cached Exchange mode

Microsoft argues that cached Exchange mode improves client performance because Outlook works with local data and only delays the user to execute a transaction with the server over the network if some required data is not available in the local cache. This statement is absolutely true and user perception of Outlook performance is generally much better when they configure Outlook to run in cached Exchange mode. Microsoft also says that cached Exchange mode aids server performance by normalizing the demands that Outlook clients would otherwise make in a fairly arbitrary fashion over the day with a more predictable pattern of network traffic generated by background synchronization. This statement is also true, but do not imagine that cached Exchange mode is the answer for every network or performance issue that an Exchange server can have. For instance, you will still see peaks in demand at times such as early in the morning, when users tend to arrive into the office close together and connect to pick up new mail. Daily OAB downloads may also contribute to early morning peaks. Working with cached Exchange mode generates different patterns of demand for the network and server, but these demands are generally easier to predict and cater for.

There are situations where cached Exchange mode does not work (in a practical sense). For example, if your users roam from PC to PC, it obviously does not make sense to configure Outlook to use cached Exchange mode because it means that Outlook will have to rebuild the cache for each user as they connect using different PCs. Not only would this requirement generate additional network and server load, users would not be happy because the local copies of their mailboxes would be in a state of constant reconstruction. Roaming users or those that use thin client solutions such as Windows Terminal Server or Citrix Metaframe are best advised to work with online mailboxes.

Another example where cached Exchange mode can cause some difficulties is for users who have very large (greater than 2–3GB) mailboxes. Given the continuing trend towards larger message sizes, cheap storage, and Microsoft's message that the 64-bit nature of Exchange 2007 means that it is okay to have massive mailboxes, we are going to see mailboxes swell in size. This would not be a problem if the OST file structure were efficient when it came to dealing with thousands of items in the file or laptop hard disks were faster than they are, but neither of these cases is true. If you have a large OST, it is likely that the OST contains thousands of items—my own contains about twenty thousand items in a 2GB file. Outlook does an increasing amount of work to insert new items into the OST as the number of items in the file grows, and the relatively slow I/O performance of laptop disks do not help. The net result is that if you have a large mailbox, be prepared for times when Outlook slows down a tad to process data in the OST. Most OST files are now in Unicode[4] format, so they can expand past the previous 2GB limit. Note that if you upgrade from a previous version of Outlook to Outlook 2003 or 2007, there is no way to upgrade your OST from ANSI to Unicode format to take advantage of the support for larger files, so you will have to

4. See http://www.unicode.org/standard/WhatIsUnicode.html for details about Unicode.

Figure 7.8
*Checking the OST
format*

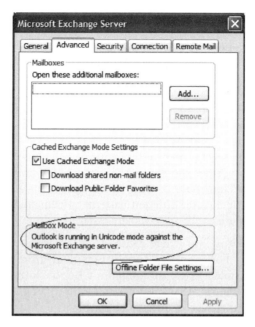

delete the existing OST and allow Outlook to rebuild a new file, which will be Unicode format. You can check the OST format by viewing the file properties through the "Advanced" tab of your Exchange mailbox, as shown in Figure 7.8.

If you decide not to deploy Outlook in cached Exchange mode, you may have to calculate the network load and performance that is necessary to support clients that depend on a direct connection. In this case, you can use the following guidelines:

1.   Ensure that the round-trip latency is acceptable by achieving <100ms between Outlook and Exchange; problems occur after a latency of >300ms and you will see RPC failures if the latency reaches 1,200ms or higher.

2.   The bandwidth load generated by users usually comes out at between 3 kbps (low usage) and 6 kbps (high user) per concurrent Outlook client connection. Note that it is possible for users who are very active or who send a lot of large attachments to soak up far more bandwidth. Also remember that Outlook creates multiple threads to communicate with Exchange across the single connection.

3.   Assess the total number of users who are likely to connect across the link and then calculate a worse case that 80% of the total user

community will connect concurrently and absorb 6 kbps each. That gives you the worst-case scenario load and you can throttle this back to a more reasonable load by estimating how many users are realistically likely to connect concurrently.

Of course, these are just rules of thumb, so your own estimation and experience will help you get to better figures.

7.1.4 Address caching

One of Outlook's convenient features is its ability to cache the names of people that you have sent messages to. Outlook uses this data to recognize names as you address messages. For example, in Figure 7.9, I have started to address a message to Jim Smith. Outlook knows that I have sent messages to Jim.Smith@xyz.com before, so as soon as I type the name, Outlook shows whatever addresses exist in its cache that match. This feature is a godsend for anyone who sends lots of email.

The downside is that address caching can lead to undelivered messages when users send messages using addresses that Outlook takes from the cache that have changed since they were cached, perhaps because the recipient has moved their mailbox to a new Exchange 2007 server. In this case, you may see a Delivery Service Notice like this:

```
Diagnostic information for administrators:


Generating server: ExchHub1.xyz.com


IMCEAEX-_O=XYZ_OU=USERS_CN=RECIPIENTS_CN=Blane@XYZ.COM
#550 5.1.1 RESOLVER.ADR.ExRecipNotFound; not found ##
```

All this means that Exchange can't resolve an address in the header despite the fact that it seems to be valid. The address is an older format X.400/X.500-style address. This isn't an issue because Exchange is quite capable of resolving these addresses, providing a matching entry exists in the Active Directory. In this case, the address cannot be resolved because the mailbox is no longer in the place where it once was. This is all very sensible from an Exchange perspective but maddening for the user. The answer is to tell the user to delete the offending entries from their cache, which they can do by creating a new message, entering the address, and using the delete key to remove the addresses from the list suggested by Outlook. The next time the user addresses a message to the recipient, Outlook will insert the correct

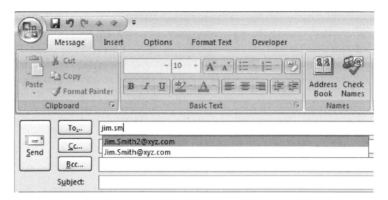

Figure 7.9
*Outlook suggests
email addresses*

MAPI address into the message header and all will be well—until the user's mailbox is moved again!

The issue of lingering old addresses is less common in pure Exchange deployments than it used to be, but is reported from time to time. A variation on the problem is where you are migrating mailboxes from one mail system to another, such as from Lotus Notes to Exchange. Users have the old Notes addresses for recipients cached in Outlook instead of the new Exchange address and can therefore meet the problem when they address messages to mailboxes that don't exist on a Notes server. The same solution applies—delete the old address and force Outlook to repopulate its cache with a newly validated address.

7.1.5   MAPI compression and buffers

MAPI clients request Exchange servers to provide data in chunks or buffers. To optimize communications, the size of the buffers generated by Exchange varies depending on the version of Outlook and the type of network in use. For example, Outlook 2003 uses large 32KB buffers on LAN-quality networks and reduces the buffer to 8KB or even 4KB if the connection is slower. Table 7.1 shows the difference in network activity between Outlook 2002 and Outlook 2003/2007 when connected to an Exchange 2000, 2003, or 2007 server. As you can see, there is a much greater degree of granularity in how Outlook 2003 communicates with Exchange.

You also notice that the latest versions of Outlook compress data to reduce network demand. Exchange 2003 and 2007 include the same compression technology[5] and so these combinations of clients and servers deliver full duplex compression. Older clients do not compress data because

---

5.   Microsoft calls the compression technology "XPRESS" and it is based on the Lempel-Ziv algorithm. Active Directory uses the same algorithm to compress RPC data sent between domain controllers.

Table 7.1 *Outlook network activity*

Version	Mode	Data Flow	Network	Client Buffer Size	Data Buffer Size	Size on Wire
Outlook 2002	Online	Download/ Upload	LAN	32KB	32KB	32KB
	Online	Download/ Upload	WAN	4KB or 8KB	4KB or 8KB	4KB or 8KB
	Offline (synch.)	Download/ Upload	Any	32KB	32KB	32KB
Outlook 2003/ 2007	Online	Download	All	32KB	32KB	<32KB
	Online	Upload	All	32KB	32KB	M 32KB
	Cached	Download	All	96KB	>96KB	96KB
	Cached	Upload	All	32KB	32KB	<32KB
	Offline	Download	All	32KB	>32KB	32KB
	Offline	Upload	All	32KB	32KB	<32KB

they do not support the code or the MAPI call that lets Exchange know that communication is compressed, so all connections between Exchange and Outlook clients earlier than Outlook 2003 are uncompressed. Clearly, there is some demand on Exchange to compress and decompress data, but Microsoft believes that the performance penalty is more than offset by the gain because the server has to process fewer network packets. You can change the way that Exchange 2003 or 2007 servers perform RPC compression for Outlook clients with the registry values described in Table 7.2, which you insert at the key:

```
HKLM\System\CurrentControlSet\Services\MSExchangeIS\
ParametersSystem\
```

Whenever possible, Exchange 2003 and 2007 compress the complete content of messages, including attachments. In much the same way that ZIP utilities achieve different compression ratios for different file formats, the compression ratios produced by Exchange vary across different message types and attachments. For example, HTML and plain text body parts compress to between 60 and 80 percent of their original size. Word documents and Excel spreadsheets compress well, while PowerPoint presentations are less amenable to compression.

Table 7.2   *Exchange RPC Compression Parameters*

Value	Description
RPC Compression Minimum Size (DWORD)	Defines the minimum size a packet is before Exchange compresses it (the default value is 1,024 bytes).
RPC Compression Enabled (DWORD)	A flag that allows or prevents compression on the Exchange server. The default value is 1, which allows compression to occur. Set the value to 0 if you want to disable compression.
RPC Packing Enabled (DWORD)	A flag that allows or prevents the Exchange server packing RPCs. The default value is 1, which allows RPC packing.

7.1.6 Conflict resolution

The nature of synchronization means that the potential exists for different versions of items to exist on the client and on the server. A conflict occurs when some action modifies a previously agreed common version of an item. For example, a user works with Outlook offline and modifies an item in the cached version of their mailbox. Later on, they connect to Exchange online using Outlook Web Access and read the same item again and take an action to modify it, such as clearing an event flag. They then connect Outlook to Exchange and synchronize and a conflict results because different versions of the same item now exist. This is a somewhat convoluted example, but given the many ways that people interact with mailboxes through Outlook, Outlook Web Access, Blackberries, Pocket PCs, and SmartPhones, conflicts do occur all the time, especially with calendar items.

Up to Outlook 2003, the approach taken is to mark items that are in conflict with a "crossed swords" icon to show the user that a conflict exists that they will have to resolve by opening the item, viewing the different versions, and deciding which version to keep. Outlook 2003 introduced a new conflict-resolution engine that Microsoft designed to resolve conflicts automatically. The engine quickly resolves spurious conflicts (two versions exist, but they are identical) and presents a more elegant interface for users to track and resolve conflicts that require user intervention. In these cases, the engine uses an algorithm to determine which copy of the item is most likely to be the version to keep and Outlook retains this version in the original folder. Outlook moves the other versions into the Conflicts folder, which is a subfolder of the Sync Issues folder in the user's mailbox. You have to click on the

Folder List shortcut to have Outlook reveal the Sync Issues folder in the folder tree view.

You can review the contents of the Sync Issues folder from time to time to see what items Outlook has moved there. There are three subfolders: Conflicts, Local Failures, and Server Failures. Outlook uses the Conflicts folder to store all the items that Outlook believes to be in conflict. You can review these items individually and decide whether you want to keep the version in the Conflicts folder by replacing the version that Outlook has retained in the original folder or you can delete the version in the Conflicts folder, which is a emphatic way of resolving the conflict. Alternatively, you can leave conflicts alone unless Outlook prompts you to resolve a conflict when you access an item. At this time, Outlook displays a conflict resolution band in the message header to present the options that a user can take. You can decide what version to keep and Outlook will update the folder with this version.

The Local Failures folder holds copies of items that Outlook was unable to synchronize with the server. Usually the problem that caused the failure is transient (such as a network interruption) and Outlook subsequently synchronized successfully. The Server Failures folder holds items that Exchange was unable to synchronize down to Outlook and again, the failure condition is usually transient. You can delete the items that you find in the Local Failures and Server Failures folders—I do this on a regular basis to free up a small amount of space in my mailbox.

It is not a sign of good synchronization health if you find more than a few items in the Local Failures and Server Failures folders and it could be an indication of an underlying problem that you need to address. If such a condition occurs, you can turn on email logging though Tools, Options, Other, and Advanced to force Outlook to begin logging more detailed results for synchronization operations, which it stores as items in the Sync Issues folder. Note that you have to restart Outlook before detailed logging begins. Some of the information that Outlook logs may help you understand why problems occur, but it is more likely that a PSS specialist will be able to decipher the data, as the information is useful but a tad cryptic.

7.1.7 Preventing MAPI clients from connecting

Exchange 2007 allows you to disable connection protocols, including MAPI, on a per-user basis by amending the protocol properties of a mailbox. If you disable MAPI, a user cannot use Outlook to connect to their mailbox.

The `Set-CasMailbox` command supports a number of parameters to control how an individual mailbox can use MAPI to connect to a mailbox on an Exchange 2007 server:

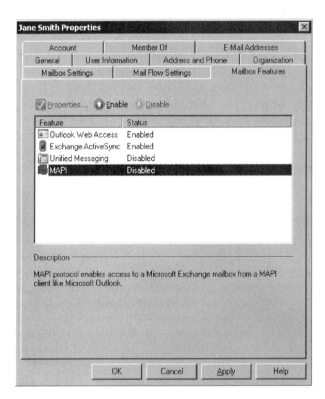

Figure 7.10
Disabling MAPI
access for a user

- MAPIBlockOutlookRPCHTTP: Allows you to determine whether you allow Outlook clients to connect over RPC over HTTP via Outlook Anywhere. Set the parameter to $True to allow RPC over HTTP access and $False to block this access.

- MAPIBlockOutlookVersions: Allows you to control what versions of Outlook can connect to Exchange 2007. You might use this setting to force users to upgrade to a more modern version of Outlook such as Outlook 2003 or 2007 because these clients are able to make efficient use of server resources. If a user attempts to use a blocked version of Outlook, they see the error message shown in Figure 7.11. Outlook clients configured for cached Exchange mode continue to work offline, but they cannot connect to the server until an administrator lifts the block.

- MAPIBlockOutlookNonCachedMode: Allows you to determine whether you allow Outlook clients to connect in online mode to the server. Set this parameter to $True to allow online access and to $False to force clients to connect in cached Exchange mode. Somewhat confusingly, users blocked from online access also see the same message shown in Figure 7.11 followed by another error message to tell them that Outlook is unable to open their default email folders. Pointing to the version of Outlook rather than the need to use cached Exchange mode may confuse the help desk when the user reports their problem.

Figure 7.11
*MAPI logon has
been blocked*

The values that you specify in the MAPIBlockOutlookVersions parameter are the same as Exchange supports on the server to block incoming MAPI client connections. See Microsoft Knowledge Base article 288894 for more information. As an example, here are two commands. The first restricts access so that the user must use Outlook 2003 or above; the second restricts access to Outlook 2007 or later. In both cases, an explicit "allow" is included for version 6.0.0 in order to support Exchange server-side MAPI connections (server connections always use MAPI version 6.0).

```
Set-CasMailbox –Id Bond –MAPIBlockOutlookVersions
'-6.0.0;10.0.0– 11.5603.0'

Set-CasMailbox –Id Bond –MAPIBlockOutlookVersions
'-6.0.0;10.0.0-12.4406.0'
```

You have to wait up to 20 minutes for the cached information about the mailbox to expire from the Store's cache. Alternatively, you can restart the Information Store service, but apart from test situations, this is definitely not the best approach because it will affect all the other mailboxes connected to the server.

You can check to see if any MAPI restrictions are in place on a server by using the Get-Mailbox command to examine the ProtocolSettings property of each mailbox. If a restriction is in place for a specific client version, you will see that version number listed. If an administrator has completely disabled MAPI access for the mailbox, you will see "MAPI" and no version number. For example:

```
Get-Mailbox –Server ExchMbxSvr1 | Where {$_.ProtocolSettings –ne $Null} | Select
Name, ProtocolSettings
```

```
Name                                 ProtocolSettings
----                                 ----------------
Tony Redmond                         {MAPI§§§-6.0.0;10.0.0-11.5603.0§§§§}
Jane Smith                           {MAPI§0§§§§§§§}
James Bond                           {OWA§1, IMAP4§0§§§§§§§§, POP3§0§§§§§...
```

Microsoft introduced the ProtocolSettings property in Exchange 2003 SP2, where administrators could use it to control MAPI access, but not other protocol. In this version, you need to use a utility such as ADSIEDIT to set the property. See the Exchange 2003 SP2 release notes for details.

You can also use the `Get-CasMailbox` command to check for MAPI blocks. On the one hand, `Get-CasMailbox` is more interesting because it also allows you to return the value of the MapiEnabled property (this will be False if the user is completely blocked from using MAPI) and to see the details of all of the protocol settings that you can set on a mailbox. On the other hand, you cannot specify a server name to check against, so `Get-CasMailbox` will be less efficient as it will scan the entire organization unless you restrict its scope by using a server-side filter to focus in on one server:

```
Get-CasMailbox —Filter {ServerName —eq 'ExchMbxSvr1'} | Where
{$_.ProtocolSettings —ne $Null} | Select Name, ProtocolSettings, MapiEnabled
```

```
Name                     ProtocolSettings                     MAPIEnabled
----                     ----------------                     -----------
Tony Redmond             {MAPI§§§-6.0.0;10.0.0-...                   True
Jane Smith               {MAPI§0§§§§§§§}                            False
James Bond               {OWA§1, IMAP4§0§§§§§§§§...                  True
```

If you want to stop all MAPI clients of a specific version connecting to Exchange, you can either use a command to loop through all the mailboxes on the server and call the `Set-CasMailbox` command to set the block as described above or implement the block through the system registry. To do this, create a value called Disable MAPI clients at:

```
HKLM\System\CurrentControlSet\Services\MSExchangeIS\
ParametersSystem
```

Set the value in the registry as above. Figure 7.12 illustrates the block in action.

In addition to imposing blocks on MAPI connections, you can use the
`Set-CasMailbox` command to disable client access to other protocols. For
example:

- To disable access to POP3: `Set-CasMailbox —Id Bond —PopEnabled`
  `$False`

- To disable access to IMAP4: `Set-CasMailbox —Id Bond`
  `—ImapEnabled $False`

- To disable access to Outlook Web Access: `Set-CasMailbox —Id Bond`
  `—OWAEnabled $False`

- To disable access to ActiveSync: `Set-CasMailbox —Id Bond`
  `—ActiveSyncEnabled $False`

Figure 7.12
Blocking MAPI
clients via the
registry

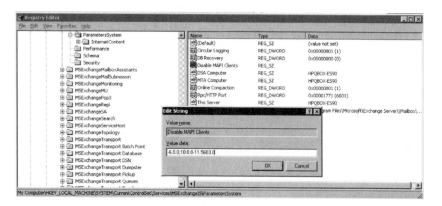

7.1.8   Outlook 2007 and Exchange 5.5

Exchange 5.5 is a great mail server that is unfortunately well past its shelf life,
at least in terms of Microsoft's desire to support it. If you still run Exchange
5.5, it is time to move into the future because Microsoft will not provide support (extended lifecycle support from Microsoft for Exchange 5.5 ended on
January 10, 2006). In addition, you cannot migrate to Exchange 2007
directly using Microsoft tools such as the `Move-Mailbox` command, and you
will struggle to deal with new demands on messaging systems such as compliance—not to mention the problems of support for whatever anti-virus, anti-
spam, backup, and other complementary products you use alongside
Exchange. The final straw may be the fact that you cannot connect Outlook
2007 to Exchange 5.5 because Microsoft has incorporated a block to prevent
Outlook 2007 connecting to a mailbox on an Exchange 5.5 server.

Microsoft's logic for the decision is that neither the Exchange nor the Outlook development team has the time or the resources to support the testing of Outlook 2007 against Exchange 5.5. Their view is that they would prefer to spend their development resources to create new features for Exchange 2007 and Outlook 2007 and to support more recent products, such as Exchange 2003 and Outlook 2003, where customers still have support contracts and expectations that bugs will be fixed quickly. Even though you might regret Microsoft's logic, you can't really argue against it because of the relatively small community that still runs Exchange 5.5 and the expectation that this community will decrease over time.

However, there is a ray of hope for those running Exchange 5.5 who want to move directly to Exchange 2007. Third-party vendors have identified this as a gap that they can fill. The first product to enable migration from Exchange 5.5 to Exchange 2007 came in Quest Software's Exchange Migration Wizard[6] and more offerings are likely to emerge over time. If you're in this situation, take the time to scan the Internet to discover what's out there and take the time to test the available products before deciding on your migration strategy.

7.2   Offline and personal Stores

The Store is the repository for messages and other items created by users. The Store has many notable attributes—high performance, a single place to impose protection against incoming virus attacks, availability from any client, and so on. However, from a user perspective, the drawbacks of server-based storage are that each mailbox has a set quota enforced by the Store, and that mailboxes are only available when the server is running and the network is available to connect clients to the server.

You can use personal folder (PST) files to provide additional storage to users, while offline folder files (OST files) enable people to work when a network link is unavailable or they cannot otherwise reach the server. Curiously, on the one hand Microsoft tells everyone that we're all heading to an era where a 2GB mailbox is common and that you will be able to store all your data in your mailbox and not have to use PSTs, while on the other they invent new ways to use PSTs, such as synchronizing SharePoint lists with Outlook to allow offline access to SharePoint data. It will be a while before we can eliminate PSTs!

---

6.   See http://www.quest.com/exchange_migration_wizard/.

7.2.1 **Personal folders**

PSTs reside on either a local drive or network drive. You can even create a PST on a USB drive, a feature that you can use to transfer small amounts of folder data from one PC to another. The concept behind PSTs is that they provide a "personal repository," and so differentiates them as a storage mechanism from the server-based mailbox and public folders. PSTs allow users to create and manage their own private document archive. All servers have some storage limitations in terms of either the total available physical disk space or the mailbox quota allocated to individual users. It is easy to run out of space, especially if you are in the habit of creating or circulating messages with large attachments. In these situations, users can reduce their mailbox under the quota by moving files to a PST.

Up to Outlook 2003, an ANSI-format PST could grow to a maximum size of 2GB. The Unicode format supported by Outlook 2003 and 2007 allows PSTs to expand to 20GB (more than enough for even the most fastidious of human packrats), although administrators can limit this to even less than 2GB by setting the registry keys described in Table 7.3 at:

```
HKEY_CURRENT_USER\Software\Policies\Microsoft\Office\12.0\
Outlook\PST
```

For Outlook 2007 use:

```
HKEY_CURRENT_USER\Software\Policies\Microsoft\Office\11.0\
Outlook\PST
```

All values are DWORDs and expressed in megabytes (Unicode format) or bytes (ANSI format). Administrators can control all these values through policies.

Table 7.3 *Registry values to control PST and OST file sizes*

Name	Value Range	Default Value	Meaning
MaxLargeFileSize	0x00000001 – 0x00005000	0x00005000 (20,480 in decimal or 20 GB)	Maximum size of a Unicode PST or OST
WarnLargeFileSize	0x00000001 – 0x00005000	0x00004C00 (19,456 in decimal or 19 GB)	Size when Outlook issues warning that a PST or OST is becoming too large

Table 7.3   *Registry values to control PST and OST file sizes (continued)*

Name	Value Range	Default Value	Meaning
MaxFileSize	0x001F4400 – 0x7C004400	0x7BB04400 (1.933 GB)	Maximum size for an ANSI format PST or OST
WarnFileSize	0x00042400 – 0x7C004400	0x74404400 (1.816 GB)	Size when Outlook issues warning that a PST or OST is becoming too large

Clearly, many older Outlook clients remain in use, so a danger exists that users could attempt to store more than 2GB in a PST and corrupt the file. Microsoft released preventative fixes in Office XP SP1 and service release 1A for Office 2000. The Office XP fix issues a warning when a PST gets to 1.8GB, while the Office 2000 fix just stops the file growing. If you get into a situation where a PST grows past the supported limit, you can use a Microsoft utility called[7] PST2GB to truncate the file. However, truncation will lose data so it is best to keep PSTs small. You cannot convert an existing PST file to Unicode format, so if you want to use a PST larger than 2GB, you have to create a new file and populate it from scratch, usually by dragging and dropping items from older PSTs. People often use PSTs to transfer documents between each other, so remember that older versions of Outlook cannot open Unicode-format PSTs and use older format files whenever you need to swap files in this fashion.

Messages are stored in two formats within a PST: RTF and ASCII, the logic being that it is conceivable that some clients will be unable to read RTF-style messages. This is largely a historical throwback to the time when some clients, such as the original DOS client shipped with Exchange 4.0, could only process plain text messages.

Unless it is password-protected, you need to provide no security credentials to open a PST. It is possible to browse a PC or network share, find a PST, and then open it with any MAPI client, even if it is not associated with your own mailbox. Note that Microsoft does not support opening a PST that is on a network share[8], but it can be done, and it's surprising how many users put PSTs on network shares as a form of backup.

You can set a password on the PST when you create the file (Figure 7.13) or by changing the properties of the PST afterwards. You must then provide the password before the client can open the file. Microsoft's official policy is that there is no way that they can recover data from a PST if the user forgets their password. However, this is a legal rather than a technical issue and you can easily break into a PST through utilities from companies such as

---

7.   Available from the Microsoft download center.
8.   See http://support.microsoft.com/kb/829971.

crackpassword.com or that circulate freely around the Internet. Of course, if an accident happens and you corrupt the PST by using an unsupported utility you are on your own and Microsoft support will be very unsympathetic.

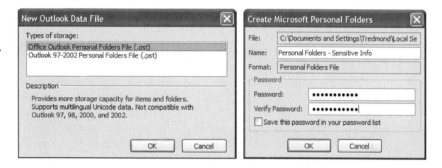

Figure 7.13

Creating a new PST

Encouraging users to work with PSTs is fine as long as they use the same PC all the time and understand their responsibilities to manage and protect data. However, if users move from one PC to another they will leave information behind them. In these situations, server-based storage (which is accessible from any PC—and from any client) is a better solution. One way to accommodate roaming users is to place their PST in their directory on a networked file server. If you do this, remember to tell users to always fully log-out from each PC they use, otherwise they will not be able to connect to their PST when they move to another PC. Microsoft did not design the internal structure of a PST to support multiple concurrent accesses.

7.2.2 Mail delivery to personal folders

You can configure Outlook to deliver new messages to a PST through the Delivery tab of the client *Tools | Options* menu option (Outlook 98 or 2000), or by selecting the PST file as the preferred Mail Delivery location (Outlook 2002 and 2003), or by selecting a PST as the default location for email as shown in Figure 7.14 (Outlook 2007). Rushing to divert messages from your mailbox to a PST is not a good idea and you should consider a few points before you make what is, to some extent, a radical change in a basic function of the messaging system. When you select the option to deliver messages to a PST, they remain in the server mailbox until you connect to the server. Outlook then transfers the messages from the server Inbox folder to an Inbox folder in the PST. After the messages transfer, Exchange deletes them from the mailbox. Some users do not expect this to happen, and are very surprised when they look at their server-based Inbox to find that all their mail has apparently disappeared! Of course, the messages are available in the PST, but users often overlook this fact, leading to any number of frantic calls to the help desk to demand the return of the missing messages.

Delivering mail to a PST is similar in concept to the traditional POP3/ IMAP4 email model provided by ISPs. This model holds some attractions if you want to build Exchange servers to host very large numbers of mailboxes with a restricted amount of storage. The economics behind hotmail.com would be very different if each user had mailbox quotas of the size seen in corporate messaging systems.

If server-based mailboxes are used, the space available to each user is constrained by their mailbox quota. If PSTs are used, then the server's storage is largely transient because Exchange only holds messages on the server until users connect to fetch messages. Users can therefore be allocated relatively small mailbox quotas (25MB or less), allowing many more users to be supported on a single server. Delivering messages to PSTs or using PSTs as secondary storage was much more common in the early days of Exchange, but cheaper hardware has reduced the attractiveness of these options. In addition, multiple client access has become increasingly important. Exchange 4.0 offered a single client and single access protocol (MAPI). Exchange now supports a huge variety of clients, but only MAPI clients can use PSTs. If you opt to deliver mail to a PST, then you immediately restrict your options for client deployment, so you lose much of the value of being able to make an occasional connection to your mailbox with Outlook Web Access as only new messages are kept there. Another issue to consider is that once messages arrive in a PST, Outlook is the only client that can access them. In other words, you completely eliminate the "Exchange Anywhere" notion of being able to access your email from a wide variety of clients from SmartPhones to web browsers.

The arrival of email-enabled viruses creates yet another problem. There are many server-based anti-virus agents, all of which are able to protect thousands of mailboxes from a single point. There are programs to scan a complete mailbox store to find and disinfect viruses, but no utilities exist to scan multiple PSTs for viruses. If a virus arrives and passes by an outdated virus detection pattern and for delivery to hundreds of PSTs, you have a huge amount of work to track down each instance of the virus and eliminate it.

You can only process messages in a PST if you have physical access to the PST. In other words, an administrator who can access the contents of server-based mailboxes cannot run utilities such as those that check for compliance or for lurking viruses against the messages unless they can access the PST. The only messages that remain in the server mailbox are those that have arrived since the last time the user connected and picked up mail. The inability to manage data centrally is probably the biggest issue that exists with PSTs today and in some respects is a major driver to move away from PSTs to adopt larger mailboxes. However, users will fill even the largest mailboxes, so PSTs will probably remain in use until Microsoft creates a better local storage repository for Outlook.

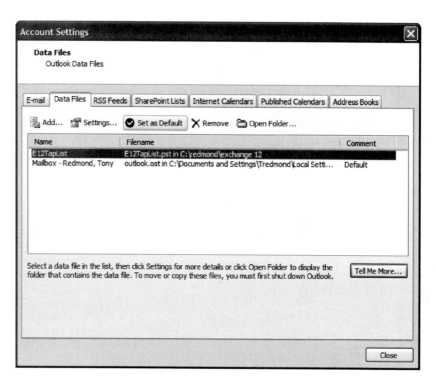

Figure 7.14

Selecting a PST as the Mail Delivery location in Outlook 2007

Table 7.4 *Pros and cons of using PSTs*

Pros	Cons
A PST can be stored on any available device, including floppy disks.	You cannot share a PST between users. For example, you cannot use a PST to share documents between a manager and a secretary. Users who leave a PC logged on can inadvertently block their own access to a PST if they move to another PC.
PSTs can be used to transfer files between users, including users in different Exchange organizations.	You can encrypt a PST to protect its content against other users, but if the password is lost, there is no supported way to recover it. However, unsupported utilities exist that can crack a PST passwords.

Table 7.4   *Pros and cons of using PSTs (continued)*

Pros	Cons
An "old format" PST can expand to any size up to a theoretical 2GB limit, subject to available disk space. The largest PST in use is well over 1GB (there is a limit of 64,000 items in a single folder). A Unicode-format PST can grow much larger than 2GB. Thus, PSTs allow users to hold more information, so it becomes a more attractive personal archive.	Delivering mail to a PST removes the benefit of single-instance storage (within a single mailbox store). In addition, unless you use Outlook 2003, double the space is required to store a message because the PST holds items in both RTF and ASCII format.
You can backup PSTs with any file-level backup utility.	If you use PSTs, you must make sure that someone is actually backing the files up on a regular basis. There is an increased chance of message corruption because there is no rollback/ transaction log mechanism available for PSTs, so you may need to go back to a backup to recover data.
PSTs are easier to restore than a complete mailbox store.	You cannot send deferred mail messages unless you connect the client to the server.
The Auto-Archive feature in the Outlook client uses PSTs to store archived items.	Inbox Assistant rules are not processed unless the client is connected to the server.
The EXMERGE utility uses PSTs to move mailbox contents between servers.	Extra network traffic is generated to move information to and from PSTs. Messages for delivery to a PST are held on the server until a client connects, and if a lot of mail is waiting the initial connect can take a long time. Microsoft doesn't support ExMerge for use with Exchange 2007, which uses the `Move-Mailbox` command to transfer mailboxes between servers. The Move-Mailbox command in Exchange 2007 SP1 will support PSTs.
	You can only access PSTs from MAPI clients.

Table 7.4 *Pros and cons of using PSTs (continued)*

Pros	Cons
	The "Move Mailbox" option in EMC or the `Move-Mailbox` command do not move items stored in PSTs (until Exchange 2007 SP1). If you move a user to a new server, you may also have to move their PSTs to a suitable local file share.
	It's difficult to come up with a good strategy to clean items infected by a virus if they are delivered to a PST.
	Microsoft does not support access to PSTs on network shares, so you cannot roam from one workstation to another and access your data. The same is true for moving from work to home, unless the PST is stored on a laptop's hard disk.

Some installations encourage users to view their server mailbox as a repository for working documents, somewhere to hold information that must be available no matter which client they use to connect to the server. In this model, users are supposed to move items to a PST once the files are no longer current or perhaps become less important. The model assumes a fair amount of discipline on the part of users, something that is not always easy to find. It also devolves responsibility for data security to users after data transfers to user control. One of the undoubted advantages of server-based storage is the assurance that someone else will take care of backing up all your important data. People are not so good when the time comes to create backups or copies of local data on a PC. Some of the features of Exchange 2007, such as managed folder policies, help users maintain their mailboxes by cleaning out old content, but a user still has to make a decision when something is important or not.

7.2.3 Configuring PSTs

Users are not limited to a single PST and can create an array of PSTs for different purposes. Some users have a separate PST for each year, some for each project they work on, and some to divide personal and business email. Each PST is configured in the MAPI profile. By default, the display name of each PST is "Personal Folders," so things can get slightly confusing if you do not change the name afterwards to reflect the intended use of the PST. For example, use names such as "Project Folders," "Archived Folders," "Mail Folders," and so on. You can easily change the display name of a PST through Outlook by selecting the PST and then bringing up its properties, as shown in Figure 7.15. Administrators are unable to configure or control PSTs through EMC or the shell. Remember – these are *personal* folders.

Training sessions clearly offer an opportunity to encourage good work habits such as the effective use of PSTs in people. Trainers can use hint or cheat sheets to brief users on how you would like them to work and so relieve some pressure on server-based resources. As with most features, there are pros and cons that you need to understand before you can make the most effective use of them. Table 7.4 summarizes the most important issues to understand about PSTs. Make sure that you understand the impact of these issues before you rush into using PSTs.

Figure 7.15
Changing the
properties of a PST

Administrators can also control PSTs with group policy. For example, you could deactivate write access to PSTs by setting the DisablePSTGrow parameter in the registry. This has the effect of allowing users to access any content that exists in PSTs but they cannot create any new items. You could take this approach if you wanted to move users away from PSTs to server mailboxes to achieve better compliance with regulatory requirements or simply to get a better handle on user data. In making such a radical change to the user environment, I assume that you complement it by providing larger mailboxes on the server.

7.2.4 PST archiving

Users, despite the suspicions of many system administrators, are only human. As such, they will accumulate mail messages and other items in their mailboxes in the same way as they collect anything else. Some people will be very neat and tidy, maintaining an efficient and effective folder structure. Others will let chaos exist with messages piling up in folders created for a purpose long forgotten. Most users exist between the two extremes. They do their best to keep their mailboxes reasonably clean, eliminating dead wood from time to time, but generally, there is a lot of excess information hanging around mailboxes, all occupying valuable space on the server.

Archiving attempts to provide automatic clean-up assistance to users by allowing them to define criteria to control when to move items from the "live" (server-based) store to a "passive" (PST) store. Archiving obsolete email helps to increase overall system performance by reducing the number of items in folders and the overall size of the mailbox stores. The more items in a folder, the slower it is to access. This is especially so for folders like the Inbox, Journal, and Calendar.

Archiving uses age-based criteria to select items. In other words, messages become archival candidates after they exceed a certain age—28 days, 15 weeks, or maybe 6 months. The net effect of moving messages from the live store is to reduce the amount of information held on the server, although you do not reduce the actual physical size of a mailbox store unless you rebuild the database with the ESEUTIL program. Of course, reducing the space occupied by the databases is good from a system administrator's point of view. More space is available for new items, optimal use is made of disks, and you reduce backup times. Archiving is client-driven and the server plays no great role, apart from processing client requests during the archival process. Outlook is the only client that includes archiving features, either on an automatic basis or on an explicit basis according to criteria defined by the user.

Outlook can archive messages in two ways. First, access the "Archive" option on the File menu to invoke the dialog shown in Figure 7.16 (Outlook 2007 running on Windows XP Professional). The default option reviews the contents of selected folders (and subfolders) and archives any items contained in the folders that are older than a specified date. The items are archived immediately into the archive file, which is a PST located on any available disk.

Alternatively (by clicking the first radio button in the dialog), you can scan all folders in the mailbox and process items according to the auto-archive settings (Figure 7.17). Auto-archive settings can be set on an individual folder-by-folder basis, or you can apply the same criteria to all folders. Note that Outlook archives items based on a message's last modified date

Figure 7.16
Setting up archiving for Outlook

rather than the received or created date. The following actions change an item's modified date:

- Forwarding
- Replying
- Replying to All
- Editing and Saving
- Moving or Copying

The second option you can take is to auto-archive, which Outlook runs according to a schedule that you create (Figure 7.17). The default interval is 28 days. When Outlook starts, it checks to see if auto-archiving is enabled and then how long it is since it archived items. If archiving is enabled and the time interval has elapsed, Outlook prompts to determine whether it should begin to process folders.

Auto-archiving can take a long time. The initial implementation of archiving (prior to Outlook 98) suffered because moving items from a server to a PST is a slow process. Users who hit the "OK" button when they were given the option to archive quickly learn that the process could take up to 30 minutes to complete (depending on the folders and the number of items in each folder), and during that time they could do nothing else. Current versions of Outlook perform archiving in a background thread, much like back-

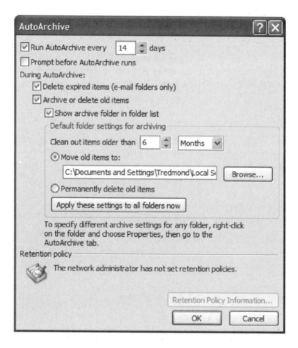

Figure 7.17
*Outlook 2007
AutoArchive
options*

ground synchronization. Users can continue to work while archiving proceeds, albeit with reduced response times.

7.3 Offline folder files

Offline folder files (OSTs) are very important to Outlook because they provide the client-side storage necessary to support cached Exchange mode. Instead of being a separate and distinct repository like PSTs where the contents of the files have no connection to anything on the server, OSTs hold replicas of server-based folders. Outlook automatically creates an OST when you configure a MAPI profile to enable to offline work. The name of the OST is visible by selecting the "Offline Folder File Settings" option when viewing details of the Exchange service in the profile. Table 7.5 contains a more exhaustive list of the basic differences between OSTs and PSTs.

MAPI clients have always used OSTs to work with items without connecting to the server. OST folders are slave replicas of server-based folders. You can compare them to snapshots of the server folders taken at a particular point in time. Essentially, an OST uses the same basic technology as a PST with the noticeable exception that they automatically encrypt their contents and so require authentication before a client can connect and use the file. The encryption key (based on the MAPIEntryID GUID for the mailbox) exists in two places: in the mailbox on the server and in the user's MAPI pro-

Table 7.5   *Differences between PSTs and OSTs*

	Personal Folders (PST)	**Offline Folders (OST)**
Valid locations	Any storage device except network shares, even including floppy diskettes (however, you need read-write access to the media).	Any storage device that supports read-write access.
Storage type	Permanent, persistent user-managed storage.	Transient storage that is inextricably linked to the contents of the master (server) folders.
Can be opened by	Any MAPI client, using any MAPI user profile.	Any MAPI client, but only using the same MAPI profile that originally created the OST.
Synchronization	None—all movement between the PST and other stores is user-initiated and performed manually.	Automatic for changes made to offline folder replicas upon each connection to the server. Specific synchronization must be set up for replicas of public folders, or of any user-created folder when connected to the server.
Encryption options	Optional encryption with a separate password (individually defined for each PST).	By default, OSTs are automatically encrypted. No password used (because of OST association with server mailbox).
Managed through	By configuring Personal Folders (see the *Tools | Account Settings | Data Files* option in Outlook 2007)	Change the Offline Folder File Settings tab for the Exchange mailbox (*Tools | Account Settings | Data Files*)
Concurrent access possible to multiple PST/OST	Yes.	No. A PST and OST can be open at the same time, but you cannot open two OSTs concurrently.

file in the PC's registry. Every time you attempt to work offline afterwards, Outlook reads the profile to determine whether the key exists in the registry and matches the value in the OST. As long as the two keys exist and match, you can open an OST with Outlook and synchronize with a mailbox. If you cause them to differ, for example by recreating a profile, the OST becomes invalid and you cannot access its contents.

Not using the right profile is the most common reason for not being able to access an OST. Deleting and recreating the server mailbox is another cause as this operation changes the master ID, even if the alias, distinguished name, account, and other account properties match. In this instance, the next time you connect to the server, the master ID for the server mailbox will not match the data held in the profile and Outlook will refuse to load the OST. You can find an "OST recovery utility" at www.officerecovery.com. The utility works by reading the OST and writing out a PST, which can then be opened as usual. No guarantee is given that you can open every OST and Microsoft does not support its use.

7.3.1 OST synchronization

When Outlook creates an OST, it automatically adds the set of special mail folders (Calendar, Tasks, Inbox, Journal, Notes, Outbox, Sent Items, and Deleted Items). These folders allow you to process messages while disconnected from the server. For example, you can create and send messages or set up meeting requests. Outlook holds the messages in the Outbox folder and automatically sends them through a synchronization process the next time you connect to the server, after which Outlook moves the messages into the Sent Items folder. Outlook automatically checks an OST for outgoing messages that are waiting to be sent each time it connects to Exchange.

When you use cached Exchange mode with Outlook 2003 or 2007, Outlook automatically synchronizes all of your mailbox folders into the OST. If you have a large mailbox, you'll have an even larger OST. Microsoft has made some changes in Outlook 2007 to make the OST more effective with large mailboxes, but even so, an OST of more than 2GB is not going to be fast because of the relatively inefficient internal structure and the slow speed of laptop disks.

If you don't use cached Exchange mode, you must select each folder you want to have in the OST individually and then change its synchronization properties. You can also apply a filter so that Outlook only synchronizes selected items. For example, you could decide that you only want to have items less than three months old in your offline folders. To do this, you create an appropriate filter for the folder. Note that you can only mark folders from your primary mailbox for synchronization. In other words, if you connect to another user's mailbox to access one of their folders (such as their calendar), you cannot replicate any of the folders in that mailbox for use offline. Using a public folder to hold shared calendar or other items is a good workaround because you can synchronize these folders.

You must first mark a public folder as a "favorite" before including it in the synchronization process. Everyone is different when it comes to making decisions about the folders they want to be able to access offline. When the

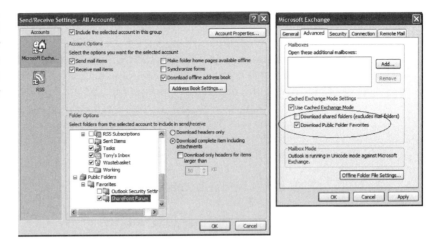

Figure 7.18
*Adding public
folders to
synchronization
settings*

disks on notebook PCs were small (under 2 GB), you certainly couldn't afford to synchronize large numbers of folders because the resulting OST could quickly fill the entire disk. Now that notebook disks are far larger, the same limitations do not exist.

You synchronize public folder favorites in the same way as mailbox folders by adding them to a send and receive group (left-hand screen in Figure 7.18) or by including them in your cached Exchange mode settings (right-hand screen in Figure 7.18). At the same time, you can specify a filter to restrict the amount of information that Outlook fetches from the public folder. For example, you may only want to synchronize the last month's contributions to a distribution list, or ignore items that have attachments larger than a specific size, and so on. The filter becomes active the next time you connect to a server.

Because OSTs are slave replicas of server folders, you can use them to recover information from accidentally deleted mailboxes. For example, assume that a system administrator deletes a mailbox, only to discover that they should not have deleted it. If an OST is available, you can ask the user to start Outlook, work in offline mode, and recover items by copying them from the OST to a PST. Once the copy is finished, log out of Outlook, delete the OST file, and reconnect to the server using a new MAPI profile. The old OST is invalid because the mailbox ID changes when you recreate the mailbox, so there is no point in attempting to use it. The recovered messages are in the PST and you can drag and drop the messages from the folders in the PST to folders on the server after you connect to the mailbox. Following that, synchronizing with the newly populated server folders will rebuild a new OST. This technique only works for folders synchronized with the OST and the server-based "Recover Deleted Mailbox" option should be your first step in situations like this.

Outlook automatically synchronizes changes you make to offline folders when it connects to a server, transmitting any waiting messages to the server for onward delivery and applying deletes or other changes in the folders marked for synchronization. Outlook also synchronizes changes made to offline replicas of public folders back to the server-based folders. If synchronization errors occur, Outlook captures details in a message in the Deleted Items folder. The most common error is caused by a client not having sufficient permissions to access the contents of a folder. Typically, this error occurs with public folders, but you can see this error for system folders such as that holding the OAB.

Apart from their obvious use in processing messages, offline folders are very useful for anyone who travels. For instance, you might want to take a copy of all documents relating to a particular project before going on a trip. During the trip, you can browse the data and make any changes that you wish, and when you get back to base, you can synchronize the changes back with the data held in the server-based folder. Conflicts can occur when synchronization is attempted. If this happens, you will have to resolve the conflicts manually by deciding which copy of an item you should keep.

7.3.2 **When things go wrong with your OST**

As already noted, the internal file structure of the OST is not particularly optimized to deal with the number of items and the size of mailboxes that we commonly see today. Over time, the efficiency of the OST degrades. There are a few reasons why this is so: the internal structures that track items become fragmented, the OST file itself may be spread over a large number of individual blocks on the disk, or software errors and operational interruptions (such as a PC losing power for some reason when Outlook was accessing the OST). All conspire to slow down Outlook's performance.

Microsoft includes the SCANPST utility with Outlook. Microsoft designed this utility, which has not changed much since Exchange 4.0, to repair problems in PST and OST files such as minor corruptions. You can run SCANPST if you feel that an OST needs it for some reason. Outlook checks for errors in an OST when it opens the file and attempts to fix any problems that are detected before it allows the user to access their mailbox. Depending on the size of your OST and the speed of your PC, you might have to wait several minutes before Outlook finishes checking the OST. Outlook 2007 is slightly smarter in this respect because it performs whatever fixes are necessary to get things going and then lets you access your mailbox at the expense of some performance degradation while Outlook continues to verify the file structure in the background. You know that this work is going on because Outlook displays a small icon featuring a set of cogs in its lower right-hand corner (Figure 7.19). While Outlook does its best to fix errors, you may have to run SCANPST afterwards to restore the OST to good health.

Every time I have run SCANPST against a PST or OST, SCANPST finds some errors in the file. I may be unlucky in that every OST and PST that I have ever used with Outlook picks up errors quickly or SCANPST might be slightly paranoid in the way that it checks for errors. In either case, SCANPST does fix problems in an OST's file structure, albeit slowly.

Figure 7.19
OST repair in progress

Sometimes an OST can become very fragmented or has some lurking problems that SCANPST cannot fix. Fragmentation often occurs for large files when Windows cannot allocate enough contiguous space on the disk to store the entire file, so the file ends up in different pieces scattered across the disk. Fragmentation poses a potential performance problem for any file, but it is much worse for an OST because of its unsophisticated internal structure and the slow nature of most laptop hard disks. If you experience unexplained "hangs" when you use Outlook and this happens on a consistent basis, it is a good indication that something is going wrong and often the root cause lies in a badly fragmented OST. In this case, the best idea is to rebuild the OST from scratch. Exit Outlook and delete or rename the OST file. When you restart Outlook, it detects that the OST is no longer available and will recreate the file. If you have a large mailbox, it can take an hour or so to repopulate the OST even with a fast network connection to the server that hosts your mailbox, so rebuilding an OST is not something to do when you're travelling and away from the office. A newly created OST is always more efficient and smaller than one that has been in use for some time. For example, a newly created OST for a 1.3GB mailbox was 1.5GB in size. After a month's use, the OST had swelled to 1.9GB but the mailbox was the same size. Maybe it is a good idea to consider a regular rebuild!

7.4   Out of Office changes

Outlook 2007 and Outlook Web Access both support different OOF messages to send to internal and external correspondents and both allow you to create a scheduled OOF message with a start and end time. The OOF message can also be in HTML format. Exchange stores the OOF messages as hidden items in the root of the mailbox. There are two items—one for internal and one for external. These items are message class IPM.Microsoft.OOF.UserOOFSettings, which is a new class introduced in Exchange 2007.

The decision whether a correspondent is internal or external depends on the authoritative domains that you have defined for the Exchange organization. See Chapter 6 for more information about how to create authoritative domains for Exchange 2007. If a user comes from an authoritative domain, then Exchange automatically considers them as internal. Exchange considers a user from any other domain as external.

The Microsoft Exchange Mailbox Assistants service runs on a mailbox server to send OOF messages. If the service is not running, Exchange cannot send OOFs in response to incoming messages. Interestingly, if the service is not running, Exchange does not queue OOFs for future dispatch.

7.4.1 The big question: Is Outlook 2007 worth the upgrade?

Microsoft has struggled with the richness of its Office applications for years. Few know how to use the power of Excel and most are happy to build simple spreadsheets. Few know how to use Word to build a book composed of many chapters, hundreds of figures, cross-references, and all the other complex document parts that professional authors depend on, but we can all generate simple documents. Word 2.0 remains my favorite release, possibly because it was my first exposure to a Windows-based word processor and I wonder if I really use all of the features and improvements that Microsoft has made to Word since. Professional programmers like the power and flexibility of Access and it is certainly easier to generate databases with Access 2007 than it was with the first few releases. Apart from anything else, each upgrade to a new desktop application is costly because of the need to touch so many PCs, to train users, and to provide the inevitable increase in help desk support through the transition.

When I wrote about Outlook 2003 for my Exchange 2003 book, I concluded that Outlook 2003 was a worthwhile upgrade in terms of the additional useful functionality that it included and the economical benefit that an organization could gain from its implementation. Features such as cached Exchange mode delivered better performance and usability for users while allowing organizations to consolidate servers into central locations and so save hardware and operational costs. The reduction in network costs in many countries made it economically feasible to connect clients over extended links back to datacenters and the ability to use RPC over HTTP connections allowed users to piggyback on standard Internet connections to get their email, assuming that the organization deployed the necessary infrastructure to support these connections. I also liked the network "smarts" included in Outlook 2003, such as better checkpointing, drizzle synchronization, and buffer packing, and compression and the junk mail filtering capability consigned spam to the wastebasket without bothering me with offers that I never wanted to accept. Overall, Outlook 2003 delivered the necessary combination of features, functionality, and value to make it a compelling upgrade.

I wish that I could say the same about Outlook 2007, but I cannot. There is no doubt that Outlook 2007 is an evolution from Outlook 2003 that includes many worthwhile improvements in the user interface as well as bug fixes. As such, you can regard Outlook 2007 as the best client for Exchange 2007, at least in terms of the total feature set and client usability. However, Outlook 2007 struggles to deliver the headline new pieces of functionality to build the financial case to back a recommendation to deploy Outlook 2007 company-wide, unless you can wrap it up all in the costs of a desktop migration where you plan to upgrade hardware, the operating system (to Vista), and applications. Sure, the AutoDiscover service is a nice way to avoid knowing the name of the server that holds your mailbox, but knowing this information has never been an intellectual or tortuous challenge for me in the past. The integrated search feature is a terrific way of finding messages and attachments quickly. The scheduling assistant makes it easier to find gaps in calendars to bring an important meeting together and probably saves time, but I cannot quite put a compelling value on this feature. The ability to cache a delegate calendar so that you can work with it offline is also good. I can make the same comment as I go through other features like support for RSS feeds. All of the new features are nice and add some value, but maybe they are not essential and certainly not enough to change either the way that I work or the way that the company deploys Exchange.

It's not all doom and gloom however. Companies will upgrade to Office 2007 and use Outlook 2007 because of two factors. First, Microsoft has signed them up for upgrades as part of license deals and many small companies will find it a logical step to proceed with an upgrade because they have a relatively small number of clients to migrate. Second, the advent of Vista presents an opportunity for a desktop refresh. It makes a lot of sense to combine an upgrade to a new operating system with a new applications suite alongside a possible hardware upgrade if everything can be accommodated by a company's regular PC refresh cycle. I think Outlook 2007 will have slower acceptance in large corporations than Outlook 2003 has enjoyed so far. Companies who deploy Exchange 2007 don't have to change their desktop clients unless they need some specific functionality or have an opportunity to reduce operating costs.

7.5   **The Offline Address Book (OAB)**

The OAB (also called the Office Address List, or OAL) is a point-in-time snapshot of the Active Directory that Outlook clients can download to enable offline validation of addresses added to messages. You need to download a copy

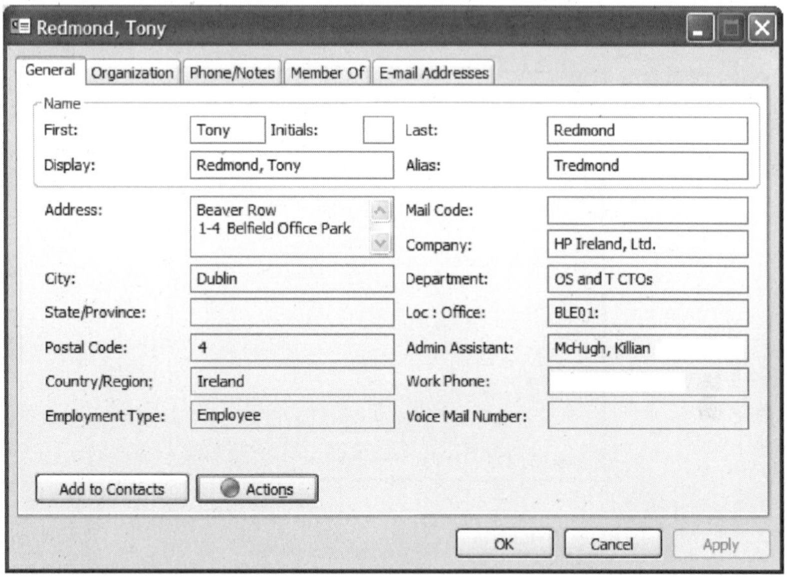

Figure 7.20
Viewing user information in the OAB

of the OAB before you can work offline, so it is an important part of the cached Exchange mode scenario for Outlook 2003 or 2007 clients.

Apart from access to a restricted set of properties, users perceive no real difference when they view details about users, groups, and contacts from the OAB to when they access the GAL online. If you opt to download full details into the OAB, all of the information presented on the pages that show General (Figure 7.20), Phone/Notes, and E-mail Addresses properties is available online or offline. However, any data that depends on pointers that connect directory objects together is unavailable offline, such as details of a user's supervisor or their direct reports. Customized attributes that you may have added to the Active Directory, such as an employee number or location code, are also unavailable unless you customize the standard address templates to present a different set of properties through the OAB.

7.5.1 Downloading the OAB

Outlook clients download the OAB with the *Tools | Send/Receive | Download Address Book* option, which invokes the dialog shown in Figure 7.21. You can minimize the amount of data downloaded by selecting the "No Details" option, but this makes the OAB much less useful. You can still validate email addresses, but other useful data, such as phone numbers, is only available when you download full details.

Like other synchronization operations, Outlook downloads the OAB using a background thread, so users can continue working while the down-

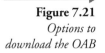

Figure 7.21
*Options to
download the OAB*

load proceeds. Clients prior to Outlook 2000 devote all their energy to the download when it is active and cannot do anything else. Downloading a large OAB can take a long time across a slow connection, so you may want to configure Outlook to avoid automatic OAB downloads if users commonly use dial-up or other slow connections. Despite the fact that high-speed connections are now available in most places, a need sometimes exists to throttle OAB downloads for users that work in cached Exchange mode (see page 630 for details). Clients must use a version of the OAB that is compatible with the server that holds their mailbox. In other words, if your mailbox is on an Exchange 2003 server, you have to download an Exchange 2003 OAB, with the same restriction applying to Exchange 2007.

7.5.2 OAB files on the PC

Exchange 2007 can generate OAB files in multiple formats to support different files. The most recent format is OAB Version 4, which uses a Unicode format instead of the older ANSI format that is used by Outlook clients prior to Outlook 2003. The difference between the two OABs is that the Unicode OAB contains some extra properties that Outlook can use internally (like the HomeMDB property, which points to a user's mailbox store) and others that are available to users. For example, home and business telephone numbers are multi-valued in a Unicode OAB instead of single valued in an ANSI OAB. You know that you have a Unicode OAB if the OAB files on your PC have a "u" prefix, as in UDETAILS.OAB instead of DETAILS.OAB. Because of the extra information held in the file, UDETAILS.OAB is between 15% and 20% larger than an equivalent DETAILS.OAB. Only Outlook clients that use a Unicode-format OST can request Unicode format OABs from Exchange and other clients continue to get the older format file.

After you download the OAB, Outlook creates a set of files on your PC. Table 7.6 lists the files and their use. These files can occupy a reasonable amount of space. For example, the six files that constitute the HP OAB total 211MB, representing approximately 260,000 entries (mailbox-enabled accounts, contacts, some public folders, and a lot of groups). From this, we can conclude that a reasonable back-of-the-envelope calculation to work out the likely size of an OAB for an organization is roughly 1MB for every 1,000 entries. Outlook downloads compressed versions of the OAB files to minimize network demand, but even so, it takes a very long time to fetch the data across slow links. Typically, the compressed files are roughly half the size of the size on disk.

Table 7.6   *OAB local data files*

File	Use
BROWSE.OAB or UBROWSE.OAB	This is the most important OAB file as it is the core index for the OAB. Records contain the object type, display name, and a pointer for the object's data in the details file.
DETAILS.OAB or UDETAILS.OAB	This file holds all of the details (if available) for objects.
RDNDEX.OAB or URDNDEX.OAB	The OAB uses this index to resolve relative distinguished names. It is used to track changes to domain names.
PDNDEX.OAB or UPDNDEX.OAB	Index file that contains domain names.
ANRDEX.OAB or UANRDEX.OAB	The OAB uses the ANR index to resolve ambiguous names using much the same approach used by the Active Directory to resolve ambiguous names.
TMPLTS.OAB or UTMPLTS.OAB	This file contains language-specific strings for dialog boxes and any other static items that the OAB uses in its templates.

Unless your OAB is very out of date or deemed by Outlook to be corrupt in some way, Outlook does not usually need to download the complete OAB from the server. Instead, Outlook downloads a set of smaller files that contain differences generated since the last OAB download. However, Outlook always downloads a full copy of the OAB if changes have been made to more than 12.5% (approximately) of the total entries in the directory that have been updated since the last full download. In a mixed environment composed of legacy Exchange servers and Exchange 2007 servers, adding a new administrative group to the organization also provokes clients to download a complete OAB, even if only a few changes have occurred to other GAL entries.

Outlook 2003 and 2007 use a "divisor" to know the percentage change must occur within the OAB before invoking a full download. The default divisor is "8," or 12.5%. You can change this value to alter download behavior. To do this, use the REGEDIT utility to create a new (or update an existing) DWORD value called "OAB Dif Divisor" under the key:

```
HKLM\Software\Microsoft\Exchange\Exchange Provider
```

Set the value of the DWORD to be the divisor you want to use to govern full OAB downloads. For example, a divisor of "4" means that you only want full OAB downloads after 25% of the full OAB changes. A value of "2" (two) means that you are happy to wait until 50% changes, and so on. If the value is set to "0" (zero), Outlook uses 16 (6.25%) to avoid any problems caused by attempting to divide by zero. Table 7.6 lists the set of files that form the OAB. The details file is the largest, followed by the ANR index.

Within the OAB, distinguished names in Exchange 5.5 format[9] (rather than AD format) are used to identify objects, and clients write the distinguished names fetched from the OAB into message headers after they validate addresses. Using distinguished names in this way allows the display name of users, contact, or group to change without rendering OAB entries invalid.

Using legacy distinguished names may seem strange, but it allows Microsoft to maintain backwards compatibility, not only in the OAB but also in MAPI profiles, and allows users to reply to messages originally sent on older servers. An attribute called *LegacyExchangeDN* provides the magic. This attribute stores the older form of distinguished name for AD objects, and participates in address validation through the ambiguous name resolution process. Therefore, when an Outlook client reconnects after creating some offline messages, Exchange revalidates the addresses by searching the AD using the *LegacyExchangeDN* attribute.

7.5.3   The evolving OAB format

Microsoft has evolved the format used for the OAB files across the different versions of Exchange and uses OAB V4 as the default format today. For many organizations, the OAB V3 format introduced in Exchange 2003 worked very well with Outlook clients running in cached Exchange mode. However, large organizations encountered difficulties that could swamp servers with client requests for OAB downloads, so Microsoft introduced OAB version 4 and a new update mechanism in Exchange 2003 SP2 to relieve the strain on servers. The mechanism is used in Exchange 2007.

---

9.   For example: /O=XYZ/OU=Central/CN=Recipients/CN=TRedmond.

We know that Outlook clients request a full download of the OAB if more than a certain percentage of the OAB has changed. As explained earlier, the default threshold is 12.5% to trigger a full download, or one-eighth of the entries in the OAB. However, even a very small change such as the update of one digit in a phone number causes Exchange to consider that a record is changed. Any organization that is upgrading from Exchange 5.5, consolidating servers, adding or removing administrative groups, or performing typical email operations, such as moving mailboxes between servers, changing physical offices, or adding new SMTP or other email proxy addresses, therefore generates a large number of changes to the OAB. In turn, this means that the default 12.5% threshold is easily surpassed, leading to many client requests for complete copies of the OAB and a subsequent heavy demand on servers. Small organizations generate small OABs, so these servers are less likely to be impacted, but large organizations felt the pain and this problem also made these organizations less willing to deploy Outlook 2003 or 2007 running in cached Exchange mode.

Microsoft's response was to introduce LZX compression to speed transfer of OAB data between server and client (this is the same technology that clients use to download Windows updates from the Web) and a mechanism called BinPatch (Binary Delta Compression) to apply updates to client OAB files. In addition, clients now generate their own sort orders for the ANR and Browse files based on the PC locale setting instead of depending on the locales that the server supports. Because of the changes to the client, only PCs running Outlook 2003 SP2 or later can download and use the OAB V4 files; clients running Outlook 2003 or 2003 SP1 will continue to use the OAB V3a format. If you browse the set of OAB files in the web distribution folder, you'll see that many of them have a .LZX extension, indicating that these files are compressed using the same algorithm. If you use web-based distribution, Outlook copies the OAB files from the distribution directory and decompresses them to build the OAB on the PC.

Because only Outlook 2007 clients can use web-based OAB distribution, it follows that these files are in the V4 format. However, if you use public folder distribution, during the OAB generation process, Exchange 2003 SP2 and 2007 servers generate two new files called BINPATCH.OAB and DATA.OAB and store these files in the OAB V4 system public folder. Each BINPATCH.OAB file contains the delta changes from the last OAB generation run, or every change to the GAL that has occurred within an organization during a day. Unlike a previous OAB changes file that contains complete updated records even if the actual change to the record is minimal, these files contain binary patches that Outlook 2003 SP2 and later clients can combine with a DATA.OAB file to create an updated OAB. For example taken from a real-life organization, the OAB V3 "full data" file for the organization is 66MB and the update for one day is 161KB, whereas the OAB V4 figures are 34MB and 153KB, respectively. The net result is that Outlook has far less data to download than in previous versions at the expense of some extra processing on the PC to decompress and reconstitute the OAB files.

7.5.4 OAB and cached Exchange mode

The ability to access information about mail-enabled users, contacts, and groups in a directory is a fundamental requirement for an email client. When you deploy Outlook in cached Exchange mode, the OAB provides the necessary access to directory information to make cached Exchange mode work, but the directory information is only useful if it is kept updated. Most companies have a reasonable churn within the directory as user details are updated, new users are added, and others are removed, so whereas a week-old OAB is usually okay because the vast majority of its entries are correct, a month-old OAB is much less satisfactory. The accuracy and usefulness of the OAB degrades rapidly as it ages past a month.

When you use Outlook 2003 and 2007 in cached Exchange mode, Outlook automatically checks for OAB updates daily, but only when you have a fast network connection. In this situation, Outlook checks for updates daily (you cannot change the frequency of this check). The time that these updates occur varies from client to client to ensure that the traffic generated by many concurrent client connections, all attempting to download the OAB, does not swamp the Exchange server. If updates are available on the server, Outlook downloads the files that contain the differences and applies them to the local OAB. If Outlook discovers that it does not have an OAB available on the PC when it first creates an OST file, it attempts to download the OAB from the server. If a download for an OAB update fails, Outlook continues to attempt to download the necessary updates every hour until it succeeds. If Outlook needs to fetch a full OAB, it will only attempt this once in a 13-hour period. In both cases, an attempt is counted if Outlook can connect to Exchange and begin a download.

Outlook attempts automatic OAB downloads only when it can connect over LAN-quality or "Fast" connections. If you connect over a slow connection like a dial-up telephone link, you must explicitly instruct Outlook to download the OAB in the normal manner. In either case, you can disable automatic OAB downloads by setting the "DownloadOAB" DWORD registry value to "0." For Outlook 2003, insert the entry at the following key:

```
HKCU\Software\Microsoft\Office\11.0\Outlook\Cached Mode
```

For Outlook 2007, use:

```
HKCU\Software\Microsoft\Office\12.0\Outlook\Cached Mode
```

Note that if a client has already downloaded the OAB, you have to delete this copy of the OAB and download a new version to ensure that Outlook respects the new setting.

Administrators can include a setting in a group policy to control OAB downloads. In this instance, for Outlook 2003, the "DownloadOAB" DWORD value is placed under the Policies section of the registry:

```
HKCU\Software\Policies\Microsoft\Office\11.0\Outlook\Cached
Mode
```

For Outlook 2007, use:

```
HKCU\Software\Policies\Microsoft\Office\12.0\Outlook\Cached
Mode
```

If this value is set, users who do not have administrative permission on the PC will not be able to affect the way that Outlook downloads the OAB. In either case, you can configure Outlook to flag a warning before it begins to download the OAB through the "Allow Full OAB Prompt" DWORD value at:

```
HKCU\Software\Microsoft\Exchange\Exchange Provider
```

Set the value to 1 (one) to see the prompt. The default setting is 0 (zero), which means that Outlook does not prompt. Administrators often configure their own PCs to prompt before they download a full copy of the OAB to receive a warning that something that occurred to force Outlook to want to refresh the complete OAB. They do this so that they know when extra demand will occur on the servers as users fetch copies of the OAB.

If your Active Directory is reasonably stable, Outlook should rarely have to download full copies of the OAB. In situations where you have very large OAB files or the Active Directory changes to such an extent that clients have to fetch large differences files or even complete OABs regularly, you may want to use the registry changes described here to limit automatic daily downloads and instead ask users to download on an as-needed basis. The problem here is that users will invariably forget to download updates and so will operate with outdated OABs, but this may be a lesser evil than having to cope with excessive demand on the server or network as they cope with client downloads. It is therefore a good idea to monitor server and network load as you add Outlook 2003 clients to your system.

A delay always exists between when an administrator adds an object to the Active Directory and when the object appears in the OAB. Users do not always appreciate the processing that occurs behind the scenes to generate the OAB updates on the mailbox server. Afterwards, Exchange distributes the updates to Client Access servers for download by Outlook, so it can be a tad frustrating for them when their personal copy of the OAB does not include a recently added user, group, or contact until Exchange incorporates the new object into an OAB update and the client downloads and applies the update. Even assuming that Exchange generates OAB updates daily and that you have configured Outlook to download updates automatically, the delay between an object's addition and its availability in the OAB can take a long time. For example, if you add a new group at 9AM on Monday and Exchange doesn't update the OAB until 4AM on Tuesday, the earliest that a client can use the new object is 19 hours after it is added. This situation would be atypical because it assumes that Outlook downloads an updated OAB immediately and Exchange populates the public folder or web distribution point. It is more likely that Outlook will check for OAB updates up to a day after they are available, so the actual delay between addition and availability can be as long as 36 hours. For any Outlook client working in offline mode (where the OAB is the only source of directory information) the solution is to use the SMTP address for the new object to send any messages that are required before the necessary OAB update is available.

7.5.5　OAB generation and distribution

Exchange 2007 controls OAB generation at the organization level. A specific server is assigned the responsibility for generating regular updates for the OAB and to distribute those updates to other servers within the organization. You assign the server to generate the OAB and other details by manipulating the properties of the Default Offline Address List object (the default OAB), which you find under the Mailbox object under the Configuration node (Figure 7.22).

When you migrate an organization from Exchange 2003, the responsibility for managing the Default Offline Address List will be assigned to an Exchange 2003 server. This server distributes OAB updates daily via public folder replication because this is the only distribution mechanism that is available within a legacy Exchange organization. If you install an Exchange 2007 organization from scratch, the first server that holds the mailbox role will automatically manage the OAB. During migration projects, you should move OAB management to an Exchange 2007 mailbox server and use it to generate the OAB and distribute it through both public folder replication and web-based access to accommodate the needs of legacy and Exchange 2007 mailboxes. You can use the Move option in the action pane to transfer OAB management to an Exchange 2007 mailbox server. After you move the

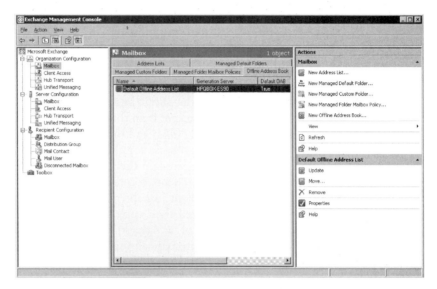

Figure 7.22
The OAB is an organization-level object

OAB to an Exchange 2007 server, you should update the properties of the Offline Address Book object to select one or more Exchange 2007 Client Access servers to participate in OAB distribution. In addition, you should take the update option to generate a new set of OAB files so that the Client Access servers can begin providing the OAB to Outlook 2007 clients via web-based distribution. Depending on the size of your organization, generating the OAB may take some time to complete. You can generate a new OAB at any time, or leave it to the default schedule, which generates updates for the OAB nightly. It's a good idea to tailor the OAB generation schedule so that this work is done outside the hours of peak demand for both users and scheduled system maintenance.

You configure the properties of the Default Offline Address List and any other offline address books that you create to support different versions of Outlook clients and to enable web-based distribution. The right-hand screen in Figure 7.23 shows how to select publication of the different format of OABs for different clients and checkboxes that control web-based and public folder distribution. Web-based distribution is the best approach for Outlook 2007 clients and Outlook 2007 will always use the web-based method if it is available and usually only ever needs to use public folder distribution if you use Exchange 2003 to generate and distribute the OAB.

To generate the OAB, Exchange calls a component called OABGEN that runs inside the System Attendant process. OABGEN reads data from the Active Directory by making a set of NSPI queries and generates the OAB files. First, it creates files in the system temp directory and then compresses the files. Depending on the choices that you make for OAB distribution,

Exchange updates the OAB public folder (if used to support Exchange 2003 servers) and the distribution point specified for web-based access. Later on, Client Access servers that are configured for OAB distribution will poll the distribution point to discover updated OAB files and copy these files to make them available to users.

When it populates the public folder, Exchange posts a full version of the OAB in one item and another item that contains the differences between the current full version of the OAB and the last. Thus, the public folder ends up containing a set of posts—one for the full OAB and a set of differences. Attachments to the posts contain the full detail information that clients can opt to download. When clients connect to request an OAB download, they fetch either the full OAB or just the posts that contain the differences since the last time they updated their copy of the OAB. The OAB system folder has a default aging limit of 30 days, so it can keep up to 30 days of changes as older generations are automatically removed. If a client therefore needs to download more than 30 days of change data they will be unable to find all the necessary data and must download a complete copy of the OAB.

Figure 7.23
*Configuring
Default Offline
Address Book
details*

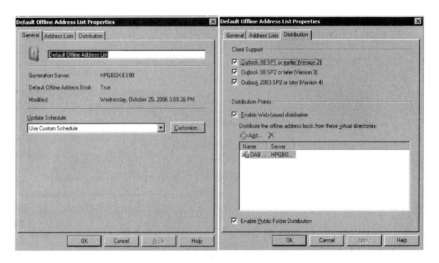

While it can use public folders to distribute the OAB, this mechanism will be eliminated in a future release of Exchange, so Exchange 2007 has to incorporate a mechanism for OAB distribution that doesn't depend on public folders. Web-based distribution means that servers can communicate together using standard HTTP commands to exchange the files necessary to publish the OAB to clients. Exchange generates a control file called OAB.XML (the OAB manifest) for clients to check to determine what differences files they need to download. The OAB manifest contains pointers to all of the files that collectively constitute the OAB including templates, a full version of the OAB, differences, and metadata such as compressed and uncompressed sizes. The OAB files are compressed and stored in the ExchangeOAB[10] file share on the mailbox server that generates the OAB. When an Outlook 2007 client needs to download the OAB from the file share, it uses the OAB distribution point information that it retrieves from the AutoDiscover service to access OAB.XML to understand the OAB data that's available on the server, compares what exists on the PC, and calculates what differences files it requires to update its copy of the OAB. Outlook then downloads the required files and applies the updates to the local OAB files. Figure 7.26 shows a set of OAB files.

While an Exchange 2007 mailbox server generates the OAB, web-based distribution to Outlook 2007 clients is controlled by Client Access servers. Each of the Client Access servers that you configure to support web distribution of the OAB poll the mailbox server that hosts the OAB to detect whether any updates exist and then pull the updated files to the local distribution directory. Exchange uses BITS (Background Intelligent Transfer Service) to copy the OAB data from the mailbox server to Client Access servers. BITS enables Exchange to transfer files in small chunks so that even large files can travel safely across over low-bandwidth, high-latency connections, making it possible for a Client Access server in a remote location to pick up new OAB files regularly, even if it might take several hours to transfer the data. All of the files must be copied and verified before Exchange determines that a new OAB is available for clients.

Outlook 2007 clients use the AutoDiscover service to determine the closest Client Access server that supports an OAB distribution point when they start up and then connect to that server over HTTP to search for OAB updates. Ideally, you should configure a Client Access server in every Active Directory site to act as a distribution point for OAB updates so that clients do not have to navigate to a remote site to fetch OAB updates. Even when you have several Client Access servers configured to pull updates across the network, the load that is generated on the mailbox server is reasonably low because each Client Access server begins the countdown for the polling interval at the time that the Exchange File Distribution service starts up. It is unlikely that all of the servers start up at the same time, so polling and copying is usually distributed across the day. Outlook clients also use BITS to copy OAB updates.

In web terms, the distribution points are IIS virtual directories. You can retrieve and update details of the OAB virtual directories through the shell with the `Get-OABVirtualDirectory` and `Set-OABVirtualDirectory` commands. The values returned allow Outlook 2007 clients to connect and retrieve the OAB files via either TCP (the internal URL) or RPC over HTTP (the external URL). By default, Outlook 2007 communicates with Exchange

---

10.   Usually equivalent to \Program Files\Exchange Server\Client Access\OAB.

over an HTTPS connection when it fetches the OAB files. You can configure this connection to be over HTTP if you disable the RequireSSL property and set the URLs to use HTTP rather than HTTPS. For example:

```
Set-OABVirtualDirectory –id 'OAB (Default Web Site)' –
RequireSSL:$False –InternalURL http://ExchMBXSvr1.xyz.com/
```

Figure 7.24

Configuring the poll interval for updated OAB files

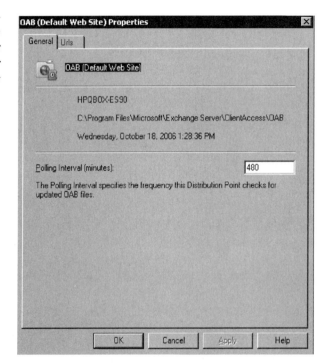

If desired, you can force an update of the OAB at any time through EMC by selecting the OAB (the Default Offline Address List or any other OAB that you have configured) and then choosing the "Update" option. Alternatively, you can use this shell command to update the Default Offline Address List.

```
Update-OfflineAddressBook –id 'Default Offline Address List'
```

Exchange logs event 9017 when it has successfully updated the OAB. After the OAB files are updated, you can then force a Client Access Server to poll for the updates through the Exchange File Distribution Service (MSExchangeFDS) with the command:

```
Update-FileDistributionService —id ExchCASvr1 —Type OAB
```

This command instructs the specified server to poll for OAB updates. You can also use the File Distribution Service to distribute updated voice prompts to Exchange Unified Messaging servers, but that's not important here.

If you add a new Client Access server to the set that handle OAB distribution, then it becomes the responsibility of the Exchange File Distribution Service running on the Client Access server to poll the generating server for updated OAB files according to the interval set as a property of its OAB web site. As you can see from Figure 7.24, the default poll interval is 480 minutes or 8 hours. When the poll interval elapses, Client Access servers fetch the OAB manifest file (OAB.XML) and check its contents to verify if any updates are available. The manifest file is usually about 20KB in size, depending on the number of OABs and the languages that are supported by the organization, so polling does not impose a great demand on the network. It is safe to increase this value to 720 minutes (12 hours) as its usual practice is to generate OAB updates nightly. You can change the poll interval through the GUI or with a one-line shell command:

Figure 7.25
OAB
synchronization
completes

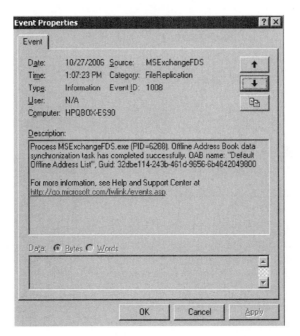

```
Get-OABVirtualDirectory | Set-OABVirtualDirectory
—PollInterval 720
```

The poll interval is specific to a Client Access server, so you have to set it on every Client Access server that participates in OAB distribution. If updates are discovered, the Exchange File Distribution service copies the OAB files to the Client Access Server using the SMB protocol. Exchange servers have write access to the OAB distribution point through their membership of the Exchange Servers security group. You can move the ExchangeOAB share from its default location on the system partition providing that you ensure that the new location allows full access to the LocalSystem account and read access to the Exchange Servers security group as otherwise the Exchange File Distribution Service will be unable to distribute updates. You can check that OAB distribution has completed successfully by looking for event 1008 for MSExchangeFDS in the application event log (Figure 7.25).

Figure 7.26
OAB files in the ExchangeOAB share

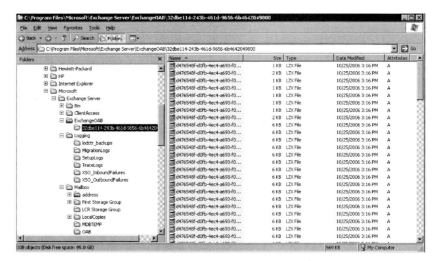

7.5.6   Creating a customized OAB

Exchange 2007 supports the ability to create and allocate different OABs to different users. While most companies will be happy to use the default OAB, you may want to create customized OABs to provide selected users with a smaller subset of the GAL. For example, hosting companies that support many different businesses within a single Exchange organization can create a separate OAB for each business and allocate that OAB to the users within that business.

Each OAB is composed of one or more Address Lists, which are objects managed at the organization level that define sets of mail-enabled Active Directory objects. If you look at the Default Offline Address List, you can see that it uses just one address list—the Global Address List. However, in some instances, it may not be appropriate to share the complete Global Address List with every user, and this is why Exchange allows you to create different address books.

When you create a new OAB, you first need to decide what Address Lists to include in the OAB (Figure 7.27). Exchange provides a default set of Address Lists such as the GAL, all rooms, all contacts, all groups, and so on, but it is likely that you need to create a customized Address List to restrict the OAB to a particular set of objects. Creating a customized Address List is explained in Chapter 3.

After you decide on the new Address Lists that are required to form the customized OAB, you can click on the New Offline Address Book option to invoke the wizard to lead you through the process of assigning the mailbox server that will generate the OAB files, the Address Lists to include in the OAB, and if Client Access servers are to provide web-based distribution points. Note that Exchange 2007 does not support public folder–based distribution for customized OABs, so you can only use these OABs with Outlook 2007 clients.

Figure 7.27
Creating a new OAB

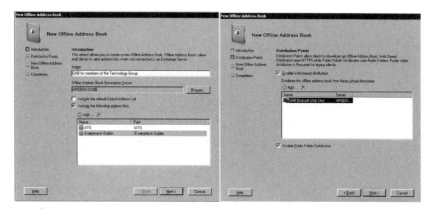

As described earlier, each OAB is represented by a set of files under a folder identified by the OAB's GUID. Figure 7.28 shows how this works. You can clearly see that this server supports three sets of OAB files under the ExchangeOAB file share (see Figure 7.26).

As mentioned above, the filters used to populate Address Lists are very similar to those used for dynamic distribution groups. You can even take a filter from a group and use it to create a new address list through the shell. For example:

```
New-AddressList —Name 'UK Employees' —RecipientFilter (Get-
DynamicDistributionGroup 'UK Employees').RecipientFilter
```

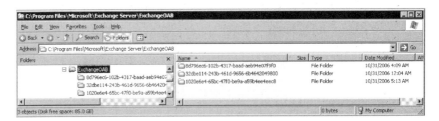

Figure 7.28
Three sets of OAB files

In this instance, we create a new address list using the same recipient filter included in a dynamic distribution group of the same name. As you'd expect, the other shell commands available to work with Address Lists are `Set-AddressList` and `Remove-AddressList` to update parameters for an existing Address List and remove an Address List, `Move-AddressList` to move an Address List to a new container, and `Update-AddressList` to update the list with recipient details that match the filter.

7.5.7   Allocating OABs to users

You can allocate an OAB on a per-database or per-user basis. Out of the box, Exchange automatically assigns the default OAB to every mailbox in a database. You can configure a new OAB through EMC by accessing the properties of the database, browsing for all available OABs within the organization, and then assigning the appropriate OAB. Figure 7.29 shows the properties of a mailbox store and you can see that the store is configured for its users to use the Default Offline Address List as their OAB. To change the OAB used by mailboxes connected to this database, click on the Browse button and select one of the OABs configured in the organization, as shown in Figure 7.30.

You can also assign an OAB to a mailbox database through EMS. First, use the `Get-OfflineAddressBook` command to determine what offline address lists exist. Here's an edited version of what returns as formatted through the `Format-List` command:

```
Get-OfflineAddressBook | Format-List

Server                             : EXCHMBXSVR1
AddressLists                       : {Default Global Address List}
Versions                           : {Version2, Version3, Version4}
IsDefault                          : True
PublicFolderDatabase               : Public Folder Store (EXCHPFSVR)
PublicFolderDistributionEnabled    : True
WebDistributionEnabled             : True
```

```
Schedule                        : {Sun.1:00 AM-Sun.3:00 AM, Mon.1:00 AM-
Mon.3:00 AM, Tue.1:00 AM-Tue.3:00 AM, Wed .1:00 AM-Wed.3:00 AM, Thu.1:00 AM-
Thu.3:00 AM, Fri.1:00 AM-Fri.3:00 AM, Sat.1:00 AM-Sat.3:00 AM}
VirtualDirectories              : {OAB (Default Web Site)}
ObjectCategoryName              : msExchOAB
Name                            : Default Offline Address List
Identity                        : \Default Offline Address List
Guid                            : 32dbe114-243b-461d-9656-6b4642049800
ObjectCategory                  : xyz.com/Configuration/Schema/ms-Exch-
OAB
ObjectClass                     : {top, msExchOAB}
OriginalId                      : \Default Offline Address List
WhenChanged                     : 10/25/2007 3:40:10 PM
WhenCreated                     : 8/2/2006 2:21:42 AM
ObjectState                     : Unchanged
OriginatingServer               : DC1.xyz.com
IsReadOnly                      : False
Id                              : \Default Offline Address List
IsValid                         : True
```

Figure 7.29
*Assigning an OAB
to a mailbox store*

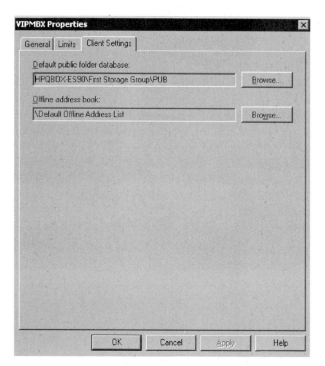

Figure 7.30

Select a new OAB for a mailbox store

This extract shows us that all three formats of OAB files (versions 2, 3, and 4) are available and that both web and public folder distribution are defined and that this OAB is based on the Default Global Address List (the GAL). We can also see the schedule used to generate updates for the OAB. Another important property is the GUID as you can tie this to the subdirectory under the ExchangeOAB share where the physical OAB files are held for web distribution. If you compare the GUID shown here to that in Figure 7.26, you'll see that they match. If multiple OABs exist, each holds its files in a separate subdirectory under the ExchangeOAB share. Now that we know what OABs are available, we check what OAB is assigned with the `Get-MailboxDatabase` command, passing the name of the database that we want to check:

```
Get-MailboxDatabase —id 'VIP Mailboxes' | Select Name,
OfflineAddressBook
```

Finally, we update the properties of the mailbox database with a new OAB:

```
Set-MailboxDatabase —id 'VIP Mailboxes' —OfflineAddressBook
'Technology Users'
```

You can also configure an individual user to use a specific OAB, but unlike configuring a mailbox database, this operation can only be done through the shell. Use the `Get-Mailbox` command to check what OAB a user is configured for:

```
Get-Mailbox —id Bond | Select Name, OfflineAddressBook
```

If the user is configured to use the default OAB, EMS returns a blank value in the OfflineAddressBook property. Use the `Set-Mailbox` command to set a new OAB, passing the name of an existing OAB in the –Offline-AddressBook parameter.

```
Set-Mailbox —id Bond —OfflineAddressBook 'Very Special
People'
```

Note that you may have to update the permissions on a customized OAB before Outlook users can access it in noncached mode. To update permissions, use commands like those shown below. You can pass the name of an individual user account or a security group in the –User parameter.

```
$OAB = Get-OfflineAddressBook 'Technology Users' |
Add-AdPermission $OAB.Identity —User Redmond
—AccessRights ReadProperty, WriteProperty
```

Assigning a customized OAB to a user is only effective in terms of applying a basic restriction to the directory if they use Outlook in cached Exchange mode. If they use another client like Outlook Web Access, they will have full access to the directory. A customized OAB will not prevent a user sending a message to someone that they can't see in the OAB because they can always generate a message using that recipient's SMTP address.

7.6   Outlook Anywhere

Outlook Anywhere is the Exchange 2007 version of the RPC over HTTP feature that Microsoft first introduced in Exchange 2003 and dramatically improved (largely by completing the functionality and making the feature much easier to deploy) in Exchange 2003 SP1. The idea behind RPC over HTTP is that you can use Outlook 2003 and 2007 clients to connect to Exchange 2003 or 2007 over any IP connection without having to create a VPN (Virtual Private Network). When you use RPC over HTTP, the RPCs generated by Outlook are "wrapped" in HTTP so that they can travel through the HTTP port (443) in your firewall.

Because of the vast differences that exist in corporate networks and security policies, describing how to set up and configure Outlook Anywhere takes many pages to cover in detail, so it is inappropriate for a book that focuses on Exchange 2007. For this reason, we only cover how to enable Outlook Anywhere for Exchange 2007 rather than the details of how to configure ISA Server.

First, you have to install the RPC over HTTP Proxy component on the Client Access server that will support Outlook Anywhere access. This part of IIS allows IIS to support RPCs that arrive in HTTP. To install the RPC over HTTP Proxy, go to the Control Panel, choose Add/Remove programs, choose Add Windows components, select Networking Services, and then select the RPC over HTTP Proxy (Figure 7.31).

Figure 7.31
Install RPC over
HTTP Proxy

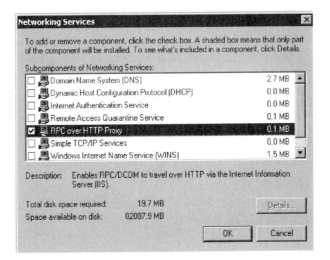

With the RPC over HTTP proxy installed, you can then enable Outlook Anywhere. In EMC, select the Client Access server that you want to enable for Outlook Anywhere, and then select "Enable Outlook Anywhere." A wizard leads you through the enabling process. All you have to do is decide what authentication method to use and the name of the external host that will support the service. If you use ISA Server 2006 as the firewall, you can specify NTLM authentication. This has the effect of suppressing the password prompt that users will otherwise see before they can connect to Exchange. As you might expect, ISA Server 2006 offers the most integrated features to support Outlook Anywhere, so it is the best choice of firewall if you want to support Outlook Anywhere. Figure 7.32 shows the wizard to enable Outlook Anywhere. The equivalent shell command generated is:

```
Enable-OutlookAnywhere -Server 'ExchCAS1'
-ExternalHostname 'mail.xyz.com'
-ExternalAuthenticationMethod 'Basic'
-SSLOffloading $False
```

If you have some legacy Exchange servers in the organization, you may see this error flagged when you enable Outlook Anywhere:

```
WARNING: Exchange versions before Exchange 2003 do not
support RPC over HTTP; the following servers cannot be
enabled:
```

■ Do not worry—this message is generated by a bug in Exchange 2007 and Outlook Anywhere will continue to function. The `Disable-Out-lookAnywhere` command is available if you want to disable Outlook Anywhere on a Client Access server.

```
Disable-OutlookAnywhere —Server 'ExchCAS1'
```

When you enable Outlook Anywhere on a Client Access server, all of the users whose mailboxes are on Exchange 2007 and Exchange 2003 SP1 servers will be able to connect via RPC over HTTP. However, if you operate a distributed environment, you should enable Outlook Anywhere on at least one Client Access server per Active Directory site so that users can always connect to a server in their home site.

If you make an error configuring Outlook Anywhere, you can select the Client Access server with EMC and then its properties, followed by the Outlook Anywhere property page. You can then change properties, such as switching from Basic to NTLM authentication or the name of the external server. You can also use the `Set-OutlookAnywhere` command to make the necessary changes. For example:

```
Set-OutlookAnywhere —id 'ExchCas1\RPC (Default Web Site)'
—ExternalAuthenticationMethod 'NTLM'
```

Notice that the identifier used to set properties for Outlook Anywhere is the name of the RPC virtual directory in IIS that the installation of the RPC over HTTP Proxy creates. You have to set the appropriate authentication mechanism on this directory (NTLM or Basic) and enable SSL if you have decided to use this with Outlook Anywhere. To view the properties of Out-

Figure 7.32
*Enabling Outlook
Anywhere*

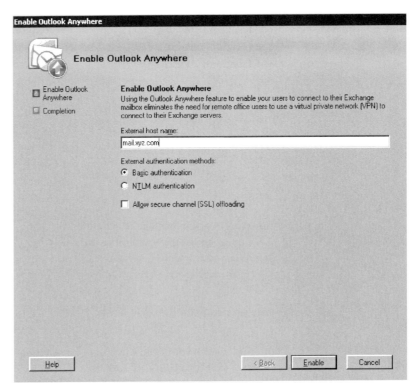

look Anywhere on a Client Access server, we use the Get-OutlookAnywhere command.

```
Get-OutlookAnywhere -Server ExchCAS1

SSLOffloading               : False
ExternalHostname            : mail.xyz.com
ExternalAuthenticationMethod : Ntlm
MetabasePath                : IIS://ExchCas1.xyz.com/W3SVC/1/
ROOT/Rpc
Server                      : ExchCAS1
ExchangeVersion             : 0.1 (8.0.535.0)
Name                        : Rpc (Default Web Site)
DistinguishedName           : CN=Rpc (Default Web
Site),CN=HTTP,CN=Protocols,CN=ExchCAS1,CN=Servers,CN=Exchange
Administrative Group (FYDIBOHF23SPDLT),CN=Administrative
Groups,CN=xyz,CN=Microsoft Exchange,
CN=Services,CN=Configuration,DC=xyz,DC=com
Identity                    : ExchCAS1\Rpc (Default Web Site)
```

You have to make sure that the public name that you provide for clients to connect to can be resolved by clients that connect from outside the company. You also have to ensure that the ISA Server or whatever method you use as a proxy can connect to the internal Client Access servers.

ISA Server performs a bridging role for incoming RPC over HTTP traffic by terminating the incoming SSL connection from Outlook, inspecting the traffic, and then creating an encrypted connection to the Client Access server. You need a certificate to secure the connections to Exchange and the name of the certificate must match the name of the Client Access server. Once you have generated the certificate, you can use the ISA New Exchange Publishing rule wizard to lead you through the steps to configure ISA Server to proxy the RPC over HTTP traffic through the firewall to Exchange. You can find details of the various parameters that you can tweak for this connection in TechNet.

Figure 7.33
Configuring an Outlook profile to use Outlook Anywhere

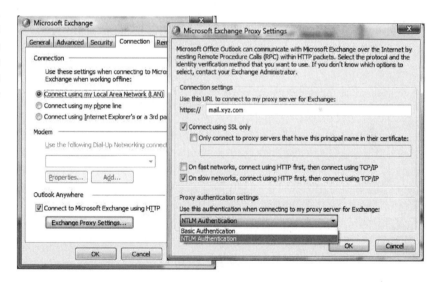

The final piece of the puzzle is to configure your Outlook profile so that it uses RPC over HTTP instead of attempting the more normal RPC connection. When you configure the profile (Figure 7.33), click on "Connection" and then set the checkbox to indicate that you want to connect to Exchange using HTTP. You will then be able to define the server that you want to connect to and the authentication mechanism to use (ensure that you match the selected authentication mechanism with one that you have configured Outlook Anywhere to support).

7.7 Outlook Web Access

Exchange 5.0 was the first version to boast a web client, reflecting the broad impetus within Microsoft to support the Internet in the 1996–97 timeframe. The web client ("Outlook WebView") worked, but it only supported basic messaging operations and you would not consider it as a client that anyone but a casual user would use. In Microsoft's defense, web development was an inexact science in 1997 and Exchange did not have the technology in the Store or other components to support web clients fully. Traditional web applications are static so any action that might cause content to change force the client to refresh the data displayed in its interface. Given the number of changes that occur in an email client, if Microsoft had followed normal development techniques, the web client would have generated a huge number of refreshes. Microsoft minimized the impact by using hidden frames to communicate with the server to maintain document context, but user navigation through the mailbox still generated a lot of client-server activity. This, together with some scalability problems in the Store, meant that Exchange could not support as many web clients as it could MAPI clients.

Over time, technology improved and the developers discovered new techniques to speed things up in the client interface and in communication between the client and server. The redesign of the Store in Exchange 2000 accommodated web clients better. WebDAV became the protocol of choice and IE5 became the target browser due to its ability to support a richer user environment. In addition, Microsoft included a component called XMLHTTP in IE5 that supported asynchronous data access to a server while preserving document state on the client. The second generation of Outlook Web Access shipped in two versions: the "rich" or premium client that delivered maximum functionality but required IE5 or better, and the "reach" or basic client that functioned much like the older client. The basic version of Outlook Web access was not pretty, but it was functional and worked pretty well on every browser. Another way of thinking about browser support is that if you use IE, you get the rich client in all its glory, but if you use anything else such as Firefox or Apple's Safari browser, you are limited to the basic client.

Exchange 2003 made further advances and Outlook Web Access now approached the functionality and appearance of Outlook more closely with features such as junk mail checking, support of themes, the ability to provide segmented features to different users, spell checking, and asynchronous polling of the server to generate notifications for reminders and new messages. The problem, of course, is that the Outlook client keeps on improving its interface and feature set, so there is a constant race for Outlook Web Access to keep up. Over the years, the Exchange developers have done a good job in this respect, and Exchange 2007 is no different as it includes a new generation of Outlook Web Access. The major differences are the introduction of the Client Access server as the component that renders objects into HTML instead of the Store process on the server that hosts the user mailbox doing this work, as is the case in Exchange 2003. The movement of code out of the Store makes it easier for Microsoft to enhance it in the future and reduces the risk that an application component can cause a problem for the Store that affects multiple parts of Exchange. At the same time, because the Client Access server provides a common touch point for all client applications that want to use Exchange, Microsoft has implemented a set of common business logic routines for subsystems such as calendaring so that you now see the same behavior no matter what client you use. Finally, the major difference on the platform side is the complete rewrite of the Outlook Web Access code base to move away from C++ to create an ASP.NET application written in managed code and to incorporate newer web technologies such as AJAX.

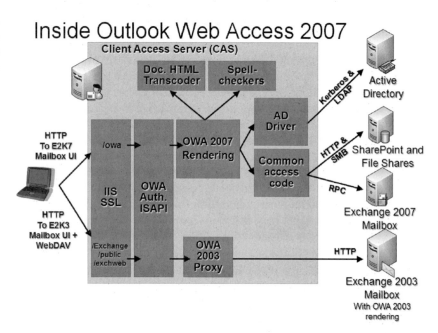

Figure 7.34

Outlook Web Access 2007 architecture

Figure 7.34 illustrates the Outlook Web Access 2007 architecture. When a browser makes a connection to a mailbox on an Exchange 2003 server, an ISAPI extension (DAVEX) running within IIS on that mailbox server takes responsibility for the generation of the HTML that creates the client user interface and then populates it with data. Behind the scenes, DAVEX communicates with the Information Store through the ExIFS file system to retrieve mailbox data. DAVEX no longer exists in Exchange 2007. In an Exchange 2007 environment, a user running Outlook Web Access connects via IIS to an ASP.NET application that runs on the Client Access server. The Client Access server supports components to handle document format conversion and rendering into HTML (while this feature is exposed to Outlook Web Access as a DLL, it runs in its own process), rendering of mailbox data, spell checking, and access to the Active Directory, SharePoint and UNC file shares, and Exchange mailbox servers. Exchange secures communications between all components as tightly as possible. For example, communication between the Client Access server and an Exchange 2007 mailbox server occurs through RPCs flowing over a secured authenticated channel.

As you look at the role that the Client Access server plays for Outlook Web Access, you might conclude that this is essentially the same way that front-end and back-end servers work in an Exchange 2003 environment. Conceptually, or perhaps when illustrated in a PowerPoint presentation, this might seem to be the case, but in fact a traditional front-end Exchange server simply proxies incoming HTTP connections from a browser to the correct back-end mailbox server, which is then responsible for generating the content and relaying it back to the browser. The Client Access server hosts the Outlook Web Access application and is responsible for content generation through its secure connection with the mailbox server. In some instances the Client Access server proxies connections, such as in the case when a client connects to a Client Access server that is outside the Active Directory site that hosts the user's mailbox server. In this case, the Client Access server that handles the original connection proxies the HTTP requests from the browser to a Client Access server that resides in the same Active Directory site as the mailbox server (if one is available). The logic here is that the first case may not have a high-speed connection to the mailbox server because they are not in the same Active Directory site, so the RPC connection over the secure channel may not work properly. It therefore makes more sense to proxy the connection over HTTP to a Client Access server in the target Active Directory site and allows the Client Access server to connect via RPC to the user's mailbox server.

7.7.1   New features in Outlook Web Access 2007

Microsoft has continuously updated the feature set for Outlook Web Access with the intention of keeping up with the pace set by their mainline Outlook client. Of course, the always-online nature of a web client creates some limitations, but even if you consider this factor, Microsoft continues to innovate in their browser client. Microsoft has made many changes across Outlook Web Access and it is difficult to list them all. My favorite new features in Outlook Web Access 2007 include:

- The improved user interface. Every software designer says that their user interface improves over time and Outlook Web Access has quite a challenge to match Outlook because of the resources that Microsoft pours into the user interface of the Outlook client and the other Office applications. In Outlook Web Access 2007, Microsoft reduces the number of key clicks and other actions required to get work done. They have incorporated actions and responses in place so that you can carry out actions without having to go through multiple dialogs or property sheets, and expanded the context-sensitive menus (right click) so that you can do things like create a new folder or rename an existing folder. New messages appear automatically in your inbox and increments the unread count, so you do not have to keep on checking that a message has arrived[11]. Interestingly, because of security concerns, best security practice for browser applications prohibit rendering items outside the browser window (which is how Outlook Web Access 2003 displays new mail notifications), so Outlook Web Access 2007 integrates the new item notification into its own window rather than using a pop-up from the Windows taskbar. Outlook Web Access 2007 tracks the count of new items in folders and updates the counts as new items arrive so you do not have to check for new mail constantly. Notifications (for new mail, faxes, and voice messages) appear in a small menu with the sender's name and message subject for five seconds before fading out from the main window. Clicking on the notification selects the new message, even if you are working with the Calendar or Contacts. Outlook Web Access 2007 is better at remembering settings, such as your domain and username so that you only have to enter your password to connect. These changes together with the new look and feel (including updates to accommodate users with poor vision) make Outlook Web Access 2007 a better place to work than previous versions.

- Support for voice messages delivered to the inbox so that Outlook Web Access can deal with voicemail as seamlessly as Outlook 2007 is able to.

- Much better name resolution. Previous versions of Outlook Web Access supported the CTRL/K function to check names typed into the address dialogs. Outlook Web Access now supports the display of properties (office, phone number, etc.) for an addressee from this list providing that it has some source (such as the GAL or a contact record) to extract the properties. You can also view organizational information (the user's manager) and a snapshot of the user's availability from their calendar. Disappointingly, you still can't update the contents of a distribution group from Outlook Web Access, so you have to use Outlook if this is something that you do often.

---

11.   This feature uses the XMLHTTPRequest method.

- Outlook Web Access 2007 adds support for a drop down set of names of addresses that you have previously used, just like the feature available in Outlook. Outlook Web Access maintains the list in a hidden item in the mailbox root that it reads into a client-side array at start-up. The array can hold up to 70 items.

- The Outlook Web Access calendar looks very similar to Outlook 2007 (and supports features like transparency during drag and drop actions) and includes redesigned views for daily, weekly, and work week, including a reading pane preview so that you don't have to open an item to see the full details. The calendar now supports a smart scheduling feature to help you set up meetings, including searching for the right conference room. One surprising feature that is missing is support for the monthly calendar view, but this may reappear in a future Exchange 2007 service pack.

- The ability to open additional mailboxes (premium client only). Outlook has long had the ability to open multiple mailboxes, including mailboxes on IMAP and POP servers such as Hotmail. The problem that Microsoft faced in the past is how to cache and transmit credentials in a secure manner to allow the Outlook Web Access to open and access multiple mailboxes. Exchange 2007 adopts a tabbed window approach to solve the problem. If you have the right to open another mailbox, you can select it from a dropdown list and Outlook Web Access then launches another window with the correct URL and performs an explicit logon for the target mailbox in that window.

  One minor nagging problem is that you are still unable to use Outlook Web Access to manage permissions on your mailbox, so you still have to do this work through Outlook or by using the `Set-Mail-boxPermission` command. Note that Outlook Web Access 2007 continues to support the ability to use URLs to access specific folders in another user's account (if you have the permission). For example, the following URL opens the calendar folder in Jane Smith's mailbox:

```
https://ExchMbxSvr1/owa/Jane.Smith@xyz.com/
?cmd=contents&f=calendar
```

- Fast search using the server-based content index built and maintained by Exchange 2007. The important point here is that Outlook Web Access is intelligent enough to feed Exchange with the necessary information to allow the server to perform efficient searches and then accept the results of the searches back from the server. The search works the same way as the similar feature in Outlook 2007 or indeed like Google: You can select the scope of the search to be the current folder, folder and subfolders, or all folders and items.

- The ability to remotely wipe a user's mobile device if it is lost or stolen. This feature should not come as a surprise because Exchange 2003 SP2 includes a web-based management interface to wipe lost devices, so this is simply a personal version of that feature.

- Outlook Web Access 2007 supports access to documents stored in folders on SharePoint Portals through a function called "Document Access" or "Link Access." This is an important feature in light of the troubled future for public folders and the need for companies to find an alternate repository. SharePoint may well be the right target for public folders and better integration with SharePoint offers an opportunity to migrate user data from PSTs to a more manageable and secure repository, not to mention one to which you can apply any restrictions required to comply with legislation.

- Troubleshooting—a much overlooked but important feature that makes deployment and support much easier for administrators finally appears in Outlook Web Access. This option allows a user to collect a set of data about their current environment such as browser version, client O/S version, Exchange mailbox name, Exchange server name, and so on in a form that it is easy to provide the data to a support technician when required. The user can either cut and paste the data into a message or read it over the phone to the support technician. There is nothing more sophisticated in troubleshooting than reporting the current environment, but it is truly astonishing how many problems are resolved from this information, so it is a good step forward.

Other popular features include the improved Out of Office Assistant (I like the ability to set a notice for a specific period of time in the future and have Exchange turn OOF on and off for me) that now allows users to create different messages for internal and external recipients. You might also like the small touches such as the way that Outlook Web Access 2007 includes availability information for users when you look them up in the GAL (Figure 7.36).

On the downside, users will notice that they cannot work with personal distribution groups any more, they cannot create and send signed S/MIME messages (you can read clear signed messages with Outlook Web Access) and they cannot work with rules (rules set by other clients still function). If you need to be able to support S/MIME signed messages for Outlook Web Access users, you will have to keep their mailboxes on an Exchange 2003 server until Microsoft provides S/MIME support in Exchange 2007 SP1, which supports S/MIME messages, but only for the premium version.

Figure 7.35
*Outlook Web Access
2007 Premium*

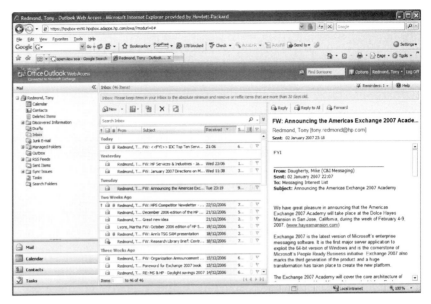

Another missing feature is that you cannot use Outlook Web Access to recover messages from the Deleted Items folder (or any other folder). This regrettable oversight may lead to additional work for administrators if users want to recover information that they have deleted in error. Fortunately, Microsoft fixes this issue in Exchange 2007 SP1. Finally, as you can see from Figure 7.35, Outlook Web Access arranges items in date groups ("Today," "Yesterday," "Last Week," and so on). This is a sensible arrangement for most users but as the result of a deliberate decision by the Exchange development group to reduce code complexity (and potential bugs), you cannot turn these date groups off by customizing the view. By comparison, you can turn date grouping off in Outlook.

Microsoft plans to address these issues in Exchange 2007 SP1 by providing support for S/MIME signed messages, access to personal distribution lists, rules, a monthly calendar view, and deleted items recovery. In addition, Outlook Web Access SP1 will support Korean and Arabic spell checking and the Office 2007 file formats, so that the Direct File Access feature can render attachments in these formats as HTML and avoid the need for users to download and open files.

Overall, the important point is that Outlook Web Access is very much a frontline client for Microsoft that receives a lot of care and attention. Inevitably, the growing feature set and usability of Outlook Web Access raises the question of which client you should deploy. Outlook Web Access is a very cost-effective client to deploy because it is easier to support and manage than Outlook or other email clients, but on the other hand, Outlook Web

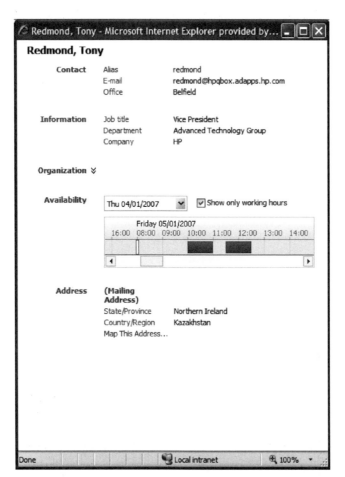

Figure 7.36
User details viewed through Outlook Web Access

Access still lacks some features when compared to Outlook. For instance, Outlook Web Access clients cannot open PST files and many users have collections of PSTs that they use as email archives. You obviously cannot use OST files with Outlook Web Access either, so offline access is impossible.

For some environments such as Internet kiosks, the answer to "which client should I use" is easy. Things get more difficult inside a corporation where users are accustomed to Outlook and they would not be happy to revert to using Outlook Web Access because of some missing features. Even with these caveats, some users could switch to Outlook Web Access and would still be able to work effectively, such as people who do not travel and use email intermittently. Every company is different and each user community is different within an organization. Deciding to change clients is not something that you can do without some careful planning and lots of involvement from your users, but Outlook Web Access 2007 does deliver the email and calendaring functionality that many people need, so it is worth looking at the question of client choice again.

7.7.2 Outlook Web Access Light

Outlook Web Access supports two versions: the "premium" version and the "light" version. Since Exchange 2000, we have been able to choose between two versions of Outlook Web Access. Initially, the requirement to support browsers with radically different capabilities was the reason for the different versions. From IE5 onwards, Microsoft's own browser supports some features such as WebDAV and DHTML that earlier browsers did not, so it was capable of delivering a richer user interface and so became the "rich" client, but you need to use IE6 or IE7 to access the premium version of Outlook Web Access 2007.

Microsoft designed the "reach" client with a simpler interface that almost any browser (that supports HTML 3.2 at a minimum) could support to allow customers to deploy Outlook Web Access across a much wider user population and ISPs to support kiosk-style environments. Today's light version is used in these environments. It is also the version used by people who prefer non-IE browsers or who cannot use IE, such as the Macintosh Safari browser or the open source browsers preferred by the Linux community. Outlook Web Access light is also the preferred version for blind or low-vision users because of its simpler design (Figure 7.37). While it is easy to understand why Microsoft prefers IE as the platform for Outlook Web Access, it is sometimes hard to understand why other feature-rich browsers such as Firefox cannot support the premium client and why Microsoft restricts support for Firefox to the light version. The answer is engineering cost—the cost to Microsoft to test and discover all of the tweaks that they would need to make to get the premium features run on non-Microsoft browsers. The premium version of Outlook Web Access uses many advanced AJAX features in its user interface. Other browsers support AJAX, but not all browsers support AJAX in exactly the same way. Thus, Microsoft has to test each feature against a browser before they can support it. The cost of testing every advanced feature against Firefox, Safari, Opera, and all the other browsers that exist today is colossal, as are the ongoing support costs as new browser versions, patches, and hot fixes arrive. For purely economic reasons, especially as Firefox and other browsers have a relatively small following in the Exchange user base, Microsoft decided that they would restrict the premium Outlook Web Access client to IE.

The first time a user connects to an Exchange 2007 server via Outlook Web Access, they see a dialog to allow them to select whether the computer is private or public and whether they want to use the light version. If you run Outlook Web Access on a public computer, such as one in an Internet café, Exchange will time your session out and disconnect from the mailbox after

10 minutes inactivity. Exchange stores these settings as properties of the user's mailbox (see discussion later). Subsequently the user can switch between interfaces through the client Options. Outlook Web Access respects the interface choice for sessions until the user elects to change it again. This is much better than the previous approach, which locked the user into a preference that was difficult to change after the initial selection.

Figure 7.37
Outlook Web Access 2007 light

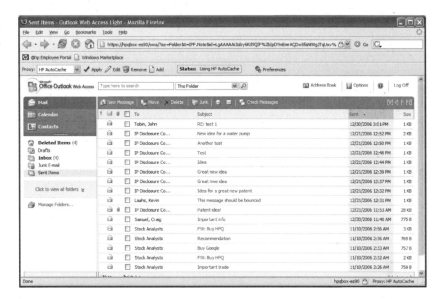

The lack of premium functionality might be bad news for non-IE users, but the positive way of looking at the issue is that Microsoft has delivered a highly functional client for Exchange in the light version of Outlook Web Access 2007 that is at a par with the "rich" version delivered in Outlook Web Access 2003. In fact, the light version of Outlook Web Access 2007 behaves very similarly to the rich version of Outlook Web Access 2003, so on the surface you could consider that the light version is roughly one development cycle behind its premium counterpart.

The major features that are missing from the light client when you compare it to the premium client are:

- No support for tasks. You can create tasks using other clients but Outlook Web Access light does not render or process tasks correctly. You can see the text of the tasks but not the task-specific properties such as the start and end dates.

- Messages are composed in plain text only, so you cannot use the HTML editor that comes along with the premium client. However, you can read HTML-formatted messages that are sent to you so that pictures and other graphic elements are rendered correctly.

- No support for flags and categories. You can set these attributes with other clients and the light version of Outlook Web Access 2007 will ignore them.

- No support for reminders.

- No support for drag and drop between folders.

- Printing is done through the browser's print option rather than a specific print option supplied as part of the Outlook Web Access user interface.

- No weekly view available in the calendar—you have to navigate using a date picker or move through your calendar day by day.

- No spell checker is available when you send messages. Some browsers (like Firefox) offer spell checking features that you can use to check text before sending a message, but it is not as convenient as the integrated version that the premium client delivers.

- Outlook Web Access light does not display any mailbox quota information when you move the mouse over the mailbox root (Figure 7.38) or information about folder quota when you access a managed folder.

Figure 7.38
Mailbox quota information

- No support for keyboard shortcuts such as CTRL/Enter to send a message and CTRL/K to check the names in a message header.

- Limited support for views, for example, you can't create a view by conversation.

- The scheduling assistant is a lot less graphical and effective in the light client than its premium equivalent—this demonstrates the effectiveness of some of the AJAX functionality in creating the premium user interface (Figure 7.39).

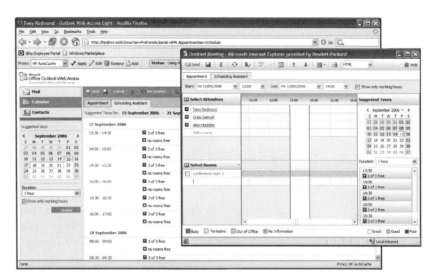

Figure 7.39
Scheduling in Outlook Web Access 2007 light and premium

While the user interface of the light client is less glitzy than the premium Outlook Web Access client, there are some advantages:

- Logon times are faster across slow connections because less data is transmitted between the server and the browser.

- Microsoft has tested the light version on many platforms including Vista, Windows XP, Windows 2000, Windows ME, Windows 98, Mac OS X, and Linux on browsers such as IE7, IE6, IE5.5, IE5.01, and IE5.2 for Mac, Firefox, Safari, Opera, and Netscape. The net result is that this is a version that you can deploy across heterogeneous environment if you want to support a single version of the Outlook Web Access client.

- Microsoft has included some nice features in the light client in an effort to overcome the lack of functionality in some of the browsers that it has to support. For example, when you create a new message, Outlook Web Access light lists your most recent email correspondents in a pick box so that you can select an address.

- Microsoft designed Outlook Web Access light for use in locked-down environments such as kiosks where pop-ups are restricted.

The relatively long list of missing features when you compare the light and premium versions of Outlook Web Access 2007 may make you think that the light version is uninteresting, but this is not the case. Relatively few large enterprises operate a completely Microsoft-centric computing environment and you are bound to find a few users who do not want to use Microsoft browsers on their desktop or even any Microsoft technology at all. You still need to connect them to Exchange so that they can participate in the corporate messaging system and Outlook Web Access light or IMAP are good solutions for these users. Outlook Web Access is best if the user likes to use a browser and is connected to the network all the time; IMAP is best when they want to work with email offline or prefer to use one of the IMAP clients rather than a browser.

7.7.3   International versions

When a user first logs on to Outlook Web Access, they have to select the regional settings that they want the client to use. These settings are stored in the root of the user's mailbox. As shown in Figure 7.40, users can change the language that they want to run Outlook Web Access through the Regional Settings option. This is a small but important change because previous versions of Exchange assumed that the language option implemented for the browser was also the user's preferred language. This is an acceptable assumption for your normal PC, but it is not a great assumption to make if you use a PC in an Internet café in a foreign country to access Exchange. Consider the difficulties faced by an English speaker who is suddenly faced with Outlook Web Access in Japanese because they use Outlook Web Access to connect from a PC in Tokyo! They may be able to navigate the Japanese prompts and options, but that is not always the case, so a change was required. In passing, I will note that you can change the accessibility option through General Settings.

Figure 7.40
Outlook Web Access
Regional Settings

Outlook Web Access supports over 40 languages, including a surprising number of regional variants. It is not possible for an administrator to restrict the languages available for selection on a server, so a user could select a language that they can't cope with, which may result in a support call when the user discovers that they can't find a way to switch back to the language that they really wanted. For example, in Figure 7.41, the user has switched language to Kazak. After they discover that Kazak is very different to English, they attempt to switch back to English. It is easy to access Options (the command button is always positioned in the same place), but not so easy to figure out how to select any variant of English, or even to select another language (such as French) that would give them a sporting chance to get back to English.

The moral of the story is that user education is important and that this is yet another thing to tell users not to do!

Figure 7.41
Outlook Web Access in Kazak

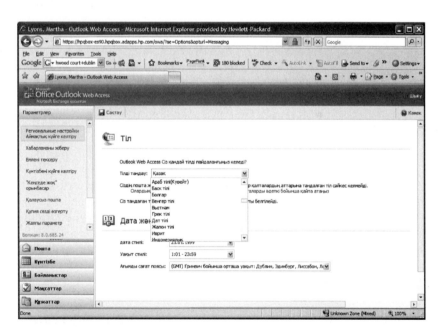

Incorrect sort order for the GAL is another international issue that can afflict Outlook and Outlook Web Access clients. This occurs when domain controllers do not have the same locales installed as clients, so the sort order that the server uses to present data to clients does not match the requests that they make. The error is most obvious when a client using one language attempts to look up the GAL. For example, if a client using the Danish locale attempts to search the GAL on a server that supports only English, the request made in Danish will not match the results provided in English. See

Microsoft Knowledge Base article 919166 for further details about how to fix the problem.

7.7.4   Accessing legacy data

It is possible for a Client Access server to connect to legacy back-end mailbox servers during the transition period when Exchange 2003 servers still exist within the organization. This allows you to begin the migration by replacing front-end Exchange 2003 servers with Exchange 2007 Client Access servers—a tactic that introduces new 64-bit Exchange 2007 servers into the organization while you prepare for the upgrade of the mailbox servers. The new Client Access servers should be more scalable and provide better performance to clients, so you gain by improving service to users with little disruption to your infrastructure. Another advantage that you gain through this approach is that you get the chance to learn more about Exchange 2007 in production before you commit to a mailbox server deployment. Note that users whose mailboxes are on Exchange 2003 servers will see the Outlook Web Access 2003 user interface. To ensure that the setup program installs the necessary ISAPI filter to support Exchange 2003 mailboxes, you should always install the Client Access role before the mailbox role on multi-role servers.

A Client Access server is able to proxy client connections to mailboxes on Exchange 2003 back-end servers. For this reason, there are two IIS virtual directories used by Outlook Web Access. The /owa virtual directory supports the Outlook Web Access 2007 application while the /exchange virtual directory is to provide backwards compatibility for connections to mailboxes on Exchange 2000/2003 servers. The /public and /exchweb virtual directories exist for the same reason. Because Exchange holds information about servers in the Active Directory, the Client Access server knows what version runs on a mailbox server, so even if someone with a mailbox on an Exchange 2007 server uses /exchange, Exchange will proxy the connection successfully. In other words, if you want to connect to a mailbox on an Exchange 2007 server, the URL is:

```
https://Client-Access-Server-Name/owa OR https://Client-
Access-Server-Name/exchange
```

By comparison, the URL to connect to a mailbox on an Exchange 2003 server using the same Client Access server to proxy the connection is:

```
https://Client-Access-Server-Name/exchange
```

You can confirm the situation with the `Get-OwaVirtualDirectory` command:

```
Get-OwaVirtualDirectory —Server ExchCAS1
Name                    Server            OwaVersion


----                    ------            ----------

owa (Default Web Site)    ExchCAS1            Exchange2007

Exchweb (Default Web Site)  ExchCAS1          Exchange2003or2000
```

The code on a Client Access server that handles client requests to connect to Outlook Web Access is contained in exprox.dll. This component is responsible for proxying traffic from the Client Access server to the appropriate mailbox server, whether that server runs Exchange 2000/2003 or Exchange 2007. It works alongside another component called davex.dll, which contains the logic to handle DAV requests to mailbox servers. Davex makes sure that users receive the appropriate version of Outlook Web Access by either pointing them to the /owa virtual directory on the Client Access server or to the /exchange virtual directory on an Exchange 2003 mailbox server.

Even if your mailbox is on an Exchange 2007 server, you can use the /public virtual directory to connect to an Exchange 2003 server to access public folders. For example, if you use the URL https://ExchCas1.xyz.com/owa to access your mailbox on an Exchange 2007 server, you can use https://ExchCas1.xyz.com/public to instruct the Client Access server to proxy the connection to an Exchange 2003 public folder server. The Client Access server is intelligent enough to understand how to redirect the connection to the Exchange 2003 server.

If you know the name of the Exchange 2003 public folder server, you can pass it directly, as in the example shown in Figure 7.42, where the URL used is http://public-folder-server1.xyz.com/public[12]. Here you can see IE7 (on a Vista client) accessing public folders on an Exchange 2003 public folder server. Note the distinct difference between the user interface shown here and that used by Outlook Web Access 2007. This is because the Exchange 2003 public folder server renders the user interface by combining data and user interface elements before transmitting them to the browser, so you see the older Outlook Web Access 2003 user interface. When you access

---

12. Reflecting the "secure by default" theme, Outlook Web Access 2007 uses https: for all of its URLs whereas Outlook Web Access 2003 uses http:.

an Exchange 2007 mailbox, the Client Access server pulls the data from the mailbox and renders the user interface to create the new Outlook Web Access 2007 user interface.

While the lack of investment in public folders across Exchange 2007 makes the lack of support in Outlook Web Access 2007 unsurprising, it is a fact that many companies have large numbers of public folders that they need to continue using until they can move their content elsewhere. As you can see from Figure 7.42, public folders often hold thousands of items. According to Microsoft, Exchange 2007 SP1 will incorporate new processing to allow access to public folders for Outlook Web Access 2007. At that point, the separate connection to the Exchange 2003 public folder server will not be required.

Figure 7.42
*Accessing Exchange
2003 public folders*

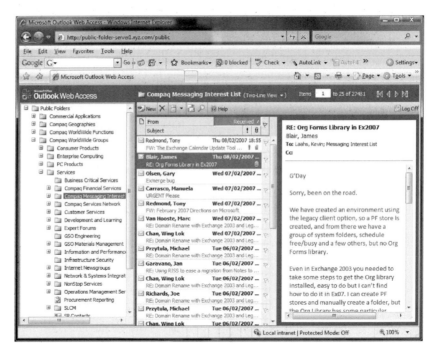

7.7.5 Managing Outlook Web Access

Administrators manage previous versions of Outlook Web Access through a mixture of ESM, IIS, and registry settings. Microsoft has integrated most of these functions into EMC (Figure 7.43) under the Client Access server role, where you manipulate the properties of the "owa (Default Web Site)" object (the OWA virtual directory). Alternatively, you can manipulate these properties through the `Set-OwaVirtualDirectory` shell command. You manage

Outlook Web Access configuration on a server-by-server basis and servers do not share configuration information across an organization. In other words, if you want to have consistent operation of Outlook Web Access, you have to make the necessary changes on every Client Access server in the organization.

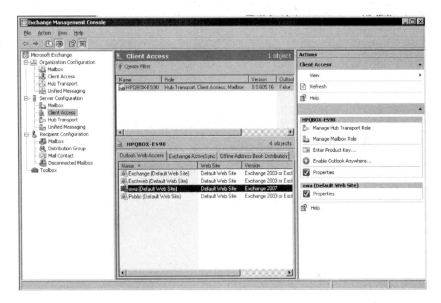

Figure 7.43
Managing Outlook Web Access

For example, the command to force all users on the ExchCAS1 server to use the light rather than the premium client is:

```
Set-OwaVirtualDirectory -Identity 'ExchCAS1\owa (Default Web
Site)'
–PremiumClientEnabled:$False
```

The name of the service specified in the –identity parameter is the same name displayed in the EMC GUI as shown in Figure 7.43.

7.7.6 **Authentication**

By default, Outlook Web Access uses forms-based authentication to present users with the ability to provide credentials necessary to logon and connect to a mailbox (Figure 7.44). The logon screen allows users to select whether the computer they are using is a public or shared computer (such as one in an Internet café) or a private computer (like the one you use at work). They can also select whether they wish to use the light version of Outlook Web Access. These options are stored in a hidden item in the root of the user's mailbox.

As we will see later on, the choice of private or public computer also influences some of the options to control a user's environment, such as their ability to download attachments. It also affects the timeout for the client, which kicks in between 15 and 23 minutes for public computers (to ensure that even if a user leaves the PC without logging off, there is a manageable risk that someone might compromise the data). By comparison, private computers have a timeout period of over eight hours.

Timeouts work through session cookies. The Client Access server sends an encrypted cookie together with the username and password back to the client. The server continues to generate encryption keys and keeps the last three in memory. Clients send the encryption key along with their requests to the server. If the encryption key is still in memory, the server responds by sending a new encryption key back to the client. However, if the encryption key has expired and the server has discarded it, the server times the session out and the client is forced to reauthenticate.

Figure 7.44
Outlook Web Access
logon screen

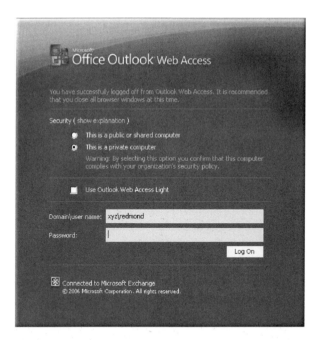

You can control how Outlook Web Access handles client authentication by amending the properties of the "owa (Default Web Site)" object. Go to the Client Access node of Server Configuration, click on the Client Access server that you want to work with, and then select the web site and click on "Properties." This reveals a set of property pages that allow you to change the way that Outlook Web Access deals with clients. We'll begin by changing the way that users authenticate themselves when they logon to Outlook Web

Access. The options available are shown in Figure 7.45. You can select from three different logon formats for forms-based authentication:

- Standard Windows Domain and username: For example, XYZ\Redmond
- User Principal Name: For example: Redmond@xyz.com
- User Name only: For example: Redmond

If you do not want users to see the standard Outlook Web Access logon screen, you can opt to use one, two, or three other standard authentication methods.

- Basic authentication uses a HTTP mechanism to encode the user name and password before Outlook Web Access sends the credentials to the Client Access server to be validated. This mechanism supports the widest range of connections to Exchange via Outlook Web Access, including browsers that run on non-Windows platform. Ideally, you should use the basic authentication mechanism with SSL so that the communications between the browser and the Client Access server is protected.
- Integrated Windows authentication, which means that the browser can use any cached credentials that exist on the client PC. This mechanism works very smoothly to achieve a fast logon if the client PC is part of the same domain as Exchange or is in a trusted domain.
- Digest authentication provides an extra level of protection by transmitting passwords over the network as hashed values.

Exchange holds all of these settings in properties that you can manipulate with the shell. To see their values, use the `Get-OwaVirtualDirectory` command. For example, the values shown in Figure 7.45 as viewed through the shell are:

```
Get-OwaVirtualDirectory —id 'owa (Default Web Site)' | Select
*auth*, *logon*

InternalAuthenticationMethods : {Basic, Fba}
ClientAuthCleanupLevel        : High
BasicAuthentication           : True
DigestAuthentication          : False
```

Figure 7.45
OWA
Authentication
Options

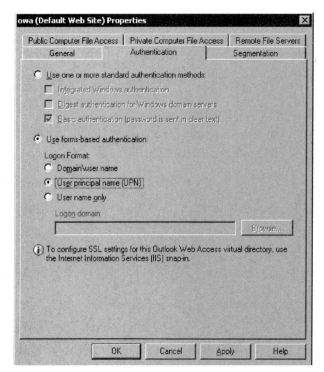

```
WindowsAuthentication              : False
FormsAuthentication                : True
ExternalAuthenticationMethods  : {Fba}
LogonFormat                        : PrincipalName
```

You can see that forms-based authentication (fba) is in use for both internal and external authentication and that the logon format is user principal name.

If multiple mechanisms are available, the client PC selects the most appropriate to use and will present the user with a standard credentials gathering dialog if it cannot find suitable credentials to use. You have to restart the IIS service to make the change effective if you enable or disable forms-based authentication. You can do this with the following shell command:

```
IISReset /Noforce
```

7.7.7 Segmentation

Segmentation is the ability to deliver selective parts of the overall Outlook Web Access client functionality to users. Application Service Providers often want to segment Outlook Web Access functionality to control the components that are available to users. For example, users who pay for calendar access can see the calendar while those who only want to use email can not. You might also decide to limit client functionality to reduce the load on the server so that all clients access the light client instead of the premium client.

Figure 7.46
*Segmenting OWA
functionality*

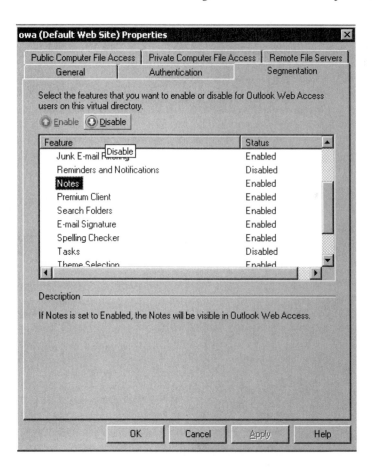

Microsoft introduced the ability to segment Outlook Web Access client functionality from Exchange 2000 SP2 onwards but never provided a user interface. Instead, you had to edit a bit mask in a value in the system registry to segment functionality on a system-wide basis or edit a user's account properties using ADSIEDIT. Either approach was highly prone to mistakes. Controlling segmentation for a server is much easier in Exchange 2007 because

EMC offers GUI support for feature selection as part of the properties of the Outlook Web Access application (Figure 7.46) running on a Client Access Server. After you make changes through EMC, Exchange stores the selected segmentation in the IIS metabase, so you have to restart IIS to force Outlook Web Access to pick up a new feature selection. The following options are available to segment Outlook Web Access client functionality:

1. Premium—disable to force users to use the light client. Note that a user can opt to use the light client (they might want to use the light client for accessibility reasons) by selecting this option through Outlook Web Access. In this case, the user-selected option overrides the option selected by the administrator.

2. Junk Email Filtering—disable to stop the user having the ability to control Junk Mail settings for their mailbox. Any settings to control junk mail filtering made from other clients such as the addition of a new safe sender are still respected by Outlook Web Access.

3. Calendar—disable access to the Calendar.

4. Contents—disable access to Contacts.

5. Notes – disable to stop users accessing the Notes folder. Outlook Web Access provides read-only access to Notes items.

6. Reminders and notifications—disable to stop Outlook Web Access polling the server for reminders and notifications and displaying these to users (premium client only).

7. Search folders – disable to stop users being able to use search folders.

8. Email signature – disable to stop Outlook Web Access displaying the option to set an email signature and to stop inserting an autosignature into new messages, even if an autosignature is set by another client (like Outlook).

9. Tasks—disable access to the Tasks folder (premium client).

10. ActiveSync—disable the ability for a user to manage their mobile devices from Outlook Web Access. For example, to wipe a lost device.

11. Address Lists—disable to block access to Exchange address lists except the GAL.

12. Spell checker – disable the option to spell check messages (premium client only).

13. Journal—disable the journal feature (premium client only).

14. Theme Selection—disable the option to allow the user to select different themes (premium client only).

15. Unified Messaging—disable the option to update unified messaging options (premium client only – only shown if user is enabled for Unified Messaging).

16. Change Password—disable the ability to change the user's Windows account password. In passing, I'll note that Outlook Web Access begins to prompt users (Figure 7.47) that their password will expire 14 days before the password actually expires. You can't change this settings as the period is hardcoded.

Figure 7.47
Outlook Web Access offers to change a password

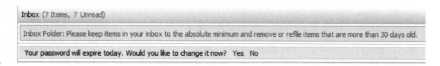

The `Set-OWAVirtualDirectory` command allows you to control these settings through the shell. You can execute this command on any computer that has the Exchange 2007 administration tools installed, providing that you have permission to administer the target computer. In this example, we disable the premium client on the Client Access server ExchCAS1:

```
Set-OWAVirtualDirectory —identity 'ExchCAS1\owa (Default Web Site)'
—PremiumClientEnabled:$False
```

If we execute the same command on the Client Access server that we want to manage, it would be sufficient to pass "owa (Default Web Site)" as the value to the identity parameter.

Like Exchange 2003, you can segment Outlook Web Access client functionality for an individual user, and if you do so, the per-user settings override the per-server settings. However, you can only make per-user settings through the shell with the `Set-CasMailbox` command. Table 7.7 lists the parameters that you can use to segment OWA functionality.

For example, this command lets the user "Bond" continue to use the premium client but restricts access to the Calendar, Notes, Journal, and Junk Mail options.

```
Set-CasMailbox —id Bond —OWAPremiumClientEnabled:$True
—OWACalendarEnabled:$False —OWANotesEnabled:$False
—OWAJournalEnabled:$False —OWAJunkMailEnabled:$False
```

Changes to segment functionality become effective after a user next logs onto Outlook Web Access or if they are logged on and inactive for 60 minutes. You can also implement changes immediately by restarting IIS on the Client Access server.

Table 7.7   *Set-CasMailbox parameters to control OWA segmentation*

Set-OWAVirtualDirectory (per-server) Parameter	Set-CasMailbox (per-mailbox) Parameter	Meaning
CalendarEnabled	OWACalendarEnabled	Controls access to the Calendar
ContactsEnabled	OWAContactsEnabled	Controls access to Contacts
TasksEnabled	OWATasksEnabled	Controls access to Tasks
JournalEnabled	OWAJournalEnabled	Controls use of the Journal feature
NotesEnabled	OWANotesEnabled	Controls access to the Notes folder
RemindersAndNotificationsEnabled	OWARemindersAndNotifications-Enabled	Controls whether OWA generates reminders of appointments and notifications of new messages
PremiumClientEnabled	OWAPremiumClientEnabled	Controls whether the premium OWA client can be used
SpellCheckerEnabled	OWASpellCheckerEnabled	Controls access to the spell checker
SearchFoldersEnabled	OWASearchFoldersEnabled	Controls access to search folders
SignaturesEnabled	OWASignaturesEnabled	Controls the ability to apply signatures to outgoing messages
ThemeSelectionEnabled	OWAThemeSelectionEnabled	Controls whether the user can select to apply different themes
JunkMailEnabled	OWAJunkMailEnabled	Controls access to the Junk Mail options
UMIntegrationEnabled	OWAUMIntegrationEnabled	Controls whether OWA loads the Unified Messaging components
WSSAccessOnPublicComputers-Enabled	OWAWSSAccessOnPublic-ComputersEnabled	Controls whether the user can access documents in WSS sites when using a public computers

Table 7.7   *Set-CasMailbox parameters to control OWA segmentation (continued)*

Set-OWAVirtualDirectory (per-server) Parameter	Set-CasMailbox (per-mailbox) Parameter	Meaning
WSSAccessOnPrivateComputers-Enabled	OWAWSSAccessOnPrivate-ComputersEnabled	Controls whether the user can access documents in WSS sites when using a private computer
UNCAccessOnPublicComputers-Enabled	OWAUNCAccessOnPublic-ComputersEnabled	Controls whether the user can access documents from file shares when using a public computer
UNCAccessOnPrivateComputers-Enabled	OWAUNCAccessOnPrivate-ComputersEnabled	Controls whether the user can access documents from file shares when using a private computer
ActiveSyncIntegrationEnabled	OWAActiveSyncIntegration-Enabled	Controls whether OWA loads the ActiveSync integration
AllAddressListsEnabled	OWAAllAddressListsEnabled	Controls whether user can see other Address Lists than the GAL.
ChangePasswordEnabled	OWAChangePasswordEnabled	Controls whether the user can set their password from OWA.

7.7.8 Notifications

Microsoft introduced the ability for Outlook Web Access clients to receive notifications about new messages and calendar events in Exchange 2003. The same basic mechanism is used to enable notifications in Exchange 2007 with the only difference being that Outlook Web Access goes through the Client Access server when it polls for new mail notifications instead of direct to the mailbox server. Notifications are supported only by the premium version and a mailbox must be enabled for this feature before it can receive notifications. You can check the ability of a mailbox to receive notifications by verifying that the Outlook Web Access notifications flag is enabled as follows:

```
Get-CasMailbox —Id Bond | Select Name,
OwaRemindersAndNotificationsEnabled
```

When Outlook Web Access connects to a mailbox that has notifications enabled, the client uses the SUBSCRIBE method to register that it wishes to receive notifications for the Inbox. A simplified form of the HTTP message sent to the server to enable new mail notification for my account is:

```
SUBSCRIBE/Exchange/Redmond/Inbox HTTP/1.1
Notification-Type: pragma/<http://schemas.microsoft.com/
exchange/newmail> Host: ExchMbxSvr1
```

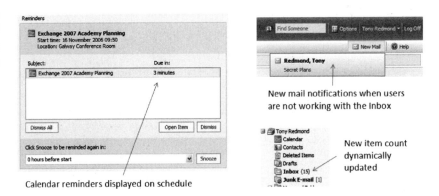

Figure 7.48
Outlook Web Access subscriptions

The request asks for a subscription on the Inbox folder that triggers notifications for new mail (and new voicemail, if you run an Exchange 2007 Unified Messaging server). In response, the server replies with an okay and gives the client a subscription identifier and a subscription lifetime (in seconds). The client must renew the subscription before it expires if it wishes to continue receiving notifications—all subscriptions taken out by Outlook Web Access have a default lifetime of one hour. It is the responsibility of the client to poll the server to receive subscription updates. The POLL command is very simple and passes the folder and subscription identifier:

```
POLL /Exchange/Redmond/Inbox
Subscription-Id: 1099
Host: Server-name
```

The response is a stream of XML data that contains reminder information. New mail notifications are straightforward – a simple indication that new mail has arrived plus the sender and message subject. Outlook Web Access displays this information when the user is not working in the Inbox (Figure 7.48). If they are working with the Inbox, then Outlook Web Access refreshes the list of messages and increments the new mail count dynamically. The light version does not support dynamic updates and folder refreshes, so you have to check for new mail before you can access these messages. In a change from previous behavior to avoid excessive network traffic, Outlook Web Access 2007 maintains a list of calendar notifications on the client PC. The list includes information about the meetings or appointments and may include multiple reminders.

By default, Outlook Web Access checks for new mail every two minutes but decreases to six minutes if the client is inactive. You can set a different default interval in seconds for new mail polling on the Client Access server with the Set-OwaVirtualDirectory command

```
Set-OwaVirtualDirectory —id "owa (Default Web Site)"
—NotificationInterval 180
```

Calendar reminders are processed differently because these are static when compared to new mail notifications. When Outlook Web Access starts up, it scans the calendar folder to detect upcoming events and creates entries for any reminders that will occur in the next day in a cache maintained on the client PC. Outlook Web Access then polls this cache to look for reminders to display rather than the Calendar folder and so avoids the network overhead. To stay up to date, Outlook Web Access updates the cache regularly, including when new calendar items are created.

7.7.9 Controlling attachments

Downloading attachments from web browsers can pose a security issue, especially for an email system that can be used on computers that people rent out for an hour or so, such as those that you find in Internet cafes or in public areas like airports or shopping malls. If users download attachments, they can end up leaving sensitive information on these PCs. In addition, they might access attachment types that you would really prefer them to avoid because the files may contain malicious content. Outlook Web Access 2007 provides administrators with a great deal of control over how users are able to access attachments that they receive. You can:

1. Allow users to open attachments of specified type using the native application for the file type. For example, use PowerPoint to open PowerPoint attachments.

2. Force users to save certain attachment types to disk before they can be opened.

3. Block unknown attachment types so that users cannot access them.

4. Force users to open attachments in a browser window using WebReady Document Viewing. This is a set of HTML transcoders that are able to render some Office document types (Word, PowerPoint, Excel) and PDF as HTML pages. Microsoft provides these transcoders with Exchange 2007[13].

5. Allow or deny users the ability to access files held on Windows file shares or Windows SharePoint Services sites.

To configure how users can deal with attachments, you access the properties of the Outlook Web Access application on a Client Access server. Exchange provides separate property pages to configure attachment handling when users access Outlook Web Access through private and public computers. Typically, your attachment policy should be looser when users work on private computers and tighter when they work on public, as obviously a greater risk exists that an attachment containing sensitive information will be compromised when if it is downloaded onto a public computer.

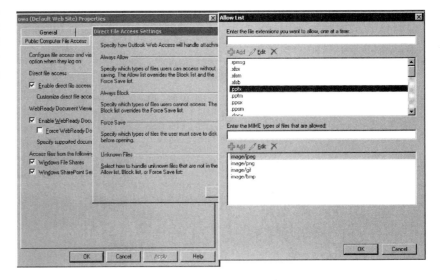

Figure 7.49
Configuring direct file access for Outlook Web Access

The Direct File Access properties allow you to specify attachment types that you will always allow the user to open with their native application, those that you always want to block, those that you will force the user to save to disk before they can process the file, and how you want to deal with unknown file types. The options for unknown file types are to allow the user to open the file, force them to save to disk, or block access com-

13.   Microsoft is working on transcoders for Office 2007 document formats that will be supported in Exchange 2007 SP1.

pletely. Figure 7.49 illustrates how you can work with the list of files that you allow users to open. As you can see, you can specify a list of file extensions (such as PPTX for PowerPoint 2007) and MIME types (such as image/bmp for bitmap images).

The WebReady Document Viewer section allows you to configure what file types you want to allow users to open in an HTML page. By default, when a user opens a message that has an attachment that supports a WebReady transcoder, they can elect to open the attachment as an HTML page (Open as Web Page option) or they can double-click on the attachment name to launch it in its native application. When you configure attachment types for WebReady Document Viewing, you can select all supported file types or focus in on a specific set. The default (shown in Figure 7.50) is to allow users to view HTML for all supported file types. You can configure Outlook Web Access to force users to view attachments as HTML pages if a transcoder is available rather than opening the file in its native application, even if you have allowed access to the file type. If you force users to view attachments as HTML, the user can save the attachment as a file and open that file afterwards. Figure 7.51 shows how Outlook Web Access renders a PDF file as an HTML page.

Figure 7.50
*Web Ready
document types*

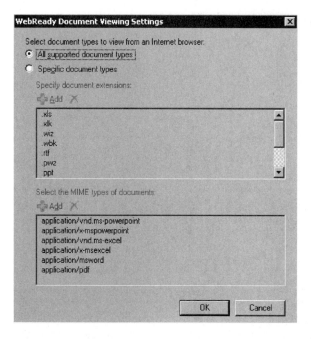

The last document access options are those that control whether Outlook Web Access will allow users to open attachments through pointers to files stored on UNC File Shares or Windows SharePoint Services (WSS) sites.

In the past, file shares were the natural information repository for a Windows infrastructure. The problem with file shares is that they quickly become completely unmanageable and this is one of the reasons why organizations welcomed public folders as they saw public folders as a replacement for shared file storage, and one that offered two major advantages in replication (so content stayed close to users) and a much better user interface in Outlook. However, as we all know, things did not work out as planned and solutions such as eRoom and Documentum gained market share.

The introduction of SharePoint Portal Server in 2001 marked a new beginning in the document management space for Microsoft. The first version of SharePoint was very attractive from an economic perspective because it was far cheaper than any other portal product on the market and while it was not well suited to the demands of large enterprise deployments, SharePoint Portal Server 2001 was great for departments. SharePoint Portal Server 2003 moved its underlying database to SQL and improved scalability and robustness and encouraged more organizations to deploy it as a document repository. The upshot of all this activity is that many documents reside on SharePoint servers. The problem is that you can only get to documents in a SharePoint site if you connect to the same network. Users can become frustrated when they receive a pointer (a URL) in a message to a document in a SharePoint site that they cannot access because they use a client like Outlook Web Access in a kiosk or a handheld device.

Document Access or "Link Access" provides one-click, read-only access to documents stored in file shares or in SharePoint sites. Outlook Web Access provides authenticated proxy access via a client access server, which connects to the repository and fetches a copy of the content to send back to the client, which then renders the information inside the browser. A user interface is also available to navigate within a set of SharePoint folders. Document access is also integrated with Outlook 2007 SharePoint folders, allowing users to copy and send links and to use links to attach files from remote servers to messages.

You can use the `Set-OwaVirtualDirectory` command to control how Outlook Web Access clients access attachments. Table 7.8 lists the parameters that you can use and their meaning.

7.7.10 Themes

Outlook Web Access supports the ability for administrators to change the basic appearance (logos and colors) of the Outlook Web Access user interface by altering the style sheet and graphic files that Outlook Web Access uses to build the interface. Outlook Web Access 2007 improves this feature by making it easier for administrators to implement a custom theme. Note that you can only customize the premium version of Outlook Web Access. You cannot customize the basic client.

Figure 7.51
Viewing a PDF attachment through a WebReady transcoder

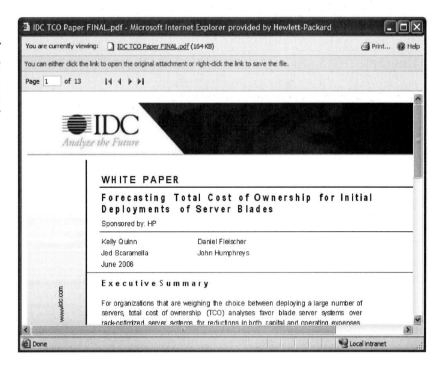

Table 7.8 *Parameters to control Outlook Web Access file handling*

Parameter	Meaning
DirectFileAccessOnPublicComputersEnabled	If true, allow access to attachments when using a public computer.
DirectFileAccessOnPrivateComputersEnabled	If true, allow access to attachments when using a private computer.
WebReadyDocumentViewingOnPublicComputersEnabled	If true, allow web-ready document viewing when using a public computer.
WebReadyDocumentViewingOnPrivateComputersEnabled	If true, allow web-ready document viewing when using a private computer.
ForceWebReadyDocumentViewingFirstOnPublicComputers	If true, force web-ready viewing on public computers if a viewer is available.
ForceWebReadyDocumentViewingFirstOnPrivateComputers	If true, force web-ready viewing on private computers if a viewer is available.
RemoteDocumentsActionForUnknownServers	Allow or deny access to attachments from an unknown server.

Table 7.8　*Parameters to control Outlook Web Access file handling (continued)*

Parameter	Meaning
ActionForUnknownFileAndMIMETypes	Action to perform for attachments of unknown file and MIME formats that are not in the allowed list (default is to force user to save).
WebReadyDocumentViewingSupportedFileTypes	List of attachment file types supported for web-ready viewing.
WebReadyDocumentViewingSupportedMimeTypes	List of MIME formats supported for web-ready viewing
WebReadyDocumentViewingForAllSupportedTypes	If true, use web ready viewing for all supported file types. If false, use a selective list.
WebReadyMimeTypes	Selective list of MIME formats used for web-ready viewing.
WebReadyFileTypes	Selective list of attachment file types used for web-ready viewing.
AllowedFileTypes	List of attachment file types that a user can access without saving. Allow lists override the Block and Force Save lists.
AllowedMimeTypes	List of MIME formats that a user can access without saving.
ForceSaveFileTypes	List of attachment file types that a user must save before they can access content.
ForceSaveMimeTypes	List of MIME formats that a user must save before they can access content.
BlockedFileTypes	List of blocked attachment file types. The block list overrides the Force Save list.
BlockedMimeTypes	List of blocked MIME formats.
RemoteDocumentsBlockedServers	List of remote servers that users cannot download files from.
RemoteDocumentsAllowedServers	List of remote servers that users can download files from.
RemoteDocumentsInternalDomainSuffixList	List of domains that Outlook Web Access should consider as internal. This list is used for WSS sites and UNC file shares.

Out of the box, Exchange ships with three themes. You can find the files for each theme in a separate folder. The folders are arranged under the \themes folder in the \owa folder. The default themes are:

- The base theme, known as "Seattle Sky" and with a blue color—this is in the \base folder.

- The black theme, known as "Carbon Black"—this is in the \1 folder.

- The mountain theme, known as "Olympic Sunrise"—this is in the \2 folder.

OWA builds a complete theme by taking custom files and layering them on top of the base files. Thus, you only have to change a single file to replace Microsoft's logo with your own design. Things get more complex when you want to change complete color schemes to comply with the palette that your company favors, but the basic point is that you don't have to do much work to create a new theme. Here's how.

- First, create a new folder under \themes. Give the folder the same name as the name of the theme you want to create. In my case, I wanted to call it "Tony's theme."

- Now copy the premium.css (the style sheet file for the Premium client) and logopt.gif from the \base folder into your new folder. You don't actually need to copy the premium.css file unless you want to change one of the colors used by Outlook Web Access.

- Edit logopt.gif to remove the Microsoft logo and replace it with your own. I used the standard Paint utility, but you'll want to use a more comprehensive graphic editor like PhotoShop to do a proper job. Don't change the size of the graphic because Outlook Web Access fits it in with other files to form the top of its title bar.

- Restart IIS to force IIS to load the new files.

- Select the new theme from Outlook Web Access and you'll see the change to the logo as shown in Figure 7.52. It's as simple as that!

Figure 7.52

A quick change to the OWA heading

There are other changes that you can make to customize the Outlook Web Access user interface. For details, see the information about building themes in TechNet or the articles that the Exchange development team has published on their blog. There is no way (automatic or manual) to convert a theme built for use with Outlook Web Access in Exchange 2003 to code that works with Exchange 2007, so if you have any Exchange 2003 themes, you will have to build new code.

7.7.11　Client settings

Outlook clients store many user settings in MAPI profiles in the system registry. This option is not open to Outlook Web Access because the whole idea is that users can move from PC to PC and use a web browser to access their mailbox. The solution is to hold user properties and settings for Outlook Web Access in an XML-formatted hidden item in the root of the user mailbox. Previous versions of Outlook Web Access used individual properties that were set on the mailbox itself and administrators could configure and manage these properties with interfaces such as CDO or WebDAV. Some settings remain properties of the mailbox because they are shared with other clients. For example, Outlook and Outlook Web Access share the Junk Mail Filter settings and these have to be available no matter what client you want to use.

A tool such as Outlook Spy allows you to view the contents of the XML item (called OWA.UserOptions). Outlook Web Access stores a number of other hidden XML items to hold data in user mailboxes such as the list of previously used addresses (OWA.AutoCompleteCache) and the set of recently used folders (OWA.FolderMRUCache).

By default, Outlook Web Access does not display public folder hierarchies, which underlines the reduced role of public folders accorded by Exchange 2007. Of course, many companies are still in a position where they have lots of information in public folders and no good way to migrate to a new repository, which means that they have to keep a public folder server within the organization. In this case, Outlook Web Access supports public folders through redirection via the Client Access server. You can continue to use URLs to public folders (such as http://server-name/public) as the Client Access server recognizes the public root and will redirect to the correct server.

7.8　Internet client access protocols

MAPI is the most functional client access protocol for Exchange, but access via MAPI is limited to clients produced by Microsoft (Outlook). If you want to use a non-MAPI client to access Exchange that is not a web browser, you have to use one of the Internet client access protocols supported by Exchange: POP3 (Post Office Protocol version 3) or IMAP4 (Internet Mail Access Protocol version 4). These protocols allow you to accommodate clients on non-Microsoft platforms, such as Linux, UNIX, and Macintosh and handheld clients that cannot connect to Exchange via ActiveSync. IMAP4 is the more functional access protocol and it is the one that is most used today. POP3 is a throwback to a simpler time for email when all users wanted to do was pick up their messages from a server. Because it is such a basic protocol and IMAP offers the same type of connectivity with a better feature set, POP3 is of little real interest to the Exchange community today and I do not know many people who use POP3 to connect to Exchange.

Exchange deals with all clients through a common funnel (the Store). Non-MAPI clients tend to generate a reduced load on the Store because they use fewer threads to connect to the Store and execute a smaller set of functions, so at first glance you could argue that it is better for performance to use non-MAPI clients. However, this argument does not take into account the on-the-wire smarts and drizzle-mode synchronization that Outlook uses to reduce load on the server, so there's not much of a difference in reality. The challenge for administrators is to support (or control) the proliferation of client types and protocols that users want to connect to Exchange. It is much easier to support a single client-type, even if, like Outlook, you have to deal with different versions of the client. It is much harder to support a mixed-client population of different types, versions, and capabilities.

When you move from simple email and want to support the use of non-Microsoft clients with Exchange for calendaring and other extended features, you will find that the Internet client access protocols do not deliver enough to support these features. Other standards, such as iCal for calendar items, are necessary to achieve a broad range of interoperability between Outlook and non-Microsoft clients. In these situations, either you can wait for Microsoft to deliver support for the protocols you require or continue to use your non-Microsoft email client to access Exchange to pick up and send email, and then use Outlook Web Access for the extended features, including setting user options such as Out of Office notices. It is not a perfect solution by any means, but it is reasonably pragmatic.

7.8.1 IMAP4

In my experience, you can connect just about any IMAP client to Exchange. Outlook Express is the most widely deployed IMAP alongside Exchange because it is cheap (free) and easily available. Outlook Express is the standard mail reader provided for Windows. It ships and installs with Internet Explorer. Outlook Express is a reasonably feature-rich email client, so it offers a combination of acceptable functionality at a great price point. There are many other IMAP clients for Windows including Thunderbird and the ever-popular Eudora and Eudora Pro, and there is a growing demand for connections from the IMAP clients that mobile devices increasingly support, including Apple Inc.'s new Apple iPhone.

Outlook Express and Outlook share a number of components, including the HTML rendering engine[14] and the IMAP protocol stack, but you cannot compare the two clients in terms of their breadth of functionality. Outlook is a much better Personal Information Manager (PIM) that you can customize in terms of electronic forms and application code whereas Outlook Express is really just an email and newsgroups client. It used to be true that Outlook Express was a better choice to use over low-bandwidth or high-latency connections because it did not have to deal with RPC timeouts and generated less network traffic to fetch and send messages, but Outlook 2003 or 2007 are equally capable across these types of connections now.

Figure 7.53
Configuring Outlook Express to connect to Exchange

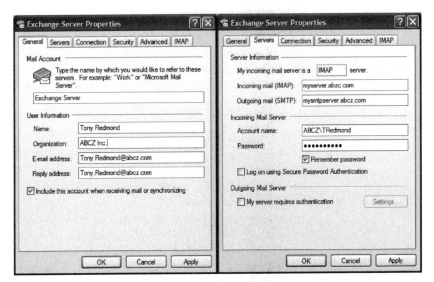

As shown in Figure 7.53, configuring Outlook Express to connect to Exchange is straightforward. Unless your mailbox is on a multi-role server, you need the name of a Client Access server in the same Active Directory site that hosts the server where your mailbox is located. The new role of the Client Access server is likely to be the thing that catches most administrators who have to support IMAP clients immediately after the migration, but it does become second nature gradually.

Input the name of the Client Access server as the server that you want to connect to via IMAP. You also need to know what SMTP server to use to relay outgoing messages, and your NT account credentials. You also need to configure access to the Active Directory if you want to look up email addresses or validate addresses before you send messages. The default option for IMAP clients is to access Exchange using port 143. Up to Exchange

14.   By comparison, Outlook 2007 uses the Word HTML engine to render HTML content.

2003, this is probably the way that most servers are configured. Exchange 2007 is secure by default, so the server uses secure connections for clients whenever possible, so it is more likely that you will connect using SSL to port 993, as shown in Figure 7.54. IMAP clients can work both offline and online, similar in some respects to Outlook. However, IMAP offline access is not the same as Outlook's cached Exchange mode—it is much more like the way that older versions of Outlook synchronize specific folders down to the client and then connect to send and receive messages on an on-demand or scheduled basis. Outlook Express and other IMAP clients offer rules processing and junk mail filters like Outlook, but they are generally not as customizable in terms of electronic forms or deployment options.

Figure 7.54
IMAP Advanced
Options

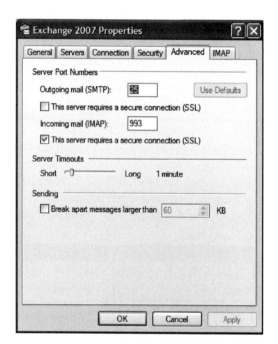

POP3 clients, by comparison, use port 110 as default or port 995 for secured SSL connections. The big difference between POP, which is now a very elderly email protocol, and almost any other way of connecting to an email server, is that POP clients usually connect and download all messages to the client before users can access them. Unless configured otherwise, POP clients do not leave messages on the server, which is something that can be a real problem if you move from workstation to workstation or want to use different clients to access your mailbox.

Exchange 2000 and 2003 both provide support for IMAP clients to access the contents of public folders (Figure 7.55), including the ability to download content from public folders for offline use. This feature disappears

Figure 7.55
*IMAP access to
public folders,
but not in
Exchange 2007*

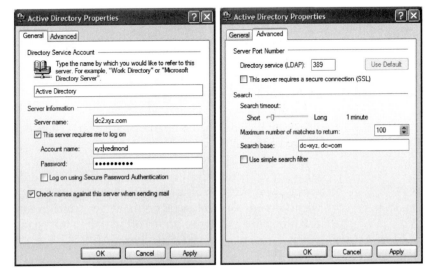

in Exchange 2007 and you can no longer use an IMAP client to access public folders. The workaround is to use Outlook Web Access if you need to support people who cannot use Outlook and still need to get to information held in public folders. Exchange 2007 supports TLS encryption and Kerberos authentication, so connecting non-Windows clients is easier to secure.

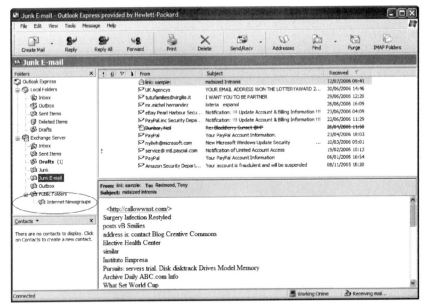

You can use the Active Directory as an LDAP directory service for IMAP (and POP) clients. When you configure Outlook Express to use the Active Directory (Figure 7.56), you have to provide the name of a Global Catalog server for the client to connect to, credentials to use, and the LDAP search base to use. By default, Outlook Express includes an entry for the Active Directory in the set of prepackaged directory services and you have to update the default settings to provide valid options for your environment. Active Directory services LDAP lookups using port number (389). You should not have to change the search timeout value (1 minute) or the maximum number of results to return from a search (100) as these values work well in most circumstances. Like any other LDAP search, it is possible to generate a lookup that causes the client to freeze and the directory server to do a lot of work. For example, looking for all accounts where the first name is "John" in any reasonably sized directory is enough to prove the point!

After you configure Outlook Express for LDAP access to the Active Directory, you can use Active Directory to check email addresses before sending messages (you can use the CTRL/K shortcut) or to look for people through the find option in the Outlook Express address book or the Find People option. Figure 7.57 illustrates the search dialog used by the Find People option together with the result of a search for any user whose name contains the string "Tony." This kind of search completes fast against a small directory, but it's exactly the kind of vague search that could last forever if executed against a large directory (more than 50,000 objects).

7.8.2   The Exchange 2007 IMAP server

IMAP clients access Exchange through an IMAP virtual server. Every Exchange 2000 and 2003 server supports a default IMAP virtual server to allow IMAP clients to connect, but only Exchange 2007 Client Access servers support IMAP connections. In some respects, connecting via IMAP is easier with Exchange 2000 or 2003 because all you need to do is to point the IMAP client at the server that holds your mailbox. As we have seen with Exchange 2007, you have to configure the client to point to a Client Access server that you may not know exists!

However, even though the IMAP server is straightforward, it is still interesting to look behind the scenes to determine whether it is worthwhile to tweak any of the server's properties. Use the Get-IMAPSettings command to discover what properties exist for the default IMAP virtual server on a specified Client Access server:

Figure 7.57
*Active Directory
search from
Outlook Express*

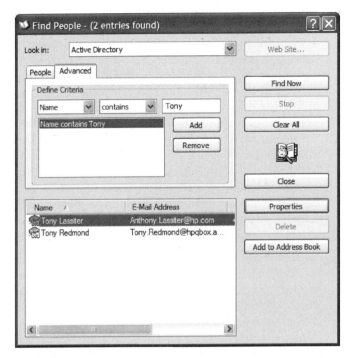

```
Get-IMAPSettings —Server ExchCAS1


ProtocolName                          : IMAP4
Name                                  : 1
MaxCommandSize                        : 10240
ShowHiddenFoldersEnabled              : False
UnencryptedOrTLSBindings              : {0.0.0.0:143}
SSLBindings                           : {0.0.0.0:993}
X509CertificateName                   : ExchCAS1
Banner                                : Microsoft Exchange Server 2007 IMAP4 service
ready
LoginType                             : SecureLogin
AuthenticatedConnectionTimeout        : 00:30:00
PreAuthenticatedConnectionTimeout     : 00:01:00
MaxConnections                        : 2000
MaxConnectionFromSingleIP             : 20
MaxConnectionsPerUser                 : 10
MessageRetrievalMimeFormat            : BestBodyFormat
ProxyTargetPort                       : 143
CalendarItemRetrievalOption           : iCalendar
```

```
ExchangeVersion                  : 0.1 (8.0.535.0)
Identity                         : ExchCAS1\1
Guid                             : 30893ecd-e4e9-444f-8ad5-783601246ff2
ObjectCategory                   : xyz.com/Configuration/Schema/ms-Exch-
Protocol-Cfg-IMAP-Server
ObjectClass                      : {top, protocolCfg, protocolCfgIMAP,
protocolCfgIMAPServer}
```

You can use the `Set-IMAPSettings` command to change any of these properties. For example, to change the banner that greets clients when they connect interactively:

```
Set-IMAPSettings —Server ExchCAS1 —Banner 'Welcome to the Friendly
IMAP Service' —MessageRetrievalMIMEFormat 2
—AuthenticatedConnectionTimeOut 00:15:00
—PreAuthenticatedConnectionTimeOut 00:00:45 —MaxConnections 4000
```

Table 7.9 lists the most interesting properties of an Exchange 2007 IMAP server and their meaning.

Table 7.9   *Properties of Exchange 2007 IMAP server*

IMAP Server property	Meaning
Name	The default IMAP server hosted by a Client Access Server is always named "1."
MaxCommandSize	Sets the maximum size of a single command acceptable to the IMAP server.
ShowHiddenFoldersEnabled	Some IMAP clients support hidden folders. The default for this setting, meaning that Exchange doesn't reveal hidden folders.
SSLBindings	Defines the IP port to use for a Secure Sockets Layer connection. The default is 993.
X509CertificateName	Specifies the host name (Exchange server) in the SSL certificate from the Associated Subject field.
Banner	Sets the welcoming message that clients see when they connect successfully to the IMAP server.

Table 7.9   *Properties of Exchange 2007 IMAP server (continued)*

IMAP Server property	Meaning
LoginType	Specifies the login method required by the server. The default is SecureLogin, but you can set the following values: 1. PlainTextLogin 2. PlainTextAuthentication 3. SecureLogin
AuthenticatedConnectionTimeOut	The period in time that Exchange waits before terminating an authenticated connection. The default is 30 minutes and the supported range is from 30 seconds to 24 hours.
PreAuthenticatedConnectionTime-Out	The period that Exchange waits before terminating a nonauthenticated connection. The default is 60 seconds and the supported range is from 10 seconds to an hour.
MaxConnections	The maximum number of connections that the server will accept. The default is 2,000 and the range is from 1 to 25,000.
MaxConnectionFromSingleIP	The maximum number of connections that the server will accept from a single IP address. The default is 20 and the range is from 1 to 1,000.
MaxConnectionsPerUser	The maximum number of connections that the server will accept for a single mailbox. The default is 10 and the range is from 1 to 1,000.
MessageRetrievalMimeFormat	Determines the format that the IMAP server provides messages to clients in. The default value is "BestBodyFormat," which means that the server attempts to provide the client with the highest fidelity of message that it believes the client can accept. Use 2 or 6 for Outlook Express clients. You can set the following values: 0 = Text Only 1= HTML Only 2 = HTML and Text 3 = Rich Text Only 4 = UUEncode 5 = UUEncodeBinHex 6 = BestBodyFormat

Table 7.9   *Properties of Exchange 2007 IMAP server (continued)*

IMAP Server property	Meaning
ProxyTargetPort	
CalendarItemRetrievalOption	

The commands to deal with the default POP3 virtual server on an Exchange 2007 Client Access server are `Get-POPSettings` and `Set-POPSettings` function in the same manner as `Get-IMAPSettings` and `Set-IMAPSettings`. If you make changes to the POP3 or IMAP4 settings, you have to stop and restart the Microsoft Exchange POP3 or IMAP4 Service before the new settings come into effect.

In addition to the POP3 and IMAP4 settings available through PowerShell, Exchange maintains two configuration files that you can change to alter the behavior of these services. If you look into the \Program Files\Microsoft\Exchange Server\ClientAccess\PopImap directory, you can see the files:

- Microsoft.Exchange.Imap4exe.Config—IMAP4 server configuration
- Microsoft.Exchange.Pop3exe.Config—POP3 server configuration

These configuration files are similar in format and use to the transport configuration file that we met in Chapter 6. Common examples of the kind of changes that you can make include:

To enable logging of all client activity (useful for debugging client connection problems) the following.

```
<add key="ProtocolLog" value="false" />
```

To allow clients to connect to a Client Access server even if their mailboxes are located on a server in another Active Directory site. This may be useful if you maintain a central Client Access server that serves many different sites:

```
<add key="AllowCrossSiteSessions" value="false" />
```

See the TechNet documentation for more details about the changes that you can make to the IMAP4 and POP3 configuration files. Configuring

Exchange's IMAP4 and POP3 virtual servers will be easier in Exchange 2007 SP1 because Microsoft plans to upgrade the EMC console to provide the UI to allow you to set server properties without having to resort to shell commands.

7.9   Mobile clients

We have seen an explosion of mobility since 2000. An administrator who took care of an Exchange server in 2000 might have to accommodate the mobility requirements of a few executives, but this was the exception rather than the rule. Handheld devices were not common, the connection costs were expensive, and functionality was not particularly great. Email worked, but synchronization was not perfect, especially around the calendar. The devices available in 2000 included the first BlackBerries, Palm devices, and early Pocket PCs. Phones were not smart, so we did not think about connecting them to Exchange except through SMS (Short Message Service) connectors that were mostly popular in Europe. Networks were slow and getting messages delivered to a handheld inbox was about all you could expect.

Given the number of mobile devices in use today from SmartPhones to BlackBerries to PDAs of all shapes and sizes and the fact that messaging, calendar, tasks, and notes are all popular applications for these devices, the need clearly exists for Microsoft to support the use of a wide range of handheld devices with Exchange. Engineers have worked through the technical difficulties and the devices are slim enough, powerful enough, intelligent enough, and robust enough to be a solid mobile platform for most users. Best of all, network speed continues to improve all the time and we are no longer limited by the anemic throughput of the original cellular networks, as high-speed variants such as EDGE (Enhanced Data rates for GSM Evolution, 100–150 kbps throughput) and EVDO (Evolution Data Optimized, 800kbps–1Mbps throughput) spread. We also have an increasing range of connection options available through metropolitan wireless networks. Even the backup service of GPRS (General Packet Radio Service) is enough to get the mail through, and as the network providers continue to invest to deploy newer technologies, we can expect a steady increase in network performance and capability.

Up to and including the time that Microsoft released Exchange 2003, third-party technology provided the necessary components to connect mobile devices to Exchange and companies such as RIM (www.rim.net) and Good Technologies (www.good.com) built large businesses around the ability to connect to and synchronize with Exchange. Microsoft then stepped into the game with the first release of the Exchange Mobile Services subsystem in Exchange 2003. Microsoft recognized the importance of the mobile market and the rapid increase in features and functionality in mobile devices by putting huge development resources into this part of Exchange ever since. The result is that the support provided by Exchange for mobile devices is now very competitive because of a rich feature set and the little additional cost required in supporting mobile devices once you have deployed the infrastructure to support Exchange. It is also worth noting that Microsoft is very proactive in licensing its Exchange ActiveSync technology to mobile device suppliers such as Nokia, Palm One, DataViz, Motorola, and Symbian.

Exchange 2003 supports mobile devices in two ways: Exchange Active-Sync Services (EAS) and Outlook Mobile Access (OMA). The two methods are very different in the way that they work and the devices that they aim to support. EAS is the full-function access method that devices such as the Pocket PC use. EAS devices use a local cache to store data, which means that you can read and process email without a network connection. OMA provides lightweight access to a restricted set of folders with limited functionality, but it covers a far wider array of devices. OMA never caches data locally and always requires a connection to the server to read and send email.

Microsoft sometimes refers to EAS as the high-fidelity choice (because of the extended feature set); another way to look at the two clients is to compare them to Outlook (EAS) and the reach variant of Outlook Web Access (OMA). Outlook is the full-feature client that uses a sophisticated protocol (MAPI) to communicate with Exchange and supports offline access to your mailbox, but you need to run Outlook on a well-equipped Windows device. The light version of Outlook Web Access runs on anything from a kiosk device and allows access to a restricted feature set. Both clients allow you to read and send email. While OMA had its unique selling point in its ability to provide Exchange data to any handheld device that supported a minimal browser, it was never very successful in the real world and its lack of success coupled with Microsoft's focus on ActiveSync as the future of handheld connections to Exchange led Microsoft to decommit from OMA in Exchange 2007.

To underline the improvement in Microsoft's mobile technology since 2003, it was interesting to see the arrival of the Windows Mobile 5.0–based Treo 700w PDA in early 2006 as this device marked the movement of the long-time major rival for Microsoft into the Windows camp. The net effect of all this licensing and platform development activity is that we have a wide array of devices that can connect to Exchange already and more arrive all the time. For example, a look at Dataviz's web site at http://www.dataviz.com reveals a rich set of mobile devices that you can connect to Exchange using a mixture of EAS and their RoadSync product[15]. Of course, the variety of choice in handheld devices that exists is a double-edged sword for administrators; users love the choice of available devices and naturally buy the phone, Pocket PC, or other form factor of handheld that attracts their attention.

---

15. RoadSync is a good alternative to Pocket Outlook.

Sometimes the look and feel of the device rather than its functionality influences their choice. Users then look to the IT department to connect the devices to Exchange. On the other hand, administrators want devices that are simple to connect to Exchange, straightforward to secure, and easy to support. Administrators usually prefer to restrict users to a certain set of handheld devices that they know to work well with their IT infrastructure. These aspects do not often factor in user choice and the result is a certain tension between the desire of users and the ability of the IT department to support that desire.

Not all Windows Mobile 5.0 devices are created equal. To work with Exchange 2003 or 2007, you need Windows Mobile 5.0 and the MSFP (Microsoft Messaging and Security Feature Pack) as this code adds not only the basic email and calendar access but also the necessary security features to allow Exchange ActiveSync to function in an enterprise messaging environment. You can download the MSFP from Microsoft's web site, but it is far more preferable to purchase devices that come with MSFP integrated out of the box. As we will see in just a few pages, Windows Mobile 6.0 devices are now available. These devices deliver the best performance and functionality when connected to an Exchange 2007 server, so they should be your device standard if possible.

Table 7.10 lists some of the features that you can use to compare the different ways to connect mobile devices into Exchange. For example, you may believe that native support for Microsoft Office documents on the mobile device is critical—in other words, that you can read a Word document or Excel worksheet on the device and see all the content and formatting. This is a desirable feature, but only if you are able to read and navigate through formatted documents with the small screen that equips so many mobile devices. In some cases, the approach taken by the Blackberry Enterprise Server, which converts Office documents to text before transmitting them to the device, saves some bandwidth and creates more readable text. However, in other cases, the conversion mangles the content and creates an interesting challenge for the reader to determine exactly what is in the document.

7.9.1 Selecting mobile devices

The choice of mobile device is very personal and as devices change all the time, your options change all the time. Some users will never move away from laptops because they like the richness of the environment and believe that a phone should be a phone and nothing else. On the other hand, many people like the Windows-based SmartPhone because this device is closest to the standard phone format. The SmartPhone supports a form of Windows, so they can run applications like GPS locators and maps as well as Mobile Office. These users do not require a full keyboard or any of the other extended options that often come with Pocket PCs because they place more

Table 7.10 *Mobile support features*

Feature	Desired Functionality
Authentication and network security	Username and password or certificate-based authentication or both to secure network traffic between devices and Exchange.
Synchronization	Ability to synchronize messages (Inbox and other folders), calendar items, tasks, and other Outlook data to and from the mobile device using pull or push update mechanism.
Support for Microsoft Office and other common document types such as PDF	Ability to read Microsoft Word, Excel, and PowerPoint files with or without server-based conversion to text.
Directory lookup	Ability to search and/or browse the GAL to validate email addresses.
Device security	Ability to wipe or erase personal data from device if it is lost or stolen; ability to wipe data from storage on device.
Range of supported devices	Example devices: ■ Smartphone ■ Pocket PC (PDA) ■ Proprietary device such as a BlackBerry ■ Mobile device with integrated Black-Berry/Good client
Connectivity	Range of supported network connections (Wi-Fi, GSM, GPRS, EDGE, EVDO, 3G, etc.)
Data store encryption	The ability for administrators to selectively encrypt all or part of the data held on mobile devices.

importance on the phone features and use the messaging capability as a triage device to know when an important message has arrived that they have to deal with. Users of the Pocket PC are often email-centric in their approach to communications and some that I know even use a separate cell phone (something that I think is a little odd) to make phone calls. If you are like me and select a Pocket PC or similar PDA-type device, you probably view messaging as a prime concern and want to keep up to date with a busy inbox. You probably also want the ability to compose more complex messages than you might attempt on the truncated keypad of a cell phone. Some cell phone providers can duplicate SIM cards so that you can put SIMs into several devices and carry a Pocket PC to process email and a Windows SmartPhone to use as your phone, if that's a good solution for you. In this case, calls go to both devices and both devices can synchronize with Exchange. No one device available today is capable of satisfying all the needs of the different types of users and I suspect that we'll be arguing about what device format is best for quite a few years yet. However, the good point is that you can deploy and manage a single infrastructure that supports many types of mobile device, so you can allow a certain amount of user choice.

As part of your deployment strategy for mobile devices, you should consider what kind of replacement cycle to deploy. Many devices that have been released in the past cannot be updated with new versions of handheld operating systems and applications. Sometimes this is because of technical limitations in the device or new requirements from the operating system; sometimes the inability to upgrade is linked to the cellular provider that you use. In any case, you need to review new releases of devices and operating systems to ensure that you can advise users whether your infrastructure can support the devices or upgrade existing devices with new software, or if you need to replace devices completely.

Cell phones have reached a stage where many consumers consider them as fashion items that should be replaced on almost an annual basis. It is not inconceivable that the same will happen with mobile devices. Of course, if users are willing to fund the upgrade or replacement of devices, then you should not have a problem—provided the infrastructure can support the new devices. However, such a situation is unlikely and it is more common for companies to establish a policy for device renewal, including the replacement of lost devices, and to set aside the necessary budget to test, qualify, and provide these devices to users.

7.9.2   Server-based ActiveSync

Until Exchange 2003 SP2, EAS was firmly in the cheap and cheerful category for mobile solutions. Its low cost was undeniable, but it suffered from a lack of functionality in some important areas. This situation has now changed and the functionality available to Pocket PC and SmartPhone clients through the combination of Windows Mobile 5.0 and EAS is sufficient for consideration by any company that wants to deploy mobile messaging to its workforce. In fact, because EAS leverages the infrastructure that you have to deploy to support features such as RPC over HTTP (ISA proxy servers and Exchange front-end servers), you can argue that EAS is essentially free of charge when compared to the additional infrastructure that you have to deploy for other solutions such as BlackBerry and GoodLink.

To go along with the improved messaging delivered by Windows Mobile 5.0, Microsoft added the following features in Exchange 2003 SP2:

- Data compression for ActiveSync connections over HTTPS using GZIP.

- Connection pooling to reduce the overhead of creating a connection between devices and network carriers.

- Certificate-based authentication.

- Security policy enforcement.

- GAL search and real-time address validation against the GAL.

- Better AUTD (always up to date) synchronization.

While it is nice to see new features delivered by EAS and in the latest version of Windows Mobile, many handheld devices are impossible to upgrade to the latest release of Windows Mobile and so cannot take advantage of the new features. It is difficult enough to upgrade a Pocket PC to a new patch release of Windows Mobile (you lose all your settings, the upgrade can only occur when the device is connected to a PC via a cradle, and the upgrade takes a long time), but moving to a brand new version causes even more difficulties. Perhaps this is because of the close connection between the hardware and the operating system, or maybe it is because handheld devices are essentially time-limited electronics that you should be prepared to upgrade ever couple of years, just like regular cell phones. The need to upgrade devices to use new features is definitely something that you need to consider when you decide how to deploy and support mobility within an organization.

AUTD is a mechanism to allow EAS to provide information to a mobile device when new information is available in a mailbox. Microsoft sometimes describes AUTD as equivalent to the way that BlackBerry and GoodLink servers push information to a device, but AUTD is really a pull mechanism that depends on server notifications to the mobile device to tell it that new data is ready for it to pull down the next time that it connects to Exchange.

From Exchange 2003 SP2 onwards, AUTD uses persistent TCP/IP connections to send notifications to devices rather than SMS (Short Message Service) messages, which helps to drive down connection costs because it is all too easy to run up a big bill through SMS message traffic, unless you have a subscription with unlimited SMS messages. In the background, messages flowed from Exchange to the mobile operator via SMTP, which then converted the SMTP traffic into SMS messages for onward delivery to the device. Apart from the cost of all the SMS messages, not all mobile operators supported an SMTP to SMS gateway, so they could not provide EAS to their subscribers.

In most cases, SMS got the messages through, albeit at a price. Microsoft changed AUTD in Exchange 2003 SP2 to use a much smarter and effective mechanism that they call "direct push." You might assume from this name that it is possible to push all kinds of data to the handheld, but in some respects, the name is more of a marketing term than anything else because EAS sends only notifications to the handheld, which synchronizes with the user's mailbox as a consequence of receiving a notification that new mail is present to be picked up.

In the direct-push environment, the handheld initiates an HTTPS connection to the server over a GPRS or other connection (that can carry the IP traffic, such as an EDGE connection) across the cell phone network, through your firewall,[16] to a front-end server that eventually connects to the Exchange server that hosts the user mailbox. To make the direct-push mechanism work, the front-end servers must run Exchange 2003 SP2 at a minimum, although the back-end mailbox servers can run older versions until they can be upgraded to Exchange 2007. The handheld uses the EAS "PING" command to establish the connection, and during the connection process, the handheld passes parameter data to the server that is registered in a document called AUTDSTATE.XML that is hidden in the user's mailbox so that the handheld does not have to continually update these settings during the course of a connection session. The device only updates AUTD-STATE.XML if the connection parameters change, for example, if the user decides to synchronize a new folder down to the handheld, an action that requires the handheld to transmit a new folders list to the server. The connection is maintained for an interval known as the "heartbeat," which is one of the parameters stored in AUTDSTATE.XML, and the client is capable of dynamically changing its own heartbeat according to network conditions such as firewall or operator network timeouts. Generally speaking, the higher the heartbeat interval, the better it is for handheld battery life because the handheld generates less interaction with the server. If required, you can change the minimum and maximum heartbeat intervals on the mailbox server by setting the MinHeartbeatInterval (minimum value of 1) and Max-HeartbeatInterval (to a maximum value of 59) under the HKLM\Current-ControlSet\Services\MasSync\Parameters registry key. In most cases, the default values work well and you can ignore these settings.

Over a period of time, the client will destroy and renew the connection as it needs to continue email flowing. Exchange uses the connection to send notifications of new messages to the handheld and to deliver the content of the messages and their attachments when the handheld chooses to synchro-

---

16.   See Microsoft Knowledge Base article 905013 for more information about configuring firewalls to use with EAS.

nize. Once a connection is established, the handheld sends a request to Exchange via HTTPS to register a DAV subscription request for updates to the inbox and any other folders that the user has marked for synchronization. The server registers the DAV subscriptions in the same way that Outlook Web Access registers notifications for new mail and calendar updates when you use it to log on to a mailbox. The request specifies a time interval (typically 15 minutes—the maximum allowed value is 59 minutes as the maximum DAV subscription is an hour) and the folders that the device wishes to monitor (typically Inbox, Calendar, Contacts, and Tasks). Exchange completes the initial part of the connection process by checking all registered folders to see if any data changes occurred between the start and end of the registration process. If the server detects a change, the server tells the handheld to initiate synchronization to retrieve the information.

Direct-push email doesn't work over a Wi-Fi connection on a Windows Mobile 5.0 device. Microsoft disabled this ability deliberately because Windows Mobile 5.0 turns Wi-Fi off automatically (to save battery life) when the device enters sleep mode. Windows Mobile 6.0 devices have a different implementation of Wi-Fi networking, so direct-mode email works with these devices.

Pocket Outlook allows users to specify what folders they want to synchronize. If data changes in these folders during the heartbeat interval, Exchange sends a UDP packet to port 2883[17] on the front-end server that the mobile device connects through and the front end server uses its open HTTP connection to relay the notification to the device. Once the device receives the notification, it issues a synchronization request back to Exchange to retrieve the new data and then sets up a new subscription. If Exchange has no updates for the device during the time interval, Exchange sends a "no data" message to the device, which can then respond to Exchange by setting up a new subscription request. Many components along the network path can interfere with the heartbeat, including carrier limitations on the duration of connections that they allow, so it's not always possible to accurately predict how the devices and Exchange connect. Indeed, moving from one cell to another in a metropolitan area can produce a great connection in one place and a dropped connection in another.

Communications between the device and Exchange are short in nature and do not consume much power, which is all-important in terms of extending battery life. Unless mail is flowing to and from the device all the time, the device can stay in a low-power listening mode rather than having to constantly poll for new messages, and because everything happens across HTTP, administrators do not have to configure anything special on the firewall.

---

17.   You can change the default port by updating the UDPListenPort value in HKLM\SYSTEM\CurrentControlSet\Services\ MasSync\Parameters in the registry.

If the network connection (such as a wireless or GPRS link) times out or is broken by the device shutting down or moving in and out of coverage, the device can reestablish communications and restart its connection to Exchange. Pocket Outlook also supports a Send/Receive function to allow the user to connect and fetch messages when they want. GPRS devices consume power only when they transmit, so the AUTD mechanism is more power efficient than if the device had to poll Exchange for updates regularly. Your mileage will vary, but some users report that they have a 20% to 30% increase in battery life with Windows Mobile 5.0 devices.

7.10 Windows Mobile 6.0 and Exchange 2007

Software that does not evolve is uncompetitive in today's market. With its focus on spreading Windows to as many devices as possible, Microsoft continues to evolve Windows Mobile. The Windows Mobile 6.0 or "Crossbow" release is the follow-on release from Windows Mobile 5.0 and delivers improvements in the operating system as well as a number of new features for applications such as Pocket Outlook. Microsoft announced the availability of Windows Mobile 6.0 at the GSM congress in February 2007. However, Microsoft does not manufacture or sell Windows Mobile devices themselves and depends on OEMs to add driver support and other features to customize devices as well as testing the devices on various networks. OEMs therefore determine the availability of devices that support Windows Mobile 6.0 and this varies from country to country. Even so, Windows Mobile 6.0 devices will be generally available worldwide by mid-2007 and it will be difficult to buy anything a Windows mobile device that does not run 6.0 thereafter.

On the server side, Exchange 2007 delivers a new version of the Active-Sync protocol and the combination of the upgraded server-side ActiveSync and Windows Mobile 6.0–powered devices deliver the widest set of new features because both server and client understand the fullest version of the synchronization protocol. Some of the Windows Mobile 6.0 features work when devices running this version connect to an Exchange 2003 SP2 server. In the same way, Windows Mobile 5.0 devices can connect to an Exchange 2007 server and pick up a little extra functionality, such as smarter downloads. Some features also work when individual handhelds synchronize through PC-based ActiveSync (version 4.5 or later), but I concentrate here on the interaction between server-mode ActiveSync and Windows Mobile 6.0 devices. Of course, you cannot upgrade every handheld device (some devices do not support this functionality), so you may have to purchase and deploy new devices if you are specifically interested in one or more of the features listed below.

The goal of the Exchange 2007 development team for ActiveSync was simple. They knew that they had made progress with Exchange 2003 SP2 and had managed to introduce some administrative functionality, but acknowledged that some features were lacking that could make users and administrators more productive. The result is that Microsoft concentrated their efforts to improve in three major areas.

Better email: The version of Pocket Outlook in Windows Mobile 5.0 is a basic email client, but it lacks many of the features that you would expect in a Windows device. Microsoft therefore added features such as:

- Users can execute search operations on the contents of their entire mailbox if it is located on an Exchange 2007 server rather than being limited to the data held in the replica mailbox on the mobile device. You can then elect to retrieve selected found items down to the device to view and work with their content.

- Reply/forward for meeting requests and the ability to review and resolve meeting conflicts on the mobile device. You can also view tracking information for attendees to know who is likely to attend a meeting.

- Better task management.

- Messages generated on the handheld have HTML message bodies rather than the fixed font used by earlier devices, so they appear "nicer" rather than the plain text messages generated by Windows Mobile 5.0. Note that HTML-format messages are bigger, so you need to increase the default size for message downloads to see the same amount of information as you would see in text-format messages.

- Support for hyperlink access to documents stored in SharePoint Portal Server and UNC folders. This feature uses the Document Access proxy service provided by an Exchange 2007 Client Access server.

- The ability to set and update out-of-office responses from the handheld, if connected to an Exchange 2007 server. However, unlike Outlook 2007, you can only set a single OOF notice that is used for both internal and external correspondents. In addition, the device forces you to create an OOF notice from scratch whereas other clients download the last text that you used to allow you to use it as the basis for the new OOF. This is a small but annoying omission.

- Better support for security certificate distribution and management. However, Windows Mobile clients still do not support S/MIME-signed messages and this feature is unlikely to arrive until a future service pack for Exchange 2007. For now, all you can do is see on the handheld that a signed message has arrived in the inbox, but you have to go to another client to be able to read it.

- Synchronization is more accurate and there are less instances of an item remaining unread on the handheld when you've read it using Outlook or another client.

Windows Mobile 6.0 adds a small set of features that you benefit from even when you use a handheld to connect to a mailbox on an Exchange 2003 server:

- Downloading of message bodies to the handheld is faster.

- "SmartFilter," a feature that allows you to search through inbox contents with a minimum number of key clicks, a feature that is important when you have limited keyboard capability on phone-style devices. Windows Mobile 6.0 also adds support for a set of keyboard shortcuts (press 1 for reply, 2 for reply all, 3 for forward, etc.)

Better and more granular control over policies: For Exchange 2003, policies that affect handheld devices are set on a global organization-wide basis so they are not very granular. In Exchange 2007, the policies that influence how a user can use their handheld device when they connect to Exchange are set where they should be—as part of general mailbox policies. Thus, you can have different policies for your executives and general users, or one policy for sales people who might absolutely have to have access to large attachments, even when they are roaming away from their home network, and another policy for other users where you want to limit their ability to rack up large data bills when they roam. Other examples include:

- The ability for administrators to set and enforce policies is expanded to accommodate additional policies, for example, to enforce data encryption for removable storage cards.

- The remote wipe command wipes data from any local storage card. This step is especially welcome because of the large amount of data that can be held on removable storage cards in mobile devices today.

- PIN expiry can be governed by policy and you can also stop people reusing old PINs, and stop them creating new PIN codes by incrementing or decrementing. In other words, users have to think to create a new PIN rather than simply increasing or decreasing an existing PIN by one.

- You can restrict users to a specific device.

The device storage encryption feature is limited to any storage card that is installed on the mobile device, such as the mini-SD cards that people commonly install. Through a policy setting, you can force any files written or updated on the card to be encrypted. However, the setting only applies to new files that are created on the device, and even if you move unencrypted files on the card after you turn encryption on, they will remain unencrypted unless you move the files off the storage device and rewrite them back onto the storage device. The encryption mechanism uses a key that is unique to the handheld that is re-initialized each time that the handheld goes through a cold boot cycle. Any encrypted content on a storage card can only be read on that handheld that originally created the content. If the device is lost or stolen the card cannot be read on another device or computer, and once the lost/stolen handheld has been remote wiped, the data on the card cannot be read even on the original handheld since the act of restoring the handheld means that an administrator has generated a new system key for the handheld.

Anti-virus for Windows Mobile is still an area that has not received much attention. The growing number of Windows Mobile devices used for email will no doubt lead to some attacks in the not too distant future, so it will be interesting to see how this area develops in the next few years, both in terms of attacks and the countermeasures deployed to protect the devices.

Windows Mobile 5.0 implements OMA[18] DM 1.1.2. Microsoft's support for OMA DM receives a significant upgrade in Windows Mobile 6.0 to bring the implementation up to the OMA DM 1.2 standard. OMA DM is a very comprehensive device management standard that is mostly used by the cell phone operators, but it is likely to evolve as the basis over time for enterprise mobile device management solutions provided by Microsoft (a mobile version of SMS perhaps) or other vendors. OMA DM uses a combination of SMS messages to trigger the management sequence that mobile devices use to upgrade their configuration by making a connection to the DM server to get and apply instructions.

Devices that support OMA DM 1.2 have FUMO (firmware update over the air) capabilities. They can receive instructions to upgrade their configuration using their normal network connection without having to be inserted into a desktop cradle. In addition, these devices can confirm back to the OMA DM server after the update is applied. Windows Mobile 6.0 adds WBXML compression to reduce the communications overhead between the OMA DM server and the mobile devices and also supports the standard IME1 device identification for the devices. To ensure that firmware upgrades can reach the devices, Windows Mobile 6.0 incorporates a more robust retry mechanism, segmented update packages that allow the

---

18. The Open Mobile Alliance Device Management standard.

server to deliver larger and more complex updates, and also supports finer granularity in delta updates.

Better reporting: You can extract some data about mobile device activity from the IIS logs in an Exchange 2003 environment and use tools like LogParser to interpret the data and generate basic reports, but you have to do all this work yourself. Microsoft addresses this problem in Exchange 2007 by giving Windows Mobile 6.0 devices more ability to report information about their configuration and by providing administrators with the ability to generate some rudimentary reports through PowerShell. We will get to the reporting functionality later on in this chapter.

Regretfully, support for Office 2007 document formats is one major missing piece of functionality in Windows Mobile 6.0. If you receive an attachment in Word 2007, Excel 2007, or PowerPoint 2007 format, you will not be able to read it on a Windows Mobile 6.0 device—at least, not until Microsoft upgrades the software to support these formats.

7.10.1   ActiveSync policies

As previously mentioned, Exchange 2007 allows you to create and deploy multiple ActiveSync policies to support the needs of different types of users instead of the single global policy that you can apply with Exchange 2003 SP2. Exchange 2007 always applies and respects ActiveSync policies on a per-user basis (each mailbox either has or has not an ActiveSync policy applied), so you can create as many policies as you need to operate within your company. As always, it's sensible to restrict yourself to as few policies as possible so as to remove complexity from the environment.

To create a new ActiveSync policy, go to the Client Access node under Organization Configuration and take the New Exchange ActiveSync Mailbox policy option, which invokes the wizard shown in Figure 7.58.

The `New-ActiveSyncMailboxPolicy` command issued to create the policy illustrated in Figure 7.58 is:

```
New-ActiveSyncMailboxPolicy -Name 'Mobile Executives'
-AllowNonProvisionableDevices $False -DevicePasswordEnabled $True
-AlphanumericDevicePasswordRequired $True -
MaxInactivityTimeDeviceLock '00:15:00' -MinDevicePasswordLength '6' -
PasswordRecoveryEnabled $True -DeviceEncryptionEnabled $True -
AttachmentsEnabled $True
-AllowSimpleDevicePassword $True -DevicePasswordExpiration
'30.00:00:00' -DevicePasswordHistory '5'
```

Table 7.11 explains the meaning of each parameter used the policy.

Figure 7.58

*Creating a new
ActiveSync policy*

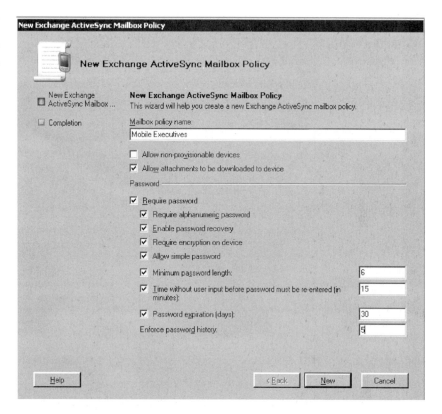

Table 7.11 *ActiveSync policy parameters*

Parameter	Meaning
AllowNonProvisionableDevices	When true, any device that supports Active-Sync can synchronize with Exchange even if the device does not support all settings.
DevicePasswordEnabled	When true, the user can set a password on the device.
AlphanumericDevicePasswordRequired	When true, the user has to set an alphanumeric password instead of a simple numeric password (often used with mobile devices).
MaxInactivityTimeDeviceLock	The length in minutes that the device can be inactive before the user is prompted for their password.

Table 7.11   *ActiveSync policy parameters (continued)*

Parameter	Meaning
MinDevicePassword	The minimum number of characters in the device password.
PasswordRecoveryEnabled	When set to True, the password for the device is stored by Exchange and can be retrieved by the user through Outlook Web Access.
DeviceEncryptionEnabled	If true, encryption is enabled on the device, but only for storage cards.
AttachmentsEnabled	If true, the device is allowed to download attachments for email messages.
AllowSimpleDevicePassword	If true, the device can be secured with a simple password, which is one that has a pattern, such as 9999 or 2323.
DevicePasswordExpiration	The time in days that the password is valid.
DevicePasswordHistory	The number of previously used passwords that Exchange stores. A user cannot reuse a password that is in the stored list.

After the policy is created, you can view details with the `Get-Active-SyncMailboxPolicy` command and amend details with the `Set-ActiveSync-MailboxPolicy` command. Once you're happy with the policy, you can begin to apply them by selecting mailboxes and then setting the policy as shown in Figure 7.59.

Naturally, you can also apply policies through the shell using the `Set-CasMailbox` command. For example:

```
Set-CasMailbox —id Bond —ActiveSyncMailboxPolicy 'Mobile
Executives'
—ActiveSyncEnabled:$True
```

Of course, we can automate this process considerably if we can identify the mailboxes that we want to apply a policy to. Let's assume that we use the CustomAttribute1 property to identify users that should come under a specific policy. The custom properties are good to use for this purpose because you can apply server-side filtering to find the mailboxes and you can use the

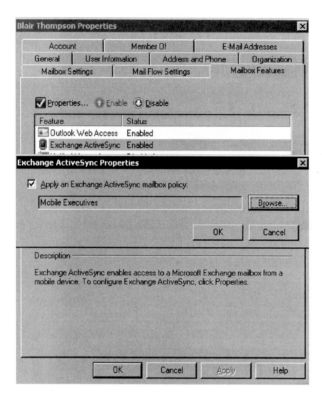

Figure 7.59
*Applying an
ActiveSync policy to
a mailbox*

same property to hold values for different mobile plans that you want to apply. For example:

```
Get-Mailbox -Filter { CustomAttribute1 -eq "Mobile Plan
1"} | Set-CasMailbox -ActiveSyncMailboxPolicy "Mobile
Executives" -ActiveSyncEnabled $True
```

Another thing that you might want to do is to make periodic checks for ActiveSync-enabled mailboxes that have no policy assigned to them and to then set a default policy on these mailboxes. This PowerShell code scans for ActiveSync-enabled mailboxes (excluding room and equipment mailboxes) that do not have an ActiveSync policy assigned. We eliminate any mailbox that is on a legacy Exchange server and apply a default policy to the remaining set:

```
Get-Mailbox | Where {$_.RecipientTypeDetails -eq
"UserMailbox"} | Get-CasMailbox | Where {$_.ActiveSyncEnabled
-eq $True -And $_.ExchangeVersion -like "*0.1*" -And
```

Figure 7.60
*Managing a mobile
device for a user*

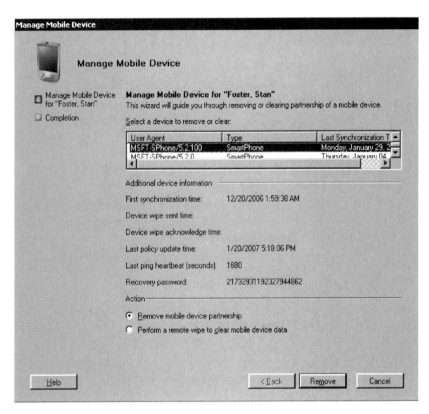

```
$_.ActiveSyncMailboxPolicy —eq $Null} | Set-CasMailbox -
ActiveSyncMailboxPolicy "Basic ActiveSync User"
```

This code works well in a small Exchange organization. In a larger organization where you have to work with thousands of mailboxes, you may want to apply a filter so that, for instance, you process only all of the mailboxes on a server.

Microsoft plans to allow administrators to control some additional features of mobile devices through ActiveSync policies in Exchange 2007 SP1. Among the features that they are considering are:

- Enforce encryption of the main memory contents of the mobile device.

- Allow or block applications from running on the mobile device.

- Enforce network capabilities, such as disabling or enabling Bluetooth or Wi-Fi or allowing use of infrared to connect devices together.

- Allow use of external storage such as Micro-SD cards connected to devices.

- Permit selective enabling of communications capabilities, such as enabling or disabling SMS (Short Message Service), MMS (Multimedia Message Service), POP3, or IMAP4 access to Exchange.

- Disable an embedded camera, if one exists on the device.

More details will become available as Microsoft works through the beta versions of SP1 to arrive at the final release. It is likely that these features will depend on the deployment of Windows Mobile 6.0 devices because earlier devices are unlikely to understand the policy instructions that Exchange will have to send to the device to enable or disable features.

7.10.2 Managing mobile devices through EMC

In addition to policies, there are some other options available to administrators to manage mobile devices. After you enable a user for ActiveSync, you will see a "Manage Mobile Device" option appear in EMC's action pane when you select the mailbox. This option calls a wizard to either remove a mobile device partnership (and force a full resynchronization) or perform a remote wipe of the device (Figure 7.60). These options are equivalent to using the `Remove-ActiveSyncDevice` and `Clear-ActiveSyncDevice` commands.

The `Get-ActiveSyncDeviceStatistics` command reports various details about mobile devices including the device type, name, model, phone carrier, device phone number, and OS version (Windows 5.0 devices report a restricted set of fields). An edited version of what you can expect to see from the `Get-ActiveSyncDeviceStatistics` command is shown below. You will notice that two devices are listed: an HP iPAQ 6915 and an HP SmartPhone.

```
Get-ActiveSyncDeviceStatistics —Mailbox Redmond

FirstSyncTime          : 12/15/2006 10:21:24 PM
LastPolicyUpdateTime   : 12/16/2006 1:15:50 AM
LastSyncAttemptTime    : 12/21/2006 10:52:00 AM
LastSuccessSync        : 12/21/2006 10:52:00 AM
DeviceType             : PocketPC
DeviceUserAgent        : MSFT-PPC/5.2.0
LastPingHeartbeat      : 480
RecoveryPassword       : ********
DeviceModel            : hp iPAQ hw6915
```

```
DeviceIMEI                    : 357533000051762
DeviceFriendlyName            : Pocket_PC
DeviceOS                      : Windows CE 5.2.297
DeviceOSLanguage              : English
DevicePhoneNumber             :
Identity                      : tony.redmond@xyz.com\AirSync-PocketPC-
C0AA69342E48E93851
                                388031415505A8


FirstSyncTime                 : 12/22/2006 8:50:43 PM
LastPolicyUpdateTime          : 1/3/2007 5:12:27 PM
LastSyncAttemptTime           : 1/29/2007 8:39:37 PM
LastSuccessSync               : 1/29/2007 8:39:37 PM
DeviceType                    : SmartPhone
DeviceUserAgent               : MSFT-SPhone/5.2.0
LastPingHeartbeat             : 780
RecoveryPassword              : ********
DeviceModel                   : HP iPAQ Mobile Messenger
DeviceIMEI                    : 446019-19-750759-01
DeviceFriendlyName            : WM_Tredmond1
DeviceOS                      : Windows CE 5.2.964
DeviceOSLanguage              : English
Identity                      : tony.redmond@xyz.com\AirSync-SmartPhone-
3EABAEF0CB94D930
                                8ACFAA131B12545F
```

You will notice that the identities returned for mobile devices are quite long and complicated. If you want to use the `Remove-ActiveSyncDevice` or `Clear-ActiveSyncDevice` commands to resynchronize or wipe a mobile device, the easiest way is to use the `Get-ActiveSyncDeviceStatistics` command to return the identity of the device associated with a mailbox and pipe this to the command that you want to use. For example:

```
Get-ActiveSyncDeviceStatistics –Mailbox Redmond | Remove-
ActiveSyncDevice
```

The `Export-ActiveSyncLog` command is available to process IIS logs to generate a set of CSV files that you can analyze and report using tools such as Excel. We will discuss the contents of these files and what use you can make of them later on in this chapter. Microsoft has also integrated ActiveSync more comprehensively into the MOM Management Pack for Exchange 2007. However, it is fair to say that Microsoft has not yet delivered the same kind of comprehensive management view of mobile devices that is available in competing products such as the BlackBerry Enterprise Server. You can take a snapshot of mobile device activity through the EMS commands and analyze the data with LogParser or other utilities, but there is no dynamically updated view of current activity for mobile devices available in EMC. The weak reporting for ActiveSync is an area of Exchange that Microsoft will probably address in a future release.

Note that there is no method to migrate Exchange 2003 policy settings for mobile devices to Exchange 2007. Exchange 2003 stores the global policies for mobile devices in the Active Directory as an XML blob that mobile devices interrogate when they connect to the server. Instead of going direct to a global policy, The Exchange 2007 Client Access server queries the Active Directory object for the user that connects to discover the value of the msExchMobileMailboxPolicyLink property, which contains a forward link to the Exchange 2007 ActiveSync mailbox policy that determines whether Exchange needs to apply a policy. There is no backward connection to older policies, so while mobile device policies for both Exchange 2003 and 2007 will co-exist inside the same organization, you need to ensure that you apply any applicable mobile device policies to users as you move their mailboxes to an Exchange 2007 server during the migration process. Failure to do this may disable some security settings that you want to apply to mobile devices and so expose confidential data should the user lose the device.

You do not have to depend solely on the features provided by Exchange to protect handheld devices. For example, RSA Security (www.rsasecurity.com) offers a protection called SecurID to increase security by requiring users to provide a PIN before they can synchronize email with the server. Providing a PIN every time you synchronized email would become boring very quickly, so you can modify the RSA Authentication Agent to set an authentication window (the default is 15 minutes) during which you do not have to re-enter the PIN. Achieving the right balance between usability and security is an important part of getting users to buy into the need for security, and if you do not, then users will look for ways to circumvent security. For this reason, if you opt to deploy enhanced security for handhelds, make sure that you can achieve the balance by configuring the server and devices to meet user needs.

7.10.3 Moving mailboxes to Exchange 2007 and ActiveSync

If you move mailboxes from Exchange 2003 servers to Exchange 2007 servers using either EMC or the `Move-Mailbox` command, you will notice that Exchange 2007 drops any security policy settings that you had on the Exchange 2003 mailbox. In addition, Exchange has enabled the mailbox for ActiveSync even if your default policy for Exchange 2003 was to enable mailboxes only for select individuals. The net result is a potential weakening of device security. Microsoft plans to address this problem by setting a default ActiveSync policy, but this will not happen until Exchange 2007 SP1 at the earliest.

The same problem occurs for new mailboxes that you create on Exchange 2007 servers, which also end up with ActiveSync enabled by default. Even stranger, if you create a room or resource mailbox with Exchange 2007, those mailboxes are enabled for ActiveSync[19]. While it would be better if an administrator could decide what the default enablement policy was for the organization, the fact that mailboxes are enabled without your consent for ActiveSync is annoying but it won't cause any great damage in the long run. It is easy to create some EMS code to scan for ActiveSync-enabled mailboxes, validate whether the mailboxes should be enabled, and disable any that should not. You could then run this code periodically.

In this example, we use one of the custom properties to track the users that should be enabled for ActiveSync. Before we scan and apply the restriction, let's ensure that all of the room and equipment mailboxes are not enabled for ActiveSync:

```
Get-Mailbox —ResultSize Unlimited —Filter
{RecipientTypeDetails —eq 'RoomMailbox' —or
RecipientTypeDetails —eq 'EquipmentMailbox'} |
Set-CasMailbox —ActiveSyncEnabled $False —OWAEnabled $False
—IMAPEnabled $False -POPEnabled $False
```

The second command scans all mailboxes using a slightly awkward combination of the `Get-CasMailbox` and `Get-Mailbox` commands. We need to use both commands because the `Get-CasMailbox` command is able to retrieve information about protocol enablement but not about the custom properties, which are accessible by `Get-Mailbox`. Thus, to be able to combine a check for ActiveSync enablement with one against a custom property, we have to use both commands. Perhaps it will be possible to use just one shell command to access any property for a mailbox in the future, but for now we have to accept the division of responsibilities across different commands.

```
Get-CasMailbox —ResultSize Unlimited | Where
{$_.ActiveSyncEnabled} | Get-Mailbox | Where
{$_.CustomAttribute13 —ne 'Mobile' -and
$_.RecipientTypeDetails -eq 'UserMailbox'} |
Set-CasMailbox -ActiveSyncEnabled $False
```

---

19.   Any room and equipment mailboxes that you create are also enabled for Outlook Web Access, POP3, and IMAP4.

These commands process all mailboxes in the organization and work well for smaller organizations. In larger organizations where you have thousands of mailboxes to work with, you may want to use a filter to reduce the amount of data processed in one run.

Another issue that occurs for ActiveSync users when their mailboxes move from Exchange 2003 to Exchange 2007 is that they have to rebuild the ActiveSync state for the mailbox as this has changed format between versions. The only way that you can rebuild the ActiveSync state is through a complete resynchronization of all mailbox data to the mobile device. The first time that you attempt to synchronize the mobile device with Exchange after your mailbox is moved, you'll see a message to tell you that an error has occurred and that ActiveSync needs to resynchronize. Apart from the additional network traffic that's generated to resynchronize the entire mailbox, the change in ActiveSync state for mailboxes isn't a big deal per se. However, the resynchronization warning may cause some users to contact the help desk to ask what's going on, so be prepared for these calls.

7.10.4 Estimating network traffic for mobile devices

Network traffic across a GPRS connection comes with a price tag, unless you subscribe to an unlimited GPRS data plan with your carrier. Even with an unlimited data plan, it's important to control the amount of data traffic that users generate when they roam from their home network as it is all too common to find a heavy bill is generated if you use the same parameters when roaming as you do when connected to the home network. For example, if you have a U.S. flat-rate plan, spending a week in Europe roaming across several networks (even if the same multi-national carrier operates in all the different countries that you roam) can result in a bill of several hundred dollars. Microsoft does not control the way that cell phone operators bill users but the way that things work today can be a deployment blocker for companies who fear that giving ActiveSync devices to users is a fast way to extra cost.

Experience of running Windows Mobile devices for a range from light to medium email users shows that they generate between 10MB and 25MB of traffic monthly, with the heaviest users reaching peaks of 300MB or more depending on mail volume, the default synchronization settings for message size, and how many attachments they download. You can discover this information by analyzing the IIS logs on the Exchange Client Access servers that support ActiveSync. The amount of traffic will vary from company to company and how people use their devices. For example, if you roam across networks, you can instruct ActiveSync to connect on a scheduled basis and elect to synchronize with your mailbox every 10 minutes rather than accept new mail as it arrives. Using a schedule for synchronization throttles back some network traffic and limits data consumption and cost, which is important especially when roaming across different international networks.

Figure 7.61
*Configuring
ActiveSync for
email
synchronization*

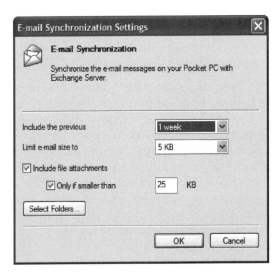

In addition to the frequency of email synchronization, other factors that influence the amount of network traffic generated by mobile devices include:

- Use of Internet Explorer. Many of the home pages for major Internet sites such as www.hp.com or www.microsoft.com generate traffic of 100KB or more. Even a Google search generates a minimum of 65KB.

- Capture and transmission of photos (as email attachments) taken using the inbuilt cameras that are common in many devices. A typical photo taken with a 1.3 megapixel camera generates an attachment of 110KB.

- Configuring ActiveSync (on the device or partner PC) to synchronize more than the standard amount of email to the device. The default settings are to synchronize three days worth of email, to limit the size of a message to 0.5KB, and to not download attachments. Because of the formatting information that is carried by HTML messages (only supported Windows Mobile 6.0 devices), they are larger than text-format messages, so if you use HTML on the device, you may increase the default size for message downloads to see the same amount of information as you see with text-format messages and so increase network traffic. As you can see from Figure 7.61, it is easy to increase these settings from any value from 0.5KB upwards. An increase from 0.5KB (hardly enough to see the message header) to 5KB dramatically affects the amount of data traffic. You can also use ActiveSync to select a wider group of folders for synchronization (see Figure 7.67) and every folder that you select for synchronization increases the amount of data traffic.

- Configuring ActiveSync (on the device) to download new messages on a schedule rather than as they arrive. You can also configure the device to use a different schedule for off-peak hours, which you can customize to fit your work day. For example, you could download new messages as they arrive during working hours and then download every 30 minutes outside working hours and at the weekend. Apart from perhaps saving your sanity by isolating you from the constant interruption caused by new messages, especially outside working hours, downloading on a schedule rather than on demand increases battery life significantly because the device uses the radio to communicate with Exchange less often. Another benefit that you gain is a radical reduction in cell phone bills. Some providers have plans that allow you unlimited data access and if this is the case, you won't have a problem (apart from battery life) synchronizing with Exchange as often as you want. At the time of writing, most of the unlimited data access plans are available only in the United States and are less common in Europe or elsewhere, so it's easy for users to run up very large bills. I manage a group of technical consultants and when we started to use Windows Mobile devices, we received many monthly cell phone bills of over a thousand dollars until the proverbial penny dropped and we instituted a more rational synchronization policy to save money. Solid education and awareness of how costs can rack up are key parts of a mobile device deployment.

Remember that increased network activity also increases battery demand, so the heaviest users will experience the shortest battery life. All of this goes to prove that it is not a good idea to hand out mobile devices without paying some attention to user education so that users know the consequences of their action in configuring and using the devices before they realize the dollar impact when they receive their bills.

7.10.5   Analyzing ActiveSync logs

The `Export-ActiveSyncLog` command can give you some insight into the amount of activity that ActiveSync imposes on a Client Access server. `Export-ActiveSyncLog` works by analyzing the ActiveSync transactions that flow through the IIS logs on the Client Access server. For example, this command instructs `Export-ActiveSyncLog` to analyze the contents of the ex070123.log file (the log generated on January 23, 2007) and to place its output into the c:\temp\ directory.

```
Export-ActiveSyncLog -FileName: 'C:\WINNT\system32\LogFiles\
W3SVC1\ex070123.log' -UseGMT:$true
-OutputPath 'c:\Temp\'
```

Export-ActiveSyncLog generates six files in CSV format:

- Users.csv: Contains details of activity by user account. This is the most interesting file because you can see who your heaviest users are.

- User-Agents.csv: Contains details of the activity generated by each user agent (operating system and build number) that connected to ActiveSync. For example, in this extract we see that 19 devices running build 5.2.0 generated 3060 "hits" against the server, whereas only two devices running the Nokia E50 O/S connected. However, on average, the Nokia devices were busier as they generated an average of 307 hits each.

```
MSFT-SPhone/5.2.0,3060,19
NokiaE50/1.0,614,2
```

- Servers.csv: Contains data about the activity for each server that hosts mailboxes connected to via ActiveSync.

- Statuscodes.csv: Not of great interest to administrators as you will not understand the cryptic codes, but Microsoft might!

- PolicyCompliance.csv: Contains data relating to the compliance level of the devices (with ActiveSync policy) that connect via ActiveSync.

- Hourly.csv: Contains an hour-by-hour analysis of the ActiveSync activity, including the number of unique devices that connected to the server. This data is interesting because it can help you to identify your hours of peak demand (if you cannot guess them anyway).

Unfortunately, Microsoft leaves the data generated by Export-Active-SyncLog entirely in your hands to interpret. Because the files are in CSV format, the easiest approach is to use Excel to open them and interpret their contents (Figure 7.62). A more sophisticated approach would be to pour the data into a SQL or Access database so that you can analyze the data over an extended period and to generate more insightful reports than you can gain from looking at a single day's activity.

As you analyze the data from Export-ActiveSyncLog, the important thing to remember is that ActiveSync records the data from the server's perspective and not from the user's. For example, if you look at the highlighted cell in Figure 7.62, you might conclude that this row is for a hyperactive user as it seems that they have sent 322 items (messages) in a single day. However, the data actually means that the server sent 322 items to the user's handheld device. In the same manner, the server received 14 items from the handheld. The natural thing is to read the column headings and assume that the data relates to user activity but a computer has its own view.

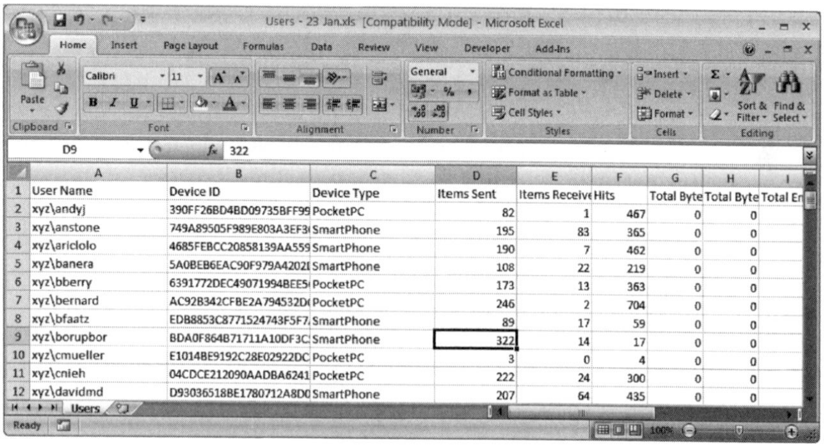

	A	B	C	D	E	F	G	H	I
1	User Name	Device ID	Device Type	Items Sent	Items Receive	Hits	Total Byte	Total Byte	Total En
2	xyz\andyj	390FF26BD4BD09735BFF99	PocketPC	82	1	467	0	0	
3	xyz\anstone	749A89505F989E803A3EF3	SmartPhone	195	83	365	0	0	
4	xyz\ariclolo	4685FEBCC20858139AA559	SmartPhone	190	7	462	0	0	
5	xyz\banera	5A0BEB6EAC90F979A4202I	SmartPhone	108	22	219	0	0	
6	xyz\bberry	6391772DEC49071994BEE5	PocketPC	173	13	363	0	0	
7	xyz\bernard	AC92B342CFBE2A794532D	PocketPC	246	2	704	0	0	
8	xyz\bfaatz	EDB8853C8771524743F5F7.	SmartPhone	89	17	59	0	0	
9	xyz\borupbor	BDA0F864B71711A10DF3C	SmartPhone	322	14	17	0	0	
10	xyz\cmueller	E1014BE9192C28E02922DC	PocketPC	3	0	4	0	0	
11	xyz\cnieh	04CDCE212090AADBA6241	PocketPC	222	24	300	0	0	
12	xyz\davidmd	D93036518BE1780712A8D0	SmartPhone	207	64	435	0	0	

Figure 7.62 *Analyzing data generated by Export-ActiveSyncLog*

7.10.6 Wiping mobile devices

Up to Exchange 2003 SP2, Microsoft supported no way to wipe or reset a mobile device (SmartPhone or Pocket PC) if it was lost. Other competing systems such as the GoodLink or BlackBerry Enterprise Servers both support features that allowed administrators to send instructions to mobile devices to wipe their contents if they became lost or are stolen. Given that mobile devices are among the easiest things to leave behind in taxis, fall out of bags, or otherwise mislay, it is a big feature to have. As an example of the problem, the security company PointSec[20] estimated that people left 5,358 Pocket PCs and PDAs (and 4,973 laptops) in the back of London taxicabs in the second half of 2004. Apart from their "loseability," today's mobile devices contain far more sensitive information than ever before, so the ability to wipe a device and deny access to whoever finds it is critical for data security.

For Exchange 2003, the Exchange wipe device functionality is basic but effective. You need to download the Exchange ActiveSync Remote Administration tool from Microsoft's web site and install it on an Exchange server to create a new IIS virtual folder called MobileAdmin. Administrators can then access the web page (https://server-name/MobileAdmin) to issue commands

20. www.pointsec.com.

to wipe devices, cancel wipe commands, and delete synchronization partnerships between devices and users. For Exchange 2007, you can either use the Manage Mobile Device option through EMC or execute the `Clear-Active-SyncDevice` command to initiate a remote wipe.

When an administrator initiates a remote wipe, the web application sends a WebDAV PROPPATCH command to the user's mailbox to set the "wipeinitiated" property of the mailbox to a nonzero value. ActiveSync notices that the property is set and sends a wipe command to the device, which then executes the appropriate command locally. The client then acknowledges the wipe command back to the server together with an indication of success or failure. Note that if you send a remote wipe request to a device that doesn't support this function, the device will not wipe its data, but synchronization of future data will fail, so you can at least prevent any more sensitive data going to the device. The different degrees of support across device types for remote wipe functionality is a good reason for you to test this feature before approving a device type for deployment.

Figure 7.63
*Outlook Web Access
2007 options for
mobile devices*

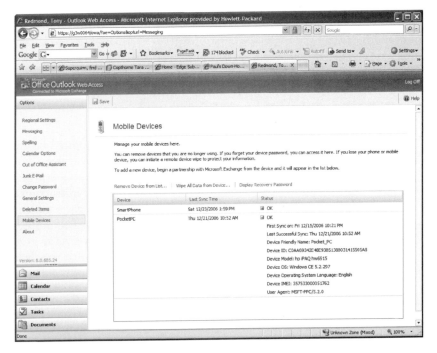

A log tracks all commands and the status reported by the device. Remote wipe commands do not erase data on any storage card in the mobile device; the only data that these commands cause the device to wipe are email and other data held in the device's fixed storage. Managing mobile devices is a lot easier for users in Exchange 2007 because users can see information about all of the devices that they have used to synchronize with Exchange, including options to wipe a device or recover a password through the "Wipe Device" feature that is included in the "Mobile Devices" options presented by Outlook Web Access (Figure 7.63). As pointed out before, I use both a SmartPhone and a Pocket PC to synchronize with Exchange, so both devices appear in the list.

7.10.7 Debugging synchronization

It is the nature of handheld devices that there is no way for users to see the interaction between client and server. All that users normally see is that messages arrive on the handheld. The more technologically aware users might fire up the ActiveSync application on their handheld and force a synchronization to occur or change the settings that control how the handheld and Exchange synchronize data, but even these users do not fully understand what happens to synchronize data. This is fine and the way that things should be until problems happen. Apart from checking that they can connect to the network (usually verified by running a browser on the handheld and connecting to a site such as hp.com), there is little an administrator can do to debug synchronization problems if a user complains that their email is not arriving on their handheld. The server logs report when successful transactions occur and not when transactions fail, so there is little information for an administrator to harvest there. However, you can enable a setting to force ActiveSync to capture details of the conversation between a handheld and the server and use that information to help debug problems. When enabled, users can take the option through the Mobile Devices options for Outlook Web Access 2007. The only issue is that Exchange 2007 does not enable the setting by default, so you have some work to do.

Figure 7.64 illustrates the option that we want to enable. When a user clicks on "Retrieve Log," Exchange grabs a copy of the latest synchronization log for the selected device and sends it as an attachment to a message to the user's mailbox. The plain text attachment contains XML-formatted data that reports all of the transactions that take place between the handheld and Exchange during a single synchronization cycle. You can see details of the messages that were downloaded (recipients, subjects, sizes) as well as the flow of communications between client and server. The user will not know what to do with this information but it is invaluable data for an administrator to have, so the user can forward the message to the help desk or administrator and ask them to help.

Three steps are necessary to enable the logging feature:

1.   Enable the mailbox to generate logging reports.

Figure 7.64
The option to retrieve an ActiveSync log

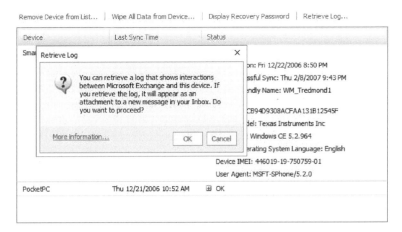

2. Change the Program Files\Microsoft\Exchange Server\Bin\Client Access\owa\web.config file on the Client Access server to enable the feature in Outlook Web Access.

3. Change the Program Files\Microsoft\Exchange Server\Bin\Client Access\sync\web.config file on the Client Access server to force the capture of the synchronization log.

You use the `Set-CasMailbox` command to enable a mailbox to generate synchronization logs. For example:

```
Set-CasMailbox —id Redmond —ActiveSyncDebugLogging $True
```

We now update the web.config file in the \owa directory. You can do this with any text editor. Search for the "<appsettings>" section and set the "EnableEmailReports" value to "true." Enter the email address that you want users to send reports to if they need help in the "MailboxLoggingAddress" value.

```
<appSettings>
        <add key="ConnectionCacheSize" value="100" />
```

```
                    <add key="MaximumIdentityArraySize" value="100" />
                    <add key="ShowDebugInformation" value="true" />
                    <add key="EnableEmailReports" value="true" />
                    <!-- Configurable email address of where to forward
          ActiveSync log messages-->
                    <add key="MailboxLoggingAddress"
          value="admin@xyz.com"></add>
          </appSettings>
```

The last step is to update the web.config file in the \sync directory. Again, make the change with a text editor. All you need to do is update the "MailboxLoggingEnabled" value to be "True."

```
          <!-- Disable Mailbox Logging by default-->
                    <add key="MailboxLoggingEnabled" value="true"></add>
          <
```

7.11 Comparing Windows Mobile and BlackBerry

Selecting a handheld device is an extremely personal choice. Some users will never move from their Palm devices, others swear by their SmartPhones, while others say that the Good client is the most effective way to process email on a Pocket PC (whether or not the Pocket PC runs the latest version of Windows Mobile). However, the largest single group of handheld email devotees use various models of RIM BlackBerry handhelds or use the BlackBerry software on a licensed device from another vendor. The number of people who use BlackBerry means that it sets the standard for handheld email connectivity, so it is important that Microsoft delivers enough functionality in Pocket Outlook to be at least competitive with BlackBerry as otherwise the cost advantages in being able to use the same Exchange and Windows infrastructure to support handheld users will be negated. Companies will pay the extra costs to deploy and manage BlackBerry Enterprise or GoodLink servers if they believe that they get value from the investment.

I was a faithful BlackBerry user for many years and enjoyed the fast, reliable, and effective email access that BlackBerry provides for Exchange. There is no doubt that BlackBerry is a very good client for Exchange and I used several BlackBerry devices, the most recent being a 7100. RIM has since introduced some very nice new BlackBerry devices that are more modern than the 7100, but their interaction with Exchange remains the same.

Breaking my always-available "CrackBerry" habit was always going to be hard and none of the Pocket PC–based devices seemed to be able to deliver the same kind of efficient email service that I was accustomed to with the

BlackBerry until Microsoft delivered their direct-push technology in Active-Sync in Exchange 2003 SP2 and coupled it with Windows Mobile 5.0. I transitioned to an iPAQ 6915 (Figure 7.65 shows the iPAQ 6915 complete with its integrated keyboard and the BlackBerry 7100, which is a smaller and lighter device, albeit not significantly). Moving my work to the iPAQ 6915 was a matter of taking my SIM (the identification card that links your phone number to a GSM network) card out of the BlackBerry, inserting it into the iPAQ, powering the device up, and waiting for ActiveSync to synchronize my email, calendar, and contacts down to the device. Since the advent of Exchange 2007 and Windows Mobile 6.0, I now use an HP SmartPhone and enjoy the experience. The SmartPhone is different to the iPAQ, but it's different in a good way and delivers a nice combination of a great phone, good battery life, and satisfactory control over my inbox.

Cell phone providers usually issue devices that are locked to specific networks, so it may not be possible to simply move your SIM if you do not have devices that are linked to the same provider or the Windows Mobile device that you want to transfer your SIM to belongs to a different provider.

Before I moved devices, I made sure that my mailbox was enabled for ActiveSync. Figure 7.66 shows how to enable a mailbox for ActiveSync using the AD Users and Computers console (for Exchange 2003—left) and through EMC (for Exchange 2007—right). I also made sure that I knew the name of the ISA server that the iPAQ would go through to connect to the HP network to synchronize my mailbox. Finally, I installed ActiveSync[21] on my PC as the PC version of ActiveSync is required if you want to download software on your PC (such as ROM updates for the device) and then transfer it to the Pocket PC. At the time of writing, the latest version of ActiveSync for the PC is 4.5.

Figure 7.66
Enabling ActiveSync for a mailbox on Exchange 2003 and 2007

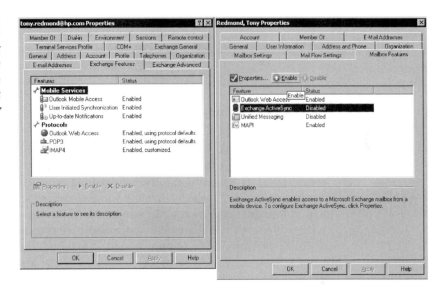

7.11.1   Processing the mail

Processing email is a similar experience on both the Pocket PC and the BlackBerry. Because it is based on Windows, the Pocket PC is a more graphical environment to work in. BlackBerry users tend to make more extensive use of keyboard commands and can often process email faster, which is an advantage if you are faced with a bulging inbox. In both cases the devices fetch the complete content of small messages and the first portion of larger messages and you can instruct the device to fetch the complete content if you decide that it is necessary. The default is that BlackBerry fetches approximately 2KB for messages and Pocket Outlook fetches 0.5KB (including the header information). However, you can edit the ActiveSync settings on the Pocket PC to set a different default download size for messages and you can also have attachments downloaded automatically if they are under a certain size. The default is not to download attachments unless requested by the user.

I normally use a default message download size of 5KB with ActiveSync, which works well for almost all the messages that I receive, even those that are part of a long email thread where some important point is buried earlier

---

21.   You can download the latest version of ActiveSync for the PC from Microsoft's web site.

in the thread. I also change the default time window for message storage from three days to two weeks to ensure that Pocket Outlook held more of my inbox on the device. These settings affect the amount of storage used on the handheld and you will need to add more storage to the device if you want to hold a lot of data locally. The iPAQ has a mini-SD slot for additional storage and you can get a 1GB mini-SD card for a reasonable amount at online stores[22]. Windows Mobile allows you to store attachments on the mini-SD card, which increases the amount of main storage available for messages. However, if you increase the default download size for messages, you also increase the amount of data that the device receives over the GPRS connect and so may end up with a larger monthly bill for GPRS connectivity. The extra network activity also increases the drain on the battery as the device makes more use of the GPRS connection to fetch the extra data.

Unlike the BlackBerry, Pocket Outlook does not automatically store copies of messages that you send. You can use Pocket Outlook to view the complete folder structure of your mailbox (and move messages to any folder) and then use the "Tools … Manage Folders" option (Figure 7.67) to select folders for synchronization to the handheld. Afterwards, Pocket Outlook will synchronize any new items that appear in these folders. Being able to synchronize selected folders to your handheld is an advantage for Pocket Outlook, as it is tremendously useful to be able to use a set of folders to hold different information on the device. Both types of device allow you to download attachments and the BlackBerry Enterprise Server (BES) will convert common document formats such as Word and Excel to a format that BlackBerry devices can read. Pocket Outlook does not have to convert the most common Microsoft Office formats because Windows Mobile includes versions of Word, Excel, and PowerPoint that can read these documents. BlackBerry fetches document contents immediately as you request them while Pocket Outlook waits for the next synchronization cycle.

Figure 7.67
Selecting folders for synchronization

22.   For example, http://www.flash-memory-store.com/mini-secure-digital.html.

After email, maintaining your schedule is the second most important application for most handheld users. Mobile Windows includes an effective calendar application and I could not see any great difference in functionality with the calendar application on the BlackBerry.

The BlackBerry supports the ability to execute lookups against your contacts and against the GAL. Windows Mobile devices can use the GALSearch feature to validate email addresses against the GAL (through the Check Names feature in Pocket Outlook) and to search the GAL (by performing an online search through the Contacts application). Even though you can perform an online search through the GAL, it is a good idea to create contacts for all your frequent correspondents so that a local entry exists for them on the handheld. The Check Names feature responds instantly if you use a contact and you gain other advantages such as the phone application recognizing the contact if they call you using a phone number that is included in their contact record. In addition, memory is at a premium on mobile devices, so it is logical that GALSearch supports a limited subset of the information that the GAL holds when compared to other clients such as Outlook, so having a local contact record means that you have direct access to much more information about the contact than you can retrieve online. Table 7.12 lists the properties that GALSearch supports and how they map against Active Directory attributes.

Table 7.12   *Mobile GAL properties*

ActiveSync property	Active Directory attribute
DisplayName	displayName
Phone	telephoneNumber
Office	physicalDeliveryOfficeName
Title	Title
Company	Company
Alias	mailNickName
FirstName	givenName
LastName	Sn
MobilePhone	Mobile
EmailAddress	Mail

GALSearch works by taking a query string supplied by the user and executing an ANR (ambiguous name resolution) indexed search on the server against mail-enabled objects in the GAL. The ANR search is similar to that executed by Outlook when it searches the GAL and attempts to return up to 100 results for GAL entries that satisfy the search string. Figure 7.68 shows the result of a search against the HP GAL. One irritation is that you cannot search the GAL for the name of a distribution group (including dynamic distribution groups) as GALSearch seems to be curiously blinded by the existence of these entries in the GAL. This is an easy problem to work around by creating a contact that points to the SMTP address of the group, which allows Pocket Outlook to use the email address of the contact, but this is not a great workaround if, like me, you work in a company that has over 50,000 distribution groups in the GAL.

GALSearch also ignores any personal distribution lists in your contacts folder. In this case, there is some logic behind the apparent omission because personal distribution lists are under the control of Outlook, which also takes responsibility for expanding the contents of the list into a set of individual email addresses before sending any message that you address to the list. Personal distribution lists do not have email addresses and are simply containers of other email addresses, but Exchange cannot expand the content of the list into individual addresses because these lists are "personal" to the user and very unlike system distribution lists, which are composed of a set of backward pointers to individual email addresses in the GAL. GALSearch solves the problem by ignoring these lists, so you cannot use a handheld to address a message to a personal address list.

Figure 7.68
Selecting a contact
from a directory
lookup

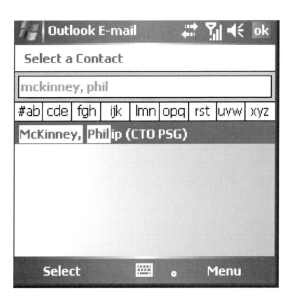

The performance of any handheld client when it checks addresses against the Active Directory depends on elements such as the connection between the handheld and the network provider, the load on any of the servers that participate in the transaction, network congestion, and the connection between the proxy server and the Active Directory. In most cases, you should have to wait no more than a few seconds for a lookup operation to complete. Clients send search requests to servers, which execute the searches and return the results to the clients. To complete the transaction, the requests pass from handheld to the server that performs the directory search and back again along the same path to deliver the results. If lookups seem extended, the first place to look is the performance of the servers along the path. For BlackBerry, the focus is on the BlackBerry Enterprise Server. For EAS, you need to check out the ISA server and Exchange front-end server. In both cases, you could also check the performance of the Global Catalog server that handles the incoming requests.

The speed of message delivery to the handheld is similar for BlackBerry and Pocket PC, although the underlying infrastructure that you deploy to support mobile users influences delivery times because the speed of delivery depends on factors such as the load placed on the servers and the complexity of network connections. In both cases, messages travel from the Exchange server that hosts your mailbox to another server that "packages" them up before it transmits the messages to the cellular provider for onward delivery to the handheld (via GPRS). In any such scheme, it is inevitable that differences in server and network configurations can influence the speed of data delivery. For example, the BES that I use is in a Dublin datacenter alongside the Exchange server that holds my mailbox, so all the interaction between the servers up to the point that messages travel to the cellular provider is local. By comparison, messages for my Pocket PC transfer from the mailbox server to a front-end server (in the United States) and then through an ISA server before they go across the GPRS network to the device. The only other characteristic of message delivery that is different between the two systems is the way that EAS groups messages for transmission to the Pocket PC. This may be a function of the notify and pull model where EAS sends any new messages that arrive since the last synchronization together rather than fetching new messages as they arrive into the inbox. The BlackBerry model processes new messages as they arrive. This is not a big difference as you swiftly get used to seeing groups of messages appear in the inbox rather than individual messages.

Discussing the speed that messages arrive to the handheld is really just of academic interest because users will not realize that messages arrive more slowly to Windows Mobile unless they can compare delivery times to Outlook and then to a BlackBerry. In addition, it is important to say that BES puts a much bigger load on an Exchange server than ActiveSync, as it has to poll mailboxes constantly to discover new email and then extract and transfer the messages to the handhelds. In some ways, BES is similar to the MAPI-based anti-virus scanners that were popular in the early days of Exchange but went out of fashion when servers scaled to support more than a few hundred concurrent connections. The MAPI-based scanners hit performance bottle-necks after servers scaled to support more than five or six hundred concur-rent mailbox connections and this factor eventually forced anti-virus vendors to move their products to use a direct connection to the Store via the Virus Scanning API (VSAPI). Experienced BlackBerry administrators recommend that you need to deploy a server to run BES to support every five or six hun-dred active BlackBerry users whereas ActiveSync is quite capable of support-ing thousands of mobile users – and you do not need an additional server to support users with ActiveSync.

7.11.2   Other messaging options for Windows Mobile

Of course, you do not have to use Pocket Outlook on a Windows Mobile device to access Exchange and many companies have chosen Good Technol-ogy's (acquired in late 2006 by Motorola, see www.good.com) client over Outlook. The Good client runs on a variety of platforms, including Black-Berry, Pocket PC, and Palm devices, and it does an excellent job of integrat-ing with Exchange. Indeed, the Good client offers a better user interface and range of functions than either BlackBerry or Pocket Outlook. However, Good is still working on its international coverage and you may not find that it is a viable option in some of the regions where your users are located. In addition, like the BlackBerry solution, Good requires a separate server infra-structure to support its devices and also suffers some of the same scalability concerns in terms of the number of handheld devices that a single GoodLink server can support, so the Good solution is more expensive to deploy and operate than Exchange ActiveSync is.

Exchange-based messaging is important for the enterprise world, but Short Message Service (SMS) is important for communication with friends and family as well as business acquaintances. The integration of SMS is bet-ter on the BlackBerry because BlackBerry treats SMS messages as just another message type and incorporates the messages into the Blackberry's inbox along with messages from Exchange. Pocket Outlook only includes messages from your Exchange inbox, and if you want to send an SMS mes-sage, you have to select a contact and then select to send an SMS message. These steps are easy, but it would be better if everything was more integrated.

Windows Mobile stores SMS messages that you have sent and received in a separate inbox and outbox that you can access through the folder struc-ture that you can navigate through Pocket Outlook. Windows Mobile han-dles incoming SMS messages well and displays most of the text in the messages as a notification that the device displays at the bottom of the screen. You can tap on the notification to see the complete message.

The first BlackBerry handhelds that incorporated a phone were not great performers as a phone when you compared their functionality and performance to a standard cell phone. The form factor of the BlackBerry did not make it comfortable for people to hold it for long calls and the clarity of communication was usually worse than a standard phone. Any of the current range of BlackBerry devices is a much better phone than the previous generations of BlackBerries were and I have used the 7100 with its earpiece for long conference calls without suffering great discomfort. The BlackBerry's inbuilt loudspeaker and microphone are also effective. I was able to connect the 7100 to the cell phone system in my car with Bluetooth and so did not have to invest in an additional (and expensive) phone connection kit for the car. The iPAQ 6915 is as good a phone as most BlackBerry devices and supports speakerphone and Bluetooth features as well. While some people insist on carrying a separate phone (perhaps so they can use the latest designer phone), I find no problem using the Pocket PC as my only communications device, although if you place more importance on the phone than email, a Windows-based SmartPhone might serve you better. SmartPhones are much closer to classic cell phones in form and function and you will find it harder to process your inbox because of the smaller screen and restrictive keyboard. However, while their form factor means that they are not as functional as the Pocket PC in some respects, such as the range of applications you can run on the device, SmartPhones are an excellent triage device. In other words, they allow you to scan your inbox and make decisions about the messages that you need to respond to and those you can discard. When you get back to a more functional device, such as your PC, you then have a filtered set of messages to process.

7.11.3   Power management

Battery life is always an issue with mobile devices and the BlackBerry has traditionally offered good battery endurance. Even with heavy email use and a fair amount of phone use, my two-year-old BlackBerry goes up to two full days and sometimes three without needing a charge, even without powering the device off overnight. Your battery life will vary depending on how old it is, how many charge cycles the battery has been through, and how much use you make of the device. The capacity of a rechargeable battery to hold a charge degrades over time and after multiple recharge cycles, so the ability of such an old device to provide extended service after hundreds of recharge cycles is very good. By comparison, a Windows Mobile device is usually hungrier for power and exhausts its battery faster than a BlackBerry does. You can expect a full day's use on the iPAQ if you are lucky, two days maximum if you are careful to conserve battery use, but if you are a heavy phone or messaging user, you may see less, perhaps six hours before you need to find an outlet to recharge the battery. Of course, one way to conserve the battery is to turn off the phone and suspend the device when you are not using it, which will stop any mail traffic until you wake the device up again and re-establish communications.

While phone calls are the best way to drain the Pocket PC's battery, using features like the Windows Media player to play music also drain power fast. In addition, if you want the battery to last, you need to disable features like Bluetooth connections, turn down the screen brightness, and set the device to hibernate after a short period of inactivity (one or two minutes). Like anything to do with power, your mileage will vary for any device with the applications that you use and how you use them. Maintaining a full charge on the road is reasonably easy as you can recharge modern mobile devices by connecting them via USB to your PC.

On versions prior to Windows Mobile 5.0, you definitely did not want a Pocket PC to run down its battery because this meant that you had to recreate any customized settings and resynchronize data after you recharge the device. Windows Mobile 5.0 stores user settings and data in solid-state memory, so they are not lost even if the device powers down completely. The BlackBerry has traditionally been more resilient to power failure and you do not have to make as many tweaks after a recharge. If you are someone who absolutely needs better battery lifetime than provided by the standard battery for your Pocket PC, there are plenty of places to buy an upgraded battery, such as http://www.lionbattery.com/. Be sure that the battery you buy is designed to fit your device and that it is a high-quality item and fits into the device properly, as you do not want to end up with a leaking battery. Searching the net for "upgraded battery" and your Pocket PC's model number is normally a good way to find plenty of opinions about the right type of battery to choose.

7.11.4   Input flexibility

Blackberry devices support two different keyboard types. Traditional Blackberry devices have keyboards with a single key per letter while the latest BlackBerry devices assign multiple letters to the majority of the keys. Not having a separate key per letter can be disconcerting to some users but predictive recognition software does a good job of figuring out what letter you mean when you type in text. When you use a Blackberry, you do everything through the keyboard or by navigating command menus with the famous BlackBerry thumbwheel. This system works well and is very effective in the hands of an expert user.

The iPAQ keyboard has more keys for individual characters, so it is easier for most people to use. Like all Windows Mobile devices, the iPAQ supports a software keyboard, voice recording, block character recognition (write letters and the device turns them into text) and handwriting recognition (write letters and the device stores them as bitmaps), so there is a wide variety of methods available to commit your thoughts electronically. Windows Mobile supports a number of keyboard shortcuts, but even so, you still need to use the supplied stylus or a pen—or a finger (after you lose the stylus) to get work done. Like any Windows device, the Pocket PC hides a lot of complexity behind the user interface and it takes time to find out just where all the settings are, but persistence and curiosity will get you there. Windows SmartPhones use the same 12-key layout as standard cell phones, so it is more challenging to compose messages until you get used to the idiosyncrasies of the T9 predictive text engine. After you have learned T9, you can compose reasonably complex messages, but a device with an integrated full keyboard will always be better when it comes to answering email. Windows SmartPhones also include the famous Windows Start button to allow you to get to applications and some command buttons that you can use to open applications, documents, and messages, use for functions required by applications, and so on.

While its browser supports graphics and it can display bitmap images, the BlackBerry does not use as graphical an interface as the version of Windows Internet Explorer supplied on the Pocket PC and SmartPhone do. I think the browser is a real strength of the Windows Mobile platform because I have used it so many times in the last year to do things like discover the time of a bus I had to catch in Paris, look for a hotel or restaurant phone number, check stock prices, airline schedules, sports scores, and so on. Google offers a very nice search page specially designed for mobile devices at www.google.com/pda and you can get to almost any information you care to from here.

The different ways that you can input data into a Windows Mobile device is indicative of the development potential for the Windows platform, which is its real strength over a BlackBerry. BlackBerry is a fast, straightforward, and powerful email client, but once you want to do more than email, you start to hit limitations that do not apply with Windows Mobile. For example, browsing is a frustrating experience on the BlackBerry because the browser struggles to cope with all but the simplest web site. You can receive attachments on the BlackBerry, and the BES server does its best to render Word and Excel documents into something that the BlackBerry can view, but BES struggles to interpret all but the simplest Office documents. The native Microsoft Office compatibility built into Windows Mobile (Figure 7.69) does a far better job of allowing the user to view the content of Office documents, including PowerPoint, than BES can.

Apart from Outlook and SMS messaging, Windows Mobile also supports MSN Messenger and a Live Communications Server client is also available, so you can use the device to IM your contacts (and include a photo of your contact so that you talk to the right person). The inclusion of Windows

Figure 7.69

Reading a Word document on the Pocket PC

Media Player will please music fans—providing that you equip the device with some additional storage (such as a large SD card). Third party media players such as TCPMP (http://tcpmp.corecodec.org/) are also available for Windows Mobile devices, and while the Pocket PC is unlikely to surpass the abilities of a purpose-built device like an iPod to play music and video, it does a passable job. The inbuilt camera on some models of Pocket PCs (the iPAQ 6915 and the HP 514 SmartPhone both incorporate a 1.3 megapixel camera) is a useful tool occasionally. Note that some companies—especially in the financial and government sectors - do not allow devices with cameras on their premises, so it may be best to select a model that does not include this feature. Many people link Global Positioning System (GPS) devices with mapping applications on the Pocket PC to create a low-cost personal navigation system. A range of games is also available for the Pocket PC, including Microsoft's popular "Age of Empires." Sites such as http://www.handmark.com/ and www.pocketgear.com are good resources to search for Pocket PC applications. In some cases, you can find add-on applications (such as IM+ for Black-Berry—see http://www.shapeservices.com/eng/im/BLACKBERRY/ for one example) to upgrade the BlackBerry's functionality. Each application costs money, so you have to be careful to select applications that you really need.

Because the iPAQ is a "pocket PC" that runs a version of Windows, it—or any other Windows Mobile device, including SmartPhone—offer much better development possibilities than a BlackBerry. This is not because you cannot develop code for the BlackBerry but rather because a wider range of development tools exists for Windows Mobile, including the Microsoft Windows Mobile Application Development Toolkit.

Just like anything else in life, it takes time to get used to new things. As an experienced BlackBerry user who had used several different BlackBerry devices, I had grown accustomed to a certain way of doing things like messaging, searching for contacts, and viewing my calendar. It took a little time to figure out how everything worked on the iPAQ, but after a while the combination of the device, Windows Mobile 5.0, and Exchange ActiveSync convinced me that I could survive withdrawal pains and make the transition away from my BlackBerry. Of course, winning over just one user does not mean that a company will decide to move from BlackBerry to EAS and Windows Mobile handhelds. Any company that has deployed BlackBerry has invested in the supporting infrastructure, including:

- Deployment and maintenance of BlackBerry Enterprise Servers (BES): This includes the costs of the licenses and the hardware necessary to support the number of users in your organization. RIM has upgraded BES to support Exchange 2007, but these servers still suffer from some scalability issues due to the way that they connect to mailboxes to intercept new messages before transmitting data to the Blackberry handhelds.

- Administrative support for the BlackBerry servers.

- Training and support for end users.

- Handhelds and the mobile phone subscriptions (some of which may need to be changed to deploy Windows Mobile devices if the cell phone provider does not include a Windows Mobile device in their supported handhelds).

The move to Exchange 2007 and the consequent refresh of the complete Windows infrastructure to deploy new servers may offer companies an opportunity to review their use of handheld devices and decide to switch over at this point.

7.12 Unified Communications

Unified Communications (UC) currently represents the single biggest area of investment for Microsoft in the server area. UC includes Unified Messaging (UM) for Exchange as well as other associated products such as Office Communications Server 2007, Office Live Meeting, and the Office Communicator 2007 client. Microsoft's view is that moving into the unified communications space is a natural evolution of their work on the Office system and follows a trend where technology in any space evolves from being hardware-centric to software-centric. Just as the typewriter evolved into a purpose-built word processor to a general-purpose PC to the software that we have today (including the software to produce great looking documents on even the simplest printer), the telephone has moved from a single-purpose essentially dumb device to multi-purpose phones to IP-based phones to a point where software such as Skype represents the state of the art. Together with more sophisticated and functional software, IP is a unifying protocol in this evolution.

While some pretty complex and sophisticated voice integration has been done in the past, it is usually engineered for bespoke applications such as call centers and normally comes with a hefty bill. Microsoft's view is that the time is now right to make telephony easier, cheaper, and more integrated to help people work together better. Making telephony easier means making some of the embedded features in phones more approachable (like figuring out how call forwarding works or how to join another user into a conference call). Making it more integrated means incorporating the ability to communicate by voice into applications like email and IM so that you can associate properties such as subjects or degrees of importance to calls, add notes to voicemail messages, initiate a call from within Outlook or Communicator or any other presence aware application (such as Share-Point), and so on. Presence information becomes very important in an integrated world because you can make a decision as to what communications method to use based on someone's presence. If you know that they're in the office, then you might call them, but if you know that they are out of the office for the next three days (because you can read their free/busy data or their OOF notice), then you're more likely to send them email. Directory integration is also important because you can now begin to use the phone information that the Active Directory has always stored, and applications can begin to identify people by name rather than their number when they call you. Another benefit is that as Microsoft builds APIs to develop these applications, the developer community can then leverage the APIs to build even better applications on top of the new platform.

The general messaging community is likely to gain a number of advantages from Microsoft's venture into the UC arena:

- As Microsoft pours in R&D dollars, the pace of innovation in UC will accelerate and will encourage the whole industry to put more focus on how their applications work in with unified communications.

- Users will become aware that the software applications they use support features that use integrated communications, such as the voicemail options in Outlook 2007. This will drive some additional demand and may encourage companies to accept the concept of UC faster.

- The support of the Windows developer ecosystem will drive acceptance through new applications that exploit the Microsoft platform.

- Because of the increase in potential business, a wider range of system integrators will be available to help companies to design, deploy, and support UC.

There will also be some challenges. For example:

- The cost of transforming outdated telephony and Windows infrastructures may cause organizations to make trade-offs as to what parts of the infrastructure they will modernize first. Some may decide to concentrate on telephony, some on Windows, and some will attack both to produce a totally integrated infrastructure.
- Demos of UC invariably get the creative juices going, but there's a lot of hard work between running a demo and running UC for a large organization.
- Some companies will resist what seems to be an invitation to put all of their UC eggs into the one Microsoft basket; heterogenous support for UC is still an issue as not everyone runs Windows.

There is too much content in the world of UC to attempt to cover it here. Instead, let's look at what Unified Messaging means in the context of Exchange 2007.

7.13 Unified Messaging

Unified Messaging has been around for a long time. The industry normally defines UM to be a system that provides access to email, voicemail, and fax services via phones and email clients. I remember visiting a Nortel development group in the late 1990s to see their latest technology for integrating voicemail with Exchange. Nortel had a special form of Windows server that incorporated about 80GB of disk space to store voicemail that fit into their PBX. An add-on to Outlook allowed users to listen to voicemail. The system worked well, but it was expensive (over $100 extra per user), required special hardware and software, would only support specific models of PBX, and created work that was very much outside the boundaries of a normal deployment of Exchange. The overall cost and complexity of deploying and supporting UM was the usual block that stopped companies from translating an initial interest in UM to an actual implementation.

Perhaps because of the cost and complexity involved in connecting email to traditional corporate telephony systems, up to the time that they started to lay out the feature set for Exchange 2007, Microsoft never really paid much attention to Unified Messaging. As older telephony systems aged (so some new features are not available), customers amortized the investment that they made to upgrade telephone systems to handle the demands of Y2K, the capacity of industry-standard servers improved in terms of their ability to handle the demands of voice processing, and standards such as SIP (Session Initiation Protocol) became more common. Microsoft's interest in UM increased, leading to a situation where you can now buy and deploy a dedicated Exchange 2007 UM server.

Increased support for SIP within telecommunications infrastructures is an important step forward in terms of UM technology because it means that you can more easily integrate telephony components together across a corporate WAN. It also eliminates the requirements to co-locate PBXs with email servers as a SIP connector (to convert TDM signalling to SIP), so you can deploy the necessary components to connect the existing telephony infrastructure with Exchange without having to re-engineer anything. A TDM to SIP gateway can support anything from 4 to 120 ports, with smaller gateways using digital set emulation and larger gateways using 24 or 30 channel T1 or E1 connections. Each gateway port handles a telephone session with the UM server to send voicemail or access UM commands that the UM server then actions. These gateway systems need to be co-located with the PBX that they serve because the signalling protocols that they use were never designed for WAN interconnection. However, over time, more companies are switching to IP-based PBXs. Newer IP-based PBXs are likely to support SIP over TCP/IP (as opposed to SIP over UDP, which still requires a gateway to communicate with Exchange) and their deployment will remove the need for the gateway systems to communicate Exchange UM. Microsoft plans to integrate Exchange UM with more PBXs (and the software that often comes with PBXs, such as Cisco Call Manager) to make the integration even easier. PBXs like Mitel's 3300 ICP (www.mitel.com <http://www.mitel.com>) that include a direct SIP connection that supports Exchange 2007 UM are likely to be popular with Exchange customers because they remove the requirement for a gateway and take some complexity out of the overall configuration.

It is too early to say just how successful Microsoft will be with UM, but it is safe to observe that Microsoft has shaken up the market by reducing the cost of deployment and by integrating voicemail much more closely with Outlook than has been done by other vendors to date. Of course, given that Microsoft has the chance and the platform to extend both email client and email server to deal with voicemail better than any add-on software can do, it is not surprising that Microsoft's integrated voicemail looks more complete and finished than anything that has gone before. The reaction of the traditional voicemail vendors such as Avaya and Cisco will be interesting in terms of the competitive products that they will now generate. However, the overall success of Exchange 2007 UM will probably be more influenced by the speed that organizations deploy Exchange 2007, the level of interest that the customer base has in delivering voicemail integration to their users, and Microsoft's success in selling the benefit that UM delivers above what users already get from Outlook. The benefits that Microsoft often cite include an increase in end-user productivity because users have more comprehensive access to messages, especially for mobile users who have enjoyed much better access to email recently through PDAs without seeing quite the same increase in functionality for voicemail or, indeed, voice access to email. When Microsoft presents UM, they often illustrate how they see people using UM through some scenarios such as:

- You are travelling and your cell phone is the only way that you can connect to the network and you need to access your inbox to check for an important message—clearly, voicemail access can be a big benefit in this situation. The benefit of being able to access your calendar via the phone is also obvious, especially as you can rearrange appointments via voice command!

- You are transiting between locations and need to check on your schedule for the rest of the day. You could look at your PDA, but this is hard to do (and illegal) if you're driving, but you can use a hands-free phone kit to call Exchange 2007 UM to check your calendar and find out where you are supposed to go. Along the same lines, if you discover that you are going to be late for your next meeting, you can ask Exchange to send a notice to meeting attendees to update them.

- You are on the road and do not want to spend time to listen to your voicemail messages on the phone before you leave the hotel. Because Outlook downloads your voicemail into the local cache along with your other email, you can listen to the messages through Outlook when you get a chance to later on, even if you do not have a network connection.

UM is often associated with Unified Communications (UC), which expands the traditional features of UM to include other modes of communication such as voice, video, and instant messaging. UC includes capabilities such as presence updates, initiating calls from IM conversations, and "find-me" or "follow-me" services.

The Exchange 2007 UM server is the basic building block of an Exchange UM deployment. This is a new server role that you can deploy anywhere within your organization, where it is available to any PBXs that you want to connect to it. The UM role can co-exist alongside other server roles and is commonly deployed on the same physical computer as a mailbox or CAS server, especially in smaller organizations where you cannot justify the expense of a dedicated UM server.

The UM server is responsible for performing any audio-related functions, such as:

- Answering a telephone call, playing the appropriate user greeting, and recording any messages that the caller leaves.

- The Outlook Voice Access (OVA) component provides speech recognition to allow remote telephone access to voicemail, email, calendaring, and contents. This includes text to speech conversion to allow users to listen to email and other mailbox content over the phone and support for natural language commands for common tasks such as "clear my calendar." If the system has problems recognizing voice commands during a session or the user wishes to, the system can switch to accept DTMF (dual tone multi-frequency signalling, or Touch Tone) commands. Outlook Voice Access works by accepting calls to the subscriber access number, asking users for a PIN, and then logging on to the user's mailbox to act as an agent on behalf of the user. Outlook Voice Access can then perform whatever actions the user selects from a voice-driven menu, such as reading new messages from the inbox, checking their calendar, or finding someone in contacts or the Active Directory. However, a potentially big issue is that Outlook Voice Access supports AVR (Automatic Voice Recognition) commands in US English only,[23] so this is obviously a problem for major markets such as France, Germany, Italy, Japan, China, and Iberia. Outlook Voice Access supports 16 languages for DTMF commands in the initial release of Exchange 2007. You can expect Microsoft to address this issue proactively as Exchange 2007 service packs roll out or through the release of modular language packs that you can download from the web.

- Auto Attendant functionality that allows users to select from a spoken menu of options to allow the user to reach the right person or other location. For example, a caller can reach a helpline with a single number and then select from a menu of options such as reset my password, access application help, reach a specific help desk team, or so on. Exchange 2007 Auto Attendants support multiple hierarchies of attendants that can be accessed through touch-tone or by voice commands. The attendants can access the GAL to find the right destination. Users can also use touch-tone phones to search the GAL for a recipient.

---

23.   Outlook Voice Access does a reasonably good job of dealing with the range of accents that you encounter in the US.

- Fax receipt and delivery to the right mailbox. While Exchange can route incoming faxes to the right mailbox, you need to install a separate fax gateway if you want to allow users to send outgoing faxes.

- Missed call notification. If a call is redirected to voicemail and the caller does not leave a message, the UM server can send an email to the recipient with a timestamp and caller ID of the caller. If the UM server can resolve the caller ID against the user's contacts or the GAL (if you share the same dialplan with the caller—cross dialplan resolution is planned for Exchange 2007 SP1), then it provides the caller name. Users can disable this feature if they want.

- Like other parts of Exchange, administrators can impose policies to control how users access UM, including options such as PIN setting, PIN lifetime, and restrictions on international calling.

This is a reasonable set of features for any voicemail system to offer, so let's move on to understand how easy Outlook Voice Access is to use in practice.

7.13.1 Client Access to voicemail

Using Outlook Voice Access is easy. You ring the number that's allocated to you for Outlook Voice Access, enter your PIN, and respond to the voice-driven menu of commands. Access to a cluttered inbox is slow because Outlook Voice Access has to scan the inbox to detect waiting voicemail. I usually have to wait about 10 seconds before Outlook Voice Access has processed the 4,000 or so messages in my inbox, which is a suitable penalty for my habit of storing anything that I might possibly ever have to respond to in the inbox.

Once connected, Outlook Voice Access tells you the number of any new voice and email messages and what your current calendar contains. You can then take the voicemail option to start dealing with voicemail, email to go directly to the inbox, or directory to look up a contact or user. You can reply to an existing message or look up someone to send a new voicemail. If you prefer to use Outlook Voice Access to go to another folder, you can select the folder you prefer through the Voice Mail options available in Outlook 2007 and Outlook Web Access 2007. The voice-driven commands offered by Outlook Voice Access make the process reasonably easy, even if the somewhat metallic female voice that is used can remind you of a teacher from time to time. It is not quite as annoying as the voices used to respond to commands in some cars, but Outlook Voice Access can get close at times. Fortunately, you quickly learn that you can interrupt Outlook Voice Access and instruct it to move to your desired command without having to listen through interminable lists of available commands.

Outlook 2007 and Outlook Web Access 2007 clients both incorporate special processing, including an embedded audio control, to provide users with a more elegant experience while they work with voicemail messages. Older clients receive voicemail messages as WMA attachments that Windows Media Player or a similar program can play.

Figure 7.70

Voicemail messages as displayed by Outlook 2007

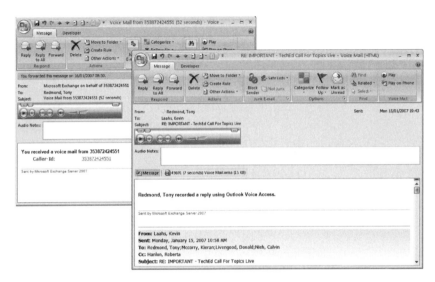

Figure 7.70 shows two voicemail messages displayed through Outlook 2007. On the left-hand side, you can see a message that has come into my mailbox from an unknown caller. The Unified Messaging server has not been able to resolve the telephone number against my contacts (it would be nice if the server was able to scan the Active Directory for the number), so it displays the number as received by the PBX in the header. The right-hand message is a reply in the form of a voicemail that I sent in response to a message that I listened to via Outlook Voice Access. In both cases, you can see that Outlook displays an audio control to allow the voice attachment to be played through the PC.

YYou can use Outlook (Figure 7.71) to change the greeting message that Exchange UM plays to callers by using Outlook to call a number and then recording a new greeting. Outlook 2007 only activates the Voice Mail property page if it detects the present of the Unified Messaging web service through its AutoConfiguration feature and your mailbox is enabled for voicemail. The URL that points to the Unified Messaging web service is of the form https://Exumserver/UnifiedMessaging/service.asmx. You can use Outlook's Test AutoConfiguration option to check whether clients can detect the UM service.

As part of its support for DTMF, Exchange converts user names to various forms that users can spell out using the keys on a touch-tone phone. You can see these values with a `Get-Mailbox` command. For example, here is the touch-tone information for my mailbox, which is quite easy to figure out because you know my name:

```
Get-Mailbox Redmond | Select umdt* | Format-List


UMEnabled : True
UMDtmfMap : {emailAddress:86697336663,
lastNameFirstName:73366638669, firstNameLastName:86697336663}
```

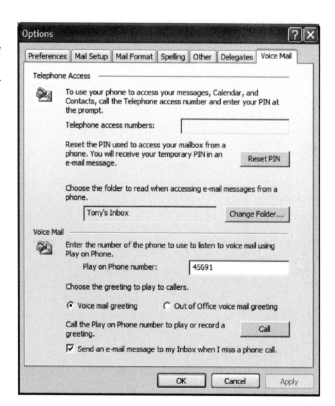

Figure 7.71
*Setting voice mail
options from
Outlook 2007*

Of course, because Unified Messaging is part of Exchange 2007, you can use a range of PowerShell commands to manage Unified Messaging components. For example, to enable a mailbox for Unified Messaging:

```
Enable-UmMailbox –id Redmond –UmPolicy 'Dublin Users'
```

—Extensions 5143 —PIN 452545 —PINExpired $True

This command enables a mailbox for Unified Messaging and specifies a policy, extension number, and PIN. The PIN is expired, so the user has to change it the next time that they connect. The command to disable Unified Messaging for a mailbox is naturally `Disable-UmMailbox`. The `Set-UmMailbox` command allows us to manipulate properties further, such as defining whether the user can use features such as fax or missed call notification. The `Get-UmMailbox` command retrieves information about the Unified Messaging properties set on a mailbox.

```
Get-UmMailbox —id Redmond | Format-List
```

```
DisplayName                          : Redmond, Tony
EmailAddresses                       : {smtp:tony.redmond@xyz.com, EUM
:45691;phone-context=Dublin Dial Plan.xyz.com,        sip:tony.redmond@xyz.com}
ServerName                           : g3w0076
UMDtmfMap                            : {emailAddress:86697336663, lastNameFirstNam
                                       e:73366638669, firstNameLastName:8669733666
                                       3}
UMEnabled                            : True
TUIAccessToCalendarEnabled           : True
FaxEnabled                           : True
TUIAccessToEmailEnabled              : True
SubscriberAccessEnabled              : True
TUIAccessToAddressBookEnabled        : True
MissedCallNotificationEnabled        : True
AnonymousCallersCanLeaveMessages     : True
AutomaticSpeechRecognitionEnabled    : True
AllowUMCallsFromNonUsers             : SearchEnabled
OperatorNumber                       :
UMDialPlan                           : Dublin Dial Plan
UMMailboxPolicy                      : Dublin Dial Plan Default Policy
Extensions                           : {45691}
CallAnsweringAudioCodec              :
SIPResourceIdentifier                :
```

The `Get-UMServer` command returns details of a Unified Messaging server and the `Set-UMServer` command allows you to set properties of the server.

```
Get-UMServer —id ExchUMSvr1 | Format-List
```

```
Name                 : ExchUMSvr1
MaxCallsAllowed      : 100
```

```
MaxFaxCallsAllowed          : 100
MaxTTSSessionsAllowed       : 50
MaxASRSessionsAllowed       : 50
Status                      : Enabled
Languages                   : {en-US}
DialPlans                   : {UM Test Lab, Dublin Dial Plan}
GrammarGenerationSchedule   : {Sun.2:00 AM-Sun.2:30 AM, Mon.2:00
AM-Mon.2:30 AM,
                              Tue.2:00 AM-Tue.2:30 AM, Wed.2:00 AM-
Wed.2:30 AM, T
                              hu.2:00 AM-Thu.2:30 AM, Fri.2:00 AM-
Fri.2:30 AM, Sa
                              t.2:00 AM-Sat.2:30 AM}
```

There are many other commands specific to Unified Messaging, such as Get-UmMailboxPIN and Set-UMMailboxPIN that retrieve details of the PINs set on a mailbox and reset a PIN respectively. These commands are probably not as interesting to the wider Exchange community, so I will leave you to investigate the full set of UM commands at your leisure, or when you deploy your first Exchange 2007 Unified Messaging server.

7.13.2 Dealing with voicemail

Apart from its ability to play voicemail directly through the embedded audio control, Outlook 2007 provides two other options to help you to deal with voice messages. As well as playing the message on the PC, you can direct it to a phone and have the message played there (Figure 7.72). This is a convenient option because you may be working in an environment where you do not want others to be able to overhear the message. We do not yet have the capability to index the content of voicemail, so you can add notes to a received or sent voicemail to help you understand what the message contains without having to open it. You can select only phone numbers that are allowed by the dialling rules in the UM policy assigned to your mailbox. For example, you could not ask Outlook to call the number of your cell phone if the policy bars access to cell phones.

The other option is the ability to add some text content to a voicemail message. Audio content is great to have but it can be very hard to find voicemail, even if you carefully move any voicemail that you receive into an appropriate folder or the sender has used a subject that clearly indicates the content and meaning of the message. Unfortunately, the default subject for any voicemail generated by Outlook Voice Access is "Voice Mail from …" and you cannot change the subject before you send the message, so that's what arrives in the recipient's mailbox. As we all know, senders are not great in composing appropriate subjects for normal messages, so even messages that contain a mixture of voice and text content can be hard to find in a cluttered mailbox. As shown in Figure 7.72, you can add text in the "Audio Notes" field to help you understand what the message contains, but only with Outlook 2007 or Outlook Web Access 2007, as other clients do not include the user interface to expose this data.

Figure 7.72

Play on phone and audio notes

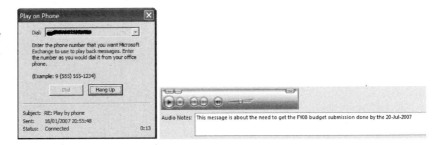

If you send voicemail to someone who uses a client other than Outlook 2007 or Outlook Web Access 2007, they receive the voice content as WMA attachments. This also applies if you forward messages containing voice content outside your organization to a messaging system where Exchange Unified Messaging is not installed. For example, the message shown in Figure 7.73 contains three WMA attachments generated as the result of a thread of voicemail between two users. This message contained some audio notes, but these are discarded when you forward a message because audio notes are deemed to be confidential to an individual.

Even if the receiving client (in this case, Outlook Web Access 2007 running in another Exchange organization) is unable to display the audio control, the voice content is perfectly accessible because you can play the attachment with Windows Media Player or another audio player.

Some legal departments have expressed concern about the effect of UM on discovery actions. Up to now, it is common for voicemail systems to clear out old messages after a month or so, partly because the systems have limited storage and partly because lawyers do not want voicemail kept around and available to be discovered. A feeling exists that users are less cautious when they send voicemail than they are when they send email and to a certain degree, this is true. After all, you do not see the content when you create a voicemail and you have less chance to review what you have created before sending voicemail, so the possibility exists that you might say something that you would prefer not to be available for discovery. When you deploy UM, users gain the advantage of being able to deal with voicemail in the same way that they can with regular email—they can forward messages, store them on PSTs, add audio notes, and so on. However, just like regular messages, voicemail then ends up on backup tapes and linger for a lot longer than if voicemail systems clear them out automatically. Even worse (from the lawyers' perspective), users can keep voicemail on personal devices that no one else knows about until the voicemail surfaces under threat of discovery. Clearly, this is a complicated issue that can create unique implications for different companies, but it is worth considering as you develop your deployment plan.

Figure 7.73
Attached voicemail

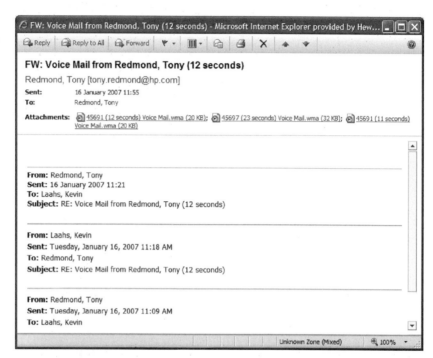

7.13.3 Voice synthesis

Having your email read to you by a machine is not new. The first time I encountered a system with this capability was in 1984, when Digital Equipment Corporation's ALL-IN-1 Office System integrated DECtalk Voice Mail Access. Of course, the integration took more work then because you had to connect all sorts of special equipment to a VAX computer to have ALL-IN-1 play email messages back to a touch-tone phone, but the system worked and the DECtalk hardware had other tricks, such as being able to sing a small number of songs. As I recall, "Moonlight in Vermont" was DECtalk's party piece. Some of the original DECtalk engineers work at Microsoft now and I am sure that they have used their 20-plus years of experience to make Outlook Voice Access work as well as it possibly can. Most of the time, Outlook Voice Access makes a pretty good job of reading the content of messages, though it has its challenges when it meets non-English names or terms embedded in a stream of English content. If you embed titles and department names in user display names, you may also raise a wry smile when you listen to Outlook Voice Access grappling with these words.

Outlook Voice Access also has great fun reading a message written in a foreign language, for example, if you receive a message in French and Outlook Voice Access attempts to read the French content as if all the words were English. This can generate some hilarious results. Outlook Voice Access is able to handle non-English content, but only if you install the necessary language packs on the UM server to support the languages that you would like Outlook Voice Access to read back to users. However, even with the necessary language packs installed, you may still have to instruct Outlook Voice Access as to what language it should use to read a message because Outlook Voice Access may not be able to detect what language it should use for best effect. For example, if you receive a message in French that you want Outlook Voice Access to read in French, you use the voice command "Set Language French." There is no way of retaining this setting with the message, so you will have to do it each time that you want it to be read in French. In some cases, Outlook Voice Access is able to detect the language contained in a message using the codepage of the message body. This is most obvious with double-byte languages, so if you receive a message in Japanese or Chinese, Outlook Voice Access is able to switch to read the message in the proper language automatically as long as the required language pack is installed on the UM server. You may not be able to understand the content, but that is another matter.

Directory access through voice commands is acceptable if not brilliant. Outlook Voice Access does its best to find the person that you want to contact. You can search through your Personal Contacts or the Active Directory and Outlook Voice Access will tell you if it finds multiple matches and allow you to select from one of the found entries, but I have a very bad record of being able to find anyone in the directory. This may be due to my accent, the way that I am pronouncing names (normally, Outlook Voice Access looks for you to ask for people by stating their first and last names), the size of the GAL (the more entries in the GAL, the more opportunity exists for name clashes), or the way that Outlook Voice Access interprets what I have said and uses it to find someone. For example, a request to find Veli-Matti Vanamo resulted in Darlene Masci, while looking for Kevin Laahs found Bob Kassam!

7.13.4 Pure voicemail

Another design point that often confuses is the way that Outlook Voice Access differentiates between voicemail and email. Every message that comes into your inbox is displayed by Outlook, but Outlook Voice Access splits the inbox into voicemail messages and email. Sounds logical, but then you see a further differentiation between "pure" voicemail messages that only contain voice content and other voicemail messages that contain a mixture of voice and text. Outlook Voice Access presents pure voicemail in the voicemail inbox and leaves other messages, even those that contain voice content, in the regular inbox. This is confusing because users think that a message is a message, and what is the point of unified messaging if voice and text aren't melded together into a unified inbox?

Of course, there is a technical reason why Outlook Voice Access deals with messages differently. When you call Outlook Voice Access, it tells you whether any new messages are waiting (the more messages are in the inbox, the longer you wait for this check to complete) and then asks you to select Voicemail or Email. If you select voicemail, Outlook Voice Access scans your inbox for any message that has a message class of "IPM.Note.Microsoft.VoiceMail.UM.*," but if you select email, Outlook Voice Access looks for any message that is not of class "IPM.Note.Microsoft.VoiceMail.UM.*." If you receive an email and then generate a voice reply, the resulting message has a class of "IPM.Note.Microsoft.VoiceMail", so it is never found by Outlook Voice Access when it scans for new voicemail! Outlook and Outlook Web Access recognize that these messages contain voicemail so it's a tad baffling why Outlook Voice Access ignores them. However, if Outlook Voice Access opens a message that contains voice content when it processes email, it accesses and reads the content properly. All of this means that Outlook Voice Access isn't quite as unified when it comes to messaging as it could be.

7.13.5 The magic of SIP

All of the UM magic depends on SIP communications between a PBX and the Exchange UM server. When a call comes in to the PBX that the recipient does not answer after a defined interval, the PBX attempts to handle the call by routing it somewhere. When you deploy Exchange UM servers, the PBX knows that it can send certain calls to Exchange for processing because you update the call coverage information on the PBX with a pilot number for the UM server so that the PBX knows where to route calls to busy or unanswered extensions for UM-enabled mailboxes. Every UM-enabled user has an associated extension (usually the same as the extension used for regular calls) that is defined as a property of the user's Active Directory object. The Exchange organization has at least one dial plan object. Figure 7.74 illustrates some of the detail that you will see in a dial plan. In this case, you can see that the default audio codec is WMA and that the default language is EN-US (American English), along with some other settings such as the maximum length of a voicemail message (30 minutes seems a tad extreme). Details defined on other property pages include the numbers required to dial an outside line or internationally.

Complex or distributed organizations can deploy several dial plans to handle different PBX configurations. Another important element is the IP gateway object that Exchange uses to figure out where calls come from and where to send calls to when it needs to transfer them. Each IP gateway is defined in a dial plan so that Exchange knows that calls will come in through the gateway. The interaction between the PBX, gateway, dial plans, and extensions requires planning before deployment and this work is usually done by a combination of the messaging and telecommunications teams.

Assuming that the extension being called is handled by Exchange, the PBX sends call signalling information including the caller's number and the destination extension to the Exchange UM server via a SIP INVITE[24] request, which is basically an invitation to create a conversation. The Exchange UM server uses the extension number to determine whether or not it is for a UM-enabled user, and if it is, the UM server retrieves the user's greeting message. The greeting message is stored as a hidden item in the root of the user's mailbox. If a greeting is available, the UM server converts the audio file and plays it back to the caller as a stream of Real-Time Protocol (RTP) packets that the gateway between UM and the PBX understands. If the caller wants to leave a message, the PBX sends Exchange another stream of information that the gateway converts to RTP packets and sends to the UM server. The UM server converts this data into an audio file and then creates a new message that Exchange routes to the user's inbox via the nearest hub transport server. During this process, Exchange checks the caller ID information against the user's contacts and the GAL to attempt to discover more information about the caller. Incoming faxes are dealt with in much the same way, with the difference being that Exchange creates a TIFF file from the incoming T.38 fax data for the new message instead of a voice audio file.

Exchange 2007 UM supports three codecs for audio storage. A codec is the encoding scheme that converts voice messages to a format that can be easily stored and accessed in a repository such as an email mailbox. Exchange 2007 supports the WMA (Windows Media Audio), GSM (Global System for Media Communication), and PCM (Pulse Code Modulation) codecs. PCM offers the highest fidelity, but uses most space. A thirty-second voice-mail message stored in PCM format is likely to occupy around 450KB while the same message in GSM occupies roughly 8 KB/second, or around 240KB. By comparison, the WMA codec generates the most compressed messages at approximately 2KB per second, so a 30-second message in WMA format will take up around 60KB. WMA will be the most likely option chosen by most organizations because of its general use in a Windows environment and because users can store and access these files on other devices, such as a hand-held device or even a Macintosh. Linux is currently the only platform that may have trouble with WMA attachments until someone in the open source community backward engineers the format to generate a Linux codec. Some administrators fear the storage requirements for voicemail, but in practice, voicemail messages tend to be 30 seconds or less and the messages that Exchange generates in mailboxes are usually far smaller than the size of

---

24.   See RFC3261.

Figure 7.74
Dial plan details

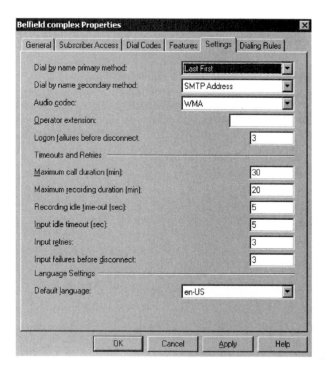

attachments that commonly circulate in large enterprise email infrastructures today. A single large PowerPoint deck or even the graphics that some users include in their autosignatures will occupy more space than many voicemails. The cumulative effect on storage requirements caused by voicemail building up in mailboxes is more of a concern. Voicemails tend to be transient information, so it is a good idea to coach users to listen and then delete voicemail to prevent them exhausting their mailboxes quotas with lots of obsolete messages. You can also create a mailbox policy to remove voice messages after a specific period.

Performance data from Microsoft indicates that a single UM server can cope with up to 100 simultaneous calls on a server with two dual-core CPUs and up to 2GB of memory. If you need to handle more traffic than this, you need to deploy more UM servers. One hundred simultaneous calls on a single UM server is an artificial limit because in theory there is no upper limit for concurrent calls that a suitably sized server can cope with, so it is likely that you will see Microsoft test well past 100 simultaneous calls in the future as new hardware becomes available. In an enterprise-class deployment, you will need to deploy dedicated UM servers and you will have to cope with issues such as how best to position the servers within the network so that you provide load balancing, failover, and suitable performance in terms of delivery of voicemail to user mailboxes. Experience with UM deployments to date demonstrates that you see an initial peak in demand as users experiment with the new technology and demonstrate to each other that they can send and receive voicemail messages with Exchange and all the other tricks that OVA allows followed by a settling down period when demand subsides to more normal levels.[25]

On the surface, a positive future seems to exist for Exchange-based UM. Microsoft has a highly functional UM server, good client and server integration, the world of telephony is changing to support SIP everywhere, server hardware is able to support more activity than ever before, and the move of Exchange to the 64-bit Windows platform allows larger mailboxes for users to store voicemail alongside all their other data. However, apart from some small missing features (such as voicemail integration with non-Microsoft systems), the big challenge may be connecting the sales cycle for Exchange with customer buyers who traditionally have never dealt with email. In most large companies, telephony is a specialized discipline for people who have the necessary training to design and implement telephone networks. These individuals probably know nothing about Exchange and would not recognize Microsoft as a provider of enterprise telephony products. For example, telephone systems usually have a 99.9999% uptime—an uptime level that a Windows-based messaging system might have some difficulty to prove that it can attain. It will take some time and a lot of effort for Microsoft to prove their worth as a UM provider and to make the necessary connections in the right places with customers to overcome the concerns of the telephony group.

7.13.6 Speech Grammars

Speech Grammars is a term that will be unfamiliar to messaging administrators, but providing a mechanism to allow users to control their mailboxes through automatic voice recognition that allows users to give commands in natural language is a big part of delivering value through unified messaging. Exchange UM uses one or more speech grammars active when it responds to a call. Some grammars are used for command and control and contain details of the basic commands that you can issue to Exchange over the phone. For example, Outlook Voice Access understands commands like "Next Meeting" or "Call Organizer" that allow users to work with their calendar and "Next Message" or "Reply All" to work with mailboxes. These commands are defined in standard speech grammars and stay the same until Microsoft updates them in a service pack or new version of Exchange. The first version of Exchange UM only supports US English,

---

25.   See http://www.newport-networks.com/pages/voip-bandwidth-calculator.html for a good calculator to assess bandwidth requirements between the IP gateway and the UM server. For the G.711 codec, the estimate is 87kbp/s for an active voice call. For G.723.1, the estimate is 22kbp/s.

so the speech grammars are encoded to allow Outlook Voice Access to recognize commands in US English, including accommodation for the many accents that make up US English and regional variations such as UK English and Australian English. Future versions may incorporate new speech grammars to support additional languages.

Coping with spoken commands so that software interprets the commands correctly is a well-understand technical problem for engineers to attack. Outlook Voice Access supports a limited set of commands and voices, and while different people speak with different accents and stress words in different ways, the software can be tuned to recognize different ways that the set of command words are spoken. Things get a lot more interesting and many times more difficult when you take on the challenge of directory lookups for user names. For example, if you want to find someone in the directory, you state their name and let the software find that person by searching the directory. This is easy to do in controlled conditions with a limited directory composed only of basic English names organized in a predictable fashion. However, Outlook Voice Access has to work against the Active Directory to locate users, and companies populate the Active Directory in different ways. Some organizations use a naming scheme for display names that is based on first name, last name; some use last name, first name; some incorporate titles; some incorporate initials; some include organizational detail such as department name or location; and some use a mixture of all of the above. Add in common surnames (how many Smiths are there in your directory?) and a heterogeneous sprinkling of names from difficult cultures and the technical challenge of supporting voice-driven lookups against the directory is a different order of complexity.

To solve the problem, Exchange UM creates speech grammars by scanning the Active Directory to discover information about the mail-enabled objects in the GAL. Because you can restrict the ability of users to contact other users through dial plans, following a schedule (normally starting at 2AM nightly), Exchange creates grammars for the complete GAL and for every individual dial plan in use within the organization. Speech grammars created from the Active Directory contain the display names of users and a unique identifier for each user (because several users can share the same name and because some names that are spelt differently sound the same). If Outlook Voice Access finds several matches for a name, it can use the identifiers to help the user to find the right person to contact. Each UM server creates its own speech grammars and the files are not shared or replicated between servers if multiple UM servers operate in an organization.

When Exchange builds speech grammars, it attempts to create forms of user names that Outlook Voice Access can match against values provided by users. This is done by processing the names through several stages that normalize names to make them easier for text-to-speech engines to handle, translate foreign characters to English, and to create values according to a pattern filter[26] that helps Outlook Voice Access understand the different forms that a name might take. For example, pattern filters help Outlook Voice Access recognize parts of names such as hyphens that are not used in the spoken form, so the text-to-speech engine does not attempt to process these elements. Several different values for a name may be generated for inclusion in the speech grammar, each of which lead to the same user. This allows Outlook Voice Access to accommodate callers who ask for users in slightly different ways. Of course, it is likely that Microsoft will receive a huge amount of feedback about the pattern files and their output as customers gain experience with UM, so you can expect greater accuracy and precision in the speech grammars as time goes by.

7.13.7   Phonetic names

The fact that different organizations have different naming conventions for display names poses a problem for Outlook Voice Access as it is inconceivable that Microsoft could force companies to change an established naming convention just to accommodate voice access. To get around the problem and to increase the probability that Outlook Voice Access can find a requested user, you can add a special attribute called the Phonetic Display Name[27] for users that may not be easily identifiable, perhaps because their name sounds differently to the way that it is written. There is no GUI for this, so you have to set these values through the Set-User shell command. For instance:

```
Set-User —Id James.Bond@xyz.com —PhoneticDisplayName 'James
Bond Super Spy'
```

Another situation that has to be dealt with is where a difference occurs between a user's formal name and the name that they are commonly known by (the name that users are more likely to ask for when they interact with Outlook Voice Access). This can happen for different reasons. My formal name is Anthony, but I am known as Tony, and no one would ever dream of asking for Anthony Redmond when they want to speak to me because even a human operator probably wouldn't know who they were looking for. Another example is where someone's formal name is in a foreign language and they are commonly referred to in an English form. For example, I know a user whose formal name (in Gaelic) is Pádraig Ó Meachair, yet he is always called Paddy Maher. Being able to assign phonetic names for Outlook Voice Access to match against is extremely useful in these situations.

26.   Defined in SpeechGrammarFilterList.XML—this file is only present on a UM server.
27.   Stored in an attribute called msDS-PhoneticDisplayName added by the Exchange 2007 schema update.

You may also have to create phonetic display names if your organization uses a naming convention that generates display names that people are unlikely to use when they look for someone. For example, if your naming convention for mailboxes is last name, first name, then your GAL displays mailboxes in this order:

```
Redmond, Andy
Redmond, James
Redmond, Tony
```

This order is extremely logical when you want to find someone in the GAL, but it is not a very natural way to refer to anyone, especially when prompted for their name. In these circumstances, it is much more natural to ask for "Tony Redmond" or "Jane Smith," which poses a problem for Outlook Voice Access because it will not be able to find these names in its speech grammar. The solution is to create a script that assigns phonetic display names to users based on the values of their first and last names. For example, here's a script that searches for users in the Legal department and assigns them a new phonetic display name:

```
$Users = Get-User -filter {Department -eq 'Legal'}
ForEach-Object ($U in $Users)
{
        $PN = $U.FirstName + " " + $U.LastName
        Write-Host "Processing " $PN
        Set-User $U.Name -PhoneticDisplayName $PN
        $PN = $Null
}
```

You can only add a single phonetic display name for each user.

Even with maximum attention paid to speech grammars, there are going to be times when Outlook Voice Access cannot understand or resolve human speech in order to find a UM-enabled user. It may be that the requested user is not in the speech grammar because their mailbox was only recently added or that the caller may have said their name indistinctly or across a bad line. Background noise may have been sufficient to transform the requested name into an unintelligible mess or the caller spoke so softly that Outlook Voice Access was not able to recognize what they were looking for. Another reason is that the caller might use an unusual form of a name for Outlook Voice Access to search for, such as asking for Joseph Louis when someone has been called Joe Louis since the day that they were born. You cannot do much about the time delay between user mailboxes being added and inclusion in the speech grammars unless you regenerate the grammars very frequently, which is not practical. You cannot do much about background noise, bad connections, or callers who don't speak clearly. All you can do is to improve the chances that Outlook Voice Access can find the right user for callers is to consider customizing the pattern filter files to accommodate the requirements of your organization or to add phonetic display names to the Active Directory for your users.

7.13.8   Cross-forest UM

While UM is not designed to work across forests, some parts of its functionality do. For example, a UM user known to one forest will not be recognized as a UM user in another forest, even if you replicate data between forests, because Active Directory replication does not include the UM attributes. Some progress may be made if Microsoft enhances the replication of Active Directory information between forests in future releases to include UM data.

Until then, it is entirely possible for a UM user to send voice messages to other forests if they know the right email addresses to use. The recipients will be able to play the voice messages through any client that knows how to handle voice attachments. You might even be able to persuade UM to dial a foreign user if you know their telephone number and the dialing plan supports it. Also, even if users from two forests share the same PBX, missed call notifications from users in a different forest won't contain anything but their calling number.

7.14   Special mailboxes

If you browse the set of mailboxes in a store on an Exchange 2003 server, you will find three that do not seem to belong to anyone. These mailboxes are special because Exchange uses them for its own purposes. Figure 7.75 illustrates a typical mailbox set with the three special mailboxes clearly shown.

The special Exchange mailboxes are:

- SMTP (plus server name and GUID): An SMTP folder is present in every mailbox store (the GUID value corresponds to the GUID of the store). Exchange's mail transport subsystem uses this mailbox as a temporary holding point for messages during routing operations. The mailbox includes MTS-IN and MTS-OUT folders used by connectors built with the EDK (Exchange Development Kit) and any other connector (such as the X.400 connector) that uses the MTA. The mail transport subsystem uses a set of other temporary folders to hold messages submitted by MAPI or Outlook Web Access clients while it

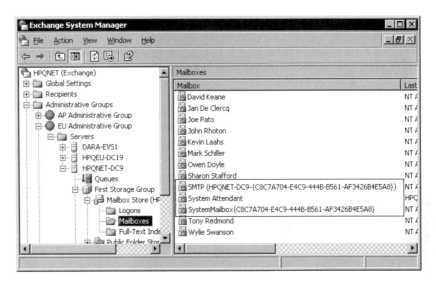

Figure 7.75
Special mailboxes

brings them through the different phases of the routing process. Messages submitted by SMTP (from another Exchange server or through the SMTP connector) are not stored in these folders.

- System Attendant: There is only one System Attendant mailbox per server, which exists in the first mailbox store on the server. Exchange uses this mailbox to publish free/busy information from Outlook Web Access 2003 clients into the store through the MSExchangeFB-Publish process. The Mailbox Move process also uses the System Attendant mailbox and you will not be able to move mailboxes if this mailbox is unavailable for any reason.

- SystemMailbox (plus GUID): This mailbox exists per mailbox store (the GUID value corresponds to the GUID of the store) and holds the structure that defines the schema used by folders. It also holds a separate hierarchy of any event sinks belonging to the mailbox store. Event sinks depend on the schema so they cannot work if the schema is unavailable. The normal size of the mailbox is 361KB (401 items), which is the space occupied by the schema.

Apart from the physical mailboxes, Exchange holds a separate entry for each mailbox in its configuration data in the Active Directory. If the SMTP mailbox is not present when the Store mounts a mailbox store, the Store recreates the mailbox based on the information from the Active Directory. If you delete the SMTP mailbox for some reason while the store is operational, Exchange will no longer be able to deliver messages locally or queue messages for outbound delivery to SMTP or to older connectors built with the

Exchange Development Kit. Users may report the problem if they notice that messages remain in the Outbox folder even when they are connected to the server. If the Active Directory entry is deleted in some way, a disconnect condition exists between the SMTP mailbox and the Active Directory and Exchange will not be able to route messages. You will see events 326 and 1194 logged into the event log and you will have to recreate the mailbox using the steps outlined in Microsoft Knowledge Base article 828938.

It is common to see that the SMTP mailbox holds some items, especially on a heavily loaded server or one that experiences transient network problems. Over time, Exchange will clear the messages out of the mailbox, so there is no need to worry about this unless you notice that the number of messages in the mailbox is growing over time and never reduces. In this case, the presence of these messages indicates that Exchange is unable to deliver messages to some destination, so it is worthwhile checking out why the problem exists.

If you attempt to delete the store that holds the System Attendant mailbox, Exchange signals a warning that you will have to restart the System Attendant process after the store deletion completes. During the restart, the System Attendant recreates its mailbox in another mailbox store and updates the mailbox entry in the Active Directory. If you do not restart the System Attendant process, Exchange will continue to operate, but Outlook Web Access 2003 clients will be unable to publish free/busy information into the store and mailbox moves will fail. One indication that a problem exists is the presence of 9175 events (failure to log on to the mailbox) in the event log.

If Exchange attempts to mount a mailbox store and cannot find a SystemMailbox mailbox in the store, it will create a new SystemMailbox mailbox by reference to the configuration data in the AD. If the configuration data is missing, Exchange cannot recreate the mailbox and you will have to recreate its entry in the Active Directory using the procedure described in Microsoft Knowledge Base article 316622.

If you feel the need to log onto the System mailboxes, you can use the MFCMAPI utility for this purpose. Microsoft Knowledge Base article 291794 explains how to use MFCMAPI to log onto a mailbox without creating an explicit profile.

Exchange 2007 takes a different approach to special mailboxes:

- There is one System mailbox per mailbox database. However, unlike the Exchange 2003 ESM console, the Exchange 2007 EMC does not list the System mailbox when you view mailbox information. The same is true if you issue a `Get-Mailbox –Server ServerName` shell command. The only time that you see the System mailbox is through the `Get-MailboxStatistics` shell command, when Exchange 2007 lists the mailbox size (normally around 350KB).

- There is no SMTP mailbox because the Exchange 2007 transport engine does not include the MTS-IN and MTS-OUT processing performed by Exchange 2003.

- There is no System Attendant mailbox because Outlook Web Access 2007 clients do not publish free and busy data via this route.

7.15 Clients and users

Behind every client, there's a user. Clients only do what they are told, so to master what happens with clients, we have to be able to influence how users behave. Some of this discussion occurred in Chapter 3 when we reviewed the basics of how to create mailboxes, but there are other things that an Exchange administrator needs to know to be able to figure out how to help users do the right thing. On we go to Chapter 8.

8

Managing Users

One of the themes that you may have picked up as you read this book is the importance that Microsoft places on policy-driven management for Exchange 2007. In other words, administrators are able to create policies to determine how users interact and gain access to the resources offered by Exchange. You see this in:

- Email Address policies, which define the email addresses that Exchange assigns to mail-enabled objects when they are created or updated. Email address policies are linked to accepted domains, which define the domains that Exchange is willing to accept email for.

- ActiveSync policies, which define how users can interact with Exchange through Windows Mobile devices.

- Unified Messaging policies, which define how users can exploit the features of the Exchange 2007 Unified Messaging server.

- Managed folder mailbox policies, which define how Exchange manages the content that users place into defined folders, both default folders such as the Inbox and Sent Items folders and custom folders that you create to hold items for business purposes. The closest we have seen to this functionality in the past was the Mailbox Manager. However, the Mailbox Manager limited its functionality to removing old messages from folders.

Exchange 2007 removes some policies that you might be familiar with from Exchange 2000/2003. System policies do not exist because PowerShell commands provide a new way to apply settings across a set of objects, including servers, and Email Address Recipient policies divide their work between Email Address policies and accepted domains to provide more flexibility.

The ability to define policies that Exchange then applies automatically is a real boon to administrators because policies ensure consistency across the board. We have already met some of the policies referred to above in earlier chapters. In this chapter, we discuss Messaging Record Management, which makes heavy use of managed folder mailbox policies as well as some of the places where you cannot depend on policies to help users do the right thing. I do not expect that you will ever be able to eradicate bad habits from users (no human being is perfect), so managing users will continue to be a struggle between the desire of administrators to run well-managed servers and the desire of users to do what they want to with the resources of the servers. It has been ever so since the first email server and so it will probably be for the next few years, unless we are swamped with a collection of policies that make Exchange management totally automatic.

8.1   Room and equipment mailboxes

Along with the mailboxes, contacts, and groups that you're familiar with from previous versions of Exchange, we now have rooms and equipment (or resource) mailboxes. These are special versions of mailboxes that you create under the Mailbox section of the Recipient Configuration in EMC. The mailboxes are special because no one ever logs onto the mailboxes and the user accounts associated with the mailboxes are disabled. Equipment mailboxes are usually associated (loosely) with room mailboxes because in real life equipment is always located in a specific room. The sole purpose of room and equipment mailboxes is to allow users to schedule resources when they set up meetings. In this respect, Microsoft has codified what many different companies have done to create this functionality in the past. We've seen mailboxes set up to support conference room bookings that had to have an Outlook client logged in all the time to process incoming reservation requests. Another tactic was to use a public folder to host a calendar for conference rooms. For whatever reason, it took Microsoft a long time to realize that customers needed this functionality and it's surprising that it took so long for resource mailboxes to make an appearance as a formal part of Exchange.

The implementation of resource mailboxes in Exchange 2007 depends on a set of properties that mark these mailboxes to be different to regular user mailboxes. In turn, these special properties identify these mailboxes to Outlook 2007 and Outlook Web Access 2007 so that these clients can display them as resources that you can schedule for meetings. For example, if you browse the GAL (Figure 8.1), you see that the mailboxes for rooms and equipment, listed among all the other entries, but they have different icons to indicate their purpose. Behind the scenes, if you use the Get-Mailbox command to examine the properties of a room mailbox, you'll find that the value of the RecipientTypeDetails property is "RoomMailbox," while an equipment mailbox has "EquipmentMailbox" in this property. You can therefore discover the list of room mailboxes with the Get-Mailbox command as follows:

```
Get-Mailbox —Filter {RecipientTypeDetails —eq 'RoomMailbox'}
```

Figure 8.1
Rooms and resources shown in the GAL

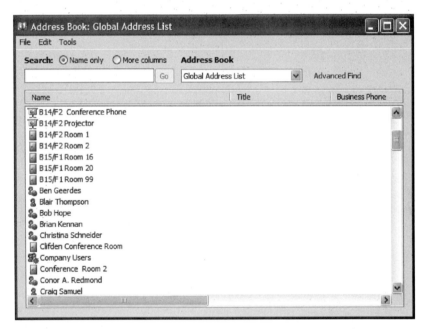

From a user perspective, room and equipment mailboxes come into play when they use the scheduling assistant feature in Outlook 2007 and Outlook Web Access 2007. These clients can distinguish rooms and equipment mailboxes from regular mailboxes and can therefore treat them differently in the user interface. Figure 8.2 shows how Outlook Web Access 2007 lists room mailboxes for a user to select from. Behind the scenes, this feature uses the standard "All Rooms" address list.

Creating room and equipment mailboxes is easy, but you can apply some simple administrative practices to make it easier for users to find rooms and resources when they browse the GAL and to manage the

Figure 8.2

Listing room mailboxes in Outlook Web Access 2007

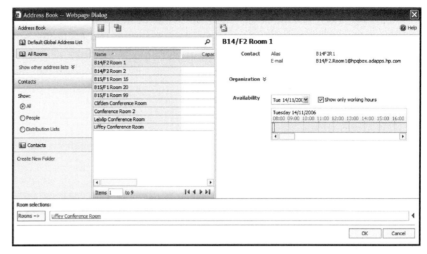

mailboxes. First, always use a logical and consistent naming convention for rooms and resources. Deciding on a logical naming convention will be unique from company to company and depends on whether the company already uses a naming convention. There is no point in changing things if a naming convention exists and is familiar to users because all you will do is confuse people. The rooms listed in Figure 8.2 use two naming conventions. The first uses a scheme that is suitable for large companies that occupy many buildings, so the name of the room includes the building number, floor number, and room number. Hence, B14/F2 Room 1 means Room 1 on Floor 2 of Building 14. The second uses the name of conference rooms but doesn't give any indication of the building or floor where you might find the room, so it's a convention that is probably more appropriate for a small company that occupies a single building where everyone knows where the "Liffey Conference Room" is located. Select whatever naming convention makes sense for you and then use it consistently as you create the room and equipment mailboxes. For example, when you create a resource that belongs to a room, use the room name as the prefix for the equipment mailbox. Thus, an equipment mailbox for a projector that belongs to B14/F2 Room 1 is called "B14/F2 Room 1—Projector."

Second, you should create a special Organizational Unit in the Active Directory to hold the equipment mailboxes and perhaps another for equipment mailboxes. This is not a requirement, but it makes sense to hold objects of a similar type together within the Active Directory.

Third, some administrators like to create a special Storage Group and mailbox database to store conference room and equipment mailboxes because they don't like to mix special mailboxes with regular mailboxes and want to implement circular logging for the storage group. The only message traffic going to equipment mailboxes are meeting requests to book times for the resources, so it makes sense to use circular logging if the equipment mailboxes are in their own storage group. In addition, isolating equipment mailboxes in their own storage group makes it easier to report mailbox usage statistics for real users.

8.1.1 Managing properties of room and equipment mailboxes

We know that an equipment mailbox is a special type of mailbox because the RecipientTypeDetails property of the mailbox contains a value of "EquipmentMailbox" while the RecipientTypeDetails property of a room mailbox is "Room Mailbox." Behind the scenes, Exchange 2007 maintains another set of properties that are specific to equipment mailboxes that allow you to more fully describe some details about the equipment to help users decide whether they want to add the equipment to their meeting request. Some of these properties are revealed through EMC while others can only be manipulated through the shell. Figure 8.3 illustrates how you can add a custom property to a room mailbox. These properties are revealed to users when they use the "Add Room" picker to add a room to a meeting request with Outlook 2007.

Figure 8.3
Adding custom properties to a room mailbox

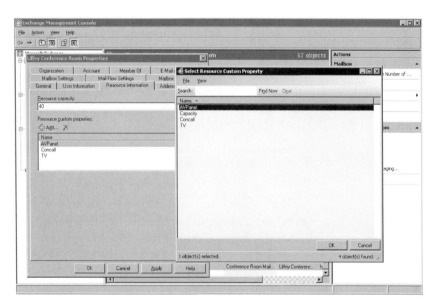

Before we discuss the Outlook "Add Room" picker, we should say that the custom properties for rooms are defined in an object called Resource Schema that you can find as part of Global Settings in the Exchange configuration container in the Active Directory. A property of the object, called MsExchResourcePropertySchema, contains the list of valid properties that you can assign to rooms. Exchange 2007 provides a default set of properties for rooms and equipment, but you can update the list with the `Set-ResourceConfig` command. For example:

```
Set-ResourceConfig —ResourcePropertySchema ("Room/TV", "Room/
Concall", "Room/Couch", "Room/Whiteboard", "Equipment/VCR",
"Equipment/ComfortableChairs")
```

You'll notice that two property lists are defined here: one for rooms and one for equipment. The values must be alphanumeric and contain no spaces, which can lead to some interesting formatting. You should always include the values that are in previous lists when you add a property because otherwise Exchange will signal an error the next time that someone edits the resource.

Figure 8.4 shows the Outlook 2007 Add Room picker. This dialog displays the content of the "All Rooms" address list and outputs the content of the Office attribute for each room in the Location column and the custom resources defined for each room in the Description column. You can also see that there is a Capacity column, the value of which is taken from the "Resource Capacity" property of the room (you can see this property in Figure 8.3).

Because it is a property that is common across user and mailbox objects, you can use the `Set-User` or `Set-Mailbox` commands to update the Office property:

```
Set-User —id 'Galway Conference Room' —Office 'Building 1,
Floor 3'
```

The capacity and custom properties are specific to equipment mailboxes, so you have to use the `Set-Mailbox` command to update these values. EMS flags an error if you attempt to pass a value for the custom property that is not defined in the schema.

```
Set-Mailbox —id 'Galway Conference Room' —ResourceCapacity 45
—ResourceCustom TV, Concall
```

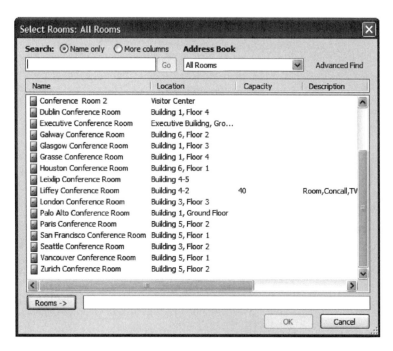

Figure 8.4
*Add Room picker
from Outlook
2007*

Outside the standard set of mailbox properties that are exposed through EMC and the `Get-Mailbox/Set-Mailbox` commands, room mailboxes have a complete new set of properties that they use to control how they can be scheduled by users. You can see these properties with the `Get-MailboxCalendarSettings` command. For example:

```
Get-MailboxCalendarSettings —id 'Galway Conference Room' |
Format-List
TestFields                        : {RequestInPolicyRecipients,
RequestInPolicy, RequestOutOfPolicyRecipients,
RequestOutOfPolicy, BookInPolicy, BookInPolicyRecipients}
AutomateProcessing                : AutoUpdate
AllowConflicts                    : False
BookingWindowInDays               : 180
MaximumDurationInMinutes          : 1440
AllowRecurringMeetings            : True
EnforceSchedulingHorizon          : True
ScheduleOnlyDuringWorkHours       : False
ConflictPercentageAllowed         : 0
MaximumConflictInstances          : 0
ForwardRequestsToDelegates        : True
DeleteAttachments                 : True
DeleteComments                    : True
RemovePrivateProperty             : True
```

```
DeleteSubject                             : True
DisableReminders                          : True
AddOrganizerToSubject                     : True
DeleteNonCalendarItems                    : True
TentativePendingApproval                  : True
EnableResponseDetails                     : True
OrganizerInfo                             : True
ResourceDelegates                         : {}
RequestOutOfPolicy                        :
AllRequestOutOfPolicy                     : False
BookInPolicy                              :
AllBookInPolicy                           : True
RequestInPolicy                           :
AllRequestInPolicy                        : False
AddAdditionalResponse                     : False
AdditionalResponse                        :
RemoveOldMeetingMessages                  : True
AddNewRequestsTentatively                 : True
ProcessExternalMeetingMessages            : False
DefaultReminderTime                       : 15
RemoveForwardedMeetingNotifications       : False
Identity                                  : xyz.com/Room mailboxes/
Galway Conference Room
```

Logically, the `Set-MailboxCalendarSettings` command is used to manipulate any of these properties. Among the more interesting properties are:

- AllowConflicts: Set to False to stop users double-booking the room. Set to True to allow double-booking to occur, in which case you probably want to define delegates who receive copies of incoming requests to resolve the conflicts.

- ScheduleOnlyDuringWorkHours: Set to True to stop Exchange accepting bookings that occur outside normal working hours (8AM to 6PM), set to False to allow 24-hour bookings.

- RemoveOldMeetingMessages: Set to True to have Exchange clean up messages from the room's mailbox after messages have been processed. The Calendar Assistant is responsible for tidying up the contents of room and equipment mailboxes.

- DeleteNonCalendarItems: Set to True to have Exchange delete any noncalendar messages that arrive into the room's inbox.

- BookInPolicy: Defines the set of users (normally groups) who have the right to schedule the room automatically if they request a free slot. Other users will have to request slots to delegates who are assigned to process requests.

- AddOrganizerToSubject: Set to True to have Exchange automatically add the organizer's name to the meeting subject.

- MaximumDurationInMinutes: Defines the maximum length of a meeting (in minutes). The default is 1,440 minutes, or 24 hours, which you might consider excessive for a room.

Figure 8.5
Outlook Web Access Resource Scheduling Options

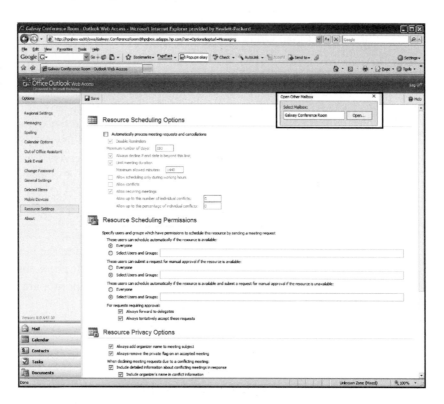

Sometimes the names of properties don't immediately communicate their meaning or the kind of values that they accept, so it's useful to be able to go to a GUI and manipulate the properties that way. The easiest way to get at the settings that control resource scheduling is to open the mailbox and use Outlook Web Access as shown in Figure 8.5. Before you can open the mailbox, you have to be able to access the mailbox and you'll recall that the account used by equipment mailboxes is normally in a disabled state. One way to gain access is to enable the account and change the password to log on and then start Outlook Web Access to make whatever changes are required. If you do this, remember to disable the account afterwards. The problem with this approach is that it's a pain to have to enable and disable accounts just to play around with the scheduling settings. The easier way to gain access to the mailbox is to give yourself the required permission to allow you to log on:

```
Add-MailboxPermission —id 'Galway Conference Room'
—AccessRights FullAccess —User 'James Bond'
```

Once you have the permission, you can use Outlook Web Access's "Open Other Mailbox" feature to connect to the equipment mailbox and make the necessary changes as shown in Figure 8.5.

8.1.2 Converting old mailboxes to rooms

The idea of assigning mailboxes to conference rooms is not new to Exchange 2007 and it is common practice to find mailboxes set aside for this purpose on Exchange 2000 and 2003 servers. Of course, the mailboxes are like any other user mailbox and don't support the custom processing that is now available in Exchange 2007, but they can accept meeting requests and are used for this purpose.

When you move these mailboxes to Exchange 2007, they are treated as user mailboxes and don't automatically assume the properties that differentiate room mailboxes from user mailboxes. It is possible to transform a user mailbox to a room mailbox by setting the appropriate properties. First, let's mark the mailbox to be a room:

```
Set-Mailbox —id 'San Jose Conference Room' —Type Room
```

Now, let's turn on auto accept for the room:

```
Set-MailboxCalendarSettings —id 'San Jose Conference Room'
—AutomateProcessing AutoAccept
```

The newly transformed room mailbox should now behave like any other room mailbox.

8.2   **Helping users to use email better**

Every email client has its own unique feature set. You have to manage them if optimum use is to be made of available system resources such as disk space and network bandwidth. In this section, we discuss some common issues that administrators should consider to help users optimize system resources, including:

- How to reduce the network load generated by clients.
- How to limit the size of messages generated by clients.
- Whether to add legal disclaimers to outgoing messages.

Your company has a work culture of its own, so some give and take is required to achieve a balance between the perfectly managed systems valued by the administrators and the desire of the users to send messages without let or interference.

8.2.1   **Eliminating bad habits**

Every Exchange design pays a lot of attention to the number of servers that are deployed and how the servers are connected together most efficiently, along with plans to control and manage public folder and directory replication. We often give less attention to the traffic generated by clients and how to reduce network demand, yet this aspect can be a very important part of a deployment project.

Users generate network load through their normal activities, like sending and reading messages. Benchmarks typically use standard messages ranging in size from 1KB to maybe 10KB that contain text, some attachments, and maybe a meeting request or two. However, real-life activity is always different to simulations and this is the reason why designs often demonstrate flaws when exposed to real-life pressure. Left to themselves, human beings are very curious and use software in ways you can never imagine. If you do not educate users to respect the need to preserve network resources, they are unlikely to consider the ramifications of, for example, dragging and dropping a large PowerPoint presentation to a message and sending it to a distribution list. I see many bad e-mail habits on a daily basis. Here are some of my personal dislikes:

Get rid of complex, object-ridden autosignature files. Far fewer dial-up connections are used today than in the past and maybe we have become too used to high-speed connections, but bloated auto signature files continue to be one of the things that annoys me most when I receive them in email. Sure, the difference in connect times across high-speed connections because people send messages that contain 2KB of useful data but end up at 50KB to accommodate a spinning, 3D, or other form of graphic-intense logo isn't going to affect you, especially when you use Outlook in cached Exchange mode, but it does become tiring to see so much space occupied by so much unwanted data. My degree of annoyance becomes infuriating when 20% or more of the messages in my inbox are similarly bloated. Apart from absorbing valuable bandwidth and slowing user ability to process email, graphics soak up storage and create pressure on mailbox quotas. I often wonder what percentage of Exchange mailbox stores is occupied by autosignatures. It would certainly be interesting to analyze some databases to try and determine just how much graphics and other useless data they contain, and then calculate how much work administrators do daily to take backups of that data, not to mention the expense required to provide and manage the storage that the data occupies.

For example, if you include a 50KB graphic in your signature, then after you send 100 messages, your mailbox contains 5MB of redundant, duplicated graphics. Would you or any other user accept a voluntary reduction of 5MB in their mailbox quota? Yet many users cheerfully accept this overhead without thinking! Moreover, if you scale this up for 1,000 users on a server, you end up with 5GB useless data. With 3,000 users, you end up with 15GB and so on.

Autosignature files convey some information about a message's sender and the feature appeared first in `sendmail`-based UNIX email systems. Normally, you add some autosignature text to each message to provide details of your return email address, telephone and fax numbers, and perhaps some witty "thought of the day." Text-based data does not occupy much space and no one can really complain about autosignatures until you meet some of the crazy ones that circulate today. Everyone is aware that cut and paste allows you to insert objects into message bodies, and it did not take people long to discover that you can do the same thing for autosignatures. We can clearly see the intention behind auto signature files in RFC1855, which covers netiquette:

If you include a signature keep it short. The rule of thumb is no longer than 4 lines. Remember that many people pay for connectivity by the minute, and the longer your message is, the more they pay.

RFC1855 appeared in 1995 and focused on a world where dial-up connects were the de facto standard and people worried about paying telephone companies by the minute, a feature of life outside the United States. The authors probably did not foresee a time when users could cheerfully include a spinning multi-color 3D logo into their email signature.

If you are determined to use a graphically rich auto signature, it is easy to include your favorite logo (which may not be the approved version of the corporate logo). Before you begin, find the logo you want to use and save it to a local directory. For Outlook, click on Tools and then Options to access the "Mail Format" properties, and then click on the Signatures command button. You can create a new signature or edit an existing signature file. When Outlook places you in the signature editor, you can click on "Advanced Edit" to force Outlook to launch an HTML editor. Outlook 2000, 2002, and 2003 launch Microsoft FrontPage and you can paste the logo directly into the HTML content. After the logo is in the signature file, you can use the standard editor to change the text information such as your phone numbers, but you must use the advanced editor to make any change to the graphics. Outlook 2007 has its own signature editor that you can paste the desired graphic into together with any other textual information that you want to include.

Figure 8.6
Adding a graphic to an autosignature file

As an example, I inserted a 4MB digital picture of an airplane taking off into my autosignature as shown in Figure 8.6. The interesting thing is that the compression algorithms in Outlook 2003 and Outlook 2007 do an impressive job of compressing the graphic data so that the 4MB original photo ended up as 56KB when Outlook inserts it into a message. Earlier versions of Outlook don't compress graphics and would therefore include the whole 4MB in every outgoing message, which would quickly fill even the largest mailbox and pose some interesting transmission challenges for Exchange. Best practice is to use a low-resolution GIF file to reduce the impact of the logo to an acceptable limit. For example, HP recommends users to include a 1.11KB GIF file in their autosignatures. This is much better for all concerned than the other variations of corporate logos that are usually designed to be used in advertising or other graphically-rich situations. Of course, even after providing a reduced graphic and making it known that the graphic is available to use, people still go and use whatever bloated graphic they can find.

Users do not realize that email gateways often negate the desired effect of the logo on external correspondents if the gateways strip out graphics in message bodies (not attachments) as messages pass through. Companies are rightly concerned about viruses and it is possible to hide a virus behind a graphic or embed instructions to launch a virus in a graphic, so it is also possible that anti-virus scanners will remove the logos too. Therefore, the result is that the only people who see the logos are internal recipients who probably already know what your company's logo looks like.

Another issue is the impact on recipients. While it may be acceptable for you to let everyone else inside the company know about what the current corporate logo looks like, it is a different matter when you send excessive data to other companies because you are now consuming their network bandwidth, their time, and their storage to hold whatever you care to transmit. People already complain about spam because these messages absorb resources that they have to pay for. Why would they not treat your graphically-intense messages in the same light?

Apart from logos, trademarks, and other public information like a URL to the company's web site, it is unwise to include corporate information in an autosignature file. Titles and the name of your group are acceptable, as long as they make sense to the recipient, but if you send this information outside the company, you always have to be aware that recruiters or other people who want to learn about the company's organization for their own purposes could use the information. In addition, the GAL already contains all of the information you may want to transmit so it is available to internal

Figure 8.7
Outlook smart tags

recipients. If required, they can click on the name of the sender or a recipient in the message header and view the properties of their entry in the GAL to discover details like phone numbers, assistants, and even reporting relationships. Of course, the GAL is sometimes out of date, but it is usually the most reliable source of corporate information. Outlook 2003 and 2007 make things even easier by using smart tags (Figure 8.7), so you can click on a recipient to find out whether they are online (through instant messaging), available for a meeting (by checking free and busy information), and what their office phone number is (from the GAL).

Don't generate mail storms with "Reply All." I'm sure that some sophisticated research into user interfaces has been conducted by messaging vendors over the years, but maybe they made the "Reply All" function a little too easy to use? The fact is, it is just too easy to reply to everyone while being blissfully unaware that thousands of people were circulated on the original memo. In addition, when many people add their own "me too" or "good idea" or "I agree" contribution to the discussion, and reply to everyone else to let them know, we then have a fully-fledged mail storm. With respect to bandwidth, two problems exist here. First, we have to deal with the sheer volume of messages generated by the contributors. Fortunately, there is an easy solution to this problem because you can use the delete key to remove all the "me too" responses from your mailbox. I find that turning on the "View.AutoPreview" function in Outlook allows me to quickly scan my inbox and identify candidate messages for instant culling.

The second issue is more invidious. Users tend to accept default options and do not want to mess too much with client settings in case they break things. By default, Outlook inserts the text of the original message into a reply, so you end up with messages that gently swell in size as Outlook adds each reply (short as it might be) to the thread. You can get rid of the "me too" replies by deleting them unseen, but this technique isn't so useful when the reply actually contains something useful and there is no real option except to download the full message, complete with the original text. As an example of the potential impact on message size generated by the "reply all syndrome," let us consider what happens in a typical email exchange.

- User A sends a message to seek opinions from 10 colleagues. The original message is 5KB.

- User B uses "Reply All" and includes User A's original text. This message is 10KB.

- User C now responds with "Reply All" and includes the text from User B's message along with his comments. The message has grown to 20KB.

The cycle continues until everyone has contributed and the final message that holds the complete thread might now be 100KB. At this point, everyone involved probably has 10 messages occupying 200KB or more in their mailbox. The single-instance storage model used by the Exchange store helps to reduce the impact of this duplication, but you could end up with up to 2MB of wasted space if the recipients' mailboxes are in different stores. While tidy users will clean up and only keep the last message in a thread, many users only remove messages when forced to by reaching their quota and they cannot send any further email. The result is a lot of redundant information that is stored from here to the end of eternity unless you use an automated tool like the Mailbox Manager to clean up the mess.

There is no harm in inserting the original text in a reply, providing you use the text to add context or as the basis for edits. There is simply no case for including the original text just because it is there, so it is best practice to take the time to remove extraneous text before sending messages.

Be careful when you attach large files. We live in a drag-and-drop world. Users expect to be able to drag a document to their email client and drop it onto a message. Unless you compress an attachment, Outlook and Outlook Express take no further action to minimize the impact of sending large files around with messages. This situation changes from the introduction of Exchange 2003/2007 and Outlook 2003/2007 where compression techniques are used.

There is no doubt that the average size of messages has grown steadily over the last decade. Ten years ago, most corporate email accounts were on "green screen email" systems and the average message contained less than a page of text. Thus, fetching a message from the server generated no more than 4–6KB traffic and we happily used 9.6kbps modems. If you track statistics from Exchange servers over a period, you will invariably find an increase in the average message size—to well over 100KB in some companies. While messages with large multi-megabyte attachments are the chief culprit, among the reasons why today's email systems handle much larger messages are:

- The power of the drag-and-drop paradigm implemented in software like Windows Explorer and Outlook makes it so easy to add an attachment to a message that people add attachments without thinking;. People use graphics more extensively to convey ideas, so documents, presentations, and spreadsheets are full of diagrams, charts, and pictures.

- A wider range of software is used and few packages compress data.

- Especially in the U.S., network bandwidth is more plentiful and far cheaper, so people have to take less care about bandwidth absorption.

- Users have better message editors (including Word), so they can include graphics in message content.

- Storage is also far cheaper so the ever-growing size of files does not have a huge cost impact and users can have larger mailbox quotas so they do not see the need to change the way they handle attachments.

You can try to educate people to use compression utilities like WinZIP to process large attachments before adding them to messages. Word and basic graphic files like bitmaps compress well, but compression utilities are less successful in reducing other file types (like PowerPoint). However, users often forget to compress attachments and the additional step makes the email system harder to use. In addition, administrators need to distribute copies of the chosen utility to all desktops.

If you are not able to deploy clients that support cached Exchange mode, you can still trade CPU cycles (to process the messages) against bandwidth and storage by installing an add-on product. For example, the Max Compression product from http://www.c2c.com/ automatically compresses and decompresses attachments as users send and receive them through Outlook. Modules of the same product are available for Outlook Web Access for earlier Exchange servers.

Examples of good email habits include the following:

- Because many people use SmartPhones, PDAs such as the Black-Berry, and Pocket PCs to read their email, it is best to write short messages or at least place the key points up front so that readers can understand what you want to say without going through multiple screens. Boring or irrelevant preambles stop people understanding what you want them to do as a result of receiving your message. It is also a good idea not to have important points or questions at the bottom of messages because readers may never see them.

- To reduce the number of messages, do not respond immediately to a request if you do not have all the necessary information. Instead, wait until you have the information and then send a complete answer.

- Don't forward a message to another user to clog up their mailbox unless they really need the information in the message.

- The volume of email continues to rise, so it is helpful to use clear subjects so that recipients can pick the most important messages out of their inboxes. Spammers pay a lot of attention to creating compelling message subjects and maybe this is something we can learn from them. If the topic being discussed changes during a message thread, alter the message subject to reflect the new discussion. Along the same lines, if a message thread splits into a number of different topics, create a new message for each topic, clearly label each message with an appropriate subject, and send the new messages to only the people who need the information. You can go too far in breaking up one message into many, so it's important to maintain a balance.

- Never use Word to compose a message and then send it as an attached document. Instead, use the advanced features of the message editor to format your text. Sending unnecessary attachments occupies valuable network bandwidth, ties up disk space, and makes the message hard for users of SmartPhones and other hand-held devices to view.

The last good habit may save your job, or at least stop you angering someone. It is always satisfying to compose the world's most cutting and sarcastic response to the inept ideas expressed in a message you receive, but it is even better to save your response as a draft and come back to it a few hours later. At that time, some mature reflection may convince you that it is a bad idea to send the text as written. Unfortunately, it is all too easy to send a message written in haste and then consider the consequences at leisure. Outlook includes a message recall function, but the speed that Exchange transmits and delivers messages plus the vast array of devices (SmartPhones, BlackBerries, etc.) that someone can use to receive the message means that the recall function has little chance of being able to retrieve the message before it is read. It is better to pause and save the message, leave it for an hour or so, and then review before sending. Do not leave the message open, waiting to be sent, because it is easy to make a mistake and send the message inadvertently. If you do leave the message open, include an undeliverable address (such as "XXX") in the TO: or CC: line so that Outlook has to display an "unresolveable address" warning first.

8.2.2 Disclaimers

The legal profession loves words. They especially love words that establish a strict limitation of liability in as many circumstances as possible. Given the high profile of court actions that have featured email as exhibits, including the Enron affair and the multiple actions taken by the US Department of Justice against Microsoft, it is reasonable to assume that companies around the world have consulted their lawyers in an effort to restrict corporate liability for the actions of their employees.

The appearance of disclaimer text on the bottom of every outgoing message is evidence that managers are listening to the lawyers, but I often wonder whether the text so faithfully appended has any effect. While the original disclaimers were blunt and to the point, some of the disclaimers are now bigger than the average size of message they seek to protect. Apart from making messages larger, the disclaimers make messages harder and less friendly to read, especially if you insert the disclaimer into every forward and reply as well.

On a purely facetious note, you might consider that implementing policies of this nature is a much-loved tactic of the PHB (a la Dibert) class. The real questions that we need to ask is whether recipients take very much notice of the dire legal warnings contained in the disclaimer, and whether the warning has any legal meaning whatsoever in some of the places where people read the message. A legal warning that is valid in the U.S. is probably not effective in Eastern Europe, so all it does is keep managers and lawyers happy. On a more fundamental point, email is not like a fax that someone can intercept who reads it as the fax arrives on a machine shared by a department or complete building. Usually, email has a more precise delivery mechanism as messages go to a known recipient who presumably must authenticate to a server before they can access the mailbox to pick up messages. However, these arguments do not usually hold much water when presented to the legal community.

Recently, the situation has become even more complex for any company that operates in the European Union because of a directive (2003/1958) aimed at forcing companies to disclose more information about their legal entities in all manner of communications. We are familiar with the requirement for companies to include details such as registration numbers and the names of directors on printed notepaper, but the effect of the European directive is to force companies to include this information in email, no matter whether the messages go to an internal or an external recipient. Each of the 27 countries in the European Union is implementing the directive through local legislation and as the directive comes into effect, companies must include the information in outgoing email. For example, the directive became law in Ireland on April 1, 2007 with a penalty for non-compliance of 2,000 per instance. As you can imagine, the thought of being charged 2,000 for every message that does not contain the necessary information made the need to add disclaimers to the attention of lawyers, managers, and messaging administrators.

Up to Exchange 2007, it was common practice for companies to use products such as Clearswift's MimeSweeper (www.clearswift.com <http://www.clearswift.com>) to add disclaimers on all outgoing messages – the alternative is to ask users to add their own version of a disclaimer in an auto-signature applied by Outlook or other clients. Exchange 2007 includes the ability to add disclaimers to outgoing messages out of the box, so you do not need to spend anything on extra software to comply with regulations such as the European Union directive. The advantage of using a transport rule to apply disclaimers is that all the work occurs in one place and that you can assure compliance. The alternate is to ask users to insert the required text in their autosignature files. Because of the human involvement, this approach is costlier, prone to error, difficult to support, hard to audit to ensure compliance, and much less efficient. In fact, deploying Exchange 2007 transport rules to address the problem of compliance in disclaimer text can be a quick win that adds real business value.

See the section on Transport Rules later on in this chapter for details about how to deploy a transport rule to include disclaimers in outgoing messages.

8.2.3   Out-of-Office Notifications

As discussed in Chapter 6, Exchange 2007 provides users and administrators with a great deal of control over Out of Office (OOF) notifications. When they are properly used, OOFs are very useful. The issue is whether to allow Exchange to send OOFs outside the company. OOFs inform correspondents that a recipient will not be able to deal with their message for some reason. As the name implies, the most common reason is that someone is travelling and will not have access to their email for an extended period. Given the ability of people to reach their email via dial-in connections when they are on the road, Out of Office notifications are most useful when they tell you that someone is away on vacation. To be effective, the text of a notification should tell the recipient:

■ A brief reason why their correspondent won't be able to respond.

■ The next time when the person is likely to be able to process email.

■ An alternate person who they can contact for specific reasons, such as management of a project or to provide information on a product, together with their contact details (email addresses and phone numbers). Obviously, you need to balance informing internal correspondents with the requirement not to provide sensitive company information to external people who receive the OOF.

See the discussion in Chapter 6 to learn how to exert administrative control over OOFs.

8.2.4   The last few bad email habits

There are many other smaller points of email etiquette that cause people grief. These include:

■ Replying to a message that you received as a BCC recipient when the author really would prefer you not to.

- Forwarding a message to a new set of recipients without permission of the original author. This becomes an especially grievous fault if you send the message to external recipients because you may disclose corporate information that should stay inside the company.

- Using an auto reply (Out of Office) message where you do not give useful information to the recipient. It is nice to know that someone is enjoying themselves on holiday, but even better to know where to go to (preferably with a telephone number and email address) in their absence.

Minor breeches of etiquette usually cause frustration only and do not absorb additional resources. However, the frustration level can be intense especially if you inadvertently tell someone about something that they should learn in another manner. For example, telling someone that you have heard that they are about to be promoted when you are not their boss is possibly acceptable; telling them that they are going to move to another job is not.

8.3   Customizing display templates

Exchange uses details (otherwise called display) templates to format and display directory information when Outlook users view details about objects in the GAL. You can customize the templates to add new fields or remove some of the data that Exchange displays by default. Customizing details templates is a relatively common occurrence in large organizations but much less so in smaller organizations as the default set of fields displayed in the templates is very functional.

Figure 8.8
Customized and standard display templates for a user object

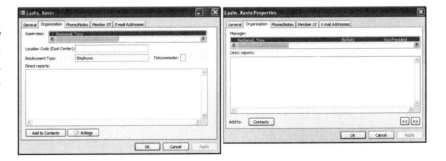

Figure 8.8 illustrates a simple customization. The right-hand screen is the standard "Organization" property page as viewed through Outlook 2003. The left-hand screen is the customized version as viewed through Outlook 2007 (all versions of Outlook can use the same template). The differences are:

1. "Manager" label changed to "Supervisor": This is an example of organizational culture in action where the term chosen by Microsoft for a label does not match the term in use within the organization.

2. Field and label added for "Location Code (Cost Center)": Most large organizations assign employees to cost centers and may wish to make information like this available to users. You can adapt one of the standard Exchange properties for this purpose by renaming it, but it is usually better to use one of the 15 extended properties provided by Exchange for customizations like this.

3. Field and label added for "Employment Type": Again, depending on the culture of the organization, you may want to display information like this to users.

4. Field and label added for "Telecommuter."

In Exchange 2000 and 2003, you modify details templates through the ESM console, where they are located under the Recipients node. You'll find details templates for the various object types contained in the GAL including users, groups, mailbox agents, public folders, and contacts along with templates for search dialogs. Search dialogs allow you to specify the fields that users can use to search the GAL. Exchange 2000 and 2003 servers also show address templates in this location in ESM, but these are no longer supported in Exchange 2007, largely because experience has shown that address templates do not need to be customized. Exchange stores all of the information about details and address templates in the Addressing section of its configuration data in the Active Directory, so once you make a change to a template, the change is replicated by the Active Directory throughout the organization. For this reason, only Exchange Enterprise Administrators can update details templates.

Microsoft did not include the ability to customize templates in EMC, perhaps because they purposely designed EMC to incorporate only the operations most commonly performed by administrators and customizing

Figure 8.9
*Adding the Details
Templates Editor to
an MMC console*

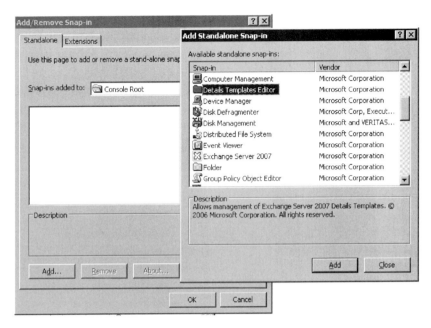

a display template is definitely not in this category. If you want to view or update a template, you have to start up MMC and then load the Details Templates Editor snap-in to the console, as shown in Figure 8.9. Exchange then reads the information about available details templates from the Active Directory and loads them into the console. As you can see from Figure 8.10, you can modify templates in any of the languages supported by Exchange. If you operate in a multi-lingual organization, you will have to make the same changes to the details templates for each language version of Outlook client that you deploy in the organization. For example, if you have deployed the Swedish, Finnish, German, and English versions of Outlook to users, then you need to update the details templates for these four languages.

The user template is most commonly customized and as we have already used it as an example, I will explain how to apply the customizations described before. To work with a template, select it from the list and double-click, at which point Exchange fetches the details of the current template from the Active Directory. The template we are interested in is the en-US\User template. This is the English language—U.S. variant—of the user details template. Despite the fact that Exchange is used in English in many other places such as the United Kingdom, Ireland, and Australia that may not share the same spelling or usage of words, you only have one English language details template to work with. The same is true of one Spanish

Figure 8.10
*MMC console
loaded with details
templates*

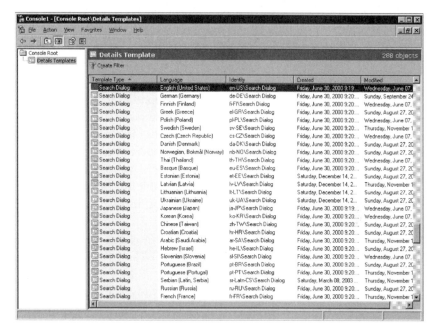

template, one Portuguese template, and so on. The rule is therefore that
whatever changes you make have to apply to the broadest possible user population that accesses Exchange in whatever language you choose.

Figure 8.11
*Customizing a user
details template*

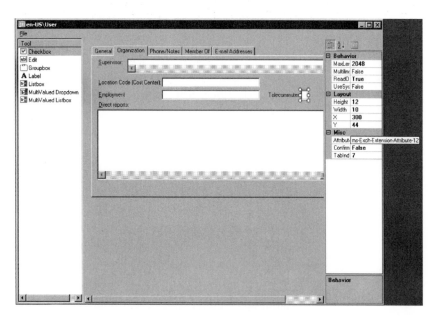

The template editor provided with Exchange 2007 is still basic by comparison to most layout editors, even if it is an improvement over previous versions. Figure 8.11 shows the "Organization" page of the user details template loaded, and you can see that the extra Telecommuter field is selected. The toolbox on the left-hand side allows you to select different types of controls for the various properties that you want to display. To add a new field, select the type that you want and drag it to the position on the page, then set its properties such as the attribute that you want to display. In this case, the Telecommuter property is a simple checkbox that uses ms-Exch-Extension-Attribute12 for storage. As shown in Figure 8.12, you can click on a dropdown list of available attributes for the user object if you want to select a different attribute for display.

Figure 8.12
Selecting an attribute to display

Apart from checkboxes, the other control types are:

- Edit: Displays only one value for an attribute. For example, users only have one first name, which comes from the Given-Name attribute.

- Listbox: Displays data for a list of attributes that come from different objects. For example, a user can be a member of many distribution groups, so the "Member Of" page has a listbox that is populated from the Is-Member-Of-DL attribute.

- Multi-valued Listbox: Displays data for an attribute that can have multiple values. For example, user objects can have multiple email addresses, so the "Email Addresses" page has a single multi-valued listbox that is populated from the Proxy-Addresses attribute.

- Label: Holds a language-dependent text string and typically appears alongside another control that holds data. You will notice that some characters in the label fields are underlined to indicate that users can navigate to these fields using the ALT + letter key combination. For example, the "Supervisor:" field has the S underlined, so you can move to it with an ALT + S combination. You include the ampersand (&) character in the label control value to set this up, so the value in the label field in this case is "&Supervisor."

- Group box: Specifies a group of fields that Outlook draws a line around when it displays the template. For example, the "General" page of the user template has a line around the First, Last, Display, and Alias fields.

Customizing details templates is easy, but you have to ask the question whether a customization adds any value before you rush to change something and there are some minor points that you need to consider. Remember that you will have to revalidate the customization after each upgrade of Exchange, as there is no guarantee that Microsoft will not overwrite your customization or make a change to the templates that is not compatible with your changes in a new version or service pack. As it happens, the transition from Exchange 2003 to Exchange 2007 was very smooth for template customizations, but this might not be the case in the future. If you operate multiple organizations, you will not be able to share template customizations directly between the organizations. Instead, you will have to export them using a tool like LDIFDE from the organization where you make (and test) the customizations and import them into the Active Directory instances that support the other organizations.

8.4   Exchange 2007 and compliance

The requirement to process all messages through one common place to provide the ability to apply compliance rules easily is one of the driving reasons behind the new transport architecture in Exchange 2007. Apart from removing the ability of the Store to deliver messages sent to local mailboxes, the separation of the mailbox and hub transport roles within the Exchange architecture gives the developers a single place to focus on to implement the rules that enable compliance. Every message that passes through the Exchange transport service is processed by a hub transport server before it is delivered to a mailbox or queue for onward transmission. Every message that goes through a hub transport server passes through the categorizer, so the categorizer provides a single point where Exchange can implement rules processing. The last stage of processing within Exchange 2007 categorizer, after all of the message recipients are known and routing is determined, is to check for and apply transport and journal rules.

Once Microsoft determined the single point of processing, they could then build the code to provide a UI for administrators to create rules and a set of commands to script rules. Exchange 2007 allows you to create journal rules, effectively simple transport rules to capture messages, as well as transport rules, to perform other more complex compliance tasks. Journaling is a matter of copying messages sent to certain addressees to another destination, so they are simple in concept and implementation. The same code applies transport rules but these are more powerful in terms of the checks that they can apply and the actions that they can take.

The intention behind transport rules is to allow administrators to apply checks on messages to comply with legal, regulatory, or company policies. For example, you may want to stop confidential information leaving your company or stop users communicating with certain individuals. You may want to capture copies of messages that meet specific conditions (such as when the message body contains a certain code word) or all messages sent by individuals or groups who may be suspected of engaging in inappropriate or illegal conduct. You may want to limit interaction between users who happen to share the same messaging infrastructure but should not be communicating with each other, such as the condition that sometimes occurs in financial companies where traders should not swap hot stock tips with brokers. This kind of restriction is often called an "Ethical Wall." Finally, you may want to mark outgoing messages by changing the subject field by adding a prefix or by appending some disclaimer text to protect the interests of your company. All of these operations are possible with Exchange 2003 but you have to write bespoke code to create the necessary transport sinks to implement whatever functionality you require.

While transport rules are basic in comparison to some of the sophisticated purpose-built archiving and journaling third-party products that are available for Exchange, they provide a decent level of functionality that will handle many regulatory requirements. However, you should understand that there are gaps that may force you to buy and deploy additional software to meet specific requirements. For example, you cannot delete all copies of messages from user mailboxes after they have been captured for archiving, so if a regulation forces you to deploy this functionality, you will need to either write some code or find an add-on product that can satisfy the need. Exchange cannot interact with Hierarchical Storage Management (HSM) systems either, so that might be another requirement that forces you to look elsewhere. There are many examples of companies who have implemented Exchange transport sinks for the reasons cited above. During their migration to Exchange 2007, these companies will have to review why they implemented the transport sinks and determine whether they can swap them out for standard transport rules or continue to need custom code.

Third-party developers have had the compliance market to themselves up to now. Given Microsoft's entry into the market, albeit with the basic functionality in Exchange 2007, you can expect that companies such as Symantec, CA, and HP will increase the features, functionality, and sophistication of their archiving and compliance products. Microsoft will probably improve their features in a future release of Exchange and the cycle of further improvement in the third-party products will kick off again. Microsoft publishes a list of companies who provide compliance products suitable for use with Exchange on their web site and a search of Microsoft.com will reveal the current state of the art.

8.4.1 The growing need for compliance

The need for email systems to comply with legislation has existed for many years. The original requirement arose through discovery actions as lawyers searched for evidence of wrongdoing through backup tapes and online repositories. The most famous early example was that of Oliver North, whose role in the Iran Contras affair became public when investigators found incriminating messages in a backup taken from an IBM PROFS system. This event seemed to whet the appetite for legal discovery (and the formation of companies who specialized in forensic discovery conducted against IT systems). We progressed from the point where we had to recover paper copies of messages by restoring backup tapes and printing off the documents to having intelligent archiving systems that can locate the necessary documents very quickly.

Legislation began with laws such as the Florida Sunshine Law, which enabled the public to read the communications of public representatives, but since 2000, the focus has been to ensure that the email systems used within companies possess the necessary features to allow the companies to comply with financial regulations. The best known of the US regulations that govern communications within financial companies is SEC 17-4A and the audit requirements that arise under the Sarbanes-Oxley act. Another important impetus for compliance systems comes from human resources, where any action taken by an employee to protest harassment, inappropriate behavior, or another problem that arises during their employment is likely to include some email among the evidence.

Of course, technology has changed greatly since the first email discovery actions. We store far more messages than ever before in far more formats. In the past, only "important" people received mailboxes, but now everyone has at least one mailbox—and maybe several business mailboxes and a couple of personal mailboxes. We use different ways to connect to our email too, with handheld devices, laptops, smart phones, web kiosks, and traditional workstations. Messages come in as voicemail, SMS text messages, from the Internet, from human beings, and from automated systems. Overall, the level of complexity that administrators deal with when they consider about how they can capture messages—or even understand the flow of messages from one part of the messaging ecosystem to another—has increased enormously in the last decade.

Because it is a popular email system, Microsoft has had to increase the features to support compliance within Exchange. The change has occurred gradually and Microsoft's initial focus was to allow administrators to journal (or capture) email traffic to an archive. The features in Exchange 2000 and 2003 are basic, but they are enough for ISVs to build sophisticated archive and retrieval systems, or indeed for companies to develop their own compliance system. Time and additional legislative requirements have increased the pressure on email and these factors have driven Microsoft to put compliance at the top of their feature list for Exchange 2007.

Having adequate software is only the first step to achieving compliance. The other challenges include:

- Agreeing reasonable and appropriate document retention policies between the legal and IT departments: The legal department (who probably do not understand technology to the necessary level of detail) want to ensure that they can produce evidence to demonstrate that the company complies with all relevant legislation. They may also want a policy that requires users not to retain email for lengthy periods. For example, some companies require users to delete all messages older than a month. Another issue that administrators often need to cover is the different requirements that exist from country to country. A solution that works in the United States may not apply in an EU country and vice versa. Privacy requirements, for instance, are quite different in countries such as France and Germany than they are in the United States. Another complicating factor is that different rules may apply to different groups of users within the company. For example, there are many regulations that govern the communications of financial traders, but the same regulations do not cover the communications of the IT department members who support the traders.

- User education: While email systems are corporate utilities, almost everyone makes some use of this facility to send personal email. This is not usually an issue but just in the same way that problems occur when people misuse business telephones to run up large cell phone bills, email systems cause difficulties when users abuse them. For example, we do not want users to send messages that contain inappropriate content inside or outside the company; we do not want users to send messages that contain confidential information outside the company; we do not want users to use email to swap material such as MP3 files with each other, and so on. Many of the problems can be addressed by defining clear policies for email usage and then communicating the policies and the consequences for infraction to users but, unfortunately this does not seem to be the case as we still see many instances where employees are fired because they misused email.

You can realize the scale of the problem from the results of a survey conducted by ProofPoint (www.proofpoint.com) and Forrester Research in mid-2006. The survey covered 294 U.S. companies and 112 UK companies, all of whom had over 1,000 employees. Among the findings were:

- 34% of U.S. companies investigated a suspected email leak of confidential or proprietary information in the last year. More than half of U.K. companies reported the same concern.

- U.S. companies estimate that 22.8% of all outgoing messages contain content that poses a legal, financial, or regulatory risk. The figure is 18.1% for U.K. companies.

- 31.6% of U.S. companies terminated an employee for violating email polices in the last year; the figure was 33.9% for U.K. companies

This is only one survey and it covered a reasonably small base of companies but even so there is enough data to indicate that email poses some problems for both companies and employees in terms of compliance. The functionality in Exchange 2007 is not a complete compliance solution, but it does much more than any other version through the provision of transport rules and basic journaling along with other Exchange 2007 features such as managed folders (see page 837). In this section, we discuss how to use transport rules to achieve a certain level of compliance. It will not be perfect, but it is a start and it's an area that third-party software providers will no doubt build on to create complete solutions.

8.4.2   Transport rules

The transport rules agent is responsible for executing transport rules as messages pass through the transport engine. Two kinds of transport rules can exist within an Exchange organization, each with a different scope:

1.   Rules executed on a hub transport server. Exchange applies these rules on all messages that circulate within the organization, including those that are destined for an external recipient. All hub transport servers in an organization share the same rules, which are stored in the Active Directory. When you add or change a transport rule, Exchange stores the new data in its configuration container in Active Directory and notifies Active Directory that the change has occurred. Active Directory then replicates the updated information around the organization so that the change becomes effective.

2.   Rules executed on an Edge server. Exchange applies these rules to messages as they enter or exit the organization through the Edge server. Administrators have to set up these rules separately on each Edge server, where they are stored in the local instance of ADAM.

There is no requirement to have the same set of rules running on hub and Edge servers. Microsoft provides a wizard-driven UI for administrators to create new transport rules in Exchange 2007 hub transport servers. If you have ever set up a rule to use with Outlook, you will be comfortable with the wizard because the process of creating a transport rule is very analogous to the thought process that a user goes through when they create an Outlook rule. The basic approach is that you:

1.   Define the conditions that will cause the transport service to apply the rule. For example, we may want to execute the rule when a specific user or members of a distribution group send a message.

2. Define any exceptions for Exchange to observe. For example, do not process messages sent by a senior executive, even if the condition exists that would otherwise cause the transport service to apply the rule.

3. Define the actions to occur when the rule fires. For example, add some text to the subject field. Rules fire when all of the conditions and none of the exceptions exist.

Exchange executes transport rules in the priority order that you set while also respecting the transport event that the rules are bound to. For example, a rule that journals messages sent by executives may fire when the OnConnect event occurs while a rule that checks for the presence of specific content in a message may have to wait until the OnReceived event fires.[1] The first rule that you create is assigned top priority and so on, but you can change rule priority by selecting the rule and then using the "Change Priority" option, giving a value from 0 (most important) to 2 (least important). EMC will not allow you to have two rules with the same priority, so if you change a rule with priority 1 and make it priority 0, EMC will downgrade the rule that used to have priority 0 and make it priority 1.

Figure 8.13

A set of transport rules

It is easy to create a situation where Exchange processes multiple rules for a message before it leaves a hub transport server. For example, there are three transport rules specified in Figure 8.13, two (the first and last) of which add different disclaimer text to outgoing messages. If a message matches the criteria set for these two rules then Exchange will append both disclaimers to the message. This isn't a disaster, but it does illustrate the point that you need to take some care to think about what transport rules to create, who to apply them to, and what priority order to set for Exchange in which it will apply the rules.

---

1. See the Exchange 2007 help file for more information on how events fire during SMTP processing.

8.4.3   **Using a rule to add disclaimer text to outgoing messages**

Companies commonly want to add disclaimers to outgoing messages to inform recipients that they have no control whatsoever over message content and that the recipient should immediately delete a message if they weren't meant to receive it. The requirement to add disclaimers steadily crept in since the late 1990s as companies realize the damage that email can do if abused by users. No version of Exchange offers out-of-the-box functionality to add a disclaimer but you can do it quickly with a simple transport rule in Exchange 2007 and avoid the need to deploy third-party software for this purpose.

Figure 8.14
*Editing a transport
rule to add a
disclaimer*

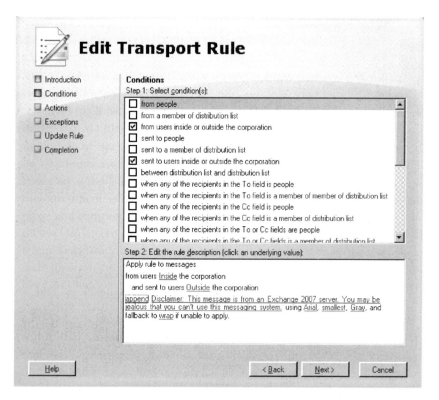

We can sketch out the rule that we need as follows:

1.   Condition: Look for any outgoing messages.

We complete the wizard by stating that there are no exceptions to the rule and that is all there is to it. Our ethical firewall is in place and active across the organization once the Active Directory replicates the rule data. Again, a simple rule like this may not meet the requirements posed by complex regulations, but it is enough to satisfy the needs of maybe 80% of all of the companies who had to write transport events for previous versions of Exchange.

8.4.7 Transport rule storage

Exchange 2007 stores transport and journal rules along with the rest of its organization configuration data in the Active Directory. You can find transport rules in the Transport Settings\Rules\ section of the Exchange configuration data in the Active Directory. Journal rules are in the \Journaling section and transport rules are in the \Transport section. After you create or update rules, the Active Directory updates servers using its normal replication mechanism. Inside the Active Directory, rules look like any other object. The properties of the rules object hold the information that Exchange needs to implement the rules. The Microsoft Exchange Active Directory Topology Service notifies the hub transport servers in the organization when new or updated rules are available and the servers then refresh their local rules cache with the new information. Active Directory replication therefore dictates the speed in which new rules are shared within the Exchange organization. Figure 8.22 illustrates the properties of the disclaimer rule that we created on page 794. As you can see, the msExchTransportRuleXML attribute holds XML-formatted data for the disclaimer text and its format (you can just see that Arial is the preferred font).

While Exchange 2007 does not impose a hard limit for the number of transport rules that can be deployed per organization, Microsoft suggests that 1,000 is about as high as you want to go. This is a figure large enough for most situations, but it might pose some problems if you wanted to use Exchange to host many different companies and you needed to apply a different disclaimer or perform another type of rules processing for each company. The limit for rules is dictated by performance and memory usage. Microsoft is confident that the performance of the transport engine is sufficient to handle the most complicated rule set that you can create. Experience will tell us soon enough, but Microsoft has done a lot of work to create wizards that guide administrators through the creation of efficient and effective rules and then to optimize the output from the wizards behind the scenes. Once created, rules are compiled and loaded into memory to maximize performance.

Figure 8.22
Active Directory
properties of a
transport rule

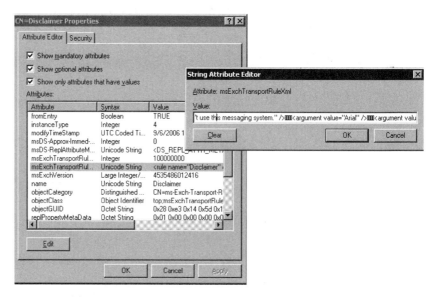

8.4.8 **Rules and the shell**

You can manipulate transport rules through the shell. For example:

```
Get-TransportRule
```

Returns a list of all the transport rules currently known within the organization and indicates their priority and whether they are enabled or disabled. You can make changes to a rule using the `Set-TransportRule` command. For example, to set the priority for the "Disclaimer" rule to 5 (higher values have lower priority, 0 (zero) has the highest priorty):

```
Set-TransportRule —Id 'Disclaimer' —Priority 5
```

This is an easy change, but outside of changing a rule's priority, you'll find that the syntax required to change a condition, action, or exception becomes more complex and it's easy to make a mistake. Part of the reason is that rule conditions, actions, and exceptions are stored as arrays and you have to be careful about manipulating the arrays, so it is not quite as simple as a straightforward command to set a single-valued property on a mailbox. An example similar to that offered in the Exchange help is as follows:

```
$Group = Get-TransportRulePredicate FromMemberOf
$Group.Addresses = @((Get-DistributionGroup 'Stock
Analysts'))
Set-TransportRule —id 'Ethical Wall' —Condition@($Group)
```

This code means:

1. Define a variable that will hold a predicate of a specific type. A predicate indicates the part of an email message that you're interested in looking at. In this case, we want to check on the members of a distribution group. You can find details of the various predicates in the Exchange 2007 help file.

2. Populate the variable with the distribution group that we want to use.

3. Update the "Ethical Wall" rule (we'll go into this later on in this chapter) so that it applies to members of the "Stock Analysts" distribution group as pointed to in the $Group variable.

Another example is where you might want to change the text of a transport rule that adds a disclaimer to outgoing messages. Let's assume that you already have created this rule, but now you want to change the text because of a particular circumstance that has occurred. Here is what you might do:

```
$New-Disclaimer = Get-TransportRuleAction ApplyDisclaimer
$New-Disclaimer.Text = 'Happy Holidays from all at XYZ
Corporation'
$New-Disclaimer.Font = 'Verdana'
$New-Disclaimer.Color = 'Black'
$New-Disclaimer.FontSize = 'Normal'
Set-TransportRule —id 'Disclaimer' —Action @($New-Disclaimer)
```

The code is explained as follows:

1. Define a variable and tell Exchange that you're going to use this to populate an action for a rule and that the action type is to apply a disclaimer. As before, you can find details of the various action types in the Exchange 2007 help file.

2.   Set the text that you want to use. Note that we also set the font, color, and font size to different values than the default (Arial, Grey, Smallest).

3.   Use `Set-TransportRule` to apply the new action.

In our final example, we will add a new action to a rule. There is a pre-defined set of actions that you can add to a rule. You can view the set of available actions with the `Get-TransportRuleAction` command:

```
Name                            Rank     LinkedDisplayText
----                            ----     -----------------
LogEvent                        0        log an event with <a id="EventM...
PrependSubject                  1        prepend the subject with <a id=...
ApplyClassification             2        apply <a id="Classification">me...
ApplyDisclaimer                 3        <a id="Location">append</a> <a ...
SetSCL                          4        set the spam confidence level t...
SetHeader                       5        set <a id="MessageHeader">heade...
RemoveHeader                    6        remove <a id="MessageHeader">he...
AddToRecipient                  7        add a recipient in the To field...
CopyTo                          8        copy the message to <a id="Addr...
BlindCopyTo                     9        blind carbon copy (Bcc) the mes...
RedirectMessage                 10       redirect the message to <a id="...
RejectMessage                   11       send <a id="RejectReason">bounc...
DeleteMessage                   12       silently drop the message
```

A rule will have a set of actions associated with it, so the first thing to do is to discover what they are. In this example, we'll use a rule that checks outgoing messages for certain code words.

```
$Actions = (Get-Transport Rule 'Check for Code
Words').Actions
```

This step loads the current set of rules into the $Action variable, so we can examine it by simply typing the name of the variable.

```
$Actions

Name                            Rank     LinkedDisplayText
----                            ----     -----------------
LogEvent                        0        log an event with <a id="EventM...
PrependSubject                  1        prepend the subject with <a id=...
```

```
ApplyDisclaimer                     3        <a id="Location">append</a> <a ...
BlindCopyTo                         9        blind carbon copy (Bcc) the mes...
```

There are four actions associated with the rule: log an event into the application event log, prepend the message subject with some text, apply a disclaimer, and blind carbon copy the message to an address. To see the full set of properties associated with an action, select it by its position in the array and use the `Format-List` command. To see the text that is prepended to the message subject, we need to do this:

```
$Actions[1] | Format-List

Prefix            : Caution!!!
Name              : PrependSubject
Rank              : 1
LinkedDisplayText : prepend the subject with <a
id="Prefix">string</a>
```

If in doubt, it is easy to check the actions set for a rule through EMC, as shown in Figure 8.23.

Figure 8.23
Checking actions on a rule

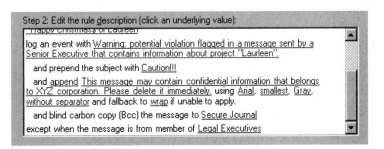

Let's say that we want to modify the disclaimer text. This is stored in position 3 in the array, so we can do this by:

```
$Actions[2].Text = 'Violation of Record Keeping Policy: Do
not Read this message unless you are a lawyer'
Set-TransportRule —id 'Check for Code Words' — Action
$Actions
```

These examples only scratch the surface of what you can do to manipulate rules programmatically through the shell. However, in most cases, unless you are very familiar with the shell and the syntax that is required to set conditions for a rule, you will be better off making whatever changes are necessary through EMC because the wizard does a good job of guiding you through the conditions, actions, and exceptions of a rule.

Curiously, you cannot use the `Set-TransportRule` command to enable or disable a rule by just setting a property of the rule. Instead, you have to use the `Disable-TransportRule` command to disable a rule and `Enable-TransportRule` to enable a rule.

8.4.9 Journal rules

Exchange 2007 supports two types of journaling: standard and premium. Standard journaling is similar to the functionality available in Exchange 2003. You enable journaling for a mailbox database by defining a journal recipient (Figure 8.24), and from that point on, Exchange will journal all messages sent and delivered to any mailbox in the database. If you can group all of the users that you need to journal messages for on one or more servers, then standard journaling may serve your purpose.

The transport service is responsible for applying journal rules after a message passes through the categorizer. This approach ensures that for all potential message recipients, including those that are added to the message as a result of distribution group expansion, Exchange 2007 puts all of the recipient data from the message into the body of a message called the journal report and attaches the original message to the report. As a change from previous versions of Exchange, Exchange 2007 marks each recipient to indicate how they were originally submitted (To:, CC:, or BCC:) by the sender and whether distribution list expansion or message forwarding added recipients. By comparison, Exchange 2003 uses BCC journaling, which means that it puts all message recipients into the BCC header of the journal report; the problem here is that you cannot tell the different types of recipients apart. Exchange 2003 SP1 changed from BCC journaling to the type of envelope journaling used by Exchange 2007 and records details of all message recipients in the body of the journal report. However, Exchange 2003 SP1 suffers from the same problem as BCC journaling in that it does not differentiate between the different recipient types.

Premium journaling requires that you have Enterprise Exchange 2007 CALs. Premium journaling allows you to create rules to capture messages for individual users or groups, to capture messages circulating within the organization or out of the organization, or both. Unlike standard journaling, premium journaling is global in scope and once you create a new journal rule, Exchange applies the rule across the entire organization. You can think of premium journal rules as being a form of very simple transport rules that capture copies of messages. Creating a new journal rule is a very simple operation and the real work occurs in the upfront decisions that are required before you enable journaling. For example:

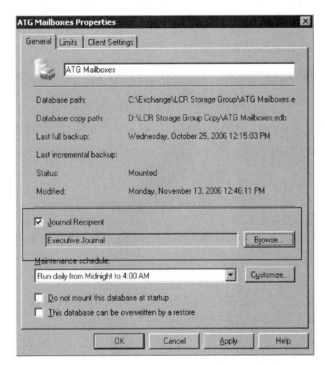

Figure 8.24
Establishing a journal recipient for a mailbox database

1.   Whose messages will the journal rule capture? Do you want to monitor a specific user or a group of users identified by a distribution group?

2.   What kind of messages do you want to capture? You can apply a journal rule to all email passing through hub transport servers, or just to internal (delivered to mailboxes in the same Exchange organization) or external (delivered to addresses outside the Exchange organization).

3.   Where will the journal rule send the captured messages? You can send the messages to any valid email recipient, so you can use a special mailbox on the same server or another server in the Exchange organization, or a contact that points to a special SMTP address that third-party software monitors and processes

Figure 8.25
*Creating a new
journal rule*

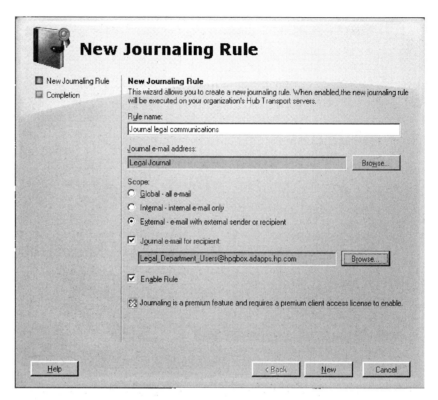

to build an archive. You could even copy all messages to a distribution group if you wanted to.

Figure 8.25 shows the dialog that captures the detail for a new journal rule. In it, you have:

1.   The name of the rule.

2.   The email address of the journal destination. This address must be in the GAL, so if you want to use an external SMTP address, you have to create a contact for the address before you create the rule.

3.   The scope of the rule.

4.   The users that you want to capture email for. You can only select recipients that exist in the GAL.

5.   Whether to enable the journal rule immediately (the default).

After you provide the necessary information, EMC executes the `New-JournalRule` command to create the new rule. As you can see, the code is straightforward:

```
New-JournalRule —Name 'Journal legal communications'
-JournalEmailAddress 'hpqbox.adapps.hp.com/Exchange Users/
Secure Journal' -Scope:'External' -Enabled:$True
-Recipient:'Legal_Department_Users@hpqbox.adapps.hp.com'
```

Other shell commands relevant to journal rules include `Get-JournalRule` to list all of the rules defined within the organization (or just a specific rule) and `Set-JournalRule` to modify a journal rule. However, the same comment about the syntax required to make changes to transport rule conditions also applies to journal rules and it is best to make whatever changes are necessary through EMC.

Once you enable a journal rule, the transport engine begins to comply with the new rule and any message that passes through the categorizer is examined to determine whether it is covered by a journal rule. When it journals messages, Exchange "wraps" a journaled message inside a separate message so that all of the header and content information is captured accurately. The outer message is known as the journal report. If Exchange did not wrap the original message in the journal report, someone who was the subject of legal action might be able to claim that Exchange or some other software rewrote the message header as part of the journaling process and therefore rendered the copy void. Another reason why Exchange journals messages in this format is that if the original message was to travel outside the Exchange organization en route to the journal destination, any intermediate gateways are quite likely to strip information from the message header. In this case, you could not state that the message that Exchange delivers to the journal is a full and absolute copy of the message as it arrives into user mailboxes. For example, Exchange 2007 supports the concept of message classifications, which we will get to later on in this chapter. When a message with a classification is originally sent, the classification is transported in the message as an x-header. X-headers are usually stripped out by gateways and replaced by x-headers generated by the receiving organization, so to preserve this information, Exchange wraps the message with an outer message that gateways can process and update as they require, meaning that messages that contain classifications or any other similar information in the x-headers are preserved. Note that when a classified message is delivered to the Store, the x-header information is promoted to be a MAPI property that contains some localized text that the user can view through Outlook.

Figure 8.26 shows the form that a journaled message arrives into a mailbox (another Exchange mailbox is a valid journal destination). The content of the message gives the header information including all of the recipient information, and you can see that the original message is contained as an attachment.

Figure 8.26
A journaled
message

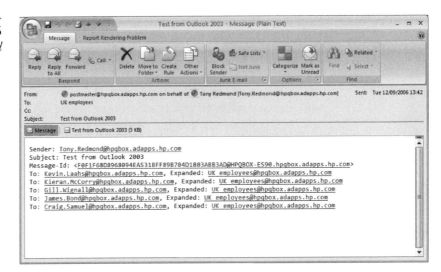

It is possible that Exchange will generate multiple journal reports for a single message. The categorizer is the component that creates journal reports, but this happens relatively late on in categorizer processing. Therefore, it is possible that something will occur to create multiple copies of a message that then result in multiple journal reports. For example, these cases may cause multiple journal reports:

1.   The categorizer bifurcates a message before the journal agent processes it.

2.   The categorizer runs transport rules before journal rules, so any processing that causes a transport rule to split a message generates multiple journal reports.

3.   A message goes to a mix of distribution groups and individual recipients. If different properties exist for the distribution group than for individual recipients (such as OOF processing), then

Exchange may create multiple copies of the message, which in turn results in multiple journal reports.

4. A third-party agent installed into Exchange may bifurcate a message before the categorizer gives it to the journal agent.

In these instances, each of the journal reports will have a different set of P1 recipients. Collectively, the set of journal reports represents the complete journal processing for the message.

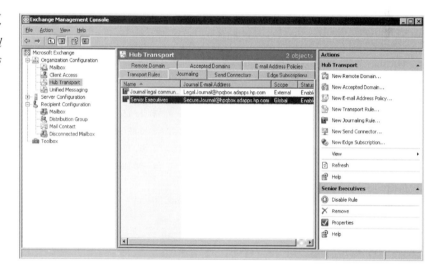

Figure 8.27
A set of journal rules

Figure 8.27 illustrates a set of journal rules as viewed through EMC. Note that it is entirely possible for an administrator to create multiple overlapping journal rules that capture multiple copies of outgoing messages to different places, so clearly you have to apply some thought to coordinate the actions applied through journal rules before you implement anything. In addition, it is a good idea to test journaling thoroughly before you start to collect messages for real. Do this to test that the rules actually journal the messages that you want (from the right users and addressed to the destinations that you need to capture messages for) and that you have the right administrative processes in place to solve problems like what to do with the messages that accumulate in the journal destination. If you use a third-party archive solution to complete processing, it's likely that the messages will be indexed and archived to something like a hierarchical storage system, but if you use mailboxes for messages, they will gradually accumulate items until they are cleaned out. For this reason, make sure that any mailbox that you use for journaling has an appropriate storage quota to allow it to store items for as long as you need to keep them around.

Apart from creating a new journal rule through EMS, you can also list, amend, or delete journal rules.

```
Get-JournalRule -id 'Senior Executives'
```

```
Recipient                                 : Senior_Executives@xyz.com
JournalEmailAddress                       : Journal, Executive
Scope                                     : Global
Enabled                                   : True
Identity                                  : Senior Executives
Guid                                      : 4f84b17f-9796-438a-a8fa-82c6cb6c88e8
Name                                      : Senior Executives
IsValid                                   : True
WhenChanged                               : 1/15/2007 1:14:54 PM
ExchangeVersion                           : 0.1 (8.0.535.0)
MaximumSupportedExchangeObjectVersion : 0.1 (8.0.535.0)
IsReadOnly                                : False
```

```
Remove-JournalRule -id 'Senior Executives'
```

```
Set-JournalRule -id 'Senior Executives' -JournalEmailAddress
'SeniorExecJournal@xyz.com'
```

Note that when you set an email address for journaled messages, Exchange must be able to validate it against the Active Directory. You can create a mailbox or contact for this purpose and pass either the SMTP address or name of the mailbox or contact in the JournalEmailAddress property.

Like transport rules, you cannot disable or enable a journal rule by setting a property of the rule with the Set-JournalRule command. If you want to disable a journal rule, you do it with the Disable-JournalRule command. To enable a journal rule, use the Enable-JournalRule command.

It is worth mentioning that Microsoft has taken a different approach to journaling in Exchange 2007 when compared to previous versions. In Exchange 2003, journaling occurs on a per-database basis, so you typically allocate all of the mailboxes that you are interested in capturing messages for into a single database. This approach works if you are able to group users in this manner, but it breaks when you want to move a user's mailbox to another database unless it is also journaled. Exchange 2007 allows you to set a more flexible scope for journaling. You can still journal on a per-database basis by creating a distribution group for all mailboxes in the database, but you can also create a distribution group that covers mailboxes from multiple databases, and as long as a mailbox is included in the group, Exchange continues to journal messages.

Exchange 2007 journaling is a simple process that allows you to capture messages for specific users or groups. Remember that journal rules are a restricted variation of standard Exchange transport rules, so if you want to do something more sophisticated in terms of more conditional control over when a rule fires to capture messages, you move to the next level and create a transport rule.

8.5 Messaging Record Management

Data retention is a big deal for many companies today because they are being forced into more stringent recordkeeping practices in order to comply with legislative or regulatory requirements. This development really isn't a surprise because it reflects the growing importance of electronic communications in business life. Discussions that once took place through letters, telexes, or faxes are now commonly resolved through email, so the filing practices that existed to record discussions through those media should logically apply to email. Of course, users can be directed to file important information in folders in their mailbox, and if they get the necessary coaching, education, and backup, a strong chance exists that they will be able to comply with these directives. However, life being what it is, users need help to know what information they should capture and where they should put the information that they capture.

In some respects, lawyers hate email because it is far too easy for people to keep messages and attachments that contain information that a company would really prefer not to reveal in a court of law. However, users need to retain messages in order to get work done and in some cases, they are required to retain all electronic communications that relate to specific activities such as financial transactions, mergers and acquisitions, and product planning that may involve contentious issues such as who owns a piece of valuable intellectual property. Users may be required to retain this information for a specific period or even indefinitely.

In previous versions of Exchange, it is difficult for administrators to manage the information contained in user mailboxes (and public folders) because apart from the Mailbox Manager, Exchange offers no facilities to enforce retention, harvest information from, or clean out mailboxes, so it is tremendously difficult to ensure that users are in fact complying with regulations. Indeed, satisfactory compliance is often only achieved through an enormous effort to educate users as to their responsibilities. And even if users comply with directives to retain information, the task of finding information when it is required is complicated because the information is scattered in a random fashion across a range of user-named and managed folders distributed in many different mailboxes. Solving the retention problem in Exchange 2003 usually requires either some custom code (which is expensive to write, test, and maintain) or deployment of a third-party archiving product. Even so, the lack of consistency in how users manage content in their mailboxes continues to complicate matters.

Microsoft's Messaging Records Management (MRM) strategy for Exchange is intended to make it easier for users to comply with company, legal, or regulatory requirements to retain specific information that circulates through the messaging system. MRM is an enterprise feature so you can't operate it unless you have enterprise Exchange licenses. According to Microsoft, MRM operates on three basic principles:

- Users classify their own messages by moving them into special folders that are intended to old information about specific topics. These folders are referred to as "Managed folders."

- Exchange can remove obsolete items from user mailboxes by implementing message expiry times that administrators can set on both default and custom folders.

- Users can retain any items that they need to keep in managed folders. If required for filing in a corporate repository, these items can be journaled (copied) by email to a mailbox or mail-enabled contact (which can be a SMTP-enabled feed for an archive or document management system). Alternatively, you can build your own processes to move content from the managed folders to a central repository or other archive system.

The process involved in deploying MRM for Exchange 2007 is pretty straightforward:

1.   Decide what default folders you want to manage and how you want to manage the contents of these folders. For example, you

might decide that messages expire and are deleted from the inbox after 60 days.

2. Decide if you need to deploy custom managed folders, what content these folders will hold, and how the content will be managed. For example, you might create custom folders for organization-wide use such as repositories for information needed for annual audits, intellectual property generation, or even a folder where users can place personal information that they want to retain indefinitely. You can also create managed custom folders that are used for specific purposes by restricted groups of users. For example, you could create a managed custom folder to hold all of the design documents for a project or customer.

3. Update the set of default folders provided by Exchange with appropriate content settings to determine how Exchange will manage the content of these folders. You may need to create new default folders.

4. Create any custom manage folders that you need and associate the content settings.

5. Create managed folder policies that cover one or more folders. You can combine default and custom folders within a policy.

6. Apply the managed folder policies to mailboxes. You do not have to apply a managed folder policy to every mailbox on a server.

7. As required, harvest information from the managed folders.

8. Periodically review whether the folders and policies meet the need of users and refine as necessary.

You can use Exchange 2007 transport rules (see the section beginning on page 792) to supplement MRM. For example, you may be in a situation where you are required to journal every message that mentions a specific code word that identifies a project. You could rely on users to file copies of these messages in a managed custom folder and journal all the messages that go into this folder, but you could create a transport rule that monitors message traffic to capture any message that refers to the project code word in the message subject or body. The combination of transport rule and managed folders may generate some duplicate copies, but it does ensure a higher degree of automation in achieving compliance.

Exchange 2007 is the first version to build MRM functionality into the product. Up to now, apart from the need to keep their mailbox under quota, users have had total control over the contents of their mailbox, so the facts that some content will expire and disappear from folders automatically and that administrators now have the ability to control how folders are used will come as a shock to some. With this point in mind, it is a good idea to communicate why MRM is necessary, how it will be implemented, what effect it will have on a user mailbox, the advantages that the company gains through MRM, and why MRM does not compromise the privacy of user data before you implement this functionality.

It is important to say that while Exchange 2007 provides administrators with much greater ability to manage the content in user mailboxes than ever before and will certainly be of huge assistance in achieving compliance, it may not satisfy the requirements of your company. You should therefore involve the personnel who are responsible for records management and compliance in any implementation so that any gaps in functionality are identified early and plugged with custom code or a third-party product.

8.5.1　Managing default folders

Exchange has had default folders, which appear in every mailbox, since its first release. The only change over the last decade is that the set of default folders has grown over the different software releases from the original group of Inbox, Sent Items, Calendar, Outbox, and Deleted Items to accommodate folders such as RSS Feeds, Sync Issues, and Junk Mail. Exchange 2007 allows administrators to create new default folders or to apply rules (called managed content settings) to existing folders. You create new default folders through EMC by selecting the mailbox node under Organization Configuration and then the "New Managed Default Folder" option. Alternatively, you can use the `New-ManagedFolder` command. For example, here's the command that creates a new folder called "Critical Documents":

```
New-ManagedFolder -Name 'Critical Documents'
-DefaultFolderType 'Mail' -Comment 'Use this folder for
critical documents" -MustDisplayComment $True
```

Figure 8.28 illustrates a set of default folders as displayed by EMC. Note that the Inbox, Sent Items, and Sync Issues folders have some additional information shown beneath their entries. This indicates that an administra-

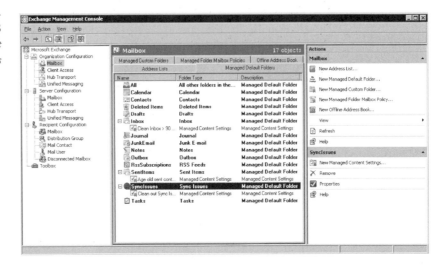

Figure 8.28
The set of default folders

tor has created a managed content setting for these folders. You can create multiple managed content settings for a folder, which allows you to define different settings for the different kinds of items that users store in folders. Content settings control:

- The message expiry time for the folder. You can define an expiry time that applies to all content types held in the folder or you can set individual expiry times for different content types. For example, you might keep calendar items for 365 days and any Exchange "missed call" items (for voicemail) only 10 days. The Managed Folder Assistant removes items that have exceeded their expiry time when it runs to ensure that users do not keep obsolete material around and you can decide whether an item's lifetime starts from when it first arrives into the mailbox or into the specific folder. You can decide to delete items permanently (a hard delete), delete the items but allow them to be recovered (a soft delete), move expired items into the Deleted Items folder (where users to recover the items from if they want to keep them—see Chapter 5 for details about deleted items recovery), move the items into another managed folder, or mark the items as being past the retention limit for the folder.

- Journal processing for the folder. You use this setting to control whether Exchange automatically copies items placed into the folder to another location, which can be a mailbox or a mail-enabled contact. You can use this feature to copy items to a mailbox that is monitored by a sophisticated archiving and categorization service that automatically refiles the content so that it complies with whatever regulatory requirements you have to satisfy.

Figure 8.29

Setting properties for a default folder

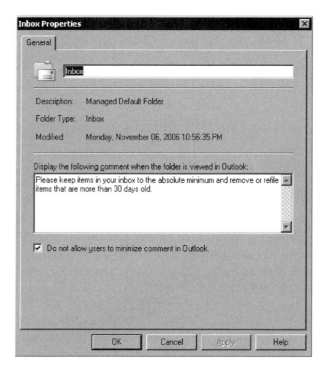

Message expiry times help users to make decisions whether or not they need to keep items by forcing them to move an item to another folder before Exchange automatically expires the item. If users know that Exchange will move items from the Inbox to the Deleted Items folder automatically after 30 days (and you point this fact out with a comment that Outlook displays when users access the folder, as shown in Figure 8.29), they soon learn that they have to decide whether to keep an item by refiling it after it first arrives or run the risk that Exchange will remove it for them. If you do decide to impose automatic aging on the Inbox, you should also do the same for the Sent Items folder because it does not make sense to clean out the messages that users receive while you allow them to accumulate messages that they send.

Users who struggle to keep their mailboxes under quota may appreciate that Exchange 2007 incorporates a Managed Folder Assistant that can clean their mailboxes out regularly, but some users won't like the fact that their data is now under the control of system processes. Of course, the usual method of deletion is to perform a soft delete, meaning that Exchange removes the item from the user's view, but retains it in the database until the deleted items retention period expires. The default deleted items retention period for new mailbox databases created for Exchange 2007 is 14 days, so even if Exchange moves expired items from a mailbox into the Deleted Items folder and the user then empties the Deleted Items folder, they'll still be able to recover an important item that they overlooked with Outlook's Recover Deleted Items option. Exchange does not impose a default message expiry time on any folder. You have to take the explicit step of deciding what content setting you want to apply to the folder, include the folder in a managed folder policy, and then apply the policy to mailboxes before Exchange starts to look for expired items in the folder actively.

Figure 8.30 illustrates the two screens that the new managed content wizard presents when you add a content setting to a folder. Note that in this case, we have defined that Exchange should journal any item added to this folder to the "Legal Journal" mailbox. Copies of the item remain in the folder. In addition, we have specified that the rule applies to items of all types that arrive into the folder. Finally, items in this folder will automatically expire 30 days after they first arrive into the mailbox. Sometimes you have to retain documents for years, so you'll have to convert years into days to enter the right value here, so if you wanted to use a four-year period, you enter 1,461 days (4×365 days + 1 for the leap year).

Figure 8.30
Setting up new managed content settings for a folder

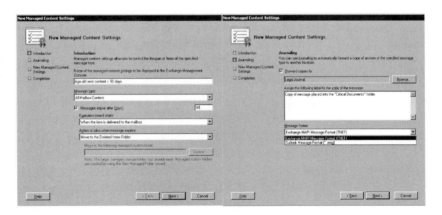

If you add a journal recipient for a folder, you can opt to journal items in Outlook message format or in Exchange MAPI message format. Figure 8.31 displays what the two types of journaled item look like. The choice as to which format to select depends on what purpose the journaled items serves. When you chose Outlook message format, Exchange essentially sends a copy of the message as an attachment to a new message, so the item is processed through the transport system. You can see that this is the case because the cover note includes a disclaimer that has been applied by a transport rule. On the other hand, the traditional MAPI-format version is a copy that is relayed by Exchange without transport rules or other processing being applied, so in some respects it is a "purer" copy of the journaled item.

The easiest way to create a new managed content setting for a folder is through EMC, but you can also use the `New-ManagedContentSettings` command to add a content setting to a folder. The same command serves the purpose of assigning a managed folder policy to both default and custom managed folders. In the example shown below, you can see that the journal destination is indicated through the Active Directory name for the mail-enabled object. You can use an SMTP address or UPN for this parameter, assuming that Exchange can find the SMTP address or UPN in the Active Directory.

```
New-ManagedContentSettings -Name 'Capture Critical Items' -FolderName
'Critical Items' -RetentionAction 'MoveToDeletedItems'
-AddressForJournaling -AgeLimitForRetention '90.00:00:00'
—JournalingEnabled:$True -MessageFormatForJournaling 'UseTnef'
—RetentionEnabled:$True -LabelForJournaling '' -MessageClass 'All Mailbox
Content' -MoveToDestinationFolder $Null -TriggerForRetention 'WhenDelivered'
-AddressForJournaling 'xyz.com/Exchange Users/Contacts/Critical Items
Journal'
—MessageFormatForJounaling UseMsg
```

The `Get-ManagedFolder` command lists all of the managed folders (default and custom) defined within the organization. You can view the complete set of properties for a folder by using a command like:

```
Get-ManagedFolder —Id 'Business Documents' | Format-List
```

The `Get-ManagedContentSettings` command lists all of the managed content settings defined in the organization. You can also use this command to look at the properties of a managed content settings as follows:

```
Get-ManagedContentSettings —id 'Business Information' |
Format-List
```

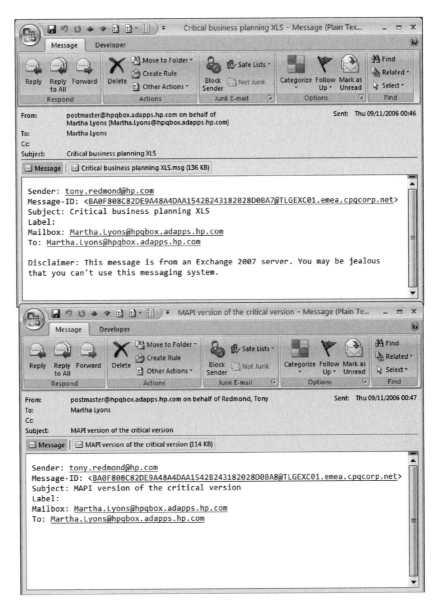

Figure 8.31
Journaled messages in Outlook and MAPI format

You can use the `Remove-ManagedContentSettings` command to remove an entry that is no longer required.

8.5.2 Managing custom folders

Exchange creates the set of default folders in a mailbox when it creates the mailbox so that every user sees a common set of default folders. By comparison, depending on the managed folder policies that you deploy, users may have different custom folders in their mailboxes. Managed custom folders are a mechanism to help users to comply by providing a known place in their mailbox where they can store items that are of interest to the organization. Another way to think about managed custom folders is to regard them as a special form of folder that administrators create so that users can store information for a particular purpose in the folder. If things go to plan and users store the right information in the right custom folder, then it should be very easy to locate the necessary information should the need arise. At least, that's the theory, but you have to realize that the sheer existence of a custom folder in a user mailbox does not mean that users will exploit the folder for its intended purpose. You still have to educate people about the expectations and correct usage of these folders if you expect them to serve their purpose.

Figure 8.32

Creating a new Managed Custom Folder

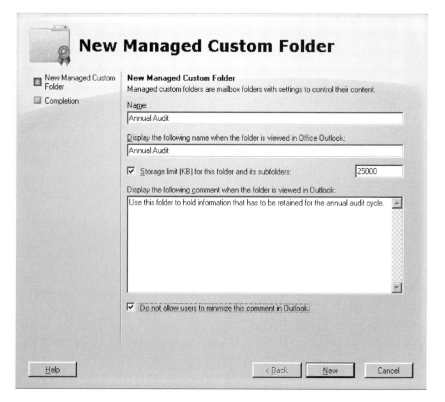

When you create a new folder (Figure 8.32), you specify the storage limit that you want to assign to the folder and some free text instructions for users to help them to understand what information to store in the folders. Outlook 2007 and Outlook Web Access 2007 display these instructions at the top of the folder when users open the folder. Exchange counts the storage occupied by managed folders against the standard mailbox quota, so these folders are not dumping grounds that users can move items into in order to stay under their quota. Clearly, there is no point in assigning a very large storage limit for managed folders if you don't allocate sufficient mailbox quota to allow users to store items in the managed folders along with a reasonable amount of information in the nonmanaged folders in their mailbox.

You can use the `New-ManagedFolder` command to create a managed custom folder through the shell. In this example, we create a custom folder called "Business Critical Documents":

```
New-ManagedFolder -Name 'Business Critical Documents'
-FolderName 'Business Critical Documents' -StorageQuota
'5000KB' -Comment 'Use this folder to store any document that
you this is of great interest to the business.'
-MustDisplayComment:$True
```

Note that Exchange 2007 does not support managed folders that have duplicate names (even display names). If you need to create several managed folders that have approximately the same purpose that might share a similar name, you will have to come up with a naming convention to distinguish the folder.

The `Remove-ManagedFolder` command is available to remove a managed folder from the organization. For example, this command removes the "Annual Audit" managed folder.

```
Remove-ManagedFolder -id 'Annual Audit'
```

If you remove a managed folder, the folder remains in any mailbox where a policy created it. However, the folder has lost its managed status, so users can work with it in the same manner as any other folder that they had created themselves, including the ability to delete the folder and its contents.

After you create whatever custom folders you require, remember to assign the necessary content settings to instruct Exchange how it should manage the items that users store in the folders.

8.5.3   Allocating managed folders with policies

Creating folders and assigning content settings prepares the scene to implement management of the folders. The next step is to allocate the folders (and their content settings) to policies that we can then assign to mailboxes. Think of policies as a way to group a collection of folders that users need to do their work. For example, you could create one managed folder policy for Senior Executives, another for members of the Legal Department, and another for users who work with a particular customer or project.

Figure 8.33
*Adding managed
folders to a policy*

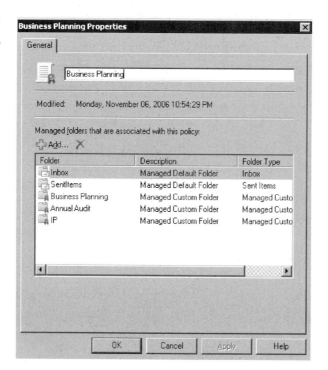

You can have as many managed folder policies as you want. These are organization-wide objects, so you can assign the policies to any mailbox within the organization. As you can see from Figure 8.33, we have created a managed folder policy called "Business Planning" that includes both custom folders and default folders that contain some custom folders that are appropriate to hold information relating to the company's business planning process. We've also included the Inbox and Sent Items default folders because we have some content settings assigned to these folders to expire messages after a set period. Exchange allows you to combine default and custom folders in a single policy because you can only apply one managed folder policy to a mailbox, so you have to ensure that the policy incorporates all of the folders that you want to assign to mailboxes.

8.5.4 Applying policies to users

With our policies defined, the final step in implementing messaging records management for Exchange 2007 is to assign the policies to mailboxes. You can select a mailbox and assign a managed folder policy to the mailbox as shown in Figure 8.34. The "Browse" button allows you to view all managed folder policies and select the right policy for the mailbox.

Figure 8.34
Assigning a mailbox with a managed folder policy

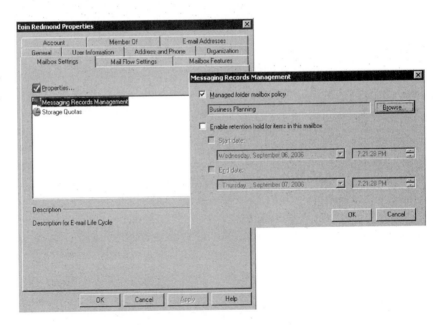

Once you have policies defined, administrators can assign the policies to mailboxes as they create the mailboxes or assign them to existing mailboxes by editing the properties of the mailboxes. The Mailbox Settings section of the New Mailbox wizard (Figure 8.35) allows you to select a managed folder policy to apply to the mailbox immediately. If you are creating mailboxes through the shell, the equivalent action is to specify the name of the policy that you want to assign as the value of the ManagedFolderMailbox-Policy property when you execute the `New-Mailbox` command:

```
New-Mailbox —Name 'John Johnson' —ManagedFolderMailboxPolicy
'Business Planning'
```

For existing mailboxes, you use the `Set-Mailbox` command to apply a managed folder policy:

```
Set-Mailbox —id 'James Bond' -ManagedFolderMailboxPolicy
'Business Planning' -RetentionHoldEnabled:$True
—StartDateForRetentionHold '6/1/2007 7:00:00 AM'
—EndDateForRetentionHold '15/2/2007 2:00:00 AM'
```

In this example, we have set the RetentionHoldEnabled property to be true, which is the equivalent of setting the "Enable retention hold for items in this mailbox" checkbox that you can see in Figure 8.34. Setting a retention hold on a mailbox instructs Exchange to retain items in the mailbox even if the managed folder policy says that they should be deleted or moved. This is an exception to the rule, so we also set a start and end date for the retention hold period.

The power of the shell now comes into play because you can use the `Set-Mailbox` command in conjunction with the `Get-Mailbox` command (with or without filters) to assign a managed folder policy to multiple mailboxes at one time. For example, this command is sufficient to loop through all of the mailboxes on the specified server and assign the same managed folder policy to every mailbox.

```
Get-Mailbox —Server ExchMbxSvr1 | Set-Mailbox
—ManagedFolderMailboxPolicy 'Business Planning'
```

Variations on the theme include using the Database parameter with the `Get-Mailbox` command to specify a database name in order to apply the policy to every mailbox in the database or even using a distribution group as the basis to apply policy. For example:

```
Get-DistributionGroupMember 'Users for Business Planning
Policy' | Set-Mailbox —ManagedFolderMailboxPolicy 'Business
Planning'
```

If you use these techniques, you may want to run a batch job on a regular schedule to ensure that the policy is applied to new users that are added

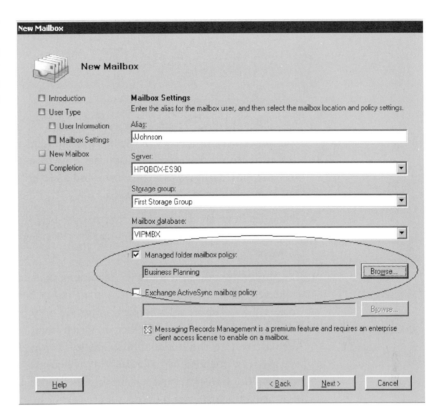

Figure 8.35
*Assigning a
managed folder
mailbox policy to a
new mailbox*

to the server, database, or distribution group. If you assign a managed folder policy to many users at one time, you may want to follow this up by invoking the Managed Folder Assistant to implement the policy on the target mailboxes.

You can list all of the available managed folder policies in the organization with the `Get-ManagedFolderMailboxPolicy` command. The `Remove-ManagedFolderMailboxPolicy` command is used to remove a managed folder policy that is no longer required.

8.5.5 The Managed Folder Assistant

Users will not see the new folders specified in a managed folder policy appear in their mailbox or any other processing occur for managed folders until the Managed Folder Assistant runs to process mailboxes. The Managed Folder Assistant runs on a scheduled basis as part of the Microsoft Exchange Mailbox Assistants service, following the schedule set through the Messaging Record Management tab of server properties (Figure 8.36). Only mailbox servers display this property tab. When the Managed Folder Assistant runs, it performs the following tasks:

- It populates new managed folders into users who come under the control of a managed folder policy.

- If a policy defines a retention or expiry period for items, the assistant stamps a MAPI property (ElcMoveDate) on items indicating the date and time from which the retention period will start. A future run of the assistant can then use this date and time to calculate when to delete an item or mark it as expired.

- It locates items in managed folders that are past their expiration date and takes whatever action is defined in the policy (delete, age out, move to another folder).

- If required by policy, it journals new items that have been placed in managed folders. In this context, journaling is different to that performed by transport rules because items are only processed when the Managed Folder Assistant is active rather than immediately when they arrive into the folder. The Managed Folder Assistant does not use the transport engine to journal items because there is no guarantee that the transport role will be installed onto the mailbox server that hosts the managed folders.

Figure 8.36
A schedule for
Messaging Record
Management on a
server

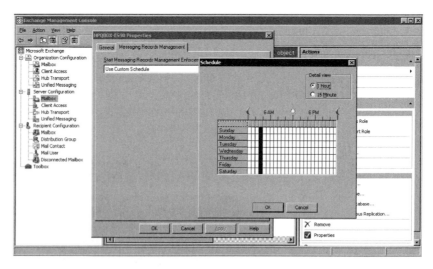

If you prefer to work through the shell, you can also manipulate the MRM schedule with the `Set-MailboxServer` command. For example, this command sets a schedule to instruct the Managed Folder Assistant to run between 9AM on Sunday and 1PM on Sunday. The assistant will continue running until all mailboxes are processed or 1PM arrives. Be aware that server load increases when the assistant runs to create new folders in user mailboxes.

```
Set-MailboxServer —Identity ExchMbxSvr1
—ManagedFolderAssistantSchedule 'Sun.09:00-Sun.13:00'
```

Depending on the work that you ask the Managed Folder Assistant to do, its processing may impose a load on the server that you prefer to schedule to occur in off-peak hours. Creating folders does not generate an excessive load, but scanning many folders in many mailboxes for items that have exceeded retention periods or need to be journaled can consume many system resources. For this reason, it is best to be cautious and keep the work of the Managed Folder Assistant outside peak demand whenever possible. Sometimes it is useful and necessary to have the Managed Folder Assistant process mailboxes immediately. For example, you may want to populate a set of new managed folders to a group of mailboxes that you have just created or you want to journal any items that are waiting to be processed. In these instances, you can use the `Start-ManagedFoldersAssistant` command to force the assistant to process all mailboxes on a selected mailbox server immediately. For example, to process all the mailboxes on a server:

```
Start-ManagedFoldersAssistant —Server ExchMbxSvr1
```

You can also instruct the assistant to process a selected mailbox. For example:

```
Start-ManagedFoldersAssistant —Mailbox 'James Bond'
```

If necessary, you can use the `Stop-ManagedFoldersAssistant` command to stop the assistant.

8.5.6   Logging Managed Folder activity

By default, Exchange 2007 does not log any details of the work performed by the Managed Folder Assistant. If you want to gain some insight into what happens when the Managed Folder Assistant runs, you can enable logging on a mailbox server with the `Set-MailboxServer` command. For example:

```
Set-MailboxServer —id ExchMbxSvr1
—JournalingLogForManagedFoldersEnable:$True
```

After you enable logging, Exchange generates daily log files in the \Program Files\Microsoft\Exchange Server\Logging\Managed Folder Assistant directory. Similar to the parameters available to control message tracking logs, you can change how Exchange manages these log files.

In this command, we set a number of parameters.

```
Set-MailboxServer —id ExchMbxSvr1
-LogDirectorySizeLimitForManagedFolders 100MB
-LogFileAgeLimitForManagedFolders 30.00:00:00
-LogFileSizeLimitForManagedFolders 25MB
-LogPathForManagedFolders "D\Logs\Managed Folder Assistant"
-RetentionLogForManagedFoldersEnabled:$True
-SubjectLogForManagedFoldersEnabled:$True
```

- The total size limit for the directory that stores the Managed Folder Assistant log files is set to 100MB. After Exchange reaches this limit, it deletes the oldest log files to make room.

- The age limit for log files is set to 30 days. Exchange deletes log files that are older than the limit.

- The maximum file size for a Managed Folder Assistant log is set to 25MB (the default is 10MB). After the log file reaches the specified size, Exchange creates a new log. Note that the 10MB default limit is more than sufficient for the vast majority of servers.

- The location where Exchange creates log files for the Managed Folder Assistant is moved away from the default on the system disk. It is best practice to move all log files generated by Exchange off the system disk.

- Exchange is instructed to log information about messages that have reached their retention limit.

- Exchange is instructed to log the subject for any message that is processed by the Managed Folder Assistant.

Figure 8.37 illustrates some example content extracted from a managed folder assistant log. Three actions are highlighted:

1. The Managed Folder Assistant has processed an item that is past its retention date.

2. The Managed Folder Assistant has journaled an item in a managed folder.

3. The Managed Folder Assistant is processing a mailbox to apply a managed folder policy.

Figure 8.37
*Managed folder
assistant log*

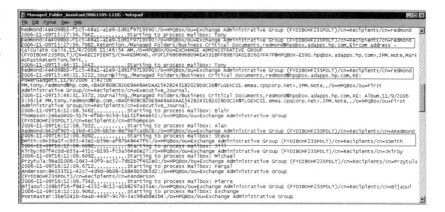

8.5.7   Using Managed Folders

Figure 8.38 shows the view that a user has of a managed folder through Outlook Web Access 2007. In this case, the Managed Folder Assistant has provisioned the managed folders covered by the policy into the user's mailbox. The folders are available for use immediately after creation. These folders behave like any other mailbox folder, so you can drag and drop information to and from them. You can create subfolders under managed folders but you cannot delete the managed folders from your mailbox. Note that both Outlook and Outlook Web Access 2007 display the comment provided by the administrator when they created the folder. Exchange also gives indication of how much storage is available in the folder. This information is not available to earlier clients.

Once populated, folders stay in user mailboxes even if you remove the policy that created the folders into the mailbox. This is logical because the folders may still contain valuable content that the user wants to retain. In

Figure 8.38
*Using a managed
custom folder*

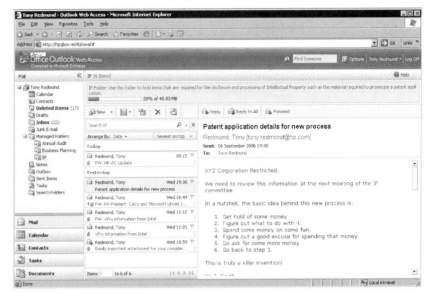

addition, you may want to add the user back to a policy in the future. Like
default folders, users cannot delete managed custom folders after Exchange
creates these folders in mailboxes (Figure 8.39). This statement is true as
long as a managed folder policy applies to the user. After you remove a policy from a mailbox, the user can first delete the folders under the "Managed
Folders" root and then remove the "Managed Folders" folder.

Figure 8.39
*Users cannot delete
a managed
custom folder*

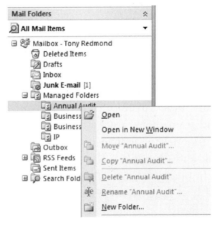

Figure 8.40 shows how Outlook 2007 displays items in a managed custom folder. You can see the information about the folder that the administrator defined on top of the folder and a number of items in the folder.

Note that the last two items are grayed out, which means that the Managed Folder Assistant has reviewed these items and detected that they exceed the retention limit (in days) for the folder. Users can still access these items, so graying them out is really just a visual indication that these items are old and are good candidates for deletion, assuming that they contain nothing of interest. You depend on users to delete expired messages, as neither Exchange nor Outlook will take any further action to remove them after they have been marked as expired, so it is entirely possible for users to accumulate hundreds of expired items in their mailboxes. If you want to delete items automatically, then the policy that you create has to delete items rather than simply marking the items as expired.

Figure 8.40
Aged out items in a managed custom folder

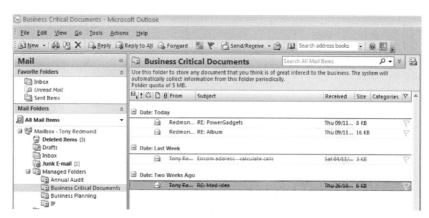

8.5.8 Harvesting information from managed folders

Once you have users accustomed to storing essential information in managed folders, you may wonder how you ever gain access to this information. Journaling is the automatic and easiest way to harvest information from managed folders. As mentioned earlier, you can journal items to a mailbox or any mail-enabled contact. Once you harvest the information from user mailboxes to a central location, it does not take much extra processing to move it to a more intelligent repository, such as HP's Record Information Storage System (RISS) or Symantec's Enterprise Vault. In fact, you can expect third-party vendors to provide their own scripts for this purpose.

Journaling is great, but it only works if you create the journal destination and implement it from the start. If you elect not to journal messages or you want to extract messages from folders created before the deployment of Exchange 2007, you have to come up with a different way to harvest information from the managed folders. The most basic approach is to ask users to move the items from selected folders into a PST on a regular basis and to send the PST to a central point for further processing. For example, you could have an administrator check all the items in PSTs that come from users to decide whether the items need to be kept. As I am sure that you realize, the problem with this approach is that it is intensely manual, time consuming, and prone to error. Nevertheless, it is cheap and might do the job for a small Exchange installation.

A better and more automated approach is to look for a way to use a third-party archiving product to move information from these folders into an archive destination. The problem here is that the connection between Exchange 2007 and the archiving product may not exist, so you either have to wait for the software vendor to write the necessary interface or come up with some code yourself.

You can use the `Export-Mailbox` command to scan user mailboxes for items that they have stored in managed folders and to export that data to a special mailbox created for this purpose. You can then have an administrator or another specialized user (such as a legal assistant, if you were scanning for documents related to Intellectual Property) check the items gathered from user mailboxes to decide what is important and should be kept and what should be deleted. Ideally, the items that are kept should be moved from the target destination used by `Export-Mailbox` so that only new items appear there.

For example, this shell command uses the `Get-Mailbox` command to fetch a list of mailboxes from a database, checks for those that are under the control of a specified mailbox policy, and then exports the content of two managed folders (note the syntax to specify the folder names) to a mailbox specially created to harvest items. We specify start and end dates so that previous items are not collected.

```
Get-Mailbox -Database 'Executive Mailboxes' | Where
{$_.ManagedFolderMailboxPolicy -like 'Business Planning'} |
Export-Mailbox —TargetMailbox 'IP Collection' -TargetFolder
'IP'     —IncludeFolders '\Managed Folders\IP', 'Managed
Folders\Business Planning' —StartDate '12/1/2007'
—EndDate '12/31/2007'
```

Because it will be unable to find the folders, the `Export-Mailbox` command will fail with a MAPI error if the source folders have not been created in the mailboxes that you process.

8.6   Message classifications

Managed folders and managed folder policies allow administrators to define some degree of control over how users store and manage items. However, apart from a set of managed folders appearing in a mailbox and the labels that you can assign to these folders, users receive little guidance as to what they should do with the information that flows around in messages. The vast bulk of email is unclassified and up to Exchange 2007. The only classification that you could apply to messages is primitive insofar as you can say that a message is urgent or add a flag or reminder to it.

Exchange 2007 introduces a new way to apply classifications to items in the form of metadata that Exchange transports along with the message. It is possible to transport the metadata to support classifications between Exchange 2007 organizations if you configure the connector between the organizations to support this feature. In addition, you can create transport rules to apply some intelligence to how users handle classified messages.

By default, Exchange 2007 includes four message classifications:

- Company Confidential: In other words, this message contains information that is proprietary and should not be disclosed without authorization. Most companies have well-defined policies that govern the handling of confidential information.

- Company Internal: Information that is sensitive and should not be shared with external recipients.

- A/C Privileged: "A/C" means "Attorney/Client" and indicates that this message is part of a conversation between a lawyer and their client. For example, if a lawyer from a company's legal department sends a note to an executive relating to a potential acquisition target, the message is usually marked with this designation in the text.

- No restriction: This classification means what it says.

Outlook Web Access 2007 clients can use the default classifications immediately, but you have to update the system registry with details of the classifications, both default and any customized classifications that you add, before Outlook 2007 clients can set classifications on messages. Older Outlook clients cannot use this feature, so it is clearly something that can only be truly effective after you have upgraded a complete infrastructure to Exchange 2007 and Outlook 2007. Microsoft might say that this is an example of how Exchange 2007 and Outlook 2007 work together to deliver new functionality, but some might wonder why Microsoft has not provided backwards compatibility if they really want to make the message classification feature useful.

The default set of message classifications are a useful start to get accustomed to how classifications work and how they might fit into the way that your company handles sensitive and confidential information. After you make this assessment, you will probably find that you need a couple of extra classifications to fit with your company's procedures or the regulatory or legislative environment that the company functions under. To bridge the gap, you can add new message classifications to Exchange 2007, and if you operate a multilingual organization, you can define the customized message classifications in whatever languages you need to support. You do all of this work through EMS, as EMC includes no UI to create or modify message classifications.

First, let's see how to find out what message classifications exist. All of the tasks to work with message classifications occur on a hub or multi-role server (that supports the hub role):

```
Get-MessageClassification

Identity                        Locale              DisplayName
--------                        ------              -----------
Default\ExACPrivileged                              A/C Privileged
Default\ExAttachmentRemoved                         Attachment Removed
Default\ExCompanyConfidential                       Company Confidential
Default\ExCompanyInternal                           Company Internal
```

Exchange uses the Default\ExAttachmentRemoved classification to indicate a message that has had an attachment removed because an antivirus agent deemed the attachment as a potential security threat. You will not use this classification from Outlook or Outlook Web Access. To see more detail about a selected classification, pass its identity and use the Format-List command to expose the detail:

```
Get-MessageClassification –id 'Default\ExACPrivileged' | Format-List

ClassificationID         : d74dbde8-4cb0-4043-ae4b-2a1b5686c9dc
DisplayName              : A/C Privileged
DisplayPrecedence        : Medium
Identity                 : Default\ExACPrivileged
```

```
IsDefault                : True
Locale                   :
RecipientDescription     : This message is either a request for legal
advice from an attorney or a response by an attorney for legal advice. It
should be treated confidentially, should only be sent to people with a need to
know, and should only be forwarded by an attorney.
RetainClassificationEnabled : True
SenderDescription        : This message is either a request for legal advice
from an attorney or a response by an attorney for legal advice. It should be
treated confidentially, should only be sent to people with a need to know, and
should only be forwarded by an attorney.
UserDisplayEnabled       : True
Version                  : 1
```

Table 8.1 describes the most interesting parameters and their meaning.

Now that we know the kind of information that a message classification contains, let's go ahead and create a customized classification. I am quite familiar with the patent application process because I have worked on it at both Compaq and HP. The process requires inventors to make disclosures of their work to patent coordinators (lawyers and experienced technologists) who assess the work and decide whether to process with a patent application. I can create a "Patent Disclosure" message classification with the New-MessageClassification command, passing suitable values to the parameters explained in Table 8.1.

Table 8.1   *Parameters for message classification*

Parameter	Meaning
SenderInformation	This parameter contains the information that Outlook or Outlook Web Access will display when a user adds the classification to a message. It can be up to 1,024 characters long and should include whatever instructions the user needs to comply with before they send the message.
RecipientInformation	This is the information that a recipient sees when a message with this classification arrives. You should populate this parameter with whatever instructions are necessary to inform the user what to do with the message.

Table 8.1   *Parameters for message classification (continued)*

Parameter	Meaning
Locale	This parameter indicates the language that the classification is used for. If blank, it can be used for all languages.
Display Name	This is the name that the user sees when they view available classifications that they can apply to messages.
RetainClassificationEnabled	Defines whether the classification persists if the message is forwarded or replied to. Naturally, this setting is only valid if the recipient uses a client that understands classifications and the metadata is transported during the delivery process. The default setting is $True.
DisplayPrecedence	Clients can only display a single classification for a message. The default precedence is Medium, but you can increase or decrease it (or this can be done by a transport rule) if you want to ensure that a certain classification is retained.

```
New-MessageClassification —DisplayName 'Patent Disclosure'
—Name 'Patent Disclosure' —SenderInformation 'Use this
classification for messages that are related to the patent
disclosure process; messages must be sent to a member of the
IP Disclosure Committee group'
—RecipientDescription 'This message contains information that
relates to a patent disclosure. Please process it promptly and
ensure that all records are maintained in accordance with
company policy'
```

We can then check that the classification looks correct with a call to Get-MessageClassification:

```
ClassificationID        : 036a61a3-1154-42f8-87d3-321804ffa422
DisplayName             : Patent Disclosure
DisplayPrecedence       : Medium
Identity                : Default\Patent Disclosure
IsDefault               : True
Locale                  :
```

```
RecipientDescription          : This message contains information that relates
to a patent disclosure. Please process it promptly and ensure that all records
are maintained in accordance with company policy
RetainClassificationEnabled : True
SenderDescription             : Use this classification for messages that are
related to the patent disclosure process; messages must be sent to a member of
the IP Disclosure Committee group
UserDisplayEnabled            : True
Version                       : 1
```

With the new classification in place, we can add it to a new message. In Figure 8.41, I have created a new message with Outlook Web Access 2007 and added the classification by selecting "Patent Disclosure" from the drop-down list revealed from the circled "message classification" button. Immediately, Outlook Web Access displays the sender information defined for the classification.

Figure 8.41

Creating a new patent disclosure

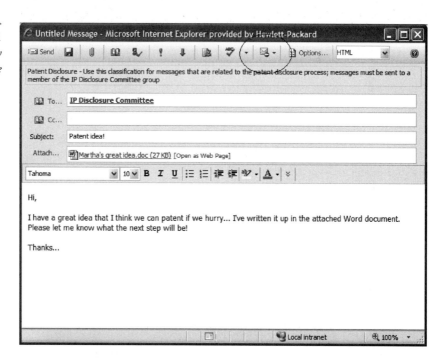

When Exchange delivers the message, the recipient sees different information. Figure 8.42 shows how Outlook 2007 displays a message classified as a patent disclosure. It is the same message as shown in Figure 8.41, but the instructions are quite different. We may want to tell users that they should store the message in a managed folder, begin another process with a

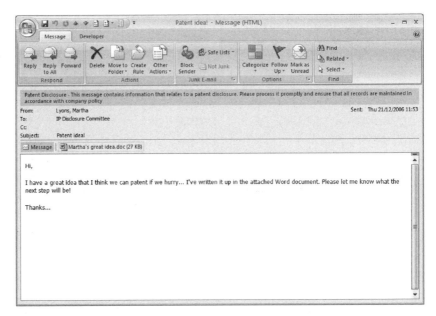

Figure 8.42
*How a recipient
sees a messaged
classified as a
patent disclosure*

different application, tell someone that a message has arrived that requires processing, or take some other action.

Outlook Web Access 2007 picks up new message classifications automatically, but you have to make Outlook 2007 aware that a new classification exists. Unfortunately, this is a manual process that requires you to export information about the new classification from Exchange and then instruct Outlook to use the information by making a change to the system registry. The exported information is in XML format, and you can see the kind of information that Exchange exports in Figure 8.43.

Figure 8.43
*Exported XML
data for a message
classification*

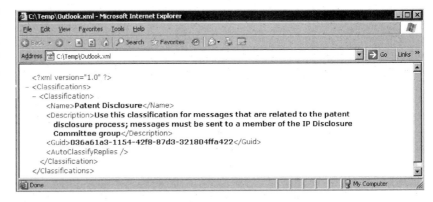

To generate the XML, you have to run a script on an Exchange 2007 hub transport server. For example, to export the information shown in Figure 8.43, I used the following command:

```
'Patent Disclosure' | Get-MessageClassification | /
.ExportOutlookClassification.ps1 > c:\temp\Outlook.XML
```

This command instructs Exchange to export details of the Patent Disclosure classification by piping the data through the `Get-MessageClassification` command into the ExportOutlookClassification.ps1 script to output into a file called Outlook.XML. Simple! Or maybe not.... The good news is that you will not have to perform this task very often unless you are in the habit of adding new classifications at frequent intervals. Remember that the client UI will be able to display a limited number of message classifications (approximately 20, depending on the client), so some thought has to go into how many classifications you want to deploy within the organization. If you need to include details of several classifications, you specify them in a comma-separated list like so:

```
"Patent Disclosure", "Tax Form", "Interesting Information" |
Get-MessageClassification…
```

Once you have created the XML file, you have to make it available to Outlook 2007 clients. You can do this by copying the file to a network share or you can copy and apply the update to every client using whatever distribution mechanism is available to you, such as SMS. Copying to the client PC is better because it ensures that the classifications are available even when disconnected from the network. Remember that every time you make a change to message classifications, you will have to distribute the XML files that contain updated message classification data to client PCs. This is a management overhead that administrators could do without. Hopefully, Microsoft will do something to make the process to distribute new and updated message classifications more automatic in future. After copying the file, you then have to update the system registry to let Outlook know that it should read the XML file the next time the client starts up. Go to HKCU\Software\Microsoft\Office\12.0\Common\Policy (you may have to create the Policy key if it does not already exist) and create the values listed in Table 8.2.

Note that if you import a classification to an Outlook client that is not registered within the organization and subsequently attempt to send a mes-

Table 8.2 *Values to enable classifications for Outlook 2007*

Value	Type	Meaning
EnableClassifications	DWORD	1
TrustClassifications	DWORD	1 (this key indicates whether the client is willing to trust classifications that come from other forests).
AdminClassificationPath	STRING	Path to where the XML file is available

sage marked with that classification, the transport service will refuse to process the message because it contains an unknown classification and the sender will receive a DSN with code:

```
#550 5.7.3 Message classification was not recognized ##
```

8.6.1 Adding intelligence to classification through rules

All the work that we have done to date is enough to create classifications for users to apply to messages, but users have to respond to the classifications or else the whole exercise is of little real value. It is true that users can set up rules to process incoming messages according to classification, but that is something that will have to be performed by each user and it is likely that many different rules will be created. We need something else to enforce policy, and that is where transport rules can help.

You will recall that transport rules are analogous to Outlook rules in that they can interact with messages based on the properties of messages. The classification of a message is something that a transport rule can examine and take action on. In our case, the instructions that we have given to users are that patent disclosures should be sent to a member of the "IP Disclosure Committee" group, but we have no way to enforce this directive unless we create a transport rule. Consider the rule illustrated in Figure 8.44. The steps performed in this rule are:

1. Look for any message marked with the "Patent Disclosure" classification.

2. Reject any message back to the user with a polite note to say that items marked with this classification can be sent only to the

members of the IP Disclosure Committee—except for messages that are actually sent to the IP Disclosure Committee or a member of that committee.

Figure 8.44

A rule to enforce a message classification

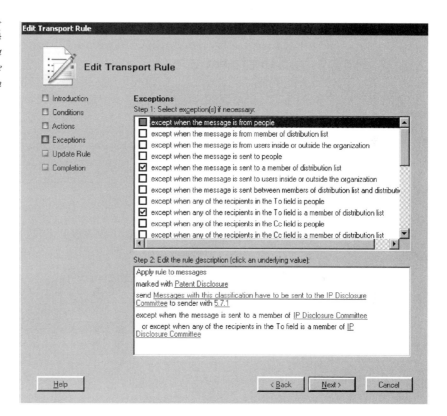

This is a simple rule, but it's a very effective way of enforcing the policy that we set out to achieve by creating a message classification for patent disclosures. Note that if you apply a transport rule like this, it will prevent users forwarding the message to any other user outside the permitted recipients unless they remove the message classification. This may be what you want to accomplish, but on the other hand, it might not be.

To take things a little further, we can combine rules to make our point about how to process patent disclosures even more forcibly. Some users need a lot of help to understand what they need to do with different types of messages, so let's create another transport rule to add a disclaimer and a special subject prefix to patent disclosures. You can't do this in the transport rule that we've just created because its first motion is to reject everything with the patent disclosure classification and to only let through messages on an exception basis to the IP Disclosure Committee. We need to apply some actions to messages and we can't when they pass on an exception basis.

Our second rule is shown in Figure 8.45. Again, the rule is very simple:

1.   Look for any message marked with the "Patent Disclosure" classification.

2.   Prepend the message subject with a string—"Patent Disclosure:" to make the recipient quite certain that they are dealing with a particular type of message.

3.   Apply a disclaimer to the message with some text to help the recipient understand what they have to do. Make the disclaimer as large as Exchange will let us and put it in Purple to create a huge impression on the recipient.

Figure 8.45
Making patent disclosures very apparent!

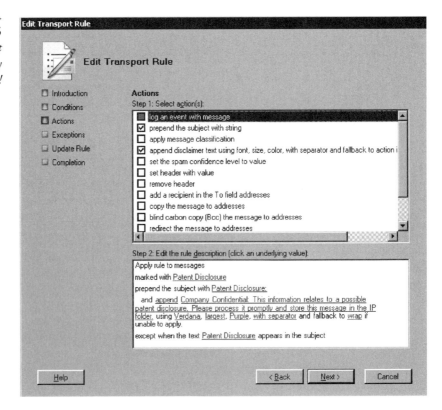

The final result after messages are processed by both transport rules and delivered to the members of the IP Disclosure Committee is illustrated in Figure 8.46. No one could ignore such a message.

Figure 8.46
The final message as delivered to a recipient

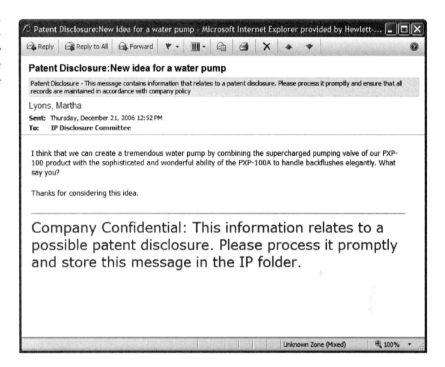

It's hard to say just how many organizations will want to use message classifications, especially because of the requirement to deploy Exchange 2007 and Outlook 2007 before they can take full advantage of the feature. However, the fact that you can combine message classifications and transport rules to help users comply with policy is a real plus. On the other hand, rules-based processing doesn't remove the fundamental flaw that exists in that you depend on people to actually use the message classifications that you create, obey the instructions, and use managed folders to retain important data, but it's a start. The flaw is not unique to Exchange as any software system has to accommodate user behavior. As always in cases where you want people to comply with policies, if you want to succeed, there's a huge need for good user education and support.

8.7   **Copying user mailboxes**

Journaling and transport rules allow administrators to monitor message traffic as it is generated. Another aspect of compliance is the need that sometimes arises to allow investigators to access a complete copy of a user's mailbox so that they can check its contents for evidence. In previous versions of Exchange, you would have to restore a backup to another server and recreate the mailbox there. Alternatively, an administrator would have to elevate their permissions to log onto the mailbox and export the information to a PST using the ExMerge tool. Microsoft doesn't support running ExMerge on an Exchange 2007 server because ExMerge uses the old 32-bit server-side version of MAPI that Microsoft has not ported to the 64-bit platform. However, it is possible to use ExMerge on an Exchange 2003 server and export a mailbox from an Exchange 2007 server, assuming that the network connection between the two servers supports this type of activity.

With Exchange 2007, you can copy one or more mailboxes to another mailbox on the same server or to another server with the `Export-Mailbox` command, which Exchange only supports when run on mailbox servers. However, while you can only run `Export-Mailbox` on a mailbox server, you can extract mailbox data from servers running Exchange 2000 (SP3 or later), Exchange 2003 (SP2 or later), or Exchange 2007. The account that you use must have administrative permission over both the source and target servers and you cannot use `Export-Mailbox` to transfer data between mailboxes in different forests, even if a trust exists between the two forests. Users are unaware that the contents of their mailboxes have been exported.

Unlike ExMerge, you cannot use `Export-Mailbox` to transfer data from a mailbox direct to a PST. You can do this in a two-step process by first exporting the data to a server mailbox and then moving the data to a PST, or if you still have an Exchange 2003 server in the organization, you can run ExMerge on that server to export the data to a PST. Microsoft plans to allow the `Move-Mailbox` command to export and import data from PSTs in Exchange 2007 SP1.

As an example of what we can do with the `Export-Mailbox` command, let us assume that you suspect that the user "Jane Smith" has been conducting some personal and inappropriate business through email. You want to check the kind of messages that she has been sending but you do not want to log onto the mailbox because you might leave a trace behind, such as reading a new message that generates a read receipt back to the sender. You have approval from the legal department to begin an investigation, so you take a copy of her mailbox as follows:

```
Export-Mailbox -id 'Jane Smith' -TargetMailbox 'Legal Review'
-TargetFolder 'Reviews' -Confirm
```

This command exports a complete copy[2] of Jane Smith's mailbox to the Legal Review mailbox. Because you can use a single target mailbox to recover data from many mailboxes, Exchange copies the information to a set of folders that it creates under the "Legal Review" folder and places all the data into an exact set of folders corresponding to the folders that exist in Jane Smith's mailbox. All of the default folders such as the Inbox, Calendar, and Deleted Items are automatically included in the export. Another example is where you want to capture information from every mailbox on a server that has been marked as belonging to an executive.

```
Get-Mailbox -Server ExchMbxSvr1 | Where {$_.CustomAttribute1
-eq 'Executive'} | Export-Mailbox -TargetFolder 'Executive
Data'
-TargetMailbox 'Executive Archive'
```

When you ask `Export-Mailbox` to process multiple mailboxes, like the `Move-Mailbox` command, it uses up to four threads to reduce processing time. A variation on the theme searches for all users who belong to a department and exports their mailboxes:

```
Get-User -Filter {Department -eq 'Technology'} | Export-
Mailbox
-TargetFolder 'Technology Users' -TargetMailbox 'Technology
Archive'
```

Another way that you can use the `Export-Mailbox` command effectively is to scan all of the mailboxes in a database to look for some specific terms that occur in message content, perhaps because you have to respond to a legal discovery action. In this case, we look for any item that mentions the words "Research," "Project Laurleen" or "Secret" in the content of any message in the database. You can see the result of the search in Figure 8.47.

---

2.   Unfortunately, the `Export-Mailbox` command does not offer the option to generate a report on what it finds inside a mailbox. You have to export the data to review the contents of the mailbox.

```
Get-Mailbox —Database 'ATG Mailboxes' | Export-Mailbox
—ContentKeywords 'Research', 'Project Laurleen', 'Secret'
—TargetMailbox Redmond —TargetFolder 'Discovered Information'
```

Figure 8.47
*Results of a search
for content*

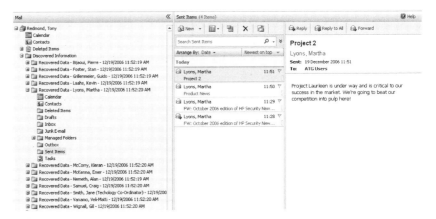

To allow you to identify the exported data for a specific user, Exchange creates a top-level folder for the copy called

```
Recovered Data — <Mailbox Name> — <Date and time>
```

The date and time stamp is part of the folder name to allow you to take multiple snapshots of a mailbox at different points in time, as you can see in Figure 8.48.

Figure 8.48
*Recovered
mailboxes*

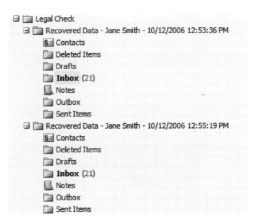

Exchange logs details of every `Export-Mailbox` operation in the \Program Files\Microsoft\Exchange Server\Logging\MigrationLogs directory where you will find a text log that describes each successive step taken by `Export-Mailbox`. This file is very useful if you need to troubleshoot an `Export-Mailbox` problem. You will also find an XML file that reports the overall outcome of the operation.

Just like moving mailboxes, Exchange uses four threads to process mailbox content when you export them. However, exporting large mailboxes can take a long time, so Exchange allows you to filter the data that you extract. You can filter on:

- Words that appear in message content with the –ContentKeywords parameter. This filter does not process the content of attachments. Exchange uses its content indexes to locate information if you enable this feature for your mailbox databases. See Chapter 5 for more information on Exchange 2007 content indexing.

- Words that appear in a message subject or title with the –SubjectKeywords parameter.

- A specific date range using the –StartDate and –EndDate parameters. Note that you pass dates in short date format and use the format that applies on the server. On U.S. servers, 1 October 2007 is "10/1/2007" whereas this would be 10 January 2007 on a U.K. server.

- Specific attachment types using the –AttachmentFilenames parameter. This supports wildcard characters, so you can state something like "*.PPT" to search PowerPoint attachments.

- Specific folders using the –IncludeFolders parameter. By default, `Export-Mailbox` processes all folders in the source mailbox. You can exclude specific folders with the –ExcludeFolders parameter. Using the –IncludeFolders parameter is particularly useful if you want to extract information from a set of managed folders in one or more mailboxes.

For example, to filter for messages that contain "Secret" or "Important" that also have a Word attachment received between 1 September 2007 and 1 October 2007, you would specify:

```
Export-Mailbox —id 'Jane Smith' —TargetMailbox 'Legal Review'
—TargetFolder 'Reviews' —ContentKeywords 'Secret',
'Important'
```

```
—AttachmentFilenames '*.DOC' —StartDate '9/1/2007' —EndDate
'10/1/2007'
```

Another example of when you would want to use a relatively complex filter statement is to exclude specific folders (in this case, anything in the Deleted Items and Junk E-Mail folders) and only take information that is in a certain language (in this case, Japanese):

```
Export-Mailbox -id 'Shoji Goto' -ExcludeFolders '\Deleted
Items', '\Junk Mail' -Locale ja-jp -TargetFolder 'Goto
Japanese Items'
-TargetMailbox 'Japanese Information'
```

To clean up after the export operation or to eliminate unwanted content from mailboxes, you can instruct Exchange to delete the content of the source folder after the content is successfully exported by specifying the —DeleteContent parameter. For example, let us assume that you want to scan all the mailboxes on a server to locate .MP3 files that users may be unwise enough to store in their mailboxes. You want to move these files into a special mailbox for examination (and potential reporting to a manager) and you want to clean up these files from the server. Here is the command that you might execute:

```
Get-Mailbox -Server 'ExchMbxSvr1' | Export-Mailbox
—AttachmentFilenames '*.MP3' -TargetFolder 'MP3 Files'
-TargetMailbox 'MP3 Journal' —DeleteContent
```

You could even use this command as a primitive cleansing mechanism to remove infected messages from mailboxes. Here is a command that could remove all of the messages from the infamous Melissa "I Love You" virus:

```
Get-Mailbox —Server 'ExchMbxSvr1' | Export-Mailbox
-SubjectKeywords 'I love you' -TargetFolder 'Infected
Messages'
-TargetMailbox 'Quarantine' —DeleteContent
```

Exchange only exports items that exist in the mailbox, so you cannot use this command to recover deleted items. If you need to recover deleted items, you will have to log onto the mailbox and use the "Recover Deleted

Items" feature. Alternatively, you could also restore a copy of the mailbox database to another server and recover the data from that copy.

8.7.1   Auditing

Somewhat surprisingly, Exchange does not provide a way to audit the use of the `Export-Mailbox` command, so it is possible for an administrator to select the mailbox of someone important (or interesting) and run a job to export data without leaving any trace that they cannot erase quickly afterwards. Apart from the log files that Exchange creates for every `Export-Mailbox` operation, the only other trace that an administrator has accessed someone's mailbox is in event 1006 logged by the Exchange Migration component (Figure 8.49). For this reason, it is important that you set out clear guidelines as to when an administrator can use the `Export-Mailbox` command in the same way that guidelines exist to permit other administrator access to user mailboxes.

Figure 8.49
Export mailbox event

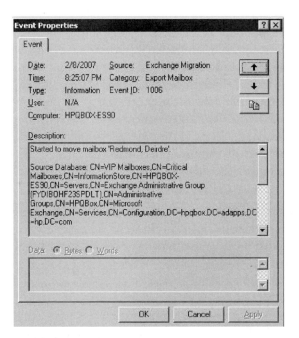

8.8   Free and busy

Free and busy data is the mechanism used by Exchange and its clients to track the availability of users for meetings. All versions of Exchange prior to Exchange 2007 store the data used by clients to calculate when users are available in a public folder, but Exchange 2007 introduces the new Availability Service to replace the need to hold data in a public folder in favor of direct publication of free and busy data by Outlook 2007 clients as properties of user mailboxes. However, it is going to take some time before any organization is able to deploy Exchange 2007 everywhere, so we will have to deal with the public folder-based implementation for quite some time to come.

Outlook is responsible for updating the data in the public folder and does so according to user-specific options as shown in Figure 8.50. The default is for Outlook to connect and update free and busy data every 15 minutes and to publish 2 months of availability data. In other words, if every user in the organization uses the default publication options, you will not be able to see the availability of another user's calendar past the next 2 months, even if they have scheduled meetings and other appointments past that time. You can publish a maximum of 36 months free and busy data and update the server as often as every minute.

Free and busy data describes when a user is busy over a period of time but does not hold any other information, such as whether they are at a meeting or have a personal appointment, the location, or any other indication of why they might be busy. Thus, when you view another user's calendar and see that they are busy between 10AM and 5PM, the time might be taken up by one long appointment or occupied by several shorter meetings. In addition, the items in the other user's calendars may have different status such as busy or tentative. Essentially, Exchange treats any slot that a user creates in their calendar as busy and any that is vacant as free.

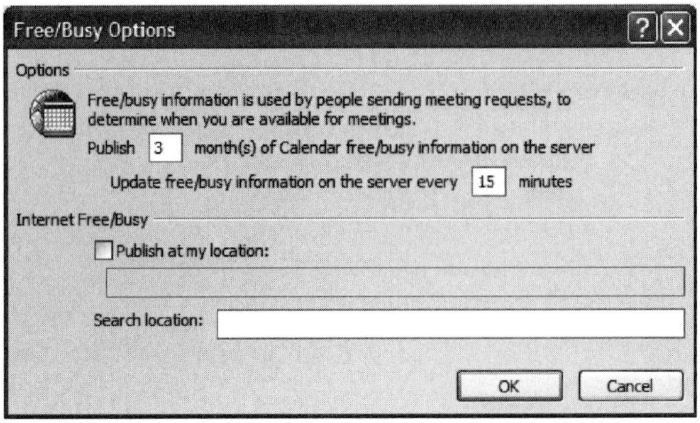

Figure 8.50
*Outlook free/busy
publication options*

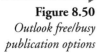

Outlook Web Access users update their free and busy data as they work with the calendar, but IMAP or POP clients do not support this functionality. No version of the Outlook Web Access client offers users the option to change the publishing period for free and busy data and the client always publishes 2 months free and busy data. The only way to change this is to update the publishing period through Outlook as this will force Outlook Web Access to use this value. Note that if you use two different clients (or the same client on two different PCs), it is entirely possible that the clients will use different publishing periods for free and busy data, so if you want consistency everywhere, you have to make sure that the same period is set on all the clients that you use.

Exchange updates the data for Outlook Web Access clients through the MSExchangeFBPublish process, which runs as part of the System Attendant. When an Outlook Web Access user updates their calendar, the Store processes the calendar data and then submits a message to the System Attendant mailbox on the server. A polling thread that runs inside the MSExchangeFBPublish process checks the System Attendant mailbox every 5 minutes to pick up free and busy messages and applies these updates to the public folder on behalf of the user. You can adjust the polling interval for MSExchangeFBPublish from anything from 30 seconds (the most frequent interval that you can set) upwards. To change the polling interval, update or insert the PollingInterval registry key (a DWORD value) at:

```
HKLM\System\ CurrentControlSet\ Services\MSExchangeFBPublish\
Parameters\<Server Name>³
```

You have to restart the System Attendant service for the new polling interval to take effect.

8.8.1 **Looking at free and busy data**

On Exchange 2003 and 2000 servers, free and busy data is stored in the SCHEDULE+ FREE BUSY\<Admin Group> public folder. For example, if the server that your mailbox is on belongs to the London administrative group, your free and busy information is stored in the SCHEDULE+ FREE BUSY\London public folder. There is one folder for each administrative group and one item in the folder for each mailbox in that administrative group. The data in the free and busy items is reasonably compact, so no great load is generated on a server to store, manage, and replicate this data

---

3. Insert the physical server name here or the virtual server name for clusters.

and you can expect that Exchange will generate about 2MB of data for every thousand users if you store 6 months of data, or 3MB of data for 12 months. While the actual amount of space used for free and busy data varies with the number of users who publish data and the period that their data covers, you can see that the actual storage requirements are not very high, especially in today's environment where a single PowerPoint presentation can take up the same storage as a year's free and busy data for thousands of users. Microsoft Knowledge Base article 197712 provides some guidance on this point.

Replication of free and busy data has an impact on the up-to-date accuracy of the data viewed by users when they schedule meetings. If you hold a single copy of the free and busy information for a user, then Outlook has to connect to the folder that holds the data on a specific server in the organization. If that server is close (in network terms) then performance will be acceptable and the data is accurate. However, in a distributed organization, you may want to replicate free and busy data to several public folder servers so that users can access local copies of the data. This will certainly improve performance, but now there is always a chance that the free and busy data will be outdated because of replication lag when a user consults it to schedule a meeting. To avoid problems caused by users publishing different amounts of free and busy data, it is best to settle on a common amount that everyone uses.

Inside the item that holds a user's free and busy data, you find records that represent chunks of occupied time. The format of the time chunk is represented by the number of minutes from the beginning of the month to the start of the chunk and from the start of the month to the end of the chunk. These two points in time are called the DTStart and DTEnd properties. All times are held in GMT to ensure that meetings scheduled across time zones occur at the right time. I am sure there is a reason for such a complex scheme of calculating start and end times but I can't quite come up with the reason now. In any case, let's assume that you have an appointment booked from July 14, 2007 from 9AM to 10AM GMT. Outlook calculates the DTStart property as follows:

- From the start of the month (July 2007) to the end is 31 days or 44,640 minutes.

- The appointment start time is 13 full days plus 9 hours = 321 hours or 19,260 minutes. A GMT offset applies if you are not in the GMT time zone.

- DTStart is 19,260 (minutes from the start of the month) and DTEnd is 19,320. Outlook converts these values to hex, so DTStart is 4B3C and DTEnd is 4B78.

- Outlook now calculates a value for the month (July 2007) using the algorithm:

  - Month = (Year × 16) + number of month in year
  - Or: (2007 × 16) + 7 = 32,119

- We now have some free and busy data to post into the item in the public folder.

  - 32,119 4B3C 4B78

Updating free and busy information is not quite as simple as posting the new information because there are different types of records in the item in the folder depending on the type of entry that the user has made in their calendar. Entries can be busy, out of the office, or tentative. Each of the different types of data has its own prefix:

- 0X684F = merged month

- 0X6850 = merged day

- 0X6851 = tentative month

- 0X6852 = tentative day

- 0X6853 = busy month

- 0X6854 = busy day

- 0X6855 = OOF month

- 0X6856 = OOF day

For efficiency's sake, Outlook also merges month and daily data together where it can. If adjacent appointments overlap, Outlook merges them together into a single record because the same time slot is occupied. For example, if you had these appointments in your calendar:

1.   10AM to 11AM Busy

2.   10:30AM to 12 noon Busy

3.   2PM to 4PM Tentative

4.   3PM to 5PM Busy

Records 1, 2, and 4 are the same type (busy), so Outlook sorts them by start time before merging them into a single record to minimize data storage. After being merged there will be two Start/End pairs: 10AM–Noon and 3PM–5PM for Busy. In addition, there will be one pair for Tentative. Assuming that Outlook has only one piece of data for the time slot that we have just occupied, the data now looks like this:

```
0X684F 32119
0X6850 3C 4B 78 4B
0X6853 31994
0X6854 3C 4B 78 4B
```

Because the free and busy data is reasonably complex, Outlook does not attempt to merge new data into existing data. Instead, Outlook deletes the user's existing free and busy data and writes brand new data that represents the current state of their calendar.

To get a programmatic insight into the data, you can use the Collaborative Data Objects (CDO 1.2 or later[4]) interface to query free and busy information for a specific mailbox (that you have access to) for a date and time period in specified time increments. For example, you could ask for free and busy data for Monday, August 28, 2006 between 1PM and 3PM in 30 minute increments. The result will be a string of numbers, each of which indicates a status for a 30 minute block. In this case you have asked for 2 hours worth of data in 30 minute increments, so CDO would return something like 1022, where 1 means that this block contains tentative data, 0 means that the next 30 minute block is free, 3 means that the next two blocks are busy. If you see a 3 value, it means that a block of time is marked as out of office, while 4 indicates that no data is available. If you don't want to write any code, you can use a query based on Outlook Web Access to query free and busy data. For example, the web query shown below looks for the same free and busy data.

---

4.   See Microsoft Knowledge Base article 186753 for more information.

```
http://Server-Name/public/?cmd=freebusy&start=2006-08-
28T13:00:00&end=2006-08-
28T15:00:00&interval=30&u=Tony.Redmond@ZYX.com
```

Exchange responds with XML-formatted data:

```
-<a:response xmlns:a="WM">
- <a:recipients>
-  <a:item>
    <a:displayname>All Attendees</a:displayname>
   <a:type>1</a:type>
   <a:fbdata>0022</a:fbdata>
    </a:item>
-  <a:item>
   <a:displayname>Redmond, Tony</a:displayname>
   <a:email type="SMTP">tony.redmond@ZYX.com</a:email>
   <a:type>1</a:type>
   <a:fbdata>1022</a:fbdata>
    </a:item>
  </a:recipients>
  </a:response>
```

Reviewing this data, you can see that the fbdata item holds the same information that CDO returns. Note that if you query for a user who has not published any free and busy data, the fbdata item will contain all 4s.

Figure 8.51
*Free and busy data
viewed through
MDBVU32*

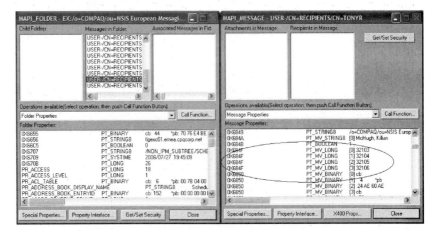

The MDBVU32 program provides the best way to gain an insight into the type of data held in a free and busy folder. When MDBVU32 starts, it asks for a profile. You can use any MAPI profile to access the free and busy data. To access the free and busy information, follow these steps:

- Select "OpenMessageStore" from the MDB menu

- Select "Public Folders" and click the Open button

- Select "Open Root Folders" from the MDB menu. Two folders are displayed: IPM_SUBTREE and NON_IPM_SUBTREE. The first root hosts all the normal public folders that users expect to see; the second is used for system folders like the free and busy information. Select NON_IPM_SUBTREE.

- Select "SCHEDULE+ FREE BUSY." You should now see all of the administrative groups in your organization in the child folders window. Select the name of the administrative group you want to examine. If you select an administrative group that does not replicate its free and busy information to your server, the folder will be empty.

You should now be able to see the items in the free/busy folder in the "Messages in Folder" pane. You can now select the free and busy information for a user by double-clicking on the item (using the name as explained earlier), after which you can look at its properties and so on. Figure 8.51 shows the kind of view you get after you open the SCHEDULE+ FREE BUSY folder for an administrative group. The left-hand screen shows the records for each user, identified by a value based on their LegacyExchangeDN property. Technically speaking, Exchange treats the item as a "note" (IPM.Note) and identifies it through its subject, following the convention:

```
USER-/CN=<recipients container>/CN=<mailbox alias>
```

For example, the free and busy item for my user account has a subject line of:

```
USER-/CN=RECIPIENTS/CN=REDMOND
```

The right-hand screen shows the properties of a selected user's record (in this case, my own). You can see four 0X684F records for different months followed by some 0X6850 records for individual days. For further information about how to use the MDBVU32 program to interrogate free and busy data, see the Word document that comes along in the MDBVU32 download.

All versions of Outlook support the /cleanfreebusy switch to force the client to recalculate and republish free and busy information should the need arise. Using /cleanfreebusy can fix the problem if users cannot access free and busy data for some reason.

8.8.2 Free and busy in Exchange 2007

The public folder model for free and busy storage and replication worked reasonably well for Exchange 2000 to 2003, but Microsoft's deemphasis of public folders requires a new mechanism for Exchange 2007. The new Availability service, which only runs on servers that support the Client Access Server (CAS) role, is responsible for making the free and busy data maintained by Outlook and Outlook Web Access 2007 clients available to other clients when they want to schedule a meeting. When they connect to an Exchange 2007 server, these clients store their free and busy data in their calendar folders instead of public folders.

Every Active Directory site that supports an Exchange 2007 mailbox server must also have a CAS present. Outlook 2007 and Outlook Web Access 2007 clients use the AutoDiscover service running on the Client Access Server to obtain the URL for the Availability service. When these clients request free and busy data to create a meeting, the Availability service reads the necessary data directly from the calendar folders in user mailboxes for anyone that uses Outlook 2007 or Outlook Web Access 2007. Outlook Web Access is less susceptible than Outlook is to a badly configured Auto-Discover service. Because of its direct connection to the server, Outlook Web Access will continue to work even if the AutoDiscover service is not functioning properly. This is not the case for Outlook, which will have real problems finding resources if AutoDiscover does not work properly.

Note that when Outlook and Outlook Web Access 2007 clients operate inside a mixed-mode organization, they continue to publish free and busy data into a public folder so that it can be shared with older clients, and the Availability service is also able to access this data along with any other free and busy data published by older clients that are present inside the organization. The Availability service can retrieve information about attendee working hours (so that you don't attempt to schedule meetings when someone is out of the office), but only for Outlook 2007 and Outlook Web

Table 8.3   *Accessing free and busy data from different clients*

Client	Scheduling Mailbox On	Meeting Requested to Target Mailbox On	Free/Busy Retrieval
Outlook 2007	Exchange 2007	Exchange 2007	Availability service reads free and busy data from the target calendar folder.
Outlook 2007	Exchange 2007	Exchange 2003	Availability service makes HTTP request to /public virtual directory on Exchange 2003 server to read the free and busy data in the public folder.
Outlook 2003	Exchange 2007	Exchange 2007	Client reads and publishes free and busy data using public folders.
Outlook 2003	Exchange 2007	Exchange 2003	Client reads and publishes free and busy data using public folders.
Outlook Web Access 2007	Exchange 2007	Exchange 2003	Outlook Web Access calls the Availability service API, which makes an HTTP request to the /public virtual directory on the Exchange 2003 server to read the free and busy data in the public folder.
Outlook Web Access 2003	Exchange 2003	Exchange 2007	Client reads and publishes free and busy data using public folders.

Access 2007 clients. Finally, the Availability service works with the Scheduling Assistant to suggest meeting times that may suit everyone involved in the meeting.

Table 8.3 summarizes the connections that different combinations of clients and servers create to access free and busy data. As an example of how things work, let's assume that an Outlook 2007 client connected to a mailbox server in London wants to schedule a meeting with users located in San Francisco and New York. Each city has an Active Directory site and there is an Exchange 2007 server in each Active Directory site. To begin, Outlook connects to a Client Access Server in the London Active Directory site. In many cases, the Client Access role runs on is the same Exchange server that hosts the user's mailbox, because an Exchange 2007 server can concurrently host the Client Access, mailbox, and hub transport server roles. The available Client Access servers are published in the Exchange configuration data within the Active Directory, so if the site supports more than one Client Access server, the Availability Service selects from the list of available servers using a round-robin algorithm. The Client Access server in the scheduling user's site proxies the request for free/busy data over an HTTPS connection to a Client Access server in the Active Directory sites that host the other users with whom we want to schedule a meeting, so separate requests go to Client Access servers in San Francisco and New York. The Client Access servers that receive the incoming requests are responsible for looking up the calendar data for the specified users and access either the user mailbox or a local copy of the public folder to retrieve this data. In either case, the Client Access server communicates with the mailbox server over MAPI. They then return the data via HTTPS to the original Client Access server, which collates the free and busy data and responds to the user who needs the information to schedule the meeting.

The big advantage of the new mechanism is that the data that Client Access returns to the user who's scheduling the meeting is guaranteed to be up to date. Free and busy data fetched by the Availability service from user calendars is "live" because it does not suffer from the potential time-lag experienced by the data published by older clients into a public folder, which may be out of date because of the time required to replicate between public folder servers. On the downside, the potential exists that the scheduling user might have to wait longer before they can see free and busy data because of the interserver communication that occurs to fetch data from around the organization. After all, it's much simpler to go to one place (the local replica of the public folder) than to make a number of network connections. Microsoft is confident that they have optimized the way that the CAS collects free and busy data and don't think that users will notice much of a difference.

Of course, it will take time for companies to deploy Outlook 2007 and Exchange 2007 and it is likely that mixed-mode organizations will persist for a number of years, so Outlook 2007 and Exchange 2007 will continue to use the free and busy public folder for backwards compatibility.

8.8.3 Changes in Outlook 2007

Outlook 2007 includes two important changes that help users to work with calendars more effectively. First, you can send your calendar by email. The default option is to send a snapshot of free and busy information that shows where free slots exist in your calendar, which is very similar to how the Availability service looks at the free and busy data to figure out the best times for a meeting. However, you can choose to send additional information to a correspondent, no matter what version of Exchange server hosts your mailbox. Figure 8.52 shows an example of the kind of information that you can send.

Figure 8.52

*Free and busy data
published from
Outlook 2007*

Tony Redmond Calendar
redmond@hpqbox.adapps.hp.com
On 14 November 2006
Time zone: (GMT) Greenwich Mean Time : Dublin, Edinburgh, Lisbon, London
(Adjusted for Daylight Saving Time)

November 2006

M	T	W	T	F	S	S
		1	2	3	4	5
6	7	8	9	10	11	12
13	**14**	15	16	17	18	19
20	21	22	23	24	25	26
27	28	29	30			

■ Busy ▨ Tentative ■ Out of Office ☐ Free ▨ Outside of Working Hours

November 2006

▲ **14 Nov**

	Before 08:00	**Free**
	08:00 – 15:00	**Free**
■	15:00 – 15:30	Project "Big-Play" Meeting Liffey Conference Room Tony Redmond
▨	15:00 – 19:30	Project Beta meeting Liffey Room Martha Lyons
■	17:00 – 19:00	Salary Planning B15/F1 Room 20 Tony Redmond
	After 19:30	**Free**

Details

The second change is that you can allow people who share your calendar to see more information about calendar items. If your mailbox is on an Exchange 2003 server, Outlook 2007 supports these options:

- None

- Full Details (apart from private items)

If your mailbox is on an Exchange 2007 server, you have these options (Figure 8.53):

- None

- Free/busy time

- Free/busy time, subject, and location

- Full details (including the free text notes for calendar items)

Be careful about turning the last option on because it does mean that Outlook makes a complete snapshot of your meetings available to users, including those who might casually browse your calendar to locate a suitable time for a meeting. You may not want everyone in the organization to know exactly what you are up to during your working day. This aspect of the feature came home to me when one of my direct reports pointed out just how interesting they found my calendar!

Another neat feature supported by Outlook 2007 is the option to create a special message to invite another user to share your calendar. This option allows you to optionally request that the other user also shares their calendar with you.

Figure 8.53
*Expanded calendar
permissions in
Outlook 2007*

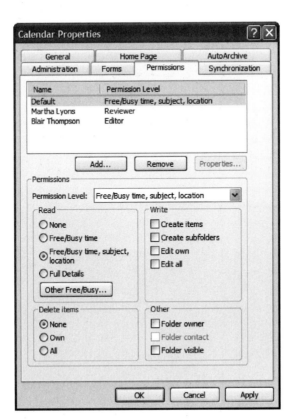

8.8.4   Cross-forest free and busy

The Availability service is able to provide access to free and busy data between trusted or untrusted Active Directory forests. The granularity of the free and busy data exchanged between the forests is determined whether you configure free and busy on a per-user or organization-wide basis. Per-user exchange is only possible when trusts exist between the forests, making it possible for the Availability service to make a cross-forest request on behalf of a user who has been granted the permission to see detailed free and busy information in another user's calendar.

Even in an untrusted forest, the Availability service can make requests from one organization to another. However, without the ability for users to set permissions on their calendars to permit access to granular free and busy data, the only data that the Availability service can return is like the situation that pertains in Exchange 2003 and indicates whether the target user is free or busy at a specific time.

9

Hardware and Performance

Exchange has always made demands on server hardware. As a complex database application, Exchange generates demand for CPU, memory, and storage—the trinity of system resources that a server must be able to provide before Exchange can perform. Exchange also generates load on the network, so that is another thing to take into account when you look at the overall system. In this chapter, we discuss how to achieve a balanced system configuration for Exchange.

In some respects, any attempt to give advice about what type of hardware to use for Exchange 2007 is a mug's game. Advice given in mid-2007 is doomed to failure because hardware specifications change so rapidly and the workload differs so much from company to company. Please keep this point in mind as you go through this chapter.

9.1 Moving toward 64-bit Exchange

Microsoft supports Exchange 2007 only on the 64-bit version of Windows running on an x64 server, so you will end up running some or all of your infrastructure on 64-bit hardware, including any third-party products that you need to support Exchange. The big that question you have to answer as you approach a deployment of Exchange 2007 is when to make the changeover to the 64-bit platform. If you run large enterprise Exchange 2000 or 2003 servers, you are probably interested in moving early so that you can take advantage of the higher scalability and consolidation opportunities that Exchange 2007 permits. However, if you are not in that league, the answer about when to move depends on your own situation and you have to analyze what benefit the 64-bit Windows platform and its associated applications will deliver for you. Here are some items to consider:

- Is your server hardware platform due for a refresh? If yes, as both the AMD and Intel server platforms have been 64-bit capable since mid-2005, then you probably have suitable servers anyway. Buying and deploying suitable hardware now even if you do not plan to deploy Exchange 2007 or another 64-bit application is a sensible first step towards a full 64-bit environment.

- Do you need the extra performance? If your current Exchange 2003 servers are running smoothly and do not need any performance boost, then you may not need to go to 64-bit in the short term. Of course, maintenance contracts and the availability of support for Exchange 2003 will eventually force the upgrade.

- Have you encountered some scalability problems such as I/O bottlenecks, kernel mode exhaustion, or virtual memory fragmentation (especially on clusters)? If so, then an early move to Exchange 2007 is a good idea.

- Do you have the opportunity to consolidate servers during your Exchange 2007 deployment? A single 64-bit Exchange 2007 server can host the load of several 32-bit Exchange 2003 (or earlier) servers, so you may have the chance to reduce costs and the overall complexity of your IT infrastructure through server consolidation. However, remember the wisdom to avoid putting all your eggs in one basket and consider how any consolidation project will affect your ability to recover from a hardware failure.

- Will your software license costs increase? Assuming that you are not going to save money through server consolidation (and so require fewer server licenses for Windows, Exchange, and other software), introducing some new 64-bit Windows and Exchange servers may increase your costs. Note that you do not need the Enterprise Edition of Windows in most cases as the standard edition of Windows supports up to 4 processors and up to 32GB of memory, which is more than enough to handle most requirements.

- Can the rest of your supporting environment for Exchange run on the Windows 64-bit platform? Microsoft has done a good job of ensuring that Windows and Exchange can both exploit a 64-bit server, but the vast majority of Exchange servers use other software from anti-virus packages to fax connectors. Before you deploy Exchange on a new platform, you have to be sure that the complete picture exists. While there is no doubt that ISVs will upgrade their software to support the 64-bit platform, they may not be as fast as

Microsoft and some software may continue to run in 32-bit mode, so you will not get as much extra performance as you want. This underlines the necessity of testing your desired environment fully before you put it into production.

Kernel-mode exhaustion has become a real issue for high-end Exchange servers in the recent past because of the many different ways that users connect to their mailboxes. In the past, you could say that each mailbox generated one connection, but now we have many other ways to connect to Exchange. All of these connections soak up kernel-mode memory. The additional headroom that 64-bit Windows affords allows Exchange to accommodate more client connections than ever before.

You cannot install Exchange 2003 (any service pack) on the 64-bit version of Windows 2003 server, but you can install Exchange 2003 on the 32-bit version of Windows running on 64-bit capable hardware, such as AMD Opteron or Intel EM64T systems. This all sounds a little confusing, but the reason is that all of the kernel mode drivers on a 64-bit Windows system must be native 64-bit programs. Exchange 2003 includes a kernel mode driver in ExIFS, but only in a 32-bit version that cannot run on 64-bit versions of Windows (even under the WOW64 subsystem). Accordingly, the only version of the ExIFS kernel mode driver you can run under 64-bit Windows would be that from the 64-bit version of Exchange 2007. The only problem is that Microsoft has not created a 64-bit version of the ExIFS kernel driver because they have removed this feature from the product![1]

One issue that immediately comes into focus is the mechanism required to upgrade an infrastructure to Exchange 2007. Unlike previous versions of Exchange, you cannot perform an in-place installation to upgrade a previous version of Exchange to Exchange 2007 on the same server. There is no way to upgrade from Exchange 2003 to Exchange 2007, even if you run Exchange 2003 on a brand-new 64-bit Windows server. Instead, you have to install brand new versions of Windows and Exchange on a new 64-bit server, plus any other supporting technology, and then move mailbox data across from a legacy Exchange server. Microsoft's problem is that it is very difficult to upgrade a server running Windows 2003 and Exchange 2003 in one motion. The problem becomes even more difficult when you factor in service packs, different languages, hot fixes and patches, different software

---

1. Apart from their desire to eliminate SMB access to Exchange data, Microsoft has removed the streaming database from Exchange 2007, which was the major consumer of the ExIFS driver.

products from third parties, and so on. No one Exchange server is likely to be quite the same as another, so the engineering problem of having to figure out how to perform a software upgrade is "interesting," or maybe impossible. It is certainly easier all round to say that you need to perform installations from scratch to deploy Exchange 2007, but only if you have multiple servers. If you only have the one Exchange server, then you will have to buy (or borrow) a new server and arrange to use it as the fulcrum for the upgrade. For example, you can install Windows 2003 and Exchange 2007 on the new server and then run it alongside the old server. When you are happy that everything runs smoothly, you can then move mailboxes over to the new server. Finally, after all the mailboxes are on the new server, you can decommission the old server and remove it from the organization.

If you want to avoid the inherent complexity that arises when you have to run two different operating system environments alongside each other, the best idea is to achieve a pure 64-bit infrastructure as quickly as you can. This approach allows you to operate common versions of software and tools everywhere. There may be some situations where it is difficult to move off 32-bit Windows or 32-bit Exchange. For example, some people still run Windows NT 4.0 because they depend on a specific version of a server application that only runs on NT 4.0. You may find that you have an application that functions perfectly well on the Windows 32 platform and you can see no gain and only work if you upgrade this application to Windows 64. There are other situations where you have to wait until a third party has upgraded their software to be able to run on Windows 64. You cannot avoid these situations, but you can aim to minimize the impact by making a policy decision to move to the 64-bit platform as quickly as possible.

9.2   Buying servers for Exchange 2007

The problem with server hardware is that models, performance, and features change all the time as manufacturers seek an advantage in the market. The best advice that you can therefore receive is to keep a careful eye on recent developments in the hardware market any time that you are interested in buying new servers. Most people want more exact guidelines than an exhortation to research hardware, so here are a few guidelines that you can use to plan hardware purchases for Exchange 2007. You can find explicit guidelines about server hardware on the web sites of server vendors such as www.hp.com/products/servers/platforms/. Note that the guidelines are most applicable for the enterprise market where servers have to take the heaviest load. It is easier to configure for the small to medium market because almost every server available today is capable of supporting hundreds of Exchange mailboxes or to act as a hub or edge server for a small organization.

- Buy and deploy standard server configurations. If you are going to deploy servers for an entire organization, it makes sense to build some standard configurations and use them as the basis for every server that you deploy. For example, you can have a "small" server configuration for branch offices, a "medium" server configuration for regional offices, and a "large" server configuration for large sites or head office. Ideally, each configuration will use as many common building blocks as possible to allow you to swap components between servers.

- Always buy 64-bit ready hardware, even if you plan to wait some time before you deploy Exchange 2007. Given the success of the AMD Opteron and Intel Xeon with EMD64 CPUs, it is now difficult to buy servers that can only support 32-bit software. It may seem that you can save a few dollars by buying servers equipped with an older generation of Intel Xeon CPUs, but this is only correct if you plan to discard the servers in the short term or have other work (such as running Linux) that you can assign to them.

- In general, unless you run Exchange to support small user communities (200 mailboxes or less), servers equipped with multi-processor and multi-core processors are a better choice for Exchange 2007 than servers equipped with single CPUs. Multi-processor servers handle a varied workload more easily and provide extra performance at a reasonable cost. It is easier to equip a server with multiple processors from the start than to have to take the server offline for an upgrade when it is in production. Multi-core processors deliver better performance than single-core processors and the Exchange benchmarks demonstrate that the multi-threaded nature of the Exchange code means that the application can take advantage of the extra processor cores. However, it is possible that front-side bus contention can negate some of the performance advantage gained by adding extra processor cores to a server and it is true that hyper-threading loses its effect for servers with more than eight processor cores. Not all processors are equal in terms of performance and there are many variations of multi-core processors available from Intel and AMD. Check with a server performance expert to establish what configuration delivers you the best combination of performance and cost. Remember that you may not need the absolute fastest processor for all your servers.

- While the front-side bus of a server determines the maximum speed that it can access memory at, it is also true that fast memory is more expensive but can deliver better performance than slow memory. Of course, the first issue is to have enough memory on the server to allow Exchange to trade expensive disk I/O for fast access to cached data, but after that, you should look at equipping servers with high-speed memory to ensure that you maximize the benefit of cached data. For example, PC3200 memory chips operate at 400MHz while PC2700 memory chips operate at 266MHz. A high-end server will certainly operate with PC2700 memory, but it will go faster with PC3200 memory. Another point to take into consideration is that a multi-core server may require a specific type of memory, so make sure that you check the server hardware specifications thoroughly before deciding on the type of memory to deploy.

- In general, more memory is better than less memory and an Exchange 2007 server will use much more memory than its Exchange 2003 equivalent because of the way that it caches data. A high-end Exchange 2003 mailbox server is happy with 4GB of memory; the equivalent Exchange 2007 mailbox server will use 32GB or more (or as much memory as you can afford). For example, Microsoft IT has configured its large mailbox servers with 24GB to support 3,600 mailboxes and smaller mailbox servers with 12GB to support 2,000 mailboxes. Even 12GB is a huge amount of memory to consider in the context of an Exchange 2003 server so these figures serve to illustrate the fundamental trade-off that Exchange 2007 makes by using more memory to reduce disk I/O operations.

- When configuring a server to give it enough memory, you have to juggle expense and slots to install the right number and type of memory modules. 2GB modules are more expensive than 1GB modules, sometimes you have to install memory modules in pairs, and sometimes you can only populate a certain number of slots in memory boards.

- Exchange servers support heavy network loads, so you need to equip servers with enough capacity to handle whatever load you want them to support. Mailbox servers may have to support thousands of concurrent client connections as well as connections to hub transport servers. Hub transport servers make connections throughout your organization to transmit messages. Client Access servers handle the connectivity load generated by Outlook Web Access clients, whereas POP3 and IMAP4 clients, mobile devices through ActiveSync, and multi-role servers have to cope with a mixture. With this activity in mind, it is wise to specify NICs (Network Interface Controllers) capable of handling Gigabit (or better) loads. You can also deploy intelligent NICs[2] that function as a single virtual NIC to handle heavy network loads. You can also deploy multi-function NICs that optimize TCP/IP processing and offload network frame processing from the CPU.

- Reliable disk battery backup is still important. With an increased amount of cached data, you need to be sure that the data can survive a sudden power down of the server. Good battery backup is necessary to protect the contents of the cache through failures. The last thing that you want is to find that you have a corrupted database because some data in the cache was lost due to a power outage.

- Be careful with any benchmark and learn as much as you can about the benchmark environment before you place any value on the reported figures. For example, running anti-virus software on a mailbox or hub transport server can place a surprising demand on the server, even if the anti-virus software applies the "Never scan an item twice" principle to ensure efficient processing. Archiving software can consume a surprising amount of resources as it retrieves information from mailboxes. You also have to take the client workload used for the benchmark into account to understand what the workload involved and what clients generated the workload because the clients and workload may not match your requirements. For instance, a benchmark generated with Outlook clients operating in online mode is not much use to you if you plan to deploy Outlook in cached Exchange mode.

These are broad recommendations that have to be refined through consultation with hardware vendors to ensure that you are up to date with the latest hardware developments. Table 9.1 lists Microsoft's basic configuration guidelines for Exchange 2007 servers. Adjustments you may have to make include:

- Configure one Client Access processor core[3] per four Mailbox processor cores. For example, if a site supports two physical mailbox servers,

---

2.   See http://www.hp.com/products/servers/networking/teaming.html for information about NIC teaming for HP ProLiant servers.

each configured with four dual-core processors, you should match the eight processor cores dedicated to mailboxes with a Client Access server with at least two processor cores equipped with 2GB of memory. However, to get a longer life from the server, you would probably upgrade it to two dual-core processors and install 4GB of memory.

- Microsoft suggests that you can assign up to 1,000 mailboxes per processor core on a dedicated mailbox server. If you install multiple roles on a server, you need to reduce the number of supported mailboxes by at least 20%. If you want to deploy continuous log replication on a dedicated mailbox server, you have to assign extra memory and processing power to handle the load generated by log copying and replay.

- Configure one hub transport server processor core per three mailbox processor cores. For example, if your site has four mailbox servers, each with four dual-core processors, you should probably match the sixteen mailbox processor cores with five processor cores assigned to hub transport servers. In reality, you'd probably adjust this down to a single dual-processor dual-core server as it is likely that such a powerful system will be able to handle the load generated by the mailbox servers (at least initially) and only introduce a new hub transport server when the load grows to a point where the additional power is necessary.

- Benchmarks published by Microsoft and other vendors do not usually cover exactly the same software configuration that you plan to deploy into production. For example, Microsoft prefers that you use ActiveSync to support mobile devices, but many companies prefer to use BlackBerry devices and therefore have to deploy the BlackBerry Enterprise Server. Every application requires some CPU, disk, memory, and network resources, and you have to consider this factor when you determine the real-life loading for servers.

- The memory assigned to a mailbox server is also influenced by the size of the mailbox quotas that you assign to users and the workload generated by users. Clearly, a server that has to handle the workload generated by one thousand heavy users who have 2GB mailbox quotas will require more memory than a server that supports light users with small mailboxes. Apart from being small, the mailboxes specified

---

3.   Modern CPU technology has moved far beyond the point where it was useful to discuss the speed of a single processor installed into a single motherboard socket. The servers you will buy to deploy Exchange 2007 are likely to have multiple processors with multiple cores. Expect to spend some time figuring out the different performance data from server vendors before you can decide what servers to use.

for benchmarks tend not to have the same number of folders that real-life users create, nor do they have folders that store thousands of items. The reason why this is important is that the Store has to work harder when mailboxes have many folders or folders hold many items. The type of client used in the benchmark is also critical. Online Outlook clients generate more work than clients operating in cached Exchange mode. Web browser clients have different characteristics than Outlook, and so on. Unfortunately, the nature of benchmarks over the years is that they use workloads that a real-life administrator might not recognize as realistic.

- Mailbox servers are the only role that you can deploy on a cluster. If you deploy clusters, you need to ensure that you generate balanced systems so that you do not run the risk of compromising cluster state transitions by forcing workload onto an underpowered server. Running LCR for a storage group automatically increases the CPU, memory, and disk above the level that you see on a mailbox server that does not use LCR. In the same way, if you decide to deploy CCR on an MNS cluster, Exchange consumes some additional CPU, memory, and disk on the passive node to copy and replay transaction logs into the passive copy of the database.

Table 9.1   *Microsoft's configuration guidelines for Exchange 2007 servers*

Role	Processor Core	Memory
Client Access	4	1GB/core
Mailbox	4	2GB + 3MB/user
Hub	4	1 GB/core
Edge	2	1 GB/core
Unified Messaging	4	512MB/core
Multi-role (CAS, MBX, HT)	4	4GB + 3MB/user

If you are in doubt about the kind of configuration that is best, you can use the Microsoft performance tools (which Microsoft has upgraded for Exchange 2007) to stress test hardware with the load that you consider appropriate. See Chapter 10 for information about tools such as JetStress and the Performance Load Generator.

9.3   **The storage question**

Microsoft makes a lot about the ability of Exchange 2007 to exploit relatively low-cost storage, so does this mean that we should eliminate the expensive SANs that many organizations have used as the basis of their Exchange 2003 deployment? The answer is an emphatic "no". Exchange 2007 is a great performer on SANs and performs better on storage configurations such as direct-attached or local[4] storage that Exchange 2003 did not work so well on. The Exchange development group is extremely sensitive to the criticism that the storage required for high-end Exchange 2003 deployments was expensive and difficult to manage because in most cases a SAN is required. Many of the problems experienced in Exchange 2003 deployments were not due to software problems or hardware capabilities but were due to the lack of expertise. It is one thing to configure or replace a direct-attached disk; it takes a vast increase in expertise to be able to configure a SAN or replace a disk in a SAN array in such a way that you do not affect operations.

A SAN is a different beast than direct-attached storage. It is more expensive to buy, probably includes features such as online volume growth that you may not want to use immediately, and it requires more expertise to configure and manage. Even granting all of these points, the problem that system designers faced with Exchange 2003 is how to deliver the necessary I/O capacity to handle the needs of thousands of concurrently connected mailboxes. In most cases, only a properly configured SAN can supply the necessary I/O capacity and performance to support the workload. When a SAN is deployed properly, configured for effective performance, and managed to provide the necessary storage and performance for all the various applications that companies typically deploy on the SAN (very few SANs support just Exchange), then you don't have a problem. However, in some situations, a lack of knowledge about the I/O patterns and demands of Exchange 2003 allied to a desire to maximize the use of the SAN led to horrible performance and failures. From the Exchange development team's perspective, it therefore makes a lot of sense to avoid SAN deployments whenever possible and utilize the better I/O characteristics enabled by the change to the 64-bit platform to favor direct-attached storage as the basis for Exchange 2007 deployments.

There is no doubt that Exchange 2007 is a different application with different storage requirements to Exchange 2003. However, as you con-

---

4.   Even when you deploy Exchange 2007 with direct-attached or local storage, you still need to take advantage of storage technologies such as intelligent RAID controllers to protect essential data.

sider what type of storage to use with Exchange 2007, the real question is
not whether to move from one type of storage to another. Instead, the fundamental issue that faces the architect for any Exchange deployment is to
select the best possible storage configuration to support the needs of both
Exchange and the other applications that need to use the storage infrastructure. The overall business situation will also provide guidance as there
is little to gain in ignoring a SAN and moving to another technology if the
business has invested in SAN technology heavily to support a wide array of
applications. Exchange 2007 gives you more options to exploit existing
storage infrastructures and to deploy new storage technology. My view is
that large organizations will continue to use SANs because they see the
advantage of shared storage infrastructures, especially when deployed with
the latest blade server technology, while smaller companies will be
delighted with the performance of Exchange 2007 on servers with direct-
attached storage.

A review of your storage infrastructure and storage technologies is likely
to be part of any deployment of Exchange 2007. You know that I/O
demand is lower with Exchange 2007 than it is with Exchange 2003 (for
the same size of mailboxes—deploying larger mailboxes may produce different I/O results), so that is one plus point on the balance sheet. Other
issues to consider include:

- Where you will deploy the servers: You can only deploy blades into a
  datacenter-like environment that supports the necessary space,
  power, and cooling to support the racks that support the blade servers. If you want to deploy servers into a standard office environment,
  you are going to have to use standard servers.

- What server form factor you want to use: The first generation of
  blade servers were limited by the amount of internal storage that
  they could accommodate, restricted network connectivity, and lack
  of expansion within the blade format, so Exchange 2003 deployments in the 2003–2005 timeframe ignored blades and used standard servers as their basic building block. Vendors such as HP have
  invested large amounts of R&D into blade systems since 2003 and
  the result is that blade servers are now a great platform for Exchange
  2003 or 2007. The latest blade server technology, such as HP's c-
  class BladeSystem servers, allows you to build dense stacks of 64-bit
  AMD or Intel servers that deliver incredible power. However, if you
  deploy blades, perhaps as part of an overall datacenter consolidation
  or redesign project, you are likely to deploy a SAN alongside

because you will want to use features such as remote boot to gain maximum advantage from the blades. In other cases, for example if you only need to deploy a single server in a branch office, a blade server is probably an inappropriate choice and you'll select a traditional server form factor and will therefore be directed toward direct-attached storage.

Different kinds of storage technology that Exchange can use: storage technology changes all the time, so this is an area that you should invest some time and probably money to investigate what is available and what trade-offs exist between the different technologies. For example, you might consider:

- Serial Attached SCSI (SAS): This technology supports high bandwidth (~ 300MB/sec) per link and full duplex connections. The latest SAS drives deliver better I/O performance than similar speed parallel SCSI drives and smart controllers can use the performance to deliver faster array rebuild times should problems occur.

- SATA (Serial Advanced Technology Attachment): Traditionally, SATA drives were viewed as only being suitable for secondary storage. You could use them to hold archive information, such as the backups for Exchange, but you would never use them for your primary storage and Exchange databases. The reduced I/O demands of Exchange 2007 may make SATA drives an inexpensive choice for some low-end hub transport and Client Access servers.

- SFF (Small Form Factor) are 2.5-inch-size drives, use less power, require less cooling, and deliver comparable performance to the traditional 3.5 inch size drives, albeit at a small price premium that will disappear over time. You can take advantage of SFF drives to create dense arrays of SAS drives that deliver great I/O performance because the array will have more spindles to handle the I/O than is possible with larger-format drives. SFF disks also use less power and operate at lower temperatures so they may prove to be more reliable over the long term.

- iSCSI (also known as IP SAN). This technology builds on the principle of SAN storage using a cost-effective TCP/IP interconnect. You are likely to find iSCSI in environments when you want to benefit from the versatility and flexibility of SAN without the cost and management overhead and expertise required to run a Fibre Channel-based SAN.

These are just three examples of storage technology to consider and the exact details of their implementation and effectiveness varies from vendor to vendor because controller intelligence can influence the suitability for a specific deployment. Given the rate of change in storage technology, you can bet that new opportunities to exploit technical advances will appear during the lifetime of your Exchange 2007 deployment. As you look at different disk technologies, consider the expected lifetime too. The old adage of "there are only two types of disk drives—those that have failed and those that are yet to fail" comes into mind here. For example, SAS drives have an expected MTBF of 1.7 million hours[5] based on a 24/7 duty cycle. However, SATA drives have a MTBF of 500K hours based on a 50% duty cycle, and they may have a reduced warranty if you want to exceed the 50% duty cycle. Remember that Exchange servers deal with user load during the day and regular background database maintenance at night, so the reduced duty cycles for SATA disks makes them a very bad choice as the location for databases on mid-range to high-end servers. There is quite a difference in these expected lifetimes if you are designing for a datacenter deployment that features high-density stacking, but it is of less concern if you are looking at low-end servers that support small user communities.

Disk speed is another issue to factor in. There is no point in having large amounts of storage if users cannot access their mailbox contents fast. Ideally, the storage that you deploy has to be able to provide a read latency below 20 milliseconds when it is under load. On high-end servers that have to support thousands of mailboxes, your preference is therefore likely to be for high-performance disks that can satisfy user demand. On smaller servers, you can probably deploy lower-performance disks.

The next item to consider is what RAID (Redundant Array of Inexpensive Disks) level you will deploy to protect Exchange databases and transaction logs. In Exchange 2003 deployments, the classic advice is to use RAID1 to protect the disks that hold transaction logs and RAID0+1 to protect the disks that hold databases. The problem with RAID0+1 is that it can be expensive to implement because you need a minimum of four disks to begin with. RAID5 delivers the same tolerance to a single disk failure as RAID0+1, but it is cheaper because it requires fewer disks. However, RAID5 delivers worse I/O performance, typically measured at about 66%

---

5.   HP assessment—see storage product specifications on www.hp.com.

of a RAID0+1 array. The question therefore is whether you can take advantage of the reduced I/O demands of Exchange 2007 and save on storage by moving from RAID0+1 to RAID5 to protect production databases. If you deploy Exchange on a SAN infrastructure, you may be able to take advantage of features such as virtualized RAID, which supports more the efficient use of available storage capacity.

Fast drives are important, but so is their capacity to deliver the necessary I/O performance in terms of the read-write ratio that Exchange generates. The published data available to date indicates that Exchange 2007 has moved its ratio of read-write I/O operations from the 2:1 ratio experienced on Exchange 2003 to much closer to a 1:1 ratio. There are many contributory factors, including a larger ESE buffer, increasing caching, delayed writes, and the change in database page size from 4KB to 8KB. If you assume that each concurrent user generates 0.33 I/OPS, then a server that supports 3,000 users generates 1,000 I/OPS in total. With a 1:1 ratio, that means 500 reads and 500 writes. If you use RAID0+1, the controller performs two data transfers to disk for every write operation, so the total load is actually 1,500 I/OPS. You then have to divide this load across the available disks. If a disk can handle 150 transfers per second, you need at least 10 disks to handle the load. Clearly, this is a very simple example to illustrate a complex issue and you are advised to take advice from a storage expert before you make any decisions. You can also use the JetStress tool (see Chapter 10) to test a storage configuration and establish how well it works under load.

However, there is more to the RAID question than cost of disks and their capacity to handle a stated load of I/O operations. You create RAID arrays to protect information, but RAID5 exposes you to problems if more than one disk fails in the array. This may not be an issue with small arrays used by small servers, but it is certainly a big problem for large servers that support large amounts of data. Another point to consider is the time required to rebuild the array any time you need to replace a drive as this can have quite a performance impact on a server, especially when you have to rebuild a drive that holds a very large mailbox database. Other issues that storage consultants worry about include the stripe size to use for data LUNs (which differ depending on the RAID level you deploy), the NTFS cluster size to use (64k recommended), the right tool to use for disk partitioning (DISKPART or something else), and whether to align sector tracks to track boundaries (potentially a performance gain). Overall, the degree of complexity and the interaction between the different parts of the storage equation means that you should consult an expert or take the time to do your own research before you decide what is best for your Exchange 2007 implementation.

9.4 RPC pop-ups

Sometimes users report that their Outlook client is not responding as well as it should (all users believe that response should be immediate at all times, so maybe that last statement should read somewhat differently). The report might be that Outlook is slow today and that the user sees pop-ups (small dialog boxes) that report that Outlook is requesting or retrieving data from Exchange. The question is why does Outlook generate these pop-ups and what can you do about them?

First, I should state that you will not see the pop-ups if you use a version of Outlook older than XP. This is because older clients have the charming habit of hanging any time communications to the server slow down. Obviously, this is not a good thing, so Outlook now generates the pop-ups if the client detects that the server is not responding to RPCs within five seconds and clients can opt to cancel the RPC if they choose. Issuing messages to reassure users that something is happening is an age-old programming technique that I took full advantage of in code that I wrote for the ALL-IN-1 Office Automation product in the 1980s!

Normally the problem that causes Outlook to issue the pop-ups is transient and goes away of its own accord, but the issue deserves closer investigation if many clients report the same problem and it persists. The first thing to establish is the scope of the problem, so you need to ask questions such as if problems are confined to clients that connect to one server, across a specific network segment, of a certain type, when they access a specific resource, and so on.

If a specific server appears to be the root of the problem, you can focus on that server's performance. The usual items to check include:

- Network traffic to the server and the ability of the server to handle that traffic (check that the network adapter is functioning correctly);

- The I/O load on the server (I/O bottlenecks slow client response very quickly); and

- If the problem occurs with GAL lookups, check the ability of the domain controller and Global Catalog selected by the Exchange server to handle the load generated by Exchange.

Note that CPU and physical memory shortages are not normally a cause of concern, as disks are the slowest part of any Exchange server. Virtual memory problems do cause an issue for heavily loaded Exchange 2000 and 2003 servers.

From the client side, the user may be attempting to access a folder that holds many items and it takes time for Outlook to establish the initial collection of items through a series of requests to the folder. This issue is not usually a problem for Outlook 2003 *or* 2007 clients that run in cached Exchange mode as the folder contents are available locally, but even Outlook can have a problem if you ask it to open a public folder that holds thousands of items. Accessing a replica of a public folder that is on a server in a remote site can also result in bad performance, as can an attempt to look up free/busy information in a public folder when you operate in a mixed-mode Exchange organization.

Once you know what operations cause the problem to appear, you can determine whether the problem is due to an underlying hardware issue, the Exchange configuration, or user error. The ExMon tool is a good way to investigate overall server performance.

9.5   Clusters and Exchange

The interesting thing about mailbox data is that it is the only data that Exchange processes that is stored in a single place. Directory information is replicated by the Active Directory, including all of the configuration data required by Exchange to function within the organization, and public folder data is replicated by Exchange among public folder servers. Mailbox data remains unprotected by duplication and is therefore prone to being affected by hardware failure. This has been the Achilles Heel of Exchange since its first version and it is the reason why Microsoft has done so much work to add protection for mailbox servers in Exchange 2007.

Of course, it's also important that Exchange remains competitive. Lotus Notes has been the major competitor for Exchange for the entire lifetime of the product, but unlike Notes, Exchange never could support continuous replication to protect mailbox data unless you invested in a third-party solution that uses intelligent software to replicate databases and logs to a remote host or storage array, or you arranged for data to be copied and restored regularly in a remote location. The advent of continuous log replication in Exchange 2007 reduces or eliminates the competitive advantage enjoyed by Notes for many years in database replication.

The first Exchange clusters used the "Wolfpack" technology for Windows NT 4.0 and ran the Enterprise Edition of Exchange 5.5. Companies deployed the first Exchange clusters in 1998–99 and found that clusters delivered better resilience to server outages by protecting Exchange against some basic hardware errors such as storage or motherboard failures. However, Exchange 5.5 clusters only support two nodes. One node was active (users could connect and use mailboxes on the server) while the other node was passive. When the active node experienced a problem, Exchange transferred its workload to the passive node to allow users to continue working. Clusters were very new in Microsoft shops and much of the supporting Exchange ecosystem of third-party software did not support clusters, so it became quite difficult to create a cluster-based production messaging environment. Because of these difficulties and the underlying costs, relatively few Exchange 5.5 clusters went into production.

Cluster technology improved with the introduction of Exchange 2000 and Windows 2000 to a point where Exchange supported four nodes in a cluster. Exchange 2000 uses the storage group as the unit of workload for an Exchange cluster. When problems occurred on a cluster node, the cluster transferred the complete storage group to another node in the cluster. Microsoft's initial thought was that the four nodes could be active simultaneously. This was obviously a good thing because keeping the four nodes working decreased the cost per mailbox for a cluster deployment. Virtual memory fragmentation imposed a performance ceiling and in practice, administrators had to take great care that a cluster transition would not overload a node by requiring it to support more than four storage groups. Cluster-aware software was easier to find, but customers still encountered problems with virtual memory management that prevented clusters scaling up to desired levels.

Cluster technology took another leap forward in the combination of Exchange 2003 and Windows 2003. Exchange clusters had a better reputation, were generally cheaper to deploy because you could make better utilization of the hardware, delivered reliable performance, and became more popular within Exchange's customer base. However, on the down side, virtual memory management problems persisted and this led Microsoft to advise customers that they would not support full active-active clusters. You always had to keep one passive node in a cluster so that it could accept the work if another node failed. This is clearly more of a problem in a two-node cluster than it is in an eight-node cluster, but the lack of true active-active clustering for Exchange remains a frustration.

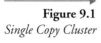

Figure 9.1
Single Copy Cluster

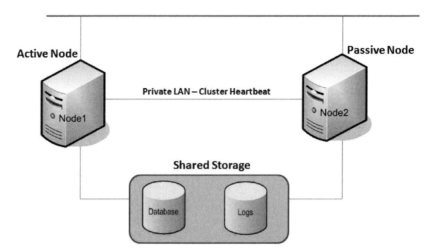

The classic implementation of Microsoft clusters and the type that Exchange has supported since Exchange 5.5 involves servers and storage co-located in the same physical place, so a catastrophic disaster can wipe everything out. Microsoft now refers to this type of cluster as a Single Copy Cluster, or SCC. Figure 9.1 shows the major components of an SCC. All of the Exchange mailbox data—databases, transaction logs, SMTP folders, content indexing, and so on—goes on shared storage that the cluster can move between the nodes in the cluster. The simplest SCC has two nodes, one active and one passive. Exchange runs as a virtual server (now called a CMS, or Clustered Mailbox Server) that can move between the nodes just like a physical resource such as storage.

Companies working in the financial services industry are especially sensitive to physical catastrophic outages because email often serves as part of the record for transactions, such as communications between traders and customers. The events of September 11, 2001 served to confirm the worst fears and demonstrated the advantages of maintaining a separate copy of data away from a computer center. Of course, the IT industry has maintained off-site storage for years, but this is typically done by sending backup tapes to an off-site vault from where they can be retrieved if ever necessary. This process is often referred to as moving cold data off-site, whereas much of the interest now is in live or hot data replication to an off-site location. The advantage gained from maintaining hot off-site copies is that the data is available much faster should a disaster occur at the production datacenter.

Unlike other database systems, Microsoft did not design the ESE engine to incorporate the capability to perform online "hot" replication. This means that Exchange cannot manage the distribution of replicated transactions to multiple locations (servers) as the Store commits data to its databases. Instead, other components that run at the server or storage level must take responsibility to replicate data that the Store writes to an off-site location. You can deploy stretched clusters for Exchange 2003 providing you use third-party technology to complement Exchange. The same situation is true for Exchange 2007 with the big difference being that Exchange 2007 supports continuous log replication.

Data replication solutions normally fall into two categories. Synchronous replication means that the host receives a write complete notification from the storage subsystem when the write operation is complete in both the local and remote storage locations. By contrast, asynchronous replication means that the host receives the write complete notification as soon as it is committed to local storage, so the host does not have to wait for the operation to complete remotely.

There are two types of replication: host and storage. In host-based replication, an I/O filter driver manages the I/O stream to perform replication. In storage-based replication, replication occurs under the control of the storage subsystem at the device level. No one wants to deploy a solution that Microsoft will not support, so it is important to understand that Microsoft does not support asynchronous replication for Exchange 2003 (see Microsoft Knowledge Base article 895847). The only category of data replication solutions that Microsoft supports for Exchange 2003 is synchronous replication, probably because of write ordering of operations into the database, something that is more difficult to ensure with asynchronous replication. You need to preserve the write I/O order so that any I/Os that arrive at the replication destination are in the same order as Exchange provides them to the original mailbox. Microsoft's policy is unlikely to change for Exchange 2003 but may change over time as storage technologies evolve, networks improve, and they improve their store engine.

Storage vendors like HP that incorporate asynchronous replication into solutions for Exchange support the implementation of their technology, so it is possible that you can find a solution that meets your needs and that you are happy to go forward with because of the support provided by the vendor. However, in case of problems, Microsoft will only provide support up to the point where they can reasonably say that the source of the problem is in the storage subsystem (such as a potential database corruption) and Microsoft may require you to remove the replication feature before they will help you. For these reasons, if you deploy an asynchronous replication solution for Exchange, make sure that you have good knowledge of the storage subsystem on staff and that everyone understands the appropriate disaster-recovery techniques, just in case.

Synchronous replication solutions can be based locally or geographically distributed (also known as geo clusters), which is the approach that has attracted most attention within the Exchange community. In this scenario, the nodes in the cluster are distributed across different physical sites. The active Exchange servers are usually located in one site and if failover occurs, passive servers in the other site take on the load. To allow this to happen, the storage subsystem must replicate data between the two sites as otherwise the cluster cannot transfer the Exchange virtual servers from one site to the other. Microsoft requires that the hardware configuration for a geo cluster is tested and listed in the geo cluster hardware compability list. See http://www.microsoft.com/technet/prodtechnol/exchange/2003/geocluster.mspx for more information on Exchange 2003 geo clusters. You can find another good source of data about Exchange 2007 clusters at http://www.microsoft.com/exchange/evaluation/editions.mspx.

The decision to deploy a geo cluster is complex, involves your own data resiliency requirements, the functionality, and features currently available from different storage vendors, and the software used to control the replication, the version of Exchange that you deploy, and so on. In other words, there are no easy answers in this space and you should consult experts to

Table 9.2   *Exchange 2007 LCR, CCR, and SCC*

Option	LCR	CCR	SCC
Database/SG	Single database per storage group	Single database per storage group	Up to five databases per storage group
Server roles	Multi-role servers	Only mailbox servers	Only mailbox servers
Public folders	Unsupported in the storage group*	Unsupported by the storage group	Supported
Data	Two independent copies of the data held in different locations on a single server	Two independent copies of the data held in different locations on two servers	Single copy of the data shared by multiple servers in the cluster
Nodes	One	Two (one active, one passive)	Up to eight (no support for active-active clusters)
Location	Single datacenter	May span two separate datacenters	Single datacenter

Table 9.2 *Exchange 2007 LCR, CCR, and SCC*

Failover	Manual transition to passive copy of database	Transition of workload to the passive server—this transition is not automatic in the case of database failure.	Transition of the Clustered Mailbox Server from the failed node to an active node
Hardware requirements	Single server; sufficient disk to host multiple copy of databases and logs; sufficient CPU and memory to handle log copy and replay	Two servers, which should be balanced but don't have to be; sufficient disk space to host copy of database and logs; sufficient CPU and memory to handle log copy and replay	Balanced server configurations for each active node; possible to have servers with other configurations dedicated to management tasks
Software	Windows 2003 SP1/R2	Windows 2003 Enterprise with SP1/R2	Windows 2003 Enterprise with SP1/R2
Protects Exchange against	Local failure on the drives supporting databases	Complete failure of the active node or a storage failure on the active node	Multiple server or disk failures within cluster

* *There is an exception that allows LCR and CCR servers to support a public folder database.*

ensure that the selected solution can deliver the necessary storage reliability and performance under stress and that it fits into your backup strategy and disaster-recovery plans.

We now have the option to deploy continuous replication for Exchange 2007 in either a single-server (LCR) or dual-server (CCR) configuration. As discussed earlier, Exchange 2007 also supports the traditional mailbox cluster model (SCC). All are options for mailbox servers—Exchange does not support any other server role on a cluster. Table 9.2 illustrates the basic differences between these configurations.

You cannot extend a CCR cluster past two nodes (you can have an MNS cluster with more than two nodes, but only two of the nodes can run Exchange 2007). This option may appear in the future, but for now if you have four servers available, you can create two CCR clusters, a single CCR cluster, and two standalone servers, or four standalone servers.

All types of Exchange 2007 clusters support only the mailbox role, which is a change for customers who have deployed traditional (SCC) Exchange clusters. These customers have been able to run small clusters that do everything from mailbox to transport to client access. For example, it is reasonably common for small companies to deploy a single two-node

Exchange 2003 cluster that delivers the necessary protection against failure while also being able to support mailboxes, route messages, and provide access to multiple clients using multiple protocols. For many reasons, the division of work into different server roles is a generally welcome move for Exchange 2007. In this instance, it results in additional expense because you need to deploy a two-node SCC mailbox cluster alongside another server to host the hub transport and Client Access roles to get the same functionality as an Exchange 2003 two-node cluster delivers. Of course, LCR and CCR provide deployment options that were not available in previous versions and you can deploy multiple server roles on an LCR server. However, you can only deploy the mailbox role on a CCR cluster. Overall, the lack of multi-role support for small clusters is a curious retrograde step when you consider that one of the prime advantages of moving to the Windows 64-bit platform is the potential to consolidate many small servers into fewer larger servers.

9.6   Continuous replication and Exchange 2007

In the past, users were satisfied if administrators got their mailbox data back online in a couple of hours. It did not matter that you had to fix the hardware or software problem that caused the outage and then restored whatever data was required. The size of the Exchange databases that were in use were usually less than 10GB so the restore didn't take too long, even with slow restores from tapes. It was just a slower, less demanding world. Things have certainly changed, and given that email has become so critical to the functioning of many businesses and the obvious competitive disadvantage with Notes, it is surprising that it has taken Microsoft so long to provide the ability for the Store to replicate its data. With Exchange 2007, you can duplicate transaction logs on a local server basis (Local Continuous Replication, or LCR) or to the other server in a two-node cluster (Cluster Continuous Replication, or CCR).

Data outages are expensive to recover from because restoring from backup takes a long time and the possibility of data loss exists if transaction log files are missing, corrupted, or cannot be replayed into the recovered database. The logical conclusion from this statement is that it is best to keep a copy of critical data that is up to date and available to be switched to take the place of production data if a problem occurs. Two possible solutions exist. You can keep a copy of the data on the same computer or keep the copy on a different computer, and that is what LCR and CCR do by using the principle of log shipping to enable loose synchronization[6] of mailbox data through continuous replication. Log shipping is the same technique that is used by SQL Server and Lotus Notes to provide continuous replication.

Continuous replication is an important feature to have in any enterprise application because copying the transaction logs and applying them against a copy of the live database ensures that you will not lose data following a failure. You are able to switch in an up-to-date copy of the failed database and restore service without having to deal with the complexities involved in restoring the database from a backup. There have been too many examples of restores failing because of unavailable or corrupt transaction logs on Exchange servers in the past for Microsoft not to include continuous replication in Exchange 2007. Another advantage gained by the introduction of continuous replication as part of Exchange is that administrators don't have to worry about the interaction and potential dependencies between third-party storage add-ons and the base product, especially after Microsoft updates Exchange or Windows with hot fixes or service packs.

Microsoft also states that because of continuous replication, you may not need to take full daily backups of databases. The logic here is that full daily backups are taken to provide a known good starting point for restore operations should a problem occur. If you deploy LCR or CCR, you have a new starting point to begin to restore service (the copy of the database), so you do not need to take full daily backups. I understand the logic and it's true that a new starting point exists, but this ignores the fact that full daily backups also provide copies of data that can be taken offsite to media vaults to be used for restore operations in the case of catastrophic failure or to satisfy audit requirements. These needs still exist, so I think that most companies will continue to take full daily backups.

Like management operations across the rest of Exchange 2007, you can automate LCR and CCR functions with EMS commands (such as `Restore-StorageGroupCopy`), so it is possible to create scripts to perform operations such as creating a new replication set, suspend or resume replication, or perform a recovery using a replica database.

9.6.1 Concepts

The theory behind continuous replication is that you start with a copy of the production data and then keep the copy updated by applying the same

---

6.   The ability to replicate data tightly rather than loosely implies that Exchange would be able to update two databases (the target mailbox store and a copy) concurrently.

modifications that are applied to the production data. The copy and continual update method is less expensive in terms of CPU processing and time than taking snapshot copies every so often. Exchange 2007 implements the theory by first taking a copy of the mailbox database (to "seed" the database replica). Afterwards, every time the Store creates a new transaction log, the Microsoft Exchange Replication Service (which is installed by default on all mailbox servers) copies the log file that the Store has just closed to the target location and applies the transactions in the log to the passive copy of the database. Exchange applies transactions from the logs to the replica database in the same way that it has performed soft recoveries for Store databases since its first release, so there is nothing strange or new here. The net result is that you maintain a second copy of your live database in an almost up-to-date condition as the copy of the database only lacks the transactions in the current log file to make it completely up to date. As illustrated by Figure 9.2, the major difference between LCR and CCR is that all of the processing done by LCR is on a local server whereas Exchange copies the logs to a remote server for processing when you use CCR. However, the concepts behind the two operations are very similar.

Because LCR and CCR allow you to have an always up-to-date copy of the database available, you can use it for backup or recovery purposes. While Microsoft anticipated that many large Exchange 2003 deployments would use VSS (Windows Volume ShadowCopy Services) to take a snapshot copy of a mailbox or public folder database, this has not been the case across the wider Exchange community, possibly due to the slowness of storage and backup software vendors to provide products that support VSS. Those companies who have deployed VSS can take a snapshot copy of a database and then move that copy to another server where it is available for

Figure 9.2
LCR and CCR

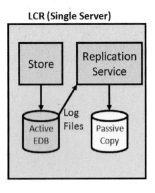

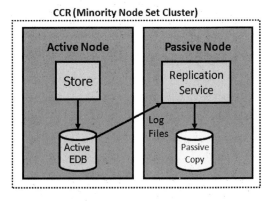

recovery operations, so log shipping continues a trend to allow companies to be more resistant to email outages.

LCR protects against hardware failures that affect the storage that hosts the production database as well as some types of on-disk corruption (a corruption that affects the database and the logs requires a hard recovery). LCR allows you to recover from local disk failures quickly because you have a complete and up to date replica of the mailbox database ready to be switched over into production. Moving a pointer so that Exchange can pick up a different copy of a database and restart is obviously much faster than the traditional restore from backup approach to disk failures, so LCR and CCR allow you to get a database back online and to restore service to users faster. Restoring services to users faster is attractive, but you can only switch databases on an LCR server if the problem that afflicted the original database does not affect the local copy. For example, you cannot switch databases if your server is still experiencing a fundamental storage problem. By comparison, CCR provides a further level of protection by allowing you to fail over to a completely different server so that you can recover operations if the original server fails completely.

Nothing comes free of charge, and if you want to use LCR or CCR, you will have to configure servers with sufficient storage capacity to hold the copies of the databases and transaction logs and sufficient I/O capability to move the logs to the target location and apply them to the replica database. In addition, you need to plan the storage so that a single failure does not effect both the active and replica databases and ensure that the I/O consumed by log shipping does not impact server responsiveness for users. You will have to update your operational procedures to take LCR or CCR into account so that administrators know exactly what to do when servers experience outages that affect the storage groups protected with log replication. CCR only supports one clustered mailbox server and all of its databases are online on the same cluster node. CCR switches databases automatically if the cluster detects that the active node has gone offline, but you have to understand how to perform (and perhaps script) other transitions, such as when you want to move databases between nodes in the cluster to apply service packs and other updates. LCR transitions are manual, so your administrative procedures have to include the necessary steps to switch databases if problems occur.

Meeting the hardware requirements incur some expense, but given the declining cost of storage (in particular), you can argue that the investment to deploy continuous replication will be realized through the avoidance of a single incident of unproductive user time generated by one significant outage. It is faster and more convenient to bring back data online from a replica than to have to go through a complicated and long restore procedure.

9.7   Deploying Local Continuous Replication (LCR)

LCR is available for all editions of Exchange 2007 and provides a resiliency option to protect against database failure caused by a disk outage that you can deploy for small to medium servers at a low price point. You can deploy LCR on any Exchange 2007 mailbox server except a cluster (CCR or SCC). Unlike an SCC cluster, you can run the hub transport and Client Access roles on a server that uses LCR. If you want to deploy a cluster to gain extra resilience against server failure, then you have the option of deploying a new CCR server on an MNS cluster or a traditional SCC configuration.

Figure 9.3
A mixture of LCR and "normal" storage groups

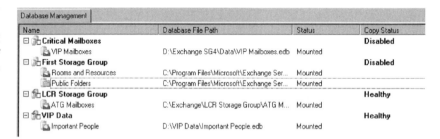

As with other Exchange 2007 servers, you can configure up to 50 storage groups on a mailbox server that uses LCR. You can deploy a mixture of storage groups, some that use LCR and some that do not. For example, you might have a storage group configured to use circular logging because it holds transient data and does not require the kind of protection offered by LCR. Figure 9.3 shows a server that supports four storage groups. You can see that the default storage group (First Storage Group) contains a public folder database and has a copy status of "Disabled," meaning that it does not use LCR. The storage group at the top of the display also has a copy status of "Disabled" although given its name ("Critical Mailboxes"), it is probably a good candidate to use LCR. The other two storage groups show their copy status as "Healthy," so you know that they use LCR. In passing, it is worth noting that the storage groups and databases on this server do not follow any naming convention. A server running LCR can become a complex environment, especially with multiple storage groups when some operate LCR and some do not. It is in these situations that you see the true value of a consistently applied naming convention.

Any storage group that uses LCR can only have one mailbox database whereas the storage groups that do not use LCR can support multiple databases, including public folder databases. The exception to this rule is that you can enable a storage group that contains a public folder database for LCR or CCR if it is the only public folder database in the organization. Apart from their desire to eliminate public folders from Exchange as soon as they can, Microsoft's logic for not supporting public folder databases for continuous replication is that the mixture of replication models (log shipping and public folder replication) may cause problems if you have to revert to a database copy. In this scenario, there is a possibility that some transactions that contain public folder replication data will be lost and this could then have an unpredictable effect on public folder contents. The meaning is clear here—do not enable continuous replication for a storage group that contains a public folder database, even if you fall into the small minority of the Exchange community that deploys Exchange 2007 from scratch.

The necessary prerequisites to operate LCR are enough disk space to hold a copy of the database and transaction logs and enough available CPU and memory to validate and then to replay the logs into the database copy to keep it updated. For planning purposes, you should assume that LCR will consume 1GB of memory and between 15–20% additional CPU. In addition, LCR generates read I/O operations on the disk volume that holds the transaction logs to copy the logs followed by a set of read and write I/O operations generated as the Replication Service inspects and validates the copied transaction logs and then replays the data from the logs to update the passive database. The exact amount of I/O operations generated depends on the load generated by users, but you can assume that LCR requires the storage system to accommodate at least twice the I/O operations that a regular server handles to support the same load. Because of the way that the Store creates the replay instance to handle sets of transaction logs, LCR is not as effective as the Store in caching data during the normal commitment process, so it generates more I/O operations than the norm.

One issue with LCR is that we do not yet know where its performance limits are. For example, you can enable LCR for a server that supports 4,000 mailboxes, but what will the performance impact be from the additional CPU, memory, and I/O resources necessary to support the load generated by 4,000 mailboxes? The lack of performance data and real-life experience about LCR in production is likely to place a restriction on the maximum number of mailboxes that anyone will deploy on an LCR server to small to medium populations. Once the data is available, administrators will be better able to decide whether LCR is an appropriate solution for their mailbox servers.

LCR supports direct-attached storage as well as storage connected by Fibre Channel (to a Storage Area Network) or iSCSI. Given the available power and storage available to most Exchange servers today, it is unlikely that LCR will apply enough strain on any production-class server to make its deployment impracticable. LCR is an important evolution for Exchange because in previous versions the available resiliency options focused on high-end servers where administrators were willing to spend the necessary money to protect databases that supported thousands of mailboxes.

Figure 9.4
Enabling LCR for a storage group

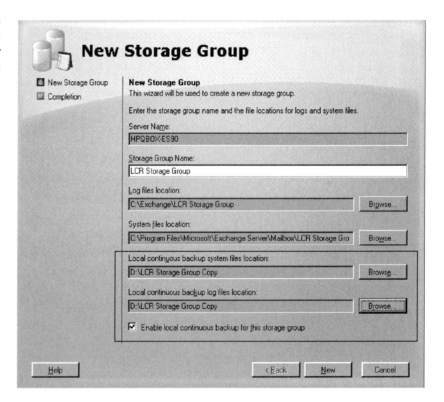

To begin to use LCR on a server, you have to configure a storage group to have a replica. You can enable LCR for a storage group when you create it (Figure 9.4) or by selecting an existing storage group and then selecting the "Enable Local Continuous Replication" option from the action pane. Below, you can see the equivalent New-StorageGroup command to create a new storage group that has LCR enabled. The important elements are setting the HasLocalCopy parameter to $True and passing values for the CopyLogFolderPath and CopySystemFolderPath parameters.

```
New-StorageGroup -Server 'ExchMbxSvr1' -Name 'VIP Data'
-LogFolderPath 'C:\VIP Data\Logs' -SystemFolderPath 'C:\VIP
Data'
-HasLocalCopy $True -CopyLogFolderPath 'D:\VIP Data\Logs'
-CopySystemFolderPath 'D:\VIP Data\'
```

You should place the database copy on a separate physical storage device to the live database to avoid the possibility that a hardware failure will take out both copies. Of course, you should also separate the two sets of transaction logs. Separation on different volumes provides an additional benefit of better I/O performance, but it does mean that before you can deploy LCR on a small server, you need at least five physical volumes as follows:

Drive 1: Windows, Exchange binaries, other operating system files

Drive 2: Active database

Drive 3: Transaction logs for active database

Drive 4: Copy database

Drive 5: Copy of transaction logs

Make sure that the selected locations for the LCR copies have enough space to hold the copies of the database and the transaction logs that will accrue over time. Exchange removes transaction logs that are no longer required automatically after a full backup, but it is still wise to keep an eye on the disk space.

After you create an LCR-enabled storage group, the next step is to create and mount a mailbox database in the storage group. We can do this through EMC or by issuing `New-MailboxDatabase` and `Mount-Database` commands.

```
New-MailboxDatabase -StorageGroup 'ExchMbxSvr1\VIP Data'
-Name 'Important People'
-EdbFilePath 'C:\VIP Data\Important People.edb'
-HasLocalCopy $True -CopyEdbFilePath 'D:\VIP Data\Important
People.edb'
```

```
Mount-Database -Identity 'ExchMbxSvr1\Important People'
```

Figure 9.5

*LCR status for a
storage group*

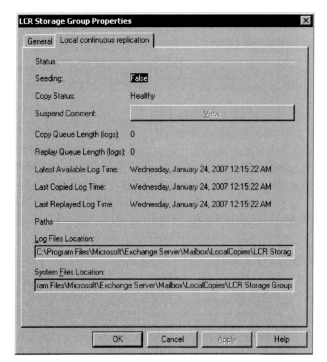

When you enable LCR for a storage group, Exchange automatically seeds the active mailbox database by copying it to the LCR location using a streaming backup. An automatic copy is possible only if the initial log file (E01000001.log in the case of the default storage group) is available. If you enable LCR for a storage group that has been in operation for some time, you will have to dismount the database and copy it manually to perform the seed operation.

The copy of the database becomes the new baseline for the replica and Exchange will copy the transaction logs for the storage group asynchronously from this point onwards and replay and commit to keep the replica database synchronized. It is possible that problems such as data corruption will force you to reseed the replica database. In this case, you can use the Update-StorageGroupCopy command to recopy the active database to the LCR location and restart the synchronization process. In fact, if you take the active database offline and perform a database rebuild with the ESEUTIL utility, you will also have to reseed the passive database because you have created a brand-new database that has no connection to the passive copy. The same restriction applies for databases on CCR servers.

You can change the locations for either the production or replica databases at any time, but you have to suspend continuous replication and dismount the databases before you can move them.

Once enabled for LCR, you can check on the LCR status for a storage group by viewing its properties and clicking on the "Local Continuous Replication" property page (Figure 9.5).

9.7.1   How LCR works

The Replication service is the core of LCR and is composed of a set of components, each of which takes responsibility for a different step in the replication process. Figure 9.6 illustrates the flow of continuous log replication to take logs generated by the active database and apply them to update the passive copy.

- The copier copies closed log files from the live database to the inspector location for the replica database. This process is asynchronous and occurs on a continual basis as new logs are created. A log file is available to be copied when the Store closes off the current log file (called E00.log for the first storage group), renames it, and creates a new current log.

- The inspector checks its directory regularly to detect newly copied logs and then verifies that the logs are valid. If valid, the inspector moves the logs to the replay directory. If a log fails validation, the inspector copies it again to ensure that temporary conditions (such as a network glitch) do not stop continuous replication working. If Exchange cannot recopy a log, then the passive copy of the database will have to be reseeded.

- The log replayer replays the contents of the copied logs to update the database replica using the same kind of processing that the Store executes for soft database recoveries following an unexpected server outage. The Store replays logs every 60 seconds or after 10 new logs are available. In LCR, the update occurs on the local system, whereas with CCR, it occurs on a remote system. This means that LCR incurs a higher performance penalty on a local server than CCR does.

- The truncate deletor deletes log files that the log replayer has successfully used to update the replica database. Full online backups of

Exchange databases have traditionally removed log files, but when continuous replication is used, the truncate deletor makes sure that the log files that the Replication services has not copied and replayed into the replica database are not deleted. Exchange does not delete a transaction log unless it is sure that it is not required for recovery purposes, so they are not deleted until after they have been backed up.

- The incremental seeder is responsible for ensuring that the active and replica databases are not in a diverged state after a restore has been performed or after a failover in a CCR environment.

- The replay manager keeps track of all replica instances on a server to ensure that the configuration for the replicas is consistent. Periodically, the replay manager verifies that the configuration data held in Active Directory matches the actual database status on the server.

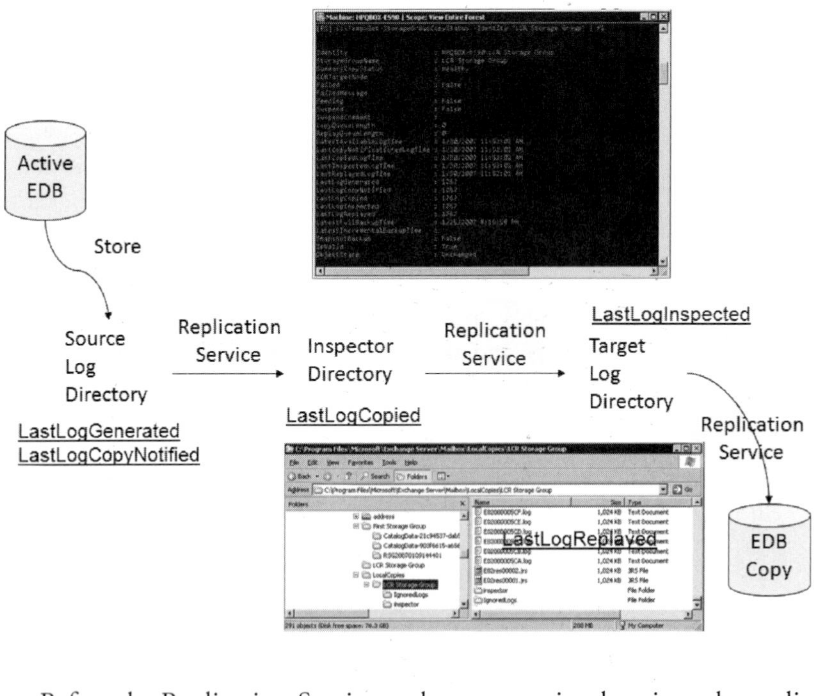

Figure 9.6
Flow of continuous log replication

Before the Replication Service replays transaction logs into the replica database, it verifies the checksum and database signature of the logs to ensure that they are valid. This is equivalent to running the ESEUTIL against the log using the /K switch. The Replication Service is responsible for copying the transaction logs to the Inspector directory. If the checksum fails, Exchange recopies that log. If Exchange fails to copy and validate the log a third time, it is an indication that something very bad is happening within the storage subsystem and you will probably end up reseeding the database.

Once the Replication Service verifies logs, it moves the logs into the log directory and then proceeds to use the data in the logs to update the mailbox database replica in the background using a transaction replay process similar to the soft recovery process that occurs when Exchange needs to update a production database when it is mounted. The log replay is similar to the processing performed when you run ESEUTIL /R to replay logs to a database, but it is faster because Exchange attempts to batch log files together to stream transactions into the database.

The Store replays logs immediately after the Replication Service has copied and validated them. A separate instance of ESE that runs inside the Information Store process is responsible for log replay. The need to run a separate instance of ESE is the reason why LCR and CCR use additional memory. Each time a set of logs is available for replay, the Store creates a new replay instance, which takes responsibility for replaying the logs into the copy database. The Store destroys the replay instance after its work is complete. The Store replays logs in generation order. For example, if LCR copies log generation 1876 and the Store is replaying log generation 1873, it is logical that generation 1876 has to wait until the Store has replayed logs 1874 and 1875. If this did not happen then transactions that span several log generations could not be replayed accurately.

The Replication service may detect logs that it ignores for updates. For example, for some reason a copied log file may be too old to apply to the replica database or it might be corrupt. These logs are moved into the IgnoredLogs directory and can be deleted. The IgnoredLogs directory may have two subdirectories: E00OutOfDate and InspectionFailed. The first directory holds any E00.log file that is present in the replica directory when a failover occurs. The file was probably created because the replica copy was previously run as the active copy. When a failure occurs, the Store creates a new E00.log file to act as the current transaction log, so if it finds an E00.log file in place, it simply moves it into the E00OutOfDate directory to get the old file out of the way. The InspectionFailed directory is there to hold log files that the inspector rejects because of some reason, perhaps because the Store cannot read the file or believes that the signature in the header is invalid.

9.7.2   LCR operations

You can use the `Get-StorageGroup` command to discover whether log replication is in use within the organization. Local replication indicates LCR, Clustered means CCR. As you can see, the ExchMbxSvr1 server supports three storage groups, two of which use LCR.

```
Get-StorageGroup | Sort-Object Server
```

Name	Server	Replicated	Recovery
First Storage Group	ExchMbxSvr1	None	False
LCR Storage Group	ExchMbxSvr1	Local	False
VIP Data	ExchMbxSvr1	Local	False
First Storage Group	ExchMbxSvr2	None	False
First Storage Group	ExchMbxSvr3	Clustered	False

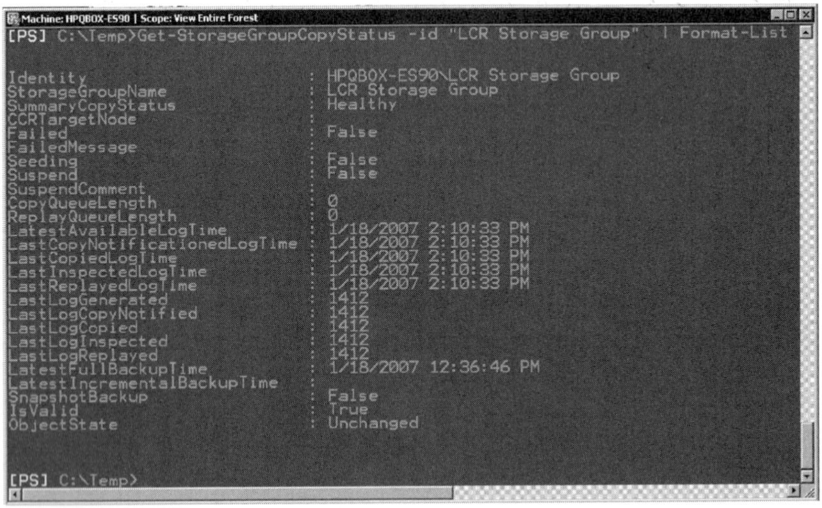

Figure 9.7
Output from the Get-StorageGroupCop-Status command

LCR adds no overhead to daily administrative operations because the copying, validation, and application of logs into the database copy proceeds automatically. In six months of running LCR on a server, I cannot recall a single instance when I had to change a setting or take another action. The only administrative functions that I performed were occasional checks using the `Get-StorageGroupCopyStatus` command, and these were only because I was curious whether everything was still working.

The `Get-StorageGroupCopyStatus` command reports on the current replication status for a storage group. Figure 9.7 shows the complete set of information returned by `Get-StorageGroupCopyStatus` for an LCR-enabled storage group on a server. You can see that all of the log generation numbers for the different stages in the replication cycle show the same value, so you know that the Store is in a relatively quiet state and that everything is synchronized. You can also view this information by looking at the properties of the storage group through EMC. The log generation properties shown here mean:

LastLogCopyNotified: Returns the last generation of log file seen by Exchange in the source (production) directory. The file may not yet been copied but it has been noted by the Replication service.

LastLogCopied: Returns the last generation of log file copied by the Replication service to the Inspector directory.

LastLogInspected: Returns the last generation of log file that Exchange has inspected, validated the checksum, and moved to the replication log directory.

LastLogReplayed: Returns the last generation that Exchange has replayed into the copy of the database.

As well as using the `Get-StorageGroupCopyStatus` command to check on the current state of health for continuous replication, you can look into the registry to see the information that the service records to track its progress. Each storage group enabled for continuous replication has a separate section in the registry, which is updated by the Replication service. Figure 9.8 illustrates the registry values as viewed at approximately the same time as the status shown in Figure 9.7, so you can compare the values and see how they match up.

Apart from `Get-StorageGroupCopyStatus`, the other commands that you can use to control LCR are:

- `Suspend-StorageGroupCopy`: Suspend LCR for a period.
- `Resume-StorageGroupCopy`: Resume LCR processing after a suspension.

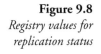

Figure 9.8
Registry values for
replication status

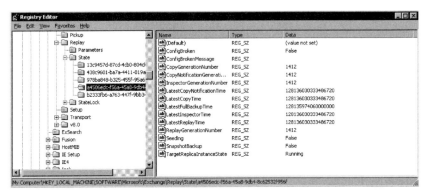

- `Update-StorageGroupCopy`: Restart LCR processing for a storage group with a new copy (seed) of the active database.

- `Restore-StorageGroupCopy`: Terminates replication activity and makes the copy of the database available to be mounted as the production copy. After the command completes, you use the `Mount-Database` command to mount the database. This command is also valid for CCR servers and can be used when the cluster does not make an automatic transition from live to copy database following a failure of the live database.

- `Enable-StorageGroupCopy`: Enable LCR processing for a storage group.

- `Disable-StorageGroupCopy`: Disable LCR processing for a storage group.

The suspend, resume, enable, and disable options are also available through EMC.

One interesting challenge that faced the Exchange engineers is how to coordinate backups across database copies. When you take a backup of a database, the Store writes information about the backup into the database header. When you use continuous replication, you create a replica copy that you may want to backup, but you cannot update the header of the replica because that would then create divergence between the replica (with its updated header) and the active databases. Taking a backup of the active copy is not a problem because the Exchange synchronizes the backup information into the replica through normal replication.

The solution that Microsoft implemented is to use the Replication service to coordinate backup information between the two copies. The coordination stops you taking backups at the same time on both copies to prevent update clashes and to transmit the header updates generated by the backup of the passive database back to the active database. The Store then applies the updates to the active database and normal replication synchronizes the change back to the passive.

Another interesting issue relating to backups is the definition of what log files are required to make a database consistent through a soft replay. For all versions of Exchange, if you take a full backup of a database, the backup process removes all of the log files that have been committed to the database. With continuous replication, some of the log files may still be in motion to be applied to the replica database, so you cannot necessarily delete them all. To solve the problem, the replication service contacts the Store after it replays some logs to update the Store with its status. The Store therefore knows how up to date the replica is and can work out what log generation it needs to keep. When a full backup occurs, the Store can then accurately delete unneeded log files.

9.7.3 LCR restrictions

Once you get to know it, you will appreciate that LCR is reasonably simple and straightforward. However, LCR has some restrictions:

- The storage group that LCR supports can only include one database. After you enable LCR for a storage group, EMC will not allow you to create another database in that storage group because LCR does not support continuous replication for multiple databases.

- The single database in the storage group must be a mailbox store. LCR does not support public folder stores because public folders have their own replication mechanism.

- There is no GUI option available to make the replica database the active database after a failure. You have to do this by updating the database paths so that the Store picks up the replica database instead of the failed active database and then switch paths again after you fix the storage problem.

- You cannot deploy LCR on a cluster. CCR is available for these configurations, so you should deploy CCR when you want to take advantage of both continuous replication and clustering.

- You can use circular logging with both LCR and CCR.

- You can take a backup of the copy database, but you cannot use NTBACKUP for this purpose. Instead, you have to use a third-party backup solution that uses Volume ShadowCopy services to take a clone or snapshot copy of the database. If you need to, you can restore a backup taken in this manner to replace the active database, put it into the recovery storage group, or use database portability to move it to another server.

- LCR only copies mailbox data; it does not cater for other important data, such as the catalog data used by Exchange search. Replacing an active database with its replica after an outage will force Exchange to rebuild its search catalog. Depending on the size of the restored database, this process will take some time to complete and impose a performance penalty on the server while the rebuild is active. See Chapter 6 for more details about how content indexing works on an Exchange server.

As shown in Figure 9.9, you can enable circular logging for a storage group that uses either LCR or CCR. Circular logging works slightly differently because the replication service takes care of managing the logs instead of the Store. When the replication service copies a log, it deletes the log in the active location and then deletes it in the passive location after the replication service has replayed its contents into the passive database. It does not seem to make much sense to couple replication with log reuse and it is certainly not recommended for production environments. Instead, you should only do this for test systems where you want to use LCR or CCR without incurring the overhead of managing large numbers of transaction logs.

9.7.4   LCR database transition

LCR database transitions are not automatic. An administrator has to perform all of the steps required to switch the copy database to take the place of the active in case of problems. The sequence is as follows:

1.   If the active database has not been taken offline by whatever problem is causing you to perform the transition, you have to dismount it:

```
Dismount-database —id 'Important People'
```

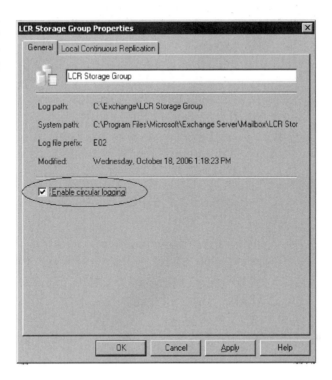

Figure 9.9
*Enabling circular
logging with LCR*

2.   Once you have dismounted the database, you can switch the loca-
      tions. This operation switches the database paths in the Exchange
      configuration data in Active Directory so that when Exchange
      accesses the database again, it will look for the files in the copy
      location.

```
Restore-StorageGroupCopy –id 'ExchMbxSvr1\VIP Data'
–ReplaceLocations
```

3.   To restore service to users, mount the database:

```
Mount-database –id 'Important People'
```

You are now back online and users should have full access to their mailboxes. LCR is now inactive for the database and the storage group is in the
same state as it would have been if you had never enabled LCR. You can
confirm this with the Get-StorageGroup command, which will report that

Exchange is no longer applying continuous replication for the storage group.

```
Get-StorageGroup —id 'VIP Data'
```

After the problem that caused the active database to go offline is fixed, you can now reseed the database to prepare to reactivate LCR. You can use the GUI option to enable LCR or you can do the following:

1.   Delete all files in the location that you want to reseed the database to.

2.   Prepare to reseed the database to the copy location with the `Enable-DatabaseCopy` command. This command does not copy the database. It merely updates the Exchange configuration data to prepare for the copy.

```
Enable-DatabaseCopy —id 'Important People' —CopyEdbFilePath
'C:\VIP Data\Important People.Edb'
```

3.   Reseed the database with the `Enable-StorageGroup` command. Note that the identifier passed is that of the storage group, not the database.

```
Enable-StorageGroup —id 'VIP Data'
```

Exchange performs a streaming copy of the database and enables replication immediately.

9.8   Deploying Cluster Continuous Replication (CCR)

LCR handles the situation when the disk that holds an Exchange database or transaction log fails. The next issue is when a complete server fails, and this is what Microsoft has designed CCR to protect against. CCR combines continuous log replication with Windows (MNS) clusters. In a CCR scenario, you create a replica database on the disks attached to another server in the same cluster and Exchange replicates the logs by copying them across the network to the disks on the other server to update the passive copy of the database. The disks can be direct attached (DAS) and do not need to be part of a SAN, as you might assume. However, while DAS offers a very cost-effective way to provide the necessary storage to host replicated data, placing critical data on your most fault-tolerant storage is obviously a good thing to do.

Conceptually, CCR uses the same replication pipeline and directory structure as LCR with one exception—CCR creates a content index catalog directory for the replica database. Of course, the big practical difference between LCR and CCR is that the passive node needs to copy the transaction logs from the active server before it can update its copy of the database. The separation between source and target server provides CCR with the extra degree of resilience to failure.

CCR uses a majority node set (MNS) cluster configuration with either two or three nodes, which uses a feature called the file share witness[7]. The file share witness lets you deploy a file share that is installed on a computer external to the cluster as an additional "vote" to determine the status of the cluster in a two-node MNS quorum cluster deployment. A single Windows server can provide the file share for multiple clusters and Microsoft recommends that the file share witness is installed on a hub transport server in the same Active Directory site as the cluster. The idea behind the file share witness is to provide extra resilience in the case of a failure in the cluster. With two-node MNS quorum clusters, the cluster is unable to handle the failure of one of the nodes because the majority of the cluster must be present to operate, which means that two "votes" have to be available. The file share witness provides the necessary second vote for a two-node cluster to continue operating if a server fails. Figure 9.10 illustrates Exchange 2007 running on typical MNS clusters as viewed through the Cluster Administrator utility. The cluster is named HPQBOX-ESCL1 and its two nodes are named HPQBOX-ESNODE1 and HPQBOX-ESNODE2. The Exchange virtual server is named HPQBOX-ES91 and it is currently active on node HPQBOX-ESNODE1. You can see the set of Exchange resources that are active on the node. Because mailbox servers are the only server role supported on Exchange 2007 clusters, the set of resources that run on a cluster is smaller when compared to Exchange 2003 clusters. You can see that no element of the transport service is present as all a mailbox server requires to run is the Mail Submission service to flag the presence of new messages to a hub transport server in the same Active Directory site.

You can associate the active resources shown by the Cluster Administrator to services that run on the computer. For example, the Information

---

7. See Microsoft Knowledge Base article 921181.

Figure 9.10
*Exchange 2007
running on an
MNS cluster*

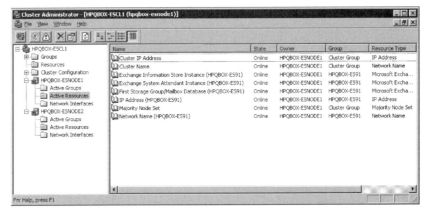

Store instance is obviously associated with the Information Store service because this is required to support the single storage group that runs on the cluster. The same is true of the mailbox database. The System Attendant instance can be associated with the System Attendant service.

Figure 9.11
*Microsoft Exchange
services running on
an MNS cluster*

A number of other services run that are not cluster resources. Figure 9.11 shows the Information Store and System Attendant running alongside the Mailbox Assistants, Mail Submission, Monitoring, Search, and Transport Log service. We can also see the Replication service, which is the critical component that underpins CCR because it is responsible for shipping and replaying the logs within the cluster nodes.

Running the `Get-ClusteredMailboxServerStatus` command on the active node generates this output:

```
Get-ClusteredMailboxServerStatus


Identity                     : HPQBOX-ES91
ClusteredMailboxServerName   : HPQBOX-ES91.hpqbox.adapps.hp.com
```

```
State                     : Online
OperationalMachines       : {HPQBOX-ESNODE1 <Active, Quorum Owner>, HPQBOX-
ESNODE2}
FailedResources           : {}
IsValid                   : True
ObjectState               : Unchanged
```

If any resources are causing problems for the cluster, you will see them listed in the FailedResources property. You can run the `Get-Clustered-MailboxServerStatus` command from another Exchange server to check the current status of a cluster. In this case, you need to pass the name of the cluster:

```
Get-ClusteredMailboxServerStatus —id Cluster1
```

If you want to scan the organization to discover what types of clustered servers are deployed, you can use the `Get-MailboxServer` command to look at the clustered storage type on the mailbox servers across the organization.

```
Get-MailboxServer

Name                      ClusteredStorageType
----                      --------------------
ExchMbxSvr1               Disabled
ExchMbxSvr2               Disabled
ExchMbxSvr3               NonShared
```

The values that you will see are:

- Disabled: Nonclustered mailbox server
- NonShared: Continuous Log Replication
- Shared: Traditional shared cluster

In the example shown above, we can see that the server ExchMbxSvr3 is a CCR cluster while the other servers are regular mailbox servers.

9.8.1 Comparing CCR and traditional clusters

A traditional Exchange cluster (SCC) operates multiple nodes that run Exchange around a core of shared storage. CCR clusters are very different for many reasons. Here are some of the major differences between the two implementations.

- Exchange 2007 runs two nodes in a CCR cluster. One is active and one is passive. Traditional clusters can have up to eight nodes deployed in an active-passive configuration.

- CCR clusters can use a range of disk technology from SAN to local disks to hold copies of the database and transaction logs. Traditional clusters use shared-disk resources to host the Exchange databases and transaction logs where only one server accesses the resource at one time.

- CCR clusters are relatively low-cost compared to traditional clusters because they can be created using relatively simple storage configurations and do not need to use the complex storage configurations that are qualified for deployment on traditional clusters on the Windows Catalog.[8]

- Because CCR clusters work using Exchange base technology, it may be easier to find third-party software that works on these servers. It is common to find that third-party software does not support traditional clusters because the vendors have not dedicated the time and financial resources to test their software for clustered environments. However, a cluster is a cluster and third-party software vendors have to test their software to ensure that it works properly for CCR. You cannot assume that software that works on a regular mailbox server will run on CCR.

- CCR clusters support storage groups that include one database. Storage groups on traditional clusters can support multiple databases.

- CCR clusters use the replication service to copy and replay logs on the passive server. As we have discussed, the Store consumes some I/O and CPU on the passive node to keep the database copy updated. The active node experiences a small and insignificant additional load to transfer the logs to the passive via an SMB share. Traditional clusters do not use Exchange-based replication.

---

8.   See http://www.microsoft.com/windows/catalog/server/default-v1.aspx.

- CCR clusters do not move disks between nodes during a failover because each node has its own disks and own copy of the database and logs. Traditional clusters failover by moving complete storage groups between cluster nodes. No disk I/O is required to move a storage group on a traditional cluster because the storage groups are located on shared storage that all the cluster nodes can access.

- The ability of CCR servers to recover from failures depends on the latency between the active and passive servers. On heavily loaded clusters that have high latency (> 20ms) between the nodes, you may see that Exchange cannot copy transaction logs quickly enough to keep the passive database in a situation where a failure will not cause data loss. Keeping the latency to 15ms or less is critical to the overall health of the cluster and this can sometimes be difficult to achieve in a stretched cluster. If Exchange cannot copy the logs to the passive server, it cannot replay the logs into the passive database, and if a failure occurs, the passive database may be 10 or 15 logs behind the active. Exchange may not be able to recover from such a wide divergence and you therefore experience data loss. SCC clusters do not experience this scenario because a failure forces the cluster to move a complete CMS to another node in the cluster, where the Store replays any outstanding data in the logs before it mounts the database.

- Both cluster types have some capability to perform automatic failovers. CCR handles the situation when the cluster detects that the active node is unavailable. SCC performs a failover when problems in the IP address or network name resource for the CMS fails. The time required for a transition to occur on either cluster type depends on how quickly it can move disk resources (within a traditional cluster) or how quickly the passive node in a CCR cluster can bring the database up to date by log copy and replay.

- CCR clusters allow you to backup the passive database copy and offload this processing from the active node. You cannot use NTBackup to take a copy of the passive database. Instead, you have to use a VSS-capable backup utility. When you take a backup on a traditional cluster, you always backup the live data and the node that supports the storage group that runs the backup takes the load generated by backup processing.

You cannot run a mixture of CCR and traditional cluster technology to build a mix-and-match cluster where continuous replication copies databases located on the shared-disk resources.

The deployment and operation of CCR clusters is much simpler than traditional Exchange clusters. However, it is unlikely that companies that have deployed traditional Exchange clusters in the past will rush out to replace them all with CCR clusters if only because of some of the differences listed above such as the two-node restriction for CCR clusters. Another issue is that the sophisticated storage technologies used in traditional clusters can prevent a higher degree of data loss in the event of failover than the simple asynchronous log shipped used by CCR. For example, if a disk fails in a traditional cluster, there is a high likelihood that all of the affected data can be retrieved from the cache. In a CCR environment, some data may be in a missing log. The use of the transport dumpster provides some mitigation against data loss, but it cannot recover every update to a database that may be in a missing transaction log.

The more likely scenario is that CCR will introduce mailbox clusters to a range of customers who have not deployed clusters in the past because of their undoubted complexity and cost. These customers can gain the additional resilience that CCR allows at a relatively low cost and with a low administrative overhead and that's an attractive proposition especially when the two cluster nodes can be placed in separate facilities to guard against physical disasters.

9.8.2   CCR in practice

Like LCR, CCR only supports storage groups that contain a single mailbox database, but like LCR, you can deploy up to 50 storage groups on a single CCR server. CCR uses the passive cluster node to pull the log files from the active node (recall that Exchange 2007 does not support active-active clusters, so one node in the cluster is always passive) and then replays the transactions in the log files to update the passive copy of the database. The same type of processing in terms of checksum validation occurs as with LCR. Exchange copies the log files using the SMB protocol and the data is unencrypted by default. The Replication service runs remotely but it needs access to the log files on the active node, so a share is created on the active node that is readable by any object in the "Exchange Servers" group. This group contains the machine accounts of all Exchange servers, so the Replication Service running on the passive node (under the LocalSystem account) is able to access the transaction logs.

Microsoft designed CCR to be a solution to server failure, even at extended distances. However, Windows 2003 requires the servers in an MNS cluster to be located on the same subnet and within the same Active Directory site, which limits the "stretch" aspect of cross-site failover. Along the same lines, Exchange 2007 is already pretty demanding in terms of network connectivity within a site because of its use of Exchange RPCs to transport messages between mailbox and hub transport servers. If you want to deploy an MNS cluster, some requirements exist in terms of network connectivity and latency that may limit the distance that you can place the two servers apart. It is possible that these limitations will disappear over time, but they are certainly a factor to consider for the Exchange 2007/Windows 2003 combination.

A CCR failover depends on the cluster service, which monitors the Exchange resources and decides whether a failover is required. For example, if the cluster service determines that the IP address or net name of the active node is no longer available, it will invoke a failover because these signs indicate that the active system has failed. On the other hand, an Exchange service failure does not necessarily mean that a physical problem exists on the active server, so the cluster service will attempt to restart the service if possible. Another example is a failure of an individual database. You may have 25 databases on an active server and the failure of one may not be a good reason to attempt to transition the other 24, especially if they are not experiencing any problems. Because of the additional overhead caused by CCR, you are recommended not to configure more than 30 databases (in 30 storage groups) on a CCR server.

The Exchange virtual server that runs on a CCR cluster expects identical logical drive letters for the system disk, the disk that holds the Exchange binaries, the disk that holds the message tracking logs, and the disks that hold the database and transaction logs on both nodes of the cluster. This is because the virtual server looks for these files in the same location after the cluster moves work from one node to the other during a failover.

Clusters are special environments for continuous replication. Because Exchange copies log files between the active and passive servers, the potential exists for a "lossy failover," which means that a failover has happened with incomplete data replicated to the passive node because some logs were being copied when the fail occurred. The passive copy of the database is therefore not completely up to date and cannot be updated because not all of the necessary transaction logs are available. Therefore, a lossy failover generates a condition called database divergence where data exists in one of the databases that is not in the other. Of course, other conditions such as a cluster "split-brain" operation can cause divergence as indeed can an administrative error (running ESEUTIL/R against one of the databases). CCR uses the file share witness to avoid the split-brain syndrome, which occurs when heartbeat signals fail within a cluster.

The Replication service is responsible for detecting when a data divergence condition exists between the production and copy log sets. The Replication Service checks for data divergence every time the Store creates a new transaction log to ensure that the two log sets stay synchronized. If the log sets differ, one database will differ from the other and you run the risk of data loss if you have to swap the copy database into production after an outage. Obviously, in production clusters that support very large databases, it would be too costly in terms of the processing required or the time necessary to complete the task to compare the complete content of the production and copy databases to detect where they might diverge. Instead, the Replication service compares the last log file for the copy with the last log file for the production. As we know, the header in every log file contains a generation number and creation time that allows Exchange to track the log file sequence accurately. Exchange can therefore take action to recover from the divergence by reference to the log files that are available in the production directory using a process called "Lost Log Resiliency" (LLR). First, Exchange compares the log files until it establishes the point where the log files in the production and copy directories match. Exchange performs this action by starting from the last log file and working backwards. Exchange knows a waypoint (the last log file required for recovery) as no modifications after this point have actually been written into the database. It also knows the last log file committed to the database. Using these points, Exchange can figure out what data is not committed into the recovery database and what log files are required to copy across and then replay to resynchronize the recovery database, which it then proceeds to do.

CCR processing also includes the recovery of messages in transit after a node failure. As soon as the passive node switches in to take over the work of a failed node, it checks to see whether data divergence exists between the database copies. If this is the case, CCR queries every Exchange hub transport server in the same Active Directory site for any messages that were in transit when the failure occurred using a feature called the "transport dumpster." The transport dumpster feature is only enabled for traffic going to mailboxes on CCR servers. We will discuss this point in some detail later on in this chapter. For now, it is enough to say that hub transport servers have the ability to resend messages that they hold in a queue of recently delivered mail to the CCR server, which then processes the messages and updates mailboxes with any that are not present in a mailbox. This step ensures that messages are recoverable in the case of geographically dispersed clusters, unless some messages were in transit through a hub transport server in the same physical site as the failed cluster node and that site is physically destroyed. Fortunately, this is not a situation that occurs frequently, and if it did, you will probably have other more important issues to deal with than a couple of missing messages.

Because log replication is going on, if you need to move databases or logs between disks on the server, you cannot use the normal "Move Database Path" option in EMC. Instead, you have to dismount the database, move the files manually, update the configuration data for the database in Active Directory, and then mount the database again. For example, let's assume that you want to move the transaction logs for a storage group to a new location. After you dismount the database, you then need to execute a `Move-StorageGroupPath` command. In this case, because you are going to move the files manually, you specify the `–ConfigurationOnly` command so that Exchange knows that you simply want to update Active Directory:

```
Move-StorageGroupPath -Identity 'ExchMbxSvr3\VIP Data'
-LogFolderPath 'G:\CCRDB\VIP Data' -ConfigurationOnly
```

9.8.3 CCR failovers

CCR failovers can take different forms. A scheduled outage is the easiest because you expect it to happen. For example, let's assume that you want to transfer the clustered mailbox server from one node to another so that you can apply some urgent hot fixes. You can do this through the EMC console or with the `Move-ClusteredMailboxServer` command as follows:

```
Move-ClusteredMailboxServer –id ExchMbxCluster –TargetMachine
ExchMbxNode2 –MoveComment 'Scheduled move from ExchMbxNode1
to ExchMbxNode2 to apply hot fixes'
```

This command moves the clustered resources to the ExchMbxNode2 system and writes a comment into the event log. The resources are transferred in a structured and orderly manner so that databases and transaction logs are closed off correctly. After a couple of moments, you should find that the services are all up and running on ExchMbxNode2. Users will automatically failover to connect to ExchMbxNode2. Similar types of transitions occur when the cluster service resource monitor detects that some resources are unavailable. For example, if the IP address or network name resource is unavailable, the resource monitor assumes that a machine has failed and the set of Exchange services will move from the passive to the active node. Figure 9.12 shows how to use the `Move-ClusteredMailbox-Server` command. You can see that we first check that the node that we want to move the cluster to is responding, we then verify that everything is OK with the cluster status, and then call `Move-ClusteredMailboxServer` to perform the transition.

Figure 9.12   *Performing a cluster transition with Move-ClusteredMailbox-Server*

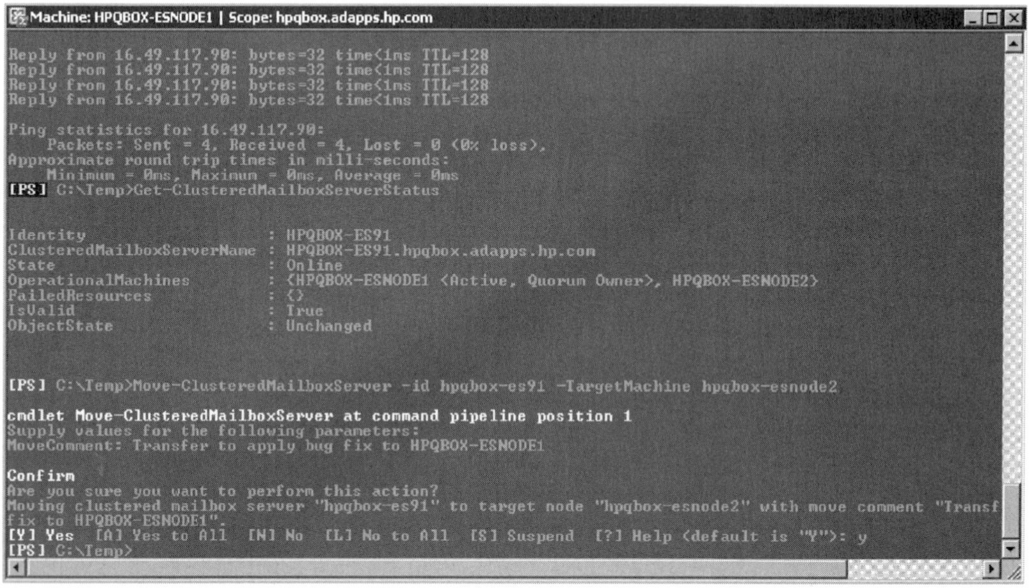

Figure 9.13 shows the event logged in the application event log when a transition is complete. As you can see, in this case the transition occurred very quickly, probably because the cluster was lightly loaded. In normal circumstances and given a reasonable load, the transition should take no more than a couple of minutes. If you are scheduling a transition, it's best to do this when clients will be least affected, such as lunchtime or after work hours. In any case, Outlook clients that work in cached Exchange mode will hardly notice the transition because Outlook will restore the connection automatically after the cluster comes back online. Outlook Web Access and other clients that work online will notice an interruption of their connection to the server, but once the cluster is online again they should be able to resume working as normal.

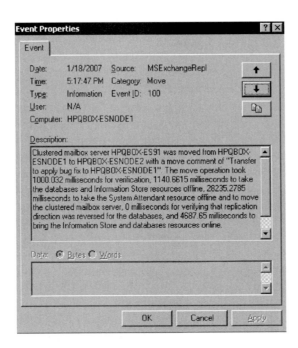

Figure 9.13
Event to report a CCR transition

Once the passive database takes over as the active database, transactions begin to flow and the replication engine begins to replay them into the copied database. In Figure 9.14, you can see the transaction logs have begun to start to build again from the time that the cluster transition occurred.

Figure 9.14
Transaction logs after a transition

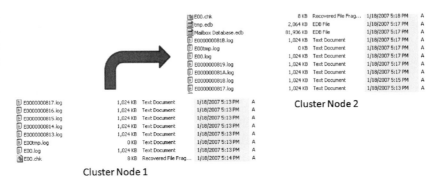

It is possible that some of the transaction logs on the active and passive node may have the same generation numbers. This situation occurs if CCR is unable to copy some transaction logs and apply to the passive database before it became active. When the failed node comes online again, it hosts the passive database and CCR will begin to copy log files from the active node to bring the passive database up to date. We now have a situation where data divergence may occur in the log generations. You can expect some divergence in a log replication scenario because the active database is always likely to be ahead of the passive database unless no transactions are occurring. However, a lossy situation is different because the divergence cannot be resolved when CCR copies and plays the transaction logs into the passive database. It is also important to point out that divergence can occur even if no clients are connected to the database because the Store could be performing background maintenance operations that cause database transactions. For example, the Store removes deleted items that have exceeded their retention period every night and each deletion results in a database transaction.

The replication service is responsible for detecting divergence conditions. Because databases can be very large, it is impracticable to compare the active and passive databases, so the Store has to calculate any divergence from the available log files. The replication service compares the last log file on the passive node with the equivalent on the active node. If the log files are the same, then operations can proceed because we have two synchronized log sets. If this is not the case, then we have to either reseed the complete database (this will always correct a divergence condition, but it can take a long time for large databases) or attempt to resolve matters using a technique called Lost Log Resilience (LLR).

There are circumstances where a cluster transition does not occur smoothly. If one of the Exchange services fails or times out, the resource service restarts it. If a database fails or if a disk used by a database suddenly becomes unavailable, the cluster will not force a failover because a single Exchange 2007 server can support up to 50 databases, and it does not make sense to close down all the other databases and move them to the passive node just because one database has failed. In this instance, it is up to the administrator to assess the seriousness of the underlying problem that caused the database outage and decide whether they should start a manual transition.

In all of the failover situations encountered so far, it is likely that the passive node has been able to come online and recover all the data from the previously active node. In other words, no data is lost. A catastrophic failure that causes the active node to be suddenly unavailable so that the passive node is not able to recover all data results in a lossy failover. For example, the replication service is unable to copy the current transaction log file from the active database to apply it to the replica database before it moves the replica database to become the active. Because the active node is unavailable, there is no possibility that Exchange can copy and apply any outstanding log files to the passive database before it resumes operations. A disk failure may cause a lossy failure to happen for LCR and a server outage can cause it to happen for CCR.

9.8.4 Lost Log Resilience

Lost Log Resilience (LLR) is a new database feature in Exchange 2007 that is used by LCR and CCR that is linked to the reduction in log file size that Microsoft has made in Exchange 2007 from 5MB to 1MB. The logic is that the smaller a log file, the less data it contains, and the easier it is to recover the data. However, while it is absolutely true that it is easier to ship around smaller log files and so be more resilient to disk failure, the way that Exchange logs transactions means that a 1MB missing log can be as important as a 5MB missing log if it contains information that is needed to commit a transaction. For example, if a user sends a message with a 6MB attachment, the transaction spans at least seven if not more transaction logs. This is because the Store interleaves all of the transactions for a storage group with each other inside the logs. A transaction log may start with transactions for many other messages before it gets to the start of the message with the 6MB attachment. The Store splits the rest of the large message and its attachment across as many more transaction logs as needed to write the entire message to disk. In most cases, a message with a 6MB attachment will spread across seven logs. Therefore, if you were to have the first six logs but not the seventh, the Store will have to roll back the entire transaction because it is incomplete.

With previous versions of Exchange, the implementation of write-ahead logging allows the Store to commit transactions to the database as soon as it has written their log records. LLR, which only runs in the Store process on the active node of a CCR server, holds transactions longer in memory to allow additional log generations to be created. Holding data longer in memory is the reason why it sometimes appears that Exchange 2007 is slower to write transaction logs to disk than Exchange 2003. The passive database is always up to date because the replication service applies transactions directly from the log and not from memory. LLR makes recovery slightly more complicated. All versions of Exchange use a database checkpoint (the minimum generation of log file required to replay transactions). LLR introduces the waypoint, or the maximum log required for recovery. Without this generation, you cannot recover, even if all the other log files are available. LLR also uses the committed log, specially created data that is not technically required to recover the database. If you lose these logs, you can still recover a database, but some data is lost.

When the replication service attempts to correct a divergence, it examines the available logs on the passive node to detect the point of divergence or the first log file where divergence occurs. The replication service starts with the highest log generation and works backwards until it finds a log file that is exactly the same log file on the active server. The next log above the matched log is the first diverged log file. It may be that the database does not need the diverged log file (see the note on the committed log above), so it can be discarded. However, if the first diverged log file is not available, you will have to reseed the database on the passive node to recover from the divergence.

The replication service now calculates how many log files might be required to correct matters. The replication service tracks the last log file that the Store generates and the Store writes this information into the cluster database in case the replication service is unavailable. You can see the last log generated by executing the `Get-StorageGroupCopyUpdate` command and noting the number shown in the LastLogGenerated property. The active database that failed now becomes the passive database. When the passive is available (not fully mounted but online), the replication service attempts to copy the outstanding log files to reduce the amount of data lost to as close to zero as possible. Exchange uses a setting called AutoDatabaseMountDial to determine how close to zero (in terms of unavailable logs—otherwise known as the copy queue length) it has to get before the Store can bring the database online. Essentially, the copy queue length is the number of logs that the passive node believes that it needs to replicate and replay before it is in a fully synchronized state. If the number of logs in the copy queue length is equal or less than the setting specified in the Auto-DatabaseMountDial property, Exchange will mount the passive database automatically. If the number of logs is higher, then a situation exists that requires manual administrator intervention as some data has potentially been lost during the transition. You use the `Set-MailboxServer` command to manipulate the AutoDatabaseMountDial property. There are three settings: Lossless (all logs are available, no data lost), Good Availability (up to three logs unavailable, some data is likely to be lost), and Best Availability (up to five logs unavailable, meaning that some data will be lost). Best Availability is the default for a storage group, so the Store can mount the passive database as long as fewer than six logs are lost. Exchange enables LLR for LCR servers and SCC clusters, but the depth is set to "1" (one) and you cannot change this value. Note that CCR servers generate transaction log files even when the server appears to be inactive. It is normal to see a log file created every two to three minutes even if no user is connected to the server. CCR creates these logs as the Store flushes dirty pages from the cache.

If you arrive at a situation where some logs are unavailable that you cannot recover from a backup or from disk, you will not be able to mount the database. In this situation, you can use a special mode for the ESEUTIL utility to force the Store to repair the database to a point where the Store can mount it again. To perform this recovery, you run ESEUTIL with the "/A" switch. For example, to force a recovery of the default storage group (with storage group prefix "E00") on a CCR server, you use this command:

```
ESEUTIL /R E00 /A
```

After ESEUTIL completes processing, you should be able to mount the database and continue operations.

If you insist, you can disable LLR on a CCR server. This should only be done if you need to troubleshoot an issue and preferably under the advice of Microsoft PSS. To disable LLR, create a new DWORD value called "Disable LLR" in the system registry at HKLM\System\CurrentControlSet\Services\MSExchangeIS\ParametersSystem. Set the value to "1" (one) to disable LLR and to "0" (zero) to enable LLR again.

9.8.5 The transport dumpster

After a lossy failover, you may lose some database transactions (moving messages to a new folder, marking them as read, deleting them, etc.) for a CCR server that the Store wrote into a lost transaction log. Exchange 2007 can recover some of the missing information in the form of inbound messages by replaying them from a cache on a hub transport server called the transport dumpster. The replication service knows the timestamp from the last log that it was able to copy, so it can request the hub transport server to resend any messages for users in the affected storage group that arrived after that time.

The transport dumpster is a new feature of Exchange 2007 that allows hub transport servers to retain a certain amount of messages in their queues in case Exchange needs to redeliver the messages in the future to compensate for lost transactions detected when a CCR server fails over from an active to a passive database. The feature only works for messages going to CCR servers and the transport server captures any message where at least one recipient has their mailbox on a CCR server. Even though messages in the dumpster queue exist for recipients on other types of mailbox servers,

Exchange cannot use the messages to recover data if failures occur on those servers. In the event of a lossy failure, the replay service on the CCR server can request the hub transport server to resubmit messages from the dump-ster queue for a specific date range in an attempt to bring mailboxes up to date. In this situation, you will see event 2099 logged to indicate that a request to resubmit messages has been made. The Store discards any resub-mitted messages that already exist in mailboxes.

It is obvious that the transport dumpster can only capture messages that pass through the transport service, so any other database updates that the Store records in transaction logs are not available to the transport dumpster and can therefore not be used for recovery. For example, if you are editing a new message, Outlook can store a copy automatically every five minutes (a user-configurable setting). Storing a draft copy generates a database update because the draft is stored in a folder in the Store and therefore results in a transaction that ends up in a log file, but as this transaction does not generate a message through the transport service, the transport dumpster does not capture the transaction. The same is true for appointments that you add to your calendar. However, the transport dumpster does capture meeting requests if you send them to recipients on a CCR server. Outgoing messages sent by clients on the CCR server may also be lost if they are still on the Submission queue and have not yet been accepted by a hub transport server.

The configuration settings for the transport dumpster are organization wide, so all hub transport servers behave the same way. You can view the settings with the `Get-TransportConfig` command:

```
Get-TransportConfig | Select *dumpster* | Format-List

MaxDumpsterSizePerStorageGroup : 18MB
MaxDumpsterTime                : 7.00:00:00
```

These settings are:

- MaxDumpsterSizePerStorageGroup: This is the maximum size of queued messages that the dumpster can hold for a single storage group. You cannot have a specific size for a selected storage group as all storage groups are treated the same. The default value is 18MB and Microsoft recommends that you should size this setting at three times the largest message that you expect to process. In other words, if you allow users to send messages of up to 10MB, you should set the dumpster to be 30MB. The more paranoid administrators will add another 20% on the basis that the extra space might be useful sometime. Exchange removes messages from the queue on a first-in, first-out basis.

■ MaxDumpsterTime: This is the maximum time that the transport service will retain a message on a dumpster queue, even if space exists in the queue. The default value is seven days with the logic for this value being that this allows Exchange to retain messages for long enough to allow administrators to recover a server from even a catastrophic hardware failure. Once the server is back online, Exchange can provide the messages from the dumpster to update mailboxes. However, the problem with this theory is that on a busy server, it is likely that messages will disappear from the dumpster long before they expire because Exchange will have to move them out of the dumpster to make room for new messages. The solution for this problem is to increase the size of the dumpster.

Use the `Set-TransportConfig` command to amend the dumpster settings. For example:

```
Set-TransportConfig —MaxDumpsterSizePerStorageGroup 50MB
```

The presence of the dumpster affects the disk space required by hub transport systems. For example, if you have four storage groups on CCR servers and set the dumpster size to be 100MB, then 400MB of space is required on the hub transport server that the CCR servers use to allow the dumpster to function. As you configure more storage groups on the CCR servers, you automatically increase the disk space requirement for the transport dumpster on the hub transport server. The same increase occurs for every hub transport server in the Active Directory site that hosts the CCR servers, so if you have 100MB allocated to the dumpster and you want to support five storage groups on two hub transport servers, the transport dumpster occupies an aggregate of 1GB. Another thing to take into account is that if you change the size of the dumpster cache through the Set-TransportConfig command, Exchange applies the change to every hub transport server within the organization. If you set either of the dumpster settings to zero, you will disable the dumpster.

9.8.6 Standby Continuous Replication

Exchange 2007 SP1 includes a variation on CCR in a new feature that Microsoft calls SCR, or Standby Continuous Replication. Where CCR uses two nodes in an MNS cluster, SCR uses two nodes in different datacenters. The idea is to allow Exchange to survive even a catastrophic datacenter outage by allowing a standby node in a different datacenter to take on the load of the active node if an outage stops the active node working.

SCR depends on the same basic principle as CCR in that the standby node has to copy (or pull) transaction logs from the active node on an asynchronous basis and apply them to its copy of the database. Like CCR, you have to ensure that a reliable link exists between the two servers to allow the passive node to copy logs in a timely manner. If the network between the two servers suffers from high latency or low throughput, then the passive node may not be able to copy logs quickly enough to ensure that it can replay sufficient logs to stay within the lost log resilience threshold in the event of a failover. Again like CCR, the transport dumpster plays a role in providing a cache of messages that Exchange can replay to bring mailboxes up to date after a failure.

Clearly, it is far too early to be able to make a reasoned assessment of how well SCR will function in production environments and the necessary hardware and network prerequisites that you will have to put in place to use SCR successfully. What we can say now is that SCR is another deployment option for administrators to consider to attain maximum resilience for your Exchange servers.

9.9 Continuous Log Replication: Good or bad?

Even with the relatively minor set of restrictions, both LCR and CCR are welcome additions to Exchange that provide new ways to protect mailbox databases by providing an extra layer of resilience to disk failure. LCR does nothing to handle the issues posed by server failures, but even so, it is a feature that anyone who is running a small to medium Exchange 2007 server should consider to help protect their mailbox database. The only other practical option for small to medium deployments is to run a multi-role Exchange server (for example, in a branch office), in which case you cannot use any form of continuous replication.

Unless you already run an Exchange 2003–based stretch cluster and want to replace the third-party technology that makes the cluster work with out-of-the-box Microsoft code, the case for continuous replication is harder to make for larger and more complex servers where better management and automation practices are required to deal with larger databases. It is also the case that continuous replication is a relatively new technology for both Exchange and administrators. We do not know how it will react in the chaos and confusion that surrounds any database failure. Best practice is still evolving in terms of how to manage continuous replication effectively, whether on a single server or in an MNS cluster. We do not know where the edge of the performance envelope lies for LCR—what the real performance impact in terms of CPU and memory use on production systems and at what point continuous replication runs out of steam in terms of the number of mailboxes that it can support on a single server. Until the technology is better proven, traditional shared copy clusters may be a better bet for those who want the most resilient Exchange configuration, and indeed, a strong case can be made for blade servers that are grouped around a SAN, especially when coupled with good server provisioning and data recovery procedures.

Whatever you may think of LCR and CCR, there is no doubt that they mark an important and fundamental evolution for the Exchange Store and that Microsoft will evolve this technology over time to improve automation and manageability and to remove the inevitable kinks that creep into a first release.

9.10 Virtual Exchange

Virtualization is a relatively new deployment option for Exchange. Hardware virtualization lets you run multiple virtual operating systems and application instances (the guests) concurrently on a single physical computer (the host). When Exchange 2003 appeared, Microsoft would not support any installation of Exchange on a virtual server. You could certainly install Exchange 2003 on a virtualization platform such as VMware ESX, but Microsoft would not support any problems that you encountered, so the only way that you could get support was to reproduce the problem on a "normal" Exchange server. Flipping back and forth between standard and virtual servers to solve problems was not a good approach for running a production email service, so virtualization remained in the back room and was used mainly for testing new versions of software and patches.

Microsoft's stance was understandable because the test matrix that they have to go through to test new versions of Exchange, service packs, and patches becomes a lot more complex when you have to test on both standard and virtual servers. Microsoft never had the inclination to take on the extra testing load until they bought in their own hardware virtualization product (Microsoft Virtual Server). Suddenly you had the situation where Microsoft did not support the deployment of their own applications on their own virtualization platform, and after some hard thinking in Redmond, Washington, Microsoft released a new support policy for Exchange in November 2005 (described in Microsoft Knowledge Base article 320220). You could now run supported virtual Exchange 2003 servers as long as the host operating system was Microsoft Virtual Server 2005 running on Windows 2003 R2. Other restrictions apply, such as no support for clusters and the requirement to use the Microsoft PCI Controller SCSI driver. Microsoft continued to impose the original support policy for non-Microsoft virtualization platforms (in effect, VMware) as per Knowledge Base article 897615.

In some respects, the change in support policy was a lot of fuss and bother about nothing. Few companies moved to deploy Exchange 2003 mailbox servers on virtual servers for two reasons. First, VMware is the market leader and the Microsoft Virtual Server product was not a compelling platform to deploy on. Second, the I/O limitations of some versions of virtual server software made it difficult to support the I/O demands of mailbox servers. This issue has been addressed in VMware ESX 3.0, which allows virtual machines to have direct access to storage and so speeds up I/O performance to an acceptable level.

Some companies have deployed SMTP servers, front-end Exchange 2003 servers (anything that only held transient data), and other parts of their Windows infrastructure, such as domain controllers and DHCP servers on virtual servers, but not a lot else happened in production. Resilience to failure was another issue—after all, if a hardware failure brings down a single server that supports four virtual servers, you affect many users. Behind the scenes, companies use many virtual servers for testing because virtualization allows you to replicate large parts of the production infrastructure on a few large physical servers.

When Microsoft released Exchange 2007, they could not support its deployment on a virtual platform for production environments because Microsoft Virtual Server does not support 64-bit guest systems (VMware does, but then you get into the support argument again). Microsoft plans to support Exchange 2007 64-bit virtual guest servers running under the Hypervisor technology on the Longhorn platform, so you will have to wait until this combination of software is available before you can consider deployment of 64-bit virtual Exchange 2007 servers. In the meantime, you can continue to use the 32-bit version of Exchange 2007 to test Exchange 2007 on Microsoft Virtual Server 2005 (or VMware).

Cost is the most compelling argument for virtualization. There is something compelling about the potential of maximizing the investment in hardware by deploying multiple virtual servers on a single large physical computer instead of using multiple physical servers. The claim is that virtual servers allow you to deploy servers faster and allocate resources dynamically. Most modern dual-processor computers equipped with 1GB or more of memory are quite capable of handling the load of thousands of concurrently connected clients and still be only 30–40% utilized. In an Exchange 2003 environment, few companies put more than 4,000 mailboxes on a single server because of the I/O load and the difficulty of meeting restore SLAs in a timely manner after a database outage. The I/O characteristics of Exchange 2007 are very different and it has new capabilities (such as continuous log replication) that you can deploy to minimize database downtime, so virtualization is more interesting, especially on the 64-bit hardware platform. However, it will still take time and a lot of testing to determine exactly where the sweet spot is for Exchange 2007 on virtual servers and for Microsoft to evolve its support policies to cope with non-Microsoft platforms.

Convenience is another factor that administrators often cite to support the use of virtualization. You can build a new virtualized server from a template in a matter of minutes—certainly far faster than it is possible to create a new physical server.

There is no doubt that virtual Exchange servers will become far more common in the next few years. Virtualization is a technology that exploits the raw power of hardware and allows companies to extract more value from their investment in server technology than they can get by deploying physical servers. On this own, this factor is enough to move virtualization onto any CIO's agenda.

10

More useful things to Know about Exchange

One of the essential truths about living in the Internet world is that while information may be at our fingertips, too much information exists for any one human to make sense of it all. The information relating to Exchange is clearly a very small part of the overall knowledge pool, but it is advantageous for an administrator to know where to find help to get their job done. This chapter covers some of the places where you can go to get help and some of the tools that do not come with the Exchange kit that make Exchange easier to work with. It is by no means an exhaustive list as new items appear all the time. Think of it as a "tried and trusted" list that is worthy of your investigation.

10.1 Automated analysis

Exchange is a complex product that requires administrators to have substantial knowledge of the environment that a server operates within—network connections, Windows configuration, third-party products, the Exchange organization, and operational procedures all influence how efficiently and effectively a server operates. It is genuinely difficult, even for the most experienced Exchange administrator, to keep up to date with every technical development that affects Exchange, including updates to Microsoft's knowledge base, new patches, independent commentary, and other sources of data. The result is that there is a huge difference in how administrators manage servers and management disciplines range from the very good to the very bad.

Administrators are not solely to blame for this somewhat confused state of affairs. Microsoft owns much of the responsibility as it would seem appropriate for them to incorporate automated management in Exchange to drive down the cost of owning and operating the software. I have frequently been critical of Microsoft in the way that they develop administration utilities for products like Exchange where it seems that developers like to complete features that users see. However, when it comes to building management utilities, less eagerness seems to exist within the development team to ensure that all of the features work as expected. Exchange is no better or no worse in this respect, but it is disappointing that the management utilities and capabilities did not improve in Exchange 2000 or Exchange 2003. Fortunately, we have seen a change since late 2004 as Microsoft began to improve the wizards included in Exchange to perform common management tasks and the release of the first versions of utilities such as the Exchange Best Practice Analyzer (ExBPA) and the Exchange Performance Troubleshooting Analyzer (ExPTA). These steps are important because automation builds on best practice and stops administrators making mistakes. Any manual procedure is more prone to mistake than an automated equivalent, so seeing more wizard-like procedures in the product and the analyzers is a great step forward.

Since 2004, Microsoft has generated additional troubleshooting tools in the Exchange Disaster Recovery Analyzer (ExDRA), which takes care of the steps required to make a database consistent again after a recovery operation, and the Exchange Mailflow Troubleshooter (ExMFA), which looks at all of the issues that may cause email to stop flowing or just slow down. The array of three letter acronyms confused customers, so Microsoft took the logical step of combining the three problem solving tools (ExDRA, ExMFA, and ExPTA) into one, the Exchange Troubleshooting Assistant, or ExTRA. No further comment is required about the introduction of yet another acronym, but at least it's only one instead of three. Exchange 2007 provided another set forward by integrating these tools directly into EMC under the Toolbox node so that they are part of the supported product and available to every Exchange 2007 installation.

ExBPA and ExTRA are both based on a simple concept – that you can encapsulate knowledge in a set of rules and use that knowledge to analyze a target environment and produce some conclusions by comparing the information gathered from the target against the rules. Microsoft builds the rules from knowledge gathered from sources such as their problem database, observations of how systems run in production, the insight of the engineers who develop Exchange, and customer feedback. As such, it is reasonable to refer to the rules used by ExBPA and ExPTA as "best practice," although you also have to remind yourself that best practice changes over time and that personal experience and analysis of an Exchange deployment by a human expert is usually more insightful than the output of an automated utility. In fact, the reports and data generated by these utilities are sometimes of more value than the recommendations that the utilities generate. You can provide the reports to a human expert for their analysis or use them as the basis for tracking the overall evolution of your messaging system over time—and perhaps to identify likely problems in the future if you do not take action, such as upgrading hardware.

Running ExBPA on an Exchange 2007 server is very simple. Invoke the Best Practice Analyzer option from the Toolbox. The program starts and checks for any updates that are available on Microsoft's web site. You then select the servers that you want to scan (Figure 10.1) and start processing. You can include legacy Exchange servers in the scan. ExBPA contacts the servers and fetches information from performance counters, WMI, the system registry, and other sources to build up a picture that it then compares against its database of best practice before generating an output report.

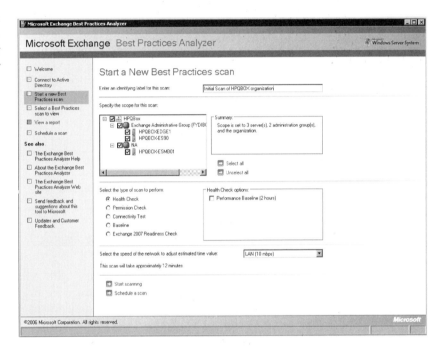

Figure 10.1
Exchange Best Practice Analyzer

After the scan is complete, ExBPA generates a set of observations and recommendations that you can view on screen or export to HTML, CSV, or XML format. Figure 10.2 shows the HTML output from an "All Issues" report taken from a small Exchange 2007 organization. You can see that ExBPA reports that it couldn't contact an Exchange server. In this case, the missing server is an Edge server that exists outside the forest that the Exchange organization belongs to, so it's quite logical that ExBPA can't access it. You can also see that ExBPA is capable of detecting problems with drivers, if its database has been tweaked to check for a particular situation.

You can find the XML-format output files from ExBPA and ExTRA in the Documents and Settings\UserName\Application Data\Microsoft\ExBPA and \ExTRA folders.

Microsoft continues to update the knowledge base that the rules in these utilities use to decide on their recommendations and it is fair to say that the output has improved greatly since the first versions. Because the information

Figure 10.2
*HTML output
from ExBPA*

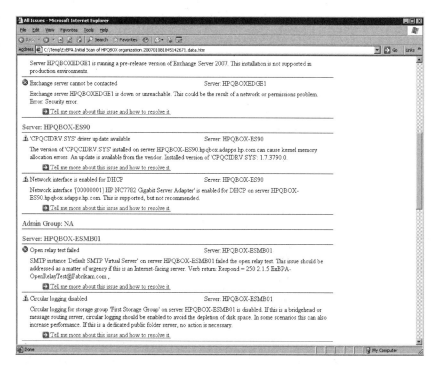

is updated, it is worthwhile to check back with Microsoft to download updates for ExBPA in particular and then scan your organization to see if the updated information reveals any lurking problems that you need to address. The readiness check feature that reviews an existing Exchange 2000/2003 organization to check for any problems that have to be addressed before you can migrate to Exchange 2007 is especially welcome for any administrator who is preparing for an Exchange 2007 deployment.

It is fair to say that an automated utility is more systematic and faster in its analysis than a human will be, so the ideal combination is to use the automated utilities to analyze and then apply human intelligence to interpret the output. In other words, never accept the output of an automated utility as the absolute truth as it is likely that anything but a relatively simple target environment has some quirk that the rule set cannot accommodate.

10.1.1 SSCP

Another interesting attempt to automate planning for the Exchange environment is Microsoft's System Center Capacity Planner (SSCP), which is only available through MSDN or a TechNet subscription. At the time of writing, SSCP does not cater for Exchange 2007, but Microsoft is working on an update.

SSCP is unlike ExBPA or ExTRA because it is a modelling tool that is designed to help figure out what a new Exchange organization might look like rather than a program that extracts and analyzes information from your current operating environment. In some respects, SSCP is an evolution from other Microsoft-provided tools such as LoadSim (now replaced with the Exchange Load Generator tool for Exchange 2007) and JetStress that selectively test the performance and capacity of different server configurations to provide data that you can interpret to help plan production servers. These utilities remain valuable tools because they generate data from real performance tests, but the results that you get from these utilities is often difficult to use outside the context of a single server, and that's what SSCP aims to address.

The basic concept behind SSCP is that you provide details of the kind of Exchange organization that you want to build in terms of the expected user load, server configurations, locations, client types, and network links. This data is gathered by SSCP into a model that it then analyzes and simulates how the model should work in production. Generating anything that is remotely accurate in terms of how a model can simulate how a configuration works in real life is terrifically complex and probably too much to expect in the first or even the first three releases of a modelling utility, and that's the case with SSCP. SSCP is capable of delivering acceptable results for reasonably simple and straightforward Exchange organizations, but any experienced Exchange administrator can probably get the same results from a pencil and paper exercise. SSCP runs out of steam with large, complex, distributed messaging infrastructures because it cannot deal with the subtleties and ambiguities that often are the trademarks of these deployments. Microsoft will improve SSCP over time and it will be interesting to see how they take this tool forward in the future.

10.1.2   Microsoft's Release to Web (RTW) strategy

Release to Web, or RTW, is the route used by the Exchange development group to make new utility programs available without including them into the base product. The advantages of making programs available like this are that the programs can follow a faster release cycle and can be updated more often, they are not tied to a specific version of Exchange, and they do not have to go through as much engineering overhead before Microsoft can release them to users. In addition, Microsoft can respond faster to feature requests from customers and test new ideas for features before formally incorporating them into a future version of Exchange. For more information about RTW programs, visit the Microsoft Exchange web site at http://www.microsoft.com/exchange.

The storage calculator for mailbox servers (Figure 10.3) is a good example of the kind of useful tool that Microsoft releases via the Web. The calculator is an Excel worksheet that you can download from the Exchange team's blog (the original note was posted on January 15, 2007). The worksheet encapsulates the guidelines that the Exchange team has given administrators around storage (database sizing, I/O requirements, and LUN layout) for Exchange 2007 and allows you to plug in your own numbers to see what kind of sizing information results. Like any utility, the output is only as good as the calculations can generate, and the calculations are limited by the input that you provide plus the knowledge and experience of the authors. However, the authors have no knowledge of your installation and business conditions, so be prepared to do some work to refine the input so that it is as accurate as possible and to put the results into context so that they make sense for your installation.

Figure 10.3

Exchange 2007 Storage calculator

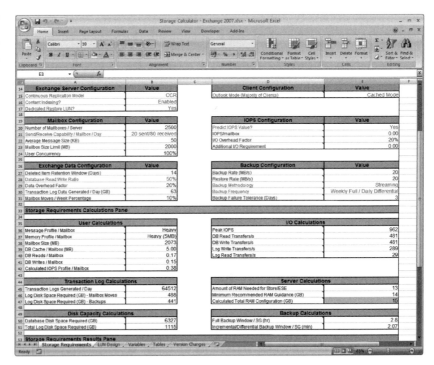

You do not have to depend on Microsoft for help with hardware recommendations as the hardware vendors will provide their own views on the subject and may also provide you with some tools to help size an Exchange deployment. For example, HP offers a storage and server sizing tool that incorporates the performance characteristics of HP storage and server solutions, including SANs and blade servers, which will often generate a more specific recommendation in terms of suggested configuration. See www.hp.com/

ActiveAnswers <http://www.hp.com/ActiveAnswers>   for more information about HP sizing utilities.

10.2   The Exchange Toolbox

The Toolbox (Figure 10.4) is the bottom node in EMC and serves as a container for a set of utilities that deliver lots of value for Exchange administrators. Some of these utilities (such as ExBPA and ExTRA) are available from Microsoft in standalone versions so that you can run them against Exchange 2003 servers, and some of the options presented are simply signposts to utilities that already exist on the server.

Figure 10.4
The Exchange Toolbox

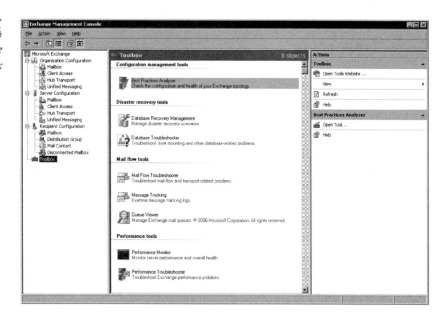

The contents of the Toolbox are:

- Exchange Best Practice Analyzer: A utility to analyze one or more Exchange servers and reports its findings compared against a database of best practice built and maintained by Microsoft. See page 1 for more details.

- Database Recovery Management: These tools assist administrators to recover from database problems.

- Database Troubleshooter: This option scans the Windows application event log for evidence of problems that might affect Exchange databases.

- Mail Flow Troubleshooter.

- Message Tracking: Tools to track the path of a message through the Exchange 2007 organization to the point where it goes to a legacy Exchange server or leaves the organization via an external gateway. See page 944 for details about how to interrogate the message tracking logs using the GUI and shell commands.

- Message Queue Viewer: A viewer that shows details of the messages that are on the transport queues of a hub transport server. Details of how to use the Queue Viewer are available in Chapter 6..

- Performance Monitor: A short-cut to start off the standard Performance Monitor utility preconfigured with the most important performance counters that are necessary to monitor the good health of an Exchange 2007 server.

- Performance Troubleshooter: This option uses tools such as the Exchange User Monitor utility (ExMon) to collect and report performance information from a server depending on the symptoms reported by the administrator.

Most of the utilities are accessed through a framework called the Microsoft Exchange Troubleshooting Assistant to deliver a consistent look and feel for troubleshooting operations. Configuration data that describes the Exchange organization is fundamental to many of the options, so be prepared to provide the names of both an Exchange server to work with and a Global Catalog server to fetch data from the Active Directory.

10.2.1   Updates

Every time you start the Troubleshooting Assistant, it attempts to contact the web downloads site for Microsoft Exchange to determine whether updated configuration or other information is available, such as a refresh of the best practice data used by ExBPA.

Figure 10.5
Fetching updates from Microsoft

The check only takes a minute or so and ensures that you run the troubleshooting assistant with the latest available information. You can cancel the check at any time and proceed. If the Assistant finds an update, it downloads the new data as shown in Figure 10.5 and then continues. Because the Troubleshooting Assistant uses language-specific information, separate updates are downloaded for each language that you use. You can find the XML-format configuration files that drive the Troubleshooting Assistant in the appropriate directory under \Exchange Server\bin as shown in Figure 10.6.

Figure 10.6
English language versions of the Troubleshooting Assistant files

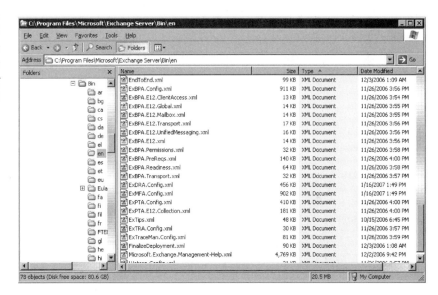

10.2.2 Database Recovery Management

The Database Recovery Management tool is designed to perform many different tasks that help administrators maintain Exchange databases and their associated files. The first set of options focus on the currently active databases:

- Analyze database and transaction log files to determine why databases cannot be mounted successfully.

- Verify database files after a restore to ensure that all files required are now available.

- Analyze the available disk space for transaction log files to report on current usage and to determine whether it is likely that a server will exhaust disk space for logs in the future (Figure 10.7).

- Reset transaction log generation number if a storage group runs out of transaction log file names (unlikely on most servers, possible on very heavily used servers that create more than two billion log files).

- Repair a database to remove problems that may cause the Store to be unable to mount a database. This option is functionally equivalent to fixing a database with the ESEUTIL and ISINTEG utilities as described in Chapter 5. You can only repair a dismounted database and the database must be dismounted before you begin the procedure as the Troubleshooting Assistant reads the current database status from the Active Directory when it starts and does not refresh this information afterwards. You have to mount the fixed database after a successful repair and you have to take a full backup after the database is mounted to ensure that the fixed data is secured in a backup.

- Review database-related event logs to make it easier for administrators to isolate events that have been logged that might indicate future database problems (Figure 10.8).

Figure 10.7
Checking for adequate disk space for transaction logs

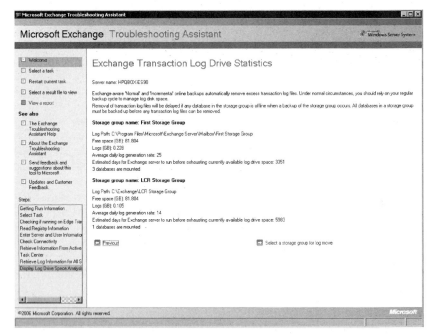

All of these operations can easily be done by administrators themselves without recourse to a Troubleshooting Assistant. The value of what Microsoft has done is to create an approachable wizardlike utility that guides inexperienced administrators through the steps necessary to get work done while at

Figure 10.8
*Checking database-
related event log
entries*

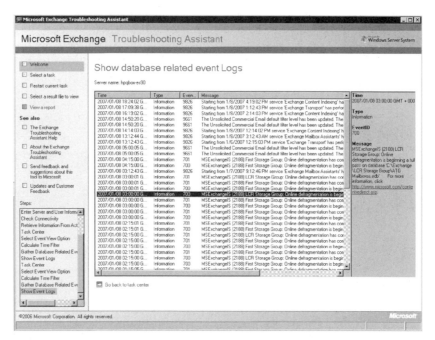

Figure 10.8
*Checking database-
related event log
entries*

the same time providing experienced administrators with enough value in the options for them to want to use the utility.

The second set of choices presented by the Database Recovery Management option cover the Recovery Storage Group (RSG). The RSG was introduced in Exchange 2003 to allow administrators to mount backup copies of databases into a special storage group. The idea is that you can restore service to users very quickly by swapping in new (blank) mailboxes so that they can receive and send new messages while you work on restoring the failed database behind the scenes. This is often called a dial-tone recovery operation because you concentrate on restoring the basic service. Later on, when you have restored the failed database into the RSG, you can merge the information from the recovered database into the online copies of user mailboxes to build up a complete copy of the mailboxes. The options available here are:

- Create the Recovery Storage Group. A server can support only one RSG.

- Mount or dismount mailbox databases in the Recovery Storage Group. Only the Exchange management utilities can access the contents of these databases (using MAPI RPCs) through either EMC or shell commands. You can mount multiple databases in the RSG as long as the databases belong to the same storage group (because they share the same set of transaction logs). Database portability allows you to mount a database on another server anywhere in the organization. However, you cannot take a database from one organization and mount it in the RSG of a server in another organization.

■ Remove the Recovery Storage Group.

■ Merge or copy mailbox content from the databases in the Recovery Storage Group into the online copies of user mailboxes. Note that you cannot access public folder data through the RSG. This is because public folder data supports its own replication mechanism to provide redundancy against failure.

■ Set the necessary flag on the database so that the files can be overwritten by a recovery operation.

The last four options are only available after you create the RSG. After you create the RSG, you can restore mailbox database and the associated transaction logs into the folders created for the RSG using your normal backup/restore utility. The next step is to extract information from the recovered database. Figure 10.9 shows how to define the merge options for the RSG to move content from the recovered database into online mailboxes.

Figure 10.9
Selecting merge operations for the RSG

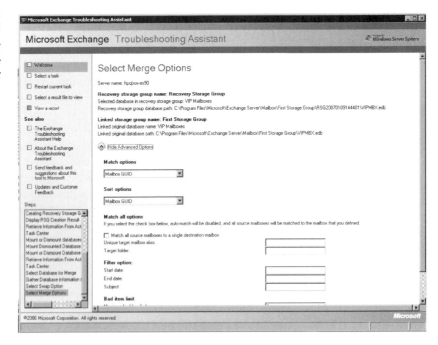

Working with the RSG is not simple and caused many problems after Microsoft first introduced the feature in Exchange 2003, so much so that the feature was overhauled completely for Exchange 2003 SP1. Putting the complexity of something like a database swap and merge into the comfort zone extended by a wizardlike step-by-step operation is a great example of how automation through a good GUI can prevent administrators making mistakes. However, working with RSGs is still not a simple matter and this option deserves some solid testing and documentation (in your own environment) so that you know exactly what to do if you ever have to use the RSG.

While the easiest and safest (because the GUI stops you making errors) way to work with the RSG is through the GUI, you can perform all of the RSG operations through shell commands. For example, the command to create the RSG is similar to the command that you use to create a regular storage group, with the exception that you specify the –Recovery parameter:

```
New-StorageGroup —Server ExchMbxSvr1 —LogFolderPath
'D:\Exchange\RSG\Logs' —Name 'Recovery Storage Group'
—SystemFolderPath 'D:\Exchange\RSG' —Recovery
```

If you now use the Get-StorageGroup command to examine the properties of the RSG, you will see that both the Recovery and the Recovery-Enabled properties are set to $True. The next step is to create a dummy mailbox database in the RSG. We are going to overwrite the database with a restore later on, so we first create the database and then set its properties to allow the restore operation to overwrite the files.

```
New-MailboxDatabase—MailboxDatabaseToRecover 'VIP Mailboxes'
—StorageGroup 'Recovery Storage Group' —EDBFilePath 'D:\
Exchange\RSG\VIP Mailboxes.edb'
Set-MailboxDatabase -Id 'ExchMbxSvr1\Recovery Storage Group\
VIP Mailboxes' -AllowFileRestore $true
```

You now proceed to restore the mailbox database and its transaction logs to the locations that you have created for the RSG. The restore operation overwrites the dummy mailbox database that you created. Once the restore is complete, you can mount the restored database in the RSG.

```
Mount-Database —Id 'ExchMbxSvr1\Recovery Storage Group\VIP
Mailboxes'
```

After the database mounts, you can perform whatever operations you require. For example, to check the mailboxes that exist in the database:

```
Get-MailboxStatistics —Database 'ExchMbxSvr1\Recovery Storage
Group\VIP Mailboxes'
```

The most interesting command is `Restore-Mailbox`, which allows you to extract information from the database mounted in the RSG and merge it into a dial-tone database that you created to replace the failed database and restore dial-tone service to users. For example, this command scans the database in the RSG to look for any information for user "Redmond" and merges it into the user's current mailbox.

```
Restore-Mailbox —Id 'Redmond'-RSGDatabase 'ExchMbxSvr1\
Recovery Storage Group\VIP Mailboxes'
```

Naturally, you can select all of the mailboxes from a database in the RSG and tell Exchange to restore them in one operation:

```
Get-Mailbox —database 'ExchMbxSvr1\Recovery Storage Group\VIP
Mailboxes' | Restore-Mailbox
```

After you have restored whatever data is required, you can clean up by dismounting the databases from the RSG, deleting the database, and then deleting the RSG. You can then remove all of the files from the RSG location.

```
Dismount-Database —id 'ExchMbxSvr1\Recovery Storage Group\VIP
Mailboxes'
Remove-MailboxDatabase —id 'ExchMbxSvr1\Recovery Storage
Group\VIP Mailboxes'
Remove-StorageGroup —id 'ExchMbxSvr1\Recovery Storage Group'
```

10.2.3   Database Troubleshooter

The Database Troubleshooter tool is designed to locate problems that cause the following problems for Exchange databases:

- Databases will not mount.
- Log files are inconsistent.
- The transaction log file generation code has exceeded the range of available numbers to create new log files.
- Disk space is unavailable.

The Database Troubleshooter works by scanning the application event log for any entries that relate to the Exchange Store and then analyzing the results that it retrieves. You give the troubleshooter a time range to scan (the default is 120 minutes; setting a value of 0 (zero) means scan all available events) and if it returns with no events found, you know that you've got a clean server. If not, you should use the options available through Database Recovery Management to take the necessary corrective action.

10.2.4 Mail Flow Troubleshooter

Microsoft designed the Mail Flow Troubleshooter to detect and report common problems that interfere with the flow of messages across an Exchange organization and some aspects of communicating with external systems. Common problems include:

■ Messages accumulate in delivery queues because DNS settings (for smart hosts or external gateways) are incorrect.

■ Messages accumulate in Exchange's categorizer queue because Exchange can't resolve the addresses against the Active Directory or system load is causing difficulties in resolving large distribution groups (or dynamic distribution groups).

■ Messages cannot be received from the Internet or through another gateway.

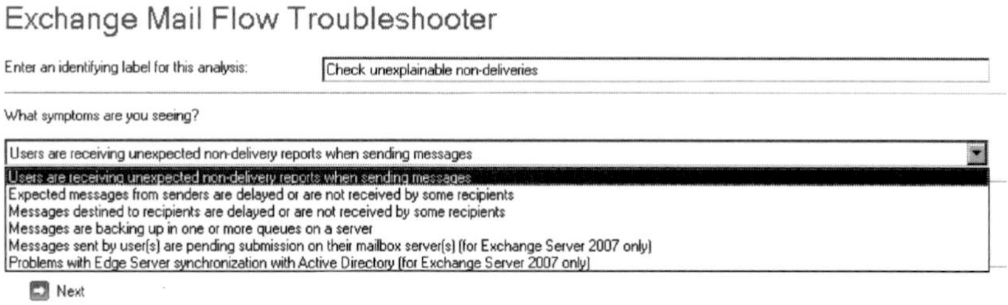

Figure 10.10
Symptoms that the Mail Flow Troubleshooter can check for

Exchange Mail Flow Troubleshooter

Enter an identifying label for this analysis: Check unexplainable non-deliveries

What symptoms are you seeing?

Users are receiving unexpected non-delivery reports when sending messages

Users are receiving unexpected non-delivery reports when sending messages
Expected messages from senders are delayed or are not received by some recipients
Messages destined to recipients are delayed or are not received by some recipients
Messages are backing up in one or more queues on a server
Messages sent by user(s) are pending submission on their mailbox server(s) (for Exchange Server 2007 only)
Problems with Edge Server synchronization with Active Directory (for Exchange Server 2007 only)

➦ Next

To begin, you select the kind of symptom that you are experiencing that causes you to believe that you have a mail flow problem. Figure 10.10 shows the dropdown list that you select a symptom from.

These symptoms include:

■ Users receive unexpected nondelivery reports when they send messages: Selecting this symptom will prompt the troubleshooter to ask you to provide the DSN code contained in the nondelivery reports.

- Expected messages from senders are delayed or are not received by recipients: This might be the symptom if you realize that mail flow from the Internet or another gateway has ceased or is much lower than usual. There are many reasons why this symptom might occur, including network outages and errors in SMTP configuration.

- Messages are delayed or not received by their recipients: This is the opposite symptom to the last and indicates a problem with outgoing mail flow. Perhaps you can't send messages to the Internet or maybe it's only the messages sent to a specific domain that have a problem.

- Messages are backing up in one or more queues on a server. As we'll see in a little while, many reasons including bad configurations can cause queues to build, so the troubleshooter has a range of tests that it applies to attempt to determine the root cause including the availability of the Active Directory (to resolve recipients), connectivity to remote hosts over port 25, DNS, and so on.

As an example of the Mail Flow Troubleshooter in action, when we discussed viewing transport queues in Chapter 7, we looked at how to use the Get-Queue command to help diagnose a problem with a smart host server that caused a queue of messages to accumulate. Figure 10.11 shows what the the Mail Flow Troubleshooter indicates in the same situation when it is told to check why the queue has accumulated. To discover this fault, the troubleshooter has checked DNS and discovered that no MX record exists for the smart host server that our SMTP connector points to, but it's also performed a number of other tests to get to this point and determine the likely root cause of our problem.

Figure 10.11
A potential problem is found

Once it is finished, the Mail Flow Troubleshooter presents its assessment in a summary screen (Figure 10.12). It is true that the Mail Flow Troubleshooter does not do anything that an experienced Exchange administrator would not if they were asked to find out why a problem existed in the mail flow. The value here is that a lot of the mundane checks are done for you automatically and in a consistent manner, so you know that something weird is going on if the Mail Flow Troubleshooter can't find the problem. One way of looking at this is that experience and intuition come to the fore when the troubleshooter can't find a problem, which is the reason why we still have human administrators. And in any case, you'll still have to fix the problems once they are detected, but at least you'll know where to look.

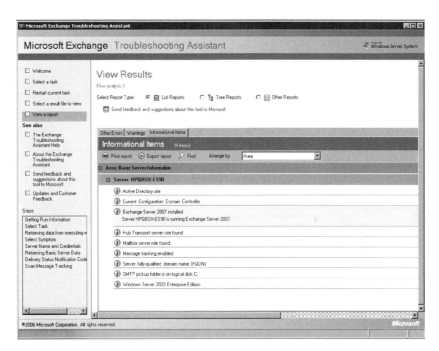

Figure 10.12
Summary report from the Mail Flow Troubleshooter

10.3 Messaging tracking logs

Like all previous versions, Exchange 2007 generates entries in message tracking logs to record the progress of messages through the system. Exchange records information about messages as the clients submit them via the Store on mailbox servers and the transport service subsequently processes the messages onwards to their eventual delivery. The logs capture information about all message activity, including incoming messages public folder replication, nondelivery notifications, and so on. Many companies use the data captured by these logs to analyze message traffic so that they can predict future demand, or indeed, for forensic purposes if they need to validate that a message went from one user to another. Some differences exist in the implementation of message tracking logs in Exchange 2007 that we need to know about before we can work with this data.

- Exchange 2007 hub, mailbox, or Edge servers can generate message tracking logs and this functionality is enabled by default. Client Access servers do not generate message traffic logs because these servers do not participate in message transport unless a server also hosts one of the other roles.

- The UI that is available in Exchange 2000 and 2003 to control various aspects of message tracking by setting them as properties of individual servers or through system policies is not provided in Exchange 2007. Instead, you use a set of shell commands to control how Exchange 2007 generates message tracking logs, where the logs are stored, and the data that the logs hold.

- The message tracking center is not part of EMC as it was in EMS. Instead, message tracking functionality is part of the Toolbox node of EMC.

- To improve security, Exchange 2007 does not make its message tracking logs not accessible via a file share as they are in Exchange 2000 and 2003. You need at least view-only administrative permission on all the servers that you want to search through to be able to access message tracking logs through the Microsoft Exchange Transport Log Search service.

- The format of the message tracking logs, the data that they contain, and the naming convention for the logs are different to the format used in Exchange 2000 and 2003.

The last point is important if you have deployed your own software or third-party packages to analyze and report on message tracking data. For example, if you wrote some scripts to use the LogParser utility to analyze message tracking logs to perform mail traffic analysis, you won't be able to use those scripts on an Exchange 2007 server. Exchange 2007 uses a common schema for all of the logs that it generates including the agent log, protocol log, and message tracking log. This is a good idea, but the format change from IIS3WC to something that is close to CSV but isn't quite (because the logs contain some header information) means that any tool that was written to analyze message tracking logs from Exchange 2000 or 2003 servers is useless for Exchange 2007.

The difference in format also means that you can only track messages within the environment that understands the message tracking log format. Exchange 2007 servers can track a message to the boundary where the message is transferred to a legacy server and Exchange 2003 servers can track messages until they move to Exchange 2007. If you need to track a message through its complete path in a mixed organization, you need to perform one trace through Exchange 2007 and another with Exchange 2003 and then match the two traces to complete the picture.

Once you connect an Exchange server to a network, traffic flows and the message tracking logs are populated. Even on a quiet day, Exchange logs message traffic. For example, on Christmas Day 2006, my Exchange server built a message tracking log of 584KB. Not many humans connected to the server to send and receive mail that day, but the background static generated by public folder replication (this won't happen unless you support public folders), incoming messages from various message lists that send daily digests, and spam was enough to accumulate the log. By comparison, the usual volume of traffic on the same server generates a log of between 10MB and 15MB daily and a large mailbox server can easily generate up to 500MB/day while a busy hub transport server may generate 1GB daily. The problem of analyzing such a large amount of data to extract message load statistics is obvious.

10.3.1 Generating message tracking logs

Unless you disable their generation, Exchange 2007 servers produce message tracking logs automatically. According to Microsoft, the generation of message tracking logs consumes approximately 2%–4% I/O overhead for a server, so if you want to disable the generation of messaging tracking logs, use the `Set-TransportServer` command for a hub or Edge server or the `Set-MailboxServer` command for a mailbox server. You will find that you also use the same two commands if you want to change many other message tracking parameters. Here are the commands to disable message tracking log generation on a hub transport or Edge server and on a mailbox server:

```
Set-TransportServer —id ExchEdge1
-MessageTrackingLogEnabled:$False
Set-MailboxServer —id ExchMbxSvr1
-MessageTrackingLogEnabled:$False
```

You can scan the organization to discover the hub and mailbox servers that have message tracking log enabled with these commands:

```
Get-TransportServer | Where {$_.MessageTrackinglogEnabled -eq
$True}
Get-MailboxServer | Where {$_.MessageTrackinglogEnabled -eq
$True}
```

By default, Exchange stores message tracking logs in the C:\Program Files\Microsoft\Exchange   Server\TransportRoles\Logs\MessageTracking folder. While convenient, it is probably best to move this location to a non-system disk. For example, to move the folder on a mailbox server:

```
Set-MailboxServer —id ExchMbxSvr1 -MessageTrackingLogPath
'D:\MailLogs'
```

You can find details of the current message tracking parameters for a server by issuing this command:

```
Get-MailboxServer —id ExchMbxSvr1 | Select *Track*
```

```
MessageTrackingLogEnabled              : True
MessageTrackingLogMaxAge               : 30.00:00:00
MessageTrackingLogMaxDirectorySize     : 250MB
MessageTrackingLogMaxFileSize          : 10MB
MessageTrackingLogPath                 : C:\Program Files\Microsoft\Exchange
Server\TransportRoles\Logs\MessageTracking
MessageTrackingLogSubjectLoggingEnabled : True
```

Exchange 2007 creates new message tracking logs daily. The logs are created when the first message traffic occurs on the server. Unlike previous versions, Exchange 2007 generates two different types of message tracking logs. The first type is generated by mailbox servers and contains details of messages that originate on the server and is named MSGTRKMyyyymmdd-1.LOG, where "yyyymmdd" is the current date. For example, the message tracking log created on July 20, 2007 is named MSGTRKM20070720-1.LOG. Because this log reflects the work done by a mailbox server, you will find that it is full of entries from the Store driver as it submits messages on behalf of users. For example, if we used the Get-MessageTrackingLog command to look at an entry for a message, we might see:

```
Timestamp       : 1/16/2007 2:04:14 PM
ClientHostname  : ExchMbxSvr2
ServerHostname  : ExchHub1
SourceContext   : MDB:28585bf7-affd-4e2e-b4e2-1ee310949448, Mailbox:1f1
                  d0e61-b12c-4e22-8a32-093b4dca0f77, Event:1432, Messag
                  eClass:IPM.Note, CreationTime:2007-01-16T14:04:13.576
                  Z, ClientType:OWA
Source          : STOREDRIVER
EventId         : SUBMIT
MessageId       : <6DF982B79886DF449CDB77A1F794D07F3C72@ExchMbxSvr2.xyz
                  .com>
Recipients      : {}
```

```
RecipientStatus        : {}
TotalBytes             :
RecipientCount         :
MessageSubject         : Buy HPQ!
Sender                 : Shane.Jennings@xyz.com
```

You can see that this message was submitted on a server called ExchMbxSvr2 and was handed over to a hub transport server called ExchHub1 for processing. The user generated the message with the Outlook Web Access client. No recipient information is yet available because this message will pass through the categorizer and have its set of recipients established only when it reaches the hub transport server.

The second message tracking log is created on hub transport and Edge servers to contain details of how a message is routed from the time that it is submitted to the transport engine to delivery to the next hop or to a mailbox server en route to a user. This log is named MSGTRKyyyymmdd-n.LOG, so the equivalent log for July 20, 2007 is MSGTRK20070720-1.LOG. Multi-role servers generate both types of logs because you have users sending messages and transport services routing messages onward and receiving incoming messages. When a hub transport server processes the message originally generated on server ExchMbxSvr1, additional detail becomes available about the message that Exchange captures in events written into the message tracking log on the hub transport server. If we use the `Get-MessageTrackingLog` command to look at the entries written into the message tracking log on the hub transport server, we can see that the recipients for the message have been expanded by the categorizer and are available. We also see that the same message identifier persists as messages flow from server to server.

```
Timestamp              : 1/16/2007 2:04:15 PM
ClientHostname         : ExchHub1
ServerHostname         : ExchMbxSvr2
SourceContext          :
Source                 : STOREDRIVER
EventId                : DELIVER
InternalMessageId      : 36
MessageId              :
<6DF982B79886DF449CDB77A1F794D07F3C72@ExchMbxSvr1.xyz.com>
Recipients             : {Marcus.Horan@xyz.com, Leo.Cullen@xyz.com,
Peter.Smyth@xyz.com, Shane.Jennings@xyz.com}
RecipientStatus        : {}
TotalBytes             : 4536
RecipientCount         : 4
MessageSubject         : Buy HPQ!
Sender                 : Shane.Jennings@xyz.com
ReturnPath             : Shane.Jennings@xyz.com
```

10.3.2 Log sizes and ages

The default file size for a message tracking log is 10MB and after Exchange writes this amount of data to the file, it creates a new file. In our example, the second log generated on a mailbox server on July 20, 2007 would be called MSGTRKM20070720-2.LOG. Unlike Exchange 2000 or 2003, which typically keep message tracking logs for 7 or 10 days, Exchange 2007 keeps log files until the folder assigned to hold the logs reaches a maximum specified size (by default, Exchange keeps 250MB of message tracking logs) or they age out (the default is 30 days). This limit is sufficient for most small to medium companies, but larger organizations may want to increase the limit to ensure that they keep logs for at least a week. Microsoft reports that they generate 220MB of logs every business day and less on the weekend, so they need to store approximately 1.5GB of logs for a week's work. This load is spread across hub transport servers and no one hub transport server will have to store the entire 1.5GB, but the busiest servers in core routing sites may have to handle nearly this amount of logs. Data from previous versions of Exchange are very valuable when it comes to estimating the correct configuration for message tracking log storage. If you take the amount generated on your busiest Exchange 2003 server and add 20% to reflect the fact that hub transport servers deal with messages from a set of mailbox servers, you will not be far wrong.

After the maximum size or age limit is reached, Exchange applies the principle of circular logging to remove the oldest log files from the server. The System Attendant process removes obsolete logs during its regular background maintenance operations. A busy mailbox server can easily generate several hundred megabytes of message tracking log data daily.

You can alter the default settings for message tracking logs as follows. To double the maximum size of a single message tracking log on a mailbox server:

```
Set-MailboxServer —id ExchMbxSvr1
-MessageTrackingLogMaxFileSize 20MB
```

To increase the total amount of message tracking log data that Exchange retains on a hub or Edge server to a size that is more appropriate for a busy server:

```
Set-TransportServer —id ExchHub1
-MessageTrackingLogMaxDirectorySize 1GB
```

To increase the age limit for message transport logs from 30 days to 60 days on a mailbox server:

```
Set-MailboxServer —id ExchMbxSvr1 -MessageTrackingLogMaxAge
60.00:00:00
```

10.3.3 Keeping track of message subjects

The default for an Exchange 2007 server is to capture the subjects of messages into message tracking logs. Some companies believe that this is not appropriate because of concerns that user privacy could be compromised if administrators are able to browse message tracking data to glean information about the subjects of messages that are being sent. On the other hand, other companies believe that an email system has to be used appropriately and in line with standards of business conduct, and if an administrator notices that a user has sent a message titled "Foxy Hot Ladies," then you might conclude that the user is paying undue attention to noncompany matters. I do not really get too worried about capturing message subjects because you can interpret the recipients of a message to learn something about the kind of traffic that flows through the system and that Exchange automatically captures data about the messages. After all, a user who sends messages to "hotgals.com" may not be spending a lot of time thinking about business. Nevertheless, if you want to disable the capture of message subjects, you can do this with a command like this:

```
Set-MailboxServer —id ExchMbxSvr1
—MessageTrackingLogSubjectLoggingEnabled:$False
```

Now that we have configured how we want Exchange to generate message tracking logs, we can move on to discuss how to make use of the data that accumulates. Every version of Exchange includes an administrative GUI option to search through the message tracking logs to track the progress of messages and there are programs like LogParser (see page 973) to help analyze the logs generated by Exchange 2000 and 2003, not to mention some commercial products that do the same thing. The difference is that Exchange 2007 provides some shell commands that make it easier.

10.3.4 Accessing message tracking logs

There are multiple ways to access message tracking data:

- Use the Message Tracking option in the Toolbox node in EMC: This option is similar in concept to the Message Tracking Center feature in Exchange 2003.

- Open the message tracking logs with a program such as Excel or Access that can read CSV-formatted files.

- Analyze the logs with LogParser to create summary data.

- Buy and deploy a commercial product such as Promodag Reports (www.promodag.com), which use message tracking log data as input to an overall analysis of an Exchange server. Commercial products cost money, but they save a lot of time and deliver guaranteed results. Note that the format and content of Exchange 2007 message tracking logs is very different to Exchange 2003, so you need updated versions of software to process Exchange 2007 logs. See Appendix 1 for details of the fields and content of Exchange 2007 message tracking logs.

- Use the `Get-MessageTrackingLog` shell command to query the tracking log data. This is the roll-your-own approach to log analysis.

One significant change from Exchange 2003 is the disappearance of the file share for the message tracking logs that allowed administrators who had view-only permission to track messages from server to server. Exchange 2007 requires users to have administrative rights over servers before they can access the message tracking logs. If you want to continue using the same approach to message tracking, you will have to assign administrative access to servers to more users than you probably want to. One alternate approach is to copy logs from all servers to a central location and perform any tracking operations there. This certainly works, but is not as convenient as the previous arrangement.

10.3.5 Using the Troubleshooting Assistant to track messages

We have already explored the Troubleshooting Assistant framework to perform tasks such as database recovery management and mail flow analysis. The same approach is used when the Troubleshooting Assistant interrogates message tracking logs.

As you can see from Figure 10.13, the first step is to provide some basic information to allow a search to begin. The most commonly used fields are:

- Who sent or received the message. The Troubleshooting Assistant resolves this information to SMTP addresses because the message tracking logs contain SMTP addresses. You can put SMTP addresses

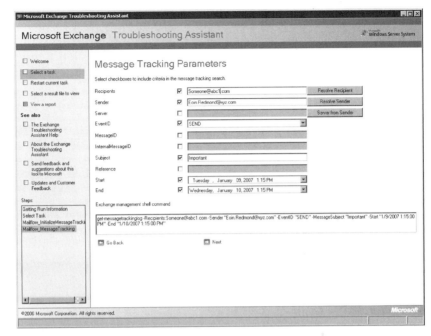

Figure 10.13

*Setting message
tracking parameters*

in these fields, but do not select the "Resolve Sender" or "Resolve Recipient" options, because these will cause Exchange to attempt to resolve the SMTP address against the Active Directory, and this will not work if they are not mail-enabled recipients.

- What server generated the event for the message? You can pass the name of any Exchange 2007 server that you think might have processed the message.

- What is in the message subject field? You cannot search based on the contents of a message because this information is obviously not captured in the message tracking logs. In addition, you can search message subjects only if the servers capture this information.

- What event do you want to look for? If you check this field, you are restricted to pick just one event to search for. It may be the SEND event to look for messages that a user has sent or the RECEIVE event to look for incoming messages that have been delivered to someone's mailbox.

- What period do you want to search from? The default is to insert today's date and time in both fields, so either uncheck the fields so that they are not used in the search or set the desired period.

The message identifier and internal message identifier are not often used at this point, but as we will see, they become more important as the search narrows in to find the message that we are interested in. Figure 10.13 shows how the search parameters come together. Notice that the Troubleshooting Assistant assembles a shell command from the parameters that you provide. In this case, the shell command is:

```
Get-MessageTrackingLog -Recipients:Someone@abc1.com -Sender
'Eoin.Redmond@xyz.com' -EventID 'SEND' -MessageSubject
'Important'
-Start '1/9/2007 1:15:00 PM' -End '1/10/2007 1:15:00 PM'
```

You can cut and paste the shell command and use it as the basis for a script that you may want to execute to find messages on a regular basis.

Figure 10.14
*Results of our
initial search*

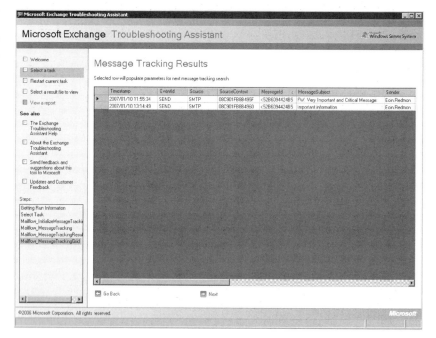

If we are lucky, we will end up with results like those shown in Figure 10.14 and only have a couple of messages that match the search criteria. Notice that you can click on any of the field headings to sort by that field. Our search might be complete at this point, but if we decide that we need more details of exactly where the message went, we can click on the message and then select Next. The Troubleshooting Assistant takes the internal message identifier (see an example below) and uses it to build a new Get-

`MessageTrackingLog` command to interrogate the logs further and determine where the message went.

<52B6094424B59C46A6C75AA5D1084FD40DC628A24B@ExchMbxSvr1.xyz.com>

Figure 10.15
*The final result of
a search*

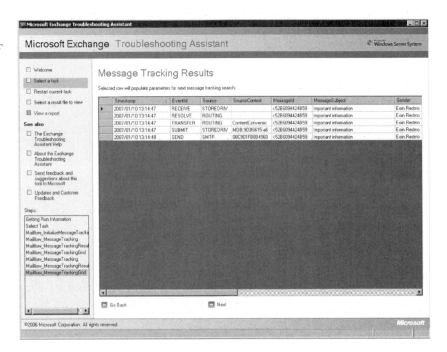

The final result of our search is shown in Figure 10.15. You may need to sort the results by the timestamp to get an accurate picture of the message's progress over time. We know it's final because the last step reported is an SMTP transfer and if we scroll across to reveal other fields, we can see that the ConnectorId field (Figure 10.16) contains a connector that we know is an external SMTP connector, and we can see that the message was transferred successfully (status 250).

Figure 10.16
*Transfer via a
connector*

ConnectorId	RecipientStat	TotalBytes	RecipientCou
		4016	1
		4016	1
		1982	1
		(null)	(null)
HPQBOX to the Internet	250 0k	2398	1

If the message passed to another Exchange 2007 server, we can continue to track it as long as the account that we have logged into has at least view-only administrative permission for the other Exchange servers.

10.3.6   Tracking messages with EMS

We have seen how the `Get-MessageTrackingLog` command underpins the Troubleshooting Assistant when it tracks messages, so now we should dive in and understand how the `Get-MessageTrackingLog` command works when it extracts and returns information from message tracking logs. Just like the other EMS commands that potentially deal with large numbers of objects, the default is to return up to 1,000 items for a search. If you need to access more data, specify the –ResultSize parameter to increase the number of returned items to the desired size. Any moderately active server will generate many tracking log entries, so you will need to apply a filter to get to the data that you want. The most common filter is to apply a date and time range. For example, here is the command to look for messages tracked between 9AM and 10AM on January 1, 2007:

```
Get-MessageTrackingLog –Start '7/1/2007 9:00AM' –End '7/1/
2007 10:00AM' | Sort Timestamp
```

Note that I have sorted the returned data by the timestamp to ensure that Exchange returns it in date order. Remember that message tracking log data can come from two different files, depending on whether you look on a single-role mailbox server or hub transport server or a multi-role mailbox/hub transport server. Sorting the data by the timestamp ensures that we see all of the entries for individual messages together. As a command that searches for data for an hour might still return many entries on a heavily trafficked server, you can combine parameters to apply a tighter filter. For example, here is how to look for messages sent by a specific user:

```
Get-MessageTrackingLog –Sender 'Tony.Redmond@hp.com' –Start
'7/1/2007 9:00AM' –End '7/1/2007 10:00AM' | Sort-Object
Timestamp
```

Another common filter is to look for specific events that occur during the lifecycle of a message. You can apply such a filter by specifying the –EventID parameter together with the name of the event that you want to look for, such as RECEIVE (new message submitted by a user) or SEND (message dispatched via SMTP). You might also be interested in looking for messages sent to a specific recipient, so you can do this by specifying the SMTP addresses that you want to look for in the –Recipients parameter. Here is an example:

```
Get-MessageTrackingLog —Recipients 'BadPerson@xyz.com',
'Anotherbadperson@xyz.com'
```

You can search the message tracking logs on another server if you have administrative permissions to manage the target server. To search on another server, we pass the server name in the –Server parameter. Putting things all together, here is the kind of focused search that we might execute:

```
Get-MessageTrackingLog —Sender 'Tony.Redmond@hp.com' —Start
'7/1/2007 9:00AM' —End '7/1/2007 10:00AM' -Recipients
'BadPerson@xyz.com', 'Anotherbadperson@xyz.com'-Server
ExchMbxSvr2 -EventId SEND | Sort-Object Timestamp
```

After you have settled on the search that you need to conduct, Figure 10.17 shows the output you can expect from the `Get-MessageTrackingLog` command. We can see four different kinds of message lifecycles. The first is a message sent to an external recipient that goes through three steps: client submission to the Store, Store submission to the SMTP transport engine, and sending to the final destination. The second situation is a message sent to a local recipient. The client submits the message and the Store accepts it before the transport engine resolves the address to decide how to deliver the message. The Store then delivers the message to the recipient's mailbox. The third example illustrates what happens when a message goes to a mailbox that has an alternate recipient. In this case, you can see that a new REDIRECT event occurs as the transport engine realizes that an alternate recipient exists and that it has to deliver to both the original and the alternate recipients. The last case is for a message sent to a distribution group and you can see that the membership of the distribution group is resolved before Exchange can deliver the message. In fact, the group is a dynamic distribution group, so you never see the recipient list.

Figure 10.17
Output from Get-Message Tracking-Log command

```
EventId    Source   Sender                 Recipients              MessageSubject
-------    ------   ------                 ----------              --------------
RECEIVE    STORE... Tony.Redmond@xyz....   {tony.redmond@xy....    Outgoing to SMTP
SUBMIT     STORE... IMCEAEX-_O=XYZ_OU...   {}                      Outgoing to SMTP      1
SEND       SMTP     Tony.Redmond@xyz....   {tony.redmond@xyz...    Outgoing to SMTP
RECEIVE    STORE... Tony.Redmond@xyz....   {IMCEAEX-_O=XYZ_O...    Local delivery t...
SUBMIT     STORE... IMCEAEX-_O=XYZ_OU...   {}                      Local delivery t...
RESOLVE    ROUTING  Tony.Redmond@xyz....   {Ailbhe.Redmond@x...    Local delivery t...   2
DELIVER    STORE... Tony.Redmond@xyz....   {Ailbhe.Redmond@x...    Local delivery t...
SUBMIT     STORE... IMCEAEX-_O=XYZ_O....   {}                      Alternate   alter...
RESOLVE    ROUTING  Tony.Redmond@Xyz....   {Fergal.Anderson@...    Alternate   alter...
RECEIVE    STORE... Tony.Redmond@xyz....   {IMCEAEX-_O=XYZ_O...    Alternate   alter...
TRANSFER   ROUTING  Tony.Redmond@xyz....   {Alan.Nemeth@xyz....    Alternate   alter...
TRANSFER   ROUTING  Tony.Redmond@xyz....   {Fergal.Anderson@...    Alternate   alter...   3
REDIRECT   ROUTING  Tony.Redmond@xyz....   {Fergal.Anderson@...    Alternate   alter...
REDIRECT   ROUTING  Tony.Redmond@xyz....   {Fergal.Anderson@...    Alternate   alter...
DELIVER    STORE... Tony.Redmond@xyz....   {Alan.Nemeth@xyz....    Alternate   alter...
DELIVER    STORE... Tony.Redmond@xyz....   {Fergal.Anderson@...    Alternate   alter...
RECEIVE    STORE... Tony.Redmond@xyz....   {IMCEAEX-_O=XYZ_O...    To large DL
SUBMIT     STORE... IMCEAEX-_O=XYZ_OU...   {}                      To large DL
RESOLVE    ROUTING  Tony.Redmond@xyz....   {Everyone@xyz.co....    To large DL           4
SEND       ROUTING  Tony.Redmond@xyz....   {Everyone@xyz.co....    To large DL
EXPAND     ROUTING  Tony.Redmond@xyz....   {}                      To large DL
```

Message tracking also captures the path of messages that journal rules process. Figure 10.18 shows how the events unfold from the time that a user sends a message to a distribution group that is monitored by a journal rule, through the resolution and expansion of the group into individual addresses, through to delivery to both the individual recipients in the local Store and to the journal recipient.

Figure 10.18
The path of a
journaled message

```
RECEIVE    STORE...  Tony.Redmond@xyz....  {IMCEAEX-_O=XYZ_O... Executive email
SUBMIT     STORE...  IMCEAEX-_O=XYZ_OU...  {}                  Executive email
RESOLVE    ROUTING   Tony.Redmond@xyz....  {Senior_Executive... Executive email
EXPAND     ROUTING   Tony.Redmond@xyz....  {Tony.Redmond@xyz... Executive email
TRANSFER   ROUTING   Tony.Redmond@xyz....  {Donald.Livengood... Executive email
SEND       ROUTING   Tony.Redmond@xyz....  {Senior_Executive... Executive email
RECEIVE    AGENT     postmaster@xyz.co...  {secure.journal@x... Executive email
DELIVER    STORE...  Tony.Redmond@xyz....  {Mary.Jones@xyz.c... Executive email
DELIVER    STORE...  postmaster@xyz.co...  {secure.journal@x... Executive email
```

Exchange records details of incoming messages in two records. First, a RECEIVE event is logged from the SMTP source (because all incoming messages flow in through the SMTP transport engine) followed by a DELIVER event to the STORE as Exchange delivers the message to a mailbox. Figure 10.19 shows the detail that `Get-MessageTrackingLog` reports if you look at a record by piping it through the `Format-List` command. You can see the IP addresses for the sending and receiving servers, the server that received this message and the connector that it used, whom the message is addressed to, the time when it arrived, who sent it, and the size (6,637,143 bytes or 6.33MB).

Figure 10.19
Details of an
incoming message

```
Timestamp                  : 7/20/2007 1:34:53 PM
ClientIp                   : 11.93.28.84
ClientHostname             :
ServerIp                   : 11.49.117.25
ServerHostname             : EXCHMBXSVR1
SourceContext              : 08C8C181848FA39F;2007-07-20T12:32:52.802Z;0
ConnectorId                : EXCHMBXSVR1\Default EXCHMBXSVR1
Source                     : SMTP
EventId                    : RECEIVE
InternalMessageId          : 31
MessageId                  : <BA0F808C82DE9A48A4DAA1542B2431820282D1D9@TLGEXC01
Recipients                 : {Tony.Redmond@xyz.com}
RecipientStatus            : {}
TotalBytes                 : 6637143
RecipientCount             : 1
RelatedRecipientAddress    :
Reference                  :
MessageSubject             : FW: Updated strategy slides
Sender                     : tony.redmond@xyz.com
ReturnPath                 : tony.redmond@xyz.com
MessageInfo                : 0bA:
```

It is possible to track messages across servers using shell commands, providing that all the servers have the Exchange Transport Log Search service running and that you have enough administrative access to support the search. To execute a search across servers, you have to use the MessageId of the message that you want to track because this is the only property that remains consistent across servers. Assuming that the MessageId for the message that you want to locate is stored in the $MsgId variable, you can search across servers using a command like:

```
Get-ExchangeServer | Where {$_.IsHubTransportServer -or
$IsMailboxServer} | Get-MessageTrackingLog -MessageId $MsgId
| Select TimeStamp, ServerHostName, Source, Recipients | Sort
TimeStamp
```

This command looks across in the message tracking logs on all hub transport and mailbox servers for any message that matches the value of $MsgId. Tracking a message like this through the shell is not easy because of the complex commands and unwieldy format of the MessageId, so this may be one situation where EMC scores over EMS.

10.3.7 Message delivery latency

Some administrators like to use message tracking log data to track the speed that Exchange delivers messages. The theory is that you can find all of the entries for a particular message and use the timestamps on the entries to track its passage and find out how long it takes the message to pass from place to place within the messaging system. The net result should be the end-to-end delivery time and you can use this value to assess whether Exchange is performing as expected. The theory is valid, but the message tracking log data is not, at least not in Exchange 2007.

Exchange is supposed to stamp the MessageInfo field with the date and time that a client originally submitted a message for processing. Unfortunately, the data is incorrect for many reasons, including incorrect clock synchronization on clients and the fact that Exchange takes the time that Outlook reports that it sent a message and uses that for the value. On the surface, this looks correct, but then you have to consider what happens when Outlook sends a message, a cached Exchange mode. The timestamp at this point is hardly correct—what you need is the time when Outlook was actually able to submit the message to Exchange. In any case, Microsoft recognizes that the problem exists and the bug is scheduled to be fixed in Exchange 2007 SP1. In the meantime, you can go to the Exchange team's blog and pick up a copy of a program called MSGAnalyzer. This program will read your message tracking logs and generate accurate end-to-end delivery statistics.

10.4 Management frameworks

Exchange 2000 and 2003 servers support some basic monitoring options that are incorporated into the ESM console. No equivalent options exist in

Exchange 2007 as some of the WMI classes that these options depend on are not in Exchange 2007. The emphasis is now on using PowerShell to interrogate information about Windows, Exchange, the event log, and other sources to build a picture of system health. If you've depended on the monitoring features built into Exchange 2000/2003, you will need to either write your own monitoring tools based on PowerShell or invest in a management framework. The latter option is probably overkill if you only operate a few Exchange servers because it is relatively easy to keep track of what's happening, even if it can get boring from time to time. Once you have to operate more than five or so servers, it is easier to justify the investment in a management framework because the automated data gathering and analysis capabilities will make it easier to identify and resolve faults earlier. The decision to use a management framework may also be mandated by a decision to use a framework for monitoring the network, other Windows applications such as SQL, or other platforms such as UNIX or Linux.

The two big management frameworks in use with Exchange today are Microsoft Operations Manager (MOM) 2005 (and soon, MOM 2007) and HP OpenView. Both products have updates available to support Exchange 2007 and both exploit PowerShell for their integrations with Exchange 2007. The frameworks also take up the concept of server roles and use this as the basis for their policies and rules.

MOM's ace card is that it is Microsoft's management framework, which makes people assume that MOM has an implicit tight association with the groups that engineer products such as Exchange and SQL. This is true insofar that the MOM team has access to the other Microsoft engineering teams and the knowledge that these groups have about how their products work. The MOM team also has access to Microsoft's knowledge base and the databases that track problems reported to Microsoft PSS. These are undoubted advantages that MOM leverages when it interprets conditions that it detects in the event log or by direct interrogation of Windows or Exchange through PowerShell. For example, Figure 10.20 shows that MOM has detected that a backup has not been performed for a public folder database on a server for 15 days. In this case, MOM has used a rule from ExBPA to assess a condition against best practice and then generate a warning. You can see that MOM also suggests a Microsoft knowledge base article for the administrator to read more about the condition that provoked the alert.

Figure 10.21 shows details of a problem as reported by MOM and the equivalent event logged in the application event log. The underlying problem is that the Managed Folder Assistant has failed to provision a mailbox because of an error in a managed custom folder where the content settings specify a nonexistent journal destination. If you scan the event logs for errors relating to Exchange, you probably look for events that you consider critical, such as problems that affect a database, so this is a good example of how

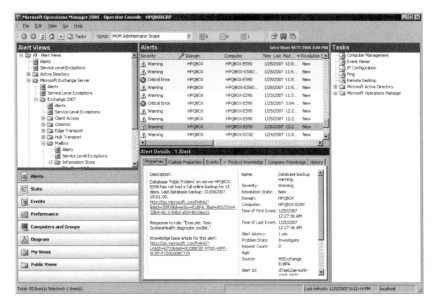

Figure 10.20
Microsoft Operations Manager 2005

MOM can bring more subtle problems to the attention of an administrator. In this case, the fix is easy (update the managed content settings for the affected folders to add a valid journal recipient) and you can do this through EMC or with shell commands. The point is that you probably wouldn't even know that you had a problem to fix unless something like a management framework brought the issue to your attention.

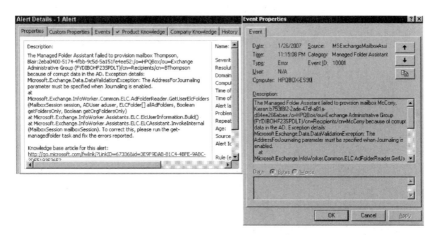

Figure 10.21
Comparing MOM details and the Event log

HP OpenView takes a more network-centric and less product-centric approach, which is unsurprising given OpenView's heritage and success as a network management framework. OpenView is also more appropriate for deployment within a heterogeneous operating environment where you want to deploy a single management framework to cover multiple operating systems, networks, and applications. Figure 10.22 shows the HP OpenView management console displaying the Active Directory structure that underpins an Exchange organization.

Figure 10.22
HP OpenView

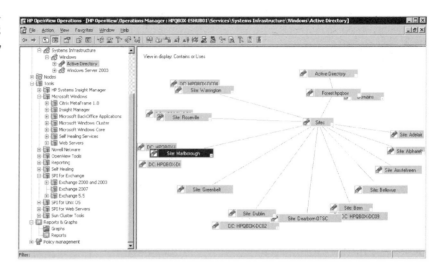

In addition to its ability to manage the Windows infrastructure (together with other platforms such as IBM AIX and HP-UX), the Open-View framework includes an SPI (Smart Plug-In) for Exchange that is completely rewritten for Exchange 2007. The SPI monitors over 100 indicators (such as SMTP queues and log shipping data) for Exchange 2003 and 2007 servers to detect and report problems to administrators. Out of the box, the OpenView SPI includes over 70 policies that administrators can use as the basis for monitoring and you can add customized policies through a configuration wizard if you want to gather specific information. Data extracted as the result of applying selected policies is integrated with other information in the OpenView console to provide administrators with a single view of the network, Windows, and Exchange. The SPI includes a set of precanned graphs and reports to help administrators understand the usage and demand trends for Exchange. Finally, the OpenView SPI is integrated with ExBPA so that it can flag issues raised by ExBPA.

The rules used by management frameworks tend to focus on the analysis and reporting of problems rather than attempting to correlate problems with advice as to what you should do to address the root cause. There are other products on the market such as Zenprise (www.zenprise.com) that specialize in analyzing the management data and events generated by Exchange servers against their own rule sets, which usually incorporate Microsoft resolutions for problems together with their own view of what best practice is used to resolve certain issues.

The value of frameworks is pretty simple to understand. They provide administrators with a method to monitor large numbers of components in an IT environment in an automated manner. Human administrators cannot physically check every single error or advisory condition flagged by every computer, network component, and application that they have to manage, so management frameworks provide the necessary automation to filter out the interesting but perhaps unimportant information and to bring the critical faults to the attention of administrators fast. You can certainly build your own monitoring utilities and tailor them to your precise requirements, but it is unlikely that you will match the depth of sophistication and precision that the leading management frameworks can provide you out of the box without investing huge amounts of money and development time.

10.5 Utilities

While Exchange 2007 is much stronger than any previous version in terms of its out-of-the-box administrative capabilities, there's always room for some specialized utility programs that may help to solve specific problems. This section describes some of the more common utilities that Exchange administrators use.

10.5.1 Performance testing

Microsoft offers a suite of utilities that you can download from their web site and use to simulate Exchange 2007 performance. These utilities are:

- JetStress: This utility tests the ability of storage subsystems to handle the I/O load generated by Exchange servers. I/O capacity is a critical success factor for any medium to large Exchange server and JetStress allows administrators to generate different I/O loads and then to measure how the storage subsystem copes with the workload. Microsoft operates a program called ESRP (Exchange Solution Reviewed Program) that allows selected partners to document the results of testing storage solutions with JetStress according to guidelines set by Microsoft. The documents published through ESRP provide useful information about how storage vendors test their solutions with Exchange and the performance data that they obtain.

- Load Generator: This utility replaces the "LoadSim" program that Microsoft first released in 1997 to allow administrators to test the performance of early Exchange servers by generating a load from simulated MAPI users. Over time, the complexity of Exchange servers has grown enormously through different client types, different workloads, and different types of servers. The Exchange Load Generator is a modern performance simulation tool that allows administrators to model workloads and to see how hardware configurations deal with the workloads that you specify. This utility (Figure 10.23) focuses on MAPI client workload and supports the kind of operations generated by Outlook 2003 and 2007 clients, including when these clients work in cached Exchange mode.

- Server Stress and Performance (ESP): Microsoft first launched targeted Exchange at the ISP community with Exchange 2000, so they needed a workload simulator that accommodated non-MAPI protocols. MAPI delivers the highest functionality to clients, but ISPs need to understand the load generated by web browsers, POP3, IMAP4, and LDAP clients, and that is what ESP does.

- Profile Analyzer: This utility allows administrators to collect data from servers in their organization in a structured manner so that the data can then be used as an input for a performance capacity model.

Figure 10.23
Load Generator
utility

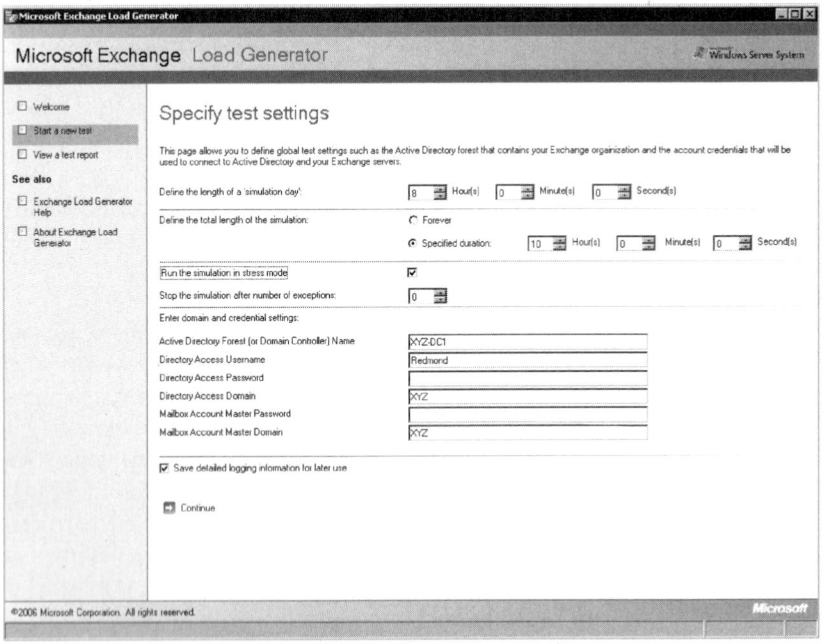

Collectively, these tools form a comprehensive set that you can use to determine whether hardware configurations can handle a selected Exchange workload. Over time, the problem areas for Exchange have tracked the evolution in hardware capabilities and cost. We have seen a move from sheer CPU (the initial servers) to CPU (first Exchange 2000 deployments) to I/O (Exchange 2003). The Microsoft tools have kept reasonable pace with changing requirements and the only deficiency now present is in the area of mobility, where it is still difficult to predict with accuracy how ActiveSync will impact a server. Microsoft is working on new modules for the Load Generator utility, so this is good reason to check back with their web site to pick up new versions as they become available.

10.5.2 The MFCMAPI utility

If you are not a programmer, a programmer who is not literate in Microsoft programming techniques, or like me—someone whose best programming days are long behind them—MAPI is a challenge. MAPI is a very comprehensive and powerful application programming interface that has proved to be very durable since Microsoft introduced the full-blown MAPI version in the original Exchange "Capone" client in 1996. Certainly, no equivalent messaging API has come about since and nothing is on the horizon to displace MAPI as the basis for the most functional client interaction with Exchange. However, while Outlook provides a good user interface that masks the complexities of client-server MAPI communication, behind the scenes, MAPI wraps up its power in a complex web of items, properties, and values that make it somewhat difficult to approach unless you take the time to become well versed in the interface. Some people in Microsoft must have felt the same way and ended up by writing MFCMAPI, a sample application written using Microsoft C++ and Microsoft Foundation Classes to interrogate the contents of a MAPI folder structure (mailbox or public folder). Begun as a learning project, MFCMAPI now provides a window into the internal structure of Exchange and that you can also use to alter properties and values of items in mailboxes, if the need arises.

You can download a copy of MFCMAPI (now known as the Microsoft Exchange Server MAPI editor—a name that's just too long to use) by following the directions in Microsoft Knowledge Base article 291794. It is a good idea to check to see whether an updated version is available as Microsoft posts new versions from time to time. By default, MFCMAPI uses your normal profile to log onto your mailbox, but you canuse another profile to connect to a different mailbox if you have the necessary permission. Microsoft Knowledge Base article 262054 explains how to grant access to your Windows account to access other Exchange mailboxes, but be sure that you follow your company's security and privacy policies before you access anyone else's mailbox.

After you start MFCMAPI, select the "Session," "Logon," and "Display Store Table" options to access your mailbox. You can then expand the contents of the mailbox by clicking on the IPM_SUBTREE root. Figure 10.24

Figure 10.24
*MFCMAPI lists
folder contents*

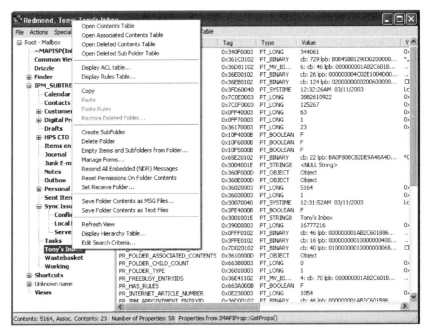

shows the options that are available after selecting a folder from the mailbox. For example, if you select "Open Contents Table," MFCMAPI lists the contents of the folder, whereas if you select "Open Deleted Contents Table," MFCMAPI lists the items deleted from the folder that are in the deleted items cache.

Figure 10.25 shows what you can expect to see after you open a folder table with MFCMAPI. In this case, it is the deleted items content table. The items are listed in the top pane and the properties of the selected item appear in the bottom pane. The reason why so many question marks and other special characters appear in the properties of the selected item is that the item is a spam message containing Cyrillic characters that MFCMAPI cannot display properly.

Being able to view information is interesting, but it is more interesting to be able to alter properties or delete items. For example, let's assume that a user is on vacation and has created a wrong out-of-office message. You could change their Windows password and log into their account to run Outlook to change the OOF message, but that means that the user will have to change their password when they return to the office. In addition, some users may be upset that an administrator has logged onto their account, even with good reason.

To change an OOF message with MFCMAPI, you:

Figure 10.25
*MFCMAPI lists
items in a folder*

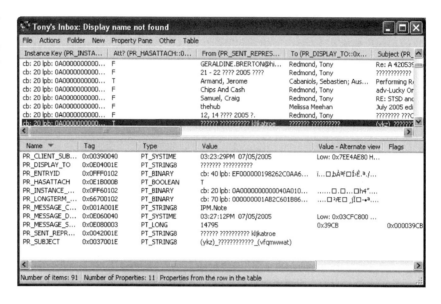

- Ensure that your Windows account has permissions to access the mailbox.

- Create a profile to access the mailbox.

- Start MFCMAPI and select the profile to log onto the mailbox.

- Expand the mailbox folders, select the inbox folder, then right click and select "Open Associated Contents Table" to display the hidden items for the folder. Exchange stores rules as hidden items, so you can then look in the Message Class column in the top pane to locate the IPM.Note.Rules.OofTemplate.Microsoft item.

- Click on the item in the top pane and select the PR_BODY property in the bottom pane. Right click and select "Edit Property" to access the current OOF message. Edit to the desired value and click on okay to set the new value.

This is a simple but effective example of the power of MFCMAPI and it is great to have a tool that you can use to interrogate and change mailbox contents. However, on a note of caution, you should not perform surgery on user mailboxes with tools like MFCMAPI if you do not know exactly what the result of the surgery will be. It is too easy to select something important and either delete or alter it with unknown consequences. Try MFCMAPI out on a test mailbox first before you apply your scalpel to your boss's mailbox.

10.5.3   MDBVU32

Figure 10.26
MDBVU32

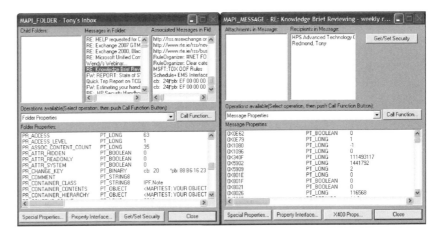

At this point, MDBVU32 (otherwise known as the Information Store Viewer) is an old utility that has been around for many years. It is a MAPI utility that can open mailboxes, public folders, and PSTs. In some respects, you can regard MFCMAPI as a more sophisticated and developed version of MDBVU32. Someone in the team who wrote MDBVU32 has a sense of humor because the program icon is a flaming drum of toxic waste. The reason why the icon was chosen is clear enough when you use the program to navigate within a MAPI store and realize that you're playing with raw MAPI information such as folder and item properties, and if you make a mistake and change something that you shouldn't have, there is no user-friendly undo command available. Figure 10.26 illustrates a typical MDBVU32 session. In the left-hand screen, I have navigated to my Inbox folder and am viewing the various items found there. The properties of the currently selected item are shown and I can move through the folder until I find an item that interests me. The properties of the selected item open in another dialog (the right-hand screen) and once again, I have the freedom to examine (or alter) values.

MDBVU32 is referenced in a number of Microsoft Knowledge Base articles as something that you can use to fix various problems that can creep into mailboxes. If you need a copy and want to live dangerously, you can download a copy of MDBVU32 from Microsoft's web site.

10.5.4   ExMon—Exchange User Monitor

ExMon is a program that allows administrators to monitor the activity of users who connect to a server with MAPI to determine the load that the users put on the server and so be able to respond to user queries if a server runs slowly. ExMon relies on the Windows Event Tracing subsystem (ETW), which Microsoft created to support low-overhead performance analysis of Windows applications. ExMon works with any version of Exchange from Exchange 2000 SP2 onwards and supports two modes: data capture and data view. In data capture mode, you can either launch the ExMon executable to capture and view data or use the standard Windows Systems Monitor tool to capture performance data that you later view with ExMon. Figure 10.27 shows ExMon in action as it monitors the performance of a relatively lightly loaded Exchange server.

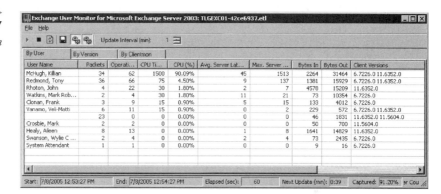

Figure 10.27

ExMon in action

The normal sampling rate is to snapshot performance data once a minute. As you can see from Figure 10.27, ExMon lists the users who are connected currently to the server with a MAPI client, together with some performance information for each user. The data includes:

- The client version used to connect. In Figure 10.27, some users are listed as connecting with two clients. This is accounted for by the fact that these users are connected with Outlook and with a BlackBerry mobile device. The Outlook client is indicated with a build number beginning with 11 (Outlook 2003), while the BlackBerry Enterprise Server logs on to the users' mailboxes to forward new messages with a server-side MAPI connection, shown as a client version of 6.7226.0. ExMon does not capture performance data for clients that connect via Outlook Web Access, POP3, or IMAP4. The data for Outlook also includes some resources absorbed by Microsoft Communicator when it connects to a mailbox to retrieve information about a user's status from the calendar.

- The amount of CPU used by each user, or rather, the percentage of the CPU consumed by the Exchange Store process. In Figure 10.27, you can see that one user seems to take up more than 90% of the CPU. While this seems to be startling, you can explain the 90% figure by realizing that the overall demand that the Store makes on the system when the snapshot was taken might be low and the user might be performing a CPU-intense operation (such as the initial log on and synchronization of a cached mode mailbox) while all the other clients are inactive. While you can ignore abnormal peaks, if a specific user persists in using a high percentage of CPU over a period then this is something that you should investigate to understand what they are doing to consume so much CPU.

■ There is a blank entry for clients that are in the process of connecting to Exchange during the sampling period.

■ The System Attendant logs on to the Store to perform updates to special folders.

The status line at the bottom of the ExMon window displays other details including the percentage of the CPU used by the Store that ExMon has captured relative to the overall CPU used by the Store. The difference between this figure and 100% represents the CPU used by non-MAPI clients.

While it is interesting to view user demand in almost real time, the fact is that different user activities will generate peaks that may mask the underlying performance of the system. If you suspect that a performance problem exists, it is better to collect data over a period and then use ExMon to analyze the information. For example, Figure 10.28 shows how ExMon displays data gathered from an Exchange server over nearly four days. To get this information, I used ExMon to interpret an ETL file generated by the System Monitor with a command like:

```
C: EXMON C:\LOGS\Exchange-Performance-July.ETL
```

One snapshot of data like this is not too helpful, but you can use ExMon's export mode to output the data to a CSV file after you have checked that there is no obvious problem to resolve. You can then import the CSV data into a database such as Access to perform analysis over time, or import the data into Excel to compare different periods against each other. Some administrators like to take regular performance snapshots with ExMon to track demand on their servers so that they can predict when a hardware refresh or upgrade is required.

Microsoft plans to have an upgraded version of ExMon available for Exchange 2007 soon after product release. It is a useful utility to have in an administrative toolbox for any time when Exchange seems to be sluggish. It will not fix performance problems, but it might tell you where they originate from.

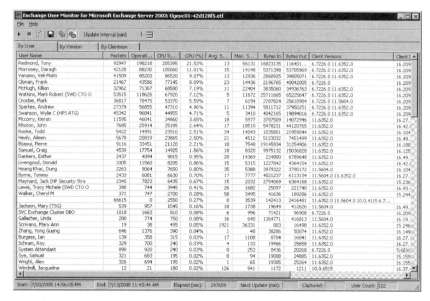

Figure 10.28
Viewing ExMon data extracted over a period

10.5.5 PFDavAdmin

PFDavAdmin is a utility that administrators run on Exchange 2003 servers to extract details of the public folders within an organization. You cannot run PFDavAdmin on an Exchange 2007 server because Exchange 2007 uses a new version of server-side MAPI that doesn't support 32-bit applications. The value of PFDavAdmin is therefore in helping you to understand what data exists in public folders within the organization so that you can better prepare for an eventual migration.

You can report on all public folders in the hierarchy or just the folders in a selected branch of the hierarchy. The report lists permissions and counts for content plus information about when a user last updated content in the folders. You can download the PFDavAdmin kit from Microsoft's web site and then unpack the contents of the kit (a compressed file containing all the necessary files) into a suitable folder where you can store and unpack the kit. You run PFDavAdmin.exe interactively (Figure 10.29) or in batch mode to create reports about public folder content. It is best to run the report on a server that hosts replicas of the folders that you want to generate the report for as otherwise the report will contain a lot of blank information, such as zero counts for items. The zero count in a folder is probably because Exchange replicates the complete public folder hierarchy but only the content for the folders that you select for replication. Thus, you end up with a list of folders that seem to contain nothing whereas in fact you have generated a report of the folder hierarchy. Further details of how to run the program are included in a document in the kit.

Figure 10.29

*Running
PFDavAdmin*

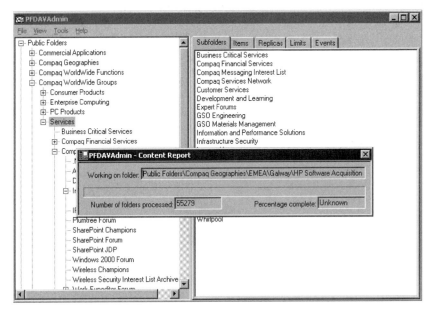

Because public folders are now in a transition phase toward an eventual phase out from Exchange, many administrators want to know what content exists in their public folders. You can run PFDavAdmin to generate a report and then load the file that the program generates into a spreadsheet for easier analysis. For example, you can sort the data by size to see the biggest folders (or those that are empty) or by "newest creation date" to look for folders that have not been active in a while. Empty folders are good candidates for immediate deletion, unless someone has created them recently and has not had a chance to use them yet. Be careful with the last accessed date because programs that analyze or index public folders may influence the last accessed date, leading to a situation where you think that users are regularly accessing obsolete folders.

Possibly the more interesting folders are the ones that have been around for a while but have not been active in the last few years. Many companies that deployed Exchange in the 1996–2000 period embraced public folders enthusiastically and ended up with large numbers of public folders. Some of the folders had associated applications, others hold archives for distribution lists, and others are repositories where teams share documents. Some are just dumping grounds for material that accumulated over time that no one really knows to exist. After you analyze the results from scanning your public folder hierarchy and identify likely candidates for deletion, you need to:

- Note the owner of the folder and advise them that you will delete their folder at some point in the future unless they can provide a good reason for its retention. Give them a week or so to respond. If you do not receive a reply, the owner probably does not want the folder.

- Decide what to do with folders who do not have an owner (usually because the original owner has left the company). In most cases, you can delete these folders if no one is using them.

- Decide whether to archive information before you delete the folders. Your legal department may require you to archive information just in case it is required to support a legal action. It is usually best to archive contents to something like a PST (for a small number of folders that are not very large) or to a more complex (and costly) archiving solution.

- Decide whether you want to set item retention limits for remaining folders. This is a good idea because it means that Exchange will automatically remove old material from folders during its regular Store housekeeping runs.

- Decide how often you will run public folder analysis so that you detect and clean out unwanted folders on a regular basis.

Like any utility, PFDavAdmin is not a magic bullet and it will definitely not solve any problems with public folder management. However, it will give you an insight into the contents of the folders and provide you with enough information to make an intelligent decision about how to clean up what can be a mess before you decide what future public folders have within your organization.

10.5.6 LogParser

LogParser is a free Microsoft utility that is unsupported apart from the best effort of its author through www.logparser.com. You can read more about LogParser at http://www.microsoft.com/technet/scriptcenter/tools/logparser/default.mspx and get a copy of LogParser from Microsoft's web site. The best presentation ever made on how to exploit LogParser for all kinds of administrative purposes was by Mike Ireland, who's presented on this topic at TechEd and the Exchange Connections conferences. If you can get a copy of his presentation, it'll be invaluable to you to understand just what potential exists in this utility.

The charm of LogParser is that it provides SQL-like access to a variety of data sources including the Windows event log, the system registry, the Active Directory, and Exchange 2000/2003 message tracking logs. LogParser can interrogate these data sources and output the results in a variety of formats, including plain text, HTML, charts, and into an SQL database. A powerful and flexible utility capable of processing a lot of message tracking data quickly, LogParser deserves some attention from Exchange administrators, because you can use LogParser to interrogate data sources such as IIS logs and Exchange 2000/2003 message tracking logs, both of which contain much valuable and interesting information about the way your servers are used. For example, you can analyze the IIS logs from an ISA server that provides access to Windows Mobile devices to determine how much data is transmitted to each device, what kind of email synchronization operations (download, send message, etc.) they perform, and how often devices connect to Exchange via ActiveSync. You can find some useful scripts to help you interrogate the IIS logs for ActiveSync activity on the Exchange team blog site (see page 978).

As an example, we will look at how to use LogParser to extract some useful information about message traffic on an Exchange 2003 server. Recall that Exchange 2007 supports shell commands to analyze message tracking logs, so you do not need to use LogParser for Exchange 2007 for basic interrogation such as finding the records for a particular message. LogParser has better capabilities than PowerShell when it comes to counting and analyzing records, so it's still a useful tool to have available if you want to use message tracking log data as the basis for mail traffic analysis.

After you download the LogParser kit, you will find that the installation procedure is rudimentary but functional and normally completes in less than a minute. The installation creates a folder called \Program Files\LogParser 2.2 and stores all the LogParser files there, including the executable, Log-Parser.exe. If you have ever used SQL, the syntax used by Log Parser should be familiar. For example, to count all the messages received on a server, you issue the command:

```
C:> LogParser "SELECT COUNT(*) FROM C:\TEMP\server.log WHERE
[Event-ID] = 1028" —i:W3C
```

This command generates output like this:

```
COUNT (ALL *)
------------
20623


Statistics:
-----------
Elements processed: 1088985
```

```
Elements output:     1
Execution time:      16.50 seconds
```

All you asked LogParser to do is to count the number of records in the log file that you specified as input. You can pass parameters such as c:\Logs\ *.log to instruct LogParser to process a group of message tracking logs in a folder. In this example, we looked for records with an event ID of 1028, which is the identifier that Exchange writes into the message tracking log when a message is delivered to a local mailbox on a server. The "-i:W3C" parameter means that the input file is in W3C format, which is the format supported by Exchange 2000/2003 message tracking logs. Note that Log Parser processed over one million records in 16.5 seconds—this is not a slow utility and you should be able to process even very large message tracking logs very quickly. Knowing how many records are in one or more message tracking logs is not very interesting, so we can execute a more sophisticated query to look for the top 10 recipients of the messages delivered to mailboxes on our server. First, we need to know what fields exist in the source logs. You can ask LogParser to parse a file and report what it finds as follows:

```
C:>LogParser –h –i:w3c C:\TEMP\Tracking.Log
```

LogParser treats fields in message tracking logs as either strings (S) or integer (I).

The query that we need to create a collection of 1028 events, group them by recipient, and then output a listing is:

```
C:> LogParser "SELECT TOP 10 Recipient-Address, COUNT(*) as
[#Messages] FROM %logs%
WHERE [Event-ID] = 1028
GROUP BY Recipient-Address
ORDER BY [#Messages] DESC"
```

This query is obviously more complex and wraps over several lines in a command window. For the purpose of debugging and ease of use, it is more convenient to create queries like this in a text file that you can then feed to LogParser by passing the name of the text file as a parameter. As we are discussing parameters, I have included a parameter called "logs" in the query to allow me to specify the location of the input logs. We can take the complete query into a file called recipients.sql and then execute it as follows:

```
C:>LogParser file:recipients.sql?logs=c:\temp\*.log –i:w3c
```

By default, LogParser outputs results to the screen and pauses output after every 10 lines. Normally, I pipe the output to a text file by including something like "> c:\temp\output.txt" at the end of the command, but if you output to a file, there is no point in specifying anything other than "TOP 10" in your query as LogParser pauses after every 10 lines and the command will never complete. In either case, the result is something like this:

```
Recipient-Address              #Messages
----------------------------   ---------
kmc@xyz.com                    3409
alerts@xyz.com                 2880
ajr@xyz.com                    1636
bij@xyz.com                    1269
kal@xyz.com                    1223
jrr@xyz.com                    1074
vmv@xyz.com                    789
djl@xyz.com                    725
Server-IS@xyz.com              737
User1@xyz.com                  722
```

This information is interesting, but we can refine things a little more. Note an entry for Server-IS@xyz.com, which is the address of the local Public Folder replication agent. We may be interested in knowing how many incoming replication messages arrived on our server, but it is more likely that we want to know about the activity of real people, so we need to exclude public folder replication messages. You can suppress the count of public folder replication messages by excluding any message sent to an address that includes the string "-IS@" as shown below. The full query is:

```
SELECT TOP 10 Recipient-Address, COUNT(*) as [#Messages]
FROM %logs%
WHERE [Event-ID] = 1028 AND Recipient-Address NOT LIKE '%-
IS@%'
GROUP BY Recipient-Address
ORDER BY [#Messages] DESC
```

Knowing how many messages a user receives is interesting, but what about knowing the total size of the messages that they receive? We can tweak our script to do the necessary work by computing the size of the total bytes field that Exchange logs for each message. Reporting the size in megabytes is more readable than bytes, so we can use a combination of the DIV and SUM commands to do the work. Notice that we divide the computed value by 1,048,756 to get the value in megabytes.

```
SELECT TOP 10 Recipient-Address, COUNT(*) as [#Messages],
DIV(SUM(Total-Bytes),1048756) AS [MB Incoming]
FROM %logs%
WHERE [Event-ID] = 1028 AND Recipient-Address NOT LIKE '%-
IS@%'
GROUP BY Recipient-Address
ORDER BY [#Messages] DESC
```

The output is:

```
Recipient-Address          #Messages MB Incoming
------------------------   --------- -----------
kmc@xyz.com                3409      94
alerts@xyz.com             2880      8
ajr@xyz.com                1636      98
bij@xyz.com                1269      88
kal@xyz.com                1223      63
jrr@xyz.com                1074      43
vmv@xyz.com                789       21
djl.com                    725       41
user1@xyz.com              722       39
tr@xyz.com                 701       80
```

If you set up Client Access servers to provide access for Outlook Anywhere, Outlook Web Access, or ActiveSync, the IIS logs on these servers contain a lot of information about the traffic that these clients generate as they access Exchange. IIS logs all of the data in its logs in IISW3C format. You can use LogParser to interrogate the IIS logs and extract the relevant information and then analyze it to discover statistics such as who are the heaviest users of the service, what kind of transactions (send mail, read mail, etc.) they generate, and so on. The trick to finding information for particular Exchange components is to filter on the cs-uri-stem, where you can use these values:

- Exchange ActiveSync: cs-uri-stem = "/Microsoft-Server-ActiveSync"

- Outlook Web Access: cs-uri-stem LIKE "/exchange%"

- RPC over HTTP: cs-uri-stem = "/rpc/rpcproxy.dll"

The reason why Outlook Web Access requires a LIKE comparison is that Outlook Web Access generates a different URL value for each user and folder that it accesses.

Exchange ActiveSync extends the standard log entry by adding some additional fields to record data about client activity, which makes these logs even more interesting as a data source for analysis. For more information on this topic, see the blog post at http://blogs.technet.com/exchange/archive/2005/03/28/403047.aspx. The only issue that I can think of about using LogParser to analyze data such as message tracking logs and IIS logs is that Microsoft will probably change the format of these logs in the future and you should therefore be prepared to test and perhaps update your scripts for each new release of Exchange or Windows.

LogParser has a lot more functionality that we cannot explore in detail here. For example, you can output in chart format rather than simple text (to do this, you need to have Excel installed on your system) or write data into an SQL database so that you can do more sophisticated queries or combine message tracking data into other reports. If you are interested in expanding your use of LogParser, check out the examples posted on www.logparser.com and the information contained in TechNet.

10.5.7 Outlook Spy

Outlook Spy (see http://www.dimastr.com/outspy/) is a utility that allows you to get a behind-the-scenes view into the Outlook object mode. It is a useful tool for any Exchange administrator to have at their disposal, especially if you need to examine details of mailbox properties. It is an alternative to the MFCMAPI or MDBVU32 utilities.

10.6 Bits and pieces

People ask me all the time what web sites do I visit, what conferences do I attend, and what books and magazines do I read to learn about Exchange. This section gives you a brief overview of some of the information sources that I use, together with all the useful bits and pieces that I cannot find anywhere else in the book.

10.6.1 Where the Exchange team hangs out

For years, the Exchange development group received a lot of criticism because they did not make a lot of information available about how Exchange worked (or as some said, how Exchange really worked) outside the formal product documentation. The lack of documentation allowed a book industry to develop around Exchange, with books appearing from quick administrator guides to in-depth descriptions of how to write server-based applications. Since Exchange 2003 appeared, the development team has done a much better job to communicate with the technical community that buys and supports their product, so it is now possible to find a great deal of insightful information without having to buy a book.

Apart from the formal Exchange product site at www.microsoft.com/exchange, where you will find white papers and downloads, the Exchange developers and other interested parties, such as Microsoft PSS engineers who support Exchange, maintain a blog at http://msexchangeteam.com/default.aspx. You should bookmark this blog and browse it from time to time to discover new developments. The Exchange team blog also links to other web sites and blogs that contain interesting information about Exchange, including local language sites dedicated to Exchange in several countries and a site dedicated to Exchange 2007 at http://www.theexchangewiki.com/. As always, don't believe everything that you read on the Internet until you have validated it in action within your environment.

10.6.2 Online Forums

If you need help, you can ask a question on the Exchange Forum on TechNet at http://forums.microsoft.com/TechNet/default.aspx?Forum-GroupID=235&SiteID=17. The forums are reasonably active and you may well find an answer to your question there.

Another good place to look is the MSExchange.org site at http://www.msexchange.org/. This offers a set of articles on all versions of Exchange, forums, white papers, and other material.

10.7 Conferences

Technologists love conferences. Maybe it is the new bag that we receive at every event, stuffed full of material that we can discard at our leisure, or maybe it is the conference proceedings that attract us to attend these events. Up to 2002, Microsoft ran the Microsoft Exchange Conference (MEC), which was dedicated to all things related to Exchange. MEC, which ran in both the United States and EMEA, attracted the hard-core Exchange fans and was an excellent place to get updates about the latest technical information about the product. Unfortunately, Microsoft decided that MEC was not required and stopped running the event in favor of an expanded TechEd, which became Microsoft's premier technical event.

TechEd is an excellent event to attend and there is no doubt that you can find enough high-quality material at a TechEd to justify attendance. However, the problem with TechEd is that it is just too big, especially in the United States, and the Exchange sessions tend to be swamped by the whole mass of sessions dedicated to anything and everything related to Microsoft technology. The pressure to get a session on the TechEd agenda means that many good session ideas are never presented and you will only ever hear a small part of the technical discussions that could occur about any product there. In addition, for many reasons, the quality of some of the sessions delivered at TechEd events outside the United States is not as high as those delivered in the United States.

The demise of MEC created a vacuum for the Exchange community that conferences such as the Exchange Connections event (www.devconnections.com) have filled. Exchange Connections (and its companion Windows Connections event) is a much smaller gathering than TechEd or an MEC and there are not as many sessions on the agenda. However, the event is dedicated to Exchange and you will be able to listen to a range of speakers from Microsoft, independent consultants, and some of Microsoft's top partners such as HP. The sessions are not marketing fluff and focus on the practical side of how to get things done with Exchange rather than product futures. Overall, while Exchange Connections is not MEC, it is the closest thing that we have to an Exchange community event today and is a worthy venture for that reason.

10.7.1 Magazines

Over the years, I have read many magazine articles about Exchange and many of those articles were in magazines that no longer exist. The magazine publishing world is a tough place with editors in a constant struggle to find and publish high-quality material balanced by the commercial reality of generating income from ads and sales. My personal favorite is the Exchange Administrator newsletter, a monthly publication that I have written for since 1997. The newsletter is now published online, which is something that I regret a little because I like reading technical material on paper.

I like magazines that have exacting editorial standards that force writers to provide interesting material with all their facts checked and accurate, and that is what the staff of Exchange Administrator has done. Its parent magazine, Windows IT Pro (www.windowsitpro.com) differs from the newsletter in that its articles are less "how-to" and more "this is why" in style, but the content is equally good. Both publications are recommended for their quality and durability.

10.7.2 How Exchange uses registry keys

No matter what you do, an Exchange administrator is unlikely to get away from the need to interfere with the system registry at some time during his or her career. As a product, Exchange has always seemed to have an irresistible temptation to use registry settings, and as a development group, the engineers just love going to the registry to store settings that tweak how Exchange works. PSS may recommend that you change a setting to fix a problem, or you will discover a knowledge base article that tells you how to enable new functionality through a registry setting, or you will read about something in a magazine article or book. The list of registry settings that Exchange uses is endless and the worse thing is that outside the source code, no comprehensive list exists of all settings and their values.

Figure 10.30
The Store accesses the registry as it starts up

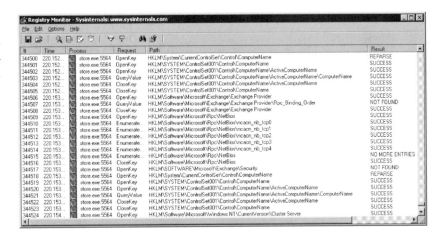

If you doubt that Exchange makes extensive use of the registry or just want to peek behind the scenes, go to http://www.microsoft.com/technet/sysinternals/default.mspxand and download a copy of the RegMon utility and run it (Figure 10.30) to observe the interaction between Exchange components such as the Store and System Attendant and the registry.

10.8   Good reference books

When you work with a product as complex as Exchange, you always have the need for knowledge about many different subjects. This is a small list of the books that I have read and enjoyed that have helped me understand the technologies that surround Exchange. While some cover Exchange 2003, their content is still valuable for Exchange 2007.

Windows PowerShell in Action—Bruce Payette (2007), ISBN 978-1932394900

Monad (PowerShell)—Andy Oakley (2006), ISBN 0-596-10009-4

Secure Messaging with Microsoft Exchange Server 2003—Paul Robichaux (2004), ISBN 0735619905

Microsoft® Exchange Server 2003 Scalability with SP1 and SP2—Pierre Bijaoui (2006), ISBN 1555583008

Microsoft SharePoint Technologies: Planning, Design and Implementation—Kevin Laahs, Emer McKenna, and Veli-Matti Vanamo (2004), ISBN 1555583016

Microsoft Windows Security Fundamentals: For Windows 2003 SP1 and R2—Jan De Clercq and Guido Grillenmeier (2006), ISBN 1555583407

Appendix

A.1   Message Tracking Log Format

Field	Type	Description
Client-IP	IPAddress	The IP address of the submitting server, which could be a remote Messaging Client/MTA.
Client-hostname	string	The name of the messaging client application that submitted the message.
Connector-ID	string	The ID of the connector that this message was received/sent from
Message-ID	string	Internet message ID – from the P2 headers of the message. If none is present on an inbound message, Exchange stamps a unique Message ID on the message
Source	string	The component that submitted this message to the system. It can be one of the following: ■ SMTP ■ Pick-Up ■ Gateway (Notes Connector or any other third party application to Exchange 2007) ■ Store Driver ■ Routing ■ DSN ■ Agent ■ Admin
Event	string	The transport action (such as SUBMIT) carried out on this message

Field	Type	Description
Internal-message-id	Long	A unique identifier for the message that is generated by the Exchange 2007 server. Unlike the Message identifier, which remains constant for the message lifetime, this identifier is unique for every hop the message takes in the system.
Message-subject	string	Subject of the message
Source-context	string	A hint associated with source to provide some extra information while troubleshooting. The protocol session ID for the "SMTP" source. The pickup file name and email file name for "PickUp" and "Gateway" source. The Agent name for the "Agent" source
Sender Address	string	The email address in the RFC 822 From: header
Recipient Address	Collection of strings	The e-mail addresses of the recipients in a message. This could be a group address and not the addressees of the individual recipients.
Related-recipient-address	string	Related-Recipient-Address is used with the Resolve event to indicate the secondary SMTP address or in the Expand case it is the expanded address.
Recipient-count	Integer	The number of recipients in the message
Recipient status	string	This field is only populated for the Send Event and contains the SMTP Response that the server generates when the message is sent or relayed to another server.
Reference	Collection of strings	Reference is a field to provide administrators with more information about the event: ■ For Send Events, it contains the Internet-Message-Id of the DSN, if any ■ For Transfer Events, it contains the Internal-Message-Id of the message being forked ■ For DSN Events, it contains the Internet-Message-Id of the message that caused the DSN
Server-hostname	string	The name of the server instance that created the message tracking log entry.
Server-IP	IPAddress	**The IP address of the Exchange server. In case of IP Load balancing this** is the connecting IP not the server static IP
Time	DateTime	The date and time, (in UTC) the message tracking log entry was created

Field	Type	Description
Total-bytes	long	Message size, including attachments, in bytes
Security Info	string	The mechanism (if any) used to authentication the message
MessageInfo	DateTime	Timestamp when the message passes from one point to another in the messaging system

A.2   Events noted in Message Tracking Logs

Event	Description
Receive	ACTION: Message received and has been committed into the database SOURCE: SMTP, Pickup, Gateway, Store Driver and Agents
Send	ACTION: Message relayed via SMTP to another server SOURCE: The only source is "SMTP"
Fail	ACTION: Message failed somewhere in the system SOURCE: SMTP (outbound), Store Driver, DNS and transport Agents
DSN	ACTION: A delivery status notification was generated. SOURCE: DSN Generator Logic in the system
Deliver	ACTION: Message was delivered to destination mailbox SOURCE: Only Storedriver
Badmail	ACTION: Message was deleted permanently, because it was a DSN of a DSN. Possible Source – DSN/Pickup SOURCE: DSN Generator Logic in the system
Resolve	ACTION: Recipients have been resolved to another address after an AD lookup SOURCE: Routing
Expand	ACTION: A DL was expanded by the system SOURCE: Routing
Redirect	ACTION: Message that was intended for a recipient was redirected to an alternate recipient after an AD lookup SOURCE: Routing
Transfer	ACTION: Some recipients are moved to a forked message. This can happen due to many reasons like Content Conversion, limiting the number of recipients per message and Agents need to fork when a recipient-specific rule hits and content modification is required. This information is great for troubleshooting. SOURCE: Routing, Agent

Event	Description
Submit	ACTION: Message submitted by the Mailbox into transport server SOURCE: Store

B

Important Exchange PowerShell commands

I mention the commands listed in this appendix somewhere in the book, so they must be reasonably important. If you're missing a PowerShell command that you think you need, check the PowerShell Community Extensions site at http://www.codeplex.com/PowerShellCX/Release/ProjectReleases.aspx to see all the commands that people have created and shared. You may find the command of your dreams there!

Get-Command	Query all of the shell commands available (including standard Windows PowerShell commands)
Get-ExCommand	Query all of the Exchange 2007 shell commands that are available. Get-ExCommand *Connector* reports all of the shell commands that mention "Connector" in their name

B.1 Recipient management commands

New-Mailbox	Creates a new mailbox (see Chapter 4 for examples)
Set-Mailbox	Sets properties on an existing mailbox
Get-Mailbox	Retrieves properties of an existing mailbox Get-Mailbox –id Redmond retrieves properties of Redmond's mailbox Get-Mailbox –server 'XYZ1' retrieves all mailboxes on server XYZ1
Disable-Mailbox	Disables a mailbox Disable-Mailbox –id 'Jane Smith'
Remove-Mailbox	Removes a mailbox and its Active Directory object Remove-Mailbox –id 'Jane Smith'

Connect-Mailbox	Reconnect a disconnected mailbox with an Active Directory account
	Connect-Mailbox –id 'Smith, JP' –User JPSmith
Restore-Mailbox	Restore information from a mailbox in a database mounted in a Recovery Storage Group.
	Restore-Mailbox –Id 'Redmond'-RSGDatabase 'ExchMbxSvr1\ Recovery Storage Group\VIP Mailboxes'
Get-MailboxStatistics	Returns mailbox statistics for a server, database, or mailbox
	Get-MailboxStatistics –id Redmond
	Get-MailboxStatistics –Server ExchMbxSvr1
	Get-MailboxStatistics –Database 'VIP Mailboxes'
Move-Mailbox	Moves a mailbox to another database or server. You can pass the –ConfigurationOnly parameter to update the mailbox information in Active Directory without moving the mailbox contents.
	Move-Mailbox –id Redmond –TargetDatabase 'ExchMbxSvr3\VIP Mailboxes'
Add-MailboxPermission	Assign permission to a user over a mailbox. For example, to allow a user to open another user's mailbox
Get-MailboxPermission	Retrieves details about permissions held over a mailbox
Set-MailboxCalendarSettings	Set calendar properties on a room mailbox
Get-MailboxCalendarSettings	Retrieves information about the calendar properties on a room mailbox
	Get-MailboxCalendarSettings –id 'Liffey Room'
Set-ResourceConfig	Set resource configuration on an equipment mailbox
	Set-ResourceConfig –ResourcePropertySchema ("Room/TV", "Room/Concall", "Room/Couch", "Room/Whiteboard", "Equip-ment/VCR", "Equipment/ComfortableChairs")
Get-Recipient	Returns a full set of properties for Active Directory recipient objects.
	Get-Recipient –RecipientType MailUniversalSecurityGroup
New-Mailcontact	Creates a new mail-enabled contact
Get-Mailcontact	Retrieves the properties of a mail-enabled contact
	Get-MailContact –id Smith
Set-MailContact	Sets properties on a mail-enabled contact
	Set-MailContact –id Smith –UseMapiRichTextFormat Always

Remove-MailContact	Deletes a mail-enabled contact Remove-MailContact –id Smith
Enable-MailContact	Mail-enables an existing Active Directory contact Enable-MailContact –id 'JFS' –ExternalMailAddress 'jfs@xyz.com'
Disable-MailContact	Disable a mail contact by removing the Exchange attributes. The contact reverts to being a "normal" contact Disable-MailContact –id 'JFS'
New-DistributionGroup	Creates a new distribution group
Set-DistributionGroup	Sets properties on a distribution group Set-Distribution Group –id 'Senior Executives' –ExpansionServer ExchHub1
Get-DistributionGroup	Retrieves properties of a distribution group
Remove-DistributionGroup	Deletes a distribution group Remove-DistributionGroup –id 'Senior Executives'
Get-DistributionGroupMember	Retrieves the membership of a distribution group Get-DistributionGroupMember -id 'Senior Executives'
New-DynamicDistributionGroup	Creates a new dynamic distribution group
Set-DynamicDistributionGroup	Sets properties on a dynamic distribution group Set-DynamicDistributionGroup –id 'Irish Employees' –CustomAttribute1 'Important'
Get-DynamicDistributionGroup	Retrieves properties of a dynamic distribution group Get-DynamicDistributionGroup –id 'Irish Employees' | Format-List
Remove-DynamicDistribution-Group	Deletes a dynamic distribution group Remove-DynamicDistributionGroup –id 'Company Users'
Set-CasMailbox	Sets properties of a mailbox for a Client Access Server Set-CasMailbox –id Redmond –ActiveSyncMailboxPolicy 'Mobile Users'
Get-CasMailbox	Retrieves properties of a mailbox from a Client Access server Get-CasMailbox –id Redmond | Format-List
Export-Mailbox	Exports the contents of a mailbox to another mailbox. Export-Mailbox –id 'Jane Smith' –TargetMailbox 'Legal Review' –TargetFolder 'Reviews'

Enable-UmMailbox	Enable a mailbox for Unified Messaging Enable-UmMailbox –id Redmond –UmPolicy 'Dublin Users' –Extensions 5143 –PIN 452545 –PINExpired $True
Disable-UmMailbox	Disable a mailbox for Unified Messaging Disable-UmMailbox –id Redmond
Get-UmMailbox	Retrieve properties for a mailbox that is enabled for Unified Messaging Get-UmMailbox –id Redmond | Format-List
Set-UmMailbox	Set Unified Messaging properties on a mailbox Set-UmMailbox –id Redmond –FaxEnabled $True
Get-UmMailboxPIN	Retrieve PIN information for a Unified Messaging mailbox Get-UmMailboxPIN –id Redmond
Set-UmMailboxPIN	Set PIN information for a mailbox Set-UMMailboxPIN –id Redmond –PIN 174646 –PINExpired $True

B.2   Exchange server administrative Commands

Get-ExchangeServer	Retrieves details of an individual server or the servers in the organization Get-ExchangeServer –id ExchMbxSvr1 Get-ExchangeServer –Status (include AD information)
Add-ExchangeAdministrator	Add a new Exchange administrator Add-ExchangeAdministrator –id Redmond –Role ServerAdmin –Scope ExchMbxSvr1
Get-ExchangeAdministrator	Retrieves details of users who hold some administrative permission over Exchange Get-ExchangeAdministrator –id Redmond | Format-List
Remove-ExchangeAdministrator	Remove administrative permission over Exchange from a user Remove-ExchangeAdministrator –id Redmond –Role OrgAdmin
Get-ExchangeCertificate	Views details of the certificates used by Exchange that are in the local certificate store Get-ExchangeCertificate
Get-MailboxServer	Retrieve properties of a selected or all mailbox servers Get-MailboxServer –id ExchMbxSvr1

Set-MailboxServer	Sets a property on an Exchange mailbox server Set-MailboxServer –id ExchMbxSvr1 –MessageTrackingEnabled $False
Get-TransportServer	Retrieves details about a selected or all transport servers Get-TransportServer –id ExchHub1
Set-TransportServer	Sets a property on an Exchange hub transport or Edge server Set-TransportServer –id ExchEdge1 –MessageTrackingEnabled $False
Get-MessageTrackingLog	Search the message tracking log for messages Get-MessageTrackingLog –Start "7/1/2007 9:00AM" –End "7/1/ 2007 10:00AM" | Sort Timestamp
Get-MailboxFolderStatistics	Retrieve information about the folders in a mailbox Get-MailboxFolderStatistics –id Redmond
Move-ClusteredMailboxServer	Move Exchange resources from one node to another in a shared storage cluster.
Get-OWAVirtualDirectory	Retrieve details of Outlook Web Access settings.
Set-OWAVirtualDirectory	Set properties for Outlook Web Access
Get-UMServer	Retrieve properties for a Unified Messaging server. Get-UMServer –id ExchUM1 | Format-List
Set-UMServer	Set properties for a Unified Messaging server.
Get-ClientAccessServer	Retrieve properties for a Client Access server.
Set-ClientAccessServer	Set properties for a Client Access server
Get-OrganizationConfig	Retrieve configuration settings for the organization Get-OrganizationConfig
Set-OrganizationConfig	Set a property for the organization Set-OrganizationConfig –SCLThreshold 7
Get-EventLogLevel	Return the current diagnostics level for an Exchange component Get-EventLogLevel –id 'MSExchangeIS'
Set-EventLogLevel	Set a diagnostics level for an Exchange component Set-EventLogLevel –id 'MSExchangeTransport\Categorizer' –Level High
Get-ManagedFolder	Retrieve the properties of a managed folder Get-ManagedFolder –id 'Business Critical Documents'

Set-ManagedFolder	Sets the properties of a managed folder.
	Set-ManagedFolder –id 'Business Critical Documents' –Storage-Quota 1GB
Remove-ManagedFolder	Removes a managed folder
	Remove-ManagedFolder –id 'Business Critical Documents'
New-ManagedFolder	Creates a new managed folder
Get-ManagedContentSettings	Retrieve the content settings for a managed folder.
	Get-ManagedFolderContentSettings –id 'Age out calendar items'
Set-ManagedContentSettings	Set the properties of a content setting for a managed folder.
	Set-ManagedFolderContentSettings –id 'Age out calendar items' –AgeLimitForRetention 45.00:00:00
Remove-ManagedContentSettings	Remove a content setting for a managed folder.
	Remove-ManagedFolderContentSettings –id 'Age out calendar items'
New-ManagedContentSettings	Create a new content setting for a managed folder.
Start-ManagedFoldersAssistant	Start the managed folders assistant to process mailboxes
	Start-ManagedFoldersAssistant
Stop-ManagedFoldersAssistant	Force the managed folders assistant to stop processing mailboxes
	Stop-ManagedFoldersAssistant
Update-FileDistributionService	Force a Client Access Server to poll for OAB updates through the Exchange File Distribution service.
	Update-FileDistributionService –id 'ExchCAS1' –Type 'OAB'
Enable-OutlookAnywhere	Enable Outlook Anywhere on a Client Access server.
	Enable-OutlookAnywhere –Server ExchCas1
	–ExternalAuthenticationMethod 'NTLM'
	–ExternalHostName 'Mail.xyz.com'
Disable-OutlookAnywhere	Disable Outlook Anywhere on a Client Access server.
	Disable-OutlookAnywhere –Server 'ExchCas1'
Get-OutlookAnywhere	Retrieve the properties of Outlook Anywhere on a Client Access server.
	Get-OutlookAnywhere –Server 'ExchCAS1'
Set-OutlookAnywhere	Set the properties of Outlook Anywhere on a Client Access server.
	Set-OutlookAnywhere –id 'ExchCAS1\rpc (Default Web Site)' –ExternalAuthenticationMethod 'NTLM'

Get-UMServer	Retrieve details of an Exchange 2007 Unified Messaging server
	Get-UMServer –id 'ExchUMSvr1' | Format-List
Set-UMServer	Set properties for an Exchange 2007 Unified Messaging server
	Set-UMServer –id 'ExchUMSvr1' –MaxCallsAllowed 120

B.3   Databases and Storage Groups

Get-MailboxDatabase	Return properties for one or more mailbox databases
	Get-MailboxDatabase –Server ExchMBXSvr1
Set-MailboxDatabase	Set properties on a mailbox database
	Set-MailboxDatabase –id 'SG1\Mailboxes'
	–ProhibitSendQuota 1GB
New-MailboxDatabase	Create a new mailbox database
Remove-MailboxDatabase	Delete a mailbox database
	Remove-MailboxDatabase –id 'SG1\Mailboxes'
Clean-MailboxDatabase	Search for disconnected mailboxes that are not properly marked and correct their status
	Clean-MailboxDatabase –id 'SG1\Mailboxes'
New-PublicFolderDatabase	Create a new public folder database
Get-PublicFolderDatabase	Return properties of a public folder database
	Get-PublicFolderDatabase –id 'Public Folders'
Set-PublicFolderDatabase	Set a property on a public folder database
	Set-PublicFolderDatabase –id 'Public Folders'–MaxItemSize 10MB
Remove-PublicFolderDatabase	Remove a public folder database
	Remove-PublicFolderDatabase –id 'SG2\PFDB'
New-StorageGroup	Create a new storage group
Get-StorageGroup	Retrieve properties of a storage group
	Get-StorageGroup –id 'ExchMbxSvr2\SG1'
Set-StorageGroup	Set properties of a storage group
	Set-StorageGroup –id 'ExchMbxSvr2\SG1'
	–CircularLogEnabled $True
Remove-StorageGroup	Remove a storage group
	Remove-StorageGroup –id 'ExchMbxSvr2\SG3'

Get-StorageGroupCopyStatus	Return the LCR status for a storage group Get-StorageGroupCopyStatus
Suspend-StorageGroupCopy	Suspend LCR processing for a storage group Suspend-StorageGroupCopy –id 'ExchMbxSvr2\SG3' –Suspend-Comment 'Moving to new disks'
Resume-StorageGroupCopy	Resume LCR processing after suspension Resume-StorageGroupCopy –id 'ExchMbxSvr2\SG3'
Update-StorageGroupCopy	Restart LCR processing for a storage group with a new seed copy of the production database Update-StorageGroupCopy –id 'ExchMbxSvr2\SG3'
Restore-StorageGroupCopy	Terminates replication activity and prepares a copy database to be mounted as the production copy Restore-StorageGroupCopy –id 'ExchMbxSvr2\SG3'
Enable-StorageGroupCopy	Enable LCR processing for a storage group Enable-StorageGroupCopy –id 'ExchMbxSvr2\SG3' –CopyLog-FolderPath 'L:\Logs\SG3\' –CopySystemFolderPath 'D:\Exchange\System\'
Disable-StorageGroupCopy	Disable LCR processing for a storage group and remove the copy files. Disable-StorageGroupCopy –id 'ExchMbxSvr2\SG3'
Get-ClusteredMailboxServerStatus	Return the status of a clustered mailbox server. Get-ClusteredMailboxServerStatus
Move-ClusteredMailboxServer	Move a mailbox server from one node of a cluster to another Move-ClusteredMailboxServer –id ExchCluster1 –TargetServer ExchCluster2 –MoveComment 'Apply patches to ExchCluster2
Mount-Database	Mount a database. Mount-Database –id 'Critical Mailboxes\VIP Mailboxes'
Dismount-Database	Dismount a database. Dismount-Database –id 'Critical Mailboxes\VIP Mailboxes'
Move-StorageGroupPath	Move the disk location for a storage group's transaction logs, system files, or the copy locations (for LCR). Note that you can pass the –ConfigurationOnly parameter to update the location in Active Directory Move-StorageGroupPath –id 'ExchMbxSvr3\VIP Data' –Log-FolderPath 'G:\Logs\'

| Move-DatabasePath | Move the disk location for an EDB database or its LCR copy. The ConfigurationOnly option is also available for this command. Move-DatabasePath –id 'ExchMbxSvr1\VIP Mailboxes' –EdbFile-Path 'D:\Databases\VIP' |

B.4   Address Lists and Email Policies

Get-AddressList	Retrieve properties for all Address Lists in the organization or a specific address list Get-AddressList –id 'All Users' | Format-List
Set-AddressList	Set properties for an Address List Set-AddressList –id 'All Groups' –IncludedRecipients MailGroups
New-AddressList	Create a new Address List
Remove-AddressList	Remove an Address List Remove-AddressList –id 'NewAddressList'
Get-GlobalAddressList	Retrieve properties for the Global Address List Get-GlobalAddressList | Format-List
Set-GlobalAddressList	Set properties for the Global Address List
Get-EmailAddressPolicy	Retrieve properties for all Email Address Policies in the organization or a specific policy Get-EmailAddressPolicy –id 'Default Policy'
Set-EmailAddressPolicy	Set properties on a specific Email Address Policy
New-EmailAddressPolicy	Create a new Email Address Policy
Remove-EmailAddressPolicy	Remove an Email Address Policy
Get-OfflineAddressBook	Retrieve properties for one or more Offline Address Books
Set-OfflineAddressBook	Set properties for an Offline Address Book
New-OfflineAddressBook	Create a new Offline Address Book

B.5   Queues and Messages

| Get-Queue | Show all the messages on one or more queues Get-Queue –id Submission \| Format-List |

Suspend-Queue	Suspends processing of messages on the selected queue Suspend-Queue –id 'ExchHub1\57'
Resume-Queue	Resumes processing of messages on the selected queue Resume-Queue –id 'ExchHub1\57'
Retry-Queue	Forces a connection attempt for a queue that is in retry status Retry-Queue –id 'ExchHub1\57'
Get-Message	Retrieve details of one or more messages on a queue Get-Message –id 'ExchHub1\40\26' | Format-List
Suspend-Message	Suspends processing of a message that's on a queue Suspend-Message –id 'ExchHub1\40\26'
Resume-Message	Releases a suspended message and makes it active again Resume-Message –id 'ExchHub\40\26'
Remove-Message	Removes a message from a queue, with or without sending an NDR Remove-Message –id 'ExchHub\40\26' –WithNDR $True

B.6   Edge Synchronization

New-EdgeSubscription	Exports or imports an XML file containing details of a synchronization subscription between an Edge server and a hub transport server New-EdgeSubscription –Filename c:\Edge.XML New-EdgeSubscription –Filename c:\Edge.XML –Site 'New York'
Get-EdgeSubscription	Retrieves details of an Edge subscription Get-EdgeSubscription | Format-List
Remove-EdgeSubscription	Removes an Edge subscription from a hub transport server Remove-EdgeSubscription –Id ExchEdgeServer1
Test-EdgeSubscription	Tests whether subscribed servers have an accurate directory Test-EdgeSubscription
Update-SafeList	Update the safe list data in Active Directory from the information gathered by users and prepare to synchronize with an Edge server. Update-SafeList –Type SafeSenders
Start-EdgeSynchronization	Begin a synchronization between a hub transport server and its subscribed Edge server Start-EdgeSynchronization

B.7 Routing

New-RoutingGroupConnector	Creates a routing group connector to link Exchange 2007 to an Exchange 2000/2003 routing group.
Get-RoutingGroupConnector	Retrieve properties of a routing group connector Get-RoutingGroupConnector –id 'Link to Exchange 2003'
Set-RoutingGroupConnector	Set properties for a routing group connector Set-RoutingGroupConnector –id 'Link to Exchange 2003' –Cost 100
Remove-RoutingGroupConnector	Remove a routing group connector Remove-RoutingGroupConnector –id 'Link to Exchange 2003'
New-ReceiveConnector	Create a new receive connector
Get-ReceiveConnector	Returns properties of one or more receive connectors that are active in the organization. Get-ReceiveConnector –Server ExchHub1
Set-ReceiveConnector	Set a property of a selected receive connector. Set-ReceiveConnector –id 'Internet Connector for Organization' –MaxRecipientsPerMessage 250
Remove-ReceiveConnector	Remove a receive connector Remove-ReceiveConnector –id 'Internet Connector'
New-SendConnector	Create a new send connector
Get-SendConnector	Returns properties of one or more SMTP send connectors that are available within the organization. Get-SendConnector –id 'SMTP to the Internet' | Format-List
Set-SendConnector	Sets a property on a send connector Set-SendConnector –id 'SMTP to the Internet' –ConnectionInactivityTimeOut "00:07:30"
Remove-SendConnector	Removes a send connector Remove-SendConnector 'SMTP to the Internet'
Get-TransportServer	Returns the properties of the transport server configuration on a server Get-TransportServer –Server ExchHub1 | Format-List
Set-TransportServer	Sets a property for a hub transport server. Set-TransportServer –id ExchHub1 –MessageTrackLogPath 'L:\Logs\MessageTracking'

Get-TransportConfig	Retrieves details of the default transport configuration for the organization. Get-TransportConfig | Format-List
Set-TransportConfig	Sets a value for a property of the default transport configuration for the organization Set-TransportConfig –MaxSendSize 50MB
Get-TransportAgent	Retrieves details of one or all transport agents that are active Get-TransportAgent –id 'Content Filter Agent'
Set-TransportAgent	Sets properties for a transport agent Set-TransportAgent –id 'Content Filter Agent' –Priority 6
Get-TransportPipeline	Reports the 17 SMTP events that are available for transport agents to fire upon and the associated transport agents Get-TransportPipeline
Get-AgentLog	Retrieve information from the log that tracks the processing performed by anti-spam agents Get-AgentLog –StartDate '2/21/2007'
New-AcceptedDomain	Define a domain for Exchange New-AcceptedDomain –Name 'XYZ' –DomainName 'xyz.com' – DomainType 'Authoritative'
New-SystemMessage	Define a new system message New-SystemMessage –DSNcode 5.7.1 –Language En –Internal $True –Text 'Unable to send'
Get-SystemMessage	Retrieve properties of system messages Get-SystemMessage

B.8   ActiveSync

Get-ActiveSyncDeviceStatistics	Return statistics about one or more devices used by a mailbox Get-ActiveSyncDeviceStatistics –mailbox Redmond
Get-ActiveSyncMailboxPolicy	Returns the properties of one or more ActiveSync mailbox policies Get-ActiveSyncMailboxPolicy –id 'Roaming Users'
Set-ActiveSyncMailboxPolicy	Set a property of an ActiveSync mailbox policy Set-ActiveSyncMailboxPolicy –id 'Roaming Users' –MinDevice-PasswordLength 10
New-ActiveSyncMailboxPolicy	Create a new ActiveSync mailbox policy

Remove-ActiveSyncMailboxPolicy	Remove an ActiveSync mailbox policy Remove-ActiveSyncMailboxPolicy –id 'Roaming Users'
Export-ActiveSyncLog	Export data collected about ActiveSync activity from the IIS logs
Get-ActiveSyncVirtualDirectory	Returns properties of the virtual IIS directory used by ActiveSync Get-ActiveSyncVirtualDirectory
Set-ActiveSyncVirtualDirectory	Sets a property for an Active Sync virtual directory
New-ActiveSyncVirtualDirectory	Creates a new virtual IIS directory for ActiveSync
Remove-ActiveSyncVirtualDirectory	Removes an IIS virtual directory used by ActiveSync
Clear-ActiveSyncDevice	Force a complete resynchronization of a device and a mailbox by removing a partnership Clear-ActiveSyncDevice –id 'WM-Redmond'
Remove-ActiveSyncDevice	Wipe all data from a mobile device Remove-ActiveSyncDevice –id 'WM-Redmond'

B.9   Public folders

New-PublicFolder	Create a new public folder New-PublicFolder –Name '\Exchange 2007' –Path '\Discussions' –Server ExchPF1
Get-PublicFolder	Retrieve properties of a public folder Get-PublicFolder –id '\Exchange 2007'
Set-PublicFolder	Set properties for a public folder Set-PublicFolder –id '\Exchange 2007' –UseDatabaseReplicationSchedule $True
Remove-PublicFolder	Remove a public folder Remove-PublicFolder –id '\Exchange 2007'
Get-PublicFolderStatistics	Retrieve information about public folders Get-PublicFolderStatistics
Add-PublicFolderClientPermission	Add a permission for a client to access a public folder Add-PublicFolderClientPermission –id '\Exchange 2007' –AccessRights 'Owner' –User 'Bond'
Get-PublicFolderClientPermission	Return information about permissions on a public folder Get-PublicFolderClientPermission –id '\Exchange 2007'

Remove-PublicFolderClientPer-mission	Remove a permission for a client from a public folder Remove-PublicFolderClientPermission –id '\Exchange 2007' –AccessRights 'Contributor' –User 'Smith'
Add-PublicFolder Administrative-Permission	Add an administrative permission to a public folder Add-PublicFolderAdministrativePermission –id '\Exchange 2007' –AccessRights AllStoreRights –User Bond
Get-PublicFolder AdministrativePermission	Retrieve administrative permissions for a public folder Get-PublicFolderAdministrativePermission –id '\Exchange 2007'
Remove-PublicFolder AdministrativePermission	Remove an administrative permission from a public folder Remove-PublicFolderAdministrativePermission –id '\Exchange 2007' –AccessRights AllStoreRights –User Bond
Enable-MailPublicFolder	Enable a public folder so that users can send email to it Enable-MailPublicFolder –id '\Exchange 2007'
Disable-MailPublicFolder	Disable the email address for a public folder Disable-MailPublicFolder – id '\Exchange 2007'
Get-MailPublicFolder	Return a list of mail-enabled public folders Get-MailPublicFolder
Update-PublicFolderHierarchy	Force Exchange to replicate the public folder hierarchy Update-PublicFolderHierarchy
Suspend-PublicFolderReplication	Suspend public folder replication between servers Suspend-PublicFolderReplication
Resume-PublicFolderReplication	Resume public folder replication Resume-PublicFolderReplication

B.10　Transport and journal rules

Get-TransportRule	Returns properties for a selected transport rule or all transport rules defined for the organization Get-TransportRule –id 'Disclaimer' | Format-List
Set-TransportRule	Sets a property for a transport rule. Set-TransportRule –id 'Disclaimer' –Priority 4
Remove-TransportRule	Deletes a transport rule Remove-TransportRule –id 'Disclaimer'
New-TransportRule	Creates a new transport rule

Enable-TransportRule	Enable a transport rule.
	Enable-TransportRule –id 'Ethical Firewall'
Disable-TransportRule	Disable a transport rule
	Disable-TransportRule –id 'Ethical Firewall'
Get-TransportRuleAction	Returns a list of available actions that can be defined for a transport rule
	Get-TransportRuleAction
Get-TransportRulePredicate	Returns a list of available predicates that can be used with actions defined in a transport rule
	Get-TransportRulePredicate
Get-JournalRule	Returns properties for a selected journal rule or a list of all journal rules within the organization.
	Get-JournalRule –id 'Senior Executives' | Format-List
Set-JournalRule	Sets a property for a journal rule
	Set-JournalRule –id 'Senior Executives'
	–JournalEmailAddress 'SeniorJournal@xyz.com'
Remove-JournalRule	Removes a journal rule.
	Remove-JournalRule –id 'Test Journal Rule'
New-JournalRule	Creates a new journal rule
Enable-JournalRule	Enable a journal rule
	Enable-JournalRule –id 'New Rule'
Disable-JournalRule	Disable a journal rule
	Disable-JournalRule –id 'New Rule'
New-MessageClassification	Add a new message classification
Get-MessageClassification	Returns details of one or more message classifications that are defined
	Get-MessageClassification
Remove-MessageClassification	Remove a message classification
	Remove-MessageClassification –id 'Patent Disclosure'

B.11 IMAP and POP

Get-IMAPSettings	Retrieve current settings for the IMAP4 virtual server on a Client Access Server
	Get-IMAPSettings –Server ExchCAS1

Set-IMAPSettings	Change an existing property for the default IMAP4 virtual server on a Client Access Server Set-IMAPSettings –Server ExchCAS1 –Banner 'Welcome to the Friendly IMAP Service'
Get-POPSettings	Retrieve current settings for the POP3 virtual server on a Client Access Server Get-POPSettings –Server ExchCAS1
Set-POPSettings	Change an existing property for the default POP3 server on a Client Access Server Set-POPSettings –Server ExchCAS1 –Banner 'POP3 is an outdated email protocol – you shouldn't use it!'

B.12 Active Directory commands

Set-AdSite	Overrides the default routing function for an Active Directory site. Set-AdSite –HubSiteEnabled:$True –id London
Get-AdSite	Returns the properties of an Active Directory site and reveals whether it is a hub site for Exchange 2007 routing Get-AdSite –id Dublin | Format-List
Set-AdSiteLink	Set a routing cost for an Active Directory site that overrides the normal site link cost for the purpose of routing calculations Set-AdSiteLink –id 'London to Paris' –ExchangeCost 1
Get-AdSiteLink	Returns details of the current site link cost and routing cost (if set) Get-AdSiteLink | Format-List
Get-AdPermission	Returns the set of permissions over an object Get-AdPermission –id ExchMbxSvr1
Add-AdPermission	Adds a permission on an object Add-AdPermission –id 'Shane Smith' –User Redmond –ExtendedRights Send-As
Remove-AdPermission	Removes a permission from an object Remove-AdPermission –id 'Shane Smith' –User Redmond –ExtendedRights Send-As
New-User	Create a new Active Directory account
Get-User	Return properties of an Active Directory Account Get-User id Redmond | Select Name, Department

Remove-User	Delete an Active Directory account.
	Remove-User –id Redmond
New-Group	Create a new distribution or security group.
Get-Group	Retrieve the properties of a distribution or security group.
	Get-Group –id 'Sales Executives' | Format-List
Remove-Group	Delete a distribution or security group
	Remove-Group –id 'Sales Executives'

B.13   Testing Exchange 2007

Test-SystemHealth	Test the overall system health for an Exchange 2007 server
	Test-SystemHealth
Test-ServerHealth	Test that all essential services are functioning properly on an Exchange 2007 server
	Test-ServerHealth –Server ExchMbxSvr1
Test-ExchangeSearch	Test that Exchange's server-based content indexing is working properly for a specific mailbox
	Test-ExchangeSearch 'James Bailey'
Test-MAPIConnectivity	Test MAPI connectivity to a server
	Test-MAPIConnectivity –Server ExchMbxSvr1
Test-POPConnectivity	Test that POP3 clients can connect to a Client Access server
	Test-PopConnectivity –ClientAccessServer ExchCAS1 –Mailbox-Credential(Get-Credential XYZ\Redmond)
Test-IMAPConnectivity	Test that IMAP4 clients can connect to a Client Access Server
	Test-IMAPConnectivity –ClientAccessServer ExchCAS1 –MailboxCredential(Get-Credential XYZ\Redmond)
Test-OWAConnectivity	Test that a client can use Outlook Web Access to connect to a mailbox
	Test-OWAConnectivity –MailboxCredential(Get-Credential Xyz\Redmond) –MailboxServer ExchMbxSrv1
Test-UMConnectivity	Test that you can connect to a Unified Messaging server
Test-OutlookAnywhereConnectivity	Test that Outlook Anywhere connections function properly.
Test-MailFlow	Test that the transport service can send a message to a target destination
	Test-MailFlow –TargetEmailAddress Tony.Redmond@xyz1.com

Test-OutlookWebServices	Test that Outlook Web Services are working properly on a Client Access server
	Test-OutlookWebServices –ClientAccessServer ExchCAS1 –Identity Tony.Redmond@xyz.com
	–TargetAddress James.Bond@xyz.com
Test-IPAllowListProvider	Test that the selected IP Allow List provider is functional
	Test-IPAllowListProvider
Test-IPBlockListProvider	Test that the selected IP Block List provider is functional
	Test-IPBlockListProvider
Test-SenderID	Test that Sender ID checks are functioning correctly
	Test-SenderID –PurportedResponsibleDomain Microsoft.com –IPAddress 65.55.238.126

B.14   Basic PowerShell

Get-Alias	Return a list of all the current command aliases known to PowerShell
	Get-Alias
Where-Object	Apply a client-side filter to a data set. "Where" is an alias for this command.
	Where-Object {$_.Name –Like '*Tony*'}
Select-Object	Select properties to output from a data set. "Select" is an alias for this command.
	Select-Object Name, TotalItemSize
Format-List	Format output in a list. Fl is an alias for this command.
Format-Table	Format output in a table. Ft is an alias for this command.
ForEach-Object	Loop through the objects in a data set.
Sort-Object	Sort records in a data set. Sort is an alias for this command.
Group-Object	Groups objects that share the same value for specified properties. "Group" is an alias for this command.
	Get-Mailbox | Group ServerName
Measure-Object	Measure the properties of an object
	Get-MailboxStatistics –Database 'VIP Mailboxes' | Measure-Object –Average TotalItemSize
Import-CSV	Import data from a CSV format file.

Export-CSV	Export data to a CSV format file.
Export-CliXML	Export data to an XML format file.
ConvertTo-SecureString	Convert a plain text string to a secure string.
New-Object	Create a new object of a specific type, such as COM
Invoke-Item	Invoke an application to process a file. Windows launches the default application for the file extension. Invoke-Item 'c:\temp\Stats.htm'
Get-Content	Read an item in from a file Get-Content 'c:\temp\Items.Txt'
Get-Service	Return details of Windows services Get-Service *Exch*
Get-Credential	Ask a user for their Windows credentials $Credentials = Get-Credential
Get-EventLog	Return entries from the event log Get-EventLog –LogName Application –Newest 10
Read-Host	Accept input.
Write-Host	Write something out to the current display. Write-Host 'Hallo World'

B.15 PowerShell control commands

Add-PSSnapin	Add a PowerShell snap-in to extend the PowerShell environment with new commands, such as the set provided by Exchange 2007: Add-PSSnapin Microsoft.Exchange.Management.Power-Shell.Admin
Get-PSSnapin	List the current PowerShell snap-ins that are loaded.
Remove-PSSnapin	Remove a PowerShell snap-in
Set-ExecutionPolicy	Set the execution policy for PowerShell scripts Set-ExecutionPolicy –ExecutionPolicy AllSigned
Get-PSProvider	Return a list of the namespace providers that are available. Get-PSProvider
Get-ExecutionPolicy	Return the current execution policy for PowerShell scripts
Set-PSDebug	Set debug level for PowerShell commands

Index

64-bit hardware, 871
64-bit Windows platform, 868
64-bit Windows servers, 22, 868,
   869

Accepted domains, 460–61
   creating, 462
   defined, 460
   See also Domains
Access Control Entry (ACE), 89
ACID (Atomicity, Consistency,
   Isolation, and Durability)
   test, 303, 304
Acquisitions, 272
Active-active clusters, 8
Active Directory
   changes to, 54
   connectivity assumption, 66
   custom attributes, 85
   database size, 70
   deleted accounts, recovering,
     78–80
   design, 48
   in Exchange 2007, 10
   Exchange and, 47–50
   Exchange configuration data in,
     48
   Exchange connection with, 10–
     11
   extended rights, 87
   functional level, 21
   internal GUIDs, 54–55
   migration to 64-bit Windows
     servers, 75
   naming contexts, 55–58

propagation dampening
   mechanisms, 68
replication, 50–71
schemas, 80–90
sites, 24
site topology, 437
user tables, 61, 62, 63
USNs, 52–53
write operations, 54
Active Directory Topology service,
   33, 71–78, 472
   attribute stamping, 71
   attribute value verification, 71–
     72
   Net Logon service and, 72
   in policy refreshment, 174
   transport service, 436
ActiveSync, 698–702
   configuring for email
     synchronization, 716
   default message download size,
     725
   defined, 582
   disabling access to, 607
   enablement, 714
   enabling for mailboxes, 725
   logs, analyzing, 717–19
   moving mailboxes to, 713–15
   resynchronization, 715
   server-mode, 702
   state, rebuilding, 715
ActiveSync policies, 706–11, 761
   applying, 709
   creating, 706–8
   defined, 761
   parameters, 707–8
ADAccess, 72–75

data returned by, 73–74
defined, 72
role, 72–73
services relying on, 74
ADAM (Active Directory
   Application Mode), 31–32,
   33
   database, 510
   safelist synchronization to, 547
Add-AdPermission command,
   119
Add-AttachmentFilterEntry
   command, 562–63
Add-DistributionGroupMember
   command, 204, 254, 256
Add-ExchangeAdministrator
   command, 266
Add-IPBlockListEntry
   command, 537
Add-MailboxPermission
   command, 249, 770
Add-
   PublicFolderAdministr
   ativePermission
   command, 401
Add-
   PublicFolderClientPer
   mission command, 400
Address caching, 599–600
Address lists, 183–88
   concept, 183
   creating, 185–86
   creation illustration, 186
   customized, 186, 188
   Default Global, 187–88
   global, 183
   illustrated, 183

management, 185
Outlook view, 184
properties, 185
Public Folders, 187
upgrading to Exchange 2007
    format, 187–88
Address Rewrite agent, 539–40
ADMIN.EXE, 195
Administration, restricting, 127
Administrative groups, 17
Exchange View Only, 25
hidden, 433–35
ADSIEDIT utility, 57, 81, 93–98
Active Directory data access, 95
adding, 93–94
connecting to naming context,
    94
default, 94
defined, 93
as double-edged sword, 93
in object property examination,
    95, 96
uses, 96
viewing distinguished names
    with, 91
Windows Support Tools and,
    93
AD Users and Computers, 113–
    16, 148, 271
Agents, 532–35
Address Rewrite, 539–40
Attachment Filter, 531, 561–63
Connection Filter, 536
Content Filter, 538, 547–50
defined, 532
"fire" order, 532–33
function, 532
on hub transport server, 534
logs, 535–36
Recipient Filter, 559–60
Sender Filter, 537
Sender ID, 540–47
Sender Reputation, 556–59
viewing, 533
AJAX, 658
ALL-IN-1 Office System, 747
Alpha, 307–8
"Always up-to-date" model, 378
Ambiguous Name Resolution
    (ANR), 83, 727–28
allowing, 86–87

defined, 86
Anti-spam software, 522, 564
Anti-spam updates, 550
automatic, 551
enabling on Edge server, 551
Anti-Spam Update service, 34, 551
Anti-virus software, 522
Archiving
PST, 617–19
selected messages, 795
setup in Outlook, 618
Attachment Filter agent, 531, 561–
    63
defined, 561
function, 561–62
Attachments
blocking, 560–61
block types, 561
compression, 776–77
content indexing and, 376
filtering, 531
large files, 776–79
OWA, controlling, 677–80
as security issue, 677
splits, 313
table, 320
viewing through WebReady,
    681
WMA, 742, 746
Attribute-level replication, 51, 143
Attributes
adding, 83
custom, 85
hidden, 95
LegacyExchangeDN, 91–93
marking for ANR, 86–87
populating, 274
property sets, 89
single-valued, 83
verifying, 84
Auditing, 853
AUTD, 699
AUTDSTATE.XML, 700
Authentication, 590–91
basic, 669
digest, 669
forms-based, 667, 669, 670
integrated Windows, 669
MAPI clients, 590
NTLM, 590
Outlook modes, 591

Outlook Web Access (OWA),
    667–70
Authorization, 460
Auto Attendants, 740
AutoDatabaseMountDial setting,
    920
AutoDiscover service, 346, 585–90
AutoConfiguration option, 586
Client Access servers and, 587,
    637
defined, 585
process, 587
SCP, 588
Automated analysis, 929–35
Autosignature files, 772–75
bloated, 772
corporate information, 774
defined, 772
graphics, 773
impact on recipients, 774
viruses and, 774
Availability service, 585, 861, 862,
    863

Background Intelligent Transfer
    Service (BITS), 637
Background maintenance, 360–68
backups during, 361–62
deleted folders and, 366
running, 365
scheduling, 362–63
Store control, 361
tasks, 360–61, 364–67
tracking, 367–68
Back pressure, 494–96
condition existence, 495
effect, 495
Backup agent, 417, 418
Backups, 409–26
background maintenance and,
    361–62
block-level, 426
checking, 420
checkpoint file, 421–26
continuous replication and, 889
daily, 410
differential, 419
disk battery, 873
ESEBACK2.DLL, 411
ESEBCLI2.DLL, 411

full, 374, 417
full online, 374
incremental, 410, 419
media movement, 416
NTBackup, 410
online, 409
operations, 416–21
set, 419
as snapshots, 409
storage groups and, 416–21
strategies, creating, 413–16
streaming, 426
third-party products, 412
timestamp, 421
Bastion servers, 522
Benchmarks, 873
education, 873
published, 874
Bifurcation, 475
BlackBerry
device illustration, 724
form factor, 731
input flexibility, 732–35
lookup execution support, 727
message delivery speed, 729
power management, 731–32
sent message storage, 726
Windows Mobile comparison, 723–35
BlackBerry Enterprise Server (BES), 713, 726, 729
deployment, 735
support, 730
BLAT, 228
Blocked Senders list, 571
adding email addresses to, 571
Store checking, 572
Block-level backups, 426
Books, reference, 981–82
B-tree structure, 303
Buffer manager, 312
Bulk updates, 270–75
Buying servers, 870–75

Cached Exchange mode, 592
deploying, 596–99
difficulties, 597–98
OAB and, 632–34
Outlook configuration, 597
Calendars

Outlook 2007 changes, 863–65
permissions, 865
Categorizer, 438–39
CCR clusters, 887–88
automatic failovers, 911
deployment, 912
disk technology, 910
identical logical drive letters, 913
low cost, 910
MNS configuration, 907–9
operation, 912
storage group support, 910
See also Cluster Continuous Replication (CCR)
CDOEXM, 207, 271
Cell phones, 698
Checkpoint file, 421–26
database restoration, 422–26
defined, 421–22
primary role, 422
Checkpointing, 316
Circular logging, 335–37
with CCR, 904
defined, 335
disabled, 337
enabling, 337
equipment mailboxes and, 765
golden rule, 336
with LCR, 904, 905
See also Logging
Clean-MailboxDatabase command, 330
Clear-ActiveSyncDevice command, 712
Client access licenses (CALs), 36
enterprise, 36
functionality gained through, 37
standard, 36
Client Access servers, 30
AD use, 32
in AutoDiscover service, 587
closest, 637
OAB distribution, 635
OAB poll interval, 640
proxy client connections, 664
RPC over HTTP Proxy component, 646
Client-based indexing, 375
Client-side filters, 267

Client-side spam suppression, 567–79
Cluster Continuous Replication (CCR), 9, 906–23
circular logging and, 904
clusters, 887–88
copies, 918
defined, 906
deploying, 906–23
directory structure, 907
failovers, 913, 915–19
as failure solution, 913
illustrated, 890
LLR and, 919–21
managing, 120
processing, 914
queries, 914
replication pipeline, 907
servers, 914, 920
storage group support, 912
switches, 891
traditional clusters comparison, 910–12
transitions, 917
transport dumpster and, 921–23
See also CCR clusters; Continuous replication
Clusters, 8, 882–88
active-active, 8
CCR, 887–88, 910
classic implementation, 884
geo, 886
LCR deployment and, 903
MNS, 906, 907
SCC, 920
single copy, 884
technology, 883
"traditional," 9
Cmdlets, 198–99
defined, 198
as .NET classes, 199
Collaborative Data Objects (CDO), 858
Columns
changing, 116
for send connectors, 117
Command line installations, 24–25
Commands, 100
all-purpose, 251

editing, 208–10
help, 205–6
PowerShell, 199–204
server-side filters, 268
shell, 204–7
Unified Messaging
    management with, 743–45
See also specific commands
Command validation, 287–90
    information capture, 289–90
    `Move-Mailbox` command, 287
    with non-Exchange commands,
        288
COM objects, 196
Compliance, 433
    challenges, 790–91
    Exchange 2007 and, 787–815
    growing need, 789–92
Compression
    attachments, 776–77
    LZX, 631
    MAPI, 600–602
    RPC, 601
    WBXML, 705
Conflicts folder, 602
Connection Filter agent, 536
Connection filtering, 536–37
Connection objects, schedule, 68
Connections
    bypassing, 472–73
    GPRS, 715
    HTTP, 652, 701
    Outlook status, 595
    RPC over HTTP, 596
    RPC over NetBIOS, 591
    RPC over TCP/IP, 591
`Connect-Mailbox` command,
        331
Connectors
    closest proximity, 467, 469–70
    cost, 467, 469
    Edge server, 509, 515
    Exchange 2007, selection, 467
    foreign, 459–60
    listing, 480
    most specific, 467–68
    receive, 440–47
    routing group, 111, 436
    scoping, 469
    send, 447–53
    SMTP, 468, 492

X.400, 474
Consolidation, 309
Contacts, 253
    disabling, 253
    mail-enabled, 253
    managing, 110
    working with, 114
Content Filter agent, 526, 538,
        547–50
    blocking/allowing words, 548
    defined, 547
    output, 548–49
    safelist availability, 554
    thresholds, 549
    updates, 550–52
Content indexing, 375–83
    advantages, 376
    database operation effects, 379
    reenabling, 380
    services, 377–78
    spam and, 379–80
    testing, 381
    using, 380–83
Continuous replication, 882, 888–
        92
    advantages/disadvantages, 924–
        25
    backups and, 889
    concepts, 889–92
    flow, 898
    importance, 889
    standby (SCR), 924
    See also Cluster continuous
        replication (CCR); Local
        continuous replication
        (LCR)
Credential service, 34
Cross-forest free and busy, 866
Cross-forest UM, 756
CSV, 239, 272
    data export in, 239
    file, reading, 274
    hourly.csv, 718
    input file, 273
    load file, 274–75
    output, 240
    servers.csv, 718
    statuscodes.csv, 718
    user-agents.csv, 718
    users.csv, 718
CSVDE, 270

Custom folders, managing, 824–
        26

Database pages, 349
Database portability, 345–49
    defined, 345
    importance, 345–46
Database Recovery Management,
        937–42
    currently active database
        options, 937–38
    defined, 935
    RSG options, 939–40
Database repair, 368–75
    with ESEUTIL, 370–73
    full online backup, 374
    with ISINTEG utility, 373–74
    rebuilding and, 373
    results, 375
    starting, 370
Databases
    creating, 327–29
    dismounting, 347
    ESE, 302, 303, 312
    failed, fixing, 368–75
    maximum size, 343–45
    multiple, 323–24
    public folder, 321, 365, 396
    rebuilding, 360, 361
    reseeding, 906
    restoring, 422–26
    shrinking, 408
    size limits, removing, 408–9
    Store check, 331
    working with, 329–31
Database Troubleshooter, 942–43
    defined, 935
    functioning, 943
    problems, 942
Data Definition Language (DDL),
        302
Data Manipulation Language
        (DML), 302
DAVEX, 651
DCPROMO procedure, 82, 96
Default-first-site, 65
Default folders
    administrator creation, 818
    creation, 824
    growth of, 818

illustrated, 818
journal processing for, 819–20
managed content settings, 819–
    20
managing, 818–23
message expiry time, 819, 820
See also Folders
Default Global Address List, 187–
    88
Default Offline Address List, 635
    configuring, 636
    selecting, 638
    use as OAB, 642
    See also Offline Address Book
        (OAB)
Default storage group, 349, 395
Defense in depth, 522–23
Delegation model, 124–28
Deleted item recovery, 357–60
    default, 358
    enabling, 358–59
Deleted Items cache, 350–60
    cleaning, 356–57
    defined, 350
    item recovery, 357–60
    item size, 356
    mailbox recovery, 357–60
    removing items from, 356–57
Deleted Items folder, 350
    default retention period, 353–
        54
    deleted items retention period,
        353–56
    empty option, 352
    function, 350
    item recovery, 358
    items, 353
Deleted items retention period,
        353–56
    changing, 353–54
    default, 353
    setting through shell, 354–55
Deleted mailboxes, 359–60
    list, 359
    reconnecting, 359–60
Delivery reports, 262
Delivery Service Notice, 599
Delivery Status Notifications
        (DSNs), 496–505
    capturing, 498
    categories, 496–97

collecting copies of, 498
control parameters, 497
customizing, 501–4
diagnostic section, 499–500
error, 501
layout, 499
re-rendering, 498
user information, 498
Details templates
    attribute selection, 786–87
    customizing, 782–87
    illustrated, 782
    MMC console loaded with, 785
    modifying in ESM console, 783
    user, 784–87
Details Templates Editor, 784
DHCP servers, 19
Diagnostic logging, 367
Differential backups, 419
Differential restores, 425
Digest authentication, 669
Digital Alpha 64-bit platform,
        307–8
Direct-attached storage (DAS),
        894
Direct-push
    email, 701
    technology, 724
Direct Trust, 518
`Disable-Mailbox` command,
        204
`Disable-MailContact`
        command, 253
`Disable-MailPublicFolder`
        command, 399
`Disable-OutlookAnywhere`
        command, 647
`Disable-StorageGroupCopy`
        command, 902
`Disable-UmMailbox` command,
        744
Disclaimers, 779–81
    adding with transport rules,
        794–95
    S/MIME messages and, 795
    text applied by message, 796
Disk battery backup, 873
Disk I/O, optimizing, 327
DISKPART, 880
Disk speed, 879

`Dismount-Database` command,
        330, 904
Display templates
    attribute selection, 786–87
    customizing, 782–87
    details, 783–84
    illustrated, 782
    modifying in ESM console, 783
    user, 784–87
Distribution groups. *See* Groups
Distribution lists
    expanding, 147–48
    hiding groups from, 262
    maintainer details, 150
    personal, 147
    preferred expansion, 148
    See also Groups
DMZ
    deployment inside, 507
    Edge server deployment in, 518
    infrastructure, 508
DNS, 487, 564
Domain controllers
    deploying in two different sites,
        79
    Global Catalog property, 59
    read-only, 91
    transforming into Global
        Catalogs, 58–60
    Windows 2003 server, 70
Domain local groups, 141
Domains
    accepted, 460–61, 462
    designs, 48–50
    multiple user, 49
    OOF settings, 579
    as partitions, 55
    preparing, 20, 21
    root, 48
Drag-and-drop paradigm, 777
Drizzle synchronization, 593
DSAccess. *See* ADAccess
DSProxy, 155
DTMF (dual tone multi-frequency
        signaling), 740
DTStart/DTEnd properties, 856–
        57
Dual-phase commit, 304
DWORD registry value, 630, 632,
        633

Dynamic distribution groups,
    156–68
    creating, 162–67
    defined, 156
    EMC generation, 257
    existence, 167
    filters, 157–59, 260
    LDIFDE output, 158
    membership discovery, 262
    organizational units (OUs) for,
        162
    as recipient objects, 259
    restricting, 260
    self-maintaining groups and,
        168
    UI, 160–62
    using, 167–68
    viewing, 167
    Windows security principals
        and, 168
    working with, 257–62
    See also Groups
Dynamic routing, 459

E2003Svr1, 456
EAS, 695
    PING command, 700
    solution, 698
EDB
    MAPI properties in, 318
    STM file, 319
EDGE, 694
Edge Connection Manager, 466
Edge servers, 30–31, 507–67
    AD use, 32
    as anti-spam software
        appliances, 564
    anti-spam updates on, 551
    components, 509–11
    configuring, 511
    connectors on, 509, 515
    deployment, 507
    deployment within DMZ, 518
    domain membership, 514
    FQDN, 512
    general options, 531
    hub transport servers versus,
        508–9
    information held in ADAM
        instance, 516

Internet outage and, 565–66
    properties, 552
    recovering, 566
    roles, 508
    running Forefront, 530
    simplicity, 509
    subscriptions, 514
    synchronization, 511–17
    TCP ports, 511
    traffic load, 517
    transport rules, 563–64, 792
Edge subscription XML files, 153,
    512
EdgeSync, 34, 511–17
    process, 510
    successful, 516
EdgeTransport.Exe.Config, 481
Electronic Forms Designer (EFD),
    7, 383
Email
    direct-push, 701
    etiquette, 781–82
    good habits, 778–79
    as propagation mechanism, 521
    sending from shell, 226–29
    See also Messages
Email address policies, 173–82,
    761
    in Active Directory, 174
    applying, 175–76
    conflict, 176
    creating, 175
    custom recipient filter, 182
    default, 179
    defined, 173, 761
    defining, 174
    illustrated, 174
    legacy, EMC detection, 180
    mailbox moves and, 178
    objects, 175
    OPATH syntax, 181
    at organizational level, 174
    queries driving, 178–82
    recipient filters, 181
    sorting queries for, 182
    upgrading, 187
Email scam, 520
Email viruses
    autosignature file, 774
    defense in depth, 522–23
    fighting, 518–22

reporting, 532
Enable-DistributionGroup
    command, 254
Enable-JournalRule command,
    814
Enable-MailPublicFolder
    command, 399
Enable-OutlookAnywhere
    command, 647
Enable-StorageGroup
    command, 906
Enable-StorageGroupCopy
    command, 902
Enable-UmMailbox command,
    743–44
Enterprise Vault, 835
Equipment mailboxes, 762–70
    circular logging and, 765
    creating, 231–32, 763–64
    defined, 132
    holding, 764
    icon, 763
    message traffic, 765
    properties, managing, 765–70
    user perspective, 763
    See also Mailboxes
ESEBACK2.DLL, 411
ESEBCLI2.DLL, 411
ESE databases
    B-tree structure, 303
    internal structure, 303
    page arrangement, 302
    page hierarchy, 312
ESE (Extensible Storage Engine),
    301–2, 360
    characteristics, 302
    dual-phase commit, 304
    transaction logs and, 332
ESEUTIL utility, 332
    in database rebuild, 360, 361
    defined, 369
    /MS, 372
    operation, 369
    output, 333, 372
    /P, 370, 372
    in repair mode, 370
    running, 371
    slowness, 372
    warning from, 373
    white space removal, 408
Ethical firewall

creating, 800–803
transport rule, 802
EVDO (Evolution Data
    Optimized), 694
Event notifications list, 362
ExBPA, 23, 930
    concept, 930
    defined, 21, 935
    HTML output, 932
    illustrated, 931
    output files, 931
    rules, 930
    running, 21–22, 930–31
Exchange 2000
    backwards compatibility, 16–17
    multiple folder hierarchies, 7
Exchange 2003
    ESM, 100–101
    functionality, 14–15
    linking Exchange 2007, 453–
        57
    link state updates, handling,
        458–59
    multiple routes into, 458
    public folders, accessing, 666
    public folders, improvements,
        386–87
    referrals, 406
    routing groups,
        decommissioning, 458
    storage groups, 315
Exchange 2007
    32-bit, 41
    Active Directory, 10
    administrative model, 13
    buying servers for, 870–75
    challenges, 42–45
    client support, 13
    compliance and, 787–815
    content indexing, 375–83
    continuous replication, 888–92
    delegation model, 124–28
    free and busy in, 861–63
    installation program, 23
    installing, 22–28
    Internet protocols, 13
    linking Exchange 2003, 453–
        57
    Longhorn and, 90–91
    manageability, 15
    managing, 99–194

MAPI.Net, 3
notification mechanism, 22
preparing for, 20–22
public folder phase-out, 7
public folders and, 384–86
services, 32–36
SMTP stack, 21
storage groups, 315
store differences, 306–18
support, 42
system messages, 16
testing, 292–97
third-party product support, 29
transport architecture, 435–64
transport engine, 432–33
Unified Messaging server, 14
Windows Mobile 6.0 and, 702–
    23
x86-64 Windows platform, 5
Exchange 2007 servers
    buying, 870–75
    configuration guidelines, 875
    in ESM, 110
    Exchange 2003 server upgrade
        and, 19–20
    installation location, 21
    installations, 26–27
    memory recommendations, 12
    memory usage, 872
    modifying, 27
    removing, 27
    roles, 28–36
    in single routing group, 457
    See also Servers
Exchange Best Practice Analyzer.
    See ExBPA
Exchange Development Kit
    (EDK), 459
Exchange Disaster Recovery
    Analyzer (ExDRA), 930
Exchange Information property
    set, 89
Exchange Mailflow Troubleshooter
    (ExMFA), 930
Exchange Management Console
    (EMC), 99, 100–124
    column changing, 116
    defined, 100
    design philosophy, 276
    Exchange Toolbox, 103, 374,
        935–45

filters, 104–9
"get everything" default filter,
    104
GUI, 122
illustrated, 101
IP blocks, 537
layout, 103
learning from, 229–32
legacy email address policy
    detection, 180
"list view virtual page" feature,
    104
mailbox management, 114–16
mixed organization
    management, 109–12
mobile device management,
    711–13
nodes, 101–3
option disappearance, 118–24
Organization Configuration,
    101
PowerShell code from, 230
Recipient Configuration, 102–
    3
for recipient filter editing, 261
recipients and, 275
remotely running, 112–13
scopes, applying, 105
Server Configuration, 102
tabbed view, 104
Toolbox node, 374
user statistics display, 275
visual effects, 116–18
wizard, 259
on workstation, 112–13
Exchange Management Shell
    (EMS), 20, 195–299
    bulk updates, 270–75
    commands, 204–7
    delegation through, 265–66
    editing from within, 222
    execution policies, 224–26
    information capture, 289–90
    management tasks, 284–87
    message tracking with, 956–59
    pervasive nature, 207
    profiles, 221–23
    properties, 222
    range of commands supported
        by, 284–87
    scope and, 221

sending email from, 226–29
Exchange Organization
    Administrator role, 125–26
Exchange Performance
    Troubleshooting Analyzer
    (ExPTA), 930
Exchange Personal Information
    property, 89–90
Exchange Recipient Administrator
    role, 126
Exchange Search Indexer, 377
Exchange Server Administrator
    role, 126
Exchange System Manager (ESM),
    99, 100
    command syntax, 123
    default behavior, 342
    editing objects and, 111
    Exchange 2007 servers in, 110
    GUI, 119
    value, 122–23
Exchange Transport Log Search
    service, 958
Exchange Troubleshooting
    Assistant. *See* ExTRA
Exchange Unified Messaging,
    testing, 297
Exchange User Monitor. *See*
    ExMon
Exchange View-Only
    Administrator role, 126
ExchMbxNode2, 915
ExchMbxSvr1, 286, 949
ExchMbxSvr2, 949
ExDRA, 930
Execution policies, 224–26
    changing, 225–26
    defined, 224
    list of, 224
    Restricted, 224
ExIFS, 318
ExMerge, 848
ExMFA, 930
ExMon, 968–71
    data extraction, 971
    defined, 936, 968
    ETW, 968–69
    illustrated, 969
`Export-ActiveSyncLog`
    command, 712, 717
`Export-Mailbox` command, 836

-AttachmentFilenames
    parameter, 851
auditing use of, 853
copying mailboxes with, 849
-DeleteContent parameter, 852
-IncludeFolders parameter, 851
in processing multiple
    mailboxes, 849
in transferring data to PST, 848
`Export-`
    `TransportRuleCollecti`
    `on` command, 563
Expressions, filter, 109
ExPTA, 930
ExSetup program, 128
Extended rights, 87
Extended Type System (ETS), 198
ExTRA
    defined, 930
    output files, 931

Fail-first pass tests, 521
File Distribution Service, 34
File Replication Services (FRS), 71
Filtering
    connection, 536–37
    content, 547–50
    recipient, 559–60
    sender, 537–39
Filters
    applying, 107
    client-side, 267
    client-side junk mail, 526
    client-side spam, 522
    dynamic distribution groups,
        157–59, 260
    efficient, creating, 267–70
    EMC, 104–9
    expressions, 109
    LDAP, 56, 179
    OPATH, 158, 159
    properties, 107–8, 260–61
    recipient, 181, 559–60
    server-side, 267–70
    specification, 270
    tweaking programmatically,
        259
Firewalls, ethical, 800–803
Florida Sunshine Law, 789
FMSO servers, 48

Folders
    custom, managing, 824–26
    default, managing, 818–23
    deleted, 366
    header information, 321
    journal processing for, 819–20
    journal recipients, 821
    message expiry time for, 819,
        820
    nested, 322
    table, 320
    tree, 322
    See also specific folders
"Forced" replication, 64
Forefront, 528–32
    anti-virus engine configuration,
        529
    defined, 528–29
    deployment, 530
    Edge server running, 530
    manual scans, 530
    Scanner Update options, 529
Foreign connectors, 459–60
Forests
    Active Directory functional
        level, 21
    details, 77–78
    GALs, 56
    mailbox moves between, 249
    multi-domain, 219–21
    preparing, 20
`Format-List` command, 203,
    210, 211, 642
`Format-Table` command, 210,
    277
Forms-based authentication, 667,
    669, 670
Free and busy, 853–66
    accessing from different clients,
        862
    data, free and busy, 855–61
    data complexity, 858
    defined, 853
    in Exchange 2007, 861–63
    MDBVU32 view, 859
    Outlook 2007 changes, 863–65
    publication options, 854
    recalculating/republishing, 861
    replication, 856
    updating, 857
FSMO servers, 50

Full online backups, 374

GALSearch, 727, 728
Geo clusters, 886
Get-ActiveSyncDeviceStatistics command, 711, 712
Get-ActiveSyncMailboxPolicy command, 708
Get-AddressList command, 183–84
Get-AddressRewriteEntry command, 540
Get-AdPermission command, 120
Get-AdSite command, 470
Get-Alias command, 201, 202
Get-AttachmentFilterEntry command, 562
Get-AttachmentFilterListConfig command, 562
Get-CasMailbox command
  in checking for MAPI blocks, 606
  defined, 251
  when to use, 252
Get-ClientAccessServer command, 286, 588
Get-ClusteredMailboxServerStatus command, 908–9
Get-Connector command, 441
Get-Contact command, 253
Get-Credential command, 295
Get-DistributionGroup command, 209, 255
Get-DistributionGroupMember command, 828
Get-EmailAddressPolicy command, 179
Get-EventLog command, 204, 210
Get-ExBlog command, 205
Get-ExchangeAdministrator command, 265
Get-ExchangeServer command, 204, 279, 285

Get-ExCommand command, 288
Get-ExecutionPolicy command, 225
Get-IMAPSettings command, 689, 690–91
Get-IPBlockListEntry command, 537
Get-LogonStatistics command, 275, 282
Get-MailboxCalendarSettings command, 767–68
Get-Mailbox command, 211, 212, 213, 235–36, 251, 555
  -ContentKeywords parameter, 851
  -Database parameter, 828
  Format-List command after, 211–12
  in getting list of mailboxes, 836
  in managed policy assignment, 828
Get-MailboxDatabase command, 236–37, 355, 362, 363
  in database status check, 330
  defined, 204
  legacy Exchange servers and, 292
  -Server parameter, 237
  -Status parameter, 420–21
Get-MailboxFolderStatistics command, 239, 240
Get-MailboxPermission command, 244, 250
Get-MailboxServer command, 223, 286, 472
Get-MailboxStatistics command, 172, 205, 223, 241, 279, 347
  deleted mailbox list, 359
  example use, 279
  HTML output, 280
  reports, 281
  Where-Object command combination, 282
Get-ManagedContentSettings command, 822

Get-ManagedFolder command, 822
Get-ManagedFolderMailboxPolicy command, 829
Get-Member command, 244, 269
Get-MessageClassification command, 838–39
Get-Message command, 486, 489
Get-MessageTrackingLog command, 954–55, 956
  -EventID parameter, 956
  output, 957
  -Server parameter, 957
Get-OfflineAddressBook command, 642–43
Get-OutlookAnywhere command, 648
Get-OutlookProvider command, 589
Get-OwaVirtualDirectory command, 665, 669–70
Get-POPSettings command, 693
Get-Process command, 200, 201, 290
Get-PSSnapin command, 200
Get-PublicFolderAdministrativePermission command, 401
Get-PublicFolder command, 395–96, 397
  deleting folders and, 402
  -GetChildren parameter, 398
  -Identity parameter, 399
  -Recurse parameter, 398
Get-PublicFolderDatabase command, 330, 362, 395
Get-PublicFolderPermission command, 400
Get-PublicFolderStatistics command, 404
Get-Queue command, 485–86
  in checking for poison messages, 494
  defined, 485
Get-ReceiveConnector command

in listing current connectors, 480
output, 445
Get-Recipient command, 245
Get-RoutingGroupConnector command, 456
Get-SendConnector command, 452–53, 469–70
defined, 452
in listing current connectors, 480
Get-SenderFilterConfig command, 538
Get-SenderIDConfig command, 546
Get-SenderReputationConfig command, 557–58
Get-StorageGroupCopyStatus command, 900–901
defined, 901
output, 900
uses, 901
Get-StorageGroupCopyUpdate command, 920
Get-SystemMessage command, 502, 503
Get-TransportAgent command, 505–6, 533, 534
Get-TransportConfig command, 205, 476–77, 922
Get-TransportPipeline command, 534, 535
Get-TransportRuleAction command, 806
Get-TransportRule command, 804
Get-TransportServer command, 286, 447–48
in changing properties, 448
hub transport server connections, 466
in updating properties, 448
Get-UmMailbox command, 252, 744
Get-UmMailboxPIN command, 745
Get-UMServer command, 286, 744
Get-User command, 219, 251, 270

Set-Mailbox command combination, 271
-ValidateOnly parameter, 248
Global Address Lists (GALs), 183
forests, 56
incorrect sort order, 663
mobile, properties, 727
sorting, 189
well-ordered, 191
Global Catalogs
64-bit, 75, 76
consistent availability, 59
domain controller transformation into, 58–60
full synchronization, 71
location, 76–78
outage, 76
placement, 76
Global Catalog servers, 20, 21
number needed, 75–76
read-out copy of objects, 51
in remote domain, 221
Global groups, 141
Global Positioning System (GPS) devices, 734
Global Unique Identifiers. *See* GUIDs
Google Desktop, 375
GPRS
connections, 715
network, 729
Groups
access, restricting, 263
administrative, 435
advanced properties, 262–65
domain local, 141
dynamic distribution, 133
Exchange 2007, 145–47
forming, 142–45
global, 141
hiding, 262
limiting to authenticated users, 153
list, 141
mail-enabled, 142
managing, 111
managing from Outlook, 154–56
members, adding, 149
members, importing, 263
members, removing, 151

membership, 143
membership, listing, 151
membership, managing, 149–52
membership, viewing, 144
nonuniversal, 133
permission, 154–56, 441–42
properties, 143, 152
properties, comparing, 146
protected, 152–54
query-based, 141, 158
regenerating, 257
routing, 433–35
self-maintaining, 168
SMTP address, 152
transport rules with, 797
universal, 140, 141
universal distribution, 133
universal security, 133
using, 140–54
working with, 114, 254–65
GSM (Global System for Media Communication), 750
GUIDs, 91, 641
GWART (Gateway and Routing Table), 431, 459

Hashing, 517
Header firewalls, 476
Hierarchical Storage Management (HSM), 788
High-watermark vector table, 69
HP OpenView, 6, 961–63
HTTP, 13
clients, 309
connections, 652, 701
defined, 582
requests, 652
HTTPS connections, 309
Hub routing sites
enabling, 470
role, 470–71
routing groups and, 471
Hub transport servers, 30, 436
AD use, 32
anti-spam agents on, 534
back-pressure settings effect, 495
common configuration, 437
connections, 466

connectors, 509
critical role, 438–40
default configuration, 442
edge servers versus, 508–9
message flow into, 438
point-to-point connections, 464
processor core, 874
protection, 439
roles, 508
on round-robin basis, 496
transport rules, 792
unavailable, 464

Identities, 217–19
defined, 217
in group membership discovery, 219
mailbox, 218
IIS logs, 977
IMAP4, 13, 34, 685–89
clients, 7, 294–95
configuration files, changing, 693
defined, 582
disabling access to, 607
virtual servers, configuring, 694
IMAP clients, 685
default option, 686
public folder access, 687–88
rules processing, 687
support, 686
IMAP server, 689–94
defined, 689
properties, 691–93
Importing, group members, 263
Incremental backups, 410, 419
Incremental Change
Synchronization (ICS), 594
Incremental restores, 425
Incremental seeder, 898
Independent software vendors
(ISVs), 42, 45
Indexes
content, unavailable, 380
populating with full crawl, 378
Indexing
client-based, 375
content, 375–83

database operation effects on, 379
engine, 377, 379
server-based, 375
services, 377–78
Information capture, 289–90
Information Store. See Store
Initialization (.INI) files, 584
Installation
command line, 24–25
Exchange 2007, 22–28
procedure logs, 27
updating schemas with, 80–82
validating, 27–28
In-Store searches, 376
Intelligent Message Filter (IMF),
507, 525, 547
PCL calculation, 525
SCL calculation, 525
SmartScreen technology, 525
Internet Message Filter (IMF), 13
Internet service providers (ISPs),
6–7
Inter-Site Messaging (ISM-
SMTP), 67
Intersite replication, 65–68
Inter-Site Topology Generator, 66
Intrasite replication, 65–68
I/Os
coalescing, 316
demand, 314, 318
disk, 315, 327
filter driver, 885
generated per mailbox, 317
operations, 314, 317
performance testing, 317
profile, 327
requirements, 318
stream management, 885
trading memory for, 312–17
transaction log, 341
iPAQ 6915, 724, 731
input flexibility, 732
as pocket PC, 734
Windows, 734
See also Windows Mobile
devices
IP blocks, setting, 537
ISA Server 2006, 646, 649
iSCSI, 878–79
ISINTEG utility

defined, 369
operation, 369
running, 373–74

Jet (Joint Engine Technology)
data organization, 313
defined, 301–2
implementation, 302
technology use, 302
JetStress, 963
Journaled messages, 823
illustrated, 812
path, 958
Journaling, 815
BBC, 808
on per-database basis, 814, 815
premium, 808–9
process, 811
standard, 808
types, 808
Journal reports, 812
Journal rules, 808–15
application, 808
capture, 810
creating, 809–10
enabling, 811, 814
illustrated, 813
storage, 803
Junk E-Mail folder, 380, 519, 568,
570
Junk mail detection, 567
Junk Mail Filter, 567–72
check order, 569
defined, 567
effectiveness, 569–70
functioning, 568
ranking, 569

Kerberos tickets, 64
Kernel-mode exhaustion, 869
Knowledge Consistency Checker
(KCC)
functions, 58
intrasite topology management,
66

LDAP, 13, 157
filters, 56, 179

lookups, 689
Outlook Express access, 688–89
picker, 157
queries, 166
search base, 689
LDIFDE utility, 270–71
defined, 98
output for dynamic distribution group, 158
LDP utility, 96–97
defined, 96–97
illustrated, 97
Least Recently Used Reference Count (LRU-K), 312
LegacyExchangeDN attribute, 91–93, 630
defined, 92
index, 92
Legacy mailboxes, 133
Legacy servers, 457
Licensing, 36–41
CALs, 36–37
unlicensed editions and, 38
version numbers, 40–41
Volume Licensing Program, 37
Linked mailboxes, 231–32
creating, 231–32
defined, 133
See also Mailboxes
Linked value replication (LVR), 143, 144
Link state propagation, stopping, 459
Link state updates, 458–59
Load Generator utility, 963–64
defined, 963–64
illustrated, 964
Local continuous replication (LCR), 9, 35
availability, 892
circular logging and, 904, 905
cluster deployment and, 903
database transition, 904–6
deploying, 892–906
direct-attached storage support, 894
disabling processing, 902
enabling for storage groups, 894
enabling processing, 902

flow, 898
functioning, 897–99
hardware failure protection, 891
illustrated, 890
incremental seeder, 898
log replayer, 897
mixture of storage groups, 892
operations, 900–903
overhead and, 900
prerequisites, 893
replay manager, 898
Replication service, 897, 898, 899
restart processing, 902
restrictions, 903–4
resuming, 901
servers, 891, 892
storage group usage, 893
suspending, 901
transitions, 891
truncate deletor, 897–98
See also Continuous replication
Local Failures folder, 603
Local queues, 485
Log files
installation program, 25
reserved, 338
temporary, 338
Logging
circular, 335–37
diagnostic, 367
mailbox moves, 138–40
managed folder activity, 831–33
protocol, 473–74
LogParser, 973–78
defined, 973
downloading, 974
functionality, 978
functions, 973–74
in IIS log interrogation, 977
message tracking log fields, 975
output, 976
record counting/analysis, 974
Log replayer, 897
Logs
ActiveSync, 717–19
agent, 535–36
committed, 919
IIS, 977

managed folder assistant, 833
routing, 483–85
synchronization, 722
Longhorn
defined, 90
Exchange 2007 and, 90–91
read-only domain controller support, 91
LookOut add-in, 375
Lookups, 221
execution support, 727
scope, setting, 220
Lost Log Resiliency (LLR), 914, 918, 919–21
committed log, 919
defined, 914, 918
recovery and, 919
waypoints, 919
LRCK (Log Record Checksum), 342
LZX compression, 631

Magazines, 980
Mailbox Assistants, 34
Mailboxes
ActiveSync-enabled, 709
another, opening with OWA, 250
bigger, 310
copying, 848–53
count, 240
creating, 116, 231–32
creating, with template, 232–33
data, reporting, 275–84
deleted, 359–60
details, viewing, 122
disabled, checking for, 242
disabling, 235
editing, 110
email addresses for, 177
EmailAddressPolicy Enabled property, 178
EMS and, 232–53
equipment, 132, 762–70
forwarding address, 243
identity, 218
interacting with, 244–45
legacy, 133
linked, 133, 231–32
list of, 123

list of, creating, 347
new, SMTP address, 233
permissions, adding, 249–50
permissions, removing, 251
permissions, viewing, 250
per processor core, 874
PrimarySmtpAddress property, 213
quarantine, 549
recovered, 850
recovering, 357–60
removing, 110
resource, 762
room, 132, 762–70
searching for, 236
sets, creating, 273–75
shared, 133, 231–32
size, 308
snapshots, 850
special, 756–59
statistics, 279
storage limits, 170
updating, 233, 244
user, 132
user, access, 249–51
working with, 114
working with (EMS), 232–53
Mailbox moves, 110, 111, 134–38, 245–49
  to ActiveSync, 713–15
  email address policies and, 178
  between forests, 249
  logging, 138–40
  schedule, 136
Mailbox properties, 114
  retrieving, 234–44
  setting, 234–44
Mailbox quotas, 168–73
  applying, 171
  event logging, 172
  growth, 324
  OWA flag, 173
  setting, 170–73
Mailbox servers, 30, 436
  AD use, 32
  configuring, 472
  instructing, 472
Mailbox table, 320
Mail Flow Troubleshooter, 936, 943–45
  defined, 943

example, 944–45
problems, 943
summary report, 945
symptoms, 943–44
Mail hygiene, 523–28
Mail.que, 461
Mail storms, 775–76
Mail submission service, 34
Maintenance
  background, 360–68
  tasks, 360–61
  tombstone, 365
Majority node set (MNS) clusters, 906, 907
  Exchange 2007 running on, 908
  Microsoft services running on, 908
  See also Clusters
Managed content settings, 818
  control elements, 819–20
  creating, 822
  setting up, 821
Managed Folder Assistant, 829–31
  log, 833
  schedule, 829, 830
  starting, 831
  tasks, 830
Managed folder policies
  allocating, 826–27
  applying, 827–29
  assigning mailboxes with, 827, 829
  defined, 761
  number of, 826
Managed folders
  activity, logging, 831–33
  creating, 824–25
  defined, 824
  deletion and, 834
  grayed out, 835
  harvesting information from, 835–36
  removing, 825
  storage limit, 825
  using, 833–35
Management frameworks, 959–63
  HP OpenView, 961–63
  MOM, 960–61
MAPI, 2–4, 581, 695
  access, disabling, 604

buffers, 600–601
client-side, 10
compression, 600–602
connections, 349–50, 351
connections, testing, 294
defined, 581
in Exchange 2003, 3
logons, 351
as message format, 3
profiles, 584, 586
properties, 305, 318
as protocol, 2–3
restrictions, 605
RPC combination, 581
server-side, 10
sessions, 349
MAPI clients, 306, 318, 582
  authentication, 590
  blocking via registry, 607
  disabling, 606–7
  OST use, 619
  preventing from connecting, 603–7
MAPI.Net, 3
MAPISend, 228
Maximum database size, 343–45
MDBVU32 program, 968
  defined, 860, 968
  documentation, 861
  free and busy data view, 859
  illustrated, 968
  sessions, 968
Memory
  kernel-mode, 311
  mailbox server, 874
  management overhead, 323
  trading for I/O, 312–17
  virtual, 311, 883
Mergers, 272
Message categorization, 438–39
Message classifications, 837–47
  A/C Privileged, 837
  Company Confidential, 837
  Company Internal, 837
  default, 837–38
  enabling values, 844
  exported XML data for, 842
  importing, 843–44
  intelligence, adding, 844–47
  no restriction, 837
  parameters, 839–40

viewing, 838
Message delivery, 439
    failure causes, 500–501
    latency, 959
    to PSTs, 611–15
Message/folder tables
    contents, 321
    defined, 320
    message identifier, 321
    See also Tables
Message identifier, 954
Message policies, 437
Message recovery, 439
Messages
    average size, 777
    capturing, 795–97
    DSN, 496–505
    expiry time, 819, 820
    journaled, 812, 823
    maximum size, 479
    original text in, 776
    poison, 432, 493–94
    postmaster, 504–5
    queued, 490
    quota, 504
    reducing number of, 778
    removing, 490–91
    size, 308
    size fluctuation, 480
    SMS, 699, 730
    suspending, 490
    system, 601–3
Message table
    contents, 322
    defined, 320
    generating, 947–50
    See also Tables
Message tracking, 433, 945–59
    center, 946
    defined, 936
    with EMS, 956–59
    message subjects, 951
    parameters, setting, 953
    with Troubling Assistant, 952–
        56
Message tracking logs, 448, 945–
    52
    accessing, 951–52
    age, 951
    default size, 950
    generating, 947–50

LogParser and, 975
    removal, 950
Messaging records management
        (MRM), 439–40, 815–36
    custom folder management,
        824–26
    default folders management,
        818–23
    defined, 816
    deploying, 816–17
    managed folder activity logging,
        831–33
    manipulating through shell,
        830–31
    principles, 816
    transport rules and, 817
MFCMAPI utility, 965–67
    changing OOF messages with,
        966–67
    defined, 965
    downloading, 965
    folder contents, 966
Microsoft Exchange Conference
        (MEC), 979
Microsoft Exchange
        Troubleshooting Assistant
    defined, 936
    files, 937
    updates, 936–37
Microsoft Management Console
        (MMC), 100
Microsoft Operations Manager
        (MOM), 960–61
    defined, 960
    details, comparing, 961
    illustrated, 961
Migrations, 18–20
    public folder content, 406–8
    speed, 28
MimeSweeper, 780
Mixed organizations
    managing, 109–12
    message path calculations, 473
MobileAdmin, 719
Mobile devices, 694–702
    deployment strategy, 698
    feature control, 710–11
    managing, 710
    managing through EMC, 711–
        13

network traffic estimation,
        715–17
    OWA options, 720
    power management, 731–32
    selecting, 696–98
    support features, 697
    wiping, 655, 719–21
Mobility, 4–5
MOM Management Pack, 712
Most-specific connector, 467–68
Mount-Database command,
        329–30, 895, 896, 905,
        941
Move-AddressList command,
        642
Move-
        ClusteredMailboxServe
        r command, 916
Move-DatabasePath command,
        330
Move-Mailbox command, 204
    database portability and, 346
    defined, 245
    example, 247
    parameters, 245–46
    syntax, 246
    validation, 287
Move Mailbox wizard, 134
    checks, 134–35
    illustrated, 135
Move Mailbox XML report, 139
Move-StorageGroupPath
        command, 915
MSExchangeFBPublish process,
        855
MSExchange.org, 979
Ms-Exch-SMTP-Accept-
        Authoritative-Domain-
        Sender, 153
MSFTEFD.EXE, 378
MSFTESQL.EXE, 378
MTBF (Mean Time Between
        Failures) rate, 414
Multi-core processors, 871
Multi-domain forests, 219–21
Multi-domain model, 49
Multiple databases, 323–24
    allocation to storage groups,
        323
    splitting user load across, 324

Naming contexts (NC), 55–58
connecting ADSIEDIT to, 94
defined, 55
in replication boundaries, 56
Naming conventions
function indicator, 193
geographic names, 192–93
identifier, 193
office or location codes, 192
server, 192–94
user, 188–92
Net Logon service, 72
.NET
framework, 432
objects, 196
programming, 197
New-
ActiveSyncMailboxPoli
cy command, 706
New-AddressRewriteEntry
command, 540
New-Contact command, 253
New-DistributionGroup
command, 254
New-
DynamicDistributionGr
oup command, 258, 261
New-EdgeSubscription
command, 511, 512
New-EmailAddressPolicy
command, 181
New-JournalRule command,
811
New-Mailbox command, 232–33
New-MailContact command,
253
New-ManagedContentSettings
command, 822
New-ManagedFolder command,
825
New-MessageClassification
command, 839–40
New-Object command, 280
New-PublicFolder command,
395
New-PublicFolderDatabase
command, 330, 394–95
New-RemoteDomain command,
577
New-RoutingGroupConnector
command, 255

New-StorageGroup command,
329, 894, 895
New-SystemMessage command,
503
NextHopDomain property, 487
Nondelivery reports (NDRs), 496
Non-Exchange 2007 servers, 290–
92
Notifications
Outlook Web Access (OWA),
675–77
restricting, 574–79
NSLOOKUP utility, 77
NTBackup, 410
as choice for Exchange
deployments, 426
enhancements, 413
See also Backups
NTDS.DIT, 89
NTDSUTIL program, 79
NTLM authentication, 590

OABGEN, 635
OAB.XML, 636, 639
Object identifiers (OIDs), 83
Objects
COM, 196
connection, scheduling, 68
editing, 110–11
fetching, 218
grouping, 237
list, retrieving, 217
number limit in groups, 148–
49
properties, examining, 95
Offline Address Book (OAB), 186,
626–45
allocating to users, 642–45
assigning to mailbox store, 643
automatic downloads, 632
automatic management, 634
cached Exchange mode and,
632–34
customized, creating, 640–42
default, 634
defined, 626–27
distribution, 585, 634–40
downloading, 627–28
download options, 628
file compression, 637

file generation, 628
files in ExchangeOAB share,
640
files on PC, 628–30
format evolution, 630–32
generation, 634–40
GUID, 641
invalid entries, 630
local data files, 629
manifest, 636
as organization-level object, 635
outdated, 633
Outlook use, 595
poll interval, 638
public folder, 636
synchronization, 639
update failures, 632
updates, 634
updates, forcing, 638
user information in, 627
V3 format, 630
V4 format, 631
web-based distribution, 637
Online backups
full, 374
support, 409
See also Backups
Online defragmentation, 362
Online forums, 979
OPATH filters, 158, 159
recipient, 166
specification, 166
syntax, 159–60
OPATH queries
construction, 160
as replacements, 166
results, previewing, 165
OpenView, 6, 961–63
console, 962
defined, 961–62
illustrated, 962
SPI, 962
OpenVMS, 198
Organizational units (OUs), 162
Organizations, mixed, 109–12
OSPF (Open Shortest Path First),
431
OSTs, 619–24
defined, 608
file size registry values, 609–10
format, changing, 598

MAPI client use, 619
moving, 593
opening, 620
problems, 623–24
PSTs versus, 620
rebuilding, 622, 624
recovery utility, 621
repair in progress, 624
size, 592
as slave replicas, 622
synchronization, 621–23
Out-Chart command, 281
Outlook, 583–608
2007 version upgrade, 625–26
address caching, 599–600
address lists view, 184
Add Room picker, 766, 767
archiving setup, 618
authentication modes, 591
AutoArchive options, 619
Automatic Picture Download
setting, 572
cached Exchange mode, 592,
596–99
clients in cached Exchange
mode, 382
conflict resolution, 602–3
connection status, 595
default behavior, 308
defined, 583
drizzle synchronization, 593
email address suggestions, 600
Exchange 5.5 and, 607–8
Exchange relationship, 591–96
free and busy changes, 863–65
Incremental Change
Synchronization (ICS), 594
Junk Mail Filter, 567–72
managing distribution groups
from, 154–56
multiple connectivity threads,
309
network activity, 601
OAB use, 595
Out of Office changes, 624–25
RPC over HTTP connection
support, 596
Search Options, 382
signature editor, 773
smart tags, 775
synchronization settings, 593

web services, 585–91
Outlook Anywhere, 645–49
configuration error, 647
defined, 645
enabling, 646–47, 648
Outlook profile configuration,
649
properties, viewing, 647–48
RPC over HTTP Proxy
component, 646
support, 646
testing, 297
Outlook Express
AD search from, 690
Exchange connection
configuration, 686
LDAP access configuration,
688
Outlook Mobile Access (OMA),
695
support, 705
Windows Mobile
implementation, 705
Outlook Spy, 684, 978
Outlook Voice Access (OVA), 740,
741, 747–48
calling, 749
inbox, 748
pattern filter, 754
Outlook Web Access (OWA), 4,
650–84
additional mailboxes capability,
654
architecture, 651
attachments, controlling, 677–
80
authentication, 667–70
authentication options, 670
basic authentication, 669
calendar, 654
client functionality options,
672–73
clients, 657
client settings, 684
connections, testing, 295
connections via HTTPS, 17
default mail interval, 677
defined, 650
digest authentication, 669
Direct File Access properties,
678

disabling access to, 607
file handling parameters, 681–
82
forms-based authentication,
667, 669, 670
hidden XML items, 684
illustrated, 16
integrated Windows
authentication, 669
international versions, 662–64
language support, 663
legacy data access, 664–66
light version, 658–62
light version advantages, 661
logon screen, 668
mailbox quota information,
660
managing, 666–67
mobile devices, options, 720
mobile devices, wiping, 655
name resolution, 653
names of addresses support,
654
new features, 652–58
notification flag, enabling, 675
notifications, 675–77
OOF settings in, 577
opening mailboxes with, 250
Out of Office Assistant, 655
premium client, disabling, 673
premium version, 656, 658
public folder hierarchies, 684
quota problem flag, 173
regional settings, 662
scheduling in, 661
searches, 654–55
segmentation, 671–75
SharePoint Portal document
access, 655
subscriptions, 676
themes, 680–84
troubleshooting, 655
user interface, 652–53
user interface, customizing,
683–84
voice message support, 653
WebReady Document Viewer,
679
Outlook WebView, 650
Out of Office Assistant, 575–76

Out of Office (OOF) notifications,
    262, 585, 781
    configuration, 574
    contents, 781
    disabling, 575
    effective, 781
    email etiquette and, 782
    generation, reenabling, 577
    message format, 576
    messages, changing with
        MFCMAPI, 966–67
    message support, 576
    organizational data, 574
    Outlook 2007 changes, 624–25
    response security, 578–79
    restricting, 574–79
    settings for domains, 579
    settings in OWA, 577
    suppression types, 578
    system-wide settings, 576

Parent disclosures
    creating, 841–44
    exporting details of, 843
    making apparent, 846
    message view as, 842
PCM (Pulse Code Modulation),
    750
Permission groups, 441–42
Permissions
    administrative, 134
    calendar, 865
    checking, 400
    Exchange-specific, 87–88
    groups for, 154–56
    mailbox, adding, 249–50
    property page, 119
    public folder, 400–401
    top-level folders, 405–6
    working with, 119–20
Personal folder files. See PSTs
Personal Information Manager
    (PIM), 686
Per-value replication, 71
PFDavAdmin, 387, 406, 971–73
    defined, 971
    downloading, 971
    running, 972
Phishing confidence level (PCL),
    525

Phonetic names, 754–56
PING, 487
Pocket Outlook, 701, 702
    sent message storage and, 726
    synchronization specification,
        701
Pocket PC, 697
    GPS device links, 734
    mail processing, 725–30
    message delivery speed, 729
    power management, 731–32
    Word documents, 734
Pointers, 321
PointSec, 719
Poison messages, 432, 493–94
    checking for, 494
    defined, 493
    exporting, 494
    queue, 493–94
Policies
    ActiveSync, 706–11, 761
    defining, 762
    email address, 173–82, 761
    managed folder mailbox, 761
    UM, 761
POP3, 35
    clients, 7, 294–95, 582, 687
    configuration files, changing,
        693
    defined, 582
    disabling access to, 607
    virtual servers, configuring, 694
Postmarks, 572–74
    generation, 573
    illustrated, 573
    processing, 574
Postmaster addresses, 504–5
PowerGadgets, 280, 281
Power management, 731–32
PowerShell, 10, 39, 197
    in batch, 223–24
    commands, editing keystrokes,
        208
    commands, working with, 199–
        204
    error handling, 264
    evolution, 298–99
    for Exchange administrators,
        297–99
    execution policies, 224–26

F7 keyboard command, 208,
    209
    installing, 200
    object support, 196
    OPATH filtering syntax, 158
    power of, 198–99, 298
    provider support, 292
    runtime engine, 198
    scripts, 26, 216, 217, 298
    snap-ins, 280–81
    support, 195–96
    tab completion, 208–10
    uses, 202–4
    in Windows management, 299
    See also Commands
Premium journaling, 808–9
Profile Analyzer, 964
Profiles
    EMS, 221–23
    I/O, 327
    MAPI, 584, 586
    personal, 223
ProofPoint, 791
Propagation dampening, 68–69
Property sets, 88–90
    attributes, 89–90
    Exchange Information, 89
    Exchange Personal Information,
        89–90
Protected groups, 152–54
Protection layers, 523–27
    layer 0, 524
    layer 1, 524
    layer 2, 524–25
    layer 3, 525–26
    layer 4, 526
    layer 5, 526–27
Protocol logging, 473–74
    disk space consumption, 474
    output, 475
    setting, 474
    PS command, 201
PSTs, 609–19
    administrator control, 616, 836
    archiving, 617–19
    configuring, 615–16
    creating, 611
    data transfer to, 848
    defined, 608
    effective use, 616
    file size registry values, 609–10

limitations, 169
mail delivery to, 611–15
message processing, 612
OSTs versus, 620
passwords, 610
properties, changing, 616
pros/cons, 613–15
security problem, 169
selecting as Mail Delivery
    location, 613
use, disabling, 169
Public folder databases, 321, 365
organization, 321
properties, 396
Public folder replication, 367,
    388–92
as black art, 388
disabled, 390
schedule, 391
start, 391
stop ability, 389, 390
storms, 388–92
verification, 391
Public folders, 383–408
adding, to synchronization
    settings, 622
administration changes, 386–
    88
age limit, 366
backwards compatibility and,
    385
content, 392
content, migrating, 406–8
content, viewing, 404
customer guidance, 386
data, 383
database properties, 392
defined, 383
deleted, 366
deleting, 401–2
Exchange 2003, accessing, 666
Exchange 2003 improvements,
    386–87
Exchange 2007 and, 384–86
as "favorite," 621
hiding, 400
hierarchy, 396, 684
limits, setting, 402–3
mail-enabling, 399
managing, 392–405

managing, on remote server,
    403–4
nonsystem, 398
OAB, 636
permissions, 400–401
phase-out, 7
proliferation management, 384
referrals, 406
sample management scripts,
    394
sizes, viewing, 393
"standard," 384
statistics, 404–5
system, 398
top-level, 396
top-level, permissions, 405–6
types, 398
viewing, 399
Public Folders Address List, 187

Quarantines, 549
Queries
CCR, 914
driving email address policies,
    178–82
LDAP, 166
NSPI, 635
OPATH, 160, 165, 166
parameters, setting, 164
results, previewing, 165
sorting, for email address policy,
    182
Query-based groups, 141, 158
Quest Software, 6
Queues, 485–94
finding messages in, 489
information, 485–86
local, 485
poison, 493–94
remote, 485
smart host, 487
submission, 486
as transient objects, 488
types, 485
Unreachable, 491–93
Queue Viewer, 432, 488–91
defined, 488, 936
filter support, 488
illustrated, 489
Quota messages, 504

Quotation marks, 215

RAID (Redundant Array of
    Inexpensive Disks), 879–80
RAID0+1, 879, 880
RAID1, 879
RAID5, 341–42, 879, 880
RAM, 313, 315
Real-time block lists (RBLs), 536
Receive connectors, 440–47
creating, 443–44, 449
default, 441, 515
default, updating, 443
illustrated, 440
properties, 440
properties, viewing, 441
updating, 443, 446
usage types, 444
See also Send connectors
Recipient Administrator role, 90
Recipient Filter agent, 559–60
Recipient filters, 181, 559–60
editing, 261
setting up, 559
Recipients
EMC treatment, 275
management, 128–33
management console, 129–30
types, 132–33
Recipient Update Service (RUS),
    125, 130–32
changing/removing, 131
function, 130
Record Information Storage
    System (RISS), 835
Recovery Storage Group (RSG),
    120, 328
defined, 939
merge options, 940
options, 939–40
working with, 941
Referrals, 406
REGEDIT utility, 584, 630
Registry keys, 980–81
Release to Web (RTW) strategy,
    933–35
Remote queues, 485
Remote servers
public folder management on,
    403–4

working with, 290
See also Servers
Remove-ActiveSyncDevice
command, 712
Remove-AddressList command,
642
Remove-AdPermission
command, 120, 204
Remove-
DistributionGroupMemb
er command, 256
Remove-
ExchangeAdministrator
command, 266
Remove-IPBlockListEntry
command, 537
Remove-Mailbox command,
240–41
Remove-MailboxPermission
command, 251
Remove-MailContact command,
253
Remove-
ManagedContentSetting
s command, 823
Remove-ManagedFolder
command, 825
Remove-
ManagedFolderMailboxP
olicy command, 829
Remove-Message command,
490–91
Remove-
PublicFolderAdministr
ativePermission
command, 401
Remove-PublicFolder
command, 401
Remove-
PublicFolderPermissio
n command, 400
Remove-StorageGroup
command, 330
Replay manager, 898
Replication, 35
    Active Directory, 50–71
    asynchronous, 67
    attribute-level, 51, 143
    basics, 51–53
    changes in Windows 2003, 70–
        71

characteristics, 67
configuration data, 50
"forced," 64
free and busy data, 856
FRS, 71
host, 885
intersite, 65–68
intrasite, 65–68
linked value (LVR), 143, 144
load, reducing, 145
monitor and control, 52
naming contexts (NC) and, 55–
    58
occurrence, 53–55
per-value, 71
public folder, 367, 388–92
SMTP, 67
storage, 885
synchronous, 67
unnecessary, elimination, 69
urgent, 64–65
USNs and, 60–64
REPLMON utility, 77
Reports
    delivery, 262
    Get-MailboxStatistics
        command, 281
    journal, 812
    Move Mailbox XML, 139
    nondelivery (NDRs), 496
Reserved logs, 338
Restores, 415
Restore-StorageGroupCopy
    command, 902, 905
Restoring databases, 422–26
    database selection, 422–23
    differential restores, 425
    incremental restores, 425
    parameters, 423
    steps, 423–25
Resume-
    PublicFolderReplicati
    on command, 405
Resume-StorageGroupCopy
    command, 901
RIM, 694
RoadSync, 695
Roles, 28–36
    Exchange Organization
        Administrator, 125–26

Exchange Recipient
    Administrator, 126
Exchange Server Administrator,
    126
Exchange View-Only
    Administrator, 126
out-of-the-box, 124
services and, 32
Room mailboxes, 762–70
    converting mailboxes to, 770
    creating, 231–32, 763–64
    defined, 132
    icon, 763
    listing, 764
    properties, adding, 765
    properties, managing, 765–70
    user perspective, 763
    See also Mailboxes
Root domain, 48
Routing, 464–76
    closest proximity, 467, 469–70
    connector cost, 467, 469
    costs, 471–72
    diagram, 465
    dynamic, 459
    evolution of, 429–30
    hub sites, 470–71
    most specific connector, 467–
        68
    path resolution, 467
    paths, 437
    SMTP messages, 451
    topology, 432, 437, 467
Routing group connector, 111,
    436
Routing groups, 406
    Exchange 2003,
        decommissioning, 458
    hidden, 433–35
    hub routing sites and, 471
    special, 454
Routing logs, 483–85
    content, 485
    sections, 483–84
    understanding, 484
Routing table calculation, 483
RPCs
    compression, 601
    hanging, 592
    over HTTP connection, 596,
        649

over NetBIOS connection, 591
over TCP/IP connection, 591
pop-ups, 881–82
RSA Authentication Agent, 713
RSA Security, 713
Rule-based processing, 847

Safelists, 547
    aggregation, 553–56
    anti-spam checking and, 556
    availability, 554
    data, 555
    hashing, 555, 556
    populating, 553, 554
    synchronizing, 553
Safe Senders list, 571
SCANPST, 623, 624
Schemas, 80–90
    attribute verification, 84
    change arbitration, 82
    changing, 81, 82–84
    defined, 80
    extending, 80
    updating to allow ANR, 86–87
    updating with installation, 80–
        82
Scope
    EMS and, 221
    setting, 220
Scripts, 26, 228
    accumulation, 298
    calling, 216
    creating, 231
    debugging, 217
    loops, 242
    as programs, 298
    public folder management, 394
Search, 35
Search Indexer, 35
SEC 17-4A, 789
SecurID, 713
Security
    attachments, 677
    dynamic distribution groups,
        168
    Edge server, 518
    PSTs, 169
    universal groups, 133
Security Configuration Wizard
    (SCW), 26, 507

Segmentation
    defined, 671
    Outlook Web Access (OWA),
        671–75
Select-Object command, 212
Self-maintaining groups, 168
Send connectors, 447–53
    address space support, 450
    configuration, 449
    creation, 449
    default, 447
    properties, 447–48
    properties, viewing, 452–53
    shell command to create, 452
    source servers for, 450
    usage, 450
    See also Receive connectors
Sender Filter agent, 537–39, 540
Sender filtering, 537–39
Sender ID agent, 540–47
    adoption, 544
    configuration options, 546
    configuring settings for, 545
    defined, 540
    domain support, 543
    _ep subdomain, 543
    implementation, 541–42
    message validation process, 543
    problem addressed by, 541
    running, 546–47
    selecting, 546
    SMTP servers and, 544
    status, 547
    valid PRA determination, 543–
        44
Sender Policy Framework (SPF),
        540
Sender Reputation agent, 556–59
Sender Reputation Level (SRL)
    defined, 556–57
    Microsoft list, 557
    threshold, 557
Serial Advanced Technology
        Attachment (SATA), 878,
        879
Serial Attached SCSI (SAS), 878,
        879
Server-based indexing, 375
ServerLegacyDN property, 283–84
ServerName property, 283
Server refresh, 19

Servers
    64-bit hardware, 871
    bastion, 522
    buying, for Exchange 2007,
        870–75
    CCR, 914
    Client Access, 587
    configuring, 872
    consolidation, 20
    Edge, 30–31, 32, 507–67
    full crawl of, 378
    Global Catalog, 20, 21, 51, 75–
        76
    hardware guidelines, 870
    hub transport, 436, 437
    IMAP, 689–94
    information, getting, 210–13
    legacy, 457
    mailbox, 436, 472
    memory usage, 872
    naming conventions, 192–94
    network load support, 872
    non-Exchange 2007, 290–92
    properties, 119
    remote, 290, 403–4
Server-side filters, 267–70
    commands, 268
    execution speed, 267–68
    See also Filters
Server Stress and Performance
        (ESP), 964
Service Connection Point (SCP),
        587, 588
Service Host, 35
Services, 32–36
    list of, 33–36
    relying on ADAccess, 74
    roles and, 32
    See also specific services
Session cookies, 668
Session state manager, 198
Set-AddressList command,
        642
Set-AdSite command, 470
Set-
    AttachmentFilterListC
    onfig command, 562
Set-CasMailbox command,
        244–45, 603
    in ActiveSync policies, 708
    defined, 251

MAPIBlockOutlookNonCa chedMode parameter, 604–5

MAPIBlockOutlookRPCH TTP parameter, 604
MAPIBlockOutlookVersions parameter, 604, 605
when to use, 252
Set-ClientAccessServer command, 286
Set-ContentFilterConfig command, 549
Set-DistributionGroup command, 255, 263
Set-EmailAddressPolicy command, 179–80
Set-EventLogLevel command, 367
Set-ExecutionPolicy command, 225
Set-Group command, 141, 255
Set-IMAPSettings command, 691
Set-JournalRule command, 811
Set-MailboxCalendarSettin gs command, 768–69, 770
AddOrganizerToSubject property, 769
AllowConflicts property, 768
BookInPolicy property, 769
DeleteNonCalendarItems property, 768
MaximumDurationMinutes property, 769
RemoveOldMeetingMessages property, 768

ScheduleOnlyDuringWork Hours property, 768
Set-Mailbox command, 204, 234, 244, 251
Get-User command combination, 271
-OfflineAddressBook parameter, 645
in OOF suppression, 576

SCLJunkThreshold property, 553
Set-MailboxDatabase command, 330, 354
Set-MailboxServer command, 286, 830–31
in logging managed folder activity, 832
in mailbox server configuration, 472
Set-MailContact command, 253
Set-OABVirtualDirectory command, 638
Set-OrganizationConfig command, 505
Set-OutlookAnywhere command, 647
Set-OwaVirtualDirectory command, 667, 673
attachment access control, 680
default interval, 677
OWA segmentation parameters, 674–75
Set-POPSettings command, 693
Set-PublicFolder command, 403
Set-PublicFolderDatabase command, 330, 365, 403
Set-ReceiveConnector command, 446–47
Set-RemoteDomain command, 577, 579
Set-ResourceConfig command, 766
Set-SendConnector command, 469
Set-SenderFilterConfig command, 539
Set-SenderIDConfig command, 546
Set-SenderReputationConfig command, 558
Set-StorageGroup command, 349
Set-SystemMessage command, 501, 502
Set-TransportConfig command, 477–78, 482, 923

Set-TransportRule command, 804, 808
Set-TransportServer command, 286, 504–6
Set-UmMailbox command, 252, 744
Set-UmMailboxPIN command, 745
Set-UMServer command, 286, 744–45
Set-User command, 251, 766
Shared mailboxes
creating, 231–32
defined, 133
See also Mailboxes
SharePoint, 386
lists, synchronizing, 608
moving to, 407
Portal Server, 388, 680
Server, 386
sites, 680
Short Message Service (SMS), 694
gateway, 700
messages, 699, 730
Shutdowns, clean, 331
Single Copy Cluster (SCC), 884, 920
SIP
communications, 749–52
INVITE, 750
Site links
costs, 471–72
schedule, 68
Small Form Factor (SFF), 878
SmartFilter feature, 704
Smart host queues, 487
SmartPhone, 696, 724, 778
SmartScreen, 548
Smart tags, 775
S/MIME, 655, 656
SMTP, 2, 13, 429–30
commands, 226
connectors, 468, 492
as de facto standard, 460
as default transport protocol, 432
extended, 446
extensions (ESMTP), 2
external, 446
folder, 756
message routing, 451

message transfer, 955
pickup directory, 228
replication, 67
routing engine, 17
servers, 226, 544
stack, 24
support, 430
transport engine, 957
SMTP addresses, 168, 177
    for new mailboxes, 233
    patterns, 188
    user accounts with, 234
Soft recoveries, 422
Spam
    in circulation, 521
    client-side filters, 522
    client-side suppression, 567–79
    defense in depth, 522–23
    fighting, 518–22
    reporting to Microsoft, 527
Spam confidence level (SCL), 525
    per-user processing, 552–53
    ratings, 557
    support, 556
    thresholds, 549, 550
Special mailboxes, 756–59
    Exchange 2007 approach, 758–
        59
    SMTP, 756–57
    System, 757, 758–59
    System Attendant, 757
    See also Mailboxes
Speech grammars, 752–54
    building, 753–54
    creation, 753
    defined, 752
SQL 2005, 306
Standby continuous replication
    (SCR), 924
Start-
    ManagedFolderAssistan
    t command, 831
Statistics
    mailbox, 279
    public folder, 404–5
    user, display of, 275
STM file, 319
Storage
    costs, 317–18
    direct-attached, 894, 906
    low-cost, 343–44

single-instance model, 367
transport, 461–63
transport rule, 803–4
vendors, 885
Storage Area Networks (SANs), 8
    deployments, 307, 876
    expense, 876
    exploitation, 19
    performance on, 876
Storage calculator, 933–34
Storage controller caches, 313
Storage groups, 310, 323–31
    after creation, 328
    approaches, 325
    backups and, 416–21
    calculation, 325–26
    creating, 327–29
    default, 349, 395
    defined, 323
    deployment considerations,
        324–25
    enabling LCR for, 894
    in Exchange 2003, 315
    in Exchange 2007, 315
    location, 327
    mailbox sizes and, 326
    multiple database allocation to,
        323
    position, 328
    root directory, 329
    support, 323, 326
    transaction logs, 332
    working with, 329–31
Store, 34, 301–427
    background maintenance
        control, 361
    background maintenance tasks,
        356
    Blocked Senders list check, 572
    buffer manager, 312
    circular logging, 335–37
    cleanup process, 357
    database check, 331
    defined, 301
    ESE and, 304–5
    event notifications list, 362
    Exchange 2007 differences,
        306–18
    header information, 321
    management tasks, 284
    overview, 301–6

page size, 313
permissions, 47
pointer management, 321
replaying logs, 899
restore operations, 422–26
single-instance storage model,
    367
transactions replay, 340
Streaming backups, 426
Submission queue, 486
Subscriptions, 676
Suspend-Message command,
    490
Suspend-
    PublicFolderReplicati
    on command, 405
Suspend-StorageGroupCopy
    command, 901
Sybari, 528
Synchronization
    debugging, 721–23
    drizzle, 593
    Edge servers, 511–17
    folder selection for, 726
    logs, 722
    OAB, 639
    OSTs, 621–23
    Outlook settings, 593
    safelist, 547
    Windows Mobile, 704
Sync Issues folder, 603
System Attendant, 35
    log removal, 950
    mailbox, 757
    restarting, for new polling
        interval, 855
System Center Capacity Planner
    (SCCP), 932–33
    concept, 932
    defined, 932
System failure categories, 413–14
System mailboxes, 757, 758–59
System messages, 501–3
    customized, example, 503
    customizing, 501–2
    viewing, 502
SystemX.xyz.com, 450

Tab completion, 208
Tables, 320–22

attachments, 320
folders, 320
interaction, 322
mailbox, 320
message, 320
message/folder, 320
vector, 69–70
Tarpitting, 560
TechEd, 979–80
TechNet, 979
Technology Adoption Program
    (TAP), 43
TELNET, 487
Temporary log files, 337
Test-ExchangeSearch
    command, 297
Test-IMAPConnectivity
    command, 294–95
Testing
    client connections, 294–95
    content indexing, 297, 381
    Exchange 2007, 292–97
    Exchange Unified Messaging,
        297
    I/O performance, 317
    mail flow, 295–96
    MAPI connections, 294
    Outlook Anywhere, 297
    OWA connections, 295
    system health, 293–94
Test-IPAllowListProvider
    command, 297
Test-MailFlow command, 295–
    96
Test-MapiConnectivity
    command, 294
Test-
    OutlookAnywhereConnec
    tivity command, 297
Test-OutlookWebServices
    command, 296–97
Test-OWA-Connectivity
    command, 295
Test-PopConnectivity
    command, 294–95
Test-SenderID command, 297
Test-SystemHealth command,
    293–94
    defined, 293
    illustrated results, 293–94

Test-UMConnectivity
    command, 297
Themes
    default, 682–83
    Outlook Web Access (OWA),
        680–84
Third-party products, 6
Timestamps, 62
    backups, 421
    last logon, 71
Tombstone maintenance, 365
Toolbox, 103, 374, 935–45
    contents, 935–36
    Database Recovery
        Management, 935, 937–42
    Database Troubleshooter, 942–
        43
    defined, 935
    ExBPA, 935
    illustrated, 935
    Mail Flow Troubleshooter,
        943–45
    message tracking logs, 945–59
    Performance Monitor, 936
    Performance Troubleshooter,
        936
    Queue Viewer, 488–91, 936
Top-level folder hierarchies
    (TLHs), 384
Top-level public folders, 396, 405–
    6
TotalItemSize property, 282
Transaction logs, 331–45
    after CCR transition, 917
    checksum, 342–43
    circular logging, 335–37
    creating, 337–38
    data, 339
    directories, 328
    disk space, checking for, 938
    ESE and, 332
    file names, 333
    illustrated, 334
    I/O, 341
    location, 327
    mixed, 348
    naming prefix, 334, 335
    protecting, 341–42
    replay time, 325
    reserved, 338
    sets, 324

Transport, 36
Transport architecture, 435–64
    message flow, 435
    receive connectors, 440–47
    send connectors, 447–53
Transport configuration, 476–85
    file, 481–83
    properties, 477–78
Transport dumpster, 921–23
    configuration settings, 922–23
    defined, 921
        MaxDumpsterSizePerStorag
        eGroup, 922–23
    MaxDumpsterTime, 923
    message capture, 922
    queue, 921
Transport engine
    advantages, 432–33
    "poison" messages and, 432
    SMTP, 957
Transporter agents, 505–6
Transport Log Search, 36
Transport queue files, 463
Transport rules, 792–93
    actions, adding, 806
    actions, checking, 807
    to add disclaimer text, 794–95
    AD properties, 804
    application default, 795
    classification intelligence with,
        844–47
    complicated, 797–800
    creating, 792–93
    on Edge server, 792
    editing, 794
    enforcing message
        classifications, 845
    for ethical firewall, 800–803
    execution, 793
    functionality, 788
    groups with, 797
    on hub transport server, 792
    illustrated, 793
    intention, 788
    loading groups for, 799
    managed folders combination,
        817
    manipulating, with shell, 804–8
    for message refiling, 798
    as MRM supplement, 817

number limit, 803
in selected message capture, 795–97
storage, 803–4
Transport storage, 461–63
Troubling Assistant, 952–56
Truncate deletor, 897–98
Two-phase deletes, 352

Unified Communications (UC), 735–37
advantages, 736–37
challenges, 737
defined, 735
demos, 737
UM and, 739
Unified Messaging server, 31
AD use, 32
as building block, 739
functions, 740–41
performance, 751
Unified Messaging (UM), 36, 585, 737–56
client access to voicemail, 741–45
cross-forest, 756
deployments, 746, 751–52
deployment/support cost, 737
integration, 738
managing with PowerShell commands, 743–45
Microsoft interest in, 738
phonetic names, 754–56
policies, 761
speech grammars, 752–54
UC and, 739
use scenarios, 739
Unique serial numbers (USNs), 52–53
incremented, 64
originating, 63, 64
replication and, 60–64
server, 60
Universal groups, 140, 141
availability, 140
distribution, 133
mail-enabled, 142
security, 133
See also Groups
Unreachable queue, 491–93

defined, 491
reason for messages in, 491–92
See also Queues
Update-AddressList command, 642
Update-FileDistributionServi ce command, 639
Update-OfflineAddressBook command, 638
Update-StorageGroupCopy command, 896, 902
Up-to-date vector table, 69–70
Urgent replication, 64–65
User-defined variables, 214–17
User details templates, 784–87
User mailboxes, 132
Users
authenticated, limiting groups to, 153
better email use, 771–82
clients and, 759
default options acceptance, 776
managing, 761–866
moving, 133–40
naming conventions, 188–92
returning list, 219–20
statistics display, 275
updating, 272
User tables, 61, 62, 63

Variables, 214–17
common, 214–17
decimal, 216
$ExBin, 214
$ExInstall, 214
$ExScripts, 214
global, 215
integer, 216
string, 215
user-defined, 214–17
VAXmail, 581
Vector tables, 69–70
high-watermark, 69
up-to-date, 69–70
Version numbers, 40–41
View-Only Administrator permissions, 491
Virtual Hard Disk (VHD), 426
Virtualization, 925–27

Virtualized servers, 79
Virtual memory, 311
consumption, 311
management problems, 883
Virus Scanning API (VSAPI), 437, 730
Visual effects
EMC, 116–18
illustrated, 118
VLV (Virtual List View), 22
VMware, 926
Voicemail, 741–47
attached, 747
client access, 741–45
dealing with, 745–47
message display, 742
notes, 745
pure, 748–49
Voice synthesis, 747–48
Volume Licensing Program, 37
Volume ShadowCopy Services (VSS), 426

WBXML compression, 705
Web.config file, 723
WebDAV, 10, 14, 650, 658, 720
WebReady Document Viewer, 679
Where-Object command, 279, 282
Windows
32-bit, 311
64-bit, 312
Backup Wizard, 417
Desktop Search, 375, 382, 383
Event Tracing (ETW) subsystem, 968–69
kernel memory, 311
Media Audio. See WMA
Remote Desktop Connection, 117
SharePoint Services (WSS), 679
Support Tools, 93
Team Services, 408
Volume Shadow Copy Services, 410, 426
Windows Management Instrumentation (WMI), 195
CDOEXM and, 207
objects, 196

Windows Mobile, 699
    attendees tracking information,
      703
    email, 703
    Exchange 2007 and, 702–23
    hyperlink access support, 703
    messaging, 699
    OMA implementation, 705
    out-of-office responses, 703
    reporting, 706
    search operations, 703
    security certificate support, 703
    SmartFilter feature, 704
    SMS message storage, 730
    synchronization, 704
    task management, 703
    version 6.0, 702–23

Windows Mobile devices, 696, 724
    BlackBerry comparison, 723–
      35
    features, 702
    input flexibility, 732–35
    Live Communications Server
      support, 733
    mail processing, 725–30
    messaging options, 730–31
    MSN Messenger support, 733
    power management, 731–32
    Windows Media Player, 733–
      34
WinZIP, 777
Wiping mobile devices, 655, 719–
    21
WMA

    attachments, 742, 746
    format, 750
    support, 750
"Wolfpack" technology, 883
Workstations, running EMC on,
    112–13

X.400 protocol, 429, 474–75
X-headers, 811
XML files
    Edge subscription, 153, 512
    hidden, 684
    importing, with rule collection,
      563